1 MONTH OF
FREE
READING

at

www.ForgottenBooks.com

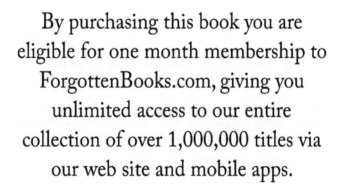

By purchasing this book you are eligible for one month membership to ForgottenBooks.com, giving you unlimited access to our entire collection of over 1,000,000 titles via our web site and mobile apps.

To claim your free month visit:
www.forgottenbooks.com/free953980

ISBN 978-0-260-52585-7
PIBN 10953980

For support please visit www.forgottenbooks.com

56TH CONGRESS, | SENATE. | Doc. No. 231,
2d Session. | | Part 7.

COMPILATION

OF

REPORTS

OF

COMMITTEE ON FOREIGN RELATIONS,

UNITED STATES SENATE,

1789-1901,

First Congress, First Session, to Fifty-sixth Congress, Second Session.

DIPLOMATIC RELATIONS WITH FOREIGN NATIONS—
AFFAIRS IN CUBA.

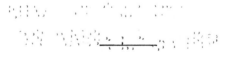

VOL. VII.

WASHINGTON:
GOVERNMENT PRINTING OFFICE.
1901.

In the Senate of the United States,
January 15, 1901.

Resolved, That there be printed as a Senate document the Compilation of Reports of the Committee on Foreign Relations of the United States Senate from seventeen hundred and eighty-nine to nineteen hundred, prepared under the direction of the Committee on Foreign Relations, as authorized by the Act approved June sixth, nineteen hundred, entitled "An Act making appropriations to supply deficiencies in the appropriations for the fiscal year ending June thirtieth, nineteen hundred, and for prior years, and for other purposes."

Attest:

Charles G. Bennett,
Secretary.

2

DIPLOMATIC RELATIONS WITH FOREIGN NATIONS.

DIPLOMATIC RELATIONS WITH FOREIGN NATIONS.

FIFTY-THIRD CONGRESS, THIRD SESSION.

January 16, 1895.

[Senate Report No. 772]

Mr. Davis, from the Committee on Foreign Relations, submitted the following report:

The Committee on Foreign Relations (through Mr. Davis), to whom was referred the bill (S. 1309) to provide for the provisional government of foreign countries and places acquired by treaty or otherwise, recommend the passage of said bill with the following amendments:

Strike out the words "with the advice and consent of the Senate" in lines 6 and 7.

In line 8 strike out "five" and insert "three."

[See pp. 33, 979, and p. 120, Vol. VI.]

February 6, 1895.

[Senate Report No. 886]

Mr. Morgan, from the Committee on Foreign Relations, submitted the following report:

The consular service of the United States, like that of other nations, developed gradually out of the necessities of commerce and the willingness of merchants in foreign countries to represent other governments than their own and to discharge certain fiscal and other duties for the sake of the fees to be collected for such services. While the other great commercial nations of the world have at intervals down to recent times been active in the improvement of their consular service, in order to meet satisfactorily the exigencies of a steadily increasing competition in international trade, the consular system of the United States has remained practically unchanged since the time it was called into existence on a small scale by the acts of July 1, 1790, and of April 14, 1792, and kept alive by a number of subsequent unimportant acts.

The act "to remodel the diplomatic and consular system" of March 1, 1855, is entitled to be regarded as an improvement only so far as it slightly enlarged the service and corrected certain abuses therein by a closer supervision of the fees. It in no way, however, effected a change in the principle of consular representation or in the system of appointment. Apart, therefore, from the act of June 20, 1864, which provided for the establishment of a small body of thirteen consular clerks with a permanent tenure of office, a measure which at its inception was intended to form the nucleus of an entire reform of the

5

service on that basis, this institution, so important to our foreign trade, has suffered the oversight and indifference of Congress.

This neglect is the more striking and the less excusable when our foreign trade of half a century ago is contrasted with that of to-day. In 1850 the combined value of our imports and domestic exports amounted to $308,409,759; in 1893 it reached the figure of $1,697,431,707. But notwithstanding these present vastly increased and far more intricate commercial relations indicated by these figures, no step whatever to increase the efficiency of the consular service, to which the direction and fostering of these relations are intrusted, has been taken. That this has entailed a great loss annually to our foreign trade can not be questioned; that there is also an urgent necessity to correct this want of efficiency is equally apparent.

Even more applicable to the industrial and commercial conditions of to-day, but with reference to those of a decade ago, Secretary Frelinghuysen said in 1884:

Until recently the demands of Europe. which consumed the greater portion of our exports, and the condition of the producing countries, were such as to give us control in the supply of certain products, such as breadstuffs, provisions, cotton, petroleum, etc. The demands of Europe for all these products, and of the other continents for petroleum especially, were so positive, and our p oducing conditions so favorable, as to give us practically a monopoly for their supply.

These conditions of international demand and supply are undergoing radical changes which the near future will intensify.

The efforts which have been made and which are being made by Europe to enlarge the field of supply in the above-mentioned products, aided by the ambition which prevails in all countries for the development of natural and artificial resources to meet their own wants and to supply the wants of others, have resulted in awakening competition for the supply even of those products which we have heretofore controlled. It is true that thus far this competition has not affected our trade to any appreciable extent, but the desire for development which is now abroad and the ambition which prevails to increase the production (outside of the United States) of the foregoing articles render consular supervision of absolute importance. The complex commercial relations and industrial interests which now prevail in Europe have originated hostility to American products in many countries. and afford additional reasons for the enlargement and perfection of the consular service.[1]

In 1888 Mr. Cleveland, in his message to Congress, expresses himself to the same effect when he says: "The reorganization of the consular service is a matter of serious importance to our national interests," and in 1893 he again refers to the subject, as follows:

During my former administration I took occasion to recommend a recast of the laws relating to the consular service, in order that it might become a more efficient agency in the promotion of the interests it was intended to subserve. The duties and powers of consuls have been expanded with the growing requirements of our foreign trade. Discharging important duties affecting our commerce and American citizens abroad, and in certain countries exercising judicial functions, these officers should be men of character, intelligence, and ability.

In addition to these expressions from a high official source, the necessity of a reform has been recognized by men of letters, eminent statesmen, journalists, and important boards of trade of this country.

It must be admitted that the present management of our foreign service is burdened with many drawbacks to its efficacy by considerations that relate to domestic politics. Partisan policy, when strictly carried out in making appointments in our foreign service, has no other meaning than that the consular offices are primarily regarded as rewards for political services. The real capacity and usefulness of a consul is too often a secondary consideration.

---

[1] Communication of the Secretary of State to the President, March 20, 1884.

This important and indispensable part of the machinery by which our foreign intercourse is conducted is often employed to pension political favorites. That to subserve the interests of the service ought to be the sole end in view in the selection of incumbents can not be disputed. To consider the offices merely as sources from which these partisan officeholders may derive four years of maintenance is as absurd as it would be to construct a navy to defend the country and to intrust its command to landsmen without experience for whom we might desire to provide a living and comfortable quarters.

Such a purpose, or one not more gratifying, has often been put into practice in our diplomatic and consular service. To protect and promote in time of peace our varied foreign interests through the agency of a trained personnel is not a less-important subject for legislative consideration and provision than in time of war to defend them by the most efficient means at our command.

The object of this act is to provide a system by which persons shall be trained for the duties of the consular service, so that they shall be able to perform them in the best possible way at a reasonable expense to the Government. That this can not be obtained without removing the selection of persons for this service from the control of party politics is shown by our experience, if any proof were required to establish a conclusion so entirely true and indisputable.

Fitness of the candidate, permanency of tenure during good behavior, and an impartial method of selection and to govern promotion as reward for efficiency are the principles on which a useful consular service can alone be based, with an expectation of the best results.

Under our present system a consular or diplomatic officer has no sooner familiarized himself with the duties of his office and begun to acquire a knowledge of its business and fitness for his duties than he is removed to make room for another novice, who is likewise superseded as soon as his experience begins to enable him to discharge the duties of his office to the satisfaction of himself and others. Thus, in one generation the same post is frequently filled by a number of men, who are successively displaced as soon as they have learned to transact the business of their offices with something of professional knowledge and skill.

This system is not only unjust to the people, but it is equally unjust to the agents, who are thrown back upon their own resources just at the time when a three or four years' preparation has fitted them to devote their energies and capacity with advantage to the foreign service.

To compete successfully with the agents of foreign powers, and to conduct advantageously the political and commercial affairs of our own country, the appointees to this service should be familiar not only with the laws, customs, industries, manufactures, and natural products of our own land, but they should be instructed in the laws, pursuits, language, the contributions to commerce, and the character of the people to whom they are accredited. To this should be added a competent knowledge of the law of nations and of commercial law. As long as these officers are transferred from pursuits and associations which have no connection with commerce or the foreign service, however able and skillful they may be in other things, they can not possess the special knowledge and skill which will render their labors either useful or creditable to the consular service.

The foreign service of European governments for many years has been the object of careful solicitude on their part. An outline statement of them will better enable us to understand the disadvantage we suffer from a defective system.

The French consular service is composed of—

40 consuls-general, at a salary each	$3,600
50 consuls of the first class, each	2,800
80 consuls of the second class, each	2,000
100 Vice-consuls	1,400
24 pupil consuls	800

The conditions for admission to the diplomatic and consular service of France are prescribed in a decree of October 15, 1892, and, to show how important France considers its foreign service, attention is called to the fact that over thirty decrees have been issued since 1880 tending to perfect the system.

The pupil consuls are appointed by the minister of foreign affairs. They can only be drawn from the body of attachés on probation who have passed a competitive examination for admission into the service and who have served not less than one year in the home office.

Before being assigned to a diplomatic or consular post they are required to spend at least one year at one of the principal chambers of commerce, where they are to acquire a thorough knowledge of the methods and needs of commerce, and whence they must send the minister periodical reports on the trade of the district. After three years of service, half of which time must be rendered abroad, the pupil consul becomes eligible for vice-consul, and after a service of three years in each subsequent grade he becomes eligible for promotion to a higher one.

Candidates for admission in the French diplomatic and consular service must be under 27 years of age, and must have taken a collegiate degree in law, science, or letters, or must have passed certain other examinations, or be the holders of commissions in the army or navy.

The examination for entrance into the service is either written or oral, as may be required.

The written test consists of a composition on public and private international law, and a translation into French from English and German, which is dictated. Those candidates who aspire to the diplomatic career are to write also a composition on a subject of diplomatic history that occurred since 1648; those destined for the consular service must write a composition on a subject of political economy or of political and commercial geography.

Those whose papers are sufficiently creditable in the opinion of the examiners to warrant their going any further are then subjected to a public oral examination on public and private international law, political and commercial geography, political economy, and a conversation in English and German. Candidates for the diplomatic career are further examined orally in diplomatic history since 1648, and candidates for the consular service are examined on maritime and customs laws.

The French foreign service is under very strict discipline, and for misconduct or inefficiency there are the following penalties:

(1) Reprimand.

(2) Withholding a part of the salary, not exceeding one-half thereof and not for a longer period than two months.

(3) Suspension from the service, without salary, for two or more years.

(4) Dismissal.

The last three penalties are imposed by the minister of foreign affairs, with the consent of the council of directors, and after a written or oral hearing of the party under censure.

In addition to their regular salaries, the French consular officers are entitled to traveling expenses and allowances for house and office rent, and for entertaining where it is necessary.

Such a course of training and discipline must produce thorough efficiency, and the generous rewards given for faithful and profitable service must encourage a good class of men to adopt such employment as a profession to which all their energies and abilities are industriously devoted. The permanency of employment during good behavior gives confidence to the officer and constantly increasing benefit to the Government.

The British system of regulations for the admission of applicants to the consular service are as follows:

Persons selected for the consular service, whenever the circumstance of their being resident in England, on their first appointment, or of their passing through England on their way to take up such first appointment, may admit of their being subject to examination, will be expected to satisfy the civil service commissioners—

(1) That they have a correct knowledge of the English language so as to be able to express themselves clearly and correctly in writing.

(2) That they can write and speak French correctly and fluently.

(3) That they have a sufficient knowledge of the current language, as far as commerce is concerned, of the port at which they are appointed to reside to enable them to communicate directly with the authorities and natives of the place—a knowledge of the German language being taken to meet this requirement for ports in northern Europe; of the Spanish or Portuguese language, as may be determined by the secretary of state, for ports in Spain. Portugal, Morocco, and South or Central America, and of the Italian language for ports in Italy, Greece, Turkey, Egypt, and on the Black Sea or Mediterranean, except those in Morocco or Spain.

(4) A sufficient knowledge of British mercantile and commercial law to enable them to deal with questions arising between British shipowners, shipmasters, and seamen. As regards this head of examination, candidates must be prepared to be examined in "Smith's Compendium of Mercantile Law."

(5) A sufficient knowledge of arithmetic for the nature of the duties which consuls are required to perform in drawing up commercial tables and reports. As regards this head of examination, candidates must be prepared to be examined in Bishop Colenso's Arithmetic.

Moreover, all persons on their first nomination to consulships, and after having passed their examination before the civil service commissioners, will be required, as far as practicable, to attend for at least three months in the foreign office, in order that they may become acquainted with the forms of business as carried on there.

Limit of age for candidates, 25 and 50, both years inclusive. (Fee for examination, £1 to £6.)

Mr. Henry White, formerly secretary of legation at London, in an article contributed to the North American Review makes the following instructive statement concerning the British consular service:

The British service was established in its present form by act of Parliament in 1825 (6 Geo. IV, cap. 87). Up to that time its members had been appointed, on no regular system, by the King, and were paid from his civil list. This act placed the service under the foreign office, and provided for its payment out of funds to be voted by Parliament. Since then it has been the subject of periodical investigation by royal commissions and Parliamentary committees, with a view to the improvement of its efficiency. The evidence taken on these occasions is published in voluminous blue books, the perusal of which I recommend to those interested in the reform in our service.

Appointments are made by the secretary of state for foreign affairs. Candidates must be recommended by some one known to him, and their names and qualifications are thereupon entered on a list, from which he selects a name when a vacancy occurs. The candidate selected, whose age must be between 25 and 50, is then required to pass an examination before the civil service commissioners.

The salaries of British consular officers are fixed, under the act of Parliament of July 21, 1891 (54 and 55 Vict., cap. 36), by the secretary of state, with the approval of the treasury, and no increase can be made in any salary without the approval of the latter. They average about £600 ($3,000) a year, but, of course, some of the important posts are much more highly paid, the salary of the consul-general at New York being £2,000 (nearly $10,000), with an office allowance besides of £1,660, and a staff consisting of a consul at £600, and two vice-consuls at £400 and £250, respectively; that of the consul at San Francisco, £1,200 (nearly $6,000), with an office allowance of £600 besides.

British consular officials are retired at the age of 70 with a pension.

There is also an unpaid branch of the service, consisting chiefly of vice-consuls, appointed at places which are not of sufficient importance to merit a paid official. They are usually British merchants, but may be foreigners. They are not subjected to an examination, and are rarely promoted to a paid appointment.

Consular clerks are required to pass an examination in handwriting and orthography, arithmetic, and one foreign language (speaking, translating, and copying).

Mr. White through a series of years was our secretary of legation at London, and is thoroughly informed on the subject of consular duties and the acquirements that are essential to an efficient and respectable service. His approval of the plan adopted in this bill for the reformation of our consular system and service is a strong recommendation of its future advantages.

In Germany persons are appointed to the office of consular chancellor who have passed their examinations as "referendary," a title which requires graduation at a German university and requires a thorough knowledge of law, political science, statistics, etc. The chancellor of the consulate is promoted gradually until he reaches the rank of consul-general.

As a rule the personnel of our consular establishment is not in unfavorable contrast with that of the leading European States as to intelligence and sagacity; but our consuls have not usually the liberal education characteristic of the consular representatives of the great European States, nor are they so well informed as to commerce and its great variety of contributory pursuits, or with the exact business methods employed in conducting the commerce of the leading nations. This seems to be our point of most serious deficiency.

It is proper, and may be necessary, that the laws should designate the places at which consulates are established, but discretion should be given to the President to send consuls to other places, at least temporarily, to meet the demands of trade and intercourse that may arise in new and unexpected quarters. Especially is this necessary in cases where other countries are engaged in war and a sudden emergency calls for the protection of our citizens in places which are not designated by law as the location of consular establishments.

But the laws should not designate the individual who is to be the consul at any particular locality. That matter should be left to the discretion of the President, so that he can at all times have the right man at the right place, to meet any demand of trade, or to secure the adequate protection of the persons and property of our citizens in any emergency, or for any public reason.

The arrangement of the fixed residences of consuls of the several classes is not attempted in this bill. The laws and the practice of the Department of State are, for the present at least, a sufficient guide in that matter.

The President should, however, be left free in his authority to send a consul of any class to any consulate when he may consider that the demands of the public service require such transfers.

The reasons for such a provision of law are many and cogent, and they are so obvious as not to require any elaboration in this report. They relate as well to the fitness of consular officers for the particular duties of the occasion as to their usefulness because of their experience as to the condition of the people, the trade, and the language of the particulr locality where their services are required.

The consular establishments thus mobilized would soon show a great growth in useful knowledge of the affairs of various parts of foreign countries, and our trade with many foreign countries would be greatly increased and rendered more secure.

The following statements, showing the present condition of our consular service, will show that the change in the organization of the system will add materially to the revenue derived from that source, without a material increase of the expenditures:

Expenditures for salaries of consular officers and amount of compensation in fees, where the officer has no salary, for the year 1894.

26 consuls-general (not including those also commissioned ministers resident)	$98,000.00
188 salaried consuls	371,500.00
11 salaried commercial agents	22,000.00
13 salaried consular clerks	15,000.00
62 feed consuls (personal perquisites in official fees)	36,152.85
33 feed commercial agents (personal perquisites in official fees)	36,505.53
Notarial and unofficial fees retained by consular officers as personal perquisites (lowest estimate)	250,000.00
333 Total	829,158.38

Officers of the diplomatic service embraced in this bill.

6 secretaries of embassy	$13,875.00
17 secretaries of legation	31,975.00
23 Total	45,850.00

According to the Annual Report of the Fifth Auditor of the Treasury for the year ended June 30, 1894—

The expenses for last year of the consular service were	$1,055,417.43
The consular fees received for official services were	758,410.81
Excess of expenditures over receipts	297,006.62

This excess of expenses is larger than it has been for ten years. In 1893 it only amounted to $96,042. The difference is not due to an increase of expenditures, but, no doubt, may be found to a great extent in the changes of our tariff laws. This excess, though larger than customary, is, after all, a small sum when considered with reference to the important purposes for which it is disbursed, and, with the payment into the Treasury of the unofficial fees, as proposed under this bill, it is likely to be greatly reduced, if not changed into a balance in favor of the income from that source.

The entire excess of expenditures for salaries in the Department of State and in the diplomatic and consular service over the receipts amounts to only $615,909.19, the smallest amount expended by any of the great powers of the world. The expenditures of the foreign service of Great Britain, Russia, Germany, Italy, and Spain exceed this amount by very considerable figures, and the report of the ministry of foreign affairs of France for the year 1893 shows only $240,000 receipts and $3,266,960 expenditures, a sum almost double that expended by the United States, including even the incidental and contingent expenses of the consular and diplomatic service of the latter country.

This bill adopts the principle of permanent official tenure, so far as the laws can control that subject, but permanent only as it is of benefit to the service. It leaves the power of removal from office to the discretion of the President. The position of each employee of the service is protected against the uncertain and demoralizing effects of changes for merely political reasons in the administration of the Government as far as Congress can control the subject. But this protection is as necessary in practice for efficient work as it is just in theory, and if the plan is adopted of appointing consuls after they are found to be qualified for the respective classifications of the consular service they will seldom, if ever, be dropped from the service for the purpose of supplying their places with political favorites.

The required examination for appointment and promotion creates an impediment in the way of those who may demand office as a reward for political partisanship, without having adequate knowledge of the duties of this peculiar branch of the public service.

Each consul must on frequent occasions be the judge of his proper line of action without aid or direction from the minister to whom he is required to report or from the Department of State. In such cases it is requisite to the honor and security of the Government that the consul should be well informed as to his duties.

The right of the President to select from the whole body of consuls any man for any place he may prefer, and to assign him to such place for duty, and to transfer him at pleasure to another place, is the full equivalent of the power of appointment to a particular office.

These functions are to be exercised in foreign countries, for the most part distant from the United States, and disconnect the incumbents from participation in our home politics.

In so far as they may be given as rewards for party services, they are a sort of pension system for men who have not been successful in getting offices at home, or who have failed of success in the usual channels of business.

The consular system should be based upon the plan of personal qualification for its important and peculiar duties, ascertained by the examination and experience of those employed in it, rather than upon the plan of selecting those for this service who have failed in other pursuits, or those who desire to go abroad for purposes of travel, recreation, or amusement.

This is the only branch of the public service that has been used, to any great extent, for the gratification of the incumbents, without regard to their capacity to render efficient service to the country, and it is time that our policy in respect of these offices was changed.

Taken in the aggregate, there is no class of representatives of our Government who can so seriously affect our commerce with other countries, in their actual and direct conduct and dealings, as our consuls and commercial agents.

We should encourage our best classes of people to qualify themselves for this important service by giving them just compensation for their work, and by securing them in these offices during good behavior.

They have much to do with the dignity of our Government, its credit in foreign lands, the honor of its flag, and the safety of its citizens.

[See pp. 40, 143, 187, 321, and pp. 119, 199, 276, Vol. VI.]

FIFTY-FOURTH CONGRESS, FIRST SESSION.

January 29, 1896.

[Senate Report No. 141.]

Mr. Morgan, from the Committee on Foreign Relations, submitted the following report:

The Congress of the United States, deeply regretting the unhappy state of hostilities existing in Cuba, which has again been the result of the demand of a large number of the native population of that island for its independence, in a spirit of respect and regard for the welfare of both countries, earnestly desires that the security of life and property and the establishment of permanent peace and of a government that is satisfactory to the people of Cuba should be accomplished.

And to the extent that the people of Cuba are seeking the rights of local self-government for domestic purposes, the Congress of the United States expresses its earnest sympathy with them. The Congress would also welcome with satisfaction the concession, by Spain, of complete sovereignty to the people of that island, and would cheerfully give to such a voluntary concession the cordial support of the United States. The near proximity of Cuba to the frontier of the United States, and the fact that it is universally regarded as a part of the continental system of America, identifies that island so closely with the political and commercial welfare of our people, that Congress can not be indifferent to the fact that civil war is flagrant among the people of Cuba.

Nor can we longer overlook the fact that the destructive character of this war is doing serious harm to the rights and interests of our people on the island, and to our lawful commerce, the protection and freedom of which is safeguarded by treaty obligations. In the recent past and in former years, when internal wars have been waged for long periods and with results that were disastrous to Cuba and injurious to Spain, the Government of the United States has always observed, with perfect faith, all of its duties toward the belligerents.

It was a difficult task thus forced upon the United States, but it was performed with vigor, impartiality, and justice, in the hope that Spain would so ameliorate the condition of the Cuban people as to give them peace, contentment, and prosperity. This desirable result has not been accomplished. Its failure has not resulted from any interference on the part of our people or Government with the people or government of Cuba.

The hospitality which our treaties, the laws of nations, and the laws of Christianity have extended to Cuban refugees in the United States has caused distrust on the part of the Spanish Government as to the fidelity of our Government to its obligations of neutrality in the frequent insurrections of the people of Cuba against Spanish authority.

This distrust has often become a source of serious annoyance to our people, and has led to a spirit of retaliation toward Spanish authority in Cuba, thus giving rise to frequent controversies between the two countries. The absence of responsible government in Cuba, with powers adequate to deal directly with questions between the people of the United States and the people and political authorities of the island, has been a frequently recurring cause of delay, protracted imprisonment, confiscations of property, and the detention of our people and their ships, often upon groundless charges, which has been a serious grievance.

When insurrections have occurred on the Island of Cuba the temptation to unlawful invasion by reckless persons has given to our Government anxiety, trouble, and much expense in the enforcement of our laws and treaty obligations of neutrality, and these occasions have been so frequent as to make these duties unreasonably onerous upon the Government of the United States.

The devastation of Cuba in the war that is now being waged, both with fire and sword, is an anxious and disturbing cause of unrest among the people of the United States, which creates strong grounds of protest against the continuance of the struggle for power between Cuba and Spain, which is rapidly changing the issue to one of existence on the part of a great number of the native population.

It is neither just to the relations that exist between Cuba and the United States, nor is it in keeping with the spirit of the age or the rights of humanity that this struggle should be protracted until one party or the other should become exhausted in the resources of men and money, thereby weakening both until they may fall a prey to some stronger power, or until the stress of human sympathy or the resentments engendered by long and bloody conflict should draw into the strife the unruly elements of neighboring countries.

This civil war, though it is great in its proportions and is conducted by armies that are in complete organization and directed and controlled by supreme military authority, has not the safeguard of a cartel for the treatment of wounded soldiers or prisoners of war.

In this feature of the warfare it becomes a duty of humanity that the civilized powers should insist upon the application of the laws of war recognized among civilized nations to both armies. As our own people are drawn into this struggle on both sides, and enter either army without the consent of our Government and in violation of our laws, their treatment when they may be wounded or captured, although it is not regulated by treaty and ceases to be a positive care of our Government, should not be left to the revengeful retaliations which expose them to the fate of pirates or other felons.

The inability of Spain to subdue the revolutionists by the measures and within the time that would be reasonable when applied to occasions of ordinary civil disturbance is a misfortune that can not be justly visited upon citizens of the United States, nor can it be considered that a state of open civil war does not exist, but that the movement is a mere insurrection and its supporters a mob of criminal violators of the law, when it is seen that it requires an army of 100,000 men and all the naval and military power of a great kingdom even to hold the alleged rebellion in check.

It is due to the situation of affairs in Cuba that Spain should recognize the existence of a state of war in the island, and should voluntarily accord to the armies opposed to her authority the rights of belligerents under the laws of nations.

The Congress of the United States, recognizing the fact that the matters herein referred to are properly within the control of the Chief Executive until, within the principles of our Constitution, it becomes the duty of Congress to define the final attitude of the Government of the United States toward Spain, presents these considerations to the President in support of the following resolution:

Resolved by the Senate (the House of Representatives concurring), That the present deplorable war in the Island of Cuba has reached a magnitude that concerns all civilized nations to the extent that it should be conducted, if unhappily it is longer to continue, on those principles and laws of warfare that are acknowledged to be obligatory upon civilized nations when engaged in open hostilities, including the treatment of captives who are enlisted in either army; due respect to cartels for exchange of prisoners and for other military purposes; truces and flags of truce; the provision of proper hospitals and hospital supplies and services to the sick and wounded of either army.

Resolved further, That this representation of the views and opinions of Congress be sent to the President; and if he concurs therein that he will, in a friendly spirit, use the good offices of this Government to the end that Spain shall be requested to accord to the armies with which it is engaged in war the rights of belligerents, as the same are recognized under the laws of nations.

FEBRUARY 5, 1896.—Mr. MORGAN, from the Committee on Foreign Relations, reported the following

CONCURRENT RESOLUTION

As a substitute for Concurrent Resolution No. 19, reported January 29, 1896:

Resolved by the Senate (the House of Representatives concurring), That, in the opinion of Congress, a condition of public war exists between the Government of Spain and the Government proclaimed and for some time maintained by force of arms by the people of Cuba; and that the United States of America should maintain a strict neutrality between the contending powers, according to each all the rights of belligerents in the ports and territory of the United States.

Mr. CAMERON, from the Committee on Foreign Relations, submitted the following as the

VIEWS OF THE MINORITY.

After the cessation of our civil war we were called upon to take notice of the struggle in Cuba against Spanish rule which broke out in October, 1868. It is said that early in the year 1869 a proclamation was actually signed by President Grant recognizing the Cubans as belligerents, although the fact was known to very few persons. This proclamation was not promulgated owing to the opposition of Secretary Fish. In December, 1869, President Grant, in his first annual message, called the attention of Congress to this struggle. He said:

> For more than a year a valuable province of Spain, and a near neighbor of ours, in whom all our people can not but feel a deep interest, has been struggling for independence and freedom. The people and Government of the United States entertain the same warm feelings and sympathies for the people of Cuba, in their pending struggle, that they manifested throughout the previous struggles between Spain and her former colonies in behalf of the latter. But the contest has at no time assumed the conditions which amount to a war in the sense of international law, or which would show the existence of a de facto political organization of the insurgents sufficient to justify a recognition of belligerents. The principle is maintained, however, that this nation is its own judge when to accord the rights of belligerency, either to a people struggling to free themselves from a government they believe to be oppressive, or to independent nations at war with each other.

He concluded that in due time Spain must find it for its interest to establish its dependency as an independent power which could then exercise its right of choice as regarded its future relations with other powers.

The Cuban war which broke out in 1868 had been in existence for only nine months when our Government felt the necessity of interference. Mr. Sickles was appointed our minister to Madrid in 1869, and instructions were given to him to submit propositions on the part of our Government, in order to bring to a close the "civil conflict" raging in Cuba. The part taken by our Government at that time in Cuban affairs is full of interest, not only as regards the engagement into which the authorities were willing to enter, but also as respects the status which the instructions gave to the Cuban conflict. Our minister was directed to impress upon the Spanish mind "the advancing growth of that sentiment which claims for every part of the American hemisphere the right of self-government and freedom from transatlantic dependence." The good offices of the United States were offered to the cabinet at Madrid for the purpose of bringing to a close "the civil war now ravaging the island of Cuba." The bases of settlement were:

1. The independence of Cuba to be acknowledged by Spain.
2. Cuba to pay Spain an indemnity for her relinquishment of all her rights in the island.
3. The abolition of slavery.
4. An armistice pending negotiations of settlement.

Our minister was also authorized to state that if Spain insisted, our Government might guarantee the payment of the indemnity by Cuba.

His attention was called particularly to the expression used in the instructions "the civil war now ravaging the island."

While this expression is not designed to grant any *public recognition* of belligerent rights to the insurgents, it is nevertheless used advisedly and in recognition of a state and condition of the contest which may not justify a much longer withholding of the concession to the revolutionary party of the recognized rights of belligerents. Should the expression, therefore, be commented upon you will admit what is above stated with reference to it, and may add, in case of a protracted discussion, or the prospect of a refusal by Spain to accept the proposed offer of the United States, that an early recognition of belligerent rights is the logical deduction from the present proposal, and will probably be deemed a necessity on the part of the United States unless the condition of the parties to the contest shall have changed very materially.

Negotiations were at once entered upon by our minister with the Spanish Government and the proposition of the United States was submitted to General Prim, the president of the council of state, who was then at the head of Spanish affairs and practically dictator in Spain. Prim asked how much Cuba would give and it was suggested that $125,000,000 might be arranged. Prim intimated that autonomy to Cuba would be conceded as soon as hostilities ceased, but that Spain could not entertain the question of the independence of Cuba as long as the Cubans were in arms against the Government. He also declined to consider the Cubans as parties to be consulted in the negotiation. He was willing to assure Cuban independence, if, after laying down their arms, the Cubans should vote for a separation, although he would not insist upon the necessity of such a vote. That for his part, if he alone were consulted, he would say to the Cubans " go, if you will; make good the treasure you have cost us, and let us bring home our army in peace, and consolidate the liberties and resources of Spain." He added that he had no doubt that whatever might be the result of the conflict Cuba would eventually be free; that he recognized without hesitation the manifest course of events on the American continent, and the inevitable termination of all colonial relations in their autonomy as soon as they were prepared for independence; but he repeated that no consideration would reconcile Spain to such a concession until hostilities ceased. His language was:

I do not flatter myself that Spain will retain possession of the island. I consider that the period of colonial autonomy has virtually arrived. However the present contest may end, whether in the suppression of the insurrection, or in the better way of an amicable arrangement through the assistance of the United States, it is equally clear to me that the time has come for Cuba to govern herself; and if we succeed in putting down the insurrection to-morrow, I shall regard the subject in the same light, that the child has attained its majority and should be allowed to direct its own affairs. We want nothing more than to get out of Cuba, but it must be done in a dignified and honorable manner.

Our Government saw the futility of accepting the conditions suggested by Spain. They recognized that nothing could be effected by a plebiscite and that the Cubans could not be induced to lay down their arms and trust the Spaniards to carry out their promises. Moreover, while the negotiations were in progress the public became informed of them. Immediately a great excitement arose, communicated by the press, which disinclined the Spanish administration to pursue the matter, and our Government, finding itself unable to effect any good purpose, withdrew its offer of mediation.

Mr. Sickles wrote Mr. Fish that Spain deprecated the expression of the sympathy of the Government and people of the United States for the cause of the revolutionists, as well as the President's declaration of the right of the Government of the United States to determine when it may rightfully proclaim its neutrality in the conflict between a

colony struggling for independence and the parent state. It is remarkable, was the comment of Mr. Sickles, that in all these discussions the
fact is overlooked that Spain conceded the rights of belligerents to the
Confederates without waiting for the outbreak of hostilities—

The Queen's proclamation of June, 1861, is forgotten; and the large and profitable
commerce carried on between Havana and the blockaded ports of the South in enemies' ships, which changed their flags in Cuban waters is quite ignored.

On the failure of negotiations, the logical result of our action was to
recognize the Cubans as belligerents engaged in a "civil war." As
was said by Secretary Fish, the mere offer on our part to mediate as
between the contending forces was in itself a concession of belligerency
and a recognition of that condition. But for various reasons this
argument was not pressed by our Government. Although from month
to month the aggressiveness of the revolutionists increased and their
power extended. our Government, speaking through the State Department and the President, continued to inform the country that the
Cubans had not reached such a condition as entitled them to be recognized as belligerents, although the administration had already in
instructions to our own minister to Spain recognized that condition at
a time when the revolution had hardly attained any headway.

One of the reasons for this inconsistency was the expectation felt
by our Government that Spain would voluntarily concede to the Cubans
much that they were struggling for. Liberal ministries succeded one
another in Spain, each of which was more liberal than its predecessor
in *promises* of reform and recognition of the rights of the Cubans.
Civil war broke out in Spain, and its Government became involved in
such difficulties that ours was loath to press the subject of Cuba, or to
insist upon a speedy solution of the question. Mr. Fish was irritated
by the operations of the Cuban junta in this country, which at times
infringed our neutrality laws. He thought they should have confined
their activity to sending to the insurgents arms and munitions of war,
which he says they might have done "consistently with our own statutes
and with the law of nations." At home the Federal Administration
had to deal with the pressing question of the reconstruction of the
South. The negro problem in this country was of such importance
that the Administration had no desire to add difficulties by undertaking
to settle the negro question in Cuba.

The action of our Government was in striking contrast to that of
Spain in recognizing the Confederates as belligerents. Mr. Fish refers
to this in a letter to Senor Roberts, the Spanish minister, in 1869:

The civil war in Cuba has continued for a year; battle after battle has been fought;
thousands of lives have been sacrificed, and the result is still in suspense. But the
United States have hitherto resisted the considerations which in 1861 controlled the
action of Spain and determined her to act upon the occurrence of a single bloodless
conflict of arms and within sixty days from its date.

Six years later, in 1875, this Government was again on the point of
intervening. In a dispatch from Mr. Fish, Secretary of State, to Mr.
Cushing, then minister to Spain, the Secretary said that the condition
of Cuba was the one great cause of perpetual solicitude in the foreign
relations of the United States. He informed the minister that the
President did not meditate the annexation of Cuba to the United States
but its elevation as an independent republic—

The desire of independence [the Secretary says] on the part of the Cubans is a
natural and legitimate aspiration of theirs, because they are Americans. That the
ultimate issue of events in Cuba will be its independence, however that issue may be
produced, whether by means of negotiation, or as the result of military operations,
or of one of those unexpected incidents which so frequently determine the fate of

nations, it is impossible to doubt. If there be one lesson in history more cogent in its teachings than any other, it is that no part of America large enough to constitute a self-sustaining state, can be permanently held in forced colonial subjection to Europe. Complete separation between the metropolis and its colony may be postponed by the former conceding to the latter a greater or less degree of local autonomy, nearly approaching to independence. But in all cases where a positive antagonism has come to exist between the mother country and its colonial subjects, where the sense of oppression is strongly felt by the latter, and especially where years of relentless warfare have alienated the parties one from another more widely than they are sundered by the ocean itself, their political separation is inevitable. It is one of those conclusions which have been aptly called the inexorable logic of events.

Thus we have shown that already, in 1869, when the revolution of the preceding year had attained but inconsiderable proportions, President Grant expressed his firm conviction that the ultimate result of the struggle for independence would be to break the bonds which attached Cuba as a colony to Spain. President Grant announced the determination of our Government to intervene if the struggle in Cuba was not speedily terminated. It was pointed out that while the Spanish authorities insisted that a state of war did not exist in Cuba, and that no rights as belligerents should be accorded to the revolutionists, they at the same time demanded for themselves all the rights and privileges which flowed from actual and acknowledged war. That Cuba exhibited a chronic condition of turbulence and rebellion was due to the system pursued by Spain and the want of harmony between the inhabitants of the island and the governing class. That should it become necessary for this Government to intervene it would be moved by the necessity for a proper regard to its own protection and its own interests and the interests of humanity.

The inhuman manner in which the war was waged, and the shocking executions of natives and citizens of this country made an impression of horror on the world.

The nicest sense of international requirements can not fail to perceive that provocation from Spain was overlooked by our Government for a longer period and with greater patience than any other Government of equal power would have tolerated. A writer in the London Times, in 1875, reflecting upon the possibility of Spain's overcoming the then insurrection, and on the prospect of our interference, said:

Were Cuba as near to Cornwall as it is to Florida we should certainly look more sharply to matters of fact than to the niceties of international law. But everything, we repeat, depends upon these matters of fact. If Spain can suppress the insurrection and prevent Cuba from becoming a permanent source of mischief to neighboring countries, she has the fullest right to keep it. But she is on her trial, and that trial can not be long. When she is made to clearly understand that the tenure of her rule over Cuba depends upon her ability to make that rule a reality, she will not be slow to show what she can do, *and the limits of her power will be the limits of her right.*

In 1869 Gen. Martinez Campos, the greatest soldier Spain possessed, was sent to Cuba to make a final effort to bring hostilities there to a termination. He was not only a great soldier but was believed to be a great administrator, and had the respect of all parties on account of his patriotism and integrity. He was afforded all the aid in the way of men and money which Spain could furnish. In 1878 he succeeded in the so-called pacification, for which service he was raised to the highest pinnacle in Spain and made prime minister. He did not conquer the insurgents but induced them to lay down their arms on conditions of peace which, as the Spanish administrator, he undertook for his Government should be faithfully carried out. A treaty of peace was negotiated with the leaders of the revolution. In 1879 General Campos wrote a long dispatch to his Government from the seat of his triumph, which at this day is extremely interesting, owing to the fact that the present war owes its origin to the same circumstances as caused the former outbreak. In this dispatch, stating the particulars of the pacification, General Campos gave an extended review of the situation in Cuba, and of the terms of the treaty of peace and the negotiations which led thereto. This recital shows that General Campos believed, as was afterwards said by our minister, James Russell Lowell, that the reforms he stipulated were necessary if Cuba was to be retained as a dependency of Spain, and, Mr. Lowell remarked, all intelligent Spaniards admitted that the country could not afford another war. As a reason for according conditions to the Cubans General Campos sketched the motives of his policy:

Since the year 1869, when I landed on this island with the first reinforcements, I was preoccupied with the idea that the insurrection here, though acknowledging as its cause the hatred of Spain, yet this hatred was due to the causes that have separated our colonies from the mother country, augmented in the present case by the promises made to the Antillas at different times (1812, 1837, and 1845), promises which not only have not been fulfilled, but, as I understand, have not been permitted to be so by the Cortes when at different times their execution had been begun.

While the island had no great development, its aspirations were confined by love of nationality and respect for authority; but when one day after another passed without hopes being satisfied, but, on the contrary, the greater freedom permitted now and then by a governor was more than canceled by his successor; when they were convinced that the colony went on in the same way; when bad officials and a worse administration of justice more and more aggravated difficulties; when the provincial governorships, continually growing worse, fell at last into the hands of men without training or education, petty tyrants who could practice their thefts and sometimes their oppressions, because of the distance at which they resided from the supreme authority, public opinion, until then restrained, began vehemently to desire those liberties which, if they bring much good, contain also some evil. * * *

The 10th of October, 1868, came to open men's eyes; the eruption of the volcano in which so many passions, so many hatreds, just and unjust, had been heaped up was terrible, and almost at the outset the independence of Cuba was proclaimed.

He showed the gains speedily made by the insurgents and the advantages they had by reason of the familiarity with the country, so that "they defeated large columns with hardly a battalion of men. They almost put us on the defensive, and as we had to guard an immense property the mission of the army became very difficult." He recounted his efforts to reestablish the principle of authority, but said that he had against him a "public spirit without life. Nobody had higher aspirations than to save his crop of sugar. In official regions the enemy was thought inferior, but the commanders generally believed it unsafe to operate with less than three battalions; there was no venturing beyond the highways." He said little was gained by beating the enemy. What he needed was to exterminate them and that he could not do. That had his responsibility been free of the Cortes and the Government he would in the beginning have ventured everything to secure peace—the disembargo of estates, a general pardon, the assimilation of Cuba with Spain, orders to treat prisoners well, and to show that this was not weakness but strength there was "the argument of his *one hundred thousand bayonets.*" He finally related the terms by which he induced the Cubans to lay down their arms. All desired reforms were promised. Municipal law, the law of provincial assemblies, and representation in the Cortes should be established; the jurisdiction of the courts defined, tax laws settled, the form of contribution and assessments determined, schools established, the people to be consulted through their representative as to all these reforms and others, and they were not to be left to the will of the captain-general or the head of a department. This summary is sufficient to indicate what was stipulated between the parties. Said General Campos:

I do not wish to make a momentary peace; I desire that this peace be the beginning of a bond of common interest between Spain and her Cuban provinces, and that this bond be drawn closer by the identity of aspirations and the good faith of both. Let not the Cubans be considered as pariahs or children, but put on an equality with other Spaniards in every thing not inconsistent with their present condition. Perhaps [he concluded] the insurgents would have accepted promises less liberal and more vague than those set forth in this condition; but even had this been done, it would have been but a brief postponement, because those liberties are destined to come for the reasons already given, with the difference that Spain now shows herself magnanimous, satisfying just aspirations which she might deny, and a little later, probably very soon, would have been obliged to grant them, compelled by the force of ideas and of the age. Moreover, she has promised over and over again to enter on the path of assimilation, and if the promise were more vague, even though the fulfillment of this promise were begun, these people would have a right to doubt our good faith, and to show a distrust unfortunately warranted by the failings of human nature itself. The not adding another one hundred thousand to the one hundred thousand families that mourn their sons slain in this pitiless war, and the cry of peace that will resound in the hearts of the eighty thousand mothers who have sons in Cuba or liable to conscription, would be a full equivalent for the payment of a debt of justice.

This debt of justice has not yet been paid.

The highest Spanish authorities have been obliged to confess that the grievances of the Cubans are just and their aspirations for liberty legitimate.

Marshal Serrano, in his official report to the Spanish Government of the 10th of May, 1867, said:

We are forced to acknowledge that in the last years the treasury of Cuba has been used abusively, which is partly the cause of the crisis the islands go through now and of the exhaustion of its resources.

Castelar, in 1873, while president, endeavored to convince Spain of the necessity of making reforms demanded alike by "humanity and civilization," and he deplored making Cuba a "transatlantic Poland." In 1874 our minister to Spain informed our Government that the entire unwillingness of Spain to do anything toward the amelioration of Cuba was shown by the fact that all the governments since the breaking out of the revolution in 1868 had promised to reform the administration, but that the situation of the island was worse than ever. And Secretary Fish informed the Spanish Government that most of the evils of which Cuba was the scene were the necessary results of harsh treatment and of the maladministration of the colonial government.

In 1875 Mr. Cushing, then minister to Madrid, communicated to our Government a large amount of evidence from Spanish sources showing the demoralization existing in the administration in Cuba. The Spanish journals of that date openly informed the central government that war in Cuba could never be ended until the vices of the ultra-marine administration were corrected and its moral tone raised. Spain was exhorted to make one supreme effort for the pacification of Cuba and its moralization. "The journals of all shades of opinion speak of the official corruption," said Mr. Cushing, "and peculations of the public employees in Cuba as a eature of the situation not less calamitous than the insurrection." He remarked that the burden of taxation had become intolerable, aggravated as it was by the frauds and wastes committed by almost everybody connected with the collection or expenditure of the public moneys; that the abuses of administration, of which so much was being said at that time, were old, chronic, deep-rooted, *and impossible of eradication under the colonial régime.* "It would seem that each of the ephemeral parties on attaining power, with a crowd of eager partisans behind it like troops of howling wolves, shakes off as many as it can upon Cuba."

Notwithstanding that the public press did not cease to advise the Government that the immorality of the public administration of the island offered a vast field to censure, nothing was done to improve its condition. It was thought by the central government that it was only necessary by force to save Cuba to Spain. It was common remark, however, that the Government ought to sustain two campaigns in Cuba—one against insurrection and the other against corruption. Said Mr. Cushing:

So merely mercenary and so regardless of duty and the public weal are many of the public officers who go out to the island as to cause the saying to become current that on embarking they leave all sense of shame behind them in Cadiz.

And he observed that all testimony was unanimous as to the corruptions and the embezzlements of the administrations of Cuba.

The testimony of Mr. Cushing is of the most convincing character, as he has never been accused of being unfriendly to Spain. That he did not draw a too highly colored picture of Spanish misrule is shown by the declaration of the minister of transmarine affairs at Madrid, in an official paper quoted by Mr. Fish in 1874:

A deplorable and pertinacious tradition of despotism which, if it could ever be justified, is without a shadow of reason at the present time, intrusted the direction and management of our colonial establishment to the agents of the metropolis, destroying, by their dominant and exclusive authority, the vital energies of the country and the creative and productive activity of free individuals. And although the system may now have improved in some of its details, the domineering action of the authorities being less felt, it still appears full of the original error, which is upheld by the force of tradition, and the necessary influence of interests created under their protection. A change of system, political as well as administrative, is therefore imperatively demanded.

It is needless to say no such change has been made.

The Spanish Government to-day in Cuba is of the same character as it was when Richard Henry Dana visited the Island in 1854, "an armed monarchy encamped in the midst of a disarmed and disfranchised people; an unmixed despotism of one nation over another." Dana warned the public against the testimony of Americans and other foreigners engaged in business in Cuba as to the condition of affairs there:

Of all classes of persons I know of none whose situation is more unfavorable to the growth and development of sentiments of patriotism and philanthropy and of interest in the future of a race than foreigners temporarily resident, for purposes of money making only, in a country with which they have nothing in common in the future or the past. This class is often called *impartial*. I do not agree to the use of that term. They are indeed free from the bias of feeling or sentiment, but they are subject to the attractions of interest. It is for their immediate advantage to preserve peace and the existing order of things.

That the condition of Cuba had not improved prior to the present war is shown by a report of our consul-general at Havana to the State Department in 1885. This stated that the entire population, with the exception of the official class, was living under a tyranny unparalleled at this day on the globe:

There is a system of oppression and torture which enters into every phase of life, eats into the soul of every Cuban, mortifies, injures, and insults him every hour, impoverishes him and his family from day to day, threatens the rich man with bankruptcy and the poor man with beggary. The exactions of the Spanish Government and the illegal outrages of its officers are in fact intolerable. They have reduced the island to despondency and ruin.   *   *   *   The Government at Madrid is directly answerable for the misery of Cuba and for the rapacity and venality of its subordinates.   *   *   *   No well-informed Spaniard imagines that Cuba will long continue to submit to this tyranny, or at least that she will long be able to yield this harvest to her oppressors. Spain cares nothing whatever for the interests, the prosperity, or the sufferings of her colony. The Government does almost nothing to ameliorate any of the evils of the country. The police are everywhere insufficient and inefficient. The roads are no roads at all. Every interest which might enrich and improve the island is looked upon by the officials as one more mine to exploit. * * * Cuba is held solely for the benefit of Spain and Spanish interests, for the sake of Spanish adventurers. Against this all rebel in thought and feeling if not yet in fact and deed. * * * They wish protection from the grasping rapacity of Spain and see no way to attain it except by our aid.

He concluded, that from the general misery, war must ensue, of such a savage character that the world would be shocked, and the United States would be compelled from sheer humanity to interfere and save a country which Spain would be unable either to control or to preserve. He had learned from many quarters that in any future attempt to change the condition of affairs all the inhabitants would go hand in hand; "it is generally understood that the permanent white population is of one mind."

While some of the reforms stipulated for by the Cubans and engaged to be carried out by General Campos in 1879 were nominally granted, they were all substantially withheld. The central government did not feel itself bound after the cessation of hostilities was secured to perform the conditions by which that result was brought about. Our consul-general reported (1885) "that the island is worse governed than at any previous period of its history."

Cuba it was determined must pay the entire cost of the war. At the time when the fostering care of the Government was most needed to heal the wounds inflicted by the war, when every interest was prostrate and every business suffering, new and enormous taxes were imposed. * * * A war tax of the most exaggerated character was laid. Every business, trade, art, or profession is taxed in the proportion of from 25 to 33⅓ per cent of its net income. * * * All ordinary mercantile business and all the petty trades and employments of the country are separately suffering. All participate in the common distress.

He stated that the absolute legal tax imposed on the island was only a part of what the wretched and impoverished inhabitants were compelled to pay.

It is a matter of notoriety that illegal charges are constantly made and then taken off for a bribe. The hordes of officials who batten like hungry beasts on the vitals of Cuba make no pretense of honesty except on paper. The highest officers, when they chance to be better than their subordinates, admit the character of their inferiors; more often they share it. * * * The present state of things can not continue. Some change amounting almost to revolution is inevitable. What with governmental oppression and illegal tyranny, emancipation, brigandage, low prices for sugar and high taxes on everything, the ruin of the island is already almost consummated. She is absolutely incapacitated for rendering the revenue demanded or supporting the army of officials who keep her prostrate in her agony.

Shortly after Mr. Blaine became Secretary of State, in the administration of President Harrison, it was the subject of consideration whether Spain could be induced to acknowledge Cuba as independent should the United States agree to guarantee the sum to be paid by Cuba for the relinquishment of all Spanish rights in the island This movement was made by the sugar planters and it was thought that the entire sugar interest would support it. Mr. Blaine announced himself warmly in favor of the project, but after long conferences it was ascertained that the consent of Spain could not be obtained.

In truth, the pacification effected by Martinez Campos in 1878 was hardly efficient even as a truce. The reports of our consular agents, the testimony of travelers, the avowals made in the Spanish press, and the constant evidence almost daily recurring in the Cuban press, show that between 1878 and 1895 Cuba enjoyed little peace or repose. Brigandage, which was merely one form of public discontent, never ceased. Only the presence of a very large Spanish army prevented organized war.

The danger and the scandal of the Cuban situation have been such as can be compared with nothing but the condition of Armenia. So serious did they become, and so imminent was the peril, that in 1894–95 the Spanish Government at last adopted measures looking to the partial satisfaction of Cuban demands. These measures we need not discuss. They were held by the old insurgent party to be illusory and deceptive. Another attempt at independence was decided upon, and in February, 1895, the present "sanguinary and fiercely conducted war" broke out, "in some respects more active than the last preceding revolt." In thus characterizing the situation in Cuba as a state of war, President Cleveland, like Secretary Fish, has cleared the subject of all preliminary doubts. A state of war exists in Cuba. With that, and with that alone, we have to deal.

The precedents are clear, and if our action were to be decided by precedent alone, we should not be able to hesitate. The last great precedent was that of the civil war which broke out in the United States in the spring of 1861. In that instance, without waiting for the outbreak of actual hostilities, further than the bloodless attack on Fort Sumter and its surrender, April 13, 1861, the British Government issued its proclamation of neutrality on the 13th of May following, before it had received official information that war existed, except as a blockade of certain insurgent ports. The French Government acted in concert with Great Britain, but delayed the official announcement until June. The Spanish Government issued its proclamation of belligerency June 17; and the first battle of our war was not fought until July 21, or known at Madrid until August.

In this great instance the outbreak of insurrection and the recognition of belligerency were simultaneous. The United States protested against the precipitancy of the act, and have never admitted its justice or legality. Neither in 1869 nor in 1895 did the President enforce the precedent against Spain in regard to the insurrection in Cuba. Not even in 1875, when the insurgents held possession of a great part of the island and seacoast, with no restraint but the blockade, did the United States recognize their belligerency.

Yet belligerency is a question of fact, and if declared at all it should be declared whenever the true character of neutrality requires it or the exigencies of law need it. The nature of such action may be political or legal or both. As a political act, impartiality requires that belligerency should be recognized whenever, existing in fact, its denial is equivalent to taking part with one of the belligerents against the other. In such cases the unrecognized belligerent has just ground for complaint. The moral support of the neutral government is given wholly to its opponent. That the Cuban insurgents were belligerents in fact as early as 1869 was expressly stated by Mr. Fish when he explained the meaning he attached to his phrase regarding "the civil war now ravaging the island." The word war in such conditions necessarily implies the fact of belligerency. President Cleveland, in his annual message of last month, informs us that the present war is more active than the preceding one.

Nevertheless, our Government has still refrained from what Mr. Fish called "any public recognition of belligerent rights to the insurgents." No legal necessity arose to require it, and the political exigency was not absolute. Yet, after the victory of Bayamo in the month of July last, when the insurgents defeated and nearly captured the captain-general, Martinez Campos, and gained military possession of the whole eastern half of the island, the fact of their belligerency was established, and if further evidence was needed it was fully given by the subsequent victory at Coliseo on the 24th of December, when the insurgents drove the captain-general back to Havana and gained military control of the western provinces.

If the Government of the United States still refrained from recognizing the belligerency of the insurgents after this conclusive proof of the *fact*, the reason doubtless was that in the absence of any legal complications the question became wholly political, and that its true solution must lie not in a recognition of belligerency, but in a recognition of independence.

In 1875, when the situation was very far from being as serious as it is now, President Grant, after long consideration of the difficulties involved in public action, decided against the recognition of belligerency as an act which might be delusive to the insurgents and would certainly be regarded as unfriendly by Spain. He decided upon a middle course. The documents above quoted show that he proposed to the Spanish Government a sort of intervention which should establish the independence of Cuba by a friendly agreement. In doing so he not only necessarily recognized both parties to the conflict as on an equal plane, but he also warned Spain that, if such mediation should not be accepted, direct intervention would probably be deemed a necessity on the part of the United States.

Spain preferred to promise to the insurgents terms so favorable as to cause for a time the cessation of hostilities. Since then twenty years have passed. The insurrection, far from having ceased, has taken the proportions of a war almost as destructive to our own citizens as to the contending parties. The independence of Cuba was then regarded by the President of the United States as the object of his intervention, and has now become far more inevitable than it was then. Evidently the Government of the United States can do no less than to take up the subject precisely where President Grant left it, and to resume the friendly mediation which he actually began, with all the consequences which necessarily would follow its rejection.

Confident that no other action than this accords with our friendly relations with Spain, our just sympathy with the people of Cuba, and with our own dignity and consistency, I recommend the following resolution to the consideration of the Senate:

Resolved, That the President is hereby requested to interpose his friendly offices with the Spanish Government for the recognition of the independence of Cuba.

FIFTY-FOURTH CONGRESS, FIRST SESSION.

April 29, 1896.

[Senate Report No. 821.]

Mr. Sherman, from the Committee on Foreign Relations, submitted the following report:

The Committee on Foreign Relations have considered the proposed amendment to the bill (H. R. 8293) "making appropriations to supply deficiencies in the appropriations for the fiscal year ending June 30, 1896, and for prior years, and for other purposes," appropriating $5,000, or so much thereof as may be necessary, to remove from the State of Montana, and to deliver to the Canadian authorities at the international boundary line, the refugee Canadian Cree Indians, and recommend the passage of the same.

The recommendation of the Secretary of State, with accompanying papers, is herewith submitted.

DEPARTMENT OF STATE,
Washington, April 29, 1896.

SIR: I have the honor to acknowledge yours of the 29th instant.

House Ex. Doc. No. 341, Fiftieth Congress, first session, shows the circumstances under which the Canadian Cree Indians first crossed the boundary line of the State of Montana and something of their history since that time. Your remaining inquiries will, I believe, be fully answered by certain correspondence, copies of which are hereto annexed.

It will be observed that the Canadian authorities have now for the second time agreed to accept and take charge of these refugee Indians upon their being delivered to them at the frontier. A third offer of the same kind can hardly be expected, and in my judgment it would be a great mistake if the present favorable disposition of the Canadian authorities were not at once availed of. The number of Indians to be deported is said to now amount to something like 500.

Undoubtedly they can be removed by the President, with such aid from the Army as may be necessary, more expeditiously and cheaply than any other way. But he is at present without any authority to take any steps in the matter and without any funds to meet the necessary expenditures. I recommend, therefore, that you obtain appropriate legislation, if practicable, either by independent bill or resolution, or by some amendment to an appropriation bill. The legislation should expressly authorize the President to remove and deliver the Indians, with the aid of the Army, if necessary, and should appropriate a sum not exceeding $5,000 to defray the necessary charges.

I am, very truly, yours,   RICHARD OLNEY.

Hon. THOMAS H. CARTER,
United States Senate.

THE STATE OF MONTANA, EXECUTIVE OFFICE,
Helena, January 21, 1896.

SIR: This office has had previous correspondence with the Department of State in relation to the presence of a number of Cree Indians in our State. These Indians, as you may know, are wards of the British Government, and generally referred to as refugees of the Riel rebellion. In default of a reservation and the restrictions of the Federal Government they have become an intolerable nuisance, constantly violating our game laws, foraging upon our herds, and not infrequently looting isolated cabins. The patience of our people has been sorely tried, and I have at times feared that bloodshed would result. The police power of the State is not equal to the task of protecting the people from these marauding bands. This condition of affairs can not be allowed to continue indefinitely.

I desire to call your attention to the very serious fact that the number of these Crees in our State is increasing very rapidly through accessions annually from their relatives in Canada.

Investigation shows that only about 100 of them crossed our border as refugees at the close of the Riel rebellion.

In a letter bearing date November 1, 1887, from J. D. C. Atkins, Commissioner of Indian Affairs, addressed to the Secretary of the Interior, he said: "The fugitives number about 200—men, women, and children." I learn from a conference with their chief, "Little White Bear," that they number now about 500. Hence we should not only get rid of these now annoying us, but prevent others from coming.

The question of supreme importance is the adoption of some plan by which these Indians can be deported across the boundary line to the British Possessions from whence they came.

Let me indulge the hope that you can in some manner afford us relief in this matter.

I have the honor to be, yours, very respectfully,

J. E. RICKARDS, *Governor of Montana.*

Hon. RICHARD OLNEY,
Secretary of State, Washington, D. C.

DEPARTMENT OF STATE, *January 30, 1896.*

SIR: I have the honor to acknowledge the receipt of your letter of the 21st instant, relative to making arrangements for the removal of certain British Cree Indians from Montana to the Dominion of Canada.

In reply, I inclose for your information a copy of a note to this Department, dated April 6, 1892, from the British ambassador at this capital, from which it appears that the authorities of the Dominion of Canada were then willing to receive the above-named Indians. A copy of the note was sent to your predecessor, but the Department is not informed as to why it was not acted upon at that time.

The Department has now recalled the subject to the attention of the British embassy with the request that the authorities of the Dominion of Canada may be informed of your readiness to deliver the Indians to them, and that this Government may be informed as to when and where Her Majesty's authorities will be ready to receive them.

The Department expects an early response to its inquiries, and it is hoped that the authorities of Montana will be prepared to take prompt action if a favorable reply shall be received from the embassy.

I have the honor to be, sir, your obedient servant,

RICHARD OLNEY.

The GOVERNOR OF MONTANA,
Helena, Mont.

STATE OF MONTANA, EXECUTIVE OFFICE,
Helena, April 8, 1896.

SIR: I have the honor to inclose herewith communication received from the honorable commissioner of Indian affairs, Northwest Territories, relative to the matter of the removal of the Cree Indians from the State of Montana. Your attention is called to the willingness of the Canadian Government to receive these Indians provided they are delivered to its agents no later than the 10th of May at Coutts Station, on the Great Falls and Canada Railway. This being an international matter the authority to deliver these Indians to the Canadian authorities rests wholly in the Federal Government, and does not repose in the State of Montana. I earnestly request that your Department take up this matter with the Canadian authorities with a view to acting on the plan proposed by the commissioner, and see that the Cree Indians are delivered as suggested.

With great respect, yours, very truly,

J. E. RICKARDS, *Governor of Montana.*

The SECRETARY OF STATE,
Washington, D. C.

OFFICE COMMISSIONER OF INDIAN AFFAIRS,
NORTHWEST TERRITORIES,
Regina, April 1, 1896.

SIR: With reference to negotiations which have recently been pending between the United States Federal authorities and the Government of the Dominion of Canada relative to the removal from the State of Montana of certain refugee Cree Indians who entered the territory of that State during and since the Canadian Northwest rebellion of 1885, I have the honor to inform you that the Dominion Government having decided to cooperate with that of Washington in bringing about this end, I have been instructed to place myself in communication with you for this purpose.

I should therefore be pleased to learn whether your arrangements for the delivery of these persons at the international boundary will admit of such being done not later than, say, May 10 next, and at Coutts Station, on the Great Falls and Canada Railway. I may say that if you can secure their being brought to that point by rail it will very greatly facilitate the transfer being effectively made, as I would take them on immediately by the same train to Lethbridge, a distance of about 50 miles toward the interior, thus minimizing the chance of straggling parties breaking away from the main body and returning secretly to the South.

We are desirous of effecting the transfer at the earliest possible date, in order that they may be distributed to their various reserves in time for agricultural operations.

In conclusion I would invite your attention to the fact that not a few of those who passed from this country to your territory as Indians have during the interval changed their status by legal process provided by laws of the Dominion governing the discharge of half-breeds from our Indian treaties. Many of these persons are now therefore not Indians in the eye of the law, as while residing abroad they applied for, through attorneys, and received from the Dominion Government, certificates of the termination of their disabilities as treaty Indians. These persons having now resided for ten years (more or less) on United States soil (principally in Choteau County, Mont., I believe), it is assumed that it is not the intention of the United States Government to disturb them.

I send you, under separate cover, a map which may be of service to you in this connection.

I have the honor to be, sir, your obedient servant,

A. E. FORGET, *Commissioner.*

The GOVERNOR OF THE STATE OF MONTANA,
Helena, Mont., United States of America.

BRITISH EMBASSY,
Washington, April 23, 1896.

SIR: With reference to your note, No. 309, of January 30 last, relative to the desirability of effecting the removal of certain Cree Indians from Montana to Canadian territory, I have the honor to inform you that I am in receipt of a dispatch from the Governor-General of Canada, expressing the willingness of his Government to cooperate with the State authorities for that purpose.

His excellency states that when the necessary arrangements have been made, the Canadian department of Indian affairs will communicate with the governor of Montana as to the manner and time to be appointed for the removal of the Indians.

I have the honor to be, with the highest consideration, sir,

Your most obedient, humble servant,

JULIAN PAUNCEFOTE.

Hon. R. OLNEY, etc.

[House Ex. Doc. No. 341, Fiftieth Congress, first session.]

DEPARTMENT OF THE INTERIOR,
Washington, May 31, 1888.

SIR: I am in receipt of a communication from the Commissioner of Indian Affairs, dated April 18, 1888, calling my attention to the condition of the Cree Indians now near Fort Assinniboine, Mont. In this communication he requests that he be authorized to instruct the agent that these Indians be allowed to come to the agency at Fort Belknap, Mont., and to cultivate such land as they may require to support themselves, and that the agent render them such assistance as he will be able to give without injury to the welfare of his own Indians.

I question my authority to comply with this request in the absence of Congressioual action, and I now submit the information in relation to the condition of these Indians in the possession of this Department, in order that Congress may, by legislation, give such authority as it may consider proper in regard to the matter.

In October, 1885, this Department received official information that a band of British Cree Indians, then stated as numbering about 137 souls, had crossed the international boundary line and were located near the Fort Belknap Agency, Mont. They had in their possession property, the character of which clearly indicated that they had been engaged in the then recent outbreak in the British Possessions known as the "Riel rebellion."

This information was laid before the Department of State with the suggestion that some arrangements be made with the Dominion authorities for the return of these Indians to their homes in the British territory. The Secretary of State replied that unless there should be a specific demand from the Dominion authorities, the Indians can not be returned by the United States to Canada, nor can the United States authorities, civil or military, properly connive at their being kidnaped and sent over the line.

On April 26, 1886, the Commissioner of Indian Affairs called the attention of the Department to the destitute condition of these Indians, and requested decision whether the $50,000 appropriated by act of March 3, 1885 (23 Stat. L., 379), for relieving distress among Indians not having treaty funds, etc., is applicable for the purchase of supplies for them. The Department in reply directed that the facts in the case be reported, and a clause prepared to be submitted to Congress asking for a special appropriation for the purpose. The report and estimate for $5,000 were sent to the Secretary of the Treasury May 3, 1886, for presentation to Congress. Copies were subsequently, on July 2, 1886, sent by this Department to the Senate and House Committees on Indian Affairs, but no appropriation was made. January 24, 1887, War Department reported a deplorable condition of a portion of these Crees then camped on South Fork of the Sun River, Montana, and urged relief for them; whereupon the Commissioner of Indian Affairs recommended that $1,000 be taken from the "distress fund" of $50,000 above referred to. This was submitted by the Department to the President, requesting his authority to so use the amount stated from that fund, and was approved by him February 11, 1887. The War Department was then requested to furnish the Indians with such supplies as were necessary to relieve distress among them, and reimbursement was made out of the $1,000.

On December 2 1887, the President was requested, on recommendation of the Commissioner of Indian Affairs, to authorize a further expenditure of $3,000 from the "distress fund" above referred to for relief of these Indians; approved December 3, 1887. The relief was afforded by the War Department and reimbursement made as in previous case.

There has been reimbursed to the War Department to this date, for supplies furnished those Indians under the authorities above granted, the sum of $3,374.25.

The commanding officer at Fort Assinniboine, Mont., in report herewith, of February 4, 1888, urges that some disposition be made of these Indians now encamped near that post, numbering 160 souls; says that they have been fed under the direction of the military during winter months; that they earn their living by working and hunting during the summer months; that they are workers, eager to have land assigned to them for cultivation, and have some knowledge of soil tillage; and says the agent at Fort Belknap has signified his willingness to receive and assist these Indians.

General Ruger, commanding the Department of Dakota, in forwarding the report above referred to, says that the Indians should either be compelled to go north of the boundary line or be assigned to the care, if temporarily only, of some agency.

The Commissioner of Indian Affairs, in report of April 18, 1888, while recognizing that the refugees are not native Indians and have no rights on any of our Indian reservations, thinks that humanity demands that they be given a chance to earn their bread, which he says is all they ask. He recommends, as before stated, that he be authorized to direct the Fort Belknap agent to allow them to come to that agency and cultivate as much land as may be required to support themselves, and to render them such assistance as he may be able to give without injury to the welfare of the Indians belonging to that agency; thinks it may be proper that they be informed that they will acquire no rights in or to the soil by reason of the privilege extended to them.

In 1862, when a portion of the Sioux tribe fled to Canada after the Indian massacre in Minnesota, the Canadian Government assigned them to a reservation within her territory, and while since then she has endeavored to persuade them to return to the United States, they still continue to occupy, with the consent of that Government, the reservation set apart for them. I allude to this to show the action of that Government in dealing with Indians from the United States who had fled to her territory under circumstances similar to those which induced the Cree Indians to flee to the United States.

This band of Cree Indians doubtless is to remain, unless forcibly driven across the border, and even if so driven, will probably return.

I am impressed that some Congressional action should be had without delay to enable this Department to deal with this problem. It is therefore respectfully suggested that authority be granted to place them on lands of some of our own Indians who are willing to receive them, if such can be found; and if not, to set apart a small reservation for their temporary benefit, and that the sum of $5,000 be appropriated to be used, as far as necessary, to relieve any destitution which may exist among them during the next fiscal year.

For the information of Congress I send herewith a letter from Col. E. S. Otis, Twentieth Infantry, indorsed by Brig. Gen. Thomas H. Ruger; also two letters from the Commissioner of Indian Affairs, dated, respectively, November 1, 1887, and April 18, 1888, all relating to this subject.

I have the honor to be, very respectfully,

WM. F. VILAS, *Secretary.*

The SPEAKER OF THE HOUSE OF REPRESENTATIVES.

DEPARTMENT OF THE INTERIOR, OFFICE OF INDIAN AFFAIRS,
Washington, April 18, 1888.

SIR: I have the honor to return herewith the report of Col. E. S. Otis, commanding the post of Fort Assinniboine, Mont.—bearing indorsements of the department (Dakota) and division (Missouri) commanders—which was received here by your reference March 1, 1888, regarding the British Cree refugees who fled to this country after the Riel rebellion, and who, it appears, are now encamped near Fort Assinniboine.

The history of this little band of refugees is so well known to the Department as to need no recital.

Colonel Otis thinks that they ought to be placed at some agency and assisted. He speaks in praise of them; says they are workers and eager to have land assigned to them; that they have some knowledge of tillage, and would under favorable conditions raise enough to meet their wants; that they would set a good example to other Indians and be a positive benefit to them; and furthermore, that the agent at Fort Belknap has signified to him his willingness to receive and assist them at his agency.

I am aware that these refugees are not native Indians of the United States, nor have they any rights on any of our Indian reservations, but as a simple act of humanity I think they should be given a chance to earn their bread when that is really all that they ask. They have been wandering about from place to place now for nearly three years, homeless and hopeless, and but for the little assistance they have received from the military (for which reimbursement has been made by this Department) they would certainly have starved to death long ago.

Bad as they may have been at home, they have committed no offense since they have been on our soil, and it is known that some of them have starved to death when they could easily have supplied their wants from the cattle ranges of northern Montana. No complaint has ever been made against them; but, on the contrary, their conduct has called forth the warmest expressions of praise and sympathy from the white people of the Territory.

It is not likely that they will ever go back to the British Possessions, and instead of longer treating them as felons and outcasts to be driven away on sight, I think the dignity of the Government requires that they be given a place somewhere, where they can raise food enough to keep them from starvation at least.

The fact that the agent at Fort Belknap Agency has expressed his willingness to receive and care for them at his agency would seem to indicate that his own Indians would make no objections to having them in their midst, and I therefore have the honor to recommend that this office be authorized to direct him to allow the refugees (numbering, as it appears, 160 souls) to come to his agency and cultivate as much land as they may require to support themselves, and to render them such assistance as he may be able to give without injury to the welfare of his own Indians.

If the Department thinks proper, the refugees can be given to understand that they will acquire no rights in the soil by reason of the privileges extended to them; and they should be told that they will not be fed in idleness, but must earn their own living with what little assistance the agent may be able to give them.

Very respectfully, your obedient servant,

J. D. C. ATKINS, *Commissioner.*

The SECRETARY OF THE INTERIOR.

FORT ASSINNIBOINE, MONT., *February 4, 1888.*

SIR: I have the honor to invite the attention of the proper authorities to the importance and necessity of making some disposition of the band of Cree Indians encamped near this post, having in view their permanent establishment in some designated locality if they are to be permitted to remain on this side of the international boundary line. The band numbers 160 souls.

It arrived here during the summer of 1885, since which time it has been encamped either in this neighborhood or in the vicinity of Fort Shaw. The War Department has been obliged to issue to it subsistence stores to prevent starvation during the winter seasons, but during the warmer months it has earned its food for the most part by working for Government wood contractors and in hunting small game on the prairies. The War Department has now issued to it subsistence stores amounting to $1,900, of which about one-half was distributed during the winter of 1885–86— stores of the value of $380 at Fort Shaw, and the remainder during the present winter at this point. These Indians are workers, are eager to have land assigned to them for cultivation, and have some knowledge of soil tillage.

I believe that if placed at some agency and properly assisted they would in propitious seasons raise sufficient produce for their consumption, and would at the same time encourage, by example, other Indians among whom they might be placed to greater exertions in farming. The agent at Fort Belknap has signified to me his willingness to receive and assist these Crees. He has a large amount of land broken up, and it seems to me that should they be sent there in the early spring it would result in mutual benefit to all the Indian bands there assembled.

Very respectfully, your obedient servant,

E. S. OTIS,
Colonel Twentieth Infantry, Commanding.

The ASSISTANT ADJUTANT-GENERAL,
DEPARTMENT OF DAKOTA,
St. Paul, Minn.

[First indorsement]

HEADQUARTERS DEPARTMENT OF DAKOTA,
St. Paul, Minn., February 13, 1888.

Respectfully forwarded through the headquarters Division of the Missouri.

I concur in the opinion of the commanding officer Fort Assinniboine, and that disposition should be made of these Cree Indians, either by compelling them to go north of the boundary line, or else assigning them to the care, if temporary only, of some agency. Last fall the commanding officer Fort Assinniboine was directed to put north of the boundary all Cree Canadian Indians who might have joined those allowed asylum on our territory in 1885; also, that none should be permitted hereafter to join them.

It is believed that all those now in the vicinity of Fort Assinniboine were of the original party of refugees.

In this connection attention is invited to the views as expressed by papers heretofore forwarded from these headquarters.

THOS. H. RUGER,
Brigadier-General, Commanding.

[Second indorsement]

HEADQUARTERS DIVISION OF THE MISSOURI,
Chicago, February 17, 1888.

Respectfully forwarded to the Adjutant-General of the Army.

P. H. SHERIDAN,
Lieutenant-General, Commanding.

———

DEPARTMENT OF THE INTERIOR, OFFICE OF INDIAN AFFAIRS,
Washington, November 1, 1887.

SIR: I have the honor to acknowledge the receipt of your letter of October 27, 1887, in reply to office letter of October 24, 1887, submitting a memorandum of information concerning the British Cree refugees now in Montana, in which you were pleased to observe as follows:

"The Cree Indians are not native Indians of the United States, and they have no rights on any existing reservation, and are not under the care of any agent of this Department. Heretofore subsistence and other supplies have been provided by the military authorities to relieve suffering among them, and reimbursement made by this Department upon accounts presented.

" If the military authorities shall find it necessary to furnish these Indians with food and supplies to prevent starvation among them while they continue to remain away from their home and wander about within the territory of the United States this Department will take such action as the facts then reported will warrant, and especially on the question of reimbursement of the expense which may be incurred on that account."

While it is true that these Indians have no rights on this side of the international line, and are not under the care of any agent of the Indian Department, still I regard it as the special province and duty of this office, not only to notice their presence and be watchful of their doings on this side of the line, but to pay suitable regard to the pitiable stories told of their poverty and suffering, especially as they are to some extent related by blood to our Indians, and hold constant communication with them in their wanderings through the country, and I think a generous public sentiment would sustain any efforts that might be made by this Department tending to relieve their sufferings even though they are not natives of our soil; and I think it is fitting that this office should take the initiative in providing some way for their very pressing needs, or at least in proposing such relief. Therefore, I have to respectfully suggest that the case of these refugees be called to the attention of the War Department, and that the Honorable Secretary of War be advised of the willingness of the Department to reimburse any proper expenditure that may be incurred by that Department in furnishing food and supplies to prevent starvation among them, upon the presentation of proper accounts therefor, as expressed in your letter to this office of October 27, 1887.

The fugitives number about 200—men, women, and children—and are reported to be on Dupuyer Creek, about 75 miles northwest from Fort Shaw, Mont., and not far from the Blackfeet Agency, though not, I believe, on the reservation.

I inclose a copy of this report.

Very respectfully, your obedient servant,

J. D. C. ATKINS, *Commissioner.*

The SECRETARY OF THE INTERIOR.

[See pp. 5, 979, and p. 120, Vol. VI.]

FIFTY-FOURTH CONGRESS, FIRST SESSION.

May 27, 1896.

[Senate Report No. 1073.]

Mr. Lodge, from the Committee on Foreign Relations, submitted the following report:

The Committee on Foreign Relations, to whom was referred the bill (S. 1187) to provide for the reorganization of the consular and diplomatic service, submit the following report:

The following report was made by Mr. Morgan on February 6, 1895, to accompany this bill when it was reported to the Senate at that time. It covers entirely all the essential points in regard to the proposed reorganization:

The consular service of the United States, like that of other nations, developed gradually out of the necessities of commerce and the willingness of merchants in foreign countries to represent other governments than their own and to discharge certain fiscal and other duties for the sake of the fees to be collected for such services. While the other great commercial nations of the world have at intervals down to recent times been active in the improvement of their consular service, in order to meet satisfactorily the exigencies of a steadily increasing competition in international trade, the consular system of the United States has remained practically unchanged since the time it was called into existence on a small scale by the acts of July 1, 1790, and of April 14, 1792, and kept alive by a number of subsequent unimportant acts.

The act "to remodel the diplomatic and consular system" of March 1, 1855, is entitled to be regarded as an improvement only so far as it slightly enlarged the service and corrected certain abuses therein by a closer supervision of the fees. It in no way, however, effected a change in the principle of consular representation or in the system of appointment. Apart, therefore, from the act of June 20, 1864, which provided for the establishment of a small body of thirteen consular clerks with a permanent tenure of office, a measure which at its inception was intended to form the nucleus of an entire reform of the service on that basis, this institution, so important to our foreign trade, has suffered the oversight and indifference of Congress.

This neglect is the more striking and the less excusable when our foreign trade of half a century ago is contrasted with that of to-day. In 1850 the combined value of our imports and domestic exports amounted to $308,409,759; in 1893 it reached the figure of $1,697,431,707. But notwithstanding these present vastly increased and far more intricate commercial relations indicated by these figures, no step whatever to increase the efficiency of the consular service, to which the direction and fostering of these relations are intrusted, has been taken. That this has entailed a great loss annually to our foreign trade can not be questioned; that there is also an urgent necessity to correct this want of efficiency is equally apparent.

Even more applicable to the industrial and commercial conditions of to-day, but with reference to those of a decade ago, Secretary Frelinghuysen said in 1884:

"Until recently the demands of Europe, which consumed the greater portion of our exports, and the condition of the producing countries, were such as to give us control in the supply of certain products, such as breadstuffs, provisions, cotton, petroleum, etc. The demands of Europe for all these products, and of the other continents for petroleum especially, were so positive, and our producing conditions so favorable, as to give us practically a monopoly for their supply.

"These conditions of international demand and supply are undergoing radical changes, which the near future will intensify.

"The efforts which have been made and which are being made by Europe to enlarge the field of supply in the above-mentioned products, aided by the ambition which prevails in all countries for the development of natural and artificial resources to meet their own wants and to supply the wants of others, have resulted in awakening competition for the supply even of those products which we have heretofore controlled. It is true that thus far this competition has not affected our trade to any appreciable extent, but the desire for development which is now abroad, and the ambition which prevails to increase the production (outside of the United States) of the foregoing articles, render consular supervision of absolute importance. *The complex commercial relations and industrial interests which now prevail in Europe have originated hostility to American products in many countries, and afford additional reasons for the enlargement and perfection of the consular service."* [1]

In 1888 Mr. Cleveland, in his message to Congress, expresses himself to the same effect when he says: "The reorganization of the consular service is a matter of serious importance to our national interests," and in 1893 he again refers to the subject as follows:

"During my former administration I took occasion to recommend a recast of the laws relating to the consular service, in order that it might become a more efficient agency in the promotion of the interests it was intended to subserve. The duties and powers of consuls have been expanded with the growing requirements of our foreign trade. Discharging important duties affecting our commerce and American citizens abroad, and in certain countries exercising judicial functions, these officers should be men of character, intelligence, and ability."

In addition to these expressions from a high official source, the necessity of a reform has been recognized by men of letters, eminent statesmen, journalists, and important boards of trade of this country.

It must be admitted that the present management of our foreign service is burdened with many drawbacks to its efficacy by considerations that relate to domestic politics. Partisan policy, when strictly carried out in making appointments in our foreign service, has no other meaning than that the consular offices are primarily regarded as rewards for political services. The real capacity and usefulness of a consul is too often a secondary consideration.

This important and indispensable part of the machinery by which our foreign intercourse is conducted is often employed to pension political favorites. That to subserve the interests of the service ought to be the sole end in view in the selection of incumbents can not be disputed. To consider the offices merely as sources from which these partisan officeholders may derive four years of maintenance is as absurd as it would be to construct a navy to defend the country and to intrust its command to landsmen without experience for whom we might desire to provide a living and comfortable quarters.

Such a purpose, or one not more gratifying, has often been put into practice in our diplomatic and consular service. To protect and promote in time of peace our varied foreign interests through the agency of a trained personnel is not a less important subject for legislative consideration and provision than in time of war to defend them by the most efficient means at our command.

The object of this act is to provide a system by which persons shall be trained for the duties of the consular service, so that they shall be able to perform them in the best possible way at a reasonable expense to the Government. That this can not be obtained without removing the selection of persons for this service from the control of party politics is shown by our experience, if any proof were required to establish a conclusion so entirely true and indisputable.

Fitness of the candidate, permanency of tenure during good behavior, and an impartial method of selection and to govern promotion as reward for efficiency are the principles on which a useful consular service can alone be based, with an expectation of the best results.

Under our present system a consular or diplomatic officer has no sooner familiarized himself with the duties of his office and begun to acquire a knowledge of its business and fitness for his duties than he is removed to make room for another novice, who is likewise superseded as soon as his experience begins to enable him to discharge the duties of his office to the satisfaction of himself and others. Thus, in one generation the same post is frequently filled by a number of men, who are successively displaced as soon as they have learned to transact the business of their offices with something of professional knowledge and skill.

---

[1] Communication of the Secretary of State to the President, March 20, 1884.

This system is not only unjust to the people. but it is equally unjust to the agents, who are thrown back upon their own resources just at the time when a three or four years' preparation has fitted them to devote their energies and capacity with advantage to the foreign service.

To compete successfully with the agents of foreign powers, and to conduct advantageously the political and commercial affairs of our own country, the appointee to this service should be familiar not only with the laws, customs, industries, manufactures, and natural products of our own land, but they should be instructed in the laws, pursuits, language, the contributions to commerce, and the character of the people to whom they are accredited. To this should be added a competent knowledge of the law of nations and of commercial law. As long as these officers are transferred from pursuits and associations which have no connection with commerce or the foreign service, however able and skillful they may be in other things, they can not possess the special knowledge and skill which will render their labors either useful or creditable to the consular service.

The foreign service of European governments for many years has been the object of careful solicitude on their part. An outline statement of them will better enable us to understand the disadvantage we suffer from a defective system.

The French consular service is composed of—

40 consuls-general, at a salary each	$3,600
50 consuls of the first class, each	2,800
80 consuls of the second class, each	2,000
100 vice-consuls	1,400
24 pupil consuls	800

The conditions for admission to the diplomatic and consular service of France are prescribed in a decree of October 15, 1892, and, to show how important France considers its foreign service, attention is called to the fact that over thirty decrees have been issued since 1880 tending to perfect the system.

The pupil consuls are appointed by the minister of foreign affairs. They can only be drawn from the body of attachés on probation who have passed a competitive examination for admission into the service and who have served not less than one year in the home office.

Before being assigned to a diplomatic or consular post they are required to spend at least one year at one of the principal chambers of commerce, where they are to acquire a thorough knowledge of the methods and needs of commerce, and whence they must send the minister periodical reports on the trade of the district. After three years of service, half of which time must be rendered abroad, the pupil consul becomes eligible for vice-consul, and after a service of three years in each subsequent grade he becomes eligible for promotion to a higher one.

Candidates for admission in the French diplomatic and consular service must be under 27 years of age and must have taken a collegiate degree in law, science, or letters, or must have passed certain other examinations, or be the holders of commissions in the army or navy.

The examination for entrance into the service is either written or oral, as may be required.

The written test consists of a composition on public and private international law and a translation into French from English and German, which is dictated. Those candidates who aspire to the diplomatic career are to write also a composition on a subject of diplomatic history that occurred since 1648; those destined for the consular service must write a composition on a subject of political economy or of political and commercial geography.

Those whose papers are sufficiently creditable in the opinion of the examiners to warrant their going any further are then subjected to a public oral examination on public and private international law, political and commercial geography, political economy, and a conversation in English and German. Candidates for the diplomatic career are further examined orally in diplomatic history since 1648, and candidates for the consular service are examined on maritime and customs laws.

The French foreign service is under very strict discipline, and for misconduct or inefficiency there are the following penalties:

(1) Reprimand.
(2) Withholding a part of the salary, not exceeding one-half thereof and not for a longer period than two months.
(3) Suspension from the service without salary for two or more years.
(4) Dismissal.

The last three penalties are imposed by the minister of foreign affairs, with the consent of the council of directors, and after a written or oral hearing of the party under censure.

In addition to their regular salaries. the French consular officers are entitled to traveling expenses and allowances for house and office rent, and for entertaining where it is necessary.

Such a course of training and discipline must produce thorough efficiency; and the generous rewards given for faithful and profitable service must encourage a good class of men to adopt such employment as a profession to which all their energies and abilities are industriously devoted. The permanency of employment, during good behavior, gives confidence to the officer and constantly increasing benefit to the Government.

The British system of regulations for the admission of applicants to the consular service are as follows:

"Persons selected for the consular service, whenever the circumstance of their being resident in England, on their first appointment, or of their passing through England on their way to take up such first appointment, may admit of their being subject to examination, will be expected to satisfy the civil-service commissioners—

"(1) That they have a correct knowledge of the English language, so as to be able to express themselves clearly and correctly in writing.

"(2) That they can write and speak French correctly and fluently.

"(3) That they have a sufficient knowledge of the current language, as far as commerce is concerned, of the port at which they are appointed to reside, to enable them to communicate directly with the authorities and natives of the place; a knowledge of the German language being taken to meet this requirement for ports in northern Europe; of the Spanish or Portuguese language, as may be determined by the secretary of state, for ports in Spain, Portugal, Morocco, and South or Central America; and of the Italian language for ports in Italy, Greece, Turkey, Egypt, and on the Black Sea or Mediterranean, except those in Morocco or Spain.

"(4) A sufficient knowledge of British mercantile and commercial law to enable them to deal with questions arising between British shipowners, shipmasters, and seamen. As regards this head of examination, candidates must be prepared to be examined in 'Smith's Compendium of Mercantile Law.'

"(5) A sufficient knowledge of arithmetic for the nature of the duties which consuls are required to perform in drawing up commercial tables and reports. As regards this head of examination, candidates must be prepared to be examined in Bishop Colenso's Arithmetic.

"Moreover, all persons on their first nomination to consulships, and after having passed their examination before the civil-service commissioners, will be required, as far as practicable, to attend for at least three months in the foreign office, in order that they may become acquainted with the forms of business as carried on there.

"Limit of age for candidates, 25 and 50, both years inclusive. (Fee for examination, £1 to £6.)"

Mr. Henry White, formerly secretary of legation at London, in an article contributed to the North American Review, makes the following instructive statements concerning the British consular service:

"The British service was established in its present form by act of Parliament in 1825 (6 Geo. IV, cap. 87). Up to that time its members had been appointed, on no regular system, by the King, and were paid from his civil list. This act placed the service under the foreign office, and provided for its payment out of funds to be voted by Parliament. Since then it has been the subject of periodical investigation by royal commissions and Parliamentary committees, with a view to the improvement of its efficiency. The evidence taken on these occasions is published in voluminous blue books, the perusal of which I recommend to those interested in the reform in our service.

"Appointments are made by the secretary of state for foreign affairs. Candidates must be recommended by some one known to him, and their names and qualifications are thereupon entered on a list, from which he selects a name when a vacancy occurs. The candidate selected, whose age must be between 25 and 50, is then required to pass an examination before the civil-service commissioners.

"The salaries of British consular officers are fixed, under the act of Parliament of July 21, 1891 (54 and 55 Vict., cap. 36), by the secretary of state, with the approval of the treasury, and no increase can be made in any salary without the approval of the latter. They average about £600 ($3,000) a year, but, of course, some of the important posts are much more highly paid, the salary of the consul-general at New York being £2,000 (nearly $10,000), with an office allowance besides of £1,660, and a staff consisting of a consul at £600, and two vice-consuls at £400 and £250, respectively; that of the consul at San Francisco, £1,200 (nearly $6,000), with an office allowance of £600 besides.

"British consular officials are retired at the age of 70 with a pension.

"There is also an unpaid branch of the service, consisting chiefly of vice-consuls, appointed at places which are not of sufficient importance to merit a paid official. They are usually British merchants, but may be foreigners. They are not subjected to an examination, and are rarely promoted to a paid appointment.

"Consular clerks are required to pass an examination in handwriting and orthography, arithmetic, and one foreign language (speaking, translating, and copying)"

Mr. White through a series of years was our secretary of legation at London, and is thoroughly informed on the subject of consular duties and the acquirements that are essential to an efficient and respectable service. His approval of the plan adopted in this bill for the reformation of our consular system and service is a strong recommendation of its future advantages.

In Germany persons are appointed to the office of consular chancellor who have passed their examinations as "referendary," a title which requires graduation at a German university and requires a thorough knowledge of law, political science, statistics, etc. The chancellor of the consulate is promoted gradually until he reaches the rank of consul-general.

As a rule the personnel of our consular establishment is not in unfavorable contrast with that of the leading European States as to intelligence and sagacity; but our consuls have not usually the liberal education characteristic of the consular representatives of the great European States, nor are they so well informed as to commerce and its great variety of contributory pursuits, or with the exact business methods employed in conducting the commerce of the leading nations. This seems to be our point of most serious deficiency.

It is proper, and may be necessary, that the laws should designate the places at which consulates are established, but discretion should be given to the President to send consuls to other places, at least temporarily, to meet the demands of trade and intercourse that may arise in new and unexpected quarters. Especially is this necessary in cases where other countries are engaged in war, and a sudden emergency calls for the protection of our citizens in places which are not designated by law as the location of consular establishments.

But the laws should not designate the individual who is to be the consul at any particular locality. That matter should be left to the discretion of the President, so that he can at all times have the right man at the right place, to meet any demand of trade, or to secure the adequate protection of the persons and property of our citizens in any emergency, or for any public reason.

The arrangement of the fixed residences of consuls of the several classes is not attempted in this bill. The laws and the practice of the Department of State are, for the present at least, a sufficient guide in that matter.

The president should, however, be left free in his authority to send a consul of any class to any consulate when he may consider that the demands of the public service require such transfers.

The reasons for such a provision of law are many and cogent, and they are so obvious as not to require any elaboration in this report. They relate as well to the fitness of consular officers for the particular duties of the occasion as to their usefulness because of their experience as to the condition of the people, the trade, and the language of the particular locality where their services are required.

The consular establishments thus mobilized would soon show a great growth in useful knowledge of the affairs of various parts of foreign countries, and our trade with many foreign countries would be greatly increased and rendered more secure.

The following statements, showing the present condition of our consular service, will show that the change in the organization of the system will add materially to the revenue derived from that source, without a material increase of the expenditures:

Expenditures for salaries of consular officers and amount of compensation in fees, where the officer has no salary, for the year 1894.

26 consuls-general (not including those also commissioned ministers resident)	$98,000.00
188 salaried consuls	371,500.00
11 salaried commercial agents	22,000.00
13 salaried consular clerks	15,000.00
62 feed consuls (personal perquisites in official fees)	36,152.85
33 feed commercial agents (personal perquisites in official fees)	36,505.53
Notarial and unofficial fees retained by consular officers as personal perquisites (lowest estimate)	250,000.00
333 Total	829,158.38

Officers of the diplomatic service embraced in this bill.

6 secretaries of embassy	$13,875.00
17 secretaries of legation	31,975.00
23 Total	45,850.00

According to the Annual Report of the Fifth Auditor of the Treasury for the year ended June 30, 1894—

The expenses for last year of the consular service were $1,055,417.43
The consular fees received for official services were................... 758,410.81

Excess of expenditures over receipts............................ 297,006.62

This excess of expenses is larger than it has been for ten years. In 1893 it only amounted to $96,042. The difference is not due to an increase of expenditures, but, no doubt, may be found to a great extent in the changes of our tariff laws. This excess, though larger than customary, is, after all, a small sum when considered with reference to the important purposes for which it is disbursed, and, with the payment into the Treasury of the unofficial fees, as proposed under this bill, it is likely to be greatly reduced, if not changed into a balance in favor of the income from that source.

The entire excess of expenditures for salaries in the Department of State and in the diplomatic and consular service over the receipts amounts to only $615,909.19, the smallest amount expended by any of the great powers of the world. The expenditures of the foreign service of Great Britain, Russia, Germany, Italy, and Spain exceed this amount by very considerable figures, and the report of the ministry of foreign affairs of France for the year 1893 shows only $240,000 receipts and $3,266,960 expenditures, a sum almost double that expended by the United States, including even the incidental and contingent expenses of the consular and diplomatic service of the latter country.

This bill adopts the principle of permanent official tenure, so far as the laws can control that subject, but permanent only as it is of benefit to the service. It leaves the power of removal from office to the discretion of the President. The position of each employee of the service is protected against the uncertain and demoralizing effects of changes for merely political reasons in the administration of the Government as far as Congress can control the subject. But this protection is as necessary in practice for efficient work as it is just in theory, and if the plan is adopted of appointing consuls after they are found to be qualified for the respective classifications of the consular service they will seldom, if ever, be dropped from the service for the purpose of supplying their places with political favorites.

The required examination for appointment and promotion creates an impediment in the way of those who may demand office as a reward for political partisanship, without having adequate knowledge of the duties of this peculiar branch of the public service.

Each consul must, on frequent occasions, be the judge of his proper line of action without aid or direction from the minister to whom he is required to report or from the Department of State. In such cases it is requisite to the honor and security of the Government that the consul should be well informed as to his duties.

The right of the President to select from the whole body of consuls any man for any place he may prefer, and to assign him to such place for duty, and to transfer him at pleasure to another place, is the full equivalent of the power of appointment to a particular office.

These functions are to be exercised in foreign countries, for the most part distant from the United States, and disconnect the incumbents from participation in our home politics.

In so far as they may be given as rewards for party services, they are a sort of pension system for men who have not been successful in getting offices at home or who have failed of success in the usual channels of business.

The consular system should be based upon the plan of personal qualification for its important and peculiar duties, ascertained by the examination and experience of those employed in it, rather than upon the plan of selecting those for this service who have failed in other pursuits or those who desire to go abroad for purposes of travel, recreation, or amusement.

This is the only branch of the public service that has been used, to any great extent, for the gratification of the incumbents, without regard to their capacity to render efficient service to the country, and it is time that our policy in respect of these offices was changed.

Taken in the aggregate, there is no class of representatives of our Government who can so seriously affect our commerce with other countries, in their actual and direct conduct and dealings, as our consuls and commercial agents.

We should encourage our best classes of people to qualify themselves for this important service by giving them just compensation for their work and by securing them in these offices during good behavior.

They have much to do with the dignity of our Government, its credit in foreign lands, the honor of its flag, and the safety of its citizens.

Since Mr. Morgan made the report just given a portion of the consular service has been classified in accordance with an Executive order, which is as follows:

EXECUTIVE ORDER.

It being of great importance that the consuls and commercial agents of the United States shall possess the proper qualifications for their respective positions, to be ascertained either through a satisfactory record of previous actual service under the Department of State or through an appropriate examination:

It is hereby ordered that any vacancy in a consulate or commercial agency now or hereafter existing, the salary of which is not more than $2,500 nor less than $1,000, or the compensation of which, if derived from official fees, exclusive of notarial and other unofficial receipts, does not exceed $2,500 nor fall below $1,000, shall be filled (a) by a transfer or promotion from some other position under the Department of State of a character tending to qualify the incumbent for the position to be filled; or (b) by appointment of a person not under the Department of State but having previously served thereunder to its satisfaction in a capacity tending to qualify him for the position to be filled; or (c) by the appointment of a person who, having furnished the customary evidence of character, responsibility, and capacity, and being thereupon selected by the President for examination, is found upon such examination to be qualified for the position.

For the purposes of this order notarial and unofficial fees shall not be regarded, but the compensation of a consulate or commercial agency shall be ascertained, if the office is salaried, by reference to the last preceding appropriation act, and if the office is not salaried, by reference to the returns of official fees for the last preceding fiscal year.

The examination hereinbefore provided for shall be by a board of three persons designated by the Secretary of State, who shall also prescribe the subjects to which such examinations shall relate and the general mode of conducting the same by the board.

A vacancy in a consulate will be filled at discretion only when a suitable appointment can not be made in any of the modes indicated in the second paragraph of this order.

GROVER CLEVELAND.

EXECUTIVE MANSION, *September 20, 1895.*

It will be seen that this provides only partially for the consular service and does not diminish the need of the comprehensive reorganization proposed by the accompanying bill; in fact the scheme proposed in the bill is an extension of that established by the Executive order, and gives not only complete reorganization but the authority of law to the classification, which now rests merely on a departmental order.

[See pp. 13, 143, 187, 321, and pp 72, 119, 199, 276, Vol. VI.]

FIFTY-FOURTH CONGRESS, SECOND SESSION.

December 21, 1896.

[Senate Report No 1160]

Mr. Cameron, from the Committee on Foreign Relations, submitted the following report:

Congress, at its last session, after long and patient consideration, adopted with practical unanimity the view expressed by your committee that the time had come for resuming intervention with Spain for the recognition of the independence of Cuba. Spain having declined to listen to any representation founded on an understanding between herself and the insurgents, and Congress having pledged itself to friendly intervention, the only question that remains to be decided is the nature of the next step to be taken, with proper regard to the customs and usages of nations.

Before deciding this question, your committee has preferred to examine with some care all the instances which have occurred during this century of insurgent peoples claiming independence by right of revolt. The inquiry has necessarily led somewhat far, especially because the right of revolt or insurrection, if insurrection can be properly called a right, seems, in every instance except one, to have carried with it a corresponding intervention. For convenience, we have regarded both insurrection and intervention as recognized rights, and have attempted to ascertain the limits within which these rights have been exercised and their force admitted by the general consent of nations.

The long duration of the French revolutionary wars, which disturbed the entire world for five and twenty years, and left it in a state of great confusion, fixed the beginning of our modern international systems at the year 1815, in the treaties of Vienna, of Paris, and of the Holy Alliance. The settlement of local disturbances, under the influence of the powers parties to these treaties, proceeded without serious disagreement until 1821, when the Greeks rose in insurrection against the Sultan. The modern precedents of European insurrection and intervention, where independence was the issue involved, began with Greece.

1. GREECE, 1821-1827.

The revolution broke out in Greece at the end of March, 1821. Within a month the rebels got possession of all the open country and all the towns, except so far as they were held by Turkish garrisons. The Sultan immediately called all Mussulmans to arms; the Greek Patriarch was hanged at the door of his own church at Constantinople; several hundred merchants were massacred; several hundred Christian churches were destroyed, and the Russian ambassador was insulted.

Russia was then the head of the "Holy Alliance," the union of Russia, Austria, and Prussia, which had crushed Napoleon and guaranteed the peace of Europe. The Greek revolution was the work of liberal forces which had produced the disturbances of 1789, and which the Holy Alliance existed chiefly to combat. No government in Europe sympathized with the Greek rebels. Austria was entirely hostile. England and Prussia followed the same impulse. France feared intervention on account of her royalist dynasty. Even Russia, the only power which must profit by weakening Turkey, was interested in revolutionizing the principalities, but not in revolutionizing Greece.

This universal fear of innovation caused no small part of the interest suddenly developed in the practice of international law and its limitations for the advantage of legitimate Governments. The neutrality acts of the United States and of England took shape in 1818 and 1819. The great powers of Europe held congress after congress for the international settlement of political and even social difficulties; at Aix in 1818; at Carlsbad in 1819; at Vienna in 1820; at Troppau, October–December, 1820; at Laibach from January to May, 1821; and subsequently at Vienna and Verona in the last six months of 1822. At Troppau, in November, 1820, the three powers of Russia, Austria, and Prussia united in signing a protocol expressly intended to assert the right of intervention in all cases where a European power "should suffer, in its internal régime, an alteration brought about by revolt, and the results of which are menacing for other States." The language of this protocol had much to do with the subsequent course of events.

Faithful to the principles they have proclaimed and the respect due to the authority of every legitimate Government, as well as to every act which emanates from its free will, the Allied Powers will engage to refuse their recognition to changes consummated by illegal methods. When States where such changes shall have been effectuated shall cause other countries to fear, by their proximity, an imminent danger, and when the Allied Powers can exercise in regard to them an efficacious and beneficent action, they will employ, in order to restore them to the bosom of the Alliance, at first friendly processes; in the second place, a coercive force, if the exercise of that force becomes indispensable.

England and France did not join in this declaration, or in the intervention in Naples which was its immediate object; but the Alliance acted systematically on the principle thus laid down, which was in the full energy of its operation, when, four months afterwards, the Greeks broke into revolt.

For these reasons the Greek insurrection assumed great importance in the eyes of all the civilized world and in the history of international relations. Other revolts were directed merely against a local authority, and aimed to subvert a dynasty or an oppressive rule. The Greeks fought for independence, and since the Declaration of Independence by the United States in 1776, no new nationality, based on successful insurrection, had been recognized by Europe.

Russia almost instantly began by calling the attention of the allies to her claim that the whole Greek race, whether in Greece proper, or in the islands, or in the principalities, were of right under Russian protection. This declaration was made June 22, 1821, within three months of the outbreak of the revolution, and two years before the Monroe doctrine took shape. It was coldly received by all the powers except Prussia, while the Turkish Government rejected with indignation a simultaneous warning from Russia in the form of an ultimatum, dated June 28, that the further coexistence of Turkey with other European States would depend on her conduct in this matter, which was a European and universal interest that Russia claimed the peculiar right to defend. Under these circumstances the Russian ambassador left Constantinople, August 10, 1821.

The concessions demanded by Russia in her ultimatum did not then include any settlement of the Greek insurrection. They chiefly concerned the principalities. An entire year passed before the other powers succeeded in bringing Turkey to concessions that opened a possibility of restoring her diplomatic relations with Russia and dealing with the subjects in dispute. Only when at last the powers induced Turkey to consent to allow her affairs to be discussed in a general conference did Russia insist that the Greek insurrection should be included among the subjects of mediation. The Turkish Government declared in the most energetic language that it would never admit of such interference, or consent to make the affairs of Greece a subject of negotiation with Russia. In the face of this declaration, made in July, 1822, the other powers, led by Austria and supported by England, under the horror roused by the massacre of Chios, abandoned their jealousy of Russia and their dread of insurrection so far as to join in insisting that Turkey should yield, and that the affairs of Greece should be made the subject of joint intervention; but in spite of this pressure, Turkey did not yield, and the powers held new conferences at Vienna and at Verona, which lasted till December, 1822, and which, while deciding on intervention in Italy and Spain, ended by yielding to Turkey an indefinite postponement of the Greek dispute. In this postponement Russia seemed cordially to acquiesce. The dread of revolution overcame for the moment the other interests of the Russian people.

In the whole discussion, from March, 1821, until January, 1823, the right of intervention was never disputed, except by Turkey. On that point the whole law was stated in conversation between the British ambassador and the Turkish minister. The Turk took the ground that everything had been done by Turkey if she had satisfied her treaty obligations. "Everything as against Russia," replied Strangford, the British ambassador, "but not as regards the allies and friends of the Porte. According to Turkish law, it was not allowed to leave a house in a condition that endangered a neighbor's safety. The Turkish Government believed it had restored the old solidity of the wall, but he (Lord Strangford) feared they were mistaken." "God forbid!" said the Turk; "but in any case this would be our affair, not yours!" "God forbid!" repeated Lord Strangford; "for this is our affair as well as yours."

This was the situation when Lord Castlereagh died, and George Canning became prime minister of England. Down to that moment the British Government had identified itself with the Turkish Government, and had overstepped the line of neutrality in order to assist the Turkish campaigns by sea and land. Lord Castlereagh and Lord Strangford avowedly considered the Greeks as a worthless and mongrel race, incapable of self-government, whose claims were to be wholly rejected. George Canning held that the greater danger to the peace and welfare of Europe was the Holy Alliance and its system of political interference; but in the case of Greece, where the Holy Alliance had refrained from interfering, while it was actively repressing disturbances in Spain and Italy, Canning held that intervention was proper and that the duties and interests of England required her to intervene. His chief anxiety was to bring about his object without war between any of the parties.

He began by recognizing Greek belligerency. The Greeks issued a proclamation declaring a strict blockade of the ports of Patras and Lepanto; and thereupon the Ionian high commissioner, on the 17th of November, 1824, recognized this "communication from persons exercising the functions of government in Greece," and ordered "all ships and boats of whatever description, bearing the Ionian flag 'to respect the same in the most strict and exact manner.'"

This seems to have been the step which led to Canning's somewhat famous definition of the nature of belligerency, in 1825. "The Turkish Government," we are told, "complained that the British Government allowed to the Greeks a belligerent character, and observed that it appeared to forget that to subjects in rebellion no national character could properly belong." To this remonstrance Canning replied, through the British resident at Constantinople, that "the character of belligerency was not so much a principle as a fact; that a certain degree of force and consistency acquired by any mass of. population engaged in war entitled that population to be treated as a belligerent, and, even if their title were questionable, rendered it the interest, well understood, of all civilized nations so to treat them."

This proposition must have seemed somewhat broad, even to Canning, for in applying it to the special case of Greece he added that "a power or community, call it which you will, which was at war with another and which covered the sea with its cruisers, must either be acknowledged as a belligerent or dealt with as a pirate." At that time no other power than England, and Turkey, least of all, admitted the necessity of this alternative, since the war had then lasted four years without producing it; but what no other power was ready to admit in 1825 became the accepted law of all Europe in 1861 in a form much more pronounced. Although this dictum of Canning's was never, so far as we know, officially published, it was quoted by Lord John Russell, then Her Majesty's principal secretary of state for foreign affairs, in the speech which he made in the House of Commons May 6, 1861, as his single and sufficient authority to justify the step upon which he and his colleagues in the Government had decided, of recognizing the belligerency of the "power or community," which he officially called "the Southern Confederacy of America," and which at that time had not a ship at sea or an army on land, and which had given as yet no official evidence of a war to the British Government. Simultaneously the same action was adopted by the Government of France, which "concurred entirely in the views of Her Majesty's Government," and whose concurrence, in the absence of protest or objection by any other power, made Russell's view the accepted practice of Europe.

Canning's recognition of Greek belligerency in 1825, as well as the joint recognition of "the Southern Confederacy of America" in 1861, was only the first step toward an anticipated system of intervention. To this subject we shall be obliged to return, after the further story of the Greek precedent has been told. Canning followed up the recognition of belligerency by making a direct offer of assistance to the Greeks· Early in the year 1824 a paper purporting to be a plan of pacification for Greece, drawn up by the Court of St. Petersburg, had appeared in the European Gazettes, and, although no one knew from what source the Gazettes had received it, no one seriously disputed its authenticity. The plan suggested the division of Greece into three Principalities, under Turkish garrisons, with an internal organization to be guaranteed by the combined powers. The Greek Government, alarmed at this suggestion, wrote to Canning a strong remonstrance and an appeal to the help and protection of England. The letter reached Canning November 4, just at the moment when he was considering the Greek blockade. His reply, dated December 1, 1824, contained a paragraph which invited the Greeks to place their interests in his hands:

> If they should at any time hereafter think it fit to solicit our mediation, we should be ready to tender it to the Porte; and, if accepted by the Porte, to do our best to carry it into effect, conjointly with other powers. * * * This appears to the British Government all that can reasonably be asked of them.

The Greeks, whose military position was desperate, at length decided not only to act on Canning's suggestion, but to place themselves absolutely in the hands of Great Britain. This they did by a formal act in June, 1825. The trust was declined, but Canning, strengthened by this authority, was enabled to draw Russia away from Austrian influence, and to negotiate in St. Petersburg, in the form of a protocol, dated April 4, 1826, an agreement for a joint offer of mediation to Turkey for the pacification of Greece. Upon this protocol rests the diplomatic value of the subsequent intervention.

> His Britannic Majesty, having been requested by the Greeks to interpose his good offices in order to obtain their reconciliation with the Ottoman Porte, having in consequence offered his mediation to that power, and being desirous of concerting the measures of his Government with His Majesty the Emperor of all the Russias, and His Imperial Majesty, on the other hand, being equally animated by the desire of putting an end to the contest of which Greece and the archipelago are the theater by an arragement which shall be consistent with the principles of religion, justice and humanity, have agreed—
> 1. That the arrangement to be proposed to the Porte, if that Government should accept the proffered mediation, should have for its object to place the Greeks toward the Ottoman Porte in the relation hereafter mentioned:
> Greece should be a dependency of that Empire, etc. * * *

Canning wished to save Turkey from Russian aggression, but Turkey refused to be saved. The Sultan would listen to no mediation between himself and his revolted subjects, least of all at a moment when his military position warranted him in feeling sure of success in subduing the revolt. Another year passed without bringing the issue to a point. Then France joined with England and Russia, and the three powers, on the 5th of July, 1827, united in a formal treaty signed in London, which committed them to armed intervention in case the Sultan should still reject their proffered mediation, within the space of one month. The preamble to this treaty set forth the motives which led the three sovereigns to intervene:

> Penetrated with the necessity of putting an end to the sanguinary contest which, by delivering up the Greek provinces and the isles of the archipelago to all the disorders of anarchy, produces daily fresh impediments to the commerce of the European States and gives occasion to piracies which not only expose the subjects of the high contracting parties to considerable losses, but besides render necessary burdensome measures of protection and repression, His Majesty the King of the United Kingdom of Great Britain and Ireland and His Majesty the King of France and Navarre, having besides received on the part of the Greeks a pressing request to interpose their mediation with the Ottoman Porte, and being, as well as His Majesty the Emperor of all the Russias, animated by the desire of stopping the effusion of blood and of arresting the evils of all kinds which might arise from the continuance of such a state of things, have resolved to unite their efforts and to regulate the operation thereof by a formal treaty, with a view of reestablishing peace between the contending parties by means of an arrangement which is called for as much by humanity as by interest of the repose of Europe.

The treaty proceeded to bind the three parties to offer their mediation immediately on the basis of Turkish suzerainty and Greek self-government, and in case Turkey should not accept within one month the proposed mediation the powers should prevent further hostilities by ordering their squadrons to interpose.

The Turkish Government August 30 reiterated its decided, uncon-ditional, final, and unchangeable refusal to receive any proposition on behalf of the Greeks. The next day the ambassadors sent the neces-sary orders to their squadrons, and in attempting to carry out these orders the admirals, much to the regret of the British Government, brought on the battle of Navarino, October 20, 1827.

2. BELGIUM, 1830.

The next European nation that claimed its independence on the ground of the right of revolution was the Belgian.

By a provision of the general European settlement of 1815 Holland and Belgium were united in one kingdom, known as that of the Neth-erlands, over which was placed the son of the last Stadtholder of Hol-land, as King William I of the Netherlands.

When the French Revolution of July, 1830, occurred, it spread instantly to the Netherlands. Toward the end of August, 1830, dis-turbances began, and soon became so serious as to threaten grave com-plications abroad as well as at home.

King William sent a formal note, dated October 5, to the British Government, identical with notes to Prussia, Austria, and Russia, the four contracting parties to the treaty of 1815, calling on them to restore order, since all were bound "to support the Kingdom of the Nether-lands and the actual state of Europe."

Representatives of the four powers, and with them the representative of France, met in London, November 4, 1830, and adopted a protocol:

His Majesty the King of the Netherlands having invited the courts of Great Britain, Austria, France, Prussia, and Russia, in their quality of powers signatory to the treaties of Paris and Vienna, which constituted the Kingdom of the Nether-lands, to deliberate in concert with his Majesty on the best means of putting an end to the troubles which have broken out in his states; and the courts above-named having experienced, even before receiving this invitation, a warm desire to arrest with the shortest possible delay the disorder and the effusion of blood, have con-certed. * * *

This protocol at once set aside the King of the Netherlands, ignoring his exclusive claim to support, and "to deliberate in concert." With-out concerting with or supporting King William, the five powers imposed an immediate armistice on both parties.

Naturally the Belgian rebels then declared themselves independent. With such encouragement their safety was guaranteed almost beyond the possibility of risk. The claim of independence was made November 18, 1830, and was recognized one month later by the powers in their seventh conference, December 20. The representatives of the five powers, whose names were among the most famous in diplomacy—Tal-leyrand, Lieven, Esterhazy, Palmerston, Bulow—adopted, without the adhesion or even an invitation to be present of the Netherlands min-ister, a protocol which announced intervention pure and simple, begin-ning with the abrupt recognition of the revolutionary government:

The plenipotentiaries of the five courts, having received the formal adhesion of the Belgian Government to the armistice proposed to it, and which the King of the Netherlands has also accepted, * * * the conference will occupy itself in discuss-ing and concerting the new arrangements most proper to combine the future inde-pendence of Belgium with the interests and the security of the other powers, and the preservation of the European equilibrium.

The Netherlands minister immediately recorded, December 22, a formal protest, and a reservation of King William's right to decide on "such ulterior measures as should be taken in the double interests of his own dignity and the well-being of his faithful subjects."

A few days later, January 4, 1831, Holland entered a still more formal protest. In this strong and dignified paper the King's Government pointed out to the five powers the extreme importance of the new precedent they had established in international law.

As King, called to guard the well-being of a fraction of the European population, His Majesty has been deeply concerned to remark that the complications arisen in Europe have appeared so grave that it has been thought proper, as the only remedy, to sanction the results of a revolt which was provoked by no legitimate motive, and thus to compromise the stability of all thrones, the social order of all States, and the happiness, the repose, and the prosperity of all peoples.

Independent of the solidarity established between the different members of the European system, His Majesty, as sovereign of the Kingdom of the Netherlands, has seen in it an attack directed against his rights.

If the treaty of Paris of 1814 placed Belgium at the disposition of the high allies, these, from the moment they fixed the lot of the Belgian provinces, renounced, according to the law of nations, the faculty of returning on their work, and the dissolution of the bonds formed between Holland and Belgium under the sovereignty of the House of Orange Nassau, became placed beyond the sphere of their attributes. The increase of territory assigned to the united provinces of the Netherlands was, moreover, acquired under burdensome conditions, for valuable consideration, requiring the sacrifice of several of their colonies, the expense required to fortify several places of the southern provinces of the Kingdom, and other pecuniary charges.

The conference assembled, it is true, at the request of the King, but that circumstance did not confer on the conference the right to give its protocols a direction at variance with the object for which its assistance had been asked, and, instead of cooperating in the establishment of order in the Netherlands, to make them tend to the dismemberment of the Kingdom.

Without noticing this protest, the conference proceeded on January 27, 1831, to fix the boundaries and other conditions of the new State. The Belgians, on the 4th of June, elected a king who was instantly recognized by the powers. On the 26th of June the conference adopted another series of eighteen articles. The King of Holland replied, July 12, that these new articles were very important changes, wholly in the interests of Belgium and to the injury of Holland.

The Belgians meanwhile continued to organize their Government on a basis, diplomatic and territorial, that assumed in their favor all the points in dispute. The King of Holland, therefore, put an end to the armistice and marching forward routed the Belgian forces, August 11, and moved on Brussels. Belgium was then at his mercy. The King of the Belgians meanwhile wrote directly to the King of France requesting the immediate succor of a corps of French troops, and without waiting for concert with other powers the French Government marched 40,000 men across the frontier. (Granville to Palmerston, August 4, 1831. British State Papers, 1833.)

Thus within less than a year, after rebellion had broken out and without waiting for evidence of the right or the military force of the insurrection, every sort of intervention took place—diplomatic and military, joint and separate. Nor did the intervention stop with the measures taken for the succor of Belgium. As King William of Holland continued to reject the conditions imposed by the powers and held Antwerp as a pledge for more favorable conditions of peace, the Governments of France and England, abandoning the European concert, announced that they should put their naval and military forces in motion, and accordingly the British Goverment, November —, 1832, embargoed Dutch ships and blockaded the Dutch coast, while the French army, November 14, formally laid siege to Antwerp.

3. POLAND, 1831.

While the Belgian revolution was going on a rebellion broke out in the ancient Kingdom of Poland, and on January 25, 1831, the Polish Diet declared the Czar Nicholas no longer King of Poland, and elected a regency of five members, with Prince Adam George Czartoriski at its head.

The Czar instantly gave notice to the minister of the new French King, Louis Philippe, that he would tolerate no intervention in Poland. Louis Philippe, who owed his own crown to the right of revolution, was the only sovereign in Europe who could be supposed likely to interpose; but, for the moment, his interest in France and Belgium absorbed all his energy. Much popular sympathy was felt for the Poles, and Lafayette, then near the end of his life, founded a Polish committee, and raised money for their assistance. Before the question could acquire diplomatic importance by establishing a claim founded on the power of the rebels to maintain themselves, the Russian armies crushed the rebellion, and on September 8 regained possession of Warsaw. The entire struggle lasted barely nine months, and from the first its result was universally regarded as inevitable, or in the highest degree unpromising to the success of the revolution. As a diplomatic precedent, it seems to have no value, except as far as it offered an example of the power of Russia as the Belgian insurrection had shown the power of England and France when in union.

4. HUNGARY, 1849.

The next European people who claimed recognition as an independent member of the family of nations seems to have been the Hungarians.

On the 14th of April, 1849, the Hungarian Diet formally declared Hungary an independent State, and the Hapsburg dynasty forever deposed from the throne. The next day the Diet elected Louis Kossuth provisional president.

In regard to history, geographical importance, population, and military resources, this people had no occasion to excuse or explain their claims or their rights. Hungary was not a new country. Its government existed from time immemorial, and its right to change its sovereign was as complete as that of England or of France. The provisional government had nearly 150,000 men in arms at that moment. The Austrian Emperor could hardly dispose of a larger force for the purpose of conquest.

The young Emperor (Francis Joseph) instantly appealed for aid to the Czar (Nicholas) of Russia, who instantly intervened. The Czar issued a manifesto April 27, stating the facts and the grounds on which his intervention was believed to be legitimate. This paper founded the right of intervention, not on the weakness of the belligerent, but on his strength. Russia asserted as a principle that she must intervene because if she did not intervene Hungary would establish her independence:

The insurrection in Hungary [began the manifesto of April 27, 1849] has of late made so much progress that Russia can not possibly remain inactive. * * * Such a state of things endangers our dearest interests, and prudence compels us to anticipate the difficulties it prepares for us. The Austrian Government being for the moment unable to oppose a sufficient power to the insurgents, it has formally requested His Majesty the Emperor (Nicholas) to assist in the repression of a rebellion which endangers the tranquillity of the two Empires. It was but natural that the two cabinets should understand one another on this point of common interest, and our troops have consequently advanced into Galicia to cooperate with Austria against the Hungarian rebellion. We trust the Governments that are equally interested in the maintenance of tranquillity will not misunderstand our motives of action. The Emperor (Nicholas) is sorry to quit the passive and expectant position which he has hitherto maintained, but still he remains faithful to the spirit of his former declarations, for, in granting to every State the right to arrange its own political constitution according to its own mind and refraining from interfering with any alterations of their form of government which such States might think proper to make, His Majesty reserved to himself his full liberty of action in case the reaction of revolutions near him should tend to endanger his own safety or the political equilibrium on the frontiers of his Empire.[1]

This precedent tended to establish the right of every Government to intervene in the affairs of foreign States whenever their situation should "tend to endanger its own safety or the political equilibrium on its frontier." As far as is known, every other Government in the world tacitly acquiesced in the establishment of this precedent.

If any Government recorded a protest, it was that of the United States, but even the United States protested only by inference from the acts and language of the President. On March 4, 1849, the administration of President Taylor began, and the Russian intervention in Hungary took place a few weeks aftewards, before the new President had time to consult other Governments in regard to possible action in European affairs. Without alliance or consultation, President Taylor instantly appointed an agent to inquire into the situation in Hungary. Secretary Clayton signed his instructions June 18, 1849, six weeks after the Russian troops had been ordered to enter Hungary. The language of these instructions was as emphatic and as decisive as that of the Czar's circular:

Should the new government prove to be, in your opinion, firm and stable, * * * you might intimate, if you should see fit, that the President would, in that event, be gratified to receive a diplomatic agent from Hungary to the United States by or before the next meeting of Congress, and that he entertains no doubt whatever that, in case her new government should prove to be firm and stable, her independence would be speedily recognized by that enlightened body.

The Russian intervention brought the Hungarian war so quickly to an end that before October all resistance was over, and when Congress met, early in December, 1849, President Taylor's annual message could only proclaim what would have been American policy:

During the late conflict beween Austria and Hungary there seemed to be a prospect that the latter might become an independent nation. However faint that prospect at the time appeared, I thought it my duty, in accordance with the general sentiment of the American people, who deeply sympathized with the Magyar patriots, to stand prepared upon the contingency of the establishment by her of a permanent government, to be the first to welcome independent Hungary into the family of nations. For this purpose I invested an agent, then in Europe, with power to declare our willingness promptly to recognize her independence in the event of her ability to sustain it. The powerful intervention of Russia in the contest extinguished the hopes of the struggling Magyars. * * *

To this paragraph, and to some expressions in the instructions, the Austrian minister was ordered to take exception. He protested accordingly. Daniel Webster had then become Secretary of State, and replied to the protest in a paper known as the Hulsemann letter, in which he declared what he believed to be the American policy and the law in regard to new nationalities claiming recognition:

Of course, questions of prudence naturally arise in reference to new States brought by successful revolutions into the family of nations; but it is not to be required of neutral powers that they should await the recognition of the new government by the parent State. No principle of public law has been more frequently acted upon within the last thirty years by the great powers of the world than this. Within that period eight or ten new States have established independent Governments within the limits of the colonial dominions of Spain on this continent, and in Europe the same thing has been done by Belgium and Greece. The existence of all these Governments was recognized by some of the leading powers of Europe, as well as by the United States, before it was acknowledged by the States from which they had separated themselves. If, therefore, the United States had gone so far as formally

---

[1] Annual Register, 1849, p. 333.

to acknowledge the independence of Hungary, although, as the event has proved, it would have been a precipitate step, and one from which no benefit would have resulted to either party, it would not, nevertheless, have been an act against the law of nations, provided they took no part in her contest with Austria.

Secretary Webster's view of the rights of intervention did not cover ground so wide as that taken by the Czar in his circular of April, 1849, but the attitude of President Taylor seems to have been intended as a counteraction, or a protest, as far as the influence of America extended, not so much to the claims of right or law asserted by the Czar, as to the object of his intervention. The instructions of June 18, 1849, expressly said that Russia " has chosen to assume an attitude of inter-ference, and her immense preparations for invading and reducing the Hungarians to the rule of Austria, from which they desire to be released, gave so serious a character to the contest as to awaken the most painful solicitude in the minds of Americans."

Thus, on both sides the right to intervene, both for and against the Hungarians seems to have been claimed and not expressly denied by either; and no other power appears to have offered even so much oppo-sition as was shown by President Taylor to the principles or to the acts of Russia, which settled the course of history.

5. STATES OF THE CHURCH, 1850.

Besides the four precedents of Greece, Belgium, Poland, and Hun-gary, where new nationalities were in question, a much larger number of interventions occurred in Europe in the process of disruption or con-solidation which has, on one hand, disintegrated the ancient empires of the Sultan, of Spain, of the Church; and on the other, concentrated the new systems of Germany, Russia, and Italy.

Interventions have occurred most conspicuously in Spain, by France, in 1823; in Portugal, by England, in 1827; again in Spain and Portugal in 1836, by England and France, under what was called the quadruple treaty; in Piedmont and Naples, by the Holy Alliance, in 1821; and in so many instances since 1848 that the mere enumeration would be long and difficult; but none of the disturbed countries claimed permanent independence under a form of revolution, unless it were perhaps the States of the Church, or Rome, which, on February 8, 1849, declared the Pope to be deposed, and set up a provisional government under a revolutionary triumvirate. The National Assembly of France, which was then a Republic, hastened to adopt, March 31,1849, a resolution that if, "in order better to safeguard the interests and honor of France, the Executive should think proper to support its negotiations by a partial and temporary occupation in Italy, it would find in the assembly the most entire agreement." The assembly doubtless intended to inter-vene in Italy in order to protect the revolutionary movement there from the threatened intervention of Austria. The French Executive, Louis Napoleon, gave another direction to the policy of France. He immedi-ately sent a French army to Civita Vecchia, which landed there April 26, and after a bloody struggle drove the republican government out of Rome. The French entered Rome July 3. Pope Pius IX returned there in April, 1850, and during the next twenty years Rome remained under the occupation of a French army.

The only reason given by France, in this instance, for intervention was that the occupation of Rome was necessary in order to "maintain the political influence of France." This was the ground taken by President Louis Napoleon in explaining his course to the Chambers in 1850.

S. Doc. 231, pt 7——4

The British Government acquiesced in this rule of European law or practice. On May 9, 1851, Lord Palmerston, then foreign secretary, said in Parliament, in reply to a formal inquiry, that the occupation of Rome was "a measure undertaken by France in her own discretion and in the exercise of her own judgment. The British Government had been no party to this measure. France had exercised her own rights in regard to it, and it was not at all necessary that the previous concurrence of the British Government should have been obtained in this matter. The British Government had been no party to this aggression and could not therefore be said to have concurred in it. It was a matter on which they might have an opinion, but in which they had no particular right, by treaty or otherwise, to interfere."

6. THE OTTOMAN EMPIRE, 1878.

Since the year 1827 intervention in the affairs of the Ottoman Empire has been so constant as to create a body of jurisprudence, and a long series of treaties on which the existence of all political systems of southeastern Europe seems now to be more or less entirely based.

Not only Greece, Montenegro, Roumania, Bulgaria, Roumelia, Servia, and Egypt have been the creations of such intervention, or the objects of its restraints, but also Samos, Crete, and even the Lebanon owe their legal status to the same source.

An authority so great must assume some foundation in law, seeing that the entire world acquiesced not only in the practical exercise of the force but also in the principle on which it rested, whatever that principle was.

The treaty of Berlin in 1878 was a broad assertion of the right of the European powers to regulate the affairs of the Ottoman Empire, but the treaty contains no statement of the principle of jurisprudence on which the right rests.

The preamble merely declares that the powers, "being desirous to regulate, with a view to European order, the questions raised in the East by the events of late years and by the war terminated by the preliminary treaty of San Stefano, have been unanimously of opinion that the meeting of a congress would offer the best means of facilitating an understanding."

In effect, the treaty of Berlin reduced the Ottoman Porte to tutelage, extinguished its sovereignty over certain large portions of its dominions, and restrained its rights over other portions. It recognized the independence of Servia, Roumania, and Montenegro, and fixed their boundaries. It established Bulgaria as "an autonomous and tributary principality under the suzerainty of the Sultan." It created the province of Eastern Roumelia "under conditions of administrative autonomy." It stipulated an organic law for Crete. It interfered in all directions with the internal arrangements of the Ottoman Empire.

Perhaps the most typical instance of assumption of power by the combined governments was Article XXV of the treaty, which began: "The provinces of Bosnia and Herzegovina shall be occupied and administered by Austria-Hungary."

So liberal a use of the right of intervention has seldom been made, but the principle of jurisprudence on which it rested has never been officially declared. Nothing in the treaties expressly limits to the Ottoman Empire the right of intervention which was exercised in its case. The only principle jealously insisted upon, seemed to be that of joint, as against separate, intervention by the European powers. With this implied restriction, the right of intervention "with a view to European order" appears to be the only foundation for the existing status of southeastern Europe, and equally applicable to the rest of the world.

—

These six precedents include, as far as is known, every instance where a claim to independence has been made by any people whatever in Europe since the close of the Napoleonic wars in 1815. Other successful revolutions, such as those of Tuscany and the States of the Church in 1859, were the immediate results of intervention, and that of Naples in 1860 was, from first to last, perhaps the most striking example of intervention in modern times, although Naples hardly. thought necessary to pass through any intermediate stage of recognition as an independent authority.

The six precedents, therefore, constitute the entire European law on the subject of intervention in regard to European peoples claiming independence by right of revolution. There is no other authoritative source of the law; for the judicial courts of Europe were bound to follow the political decision; and the opinions of private persons, whether jurists or politicians, being without sanction, could not be accepted as law.

From this body of precedent it is clear that Europe has invariably asserted and practiced the right to interfere, both collectively and separately, amicably and forcibly, in every instance, except that of Poland, where a European people has resorted to insurrection to obtain independence.

The right itself has been based on various grounds: "Impediments to commerce," "Burdensome measures of protection and repression," "Requests" of one or both parties "to interpose," "Effusion of blood," and "Evils of all kinds," "Humanity" and "The repose of Europe" (Greek treaty of 1827); "A warm desire to arrest, with the shortest possible delay, the disorder and the effusion of blood" (Protocol of November 4, 1830, in the case of Belgium); "His own safety or the political equilibrium on the frontiers of his Empire" (Russian circular of April 27, 1849, in the case of Hungary;) "To safeguard the interest and honor" and to "Maintain the political influence" of the intervening power (French declarations of 1849–50 in regard to the States of the Church). Finally, in the latest and most considerable, because absolutely unanimous act of all Europe, simply the "desire to regulate" (Preamble to the Treaty of Berlin in 1878, covering the recognition of Servia, Roumania, Montenegro, and Bulgaria).

ASIA.

There remains the experience of Asia and America.

In regard to Asia, probably all authorities agree that the entire fabric of European supremacy, whether in Asiatic Turkey, Persia, Afghanistan, India, Siam, or China, rests on the right of intervention.

The exercise of this right constitutes another large but separate branch of public law which, by common consent, is not regarded as applicable to nations of European blood.

Furthermore, although many governments in Asia have been extinguished by means of the right of intervention, none is known to have claimed independence founded on the right of insurrection. Certainly none has been recognized by Europe or America on that ground.

AMERICA, 1822-23.

America, both North and South, has always aimed to moderate European interventon and to restrict its exercise. On this point we have the evidence of George Canning in a celebrated speech on the foreign-enlistment act in 1823

We have spent much time [said Canning] in teaching other powers the nature of a strict neutrality, and generally speaking we found them most reluctant scholars. * ᐧ * If I wished for a guide in a system of neutrality I should take that laid down by America in the days of the presidency of Washington and the secretary-ship of Jefferson.

In fact, the British Government did take that guide. The American neutrality act of 1794, revised and reenacted in the act of April 20, 1818, served as the model for the British foreign-enlistment act in 1819. The cause of that act of 1819 was stated by Canning in the speech just cited:

When peace was concluded between this country and Spain in 1814, an article was introduced into the treaty by which this country bound itself not to furnish any succors to what were then denominated the revolted colonies of Spain. In process of time, as those colonies became more powerful, a question arose of a very difficult nature, to be decided on a due consideration of their de jure relation to Spain on the one side, and their de facto independence of her on the other. The law of nations was entirely silent with respect to a course which, under a circumstance so peculiar as the transition of colonies from their allegiance to the parent state, ought to be pursued. It was difficult to know how far either the statute law or the common law was applicable to colonies so situated. It became necessary, therefore, in the act of 1818, to treat the colonies as actually independent of Spain. * * *

Apparently Canning did not consider that the revolt of the American colonies in 1776 offered a precedent for "a circumstance so peculiar as the transition of colonies from their allegiance." He regarded the situation as so peculiar that it needed to be met by measures in regard to which "the law of nations was entirely silent." He seemed to regard the foreign-enlistment act as a recognition of independence.

The Government of the United States was not so much perplexed in regard to the steps by which colonies achieved independence; but in the actual condition of Europe, where the Holy Alliance held entire control and intervened everywhere against claims based on the right of insurrection, the President had the strongest reasons for moving slowly, and, if possible, only in concert with England.

The disturbances in the Spanish colonies in America had begun as a consequence of the overthrow of the Bourbon dynasty by Napoleon and the establishment of Joseph Bonaparte as King of Spain in 1808; but the movements for independence took serious form at a much later time.

In Mexico, the first national congress met at Chilpancingo in 1813, and formally declared the independence of Mexico on the 6th of November of that year. It was practically suppressed by the execution of Morelos, December 22, 1815, and did not revive until Iturbide, in January, 1821, joined Guerrero in the so-called plan of Iguala. Iturbide made his triumphal entry into the City of Mexico September 27, 1821.

Venezuela first declared independence on July 15, 1811, but the Spanish forces continued the war until General Bolivar drove them from the interior in 1821, and General Paez captured Puerto Cabello in 1823.

Chile began her revolution in 1810, but did not declare independence until January 1, 1818, and then only by proclamation of the executive authority, "the actual circumstances of the war not permitting the convocation of a national congress."

Buenos Ayres also began her revolution in 1810, but did not declare independence and claim recognition until October 25, 1816.

The question of intervention began in 1817. The Spanish Government appealed to the European powers for aid. The Czar openly took sides with Spain, and when, in September, 1817, the Spanish Government asked permission to build several ships of war in the Russian dockyards, the Czar suggested that Spain should buy five ships of the line and three frigates belonging to the Russian navy. This was done, and the ships were sent to the seat of war. At the same time, in October, 1817, the Russian Government instructed its ambassador in London to press on the British Government the great importance of European intervention.

Great Britain declared energetically that she would have no part in trying to force back the subjects of Spain under the domination of an oppressive Government. In fact, Lord Castlereagh had already assured President Monroe that if Great Britain intervened at all it would be on a system of perfect liberality to the Spanish provinces, and the President decided, as early as April, 1818, to discourage European mediation and to take the ground that there could be no rational interference except on the basis of the independence of the South Americans. In August he made a formal proposal to the British and French Governments for a concerted and contemporary recognition of Buenos Ayres, whose de facto independence made that country the natural object of a first step toward the establishment of a general policy. In December he notified both Governments that he had patiently waited without interfering in the policy of the allies, but as they had not agreed upon anything, and as the fact of the independence of Buenos Ayres appeared established, he thought that recognition was necessary. In January, 1819, he announced to them that he was actually considering the measure.

Thus, all parties had agreed, as early as 1817 and 1818, upon the propriety of intervention between Spain and her colonies. Both the United States and Europe asserted that the time had come; they disagreed only as to the mode. When Lord Castlereagh, at the Congress of Aix-la-Chapelle, in October, 1818, proposed to the four other powers "to intervene in the war between Spain and her American colonies by addressing offers of mediation to the two belligerents," Russia energetically opposed and rejected the scheme, not because it was intervention, but apparently because it was mediation, and to that extent recognized rights in the insurgents. When President Monroe interposed his fiat that no interference could be countenanced by him except on the basis of independence, he dictated in advance the only mode of intervention which he meant to permit. If he waited before carrying it out it was only because in the actual balance of European and American power he felt that isolated action might injure the cause he had determined to help.

He waited in vain. Neither England nor any other power moved again. No information came from Europe. No further attempt to subject the revolted colonies was probable, and even the declaration of the Congress of Troppau in November, 1820, which announced a general and active intervention against all "illegitimate" authorities, caused little alarm as long as England and France were not parties to it. Delay was not dangerous. The system which Monroe aimed to establish could not be firm or broad as long as it rested on the recognition of a single country like Buenos Ayres or on the isolated action of the United States. That system included all American communities which

rejected foreign authority; it was to be taken as a whole, and referred
to every part of the contest, from the recognition of the flag at the
outset to the recognition of independence at the close. Therefore,
Monroe waited until the effect of his action should settle the whole
question and cover all the ground. After a delay of four years from
the time when he began his policy, the Greek revolt in Europe and the
military successes of Bolivar and Iturbide in America gave the desired
opportunity, and Monroe sent to Congress his celebrated message of
March 8, 1822, recommending the recognition of all the revolted colonies of Spain—Mexico, Colombia, Chile, and Buenos Ayres.

These countries asked no more. They based their claim on their
independence de facto, and Monroe admitted its force. "The provinces," he said, "which have declared their independence and are in
the enjoyment of it, ought to be recognized." He added that "the
measure is proposed under a thorough conviction that it is in strict
accord with the law of nations." In reality, it created the law, so far
as its action went, and its legality was recognized by no European
power. All waited in open or tacit disapproval of Monroe's course.
England herself, even after Canning succeeded Castlereagh, refused to
approve. Spain protested vigorously; and, as far as concerned objections, the Spanish minister in Washington offered them in great numbers and with sufficient energy. He instantly protested, not only on
grounds of morality and fact, but also of policy. "Buenos Ayres," he
said, was "sunk in the most complete anarchy;" in Peru, "near the
gates of its capital," a rebel and a Spanish army divided the inhabitants;
in Chili, "an individual suppresses the sentiments of its inhabitants;"
"on the coast of Terra Firma, also, the Spanish banners wave;" "in
Mexico, too, there is no government;" and he concluded, with force:
"Where then are those governments which ought to be recognized?"

The question was not without difficulties, as Monroe knew; and on
this point all Europe supported the Spanish contention. Although
Congress unanimously approved and adopted the President's views,
and immediately appropriated $100,000 for diplomatic expenses; and
although Mexico, Colombia, Chile, and Buenos Ayres were in consequence admitted into the family of nations by the sole authority of the
President of the United States, with the approval of Congress, two
years passed before the British Government consented even to discuss
the subject in Parliament as a serious measure of policy.

Then, on June 15, 1824, a motion was made by Sir James Mackin-
tosh, and Canning replied. His speech made no allusion to the action
of the United States; it denied the de facto right of recognition so far
as to say that "we ought not to acknowledge the separate and independent existence of any government which is so doubtfully established
that the mere effect of that acknowledgment shall be to mix parties
again in internal squabbles if not in open hostilities." Canning still
thought "that, before we can act, information as to matters of fact
is necessary."

Nevertheless, Monroe's act, which extinguished the last hopes of the
Holy Alliance in America, produced the deepest sensation among European conservatives, and gave to the United States extraordinary consideration. England used it as a weapon at the Congress of Verona to
threaten the other powers when they decided on intervention in Spain.
Slowly Canning came wholly over to the side of Monroe as France and
Austria forced his hands in Spain. As early as October, 1823, he sent
consuls to all the chief cities in rebellion throughout Mexico and Central and South America. Immediately after his speech in Parliament

of June 15, 1824, he authorized his consul at Buenos Ayres to negotiate a commercial treaty with that Government. On the 1st of January, 1825, he notified other powers that England had determined to recognize the independence of Colombia, Mexico, and Buenos Ayres. In a speech in Parliament on the 15th of February, 1825, he explained and defended his conduct, blaming the United States, by implication, for pursuing "a reckless and headlong course," and claiming credit for following one "more strictly guarded in point of principle." "The whole question was one of time and mode."

Notwithstanding Canning's explanation, the principle of intervention on which he acted was not clear. Nothing in his act of recognition revealed a rule of any general value. He considered that "any other period or mode than that chosen would have been liable to some objection." Yet the period and mode he chose were strongly objected to throughout Europe, and met with energetic protest from Spain. Nearly two years more passed before he cleared up the mystery. Then, when driven to armed intervention in the affairs of Spain and Portugal, he made, on the 12th of December, 1826, a speech in Parliament which was perhaps the most celebrated of his life. At the very end of this speech he explained the "principle" on which he had acted in regard to the independence of the Spanish colonies, and the "time and mode" of recognition. It was the moment when a French army took possession of Spain:

If France occupied Spain, was it necessary, in order to avoid the consequences of that occupation, that we should blockade Cadiz? No! I looked another way. I sought materials of compensation in another hemisphere. Contemplating Spain, such as our ancestors had known her, I resolved that if France had Spain, it should not be Spain "with the Indies." I called the New World into existence to redress the balance of the Old.

The principle thus avowed by Canning added little to the European law of intervention; but the principle avowed by Monroe created an entire body of American jurisprudence. As an isolated act it meant little, but in Monroe's view it was not an isolated act; it was part of a system, altogether new and wholly American; and it was to be justified on grounds far wider than itself. The European law and practice of intervention, extending, as it did, its scope and energy with every new step in European development, could be met only by creating an American law and practice of intervention exclusive of the European within the range of its influence. This Monroe did not hesitate to do. With boldness which still startles and perplexes the world, he lopped off one great branch of European intervention and empire and created a new system of international relations. His opportunity was given by Canning, who, in the midst of his European difficulties in 1823, intimated that England would be well pleased to see the United States take ground even more advanced than in the recognition of the South American revolted States. Monroe lost no time in doubts or hesitations. In his annual message of December, 1823, he announced the principle that the new nations which his act alone had recognized as independent were by that act placed outside of the European system, and that the United States would regard any attempt to extend that system among them as unfriendly to the United States.

With the Governments who have declared their independence, and maintained it, and whose independence we have, on great consideration and on just principles, acknowledged, we could not view any interposition for the purpose of oppressing them, or controlling in any other manner their destiny, by any European power in any other light than as the manifestation of an unfriendly disposition toward the United States. * * * It is impossible that the allied powers should extend their political system to any portion of either continent without endangering our peace and happiness. * * * It is equally impossible, therefore, that we should behold such interposition in any form with indifference.

So sweeping a right of intervention had never been claimed unless by Russia in regard to the Greeks in 1821, and has never been exercised by any other single power; but the claim rested on the same general ground as that of the innumerable interventions of Europe. "Danger to our peace and happiness" was not essentially different from "danger to peace, honor, political power, and interests" which European nations had alleged as just reasons for intervention, and while the right of intervention on this ground was so energetically maintained, the right of deciding absolutely as to the time and mode of intervention was as energetically exercised by Monroe.

From that day to this the American people have always, and unanimously, supported and approved the Monroe doctrine. They needed no reasoning to prove that it was vital to their safety. The enormous and rapidly increasing force developed by Europe in her system of joint action, from the treaty of Verona to the overwhelming authority, hitherto unknown to mankind, which was exhibited in the treaty of Berlin; the rapid extension of her system over the rest of the world, and the inevitable pressure of its expansion; her immense superiority in wealth and mechanical resources; the irresistible energy of her enormous naval and military armaments when concentrated, as under the Berlin treaty, in a single mass, left no doubt that America must abandon the hope of independence if she could not maintain a system of her own. Europeans, indeed, sometimes expressed fear of America, but their fears rested only on the assumption that America could stand apart. Even the celebrated historian Niebuhr complained because the Czar did not conquer the Turkish Empire and found Christian states in Asia Minor in order to balance the growing power of America. Europe did not, it is true, adopt Niebuhr's advice and colonize Asia Minor, but she conquered, or subdued under her system, all the rest of Asia, and used this accession of strength for her common objects. She spread her system over all Asia, all Africa, all Australasia, and all Polynesia. America made no contest, even within America, except in regard to those countries or communities which expressly declared their will and their power to be American.

Within that limited range President Monroe attempted to build up an American system. He disclaimed the right or the intention to interfere with actual European possessions in America, so long as these communities were contented to remain European; but he claimed and exercised, under the broadest principle, the right to intervene in favor of communities that plainly displayed their wish and their power to be American; and, what was vital to the exercise of his claim, he asserted and used in its fullest extent the right to judge for himself, and finally, both as to "time and mode,"—both when and how—any particular community had proved its will and its right to claim admission into the American system. Against the opposition of all Europe, and at the risk of many and serious embarrassments, Monroe took and successfully held ground which his successors have struggled with varying fortune to maintain.

The right of intervention lay necessarily at the bottom of the strife of forces, and the United States exercised it freely, although usually striving to exercise it for the common good of an American system. In the case of Texas, the United States Government, as is notorious, exercised the whole right of intervention against an American power; but the case of Texas did not differ in principle from that of Colombia, except in being wholly an American and domestic affair.   In both instances the intervention rested on the claim of the Executive and the Legislature to be absolute and final judge of the "time and mode" of interference.   In no case were other governments expected to sanction the decision in order to give it validity.

In the case of Texas, however, we have to call attention to a subject on which the proposed action of Congress necessarily depends.

In a report made June 18, 1836, by Mr. Clay, from the Senate Committee on Foreign Relations, in respect to the recognition of the independence of Texas (Senate Doc. 406, Twenty-fourth Congress, first session), are the following passages:

*   *   *   *   *   *   *

The recognition of Texas as an independent power may be made by the United States in various ways: First, by treaty; second, by the passage of a law regulating commercial intercourse between the two powers; third, by sending a diplomatic agent to Texas with the usual credentials; or, lastly, by the Executive receiving and accrediting a diplomatic representative from Texas, which would be a recognition as far as the Executive only is competent to make it.   In the first and third modes the concurrence of the Senate in its executive character would be necessary, and in the second in its legislative character.

The Senate alone, without the cooperation of some other branch of the Government, is not competent to recognize the existence of any power.

The President of the United States, by the Constitution, has the charge of their foreign intercourse.   Regularly he ought to take the initiative in the acknowledgment of the independence of any new power, but in this case he has not yet done it, for reasons which he, without doubt, deems sufficient.   If in any instance the President should be tardy, he may be quickened in the exercise of his power by the expression of the opinion, or by other acts, of one or both branches of Congress, as was done in relation to the Republics formed out of Spanish America.   But the committee do not think that on this occasion any tardiness is justly imputable to the Executive.   About three months only have elapsed since the establishment of an independent government in Texas, and it is not unreasonable to wait a short time to see what its operation will be, and especially whether it will afford those guaranties which foreign powers have a right to expect before they institute relations with it.

Taking this view of the whole matter, the committee concluded by recommending to the Senate the adoption of the following resolution:

Resolved, That the independence of Texas ought to be acknowledged by the United States whenever satisfactory information shall be received that it has in successful operation a civil government capable of performing the duties and fulfilling the obligations of an independent power.

President Andrew Jackson, in his Texas message of December 21, 1836, began by calling attention to these resolutions passed by "the two Houses at their last session, acting separately, ' that the independence of Texas ought to be acknowledged by the United States whenever satisfactory information should be received that it had in successful operation a civil government capable of performing the duties and fulfilling the obligations of an independent power.' "   After treating shortly the principles of recognition, President Jackson continued:

Nor has any deliberate inquiry ever been instituted in Congress, or in any of our legislative bodies, as to whom belonged the power of recognizing a new State—a power the exercise of which is equivalent, under some circumstances, to a declaration of war; a power nowhere expressly delegated, and only granted in the Constitution, as it is necessarily involved in some of the great powers given to Congress; in that given to the President and Senate to form treaties with foreign powers, and to appoint ambassadors and other public ministers, and in that conferred upon the President to receive ministers from foreign nations.   In the preamble to the resolution of the House of Representatives it is distinctly intimated that the expediency of recognizing the independence of Texas should be left to the decision of Congress. In this view, on the ground of expediency, I am disposed to concur, and do not therefore consider it necessary to express any opinion as to the strict constitutional right of the Executive, either apart from or in conjunction with the Senate over the subject. It is to be presumed that on no future occasion will a dispute arise, as none has heretofore occurred, between the Executive and the Legislature in the exercise of the power of recognition. It will always be considered consistent with the spirit of the Constitution and most safe that it should be exercised, when probably leading to war, with a previous understanding with that body by whom war can alone be declared, and by whom all the provisions for sustaining its perils must be furnished. Its submission to Congress, which represents in one of its branches the States of this Union and in the other the people of the United States, where there may be reasonable ground to apprehend so grave a consequence, would certainly afford the fullest satisfaction to our own country and a perfect guaranty to all other nations of the justice and prudence of the measures which might be adopted.

The initiative thus asserted by Congress and conceded by President Jackson to Congress in the case of the recognition of Texas was followed in the case of Hungary by President Taylor in the instructions already quoted, which authorized his agent to invite the revolutionary government of Hungary to send to the United States a diplomatic representative, since the President entertained no doubt that in such case at the next meeting of Congress "her independence would be speedily recognized by that enlightened body."

Until now no further question has been raised in regard to the powers of Congress.

So much space has been taken by this historical summary that the case of Texas must be passed over without further notice, and the cases of Haiti and Santo Domingo may be set aside as governed by peculiar influences. The record shows that in every instance except Poland down to 1850 where any people has claimed independence by right of revolt the right of intervention has been exercised against the will of one or the other party to the dispute. In every instance the only question that has disturbed the intervening powers has regarded neither the right nor the policy so much as the "time and mode" of action. The only difference between the European and American practice was that the United States aimed at moderating or restricting the extreme license of European intervention, and this was the difference which brought the United States nearly into collision with Europe in 1861 and 1862. Lords Palmerston and Russell, as well as the Emperor Napoleon and his ministers, entertained no doubt of their right to intervene even before our civil war had actually commenced, and accordingly recognized the insurgent States as belligerents in May, 1861, although no legal question had yet been raised requiring such a decision. The United States Government never ceased to protest with the utmost energy against the act as premature and unjust, and this last and most serious case of interference, in which the United States was concerned as an object of European intervention, revealed the vital necessity of their American system at the same time that it revealed the imminent danger of its destruction.

THE UNITED STATES AND MEXICO, 1861–1866.

Allusion has been already made to the declaration of Lord John Russell on the part of the British Government in the House of Commons May 6, 1861, in which he announced that the law officers of the Crown had already "come to the opinion that the Southern Confederacy of America, according to those principles which seem to them to be just principles, must be treated as a belligerent." This astonishing promise of belligerency to an insurrection which had by the latest advices at that time neither a ship at sea nor an army on land, before the fact of war was officially known in England to have been proclaimed by either party, was accompanied by a letter of the same date from Lord John

Russell to the British ambassador at Paris, in which he said that the accounts which had been received from America were "sufficient to show that a civil war has broken out among the States which lately composed the American Union."

Other nations have therefore to consider the light in which, with reference to that war, they are to regard the Confederacy into which the Southern States have united themselves; and it appears to Her Majesty's Government that, looking at all the circumstances of the case, they can not hesitate to admit that such Confederacy is entitled to be considered as a belligerent, invested with all the rights and prerogatives of a belligerent.

Under these circumstances, Lord John Russell invited the Emperor of France to cooperate with England in "a joint endeavor" to obtain "from each of the belligerents" certain concessions in favor of neutrals. On May 8 the French minister "concurred entirely in the views of Her Majesty's Government" and pledged himself to the joint action. On May 13 the British Government issued its formal proclamation of neutrality between the United States and "certain States styling themselves the Confederate States of America."

Lord John Russell justified this action on the ground of "the size and population of the seceding States" and "the critical condition of our (British) commerce." He denied that the British Government had any thought of giving assistance to the South.

Nevertheless, the language of Lord John Russell showed that he considered the issue as decided in advance and that his measures were shaped on that assumption. His speech of May 6 characterized the insurgents without qualification as "the Southern Confederacy of America." In his official correspondence with his official agents he used the term "Northern or Southern confederation of North America," or "the Confederate States of America," as though their independence were fully established. All his expressions and acts warranted the belief that the recognition of belligerency was in his mind only a preliminary step to the recognition of independence as an already accomplished fact, and that he had hurried the declaration of belligerency in order to avoid the remonstrances certain to be made by the new American minister about to arrive. More serious still as a symptom of European temper was the joint action concerted between England and France, which soon proved that England, while waiting for the dissolution of the Union, meant, in recognizing the independence of the Southern Confederacy, to revive her old belligerent claims of 1812, which had never been expressly abandoned.

This threatened wreck of all American rights was even more imminent than our highest officials supposed. Only by slow degrees have we learned how narrow an escape we made, and even at this day much remains to be revealed. We know that as early as March, 1861, the French minister at Washington advised his Government to recognize the Confederate States, and in May he advised it to intervene by forcibly raising the American blockade. Mercier's recommendation was communicated to Russell, who entertained no doubts as to the right of intervention, either diplomatic or military, even at that early moment when the serious operations of war had hardly begun.

There is much good sense in Mercier's observations [wrote Russell to Palmerston, October 17]. But we must wait; I am persuaded that, if we do anything, it must be on a grand scale. It will not do for England and France to break a blockade for the sake of getting cotton; but in Europe powers have often said to belligerents: "Make up your quarrels. We propose to give terms of pacification which we think fair and equitable. If you accept them, well and good. But if your adversary accepts them, and if you refuse them, our mediation is at an end, and you must expect to see us your enemies."

France would be quite ready to hold this language with us. If such a policy were to be adopted, the time for it would be the end of the year, or immediately before the meeting of Parliament.

Already (on May 6) Russell had officially announced the Greek prece-dent as his rule of law. In October he was ready to take the last step but one in the line of the Greek example. The five years of 1821 counted as five months in 1861. Palmerston was not yet ready. And the concession of the United States in the Trent affair, in the follow-ing winter, made an aggressive movement less popular in England. But in the autumn of 1862 Palmerston also thought the moment had arrived. Neither of these two powerful statesmen, the highest English authorities of their times on the subjects of foreign relations, doubted the right or the expediency of intervention after the second campaign in Virginia. On September 14, 1862, Palmerston wrote to Russell suggesting a joint offer by England and France of what is diplomati-cally called "good offices," as in the Greek protocol of 1826. Russell eagerly approved:

Whether the Federal Army is destroyed or not [replied Russell to Palmerston, September 17, 1862] it is clear that it is driven back to Washington and has made no progress in subduing the insurgent States. Such being the case, I agree with you that the time is come for offering mediation to the United States Government with a view to the recognition of the independence of the Confederates. I agree, further, that in case of failure we ought ourselves to recognize the Southern States as an independent State. For the purpose of taking so important a step I think we must have a meeting of the Cabinet. The 23d or 30th would suit me for the meeting.

We ought then, if we agree on such a step, to propose it first to France, and then, on the part of England and France, to Russia and other powers, as a measure decided upon by us.

We ought to make ourselves safe in Canada. * * *

In this scheme of intervention Russell once more advanced beyond the Greek precedent. Canning would move only in concert with Russia. Russell proposed to move in concert with France alone.

Palmerston replied September 23:

Your plan of proceedings about the mediation between the Federals and Confed-erates seems to be excellent. Of course the offer would be made to both the contend-ing parties at the same time, for, though the offer would be as sure to be accepted by the Southerns as was the proposal of the Prince of Wales to the Danish princess, yet in the one case, as in the other, there are certain forms which it is decent and proper to go through.

A question would occur whether, if the two parties were to accept mediation, the fact of our mediating would not of itself be tantamount to an acknowledgment of the Confederates as an independent State.

Might it not be well to ask Russia to join England and France in the offer of mediation? * * *

We should be better without her in the mediation, because she would be too favor-able to the North; but, on the other hand, her participation in the offer might render the North the more willing to accept it.

The middle of October was the time suggested by Palmerston for action.

If the Federals sustain a great defeat they may be at once ready for mediation, and the iron should be struck while it is hot. If, on the other hand, they should have the best of it, we may wait awhile and see what may follow.

Fortunately for the United States, Russell and Palmerston found their serious difficulties not in France or in the law, but in the political division of their own party. These two powerful statesmen, who had been both honored with the position of prime minister of England, had united their influence to create the exising ministry. They seem to have supposed that their united authority was sufficient to control the ministry they had created, but the moment Russell opened the subject to others he received a check. He persevered; he issued a confidential memorandum suggesting his idea; he brought the subject before a cabinet meeting October 23, 1862, and the division of opinion proved to be so serious that the subject was postponed. The question became one of internal politics, social divisions, and party majorities.

The scheme of intervention was embraced by the Emperor of France as seriously as by Russell and Palmerston. Long before the two English statesmen decided to act, Napoleon III had given his first interview to the Confederate agent accredited to his Government. News of the defeat of the Union army before Richmond reached Paris on the 15th of July, 1862, and the next day Mr. Slidell asked and received an interview. The Emperor talked with exceeding frankness, according to the report made by Mr. Slidell to Mr. Benjamin:

> The Emperor received me with great kindness and [said] * * * that he had from the first seen the true character of the contest, and considered the reestablishment of the Union impossible and final separation a mere question of time; that the difficulty was to find a way to give effect to his sympathies; that he had always desired to preserve the most friendly relation with England, and that in so grave a question he had not been willing to act without her cooperation; that he had several times intimated his wish for action in our behalf, but had met with no favorable response, and that, besides, England had a deeper interest in the question than France; that she wished him to draw the chestnuts from the fire for her benefit; * * * that he had committed a great error which he now deeply regretted; France should never have respected the blockade; that the European powers should have recognized us last summer when our ports were in our possession and when we were menacing Washington, but what, asked he, could now be done?

Napoleon's language was not official, but he had committed himself beyond recall by the policy he described, for hardly had the civil war broken out than he had plunged into a scheme of armed intervention in Mexico. Perhaps the ultimate salvation of America, in this crisis, was due to the mistake of judgment which led Europe to attack the Monroe doctrine and the American system in Mexico instead of attacking its heart. He made no secret of his wish to substitute French influence on the Gulf of Mexico in the place of American. This had been the dream of every great French ruler, and Napoleon III had a "doctrine" of his own, far more ancient than that of Monroe and backed by more formidable military force. Europe did intervene by arms in the American civil war, but fortunately she attacked our ally and only indirectly ourselves. Fortunately, too, in betraying his ultimate objects in Mexico, Napoleon alienated England and did not conciliate Spain.

Yet the attack was made, violently in Mexico, more cautiously at Washington, and as systematically as the mutual jealousies of Europe permitted. At the moment when Russell and Palmerston brought their scheme of intervention before the British cabinet, Napoleon sent reenforcements of 35,000 men to his force in Mexico, with orders to occupy the country, and simultaneously sent a formal invitation to England and Russia to intervene in the American civil war.

These papers have not been published, and we do not know the express grounds on which the invitation was offered or declined. To the fact that Russia was avowedly friendly, and that the two most powerful British prime ministers of their time were outvoted in their own cabinet, America owed her escape from European domination. Mexico, indeed, suffered severely, but only while our civil war was in doubt. From the moment the authority of the Union was wholly restored in 1865, the entire influence of the United States Government was exerted to reestablish also the authority of the Monroe doctrine. The life of the one was dependent on the life of the other.

CUBA.

Into this American system, thus created by Monroe in 1822–23, and embracing then, besides the United States, only Buenos Ayres, Chile, Colombia, and Mexico, various other communities have since claimed, and in most cases have received admission, until it now includes all South America, except the Guianas; all Central America, except the British colony of Honduras, and the two black Republics of Spanish Santo Domingo and Haiti in the Antilles.

No serious question was again raised with any European power in regard to the insurrection or independence of their American possessions, until in 1869, a rebellion broke out in Cuba, and the insurgents, after organizing a government and declaring their independence, claimed recognition fiom the United States.

The Government of the United States had always regarded Cuba as within the sphere of its most active and serious interest. As early as 1825, when the newly recognized States of Colombia and Mexico were supposed to be preparing an expedition to revolutionize Cuba and Puerto Rico, the United States Government interposed its friendly offices with those Governments to request their forbearance. The actual condition of Spain seemed to make her retention of Cuba impossible, in which case the United States would have been obliged, for her own safety, to prevent the island from falling into the hands of a stronger power in Europe. That this emergency did not occur may have been partly due to the energy with which Monroe announced "our right and our power to prevent it," and his determination to use all the means within his competency "to guard against and forefend it."

This right of intervention in matters relating to the external relations of Cuba, asserted and exercised seventy years ago, has been asserted and exercised at every crisis in which the island has been involved.

When the Cuban insurgents in 1869 appealed to the United States for recognition, President Grant admitted the justice of the claim, and directed the minister of the United States at Madrid to interpose our good offices with the Spanish Government in order to obtain by a friendly arrangement the independence of the Island. The story of of that intervention is familiar to every member of the Senate, and was made the basis of its resolution last session, requesting the President once more "to interpose his friendly offices with the Spanish Government for the recognition of the independence of Cuba."

The resolution then adopted by Congress was perfectly understood to carry with it all the consequences which necessarily would follow the rejection by Spain of friendly offices. On this point the situation needs no further comment. The action taken by Congress in the last session was taken "on gieat consideration and on just principles," on a right of intervention exercised twenty-seven years ago, and after a patient delay unexampled in history.

The interval of nine months which has elapsed since that action of Congress, has proved the necessity of carrying it out to completion. In the words of the President's Annual Message: "The stability two years' duration has given to the insurrection; the feasibility of its indefinite prolongation in the nature of things, and as shown by past experience; the utter and imminent ruin of the island unless the present strife is speedily composed" are, in our opinion, conclusive evidence that "the inability of Spain to deal successfully with the insurrection has become manifest, and it is demonstrated that the sovereignty is extinct in Cuba for all purposes of its rightful existence, * * * a hopeless struggle for its reestablishment has degenerated into a strife which means nothing more than the useless sacrifice of human life and the utter destruction of the very subject-matter of the conflict."

Although the President appears to have reached a different conclusion from ours, we believe this to be the actual situation of Cuba, and, being unable to see that further delay could lead to any other action than that which the President anticipates, we agree with the conclusion of the message, that, in such case, our obligations to the sovereignty of Spain are "superseded by higher obligations which we can hardly hesitate to recognize and discharge." Following closely the action of President Monroe in 1818, Congress has already declared in effect its opinion that there can be no rational interference except on the basis of independence.

In 1822, as now, but with more force, it was objected, as we have shown, that the revolted States had no governments to be recognized. Divisions, and even civil war, existed among the insurgents themselves. Among the Cubans no such difficulty is known to exist. In September, 1895, as we know by official documents printed on the spot, the insurgent government was regularly organized, a constitution adopted, a president elected, and, in due course, the various branches of administration set in motion. Since then, so far as we are informed, this government has continued to perform its functions undisturbed. On the military side, as we officially know, they have organized, equipped, and maintained in the field, sufficient forces to baffle the exertions of 200,000 Spanish soldiers. On the civil side they have organized their system of administration in every province for, as we know officially, they "roam at will over at least two-thirds of the inland country." Diplomatically they have maintained a regularly accredited representative in the United States for the past year, who has never ceased to ask recognition and to offer all possible information. There is no reason to suppose that any portion of the Cuban people would be dissatisfied by our recognizing their representative in this country or that they disagree in the earnest wish for that recognition. The same thing could hardly be said of all the countries recognized by Monroe in 1822. Greece had no such stability when it was recognized by England, Russia, and France. Belgium had nothing of the sort when she was recognized by all the powers in 1830. Of the States recognized by the treaty of Berlin in 1878, we need hardly say more than that they were the creatures of intervention.

The only question that properly remains for Congress to consider is the mode which should be adopted for the step which Congress is pledged next to take.

The Government of the United States entertains none but the friendliest feelings toward Spain. Its most anxious wish is to avoid even the appearance of an unfriendliness which is wholly foreign to its thought. For more than a hundred years, amidst divergent or clashing interests, and under frequent and severe strains, the two Governments have succeeded in avoiding collision, and there is no friendly office which Spain could ask, which the United States, within the limits of their established principles and policy, would not be glad to extend. In the present instance they are actuated by an earnest wish to avoid the danger of seeming to provoke a conflict.

The practice of Europe in regard to intervention, as in the instances cited, has been almost invariably harsh and oppressive. The practice of the United States has been almost invariably mild and forbearing.

Among the precedents which have been so numerously cited there can be no doubt as to the choice. The most moderate is the best. Among these, the attitude taken by President Monroe in 1822 is the only attitude which can properly be regarded as obligatory for a similar situation to-day. The course pursued by the United States in the recognition of Colombia is the only course which Congress can consistently adopt.

We recommend, therefore, the joint resolution, with amendments to read as follows:

"*Resolved by the Senate and House of Representatives of the United States of America in Congress assembled*, That the independence of the Republic of Cuba be, and the same is hereby, acknowledged by the United States of America.

"*Be it further resolved*, That the United States will use its friendly offices with the Government of Spain to bring to a close the war between Spain and the Republic of Cuba."

ADDITIONAL VIEWS PRESENTED BY MR. MORGAN AND MR. MILLS IN SUPPORT OF THE REPORT OF THE COMMITTEE.

The report of the committee has the unqualified approval of the undersigned members of that body, but they conceive that it is well to present therewith the former action of the Committee on Foreign Relations, in 1859, on the same subject and on some of the same points that are discussed in the present report.

On January 24, 1859, the Senate Committee on Foreign Relations had under consideration a Senate bill "making appropriations to facilitate the acquisition of the island of Cuba by negotiation," and made a report, which is hereto appended and designated as Appendix No. 1.

That report covers a period of fifty-nine years, and sets forth the political conditions then existing in Cuba, and the disastrous effects of Spanish rule in Cuba, during that time. They were the same, in their leading characteristics, that existed at the beginning of the insurrection that was set on foot by the native population in 1868, in the outbreak at Yara, which was followed by ten years of internecine warfare attended with horrible butcheries.

The causes that provoked that uprising of the native Cubans were the same that are stated in the report of the committee, made ten years previously, in 1859. They are summed up in the following general statement of that committee:

There can be no doubt that an immense majority of the people of Cuba are not only in favor but ardently desirous of annexation to the United States.

It would be strange, indeed, if they were not so. Deprived of all influence even in the local affairs of the island; unrepresented in the Cortes; governed by successive hordes of hungry officials sent from the mother country to acquire fortunes to be enjoyed at home, having no sympathy with the people among whom they are mere sojourners and upon whom they look as inferiors; liable to be arrested at any moment on the most trifling charges; tried by military courts or submissive judges, removable at pleasure, punished at the discretion of the captain-general, they would be less than men if they were contented with their yoke.

The "mother country," as it is styled by the committee, is thus described in their report:

Spain is a country of coups d'état and pronunciamentos. The all-powerful minister of to-day may be a fugitive to-morrow. With the forms of a representative government, it is in fact a despotism sustained by the bayonet—a despotism tempered only by frequent, violent, and bloody revolutions. Her financial condition is one of extreme embarrassment.

Spain is not the "mother country of Cuba" even in the sense of having supplied that island with a large part of the ancestors of her present population. She is a cruel stepmother, whose introduction into the Cuban family has been the immediate cause of the robbery of the stepchildren of their inheritance and their cruel persecution to keep down revolt.

The committee were engaged, in 1859, in providing for the purchase of Cuba by negotiations with Spain, and were as gentle in their description of Spanish rule in Cuba as a decent respect for the world's knowledge of the truth of the actual situation of the people there would permit. It is dark enough without the illumination of the fires of devastation these succeeding years have witnessed in Cuba.

Among the great debates in Congress upon that report of the Committee on Foreign Relations, the part of a speech that relates to Cuba and the report of the committee above referred to, made by Hon. Judah P. Benjamin, in the Senate, on February 11, 1859, is appended hereto, marked appendix No. 2. Mr. Benjamin gives an accurate and much more complete statement of the condition of the people of Cuba and the methods of Spanish government in that island than is stated in the report of the committee.

The relations of Spain and the United States were not then strained by the disturbances of actual insurrection in Cuba, as they were afterwards, from 1868 to 1878, and have been almost ever since, and are now, by the excessive and inhuman abuses of power in Cuba, to which no limit can be now anticipated, either as to the time when they will end or the increased cruelty that is now a settled feature of the present Spanish war of extermination.

The President recognizes the fact that the present war is for independence on the part of the Cubans and not for the gratification of personal ambition, or alone for the redress of personal or political grievances with which the painful history of their sufferings is crowded. For the sake of liberty and the independence of their country they are willing to forget the recompense that is due them for their individual sufferings.

Hon. T. Estrada Palma was duly accredited as diplomatic delegate plenipotentiary to the United States, under an appointment by the Constituent Assembly of the Republic of Cuba. He appears to have been received informally for the purpose of presenting the case of Cuba to our Government. On the 7th December, 1895, he addressed a note to the Secretary of State, accompanied by a statement of facts, in which the case of Cuba is set forth officially. That document has been printed by the order of the Senate, and is appended hereto and numbered 3.

In the papers that accompanied this note the delegate stated the causes of the revolution in Cuba; that it had reached that stage in which the issue between the contending parties "is independence or extermination."

The recent message of the President is clear on the point that he has been forced to the same conclusion.

The delegate then stated the facts, showing the preliminary organization of the revolt; the uprising; the growth of the revolution; the battles and campaigns that had already been fought, including the great and victorious campaign of Gomez against Capt. Gen. Martinez Campos, which caused him to be recalled to Spain and supplanted by Captain-General Weyler; the military organization of the Cubans; their civil government; their treatment of prisoners; that the government he represented is not a negro government; the character of the war; the protests of resident citizens of the United States in Cuba against their cruel treatment by the Spanish forces; that their lives and property are placed under the special protection of the Cuban government, and that they are exempt from taxes and contributions by the constitution of the Republic of Cuba, when that government is recognized by their respective governments.

The letter of the Cuban delegate thus addressed to our Secretary of State has appended to it several papers which set forth fully the grievances complained of by the Cuban people. In its nature it is a declaration of the independence of Cuba, stating the grounds of their united action. That declaration is in keeping with the historical narrative given by Mr. Benjamine in his speech, herewith presented, and with the report of the Committee of Foreign Relations in 1859, and with the messages of President Grant and President Hayes, and the letters of Mr. Sickles and Dr. Cushing, as ministers to Spain, and of Mr. Fish and Mr. Evarts, as Secretaries of State.

All these papers are uniform in their statements of the wrongs and grievances of the Cuban people, and of the wrongful and tyrannical course of Spain toward them. In none of them is any fact or reason stated to excuse or paliate the cruelties that Spain has inflicted upon her subjects in Cuba. In ñone of them is any bad purpose imputed to the Cuban people.

No one has contradicted those statements, or any material part of them, on the authority of the Spanish Government or before any official or other credible authority.

The tenor of the message of the President to this session of Congress is a reaffirmation of all this history, stated in all these papers. In the part of his message relating to Cuba he has laid them before Congress without any special recommendation, and has left to Congress the duty of making provision for the security of the rights, the property, and the lives of our citizens residing in Cuba, and of enforcing the right of indemnity on behalf of the legal successors of those who have been killed there. He has intimated that delay is the wisest policy, but he has refrained from saying that delay is required by our national honor, by the safety of our people in Cuba or by the interests of humanity.

A comparison of this message, which is appended hereto and marked Appendix 4, will show that it agrees with the statements of every President who has attended to the subject, and it further shows that the same spirit of tyrannical domination now prevails in Cuba that has kept the people of that island in despairing servitude during this entire century.

The message of Mr. Cleveland, who has no aversion to Spanish rule in Cuba, confirms, in all important statements, the truth of the charges made by Mr. Estrada Palma against Spain in the exposition of the case of Cuba which he presented to our Secretary of State.

The only difference in the situation in Cuba, as it is described in the report of the Senate Committee on Foregn Relations in 1859 and as it is described in the President's message in 1896, thirty-seven years later, is that as time has progressed the wrongs of Cuba have been aggravated and the means of repression employed by Spain have grown into a war against humanity—a war of annihilation of property and the extermination of the native population.

If the firm purpose of our predecessors to put an end to this condition of affairs in Cuba in the comparatively mild form of tyranny that existed fifty years ago has degenerated into doubts and misgivings as to our duty to our own people and the demands of Christian civilization, let the responsibility for this lapse from the true spirit of American liberty and our love of home rule and independence rest where it justly belongs, and not upon the people through the indifference to their will on the part of their Representatives in Congress.

Concurring in all that is said in the general report of the committee, the additional facts herein stated are presented as additional reasons for agreeing to that report, and for the passage of the resolution of the Senator from Pennsylvania (Mr. Cameron), which the committee recommends.

JOHN T. MORGAN.
R. Q. MILLS.

APPENDIX No. 1.

Senate Report No. 351, Thirty-fifth Congress, second session.

JANUARY 24, 1859.

Mr. Slidell made the following report, to accompany bill S. 497:

The Committee on Foreign Relations, to whom was referred the bill (S. 497) making appropriations to facilitate the acquisition of the Island of Cuba by negotiation, have had the same under consideration, and now respectfully report:

It is not considered necessary by your committee to enlarge upon the vast importance of the acquisition of the Island of Cuba by the United States. To do so would be as much a work of supererogation as to demonstrate an elementary problem in mathematics, or one of those axioms of ethics or philosophy which have been universally received for ages. The ultimate acquisition of Cuba may be considered a fixed purpose of the United States, a purpose resulting from political and geographical necessities which have been recognized by all parties and all Administrations. and in regard to which the popular voice has been expressed with a unanimity unsurpassed on any question of national policy that has heretofore engaged the public mind.

The purchase and annexation of Louisiana led, as a necessary corollary, to that of Florida, and both point with unerring certainty to the acquisition of Cuba. The sparse and feeble population of what is now the great West called in 1800 for the free navigation of the Mississippi and the enforcement of the right of deposit at New Orleans. In three years not only were these privileges secured, but the whole of the magnificent domain of Louisiana was ours. Who now doubts the wisdom of a measure which at the time was denounced with a violence until then unparalleled in our political history?

From the day we acquired Louisiana the attention of our ablest statesmen was fixed on Cuba. What the possession of the mouth of the Mississippi had been to the people of the West that of Cuba became to the nation. To cast the eye upon the map was sufficient to predict its destiny. A brief reference will show the importance attached to the question by our leading statesmen and the steadiness and perseverance with which they have endeavored to hasten the consummation of so vital a measure.

Mr. Jefferson, in a letter to President Madison, of the 27th of April, 1809, speaking of the policy that Napoleon would probably pursue toward us, says:

He ought to be satisfied with having forced her (Great Britain) to revoke the orders on which he pretended to retaliate, and to be particularly satisfied with us, by whose unyielding adherence to principle she has been forced into the revocation. He ought the more to conciliate our good will, as we can be such an obstacle to the new career opening on him in the Spanish colonies. That he would give us the Floridas to withhold intercourse with the residue of those colonies can not be doubted. But that is no price, because they are ours in the first moment of the first war, and until a war they are of no particular necessity to us. But, although with difficulty, he will consent to our receiving Cuba into our Union to prevent our aid to Mexico and the other provinces. That would be a price, and I would immediately erect a column on the southernmost limit of Cuba and inscribe on it a ne plus ultra as to us in that direction. We should then have only to include the north in our confederacy, which would be, of course, in the first war, and we should have such an empire for liberty as she has never surveyed since the creation; and I am persuaded no constitution was ever before so well calculated as ours for extensive empire and self-government. * * *

It will be objected to our receiving Cuba that no limit can then be drawn to our future acquisitions. Cuba can be defended by us without a navy, and this develops the principle which ought to limit our views. Nothing should ever be accepted which would require a navy to defend it.

Again, in writing to President Monroe on the 23d June, 1823, he says:

For certainly her addition to our confederacy is exactly what is wanting to advance our power as a nation to the point of its utmost interest.

And in another letter to the same, on the 24th October, 1823, he says:

I candidly confess that I have ever looked on Cuba as the most interesting addition which could ever be made to our system of States. The control which, with Florida Point, this island would give us over the Gulf of Mexico and the countries and isthmus bordering on it would fill up the measure of our political well-being.

John Quincy Adams, while Secretary of State under Mr. Monroe, in his dispatch to Mr. Nelson, our minister to Madrid, of the 28th April, 1823, says:

In the war between France and Spain, now commencing, other interests, peculiarly ours, will in all probability be deeply involved. Whatever may be the issue of this war as between those two European powers, it may be taken for granted that the dominion of Spain upon the American continents, north and south, is irrecoverably gone. But the islands of Cuba and Puerto Rico still remain nominally and so far really dependent upon her that she yet possesses the power of transferring her own dominion over them, together with the possession of them, to others. These islands, from their local position and natural appendages to the North American continent, and one of them, Cuba, almost in sight of our shores, from a multitude of considerations, has become an object of transcendent importance to the commercial and political interests of our Union. Its commanding position, with reference to the Gulf of Mexico and the West India seas, the character of its population, its situation midway between our Southern coast and the Island of Santo Domingo, its safe and capacious harbor of the Habana, fronting a long line of our shores destitute of the same advantages, the nature of its productions and of its wants, furnishing the supplies and needing the returns of a commerce immensely profitable and mutually beneficial, give it an importance in the sum of our national interests with which that of no other foreign territory can be compared and little inferior to that which binds the different members of this Union together.

Such, indeed, are, between the interests of that island and of this country, the geographical, commercial, moral, and political relations formed by nature, gathering in the process of time, and even now verging to maturity, that, in looking forward to the probable course of events for the short period of half a century, it is scarcely possible to resist the conviction that the annexation of Cuba to our Federal Republic will be indispensable to the continuance and integrity of the Union itself. It is obvious, however, that for this event we are not yet prepared. Numerous and formidable objections to the extension of our territorial dominions beyond sea present themselves to the first contemplation of the subject; obstacles to the system of policy by which alone that result can be compassed and maintained are to be foreseen and surmounted both from at home and abroad; but there are laws of political as well as of physical gravitation; and if an apple, severed by the tempest from its native tree, can not choose but fall to the ground, Cuba, forcibly disjoined from its own unnatural connection with Spain and incapable of self-support, can gravitate only toward the North American Union, which, by the same law of nature, can not cast her off from its bosom.

The transfer of Cuba to Great Britain would be an event unpropitious to the interests of this Union. This opinion is so generally entertained that even the groundless rumors that it was about to be accomplished, which have spread abroad, and are still teeming, may be traced to the deep and almost universal feeling of aversion to it, and to the alarm which the mere probability of its occurrence has stimulated. The question both of our right and of our power to prevent it, if necessary by force, already obtrudes itself upon our councils, and the Administration is called upon, in the performance of its duties to the nation, at least to use all the means within its competency to guard against and forefend it.

On April 27, 1825, Mr. Clay, Secretary of State, in a dispatch to Mr. A. H. Everett, our minister at Madrid, instructing him to use his ex- ertions to induce Spain to make peace with her revolted colonies, says:

The United States are satisfied with the present condition of those islands (Cuba and Puerto Rico) in the hands of Spain, and with their ports open to our commerce, as they are now open. This Government desires no political change of that condi- tion. The population itself of the islands is incompetent at present, from its com- position and its amount, to maintain self-government. The maritime force of the neighboring Republics of Mexico and Colombia is not now, nor is it likely shortly to be, adequate to the protection of those islands, if the conquest of them were effected. The United States would entertain constant apprehensions of their pass- ing from their possession to that of some less friendly sovereignty; and of all the European powers, this country prefers that Cuba and Puerto Rico should remain dependent on Spain. If the war should continue between Spain and the new Republics, and those islands should become the object and the theater of it, their fortunes have such a connection with the prosperity of the United States that they could not be indifferent spectators; and the possible contingencies of such a pro- tracted war might bring upon the Government of the United States duties and obligations the performance of which, however painful it should be, they might not be at liberty to decline.

Mr. Van Buren, writing to Mr. Van Ness, our minister to Spain, October 2, 1829, says:

The Government of the United States has always looked with the deepest interest upon the fate of those islands, but particularly of Cuba. Its geographical position, which places it almost in sight of our southern shores, and, as it were, gives it the command of the Gulf of Mexico and the West India seas, its safe and capacious har- bors, its rich productions, the exchange of which for our surplus agricultural prod- ucts and manufactures constitutes one of the most extensive and valuable branches of our foreign trade, render it of the utmost importance to the United States that no change should take place in its condition which might injuriously affect our political and commercial standing in that quarter. Other considerations, connected with a certain class of our population, make it the interest of the southern section of the Union that no attempt should be made in that island to throw off the yoke of Spanish dependence, the first effect of which would be the sudden emancipation of a numerous slave population, the result of which could not but be very sensibly felt upon the adjacent shores of the United States. On the other hand, the wisdom which induced the Spanish Government to relax in its colonial system, and to adopt with regard to those islands a more liberal policy which opened their ports to gen- eral commerce, has been so far satisfactory in the view of the United States as, in addition to other considerations, to induce this Government to desire that their pos- session should not be transferred from the Spanish Crown to any other power. In conformity with this desire, the ministers of the United States at Madrid have, from time to time, been instructed attentively to watch the course of events and the secret springs of European diplomacy, which, from information received from various quar- ters, this Government had reason to suspect had been put in motion to effect the transfer of the possession of Cuba to the powerful allies of Spain.

You are authorized to say that the long-established and well-known policy of the United States, which forbids their entangling themselves in the concerns of other nations, and which permits their physical force to be used only for the defense of their political rights and the protection of the persons and property of their citizens, equally forbids their public agents to enter into positive engagements, the perform- ance of which would require the employment of means which the people have retained in their own hands; but that this Government has every reason to believe that the same influence which once averted the blow ready to fall upon the Spanish islands would again be found effectual on the recurrence of similar events; and that the. high preponderance in American affairs of the United States as a great naval power, the influence which they must at all times command as a great commercial nation, in all questions involving the interests of the general commerce of this hem- isphere, would render their consent an essential preliminary to the execution of any project calculated so vitally to affect the general concerns of all the nations in any degree engaged in the commerce of America. The knowledge you possess of the public sentiment of this country in regard to Cuba will enable you to speak with confidence and effect of the probable consequences that might be expected from the communication of that sentiment to Congress in the event of any contemplated change in the present political condition of that island.

And again, on the 13th of October, 1830:

This Government has also been given to understand that if Spain should persevere in the assertion of a hopeless claim to dominion over her former colonies they will feel it to be their duty, as well as their interest, to attack her colonial possessions in our vicinity, Cuba and Puerto Rico. Your general instructions are full upon the subject of the interest which the United States take in the fate of those islands and particularly of the former; they inform you that we are content that Cuba should remain as it now is, but could not consent to its transfer to any European power. Motives of reasonable state policy render it more desirable to us that it should remain subject to Spain rather than to either of the South American States. Those motives will readily present themselves to your mind; they are principally founded upon an apprehension that if possessed by the latter it would, in the present state of things, be in greater danger of becoming subject to some European power than in its present condition. Although such are our own wishes and true interests, the President does not see on what ground he would be justified in interfering with any attempts which the South American States might think it for their interest, in the prosecution of a defensive war, to make upon the islands in question. If, indeed, an attempt should be made to disturb them, by putting arms in the hands of one portion of their population to destroy another, and which in its influence would endanger the peace of a portion of the United States, the case might be different. Against such an attempt the United States (being informed that it was in contemplation) have already protested and warmly remonstrated in their communications last summer with the Government of Mexico; but the information lately communicated to us in this regard was accompanied by a solemn assurance that no such measures will, in any event, be resorted to; and that the contest, if forced upon them, will be carried on, on their part, with strict reference to the established rules of civilized warfare.

Mr. Buchanan, in his dispatch to Mr. R. M. Saunders, of June 17, 1848, said:

With these considerations in view, the President believes that the crisis has arrived when an effort should be made to purchase the Island of Cuba from Spain, and he has determined to intrust you with the performance of this most delicate and important duty. The attempt should be made, in the first instance, in a confidential conversation with the Spanish minister for foreign affairs; a written offer might produce an absolute refusal in writing, which would embarrass us hereafter in the acquisition of the island. Besides, from the incessant changes in the Spanish cabinet and policy our desire to make the purchase might thus be made known in an official form to foreign governments and arouse their jealousy and active opposition. Indeed, even if the present cabinet should think favorably of the proposition, they might be greatly embarrassed by having it placed on record, for in that event it would almost certainly, through some channel, reach the opposition and become the subject of discussion in the Cortes. Such delicate negotiations, at least in their incipient stages, ought always to be conducted in confidential conversation, and with the utmost secrecy and dispatch.

At your interview with the minister for foreign affairs you might introduce the subject by referring to the present distracted condition of Cuba and the danger which exists that the population will make an attempt to accomplish a revolution. This must be well known to the Spanish Government. In order to convince him of the good faith and friendship toward Spain with which this Government has acted, you might read to him the first part of my dispatch to General Campbell and the order issued by the Secretary of War to the commanding general in Mexico and to the officer having charge of the embarkation of our troops at Vera Cruz. You may then touch delicately upon the danger that Spain may lose Cuba by a revolution in the island, or that it may be wrested from her by Great Britain, should a rupture take place between the two countries, arising out of the dismissal of Sir Henry Bulwer, and be retained to pay the Spanish debt due to the British bondholders. You might assure him that while this Government is entirely satisfied that Cuba shall remain under the dominion of Spain, we should in any event resist its acquisition by any other nation. And, finally, you might inform him that, under all these circumstances, the President had arrived at the conclusion that Spain might be willing to transfer the island to the United States for a fair and full consideration. You might cite as a precedent the cession of Louisiana to this country by Napoleon, under somewhat similar circumstances, when he was at the zenith of his power and glory. I have merely presented these topics in their natural order, and you can fill up the outline from the information communicated in this dispatch, as well as from your own knowledge of the subject. Should the minister for foreign affairs lend a favorable ear to your proposition, then the question of the consideration to be paid would arise, and you

have been furnished with information in this dispatch which will enable you to dis
cuss that question.

The President would be willing to stipulate for the payment of $100,000,000. This,
however, is the maximum price; and if Spain should be willing to sell, you will use
your best efforts to purchase it at a rate as much below that sum as practicable. In
case you should be able to conclude a treaty, you may adopt as your model, so far as
the same may be applicable, the two conventions of April 30, 1803, between France
and the United States, for the sale and purchase of Louisiana. The seventh and
eighth articles of the first of these conventions ought, if possible, to be omitted;
still, if this should be indispensable to the accomplishment of the object, articles
similar to them may be retained.

Mr. Everett, in his celebrated letter of December 1, 1852, to the
Compte de Sartiges, rejecting the joint proposition of the French and
British Governments for a tripartite convention with the United States,
disclaiming, severally and collectively, all intention to obtain possession of the Island of Cuba, and respectively binding themselves to discountenance all attempts to that effect on the part of any power or
individuals whatever, said:

Spain, meantime, has retained of her extensive dominions in this hemisphere but
the two islands of Cuba and Puerto Rico. A respectful sympathy with the fortunes
of an ancient ally and a gallant people, with whom the United States have ever
maintained the most friendly relations, would, if no other reason existed, make it
our duty to leave her in the undisturbed possession of this little remnant of her
mighty transatlantic empire. The President desires to do so. No word or deed of
his will ever question her title or shake her possession. But can it be expected to
last very long? Can it resist this mighty current in the fortunes of the world? Is
it desirable that it should do so? Can it be for the interest of Spain to cling to a
possession that can only be maintained by a garrison of twenty-five or thirty thousand troops, a powerful naval force, and an annual expenditure for both arms of the
service of at least $12,000,000? Cuba at this moment costs more to Spain than the
entire naval and military establishment of the United States costs the Federal Government. So far from being really injured by the loss of this island there is no
doubt that, were it peacefully transferred to the United States, a prosperous commerce between Cuba and Spain, resulting from ancient associations and common
language and tastes, would be far more productive than the best contrived system
of colonial taxation. Such, notoriously, has been the result to Great Britain of the
establishment of the independence of the United States. The decline of Spain from
the position which she held in the time of Charles V is coeval with the foundation
of her colonial system, while within twenty-five years, and since the loss of most of
her colonies, she has entered upon a course of rapid improvement unknown since
the abdication of that Emperor.

Mr. Marcy, in his dispatch of July 23, 1853, to Mr. Pierre Soulé
says:

SIR: There are circumstances in the affairs of Spain, having a connection with
this country, which give unusual importance at this time to the mission to that Government. The proximity of her remaining possessions in this hemisphere—the
islands of Cuba and Puerto Rico—to the United States, the present condition of the
former, and the rumors of contemplated changes in its internal affairs, complicate
our relations with Spain. The Island of Cuba, on account of its magnitude, situation, fine climate, and rich productions, far superior in all respects to any in the
West India group, is a very desirable possession to Spain, and, for the same reasons,
very difficult for her to retain in its present state of dependence. The opinion generally prevails among the European nations that the Spanish dominion over it is
insecure. This was clearly evinced by the alacrity with which both England and
France, on occasion of the late disturbances in Cuba, volunteered their aid to sustain the Spanish rule over it, and by their recent proposition to the United States
for a tripartite convention to guarantee its possession to Spain. Without an essential change in her present policy, such a change as she will most likely be unwilling
to make, she can not, it is confidently believed, long sustain, unaided, her present
connection with that island.

What will be its destiny after it shall cease to be a dependency of Spain is a question with which some of the principal powers of Europe have seen fit to concern
themselves, and in which the United States have a deep and direct interest.

I had occasion recently, in preparing instructions for our minister to London, to
present the views of the President in relation to the interference of Great Britain,
as well as of France, in *   *   * Cuban affairs. To spare myself the labor of again

going over the same ground, I herewith furnish you with an extract from those instructions.

The policy of the Government of the United States in regard to Cuba, in any contingency calling for our interposition, will depend in a great degree upon the peculiar circumstances of the case, and can not, therefore, now be presented with much precision beyond what is indicated in the instructions before referred to. Nothing will be done on our part to disturb its present connection with Spain, unless the character of that connection should be so changed as to affect our present or prospective security. While the United States would resist, at every hazard, the transference of Cuba to any European nation, they would exceedingly regret to see Spain resorting to any power for assistance to uphold her rule over it. Such a dependence on foreign aid would, in effect, invest the auxiliary with the character of a protector, and give it a pretext to interfere in our affairs, and also generally in those of the North American continent. In case of collision with the United States, such protecting power would be in a condition to make nearly the same use of that island to annoy us as it could do if it were the absolute possessor of it.

Our minister at Madrid, during the Administration of President Polk, was instructed to ascertain if Spain was disposed to transfer Cuba to the United States for a liberal pecuniary consideration. I do not understand, however, that it was at that time the policy of this Government to acquire that island unless its inhabitants were very generally disposed to concur in the transfer. Under certain conditions the United States might be willing to purchase it; but it is scarcely expected that you will find Spain, should you attempt to ascertain her views upon the subject, at all inclined to enter into such a negotiation. There is reason to believe that she is under obligations to Great Britain and France not to transfer this island to the United States. Were there nothing else to justify this belief but the promptness with which these two powers sent their naval forces to her aid in the late Cuban disturbances, the proposition for a tripartite convention to guarantee Cuba to Spain, and, what is more significant than either of the above facts, the sort of joint protest by England and France, to which I adverted in my instructions to Mr. Buchanan, against some of the views presented in Mr. Everett's letter of the 2d of December last to Mr. Sartiges, the French minister, would alone be satisfactory proof of such an arrangement. Independent of any embarassment of this nature, there are many other reasons for believing that Spain will pertinaciously hold on to Cuba, and that the separation, whenever it takes place, will be the work of violence.

From these and other extracts that might be presented it is manifest that the ultimate acquisition of Cuba has long been regarded as the fixed policy of the United States—necessary to the progressive development of our system. All agree that the end is not only desirable, but inevitable. The only difference of opinion is as to the time, mode, and conditions of obtaining it.

The law of our national existence is growth. We can not, if we would, disobey it. While we should do nothing to stimulate it unnaturally, we should be careful not to impose upon ourselves a regimen so strict as to prevent its healthful development. The tendency of the age is the expansion of the great powers of the world. England, France, and Russia all demonstrate the existence of this pervading principle. Their growth, it is true, only operates by the absorption, partial or total, of weaker parties—generally of inferior races. So long as this extension of territory is the result of geographical position, a higher civilization, and greater aptitude for government, and is not pursued in a direction to endanger our safety or impede our progress, we have neither the right nor the disposition to find fault with it. Let England pursue her march of conquest and annexation in India, France extend her dominions on the southern shores of the Mediterranean and advance her frontiers to the Rhine, or Russia subjugate her barbarous neighbors in Asia; we shall look upon their progress, if not with favor, at least with indifference. We claim on this hemisphere the same privilege that they exercise on the other—

"Hanc veniam petimusque damusque vicissim.'   '

In this they are but obeying the laws of their organization. When they cease to grow, they will soon commence that period of decadence which is the fate of all nations as of individual man.

The question of the annexation of Cuba to the United States, we repeat, is a question but of time. The fruit that was not ripe when John Quincy Adams penned his dispatch to Mr. Forsyth (it has not yet been severed by violence from its native tree, as he anticipated) is now mature. Shall it be plucked by a friendly hand, prepared to compensate its proprietor with a princely guerdon, or shall it fall decaying to the ground?

As Spain can not long maintain her grasp on this distant colony, there are but three possible alternatives in the future of Cuba: First, possession by one of the great European powers. This we have declared to be incompatible with our safety, and have announced to the world that any attempt to consummate it will be resisted by all the means in our power. When first we made this declaration we were comparatively feeble. The struggle would have been fearful and unequal; but we were prepared to make it at whatever hazard. That declaration has often been repeated since. With a population nearly tripled, our financial resources and our means, offensive and defensive, increased in an infinitely larger proportion, we can not now shrink from an issue that all were then ready to meet.

The second alternative is the independence of the island. This independence could only be nominal; it could never be maintained in fact. It would eventually fall under some protectorate, open or disguised. If under ours, annexation would soon follow as certainly as the shadow follows the substance. An European protectorate could not be tolerated. The closet philanthropists of England and France would, as the price of their protection, insist upon introducing their schemes of emancipation. Civil and servile war would soon follow, and Cuba would present, as Haiti now does, no traces of its former prosperity, but the ruins of its once noble mansions. Its uncontrolled possession by either France or England would be less dangerous and offensive to our Southern States than a pretended independent black empire or republic.

The third and last alternative is annexation to the United States. How and when is this to be effected? By conquest or negotiation? Conquest, even without the hostile interference of another European power than Spain, would be expensive, but with such interference would probably involve the whole civilized world in war, entail upon us the interruption, if not the loss, of our foreign trade, and an expenditure far exceeding any sum which it has ever been contemplated to offer for the purchase of Cuba. It would, besides, in all probability, lead to servile insurrection, and to the great injury or even total destruction of the industry of the island. Purchase, then, by negotiation seems to be the only practicable course; and, in the opinion of the committee, that can not be attempted with any reasonable prospect of success, unless the President be furnished with the means which he has suggested in his annual message, and which the bill proposes to give him.

Much has been said of the danger of confiding such powers to the Executive, and from the fierceness with which the proposition has been denounced it might be supposed that it was without precedent. So far is this from being the case, that we have three different acts upon the statute book placing large sums of money at the disposition of the President for the purpose of aiding him in negotiations for the acquisition of territory. The first is the act of February 26, 1803. Although its object was well known, viz, to be used in negotiating for the purchase of Louisiana, the act does not indicate it. It placed $2,000,000 unreservedly at the disposition of the President for the purpose of defraying any "extraordinary expense which may be incurred in the intercourse between the United States and foreign nations." Second. The act of February 13, 1806, using precisely the same phraseology, appropriates $2,000,000, it being understood that it was to be used in negotiating for the purchase of Florida.

The act of March 3, 1847, "making further appropriation to bring the existing war with Mexico to a speedy and honorable conclusion," has been adopted as the model on which the present bill is framed. Its preamble states that—

Whereas, in the adjustment of so many complicated questions as now exist between the two countries, it may possibly happen that an expenditure of money will be called for by the stipulations of any treaty which may be entered into, therefore the sum of $3,000,000 be, and the same is hereby, appropriated, to enable the President to conclude a treaty of peace, limits, and boundaries, with the Republic of Mexico; to be used by him in the event said treaty, when signed by the authorized agents of the two Governments and duly ratified by Mexico, shall call for the expenditure of the same, or any part thereof.

The bill now reported appropriates, under the same conditions, $30,000,000 to make a treaty with Spain for the purchase of the Island of Cuba.

It will be perceived that this bill defines strictly the object to which the amount appropriated shall be applied, and in this respect allows a much narrower range of discretion to the present Executive than the acts of 1803 and 1806 gave to Mr. Jefferson. In those cases the object of the appropriation was as well known to the country and to the world as if it had been specifically stated. The knowledge of that fact did not then in the slightest degree tend to defeat the intended object, nor can it do so now. Under our form of Government we have no state secrets. With us diplomacy has ceased to be enveloped with the mysteries that of yore were considered inseparable from its successful exercise. Directness in our policy and frankness in its avowal are, in conducting our foreign intercourse, not less essential to the maintenance of our national character and the permanent interests of the Republic than are the same qualities to social position and the advancement of honest enterprise in private life.

Much has been said of the indelicacy of this mode of proceeding; that the offer to purchase will offend the Spanish pride, be regarded as an insult, and rejected with contempt; that, instead of promoting a consummation that all admit to be desirable, it will have the opposite tendency. If this were true, it would be a conclusive argument against the bill, but a brief consideration will show the fallacy of these views. For many years our desire to purchase Cuba has been known to the world.

Seven years since President Fillmore communicated to Congress the instructions to our ministers on that subject, with all the correspondence connected with it. In that correspondence will be found three letters from Mr. Saunders, detailing conversations held with Narvaez and the minister of foreign relations, in which he notified them of his authority to treat for the purchase of Cuba, and while the reply was so decided as to preclude him from making any direct proposition, yet no intimation was given that the suggestion was offensive. And why should it be so? We simply say to Spain, " You have a distant possession, held by a precarious tenure, which is almost indispensable to us for the protection of our commerce, and may, from its peculiar position, the character of its population, and the mode in which it is governed, lead at any time to a rupture which both nations would deprecate. This possession, rich though it be in all the elements of wealth, yields to your treasury a net revenue not amounting, on the average of a series of years, to the hundredth part of the price we are prepared to give you for it. True, you have heretofore refused to consider our proposition, but circumstances are changing daily. What may not have suited you in 1848 may now be more acceptable. Should a war break out in Europe, Spain can scarcely hope to escape being involved in it. The people of Cuba naturally desire to have a voice in the government of the island. They may seize the occasion to proclaim their independence, and you may regret not having accepted the rich indemnity we offer."

But even these arguments will not be pressed upon unwilling ears. Our minister will not broach the subject until he shall have good reason to believe that it will be favorably entertained. Such an opportunity may occur when least expected. Spain is the country of coups d'état and pronunciamentos. The all-powerful minister of to-day may be a fugitive to-morrow. With the forms of a representative government, it is in fact a despotism sustained by the bayonet—a despotism tempered only by frequent, violent, and bloody revolutions. Her financial condition is one of extreme embarrassment; a crisis may arise when even the dynasty may be overthrown unless a large sum of money can be raised forthwith. Spain will be in the position of the needy possessor of land he can not cultivate, having all the pride of one to whom it has descended through a long line of ancestry, but his necessities are stronger than his will—he must have money. A thrifty neighbor whose domains it will round off, is at hand to furnish it. He retains the old mansion, but sells what will relieve him from immediate ruin.

The President, in his annual message, has told us that we should not, if we could, acquire Cuba by any other means than honorable negotiation, unless circumstances which he does not anticipate render a departure from such a course justifiable, under the imperative and overruling law of self-preservation. He also tells us that he desires to renew the negotiations, and it may become indispensable to success that he should be intrusted with the means for making an advance to the Spanish Government immediately after the signing of the treaty, without awaiting the ratification of it by the Senate. This, in point of fact, is an appeal to Congress for an expression of its opinion on the propriety of renewing the negotiation. Should we fail to give him the means which may be indispensable to success, it may well be considered by the President as an intimation that we do not desire the acquisition of the island.

It has been asserted that the people of Cuba do not desire a transfer to the United States. If this were so, it would present a very serious objection to the measure. The evidence on which it is based is that on receipt of the President's message addresses were made by the municipal authorities of Habana and other towns protesting their devotion to the Crown and their hostility to the institutions of the United States. Anyone who has had an opportunity of observing the persuasive influence of the bayonet in countries where it rules supreme will know how much value to attach to such demonstrations of popular sentiment. There can be no doubt that an immense majority of the people of Cuba are not only in favor, but ardently desirous of annexation to the United States. It would be strange, indeed, if they were not so. Deprived of all influence, even in the local affairs of the island; unrepresented in the Cortes; governed by successive hordes of hungry officials sent from the mother country to acquire fortunes to be enjoyed at home, having no sympathy with the people among whom they are mere sojourners and upon whom they look down as inferiors; liable to be arrested at any moment on the most trifling charges; tried by military courts or sub-missive judges, removable at pleasure; punished at the discretion of the Captain-General, they would be less than men if they were contented with their yoke. But we have the best authority, from the most reliable sources, for asserting that nearly the entire native population of Cuba desires annexation.

Apprehensions have been expressed by some Southern statesmen of perils resulting from the different elements composing the population, and the supposed mixture of races. They are not justified by the facts. The entire population, by the census of 1850, was 1,247,230, of which 605,560 were whites, 205,570 free colored, and 436,100 slaves.

Allowing the same annual percentage of increase for each class as shown by comparison with the previous census, the total population now is about 1,586,000, of which 742,000 are whites, 263,000 free colored, and 581,000 slaves. There is good reason to suppose that the slaves considerably exceed the estimated number, it having been, until very recently, the interest of the proprietor to understate it. The feeling of caste or race is as marked in Cuba as in the United States. The white creole is as free from all taint of African blood as the descendant of the Goth on the plains of Castile. There is a numerous white peasantry, brave, robust, sober, and honest, not yet, perhaps, prepared intelligently to discharge all the duties of the citizen of a free republic, but who, from his organization, physical and mental, is capable of being elevated by culture to the same level with the educated Cubans, who, as a class, are as refined, well informed, and fitted for self-government as men of any class of any nation can be who have not inhaled with their breath the atmosphere of freedom.

Many of them, accompanied by their families, are to be met with every summer at our cities and watering places, observing and appreciating the working of our form of government and its marvelous results; many seeking until the arrival of more auspicious days an asylum from the oppression that has driven them from their homes; while hundreds of their youths in our schools and colleges are acquiring our language and fitting themselves hereafter, it is to be hoped at no distant day, to play a distinguished part in their own legislative halls or in the councils of the nation.

These men, who are the great proprietors of the soil, are opposed to the continuance of the African slave trade, which is carried on by Spaniards from the Peninsula, renegade Americans, and other adventurers from every clime and country, tolerated and protected by the authorities of Cuba of every grade.

Were there a sincere desire to arrest the slave trade, it could be as effectually put down by Spain as it has been by Brazil. Cuba and Puerto Rico are now the only marts for this illegal traffic; and if the British Government had been as intent upon enforcing its treaty stipulations with Spain for its abolition as it has been in denouncing abuses of our flag, which we can not entirely prevent, this question would long since have ceased to be a source of irritating discussion—it may be of possible future difficulty. Those who desire to extirpate the slave trade may find in their sympathy for the African a motive to support this bill.

We have, since the conclusion of the Ashburton treaty in 1842, kept up a squadron on the coast of Africa for the suppression of the slave trade, and we are still bound to continue it. The annual cost of this squadron is at least $800,000. The cost in seventeen years amounts to $13,600,000, and this, too, with results absolutely insignificant. It appears from a report of a select committee of the British House of

Commons, made in March, 1850, that the number of slaves exported from Africa had sunk down in 1842 (the very year in which the Ashburton treaty was concluded) to nearly 30,000. In 1843 it rose to 55,000. In 1846 it was 76,000. In 1847 it was 84,000, and was then in a state of unusual activity. Sir Charles Hotham, one of the most distinguished officers of the British navy, and who commanded on the coast of Africa for several years, was examined by that select committee. He said that the force under his command was in a high state of discipline; that his views were carried out by his officers to his entire satisfaction; that, so far from having succeeded in stopping the slave trade, he had not even crippled it to the extent of giving it a permanent check; that the slave trade had been regulated by the commercial demand for slaves, and had been little affected by the presence of his squadron, and that experience had proven the system of repression by cruisers on the coast of Africa futile—this, too, when the British squadron counted 27 vessels, comprising several steamers, carrying about 300 guns and 3,000 men. The annual expense of the squadron is about $3,500,000, with auxiliary establishments on the coast costing at least $1,500,000 more—a total cost annually of $5,000,000 in pursuance of a system which experience has proved to be futile.

In 1847 the Brazilian slave trade was in full activity. It has been entirely suppressed for several years. The slaves now shipped from the coast of Africa are exclusively for the Spanish islands. It is not easy to estimate the number. From the best data, however, it is supposed now to be from twenty-five to thirty thousand per year. It would cease to exist the moment we acquire possession of the Island of Cuba.

The importation of slaves into the United States was prohibited in 1808. Since then, a period of more than fifty years, but one case has occurred of its violation—that of the *Wanderer*, which has recently excited so much attention.

Another consequence which should equally enlist the sympathies of philanthropists, excepting that class whose tears are only shed for those of ebon hue, and who turn with indifference from the sufferings of men of any other complexion, is the suppression of the infamous coolie traffic—a traffic so much the more nefarious as the Chinese is elevated above the African in the scale of creation; more civilized, more intellectual, and therefore feeling more acutely the shackles of the slave ship and the harsh discipline of the overseer. The number of Chinese shipped for Cuba since the commencement of the traffic up to March last is 28,777, of whom 4,134 perished on the passage. From that date up to the close of the year the number landed at Habana was 9,449. We blush to say that three-fourths of the number were transported under the American and British flags—under the flags of the two countries that have been the most zealous for the suppression of the African slave trade. The ratio of mortality on the passage was $14\frac{3}{4}$ per cent, and a much larger proportion of these wretched beings were landed in an enfeebled condition. Coming, too, from a temperate climate, they are not capable of enduring the exposure to the tropical sun, in which the African delights to bask. When their allotted time of service shall have been completed, the small remnant of the survivors will furnish conclusive evidence of the barbarity with which they are treated. The master feels no interest in his temporary slave beyond that of extracting from him the greatest possible amount of labor during the continuance of his servitude. His death or incapacity to labor at the end of his term is to the master a matter of as much indifference as is the fate of the operative employed in his mill to the Manchester spinner.

Another effect of this measure, which will recommend it most strongly to the humanitarians, will be the better treatment and increased happiness of the slaves now existing in the island that would inevitably flow from it. As a general rule the slave is well treated in proportion to his productiveness and convertible value, as an expensive instrument is more carefully handled than one of less cost. When the importation of slaves from abroad is arrested, the home production affords the only means of supplying the increasing demand for labor. It may be assumed as an axiom of political economy that the increase of population, if not the only true test, is the most reliable of the average well-being of the class to which it is applied. Tried by this test, the slave of the United States affords a very high standard as compared even with the white population of our favored land. But when comparison is made with the statistics of African slavery in all European colonies the results are startling. Since Las Casas, in his zeal for the protection of the Indian, originated the African slave trade, it is estimated that the whole number transported to the New World has been about 8,375,000. Of these, we, in our colonial condition, and since, have only received about 375,000. By natural increase, after deducting all who are free, we had, in 1850, 3,204,000 slaves of the African race. These, allowing the same percentage of increase for nine years, as the census returns show during the last decennial period, would now number over 4,300,000; while, from the same data, the free colored population would amount to 496,000. The British West India colonies received about 1,700,000. The whole population of those islands, including Jamaica and Trinidad, acquired from the Spaniards, and British Guiana, black, white, and mixed, is but 1,062,639. The Spanish and other West India Islands received about 3,000,000. This is very much more than their entire population to-day. The proportion may vary in some of the colonies, but the general result will be found everywhere the same—a very much less number now existing of African descent, either pure or mixed, than have been imported from Africa.

There is another aspect in which this proposition may be viewed which is deserving of serious consideration. It is forcibly put in the President's annual message that the multiplied aggressions upon the persons and property of our citizens by the local authorities of Cuba for many years past present, in the person of the Captain-General, the anomaly of absolute power to inflict injury without any corresponding faculty to redress it. He can, almost in sight of our shores, confiscate, without just cause, the property of an American citizen or incarcerate his person; but if applied to for redress we are told that he can not act without consulting his royal mistress at Madrid. There we are informed that it is necessary to await the return of a report of the case which is to be obtained from Cuba, and many years elapse before it is ripe for decision. These delays in most instances amount to an absolute denial of justice. And even when the obligation of indemnity is admitted, the state of the treasury or a change of ministry is pleaded as an excuse for withholding payment. This would long since have justified us in resorting to measures of reprisal that would have necessarily led to war and ultimately resulted in the conquest of the island. Indeed, such is the acute sense of those wrongs prevailing among our people that nothing but our rigid neutrality laws, which, so long as they remain unrepealed or unmodified, a Chief Magistrate, acting under the sanction of his official oath to see that the laws be faithfully executed, is bound to enforce, has prevented the success of organized individual enterprises that would long ere this have revolutionized the island. It is in part, probably, for this cause that the President has recommended the policy which this bill embodies, and the world can not fail to recognize in its adoption by Congress a determination to maintain him in his efforts to preserve untarnished our national character for justice and fair dealing.

The effect of the acquisition of Cuba will be no less beneficial in its commercial than in its political and moral aspects. The length of the island is about 770 miles, with an average breadth of about 40 miles, comprising an area of 31,468 square miles. The soil is fertile, climate genial, and its ports the finest in the world. Habana is more familiarly known to us, for apart from our extensive trade, which employs several hundred American vessels, thousands of our citizens have touched at that port in our steamers on their way to California or New Orleans. They have all carried away with them vivid recollections of its magnificent harbor, and have breathed ardent prayers that their next visit should be hailed by the Stars and Stripes floating from the Morro. And yet Cuba can boast of several other harbors equally safe and more extensive than that of Habana.

In 1855 the importations, by official custom-house returns, were $31,216,000, the exports $34,803,000. As duties are levied on exports as well as imports, there can be no exaggeration in these returns, and the real amount is undoubtedly considerably larger.

When we consider that more than two-thirds of the whole area of the island is susceptible of culture, and that not a tenth part of it is now cultivated, we may form some idea of the immense development which would be given to its industry by a change from a system of monopoly and despotism to free trade and free institutions. Whatever may be the enhanced cost of production, caused by the increased value of labor, it will be nearly if not quite compensated by the removal of export duties, and of those levied on articles produced in the United States, which are now by unjust discrimination virtually excluded from consumption. It is not possible within the limits which your committee have prescribed to themselves for this report to cite more than a few of the most important. Of flour, on an average of three years, from 1848 to 1850, there were imported from the United States 5,642 barrels, paying a duty of $10.81 per barrel. From other countries, and it is believed exclusively from Spain, 228,002 barrels, paying a duty of $2.52 per barrel, a discrimination against our flour of nearly 200 per cent on its present average value in our markets. On lard, of which the importation from the United States was 10,168,000 pounds, a duty is levied of $4 per quintal, while of olive oil 8,481,000 pounds were imported, which is chiefly used as its substitute, paying a duty of 87 cents per quintal. Of beef, dry and jerked, but 339,161 pounds were imported from the United States, paying a duty of $1.96 per quintal, while the importation from other quarters, principally from Buenos Ayres, was 30,544,000 pounds, paying a duty of $1.17, the difference being, in fact, a protection of the Spanish flag, which thus enjoys a monopoly of this branch of trade.

To-day, with its increased population and wealth, it is fair to presume that, were Cuba annexed to the United States, with the stimulus afforded by low prices, her annual consumption of our flour would be 600,000 barrels; of our lard, 25,000,000 pounds; of our beef, 20,000,000, and of pork, the most solid and nutritious food for the laborer, 10,000,000 pounds. The same ratio of increase would be exhibited in our whole lists of exports. Many articles that now appear not at all or in very limited quantities would force their way into general consumption.

The Spanish flag, deprived of the advantage of discriminating duties of tonnage and impost, would soon abandon a competition which it could not sustain on equal terms, and the whole carrying trade, foreign and domestic, would fall into the hands of our enterprising merchants and shipowners, but chiefly those of the Northern and Middle States, while the farmer of the West would have a new and constantly increasing market open to him for the products of the soil. With all the disadvantages under which we now labor, the American vessels entering the port of Habana alone last year numbered 958, with a tonnage of 403,479. To what figure will this be extended when ours shall be the national flag of Cuba?

The cultivation of sugar is the chief basis of the wealth and prosperity of Cuba. The average annual production, exclusive of what is consumed on the island, is about 400,000 tons; that of Louisiana about 175,000 tons. The whole amount of cane sugar, from which Europe and the United States are supplied, is estimated at 1,273,000 tons. Of this, Cuba and Louisiana now furnish somewhat more than 45 per cent. Is it extravagant to predict that, with Cuba annexed, we should in a few years have as complete control of this great staple—which has long since ceased to be a luxury and become almost a necessity of life—as we now have of cotton?

There is one other consideration, of minor importance when compared with the vast political interests involved in the question of acquisition; it is that of cost. Ten years past, as appears from the published correspondence, our minister at Madrid was authorized to offer $100,000,000 as the extreme price for the purchase of Cuba. If that was its value then, something may be added to it now. Assuming it to be twenty-five millions more, the annual interest, without reference to the probable premium which would be realized from a loan bearing 5 per cent interest, would be $6,250,000. Of the imposts of $31,216,000 in 1856, your committee have not before them the means of ascertaining the proportion coming from the United States. From the summary of Balanzas Generales from 1848 to 1854, in the report of Commercial Relations, volume 1, page 187, it may, however, be fairly assumed to be somewhat more than one-fourth, or about $8,000,000. This proportion would doubtless be largely increased. Admitting it to be $16,216,000, it would leave a balance of $15,000,000 on which duties could be levied. Under our present tariff the average rate of duties is about 18½ per cent; but as the articles on our free list are of very limited consumption in Cuba, the average there would be at least 20 per cent. This would yield a revenue from customs of $3,000,000. But under the stimulus of free trade and free institutions, with the removal of many burdens from the consumer, it would necessarily be greatly and speedily augmented. It would be a moderate calculation to say that in two years it would reach $4,000,000. On the other hand, it may be said that our expenditure would be largely increased. Such is not the opinion of your committee. On the contrary, it is believed that from the greater security of our foreign relations, resulting from the settlement of this long-agitated and disturbing question, our naval expenditure might be safely reduced, while no addition to our military establishment would be required. It has already been shown that an annual saving of $800,000 may be effected by withdrawing the African Squadron when its services will no longer be necessary. Thus our expenditure for the interest on the debt incurred by the acquisition would be credited by $4,800,000, leaving an annual balance of but $1,425,000 to the debit of the purchase. Is this sum to be weighed in the balance with the advantages, political and commercial, which would result from it? Your committee think that it should not.

A few words on the wealth and resources of Cuba, and your committee will close this report, which has swollen to dimensions not incommensurate with the importance of the subject, but which, it may be feared, will, under the pressure of other business during this short session, be considered as unduly trespassing on the attention of the Senate. The amount of taxes that can be levied upon any people without paralyzing their industry and arresting their material progress is the experimentum crucis of the fertility of the land they inhabit. Tried by this test, Cuba will favorably compare with any country on either side of the Atlantic.

Your committee have before them the last Cuban budget, which presents the actual receipts and expenditures for one year, with the estimates for the same for the next six months. The income derived from direct taxes, customs, monopolies, lotteries, etc., is $16,303,950. The expenses are $16,299,663. This equilibrium of the budget is accounted for by the fact that the surplus revenue is remitted to Spain. It figures under the head of "Atenciones de la Peninsula," and amounts to $1,404,059, and is the only direct pecuniary advantage Spain derives from the possession of Cuba, and even this sum very much exceeds the average net revenue remitted from that island, all the expenses of the army and navy employed at or near Cuba being paid by the island. The disbursements are those of the general administration of the island, those of Habana and other cities being provided for by special imposts and taxes.

It may be moderately estimated that the personal exactions of Spanish officials amount to $5,000,000 per annum, thus increasing the expenses of the Government of Cuba, apart from those which with us would be considered as county or municipal, to the enormous sum of $21,300,000, or about $13.50 per head for the whole population of the island, free and slave. Under this system of government and this excessive taxation the population has, for a series of years, steadily increased at the mean rate of 3 per cent per annum, about equal to that of the United States.

Since the reference of the bill to the committee, the President, in response to a resolution of the Senate requesting him, if not incompatible with the public interest, to communicate to the Senate any and all correspondence between the Government of the United States and the Government of Her Catholic Majesty relating to any proposition for the purchase of the Island of Cuba, which correspondence has not been furnished to either House of Congress, informs us that no such correspondence has taken place which has not already been communicated to Congress. He takes occasion to repeat what he said in his annual message, that it is highly important, if not indispensable to the success of any negotiation for the purchase, that the measure should receive the previous sanction of Congress.

This emphatic reiteration of his previous recommendation throws upon Congress the responsibility of failure if withheld. Indeed, the inference is sufficiently clear that, without some expression of opinion by Congress, the President will not feel justified in renewing negotiations.

The committee beg leave to append hereto various tables concerning statistical details of matters treated of in this report.

All of which is respectfully submitted.

No. 1.—*Commerce of the Island of Cuba with foreign nations for the years 1852, 1853, and 1854, made up from the "general balances."*

[From Ex. Doc. No. 107, first session Thirty-fourth Congress, Commercial Relations of the United States.]

Country.	1852.		1853.		1854.	
	Imports.	Exports.	Imports.	Exports.	Imports.	Exports.
Spain	$10,200,429	$3,892,634	$7,756,905	$3,298,871	$9,057,428	$3,615,692
United States..............	6,552,585	12,076,408	6,799,732	12,131,095	7,867,680	11,641,813
England	5,638,824	5,486,677	6,195,921	8,322,195	6,610,909	11,119,526
France.....................	2,203,354	1,513,368	2,177,222	3,293,399	2,558,198	1,921,567
Germany	1,102,002	1,690,165	1,115,940	1,474,018	1,420,639	1,824,074
Belgium	493,908	321,260	998,511	466,306	635,866	811,880
Spanish America	2,144,618	801,160	1,677,476	514,831	2,145,370	671,380
Portugal-Brazil...........	....	....	....	....	16,245	14,186
Holland...................	243,386	297,152	88,876	246,661	194,390	251,482
Denmark	657,554	864,366	485,422	403,085	538,824	309,949
Russia....................	....	483,218	....	253,688	....	....
Sweden-Norway	27,783	15,489	47,756	16,309	14,076	23,694
Austria...................	....	241,458	....	138,036	....	168,453
Italy.....................	32,309	380,586	69,022	651,275	24,082	313,779
Deposit...................	483,486	....	377,011	....	310,865	....
Total	29,780,242	27,453,936	27,789,800	31,210,405	31,394,578	32,683,731
Add for Prussia.......	....	....	....	....	....	5,258

No. 2.—*Statement of the aggregate of revenue and expenditure of the Island of Cuba.*

REVENUE.

Section 1.—Contributions and imports.. $3,026,833.69
Section 2.—Customs 9,807,878.87
Section 3.—Taxes and monopolies 1,069,795.44
Section 4.—Lotteries... *6,719,200.00
Section 5.—State property 119,285.94
Section 6.—Contingencies 595,928.94

Total 21,338,928.88

Deduct for sums paid as portions of the forfeitures under seizures...................... 12,972.88

Actual total.. 21,325,956.00

EXPENDITURE.

Section 1.—Grace and justice $712,755.00
Section 2.—War 5,866,538.36
Section 3.—Exchequer 7,645,145.43
Section 4.—Ordinary expenses 2,386,634.16
          Extraordinary expenses 1,190,700.37
Section 5.—Executive department 2,115,833.12
Section 6.—Attentions (remittances) of the peninsula................................... 1,404,059.00

Total 21,321,665.44

* From this sum should be deducted $5,022,000, which figures among the expenditures of the exchequer under the Government guaranty of prizes in the lotteries, and which is included in the sum of $7,645,145.43 set down as expended by that department. This leaves a net revenue from that source of $1,697,200, and a total net revenue of $16,105,956.

No. 3.—*Comparative statement of the number of seagoing vessels entering the port of Habana for the years named.*

	American.		Spanish.		English.		French.		Other nations.		Aggregate of each month.	
	No.	Ton-nage.	No.	Ton-nage.	No.	Ton-nage.	No.	Ton-nage.	No,	Ton-nage.	No.	Ton-nage.
1858.												
January	101	44,162	54	10,803	13	6,256	1	1,050	14	3,845	183	66,116
February.......	79	37,367	29	5,996	22	9,976	3	1,635	13	3,710	146	58,684
March	781	44,402	32	7,022	11	4,884	5	3,948	9	2,756	158	63,012
April	102	42,492	66	13,523	21	9,347	2	1,218	21	6,053	212	72,653
May	102	42,359	81	18,961	15	5,940	3	1,176	10	3,085	211	71,521
June...........	69	29,846	65	14,895	11	5,184	2	709	13	4,371	160	54,996
July...........	54	20,409	67	15,058	10	4,181	1	336	12	4,817	144	44,751
August........	48	20,768	83	10,256	11	5,324	1	299	10	3,928	103	40,575
September.....	60	21,097	18	4,626	10	5,443	2	1,056	12	3,371	102	35,587
October........	78	35,540	56	12,976	15	7,500	2	748	10	3,323	161	60,087
November	69	30,313	66	17,729	7	4,052	3	853	15	3,390	160	56,340
December	95	23,825	86	19,182	15	6,000	1	614	12	3,782	209	55,493
Total for 1858.	958	392,572	653	151,027	161	74,127	25	12,662	79	46,432	1,949	679,815
Total for 1857...	909	406,873	684	153,651	152	64,110	67	28,760	141	42,972	1,953	696,366
1856...	883	384,752	652	159,594	131	59,013	62	20,133	132	38,993	1,815	662,426
1855...	889	379,327	527	120,881	116	49,963	122	33,522	113	29,462	1,717	613,155
1854...	903	336,998	571	111,823	122	59,556	69	18,790	127	30,027	1,782	557,186
1853...	813	304,138	553	111,029	136	58,324	93	20,877	122	33,030	1,717	527,402
1852...	750	308,120	578	114,338	143	55,427	52	12,538	124	29,782	1,647	520,196
1851...	856	344,046	550	114,216	191	58,308	47	11,124	156	40,789	1,800	568,483
1850...	634	298,299	541	107,230	164	65,136	51	12,466	152	40,337	1,542	423,468

No. 4.—*Table of the total production of sugar, consumption, etc.*

	Tons.
Cane sugar	2,057,653
Palm sugar	100,000
Beet-root sugar..	164,822
Maple sugar..	20,247
Total	2,342,722

But the quantity of sugar from which the United States, England, Europe, and the Mediterranean are to be supplied reaches only 1,273,000 tons. Thus, for the 300,000,000 souls who are dependent on it, it gives but 8 pounds per head, while the consumption in England is triple that quantity and in the United States 20 pounds per head. The use of sugar in the world is rapidly increasing. In France it has doubled in thirty years. It has increased more than 50 per cent in England in fifteen years. In the Zollverein it has quadrupled. The following table will show the imports and production of sugar in Great Britain, France, and the United States during many years:

Consumption of sugar in Great Britain, France, and United States.

Year.	Sugar duty paid in France.				Great Britain.	United States.			Average amount.
	Colonial.	Foreign.	Beet root.	Total.		Foreign	Louisiana	Total.	
	Tons.	*Tons.*	*Tons.*	*Tons.*	*Tons.*	*Tons.*	*Tons.*	*Tons.*	*Per cent.*
1841	74,515	12,042	27,162	114,719	203,200	65,601	38,000	103,606	49.52
1842	77,443	8,210	35,070	110,723	193,823	69,474	39,200	108,674	45.42
1843	79,455	9,695	29,155	118,215	204,016	28,854	64,360	93,214	42.30
1844	87,382	10,269	32,075	129,626	206,000	83,801	44,400	128,206	41.82
1845	90,958	11,542	35,132	137,632	242,831	88,336	45,000	133,336	40.40
1846	78,632	15,185	46,845	140,662	261,932	44,974	83,028	128,002	41.85
1847	87,826	9,626	52,369	149,821	290,275	98,410	71,040	169,450	34.95
1848	48,371	9,540	48,103	106,014	309,424	104,214	107,000	211,214	29.40
1849	63,335	18,979	43,798	126,107	299,041	113,421	99,180	202,301	31.00
1850	50,996	23,862	67,297	142,155	310,391	84,813	110,600	194,413	32.22
1851	....	....	74,999	....	329,715	190,193	102,000	292,193	32.32
1852	32,030	14,882	67,445	114,357	360,720	228,772	118,273	347,045	28.00
1853	32,841	15,044	87,120	135,005	380,488	232,213	160,967	393,180	30.72
1854	40,113	18,943	85,825	144,981	475,095	227,982	224,662	452,644	....
1855	45,373	49,822	52,902	148,097	384,234	236,942	173,317	410,259	....
1856	46,767	16,456	95,103	158,326	397,448	272,631	115,713	388,344	....
1857	42,466	25,689	*132,600	200,155	367,476	388,501	36,933	425,434	....

*To close of February.

The production of beet-root sugar in France was for four years as follows:

	Number working.	Kilos.
1854	303	77,848,208
1855	208	50,180,864
1856	275	91,003,098
1857	341	132,000,000

The figures for 1857 are only to March 1, and exceed by 54,000,000 kilograms the product of last year. The production in the Zollverein in 1855 was as follows:

	Cwt.
Prussia	14,099,263
Anhalt	2,301,364
Bavaria	247,126
Saxony	131,968
Wnrtemburg	603,256
Baden	988,825
Hesse	59,137
Huringen	122,965
Brunswick	634,496

giving a total of 19,188,402. The increase in the consumption is immense. In 1841 the total for the three countries above named was 420,000 tons. This has increased to 800,000 tons, or a quantity nearly doubled, and the supply has come from Louisiana and from beet roots. The former failed considerably in the last two years, and, as a consequence, nearly convulsed the world. The value of sugar in the open market, then, seems to depend upon the precarious crop of Louisiana, since, when that fails, the prices rise all over the world.—(United States Economist.)

No. 5.—*Table of number of Chinese shipped from China from 1847 to March 23, 1858.*

The following table, derived from a reliable source, exhibits the total number of vessels that have arrived at this port since 1847 with Asiatics, their flags, tonnage, number of Asiatics shipped and landed, number and percentage of deaths, etc., which I think will not be deemed uninteresting:

Flags of vessels.	Number.	Tonnage.	Asiatics, number shipped.	Landed.	Deaths.	Percentage of deaths.
American	13	13,545	6,744	5,929	815	12
British	29	21,275	10,791	9,205	1,586	14¾
Dutch	8	5,003	2,773	2,463	310	11¼
French	7	6,037	3,655	3,154	501	13¾
Spanish	5	2,038	1,779	1,489	290	11¼
Portuguese	3	1,246	1,049	1,021	28	2¾
Peruvian	3	2,484	1,314	812	502	38¼
Bremen	1	560	249	236	13	5¼
Norwegian	1	470	221	179	42	19
Chilean	1	250	202	155	47	23¼
Total	71	53,008	28,777	24,643	4,134	14¾

From the foregoing it will be seen that the loss of life on the total number shipped actually amounts to 14¼ per cent; and while the number of deaths of those brought hither in Portuguese ships amounts to only 2¾ per cent, the number brought in American ships amounts to 12 per cent, in British ships to 14¾ per cent, and in French ships to 13¾ per cent, while in Peruvian ships the number of deaths amounts to 38¼ per cent.

No. 6.—*Population of the West Indies, as stated in Colton's Atlas of the World, volume 1.*

Haiti:		
Haitian Empire	572,000	
Dominican Republic	136,000	
Cuba (slaves, 330,425)	1,009,060	
Puerto Rico	447,914	
French islands:		
Guadalupe and dependencies	154,975	
Martinique	121,478	
French Guiana	22,110	
St Bartholomew	9,000	
Danish islands:		
St. Thomas	13,666	
Santa Cruz	23,729	
St. John	2,228	
		39,623
Dutch islands—Curaçao, etc		28,497
Dutch Guiana		61,080
British islands:		
Bahamas	27,519	
Turks Island	4,428	
Jamaica *	377,433	
Caymans	1,760	
Trinidad*	68,645	
Tobago	13,208	
Granada	32,671	
St. Vincent	30,128	
Barbados	135,939	
St. Lucia	24,516	
Dominica	22,061	
Montserrat	7,653	
Antigua	37,757	
St. Christopher	23,177	
Nevis	9,601	
Barbuda	1,707	
Anguilla	3,052	
Virgin Islands	6,689	
British Guiana	127,695	
		963,639
Total		3,575,376

*Acquired from Spain.

APPENDIX No. 2.

SPEECH OF HON. J. P. BENJAMIN, OF LOUISIANA, ON THE AQUISITION OF CUBA.

[Delivered in the Senate of the United States, Friday, February 11, 1859.]

*　　*　　*　　*　　*　　*　　*

I have thus far spoken, sir, of the beneficial results to humanity arising from the acquisition of Cuba, in the double aspect of the preservation of the island from a lapse into the barbarism and savage state of the other Antilles, and of regard for its miserable laboring population. What would be its effects on the superior race—on the white natives of the island, now numbering nearly three-quarters of a million?

In spite of pro forma petitions, recently forwarded from Habana, under the orders of the captain-general, the ardent aspirations of the Cubans for release from the grinding tyranny under which they languish are too well known for concealment. I will not appeal to a knowledge personal to us all; I will not rely on the fact that amongst the numerous Cubans with whom I have had opportunity of conversing on the subject I never yet have found one—no, not one—who did not pant for the hour of freedom, who was not ready to strike for his liberty if the remotest prospect of succor could be held out to him. I will appeal to history, and leave its teachings to the appreciation of a candid world. My sketch must be rapid.

At the close of the last and the commencement of the present century Cuba was prosperous and happy. Subjected to a colonial system identical with that then generally prevalent among civilized nations, if her commerce was restricted by the monopoly established in favor of the mother country, her own internal administration was conducted by wise rulers, guided by paternal interest in her welfare. She shared the political benefits conquered by the Spanish people, and when the constitution of 1812 was established, Cuba reaped its advantages. When, on the death of Ferdinand VII, Queen Christina threw herself into the arms of the liberal party in order to insure the triumph of Queen Isabella over the pretensions of Don Carlos, the royal statute was proclaimed in both Spain and Cuba, and the latter was represented in the national congress and enjoyed the liberties accorded by that celebrated document to the mother country. Under its provisions, the Junta de Fomento was established in Habana, with branches in all the principal cities of the island. When, in 1836, the revolution of La Granja placed the party of the Progresistas in power, subverted the royal statutes, and proclaimed the old constitution of 1812, the Queen Mother, then Regent, in convoking the Cortes, included the deputies from Cuba in the call.

In the meantime, however, the example of the other Spanish-American colonies which had succeeded in establishing their independence had not been without its effects on Cuba. In 1825 the liberator, Bolivar, offered to aid the patriots by an invasion of the island. Numerous societies were formed under the title of the "Soles de Bolivar," and everything was prepared for seconding the invasion, which might very possibly have proved successful but for the intervention of our own Government, which dissuaded the invasion. (See letters of Mr. Clay to the ministers of Colombia and Mexico, December 20, 1825.) The knowledge of this effervescence of the public mind induced, on the part of the Spanish King, one of the most extraordinary acts which ever emanated from a despot. He gave the Captain-General, by an ordinance of the 28th of May, 1825, all the powers granted to the governors of besieged towns; or, in other words, declared the whole island under martial law, with full power in the Captain-General over the lives, fortunes, and liberties of the people, and with the right of suspending all laws and royal decrees at his pleasure.

This would appear scarcely credible, but I desire to read a passage from this ordinance of 1825 of the Spanish King. I find it fortunately translated here in a little book called Cuba and the Cubans, which I would recommend to the perusal of gentlemen who may desire some additional facts in relation to the condition of the island:

On the 28th of May, 1825, the royal ordinance addressed to the Captain-General of Cuba declares: "It has pleased His Majesty, in conformity with the advice of his ministers, to authorize your excellency, fully investing you with the whole extent of power which by royal ordinances is granted to the governors of besieged towns; in consequence thereof His Majesty most amply and unrestrictedly authorizes your excellency not only to remove from the island such persons holding office from the Government or not, whatever their occupation, work, class, or situation in life may be, whose residence there you may believe to be prejudicial, or whose public or private conduct may appear suspicious to you, employing in their stead faithful servants of His Majesty. Also to suspend the execution of whatever royal orders or general decrees in all the different branches of the administration, or in any part of them, as your excellency may think conducive to the royal service."

We are told that under this system of government the whites are contented. Why, sir, independent of the conspiracies of which I have spoken, in 1823–24 and 1825, again in 1826, another conspiracy broke out, and its chiefs were arrested, and Sanchez and Aguerro were executed at Port au Prince; and again, at a later day, the conspiracy called the conspiracy of the Black Eagle broke out and was again repressed, and those engaged in it executed or exiled or imprisoned. The different conspiracies that have existed of late years are familiar to us all; the various expeditions of Lopez and his companions; and the last of which I have any memory, or, at least, authentic detail, is that of 1851, when a few Cuban patriots, worn-out, disappointed fugitives, still had courage to meet together on the 4th of July, 1851, and declared the independence of Cuba. Here is their declaration of independence. I am going to refer to this, not so much for the purpose of showing this fact, not so much for the purpose of calling attention to the signatures, including names of this same family of Aguerro, that seems to have distinguished itself in behalf of the liberties of its country, but because there is a list of grievances in this declaration of independence to which I now desire to call the attention of the Senate, and which I will lay before it, asking every man who hears it, if it be possible that human beings subjected to grievances like these can be content, can be willing to kiss the rod which smites them?

They begin, sir, by stating the horrible cruelties that are exercised upon them. It is in Spanish; I will read it as well as I can; it will be probably somewhat imperfect in the translation.

They state that "they supposed the world would refuse credence to the history of the horrible iniquities which have been perpetrated in Cuba, and would consider, with reason, perhaps, that if there existed monsters capable of committing them, it is not conceivable that there should exist men who for so long a time had submitted to them; but if those persons are few who reach the truth of particular facts, by reason of the means of which the Government disposes to obscure and disfigure them, nobody can resist the evidence of acts that are public and official."

Therefore, they go on to relate:

It was publicly, and with arms in his hands, that General Tacon despoiled the Island of Cuba of the constitution of Spain, proclaimed by all the powers of the Monarchy and which these powers had ordered to be sworn to as the fundamental law of the entire Monarchy.

It was publicly, and by the acts of the courts, that Cuba was declared to be deprived of the rights which all Spaniards enjoyed, and which are naturally conceded to persons the least civilized.

It was publicly that the decree was issued which deprived the sons of Cuba of all right of being chosen to occupy public offices or of employment in the State.

It was publicly that omni-modal faculties were granted to the Captains-General of Cuba, who may deny to those whom they desire to have punished or sentenced by the tribunals even the form of a trial before the courts.

Publicly prominent in the Island of Cuba are still those military commissions which in other countries the law permits only in extraordinary cases during a time of war, and then only for offenses against the State.

Publicly has the Spanish press threatened Cuba with tearing from it the property in its slaves, of converting the island into ruin and ashes, and of disenchanining against it all the hordes of barbarous Africans which now exist within it.

Public is the continual increase of the army and the creation of new mercenary bodies which, under pretext of public security, are only put upon us for the purpose of augmenting the burdens that lie upon Cuba and of exercising with greater vexation the system of subordination and espionage over its inhabitants.

Public are the obstacles and difficulties which are placed in the way of each individual for moving, for exercising any industry, nobody being sure that he will not be seized and fined, by reason of some defect of authorization or want of license at every step that he makes in the island.

Public are the contributions which are exhausting the Island of Cuba and the projects of other contributions which are threatened and which are to absorb all the products of its riches, there remaining nothing to its miserable inhabitants but the pain of labor.

Public are the exactions of all kinds which inferior officers impose on its inhabitants, with the greatest disregard to the opinion of mankind.

I return now, sir, to the year 1836, when the Cuban deputies were convoked to the meeting of the constituent Cortes at Madrid. The Cortes assembled in 1837, but the Cuban deputies were not admitted to their seats. Cuba was deprived of her representation; nor was this the only outrage inflicted on her rights. It was decided that she should be governed in the future by exceptional laws, and not by the laws common to the rest of the monarchy. These special laws were never passed; but the royal ordinance has continued in force to the present hour, maintaining martial law, and Cuba has thus remained ever since a helpless victim, subject to the despotic control of a single man, the extent of whose powers can only be described by the word invented to express them—omni-modas, of all kinds.

Ever since this monstrous system has been adopted Cuba has not been blessed with one hour of peace. Constantly repeated have been her efforts to shake off the yoke under which they groan, but all in vain. Twenty thousand bayonets on the land and a powerful fleet off its coasts keep the dread watch of the tyrant and suppress the first symptoms of revolt. The whites have been disarmed, and 4 companies of colored men have been added to each of the 16 regiments of peninsular troops stationed on the island, thus holding before the unfortunate inhabitants the constant threat of a war of races, a renewal of the horrors of Santo Domingo. Their pride of race has been shocked by a governor's decree authorizing marriages between the two races, except when one of the parties is a noble.

The army is maintained faithful solely by a rigorous isolation, all communication between the inhabitants and troops being interdicted. No security for life, person, or liberty against the caprice of a despot; no arms for self-defense, the size of a walking stick even being limited to dimensions small enough to pass through a ring furnished the policeman.

The Cubans have not even the idea of a trial by jury. Cases are tried before the judges of royal appointment, the venal favorites of the Spanish court, who are speedily removed to make room for more hungry aspirants. The Captain-General, himself a mere soldier, presides by law over the supreme court of justice. All offices, with the exception of a few of the lowest order, are in the hands of Spaniards. The penalty for carrying weapons of any description is six years' hard labor in the chain gangs of the penal colonies of Africa. The Cuban can not have company at home without a permit, for which he must pay $2.50, and he must be provided with a license, at the same cost, if he is to absent himself from town or from his home in the country. Neither can he change his domicile without notifying the police, obtaining a permit, and paying for the same. He can not lodge any person, whether foreigner or native, stranger, friend, or relative, in his house without previous notice to the police. Mayors of cities are not elected by the people, but by the aldermen of the common councils and under the dictation of the Spanish governors. These aldermen serve for life, and their offices are either inherited or purchased from the Crown at public auction for prices varying according to the perquisites thereof. Thus it happens that even they who should be the immediate guardians of the people often become speculaters, who, far from extending them protection, extort the full interest of the capital invested in the purchase of their offices. No affidavit is required in Cuba, but a suspicion or a secret denunciation is sufficient to tear a man from the bosom of his family at any hour of the day or night, throw him into a dungeon, there to linger for weeks or months, if it so please the authorities, and then to set him free with the bare acknowledgment of his innocence, or send him to transatlantic exile, if, though innocent, he still remains suspicious.

Such is the sad, the dreadful condition of the unfortunate islanders who are represented by the official press as hastening to lay at the feet of the Queen ardent professions of loyalty to her Government and attachment to her person. They have again and again made heavy sacrifices for freedom—nay, at this very moment, and for years past, they maintain, by secret contributions, for gratuitous circulation, public journals in the United States, repeating their constant appeal to our sympathies.

The whole of the recent wrongs committed, Mr. President, in relation to the arming of the blacks, and other similar outrages, were committed under the instigation of Great Britain, and Lord Palmerston did not blush to acknowledge his guilt in the face of the civilized world. I have here his dispatch, in which, in answer to the remonstrance of the inhabitants of the island, communicated to him through the correspondence of the Spanish minister, he replied to the effect that it was true that the measures he was recommending might not be suitable for the whites, but that they were exceedingly beneficial to the blacks—an actual recommendation to the Spanish Government to trample the white native Cuban under foot for the benefit of the Africans that had been imported in defiance of the treaties with Great Britain herself. Here is Lord Palmerston's dispatch of September 11, 1851, and it is capable of that signification alone:

With reference to that passage in M. Miraflores's note, in which he states that the Spanish Government can not understand how Her Majesty's Government can seriously recommend a measure which would prove very injurious to the natives of Cuba, when they also recommend that the Spanish Government should conciliate the affections of those Cubans, I have to instruct your lordship to observe to M. de Miraflores that the slaves of Cuba form a large portion, and by no means an unimportant one, of the population of Cuba, and that any steps taken to provide for their emancipation would therefore, as far as the black population are concerned, be quite in unison with the recommendation made by Her Majesty's Government; that measures should be adopted for contenting the people of Cuba, with a view to secure the connection between that island and the Spanish Crown; and it must be evident that if the negro population of Cuba were rendered free that fact would create a most poweiful element of resistance to any scheme for annexing Cuba to the United States, where slavery still exists.

There it is, sir. It is the white population that is to be trampled under the feet of the blacks, and such blacks as now exist in Jamaica; it is this white population that is represented in the face of the Senate and the country as desirous of continuing subjects of the rule under which they now groan.

Sir, it is very easy to say: "If the people of Cuba desire emancipation from this tyranny, why do they not rise in arms?" And we are pointed to our own condition when our forefathers resisted the tyranny of the British Crown. How unfair to them! How delusive the comparison! We were 3,000,000 men. We had the right of speech, the liberty of the press. We could assemble, combine, prepare. We could arm. We had a right to buy arms and to wear them. When Patrick Henry was urging the Virginia assembly to the declaration of American independence, his cry was that three millions of men in arms could not be vanquished by any power that our enemy could send against us. But how is the case of the miserable Cubans? Had we, as they have, a foreign army in our midst—an army composed of soldiers whose fidelity to the mother country is only secured by the system already mentioned, of strict isolation, of absolute interdiction from any communication with the inhabitants of the island—had we such a force as that among us, and, backed by the bayonets of the black race, threatening an exterminating war of races? No, sir; there is no fairness, no justice, in the reproach.

I must waive, Mr. President, all discussion of the effects that the acquisition of this island would have on the industrial, agricultural, and commercial interests of our country, these points having been already treated very satisfactorily by gentlemen who have already spoken.

I shall not even speak of its geographical position, commanding, as it does, a commerce which, before all that are now within sound of my voice shall have disappeared from the earth, will reach $1,500,000,000. Still I must call attention to the fact that it seems hitherto to have been taken for granted that this country is exposed to no risk so long as this island remains within the feeble grasp of Spain. I apprehend this is a mistake, and a very grave mistake. It is a grave mistake for several reasons: First, because those harbors, being the most capacious and the best fortified in the Gulf, offer a secure rendezvous, in case of difficulties with other foreign powers, for collecting fleets and navies with which our own unprotected coasts could be attacked; secondly, because Spain is not now an independent nation.

I deny her independence in the true sense of the word. Spain has bartered away her sovereignty in Cuba, effectually bartered it away to Great Britain. She did not yield to motives of policy or of philanthropy in abolishing the slave trade. There was a time when Spanish dignity was not insulted by the offer to buy something from her, and her pride was not touched when Great Britain paid her £400,000 for giving up the slave trade. Again and again has the Spanish nation been twitted upon the floor of the British Parliament with having cheated Great Britain by taking the money and then countenancing the traffic. It is under the controlling influence of Great Britain that Spanish pride has been so far humiliated that a mixed commission sat in the Island of Cuba; that British subjects in the town of Habana try Spanish subjects in their own colonies for breaches of the treaty, and that England had a hulk, a prison ship belonging to herself, lying in

the harbor of Habana, to enforce the edicts of British judges over
Spanish colonists; and yet we are told that this is an independent
nation, whose pride and dignity will revolt at the bare proposal for a
cession of sovereignty over the island.

The safety of our country is further involved in the acquisition of
Cuba, or at least in her independence; because her harbors not only
furnish points of rendezvous for hostile fleets, but secure harbors of
refuge in which they could refit and repair, and prepare themselves for
fresh attacks on our unprotected coasts. It was those harbors that
afforded refuge for the British fleet after its descent on New Orleans,
and in them did the French fleet refit after its bombardment of the
castle of San Juan d'Uloa. In the event of a rupture with Great
Britain, which many gentlemen around me seem to suppose inevitable
in no very distant future, Cuba would be, in her possession, a tremendous point of vantage for attack; and little would she reck of any opposition by Spain to her use of it for her own purposes in a moment of
emergency. It is for this reason that the instincts of the American
people have already taught them that we shall ever be insecure against
hostile attack until this important geographical and military position is
placed under our protection and control.

This being the relation borne to us by Cuba, the President has proposed that Congress shall give expression to the national sentiment by
sanctioning a proposition to Spain for the purchase of the island. Why
should we not do it?

First, we are told that it is an offense to the dignity of Spain to make
the offer of purchase. To that, reply has been made so often and so
victoriously that it is hardly necessary to repeat it. We have only to
say that of all the colonies that Spain ever possessed on this continent
none remain but the islands of Cuba and Puerto Rico, and, I believe,
some small islands adjacent not worth naming; and that, of all she
has lost, everything has been torn from her by violence, with the exception of Florida, that we bought, and Louisiana, that France bought.
If it was no offense for France to purchase Louisiana and no offense for
us to purchase Florida, it is a little too late to say that it is an offense
to her dignity for us to propose the purchase of Cuba. And, sir, I can
not understand the dignity and sense of honor of a country that sells
to the people of Great Britain for a sum of money an agreement to
abandon the slave trade, and under that treaty gives to Great Britain
power to hold courts in her own territory, judging her own subjects;
and then turns upon us and, on the bare indication of a desire to purchase, tells us that she considers herself insulted by the proposition.
I am afraid she will have to be insulted; I am afraid the proposition
will have to be made. This insult was offered to her dignity a good
many years ago in relation to this same island, first by Great Britain
and afterwards by us, and this is the first time we have ever heard of
her being insulted by the offer.

But, sir, we are told that England and France will object. If that
be true, it affords to my mind a controlling motive for persisting. I
wish to examine a little into this subject of the interference of England
and France; and first I desire the attention of the Senate to a fact
which has not yet been adverted to in this debate—that as far back as
1823 Great Britain tried to buy Cuba from Spain, and made her offers
of purchase, which were rejected; that then in 1825 and 1826 Great
Britain was at the bottom of the plot for declaring Cuba independent,
by an insurrection of the people, with the aid of the Colombian and
Mexican forces, her object being to get the control of the island under

a protectorate, which she thought she could establish without exciting our jealousy; and that it was these views of Great Britain which induced the interference of Mr. Clay with the Colombian and Mexican ministers, and this broke up the plot. July 10, 1823, Mr. Appleton, being then at Cadiz, wrote to Mr. Adams, our Secretary of State:

The contents of the letter of which I herewith inclose a duplicate are substantially confirmed by all that has come to my knowledge since it was written. I shall say nothing of the official declaration of England; they are documents which must long since have reached you. I have it, however, in my power to say, upon the best authority, that the sentiments she now professes in relation to acquisition of territory at the expense of Spain have not always been entertained by her.

Mr. Quadra, now deputy of the Cortes, had, when minister of ultramarine in 1820, distant overtures made to him for the cession of the eastern side of Cuba to England. These overtures were treated with great coldness, and it is supposed to have not been repeated. This fact has been communicated to me in confidence by Mr. Gener, a deputy from the Habana, who, being a European by birth, has had more access to the secrets of the cabinet than his companions, and has lately received a distinguished proof of the respect in which he is held in being called on to preside over the Cortes during an epoch of particular difficulty.

In 1827, Mr. Everett, then in Madrid, sent to Mr. Clay the following dispatch:

MADRID, *August 17, 1827.*

SIR: The inclosed copy of a confidential dispatch addressed to the minister of state by the Conde de la Alcudia, Spanish minister at London, was handed to me to-day by a private friend, and may be depended on as authentic. As the communication was made to me in the strictest confidence, and as the document is in itself unsuitable for the press, I take the liberty of transmitting it to you, for the President's information, in the form of a private letter, and request that it may not be placed on the public files of the Department of State.

Here is the letter:

[Translation.]

The Spanish minister at London to the minister of state.

LONDON, *June 1, 1827.*

MOST EXCELLENT SIR: I deem it my duty to give you notice for the information of the King, our Lord, that this Government dispatched a frigate sometime ago to the Canary Islands, with commissioners on board, who were instructed to ascertain whether any preparations were making therefor an expedition to America; and also the state of defense of those islands, and the disposition of the inhabitants. The result of these inquiries was that the said islands were in a wholly defenseless situation, provided with few troops, and those disaffected and ready for any innovation.

The frigate then proceeded to the Habana, where the commissioners found many persons disposed to revolt; but in consequence of the large military force stationed there and the strength of the fortifications, they considered it impossible to take possession of the island without the cooperation of the authorities and the army. In consequence of the information thus obtained, measures have been taken in both these islands to prepare the public opinion by means of emissaries in favor of England, to the end that the inhabitants may be brought to declare themselves independent and to solicit the protection of the British. The latter are prepared to assist them, and will in this way avoid any collision with the United States. The whole operation has been undertaken and is to be conducted in concert with the revolutionists resident here (at London) and in the islands who have designated a Spanish general, now at this place, to take command of the Habana when the occasion shall require it.

The Duke of Wellington communicated to me the above information, which is also confirmed by an intimation which he gave to Brig. Gen. Don Francisco Armentecos, when this officer took leave of him to go to the Habana. The Duke then advised him, if he should discover any symptoms of disaffection in the authorities, to give immediate notice to the King, as it would be a grievous thing for His Majesty to lose the Habana.

I have thought it my duty to make these circumstances known to your excellency. May God keep you many years.

EL CONDE DE LA ALCUDIA.

This is the same Great Britain that now, having failed in her own attempt, generously proposes to the American people an alliance of three parties—France, England, and the United States—each of whom shall say, as they are bound to do in her estimate under the law of nations, that not one of them will ever acquire Cuba. Having failed herself, both by open negotiation and secret maneuver, to obtain possession of the island, she proposes to us magnanimously to renounce what she can not get, provided we will be equally generous; for such, after all, was the real proposition made in the dispatch to which Mr. Everett made his celebrated answer; and when we respectfully declined her proposal, we were informed through another dispatch that she held herself at liberty to act as she pleased for the future; and the British secretary actually proceeded, with a grave face, to argue that England had equal interests with ourselves in the Island of Cuba, because, in a geographical line, Cuba was no nearer to the United States than to the Island of Jamaica—that delectable paradise of her negro savages.

So much, sir, as regards any objections that may be made by England.

But France, we are told, will be offended; her sense of justice will be shocked at our violation of national courtesy in desiring to acquire a neighboring isle. The reproach will come with a good grace, sir, from the present Emperor of the French, who was so particularly regardful of public law when at Bologne and at Strasburg he attempted to overthrow the constitutional Government of his own country for the purpose of acquiring that power which he has since shown was desired only for the gratification of his own selfish ambition. We are to be called on to renounce all rights of national growth in deference, forsooth, to France and England. We alone are not to grow; and the reason is that we declare our purpose in advance, which gives to these intermeddling powers an opportunity of raising an outcry; whereas in the secrecy of their cabinets projects of invasion are entertained and executed before notice is given; and, when reproached for their breaches of national law, the world is coolly informed in diplomatic jargon that the outrage is un fait accompli.

Mr. President, I trust that if the voice of England is raised on this question, the first, the prompt, the peremptory answer to be given will be to ask her to give an account of her seizure of the Bay Islands in defiance of her treaty with us; to call for her title to control the Nicaragua transit; and when she has made good in the law of nations that new title invented by Lord Clarendon, and which he calls "spontaneous settlement," then, and not till then, we shall be ready on our part to give her a reason why we want "spontaneous settlement" in Cuba.

If, sir, on the other hand, the Emperor of France shall make objection, let him be asked by what right he attempts to interfere with us in the purchase of territory from Spain, when we are only following the example of his uncle, who did the same thing? Let him be asked what greater right France had to buy Louisiana than we have to buy Cuba? And, sir, let both France and England be required to show by what principle of national law territorial acquisition is forbidden when peaceful and for a price, but permissible if effected by the exercise of violence committed by the strong against the weak.

Mr. President, there is one paramount principle affecting the whole question of annexation, which our self-respect requires us to present prominently before the world. It is that in the expansion of our system we seek no conquest, subjugate no people, impose our laws on no unwilling subjects. When new territory is brought under our jurisdiction, the inhabitants are admitted to all the rights of self-government. Let no attempt be made to confuse this subject by the use of inappropriate terms. It is the fallacy lurking under the use of the word "belongs," of which despots make use. Cuba "belongs" to Spain. True, but in what sense? New York "belongs" to the United States also, but in what sense?

Cuba is subject to Spanish sovereignty. Her people now owe allegiance to Spain; but the island does not belong to Spain as property belongs to an individual. The Cubans are not the property of the Crown. Nay, the soil of the island belongs to private proprietors. The right of Spain, as a proprietary right, extends only to the public places on the island not disposed of to private individuals, and to such revenues as she can lawfully and legitimately exact from her subjects. But, sir, from the date of our independence we have had fixed principles on the subject of the true proprietorship of countries. The fundamental theory of our Government is that the people of all countries are the true and only owners, that governments are established for their benefit, and that whenever governments become subversive of the true ends of their institution it is the right of the people to alter and abolish them. The Island of Cuba belongs not to Queen Isabella, but to the people who inhabit it, and who alone have the right to decide under what government they choose to live.

Now, Mr. President, bringing this discourse to a close, I desire to say, in a few words, what my view is in relation to the policy of this country. I would propose, as the President proposes, the purchase of the Island of Cuba from the Government of Spain. If that be refused, if it be supposed that Spanish pride or Spanish dignity is involved in the proposition to such an extent as to make it impossible for them to cede it, I would then say to Spain: "If you will not cede the island to us, grant independence to your subjects there, and we will pay you a reasonable equivalent for the abandonment of your revenues, and make settlement hereafter with the people of Cuba for our advances."

If this offer be again refused, then let us announce to Spain in advance that whenever opportunity shall occur, we are ready and resolute to offer to the people of Cuba the same aid that England offered to the other Spanish colonies; the same alliance, offensive and defensive, which France so nobly tendered to us in the hour of our darkest peril. Tell her that we shall repair the wrong by us done to the generation now passing away in Cuba when we impeded their efforts for gaining their independence by affording to the present generation our aid, countenance, and assistance. Tell her that when the Cubans shall have conquered their independence, theirs shall be the right of remaining a separate republic, if they so prefer; that we will cherish, aid, and protect them from all foreign interference, and will draw close the bonds of a mutual, social, and commercial intercourse that shall be of incalculable benefit to both. Tell her, too, that if the people of the island, with their independence once acquired and republican institutions established, shall desire to unite themselves with us, they shall be admitted to the equal benefits which our system of government secures to each independent State that enters into its charmed circle. She shall unite with us freely, the equal associate of free States; and when the union shall have been accomplished, the sword of the nation shall smite down any rude hand that shall attempt to sunder those whom the God of Freedom has united.

APPENDIX No. 3.

CUBA'S CASE.

WASHINGTON, *December 7, 1895.*

SIR: I hand you herewith a statement of the facts upon which I, as authorized representative of the Cubans in arms, ask that the rights of belligerency be accorded them by your Government.

If you so desire I can exhibit to you the originals of the documents mentioned or set forth in said statement.

Should it be necessary or desirable for me to point out the arguments, based on the facts submitted, which I deem proof that we are now in condition to ask for belligerency, it will afford me great pleasure to do so.

Begging your earliest and most favorable consideration of this subject, I have the honor to remain, very respectfully, yours,

T. ESTRADA PALMA.

To Hon. RICHARD OLNEY,
Secretary of State of the United States of America,
Washington, D. C.

WASHINGTON, D. C., *December 7, 1895.*

SIR: While admitting that, as a rule, governments do not take cognizance of the justice or injustice of a struggle in which they are called upon to grant the rights of belligerency to one of the contending parties, the revolution for the independence of the Cuban people, initiated on February 24 last, is so similar in its character to that which resulted in the establishment of the foremost Republic in the world, the United States of America, that I feel called upon to point out the causes leading to the present uprising in Cuba.

CAUSES OF THE REVOLUTION.

These causes are substantially the same as those of the former revolution, lasting from 1868 to 1878 and terminating only on the representation of the Spanish Government that Cuba would be granted such reforms as would remove the grounds of complaint on the part of the Cuban people. Unfortunately the hopes thus held out have never been realized. The representation which was to be given the Cubans has proved to be absolutely without character; taxes have been levied anew on everything conceivable; the offices in the island have increased, but the officers are all Spaniards; the native Cubans have been left with no public duties whatsoever to perform, except the payment of taxes to the Government and blackmail to the officials, without privilege even to move from place to place in the island except on the permission of governmental authority.

Spain has framed laws so that the natives have substantially been deprived of the right of suffrage. The taxes levied have been almost entirely devoted to support the army and navy in Cuba, to pay interest on the debt that Spain has saddled on the island, and to pay the salaries of the vast number of Spanish officeholders, devoting only $746,000 for internal improvements out of the $26,000,000 collected by tax. No public schools are within reach of the masses for their education. All the principal industries of the island are hampered by excessive imposts. Her commerce with every country but Spain has been crippled in every possible manner, as can readily be seen by the frequent protests of shipowners and merchants.

The Cubans have no security of person or property. The judiciary are instruments of the military authorities. Trial by military tribunals can be ordered at any time at the will of the Captain-General. There is, beside, no freedom of speech, press, or religion. In point of fact, the causes of the Revolution of 1775 in this country were not nearly as grave as those that have driven the Cuban people to the various insurrections which culminated in the present revolution.

A statement of the facts and circumstances that have forced the Cubans from peaceful to belligerent measures of obtaining that redress which they are satisfied can only come with absolute independence and republican form of government are set forth at large in the pamphlet hereto annexed, marked "A."

ABSOLUTE INDEPENDENCE OR EXTERMINATION.

Every promise of reform made to procure peace in 1878 having been broken by the Spanish Government, and subsequent peaceful endeavor in that direction having proved useless, Cuba is to-day in the condition described by Vattel (Law of Nations, sec. 291):

If his (the sovereign's) promises are not inviolable, the rebels will have no security in treating with him; when they have once drawn the sword they must throw away the scabbard, as one of the ancients expressed it, and the prince destitute of the more gentle and salutary means of appeasing the revolt will have no other remaining expedient than of utterly exterminating the insurgents; these will become formidable through despair; compassion will bestow success on them; their party will increase, and the state will be in danger.

The only solution of the revolution in Cuba is independence or extermination.

PRELIMINARY ORGANIZATION FOR REVOLT.

Years before the outbreak of the present hostilities the people within and without the island began to organize, with a view of preparing for the inevitable revolution, being satisfied, after repeated and patient endeavors, that peaceful petition was fruitless.

In order that the movement should be strong from the beginning, and organized both as to civil and military administration, the Cuban Revolutionary party was founded, with José Martí at its head. The principal objects were by united efforts to obtain the absolute independence of Cuba, to promote the sympathy of other countries, to collect funds with these objects in view, and to invest them in munitions of war. The military organization of this movement was completed by the election of Maximo Gomez as commander in chief. This election was made by the principal officers who fought in the last revolution.

THE UPRISING.

The time for the uprising was fixed at the solicitation of the people in Cuba, who protested that there was no hope of autonomy, and that their deposits of arms and ammunition were in danger of being discovered and their leaders arrested. A large amount of war material was then bought by Marti and vessels chartered to transport it to Cuba, where arrangements were made for its reception in the provinces of Santiago, Puerto Principe, and Santa Clara; but at Fernandina, Fla., it was seized by the United States authorities. Efforts were successfully made for the restitution of this material; nevertheless valuable time and opportunity was thus lost. The people in Cuba clamored for the revolution to proceed immediately, and in consequence the uprising was not further postponed. The date fixed for the uprising was the 24th of February. The people responded in Santiago, Santa Clara, and Matanzas. The provinces of Puerto Principe and Pinar del Rio did not respond, owing to lack of arms. In Puerto Principe rigorous search had previous to the 24th been instituted and all arms and ammunition confiscated by the Government. The leaders in the provinces of Matanzas and Santa Clara were imprisoned, and so the movement there was checked for the time being.

On the 27th the Governor-General of the Island of Cuba, Emilio Calleja, issued a proclamation declaring the provinces of Matanzas and Santiago in a state of siege, and fixed a period of eight days within which all those who surrendered were to be pardoned. Under these conditions, on the 3d of March, Juan Gualberto Gomez surrendered, was brought to Havana, and set at liberty, but before he could leave the palace of the Captain-General was rearrested on the ground that he had bought arms for the movement, and was subsequently court-martailed and sent in chains to the Spanish penal colony in Ceuta, Africa.

GROWTH OF THE REVOLUTION.

In the province of Santiago the revolution rapidly increased in strength under the leadership of Bartolome Masso, one of the most influential and respected citizens of Manzanillo; Guillermo Moncada, Jesus Rabi, Pedro Perez, José Miro, and others.

It was characterized by the Spanish Government as a negro and bandit movement, but many of the most distinguished and wealthy white citizens of the district flocked to the insurgent camp.

The Spanish authorities, through some of the Autonomists, attempted to persuade these men to lay down their arms. Gen. Bartolome Masso was twice approached in this behalf, but positively refused to entertain any negotiations which were not based on the absolute independence of Cuba.

On the 1st of April, Generals Antonio and José Maceo, Flor Crombet, and Agustin Cebreco, all veteran leaders in the former revolt, landed at Duaba, in the province of Santiago, and thousands rose to join them. Antonio Maceo then took command of the troops in that province, and on the 11th of April a detachment received Generals Maximo Gomez, José Marti, Francisco Borrerro, and Angel Guerra.

Captain-General Calleja was, on the 16th of April, succeeded by Gen. Arsenio Martinez Campos, the present commander in chief of the Spanish forces, who has the reputation of being Spain's greatest living general.

BATTLES AND CAMPAIGN.

Campos's first plan of campaign was to confine the revolution to the province of Santiago, and he then stated that he would crush the insurgents, establish peace, and return to Spain by the November following.

He asserted that the province of Puerto Principe would never rise in rebellion; and in order to give color to the statement and hope of labor to the unemployed, he projected a line of railway from Santa Cruz to Puerto Principe, planning also another from Manzanillo to Bayamo.

These two projects, as well as the proposed construction of wharves, were never seriously contemplated. From the very beginning of the uprising, conflicts between the Spanish troops and the Cubans were of daily occurrence, and many engagements of importance also took place, forts being captured, towns taken and raided.

It is of course useless to describe every skirmish in this province; the following are among the most important operations:

Los Negros, where General Rabi defeated the Spanish colonels Santoscildes and Zubikoski; Ramon de las Yaguas, where Colonel Garzon suprised and captured Lieutenant Gallego and 50 men, who were disarmed and permitted to leave unmolested—the troops sent to reinforce the Spaniards being also defeated; El Guanabano, where General Masso and Colonel Estrada forced Santoscildes to retreat to Bayamo, with great loss; Jarahuca, where General Maceo defeated General Salcedo, who had more than 3,000 men under him.

Combined operation of Generals Antonio and José Maceo, who captured the town of Cristo and 200 rifles and 40,000 rounds, while Colonel Garzon took the town of Cauey, and Colonel Planas attacked a military convoy on the railroad.

The town of Campechuela was attacked by Colonel Guerra and Colonel Estrada, who forced the garrisons of the two forts to surrender.

Juraguanas, where Colonel Estrada, with 1,000 men, met an equal number of Spanish regulars and defeated them.

Colonel Guerra surprised a Spanish guerrilla under Boeras; made many prisoners, whom he set at liberty.

El Cacao, where General Rabi cut to pieces the Spanish forces under Lieut. Col. U. Sanchez and obtained many rifles and ammunition.

El Jobito: This was one of the most important engagements in the east. It took place near Guantanamo, and Lieutenant Colonel Bach was killed and his troops decimated by Generals Maceo and Perez.

About the middle of July Gen. Martinez Campos, urged by the numerous complaints through the press that the Spanish forces in Bayamo were in a deplorable condition, without food or hospitals, and were cut off from Manzanillo, and wishing by a concerted movement of his lieutenants to crush the revolution at one blow, started from Manzanillo on the 12th for the purpose of relieving Bayamo, and intending thence to march west and drive Gomez into the Spanish military line between the province of Santa Clara and Puerto Principe, thus catching the Cubans between two fires. At the same time three Spanish columns were to march against Maceo and his forces from different directions, and surround and exterminate them. Campos, with 4,800 men under the command of Gen. Fidel Santoscildes, met 3,600 Cubans under Generals Maceo and Rabi on the road to Bayamo at Peralejos.

The battle which followed is known as the battle of Bayamo, Valenzuela, or Peralejo. It lasted eleven hours. General Santoscildes fell in the early part of the engagement, and thereupon Campos himself took command. The Spaniards, completely routed, were forced to kill all their mules and horses to form with them a barricade; left their convoy, the wounded, and dead on the field, and fled in disorder to Bayamo. The loss of the Spaniards was 400 killed and a larger number wounded. The Cubans' was 137 in all. Maceo took care of the Spanish wounded, and sent word to Campos to send a detachment to receive them, which was done.

General Campos, on reaching Bayamo, sent for heavy reenforcements, withdrawing a considerable number of troops from the province of Santa Clara.

Generals Roloff, Sanchez, and Rodriguez landed in that province at about this time with a large amount of war material, but not enough, as it proved, to fully arm all those who enthusiastically rushed to join them. Before the Spaniards had extricated Campos from his perilous position, the Cuban forces in the province of Santa Clara had been organized into the Fourth Army Corps, and operations were immediately begun.

Santa Clara is one of the wealthiest provinces in the island, and to protect the interest there large reenforcements were called from Spain, as they could not rely on the Spanish "volunteers." The best proof of this was that 400 Spanish volunteers, under Major Casallas, deserted and joined the Cuban ranks in a body at their first opportunity, taking with them all their arms, ammunitions, and supplies. Here, as in other provinces, skirmishes are of daily occurrence, and many fierce encounters have taken place. Among the most important engagements were the capture of Fort Taguasco by Gen. Serafin Sanchez; Las Varas, where 2,000 Spanish troops under Colonel Rubin were defeated by Generals Roloff and Sanchez; Cantabria, where Colonel Rego took many prisoners and war materials, and the raid and burning of the town of Guinia de Miranda by Colonel Perez, and Cayo Espino, where Colonel Lacret inflicted a severe defeat on the Spaniards under Colonel Molina. A most important part of the work of the forces in Santa Clara, which occupied considerable time and caused many encounters with the enemy, was the destruction of telegraph and telephone communications and railroads, of which there are many lines or branches in this district.

GOMEZ'S CAMPAIGNS.

Immediately on the landing of Generals Martí and Gomez they set out to cross the province of Santiago and enter that of Puerto Principe. It will be remembered that at about this time General Campos arrived in the island with reenforcements of over ten thousand men; the object of Gomez in marching into Puerto Principe was to lead those whom he knew were only expecting his arrival in that province in order to take the field. The citizens of Puerto Principe, or Camaguey, as it is also called, had the reputation of being rather conservative and hence both Spaniards and Cubans waited their determination with great interest.

Gen. Martinez Campos boasted that the inhabitants of Camaguey would never rise in revolt against Spain, but to make assurance doubly sure he placed a cordon of troops numbering about 10,000 on the border between Santiago and Puerto Principe to prevent the entry of Gomez into the latter district. Gomez and Marti started on their westward journey with about 300 men. In trying to pass the first line of troops at Boca de Dos Rios a severe conflict took place May 19, with a greatly superior force in which José Martí was killed. Great joy was manifested by the Spaniards, who claimed that the revolution had received its deathblow in the loss of Martí, but Gomez continued his advance westward, and ordering a feint to be made by Gen. Antonia Maceo at a point in the north of the Spanish cordon, he succeeded in eluding the enemy and entering the southern part of the province of Puerto Principe in the beginning of June. Here he was joined by Salvador Cisneros Betancourt, now the President of the Republic, the most influential Cuban of that province, together with all the young men of the city, and his forces were rapidly swelled to thousands by additions from all parts of the province. These he subsequently organized into the Third Army Corps.

Thus Gomez was successful in this first campaign of the revolution. Immediately on his arrival in Camaguey he proceeded by a series of rapid cavalry movements to increase his supply of arms and ammunition. He captured and burned Alta Gracia and captured the fort of El Mulato; he cut to pieces a Spanish guerrilla near Las Yeguas. The town and fort of San Jeronimo surrendered to him, and he attacked and raided the town of Cascorro; in all of which places many arms and ammunition as well as prisoners were taken; the latter being invariably released.

During the summer the city of Puerto Principe was constantly menaced in order to allow Gomez to complete his organization of the province.

He was much criticised by Gen. Martinez Campos for his inactivity during the summer, but the Spanish troops nevertheless did not interfere with his plans. Early in July he issued the first of the now famous orders relative to the sugar crop, and announced his intention of marching through Santa Clara and into Matanzas in the winter in order to superintend the carrying out of his decrees, increasing his military stores in the meantime, as well as securing the food supply of his army by corralling the cattle of the province in secure places.

As will be shown further on, General Gomez was upon the establishment of the Government confirmed as commander in chief of the Cuban forces.

In order to carry out his winter campaign he placed Maj. Gen. José Maria Rodriguez in command of the Third Army Corps. The Spaniards explained the wonderful progress of the revolution by the fact that it is impossible for their soldiers to operate during the wet season, and stated that as soon as the winter or dry season set in, or, as it has been expressed by one of her diplomatic representatives, after three days of a northern wind, the Cubans would be driven back from the provinces of Santa Clara and Puerto Principe in the province of Santiago, intending then, by a concentration of their entire fleet at the eastern end of the island, to cut off all basis of supplies and starve the Cubans into submission. At the beginning of the dry season Gomez had perfected all the arrangements of his march to the west; he had ordered Gen. Antonio Maceo with about 4,000 men, mostly infantry, to follow and join him at Sancti Spiritus, on the western boundary of Santa Clara, where Generals Roloff, Sanchez, Perez, and Lacret were waiting, under orders, for the advance of the commander in chief.

Between the provinces of Santa Clara and Puerto Principe there is a line of forts extending from the town of Jucaro to the town of Moron, called the Trocha. To prevent the entrance of Gomez into Santa Clara, Gen. Martinez Campos reenforced their garrisons and placed strong columns along the line to fill up the gaps. General Gomez, with a few hundred men, succeeded by a series of maneuvers into getting through this line and falling upon the town of Pelayo, and captured the forts which guarded it, together with the entire garrison and a large amount of arms and ammunition. He then moved north in the province of Santa Clara, into the district of Remedios, moved west, recrossed the Trocha, and there joined forces with Gen. Antonio Maceo. The latter had marched his soldiers through the entire province of Puerto Principe, although four large Spanish columns were sent to interrupt his progress. These he succeeded in eluding, defeating them, however, on several occasions. The combined forces of Maceo and Gomez, by a series of strategic movements, again succeeded in passing the Trocha; their rear guard defeating Colonel Segura, inflicting heavy loss and capturing nearly 200 mules laden with arms, ammunition and supplies.

On the arrival of the combined forces in Santa Clara, Gomez, taking charge of all the forces in the district, divided them, sending flying columns in advance under Generals Suarez, Perez, and Lacret, dispatching others to Sagua, in the north, and toward Trinidad, in the south. Maceo's forces made a demonstration on the city of Santa Clara, which was now Martinez Campos's headquarters, while Gomez threatened Cienfuegos. In all the operations which now followed General Gomez had ample forces in his rear, so that his retreat, if made necessary, would not be cut off.

Immediately on the threatening of Cienfuegos Gen. Martinez Campos removed his headquarters from Santa Clara to Cienfuegos, and thence dispatched a large number of troops to form a line between Cienfuegos, Las Cruces, and Lajas, to impede the westward march of the Cuban army. Still advancing westward, and ordering a concentration of his troops, Gomez outflanked the Spanish command, his rear guard distracting their attention and engaging them severely at Maltiempo, in the western part of the province.

On the border of Matanzas Gomez again radiated his troops, Gen. Quintin Bandera on the north, General Maceo in the center, General Gomez himself to the south, while Generals Suarez, Perez, Lacret, and other officers attracted the attention of the enemy by rapid marches and raids. Martinez Campos had again changed his headquarters, this time moving to Colon, in the province of Matanzas; he hoped that the Spanish forces to the rear of the Cubans would be able to cooperate with him, but every means of communication by railroad, telephone, or telegraph had been completely destroyed by the Cubans in their progress, and no word could be sent nor soldiers transported quickly enough for a combined attack of front and rear of the Cubans. From this time on fighting was very sharp, and, as the order of Gomez concerning the grinding of the sugar crop was evidently being disobeyed in Matanzas and Santa Clara, the torch was applied, and it is estimated that a very insignificant part of the sugar crop will be exported this season.

With calls for the protection of the plantations in Santa Clara and Matanzas to attend to, the cities of Santa Clara, Cienfuegos, Matanzas, Cardenas, and Colon threatened, with all communications to the east, except by water, cut off, with the Cuban forces still advancing in oblique directions to the west, Martinez Campos concentrated as many troops as possible, sending to the most easterly province, that of Santiago, all the troops that could be spared from that district, he himself again changing his headquarters with the advance of Gomez to Jovellanos, thence to Limonar, to Matanzas, and finally to Havana, where, at the present writing, he is actively engaged in fortifying the land approaches to the capital, while he has hurried to the neighborhood of Batabano as many troops as could be spared, withdrawing even a large number of the marines from the fleets, thus assigning them to shore duty. Even the line at Batabano has been broken by the Cuban forces, and all communications to the east have been cut off.

So grave has the situation become that martial law has been proclaimed in the provinces of Havana and Pinar del Rio, so that the entire island from Point Maysi to Cape Antonio is now declared to be in a state of siege. The censorship of the press has been made more rigid than ever, and an order issued for the delivery of all horses in the island to the Spanish Government at prices ranging from $18 to $35. It is not intended to pay for these in cash, as only certificates of the delivery of the horses to the Government with the value of the animal as fixed by the latter are given to the owners. Either this is an extreme war measure taken only because of absolute necessity and of the scarcity of money, or it is another example of the gentle methods of the Spanish Government in its treatment of the Cuban and his property.

While the westward march of Gomez was in progress Gens. Francisco Carrillo and José M. Aguirre landed on the eastern end of the island with a considerable supply of munitions, including some artillery, and succeeded in marching through the provinces of Santiago and Puerto Principe into that of Santa Clara, capturing several forts on the way. General Carrillo has taken command in the Remedios district, where his personal popularity has caused thousands to join him. General Aguirre reported to the commander in chief, and is now assisting in the operations of Matanzas.

It was not the intention of General Gomez when he planned his winter campaign to march on and lay siege to the capital, his only object being to prevent the grinding and export of the sugar crop and the consequent flow of treasure into the Spanish coffers, and to demonstrate to the world that he could control the provinces and enforce his orders.

While this march of the main bodies of troops westward has been carried on, the Cuban forces of the other army corps have also succeeded in carrying out the orders concerning sugar cane and preventing the establishment of Spanish lines of communication. As artillery has now been introduced into the Cuban army, forts are more easily taken. There has been constant communication from the interior to the coast; vessels of the Spanish navy have frequently been engaged by the insurgents., and in one case a small armed coast-guard vessel was captured by them

Supplies are received by the Cubans at convenient points on the coast and transferred to the interior. When it is remembered that in the revolution of 1861 to 1878 there were never more than 10,000 armed insurgents in the field; that these rarely, if ever, took the offensive, and yet compelled Spain to maintain an army of 120,000 men in the field, many of whom were Cuban volunteers in the strict sense of the term; that this little band caused Spain to spend in the ten years over $700,000,000 and to lose over 200,000 men, and that when in contrast we see in this revolution there are already more than 50,000 Cubans in the field, directed by veterans of the last war, who now are on the offensive, and that now Cuban does not fight against Cuban, the chance of ultimate success of the Cuban arms must appear to an impartial observer, especially in the light of Gomez's wonderful western march, and that in two months more the climate will again militate against the Spanish troops.

MILITARY ORGANIZATION.

The military organization of the Cubans is ample and complete.

Maj. Gen. Maximo Gomez is the commander in chief, as we have said, of all the forces, a veteran of the last revolution, as indeed are all the generals almost without exception. Maj. Gen. Antonio Maceo is second in command of the army of liberation, and was, until called upon to cooperate with the commander in chief in the late march to the western province, in command of Santiago.

The army is at present divided into five corps—two in Santiago, one in Puerto Principe, and two in Santa Clara and Matanzas. These corps are divided into divisions, these again into brigades, and finally into regiments; the forces are moreover divided into cavalry and infantry, besides having engineers, and lately artillery and a perfect sanitary corps, which latter is in command of Eugenio Sanchez Agramonte, with the grade of brigadier-general. Maj. Gen. José Maceo commands the First Santiago Corps, while Maj. Gen. Bartolome Masso commands the Second Corps in that province.

Commanding divisions and brigades in these two corps are Brig. Gens. Pedro Perez, Agustin Cebreco, Jesus Rabi, Luis Feria, Bernardo Capote, Higinio Vasquez, and Angel Guerra.

The Third Corps is in command of Maj. Gen. José M. Rodriguez. The Fourth Corps is in command of Maj. Gen. Cartos Roloff, the divisions and brigades being commanded by Maj. Gens. Francisco Carrillo and Serafin Sanchez and Brig. Gens. Tranquilino Perez, Juan B. Zayas, and Rogelio Castillo. The Fifth Corps is in command of Maj. Gen. Manuel Suarez, and the divisions and brigades are commanded by Francisco Perez, José Lacret, and José M. Aguirre.

The first two corps consist of 26,000 men, mostly infantry; the third, of about 4,000 men, mostly cavalry; the Fourth and Fifth Corps consisted before the late invasion of Gomez of over 20,000 men, both infantry and cavalry, which force has been considerably increased in these last days. Of the 50,000 men that there are at least in the field, more than half are fully armed and equipped, the rest carrying miscellaneous weapons or side arms.

The work of fully equipping the army is now proceeding rapidly. The higher grades and commissions are all confirmed by the Government.

Stations for the manufacture of powder and the reloading of cartridges are established, as well as manufacturing of shoes, saddles, and other equipments. The hospitals for the sick and wounded are also provided. Red Cross societies have offered their cooperation, but the Spanish commander in chief has refused to allow them to enter the insurgent lines.

The discipline of the army is strict and marauding is promptly punished, as was done in the case of Lieut. Alberto Castillo, an officer of the Second Corps, who was tried and shot for robbery, and as has been repeatedly done with the "Plateados," men who, taking advantage of the unsettled condition of affairs in the country, have turned bandits. The Cuban Army of Liberation is entirely volunteer, without pay

CIVIL GOVERNMENT.

As above indicated, José Martí was the head of the preliminary civil organization, and he, immediately upon landing with Gomez in Cuba, issued a call for the selection of representatives of the Cuban people to form a civil government.

His death postponed for a time the selection of these men, but in the beginning of September the call previously issued was complied with.

Representatives from each of the provinces of Santiago, Puerto Principe, Santa Clara, and the western part of the island, comprising the provinces of Matanzas and Havana, making twenty in all, were elected to the constituent assembly, which was to establish a civil government, republican in form.

A complete list of the members of the constituent assembly which met at Jimaguayu, in the province of Puerto Principe, on the 13th of September, 1895, together with an account of its organization and subsequent action, will be found in the document hereto annexed and marked B.

A constitution of the Republic of Cuba was adopted on the 16th of September, and copy of which will be found in document annexed marked B.

On the 18th of September the following officers of the Government were elected by the constituent assembly in accordance with the terms of the constitution:

President, Salvador Cisneros Betancourt, of Puerto Principe; vice-president, Bartolome Masso, of Manzanillo; secretary of war, Carlos Roloff, of Santa Clara; secretary of the treasury, Severo Pina, of Sancti Spiritus; secretary of the interior, Santiago Garcia Canizares, of Remedios; secretary of foreign relations, Rafael M. Portuondo, of Santiago de Cuba; subsecretary of war, Mario Menocal, of Mantanzas; subsecretary of the treasury, Joaquin Castello, of Santiago de Cuba; subsecretary of the interior, Carlos Dubois, of Baracoa; subsecretary of foreign relations, Fermin Valdes Dominguez, of Havana.

The installation of these officers duly followed. The election of the general in chief and the second in command, who is to bear the title of lieutenant-general, was then had, and resulted in the unanimous election of Maximo Gomez and Antonio Maceo, respectively.

On the same day the constituent assembly elected by acclamation as delegate plenipotentiary and general agent abroad of the Cuban Republic, the undersigned, Tomas Estrada Palma. The credentials issued to me are hereto annexed, marked C.

Immediately thereafter the government council proceeded to the headquarters of General Gomez, in Puerto Principe, where the latter took the oath of allegiance to the constitution of the Republic, together with his troops, who there gathered for this purpose, and was installed as commander in chief of the armies of the Republic.

The government council then proceeded to the province of Santiago, where Gen. Antonio Maceo and his forces took the oath of allegiance.

Thence the council proceeded to the province or Santa Clara to inspect and administer the oath to the troops of the Fourth and Fifth Army Corps. They are now on their way to the province of Santiago, where their permanent headquarters will be established.

The divisions of the provinces into prefectures under the supervision of the secretary of the interior and the duties which devolve in this department are fully set forth in Exhibit B, as well as the duties of the secretary of the treasury. The impositions, rate and collection of the taxes, and sources of income of the Government will also be found in Exhibit B.

All moneys collected in accordance with the laws of the Republic, as well as those received through voluntary contributions, are delivered to him or his duly authorized agent and expended under his supervision or that of his agents, to supply the present needs of the Government, which are mainly purchase of arms and ammunition.

The money thus collected has been sufficient to equip the army and keep it supplied with ammunition, although, as it is natural, from the rapid increase of the ranks and the difficulty of bringing supplies into the island, many of the new recruits have not yet been fully armed. The problem of equipping the army is not a financial one, but arises from the caution necessary to blockade running and, above all, the preventive measures taken by foreign Governments, and the notice which is in all cases given to the enemy of the embarkment of munitions. No report of the secretary of the treasury has yet been made, as he has been in office but three months.

For the purpose of properly collecting the imposts the roads to all cities, as well as the coast, are patrolled by the Cubans. The Cuban

Government publishes two newspapers, El Cubano Libre and the Boletin de la Guerra.

TREATMENT OF PRISONERS.

From the beginning of this insurrection the conduct of the Cubans
as to prisoners has been in strong contrast to that of the Spaniards;
prisoners taken by the Cubans have been invariably well treated,
cared for, and liberated, officers as well as common soldiers, as soon as
it was possible under the circumstances, and word sent to the Spanish
officers to call for them on the guaranty that the detachment would be
respected.

As instances we may recite those even admitted by the Spaniards,
namely: Ramon de las Yaguas, Campechuela, and Peralejos, in Santiago; el Mulato, San Jeronimo, and Las Minas, in Puerto Principe;
Taguasco, Pelayo, and Cantabria, in Santa Clara. After the last-mentioned engagement Colonel Rego returned his prisoners to the Spanish
lines, obtaining a receipt for their delivery signed by a lieutenant, of
which a copy is hereto annexed, marked D.

This action, in accordance with the spirit of the insurrection, which
is declared not to be against the Spaniards, of whom many are fighting
for the independence of the island, but against the Spanish Government, is echoed by the general order of the commander in chief on
this subject, of which the following is a copy:

CIRCULAR OF THE GENERAL IN CHIEF.

GENERAL HEADQUARTERS OF THE ARMY OF LIBERATION,
Camaguey, August 1, 1895.

In order to establish in a clear and precise manner the mode of procedure toward
the chiefs, officers, and soldiers of the monarchy captured in action or operations,
and toward those who voluntarily surrender to our columns or authorities, I have
deemed it convenient to order as follows:

ART. 1. All prisoners captured in action or by the troops of the Republic will be
immediately liberated and returned to their ranks, unless they volunteer to join
the army of liberation. The abandoned wounded will be gathered and attended to
with all care, and the unburied dead interred.

ART. 2. All persons who shall be arrested, charged with committing the misdemeanors in the circular of July 1, by violating or disregarding the said order, will
be summarily proceeded against.

ART. 3. Those of the prisoners who are chiefs or officers of the army of the monarchy will be respected and considered according to their rank and treated according
to the valor with which they may have resisted, and will all be returned to their
ranks if they so desire.

ART. 4. Those who volunteer to join the ranks of the republicans, and appear
before our columns and authorities, will have their option in the mode of serving the
cause of the Republic, either in arms or by more peaceful occupations, civil or
agricultural pursuits.

I communicate this to you for your instruction and for your rigid compliance.
Country and liberty.

MAXIMO GOMEZ,
The General in Chief.

On the part of the Spanish, attention is called to the order prohibiting newspaper correspondents from entering insurgent lines to prevent
accurate information being given to the world at large; the order to
shoot all who supply food or medicines to the insurgents; the order,
which in every instance has been carried out, to shoot all officers of the
Cuban army who may be captured, under which Domingo Mujica, Gil
Gonzalez, Quirina Amezago, and Acebo have been executed. At the
recapture of Baire, old men, women, and children were ruthlessly
slaughtered by the Spanish soldiery, the hospital at Gran Piedra was

captured and over seventy wounded and defenseless Cubans were killed; at Cayo Espino peaceful men and women were butchered by Colonel Molina and the outrages committed by the troops under Garrido and Tejera are legion. The action of convicts, who have been liberated by Spain to fight the Cubans under such leadership as that of the notorious Lola Benitez, who bears the title of colonel, are, as might be expected, a blot on any Christian army.

As to the treatment of Cubans suspected of sympathy with the insurgents, we have but to consider the large number of men who have lately been arrested and on bare suspicion summarily sent to the Spanish penal colonies for life; some foreign citizens have indeed escaped court martial on the interference of their Governments, but it is well known that even civil trials at this time are under the absolute control of the Government.

NOT A NEGRO MOVEMENT.

The Spaniards charge, in order to belittle the insurrection, that it is a movement of negroes. It should be remembered that not more than one-third of the entire population are of the colored race. As a matter of fact, less than one-third of the army are of the colored race. Take, for instance, the generals of corps, divisions, and brigades; there are but three of the colored race, namely, Antonio and José Maceo and Augustin Cebreco, and these are mulattoes whose deeds and victories have placed them far above the generals of those who pretend to despise them. None of the members of the constituent assembly or of the Government are of the colored race. The Cubans and the colored race are as friendly in this war as they were in times of peace, and it would indeed be strange if the colored people were not so, as the whites fought for and with them in the last revolt, the only successful purpose of which was the freedom of the slaves.

If it be true that this is merely a movement of bandits and negroes and adventurers, as the Spaniards assert, why have they not armed the Cuban people to fight against the outlaws, or why have not the Cuban people themselves volunteered to crush this handful? On the contrary, they know that giving those Cubans arms who have them not would be but to increase the number of insurgents, and they have therefore sent more than 125,000 troops from Spain, mostly conscripts; they have sent over forty of their most famous generals; they have increased their navy, and virtually, so far as the Cubans are concerned, blockaded the entire coast. They have been compelled to make many onerous loans to carry on the campaign; they have increased the fortifications of their ports; they have brought torpedoes to protect their harbors, and they have even placed armed troops on their mail steamers to prevent their capture.

Besides this large army, they have between 60,000 and 80,000 volunteers to protect their towns. These volunteers, so called, are native Spaniards and a branch of the regular army, the service being compulsory; that is, instead of serving in the regular army at home, where their entire time must be given up, they volunteer to enter this body on emigration to Cuba, where they may follow to a considerable extent their occupation; in other words, they correspond to our home guards or militia, except that the service is obligatory and that the men can not leave the island without permission.

It is not denied that a large number of what the Spaniards term the lower classes are in this revolution, but this is only a proof of how deep into the mass of the people have been implanted the seeds of discon-

tent and of republicanism. This is a movement not like our last revolution—the result of the agitation of the wealthy and the educated—
but one which is the outcome of the popular sentiment of all classes.

Much surprise has been expressed that with the immense army and
resources at hand Spain has not been able to crush the insurrection or
prevent its rapid growth. Aside from the climate, which is deadly to
the raw, ill-fed, ill-clothed, ill-treated, and badly paid Spanish troops,
the greater part of whom are mere lads, the Spaniards have to divide
their troops into an army of occupation and another of operation. These
must necessarily move in considerable numbers, because if compelled
to flee without a knowledge of the intricacies of the country they would
be decimated.

A Cuban command on dispersion is readily reorganized, as each man
is his own guide. This is one of the most valuable of Cuban movements—to disperse as if routed, to rally at a previously agreed point,
and then to fall upon and surprise the seemingly victorious enemy. The
Cuban, used to the country and the climate, marches and rides much
faster than the Spaniard. He can live and thrive, and does so in
necessity, on food that is death to the Spanish soldier. Moreover in
a friendly country the movements of the enemy are readily ascertained
by the Cuban general, who can thus select his own position or evade
the engagement, while the Spanish are never so well informed and are
at the mercy of their guides.

It must be remembered that the Cuban fights for the noblest principle of man—independence. That he does so without compulsion or pay,
but spontaneously and enthusiastically—nay, he fights the battle of
despair, knowing it is better to be killed thus than to bear the tortures
of a Spanish prison or to trust himself to the tender mercy of a Spanish commander. On the other hand, the Spanish troops fight by compulsion and for pay, which is even now months in arrears; they fight
without faith, for their heart is not with their cause. They know that
surrender means pardon and good treatment, while fighting may mean
death. Hundreds of Spanish soldiers have singly or in groups gone
over to the insurgent lines, being satisfied that they would live there
under better conditions.

CHARACTER OF THE WAR.

There was also an attempt made by the Spanish to brand the Cubans
with carrying on an uncivilized warfare because of their use of dynamite.
General Roloff before using this explosive issued a proclamation warning all persons of the danger of traveling by rail. Dynamite has been
used freely, but only as a substitute for gunpowder in the destruction
of railroad bridges, trestles, and trains which could be used and were
used for the transportation of Spanish troops. Of course it is a serious
loss to Spain to have these railroads destroyed, but no one can seriously
deny that it is a measure justified by the necessities of war. The use
of this explosive as a substitute for gunpowder in the operation of
mines is simply a proof that the Cubans are keeping pace with the
advance of inventions in the art of war.

DESTRUCTION OF PROPERTY.

The subject, however, which has caused probably the most discussion
is the order of General Gomez to prevent the grinding of sugar cane
and in case of the disobedience of said order the destruction of the crop.

General Gomez issued a preliminary warning dated July 1, of which the following is a copy:

GENERAL HEADQUARTERS OF THE ARMY OF LIBERATION,
Najasa, Camaguey, July 1, 1895.

To the Planters and Owners of Cattle Ranches:

In accord with the great interests of the revolution for the independence of the country and for which we are in arms:

Whereas all exploitations of any product whatsoever are aids and resources to the Government that we are fighting, it is resolved by the general in chief to issue this general order throughout the island that the introduction of articles of commerce, as well as beef and cattle, into the towns occupied by the enemy, is absolutely prohibited. The sugar plantations will stop their labors, and whosoever shall attempt to grind the crop notwithstanding this order, will have their cane burned and their buildings demolished. The person who, disobeying this order, will try to profit from the present situation of affairs, will show by his conduct little respect for the rights of the revolution of redemption and therefore shall be considered as an enemy, treated as a traitor, and tried as such in case of his capture.

MAXIMO GOMEZ,
The General in Chief.

Nevertheless throughout the country preparations were made for the grinding of the crop. A peremptory order, of which the following is a copy, was then issued on November 6:

HEADQUARTERS OF THE ARMY OF LIBERATION,
Territory of Sancti Spiritus, November 6, 1895.

Animated by the spirit of unchangeable resolution in defense of the rights of the revolution of redemption of this country of colonists, humiliated and despised by Spain, and in harmony with what has been decreed concerning the subject in the circular dated the 1st of July, I have ordered the following:

ARTICLE I. That all plantations shall be totally destroyed, their cane and outbuildings burned, and railroad connections destroyed.

ART. II. All laborers who shall aid the sugar factories—these sources of supplies that we must deprive the enemy of—shall be considered as traitors to their country.

ART. III. All who are caught in the act, or whose violation of Article II shall be proven, shall be shot. Let all chiefs of operations of the army of liberty comply with this order, determined to unfurl triumphantly, even over ruin and ashes, the flag of the Republic of Cuba.

In regard to the manner of waging the war, follow the private instructions that I have already given.

For the sake of the honor of our arms and your well-known courage and patriotism, it is expected that you will strictly comply with the above orders.

M. GOMEZ, *General in Chief.*

To the chiefs of operations: Circulate this.

On the 11th of November the following proclamation was issued:

HEADQUARTERS OF THE ARMY OF LIBERATION,
Sancti Spiritus, November 11, 1895.

To honest men, victims of the torch:

The painful measure made necessary by the revolution of redemption drenched in innocent blood from Hatuey to our own times by cruel and merciless Spain will plunge you in misery. As general in chief of the army of liberation it is my duty to lead it to victory, without permitting myself to be restrained or terrified, by any means necessary to place Cuba in the shortest time in possession of her dearest ideal. I therefore place the responsibility for so great a ruin on those who look on impassively and force us to those extreme measures which they then condemn like dolts and hypocrites that they are. After so many years of supplication, humiliations, contumely, banishment, and death, when this people, of its own will, has arisen in arms, there remains no other solution but to triumph, it matters not what means are employed to accomplish it.

This people can not hesitate between the wealth of Spain and the liberty of Cuba. Its greatest crime would be to stain the land with blood without effecting its purposes because of puerile scruples and fears which do not concur with the character of the men who are in the field, challenging the fury of an army which is one of the bravest in the world, but which in this war is without enthusiasm or faith, ill fed and unpaid. The war did not begin February 24; it is about to begin now.

The war had to be organized; it was necessary to calm and lead into the proper channels the revolutionary spirit always exaggerated in the beginning by wild enthusiasm. The struggle ought to begin in obedience to a plan and method more or less studied, as the result of the peculiarities of this war. This has already been done. Let Spain now send her soldiers to rivet the chains of her slaves; the children of this land are in the field, armed with the weapons of liberty. The struggle will be terrible, but success will crown the revolution and efforts of the oppressed.

MAXIMO GOMEZ, *General in Chief.*

The reasons underlying this measure are the same which caused this country to destroy the cotton crop and the baled cotton in the South during the war of the secession.

The sugar crop is a source of large income to the Spanish Government, directly by tax and export duty, as well as indirectly. The action of the insurgents is perfectly justified, because it is simply a blockade, so to speak, on land—a prevention of the gathering, and hence the export, of the commodity with, naturally, a punishment for the violation thereof.

PROTESTS OF ALIENS.

Strenuous protests have, too, been made by and on behalf of aliens residing in or having property in Cuba.

It is admitted in civilized warfare that the property of alien residents, whether they are in sympathy with the enemy or not, when in the track of war, is subject to war's casualties, and that all property which might be of aid and comfort to the enemy may be taken or destroyed, the commander in the field being the judge of the exigency and necessities which dictate such action. This proposition has been laid down by the State Department and the Supreme Court of this country in the matter of the destruction of cotton in the late war.

The provision of the constitution of the Republic of Cuba that the citizens of a country which acknowledges the Cubans as belligerents, shall be exempt from the payment of taxes and contributions to the Republic, naturally implies that the property of such citizens after the granting of belligerency by their country, even though by all the laws of war it is contraband and may be seized or destroyed, will be absolutely respected, and, I have all reason to assert, will be under the special protection of the Cuban Government and its army.

For aliens to ask this protection as a right while their Government denies the existence of the belligerency of the Cubans might well be considered by the latter as allowing aid and comfort to go to their enemy, simply on the expectation that some time in the future the Government of those aliens may, out of gratitude to the Cubans, acknowledge, what is after all but a state of fact, belligerency. In the meantime the aid and comfort thus allowed by the Cubans to flow to the Spaniards must strengthen the latter and thus draw out the struggle or weaken the former. General Gomez explains the importance of this measure in the following letter:

DISTRICT OF REMEDIOS,
Province of Santa Clara, December 8, 1895.

To TOMAS ESTRADA PALMA.

MY DEAR AND ESTEEMED FRIEND: It is not long since I wrote you, but an opportunity offers by which I may send you a few words of encouragement and good cheer. Rest assured I write you whenever I can, which is not often, owing to the great amount of work which at present falls upon my shoulders. I know the pen is mightier than the sword, but my mission at present is with the latter; others must wield the pen.

Eight days ago Gen. Antonio Maceo and myself met and fought the enemy with our forces in conjunction. The Spanish column, including infantry, cavalry, and artillery were our superiors in number, but the arms of the Cuban Republic were again victorious. I have not time at present to go into details of the battle, they will follow later. Suffice it to say, Spanish reports to the contrary notwithstanding, we won the day.

Our advance may be slow, but it will be sure and firm. If you hear of our retreat remember that it will be temporary and for a purpose. Our faces are turned toward the west and nothing will stop us. The result of my observations as we proceed is that the Spaniards are in need of almost every thing—money, sympathy, soldiers, and even leaders who have faith and courage in the righteousness of their cause.

If Cuban valor and resolution do not fail us, and if the hearts of Cuba's children do not weaken, I have every reason to believe that the close of the six months' campaign now initiated will find everything satisfactorily settled and Cuba free.

I know that unfavorable comment has been made on some of the methods we have been forced to employ in this revolution, but it will not do to listen to the complaints of the superficial and irresponsible. No sugar crop must be made this winter under any circumstances or for any amount of money. It is the source from which the enemy still hopes and dreams of obtaining its revenue. To prevent that end, for the good of our country, has been and shall be our programme.

We are Cubans and have one great aim in View, one glorious object to obtain—the freedom of our country and liberty. It is of more importance to us than glory, public applause, or anything else. Everything else will follow in time. I have never believed in or advised a sanguinary revolution, but it must be a radical one. First of all we must triumph; toward that end the most effective means, although they may appear harsh, must be employed.

There is nothing so bad, so dishonorable, so inexcusable, in the eyes of the world as failure. Victory is within our reach. To hesitate, to delay it, to endanger it now, would be stupid, would be cowardly, would be criminal. We will succeed first; the applause of the world will follow. To do otherwise would be not to love one's country. I have never felt more confident than at the present moment. You can rest assured that Cuba will soon achieve her absolute independence.

Ever your true friend,   MAXIMO GOMEZ.

As I have through various sources been approached on this subject in behalf of property of American citizens on the island, and as I know the cordial friendship which the Cubans bear to the Government and people of the United States of America, feeling assured that this country, from its very history, must likewise feel a deep sympathy with a people who are treading in their footsteps, I have written to the Government of the Republic of Cuba the following letter:

NEW YORK, *December 23, 1895.*

SALVADOR CISNEROS BETANCOURT,
    President of the Cuban Republic.

MY DISTINGUISHED FELLOW-COUNTRYMAN: There have been many complaints made to me from various sources that the property of citizens of the United States of North America has been destroyed by our army of liberation in Cuba under the order of our distinguished general in chief, Maximo Gomez. I know very well how you and all my countrymen feel toward this Republic, and that you desire to do everything in your power to demonstrate your friendship, and I deem it my duty to communicate the above facts to you so that you may consider the matter carefully and thoroughly; at the same time I know that many Spaniards intend to transfer their property, as some have done already, to American citizens or companies especially organized for their purposes, in case that you should, before or after receiving the rights of belligerents, take active measures for the protection of North American interests.

I say this because I am sure that, at least after the granting of belligerency, you will do your utmost to guard the interests of the citizens of a country which warmly sympathizes with us in our present struggle.

Hoping that you will give this subject your most thoughtful consideration, I remain your devoted friend, for country and liberty,

T. ESTRADA PALMA.

In view of the history of this revolution as herein stated, in view of the causes which led to it, its rapid growth, its successes in arms, the establishment, operation, and resources of the Government of the Cuban Republic, the organization, number, and discipline of its army, the contrast in the treatment of prisoners to that of the enemy. the territory in its control and subject to the carrying out of its decrees, of the futility of the attempts of the Spanish Government to crush the revolution, in spite of the immense increase of its army in Cuba and of its blockade and the many millions spent for that purpose, the cruelties which on the part of the Spanish have especially characterized this sanguinary and fiercely conducted war, and the·damage to the interests of the citizens of this country under the present conditions, I, as the duly accredited representative, in the name of the Cuban people in arms who have fought singly and alone against the monarchy of Spain for nearly a year, in the heart of a continent devoted to republican institutions, in the name of justice, in the name of humanity, in the name of liberty, petition you, and through you the Government of the United States of America, to accord the rights of belligerency to a people fighting for their absolute independence.

    Very respectfully, yours,

T. Estrada Palma.

The Hon. Richard Olney,
    Secretary of State of the United States of America.

A

CUBA v. SPAIN.

War is a dire necessity. But when a people has exhausted all human means of persuasion to obtain from an unjust oppressor a remedy for its ills, if it apeals as a last resource to force in order to repel the persistent aggression which constitutes tyranny, this people is justified before its own conscience and before the tribunal of nations.

Such is the case of Cuba in its wars against Spain. No metropolis has ever been harsher or more obstinately harassing; none has ever exploited a colony with more greediness and less foresight than Spain. No colony has ever been more prudent, more long-suffering, more cautious, more persevering than Cuba in its purpose of asking for its rights by appealing to the lessons of experience and political wisdom. Only driven by desperation has the people of Cuba taken up arms, and having done so, it displays as much heroism in the hour of danger as it had shown good judgment in the hour of deliberation.

The history of Cuba during the present century is a long series of rebellions; but every one of these was preceded by a peaceful struggle for its rights—a fruitless struggle because of the obstinate blindness of Spain.

There were patriots in Cuba from the beginning of this century, such as Presbyter Caballero and Don Francisco Arango, who called the metropolitan Government's attention to the evils of the colony, and pointed to the remedy by pleading for the commercial franchises required by its economical organization, and for the intervention of the natives in its government, not only as a right, but also for political expediency, in view of the long distance between the colony and the home government, and the grave difficulties with which it had to contend. The requirements of the war with the continental colonies, which were tired of Spanish tyranny, compelled the metropolitan Government to grant a certain measure of commercial liberty to the Island of Cuba; a temporary concession which spread prosperity throughout its territory, but which was not sufficient to open the eyes of the Spanish statesmen. On the contrary, prompted by suspicion and mistrust of the Americans, they began by curtailing, and shortly after abrogated the limited administrative powers then possessed by some of the corporations in Cuba, such as the "Junta de Fomento"— (a board for the encouragement of internal improvements).

As if this were not enough, the Cubans were deprived of the little show of political intervention they had in public affairs. By a simple royal decree in 1837 the small representation of Cuba in the Spanish Cortes was suppressed, and all the powers of the Government were concentrated in the hands of the captain-general, on whom authority was conferred to act as the governor of a city in a state of siege. This implied that the captain-general, residing in Habana, was master of the life and property of every inhabitant of the island of Cuba. This meant that Spain declared a permanent state of war against a peaceful and defenseless people.

Cuba saw its most illustrious sons, such as Heredia and Saco, wander in exile throughout the free American Continent. Cuba saw as many of the Cubans as dared to love liberty and declare it by act or word die on the scaffold, such as Joaquin de Aguero and Placido. Cuba saw the product of its people's labor confiscated by iniquitous fiscal laws imposed by its masters from afar. Cuba saw the administration of justice in the hands of foreign magistrates, who acted at the will or the whim of its rulers. Cuba suffered all the outrages that can humiliate a conquered people, in the name and by the work of a Government that sarcastically calls itself paternal. Is it to be wondered, then, that an uninterrupted era of conspiracies and uprisings should have been inaugurated? Cuba in its despair took up arms in 1850 and 1851, conspired again in 1855, waged war in 1868, in 1879, in 1885, and is fighting now since the 24th of February of the present year.

But at the same time Cuba has never ceased to ask for justice and redress. Its people, before shouldering the rifle, pleaded for their rights. Before the pronunciamento of Aguero and the invasions of Lopez, Saco, in exile, exposed the dangers of Cuba to the Spanish statesmen, and pointed to the remedy. Other farsighted men seconded him in the colony. They denounced the cancer of slavery, the horrors of the traffic in slaves, the corruption of the officeholders, the abuses of the Government, the discontent of the people with their forced state of political tutelage. No attention was given to them, and this brought on the first armed conflicts.

Before the formidable insurrection of 1868, which lasted ten years, the reform party, which included the most enlightened, wealthy, and influential Cubans, exhausted all the resources within their reach to induce Spain to initiate a healthy change in her Cuban policy. The party started the publication of periodicals in Madrid and in the island, addressed petitions, maintained a great agitation throughout the country, and having succeeded in leading the Spanish Government to make an inquiry into the economical, political, and social condition of Cuba, they presented a complete plan of government which satisfied public requirements as well as the aspirations of the people. The Spanish Government disdainfully cast aside the proposition as useless, increased taxation, and proceeded to its exaction with extreme severity.

It was then that the ten-year war broke out. Cuba, almost a pigmy compared with Spain, fought like a giant. Blood ran in torrents. Public wealth disappeared in a bottomless abyss. Spain lost 200,000 men. Whole districts of Cuba were left almost entirely without their male population. Seven hundred millions were spent to feed that conflagration—a conflagration that tested Cuban heroism, but which could not touch the hardened heart of Spain. The latter could not subdue the bleeding colony, which had no longer strength to prolong the struggle with any prospect of success. Spain proposed a compact which was a snare and a deceit. She granted to Cuba the liberties of Puerto Rico, which enjoyed none.

On this deceitful ground was laid the new situation, throughout which has run a current of falsehood and hypocrisy. Spain, whose mind had not changed, hastened to change the name of things. The capitan-general was called governorgeneral. The royal decrees took the name of authorizations. The commercial monopoly of Spain was named coasting trade. The right of banishment was transformed into the law of vagrancy. The brutal attacks of defenseless citizens were called "componte." The abolition of constitutional guarantees became the law of public order. Taxation without the consent or knowledge of the Cuban people was changed into the law of estimates (budget) voted by the representatives of Spain; that is, of European Spain.

The painful lesson of the ten-year war had been entirely lost on Spain. Instead of inaugurating a redeeming policy that would heal the recent wounds, allay public anxiety, and quench the thirst for justice felt by the people, who were desirous to enjoy their natural rights, the metropolis, while lavish in promises of reform, persisted in carrying on unchanged its old and crafty system, the groundwork of which continues to be the same, namely: To exclude every native Cuban from every office that could give him any effective influence and intervention in public affairs; the ungovernable exploitation of the colonists' labor for the benefit of Spanish commerce and Spanish bureaucracy, both civil and military. To carry out the latter purpose it was necessary to maintain the former at any cost.

I.

In order to render the native Cuban powerless in his own country, Spain, legislating for Cuba without restriction as it does, had only to give him an electoral law so artfully framed as to accomplish two objects: First, to reduce the number of voters; second, to give always a majority to the Spaniards; that is, to the European colonists, notwithstanding that the latter represent only 9.3 per cent of the total population of Cuba. To this effect it made the electoral right dependent on the payment of a very high poll tax, which proved the more burdensome as the war had ruined the larger number of Cuban proprietors. In this way it succeeded in restricting the right of suffrage to only 53,000 inhabitants in an island which has a population of 1,600,-000; that is to say, to the derisive proportion of 3 per cent of the total number of inhabitants.

In order to give a decided preponderance to the Spanish European element, the electoral law has ignored the practice generally observed in those countries where the right to vote depends on the payment of a poll tax, and has afforded all the facilities to acquire the electoral privilege to industry, commerce, and public officials, to the detriment of the territorial property (the ownership of real estate). To accomplish this, while the rate of the territorial tax is reduced to 2 per cent, an indispensable measure, in view of the ruinous condition of the landowners, the exorbitant contribution of $25 is required from those who would be electors as freeholders. The law has, moreover, thrown the doors wide open for the perpetration of fraud by providing that the simple declaration of the head of a commercial house is sufficient to consider all its employees as partners, having, therefore, the right to vote. This has given us firms with thirty or more partners. By this simple scheme almost all the Spaniards residing in Cuba are turned into electors, despite the explicit provisions of the law. Thus it comes to pass that the municipal district of Güines, with a population of 13,000 inhabitants, only 500 of which are Spaniards and Canary Islanders, shows on its electoral list the names of 32 native Cubans and of 400 Spaniards—only 0.25 per cent of the Cuban to 80 per cent of the Spanish population.

But, as if this were not enough, a so-called permanent commission of provincial deputations decides every controversy that may arise as to who is to be included in or excluded from the list of electors, and the members of this commission are appointed by the Governor-General. It is unnecessary to say that its majority has always been devoted to the Government. In case any elector considers himself wronged by the decision of the permanent commission he can appeal to the "audiencia" (higher court) of the district, but the "audiencias" are almost entirely made up of European magistrates; they are subject to the authority of the Governor-General, being mere political tools in his hands. As a conclusive instance of the manner in which those tribunals do justice to the claims of the Cuban electors, it will be sufficient to cite a case which occurred in Santa Clara in 1892, where 1,000 fully qualified liberal electors were excluded all at one time, for the simple omission to state their names at the end of the act presented by the elector who headed the claim. In more than one case has the same "audiencia" applied two different criterions to identical cases. The "audiencia" of Havana, in 1887, ignoring the explicit provisions of the law, excused the employees from the condition of residence, a condition that the same tribunal exacted before. The same "audiencia" in 1885 declared that the contributions to the State and to the municipality were accumulative, and in 1887 decided the opposite. This inconsistency had for its object to expunge from the lists hundreds of Cuban electors. In this way the Spanish Government and tribunals have endeavored to teach respect for the law and for the practice of wholesome electoral customs to the Cuban colonists.

It will be easily understood now why on some occasions the Cuban representation in the Spanish Parliament has been made up of only three deputies, and in the most favorable epochs the number of Cuban representatives has not exceeded six. Three deputies in a body of four hundred and thirty members! The genuine representation of Cuba has not reached sometimes 0.96 per cent of the total number of members of the Spanish congress. The great majority of the Cuban deputation has always consisted of Spanish peninsulars. In this manner the ministers of "ultramar" (ministers of the colonies), whenever they have thought necessary to give an honest or decent appearance to their legislative acts by an alleged majority of Cuban votes, could always command the latter—that is, the peninsulars.

As regards the representation in the senate, the operation has been more simple still. The qualifications required to be a senator have proved to be an almost absolute prohibition to the Cubans. In fact, to take a seat in the higher house it is necessary to have been president of that body or of congress, or a minister of the crown, or a bishop, or a grandee of Spain, a lieutenant-general, a vice-admiral, ambassador, minister plenipotentiary, counselor of state, judge, or attorney-general of the supreme court, of the court of accounts, etc. No Cuban has ever filled any of the above positions, and scarcely two or three are grandees. The only natives of Cuba who can be senators are those who have been deputies in three different Congresses, or who are professors and have held for four years a university chair, provided that they have an income of $1,500; or those who have a title of nobility, or have been deputies, provincial deputies, or mayors in towns of over 20,000 inhabitants, if they have in addition an income of $4,000, or pay a direct contribution of $800 to the treasury. This will increase in one or two dozen the number of Cubans qualified to be senators.

In this manner has legislative work, so far as Cuba is concerned, turned out to be a farce. The various Governments have legislated for the island as they pleased. The representatives of the peninsular provinces did not even take the trouble of attending the sessions of the Cortes when Cuban affairs were to be dealt with; and there was an instance when the estimates (budget) for the Great Antille were discussed in the presence of less than thirty deputies, and a single one of the ministers, the minister of "ultramar" (session of April 3, 1880).

Through the contrivance of the law, as well as through the irregularities committed and consented in its application, have the Cubans been deprived also of representation in the local corporations to which they were entitled, and in many cases they have been entirely excluded from them. When, despite the legalized obstacles and the partiality of those in power, they have obtained some temporary majority, the Government has always endeavored and succeeded in making their triumph null and void. Only once did the home-rule party obtain a majority in the provincial deputation of Havana, and then the Governor-General appointed from among the Spaniards a majority of the members of the permanent commission. Until that time this commission had been of the same political complexion as the majority of the deputation. By such proceedings have the Cubans been gradually expelled, even from the municipal bodies. Suffice it to say that the law provides that the derramas (assessments) be excluded from the computation of the tributary quotas, notwithstanding that they constitute the heaviest burden upon the municipal taxpayer. And the majorities, consisting of Spaniards, take good care to make this burden fall with heavier weight upon the Cuban proprietor. Thus the latter has to bear a heavier taxation with less representation.

This is the reason why the scandalous case has occurred lately of not a single Cuban having a seat in the "Ayuntamiento" (board of aldermen) of Havana. In 1891 the Spaniards predominated in thirty-one out of thirty-seven "Ayuntamientos" in the province of Havana. In that of Güines, with a population of 12,500 Cuban inhabitants, not a single one of the latter was found among its councilors. In the same epoch there were only three Cuban deputies in the provincial deputation of Havana; two in that of Matanzas, and three in that of Santa Clara. And these are the most populous regions in the Island of Cuba.

As, on the other hand, the government of the metropolis appoints the officials of the colony, all the lucrative, influential, and representative offices are secured to the Spaniards from Europe. The Governor-General, the regional and provincial governors, the "intendentes," comptrollers, auditors, treasurers, chiefs of communications, chiefs of the custom-houses, chiefs of administration, presidents and vice-presidents of the Spanish bank, secretaries of the Government, presiding judges of the "audiencia," presidents of tribunal, magistrates, attorneys-general, archbishops, bishops, canons, pastors of rich parishes—all, with very rare exceptions, are Spaniards from Spain. The Cubans are found only as minor clerks in the Government offices, doing all the work and receiving the smallest salaries.

From 1878 to this date there have been twenty governors in the province of Matanzas. Eighteen were Spaniards and two Cubans. But one of these, Brigadier-General Acosta, was an army officer in the service of Spain, who had fought against his countrymen; and the other, Señor González Muñoz, is a bureaucrat. During the same period there has been only one native Cuban acting as governor in the province of Havana, Señor Rodriguez Batista, who spent all his life in Spain, where he made his administrative career. In the other provinces there has never, probably, been a single governor born in the country.

In 1887 there was created a council, or board of ultramar, under the minister of the colonies. Not a single Cuban has ever been found among its members. On the other hand, such men as Generals Armiñan and Pando have held positions in it.

The predominance of the Government goes further still. It weighs with all its might upon the local corporations. There are deputations in the provinces, and not only are their powers restricted and their resources scanty, but the Governor-General appoints their presidents and all the members of the permanent commissions. There are "ayuntamientos" elected in accordance with the reactionary law of 1877, restricted and curtailed as applied to Cuba by Señor Canovas. But the Governor-General appoints the mayors, who may not belong to the corporation, and the governor of the province appoints the secretaries. The Government reserves, moreover, the right to remove the mayors, of replacing them, and of suspending the councillors and the "ayuntamientos," partly or in a body. It has frequently made use of this right for electoral purposes, to the detriment always of the Cubans.

As may be seen, the crafty policy of Spain has closed every avenue through which redress might be obtained. All the powers are centered in the Government of Madrid and its delegates in the colony; and in order to give her despotism a slight varnish of a representative régime she has contrived with her laws to secure complaisant majorities in the pseudoelective bodies. To accomplish this purpose she has relied upon the European immigrants, who have always supported the Government of the metropolis in exchange for lasting privileges. The existence of a Spanish party, as that of an English party at one time in Canada, has been the foundation of

Spanish rule in Cuba. Thus, through the instrumentality of the laws and the Government, a régime of castes has been enthroned there, with its outcome of monopolies, corruption, immorality, and hatred. The political contest there, far from being the fruitful clash of opposite ideas, or the opposition of men representing different tendencies, but all seeking a social improvement, has been only a struggle between hostile factious—the conflict between infuriated foes which precedes an open war. The Spanish resident has always seen a threat in the most timid protest of the Cuban—an attack upon the privileged position on which his fortune, his influence, and his power are grounded, and he is always willing to stifle it with insult and persecution.

II.

What use the Spanish Government has made of this power is apparent in the threefold spoliation to which it has submitted the Island of Cuba. Spain has not, in fact, a colonial policy. In the distant lands she has subdued by force Spain has sought nothing but immediate riches, and these it has wrung by might from the compulsory labor of the natives. For this reason Spain to-day in Cuba is only a parasite. Spain exploits the Island of Cuba through its fiscal régime, through its commercial régime, and through its bureaucratic régime. These are the three forms of official spoliation, but they are not the only forms of spoliation.

When the war of 1878 came to an end two-thirds of the island were completely ruined. The other third, the population of which had remained peaceful, was abundantly productive; but it had to face the great economical change involved in the impending abolition of slavery. Slavery had received its deathblow at the hands of the insurrection, and Cuban insurrectionists succeeded at the close of the war in securing its eventual abolition. Evidently it would have been a wholesome and provident policy to lighten the fiscal burdens of a country in such a condition. Spain was only bent on making Cuba pay the cost of the war. The metropolis overwhelmed the colony with enormous budgets, reaching as high a figure as $46,000,000, and this only to cover the obligations of the state, or rather to fill the unfathomable gulf left by the wastefulness and plunder of the civil and military administration during the years of war, and to meet the expenses of the military occupation of the country. Here follow a few figures: The budget for the fiscal year of 1878 to 1879 amounted to $46,594,000; that of 1879 to 1880 to an equal sum; that of 1882 to 1883 to $35,860,000; that of 1883 to 1884 to $34,180,000; that of 1884 to 1885 to the same sum; that of 1885 to 1886 to $34,169,000. For the remaining years, to the present time, the amount of the budget has been about $26,000,000, this being the figure for 1893 to 1894, and to be the same by prorogation for the current fiscal year.

The gradual reduction that may be noted was not the result of a desire to reduce the overwhelming burdens that weigh upon the country. It was imposed by necessity. Cuba was not able by far to meet such a monstrous exaction. It was a continuous and threatening deficit that imposed these reductions. In the first of the above-named years the revenue was $8,000,000 short of the budget or appropriations. In the second year the deficit reached the sum of $20,000,000. In 1883 it was nearly $10,000,000. In the following years the deficits averaged nearly $4,500,000. At present the accumulated amount of all these deficits reaches the sum of $100,000,000.

As a consequence of such a reckless and senseless financial course, the debt of Cuba has been increased to a fabulous sum. In 1868 we owed $25,000,000. When the present war broke out our debt, it was calculated, reached the net sum of $190,000,000. On the 31st of July of the current year the Island of Cuba was reckoned to owe $295,707,264 in bulk. Considering its population, the debt of Cuba exceeds that of all the other American countries, including the United States. The interest on this debt imposes a burden of $9.79 on each inhabitant. The French people, the most overburdened in this respect, owe only $6.30 per inhabitant.

This enormous debt, contracted and saddled upon the country without its knowledge; this heavy load that grinds it and does not permit its people to capitalize their income, to foster its improvements, or even to entertain its industries, constitutes one of the most iniquitous forms of spoliation the island has to bear. In it are included a debt of Spain to the United States; the expenses incurred by Spain when she occupied Santo Domingo; those for the invasion of Mexico in alliance with France and England; the expenditures for her hostilities against Peru; the money advanced to the Spanish treasury during its recent Carlist wars; and all that Spain has spent to uphold its domination in Cuba and to cover the lavish expenditures of its administration since 1868. Not a cent of this enormous sum has been spent in Cuba to advance the work of improvement and civilization. It has not contributed to build a single kilometer of highway or of railroad, nor to erect a single light-house or deepen a single port; it has not built one asylum or opened one public school. Such a heavy burden has been left to the future generations without a single compensation or benefit.

But the naked figures of the Cuban budgets and of the Cuban debt tell very little in regard to their true importance and signification as machines to squeeze out the substance of a people's labor. It is necessary to examine closer the details of these accounts and expenditures.

Those of Cuba, according to the last budgets or appropriations, amount to $26,411,-314, distributed as follows:

General obligations	$12,884,549.55
Department of justice (courts, etc.)	1,006,308.51
Department of war	5,918,598.16
Department of the treasury	727,892.45
Department of the navy	1,091,969.65
Government, administration	4,035,071.43
Interior improvements (fomento)	746,925.15

There are in Cuba 1,631,687 inhabitants according to the last census, that of 1887. That is to say, that this budget burdens them in the proportion of $16.18 for each inhabitant. The Spaniards in Spain pay only — 42.06 pesetas per head. Reducing the Cuban dollars to pesetas at the exchange rate of $95 for 500 pesetas, there results that the Cubans have to pay a tribute of 85.16 pesetas for each inhabitant; more than double the amount a Spaniard has to pay in his European country.

As shown above, most of this excessive burden is to cover entirely unproductive expenditures. The debt consumes 40.89 per cent of the total amount. The defense of the country against its own native inhabitants, the only enemies who threaten Spain, including the cost of the army, the navy, the civil guard, and the guardians of public order, takes 36.59 per cent. There remains for all the other expenditures required by civilized life 22.52 per cent.

And of this percentage the State reserves to us, what a liberality! 2.75 per cent to prepare for the future and develop the resources of the country!

Let us see now what Spain has done to permit at least the development of natural wealth and the industry of a country impoverished by this fiscal régime, the work of cupidity, incompetency, and immorality. Let us see whether that nation has left at least some vitality to Cuba, in order to continue exploiting it with some profit.

The economical organization of Cuba is of the simplest kind. It produces to export, and imports almost everything it consumes. In view of this, it is evident that all that Cuba required from the State was that it should not hamper its work with excessive burdens, nor hinder its commercial relations; so that it could buy cheap where it suited her and sell her products with profit. Spain has done all the contrary. She has treated the tobacco as an enemy; she has loaded the sugar with excessive imposts; she has shackled with excessive and abusive excise duties the cattle-raising industry; and with her legislative doings and undoings she has thrown obstacles in the way of the mining industry. And to cap the climax, she has tightly bound Cuba in the network of a monstrous tariff and a commercial legislation which subjects the colony, at the end of the nineteenth century, to the ruinous monopoly of the producers and merchants of certain regions of Spain, as in the halcyon days of the colonial compact.

The district which produces the best tobacco in the world, the famous Vuelta Abajo, lacks every means of transportation afforded by civilization to foster and increase the value of its products. No roads, no bridges, or even ports, are found there. The state in Cuba collects the taxes, but does not invest them for the benefit of any industry. On the other hand, those foreign countries desirous of acquiring the rich tobacco-raising industry have closed their markets to our privileged product by imposing upon it excessive import duties, while the Spanish Government burdens its exportation from our ports with a duty of $1.80 on every thousand cigars. Is this not a stroke of actual insanity?

Everybody is aware of the tremendous crisis through which the sugar industry has been passing for some years, owing to the rapid development of the production of this article everywhere. Every Government has hastened to protect its own by more or less empirical measures. This is not the place to judge them. What is important is to recall the fact that they have endeavored to place the threatened industry in the best condition to withstand the competition. What has Spain done in order, if not to maintain the strong position held before by Cuba, at least to enable the colony to carry on the competition with its every day more formidable rivals? Spain pays bounties to the sugar produced within its own territory, and closes its markets to the Cuban sugar by imposing upon it an import duty of $6.20 per hundred kilograms. It has been calculated that a hundredweight of Cuban sugar is overburdened when reaching the Barcelona market with 143 per cent of its value. The Spanish Government oppresses the Cuban producer with every kind of exactions; taxes the introduction of the machinery that is indispensable for the production of sugar, obstructs its transportation by imposing heavy taxes on the railroads, and winds up the work by exacting another contribution called "industrial duty," and still another for loading or shipping, which is equivalent to an export duty.

As a last stroke, Spain has reenforced the commercial laws of June 30 and July 20, 1882, virtually closing the ports of Cuba to foreign commerce, and establishing the monopoly of the peninsular producers, without any compensation to the colony. The apparent object of these laws was to establish the "cabotaje" (coasting trade) between Cuba and Spain. By the former all the Cuban products were admitted free of duty in the Spanish Peninsula, excepting, however, the tobacco, rum, sugar, cocoa, and coffee, which remained temporarily burdened. By the latter the duties on the importations from Spain in Cuba were to be gradually reduced through a period of ten years, until, in 1892, they were entirely abolished. The result, however, has been that the temporary duties on the principal, almost the only, Cuban products have remained undisturbed until now, and the duties on the Spanish products have disappeared. The "cabotage" (coasting trade) is carried on from Spain to Cuba, but not from Cuba to Spain. The Spanish products pay no duties in Cuba; the Cuban products pay heavy duties in Spain. As at the same time the differential tariffs which overburdened with excessive duties the foreign products have been retained, the unavoidable consequence has been to give the Cuban market entirely to the Peninsula producers. In order to have an idea as to how far the monopoly of Spain goes, it will be sufficient to point to the fact that the burdens which many of the foreign articles have to bear exceed 2,000 and even 2,300 per cent, as compared with those borne by the Spanish products. One hundred kilograms of cotton prints pay a duty, if Spanish, of $26.65; if foreign, $47.26. One hundred kilograms of knitted goods pay, if from Spain, $10.95; if from a foreign country, $195. One thousand kilograms of bags for sugar, when they are or are represented to be Spanish, pay $4.69; if from other country, $82.50. One hundred kilograms of cassimere, if it is a Spanish product, pay $15.47; if foreign, $300.

Still, if Spain was a flourishing industrial country, and produced the principal articles required by Cuba for the consumption of its people, or for developing and fostering its industries, the evil, although always great, would be a lesser one. But everybody knows the backwardness of the Spanish industries, and the inability of Spain to supply Cuba with the products she requires for her consumption and industries. The Cubans have to consume or use Spanish articles of inferior quality or pay exorbitant prices for foreign goods. The Spanish merchants have found, moreover, a new source of fraud in the application of these antiquated and iniquitous laws; it consists in nationalizing foreign products for importation into Cuba.

As the mainspring of this senseless commercial policy is to support the monopoly of Spanish commerce, when Spain has been compelled to deviate from it to a certain extent by an international treaty, it has done so reluctantly and in the anxious expectation of an opportunity to nullify its own promises. This explains the accidental history of the reciprocity treaty with the United States, which was received with joy by Cuba, obstructed by the Spanish administration, and prematurely abolished by the Spanish Government as soon as it saw an opportunity.

The injury done to Cuba, and the evil effects produced by this commercial legislation, are beyond calculation; its effects have been material losses which have engendered profound discontent. The "Circulo de Hacendados y Agricultores," the wealthiest corporation of the Island, last year passed judgment on these commercial laws in the following severe terms:

"It would be impossible to explain, should the attempt be made, what is the significance of the present commercial laws as regards any economical or political plan or system; because, economically, they aim at the destruction of public wealth, and, politically, they are the cause of inextinguishable discontent, and contain the germs of grave dissensions."

But Spain has not taken heed of this; her only care has been to keep the producers and merchants of such rebellious provinces as Catalonia contented, and to satisfy its military men and bureaucrats.

For the latter is reserved the best part of the booty taken from Cuba. High salaries and the power of extortion for the officeholders sent to the colony; regular tributes for the politicians who uphold them in the metropolis. The Governor-General is paid a salary of $50,000, in addition to a palace, a country house as a summer resort, servants, coaches, and a fund for secret expenses at his disposal. The director-general of the treasury receives a salary of $18,500. The archbishop of Santiago and the bishop of Havana, $18,000 each. The commander-general of the "Apostadero" (naval station), $16,392. The general segundo cabo (second in command of the Island), and the president of the "audiencia," $15,000 each. The governor of Havana and the secretary of the General Government, $8,000 each. The postmaster-general, $5,000. The collector for the Havana custom-house, $4,000. The manager of lotteries, the same salary. The chief clerks of administration of the first class receive $5,000 each; those of the second class, $4,000, and those of the third class, $3,000 each. The major-generals are paid $7,500; the brigadier-generals, $4,500, and when in command, $5,000; the colonels, $3,450, and this salary is increased when they are in command of a regiment. The captains of "navío" (the largest men-of-war) receive $6,300; the captains of frigate, $4,560; the lieutenants of "navío" of the the first class, $3,370. All these functionaries are entitled to free lodgings and domestic servants. Then follows the numberless crowd of minor officials, all well provided for, and with great facilities better to provide for themselves.

At the office of the minister of "ultramar" (of the colonies), who resides in Madrid, and to whom $96,800 a year are assigned from the treasury of Cuba—at that office begins the saturnalia in which the Spanish bureaucrats indulge with the riches of Cuba. Sometimes through incapacity, but more frequently for plunder, the money exacted from the Cuban taxpayers is unscrupulously and irresponsibly squandered. It has been demonstrated that the debt of Cuba has been increased in $50,232,500 through Minister Fabié's incapacity. At the time this minister was in power the Spanish Bank disposed of twenty millions from the Cuban treasury, which were to be carried in account current at the disposal of the minister for the famous operation of withdrawing the paper currency. Cuba paid the interest on these millions, and continued paying it all the time they were utilized by the bank. Minister Romero Robledo took at one time (in 1892) $1,000,000 belonging to the treasury of Cuba from the vaults of the Bank of Spain, and lent it to the Transatlantic Company, of which he was a stockholder. This was done in defiance of law and without any authorization whatever. The minister was threatened with prosecution, but he haughtily replied that, if prosecuted, all his predecessors from every political party would have to accompany him to the court. That threat came to nothing.

In June of 1890 there was a scandalous debate in the Spanish Cortes, in which some of the frauds committed upon the Cuban treasury were, not for the first time, brought to light. It was when made public that $6,500,000 had been abstracted from the "caja de depósitos," notwithstanding that the safe was locked with three keys, and each one was in the possession of a different functionary. Then it was known that, under the pretext of false vouchers for transportation and fictitious bills for provisions, during the previous war, defalcations had been found afterwards amounting to $22,811,516. In the month of March of the same year General Pando affirmed that the robberies committed through the issue of warrants by the "junta de la deuda" (board of public debt) exceeded the sum of $12,000,000.

These are only a few of the most salient facts. The large number of millions mentioned above represent only an insignificant part of what a venal administration, sure of impunity, exacts from Cuban labor. The network of artful schemes to cheat the Cuban taxpayer and defraud the State covers everything. Falsification of documents, embezzlement of revenues, bargains with delinquent debtors, exaction of higher dues from inexperienced peasants, delays in the dispatch of judicial proceedings in order to obtain a more or less considerable gratuity; such are the artful means daily employed to empty the purse of the taxpayer and to divert the public funds into the pockets of the functionaries.

These disgraceful transactions have more than once been brought out to light; more than once have the prevaricators been pointed out. Is there any record of any of them having ever been punished?

In August of 1887 General Marin entered the custom-house of Havana at the head of a military force, besieged and occupied it, investigated the operations carried on there, and discharged every employee. The act caused a great stir, but not a single one of the officials was indicted or suffered a further punishment. There were, in 1891, 350 officials indicted in Cuba for committing fraud; not one of them was punished.

But how could they be punished? Every official who comes to Cuba has an influential patron in the court of Madrid for whose protection he pays with regularity. This is a public secret. General Salamanca gave it out in plain words, and before and after General Salamanca all Spain knew and knows it. The political leaders are well known who draw the highest income from the officeholders of Cuba, who are, as a matter of course, the most fervent advocates of the necessity of Spanish rule in Cuba. But Spanish bureaucracy is moreover so deep-rooted in Spain that it has succeeded in shielding itself even against the action of the courts of justice. There is a royal decree (that of 1882) in force in Cuba, which provides that the ordinary courts can not take cognizance of such offenses as defalcation, abstraction or malversation of public funds, forgery, etc., committed by officials of the administration, if their guilt is not first established by an administrative investigation. The administration is, therefore, its own judge. What further security does the corrupt officeholder need?

III.

We have shown that notwithstanding the promises of Spain and the ostensible changes introduced in the government of Cuba since 1878, the Spaniards from Europe have governed and ruled exclusively in Cuba, and have continued exploiting it until they have ruined the country. Can this tyrannical system be justified by any kind of benefits that might compensate for the deprivation of actual power of which the natives of the colony complain? More than one despotic government has tried to justify itself with the material prosperity it has fostered, or with the safety it has secured to its citizens, or with the liberty it has given to certain manifestations of civilized life. Let us see whether the Cubans are indebted to the iron government of Spain for any of these compensating blessings.

Personal safety is a myth among us. Outlaws, as well as men of law, have disposed at will of the property, the peace, and the life of the inhabitants of Cuba. The civil guard (armed police), far from being the guardians, have been the terror of the Cuban peasants. Wherever they pass they cause an alarm by the brutal ill treatment to which they submit the inhabitants, who in many cases fly from their homes at their approach. Under the most trifling pretext they beat unmercifully the defenseless countrymen, and very frequently they have killed those they were conveying under arrest. These outrages became so notorious that the commander in chief of the civil guard, Brigadier-General Denis, had to issue a circular in which he declared that his subordinates, "under pretext of obtaining confidential information, resorted to violent measures," and that "the cases are very frequent in which individuals arrested by forces of the corps attempt to escape, and the keepers find themselves in the necessity of making use of their weapons." What the above declarations signify is evident, notwithstanding the euphemisms of the official language. The object of this circular was to put a stop to these excesses; it bears the date of 1883. But the state of things continued the same. In 1886 the watering place of Madruga, one of the most frequented summer resorts in the island, witnessed the outrageous attacks of Lieutenant Sainz. In 1887 occurred the stirring trial of the "componte," occasioned by the application of torture to the brothers Aruca, and within a few days were recorded in the neighborhood of Havana the cases of Señor Riveron, who was stabbed in Govea by individuals of the public force; of Don Manuel Martinez Moran and Don Francisco Galañena, who were beaten, the former in Calabazar, and the latter in Yaguajay; of Don José Felipe Canosa, who narrowly escaped being murdered in San Nicolas, and of a resident of Ceiba Mocha, whom the civil guard drove from his home.

This was far from the worst. In the very center of Havana, in the Camp de Marte, a prisoner was killed by his guards, and the shooting at Amarillas and the murders at Puentes Grandes and Alquízar are deeds of woful fame in the country. The administration of General Prendergast has left a sorrowful recollection for the frequency with which prisoners who attempted to escape were shot down.

While the armed police force were beating and murdering peaceful inhabitants, the highwaymen were allowed to escape unscathed to devastate the country at their pleasure. Although three millions are assigned in the budget to the service of public safety, there are districts, such as the Province of Puerto Príncipe, where its inhabitants have had to arm themselves and undertake the pursuit of the bandits. The case has occurred of an army of 5,000 or 6,000 troops being sent to pursue a handful of highwaymen within a small territory without succeeding in capturing them. Meanwhile a special bureau was established in Havana for the prosecution of highwaymen, and fabulons sums were spent by it. The best the Government succeeded in doing was to bargain with a bandit, and deceive and kill him afterwards on board the steamer *Baldomero Iglesias* in the bay of Havana.

Nevertheless, the existence of highwaymen has served as a pretext to curtail the jurisdiction of the ordinary courts and submit the Cubans to the jurisdiction of the courts-martial, contrary to the constitution of the state, which had already been proclaimed. In fact, the code of military laws (codigo de justicia militar) provides that the offenses against persons and the means of transportation, as well as arson, when committed in the provinces of ultramar (the colonies) and the possessions of Africa and Oceanica, be tried by court-martial.

It is true, however, than an explicit legal text was not necessary for the Government to nullify the precepts of the constitution. This was promulgated in Cuba, with a preamble providing that the Governor-General and his delegates should retain the same powers they had before its promulgation. The banishment of Cubans have continued after as before said promulgation. In December of 1891 there was a strike of wharf laborers in the Province of Santa Clara. To end it the governor captured the strikers and banished them en masse to the Island of Pinos.

The deportations for political offenses have not been discontinued in Cuba, and although it is stated that no executions for political offenses have taken place since 1878, it is because the Government has resorted to the more simple expedient of assassination. General Polavieja has declared with utmost coolness that in December of 1880 he had 265 persons seized in Cuba, Palma, San Luis, Songo, Guantánamo, and Sagua de Tánamo, and transported the same day and at the same hour to the African Island of Fernando Po. At the close of the insurrection of 1879-80 it was a frequent occurrence for the Government to send to the penal colonies of Africa the Cubans who had capitulated. The treachery of which Gen. José Maceo was a victim carries us to the darkest times of the war of Flanders and the conquest of America.

Cuba recalls with horror the dreadful assassination of Brig. Gen. Arcadio Leyte Vidal, perpetrated in the Bay of Nipe in September of 1879. War had just broken out anew in the eastern department. Brig. Gen. Leyte Vidal resided in Mayari, assured by the solemn promise of the Spanish commander in chief of that zone that he would not be molested. One month had not elapsed since the uprising, however, when having gone to Nipe, he was invited by the commander of the gunboat *Alarma* to take dinner on board. Leyte Vidal went on board the gunboat, but never returned. He was strangled in a boat by three sailors, and his corpse was cast into the sea. This villainous deed was committed in compliance with an order from the Spanish general, Polavieja. Francisco Leyte Vidal, a cousin to Arcadio, miraculously escaped the same tragic fate.

The mysterious deaths of Cubans who had capitulated long before have been frequent in Cuba. To one of these deaths was due the uprising of Tunas de Bayamo in 1879.

If the personal safety of the Cubans, in a period which the Spaniards would depict with brilliant colors, continues at the mercy of their rulers, who are aliens in the country both by birth and in ideas, have the Cubans' honor and property any better safeguard? Is the administration of justice good, or even endurable? The very idea of a lawsuit frightens every honest Cuban. Nobody trusts the honesty or independence of the judges. Despite the provisions of the constitution, without warrant and for indefinite time, imprisonments are most common in Cuba. The magistrates can tighten or loosen the elastic meshes of the judicial proceedings. They know well that if they curry favor with the Government they can do anything without incurring responsibility. They consider themselves, and without thinking it a disgrace, as mere political tools. The presidents and attorneys-general of the "audiencias" receive their instructions at the captain-general's office. Twice have the governors of Cuba aimed at establishing a special tribunal to deal with the offenses of the press, thereby undermining the constitution. Twice has this special tribunal been established. More than once has a straightforward and impartial judge been found to try a case in which the interests of influential people were involved. On such occasions the straightforward judge has been replaced by a special judge.

In a country where money is wastefully spent to support a civil and military bureaucracy the appropriation for the administration of justice does not reach $500,000. On the other hand, the sales of stamped paper constitute a revenue of $750,000. Thus the State derives a pecuniary profit from its administration of justice.

Is it, then, a wonder that the reforms that have been attempted by establishing lower and higher courts to take cognizance of criminal cases, and by introducing oral and public trials should not have contributed in the least to improve the administration of justice? Onerous services have been exacted from people without proper compensation as gratuitous services. The Government, so splendidly liberal when its own expenses are in question, haggles for the last cent when dealing with truly useful and reproductive services.

Is the Cuban compensated for his absolute deprivation of political power, the fiscal extortions, and the monstrous deficiencies of judicial administration by the material prosperity of his country? No man acquainted with the intimate relations which exist between the fiscal régime of a country and its economical system will believe that Cuba, crushed as it is, by unreasonable budgets and an enormous debt, can be rich. The income of Cuba in the most prosperous times has been calculated at $80,-000,000. The state, provincial, and municipal charges take much more than 40 per cent of this amount. This fact explains itself. We need not draw any inferences therefrom. Let us confine ourselves to casting a glance over the aspect presented by the agricultural, industrial, and real estate interests in Cuba at the beginning of the present year.

Despite the prodigious efforts made by private individuals to extend the cultivation of the sugar cane and to raise the sugar-making industry to the plane it has reached, both the colonists and the proprietors of the sugar plantations and the sugar mills (centrales) are on the brink of bankruptcy and ruin. In selling the output they knew that they would not get sufficient means to cover the cost of keeping and repairing their colonies and sugar mills. There is not a single agricultural bank in Cuba. The "hacendado" (planter, landowner) had to recur to usurious loans and to pay 18 and 20 per cent for the sums which they borrowed. Not long ago there existed in Havana the Spanish Bank, the Bank of Commerce, the Industrial Bank, the Bank of St. Joseph, the Bank of the Alliance, the Bank of Maritime Insurances, and the Savings Bank. Of these there remain to-day only the Spanish Bank, which has been converted into a vast State office, and the Bank of Commerce, which owes its existence to the railways and warehouses it possesses. None of these give any aid to the sugar industry.

The cigar-making industry, which was in such flourishing condition a short time ago, has fallen so low that fears are entertained that it may emigrate entirely from Cuba. The weekly El Tabaco came to the conclusion that the exportation of cigars from Cuba would cease entirely within six years. From 1889 to 1894 the exportation from the port of Havana had decreased by 116,200,000 cigars.

City real estate has fallen to one-half and in some cases to one-third the value it had before 1884. A building in Havana which was erected at a cost of $600,000 was sold in 1893 for $120,000.

Stocks and bonds tell the same story. Almost all of them are quoted in Havana with heavy discounts.

The cause of the ruin of Cuba, despite her sugar output of 1,000,000 tons and her vast tobacco fields, can be easily explained. Cuba does not capitalize, and it does not capitalize because the fiscal régime imposed upon the country does not permit it. The money derived from its large exportations does not return either in the form of importations of goods or of cash. It remains abroad to pay the interest of its huge debt, to cover the incessant remittances of funds by the Spaniards who hasten to send their earnings out of the country, to pay from our treasury the pensioners who live in Spain, and to meet the drafts forwarded by every mail from Cuba by the Spaniards as a tribute to their political patrons in the metropolis, and to help their families.

Cuba pays $2,192,795 in pensions to those on the retired list and to superannuated officials not in service. Most of this money is exported. The first chapters of the Cuban budget imply the exportation of over $10,600,000. Cuba pays a subsidy of $471,836.68 to the Transatlantic Company. It would be impossible to calculate the amount of money taken out of Cuba by private individuals; but this constant exportation of capital signifies that nobody is contented in Cuba and that everybody mistrusts its future. The consequence is that notwithstanding the apparently favorable commercial balance exchange is constantly and to a high degree against Cuba.

On the other hand, if Cuba labors and strives to be on the same plane as its most progressive competitors, this is the work of her own people, who do not mind any sacrifices; but the Government cares little or nothing about securing to the country such means of furthering its development as are consigned in the budget under the head of "Fomento."

And now, at the outbreak of the present war, Spain finds that, although the appropriations consigned in our budgets since 1878 amount to nearly $500,000,000, not a single military road has been built, no fortifications, no hospitals, and there is no material of war. The State has not provided even for its own defense. In view of this fact, nobody will be surprised to hear that a country 670 kilometers long, with an area of 118,833 square kilometers, has only 246½ lineal kilometers of high roads, and these almost exclusively in the province of Havana. In that of Santiago de Cuba there are 9 kilometers; in Puerto Principe and Las Villas not a single one. Cuba has 3,506 kilometers of seashore and 54 ports; only 15 of these are open to commerce. In the labyrinth of keys, sand banks, and breakers adjacent to our coasts there are only 19 light-houses of all classes. Many of our ports, some of the best among them, are filling up. The coasting steamers can hardly pass the bars at the entrance of the ports of Nuevitas, Gibara, Baracoa, and Santiago de Cuba. Private parties have sometimes been willing to remedy these evils; but then the central administration has interfered, and after years of red tape things have remained worse than before. In the course of twenty-eight years only 139 kilometers of high-roads were built in Cuba; 2 first-class light-houses were erected, 3 of the second class, and 1 of the fourth class, 3 beacon lights and 2 port lights; 246 meters of wharf were built, and a few ports were superficially cleaned and their shoals marked. This was all. On the other hand, the department of public works consumes unlimited millions in salaries and in repairs.

The neglect of public hygiene in Cuba is proverbial. The technical commission sent by the United States to Havana to study the yellow fever declared that the port of the capital of Cuba, owing to the inconceivable filth, is a permanent source of infection, against which it is necessary to take precautions. There is in Havana, however a "junta de puerto" (board of port wardens) which collects dues and spends them with the same munificence as the other bureaucratic centers.

Does the Government favor us more in the matter of education? It will suffice to state that only $182,000 are assigned to public instruction in our splendid budget. And it may be proved that the University of Havana is a source of pecuniary profit to the State. On the other hand, this institution is without laboratories, instruments, and even without water to carry on experiments. All the countries of America, excepting Bolivia, all of them, including Haiti, Jamaica, Trinidad, and Guadalupe, where the colored race predominates, spend a great deal more than the Cuban Government for the education of the people. On the other hand, only Chile spends as much as Cuba for the support of an army. In view of this it is easily explained why 76 per cent of such an intelligent and wide-awake people as that of Cuba can not read and write. The most necessary instruction among us, the technical and industrial, does not exist. The careers and professions most needed by modern civilization are not cultivated in Cuba. In order to become a topographer, a scientific agriculturist, an electrician, an industrial or mechanical engineer, a railroad or mining engineer, the Cuban has to go to a foreign country. The State in Cuba does not support a single public library.

Are the deficiencies of the Spanish régime compensated by the wisdom of its administration? Every time the Spanish Government has undertaken the solution of any of the great problems pending in Cuba it has only confused and made it worse. It has solved it blindly or yielded to the influence of those who were to profit by the change. It will be sufficient to recall the withdrawal from circulation of the bank notes, which proved to be a highly lucrative transaction for a few persons, but which only embarrassed and impaired the monetary circulation of the island. From one day to another the cost of living became 40 per cent dearer. The depreciated Spanish silver entered in circulation to drive out, as was natural, the "centen" (five-dollar gold coin) and make small transactions difficult. To reach these results the Spanish Government had transformed a debt on which it had no interest to pay into a debt bearing a high rate of interest. It is true that, in exchange, all the retail dealers whose votes it was desirable to keep derived very large profits from the operation. These dealers are, of course, Spaniards.

IV.

In exchange for all that Spain withholds from us they say that it has given us liberties. This is a mockery. The liberties are written in the constitution but obliterated in its practical application. Before and after its promulgation the public press has been rigorously persecuted in Cuba. Many journalists, such as Señores Cepeda and Lópes Briñas, have been banished from the country without the formality of a trial. In November of 1891 the writer Don Manuel A. Balmaseda was tried by court-martial for having published an editorial paragraph in El Criterio Popular, of Remedios, relative to the shooting of the medical students. The newspapers have been allowed to discuss public affairs theoretically; but the moment they denounce any abuse or the conduct of any official they feel the hand of their rulers laid upon them. The official organ of the home-rule party, El País, named before El Triunfo, has undergone more than one trial for having pointed in measured terms to some infractions of the law on the part of officials, naming the transgressors. In 1887 that periodical was subjected to criminal proceedings simply because it had stated that a son of the president of the Havana "audiencia" was holding a certain office contrary to law.

They say that in Cuba the people are at liberty to hold public meetings, but every time the inhabitants assemble, previous notification must be given to the authorities, and a functionary is appointed to be present, with power to suspend the meeting whenever he deems such a measure advisable. The meetings of the "Círculo de Trabajadores" (an association of workingmen) were forbidden by the authorities under the pretext that the building where they were to be held was not sufficiently safe. Last year the members of the "Círculo de Hacendados" (association of planters) invited their fellow-members throughout the country to get up a great demonstration to demand a remedy which the critical state of their affairs required. The Government found means to prevent their meeting. One of the most significant events that have occurred in Cuba, and one which throws a flood of light upon its political régime, was the failure of the "Junta Magna" (an extraordinary meeting) projected by the "Círculo de Hacendados." This corporation solicited the cooperation of the "Sociedad Económica" and of the "Junta General de Comercio" to hold a meeting for the purpose of sending to the metropolis the complaints which the precarious situation of the country inspired. The work of preparation was already far advanced when a friend of the Government, Señor Rodríguez Correa, stated that the Governor General looked with displeasure upon and forbade the holding of the great meeting. This was sufficient to frighten the "Círculo" and to secure the failure of the project. It is then evident that the inhabitants of Cuba can have meetings only when the Government thinks it advisable to permit them.

Against this political régime, which is a sarcasm and in which deception is added to the most absolute contempt for right, the Cubans have unceasingly protested since it was implanted in 1878. It would be difficult to enumerate the representations made in Spain, the protests voiced by the representatives of Cuba, the commissions that have crossed the ocean to try to impress upon the exploiters of Cuba what the fatal consequences of their obstinacy would be. The exasperation prevailing in the country was such that the "junta central" of the home-rule party issued in 1892 a manifesto in which it foreshadowed that the moment might shortly arrive when the country would resort to "extreme measures, the responsibility of which would fall on those who, led by arrogance and priding themselves on their power, hold prudence in contempt, worship force, and shield themselves with their impunity."

This manifesto, which foreboded the mournful hours of the present war, was unheeded by Spain, and not until a division took place in the Spanish party, which threatened to turn into an armed struggle, did the statesmen of Spain think that the moment had arrived to try a new farce, and to make a false show of reform in the administrative régime of Cuba. Then was Minister Maura's plan broached, to be modified before its birth by Minister Abarzuas.

This project, to which the Spaniards have endeavored to give capital importance in order to condemn the revolution as the work of impatience and anarchism, leaves intact the political régime of Cuba. It does not alter the electoral law. It does not curtail the power of the bureaucracy. It increases the power of the general Government. It leaves the same burdens upon the Cuban taxpayer, and does not give him the right to participate in the information of the budgets. The reform is confined to the changing of the council of administration (now in existence in the island, and the members of which are appointed by the Government) into a partially elective body. One-half of its members are to be appointed by the Government and the other half to be elected by the qualified electors—that is, who assessed and pay for a certain amount of taxes. The Governor-General has the right to veto all its resolutions and to suspend at will the elective members. This council is to make up a kind of special budget embracing the items included now in the general budget of Cuba under the head of "Fomento." The State reserves for itself all the rest. Thus the council can dispose of 2.75 per cent of the revenues of Cuba, while the Government distributes, as at present, 97.25 per cent for its expenses, in the form we have explained. The general budget will, as heretofore, be made up in Spain; the tariff laws will be enacted by Spain. The debt, militarism, and bureaucracy will continue to devour Cuba, and the Cubans will continue to be treated as a subjugated people. All power is to continue in the hands of the Spanish Government and its delegates in Cuba, and all the influence with the Spanish residents. This is the self-government which Spain has promised to Cuba, and which it is announcing to the world, in exchange for its colonial system. A far better form of government is enjoyed by the Bahama or the Turks islands.

The Cubans would have been wanting not only in self-respect but even in the instincts of self-preservation if they could have endured such a degrading and destructive régime. Their grievances are of such a nature that no people, no human community capable of valuing its honor and of aspiring to better its condition, could bear them without degrading and condemning itself to utter nullity and annihilation.

Spain denies to the Cubans all effective powers in their own country.

Spain condemns the Cubans to a political inferiority in the land where they are born.

Spain confiscates the product of the Cuban's labor without giving them in return either safety, prosperity, or education.

Spain has shown itself utterly incapable of governing Cuba.

Spain exploits, impoverishes, and demoralizes Cuba.

To maintain by force of arms this monstrous régime, which brings ruin on a country rich by nature and degrades a vigorous and intelligent population, a population filled with noble aspirations, is what Spain calls to defend its honor and preserve the prestige of its social functions as a civilizing power of America.

The Cubans, not in anger but in despair, have appealed to arms in order to defend their rights and to vindicate an eternal principle, a principle without which every community, however robust in appearance, is in danger—the principle of justice. Nobody has the right of oppression. Spain oppresses us. In rebelling against oppression we defend a right. In serving our own cause we serve the cause of mankind.

We have not counted the number of our enemies; we have not measured their strength. We have cast up the account of our grievances; we have weighed the mass of injustice that crushes us, and with uplifted hearts we have risen to seek redress and to uphold our rights. We may find ruin and death a few steps ahead. So be it. We do our duty. If the world is indifferent to our cause, so much the worse for all. A new iniquity shall have been consummated. The principle of human solidarity shall have suffered a defeat. The sum of good existing in the world, an which the world needs to purify its moral atmosphere, shall have been lessened. d

The people of Cuba require only liberty and independence to become a factor of prosperity and progress in the community of civilized nations. At present Cuba is a factor of intranquillity, disturbance, and ruin. The fault lies entirely with Spain. Cuba is not the offender; it is the defender of its rights. Let America, let the world decide where rest justice and right.

ENRIQUE JOSÉ VARONA,
Ex-Diputado a Cortes.

NEW YORK, *October 23, 1895.*

B.

COMPILATION OF THE LAWS, RULES, DECREES, CIRCULARS, AND OTHER ORDERS PASSED BY THE NATIONAL COUNCIL FROM THE 19TH OF SEPTEMBER, 1895, THE DATE ON WHICH IT COMMENCED TO EXERCISE ITS FUNCTIONS.

MANGOS DE BARAGUA.

The National Council, in a meeting held on the 16th of October, 1895, resolved that the publication in book form in an edition of 500 copies of all the laws, rules, decrees, and other orders passed by it be printed after being previously approved by the Council and sanctioned by its president.

JOSÉ CLEMENTE VIVANCO,
The Secretary of the Council.

CONSTITUENT ASSEMBLY, REPUBLIC OF CUBA.

I, José Clemente Vivanco, secretary of the National Council and chancellor of the Republic of Cuba, certify that the representatives of the different army corps, into which the army of liberation is divided, met in constituent assembly on the 13th day of September, 1895, at Jimaguayu, agreed to have a preliminary session where the character of each representative would be accredited by the respective credential of his appointment. There resulted, after the proper examination by the chairman and secretaries, who were temporarily Citizens Salvador Cisneros Betancourt and Secretaries José Clemente Vivanco and Orencio Nodarse, the following distribution:

Representatives of the First Army Corps, Citizens Dr. Joaquin Castillo Duany, Mariano Sanchez Vaillant, Rafael M. Portuondo, and Pedro Aguillera.

For the Second, Citizens Licentiate Rafael Manduley, Enrique Cespedes, Rafael Perez Morales, and Marcos Padilla.

For the Third, Citizens Salvador Cisneros Betancourt, Lopez Recio Loinaz, Enrique Loinaz del Castillo, and Dr. Fermmin Valdes Dominguez.

For the Fourth, Licentiate Severo Pina, Dr. Santiago Garcia Canizares, Raimundo Sanchez Valdivia, and Francisco Lopez Leiba.

For the Fifth, Dr. Pedro Pinan de Villegas, Licentiate José Clemente Vivanco, Francisco Diaz Silveria, and Orencio Nodarse.

They proceeded to the election of officers for the following session and the following appointments were made: Salvador Cisneros Betancourt, president; Rafael Manduley, vice-president; secretaries, Licentiate José Clemente Vivanco, Francisco Lopez Leiba, Licentiate Rafael M. Portuondo, and Orencio Nodarse.

The assembly having been organized as above, and in the presence of the above representatives, they proceeded to hold the sessions to discuss the constitution which is to rule the destinies of the Republic. These sessions took place on September 13, 14, 15, and 16, instant, and in all the articles which were to form the said constitutional charta were discussed. Every article of the projected constitution presented to the assembly by the representatives licentiate, Rafael M. Portuondo, Dr. Joaquin Castillo Duany, Mariano Sanchez Vaillant, and Pedro Aguilera, was well discussed, and, together with amendments, reforms, and additions were also discussed by the proposers. On deliberation, in conformity with the opinion of the assembly, it was unanimously resolved to refer the said constitution, with the resolutions of the said assembly, to a committee of revision of the text, composed of the secretaries and of the representatives, Dr. Santiago Garcia, Canizares and Enrique, Loynaz del Castillo, who, after complying with their mission, returned the final draft of the constitution on the 16th. It was then read, and the signature of each and every representative subscribed.

The president and other members of the assembly, with due solemnity, then swore upon their honor to loyally and strictly observe the fundamental code of the Republic of Cuba, which was greeted by the spontaneous and enthusiastic acclamations of all present; in testimony of which are the minutes in the general archive of the Government.

In compliance with the resolution passed by this council in a meeting held to-day, and for its publication, I issue the following copy, in the Mangos de Baragua on the 18th of October, 1895.

JOSÉ CLEMENTE VIVANCO,
Secretary of the Council.

The revolution for the independence and creation in Cuba of a democratic Republic in its new period of war, initiated on February 24 last, solemnly declares the separation of Cuba from the Spanish monarchy, and its constitution as a free and independent State, with its own Government and supreme authority under the name of the Republic of Cuba and confirms its existence among the political divisions of the world.

The elected representatives of the revolution, in convention assembled, acting in its name and by the delegation which for that purpose has been conferred upon them by the Cubans in arms, and previously declaring before the country the purity of their thoughts, their freedom from violence, anger, or prejudice, and inspired only by the desire of interpreting the popular voice in favor of Cuba, have now formed a compact between Cuba and the world, pledging their honor for the fulfillment of said compact in the following articles of the constitution:

ARTICLE I. The supreme powers of the Republic shall be vested in a government council composed of a president, vice-president, and four secretaries of state, for the dispatch of the business of war, of the interior, of foreign affairs, and of the treasury.

ART. II. Every secretary shall have a subsecretary of state, in order to supply any vacancies.

ART. III. The government council shall have the following powers:

1. To dictate all measures relative to the civil and political life of the revolution.

2. To impose and collect taxes, to contract public loans, to issue paper money, to invest the funds collected in the island, from whatever source, and also those which may be raised abroad by loan.

3. To arm vessels, to raise and maintain troops, to declare reprisals with respect to the enemy, and to ratify treaties.

4. To grant authority, when it is deemed convenient, to order the trial by the judicial power of the president or other members of the council, if he be accused

5. To decide all matters, of whatsoever description, which may be brought before them by any citizen, except those judicial in character.

6. To approve the law of military organization and the ordinances of the army, which may be proposed by the general in chief.

7. To grant military commissions from that of colonel upward, previously hearing and considering the reports of the immediate superior officer and of the general in chief, and to designate the appointment of the latter and of the lieutenant-general in case of the vacancy of either.

8. To order the election of four representatives for each army corps whenever in conformity with this constitution it may be necessary to convene an assembly.

ART. IV. The Government council shall intervene in the direction of military operations only when in their judgment it shall be absolutely necessary to do so to realize high political ends.

ART. V. As a requisite for the validity of the decrees of the council, at least two-thirds of the members of the same must have taken part in the deliberations of the council, and the decrees must have been voted by the majority of those present.

ART. VI. The office of councilor is incompatible with any other of the Republic, and requires the age of twenty-five years.

ART. VII. The executive power is vested in the president, and, in case of disability, in the vice-president.

ART. VIII. The resolutions of the government council shall be sanctioned and promulgated by the president, who shall take all necessary steps for their execution within ten days.

ART. IX. The president may enter into treaties with the ratification of the government council.

ART. X. The president shall receive all diplomatic representatives and issue the respective commissions to the public functionaries.

ART. XI. The treaty of peace with Spain, which must necessarily have for its basis the absolute independence of the Island of Cuba, must be ratified by the government council and by an assembly of representatives convened expressly for this purpose.

ART. XII. The vice-president shall substitute the president in the case of a vacancy.

ART. XIII. In case of the vacancy in the offices of both president and vice-president on account of resignation, deposition, or death of both, or from any other cause, an assembly of representatives for the election to the vacant offices shall be convened, the senior secretaries in the meanwhile occupying the positions.

ART. XIV. The secretaries shall have voice and vote in the deliberations of resolutions of whatever nature.

ART. XV. The secretaries shall have the right to appoint all the employees of their respective offices.

ART. XVI. The subsecretaries in cases of vacancy shall substitute the secretaries of state and shall then have voice and vote in the deliberations.

Art. XVII. All the armed forces of the Republic and the direction of the military operations shall be under the control of the general in chief, who shall have under his orders as second in command a lieutenant-general, who will substitute him in case of vacancy.

Art. XVIII. All public functionaries of whatever class shall aid one another in the execution of the resolutions of the government council.

Art. XIX. All Cubans are bound to serve the revolution with their persons and interests, each one according to his ability.

Art. XX. The plantations and property of whatever description belonging to foreigners are subject to the payment of taxes for the revolution while their respective governments do not recognize the rights of belligerency of Cuba.

Art. XXI. All debts and obligations contracted since the beginning of the present period of war until the promulgation of this constitution by the chiefs of the army corps, for the benefit of the revolution, shall be valid as well as those which henceforth the government council may contract.

Art. XXII. A government council may depose any of its members for cause justifiable in the judgment of two-thirds of the councilors and shall report to the first assembly convening.

Art. XXIII. The judicial power shall act with entire independence of all the others. Its organization and regulation will be provided for by the government counci .

Art. XXIV. The present constitution shall be in force in Cuba for two years from the date of its promulgation, unless the war for independence shall terminate before. After the expiration of the two years an assembly of representatives shall be convened which may modify it, and will proceed to the election of a new government council, and which will pass upon the last council. So it has been agreed upon and resolved in the name of the Republic by the constituent assembly in Jimaguayu on the 18th day of September, 1895, and in witness thereof we, the representatives delegated by the Cuban people in arms, signed the present instrument. Salvador Cisneros, president; Rafael Manduley, Vice-president; Pedro Pinan de Villegas, Lope Recio, Fermin Valdes Dominguez, Francisco Diaz Silveira, Dr. Santiago Garcia, Rafael Perez, F. Lopez Leyva, Enrique Cespedes, Marcos Padilla, Raimundo Sanchez, J. D. Castillo, Mariano Sanchez, Pedro Aguilera, Rafael M. Pontuondo, Orencio Nodarse, José Clemente Vivanco, Enrique Loynaz Del Castillo, Severo Pina.

ELECTION OF GOVERNMENT.

The constituent assembly met again on the 18th of the said month and year, all the said representatives being present. They proceeded to the election of members who are to occupy the offices of the Government council, the general-in-chief of the army of liberation, the lieutenant-general, and the diplomatic agent abroad. The secret voting commenced, each representative depositing his ballot in the urn placed on the chairman's table, after which the count was proceeded with, the following being the result:

President: Salvador Cisneros, 12; Bartolome Maso, 8.

Vice-president: Bartolome Maso, 12; Salvador Cisneros, 8.

Secretary of war: Carlos Roloff, 18; Lope Recio Loinaz, 1; Rafael Manduley, 1.

Secretary of the treasury: Severo Pina, 19; Rafael Manduley, 1.

Secretary of the interior: Dr. Santiago Garcia Canizares, 19; Carlos Dubois, 1.

Secretary of the foreign relations: Rafael Portuondo, 18; Armando Menocal, 1. blank, 1.

Subsecretary of war: Mario Menocal, 18; Francisco Diaz Silveira, 1; blank, 1.

Subsecretary of the treasury: Dr. Joaquin Castillo, 7; Francisco Diaz Silveira, 5; José C. Vivanco, 3; Armando Menocal, 3; Carlos Dubois, 1; blank, 1.

Subsecretary of the interior: Carlos Dubois, 13; Oreneio Nodarse, 5; Armando Menocal, 1; blank, 1.

Subsecretary of foreign relations: Fermin Valdes Dominguez, 18; Rafael Manduley, 1; blank, 1.

Therefore, the following were elected by a majority of votes:

President, Salvador Cisneros; vice-president, Bartolome Maso; secretary of war, Carlos Roloff; secretary of the treasury, Severo Pina; secretary of the interior, Dr. Santiago Garcia Canizares; secretary of foreign relations, Rafael M. Portuondo; subsecretary of war, Mario Menocal; subsecretary of the treasury, Dr. Joaquin Castillo; subsecretary of the interior, Carlos Dubois; subsecretary of foreign relations, Dr. Fermin Valdes Dominguez.

The vice-president of the assembly immediately installed the president in the office of the government council that had been conferred upon him; the latter in turn installed those of the other members elected, who were present, all entering on the full exercise of their functions after previously taking the oath.

On proceeding to the election of those who were to occupy the positions of general in chief of the army, lieutenant-general, and diplomatic agent abroad, the following citizens were unanimously elected by the assembly for the respective places: Major-General Maximo Gomez, Major-General Antonio Maceo, and Citizen Tomas Estrada Palma. All these appointments being recognized from that moment.

LAWS FOR THE CIVIL GOVERNMENT AND ADMINISTRATION OF THE REPUBLIC.

CHAPTER I.—TERRITORIAL DIVISION.

ARTICLE I. The Republic of Cuba comprises the territory occupied by the Island of Cuba from Cape San Antonio to Point Maisi and the adjacent islands and keys.

ART. II. This territory shall be divided into four portions, or states, which will be called Oriente, Camaguey, Las Villas or Cabanacan, and Occidente.

ART. III. The State of Oriente includes the territory from the Point Maisi to Port Manati and the river Jobabo in all its course.

ART. IV. The State of Camaguey includes all the territory from the boundary of Oriente to the line which starts in the north from Laguna Blanca through the Esteros to Moron, passing by Ciego de Avila, follows the military trocha to El Jucaro in the southern coast, it being understood that the towns of Moron and Ciego de Avila belong to this State.

ART. V. The State of Las Villas has for boundary on the east Camaguey, on the west the river Palmas, Palmillas, Santa Rosa, Rodas, the Hannabana River, and the bay of Cochinos.

ART. VI. The State of Occidente is bordered on the Las Villas, extending to the west to Cape San Antonio.

ART. VII. The islands and adjacent keys will form part of the states to which they geographically belong.

ART. VIII. The State of Oriente will be divided into ten districts, which shall be as follows: Baracoa, Guantanamo, Sagua de Tanamo, Mayari, Santiago, Jiguani, Manzanillo, Bayamo, and Tunas.

Camaguey comprises two—the eastern district and the western district.

Las Villas comprises seven—Sancti-Espiritus, Trinidad, Remedios, Santa Clara, Sagua, Cienfuegos, and Colon.

That of Occidente comprises sixteen—Cardenas, Matanzas, Union, Jaruco, Guines, Santa Maria del Rosario, Guanabacoa, Habana, Santiago de las Vegas, Bejucal, San Antonio, Bahia Honda, Pina del Rio, and Mantua.

ART. IX. Each of these districts will be divided into prefectures, and these in their turn into as many subprefectures as may be considered necessary.

ART. X. For the vigilance of the coasts there will be inspectors and watchmen appointed in each State according to the extent of the coasts and the number of ports, bays, gulfs, and salt works that there may be.

ART. XI. On establishing the limits of the districts and prefectures, the direction of the coast, rivers, and other natural boundaries shall be kept in mind.

CHAPTER II.—OF THE GOVERNMENT AND ITS ADMINISTRATION.

ART. XII. The civil government, the administration, and the service of communications devolve upon the department of the interior.

ART. XIII. The secretary of the interior is the head of the department; he will appoint the employees and will remove them whenever there will be justifiable cause, and will have a department chief to aid him in the work of the department.

ART. XIV. The department chief will keep the books of the department, take care of the archives, will be the manager of the office, and will furnish certifications when requested to do so.

ART. XV. The department of the interior will compile from the data collected by the civil governors the general statistics of the Republic.

ART. XVI. The civil governor will inform the department of the interior as to the necessities of his state, will order the measures and instructions necessary for compliance with the general laws of the Republic and the orders given by that department, will distribute to the lieutenant-governors the articles of prime necessity which will be delivered to them for that purpose, will communicate to his subordinates the necessary instructions for the compilation of statistics, and will have a subsecretary who will help him in the discharge of his functions.

ART. XVII. The lieutenant-governor will see that the orders of the governors are obeyed in the district, and will have the powers incident to his position as intermediary between the civil governors and the prefects. In case of absolute breach of communication with the civil governors, they will have the same powers as the latter.

ART. XVIII. The prefect shall see that the laws and regulations communicated to him by his superior authorities are complied with. All residents and travelers are under his authority, and, being the highest official in his territory, he in his turn is bound to prevent all abuses and crimes which may be committed.

He will inform the lieutenant-governor as to the necessities of the prefecture; will divide these into as many subprefectures as he may consider necessary for the good conduct of his administration; he will watch the conduct of the subprefects; he will distribute among them with equity the articles delivered to him, and he will have all the other powers incident to him in his character of intermediary between the lieutenant-governor and the subprefects.

ART. XIX. The prefect will also have the following duties: He will harass the enemy whenever possible for him to do so; will hear the preliminary information as to crimes and misdemeanors which may be committed in his territory, passing the said information to the nearest military chief, together with the accused and all that is necessary for the better understanding of the hearing. He will not proceed thus with spies, guides, couriers, and others who are declared by our laws as traitors and considered as such, for these, on account of the difficulty of confining them or conducting them with security, shall be tried as soon as captured by a court consisting of three persons, the most capable in his judgment in the prefecture, one acting as president and the others as members of the court. He will also appoint a prosecuting officer, and the accused may appoint some one to defend him at his pleasure.

After the court is assembled in this form, and after all the formalities are complied with, it will in private judge and give its sentence, which will be final and without appeal; but those who form the said court and who do not proceed according to our laws and to natural reason will be held responsible by the superior government. Nevertheless, if in the immediate territory there be any armed force, the accused shall be sent to it with the facts in order that they shall be properly tried.

The prefects will take the statistics of his prefecture, setting down every person who is found therein, noting if he is the head of a family, the number of the same, his age, his nationality and occupation, if he is a farmer the nature of his farm, and if he has no occupation the prefect will indicate in what he should be employed. He will also keep a book of civil register in which he will set down the births, deaths, and marriages which may occur.

He will establish in the prefecture all the factories that he can or may consider necessary in order to well provide the army, as it is the primary obligation of all employees of the Republic to do all possible so that the hides shall not be lost, and organizing in the best manner, and as quickly as may be, tanneries, factories of shoes, rope, blankets, and carpenter and blacksmith shops.

He will not permit any individual of his district to be without occupation. He will see that everyone works, having the instruments of labor at hand in proportion to the inhabitants of his territory. He will protect and raise bees, he will take care of abandoned farms, and will extend as far as possible the zones of agriculture.

As soon as the prefect learns that the secretary of the interior or any delegate of this authority is in his district he will place himself under the latter's orders. This he will also do on the arrival of armed forces, presenting himself to their chief in order to facilitate the needed supplies and to serve him in every possible manner. He will have a bugle to warn the inhabitants of the enemy's approach; he will inform the nearest armed force when his territory is invaded. He will collect all horses and other animals suitable for the war and lead them to a secure place, so that when the army may need them or they may be required by the civil authorities to whom they may appertain.

He will provide the forces that may be, or pass through his territory with whatever they may need, which may be within his power, and especially shall he provide guides and beeves and vegetables which the chief may require to maintain the said forces. He will also deliver the articles manufactured in the shops under his immediate inspection, demanding always the proper receipts therefor.

He will also provide the necessary means for the maintenance of all the families of the territory, especially those of the soldiers of the army of liberation.

Until otherwise decreed he will celebrate civil marriages and other contracts entered into by the residents of his prefecture; he will act in cases of ordinary complaints and in the execution of powers and wills, registering the same in a clear and definite manner, and issuing to the interested parties the certificates which they may require.

ART. XX. The subprefects will see that the laws and orders communicated to him by his superior authorities are obeyed in territory under his command; he will inform the prefect as to the necessities of the subprefecture and will see to the security and order of the public; arresting and sending to the prefects those who may travel without safe-conduct, seeing that no violation of law whatsoever is perpetrated, and will demand the signed authority of the civil or military chief who has ordered a commission to be executed.

ART. XXI. The subprefects will compile a census in which the number of inhabitants of a subprefecture will be stated and their personal description; he will keep a book of the births and deaths which will occur in his territory, and of all this he will give account at the end of the year. He will invest the means provided by the prefect to pay the public charges, and if the said resources are insufficient he will collect the deficit from the inhabitants; he will not authorize the destruction of abandoned farms, whether they belong to friends or enemies of the Republic, and he will inform the prefect of the farms which are thus abandoned.

ART. XXII. For the organization and better operation of the states manufactories a chief of factories shall be appointed in each district, who will be authorized to establish such factories which he may deem convenient, employing all citizens who, on account of their abilities can serve, and collecting in the prefectures of his district all the instruments he can utilize in his work. These chiefs will be careful to frequently inspect the factories, to report any defects which they may notice, and to provide the superintendents with whatever they may need, that the work may not be interrupted.

Together with the prefect he will send to the department of the interior the names of the individuals he considers most adapted to open new shops, and on the first day of each month he will send to that department a statement of the objects manufactured in each shop of his district, indicating the place of manufacture, what remains on deposit, what has been delivered, with the names of commanders of forces, civil authorities, or individuals to whom they were delivered.

ART. XXIII. The coast inspectors will have under their immediate orders an inspector, who will be his secretary, who will occupy his place in his absence or sickness, and as many auxiliaries as he may deem convenient. He may demand the aid of the prefects and armed forces whenever he may consider it necessary for the better exercise of his functions. The duties of the inspectors will be to watch the coasts and prevent the landing of the enemy, to be always ready to receive disembarkments and place in safety the expeditions which may come from abroad, to establish all the salt works possible, to capture the Spanish vessels which frequent the coasts on his guard, and to attend with special care to the punctual service of communications between his coast and foreign countries.

ART. XXIV. The coast guards will acknowledge the inspector as their superior, will watch the places designated to them, and will execute the orders given.

ART. XXV. The lieutenant-governors, as well as the inspectors of whatever class, will have their residence, wherever the necessity of their office does not prohibit it, in the general headquarters, so that they can move easily, furnish the necessary aid to the army, and carry out the orders of the military chief.

Country and liberty.

OCTOBER 17, 1895.

The secretary of the interior, Dr. Santiago Garcia Canizares, being satisfied with the preceding law, I sanction it in all respects.

Let it be promulgated in the legal form.

SALVADOR CISNEROS BETANCOURT,
The President.

OCTOBER 18, 1895.

LAW OF CIVIL MARRIAGE.

ARTICLE I. Males of 18 years of age and females of 14 can contract marriage.

ART. II. To contract marriage they must go to the notary of their residence, two witnesses being present who will sign the contract with the parties and the notary.

ART. III. The marriage contract may contain any agreement or convention which the contracting parties may agree upon and which is not opposed to the nature of the contract nor to law.

ART. IV. If one of the contracting parties is less than 20 years of age, the marriage can be contracted with notice to the father, the mother, or the guardian, according to the circumstances, and if these oppose the celebration of the marriage, the judge of the district, with knowledge of the facts, will decide the question.

ART. V. The following reason will prevent marriage: Consanguinity in the direct line. In the collateral, brother and sister can not marry; it is null by the relationship in said degrees, or by being contracted by fraud or by force. It is completely dissolved for incompatibility by a chronic and contagious disease, or one which will cause impotency, and by adultery; moral or physical ill treatment of the wife gives to the wife the right to demand from the husband, when they live apart, to bear the expenses of the marriage; if the woman commits adultery she loses this right.

ART. VI. In case of separation, the male children of 14 years of age and upward and female children of 12 and upward may elect between their parents as to residence. Those less than 3 years of age must remain with the mother. Those who have not yet reached the age of puberty, but are older than 3 years, remain with the parent who has not given the motive for the separation. This is in case that the separation is caused by some guilt. If it occurs on account of sickness, the children will remain with the one who did not desire the separation. If the separation is on account of incompatibility, the parents must agree as to this point. On reaching the age of 3 years, the children who until then have been with the mother, the question of their custody will be governed by the other provisions of this article.

When the male reaches the age of 14 and the female of 12, whatever may have been their previous residence, they may alter it.

ART. VII. Marriage being once dissolved, the parties may remarry, but the woman shall not do so until twelve months have elapsed, in order to avoid confusion of paternity.

ART. VIII. Civil marriage is placed on an equal footing, as to duty and effects, with that recognized by our former legislation, and celebrated by the intervention of the church.

ART. IX. The promise of marriage does not have any other result than that of the payment of the penalty, which must be stipulated by the contracting party. If no penalty is stipulated, no duty of payment is incurred.

ART. X. The seduction of a female, whether she be a minor or not, obliges the seductor to marry the seduced or to pay a penalty in proportion to the fortune of both, which the judge of the district must determine.

Country and liberty.

PROVIDENCIA, *September 25, 1895.*

GARCIA CANIZARES.
Secretary of the Interior:

Let the foregoing be promulgated in the legal form, it having my sanction.

Providencia, September 25, 1895.

SALVADOR CISNEROS BETANCOURT,
President.

CIVIL MARRIAGE.

Instructions which must be observed by the prefects of the Republic of Cuba in the celebration of civil marriage, exercising the function which is given them by the provisional law passed by the Government Council on the 25th of September, 1895.

ARTICLE I. The prefect of the residence of the wife, who is the only one competent to celebrate the marriage, will demand of the parties a copy of their certificate of birth, so that they can prove their marriageable age, which of the male is 18 years and of the female 14 years.

ART. II. If either of the contracting parties should not have that document, by the omission, suppression, or burning of the register, or for any other cause, this credential may be substituted by a certificate of the authorities as to the nationality or residence, in which certificate the cause of the absence of the original certificate shall be stated (after previous investigation and on information received as to its omission) the names of the parents, their civil status, and the year and month of the birth of the contracting parties.

ART. III. If it appears that the contracting parties are over 20 years of age the prefect will proceed to the celebration of the civil marriage without further requisite than to give it publicity, for which purpose he shall affix notices in the most frequented places of the prefecture.

ART. IV. But if either of the parties is less than 20 years of age the contract must not only be made public, as previously stated, but notice given to the father, the mother, or the guardian, so that if these oppose the marriage it may be suspended until, with a full knowledge of the facts, the question be decided by the judge, who must investigate, the prefect fixing a time for the opposing parties to establish and justify their position, which must not be longer than eight days.

ART. V. In all cases the prefect will demand from the contracting party their assurance of the consent of each other, or at least that of the bride, and of her ability to enter into the matrimonial contract, which requisite the prefect may omit if he himself possesses knowledge of the circumstances.

ART. VI. If there are no disabilities to the marriage the prefect will register in a book entitled Book of Civil Marriages Contracted in the Prefecture ———, designating on the first page the year and making an index at the end in alphabetical order.

ART. VII. The contract will be formulated in the following terms:

"Formula of the marriage of persons of 20 years and upward:

"In the prefecture of ——— on the ——— day of 189—, before me, the prefect ———, and before me, the undersigned secretary, there appeared ——— and ———, of 20 years and upward, the former born and resident of ———, son of (here the names of parents), and the latter born and resident of the prefecture ———, daughter (here the names of parents), who are known to the prefect and to myself, the secretary, or who, unknown, were presented to M. and P., who act as witnesses, who affirm that that they know them, or at least that they know her, and they so declare and affirm."

"The contracting parties thereupon say, in the presence of these witnesses and those to this instrument, A and B, called for that purpose, that of their own free will, and without any violence, they promised to marry civilly, which marriage they now celebrate, and they agree to live in complete harmony and conjugal union, and never to separate unless because of incompatibility, or for any of the other reasons allowed by law, declaring that this marriage is for the welfare and honor of both, and for their offspring, and as the laws and customs of good government require (here any agreement made between the contracting parties shall be inserted, besides the nuptial contract), and the register will thus end; and in order that this marriage shall be known, and always and in all cases have its legal force, the prefect orders the minutes of this contract to be drawn for that said terms, signing with the contracting parties, and the said witnesses (if they can write, and if they can not others, at their request, may do so), to all of which I, the secretary, certify."

FORMULA FOR THE MARRIAGE OF THOSE LESS THAN TWENTY YEARS OF AGE.

The beginning will be as in the above formula, adding that the contracting parties being minors, the father, mother, or guardian appeared, who declared their assent and signed (if they can write) the register, and if not, a person of their confidence whom they may select. The declaration as to register will be the same as in the preceding formula.

FORMULA OF CIVIL MARRIAGE TO WHICH THERE IS OPPOSITION.

After the preamble similar to the first formula in the register is declared, that the father, mother, or guardian whosoever has interposed before the competent authority, has dissented, declares the contract not to be proper, as he explains in the following declaration. As to the rest, the register will be as in the first formula to its conclusion.

But in case the father, mother, or guardian do not make any opposition, it shall be so declared in the register that the time fixed having passed and the person having the right to exercise this right having failed to do so, the marriage has been consummated.

NOTE.—Of every marriage there will be formed a file consisting of the copy of the register of birth, of the cedula, of the declaration of the opposition of father, mother, or guardian, and of the decree in which it shall be declared proper, or it is ordered that the marriage shall take place because they have not exercised that right, or because the party opposing has not complied with the law. This file shall be kept for future use.

Country and liberty.

GARCIA CANIZARES,
Secretary of the Interior.

PROVIDENCIA, <i>September 25, 1895.</i>

Let the foregoing be promulgated in its legal form, as I sanction the foregoing law in all its parts.

SALVADOR CISNEROS BETANCOURT,
President.

PROVIDENCIA, <i>September 25, 1895.</i>

EXTRACT OF THE SESSIONS.

[Republic of Cuba, Provisional Government, secretary of the council—José Clemente Vivanco, secretary of the Government Council and chancellor of the Republic.]

I certify that among the resolutions passed by this council, according to the minute book of the sessions, the following are to be found:

To give two months' time to the chiefs and officers of the last revolution to join the new army of liberation, so as to have their ranks recognized, and four months' time to those in foreign countries to place themselves in communication with the delegates. To allow the Cuban emigrants individual freedom in the nature of their contributions for the revolution. To permit the export of wooden blocks on payment of $5 in gold as tax for each piece. To prohibit absolutely the export of corn and all forage; of cattle, pigs, horses; without allowing anything to enter the towns without the previous payment of taxes.

To prohibit absolutely also the introduction in the towns of all kinds of fruits and articles of commerce which may favor the said towns and indirectly the Government which we are fighting.

San Andres de la Rioja, October 9, 1895.

(Signed)
JOSÉ CLEMENTE VIVANCO,
Secretary of the Council.

———

REGULATIONS FOR THE SERVICE OF COMMUNICATIONS.

ARTICLE 1. The secretary of the interior will be the postmaster-general of the whole island, and the civil governor the chief of his territory.

ART. 2. The postal service is established between the prefectures of the Republic and between the towns and prefectures near by.

ART. 3. In order to organize the postal service, an inspector will be named for each district; as many chiefs as there are post-offices, and as many couriers and auxiliaries as are necessary for each one.

ART. 4. The inspector is the superior chief in his district of the postal service; under his direction will be the postmasters, couriers, and auxiliaries. He shall organize the service by placing the post-offices in the most convenient places, so that the service shall be carried out with the greatest ease and with the greatest rapidity. He will employ the number of employees that are necessary. He will ask for their resignations whenever there is any justifiable cause for it. He will see that every one shall fulfill his duties, and shall name the hours when the couriers shall depart. He shall correct all defects that come under his notice, propose all modifications which he may think will give a better service, and give an account of all extraordinary services which his subalterns may render in order that they should be registered and rewarded.

ART. 5. The chiefs will reside in the post-office, from which they can not be absent during the appointed hours, and they are to act whenever possible as auxiliaries to the prefect's office. They will receive official and private correspondence, sign receipts for that delivered by mail carriers, setting down the hour of delivery, and they will deliver, under receipt in which they will also put down the time of departure, to the outgoing postman the mail matter in their hands, giving with it a memorandum stating the name of mail carried and the time of departure. They will also see that the post-offices are well attended and have in them the necessary number of horses required for the service, unless in cases where the service is carried on foot. They will report to the inspector the defects they may observe in the service, without forgetting the importance of their position.

ART. 6. The mail carriers will collect daily at the appointed hours, along the route marked out, without delaying on the way nor hurrying their horses except in urgent cases that will be pointed out by the chief. They will have a receipt for the correspondence delivered to them, and will receive in exchange for the receipt a signed memorandum stating what mail they carry; which memorandum they will present to the chief of postal department, so that he may sign it and declare that he has received them, and, after complying with this requisite, change it for a receipt which he will leave in the office of departure.

A great service will be done by the couriers, and for that reason men of known honesty and valor shall be chosen, who are capable of appreciating the service they render their country.

ART. 7. A mail service will be organized in every city occupied by the enemy, and will consist of as many chiefs and carriers as may be considered necessary.

ART. 8. The inspectors of mails will be the immediate superior officer of the service in the town of his residence, and will have under his command the postmasters and mail carriers, and they will exercise their functions in the same manner as the coast inspectors. They will have special care in the selection of employees and in keeping all possible secrecy to elude the vigilance of the enemy.

ART. 9. The postmasters will be considered as the chiefs of mail carriers and will act with the carriers, as the carriers with the drivers, always giving an account of any extra services rendered.

ART. 10. The mail carriers will have charge of receiving from the postmasters the mail matter and carry it out of the cities for delivery to the office of the nearest prefect. They will give and ask for receipts as the drivers and like these must be honest men, sharp and brave enough with courage to overcome the difficulties that may arise in the performance of their important and dangerous mission and worthy to occupy these positions of trust in which they can lend such valuable services to the sacred cause every Cuban is bound to defend.

ART. 11. The inspectors and postmasters will keep a book to record the appointments of employees and the services rendered by them and will make up their archives with this book and circulars, communications, and official documents that they receive on the copies of those they may have to transmit.

Country and liberty, September, 1895.

Dr. SANITAGO GARCIA CANIZARES,
Secretary of the Interior.

In conformity with the preceding regulations I sanction them in every part; and that it may govern and produce its corresponding effects have it published in the legal form.

Country and liberty.

Residence of the Executive in Limones, the 6th day of October, 1895.

SALVADOR CISNEROS, *President.*

LAW FOR THE ORGANIZATION OF THE PUBLIC TREASURY.

ARTICLE I. All property of whatever description situated in the territory of the Republic comes under the jurisdiction of the secretary of the treasury; therefore this department shall take charge of articles of whatever description brought to this island by expeditions from abroad; this department also has the faculty of raising public loans and general taxes.

ART. II. The secretary of the treasury will be the superior chief of his department throughout the Island of Cuba, and through him the subaltern officers will receive the orders given by the council. The duties of the secretary will be to determine, on information of the collectors, the taxes which shall be paid in each state and the form in which they shall be collected, to nominate the employees of his department and to discharge them for justifiable cause. He will deliver to the chiefs of corps and civil governors the articles which he receives from abroad; he will give a receipt for the articles or sums of money which from any source may be collected by the public treasury. He may trade with the merchandise belonging to the Republic; he may lease or sell whatever be convenient and will present an account every three months to the council of the funds belonging to the Republic.

ART. III. To facilitate the work of the treasury a chief of department will be appointed who will act as general comptroller, and in each State a collector and a secretary of the administration of the treasury, and for each district a delegate.

ART. IV. The chief of the department, or general comptroller, will have charge of the archives of the department, will keep the books in due form, and will take part in all the collections and disbursements which may occur.

ART. V. The collector will represent in each State the secretary of the treasury, he will give information as to the taxable property in his State, he will dictate the necessary measures to carry out the general orders communicated to him by the secretary of the treasury, he will collect by means of agents the taxes fixed upon, and he will send to the department as soon as possible the funds collected; nevertheless he may deliver the amounts he may deem necessary to the chiefs of the different army corps, who will give a receipt for them and justify their expenditure. The collectors will monthly send to the department a statement of their operation.

ART. VI. The secretary of the administration of the treasury will keep the archives of his respective State, will keep the books in due form, and will take part in the operations of the collector.

ART. VII. The delegates or agents will be the collectors of taxes in each distric, and the commissioners will see that the orders of the collectors of the State are carried out. They may appoint auxiliaries whenever necessary, and are authorized to demand the aid of the prefects and armed forces for the better fulfillment of their commissions.

Country and liberty.

Canaster, October 16, 1895.

SEVERO PINA,
Secretary of the Treasury.

In conformity with the previous law, I sanction it in all its parts. Let it be promulgated in legal form.

Country and liberty, October 18, 1885.

MANGOS DE BARAGUA.

SALVADOR CISNEROS BETANCOURT,
President.

INSTRUCTIONS TO THE OFFICERS OF THE DEPARTMENT OF THE TREASURY OF THE REPUBLIC OF CUBA.

ARTICLE I. According to article 18 of the constitution and the decree of the general in chief of the 20th of September last, the military chiefs shall give the necessary aid to the officers of the treasury for the better fulfillment of their duties

ART. II. With the aid of the armed forces, they will proceed to the destruction of those plantations, whatever be their nationality, which will refuse to pay the taxes decreed by the Government of the Republic.

ART. III. As a basis for the rate of tax, the production of the plantations shall serve as well as the price of their products, taking into consideration the expense of transportation.

ART. IV. The amount of the tax will be paid in advance in gold or in drafts on New York, Paris, or London in the form agreed upon.

ART. V. All kinds of traffic with the enemy is absolutely prohibited, only the following articles and products are allowed to be exported:

Coffee and cocoa, $4 per hundredweight.

Wood in blocks, $8 per thousand feet or $3 apiece, as will best suit the interests of the Republic and the functionary authorizing the exportation.

Guana (a textile palm), $4 per hundredweight.

Wax, $4 per hundredweight.

Fattened steers, $3 per head.

Cheese, $2 per hundredweight.

In regard to mines, tobacco, and plantains for exportation, it is left to the judgment of the collector of the treasury.

ART. VI. The exportation of wood or guana (the latter until December 6) will only be permitted when worked or packed by individuals who are in the confidence of our authorities.

ART. VII. The exportation of cattle will only be allowed when, in the judgment of the authority, they run imminent risk of falling into the hands of the enemy.

ART. VIII. The collector of the treasury of each State may suspend, temporarily, the exportation of the products referred to in Article V, immediately giving an account of it to the secretary of the treasury for final adjudgment.

Sabanilla del Contra Maestre, October 24, 1895.

SEVERO PINA,
Secretary of the Treasury.

In conformity with the previous law, I sanction it in all its parts. Let it be promulgated in legal form.

Sabanilla, October 25, 1895.

SALVADOR CISNEROS BETANCOURT,
President.

EXTRACT OF THE SESSIONS OF THE GOVERNMENT COUNCIL, REPUBLIC OF CUBA.

Secretary of the Government José Clemente Vivanco, secretary of the Government Council and chancellor of the Republic, I certify that in the minute books of the sessions celebrated by this council the following resolutions are found:

SEPTEMBER 19, 1895.

To appoint a secretary of the Government and chancellor of the Republic, José Clemente Vivanco. To send the appointments of general in chief, lieutenant-general, and delegate plenipotentiary abroad to Maj. Gen. Maximo Gomez, Maj. Gen. Antonio Maceo, and Tomas Estrada Palma, respectively.

To appoint as civil governor of Camaguey, Dr. Oscar Primelles, and of Oriente, Rafael Manduley.

To complete the system of the division of the territory of the island into zones, and that the subsecretary of war, in the absence of the secretary, agree with the general in chief as to the organization of the army of liberation.

SEPTEMBER 20, 1895.

To give two months' time to the chief and officers of the past revolution to join the newly organized army of liberation, for the recognition of their grades, and four months' time to those outside of the island. That each secretary of state may name a chief of his department. To appoint as director of the treasury in Oriente Diego Palacios, and in Camaguey, Col. Lope Recio Loynaz. That the secretary communicate with the general in chief so the latter may indorse the authorities, passes, and orders given by the Government and require all the forces of the army of liberation to respect and obey them.

To ask the general in chief for Capts. Francisco Garcia, Manuel Merrero, and Ensign Enrique Boza, as their services are needed by the Government. That the Cuban emigrations shall be at liberty as to the manner of contributing to the revolution.

To ask from abroad a copy of all the decrees passed by the government of the last revolution, and to order that in conformity with the minutes sent from here all documents shall be printed emanating from the Government as well as the constitution passed by the constituent assembly which shall be placed in our archives.

SEPTEMBER 24, 1895.

To publish a circular of the secretary of the interior, addressed to the prefects, subprefects, and other functionaries of civil order, recommending them to fulfill their respective duties.

To approve the order given by the general in chief as to the respect due peaceful families and their interests, excepting in cases of military necessity or on account of manifest or suspected treachery, and that the secretary of the interior address such communication to the civil governors advising them of this resolution.

To appoint chief of postal service for the eastern and western district of Camaguey, Manuel Manero, and Francisco Garcia, respectively, and to confirm the appointments of prefects temporarily made by the general in chief.

To ask the general in chief to order all the chiefs of army corps to send to the secretary of war a detailed account of the chiefs and officers under his orders, their record of service, the positions which they occupy, and their respective abilities.

To communicate to Maj. Gen. Carlos Roloff that his aides, Francisco Diaz Silveira and Orencio Nodarse remain with this Government.

SEPTEMBER 25, 1895.

To permit the export of wood in blocks after the payment of $5 in gold for each block. To absolutely prohibit the sale of corn and all kinds of forage, cows, oxen, and horses, permitting only other animals to be taken within a radius of 6 leagues from the towns on a payment of the tax.

That through the secretary of the treasury a detailed statement of the tax-paying property shall be sent to the prefects and military chiefs.

To approve the provisional law of civil marriage passed June 4, 1869, by the Chamber of Representatives of the past revolution and to put it in force on motion of the secretary of the interior.

To approve and enforce the instructions as to said law, which were passed June 21, 1869, by the said chamber.

To confirm the appointment of inspectors of coasts and coast guards made previously by the general in chief.

OCTOBER 5, 1895.

That each secretary of state shall present to the council such projects of laws and regulations as shall be in force in their respective departments, and that the secretary of foreign relations, together with the subsecretary, the acting secretary of war, shall draw a project of criminal procedure for deliberation and approval by the council.

OCTOBER 6, 1895.

To absolutely prohibit the introduction in the towns of all articles of commerce which, favoring trade indirectly, aid the enemy's Government, and to confirm the appointment of the inspector of shops and prefectures in the district of Tunas to Citizen Luis Marti, provisionally given by the general in chief of the third division José M. Capote, on September 17, 1895.

OCTOBER 16, 1895.

That the secretary of the Government shall collect all the laws, rules, decrees, and all other orders of this council and an extract of the resolutions for publication in book form for an edition of 500 copies.

To approve the project of the law for the organization of the public treasury presented by the secretary of the treasury.

To approve the law for the civil government and administration of the Republic, presented by the secretary of the interior.

OCTOBER 21, 1895.

To send a communication to the chiefs of army corps; to send the secretary of the treasury a detailed account of all the contracts made by them since the beginning of the war, in order that in conformity with article 21 of the constitution they be approved.

To give military consideration to all civil functionaries, appointing for this purpose a commission composed of the secretary of the interior and the subsecretary of war, so that they may present a report as to the rules to be followed in this behalf.

OCTOBER 24, 1895.

To approve the project as to instructions of the officers of the public treasury presented by the secretary of the treasury.

To approve the report as to the military considerations to be enjoyed by the civil functionaries, presented by the secretary of the interior and the subsecretary of war, commissioned for this purpose at the last session, which is as follows:

The president of the Republic, that of general in chief of the army; the vice-president, and the secretaries of state, of major-generals.

The secretary of the council and chancellor, brigadier-general; the chiefs of departments of states, civil governors and collectors of the treasury, colonels; the lieutenant-governor, delegate of the treasury and the secretary of administration, of the treasury, majors; the prefects, the inspectors of shops, of coast and communication, that of captains; the subprefects, and ensigns.

All these considerations shall be enjoyed by them unless they have higher rank.

OCTOBER 25, 1895.

The following decree was approved:

ARTICLE I. No one can be punished by death, or by imprisonment or reprimand, without having been previously judged by court-martial.

ART. II. The factories, barns, houses, fruit trees, and useful wood trees will be respected by all the citizens of the Republic.

ART. III. Housebreaking and unjustifiable raids will be severely punished.

ART. IV. No citizen can be dispossessed from the house he occupies without justifiable motive.

ART. V. The forces on the march, detachments, or commissions will not occupy inhabited houses without the consent of their owners, unless the exigencies of the war require it or in extraordinary cases, when it will be justified by the officer who orders it.

And for the publication thereof in accordance with the resolution of the 16th instant, I publish the present compilation, which is a true copy of the originals, on file in the archives of my secretaryship.

Country and liberty.

Sabanilla, October 25, 1895.

JOSÉ CLEMENTE VIVANCO,
Secretary of the Council.

There will soon be published the laws of organization and military ordinances drafted by the general in chief and approved by the council, which shall be joined to the present compilation, C.

[COAT OF ARMS OF CUBAN REPUBLIC.]

In the name of the Republic of Cuba by delegation of the Cuban people in arms. The constituent assembly resolved by acclamation on this day to confer on Tomas Estrada Palma, the diplomatic representative and agent abroad, the title of delegate plenipotentiary of the Republic of Cuba.

In witness whereof we have affixed our signatures in Jimaguayu on the 18th of September, 1895.

Salvador Cesneros, B., President; Rafael Manduley, Vice-President; Enrique Loinaz del Castillo, Severo Pina, Fermin Valdes Dominguez, Rafael Perez Morales, Raimundo Sanchez, J. D. Castillo, Pedro Pinan de Villegas, Pedro Aguilera, Marcos Padilla, Rafael M. Portuondo, Dr. Santiago Garcia Canizares; Lope Recio, L.; Orencio Nodarse, secretary; Franco Diaz Silveira, Enrique Cespedes, Mariano Sanchez Vaillant, F. Lopez Leiva, secretary; José Clemente Vivanco, secretary.

D.

ARMY HEADQUARTERS AT CUMANAYAGUA.

Mr. ALFREDO REGO.

MY DEAR SIR: I had the pleasure to receive your polite note. I see by it the generosity of your heart, and I thank you, in the name of my superior officers, to whom I will communicate your humanitarian act.

I send the committee desired to bring back the prisoners. It takes this letter to you and is composed of Benito Mesa and Telesforo Ramirez. I beg you to give them the necessary aid, promising you that your men will be respected by this garrison.

Yours, truly,

(Signed.) JOSÉ BRETONES, *Lieutenant.*

APPENDIX No. 4.

PRESIDENT'S MESSAGE.

The insurrection in Cuba still continues with all its perplexities. It is difficult to perceive that any progress has thus far been made toward the pacification of the island or that the situation of affairs as depicted in my last annual message has in the least improved. If Spain still holds Habana and the seaports and all the considerable towns, the insurgents still roam at will over at least two-thirds of the inland country. If the determination of Spain to put down the insurrection seems but to strengthen with the lapse of time, and is evinced by her unhesitating devotion of largely increased military and naval forces to the task, there is much reason to believe that the insurgents have gained in point of numbers, and character, and resources, and are none the less inflexible in their resolve not to succumb, without practically securing the great objects for which they took up arms. If Spain has not yet reestablished her authority, neither have the insurgents yet made good their title to be regarded as an independent state. Indeed, as the contest has gone on, the pretense that civil government exists on the island, except so far as Spain is able to maintain it, has been practically abandoned. Spain does keep on foot such a government, more or less imperfectly, in the large towns and their immediate suburbs. But, that exception being made, the entire country is either given over to anarchy or is subject to the military occupation of one or the other party. It is reported, indeed, on reliable authority that at the demand of the commander in chief of the insurgent army the putative Cuban government has now given up all attempt to exercise its functions, leaving that government confessedly (what there is the best reason for supposing it always to have been in fact) a government merely on paper.

Were the Spanish armies able to meet their antagonists in the open, or in pitched battle, prompt and decisive results might be looked for, and the immense superiority of the Spanish forces in numbers, discipline, and equipment could hardly fail to tell greatly to their advantage. But they are called upon to face a foe that shuns general engagements, that can choose and does choose its own ground, that from the nature of the country is visible or invisible at pleasure, and that fights only from ambuscade and when all the advantages of position and numbers are on its side. In a country where all that is indispensable to life in the way of food, clothing, and shelter is so easily obtainable, especially by those born and bred on the soil, it is obvious that there is hardly a limit to the time during which hostilities of this sort may be prolonged. Meanwhile, as in all cases of protracted civil strife, the passions of the combatants grow more and more inflamed and excesses on both sides become more frequent and more deplorable. They are also participated in by bands of marauders, who, now in the name of one party and now in the name of the other, as may best suit the occasion, harry the country at will and plunder its wretched inhabitants for their own advantage. Such a condition of things would inevitably entail immense destruction of property, even if it were the policy of both parties to prevent it as far as practicable. But while such seemed to be the original policy of the Spanish Government, it has now apparently abandoned it and is acting upon the same theory as the insurgents, namely, that the exigencies of the contest require the wholesale annihilation of property, that it may not prove of use and advantage to the enemy.

It is to the same end that, in pursuance of general orders, Spanish garrisons are now being withdrawn from plantations and the rural population required to concentrate itself in the towns. The sure result would seem to be that the industrial value of the island is fast diminishing, and that unless there is a speedy and radical change in existing conditions it will soon disappear altogether. That value consists very largely, of course, in its capacity to produce sugar—a capacity already much reduced by the interruptions to tillage which have taken place during the last two years. It is reliably asserted that should these interruptions continue during the current year, and practically extend, as is now threatened, to the entire sugar-producing territory of the island, so much time and so much money will be required to restore the land to its normal productiveness that it is extremely doubtful if capital can be induced to even make the attempt.

The spectacle of the utter ruin of an adjoining country, by nature one of the most fertile and charming on the globe, would engage the serious attention of the Government and people of the United States in any circumstances. In point of fact, they have a concern with it which is by no means of a wholly sentimental or philanthropic character. It lies so near to us as to be hardly separated from our territory. Our actual pecuniary interest in it is second only to that of the people and Government of Spain. It is reasonably estimated that at least from $30,000,000 to $50,000,000 of American capital are invested in plantations and in railroad, mining, and other business enterprises on the island. The volume of trade between the United States and Cuba, which in 1889 amounted to about $64,000,000, rose in 1893 to about $103,000,000, and in 1894, the year before the present insurrection broke out, amounted to nearly $96,000,000. Besides this large pecuniary stake in the fortunes of Cuba, the United States finds itself inextricably involved in the present contest in other ways both vexatious and costly.

Many Cubans reside in this country and indirectly promote the insurrection through the press, by public meetings, by the purchase and shipment of arms, by the raising of funds, and by other means, which the spirit of our institutions and the tenor of our laws do not permit to be made the subject of criminal prosecutions. Some of them, though Cubans at heart and in all their feelings and interests, have taken out papers as naturalized citizens of the United States, a proceeding resorted to with a view to possible protection by this Government, and not unnaturally regarded with much indignation by the country of their origin. The insurgents are undoubtedly encouraged and supported by the widespread sympathy the people of this country always and instinctively feel for every struggle for better and freer government, and which, in the case of the more adventurous and restless elements of our population, leads in only too many instances to active and personal participation in the contest. The result is that this Government is constantly called upon to protect American citizens, to claim damages for injuries to persons and property, now estimated at many millions of dollars, and to ask explanations and apologies for the acts of Spanish officials whose zeal for the repression of the rebellion sometimes blinds them to the immunities belonging to the unoffending citizens of a friendly power. It follows from the same causes that the United States is compelled to actively police a long line of seacoast against unlawful expeditions, the escape of which the utmost vigilance will not always suffice to prevent.

These inevitable entanglements of the United States with the rebellion in Cuba, the large American property interests affected, and considerations of philanthropy and humanity in general, have led to a vehement demand in various quarters for some sort of positive intervention on the part of the United States. It was at first proposed that belligerent rights should be accorded to the insurgents—a proposition no longer urged because untimely and in practical operation clearly perilous and injurious to our own interests. It has since been and is now sometimes contended that the independence of the insurgents should be recognized. But imperfect and restricted as the Spanish government of the island may be, no other exists there—unless the will of the military officer in temporary command of a particular district can be dignified as a species of government. It is now also suggested that the United States should buy the island—a suggestion possibly worthy of consideration if there were any evidence of a desire or willingness on the part of Spain to entertain such a proposal. It is urged, finally, that, all other methods failing, the existing internecine strife in Cuba should be terminated by our intervention, even at the cost of a war between the United States and Spain—a war which its advocates confidently prophesy could be neither large in its proportions nor doubtful in its issue.

The correctness of this forecast need be neither affirmed nor denied. The United States has nevertheless a character to maintain as a nation, which plainly dictates that right and not might should be the rule of its conduct. Further, though the United States is not a nation to which peace is a necessity, it is in truth the most pacific of powers, and desires nothing so much as to live in amity with all the world. Its own ample and diversified domains satisfy all possible longings for territory, preclude all dreams of conquest, and prevent any casting of covetous eyes upon neighboring regions, however attractive. That our conduct toward Spain and her dominions has constituted no exception to this national disposition is made manifest by the course of our Government, not only thus far during the present insurrection, but during the ten years that followed the rising at Yara in 1868. No other great power, it may safely be said, under circumstances of similar perplexity, would have manifested the same restraint and the same patient endurance. It may also be said that this persistent attitude of the United States toward Spain in connection with Cuba unquestionably evinces no slight respect and regard for Spain on the part of the American people. They in truth do not forget her connection with the discovery of the Western Hemisphere, nor do they underestimate the great qualities of the Spanish people, nor fail to fully recognize their splendid patriotism and their chivalrous devotion to the national honor.

They view with wonder and admiration the cheerful resolution with which vast bodies of men are sent across thousands of miles of ocean, and an enormous debt accumulated, that the costly possession of the Gem of the Antilles may still hold its place in the Spanish Crown. And yet neither the Government nor the people of the United States have shut their eyes to the course of events in Cuba, or have failed to realize the existence of conceded grievances, which have led to the present revolt from the authority of Spain—grievances recognized by the Queen Regent and by the Cortes, voiced by the most patriotic and enlightened of Spanish statesmen without regard to party, and demonstrated by reforms proposed by the executive and approved by the legislative branch of the Spanish Government. It is in the assumed temper and disposition of the Spanish Government to remedy these grievances, fortified by indications of influential public opinion in Spain, that this Government has hoped to discover the most promising and effective means of composing the present strife with honor and advantage to Spain and with the achievement of all the reasonable objects of the insurrection.

It would seem that if Spain should offer to Cuba genuine autonomy—a measure of home rule which, while preserving the sovereignty of Spain, would satisfy all rational requirements of her Spanish subjects—there should be no just reason why the pacification of the island might not be effected on that basis. Such a result would appear to be in the true interest of all concerned. It would at once stop the conflict which is now consuming the resources of the island and making it worthless for whichever party may ultimately prevail. It would keep intact the possessions of Spain without touching her honor, which will be consulted rather than impugned by the adequate redress of admitted grievances. It would put the prosperity of the island and the fortunes of its inhabitants within their own control, without severing the natural and ancient ties which bind them to the mother country, and would yet enable them to test their capacity for self-government under the most favorable conditions. It has been objected on the one side that Spain should not promise autonomy until her insurgent subjects lay down their arms; on the other side, that promised autonomy, however liberal, is insufficient, because without assurance of the promise being fulfilled.

But the reasonableness of a requirement by Spain of unconditional surrender on the part of the insurgent Cubans before their autonomy is conceded is not altogether apparent. It ignores important features of the situation—the stability two years' duration has given to the insurrection; the feasibilty of its indefinite prolongation in the nature of things, and, as shown by past experience, the utter and imminent ruin of the island unless the present strife is speedily composed; above all, the rank abuses which all parties in Spain, all branches of her Government, and all her leading public men concede to exist and profess a desire to remove. Facing such circumstances, to withhold the proffer of needed reforms until the parties demanding them put themselves at mercy by throwing down their arms, has the appearance of neglecting the gravest of perils and inviting suspicion as to the sincerity of any professed willingness to grant reforms. The objection on behalf of the insurgents, that promised reforms can not be relied upon, must of course be considered, though we have no right to assume, and no reason for assuming, that anything Spain undertakes to do for the relief of Cuba will not be done according to both the spirit and the letter of the undertaking.

Nevertheless, realizing that suspicions and precautions on the part of the weaker of two combatants are always natural and not always unjustifiable—being sincerely desirous in the interest of both, as well as on its own account, that the Cuban problem should be solved with the least possible delay—it was intimated by this Government to the Government of Spain some months ago that if a satisfactory measure of home rule were tendered the Cuban insurgents, and would be accepted by them upon a guaranty of its execution, the United States would endeavor to find a way not objectionable to Spain of furnishing such guaranty. While no definite response to this intimation has yet been received from the Spanish Government, it is believed to be not altogether unwelcome, while, as already suggested, no reason is perceived why it should not be approved by the insurgents. Neither party can fail to see the importance of early action, and both must realize that to prolong the present state of things for even a short period will add enormously to the time and labor and expenditure necessary to bring about the industrial recuperation of the island. It is therefore fervently hoped on all grounds that earnest efforts for healing the breach between Spain and the insurgent Cubans, upon the lines above indicated, may be at once inaugurated and pushed to an immediate and successful issue. The friendly offices of the United States, either in the manner above outlined or in any other way consistent with our Constitution and laws, will always be at the disposal of either party.

Whatever circumstances may arise, our policy and our interests would constrain us to object to the acquisition of the island or an interference with its control by any other power.

It should be added that it can not be reasonably assumed that the hitherto expectant attitude of the United States will be indefinitely maintained. While we are anxious to accord all due respect to the sovereignty of Spain, we can not view the pending conflict in all its features and properly apprehend our inevitably close relations to it, and its possible results, without considering that by the course of events we may be drawn into such an unusual and unprecedented condition as will fix a limit to our patient waiting for Spain to end the contest, either alone and in her own way, or with our friendly cooperation.

When the inability of Spain to deal successfully with the insurrection has become manifest, and it is demonstrated that her sovereignty is extinct in Cuba for all purposes of its rightful existence, and when a hopeless struggle for its reestablishment has degenerated into a strife which means nothing more than the useless sacrifice of human life and the utter destruction of the very subject-matter of the conflict, a situation will be presented in which our obligations to the sovereignty of Spain will be superseded by higher obligations, which we can hardly hesitate to recognize and discharge. Deferring the choice of ways and methods until the time for action arrives, we should make them depend upon the precise conditions then existing; and they should not be determined upon without giving careful heed to every consideration involving our honor and interest, or the international duty we owe to Spain. Until we face the contingencies suggested, or the situation is by other incidents imperatively changed, we should continue in the line of conduct heretofore pursued, thus in all circumstances exhibiting our obedience to the requirements of public law and our regard for the duty enjoined upon us by the position we occupy in the family of nations.

A contemplation of emergencies that may arise should plainly lead us to avoid their creation, either through a careless disregard of present duty or even an undue stimulation and ill-timed expression of feeling. But I have deemed it not amiss to remind the Congress that a time may arrive when a correct policy and care for our interests, as well as a regard for the interests of other nations and their citizens, joined by considerations of humanity and a desire to see a rich and fertile country, intimately related to us, saved from complete devastation, will constrain our Government to such action as will subserve the interests thus involved and at the same time promise to Cuba and its inhabitants an opportunity to enjoy the blessings of peace.

[See pp. 13, 40, 187, 321, and pp. 72, 119, 199, 276, Vol. VI.]

FIFTY-FIFTH CONGRESS, FIRST SESSION.

April 1, 1897.

[Senate Document No. 19.]

Mr. Davis presented the following papers, accompanying the report submitted by Hon. J. D. Cameron, of Pennsylvania, from the Committee on Foreign Relations, United States Senate, December 21, 1896, on the joint resolution (S. R. 163) acknowledging the independence of Cuba.

CIVIL GOVERNMENT OF THE REPUBLIC OF CUBA.

From the very inception of the revolution the Cubans provided for a civil power. The Cuban revolutionary party, which prepared and directed the movement, was a civil organization headed by Jose Marti, most zealous in establishing the paramount influence of the law over the sword. General Gomez then and throughout all the revolution has shown himself desirous that the civil authorities should have the supreme power. When he and Marti landed their first aim was to constitute a provisional government. Gomez, as well as all the other military leaders, recognized Marti as the civil head. After the meeting of Gomez, Maceo, and Marti at Mejorana, on May 4, 1895, a call for the selection of representatives of the Cuban people to form a civil government was made, and Marti and Gomez marched to the central provinces to arrange for this important event. The decrees of that time are always signed by both Gomez and Marti.

The death of Marti postponed for a time the selection of the representatives, but in the beginning of September, 1895, the call previously issued was complied with.

Representatives from each of the provinces of Santiago, Puerto Principe, Santa Clara, and the western part of the island, comprising the provinces of Matanzas and Habana, making twenty in all, were elected to the constitutent assembly, which was to establish a civil government, republican in form.

A complete list of the members of the constituent assembly which met at Jimaguayu, in the Province of Puerto Principe, on the 13th of September, 1895, together with an account of its organization and subsequent action, will be found in Exhibit 1, printed in the Cuban Government printing office, a translation of which appears in Senate Document, marked B.

A constitution of the Republic of Cuba was adopted on the 16th of September, a copy of which will be found in said document, marked B.

On the 18th of September, the following officers of the Government were elected by the constituent assembly in accordance with the terms of the constitution:

President, Salvador Cisneros Betancourt, of Puerto Principe; vice-president, Bartolome Maso, of Manzanillo; secretary of war, Carlos Roloff, of Santa Clara; secretary of the treasury, Severo Pina, of Sancti Spiritus; secretary of the interior, Santiago Garcia Cañizares, of Remedios; secretary of foreign relations, Rafael M. Portuondo, of Santiago de Cuba; subsecretary of war, Mario Menocal, of Matanzas; subsecretary of the treasury, Joaquin Castillo, of Santiago de Cuba; subsecretary of the interior, Carlos Dubois, of Baracoa; subsecretary of foreign relations, Fermin Valdez Dominguez, of Haoana.

The installation of these officers duly followed. The election of the general in chief and the second in command, who is to bear the title of lieutenant-general, was then had, and resulted in the unanimous election of Maximo Gomez and Antonio Maceo, respectively.

On the same day the constituent assembly elected by acclamation as delegate plenipotentiary and general agent abroad of the Cuban Republic, Tomas Estrada Palma. The credentials issued to him appear in said Senate document, marked C.

Exhibit 1a is a copy of El Cubano Libre, dated May 10, 1896, and contains the names of the principal civil authorities of the Republic at that date.

Besides the constitution, Exhibit 1 shows the divisions of the provinces into prefectures, under the supervision of the secretary of the interior, and the duties which devolve in this department are fully set forth in Exhibit B. That these prefectures are found throughout the Republic can be seen from the Spanish official dispatches which sometimes report their capture. In the Spanish newspaper El Imparcial, published at Madrid, dated November 20, 1896, an official telegram from General Ahumada, of November 22, 1896, says: "In operations in Villas (Santa Clara) prefecture destroyed."

Exhibit No. 2. Innumerable instances of the existence of such prefectures throughout Cuba can be presented from official dispatches of the Spanish press. The civil governors discharge their duties in their respective districts and have their subordinates and employees.

Exhibit 2a is a circular of Carlos Manuel de Espedes, governor of Oriente, as to commerce.

Exhibit 3 is an extract from La Republica Cubana of December 3, which publishes an official list of the officers of the civil government of the State of Oriente, the same as the province of Santiago de Cuba, on November 1, 1896, and Exhibit 3a is a circular of the civil governor of the State of Camaguey, which is the same as the Province of Puerto Principe. In the Boletin de la Guerra, official paper of the Republic, published in Puerto Principe, of the 10th of September, 1896, Exhibit 4, under the heading civil governor, an account is given of the resignation of the governor.

In Exhibit No. 1 can also be found the other matters pertaining to the Secretary of the Interior, such as workshops, manufactories, coast inspectors and post-office, and regulations for the said State manufactories, can be seen in Exhibit No. 5, dated July 18, 1896.

An envelope marked Exhibit No. 6, addressed to the civil governor of the State of Oriente, Carlos Mo de Cespedes, shows the seals of the post-offices and the perfect system of posts. It also has an extract of the regulations of the 8th of March, 1896, as to the mail. A translation accompanies said exhibit. A set of stamps has been issued by the Republic.

As to advertisement of dead-letter office, Exhibit 5 has a decree of September 2, 1896, of the civil government of the east. A translation is accompanied, marked Exhibt 6a.

The census is being taken in the different States; a blank for the same printed in the government printing office, shows part of the work in the subprefecture of Cayo Rey, prefecture of La Sierra, district of Mayari, State of Oriente, Exhibit No. 7.

Exhibit No. 8, shows that Ernesto Fonts Sterling was appointed on the 7th of July, 1896, by the Government council, subsecretary of the interior, owing to the absence of Dr. Joaquin Castillo.

Public schools have been established; a primer for spelling and reading is the first book published by the Government. Exhibit No. 9 is the appointment of a public school teacher on May 30, 1896. Exhibit No. 10 is also of the interior department, and contains the instructions to the prefects and rules of the mails.

The laws providing for civil marriage are in Exhibit No. 1.

In this same exhibit the laws for the organization of the public treasury are found, as well as instructions to the officers of that department. A blank used in the reports of the subdelegates of the treasury department is shown in Exhibit No. 11. A circular dated May 9, 1896, given by the secretary, Severo Pina, as to the withdrawal of cattle from the Republic, is published in La Republica of Santa Clara, issue of the 1st of July, makes Exhibit No. 12. Other circulars of the treasury department can be seen under Exhibit No. 12a and 12b.

Taxes are collected, not only in Cuba, but by orders of the secretary of the treasury, payments are made to Benjamin J. Guerra, the treasurer of Cuba, in New York; his books can be seen, as well as the confidential orders of the department. El Imparcial, of Madrid, Spain, of the 25th of November, 1896, publishes a letter of the 10th of September, 1896, to the secretary of the treasury, giving an account of the sums paid to the Republic of Cuba by sugar planters through well-known bankers in New York, as well as other items amounting to hundreds of thousands of dollars. The mere perusal of this letter shows how the property owners recognize the Cuban Republic.

A translation accompanies Exhibit No. 13. In this exhibit there is also the salaries paid the army fixed by the government council.

Exhibit No. 13a. It is a well-known fact that General Weyler has not allowed any grinding of sugar this year, because he claimed that the Cubans were paid by the planters. Exhibit 13b refers to this matter and regulates it. Exhibit No. 13c is the resolution of the Government imposing exportation tax on lumber. The nature of the communications of the Cuban state department does not allow the use of its documents, but it can be affirmed that the secretary of state is in constant communication with the agent of the Republic abroad and its minister plenipotentiary, Tomas Estrada Palma. During a leave of absence the secretary, Rafael M. Portuondo, was in this country and was met by many officials, Senators, and Representatives.

Exhibit No. 14, dated June 29, 1896, shows how Dr. Eusebio Hernandez temporarily substituted him. A few months ago the secretary of foreign relations, together with the President, sent a public appeal to the republics of Spanish America in which they clearly and eloquently laid before the world the rights of Cuba.

The war department has efficiently operated during the year. In the files of the Cubano Libre the military regulations have been published. Exhibit No. 15 shows the appointment of Rafael Manduley on the 21st of May, 1896, in place of Mario Menocal, as subsecretary.

The civil government has been in actual operation since its election. Exhibit No. 1 shows an extract of the sessions of the government council up to October 25, 1895. Exhibit 15a is an extract of the sessions of November and contains the power given to Tomas Estrada Palma as delegate of the Republic. It would be a task indeed to print all the resolutions and decrees it has passed as to the different branches of the Government and general affairs. Exhibit No. 16 shows the laws for the sanitary corps of the Cuban army, drawn by Dr. Sanchez Agramonte, head of the department, and approved by the government council, under date of March 31, 1896. Exhibit No. 17 is a decree as to military rank passed by the government council on the 20th of May, 1896. Exhibit No. 18 in Exhibit No. 4 contains several resolutions passed on the 13th of July, 1896, as to freedom of speech, proposed laws for the judiciary, and the one prohibiting the sugar crop for 1896-97. A translation of the latter accompanies the exhibit. It is to be noted in this last one that it is to be communicated to the general in chief, being a war measure, for its fulfillment. The mere reading of this document proves the subserviency of the military to the civil power of the Republic. On July 13, 1896, President Cisneros issued a manifesto inviting the Spanish to join the revolution. Exhibit 19, on September 18, 1896, on the anniversary of the constitution, President Salvador Cisneros gave a proclamation to celebrate it. Exhibit 19a. And in conclusion we can assert that the supreme military power vested in the general in chief has always upheld the constitution and civil government. Exhibit 20 is the Boletin de la Guerra, an official paper of the 20th of September, 1895, and contains the oath of allegiance to the constitution taken by the general in chief and these proclamations. On the 22d of July, 1896, he published the following circular (Exhibit No. 21):

HEADQUARTERS OF THE ARMY OF LIBERATION.

[Circular.]

This headquarters being informed of the unworthy proceedings of some chiefs and officers of the army with regard to the civil authorities of the Republic, and resolved as it is not to consent in any case nor by any person that the sacred principles of discipline, subordination, and morality of the revolution should be disregarded, but that respect should be rendered to the majesty of its democratic institutions, it reminds all chiefs and officers of the inevitable duty which they have to respect the functionaries of the civil government, according to their rank.

The military authorities are obliged to give the decisive protection of their force to the civil authorities for the better fulfillment of their duties.

The chiefs of the corps, divisions, and brigades will chastise severely all subordinates against whom any complaints may be made of their bad conduct in this respect, they being answerable to this headquarters for their leniency or indifference.

P. y L. Remanganaguas, 22 July, 1896.

The general in chief:

MAXIMO GOMEZ.

PRINTING OFFICE OF EL CUBANO LIBRE.

Exhibit No. 22 proves that the civil government was in the exercise of all its functions when the Cuban army captured the important town of Guaimaro. It is a vote of thanks given to Gen. Calixto Garcia by the Government council.

The last document is dated the 21st day of November, 1896, and is a copy of a military order of Maj. Gen. Francisco Carrillo, commanding the Province of Santa Clara. From it it can be seen that he recognizes a supreme authority—the Government council of the Republic. It is exhibit No. 23. The originals of all these exhibits, in Spanish, are on file in the Committee on Foreign Relations of the Senate.

EXHIBIT No. 1.

[Translation.]

Compilation of the laws, rules, decrees, circulars, and other orders passed by the national council from the 19th of September, 1895, the date on which it commenced to exercise its function.

MANGOS DE BARAGUA.

The national council, in a meeting held on the 16th of October, 1895, resolved that the publication in book form in an edition of 500 copies of all the laws, rules, decrees, and other orders passed by it be printed after being previously approved by the council and sanctioned by its president.

JOSÉ CLEMENTE VIVANCO,
The Secretary of the Council.

CONSTITUENT ASSEMBLY, REPUBLIC OF CUBA.

I, José Clemente Vivanco, secretary of the national council and chancellor of the Republic of Cuba, certify that the representatives of the different army corps, into which the army of liberation is divided, met in constituent assembly on the 13th day of September, 1895, at Jimaguayu, and agreed to have a preliminary session where the character of each representative would be accredited by the respective credential of his appointment. There resulted, after the proper examination by the chairman and secretaries, who were temporarily Citizens Salvador Cisneros Betancourt and Secretaries José Clemente Vivanco and Orencio Nodarse, the following distribution:

Representatives of the first army corps, Citizens Dr. Joaquin Castillo Duany, Mariano Sanchez Vaillant, Rafael M. Portuondo, and Pedro Aguillera.

For the second, Citizens Licentiate Rafael Manduley, Enrique Cespedes, Rafael Perez Morales, and Marcos Padilla.

For the third, Citizens Salvador Cisneros Betancourt, Lopez Recio Loinaz, Enrique Loinaz del Castillo, and Dr. Fermmin Valdes Dominguez.

For the fourth, Licentiate Severo Pina, Dr. Santiago Garcia Canizares, Raimundo Sanchez Valdivia, and Francisco Lopez Leiba.

For the fifth, Dr. Pedro Pinan de Villegas, Licentiate José Clemente Vivanco, Francisco Diaz Silveria, and Orencio Nodarse.

They proceeded to the election of officers for the following session and the following appointments were made: Salvador Cisneros Betancourt, president; Rafael Manduley, vice-president; secretaries, Licentiate José Clemente Vivanco, Francisco Lopez Leiba, Licentiate Rafael M. Portuondo, and Orencio Nodarse.

The assembly having been organized as above, and in the presence of the above representatives, they proceeded to hold the session to discuss the constitution which is to rule the destinies of the Republic. These sessions took place on September 13, 14, 15, and 16, instant, and in all the articles which were to form the said constitutional charta were discussed. Every article of the projected constitution presented to the assembly by the representatives licentiate, Rafael M. Portuondo, Dr. Joaquin Castillo Duany, Mariano Sanchez Vaillant, and Pedro Aguilera, was well discussed, and, together with amendments, reforms. and additions were also discussed by the proposers. On deliberation, in conformity with the opinion of the assembly, it was unanimously resolved to refer the said constitution, with the resolutions of the said assembly, to a committee of revision of the text, composed of the secretaries and of the representatives, Dr. Santiago Garcia Canizares and Enrique Loynaz del Castillo, who, after complying with their mission, returned the final draft of the constitution on the 16th. It was then read, and the signature of each and every representative subscribed.

The president and other members of the assembly, with due solemnity, then swore upon their honor to loyally and strictly observe the fundamental code of the Republic of Cuba, which was greeted by the spontaneous and enthusiastic acclamations of all present; in testimony of which are the minutes in the general archives of the Government.

In compliance with the resolution passed by this council in a meeting held to-day, and for its publication, I issue the following copy, in the Mangos de Baragua, on the 18th of October, 1895.

JOSÉ CLEMENTE VIVANCO,
Secretary of the Council.

CONSTITUTION OF THE PROVISIONAL GOVERNMENT OF CUBA.

The revolution for the independence and creation in Cuba of a democratic republic in its new period of war, initiated on February 24 last, solemnly declares the separation of Cuba from the Spanish Monarchy and its constitution as a free and independent State, with its own government and supreme authority, under the name of the Republic of Cuba, and confirms its existence among the political divisions of the world.

The elected representatives of the revolution in convention assembled, acting in its name and by the delegation which for that purpose has been conferred upon them by the Cubans in arms, and previously declaring before the country the purity of their thoughts, their freedom from violence, anger, or prejudice, and inspired only by the desire of interpreting the popular voice in favor of Cuba, have now formed a compact between Cuba and the world, pledging their honor for the fulfillment of said compact in the following articles of the constitution:

ARTICLE I. The supreme powers of the Republic shall be vested in a government council, composed of a president, vice president, and four secretaries of state, for the dispatch of the business of war, of interior, of foreign affairs, and of the treasury.

ART. II. Every secretary shall have a subsecretary of state, in order to supply any vacancies.

ART. III. The government council shall have the following powers:

1. To dictate all measures relative to the civil and political life of the revolution.

2. To impose and collect taxes, to contract public loans, to issue paper money, to invest the funds collected in the island, from whatever source, and also those which may be raised abroad by loan.

3. To arm vessels, to raise and maintain troops, to declare reprisals with respect to the enemy, and to ratify treaties.

4. To grant authority, when it is deemed convenient, to order the trial by the judicial power of the president or other members of the council, if he be accused.

5. To decide all matters, of whatsoever description, which may be brought before them by any citizen, except those judicial in character.

6. To approve the law of military organization and the ordinances of the army, which may be proposed by the general in chief.

7. To grant military commissions from that of colonel upward, previously hearing and considering the reports of the immediate superior officer and of the general in chief, and to designate the appointment of the latter and of the lieutenant-general in case of the vacancy of either.

8. To order the election of four representatives for each army corps whenever in conformity with this constitution it may be necessary to convene an assembly.

ART. IV. The government council shall intervene in the direction of military operations only when in their judgment it shall be absolutely necessary to do so to realize high political ends.

ART. V. As a requisite for the validity of the decrees of the council, at least two-thirds of the members of the same must have taken part in the deliberations of the council, and the decrees must have been voted by the majority of those present.

ART. VI. The office of councillor is incompatible with any other of the Republic, and requires the age of 25 years.

ART. VII. The executive power is vested in the President, and, in case of disability, in the vice-president.

ART. VIII. The resolutions of the government council shall be sanctioned and promulgated by the President, who shall take all necessary steps for their execution within ten days.

ART. IX. The President may enter into treaties with the ratification of the government council.

ART. X. The President shall receive all diplomatic representatives and issue the respective commissions to the public functionaries.

ART. XI. The treaty of peace with Spain, which must necessarily have for its basis the absolute independence of the Island of Cuba, must be ratified by the government council and by an assemby of representatives convened expressly for this purpose.

ART. XII. The vice president shall substitute the president in the case of a vacancy.

ART. XIII. In case of the vacancy in the offices of both president and vice-president, on account of resignation, deposition, or death of both, or from any other cause, an assembly of representatives for the election to the vacant offices shall be convened, the senior secretaries in the meanwhile occupying the positions.

ART. XIV. The secretaries shall have voice and vote in the deliberations of resolutions of whatever nature.

ART. XV. The secretaries shall have the right to appoint all the employees of their respective offices.

ART. XVI. The subsecretaries in cases of vacancy shall substitute the secretaries of state, and shall then have voice and vote in the deliberations.

ART. XVII. All the armed forces of the Republic and the direction of the military operations shall be under the control of the general-in-chief, who shall have under his orders as second in command a lieutenant-general, who will substitute him in case of vacancy.

ART. XVIII. All public functionaries of whatever class shall aid one another in the execution of the resolutions of the government council.

ART. XIX. All Cubans are bound to serve the revolution with their persons and interests, each one according to his ability.

ART. XX. The plantations and property of whatever description belonging to foreigners are subject to the payment of taxes for the revolution while their respective Governments do not recognize the rights of belligerency of Cuba.

ART. XXI. All debts and obligations contracted since the beginning of the present period of war until the promulgation of this constitution by the chiefs of the army corps for the benefit of the revolution shall be valid, as well as those which henceforth the government council may contract.

ART. XXII. A government council may depose any of its members for cause justifiable in the judgment of two-thirds of the councillors and shall report to the first assembly convening.

ART. XXIII. The judicial power shall act with entire independence of all the others. Its organization and regulation will be provided for by the government council.

ART. XXIV. The present constitution shall be in force in Cuba for two years from the date of its promulgation, unless the war for independence shall terminate before. After the expiration of the two years an assembly of representatives shall be convened which may modify it, and will proceed to the election of a new government council, and which will pass upon the last council. So it has been agreed upon and resolved in the name of the Republic by the constituent assembly in Jimaguayu on the 18th day of September, 1895, and in witness thereof we, the representatives delegated by the Cuban people in arms, signed the present instrument. Salvador Cisneros, President; Rafael Manduley, vice-president; Petro Pinan de Villegas, Lope Recio, Fermin Valdes Dominguez, Francisco Diaz Silveira, Dr. Santiago Garcia, Rafael Perez, F. Lopez Leyva, Enrique Cespedes, Marcos Padilla, Raimundo Sanchez, J. D. Castillo, Mariano Sanchez, Pedro Aguilera, Rafael M. Portuondo, Orencio Nodarse, José Clemente Vivanco, Enrique Loynaz del Castillo, Severo Pina.

ELECTION OF GOVERNMENT

The constituent assembly met again on the 18th of the said month and year, all the said representatives being present. They proceeded to the election of members who are to occupy the offices of the government council, the general in chief of the army of liberation, the lieutenant-general, and the diplomatic agent abroad. The secret voting commenced, each representative depositing his ballot in the urn placed on the chairman's table, after which the count was proceeded with, the following being the result:

President: Salvador Cisneros, 12; Bartolome Masso, 8.

Vice-president: Bartolome Masso, 12; Salvador Cisneros, 8.

Secretary of war: Carlos Roloff, 18; Lope Recio Loinaz, 1; Rafael Manduley, 1.

Secretary of the treasury: Severo Pina, 19; Rafael Manduley, 1.

Secretary of the interior: Dr. Santiago Garcia Canizares, 19; Carlos Dubois, 1.

Secretary of foreign relations: Rafael Portuondo, 18; Armando Menocal, 1; blank, 1.

Subsecretary of war: Mario Menocal, 18; Francisco Diaz Silveira, 1; blank, 1.

Subsecretary of the treasury: Dr. Joaquin Castillo, 7; Francisco Diaz Silveira, 5; José C. Vivanco, 3; Armando Menocal, 3; Carlos Dubois, 1; blank, 1.

Subsecretary of the interior: Carlos Dubois, 13; Orencio Nodarse, 5; Armando Menocal, 1; blank, 1.

Subsecretary of foreign relations: Fermin Valdes Dominguez, 18; Rafael Manduley, 1; blank, 1.

Therefore the following were elected by a majority of votes:

President, Salvador Cisneros; vice-president, Bartolome Masso; secretary of war, Carlos Roloff; secretary of the treasury, Severo Pina; secretary of the interior, Dr. Santiago Garcia Canizares; secretary of foreign relations, Rafael M. Portuondo; subsecretary of war, Mario Menocal; subsecretary of the treasury, Dr. Joaquin Castillo; subsecretary of the interior, Carlos Dubois; subsecretary of foreign relations, Dr. Fermin Valdes Dominguez.

The vice-president of the assembly immediately installed the president in the office of the government council that had been conferred upon him; the latter in turn installed those of the other members elected, who were present, all entering on the full exercise of their functions after previously taking the oath.

On proceeding to the election of those who were to occupy the positions of general in chief of the army, lieutenant-general, and diplomatic agent abroad, the following citizens were unanimously elected by the assembly for the respective places: Major-General Maximo Gomez, Major-General Antonio Maceo, and citizen Thomas Estrada Palma, all these appointments being recognized from that moment.

LAWS FOR THE CIVIL GOVERNMENT AND ADMINISTRATION OF THE REPUBLIC.

CHAPTER I.—*Territorial division.*

ARTICLE I. The Republic of Cuba comprises the territory occupied by the Island of Cuba, from Cape San Antonio to Point Maisi and the adjacent islands and keys.

ART. II. This territory shall be divided into four portions, or States, which will be called Oriente, Camaguey, Las Villas or Cabanacan, and Occidente.

ART. III. The State of Oriente includes the territory from the Point Maisi to Port Manati and the river Jobabo in all its course.

ART. IV. The State of Camaguey includes all the territory from the boundary of Oriente to the line which starts in the north from Laguna Blanca through the Esteros to Moron, passing by Ciego de Avila, follows the military trocha to El Jucaro in the southern coast, it being understood that the towns of Moron and Ciego de Avila belong to this State.

ART. V. The State of Las Villas has for boundary on the east Camaguey, on the west the river Palmas, Palmillas, Santa Rosa, Rodas, the Hannabana River, and the Bay of Cochinos.

ART. VI. The State of Occidente is bordered on the Las Villas, extending to the west to Cape Antonio.

ART. VII. The islands and adjacent keys will form part of the States to which they geographically belong.

ART. VIII. The State of Oriente will be divided into ten districts, which shall be as follows: Baracoa, Guantanamo, Sagua de Tanamo, Mayari, Santiago, Jiguani, Manzanillo, Bayamo, and Tunas.

Camaguey comprises two—the eastern district and the western district.

Las Villas comprises seven—Sancti-Espiritus, Trinidad, Remedios, Santa Clara, Sagua, Cienfuegos, and Colon.

That of Occidente comprises sixteen—Cardenas, Matanzas, Union, Jaruco, Guines, Santa Maria del Rosario, Guanabacoa, Habana, Santiago de las Vegas, Bejucal, San Antonio, Bahia Honda, Pinar del Rio, and Mantua.

ART. IX. Each of these districts will be divided into prefectures, and these in their turn into as many subprefectures as may be considered necessary.

ART. X. For the vigilance of the coasts there will be inspectors and watchmen appointed in each State according to the extent of the coasts and the number of ports, bays, gulfs, and salt works that there may be.

ART. XI. On establishing the limits of the districts and prefectures, the direction of the coasts, rivers, and other natural boundaries shall be kept in mind.

CHAPTER II.—*Of the Government and its administration.*

ART. XII. The civil government, the administration, and the service of communications devolve upon the department of the interior.

ART. XIII. The secretary of the interior is the head of the department. He will appoint the employees and will remove them whenever there will be justifiable cause, and will have a department chief to aid him in the work of the department.

ART. XIV. The department chief will keep the books of the department, take care of the archives, will be manager of the office, and will furnish certifications when requested to do so.

ART. XV. The department of the interior will compile from the data collected by the civil governors the general statistics of the Republic.

ART. XVI. The civil governor will inform the department of the interior as to the necessities of his state; will order the measures and instructions necessary for compliance with the general laws of the Republic, and the orders given by that department; will distribute to the lieutenant-governors the articles of prime necessity which will be delivered to them for that purpose; will communicate to his subordinates the necessary instructions for the compilation of statistics, and will have a subsecretary who will help him in the discharge of his functions.

ART. XVII. The lieutenant-governor will see that the orders of the governors are obeyed in the district, and will have the powers incident to his position as intermediary between the civil governors and the prefects. In case of absolute breach of communication with the civil governors, they will have the same powers as the latter.

ART. XVIII. The prefect shall see that the laws and regulations communicated to him by his superior authorities are complied with. All residents and travelers are under his authority, and, being the highest official in his territory, he in his turn is bound to prevent all abuses and crimes which may be committed.

He will inform the lieutenant-governor as to the necessities of the prefecture; will divide these into as many subprefectures as he may consider necessary for the good conduct of his administration; he will watch the conduct of the subprefects; he will distribute among them with equity the articles delivered to him, and he will have all the other powers incident to him in his character of intermediary between the lieutenant-governor and the subprefects.

ART. XIX. The prefect will also have the following duties: He will harass the enemy whenever possible for him to do so; will hear the preliminary information as to crimes and misdemeanors which may be committed in his territory, passing the said information to the nearest military chief, together with the accused and all that is necessary for the better understanding of the hearing. He will not proceed thus with spies, guides, couriers, and others who are declared by our laws as traitors and considered as such, for these, on account of the difficulty of confining them or conducting them with security, shall be tried as soon as captured by a court consisting of three persons, the most capable in his judgment in the prefecture, one acting as president and the others as members of the court. He will also appoint a prosecuting officer, and the accused may appoint some one to defend him at his pleasure.

After the court is assembled in this form, and after all the formalities are complied with, it will in private judge and give its sentence, which will be final and without appeal; but those who form the said court and who do not proceed according to our laws and to natural reason will be held responsible by the superior Government. Nevertheless, if in the immediate territory there be any armed force, the accused shall be sent to it, with the facts, in order that they shall be properly tried.

The prefects will take the statistics of his prefecture, setting down every person who is found therein, noting if he is the head of a family, the number of the same, his age, his nationality, and occupation, if he is a farmer the nature of his farm, and if he has no occupation the prefect will indicate in what he should be employed. He will also keep a book of civil register in which he will set down the births, deaths, and marriages which may occur.

He will establish in the prefecture all the factories that he can or may consider necessary in order to well provide the army, as it is the primary obligation of all employees of the Republic to do all possible so that the hides shall not be lost, and organizing in the best manner, and as quickly as may be, tanneries, factories of shoes, rope, blankets, and carpenter and blacksmith shops.

He will not permit any individual of his district to be without occupation; he will see that everyone works, having the instruments of labor at hand in proportion to the inhabitants of his territory. He will protect and raise bees; he will take care of abandoned farms, and will extend as far as possible the zones of agriculture.

As soon as the prefect learns that the secretary of the interior or any delegate of this authority is in his district he will place himself under the latter's orders. This he will also do on the arrival of armed forces, presenting himself to their chief in order to facilitate the needed supplies and to serve him in every possible manner. He will have a bugle to warn the inhabitants of the enemy's approach; he will inform the nearest armed force when his territory is invaded. He will collect all horses and other animals suitable for the war and lead them to a secure place, so that when the army may need them or they may be required by the civil authorities to whom they may appertain.

He will provide the forces that may be, or pass through his territory with whatever they may need, which may be within his power, and especially shall he provide guides and beeves and vegetables which the chief may require to maintain the said forces. He will also deliver the articles manufactured in the shops under his immediate inspection, demanding always the proper receipts therefor.

He will also provide the necessary means for the maintenance of all the families of the territory, especially those of the soldiers of the army of liberation.

Until otherwise decreed he will celebrate civil marriages and other contracts entered into by the residents of his prefecture; he will act in cases of ordinary complaints and in the execution of powers and wills, registering the same in a clear and definite manner, and issuing to the interested parties the certificates which they may require.

ART. XX. The subprefects will see that the laws and orders communicated to him by his superior authorities are obeyed in territory under his command; he will inform the prefect as to the necessities of the subprefecture, and will see to the security and order of the public; arresting and sending to the prefects those who may travel without safe conduct, seeing that no violation of law whatsoever is perpetrated, and will demand the signed authority of the civil or military chief who has ordered a commission to be executed.

ART. XXI. The subprefects will compile a census in which the number of inhabitants of a subprefecture will be stated and their personal description; he will keep a book of the births and deaths which will occur in his territory, and of all this he will give account at the end of the year. He will invest the means provided by the prefect to pay the public charges, and if the said resources are insufficient he will collect the deficit from the inhabitants; he will not authorize the destruction of abandoned farms, whether they belong to friends or enemies of the Republic, and he will inform the prefect of the farms which are thus abandoned.

ART. XXII. For the organization and better operation of the State's manufactories a chief of factories shall be appointed in each district, who will be authorized to establish such factories which he may deem convenient, employing all citizens who, on account of their abilities, can serve, and collecting in the prefectures of his district all the instruments he can utilize in his work. These chiefs will be careful to frequently inspect the factories, to report any defects which they may notice, and to provide the superintendents with whatever they may need, that the work may not be interrupted.

Together with the prefect he will send to the department of the interior the names of the individuals he considers most adapted to open new shops, and on the first day of each month he will send to that department a statement of the objects manufactured in each shop of his district, indicating the place of manufacture, what remains on deposit, what has been delivered, with the names of commanders of forces, civil authorities, or individuals to whom they were delivered.

ART. XXIII. The coast inspectors will have under their immediate orders an inspector, who will be his secretary, who will occupy his place in his absence or sickness, and as many auxiliaries as he may deem convenient. He may demand the aid of the prefects and armed forces whenever he may consider it necessary for the better exercise of his functions. The duties of the inspectors will be to watch the coasts and prevent the landing of the enemy, to be always ready to receive disembarkments, and place in safety the expeditions which may come from abroad, to establish all the salt works possible, to capture the Spanish vessels which frequent the coasts on his guard, and to attend with special care to the punctual service of communications between his coast and foreign countries.

ART. XXIV. The coast guards will acknowledge the inspector as their superior, will watch the places designated to them, and will execute the orders given.

ART. XXV. The lieutenant-governors, as well as the inspectors of whatever class, will have their residence, wherever the necessity of their office does not prohibit it, in the general headquarters, so that they can move easily, furnish the necessary aid to the army, and carry out the orders of the military chief.

Country and liberty.

October 17, 1895.

The secretary of the interior, Dr. Santiago Garcia Canizares, being satisfied with the preceding law, I sanction it in all respects.

Let it be promulgated in the legal form.

SALVADOR CISNEROS BETANCOURT,
The President.

October 18, 1895.

LAW OF CIVIL MARRIAGE.

ARTICLE I. Males of 18 years of age and females of 14 can contract marriage.

ART. II. To contract marriage they must go to the notary of their residence, two witnesses being present who will sign the contract with the parties and the notary.

ART. III. The marriage contract may contain any agreement or convention which the contracting parties may agree upon and which is not opposed to the nature of the contract nor to law.

ART. IV. If one of the contracting parties is less than 20 years of age the marriage can be contracted with notice to the father, the mother, or the guardian, according to the circumstances, and if these oppose the celebration of the marriage the judge of the district, with knowledge of the facts, will decide the question.

ART. V. The following reason will prevent marriage: Consanguinity in the direct line. In the collateral, brother and sister can not marry; it is null by the relationship in said degrees, or by being contracted by fraud or by force. It is completely dissolved for incompatibility, by a chronic and contagious disease, or one which will cause impotency, and by adultery; moral or physical ill treatment of the wife gives to the wife the right to demand from the husband, when they live apart, to bear the expenses of the marriage; if the woman commits adultery she loses this right.

ART. VI. In case of separation, the male children of 14 years of age and upward and female children of 12 and upward may elect between their parents as to residence. Those less than 3 years of age must remain with the mother. Those who have not yet reached the age of puberty, but are older than 3 years, remain with the parent who has not given the motive for the separation. This is in case that the separation is caused by some guilt. If it occurs on account of sickness, the children will remain with the one who did not desire the separation. If the separation is on account of incompatibility the parents must agree as to this point. On reaching the age of 3 years, the children who until then have been with the mother, the question of their custody will be governed by the other provisions of this article.

When the male reaches the age of 14 and the female of 12, whatever may have been their previous residence they may alter it.

ART. VII. Marriage being once dissolved, the parties may remarry, but the woman shall not do so until twelve months have elapsed, in order to avoid confusion of paternity.

ART. VIII. Civil marriage is placed on an equal footing, as to duty and effects, with that recognized by our former legislation, and celebrated by the intervention of the church.

ART. IX. The promise of marriage does not have any other result than that of the payment of the penalty, which must be stipulated by the contracting party. If no penalty is stipulated, no duty of payment is incurred.

ART. X. The seduction of a female, whether she be a minor or not, obliges the seductor to marry the seduced or to pay a penalty in proportion to the fortune of both, which the judge of the district must determine.

Country and liberty.

PROVIDENCIA, *September 25, 1895.*

GARCIA CANIZARES,
   Secretary of the Interior:

Let the foregoing be promulgated in the legal form, it having my sanction.

SALVADOR CISNEROS BETANCOURT,
President.

PROVIDENCIA, *September 25, 1895.*

CIVIL MARRIAGE.

Instructions which must be observed by the prefects of the Republic of Cuba in the celebration of civil marriage, exercising the function which is given them by the provisional law passed by the government council on the 25th of September, 1895.

ARTICLE I. The prefect of the residence of the wife, who is the only one competent to celebrate the marriage, will demand of the parties a copy of their certificate of birth so that they can prove their marriageable age, which of the male.is 18 years and of the female 14 years.

ART. II. If either of the contracting parties should not have that document, by the omission, suppression, or burning of the register, or for any other cause, this credential may be substituted by a certificate of the authorities as to the nationality or residence, in which certificate the cause of the absence of the original certificate shall be stated (after previous investigation and on information received as to its omission), the names of the parents, their civil status, and the year and month of the birth of the contracting parties.

ART. III. If it appears that the contracting parties are over 20 years of age the prefect will proceed to the celebration of the civil marriage without further requisite than to give it publicity, for which purpose he shall affix notices in the most frequented places of the prefecture.

ART. IV. But if either of the parties is less than 20 years of age the contract must not only be made public, as previously stated, but notice given to the father, the mother, or the guardian, so that if these oppose the marriage it may be suspended until, with a full knowledge of the facts, the question be decided by the judge, who must investigate, the prefect fixing a time for the opposing parties to establish and justify their position, which must not be longer than eight days.

ART. V. In all cases the prefect will demand from the contracting parties their assurance of the consent of each other, or at least that of the bride, and of her ability to enter into the matrimonial contract, which requisite the prefect may omit if he himself possesses knowledge of the circumstances.

ART. VI. If there are no disabilities to the marriage the prefect will register in a book entitled Book of Civil Marriages Contracted in the Prefecture ———, designating on the first page the year and making an index at the end in alphabetical order.

ART. VII. The contract will be formulated in the following terms:

"Formula of the marriage of persons of 20 years and upward:

"In the prefecture of —— on the —— day of 189—, before me, the prefect ——, and before me, the undersigned secretary, there appeared —— and ——, of 20 years and upward, the former born and resident of ——, the prefecture ——, daughter (here the names of parents), who are known to the prefect and to myself, the secretary, or who, unknown, were presented to M. and P., who act as witnesses, who affirm that they know them, or at least that they know her, and they so declare and affirm."

"The contracting parties thereupon say, in the presence of these witnesses and those to this instrument, A and B, called for that purpose, that of their own free will, and without any violence, they promised to marry civilly, which marriage they now celebrate, and they agree to live in complete harmony and conjugal union, and never to separate unless because of incompatibility, or for any of the other reasons allowed by law, declaring that this marriage is for the welfare and honor of both, and for their offspring, and as the laws and customs of good government require (here any agreement made between the contracting parties shall be inserted, besides the nuptial contract), and the register will thus end; and in order that this marriage shall be known, and always and in all cases have its legal force, the prefect orders the minutes of this contract to be drawn in the said terms, signing with the contracting parties, and the said witnesses (if they can write, and if they can not, others, at their request, may do so), to all of which I, the secretary certify."

FORMULA FOR THE MARRIAGE OF THOSE LESS THAN TWENTY YEARS OF AGE.

The beginning will be as in the above formula, adding that the contracting parties being minors, the father, the mother, or guardian appeared, who declared their assent and signed (if they can write) the register, and if not, a person of their confidence whom they may select. The declaration as to register will be the same as in the preceding formula.

FORMULA OF CIVIL MARRIAGE TO WHICH THERE IS OPPOSITION.

After the preamble similar to the first formula in the register is declared, that the father, mother, or guardian whosoever has interposed before the competent authority, has dissented, declares the contract not to be proper, as he explains in the following declaration. As to the rest, the register will be as in the first formula to its conclusion.

But in case the father, mother, or guardian do not make any opposition, it shall be so declared in the register that the time fixed having passed and the person having the right to exercise this right having failed to do so, the marriage has been consummated.

NOTE.—Of every marriage there will be formed a file consisting of the copy of the register of birth, of the cedula, of the declaration of the opposition of father, mother, or guardian, and of the decree in which it shall be declared proper, or it is ordered that the marriage shall take place because they have not exercised that right, or because the party opposing has not complied with the law. This file shall be kept for future use.

Country and liberty.

GARCIA CANIZARES,
Secretary of the Interior.

PROVIDENCIA, *September 25, 1895.*

Let the foregoing be promulgated in its legal form, as I sanction the foregoing law in all its parts.

SALVADOR CISNEROS BETANCOURT,
President.

PROVIDENCIA, *September 25, 1895.*

EXTRACT OF THE SESSIONS.

[Republic of Cuba, provisional government, secretary of the council—José Clemente Vivanco, secretary of the government council and chancellor of the Republic.]

I certify that among the resolutions passed by this council, according to the minute book of the sessions, the following are to be found:

To give two months' time to the chiefs and officers of the last revolution to join the new army of liberation, so as to have their ranks recognized, and four months' time to those in foreign countries to place themselves in communication with the delegates. To allow the Cuban emigrants individual freedom in the nature of their contributions for the revolution. To permit the export of wooden blocks on payment of $5 in gold as tax for each piece. To prohibit absolutely the export of corn and all forage; of cattle, pigs, horses; without allowing anything to enter the towns without the previous payment of taxes.

To prohibit absolutely also the introduction in the towns of all kinds of fruits and articles of commerce which may favor the said towns and indirectly the Government which we are fighting.

San Andres de la Rioja, October 9, 1895.

JOSÉ CLEMENTE VIVANCO,
Secretary of the Council.

REGULATIONS FOR THE SERVICE OF COMMUNICATIONS.

ARTICLE I. The secretary of the interior will be the postmaster-general of the whole island, and the civil governor the chief of his territory.

ART. II. The postal service is established between the prefectures of the Republic and between the towns and prefectures near by.

ART. III. In order to organize the postal service, an inspector will be named for each district; as many chiefs as there are post-offices, and as many couriers and auxiliaries as are necessary for each one.

ART. IV. The inspector is the superior chief in his district of the postal service. Under his direction will be the postmasters, couriers, and auxiliaries. He shall organize the service by placing the post-offices in the most convenient places, so that the service shall be carried out with the greatest ease and with the greatest rapidity. He will employ the number of employees that are necessary. He will ask for their resignations whenever there is any justifiable cause for it. He will see that everyone shall fulfill his duties, and shall name the hours when the couriers shall depart. He shall correct all defects that come under his notice, propose all modifications which he may think will give a better service, and give an account of all extraordinary services which his subalterns may render in order that they should be registered and rewarded.

ART. V. The chiefs will reside in the post-office, from which they can not be absent during the appointed hours, and they are to act whenever possible as auxiliaries to the prefect's office. They will receive official and private correspondence, sign receipts for that delivered by mail carriers, setting down the hour of delivery; and they will deliver, under receipt in which they will also put down the time of departure, to the outgoing postman the mail matter in their hands, giving with it a memorandum stating the name of mail carried and the time of departure. They will also see that the post-offices are well attended and have in them the necessary number of horses required for the service, unless in cases where the service is carried on foot. They will report to the inspector the defects they may observe in the service, without forgetting the importance of their position.

ART. VI. The mail carriers will collect daily at the appointed hours, along the route marked out, without delaying on the way nor hurrying their horses except in urgent cases that will be pointed out by the chief. They will have a receipt for the correspondence delivered to them, and will receive in exchange for the receipt a signed memorandum stating what mail they carry, which memorandum they will present to the chief of postal department, so that he may sign it and declare that he has received them, and after complying with this requisite, change it for a receipt which he will leave in the office of departure.

A great service will be done by the couriers, and for that reason men of known honesty and valor shall be chosen, who are capable of appreciating the service they render their country.

ART. VII. A mail service will be organized in every city occupied by the enemy, and will consist of as many chiefs and carriers as may be considered necessary.

ART. VIII. The inspectors of mails will be the immediate superior officer of the service in the town of his residence, and will have under his command the postmasters and mail carriers, and they will exercise their functions in the same manner as the coast inspectors. They will have special care in the selection of employees and in keeping all possible secrecy to elude the vigilance of the enemy.

ART. IX. The postmasters will be considered as the chiefs of mail carriers and will act with the carriers, as the carriers with the drivers, always giving an account of any extra services rendered.

ART. X. The mail carriers will have charge of receiving from the postmasters the mail matter and carry it out of the cities for delivery to the office of the nearest prefect. They will give and ask for receipts as the drivers, and like these must be honest men, sharp and brave enough with courage to overcome the difficulties that may arise in the performance of their important and dangerous mission and worthy to occupy these positions of trust in which they can lend such valuable services to the sacred cause every Cuban is bound to defend.

ART. XI. The inspectors and postmasters will keep a book to record the appointments of employees and the services rendered by them and will make up their archives with this book and circulars, communications, and official documents that they receive on the copies of those they may have to transmit.

Country and liberty, September, 1895.

Dr. SANITAGO GARCIA CANIZARES,
Secretary of the Interior.

In conformity with the preceding regulations I sanction them in every part; and that it may govern and produce its corresponding effects to have it published in the legal form.

Country and liberty.

Residence of the Executive in Limones, the 6th day of October, 1895.

SALVADOR CISNEROS, *President.*

LAW FOR THE ORGANIZATION OF THE PUBLIC TREASURY.

ARTICLE 1. All property of whatever description situated in the territory of the ᵣepublic comes under the jurisdiction of the secretary of the treasury; therefore this department shall take charge of articles of whatever description brought to this Island by expeditions from abroad; this department also has the faculty of raising public loans and general taxes.

ART. II. The secretary of the treasury will be the superior chief of his department throughout the Island of Cuba, and through him the subaltern officers will receive the orders given by the council. The duties of the secretary will be to determine, on information of the collectors, the taxes which shall be paid in each state and the form in which they shall be collected, to nominate the employees of his department, and to discharge them for justifiable cause. He will deliver to the chiefs of corps and civil governors the articles which he receives from abroad; he will give a receipt for the articles or sums of money which from any source whatever may be collected by the public treasury. He may trade with the merchandise belonging to the Republic; he may lease or sell whatever be convenient, and will present an account every three months to the council of the funds belonging to the Republic.

ART. III. To facilitate the work of the treasury a chief of department will be appointed who will act as general comptroller, and in each state a collector and a secretary of the administration of the treasury, and for each district a delegate.

ART. IV. The chief of the department, or general comptroller, will have charge of the archives of the department, will keep the books in due form, and will take part in all the collections and disbursements which may occur.

ART. V. The collector will represent in each state the secretary of the treasury, he will give information as to the taxable property in his state, he will dictate the necessary measures to carry out the general orders communicated to him by the secretary of the treasury, he will collect by means of agents the taxes fixed upon, and he will send to the department as soon as possible the funds collected; nevertheless he may deliver the amounts he may deem necessary to the chiefs of the different army corps, who will give a receipt for them and justify their expenditure. The collectors will monthly send to the department a statement of their operation.

ART. VI. The secretary of the administration of the treasury will keep the archives of his respective state, will keep the books in due form, and will take part in the operations of the collector.

ART. VII. The delegates or agents will be the collectors of taxes in each district, and the commissioners will see that the orders of the collectors of the state are carried out. They may appoint auxiliaries whenever necessary and are authorized to demand the aid of the prefects and armed forces for the better fulfillment of their commissions. Country and liberty.

Canaster, October 16, 1895.   SEVERO PINA,
                                           Secretary of the Treasury.

In conformity with the previous law, I sanction it in all its parts. Let it be promulgated in legal form.

Country and liberty.   October 18, 1895.

                                           MANGOS DE BARAGUA.

SALVADOR CISNEROS BETANCOURT,
                     President.

INSTRUCTIONS TO THE OFFICERS OF THE DEPARTMENT OF THE TREASURY OF THE REPUBLIC OF CUBA.

ARTICLE I. According to article 18 of the constitution and the decree of the general in chief of the 20th of September last, the military chiefs shall give the necessary aid to the officers of the treasury for the better fulfillment of their duties.

ART. II. With the aid of the armed forces, they will proceed to the destruction of those plantations, whatever be their nationality, which will refuse to pay the taxes decreed by the Government of the Republic.

ART. III. As a basis for the rate of tax, the production of the plantations shall serve as well as the price of their products, taking into consideration the expense of transportation.

ART. IV. The amount of the tax will be paid in advance in gold or in drafts on New York, Paris, or London in the form agreed upon.

ART. V. All kinds of traffic with the enemy are absolutely prohibited; only the following articles and products are allowed to be exported:

Coffee and cocoa, $4 per hundredweight.

Wood in blocks, $8 per thousand feet or $3 apiece, as will best suit the interests of the Republic and the functionary authorizing the exportation.

Guana (a textile palm), $4 per hundredweight.

Wax, $4 per hundredweight.

Fattened steers, $3 per head.

Cheese, $2 per hundredweight.

In regard to mines, tobacco, and plantains for exportation, it is left to the judgment of the collector of the treasury.

ART. VI. The exportation of wood or guana (the latter until December 6) will only be permitted when worked or packed by individuals who are in the confidence of our authorities.

ART. VII. The exportation of cattle will only be allowed when, in the judgment of the authority, they run imminent risk of falling into the hands of the enemy.

ART. VIII. The collector of the treasury of each state may suspend, temporarily, the exportation of the products referred to in Article V, immediately giving an account of it to the secretary of the treasury for final judgment.

Sabanilla del Contra Maestre, October 24, 1895.

In conformity with the previous law, I sanction it in all its parts. Let it be promulgated in legal form.

Sabanilla, October 25, 1895.

SALVADOR CISNEROS BETANCOURT,
President.

SEVERO PINA,
Secretary of the Treasury.

EXTRACT OF THE SESSIONS OF THE GOVERNMENT COUNCIL, REPUBLIC OF CUBA.

Secretary of the Government José Clemente Vivanco, secretary of the government council and chancellor of the Republic, I certify that in the minute books of the sessions celebrated by this council the following resolutions are found:

SEPTEMBER 19, 1895.

To appoint a secretary of the Government and chancellor of the Republic, José Clemente Vivanco. To send the appointments of general

in chief, lieutenant-general, and delegate plenipotentiary abroad to Maj.
Gen. Maximo Gomez, Maj. Gen. Antonio Maceo, and Tomas Estrada
Palma, respectively.

To appoint as civil governor of Camaguey, Dr. Oscar Primelles, and
of Oriente, Rafael Manduley.

To complete the system of the division of the territory of the island
into zones, and that the subsecretary of war, in the absence of the secretary, agree with the general in chief as to the organization of the army
of liberation.

SEPTEMBER 20, 1895.

To give two months' time to the chief and officers of the past revolution to join the newly organized army of liberation, for the recognition
of their grades, and four months' time to those outside of the Island.
That each secretary of state may name a chief of his department. To
appoint as a director of the treasury in Orienter, Diego Palacois, and
in Camaguey, Col. Lope Recio Loynaz. That the secretary communicate with the general in chief so the latter may indorse the authorities,
passes, and orders given by the Government and require all the forces
of the army of liberation to respect and obey them.

To ask the general in chief for Capts. Francisco Garcia, Manuel Merrero, and Ensign Enrique Boza, as their services are needed by the
Government. That the Cuban emigrations shall be at liberty as to
the manner of contributing to the revolution.

To ask from abroad a copy of all the decrees passed by the Government
of the last revolution, and to order that in conformity with the minutes
sent from here all documents shall be printed emanating from the Government as well as the constitution passed by the constituent assembly
which shall be placed in our archives.

SEPTEMBER 24, 1895.

To publish a circular of the secretary of the interior, addressed to
the prefects, subprefects, and other functionaries of civil order, recommending them to fulfill their respective duties.

To approve the order given by the general in chief as to the respect
due peaceful families and their interests, excepting in cases of military
necessity or on account of manifest or suspected treachery, and that
the secretary of the interior address such communication to the civil
governors, advising them of this resolution.

To appoint chief of postal service for the eastern and western district
of Camaguey, Manuel Manero and Francisco Garcia, respectively, and
to confirm the appointments of prefects temporarily made by the general
in chief.

To ask the general in chief to order all the chiefs of army corps to
send to the secretary of war a detailed account of the chiefs and officers under his orders, their record of service, the positions which they
occupy, and their respective abilities.

To communicate to Maj. Gen. Carlos Roloff that his aides, Francisco
Diaz Silveira and Orencio Nodarse, remain with this Government.

SEPTEMBER 25, 1895.

To permit the export of wood in blocks after the payment of $5 in
gold for each block. To absolutely prohibit the sale of corn and all
kinds of forage, cows, oxen, and horses, permitting only other animals
to be taken within a radius of 6 leagues from the town on a payment
of the tax.

That through the secretary of the treasury a detailed statement of the tax-paying property shall be sent to the prefects and military chiefs.

To approve of the provisional law of civil marriage passed June 4, 1869, by the chamber of representatives of the past revolution and to put it in force on motion of the secretary of the interior.

To approve and enforce the instructions as to said law, which were passed June 21, 1869, by the said chamber.

To confirm the appointment of inspectors of coasts and coast guards made previously by the general in chief.

OCTOBER 5, 1895.

That each secretary of state shall present to the council such projects of laws and regulations as shall be in force in their respective departments, and that the secretary of foreign relations, together with the subsecretary, the acting secretary of war, shall draw a project of criminal procedure for deliberation and approval by the council.

OCTOBER 6, 1895.

To absolutely prohibit the introduction in the towns of all articles of commerce which, favoring trade indirectly, aid the enemy's Government, and to confirm the appointment of the inspector of shops and prefectures in the district of Tunas to Citizen Luis Marti, provisionally given by the general-in-chief of the third division, José M. Capote, on September 17, 1895.

OCTOBER 16, 1895.

That the secretary of the Government shall collect all the laws, rules, decrees, and all other orders of this council and an extract of the resolutions for publication in book form for an edition of 500 copies.

To approve the project of the law for the organization of the public treasury presented by the secretary of the treasury.

To appprove the law for the civil government and administration of the Republic, presented by the secretary of the interior.

OCTOBER 21, 1895.

To send a communication to the chiefs of army corps; to send the secretary of the treasury a detailed account of all the contracts made by them since the beginning of the war in order that, in conformity with article 21 of the constitution, they be approved.

To give military consideration to all civil functionaries, appointing for this purpose a commission composed of the secretary of the interior and the subsecretary of war, so that they may present a report as to the rules to be followed in this behalf.

OCTOBER 24, 1895.

To approve the project as to instructions of the officers of the public treasury presented by the secretary of the treasury.

To approve the report as to the military considerations to be enjoyed by the civil functionaries, presented by the secretary of the interior and the subsecretary of war, commissioned for this purpose at the last session, which is as follows:

The president of the Republic, that of general in chief of the army; the vice-president, and the secretaries of state, of major-generals.

The secretary of the council and chancellor, brigadier general; the chiefs of departments of states, civil governors, and collectors of the treasury, colonels; the lieutenant-governor, delegate of the treasury, and the secretary of administration, of the treasury, majors; the prefects, the inspectors of shops, of coast and communication, that of captains; the subprefects, and ensigns.

All these considerations shall be enjoyed by them unless they have higher rank.

OCTOBER 25, 1895.

The following decree was approved:

ARTICLE I. No one can be punished by death, or by imprisonment, or reprimand, without having been previously judged by court-martial.

ART. II. The factories, barns, houses, fruit trees, and useful wood trees will be respected by all the citizens of the Republic.

ART. III. Housebreaking and unjustifiable raids will be severely punished.

ART. IV. No citizen can be dispossessed from the house he occupies without justifiable motive.

ART. V. The forces on the march, detachments, or commissions will not occupy inhabited houses without the consent of their owners, unless the exigencies of the war require it or in extraordinary cases, when it will be justified by the officer who orders it.

And for the publication thereof in accordance with the resolution of the 16th instant, I publish the present compilation, which is a true copy of the originals, on file in the archives of my secretaryship.

Country and liberty.

JOSÉ CLEMENTE VIVANCO,
Secretary of the Council.

SABANILLA, *October 25, 1895.*

There will soon be published the laws of organization and military ordinances drafted by the general in chief and approved by the council, which shall be joined to the present compilation, C.

[COAT OF ARMS OF CUBAN REPUBLIC.]

In the name of the Republic of Cuba by delegation of the Cuban people in arms, the constituent assembly resolved by acclamation on this day to confer on Tomas Estrada Palma, the diplomatic representative and agent abroad, the title of delegate plenipotentiary of the Republic of Cuba.

In witness whereof we have affixed our signatures in Jimaguayu on the 18th of September, 1895.

Salvador Cesneros, B., President; Rafael Manduley, Vice-President; Enrique Loinaz del Castillo, Severo Pina, Fermin Valdez Dominguez, Rafael Perez Morales, Raimundo Sanchez, J. D. Castillo, Pedro Pinau de Villegas, Pedro Aguilera, Marcos Padilla, Rafael M. Portuondo, Dr. Santiago Garcia Canizares, Lope Recio, L.; Orencio Nodarse, Secretary; Franco Diaz Silveria, Enrique Cespedes, Mariano Sanchez Vaillant, F. Lopez Leiva, Secretary; José Clemente Vivanco, Secretary.

————

ARMY HEADQUARTERS AT CUMANAYAGUA.

Mr. ALFREDO REGO.

MY DEAR SIR: I had the pleasure to receive your polite note. I see by it the generosity of your heart, and I thank you, in the name of my superior officers, to whom I will communicate your humanitarian act.

I send the committee desired to bring back the prisoners. It takes this letter to you and is composed of Benito Mesa and Telesforo Ramirez. I beg you to give them the necessary aid, promising you that your men will be respected by this garrison.

Yours, truly,

JOSÉ BRETONES, *Lieutenant.*

EXHIBIT NO. 1*a.*

EL CUBANO LIBRE, *May 10, 1896.*

REPUBLICA DE CUBA.

CIVIL AUTHORITIES OF THE SAME.

President: Salvador Cisneros Betancourt.
Vice-president: Gen. Bartolome Maso.
Secretary of war: Maj. Gen. Carlos Roloff.
Secretary of the interior: Dr. Santiago Garcia Canizares.
Secretary of the treasury: Licentiate Severo Bina y Marin.
Secretary of foreign relations: Licentiate Rafael Portuondo y Tamayo.
Subsecretary of war: Mario Garcia Menocal.
Subsecretary of the treasury: Dr. Joaquin Castillo Duany.
Subsecretary of the interior: Carlos Dubois y Castillo.
Subsecretary of foreign relations: Licentiate Jose Clemente Vivanco.
Head of the dispatch:
  War, Saul Alsina.
  Interior, Francisco Diaz Silveira.
  Treasury, Orencio Nodarse.
  Foreign relations, Tomas Armstrong.
Delegate plenipotentiary abroad: Tomas Estrada Palma.
Civil governor:
  Of Oriente, Carlos Manuel de Cespedes.
  Of Camaguey, Maj. Antonio Aguilar Varona.
  Of Las Villas, Licentiate Domingo Mendez Capote.
  Of Occidente, Licentiate Andres Moreno de la Torre.
Administrator of the treasury:
  Of Oriente, Dr. Tomas Padro Griñan.
  Of Camaguey, Bernabe Sanchez.
  Of Las Villas, Ernesto Fonts y Sterling.

Exhibit No. 2 in the document.

EXHIBIT NO. 2 *a.*

REPUBLIC OF CUBA, STATE OF ORIENTE,
Governor's Office, June 10, 1896.

In order to establish once for all the basis under which the internal commerce or trade of products and merchandise shall be conducted in the present circumstances, and in order to prevent and put an end to innumerable abuses, consultations, and claims which are daily committed, made, and submitted in the territory under my government, I have resolved to decree the following provisionally until the government council shall legislate as to the said matter:

ARTICLE 1. Commerce, so called, is prohibited to all citizens who shall not present an expressed authority of the secretary of the treasury, or of the administrator of the treasury in the State of Oriente.

ART. 2. The exchange or sale of certain products, such as tobacco, cocoa, and coffee, can not be made by anyone not having a document showing that he is not in arrears with the national treasury.

ART. 3. The citizens who in their spare time shall manufacture the sugar product called raspadura out of canes which do not belong to the State, and sell it where they reside or elsewhere, must have with them a certificate of the prefect of the locality declaring that they serve the country as well as their conditions and abilities permit, and that this trade does not make them or their families dependent on the other citizens, but on the contrary to reward their efforts this commerce is permitted so that they can better provide for their families. For every ten tarts manufactured they must deliver at least two to the prefecture and get a proper receipt for the same; these tarts to be devoted to the wounded and sick in the hospitals of the Republic.

Country and liberty.

CARLOS MANUEL DE CESPEDES,
The Governor

MEJIAS, *June 9, 1896.*

EXHIBIT NO. 3.

[Translation.]

THE CUBAN REPUBLIC.

[From Cuba Libre.]

With great pleasure we publish to-day the accounts which the government of the state of the east of Cuba Libre expressly sends to our paper.

By these accounts it will be seen that our civil organization is a fact, and that during the activity shown in the military operations we have not forgotten the importance of developing everything that tends to the better settling of our republican institution.

Civil government of the east: Civil governor, C. M. de Cespedes; secretary, Modesto A. Tirado; first lieutenant-governor, Herminio Figarola; second lieutenant-governor, Julio Aguado; chief of the escort, Jose Lera Marrero.

Lieutenant-governors: Baracoa, Lorenzo Conde; Sagua de Tanamo, M. B. Coyula; Mayari, Capt. F. Mastrapa; Santiago de Cuba, M. d'Espaigne; Guantanamo, Capt. E. Tamayo; Jiguani, I. Campina; Bayamo, Pedro P. Mendieta; Manzanillo, Joaquin Romen; Tunas, Major-General Varona; Holguin, Col. Luis Marti.

Employees in each government seat, secretaries of the governors, agents, inspectors of coast, chiefs of salt works, inspectors of posts and workshops, prefects and secretaries, subprefects, auxiliary sergeants, professors of public schools. Chiefs of pyrotechnia, chiefs of agriculture, heads of post-offices, postilions. Chief of the secret bureau, with the secretary of foreign relations, private postilions of the bureau. Special commissioners. Chiefs of the depots of horses. Cattle commissioners.

Note 1. Every governor of every district has an escort of 15 men.

Note 2. Territorial guards of every district consist of 10 men for every prefecture, under a sergeant.

Patria y Libertad.

JULIO AGUADO,
Second Lieutenant-Governor.

BIRAU, Nov. 1, 1896.

To the DIRECTOR OF LA REPUBLICA DE CUBA.

EXHIBIT No. 3 <i>a</i>.

CIVIL GOVERNMENT OF THE STATE OF CAMAGUEY.

[Circular]

As a basis for the organization and government, which in the future must be invariably followed in this State while this revolution lasts, I have ordered as follows:

First. Commerce is absolutely prohibited in this State, it being understood by commerce, the withdrawal of cattle, vegetables, lumber, textile and combustible merchandise belonging to the State and other towns at a higher price than the current one, and generally any abuse of gain, and having contracts and relations with the enemy; all this is in conformity with the circular of the general in chief of the 1st of July, 1895, and of the decree of the government of the 25th of October, 1895.

Second. Peaceful families and individuals will be respected and considered as heretofore, allowing them to devote themselves to their labors and care of their interests, to enter and go out of our territory, provided they have the indispensable safe conduct which will be issued to them by the superior civil and military authorities of the State.

Third. From this date, the civil Government will be separated from the treasury department; all the rights and duties being in the latter, without this preventing the first from ordering payments and asking for effects when required by the service.

Fourth. The lieutenant-governors who belong to this State, in order that they shall better accomplish their mission, will have their respective residences in the brigades corresponding to their districts, to which they will attend with preference, acting in accordance with the chief of the said brigade. They will take advantage of the camping of the brigades to visit the prefectures, so as to be informed of their condition and communicate to them whatever they deem proper.

Fifth. The prefectures will be provided with necessary armed forces according to their importance and situation, so that they shall be respected; shall attack the enemy, and shall so attack the territory and zones under cultivation; shall defend the hospitals and deposits of horses and for the carrying out of commissions, so that the effective forces of the army shall not be dispersed.

Sixth. The organization and conduct of the prefectures will be provided for in the instructions which with this date are sent them through the lieutenant-governors.

Seventh. With the approval of the superior military authority, the number of armed men corresponding to each civil authority shall be determined, they being prohibited from having a larger number. Those exceeding the number prescribed will join the army of the Government escort as ordered by the military authority.

Eighth. The treasury delegates, agents, and those bringing communications will deal directly with this office, delivering all goods received by them, which will be equitably distributed among the lieutenant-governors, so that they in turn will do so among the troops or prefectures which may need them.

Ninth. All the commissions, safe-conducts, privileges, and concessions granted before this date, which are not vised by this office, are hereby declared without effect.

Tenth. The delegates, agents, lieutenant-governors, and other authorities who directly depend on this office will present themselves to it, so that they may communicate the result of their labors and receive instructions under the new rules. All of which is published for general knowledge.

Residence of the government of Camaguey, 1st of June, 1896.

MELCHOR L. DE MOLA,
The Governor.

EXHIBIT NO. 4.

CIVIL GOVERNOR.

Lieut. Col. Melchor Loret de Mola has resigned his office of civil governor of Camaguey. For a short time only he discharged the duties of the office, but he showed courage and activity worthy of applause. He ceases in the civil command of this state to probably go into the army, where there is always room for those who do not fear danger and know how to do their duty.

The name of Mola was celebrated in the last revolution. In Camaguey and Las Villas a brave one was applauded in the defense of his country.

May he who was our civil governor repeat the feats of that warrior.

EXHIBIT NO. 5.

[Translation]

REPUBLIC OF CUBA,
Government of the State of the East.

REGULATIONS FOR WORKSHOPS.

ARTICLE 1. The inspectors, with the consent of the prefects, will establish arms, smiths, shoes, carpenters, rope, hats, and crate shops, and all these industries which they may be able to start in their territories.

ART. 2. All shops will be presided over by one master workman, who will have under him the number of auxiliaries, apprentices, and men that the inspector may deem necessary.

ART. 3. Each workshop of two or more industries will have as chief the oldest master workman, or the one which by special circumstances may be appointed.

ART. 4. Work will commence in the shops at 6 a. m. and last until 11. At 2 o'clock p. m. they will recommence and continue until 5 o'clock. The tasks will be apportioned by the inspector.

ART. 5. No employee of the shops may absent himself without the permission of his superior.

ART. 6. No chief of a workshop may absent himself without permission of the inspector.

ART. 7. The inspector will present the list of materials, instruments, irons, and other necessaries that may be needed to the lieutenant-governor. He will receive from him the implements, the money to buy them, or the order for them on the delegate of the treasury.

ART. 8. The lieutenant-governors and the delegates of the treasury will attend to all the orders given them by the inspectors, and will be responsible for all obstructions in the works that may occur by lack of raw material, if by fault of theirs.

ART. 9. With details furnished by chiefs and master workmen, the inspectors will keep books in which they will keep a record of time served by the workmen, the faults they may commit, and the merits any may contract in the fulfillment of their employment.

ART. 10. The articles made by the shops will be delivered to the prefects, who will give receipts for same, and distributed also by receipts to the national force and to the civil authorities of State.

ART. 11. The application for effects must be made through the superior civil authorities, also the military to the inspector, who will be responsible for their prompt fulfillment.

ART. 12. The lieutenant-governors will demand of the inspectors, and will send to this bureau every month a detailed account of the work done and effects made in the workshops under them.

P. y L.

C. M. DE CESPEDES,
The Governor.

CAMALOTE, *July 18, 1896.*

EXHIBIT No. 6.

[Translation.]

To the chiefs of mails and postillions:

It is recommended to you to have in mind and to comply with the dispositions of our civil government in its articles dated March 8, 1896, so you may avoid the responsibilities you may incur, the article says:

ART. 3. The service of the mails being one of great importance and of trust, the persons chosen for same must be those who offer the greater guaranty.

ART. 4. The violation of mails, official or private, the theft of documents, of papers in the mails of the Republic, will be severely punished.

EXHIBIT No. 6a.

Under this date, and as superior chief of the post offices of the State of Oriente, I have ordered the following:

Every letter, dispatch, package of papers, or any other postal matter which may be detained in the post-offices on account of nonresidence or on account of not knowing the place where the person or persons to whom they are addressed are found will be sent to the inspector-general

of the post-offices of each district, who will make a list of names and
addresses to be sent every month to the editorial rooms of the El Cubano
Libre and La Independencia, so that it shall be published.

The publication will be made every thirty days during a period of six
months, after which the correspondence will be sent to headquarters,
and from there to the secretary of the interior for him to dispose of.

All this I communicate to you for its legal effect.

P. and L.

CARLOS MANUEL DE CESPEDES,
The Governor.

MEJIA, *September 2, 1896.*

EXHIBIT No. 7.

REPUBLIC OF CUBA,
State of the East.

Census of the subprefecture of Caqo Rey, prefecture of La Sierra, district of Mayari.

Name.	Birthplace.	Condition.	Age.	Profession	Actual occupation.	Remarks.

EXHIBIT No. 8.

Jose Clemente Vivanco, secretary of the government council and
chancellor of the Republic of Cuba. I certify that on page 147 of the
minute book of the session of this council there are among other resolutions the following, taken in the meeting of the 30th day of last
June: "To declare vacant the position of subsecretary of the treasury
on account of the absence of Joaquin D. Castillo, who is on a mission
abroad, and on account of his having accepted a position in the delegation abroad, according to a letter received from him, in which he
asks the President for authority to continue in the discharge of his
duties abroad.

"To appoint subsecretary of the treasury, on motion of the secretary
of the department, Erneste Fonts Sterling." On motion of the subsecretary of foreign relations, acting as secretary, it was resolved to
declare vacant the position held by any person going abroad and accepting there another employment. And at the request of the acting
secretary of foreign affairs I give the present copy.

P. and L.

JOSE CLEMENTE VIVANCO.

SAN ANDRES, *July 7, 1896.*

Exhibit No. 9.

Republic of Cuba.

Using the faculties which the law accords to me, and hoping that you will know how to discharge the duties inherent to your charge, I appoint you professor of the public school at El Harpon, district of Mayari, of which appointment I will inform the secretary of the interior, for his approbation.

Patria y libertad.*

C. M. de Cespedes,
The Governor.

La Hormiga, *May 30, 1896.*

Exhibit No. 10.

Republic of Cuba,
Interior.

Instructions given to the prefects, and rules and regulations for the post-office service.

PRINTING PRESS OF EL CUBANO LIBRE, 1895.

Instructions given to the prefects.—The prefect is the superior authority of his territory, and the residents as well as travelers are under his authority; he is in duty bound to see that no abuses are committed nor crimes.

He shall divide his territory in as many prefectures as he may deem convenient for the best service of the administration.

He will inform the lieutenant-governor as to the necessities of the prefecture; he will watch the conduct of the subprefects. He shall distribute equally among them the articles delivered to him by the lieutenant-governor, and the ones who provide the army, and he shall have all the powers which belong to his office as an intermediary between the lieutenant-governors and the subprefects.

Until a law is established regulating the following, he shall be authorized to perform all civil marriages and all other contracts which will take place between the residents of his prefecture. He will also act in ordinary suits in the making of powers and wills, and he will state all this in a clear and comprehensive record, giving the interested parties certificates whenever they are asked.

He will commence all hearings in regard to crimes which may be committed in his territory. He shall transmit them afterwards to the nearest military chief, as well as deliver the culprit or culprits, with all the documents which may tend to give information in the case.

As to spies, guides, and mail carriers, and all those which our laws declare are to be considered as traitors, he shall judge them immediately as soon as they are made prisoners by a council consisting of three of the most prominent persons who may be in the prefecture, one acting as chairman and the other two as members of that council. This summary proceeding is to be followed on account of the difficulty of keeping in security these prisoners. He will also appoint a prosecuting attorney, and allow the accused to appoint a defender at will. After the council is assembled and all the requisites have been complied with, this court shall try the culprit and sentence him. Said sentence will be final and without appeal, but those taking part in the council shall be responsible to the superior government in case they depart from our laws and from natural justice. But in case there is near the prefecture an armed force of the republic they shall be sent to it so that they shall be tried in the proper manner.

The prefect shall make the census of the territory under him, stating the name of every person found in it, his condition, the number of members in each family, their age, their nativity, their occupation, if he is a laborer what is the nature of his labor, and if he has no occupation he shall so state it, so that the authorities shall know how to deal with him.

He shall also keep a book of civil register, to record the deaths, births, and marriages that there may be. He will establish in the prefecture as many workshops as he may consider necessary, so as to keep the army well provided, this being a principal duty of all the employees of the Republic. He shall not allow the hides to be lost, and he shall send them as soon as possible to the shoe factories, the saddle factories, and other departments. He will not allow any individual of his territory to be without occupation. He will make them all work, providing them with the instruments for their labor; he shall protect and extend the beehives, he will care for the abandoned ranches, and he will try to increase the different zones of cultivation.

As soon as he knows that in his territory the secretary of the interior has arrived, or some delegate of this department, he will immediately place himself at his orders; also whenever any armed forces, so as to provide them with whatever they may need. He will have a trumpet to advise the residents of his prefecture when the enemy is near, and he will inform the nearest armed force as soon as his territory has been invaded.

He will collect all the horses and other animals useful for war, and will keep them in a secure place, so that when the army shall need them they will be at hand, or when they may be asked by the civil authorities under whom he is.

He will provide the forces that may pass through his territory with whatever they may need, especially guides, meat, vegetables, and whatever is asked by the chief of the military forces. He will deliver also the articles manufactured in the workshop which are under his immediate inspection, always asking for a proper receipt.

He will also provide for the sustenance of the families in his territory, especially of those of the soldiers of the army of liberty. As soon as possible he will obey all the orders sent to him by the secretary of the interior or by the civil governor. These rules are to be added to the book of laws, rules, and circulars and other communications sent to him.

P. and L.

A copy.

Dr. SANTIAGO GARCIA CANIZARES,
, *Secretary of the Interior.*
FEDERICO PEREZ,
The Lieutenant-Colonel of the Staff of the First Army Corps.
September 24, 1895.

EXHIBIT No. 11.

Year 189—.] REPUBLIC OF CUBA, STATE OF ———. [Month of ———.

Delegation of the treasury in the district of ———.

Statement showing the receipts and disbursements made by this delegation during the month of ———, which is sent in duplicate to the treasury department of this State, according to what is ordered in article fifth of the law for the organization of the public treasury, passed on the 16th of October, 1895.

DR.   CR.

Date.	Number of receipt.	Receipt.	Gold.	Silver.	Date.	Number of voucher.	Disbursements.	Gold.	Silver.

Sum total, ———.   Sum total, ———.

P. and L. En ———, at ——— of ——— of 189—.

———— ————,
                                                                The Delegate.

———— ————,
                                                                The Secretary.

RECAPITULATION.

Total.	Article.	Value.
	Cheese..	
	Honey...	
	Wood..	
	Cattle..	
	Pigs	
	Coffee..	
	Cocoa...	
	Bananas...	
	Wax..	
	Total...	

EXHIBIT No. 12.

[Circular.]

Severo Pina y Marin, secretary of state in the treasury. This department, considering that the withdrawal of cattle from our fields and farms is detrimental to the revolution, and which turns into a benefit for our enemy, whom we combat, and such withdrawal has already been forbidden in the State of the East, in accordance with the Government council. I resolve the following, for the general knowledge in all the other States of the Island:

From the 1st of June the withdrawal of cattle of all and every description is absolutely forbidden from our fields and farms, and anyone infringing on this decree will be made responsible.

EXHIBIT NO. 12 *a.*

[Circular.]

TREASURY DEPARTMENT.

The number of cattle and pigs withdrawn since the beginning of the war up to date from the State of Camaguey being too large, and considering that in the future the army of liberation may need them, I have decreed as follows:

ARTICLE 1. From this date the withdrawal of cattle and pigs is absolutely prohibited, the withdrawal of those only which are 3 leagues distant from towns or in places where they are in imminent danger of falling into the hands of the enemy will be allowed, after the proper payment.

The civil as well as the military authority will proceed to enforce and make this circular obeyed.

SEVERO PINA,
Secretary of the Treasury.

DAGAMAL, CAMAGUEY, *January 1, 1896.*

And for its publication in the Boletin de la Guerra I give the present.

ORENCIO NODARSE,
The Chief Clerk of the Department.

DAGAMAL, *January 2, 1896.*

EXHIBIT No. 12 *b.*

STATE OF ORIENTE, TREASURY DEPARTMENT.

The Government council in a meeting held yesterday resolved the following:

The making of the present sugar crop is absolutely prohibited to all the plantations in the territory of the Republic. The owners of these plantations who disobey this order will be treated as enemies and tried as such when caught; the cane fields will be burned and the machinery and buildings destroyed. The employees of the said plantations who shall directly or indirectly contribute to the crop will be equally considered as enemies and prosecuted as such. The first named as well as the second, when captured, will be tried by a competent court.

I communicate this to you so that, in compliance with what has been resolved, you shall communicate it to the officers of the administration of the treasury and to the public in general.

EXHIBIT NO. 13.

Treasury of the Cuban Republic from the 5th of May to the 9th of September.

May 5, amount collected to date, as per account rendered (gold)	$271,300.00
May 8, Lawrence Tournure & Co., for account of plantation Santa Gertrudis	3,200.00
May 11, from the delegate for account of plantation Senado	3,745.79
May 14, from E. Dumois, equivalent of $21,576, Spanish gold, less $393 expenses, for account of treasury department	19,170.64
May 18, from H. Dumois, balance of his note for $8,500, Spanish gold, sent by Gen. A. Maceo	4,000.00
May 20, for account of plantation Santa Lucia, of Vita, Holguin, through Mosle Bros., for 10,723 bags of sugar through Ardemose	1,965.39

May 25, from E. Dumois—Banes—equivalent of $14,188.96, Spanish gold, less $1,392.15 exchange expenses, etc $12,796.81
May 27, remittance of Mr. Fluirioch, through Messrs. Mosle Bros 3,250.00
May 29, for account of plantation Santa Lucia, of Vita, Holguin, through Mosle Bros 1,000.00
Paid by Dr. Miranda, by order of the treasury department 50.00
June 1, from Dr. M. Ferrer, through the treasury department, to E. Rossell 50.00
June 3, from N. de Cardenas, through the treasury department, for his son, N. de Cardenas, of Benitez 100.00
From R. Nuñez, through the treasury department, for Federico Nuñez... 15.00
June 9, from S. Garcia Cañizares, delegate of the treasury exchange of Flint, Eddy & Co 7,500.00
From Mosle Bros , for account of the plantation Senado, 8,950 bags sugar 1,943.43
For account of plantation Santa Lucia, Vita, Holguin, through Mosle Bros., 4,920 bags of sugar 1,150.40
From Felix Tznaga, from Dr. Betances, to give to Herminio Feguerola, through the treasury department 19.00
June 10, from Dr. R. Menocal, given to Mario Menocal by the secretary of the treasury 100.00
June 15, from Alfredo Lopez Juyillo to offset same amount given by the treasury department to Martin Marrero 10.00
From Alfredo Figuerva to pay to Leopoldo Nuñez through the secretary of treasury 15.00
June 30, for account of plantation Santa Lucia, Vita, through Mosle Bros. 1,000.00
For account of plantation Senado, through Mosle Bros., on account 1,863 bags sugar 1,418.00
For account of plantation Santa Lucia, through Mosle Bros., on account of 11,575 bags of sugar 2,565.00
July 11, from H. Dumois & Co., balance of note of $8,500, Spanish gold, sent by General Maceo 2,650.00
From Tomas Padro Griñan, subsecretary of the treasury of the east..... 322.00
July 15, for taxes on Jaguay lumber 1,000.00
July 15, from H. Dumois & Co., on account of his note for $8,000, Spanish gold, sent by Gen. A. Maceo 5,000.00
July 23, from the delegate from V. S. Curtis, through Mrs. R. Livingston, to pay $60 in Cuba Libre to F. E. Curtis, lieutenant of Salvador Rios; also $10 to be paid same by the treasury department 70.00
July 30, sent by the President of the Republic by Señor Bernal 3,215.50
July 31, for account of plantation Santa Lucia, through Mosle Bros 1,000.00
August 3, from Dreifous, balance of taxes on Taguajay lumber 1,435.00
August 6, from Dr. Menocal, to pay to Manuel Recio 20.00
August 12, from Mosle Bros., for account of Bernabe Sanchez Adan Minces, for balance of tax on crop 2,705.84
From Mosle Bros., for account of plantation Santa Lucia on 3,305 bags of sugar 3,747.63
From Dr. R. Menocal, to pay to Guarino Lauda from treasury department. 30.00
August 15, from Mosle Bros., for account of plantation Santa Lucia for 3,000 bags of sugar 633.00
August 20, from Mosle Bros., for account of plantation Santa Lucia for 3,836 bags of sugar 867.20
August 25, from Severo Pina and Antonio Aguilera Molina, through Mosle Bros 3,826.29
August 28, received from Messrs. Lawrence Tournure & Co., for account of A. L. F. A., of Guantanamo, three bills of exchange on J. M. Andrews for account of plantations Romalie, $1,000; Isabel, $2,500; Soledad, $2,000; exchange 10 per cent, $500 .... 5,000.00
August 21, from Mosle Bros., for account of plantation Santa Lucia on 2,427 bags of sugar 550.12

    E. V. O 364,558.87

NOTE.

September 8, from Ana Quesada de Cespedes, to pay to Carlos M. de Cespedes through the treasury of the east. $150.00
September 9, from John Smith, of Guantanamo, through a bank here who wishes to remain unknown, $7,176.20, Spanish gold, at 11 per cent exchange, American gold 6,465.05
Bills from Guantanamo, indorsed "John Kay," on Coudert Bros 7,500.00

    Total 14,115.05

Exhibit No. 13a.

The government council, in session held on the 14th instant, considering that, according to the law of military organization, there is established the rank of general of division, which did not exist when, on the 2d of December, 1895, the salaries which the military and employees of the Republic should enjoy, resolved to modify the resolution of that date, which will now remain in the following form:

Major-general, monthly salary	$500
General of division, monthly salary	450
Brigadier, monthly salary	400
Colonel, monthly salary	325
Lieutenant-colonel, monthly salary	275
Major, monthly salary	220
Captain, monthly salary	130
Lieutenant, monthly salary	100
Sublieutenant, monthly salary	90
First sergeant, monthly salary	60
Second sergeant, monthly salary	50
Corporal, monthly salary	40
Soldier, monthly salary	30

P. and L.

JOSÉ CLEMENTE VIVANCO,
The Secretary of the Council and Chancellor.

SEPTEMBER, 16, 1896.

I sanction this in all its parts. Promulgate it in the legal form.

P. and L.

SALVADOR CISNEROS BETANCOURT.

Exhibit No. 13b.

OFFICIAL DEPARTMENT—GOVERNMENT COUNCIL—SECRETARY.

José Clemente Vivanco, secretary of the government council and chancellor of the Republic of Cuba, I certify that on page 84 of the minute book of the sessions of the council, among the expressed conditions required of the plantations, which on account of contracts made with military chiefs before the formation of the government, are authorized to make the present sugar harvest, according to article 21 of the constitution, they must comply, besides the special ones, with these of general application.

The plantation must not be allowed to be fortified extraordinarily by the Spanish troops. No person belonging to the army of liberation can be employed in the harvest labor.

All the labor must be entirely suspended from the 31st of May of the present year, 1896, on; the laborers must be withdrawn and the beasts taken away from the plantations.

The violation of any of the above conditions, as well as the special ones required, will be sufficient motive to rescind the contract, the transgressor being considered as an enemy.

And for general knowledge, I issue the present in Mejico, on the 6th of January, 1896.

P. y L.

JOSÉ CLEMENTE VIVANCO,
The Secretary of the Council.

Exhibit No. 13c.

The government council, in its session of the 26th instant, resolved:
"To allow the transportation of the lumber and woods which are at
present felled and ready to be shipped in the rivers of the Republic
after the payment of the corresponding tax."

Approved by the President, its publication was ordered.

P. and L.

Residence of the council, on the 29th of June, 1896.

J. C. VIVANCO,
The Secretary of the Council and Chancellor.

Exhibit No. 14.

The government council in its meeting of the 29th of last June
installed as secretary of foreign affairs, on account of the absence of
the secretary, Citizen Eusebio Hernandez, and extended to him a warm
welcome.

All this I have the honor to inform you for its legal effect.

P. and L.

En La Yaya, on the 1st of July, 1896.

JOSÉ CLEMENTA VIVANCO,
The Secretary of the Council.

To the Delegate Plenipotentiary of the Republic of Cuba Abroad.

Exhibit No. 15.

The government council, in its meeting of the 19th instant, resolved
to accept the resignation of Mario Garcia Menocal as subsecretary of
war, and appointed in his stead Rafael Manduley to occupy the said
position.

It also resolved at the same meeting to appoint as subsecretary of
foreign relations Eusebio Hernandez, on account of the resignation of
Dr. Fermin Valdes Dominguez accepted on the 6th instant.

All this I have the honor to inform you for its legal effect.

P. and L.

La Yaya, May 21, 1896.

JOSÉ CLEMENT VIVANCO,
The Secretary of the Council.

To Citizen TOMAS ESTRADA PALMA,
Delegate Plenipotentiary of the Republic of Cuba.

Exhibit No. 15a.

EL CUBANO LIBRE, *March 10, 1896.*

[October 29, page 41.]

To approve the law for military recruiting and the organization of the
reserve corps proposed by the acting secretary of war.

S. Doc. 231, pt 7——12

[November 21, page 55]

To grant Tomas Estrada Palma, delegate plenipotentiary, expressed authority to take abroad all economic steps which he may deem indispensable in favor of the revolution, giving him the following powers:

First. To personally, or by delegates, represent the Republic of Cuba before the governments and people of all nations in which he may consider convenient to name a representative, giving him whatever powers he thinks adequate.

Second. To contract for one or more loans, the proceeds of which are to be used in the service of the Republic, guaranteeing said loans with all the public property, land taxes, custom-house duties, present and future, of the said Republic, issuing bonds, registered or coupon, for an amount which he may deem convenient, payable, as well as the interests, when he may judge it opportune; empowering him also to determine the nominal value of the bonds, the interest they earn, condition of the payment of the capital and interest which he may consider most favorable in order to place the said bonds at the best price, and also to mortgage them.

Third. To issue paper money in the name of the Republic of Cuba, for the amount which he may think necessary and in the form and conditions which he considers most adequate.

Fourth. To issue postage stamps of the denominations which he may consider most convenient for the service of the Republic.

Fifth. The bonds, as well as the paper money issued, shall be signed by the delegate plenipotentiary or the person delegated by him, and by the treasurer of the Cuban revolutionary party, and must have the seal and marks which the delegate may deem most effectual to prevent forgery.

Sixth. It shall be the duty of the delegate to appoint, as soon as he receives this authority, a subdelegate, who shall have all his powers in case of the permanent incapacity or death of the delegate; but the subdelegate will have no powers whatever until one of the said cases occurs; then he will act temporarily until the government appoints a new delegate. The appointment of subdelegate may be revoked at will by the delegate, making at the same time of the revocation a new appointment.

Seventh. The delegate may substitute this authority in any of its parts, delegating special powers for the loan in any place he may deem convenient; and also establishing departments, giving them the required powers for the discharge of their business and removing the employees at will and appointing others of his confidence in their stead.

Eighth. To receive, collect, invest the funds of whatever kind coming to his hands; investing them in the way which he may deem best for the interests of the Republic. He is also empowered to grant concessions and conclude, in the name of the Republic, all the agreements and contracts which he may judge of benefit to the interests of the same, these contracts being hereby ratified by that government.

[22d of November, page 58]

To permit the entry in the towns, after being provided with a safe conduct which will be given by the superior civil authorities to prefect and by the military to lieutenant-colonel having forces under his command, each in their respective districts.

[24th of November, page 60.]

To publish a circular prohibiting the present crop of all the sugar plantations in the territory of the Republic.

[28th of November, page 63.]

"To communicate to all the chiefs of the army that whatever resolution is passed by this council shall be transcribed in the 'order of the day,' in order that—known by all—it may have a most exact fulfillment." To grant those who come from educational centers to the rank of the army of liberation the consideration and military position which their abilities will warrant, taking into account the following scale: Corporal, he who may have studied two years of philosophy; sergeant, he who may have passed four years; sublieutenant, he who may have graduated as bachelor.

EXHIBIT No. 16.

[Republic of Cuba, Army of Liberty   Headquarters of the Sanitary Department   Law of the Sanitary Department, 1896.   Camaguey.   Government Printing Office]

LAW OF SANITARY DEPARTMENT.

Article first. The sanitary corps has for its object to give its services to all the wounded and sick in campaign as well as to decide all questions in regard to the health of the army.

Article second. It will be composed of doctors or bachelors in medicine, surgery, and pharmacy.

Article third. The sanitary corps will be subject to the secretary of war.

Article fourth. Promotion shall be by service.

Article fifth. It shall be composed of the following officers: A superior chief of the department, with the rank of brigadier; as many chiefs with the ranks of colonel as there are army corps; as many head physicians as there are physicians in every army corps with the rank of lieutenant-colonel, and as many physicians of the first class as there be brigades, with the ranks of majors, and as many second physicans of the second class as there be regiments or battalions, with the rank of captains.

Article sixth. The auxiliaries of the sanitary department will consist of aids with the rank of lieutenants and of nurses which will be of first and second class with the rank of sublieutenants and sergeants.

Article seventh. The chief of the sanitary department will have under his care the organization, direction, and inspection of his department, and the provision of all the necessary material. It will be his duty to inform the general in chief of the army of all matters relating to his department, but he may resolve in urgent cases, always giving account of his decision to the general in chief.

Article eighth. The promotion from sublieutenants to colonels, inclusive, in the sanitary department, will be made after proposal by the superior chief of same to the secretary of war, said proposals to be accompanied by a certificate of their services. The appointment of the superior chief of the sanitary department belongs to the government council.

Article ninth. The appointment of nurses shall belong to the chief of the sanitary department.

Article tenth. In each army corps there will be a chief of the sanitary department whose duty shall be, first, to have under him all those belonging to his department and to make a list of them; second, the direction and inspection of the hospitals; third, to form a body of nurses; fourth, to carry a book of record in which the losses of the army of liberty shall be stated.

Article eleventh. In each division there will be a head physician whose duty shall be, first, to have under him the professional members of his division, and second, the formation of hospitals and their care.

Article twelfth. In each brigade there will be a physician of the first class whose duties are, first, to have under him the professional members of his brigade; second, to appoint those persons who are to have charge of the hospitals and to inspect the sanitary service of the regiments and battalions.

Article thirteenth. In each regiment or battalion there will be a physician of the second class whose duties are, first, to watch over the members of the hospitals and to distribute them; second, to send a detailed account of the losses which may occur in the corps and of the persons cured, always giving the proper certificate.

Article fourteenth. The sanitary aides shall have as duties not only those given to them by their chief, but also to form statements to be sent to the sanitary corps to which they belong.

Article fifteenth. The nurses shall be appointed by the chief at the proposal of the army physician, and shall be ruled by a special regulation which each chief shall make according to the necessities of the corps in which they serve.

Article sixteenth. The persons belonging to the pharmacy corps will be composed of a head pharmacist, with the rank of lieutenant-colonel in each corps, another of the first class with the rank of major in each division, and one of the second with the rank of captain in each brigade.

Article seventeenth. The chief pharmacist will reside in the headquarters of the sanitary department; the pharmacists of the first and second class shall reside in their respective divisions and brigades.

Article eighteenth. Their duties are to ask for all materials and articles of medicine and pharmacy; second, to examine them; third, to take care of them, and to replace them.

Article nineteenth. The individuals who compose the sanitary department are under the immediate orders of the chief of the military sanitary department, or of the superior chief, in regard to matters in relation to the department, and in other matters they are under the general in chief of the corps.

Article twentieth. Only with the signature of the physician will the pharmacist give prescriptions or deliver chemical products as well as material and instruments of surgery.

Article twenty-first. The individuals of the sanitary crops which for special circumstances may deserve rank, will obtain it from the general in chief without this destroying the regular order of their promotion.

Article twenty-second. To enter the sanitary department diplomas must be presented in their respective professions or certificates. In case these are wanting, it will be sufficient for five persons to testify to it.

Article twenty-third. In case that there be not physicians and druggists enough to cover the number demanded by these rules they will be appointed pro tem. from those nurses in medicine and students of pharmacy as there may be.

Article twenty-fourth. Surgeon-dentists may discharge the duty of aides in the sanitary department, with the rank of captain.

Additional article. The sanitary inspectors, the head physicians, those of the first and second class, are obliged not only to give their services to the military forces to which they belong, but also to the territory to which they are appointed.

This was submitted to the government council on the 26th of March, 1896, by the undersigned.

Dr. SANCHEZ AGRAMONTE,
The Superior Chief of the Sanitary Military Department.

It was passed on the 31st of March, 1896.

JOSÉ CLEMENTE VIVANCO,
The Secretary of the Council.

The council agreed to it and sanctioned it in all its parts. Promulgated in legal form March 31, 1896.

SALVADOR CISNEROS,
The President.

EXHIBIT No. 17.

The government council, in its meeting of this date, has resolved the following:

"To rescind the decree of the 28th of November of last year, from the 1st of next August, in reference to the residents of the Island, and from the same day of October to those coming from abroad; the said degree rescinded is in regard to military rank, to be given to students and to those who may have obtained a professional diploma. In the future these individuals shall enter the ranks in the different professional corps created for that purpose with the consideration and rank which may be granted to them by the rules and regulations so far approved, and which may in the future be adopted."

All this is made public for general information.

P. and L.

En La Yaya, 20th of May, 1896.

JOSE CLEMENTE VIVANCO,
The Secretary of the Council and Chancellor.

TOMAS ESTRADA PALMA,
Delegate Plenipotentiary of the Republic Abroad.

EXHIBIT No. 18.

[Translation to be found in Exhibit No. 4.]

In virtue of these considerations I propose to the council of the Government, that as an amplification of its resolution of the 10th of May last, it may see fit to decree that said resolution remain as follows:

First. All agricultural operations are absolutely forbidden which have a tendency to prepare for the coming sugar crop, such as the sowing or hoeing of the sugar-cane fields.

Second. The crop of 1896 to 1897, is absolutely forbidden.

Third. Anyone infringing on these orders will be considered a traitor and will be condemned to death, in the form that our penal laws prescribe.

Fourth. The cane fields will be burned. The buildings destroyed of all estates (centrals or colonias) which may cultivate sugar cane, or may prepare or intend to begin to grind, and they will be confiscated.

Fifth. Confiscation will be made effective by applying in full the value of those estates, the day the revolution will triumph, to the payment of debts the revolution may have contracted, or to any legal payment they may be destined to discharge. If this case should occur, no sale, mortgage, or embargo subsequent to the decree of May 15 ultimo will have any force or validity.

Sixth. The present resolutions will be communicated to the general in chief, so that as a measure of war he may circulate them among all the officers of the army, that they may comply with them, and they will also be made to circulate among the civil officers of the Republic, so that they may know them and may make them known to all, and cooperate in their being complied with.

Seventh. Any civil or military officer, who should not cooperate to the strict fulfillments of them to the utmost in his power, will incur the punishment which our laws provide.

Eighth. These resolutions will be published in all the newspapers of the Republic; they will be sent to foreign lands so that they may be known, and may be published extensively on loose sheets in order that they may reach in a profuse manner the territories of the enemy.

These resolutions are agreed to in all their parts.

EXHIBIT No. 19.

[Coat of arms of the Republic.]

REPUBLIC OF CUBA, *July 13, 1896.*

MANIFESTO.

We want to add and not to subtract.

Consistent with our invariable policy of attraction, without hatred nor malice, with any spirit of discord or revenge, impelled alone in this struggle by the love of our country, which, sadly, enslaved clamors for the cooperation of all her children in obtaining her liberty, it is not possible that we see with indifference acts practiced by our obsecrated brethren, who on the other side battle against the desire of liberty which guides us for the welfare of our unfortunate country and for the honor and benefit of her children.

To-day, when the revolution, owing to its power, animosity, and grandeur, does not require as a necessity for its triumph new elements to aid her; to-day, when our resources of unquestioned solidity are more than enough to obtain the aspired end—the absolute independence of Cuba; to-day is when, nevertheless, we turn our eyes to our duped and misguided brothers who continue on the side of the enemy, assisting him to combat us and the idea of happiness we wish for Cuba.

We who, guided solely by the idea of humanity, respond to the measures taken by the enemy of punishing the prisoners they make us, respond by always pardoning the vanquished; we who have declared more than once that our struggle is not inspired by race hatred, nor is it moved by the bloody intention of destroying one by one the lives of those who fight us; we who have stated that our object has always been to attract, unite, to add without considering origin or nationality;

we who receive equally in our midst the repentant Spaniard who fought us with arms, and the liberty-loving foreigner who spontaneously offers us his services; we can not feel a stoic indifference when we see far from us some sons of Cuba—certainly very few—striving to obtain the only end they can—degradation.

And since we are not indifferent, since such acts of our brethren cause us acute pain, as we feel the pleasures and misfortunes of our country; it is for those reasons that to-day the government council, which I am honored in presiding, tries by this manifesto, full of faith and fraternal love, to carry to the conscience of those brothers the conviction that it is yet time to indicate their conduct; that the country always welcomes the repentant child, and that we who represent her will receive them with open arms, so that on the day of victory for Cuba, due to her children—native and adoptive—we shall offer the glorious spectacle of having broken our chains and constituted before the civilized world a new nation worthy by its culture to figure in the international community.

Spaniards who love liberty, Cubans who hate tyranny, come with your noble hearts to intone the hymn of redemption which we sing before the sacred altar of country.

That together, without the tortures of remorse, we may celebrate with pride the glorious day of independence.

It is yet time to repent.

Cuba knows how to pardon.

Your president,

SALVADOR CISNEROS BETANCOURT.

P. y L.

LA SACRA, *Residence of the Executive, July 13, 1896.*

EXHIBIT NO. 19a.

MANIFESTO.

It is to-day exactly one year since the assembly of representatives, constituted for the formation of the fundamental code of the Republic and the election of the individuals who should form the council of government, as the supreme power of the nation, delivered into our hands its powers, giving us the difficult and thorny mission of governing the destinies of this Cuban country. One year in which, answering to the conscientious dictates of our good will, we have tried, sometimes despising and others vanquishing the numberless obstacles which, in times of construction and organization, in an armed struggle, have presented themselves. We owe such a brilliant result, not to the intelligence, ability, and abnegation of us, who constitute the highest body of the Republic, for we only claim the best intentions, but to the discipline of the army, whose abnegation and patriotism, a thousand times tested, strives to comply with the orders given by the constituted Government, giving thus an example to the civilized world of the harmony of principles which guide us and the unity in the aim that we anxiously hope to obtain.

Our representatives, yet unofficial, abroad give us every day proofs of the sympathy for our cause all over the world; and although we have not been recognized as belligerents, the opinion of foreign Governments is being matured to recognize us as an independent power.

Spain, with its nameless stupidity, thinks she can intimidate us with her numerous contingents of soldiers, driven from their unfortunate mothers to be sacrificed to the ambition of a few in a land where nature is their enemy as if nature itself would protest of the domination over cultured people. Never has any nation carried her stupidity to such an extent in the sacrifice of her children for ambition.

Two hundred thousand men on a war footing she has sent against us to subdue us; she has not been able to obtain in a year and a half, but to see her armies driven to the fortified towns, whence they do not sally but to be defeated. Millions of dollars have been spent annually to keep up this state—amounts which have injured her credit and exposed her to die of her own moral weakness.

New contingents, new millions, will be the last effort of Spain in the next winter. Let us redouble our efforts to destroy them. Let the enthusiasm and patriotism that has sustained us till this day go on in our souls; let the harmony, which is a privilege we have, continue, and Spain will again have failed, and Cuba, worthy and happy, will be able, with her forehead raised, to salute with affection the New World and offer her respects to the Old.

P. y L.

SALVADOR CISNEROS BETANCOURT.

SEBANICA, *September 18, 1896.*

EXHIBIT NO. 20.

PROCLAMATION.

HEADQUARTERS OF THE LIBERATING ARMY.

To the inhabitants of the Island of Cuba, to our brothers of free America, of unredeemed Puerto Rico, and of the civilized world:

Many times has the sun shone on wonderful scenes on this land so wet with generous blood!

On the second fortnight of the month of September, 1895, 20 men, chosen patriots, have met in Jimaguayu, department of Camaguey, on the same spot where stout Agramento fell—Camaguey's hero.

Cuba, strong and decided, battles for its freedom, to be able to exercise its rights of sovereignty. At this moment she is going to constitute the government of its redeeming revolution. The constituent assembly formed of 3,000 armed men of the three arms, have in useless advances tried to interrupt the work of so respectable an assembly.

During the battle the constituent assembly, almost wrapped up in the smoke of the combat at the side of our wounded soldiers, and hearing the roar of the enemy's cannon, has finished its work forming the supreme power of the government of the redeeming revolution of Cuba, and presents to the whole country and to the free, civilized world the most solemn and magnificent fact which, in these times of liberty and progress, could be presented in America, as this the installation of the government of the revolution of Cuba, and the promulgation of its fundamental law, all adequated to the necessities of war.

Inhabitants of the Island of Cuba, the revolution is already assured, and the struggle which must be sustained with faith and resolution will confirm with its definite triumph the future Republic of Cuba. With peace will come happiness; labor will come without rancor; for under the flag of the Republic of Cuba there will be room for all honest men.

Free countries of America, who contemplate in wonder this bloody struggle for liberty, Cuba salutes you and sends you its respects, awaiting triumph, which honors the free; she salutes you in the name of the highest majesty of the principles which she defends on her own soil, stained with so much blood, already spilled—Cuban blood and Spanish blood—flowing in torrents through Spanish stubbornness. In the name of this heroic people, armed to conquer their independence, I give the good news that the foundation of the Republic is cemented.

Long live the constitution! Long live the government! Long live the Republic!

MAXIMO GOMEZ,
The General in Chief.

Exhibit No. 21 with Senate document.

EXHIBIT No. 22.

In the town of Cuaimaro, on the 28th of October, 1896, the government council held an extraordinary session under the presidency of Citizen Salvador Cisneros Betancourt, there being present the vice-president, Citizen Bartolome Maso, and the secretaries of state, Citizen Severo Pina, of the treasury department, Rafael M. Portuondo, of foreign relations, and my secretary.

The President declares that the object of the call of the present extraordinary session is that the council of government having been present in all the operations against Cuaimaro, and having witnessed the able direction of Maj. Gen. Calixto Garcia, Iniguez, chief of the eastern department, as well as the patriotism, valor, and discipline of the general, commanders, officers, classes, and privates under him, who realized such an important operation obtaining a most complete success, wishes that the government council officially assembled will consider such a brilliant feat of arms of the army of liberation.

The other members of the council unanimously declared their conformity to what the president has declared and agreed, that the government council declares its pleasure and satisfaction for the new and notable triumph obtained by the army of liberation under the able direction of Maj. Gen. Calixto Garcia.

It is unanimously resolved that, through the war department, the government council congratulate Maj. Gen. Calixto Garcia, chief of the military department of the east, as well as the generals, commanders, officers, classes, and privates who, under his orders, have contributed with their courage and patriotism to the complete success of the capture and occupation of the town of Guaimaro, and that a certified copy of these minutes be sent to him for its insertion in the general order of the day.

At the same time this congratulation is extended to the general in chief, Maj. Gen. Maximo Gomez, for this new and notable triumph of the army of liberation.

There being no other business, the present session was declared closed.

(The signatures follow.)

EXHIBIT No. 23.

Copy of a military order of the 21st day of November, 1896.

Chief of the day, Lieut. Gil Martinez.
Outposts, Capt. Ruf. Ferrer.
Officer of the service, Lieut. José Yngarry.
Service of the pickets and explorers in charge of the chief of the day.

Owing to the irreparable misfortune which occurred in the battle in the Pass of Damas of the Zaza River, on the 18th instant, the death of Maj. Gen. Serafin Sanchez, inspector-general of the army of liberation, this general headquarters, deeply moved, has ordered:

First. To communicate the news to the government council of the Republic and to the general in chief of the army of liberation.

Second. To order nine days of mourning in all the headquarters which feels profound pain at the loss of one of the most illustrious and brave generals and honest servants of the country; and

Third. To publish in the newspaper La Republica for general information the said occurrence, reminding the soldiers of independence of the place where the distinguished leader of liberty fell, so that they will raise to morrow a monument which will remind future generations of- the prowesses of he who has already won in our hearts.

P. y L.

FRANCISCO CARRILLO,
The Major-General.

GENERAL HEADQUARTERS IN LAS CHIVAS,
November 20, 1896.

[See pp. 13, 40, 143, 321, and pp. 119, 199, 276, Vol. VI.]

FIFTY-FIFTH CONGRESS, SECOND SESSION.

February 14, 1898.

[Senate Report No. 577.]

Mr. Morgan, from the Committee on Foreign Relations, submitted the following report:

The Senate referred to the Committee on Foreign Relations an amendment intended to be proposed to the consular and diplomatic appropriation bill, passed by the House of Representatives and now under consideration by the Senate Committee on Appropriations, in these words:

That a condition of public war exists between the Government of Spain and the government proclaimed and for some time maintained by force of arms by the people of Cuba, and that the United States of America shall maintain a strict neutrality between the contending powers, according to each all the rights of belligerents in the ports and territory of the United States.

In terms this proposed amendment is identical with a joint resolution which passed the Senate on the 20th day of May, 1897. was sent to the House of Representatives and referred to a standing committee of that body, where it is still pending.

In the adoption of that joint resolution the Senate, after full debate and mature consideration, performed what it conceived to be a solemn duty to our country that was demanded by a proper regard for the rights and welfare of our own people. Their love of justice, humanity, liberty, and independence of foreign oppression constrained our people to regard the persecuted native people of Cuba with earnest sympathy, and caused them to admire and applaud their heroism in the defense of their homes and families against the most atrocious violence. In this demonstration of sympathy with the cause of the republic of Cuba our people, almost with one accord, admitted their obedience to the obligations and duties of Christian civilization, and demanded the intervention of our Government against their cruel abuse and abandonment by Spain in the war of extermination now being conducted against the Cuban people.

The committee has found no reason for suggesting the modification of the action of the Senate on that resolution in any part of the history of the war in Cuba. The necessity for that action has been made more manifest, since the passage of this resolution by the terrible and unexampled wrongs to humanity in process of perpetration by Spain against her former subjects, and now more fully realized in the extermination of noncombatants by tens of thousands, and their starvation, by military orders, in groups of hundreds of thousands, who, lingering, still live.

The Senate has nothing to regret or to modify as to the action that was taken in the adoption of the resolution now again presented for its action, and still hopefully invites the concurrence of the House of Representatives. In all parliamentary usage, and in accord with the spirit of our institutions, the Houses, in their action upon all questions presented to them, are entirely free and independent in their deliberations and votes. It is needless to say that any attempt to coerce one of the Houses of Congress by the action of the other is derogatory to the welfare of the country; and it is a high duty of each House to avoid giving to the other any reasonable ground of complaint or apprehension of such a purpose.

It is, on the contrary, an imperative duty that such a suspicion should be made fairly impossible. The Government must be supported, and the necessary appropriations for the consular and diplomatic service are of vital importance. Under existing conditions it is not an unreasonable supposition that it will be in the nature of compulsion or coercion of the House of Representatives if the Senate should place upon that bill an amendment in the same terms with the joint resolution heretofore adopted by the Senate, which is still pending in the House of Representatives.

It is more clearly a reasonable inference that such would be the purpose of the Senate, because the same effort was made in the House of Representatives, on the passage of the consular and diplomatic appropriation bill, to place this proposed amendment upon that bill, and the motion was lost through the action of that body.

The desire of the committee that the joint resolution adopted by the Senate should be adopted by the House of Representatives is earnest and unanimous, but they do not recommend that any action should be taken in the Senate that will or can in any way be considered by that honorable body as an interference with their perfect freedom and independence in their deliberations upon any measure.

The committee recommends that the proposed amendment be laid upon the table.

[See pp. 307, 1016, and pp. 11, 15, 33, 78, 199, 363, Vol. VI.]

FIFTY-FIFTH CONGRESS, SECOND SESSION.

March 16, 1898

[Senate Report No. 681.]

Mr. Davis, from the Committee on Foreign Relations, submitted the following report:

The joint resolution for the annexation of Hawaii to the United States, herewith reported to the Senate by the Committee on Foreign Relations as a substitute for Senate joint resolution No. 100 and Senate bill No. 2263, which were referred to that committee, brings that subject within reach of the legislative power of Congress under the precedent that was established in the annexation of Texas. A treaty of annexation was negotiated between Texas, as an independent State, and the United States, which was signed by the agents of the high contracting powers on the 12th day of April, 1844, and was submitted to the Senate of the United States by President Tyler, with a recommendation that it be ratified.

After mature consideration that treaty was rejected by the Senate on the 8th day of June, 1844, by a vote of 16 Senators for ratification and 35 Senators against ratification. A copy of that treaty is appended to this report, marked Appendix 1.

The people of Texas were so indignant at the rejection of this treaty that a powerful party at once sprang into existence in favor of a treaty of alliance with Great Britain, and Mexico was known to be ready to acknowledge and guarantee the independence of Texas if she would agree never to form a union with any other country.

The people of the United States became greatly aroused at the prospect of losing Texas, in consequence of the indignation of her people over the rejection of the treaty, and they demanded immediate annexation by a law that would speak the will of the majority in Congress. Afterwards, and without any further action by the Republic of Texas to signify its consent to annexation to the United States, the following joint resolution, containing two alternate sections, passed both Houses of Congress and was approved by the President on the 7th day of March, 1845. The vote in the Senate on the passage of this joint resolution was, ayes, 23; nays, 19. In the House of Representatives the vote was, ayes, 120; nays, 98. The following is a copy of that joint resolution:

No. 8. JOINT RESOLUTION for annexing Texas to the United States

Resolved by the Senate and House of Representatives of the United States of America in Congress assembled, That Congress doth consent that the territory properly included within, and rightfully belonging to the Republic of Texas, may be erected into a new State, to be called the State of Texas, with a republican form of government, to be adopted by the people of said republic, by deputies in convention assembled, with the consent of the existing government, in order that the same may be admitted as one of the States of this Union.

2. *And be it further resolved*, That the foregoing consent of Congress is given upon the following conditions, and with the following guarantees, to wit:

First, Said State to be formed, subject to the adjustment by this Government of all questions of boundary that may arise with other governments; and the constitution thereof, with the proper evidence of its adoption by the people of said Republic of Texas, shall be transmitted to the President of the United States, to be laid before Congress for its final action, on or before the first day of January, one thousand eight hundred and forty-six.

Second. Said State, when admitted into the Union, after ceding to the United States, all public edifices, fortifications, barracks, ports and harbors, navy and navy-yards, docks, magazines, arms, armaments, and all other property and means pertaining to the public defence belonging to said Republic of Texas, shall retain all the public funds, debts, taxes, and dues of every kind, which may belong to or be due and owing said republic; and shall also retain all the vacant and unappropriated lands lying within its limits, to be applied to the payment of the debts and liabilities of said Republic of Texas, and the residue of said lands, after discharging said debts and liabilities, to be disposed of as said State may direct; but in no event are said debts and liabilities to become a charge upon the Government of the United States.

Third. New States, of convenient size, not exceeding four in number, in addition to said State of Texas, and having sufficient population, may hereafter, by the consent of said State, be formed out of the territory thereof, which shall be entitled to admission under the provisions of the Federal Constitution. And such States as may be formed out of that' portion of said territory lying south of thirty-six degrees thirty minutes north latitude, commonly known as the Missouri compromise line, shall be admitted into the Union with or without slavery, as the people of each State asking admission may desire. And in such State or States as shall be formed out of said territory north of said Missouri compromise line, slavery, or involuntary servitude (except for crime) shall be prohibited.

3. *And be it further resolved*, That if the President of the United States shall in his judgment and discretion deem it most advisable, instead of proceeding to submit the foregoing resolution to the Republic of Texas, as an overture on the part of the United States for admission, to negotiate with that Republic; then,

Be it resolved, That a State, to be formed out of the present Republic of Texas, with suitable extent and boundaries, and with two representatives in Congress, until the next apportionment of representation, shall be admitted into the Union, by virtue of this act, on an equal footing with the existing States, as soon as the terms and conditions of such admission, and the cession of the remaining Texian territory to the United States shall be agreed upon by the Governments of Texas and the United States: And that the sum of one hundred thousand dollars be, and the same is hereby, appropriated to defray the expenses of missions and negotiations, to agree upon the terms of said admission and cession, either by treaty to be submitted to the Senate, or by article to be submitted to the two Houses of Congress, as the President may direct.

Approved March 1, 1845.

In this act it was left to the discretion of the President to accept annexation by treaty or by articles of agreement with the Government of Texas, which were to be valid if made with the President of Texas under legislative authority, or by the act of a convention chosen by the people of Texas, under like authority. The Government of Texas preferred the convention plan, and a convention was called. The governor submitted to the people the question of annexation and it was voted, but the act of the legislature calling the convention made no such provision.

Acting on the consent of Texas to come into the Union as a State under the provisions of section 1 of the act of March 7, 1845, Congress, on the 29th of December, 1845, declared, by joint resolution, that Texas was one of the States of the American Union.

This joint resolution clearly establishes the precedent that Congress has the power to annex a foreign State to the territory of the United States, either by assenting to a treaty of annexation or by agreeing to articles of annexation or by act of Congress based upon the consent of such foreign Government obtained in any authentic way.

No exercise of power could be more supreme than that under which Texas was annexed to the United States, either as to its scope or the manner of the annexation or the choice of conditions upon which Congress would merge the sovereignty of an independent republic into the supremacy of the United States.

This act also establishes the fact that a treaty with a foreign State which declares the consent of such State to be annexed to the United States, although it is rejected by the Senate of the United States, is a sufficient expression and authentication of the consent of such foreign State to authorize Congress to enact a law providing for annexation, which, when complied with, is effectual without further legislation to merge the sovereignty of such independent State into a new and different relation to the United States and toward its own people.

It further establishes the fact that Congress, in legislating upon the question of the annexation of a foreign State, rightfully acts upon the consent of such State as the sovereign representative of its people, and that the power of Congress to complete the annexation of such foreign State depends alone upon the sovereign will and consent of such State, given and expressed through its organized tribunals.

It further establishes the fact that Congress can not acquire the right or jurisdiction to annex a foreign and independent state through a vote of a majority of its people, in opposition to the will of its constituted authorities.

It is the constitutional power of Congress that operates to annex foreign territory. Such a proceeding on the part of Congress as the submission of the question to vote of the people of such a state would only create disorder and revolution in a foreign state applying through its constituted authorities for admission into the United States.

This important, clear, and far-reaching precedent established in the annexation of the Republic of Texas is a sufficient guide for the action of Congress in the passage of the joint resolution herewith reported. If, in the judgment of Congress, such a measure is supported by a safe and wise policy, or is based upon a national duty that we owe to the people of Hawaii, or is necessary for our national development and security, that is enough to justify annexation, with the consent of the recognized government of the country to be annexed.

THE POLICY OF ANNEXATION, as it applies to Hawaii, has been exceptional and clear since our earliest diplomatic relations with that Government.

From the beginning down to this date the idea and expectation has been constantly entertained by the people and Governments of both countries that whenever the conditions should be such as to make annexation of mutual advantage it should be consummated.

On the part of Hawaii this purpose has been sustained by two facts:

First. That no ruler of Hawaii since the time of Kamehameha I has believed that these islands, that are so tempting to the cupidity of commercial powers, could maintain an autonomous government without the interested support of some great maritime nation.

Second. That the rulers of Hawaii, on each occasion when the islands have been threatened with foreign interference or domestic violence, have at once appealed to some foreign power for help.

It was with the help of guns captured, by surprise, from the ship *Fair American* that were manned and worked by John Young, an American sailor, who was captured on shore from the crew of the *Eleanor* in 1789 and fourteen other captured sailors, that Kamehameha I was enabled to extend his dominion from the Island of Hawaii to the other islands of the group and to establish his empire and dynasty.

The King was so deeply impressed with the necessity for the aid of foreigners in maintaining his rule, and of their superiority in war, that he voluntarily ceded the supreme sovereignty of his Kingdom to Great Britain, and Hawaii became a dependency, over which he was to rule as a petty king, in consideration that Vancouver would bring him missionaries to teach him the gospel and a ship of war to fight his enemies.

In every reign since that cession, which Great Britain seems neither to have accepted or refused, when any serious trouble has arisen in the Hawaiian Islands, cession, or annexation to some foreign power, has been tendered by the Crown; and on three occasions the ownership of the islands has been eagerly offered to the United States.

This was done when Lord George Pawlett, in 1843, forced a surrender of the islands to Great Britain, as it had been done in 1839, when the French frigate *Artémise*, in command of Captain La Place, invaded Honolulu and captured the fort. Then, in 1853, followed the treaty of annexation to the United States, conducted under the direction of Mr. Marcy, as Secretary of State, which was solicited by Hawaii and signed by the negotiators, but was not ratified by the King because of his sudden death.

In February, 1874, when Kalakaua was elected king, the followers of Queen Emma, his defeated opponent, who was the granddaughter of John Young, raised an insurrection against the king, which was quelled by the marines of the United States ship *Tuscarora*, who were landed in Honolulu at the request of Kalakaua, he having no forces to defend him except a body of unarmed citizens, nearly all of them Americans.

There was just cause for the constant reliance of all these kings upon the protection of the United States and upon the Americans in the islands, for the reason that none of them could have been safe at any time in relying for protection or for the enforcement of the laws upon their native subjects.

For like reasons, and because no American called into his counsels ever wronged or deceived a Hawaiian king, they were sought out and were urgently invited to accept leading positions in their cabinets. Among these advisers were men like Mr. Richards, Dr. Judd, Mr. Wylie, Mr. Armstrong, and Mr. Ricord, who, for high character and great abilities, were seldom excelled in the cabinets of the most enlightened governments.

It was the influence of such men, with the powerful aid of the missionaries, that has created in Hawaii a civilization and a government that has no equal in the rapidity and steadiness of its progress from absolute barbarism to a very high plane of social order and enlightened liberty.

That the thoughtful people of Hawaii, who have been thus lifted up to an honorable position among the family of Christian nations, should have a firm faith in the American people and a warm attachment for them, is only an evidence of their gratitude toward their deliverers and of their intelligent appreciation of the great blessings they enjoy through the devoted labors of these Americans.

The Government of the United States, with a clear forecast as to the relations that in the future would naturally exist toward the people of Hawaii, and as to the importance of these islands to the United States, assumed toward them an attitude that from the beginning has been entirely exceptional. We have dealt with no other country in the manner that we have dealt with Hawaii.

In the first diplomatic note that defined the relations of the United States toward Hawaii, Mr. Webster, in the instructions to Commissioner

Brown, dated 15th of March, 1853, clearly stated the refusal of the Government of the United States to fully recognize the independence of the Hawaiian Islands, with reference to the United States, and quite as clearly and forcibly declared that, as to all other nations, they were "entirely independent."

In that letter of instructions, Mr. Webster says:

A commission appointing you to the office will be found among the papers you will receive herewith, and a letter from this Department addressed to that minister of the king of the islands who may be charged with foreign relations, accrediting you in your official character. The title selected for your mission has reference in part to its purposes. It is not deemed expedient, at this juncture, fully to recognize the independence of the island or the right of their government to that equality of treatment and consideration which is usually allowed to those governments to which we send and from which we receive diplomatic agents of the ordinary ranks.

By this, however, it is not meant to intimate that the islands, so far as regards all other powers, are not entirely independent. On the contrary, this is a fact respecting which no doubt is felt, and the hope that through the agency of the commissioners independence might be preserved has probably, in a great degree, led to the compliance by Congress with the recommendation of the President.

It is obvious, from circumstances connected with their position, that the United States require that no other power should possess or colonize the Sandwich Islands, or exercise over their government an influence which would lead to partial or exclusive favors in matters of navigation or of trade

One of your principal duties will be to watch the movements of such agents of other Governments as may visit the islands. You will endeavor to obtain the earliest intelligence respecting the objects of those visits, and if you should think that, if accomplished, they would be detrimental to the interests of the United States, you will make such representations to the authorities of the islands as in your judgment would be most likely to further them.

This first statement of the attitude of Hawaii to the United States, as it was so clearly made by Mr. Webster, comprehends every progressive step in the increasing closeness of our relations with those people, that has occurred in our treaties of reciprocity, in our social, commercial, and religious intercourse, and in the constant protection of our war ships, which for many years have seldom been absent from Honolulu. The purpose of the ultimate annexation of Hawaii to the United States was plainly indicated in the fact that he instructed Mr. Brown to keep a watchful outlook for such efforts on the part of the agents of other governments, and carefully withheld a recognition of that Government, as being independent of the United States, while he distinctly announced their independence of all other powers.

Other American statesmen have declared with one accord that the United States held for various good reasons a peculiar interest in Hawaii. Such has been the opinion and sentiment of the American people from that time to the present, with scarcely a dissenting voice among all of our Presidents, all of our Secretaries of State, and all of our ministers and consuls accredited to that Government.

For many years past the people of the United States and of Hawaii have looked to annexation as a manifest destiny. All legitimate business enterprises there have been based on that recognized fact, and only illegitimate ventures have opposed it.

In the treaty of reciprocity of 1875 the United States demanded, as the consideration of admitting the staple productions of Hawaii free of duty into our ports, that Hawaii should so far renounce her sovereignty over her public domain, her crown lands, and her ports, bays, and harbors, that she could not dispose of them, or of any exclusive or special privileges in them, without the consent of the United States.

The gravity of this concession of her sovereign authority over her own territory to the United States was shown in 1894, when Great Britain proposed that Hawaii should grant to her the exclusive right to land a cable on Neckar Island, to which Hawaii was willing, but both Governments fully recognized the fact that the consent of the United States was necessary to be obtained. Great Britain is still pressing for that concession. This treaty arrangement, which is permanent in its character, is a complete demonstration that in this high authority the United States is exercising a right of sovereignty over Hawaii that is utterly inconsistent with the independence of that Government in its relations with the United States.

When that treaty was renewed and extended, in November, 1887, the sovereign grasp of the United States was made firmer and more specific upon the Hawaiian Islands by the stipulation that Pearl Harbor should be in the exclusive possession and control of the United States for the purpose of establishing there a permanent naval station. Such a station, with all needful belongings, including fortifications to protect it, in the exclusive possession of the United States not only shuts out all foreign powers from the harbor, but places it so entirely under the command of our fleets and guns and our military authority that the Hawaiian Government can not enter Pearl Harbor, even with her commerce, if we choose to exclude her by arbitrary military orders.

Pearl Harbor, in a military sense, will be a fortified base for naval operations that completely dominates all the islands and virtually commands the Pacific Ocean for a distance of more than 2,000 miles in all directions.

In these situations, fixed by treaty, the power and authority of the United States over Hawaii is so great and so exclusive that nothing is wanting but the formal consent of that government, expressed in some lawful way, to increase our dominion there to the dignity of sovereign supremacy.

Following the natural course of events in the direction of the inevitable union of Hawaii, by peaceable annexation to the United States, all of our relations have grown more intimate each year until the sovereignty of the islands has thus become, in effect, the sovereignty of the United States through these treaties which are founded alone in the mutual interests of the two countries.

This close relation has been formed with the cordial consent of the sovereign powers of both Governments, as a natural growth of civilization and of progress in political and commercial development, without any plan or purpose of colonization, or of force, or coercion, or persuasion, or threat, or influence, to bring about this auspicious result.

These treaty rights of the United States, and these close and valuable commercial relations, and the social and church relations of the people of the two countries can not be changed without a shock too rude to be borne, if it can be avoided.

We also hold toward the missionaries, who have brought into Hawaii the light of the twin stars of christianity and constitutional liberty, a national debt of gratitude that good conscience will not permit us to forget; and to their worthy children we owe protection in the enjoyment of the blessings of free republican government that they have created in Hawaii, under our fostering care, with faithful labor and Anglo-Saxon courage.

To our own people who have emigrated to Hawaii under the open invitation of our national policy and under the pledges given by Congress and our Presidents that no foreign power should disturb their rights we owe all the friendly care that a father can owe to his sons who have with his consent left their home to seek their fortunes in other lands. Not many of them have gone to Cuba, Jamaica, Mexico, or Central or South America, or even to Canada, to reside with kindred people, but, under our encouragement and promises of protection, a large and splendid body of Americans have gone to Hawaii to reside, not feeling that they have expatriated themselves, and have carried with them the highest virtues and the most advanced education in art, science, agriculture, and mechanics, and have established homes there that are, many of them, equal in elegance and comfort to any in the United States.

We owe it to these people that they should not again be brought into subjection to a monarchy that has lapsed because of its corruptions and its faithless repudiation of solemn oaths. In this obligation our Government is also deeply concerned for the maintenance and enjoyment of our treaty rights in Hawaii.

To these people, and also to the preservation of the native population against a speedy destruction, involving property and life, we owe the duty of rescuing them from the silent but rapid invasion of the pagan races from Asia. This invasion is concerted, and is far more dangerous to Hawaii than if it came on ships of war with the avowed purpose of subjugating the Hawaiian Islands. It is the stealthy approach of a "destruction that wasteth at noonday." The immigrants from Japan retain their allegiance to that Empire, and yet they claim full political rights in Hawaii notwithstanding their alienage.

In this demand they have the undisguised encouragement of the Japanese Government. These privileges are demanded as rights.

Such an invasion is clearly within the prohibition that the United States, in all our solemn declarations, have thrown around Hawaii to protect that people against all foreign invasion and interference with their domestic affairs.

The time has arrived when we should make good all these pledges. Efforts of Europeans to prevent the annexation of Hawaii to the United States and to check the growth of that sentiment in Hawaii have been constantly and persistently made on every occasion when that subject has seriously engaged public attention, and our ministers and consuls there, almost without exception, have earnestly called our attention to such interferences during the past fifty years by the accredited agents of European governments, and especially those of Great Britain.

That Government has an interest in these islands that is a legitimate part of her world-embracing commercial policy, to which her great navy and many fortresses in all the seas for its reinforcement are the necessary complement. In this magnificent plan only a single gap remains to be filled. It lies between her possessions in the South Pacific and Esquimalt, on the Straits of Fuca.

It is of vast importance to her commercial power, and no less to her power to protect and defend her possessions at Hongkong and in India and the Polynesian Islands, that she should occupy Hawaii, or some island of that group, where a naval station could be placed and fortified. The initial movement in acquiring such control was the recent effort to get from Hawaii the exclusive right to land a cable on Necker Island. This could only be done with the consent of the United States, which President Cleveland recommended that Congress should give. She came dangerously close to success, but Congress refused to consider the subject, and in its profound silence indicated the resolute purpose of the United States to adhere to our supremacy in Hawaii.

This effort of Great Britain went to the heart of the subject, since a cable connection from Canada with the Orient and with Polynesia would give her the control of all electrical communications that are possible between North America and Asia, and with the islands of the Pacific south of the equator.

This wise forecast of the commercial and naval control of the Pacific Ocean from these islands as a base of operations is not a new or temporary part of the policy of that great empire; neither will it ever be abandoned by Great Britain while there is any hope of its success.

This policy accounts for the intrigues that have been constantly set on foot by British subjects and officials in Hawaii, and for the presence there at this juncture of Kaiulani, who is the daughter of an Englishman, was educated in England, and is, properly, in full sympathy with the English people and the British Government.

This Princess, by the adoption of Liliuokalani, neither of whom has the royal blood of the Kamehamehas, but are the creation of the constitution of Hawaii, is waiting in Hawaii to be crowned queen of the islands when the Congress of the United States has decreed the restoration of the monarchy by refusing annexation to the Republic of Hawaii, or has thrown open the door to insurrection in the islands through which the monarchy still has lively hopes of resurrection.

If Great Britain is not industriously and openly engaged in fomenting this concerted movement for the destruction of the Republic and the restoration of the monarchy on its ruins, her agents and the Princess—her protégé—are kept conveniently near at hand to fasten her power upon the islands, on the happening of any pretext for the protection of the lives and property of British subjects in Hawaii.

In this high and noble duty of taking care of her people, Great Britain never fails, nor is she reluctant in listening to the demands of her subjects for the protection of her flag.

It is no less than a blind confidence in the impossible to assume that Great Britain has no special interest in Hawaii, when that is the only missing link in the cordon of great fortresses with which it is her proud ambition to girdle the world.

We can not so discredit her sagacity, in justice to our common sense. She still has and will ever have a most important use for dominion in Hawaii.

JAPAN HAS OPENLY PROTESTED against the annexation of Hawaii to the United States upon grounds that indicate an unjust suspicion of our national honor in our future dealing with her subjects in those islands. The blunt refusal of the President to consider this protest caused Japan to make a formal withdrawal of it, but this diplomatic intervention can not be dissociated from its real predicate, which is the demand made by Japan upon the Republic of Hawaii, which has not been withdrawn, that her subjects in Hawaii shall have equal privileges with the natives in voting at elections and in holding offices.

Of these subjects of Japan in Hawaii the larger number were soldiers in the war with China, and are still subject to the military orders of the Emperor.

Almost the entire number of Japanese in Hawaii are coolies, who were brought there under the authority of the two Governments, and were to return to Japan at the end of their term of service.

They claim the right to remain in Hawaii under a general treaty which applied only to such persons as came for temporary or permanent residence as voluntary immigrants. This claim is disputed by Hawaii, and there is still trouble over it. Under such circumstances the presence and the constant inflow of Japanese in great numbers is an evil which threatens the native people with the loss of their means of living and the whole country with the overflow of paganism. It also threatens the overthrow of the Republic and the destruction of the lives and property of the republicans through an insurrection or combination of the lower classes of natives, who are for the most part adherents of royalty and are under the control of the Kahunas, who are sorcerers, with the Japanese.

The policy of Japan toward Hawaii will become aggressive and determined so soon as the United States refuses to annex the islands, and makes the return to monarchy possible.

France has very recently annexed Tahiti to the Republic, and has sent ships of war to Honolulu with overtures for the establishment of a cable to connect these islands with Hawaii. This may or may not look toward invasion or coercion, but it distinctly ignores the right of the United States to be consulted with reference to such an important plan.

All these powers are anxious to acquire the suzerainty over Hawaii, and they would quickly agree that either of them should occupy the islands, on a pledge of their absolute neutrality in time of war, or of the common right to resort to them for coal and for water and refreshment.

This was, in effect, the joint proposal of France and Great Britain that was twice submitted to the United States for their concurrence, and refused by us.

Like proposals were submitted by those Governments to the United States relating to Cuba, which offers were also refused.

The jealous watchfulness of these powers as to the constantly increasing influence of the United States in these islands to the south and the west of us has been manifested so often in the past fifty years that it is impossible to believe that they are not ready and anxious to occupy them, or at least to enforce their neutrality and to make their ports free whenever the United States has relaxed or has cast off the hold it has upon Hawaii by treaty and through the process of affiliation that has brought them so nearly within our sovereign dominion.

They fully understand that if we now refuse to annex Hawaii that they will be at liberty to treat with any government there, either for annexation or for protection or for reciprocal trade on terms that we now have the exclusive right to insist upon.

It is true, as a matter of fact, as well as in the logic of the situation, that the refusal to annex Hawaii will mean, and will be so intended, to revoke our treaties of reciprocity with that Government, and, in that event, the United States will give up the rights secured to us in both those treaties.

It will mean that Hawaii is thereby notified that we will terminate those treaties, and that she will have the equal right to do so and to reclaim the consideration that she gave us for agreeing to them. Whether or not such a construction of our rights under these treaties would comport with their terms, these anxious powers that crave the islands would insist upon their right to protect a weak power against the apparent injustice of our holding our exclusive rights in Pearl Harbor and over the public domain in Hawaii after we had refused the reciprocity in trade which was the express consideration paid to us for that concession.

When the concession of exclusive rights in Pearl Harbor was made to us in the last treaty of reciprocity, and after it had been ratified, but before ratifications had been exchanged, the Hawaiian minister and the minister of the United States signed a protocol which declared that our rights in Pearl Harbor would cease whenever the treaty was terminated. That protocol was no part of the treaty, it not having been submitted to the Senate for its action, but such an insistence by the United States would give offense to the public sentiment of the world, and we would abandon it, or else, if we still adhered to our rights in Pearl Harbor in disregard of that protocol, we would thereby invite the interference of other powers.

If our sugar industry or any other competitive industry drives the United States to revoke the Hawaiian reciprocity treaties, we must expect to give up all the exclusive rights we have in Hawaii, as being forfeited.

THE OBJECTIONS TO THE ANNEXATION OF HAWAII, so far as they relate to our competitive industries, are based upon the cheap labor that it is alleged exists in the islands, and the production of coarse cane sugar there, so as to reduce the market value of beet sugar in United States.

The statement of facts herein submitted shows that these objections, if they are real, are a very slight matter as compared with the benefits that have already accrued to our shipping interests, and from the production of coffee, for which we are entirely dependent on foreign countries, and from the production of rice, taro, and a variety of rich tropical fruits that our people need, with which we have only a slight competition, to say nothing of the profit that comes to our shipowners, merchants, mechanics, engineers, and professional men in Hawaii, and our men of capital and enterprise who find there a very remunerative field for investment and speculation.

Labor is not cheaper in Hawaii than it is in like pursuits in many parts of the United States, nor is it so ignorant, so difficult to control, or so lawless as it is either in our great mining or agricultural regions. The criminal statistics of Hawaii furnish ample and most creditable proofs of these facts.

THE DEBTS OF HAWAII, to the sum of $4,000,000, which we are to assume, will not foot up so large an amount when the cash assets of that Government are deducted—are not equal to one-half the value of her public property. The cost, which is less than the present cash value of public property in Honolulu and other towns, added to the present cash value of the public domain in the islands is above the sum of $9,000,000, as will appear in statements appended to this report. If this was a question of profit and loss upon a commercial dealing the United States would gain not less than $5,000,000 by the transaction.

The next objection to annexing Hawaii relates to the character of population we will acquire from those islands.

It may be safely assumed that in all respects the white race in Hawaii are the equals of any community of like numbers and pursuits to be found in any country. The success they have achieved in social, religious, educational, and governmental institutions is established in results that are not dwarfed by a comparison with our most advanced communities.

They number 22 per cent in a population of 109,000, the number of Americans being 3,000, British 2,200, Germans 1,400, Norwegians and French 479, and other nationalities 1,055. These white people are so united in the support of good government that there is no political distinction of nationalities among them, and harsh differences of opinion on public questions are seldom found.

This is the supreme governing power in the islands when that power is traced to its origin, as it is in all countries where the white and colored races are admitted, on equal terms, into the exercise of civil rights connected with government. The Portuguese, who are also recognized as white citizens, are included in this estimate of 22 per cent of the entire population of Hawaii.

They belong to the agricultural classes, as laborers and proprietors, and are thrifty and law-abiding people who have intelligent conceptions of the value of liberty regulated by law.

Their homes are uniformly comfortable, and usually vine-clad and tasteful in their surroundings. Their advancement in education and in the acquisition of substantial property is very marked, since their arrival in Hawaii, and their desire to become citizens of the "Great Republic" is very earnest.

The Japanese comprise 22 per cent of the whole population, and are equal in numbers to the whites. They do not claim to be permanent residents of Hawaii, and very few of them acquire real estate, except on leases, some of them for as much as five years. They are chiefly laborers and servants; some of them are merchants and fishermen. They are less obedient to law than the people of the other races in Hawaii.

As a rule, they return to Japan at the end of their contract terms of service, so that their numbers fluctuate as the tide of immigration ebbs and flows. They are not trustworthy as laborers, nor honest in their dealings as merchants. They come to Hawaii as coolies, having been collected from the lower classes, and very few of them bringing their wives and children to Hawaii. Their wish to participate in government is evidently inspired by their managers, who are set over them in authority by the Government agents in Japan.

Under our laws the Japanese have the full right of emigration to the United States, but few of them avail of that privilege, because they prefer to return to Japan. The native women seldom intermarry with Japanese, and their association with the natives is not apparently agreeable to either race.

In a community of ignorant people they are a dangerous element and are servile in their obedience to their overseers. It is from this race that the real danger to social order comes in Hawaii, because they act as a unit in obeying the commands of their managers, and are not prone to cowardice.

The Chinese in Hawaii have all resided there for a number of years. They were largely voluntary immigrants, who came to the country prior to 1870, when their coming was prohibited. They are the most industrious and thrifty race that has come to Hawaii. They are a higher class of people, in the main, than those who have come to the United States, and some of them have accumulated considerable estates.

They evince little desire to use the ballot, from which they are excluded. In the culture of rice, taro, and garden stuff they excel, and in fishing they conduct a profitable business. Very extensive and excellent fish ponds were built by the natives in the feudal times of the great chiefs, and many of these are leased by Chinese, who work them to great profit. It is usual for them to pay a rental of $50 per acre for rice lands and a much larger rental for fish ponds.

· The native Kanakas could never rule these other colored races under any form of government. They comprise 28 per cent of the entire population, while the other imported elements, the Portuguese, Chinese, and Japanese, either of which races is more capable in governing power than the Kanakas, comprise 57 per cent of the total number, more than double the native Kanaka population.

It is beyond question that, as a factor in government, the united white race is indispensable to the safety of the people of Hawaii; and they could not control the islands without the frequent presence, if not the constant attendance, of the warships of the United States and of the European powers. If those vessels were withdrawn for the period of a year civil strife and bloodshed would ensue and would result in the rule of some white man as dictator.

If, during such a period, a Japanese man-of-war was stationed at Honolulu, the result would be the capture of the islands by Japan or by filibusters from our Pacific coast. When the white race in Hawaii is subjected to Kanaka rule, those islands will fall into speedy ruin, unless some maritime power shall take immediate control of them.

It does not follow that the natives of Hawaii are a bad, or useless, or dangerous element to be introduced into the United States. It is true that they have not the aptitude for government that qualifies them to rule a nation in the present high state of civilized government adapted to the progress of the great commercial powers, but that does not disqualify them for useful citizenship.

We have more than twelve millions of negroes and Indians in the United States who are not unfit for citizenship; yet, if every office in the Federal Government, including the executive, legislative, and judicial departments, was filled with the best men from those races, they could not conduct the Government for a year in a proper, constitutional way. Neither could the best men in China or Japan conduct our constitutional republic safely through a single Presidential term. Yet our Indians and negroes are admitted to the full rights of the ballot and of office holding without apparent detriment to the Government.

The Kanakas are a kindly, well-disposed, and generous race, who instinctively yield to power and are easily persuaded; but those qualities do not fit them for high duties as rulers, nor do they disqualify them from a free expression of their will in a free government.

The stress laid upon the objection that the infusion of 31,000 Kanakas into our citizenship will be dangerous to the United States is quite out of proportion, when it is remembered that our basis of representation in Congress is about 75,000,000 of population.

The objection to annexation that is based upon the civil rights of the Kanakas divides itself into two repugnant parts—the first being that annexation forces upon them a new government without their consent, the second being that they are not fit for citizenship in the United States. If the latter proposition is true, we will give them a better government than they can create or conduct for themselves. The injury falls upon us, and not upon them, if we force them into the body of our citizenship and compel them to accept that blessing.

Then, if they are unfit for our citizenship, we would be wanting in duty to our own people in permitting the Kanakas to vote for annexation to the United States.

The constitution of Hawaii provides a plan for annexation to the United States by the Government without a referendum to the people. That purpose, according to that plan, has been executed on the part of Hawaii. It can not be within the constitutional power of the Government of Hawaii to undo that lawful act, and refer the decision of the question of annexation to the people, whose vote upon it, under any circumstances, is not provided for in the constitution.

If a requirement should be made by the United States of a plebiscite to determine the question of annexation, it would work a revolution in Hawaii which would abolish its constitution. The demand of the United States for a plebiscite in Hawaii is only a demand for a new constitution there, or else for the violation of the existing constitution. It would mean nothing else but a vote on the issue between the Republic and the restoration of the monarchy, with the weight of our influence to be cast into the scale in favor of the monarchy.

Those natives who have refused to qualify as voters in the Republic stand on the sole ground that they prefer the monarchy, and will not accept the Republic. If the United States now demands that they shall vote on the question of annexation, when the constitution of the Republic makes no such provision, but provides, on the contrary, for annexation by treaty, or by act of the national Legislature, such a proceeding is a denial of the autonomy of Hawaii. It is a direct interference to overthrow the constitution of the Republic and its government, and to encourage those who deny the rightful existence of the Republic. This question of the rightful existence of the Republic is the real foundation on which the demand for a plebiscite is based.

It is a matter that is quite beyond the friendly contemplation of an American, who has a sincere regard for a constitutional republic as the highest and best form of human government, that a monarchy should ever be restored, with our assistance, when it has been superseded by a constitutional Republic.

Whether the Republic is a government *de facto* or *de jure* it is entitled to American sympathy, and when it has been recognized, successively, by the United States and all other powers, first, as a government *de facto* and then as a rightful government, republican in form, and is in a successful career of constitutional authority, our national obligations and all our better sentiments compel us to admit its full power and authority to dispose of any question that concerns its sovereign will and the welfare of its people.

If it is true, as some rashly venture to assert, that the United States minister at Hawaii and the commander of the warship *Boston*, in violation of our international duty, assisted a band of revolutionists to depose the queen and to usurp the government of the islands, it is also true that President Harrison recognized that de facto and provisional government as having the rightful sovereignty in Hawaii, in so far that it could conclude a treaty of annexation with the United States, and such a treaty was duly signed and sent to the Senate.

Then President Cleveland, when he came into power, sent Mr. Blount as his special commissioner and accredited him to President Dole as the representative of the sovereignty of Hawaii. If he, or those in the Senate who still suffer from the pangs and compunctions of conscience which he is supposed to have felt when he recognized President Dole, had then renounced the actions of Minister Stevens and Captain Wiltse, and if Mr. Cleveland had sent a minister to Liliuokalani as the rightful sovereign, they would have fully established the sincerity of their objections and would have shown "the courage of their convictions." But, instead of observing that logical course, they sent Mr. Willis as minister to Hawaii and accredited him to President Dole as the chief executive of Hawaii.

Then the provisional government grew into the constitutional Republic of Hawaii, and we have fully recognized that as the rightful and permanent government of Hawaii, and have kept our minister and consul-general at Honolulu and our war ships in that bay to protect them and the Republic.

Mr. Willis, our minister to Hawaii, sent there by Mr. Cleveland, in a dispatch to the Secretary of State, says:

Fortunately the men at the head of the provisional government are acknowledged on all sides to be of the highest integrity and public spirit.

This confidential utterance of an honorable man, who was dealing at arm's length with the provisional government and in a spirit of antagonism to the men who were conducting it, ought to silence the harsh imputations that are cast upon them to defeat annexation.

Now, after the lapse of five years, it is urged that the Republic is a usurping government; that it is a fraud contrived for the personal advantage of its promoters, and that Liliuokalani is still the rightful queen of Hawaii.

The effort to cover up this issue with the assertion that the men who were alleged to have overthrown the monarchy have abused the rights and scandalized the good name of the United States still more seriously discredits our Government, by imputing to it the attitude of having been fully informed of the wrong and of silently permitting its perpetration.

This incrimination of our Government and its agents is extremely unjust, especially when it is employed as a justification of the course of Liliuokalani.

Her official life as queen depended solely upon her appointment to that office by Kalakaua, under a power conferred on him by the constitution of Hawaii, which she took her oath to support. She abdicated her office by openly renouncing the obligation of that oath and by declaring her purpose to supersede that constitution by proclaiming a different one that should emanate from her sovereign will.

Neither her title to office as queen, nor her right to absolve herself from the oath to support the constitution, which was the fountain of her power, nor her purpose to create and promulgate another constitution, was ever submitted to a vote of the people of Hawaii, or to any convention or legislature chosen by them. When she thus abdicated the throne on which Kalakaua had seated her, the people of Hawaii accepted the act as terminating her right, and supplied the office of chief executive with a provisional president chosen by them.

It was no wrong to her or to Hawaii that the United States resolved to recognize Mr. Dole as such chief executive, all the other departments and offices of the Government, established in that constitution having undergone no change.

No nation in the world has refused recognition of the Republic of Hawaii as the rightful Government, and none of them question its sovereign right to deal with any question that concerns the people of Hawaii.

The issue raised by the question of referring annexation to a vote of the people of Hawaii necessarily includes a denial of the sovereign power of that Government to agree to annexation until a majority of the people have given their consent. Such an attitude, on our part, denies to that Government a right and power that is expressly given in their constitution.

This is not a question to be decided by a popular vote, nor can a majority in such an election force upon the minority a new and unwelcome citizenship. Women and minors, who are non-voters in such elections, are not bound by them unless they are authorized by the constitution, which establishes rules of government that are supreme over all the people and under laws that none can question; nor can they be bound by a plebiscite until the consent of the Legislature is had for such elections.

Congress has never demanded a plebiscite to test the question of any annexation of territory to the United States on behalf of the people directly affected by it, nor the assent of the people of the United States to accept any people into our Union.

The constitution of Hawaii requires the assent of two-thirds of their

Senate to a treaty of annexation. That is an important safeguard for the people. If it is required that an additional safeguard shall be found in a plebiscite, it should logically be supported by a vote of two-thirds of all the people.

Other minor objections to the annexation of Hawaii have been made that have no appreciable value when they are compared with the national advantages to the United States that will result from the completion of a purpose that has all the time been settled in the public policy of the United States, and is now an imperative duty that we owe to Hawaii and to our own country.

That duty is now made imperative by the fact that the sudden influx of Asiatics, and their increasing numbers, is an ever present peril to Hawaii that no local government can escape without such assistance as we are giving with our ships of war.

It is a duty that has its origin in the noblest sentiments that inspire the love of a father for his children, or a country for its enterprising and honorable citizens, or a church for its missions and the heralds it has sent out with messages of deliverance to those in pagan darkness, or our Great Republic to a younger sister that has established law, liberty, and justice in a beautiful land that a corrupt monarchy was defiling with fraud, harassing with unjust exactions, and dragging down to barbarism. We have solemnly assumed these duties and can not abandon them without discredit.

If the Hawaiian race can be saved from extermination, or, while they exist, from being driven from their homes by the Asiatics, the United States, following up the noble efforts of the Hawaiian Republic, can accomplish that work.

If we do not interpose either to annex Hawaii or to protect her from the influx of Asiatics, the native people will soon be exterminated.

In those islands all the natives who desire homes have them or can freely obtain them under the liberal land laws of the Republic, and the fertility of the country and its abundant fisheries insure a comfortable living to more than tenfold the present population. The efforts of the Republic to fill up the public domain with white people from the United States are being rapidly responded to by a strong tide of such immigrants. The climate, soil, and the agricultural productions invite such immigrants, with inducements that no other country affords.

When those islands are a part of our territory they will soon fill up with happy homesteads, and Honolulu and Hilo will become great commercial marts. The reasons for annexation that concern our national policy, welfare, and protection are of vital importance. They relate chiefly to commerce, including our shipping interests, and to the naval defense of our Pacific coasts.

In June, 1897, our commerce with Hawaii amounted to $18,385,000, which is greater than our trade with Argentine, or Spain, or Switzerland, or Venezuela, or Austria, or Russia, or Denmark, or Colombia, or Norway and Sweden, or the British and French Guianas, or with Uruguay, or with Portugal, or Turkey, or Peru.

The people of Hawaii buy American products at the annual rate of $53.35 per capita, while South America buys from us on a per capita basis of 90 per cent, and the United Kingdom buys from us on a basis of $13.42 per capita. The per capita basis of Mexico is $1.95, of the whole of Europe is $2.12, of Australia is $3.67, and of Canada is $14 per capita in their purchases from the United States.

The percentage of Hawaiian commerce carried in American ships in 1897 was 80.72, while the percentage of the whole of our trade with all countries carried on American ships was only 11.03. The number of vessels of the United States engaged in the Hawaiian trade in 1896 was 247 (since much increased), with a tonnage of 243,983 tons—nearly double that in our trade with Great Britain, and more than that of our trade with all other foreign countries.

This heavy trade rests alone upon the agriculture of Hawaii and is the product of a total population of 109,000. If the population of Hawaii was increased by the immigration of 1,000,000 Americans, its trade with the United States would increase, in proportion, to $200,000,000. But this trade is probably only a tithe of the benefit of these islands to the commerce of the United States when a ship canal connects the Pacific and Atlantic oceans.

As the place—the only one—in the North Pacific Ocean for the concentration of cable lines; for obtaining coal, water, or provisions for ships; for the repair of vessels; or for the storage of goods in bond, or otherwise, from all countries for the purposes of trade around the whole circuit of the coasts of the Pacific Ocean; and with its numerous islands, the Hawaiian Islands are the central point of distribution which can have no possible competitor.

This enormous advantage to our trade in the islands and across the Pacific Ocean must be felt by every industry in the United States. Their separation by a distance of 2,000 miles from all other lands, and their central location as to every point on the great arc of the circle that extends from the Mexican border almost to the coast of Siberia, the Pacific frontier of Alaska, Washington, Oregon, and California, makes the Hawaiian Islands the most important point in the seas of the Western Hemisphere for the fostering and protection of our coastwise and foreign commerce.

As ships of war are the necessary complement of ships of commerce, these great advantages belonging to the geographical location of the Hawaiian Islands are equally indispensable to our Navy, as the protector of our commerce, coming from both the Atlantic and Pacific oceans.

On the commercial and military views of these questions the opinions of merchants and navigators, and of our naval officers, as to the developments and necessities of the future—as yet unknown—are our most intelligent and safest guides. The committee can appeal to these sources of information and safe forecast with the confidence that comes from their almost unanimous agreement.

Unless such men are in grievous error, the committee are safe in saying that the full ownership of the Hawaiian Islands is indispensable to the commerce of the United States in respect of its development and safety, and are equally indispensable as to the defense of our Pacific coasts.

The papers appended to this report, which were written by some of our ablest officers of the Army and Navy, with direct reference to the subject of annexation, comprise only a few of the statements made by persons of great ability and experience, which sustain the conclusions of the committee as above expressed. If we can not rely upon the opinions and experience of such men on the questions of science and strategy involved in such an inquiry, we can have no safe guides to follow in such matters.

The Senate Committee on Foreign Relations have heretofore submitted a full and exhaustive report on the subject of Hawaii and its relations to the United States, which includes the diplomatic correspondence from the earliest date relating to Hawaii, the report of Mr. Commissioner Blount, and the examination, on oath, of many witnesses under the order of the Senate.

A statement of facts of more recent occurrence and of the answers to points of objection to annexation is appended to this report, which, after careful examination, the committee finds to be entirely correct.

The Government of the Republic of Hawaii and its officials deserve the warm commendation of all who desire good government there.

It is honest, just, wise, prudent, firm, and careful in taxation and public expenditures and in all administrative conduct. The results are manifest in the peace and good order of all classes of a very mixed collection of different races. There are no mendicants or tramps in the islands, and the poor, who are unfitted for active work, are well cared for in comfortable and well provided asylums, and excellent hospitals are provided for the sick and insane.

The public road system is excellent, and railroads, telegraphs, electric and gas lights, waterworks, public baths, beautiful parks, and bands of music are provided for the people by the Government. The public health is especially the care of the Government, and is in charge of physicians who are assigned to health districts and are paid liberally by the Government. Their powers are adequate, and the closest inspection is enforced in all cases where contagious or epidemic diseases are suspected.

The wisdom and benevolent care of lepers at the sanitarium of Moloki is a living proof of public benevolence that is not surpassed in any country. Christian worship and the observance of the Sabbath are respected by all classes, and intemperance is discouraged by public opinion and by laws that meet public approval. Education is compulsory, and all classes of people are equally entitled to school privileges for their children, without distinction of color, race, or religious tenets.

The colleges are of high grade, and in all the schools the tuition is careful. The people are enterprising, public-spirited, and progressive in all their vocations. The really distinctive feature of society is that it is American in all its traits and habits, and our national holidays are celebrated in Hawaii with the same enthusiasm that is manifested in the United States. The most fatal blow at the spirit of those people and the sorest wound we could inflict upon them would be our refusal to welcome them into the Union.

C. K. DAVIS.
JNO. T. MORGAN
WM. P. FRYE.
S. M. CULLOM.
H. C. LODGE.
J. B. FORAKER.
CLARENCE D. CLARK.

Appendix 1.

TEXAS ANNEXATION TREATY.

IN SENATE OF THE UNITED STATES,
June 8, 1844.

Resolved, That the Senate do not advise and consent to the ratification of a treaty of annexation concluded between the United States of America and the Republic of Texas, at Washington, the 12th of April, 1844.

Attest: ASBURY DICKINS, *Secretary.*

A TREATY OF ANNEXATION CONCLUDED BETWEEN THE UNITED STATES OF AMERICA AND THE REPUBLIC OF TEXAS.

The people of Texas having, at the time of adopting their constitution, expressed by an almost unanimous vote their desire to be incorporated into the Union of the United States, and being still desirous of the same with equal unanimity, in order to provide more effectually for their security and prosperity; and the United States, actuated solely by the desire to add to their own security and prosperity, and to meet the wishes of the Government and people of Texas, have determined to accomplish, by treaty, objects so important to their mutual and permanent welfare:

For that purpose the President of the United States has given full powers to John C. Calhoun, Secretary of State of the said United States, and the President of the Republic of Texas has appointed, with like powers, Isaac Van Zandt and J. Pinckney Henderson, citizens of the said Republic; and the said plenipotentiaries, after exchanging their full powers, have agreed on and concluded the following articles:

ARTICLE I.

The Republic of Texas, acting in conformity with the wishes of the people and every department of its government, cedes to the United States all its territories, to be held by them in full property and sovereignty, and to be annexed to the said United States as one of their Territories, subject to the same constitutional provisions with their other Territories. This cession includes all public lots and squares, vacant lands, mines, minerals, salt lakes and springs, public edifices, fortifications, barracks, ports and harbors, navy and navy-yards, docks, magazines, arms, armaments and accoutrements, archives and public documents, public funds, debts, taxes, and dues unpaid at the time of the exchange of the ratifications of this treaty.

ARTICLE II.

The citizens of Texas shall be incorporated into the Union of the United States, maintained and protected in the free enjoyment of their liberty and property, and admitted, as soon as may be consistent with the principles of the Federal Constitution, to the enjoyment of all the rights, privileges, and immunities of citizens of the United States.

ARTICLE III.

All titles and claims to real estate, which are valid under the laws of Texas, shall be held to be so by the United States; and measures shall be adopted for the speedy adjudication of all unsettled claims to land, and patents shall be granted to those found to be valid.

ARTICLE IV.

The public lands hereby ceded shall be subject to the laws regulating the public lands in the other Territories of the United States, as far as they may be applicable; subject, however, to such alterations and changes as Congress may from time to time think proper to make. It is understood between the parties that if, in consequence of the mode in which lands have been surveyed in Texas, or from previous grants or locations, the sixteenth section can not be applied to the purpose of education, Congress shall make equal provision by grant of land elsewhere. And it is also further understood that hereafter the books, papers, and documents of the general land office of Texas shall be deposited and kept at such place in Texas as the Congress of the United States shall direct.

ARTICLE V.

The United States assume and agree to pay the public debts and liabilities of Texas, however created, for which the faith or credit of her government may be bound at the time of the exchange of the ratifications of this treaty; which debts and liabilities are estimated not to exceed, in the whole, ten millions of dollars, to be ascertained and paid in the manner hereinafter stated.

The payment of the sum of three hundred and fifty thousand dollars shall be made at the Treasury of the United States within ninety days after the exchange of the ratifications of this treaty, as follows: Two hundred and fifty thousand dollars to Frederick Dawson, of Baltimore, or his executors, on the delivery of that amount of ten per cent bonds of Texas. * * *

*   *   *   *   *   *   *

One hundred thousand dollars, if so much be required in the redemption of the exchequer bills which may be in circulation at the time of the exchange of the ratifications of this treaty. For the payment of the remainder of the debts and liabilities of Texas, which, together with the amount already specified, shall not exceed ten millions of dollars, the public lands herein ceded and the net revenue from the same are hereby pledged.

ARTICLE VI.

In order to ascertain the full amount of the debts and liabilities herein assumed and the legality and validity thereof, four commissioners shall be appointed by the President of the United States, by and with the advice and consent of the Senate, who shall meet at Washington, Texas, within the period of six months after the exchange of ratifications of this treaty, and may continue in session not exceeding twelve months, unless the Congress of the United States should prolong the time. They shall take an oath for the faithful discharge of their duties, and that they are not directly or indirectly interested in said claims at the time and will not be during their continuance in office; and the said oath shall be recorded with their proceedings. In case of the death, sickness, or resignation of any of the commissioners, his or their place or places may be supplied by the appointment as aforesaid, or by the President of the United States during the recess of the Senate. They, or a majority of them, shall be authorized, under such regulations as the Congress of the United States may prescribe, to hear, examine, and decide on all questions touching the legality and validity of said claims, and shall, when a claim is allowed, issue a certificate to the claimant, stating the amount, distinguishing principal from interest.

The certificates so issued shall be numbered, and entry made of the number, the name of the person to whom issued, and the amount in a book to be kept for that purpose. They shall transmit the records of their proceedings and the book in which the certificates are entered, with the vouchers and documents produced before them relative to the claims allowed or rejected, to the Treasury Department of the United States, to be deposited therein; and the Secretary of the Treasury shall, as soon as practicable after the receipt of the same, ascertain the aggregate amount of the debts and liabilities allowed; and if the same, when added to the amount to be paid to Frederick Dawson and the sum which may be paid in the redemption of the exchequer bills, shall not exceed the estimated sum of ten millions of dollars, he shall, on the presentation of a certificate of the commissioners, issue, at the option of the holder, a new certificate for the amount, distinguishing principal from interest, and payable to him or order, out of the net proceeds of the public lands, hereby ceded, or stock of the United States, for the amount allowed, including principal and interest, and bearing an interest of three per cent per annum from the date thereof; which stock, in addition to being made payable out of the net proceeds of the public lands, hereby ceded, shall also be receivable in payment for the same. In case the amount of the debts and liabilities allowed, with the sums aforesaid to be paid to Frederick Dawson, and which may be paid in the redemption of the exchequer bills, shall exceed the said sum of ten millions of dollars, the said Secretary, before issuing a new certificate or stock, as the case may be, shall make in each case such proportionable and ratable reduction on its amount as to reduce the aggregate to the said sum of ten millions of dollars, and he shall have power to make all needful rules and regulations necessary to carry into effect the powers hereby vested in him.

ARTICLE VII.

Until further provision shall be made the laws of Texas as now existing shall remain in force, and all executive and judicial officers of Texas, except the President, Vice-President, and heads of departments, shall retain their offices, with all power and authority appertaining thereto, and the courts of justice shall remain in all respects as now established and organized.

ARTICLE VIII.

Immediately after the exchange of the ratifications of this treaty the President of the United States, by and with the advice and consent of the Senate, shall appoint a commissioner, who shall proceed to Texas and receive the transfer of the territory thereof and all the archives and public property and other things herein conveyed, in the name of the United States. He shall exercise all executive authority in said territory necessary to the proper execution of the laws until otherwise provided.

ARTICLE IX.

The present treaty shall be ratified by the contracting parties and the ratifications exchanged at the city of Washington in six months from the date hereof, or sooner if possible.

In witness whereof we, the undersigned plenipotentiaries of the United States of America and of the Republic of Texas, have signed, by virtue of our powers, the present treaty of annexation, and have hereunto affixed our seals respectively.

Done at Washington the twelfth day of April, eighteen hundred and forty-four.

[SEAL.]	ISAAC VAN ZANDT.
[SEAL.]	J. PINCKNEY HENDERSON.
[SEAL.]	J. C. CALHOUN.

S. Doc. 231, pt 7——14

APPENDIX 2.

INDEX.

REASONS IN FAVOR OF THE ANNEXATION OF HAWAII.

FIRST REASON IN FAVOR OF THE ANNEXATION OF HAWAII.

It will prevent the establishment of an alien and possibly hostile stronghold in a position commanding the Pacific coast and the commerce of the North Pacific, and definitely and finally secure to the United States the strategical control of the North Pacific, thereby protecting its Pacific coast and commerce from attack.

The question is frequently asked, how the possession of Hawaii, 2,000 miles distant from the continent, will secure control of the North Pacific; and why Hawaii is any more necessary to the Pacific coast than are the Azores, which are about the same distance off the Atlantic coast, necessary to the protection of the United States on the Atlantic side?

The reasons why Hawaii is essential to the protection of the Pacific coast, and why the Azores are not necessary to the protection of the Atlantic, are as follows:

The distance across the Atlantic is approximately 3,000 miles.

The distance across the Pacific is from 7,000 to 9,500 miles.

Second. All of the great powers of Europe lie, or have coaling stations, within steaming distance of the Atlantic coast of the United States. On the other hand, no nation, European or Asiatic, lies, or possesses a coaling station, near enough to the Pacific coast to be practically available as a base of hostile naval operation against that coast or its commerce.

British Columbia is not a material factor in this connection; for in case of hostilities between England and the United States all Canadian territory would be so speedily overwhelmed by invasion from the United States that its ports would not cut any material figure as hostile bases of operation for any considerable length of time.

Third: On the Atlantic there are scores of islands which can be used as bases of naval supply and repair; the Azores, Madeira, Canary, Cape Verde, Bermuda, Newfoundland, and the Bahamas, and the vast number of West India Islands.

On the other hand, in the Pacific Ocean, from the Equator to Alaska, from the coast of China and Japan to the American continent, there is but one spot where a ton of coal, a pound of bread, or a gallon of water can be obtained by a passing vessel, and that spot is Hawaii.

The distance from Hongkong, through Hawaii to Panama, is 9,580 miles; as far as from San Francisco eastward across the continent, across the Atlantic, across the Mediterranean, and across Turkey to the boundary of Persia.

The distance between Unalaska and Tahiti, the nearest ports north and south of Hawaii, is 4,400 miles—as far as from the southern point of Greenland to the mouth of the Amazon River.

The Atlantic is, comparatively, so narrow, that way stations are not absolutely essential; while the islands in the Atlantic north of the Equator, capable of use as way stations, are so numerous that it is practically impossible for the United States to absorb them all.

On the other hand, the width and size of the North Pacific is so great that no naval vessel in existence can carry enough to cross the Pacific from any of the existing or possible foreign naval stations to the Pacific coast of the United States, operate there and return without recoaling. No American or Japanese battle ship, now built or building, can even cross from Japan to San Francisco without recoaling. A modern battle ship without coal is like a caged lion—magnificent, but harmless.

One of the first principles in naval warfare is that an operating fleet must have a base of supply and repair.

Any country in possession of Hawaii would possess such a base within four or five days' steaming distance of any part of the Pacific coast, and be a standing menace against not only the Pacific coast, but against all of the ocean-bound commerce to and from that coast and all American commerce on or across the North Pacific.

By simply keeping other nations out of Hawaii the United States will thereby secure almost absolute immunity from naval attack on its Pacific coast for the simple reason that their bases are too far away to be made available. For example:

The distance from San Francisco to the nearest naval station of England is 4,600 miles; France, 3,600; Spain, 4,700; Russia, 4,700; Japan, 4,500, and China, 5,500 miles.

The importance of Hawaii to the commerce of the Pacific is demonstrated by the fact that of the seven trans-Pacific steamship lines plying between the North American continent and Japan, China, and Australia, all but one make Honolulu a way station.

It is for the reasons above set forth that Hawaii is called "The Key of the Pacific," and that American statesmen, regardless of party, have consistently and persistently maintained the policy that the United States could not allow any foreign government or people to colonize or control Hawaii. (See appendix of opinions of American statesmen concerning Hawaii.)

Upon the opening of the Nicaragua or Panama Canal, practically all of the shipping bound for Asia, making use thereof, will stop at Honolulu for coal and supplies.

SECOND REASON IN FAVOR OF ANNEXATION.

The conditions are such that the United States must act NOW to preserve the results of its past policy, and to prevent the dominancy in Hawaii of a foreign people.

For over fifty years, beginning with President Pierce in 1842, Presidents, Secretaries of State, American ministers to Hawaii, and successive Congresses have continuously enunciated the principle that no other foreign nation can be allowed to possess, control, or dominate Hawaii.

Until recently the simple announcement by the United States of its policy, combined with the control given by the reciprocity treaty, has been sufficient to make it effective. The time has come when these are insufficient to effectuate the policy or retain the advantages already secured.

The native race has decreased until there are now only thirty-odd thousand of them remaining, constituting less than a third of the population of the country, and the decrease is continuing. The day when the aboriginal Hawaiian alone should own and control Hawaii has gone and gone forever. *It is no longer a question of whether Hawaii shall be controlled by the native Hawaiian or by some foreign people; but the question is, What foreign people shall control Hawaii?*

Through the medium of the reciprocity treaty American dominancy in Hawaii has been maintained, and American interests have increased to such an extent that Americans now own, approximately, three fourths of all the property in the country; consume 98 per cent of their exports; furnish 75 per cent of their imports, and carry 75 per cent of their foreign trade in American bottoms.

It is said by some, Why is not this enough? Why not let well enough alone? There are two answers.

THE TREATY MAY BE TERMINATED.

First. The treaty is terminable by either party upon a year's notice. The uncertainties of politics may at any time bring into power in Hawaii a party inimical to American interests, who can at once terminate all special privileges and powers now held in Hawaii by the United States and transfer them to rival nations. Such action would be entirely legal; and that other nations stand ready to avail themselves of the opportunity is evidenced by the fact that three years ago the English and Canadian Governments sent special agents to Honolulu to obtain the cession or lease of one of the Hawaiian Islands as a cable station. The proposition is still being urged, and all that has stood in the way of its consummation has been the reciprocity treaty and the determination of Hawaii to keep its territory intact and its face turned Americawards until the annexation question is settled.

THE AWAKENING OF JAPAN.

Second. Whether the reciprocity treaty is continued or not conditions have developed within the past few years which will as certainly evict American interests and control from Hawaii as though it were accomplished by abrogation of the treaty or by hostile guns.

The awakening of Japan has introduced a new element into the politics of the Pacific. Until recently Japan prohibited immigration. This policy has now been reversed, and emigration, particularly to Hawaii, is encouraged. So rapidly have the Japanese come to Hawaii that in 1896 the adult Japanese males outnumbered those of any other nationality.

During the latter part of 1896 and the early part of 1897 they came in at the rate of 2,000 a month. If this rate of immigration had continued for a year they would have numbered one-half of the population, and before the end of five years would have outnumbered all of the other inhabitants put together two to one. Considering the relative populations of Hawaii and the United States, it was as though a million Japanese a month were entering San Francisco. It has been well said that "this was not immigration but invasion."

Hawaii has attempted to stay this invasion by legislation against contract laborers and paupers identical with that of the United States, and has thereby become involved in its present controversy with Japan, the latter country refusing to recognize the validity of such legislation and practically claiming the absolute right of emigration by her people to Hawaii.

Even though the Hawaiian legislation referred to is sustained, immigrants who do not come within its terms will soon give an overwhelming Japanese majority of the inhabitants of the country.

Under the existing constitution of Hawaii the Japanese are not citizens and are ineligible to citizenship; but an energetic, ambitious, warlike, and progressive people like the Japanese can not indefinitely be prevented from participating in the government of a country in which they become dominant in numbers and the ownership of property.

Already they are restless under the restrictions imposed upon them, and with their growing wealth, commerce, and numbers it will be impossible for any local independent government to long withhold political privileges from them.

Even though political privileges may for some time be withheld from them, their commercial men are active and progressive and are rapidly establishing themselves in Hawaii.

Experience has shown that in Hawaii, as elsewhere, blood is thicker than water.

The American merchant buys all that he can in the United States, and what he can not get there he buys elsewhere. The Japanese merchant buys all that he can in Japan and gets elsewhere what can not be advantageously obtained from his own country. Much of the advantage heretofore obtained by the United States in Hawaii has been by reason of the strong American commercial representation in the islands. The new Japanese commercial element is in a position to compete and does destructively compete with the American merchants in Hawaii in an ever-accelerating degree.

HAWAII DRIFTING JAPANWARDS

I make no charge that the Japanese Government has hostile intentions against Hawaii. But, regardless of the declarations or intentions of the Japanese Government, the fact is that Hawaii has, against the will and efforts of its Government and people, drifted Japanwards during the past two years; and unless radical action is taken to stay the process there can be but one logical result, viz, the ultimate suprem ac or the Japanese, and *thereby* of Japan, in Hawaii. This has progressed and will be accomplished in the teeth of the American policy of exclusion of foreign control in Hawaii, and with no tangible overt act on the part of the Japanese Government.

It may be claimed that Europeans and Americans can hold their own in competition with the Japanese. The reply to this is that experience has demonstrated that there can be no competition between Europeans and Americans on one side and Japanese or Chinese on the other. The only possible result is the absolute substitution of the Asiatic in the place of the white man, by reason of the fact that the Eastern standard of civilization and living is so much lower than the Western that the Asiatic can exist and prosper on a margin of profit which means starvation and destitution to a man who attempts to feed, clothe, and educate a family in accordance with the American standard.

THE ISSUE IN HAWAII.

The issue in Hawaii is not between monarchy and the Republic. That issue has been settled. There are some persons who do not recognize this fact. There are never lacking those who set their faces backward; who mourn every lost cause and vainly hope for the restoration of abuse and forfeited power.

The present Hawaiian-Japanese controversy is the preliminary skirmish in the great coming struggle between the civilization and the awakening forces of the East and the civilization of the West.

The issue is whether, in that inevitable struggle, Asia or America shall have the vantage ground of the control of the naval " Key of the Pacific," the commercial " Cross-roads of the Pacific."

All that has held, and that is now holding, Hawaii for the United States is a handful of resolute and determined men who, against heavy odds, are doing all that is within the bounds of possibility to prevent Hawaii from retrograding into an Asiatic outpost and to hold the country to that destiny which American statesmen have for fifty years, regardless of party, outlined for it. But there is a limit to their strength, and if help from the great Republic is to come in time it must come soon. Annexation will maintain American control in Hawaii and nothing else will.

A protectorate is suggested by some.

The alternative of "annexation or protectorate" has successively been presented to Presidents Pierce, Harrison, and McKinley, and Secretaries of State Marcy, Foster, and Sherman, in 1854, 1893, and 1897, and has each time been decided in favor of annexation; for the reason that a protectorate imposes upon the United States responsibility without power to control, while annexation imposes practically no more responsibility, but is accompanied with the full-power powers of ownership.

Annexation can be consummated now with little or no friction. Events are moving rapidly in the Pacific, and no one can predict what the developments and changes of even a year may bring forth.

THIRD REASON IN FAVOR OF THE ANNEXATION OF HAWAII.

It will increase many fold and secure to the United States the commerce of the islands.

Only those who have been brought directly into contact with the commercial relations between Hawaii and the United States realize its volume or importance.

Prior to the negotiation of the Hawaiian reciprocity treaty in 1876, the commerce of the islands was inconsiderable, and was in a languishing condition. Population, exports, imports, and shipping—all were steadily decreasing, as the following figures show:

Table showing condition of the Hawaiian trade for six years prior to reciprocity treaty.

Year	Imports	Domestic exports	Customs receipts	Merchant Vessels entered	Whaling vessels entered
1869	$2,040,000	$1,743,000	$215,000	127	102
1870	1,930,000	1,514,000	223,000	159	118
1871	1,625,000	1,733,000	221,000	171	47
1872	1,746,000	1,402,000	218,000	146	47
1873	1,437,000	1,725,000	198,000	109	63
1874	1,210,827	1,622,000	183,000	120	43

From the day the reciprocity treaty went into operation the island trade in all its branches increased rapidly, and to-day Hawaii is the best customer which the Pacific coast has—the largest consumer of United States products of any single country bordering on the Pacific. The following table shows the change wrought since the treaty:

Table showing improved condition of Hawaiian trade for the last five years, the result of the reciprocity treaty.

Year.	Imports.	Domestic exports.	Customs receipts.	Merchant vessels entered.
1892	$4,684,000	$8,081,000	$494,000	262
1893	5,346,000	10,742,000	545,000	315
1894	5,713,000	9,591,000	524,000	350
1895	5,714,000	8,358,000	547,000	318
1896	7,164,000	15,515,000	656,000	386

STATEMENT SHOWING IMPORTANCE OF HAWAIIAN TRADE TO PACIFIC COAST.

While the United States as a whole is benefited by Hawaiian trade, the Pacific coast finds it one of the most profitable in which it engages.

The figures for the full year 1896 showing the trade of the Pacific coast are not yet available. The following figures are from the published statement of San Francisco's commerce for the year ending November 30, 1896:

Table showing comparative importance of San Francisco exports to Hawaii, and to some other countries, for the year ending November 30, 1896.

Australia	$3,932,000
Hawaii	3,588,000
All of Central America	3,440,000
China	2,989,000
Japan	2,270,000
Mexico	1,469,000
All Europe except Great Britain	1,446,000
All of Asia and Oceanica, except China and Japan	1,298,000
New Zealand, Samoa, Marquesas, Cook, Fiji, Friendly, Marshall, Caroline and all other Polynesian islands combined	684,000
British Columbia	431,000
All of South America	294,000

STATEMENT SHOWING COMPARATIVE IMPORTANCE OF SAN FRAN-
CISCO EXPORTS OF PRINCIPAL ARTICLES TO HAWAII AND SOME
OTHER COUNTRIES.

WINE.

Hawaii is San Francisco's *second* best foreign wine customer.　Central America is the only country which took more of San Francisco's wine than Hawaii, and all that prevents Hawaii from standing first on the list is that all the Central American Republics are grouped and treated as one country in the statistics.

SALMON.

Hawaii is San Francisco's *third* best purchaser of salmon.　The only countries that bought more than Hawaii were Australia and England. Hawaii bought more salmon from San Francisco in 1896 than all the rest of the countries of the world added together, leaving out England, Australia, and New Zealand.

BARLEY.

Hawaii was the *third* largest consumer of barley exported by San Francisco, having taken barley to the amount of $139,000.

The only countries which took more barley than Hawaii were England and Belgium.

St. Vincent is credited with more, but that is only a port of call at which to receive orders as to where to deliver the grain.

FLOUR.

In the consumption of flour Hawaii stood *sixth*, flour having been exported there to the amount of $164,000.

England took flour to the amount of only $333,000
Or barely twice the consumption of Hawaii.
The export to Japan was 123,000
To all of South America 96,000
To Mexico 31,000
To all of Africa, Polynesia, Oceanica, and Asia (excepting Japan, China, and Siberia) the export of flour amounted to only 114,569

The above statistics do not include the large shipments being made to Hawaii, direct from Washington and Oregon, by the three lines of steamers and many sailing vessels running from there to Honolulu.

TABLE SHOWING VALUES OF PRINCIPAL ARTICLES IMPORTED BY HAWAII DURING 1896.

Hawaiian imports amounted during 1896 to $7,164,561, of which $5,464,208, being 76 per cent, came from the United States.

The infinite variety of the exports to Hawaii indicates the widespread participation which the residents of the United States have in the business.　There is not an industry in the United States which is not benefited by Hawaiian trade, and which would not be injured by abrogation of the treaty, or diversion of Hawaii's trade elsewhere.

The following statement shows the value of some of the principal articles imported by Hawaii during 1896:

Ale, beer, cider, and porter $74,820.65
Animals 51,633.37
Building materials 120,638.78
Clothing, boots, and hats 292,558.82
Coal and coke 135,646.85
Crockery, glassware, lamps, and lamp fixtures 47,552.58
Drugs, surgical instruments, and dental material 68,192.06

Dry goods:

Cottons	$311,891.21
Linens	12,633.94
Silks	20,953.16
Woolens	69,368.27
Mixtures	10,932.59
Fancy goods, millinery, etc	101,285.80
Fertilizer, bone meal, etc	332,238.71
Fish (dry and salt)	80,564.21
Flour	156,999.29
Fruits, fresh	14,154.97
Furniture	91,637.73
Grain and feed	273,752.71
Groceries and provisions	520,884.69
Guns and materials	16,046.42
Gunpowder, blasting, etc	7,526.68
Hardware, agricultural implements, and tools	278,267.03
Iron, steel, etc	38,940.70
Jewelry, plate, clocks	25,341.89
Leather	41,549.28
Lumber	255,241.64
Machinery	343,104.69
Matches	15,587.32
Musical instruments, etc	21,456.82
Naval stores	47,922.34
Oil—cocoanut, kerosene, whale, etc	107,418.94
Paints, paint oils, and turpentine	53,410.86
Perfumery and toilet articles	17,149.48
Railroad material, rails, cars, etc	32,977.22
Saddlery, carriages, and material	95,007.74
Shooks, bags, and containers	199,096.78
Spirits	65,947.20
Stationery and books	92,614.67
Tea	30,860.26
Tin, tinware, and materials	10,925.67
Tobacco, cigars, etc	194,835.82
Wines, light	161,360.54
Sundry personal and household effects	24,765.12
Sundry merchandise, not included in above	227,897.01

TABLE SHOWING HOW MANY AND HOW MUCH OF CERTAIN ARTICLES WERE IMPORTED BY HAWAII DURING 1896.

An enumeration of the numbers and amounts of articles imported will convey a better idea to some, of the importance of the Hawaiian trade to the farmers and manufacturers of the United States.

The following items, taken at random from the Hawaiian table of imports for 1896, indicate the wide range of their business.

This list can be indefinitely extended, but it is sufficient to show that no narrow interest is subserved by the Hawaiian trade:

Bulls and cows	33	Yards drilling	79,000
Horses	246	Yards dress goods	94,000
Hogs and pigs	1,583	Yards duck	90,000
Mules	555	Yards flannelette	48,000
Blinds	2,223	Yards gingham	179,000
Bricks	110,872	Cotton handkerchiefs	84,000
Doors	5,016	Yards muslin	24,000
Barrels lime	22,281	Yards cotton prints	1,657,000
Tons of coal	65,000	Yards sheeting	521,000
Bottles and vials	140,000	Yards shirting	103,000
Lamps	7,400	Silk handkerchiefs	49,000
Lanterns	7,500	Pairs woolen blankets	12,000
Pounds of acids	52,000	Yards embroidery	20,000
Pounds Epsom salts	11,000	Needles	569,000
Pounds soda ash	134,000	Pieces of ribbon	20,000
Yards brown cotton	271,000	Pounds codfish	304,000
Yards denim	488,000	Barrels salt salmon	4,000

Pounds (and 550 barrels and cases of other kinds) of salt fish	644,000	Pounds (and 8,000 kegs and boxes) nails	36,000
Barrels and boxes of fresh apples, grapes, peaches, pears, and other fruits	11,500	Nuts and bolts	343,000
		Picks and mattocks	4,300
		Feet iron pipe	400,000
Chairs	11,000	Razors	2,000
Rolls wall paper	39,000	Pounds beans	1,100,000
Sets parlor and chamber furniture	575	Pots and kettles	18,500
		Plows	330
Tables	970	Refrigerators	260
Pounds of barley	18,635,000	Pounds iron and copper rivets.	30,000
Pounds of bran	12,500,000	Saws	4,000
Pounds of corn	585,000	Pairs scissors and shears	15,000
Pounds of middlings	2,155,000	Shovels and spades	4,500
Bales of hay	65,000	Stoves	2,900
Pounds of oats	3,548,000	Feet wire cloth	100,000
Pounds of meal cake	85,700	Paint and other brushes	26,000
Pounds of wheat	876,500	Clocks	3,500
Pounds dried apples and apricots	23,000	Watches	3,100
Pounds bacon	63,000	Feet northwest pine lumber	19,197,000
Pounds hard bread	264,000	Laths	800,000
Pounds butter	120,000	Fence posts	64,000
Pounds butterine	45,000	Feet redwood lumber	4,100,000
Pounds candles	51,000	Railroad ties	42,600
Pounds cheese	107,000	Feet belting	21,000
Pounds (and 16,000 tins) of cakes and crackers	197,000	Boiler tubes	1,500
		Pounds packing	246,000
Pounds hams	225,000	Sewing machines	937
Pounds lard	322,000	Typewriting machines	58
Pounds onions	477,000	Guitars	600
Tins canned oysters	38,000	Pianos and organs	79
Pounds split peas	53,000	Yards canvas	24,000
Pounds potatoes	632,000	Pounds ship chains	52,000
Pounds prunes	21,000	Pounds rope	220,000
Tins canned meats	145,000	Pounds (and 38,000 feet) wire rope	130,000
Pounds salt	477,000	Cases kerosene	64,000
Pounds and 10,000 cases of soap	193,000	Gallons lubricating oil	110,000
		Barrels tar	620
Pounds refined sugar	637,000	Gallons linseed oil	31,000
Gallons vinegar	49,000	Pounds (and 9,000 gallons) paint and varnish	493,000
Gun caps	2,932,000	Bicycles	363
Window sashes	6,709	Carriages	132
Prs. boots, shoes, and slippers	189,000	Sets harness	300
Cravats and ties	18,960	Horse combs	1,200
Boys' felt and wool hats	27,600	Saddles	1,560
Ladies' hats	6,300	Sugar bags	4,000,000
Straw hats	38,000	Paper bags	1,500,000
Undershirts	55,600	Printed books	11,000
Pairs socks and stockings	194,600	Blank books	4,200
Cartridges	350,000	Packs playing cards	41,600
Pounds rope	22,500	Envelopes	2,321,000
Pairs butts and hinges	31,000	Lead pencils	96,000
Pounds fence wire	321,000	Cigars	1,427,000
Files and rasps	40,500	Cigarettes	5,827,000
Galvanized buckets	20,000	Pounds tobacco	320,000
Kegs horseshoes	1,600	Cases (and 136,000 gallons) California wine	869
Feet rubber hose	51,000		
Hoes	26,800		
Butcher and pocketknives	23,800	Pounds fertilizer	28,800,000

COMMERCE WILL BE GREATLY INCREASED UNDER ANNEXATION.

The astonishing commercial results shown above have resulted from affording to Hawaii a free market for, practically, only three of her products, viz, sugar, rice, and bananas.

Under annexation, the country would have a free market for all its products, and, with the exception of the three products above named, the resources of the country are practically untouched.

With a population of only 109,000, Hawaii in 1896 had a foreign trade of over $208 per capita for every man, woman, and child in the country—a record almost unparalleled in the history of the world.

Less than a hundred years ago Hawaii supported a population of four hundred thousand souls with the crude methods of cultivation then known.

Artificial irrigation in its most advanced methods is now practiced in Hawaii, bringing thousands of acres into cultivation that have heretofore been waste.

There is no reason why Hawaii cannot support a population of a million as easily as it does a hundred thousand.

Islands of less area and no greater resources than Hawaii, in both the East and West Indies, are supporting populations of several millions.

An increase of the population of Hawaii to even a million will place its commerce in the front rank of American export trade.

Under existing conditions, the Hawaiian general tariff of 10 per cent has allowed about 25 per cent of Hawaiian imports to come from countries other than the United States, and if annexation does not take place an increasing proportion of Hawaiian imports will come from other countries.

If Hawaii becomes American territory, the American protective tariff of approximately 50 per cent will give to Americans practically all of its present foreign trade, and an immensely larger trade which will spring into existence as the islands develop under the stimulating influences of a stable government, fertile soil, and a free market.

FOURTH REASON IN FAVOR OF THE ANNEXATION OF HAWAII.

It will greatly increase and secure to the United States the shipping business of the islands.

To those who refer to the Hawaiian Islands as "dots in the Pacific," this may appear to be an absurd reason.

It is absurd to those only who do not know the facts.

Hawaii is to-day the main stay of the American merchant marine engaged in deep-sea foreign trade.

Table showing number of American vessels entering American ports from foreign countries other than the American continent during the year ending June 30, 1896.

[Compiled from United States Treasury records.]

Countries cleared from.	Number of vessels.	
Austria	None.	
Belgium	16	
Denmark	None.	
France	2	
Gibraltar	2	
Germany	None	All of Europe, 30 ships.
Italy	5	
Netherlands	None.	
Portugal	None.	
Russia	None.	
Spain	5	
Sweden and Norway	None.	
China	14	
Hong Kong	30	
Japan	29	All of Asia, 98 ships.
East Indies	23	
Russia	2	
Australia, Tasmania, New Zealand, Fiji, and Norfolk Islands	30	All of Australasia, 30 ships.
All other Pacific islands (except Hawaii)	30	
All of Africa	22	
United Kingdom	88	
Hawaiian Islands	191	

To summarize further, the number of American vessels entering American ports during the year ending June 30, 1896, were:

From the United Kingdom 88
From Europe, Asia, Africa, Australia, and Oceanica combined.................. 210
From Hawaii 191

Or, in other words, Hawaii furnished cargo for 191 American ships, and all the world besides, outside of the American continent, furnished cargo for only 298 American ships.

Hawaii is the banner country for promoting American shipping and spreading the American flag to the breeze, and it is submitted that she should be allowed to carry on and extend the good work.

It may be said, "We have the shipping trade already. What more will annexation give us?" The reply is that the supremacy of American shipping in Hawaii arises directly and solely from the commercial supremacy of the United States in Hawaii, which in turn is the direct outcome of the reciprocity treaty. As stated above, that treaty can be abrogated at any time, and certainly will be abrogated if a party inimical to American interests should gain control in Hawaii, a contingency not only possible but probable, if annexation does not take place, as is pointed out under the "Second reason in favor of annexation."

UNDER ANNEXATION AMERICAN SHIPPING WILL BE GREATLY INCREASED.

After annexation all exports and imports to and from the United States will have to be carried in American vessels; for, being American territory, the coasting-trade laws will apply, and freight and passengers can be carried between Hawaii and other parts of the United States in American vessels only.

As the American tariff will bar out almost all imports from foreign countries, practically the whole freighting business of Hawaii will be with the United States, and will be transacted by American vessels. With the unquestionably rapid and large increase of Hawaiian population and commerce under annexation, it is entirely within bounds to say that within ten years after annexation is completed the number of American vessels required to do Hawaiian freighting will be double that now engaged therein. That is to say, 247 American ships being required to carry Hawaiian freight in 1896, approximately five hundred will be required in 1906, if annexation is consummated, or more than all the deep-sea American ships which entered American ports during 1896 from all the world outside of the American continent.

FIFTH REASON IN FAVOR OF THE ANNEXATION OF HAWAII.

It will remove Hawaii from international politics and tend to promote peace in the Pacific by eliminating an otherwise certain source of international friction.

It is the habit of those who oppose the annexation of Hawaii to ridicule the possibility of any foreign government taking any action in or towards Hawaii inimical to the interests of the United States.

One of the best methods of judging the future is to examine the past.

Within the past eighty-five years Hawaii has been taken possession of once by Russia, once by England, twice by France.

And by reason of hostile demonstrations by foreign governments, creating the fear of foreign conquest, an absolute cession of the sovereignty of the country to the United States was executed and delivered in 1851, and a treaty of annexation negotiated in 1854.

Since 1874 on four separate occasions internal disturbances have required the landing of foreign troops from war ships for the protection of the interests of the several nations there represented.

The existing conditions in the world are not such as to guarantee that the millennium is near at hand, and more particularly are the developments in the Pacific such as to render it unsafe for any country possessing interests therein to act upon the supposition that there will be no conflict of interests in that locality.

Russia has heretofore been a European country, with but a nominal interest in the Pacific. Within the past five years it has developed Pacificwards, until it fills the northwestern horizon, and with the now rapidly progressing development of its vast empire on the Pacific coast of Siberia, the construction of its transcontinental railway from St. Petersburg to the Pacific, and the foreshadowed absorption of northern China, there can be no prediction of the limit of its interests and strength in the Pacific.

The meteor-like projection of Japan into the international sky is too recent and vivid to need any enumeration of detail. In the short space of a year Japan has become not only a Pacific, but a world power.

With its rapidly increasing population, already numbering nearly fifty million; its navy now stronger than any other in the Pacific; its demonstrated power of organization and military execution; its progressive commercial and aggressive national spirit, there is no safety in basing any calculations upon the meekness or weakness of Japan.

There is a great Anglo-Saxon community growing up in the Pacific, including Australia, New Zealand, and hundreds of islands within their sphere of influence, whose interests are so great as to radically affect and frequently control British policy. This great community, inhabiting a country larger than the United States, excluding Alaska, is in the springtide of its development. Its leading statesmen have repeatedly and publicly advanced the claim that the control of the Pacific was theirs by right. To-day their influence and strength is not sufficient to be a serious menace to other interests in the Pacific. What their power may be fifty or a hundred years from now no man can tell. The statesmen of the United States should look not to the conditions of to-day only, but should stake out and secure to the .United States the position and policy which that country may require for a hundred years to come.

The population of Hawaii is, and for years to come will be, constituted of many divers nationalities and factions.

For the immediate present the Government is under the control of those favorable to the United States. There is no certainty that this condition of affairs will continue. As long as Hawaii is independent other nationalities will naturally and legitimately seek to advance their interests at the expense of those of the United States.

It is not necessary that any foreign government should attempt to do this, as a government.

The present difficulty with Japan is an illustration of how international troubles may arise through conflict of interests of the different nationalities resident in Hawaii, without direct initiative of a foreign government and from entirely unexpected sources. To-day the friction is with Japan. To-morrow it may be with Europe, England, or China.

The population of the country is so small that individual influence is much greater than in a larger country, and it is much easier for a nationality or a faction to get control of the Government.

As long as the country is independent, with its growing wealth and importance, there is, and will be, a growing tendency to international

friction among its inhabitants, which will inevitably draw into controversy the respective Governments.

When annexation was proposed in 1893 no government objected.
To-day, by reason of the increase of the interests of Japanese subjects
in the islands, Japan interposes a vigorous objection. It may not be
considered a serious obstacle to annexation; but it is an illustration of
the rapidity with which changes are taking place in the Pacific, and of
the possibility and probability of rapid developments inimical to American control, which must be expected in the Pacific within the early
future.

Hawaii independent, but without the power to maintain its independence, is a standing invitation to international intrigue and friction, and a menace to the peace of the Pacific.

As a part of the territory of the United States, Hawaii will be climi-
nated from international politics as much so as is Florida or California.

There is no certainty that the United States will go to war; but there
is no certainty that it will *not*. In case of war the possession of Hawaii
would be of the greatest value, and its occupation by a hostile force
would be the means of occasioning incalculable injury to the Pacific
coast and commerce. Is it prudent to postpone taking out an insurance
policy until the loss has occurred? Is not the annexation of Hawaii a
proper measure of national insurance against possible danger?

A BRIEF DESCRIPTION OF THE REPUBLIC OF HAWAII, ITS PEOPLE, GOVERNMENT, LAWS, COMMERCE, FINANCES, EDUCATIONAL SYSTEM, AND RESOURCES.

LOCATION.

The Hawaiian Islands are near the middle of the North Pacific
Ocean, between 18° and 22° north latitude and 154° and 160° west
longitude.

The map on the back cover of this pamphlet shows their position
better than any description.

Without disputing Boston's claim to be the hub of the universe,
Hawaii is the hub of the Western Hemisphere.

STRATEGICAL POSITION.

Hawaii is the only spot in the Pacific, from the equator on the south
to Alaska on the north, and between America on the east and Asia on
the west, where water, food, or coal can be obtained. It is also on or
near the principal trade routes across the Pacific. Its unique position
is what has given it the name of "*The Cross Roads of the Pacific*,"
"*The Key of the Pacific*," and "*The Gibraltar of the Pacific*."

CAPTAIN MAHAN'S OPINION.

Captain Mahan, of the U. S. Navy, one of the highest authorities
on naval strategy, says that Hawaii is one of the most important
strategical points in the world; that it stands "alone, having no rival
and admitting no rival."

The distances to the principal Pacific ports are as follows:

	Miles.
Hawaii to San Francisco	2,080
Hawaii to Nicaragua Canal	4,210
Hawaii to Tahiti	2,389
Hawaii to Pagopago, Samoa	2,263
Hawaii to Auckland, New Zealand	3,850

Miles.

Hawaii to Fiji 2,736
Hawaii to Marshall Islands 2,098
Hawaii to Caroline Islands.. 2,602
Hawaii to Hongkong... 4,917
Hawaii to Yokohama, Japan 3,399
Hawaii to Unalaska, Aleutian Islands................................... 2,016
Hawaii to Sitka 2,395
Hawaii to Vancouver 2,305

(See the map on the cover of this pamphlet.)

NUMBER AND AREA OF ISLANDS.

The group contains eight inhabited islands and a large number of small uninhabited ones, of a total approximate area of 7,000 square miles, or 4,480,000 acres, being nearly the area of Massachusetts, and considerably larger than Connecticut and Rhode Island combined. The group extends east and west a distance of 1,200 miles. The eight principal islands cover 300 miles at the eastern end of the group. They are Ha-wai-i, Mau-i, O-a-hu, Kau-ai, Mo-lo-kai, La-nai, Ka-hoo-la-we, and Ni-i-hau. There are valuable guano and phosphate rock deposits on some of the western islands.

HO-NO-LU-LU.

Situated on the island of O-a-hu is the principal city and the capital of the Republic.

It is located on a small but safe harbor, and has a population of 30,000.

The business portion is well built of stone and brick; the residences are of wood.

The city has 67 miles of streets and drives, of which 20 miles are macadamized; has a street railway system; public and private electric-light systems; a telephone system extending throughout the island and using 1,300 telephones; a well-regulated State prison; handsome executive buildings, custom-house and court-house; an insane asylum, public hospitals, maternity home, old folks' home; public library, a well-equipped Y. M. C. A. building, banks, churches, public and private schools, public waterworks, both a reservoir and pumping plant, a paid fire department equipped with the most modern steam and chemical engines; has a G. A. R. post, branches of the societies of "Sons" and "Daughters" of the American Revolution, and numerous Masonic, Odd Fellows, and other similar lodges. In other words, it has the appliances and conveniences of an up-to-date American city, with the added charm of a profuse tropical vegetation and a climate unrivalled the world over for mildness and evenness.

The city lies on a level strip of land along the sea, a mile or two wide and five miles long, and extending back for several miles into five valleys, which cut deep into thickly wooded, cloud-capped mountains rising to an elevation of nearly 4,000 feet at a distance of six miles from the sea.

GENERAL PHYSICAL CHARACTERISTICS OF THE COUNTRY.

The islands are all high and mountainous, rising to a height of 4,000 feet on Oahu, to 10,000 on Maui, and 14,000 feet and perpetual snow on the island of Hawaii. The whole country is volcanic in origin, there being hundreds of extinct and two active volcanoes.

Each island consists of one or more mountains seamed with valleys and gorges, with rolling plains lying between the mountains, and generally fringed with a comparatively level belt along the sea shore.

Some portions of the coast are protected by reefs of coral, while others are sheer precipices rising out of blue water to a height of thousands of feet.

THE SOIL, consisting of decomposed lava, is fertile, but has to be irrigated in many places, the water coming from mountain streams, artesian and surface wells. Some of the largest steam pumps in the world are used, raising water to an elevation of 400 feet.

Fertilizers are used in large quantities, thousands of tons per annum being used on the sugar plantations.

THE CLIMATE is mild and even, being of an average weekly maximum of 74 in winter and 82 in summer. There are no extremes of heat or cold. The lowest temperature at sea level in winter is about 56°, and the hottest in the summer about 88°. A temperature of 90° in the shade is almost unknown. At higher elevations above the sea almost any desired temperature can be found. On two mountains there is perpetual snow.

The cool northeast trade winds blow for nine months of the year. Except when the south winds blow, the humidity of the air is low.

The country at all elevations, and throughout the year, is healthy; the death rate among whites being exceptionally small. None of the fevers and other typical diseases of tropical countries are found there, and the diseases of the temperate zone are usually of a mild character.

The climate is so balmy and natural conditions so delightful that, by common acceptance, Hawaii is known as "The Paradise of the Pacific." Although spoken of as a "tropical country," it is barely on the edge of the Tropics, and the same arctic current that cools San Francisco gives Hawaii a climate many degress cooler than in the same latitude in the Atlantic. It is a climate well suited to the physical and mental development of the Anglo-Saxon.

PRODUCTS.—The principal products are sugar, rice, coffee, bananas, pineapples, guavas, and other tropical fruits, many of which grow wild.

SUGAR.—The area cultivated with sugar cane is approximately 80,000 acres. The export of sugar in 1896 amounted to 221,000 tons. The output of sugar can not be much increased, as most of the sugar lands are already occupied.

COFFEE.—The cultivation of coffee is rapidly increasing. It will soon rival sugar in amount and value, as there are large areas of rich but yet uncultivated land, not available for sugar but peculiarly adapted to coffee. This product is the hope of the country, as it can be produced profitably by farmers with small capital.

BANANAS AND PINEAPPLES.—The principal supply of these fruits consumed on the Pacific coast is from Hawaii. It is a growing trade.

THE RAINFALL varies greatly, ranging from fifty inches in some districts to 175 inches in others. Irrigation supplements the rainfall in the drier section. Two-thirds of the sugar is produced by irrigation.

EDUCATION.—There is a highly organized system of free public schools, modeled on that of the United States, in which the English language is taught. There are also a number of private boarding schools, and schools ranking with high schools in the United States.

The public school year is eight months, and all children between six and fourteen years of age are compelled, if physically able, to attend school.

All the Hawaiian born population of all nationalities can read and write English. The number of schools in 1896 was 187; number of teachers, 426; number of scholars, 12,616.

The schools are under the control of an unpaid board of five persons, appointed by the President.

The constitution prohibits the appropriation of public funds for sectarian or private schools.

REVENUE AND EXPENDITURES.

The financial status of the Republic is strong. The country is self supporting, solvent, and prosperous.

Financial status January 1, 1897.

RECEIPTS.

The current cash on hand January 1, 1896, was.........................	$22,496.30
The current revenue for 1896 was:	
From customs..	656,895.82
From post-office...	77,488.94
From internal revenue	1,240,937.12
Total current revenue for 1896..................................	1,997,818.18

EXPENDITURES.

The current expenditures for 1896 were:	
General expenses...	$1,651,631.33
Interest on all loans...	236,459.59
Matured bonds paid..	16,100.00
Total current expense for 1896..................................	1,904,190.92
Cash on hand December 31, 1896...................................	93,627.26
	1,997,818.18

This shows that after paying all running expenses, interest on all loans, and redeeming $16,100 worth of bonds falling due, the treasury closed the year with a cash surplus over $71,000 greater than at the beginning.

TAXATION.

Revenue is raised by duties on imports, averaging 10 per cent ad valorem (except a few specific duties), and by internal taxes. The internal revenue is derived from rents of public lands, wharfage, and water rates in Honolulu; a system of licenses for different kinds of business; a stamp duty on conveyances and legal documents; a tax of one per cent on all real and personal property, and a poll tax on male adults.

PUBLIC DEBT.

The bonded debt consists of—		
7 per cent bonds	$1,500.00	
6 per cent bonds	3,073,600.00	
5 per cent bonds	255,100.00	
	3,330,200.00	
Deposits in postal savings bank.........................	882,345.29	
Total gross debt		$4,212,545.29
Less bond proceeds, cash in treasury....................	221,565.90	
And postal bank deposits	111,371.04	
		332,936.94
Total net debt, January 1, 1897.....................................		3,879,608.35

With the exception of $220,000 five per cent bonds, which are redeemable in 1901, all of the debt can be taken up at any time.

Measures to refund the debt at four per cent which were being taken are being delayed, pending action on the annexation treaty, as the United States can, of course, refund at a still lower rate.

With the exception of $1,000,000 held in London, practically all of the bonds are held in Hawaii.

PUBLIC LANDS.

The area of the public lands is 1,740,000 acres, of an estimated value in 1894 of $4,389,550. The income from the rents of public lands during 1896 was $137,773, an amount which can be largely increased.

A considerable portion of the public land is mountainous and waste, and much that is arable is under leases.

The policy of the government is to renew leases of only such portions of arable land as are in actual cultivation, cutting up all available farming lands into small farms and disposing of it on easy terms to actual settlers. It is mainly through this means that the coffee industry has become established.

A complete and extremely liberal land law has been enacted by the Republic, and is in operation under a board of land commissioners.

The lands are being surveyed and roads constructed to them as rapidly as practicable.

Public lands suitable for coffee and fruit culture can be bought by actual settlers at from $7 to $20 an acre, on easy terms.

Land of similar quality can be purchased unconditionally from private parties at from $25 to $50 per acre.

POPULATION.

The census of 1896 shows the population to be 109,020.

In round numbers the different nationalities are represented as follows:

Native Hawaiians	31,000
Japanese	24,400
Portuguese	15,100
Chinese	21,600
Part Hawaiian and part foreign blood	8,400
Americans	3,000
British	2,200
German	1,400
Norwegian and French	479
All other nationalities	1,055

Expressed in percentage, the population is as follows:

	Per cent.
Native Hawaiian	28
Japanese	22
Chinese	20
Americans, and Europeans by birth or descent	22
Mixed blood	8

FORM OF GOVERNMENT.

The Government of Hawaii was a monarchy until January, 1893, when Queen Liliuokalani attempted to abrogate the constitution and promulgate one increasing her power and disfranchising the whites.

The people thereupon overthrew the monarchy and established a Provisional Government, January the 17th, 1893.

Later a constitutional convention unanimously adopted a constitution declaring the Republic of Hawaii on July 4, 1894.

THE EXECUTIVE consists of a President and four cabinet officers.

The President is Sanford Ballard Dole; fifty years of age; Hawaiian born, of American parentage; a graduate of Williams College; a lawyer by profession. He was a judge of the supreme court under the monarchy, which position he resigned to accept the leadership of the revolution which overturned the monarchy. He is respected and admired by all classes and factions in the community.

THE ELECTORATE consists of all male adult citizens who take an oath of renunciation of the monarchy and allegiance to the Republic. *Asiatics are not eligible to citizenship or to vote.*

The required qualifications of a voter for representatives is ability to read and write Hawaiian or English, and the payment of all taxes due; and for senators, in addition thereto, an income of $600 per annum, *or* the ownership of real estate worth $1,500, *or* personal property worth $3,000.

THE LEGISLATURE consists of a Senate elected for six years, and a House of Representatives elected for two years, each consisting of fifteen members.

THE LEGISLATIVE PROCEDURE is practically the same as in the United States. Each measure, in order to become law, has to pass three readings before each house and be signed by the President.

The committee system is the same as in American legislative bodies.

The President has the power of veto, which may be overridden by a two-thirds vote of each house.

CHARACTER OF LAWS.—The foundation of the legal system of the country is the common law of England.

The penal law and practice is codified, and there are no penal offenses except those enumerated in the code.

The civil law, practice and procedure, is partially codified, and is, in general, as much like that of the several American States as the law of one State is like that of another.

The text-books and law reports of England and the United States are cited as authority in the courts in the same manner that they are in this country.

The members of the supreme and circuit court bars are nearly all Americans, or were educated in American law schools. The attorneys in the district courts are mostly native Hawaiians, educated in Honolulu.

THE COURTS.

The main judicial system consists of district and circuit courts and a supreme court.

DISTRICT COURTS.—There are about thirty district courts. They have jurisdiction over civil matters involving not more than $300, and over misdemeanors. They also commit, for trial by jury, persons accused of felony, exercising the functions of an American grand jury. The grand jury system has not been adopted.

An appeal lies from the district to the circuit or supreme court.

CIRCUIT COURTS.—There are four circuit courts, with appellate jurisdiction over appeals from the district courts and original jurisdiction over all civil suits involving more than $300; over persons committed for trial for felonies; in all equity, admiralty, and probate cases, and over special proceedings such as habeas corpus, etc. Each circuit court is presided over by one judge. All jury trials are held in the circuit courts.

JURIES.—The same class of cases are tried by jury as in the United States. Juries consist of twelve men, but nine can render a verdict in both civil and criminal cases. Jury can be waived in both civil and criminal cases, except capital cases.

THE SUPREME COURT consists of three judges, with exclusive jurisdiction to decide certain special proceedings and the validity of elections to the legislature; concurrent jurisdiction with the circuit judges concerning habeas corpus and certain other special proceedings; and appellate jurisdiction over exceptions and appeals from district or circuit courts. Cases are tried promptly, and the courts are ably and honestly conducted.

The judges are appointed by the President—district judges for two years, circuit judges for four years, and supreme court judges for life.

TWENTY OBJECTIONS TO THE ANNEXATION OF HAWAII, AND REPLIES THERETO.

FIRST OBJECTION.

It is unconstitutional, because the General Government is limited in its powers to those expressly conferred upon it by the Constitution.

The Constitution does not specifically grant power to annex territory, and therefore the power does not exist.

This objection is based upon what is known as the "strict construction theory." It was believed in by Jefferson, but was abandoned by him when he annexed Louisiana in 1803. Contemporary thought condemns the strict construction theory, as applied to annexation, and the Constitution has since then been repeatedly interpreted in favor of annexation by the Executive, Congress, and the Supreme Court of the United States.

Interpretations of the Constitution by the Executive in favor of the power of annexation.

The instances in which the Executive has interpreted the Constitution in favor of annexation are eleven in number, viz: By the negotiation of treaties for the annexation of Louisiana in 1803; Florida in 1819; California, New Mexico, and Arizona in 1849; the so-called Gadsden purchase of the southern portion of New Mexico and Arizona in 1853, and Alaska in 1867, all of which were ratified by the Senate. Treaties were also negotiated by the Executive for the annexation of Texas in 1837 and 1843, Hawaii in 1854, San Domingo in 1870, Hawaii in 1893, and Hawaii again in 1897, which treaty is now pending before the Senate.

Interpretations of the Constitution by Congress in favor of the power of annexation.

Instances of Congressional action in favor of the power of annexation are:

1. The annexation of Texas in 1844, by joint resolution passed by a majority of the two Houses of Congress.

2. A statute passed Aug. 18, 1856, by which any American citizen was authorized to take possession of any island on which guano was located, and, with the approval of the United States Government, upon taking certain preliminary action, to make the same United States territory.

3. By the ratification of the annexation of Midway Island, in the North Pacific, which had been accomplished by the Executive in 1867, by the appropriation of funds with which to convert the same into a naval station.

The legislation referred to above, concerning the annexation of guano islands, is especially pertinent at the present time, when the Hawaiian Islands are under discussion, for the reason that we find that as long ago as 1856, Congress not only approved of insular annexation, but that, under that legislation, seventy islands and groups of islands were actually annexed to the United States, fifty-seven of them being in the Pacific Ocean and thirteen in the Carribean Sea. The first annexation under this statute was in 1856 and the last in 1884.

It may be claimed that the motive for annexing these islands was simply to obtain the guano located thereon. Such undoubtedly was the motive; but the motive for annexing territory has no bearing upon the constitutionality thereof. The passage of the statute is a positive declaration by Congress that the annexation of territory, and insular territory at that, is constitutional, and that so slight a value accruing to the United States as the obtaining of a limited amount of fertilizing material is a sufficient reason for the exercise of the power of annexation.

The Executive and Congressional action concerning Midway Island is of especial interest, in that Midway Island is at the western extremity of the same group of islands of which Hawaii is the easternmost; and also from the fact that the motive for the annexation of Midway was to secure a naval station in the North Pacific, which is one of the main reasons now urged for annexing Hawaii.

The query presents itself, why, if it was proper to annex the western end of the Hawaiian group in 1867, it is not now proper to annex the eastern end of the same group? Midway Island is 1,200 miles west of Honolulu. Congress appropriated and there was spent the sum of $50,000 in trying to make it into a naval station; a United States man-of-war was wrecked and three lives lost in the attempt, which was finally abandoned. The only reason that Midway was not developed into a full-fledged naval station was that it was found that the expense was far greater than originally supposed. It nevertheless remains United States territory, and a monument constructed by the Executive and Congress in favor of the constitutionality and propriety of insular annexation.

Interpretations of the Constitution by the Supreme Court of the United States, in favor of the power of annexation.

The instances of interpretation by the Supreme Court of the United States of the constitutionality of annexation are four in number, viz, one in 1828, two in 1850, and one in 1889.

The first was in the case of the American Insurance Company vs. Canter, to be found in 1 Peters, 542. The opinion was delivered by Chief Justice Marshall, in the course of which the following words were used:

"The Constitution confers absolutely on the Government of the Union the power of making wars and of making treaties. Consequently that Government possesses the power of acquiring territory, either by conquest or treaty."

The two decisions rendered in 1850 were by Chief Justice Taney. The decision in 1889 is the case of the Mormon Church vs. the United States, contained in 136 United States Reports, page 42. In the course of the decision, the court used the following words:

"The power to acquire territory is derived from the treaty-making power, and the power to declare and carry on war."

"The incidents of these powers are those of national sovereignty and belong to all independent governments."

The foregoing decisions base their conclusions some upon one point, some upon another; but they all agree that the constitutional power to annex territory exists absolutely; and the last decision is based upon the broad ground that "the power to make acquisitions of territory is an incident of national sovereignty."

It is submitted that the foregoing acts and decisions of the Executive, Congress, and the United States Supreme Court, covering a period of nearly a hundred years, are decisive in favor of the constitutional power of the United States Government to annex territory.

SECOND OBJECTION.

It is unconstitutional because Hawaii is not contiguous to the United States.

The opponents of the constitutionality of annexation, finding the precedents and reasoning strongly against them, have fallen back from the position that annexation is directly prohibited by the Constitution, to the claim that there are certain "implied prohibitions" in the Constitution which are as binding as those which appear on its face, and that among these "implied prohibitions," is the one above stated.

The only reason presented why the annexation of noncontiguous territory is unconstitutional is that the "people of the day" did not discuss nor contemplate the annexation of such territory.

We have seen by the authoritative decision of the Supreme Court in 1889 that the power to acquire territory is an incident of national sovereignty; that is to say, the United States has the right to acquire territory, or any other property, because it is a nation. It has the same rights and powers in this respect that any other nation has—that, for example, England has. There is manifestly no limitation upon the power of England to acquire territory. How, then, can there be any limitation upon the power of the United States to do so?

The fact that territory is contiguous or noncontiguous is to be considered in reference to the policy or expediency of annexation, but it is submitted that both on principle and precedent there is all the constitutional power necessary to accomplish annexation in any case where annexation is deemed to the interest of this country.

The fact that territory is contiguous or noncontiguous can have no bearing upon the constitutionality of its acquisition; but simply goes to affect the *value* of the territory proposed to be annexed. On general principles, if it is contiguous, it is more easily governed and defended. But whether this is so or not depends upon circumstances. In these days distance is not a matter of miles, but of hours. When California was annexed it was two months distant from the center of civilization in the United States. Honolulu to-day lies only ten and a half days from Washington.

As to the arguments presented in favor of the unconstitutionality of the annexation of noncontiguous territory, it is submitted that because our forefathers of 1776 did not discuss or contemplate any given proposition is no reason, constitutional or otherwise, why their children should not discuss and contemplate any and every problem which is presented to them in 1897 upon its merits, whether their ancestors ever heard of such subject or not.

It is further submitted that the precedents in United States history are all against the unconstitutionality of the annexation of noncontiguous territory. Alaska is separated from the United States by a vast foreign territory. Midway Island is approximately three thousand miles from the American coast. The Aleutian Islands, reaching almost to the Asiatic coast, extend twelve hundred miles west of Alaska, and the guano islands are scattered all over the Pacific and the Caribbean Sea.

THIRD OBJECTION.

It is unconstitutional because its inhabitants are not homogeneous with the people of the United States.

This is another of the alleged "implied prohibitions." The same reasoning applied to the last objection applies to this one, to wit, that there is no constitutional feature involved, but it is simply a fact to be taken into consideration when the advisability of annexing any given territory is under consideration.

Is it conceivable that, regardless of the advantages of annexing any given territory, the people of the United States are absolutely prohibited from annexing such territory, simply because its inhabitants may not be up to the full American standard?

Again, it is submitted that the precedents are all opposed to the view advanced in the objection under consideration. For example, when Louisiana was annexed its population consisted of a few thousand Frenchmen and several hundred thousand Indians, reaching from the Gulf of Mexico to the Oregon coast. To say nothing about the Indians, the Frenchmen were governed by the civil law of France, and to this day the foundation of the law of Louisiana is the civil law and not the English common law.

Florida had a population of a few Spaniards and Indians. Texas, prior to the great influx of Americans, had a population solely of Mexicans, Spaniards, and Indians. At the time of its annexation California had an American population consisting of only a few traders and a military post, the great bulk of the population consisting of Mexicans and Indians, with a sprinkling of Spanish priests. Alaska had a few hundred Russians and some thirty or forty thousand Arctic Indians. Were these homogeneous populations? Were they up to the American standard of citizenship? If not, and if it is unconstitutional to annex territory unless the inhabitants of such territory are up to the American standard, then such annexations were void, for if this is a constitutional principle, it can not be varied by circumstances.

It is submitted that there is no principle, direct, or implied, in the Constitution of the United States which makes the title of the United States to the territories enumerated depend upon the quality of the people living therein at the date of annexation.

FOURTH OBJECTION.

Whether the annexation of a nonhomogenous people is constitutional or not, the population of Hawaii is unfit for incorporation into, and will be dangerous to, the American political system.

Whether the Hawaiian population is unfit for incorporation into the American system depends upon two things: First, the existing facts; and second, the outlook for the future.

First, as to the existing conditions in Hawaii: The foundation of Hawaiian law is the common law of England. The general statutes, court procedure, and legal methods of Hawaii are as much like those of Illinois as those of Illinois are like those of Massachusetts. The laws of Hawaii are based upon—many of them copies of—those of the

United States. The two statutes, for example, which Japan is now objecting to as limiting Japanese immigration, are almost exact copies of the United States immigration laws restricting the immigration of contract laborers and undesirable persons. All legal documents are modeled on those in use in the United States. Most of the lawyers and judges are either from the United States or educated therein. The public-school system is based upon that of the United States. There are one hundred and eighty-seven of them, taught by four hundred and twenty-six teachers and containing 12,600 pupils, all taught in the English language. More than one-half the teachers are Americans. English is the official language of the schools and courts and the common language of business. The railroads, cars, engines, water works, water pipes, dynamos, telephones, fire apparatus, are all of American make. United States currency is the currency of the country. All Government and private bonds, notes, and mortgages are made payable in United States money. Practically manhood suffrage among all Hawaiian citizens has existed since 1852. The Australian ballot system has been in operation since 1890. All American holidays, Washington's Birthday, Decoration Day, Fourth of July, and Thanksgiving Day are as fully and enthusiastically celebrated in Hawaii as in any part of the United States. This is not the growth of a day, but of two generations, so that even to the native Hawaiian it appears to be the natural order of things.

The people of Hawaii, as a whole, are energetic and industrious. They are annually producing and exporting more per capita than any other nation in the world. Moreover, their chief export, sugar, is an article which has to compete in the markets of the world on the smallest possible margin of profit, and can be produced only by a combination of industry, economy, and keen business ability.

No people who are leading the world in the per capita export of manufactured products can be truthfully characterized as lazy, worthless, or unreliable.

As a matter of fact there are no poorhouses, paupers, beggars, or tramps in Hawaii.

To take the different nationalties up in detail:

THE NATIVE HAWAIIANS, only 33,000 in number, are a conservative, peaceful, and generous people. The have had during the last twenty years to struggle against the retrogressive tendencies of the reigning family; but in spite of that a very large proportion of them have stood out against such tendencies and are supporters of the Republic and of annexation. The majority of the present House of Representatives, the first under the Republic, consists of pure-blood native Hawaiians, and the speaker of the House is a native Hawaiian.

The Hawaiians are not Africans, but Polynesians. They are brown, not black. There is not and never has been any color line in Hawaii as against native Hawaiians, and they participate fully and on an equality with the white people in affairs political, social, religious, and charitable. The two races freely intermarry one with the other, the results being shown in a present population of some 7,000 of mixed blood. They are a race which will in the future, as they have in the past, easily and rapidly assimilate with and adopt American ways and methods.

THE PORTUGUESE have frequently been spoken of as being a bad element, and are even spoken of as not being Europeans. This is unjust and incorrect. Seven thousand of the so-called 15,000 Portuguese of Hawaii are Hawaiian born, and all of them have been educated in the public schools, so that they speak English as readily as does the average American child. The criminal statistics show a smaller percentage of offenses committed by this class of Hawaiian population than by any other nationality in the country. They are a hard-working, industrious. home-creating, and home-loving people, who would be of advantage to any developing country. They constitute the best laboring element in Hawaii.

THE CHINESE AND JAPANESE are an undesirable population from a political standpoint, because they do not understand American principles of government. The Asiatic population of Hawaii consists largely, however, of laborers who are temporarily in the country for what they can make out of it. As soon as they accumulate a few hundred dollars they return home. Shut off the source of supply, and in ten years there will not be Asiatics enough left in Hawaii to have any appreciable effect.

Moreover, most of them are making as much or more money in Hawaii than they can in the United States, and they have no object in trying to come to this country. This is evidenced by the fact that prior to the passage of the Chinese exclusion act by Congress there were as many Chinese in Hawaii as there now are, but practically none came to California. The Japanese are now free to come to California from Honolulu, but none come.

The treaty of annexation prohibits any further Chinese immigration from the date of the ratification of the treaty; prohibits emigration of the Chinese now in Hawaii to any other part of the United States, and the treaty with Japan, which goes into effect in 1899, allows the United States to regulate the immigration of Japanese laborers.

Individually, the Chinese and Japanese in Hawaii are industrious, peaceable citizens, and as long as they do not take part in the political control of the country, what danger can the comparatively small number there be to this country? They are not citizens, and by the constitution of Hawaii they are not eligible to become citizens; they are aliens in America and aliens in Hawaii; annexation will give them no rights which they do not now possess, either in Hawaii or in the United States.

The remaining inhabitants of Hawaii are some seven or eight thousand Americans, English, and Germans; strong, virile men who have impressed their form of government upon the much larger population living there, and have acquired the ownership of more than three-fourths of all the property in the country. If they were able to do this against the hostility and in the face of an unfavorable monarchy, why is there any reason to believe that they will be any less strong under the fostering influence of the republican Government of the United States?

No territory of the United States was ever annexed with so strong a leaven of Americanism in it as exists to-day in Hawaii.

As to the future prospects. Within a hundred years Hawaii possessed a population of 400,000 people, who were supported by the lax methods of cultivation then in effect. With the advanced methods of to-day and the irrigation of the heretofore barren plains, there is no reason why Hawaii can not support a population of a million as easily as it now does 100,000. With stability of government will come immigration, development, and growth, which will as certainly take place in Hawaii as it has in all the other Territories heretofore annexed by the United States.

We do not want Hawaii as a State, with two more Senators.
The treaty does not provide for Statehood. Hawaii does not ask for
it, and the United States does not grant it. The treaty of annexation
provides that Hawaii shall come into the Union as a Territory, and
leaves the form of such Territorial government absolutely in the hands
of Congress. What more could Hawaii give or the United States ask?
It is recognized that Hawaii does not now possess the population or the
wealth to warrant Statehood, and there is no probability that it will
possess such qualifications for some time to come. It will be a question for our successors and not for us to settle. They will be dealing
with their own fortunes and fates, and not with ours. Can we not
perform the duty of the hour as it is presented to us, and leave the
future to our successors in the faith that they will be as wise and as
patriotic as we are?

*Hawaii is an outlying territory, and in time of war it will be a source
of weakness to the United States.*
Whether outlying territory is a source of weakness depends upon
circumstances. When England owned territory in France it was a
source of weakness to her. Her ownership of Gibraltar is a source of
strength. This objection involves somewhat of a technical military
question. All of the military and naval authorities of the United
States who have expressed themselves upon the subject, Generals
Schofield and Alexander; Admirals Porter, Walker, Belknap, and
Captain Mahan have declared that Hawaii would be a source of
strength to the United States in case of war. They do not base their
opinion upon any occult reasoning, only known to themselves, but
upon a plain demonstration of facts, viz:
The distance from Hongkong, on the west of Hawaii, to Panama, on
the east, is 9,580 miles—as great a distance as from San Francisco across
the American continent, across the Atlantic, across the Mediterranean,
and across Turkey to the Persian border. The distance from Unalaska,
the first port north of Hawaii, to Tahiti, the first port on the south, is
4,400 miles—a distance as great as from Greenland to the Amazon
River. In all this vast territory there is only one spot where a ton of
coal, a pound of bread, or a drink of water can be obtained, and that
spot is Hawaii.
The great powers having interests in the Pacific are so far distant
from the Pacific coast of the United States that not one of them can
operate against it with a naval force unless they have a base of operations nearer than any which they now possess.
The navies of to-day are all steamers with limited coal-carrying
capacity. There is not a war vessel in existence which can steam from
any of the ports belonging to England, France, Russia, Spain, Japan,
or China to the Pacific coast and back again without renewing its coal
supply. Hawaii is only four days' steaming from San Francisco. In
possession of Hawaii, any of the great powers mentioned would be
within easy striking distance of the Pacific coast and its commerce.
Shut out from Hawaii, all of them are forced back the entire width of
the Pacific—a distance practically prohibitive of naval operations
against the Pacific coast or its vicinity. Hawaii in the possession of

any foreign power would be a menace and a danger to the Pacific coast and its commerce. With foreign countries barred out of Hawaii, the Pacific coast and its commerce is almost absolutely safe from naval attack. Vancouver has not been mentioned in this connection, for the reason that it is taken for granted that any foreign possession which can be reached from the mainland by United States troops would be taken in case of war within a very short time after the commencement of hostilities.

SEVENTH OBJECTION.

It will necessitate heavy expenditures and a navy in order to protect Hawaii in time of war.

War between the United States and any foreign country may or may not require the fortification of Hawaii. But this question depends not in the remotest degree upon annexation. *It depends upon whether the United States is to continue its policy of the past ;fifty years, to wit, the barring out of all other nations from Hawaii.* This policy was initiated by President Tyler in 1842, when he said that "it could not but create dissatisfaction on the part of the United States at any attempt by another power to take possession."

It was reiterated by Daniel Webster a short time thereafter, when, upon being informed that the French were contemplating taking possession of the islands, he said:

"I trust the French will not take possession; but if they do, they will be dislodged, if my advice is taken, if the whole power of the Government is required to do it."

This policy has been reiterated by Presidents and Secretaries of State and other American statesmen during almost every Administration from that time to the present day.

In 1894 the House of Representatives formally adopted a resolution declaring that "intervention in Hawaii by any foreign power will not be regarded with indifference," while the Senate adopted a resolution containing stronger language, to the effect that such intervention "will be regarded as an act unfriendly to the United States."

This is the policy which will have to be defended. Annexation is only incidental to the policy of exclusion.

This policy can be defended either by guns or arguments. If it can be defended by arguments now it can likewise be so defended after annexation. If it is to be defended by guns, annexation will facilitate such defense.

Having long ago decided that its policy concerning Hawaii should be to keep other countries out, *the question now to be decided is, Can that policy best be subserved by vesting the legal title in the United States or by leaving Hawaii as an independent country?*

If the title is vested in the United States all possibility of future international complication will be at an end; and if the United States at any time hereafter decides that its policy of exclusion of other countries can best be subserved by guns it can immediately proceed to fortify Hawaii. If, however, the title to Hawaii remains in a foreign Government it is certain that in the future, as in the past, Hawaii will become involved with foreign countries and continue to be a fertile source of international complications; and if the United States in the course of time should deem that its time-honored policy required the fortification of Hawaii there might be found in control in Hawaii a government inimical to the United States, which would prohibit fortifications.

Annexation does not necessitate fortification, but if ever fortification is required title will be an essential.

Title can be obtained now. What the future may bring forth no one can tell.

EIGHTH OBJECTION.

It will be a forerunner and form a precedent for a policy of unlimited annexation of territory.

Any party in the United States which may in the future desire a precedent for annexing any country whatsoever will in the past history of the country find ample precedent for so doing without referring to Hawaii. The United States has annexed all kinds of territory, from the coral reefs and cocoanut groves of Key West to the icy barrier of northern Alaska; territories bordering on the Atlantic, the Gulf of Mexico, the Pacific, and the Arctic; islands of the Pacific and the Caribbean Sea. Its possessions extend as far west of San Francisco as Maine is east of San Francisco and as far north of Chicago as Florida is south of Chicago. So far as precedents are concerned, nothing more is required.

It is submitted, however, that the annexation of Hawaii will, if it is accomplished, forever stand unique. The area of Hawaii, approximately 7,000 square miles, is not inconsiderable. It is nearly as large as Massachusetts, and considerably larger than Connecticut and Rhode Island combined. But if it did not contain a hundred square miles its value to the United States would remain practically the same.

Its foreign commerce is wonderfully large for a country of its size. It amounted to $22,000,000 for the year 1896. But if it had no commerce its value to the United States would be practically the same.

Its value to the United States consists in its unique position in the Pacific Ocean. It is the one and only point which can be made a naval base of operations against the Pacific coast. As Captain Mahan has said, "it stands alone * * * having no rival, and admitting of no rival." In the Atlantic, on the other hand, there are a hundred islands scattered around the United States coast, any one of which can be made a base of operations. In order to secure immunity from attack on the Atlantic all of these islands must be secured by the United States. In order to secure like immunity on the Pacific, Hawaii alone needs to be secured.

If there were numerous other islands in the Pacific, as there are in the Atlantic, then the annexation of Hawaii would offer a precedent for further extension of territory. As it is, *the annexation of Hawaii will not be for the purpose of securing additional territory or additional commerce, but will simply be the securing of a strategical point for the protection of territory which the United States already owns.* It will come precisely within the same principle that would be invoked did the Farallone Islands, thirty miles off the Golden Gate, or Long Island, off New York Harbor, belong to some foreign country, and were they now proposed to be secured by the United States.

NINTH OBJECTION.

It is contrary to the Monroe doctrine to acquire territory beyond the boundaries of the American continent.

This objection is made by those who do not understand what the Monroe doctrine consists of. The Monroe doctrine is a limitation on

European powers, excluding them from participation in the affairs of the American continent and its outlying islands, but it places no limitation upon the United States.

Instead of Hawaii lying beyond the purview of the Monroe doctrine, there is no territory to which the Monroe doctrine more directly applies than to Hawaii, and in no other case has there been such continued insistence on the part of American statesmen of the application of the doctrine as in the case of Hawaii.

In addition to the immense number of general statements by American statesmen concerning American control over Hawaii, the following quotations are directly in point:

In 1881 Secretary of State Blaine, in writing to United States Minister Comly, at Honolulu, says:

"The situation of the Hawaiian Islands, giving them strategic control of the North Pacific, brings their possession within the range of questions of purely American policy, as much so as that of the Isthmus itself."

In 1894 Senator Morgan, of Alabama, in a report to the Senate concerning the Hawaiian Islands, says:

"Observing the spirit of the Monroe doctrine, the United States, in the beginning of our relations with Hawaii, made a firm and distinct declaration of the purpose to prevent the absorption of Hawaii or the political control of the country by any foreign power."

TENTH OBJECTION.

A large portion of the Hawaiian voters have been disfranchised.

No vote has been taken in Hawaii upon the question of annexation, and it is un-American to annex a territory without a popular vote of its inhabitants.

It will be noted that this is the argument most resorted to by the ex-Queen Liliuokalani and her supporters. Their objection is not based upon opposition to the American Republic, but upon opposition to any republic. They are selfishly seeking the restoration of the monarchy for their own benefit, and as long as Hawaii remains independent they hope for some internal discord or foreign complication which will restore them to power.

The reply to the objection is that it is not un-American to annex territory without a vote of the inhabitants, and that no Hawaiian voters have been disfranchised.

Whether it is un-American to annex territory without a popular vote depends upon what has been done upon like occasions in the past. In the cases of the annexation of Louisiana, with its colony of intelligent Frenchmen; of Florida, with its Spaniards; of California. New Mexico, Arizona, and Alaska, there was no semblance of a vote, and there is no indication that the subject was even so much as discussed by either of the contracting parties. All that was done, or lawfully required to be done, was the agreement of the two Governments, and the act was complete without reference to either the people of the United States or of the territory proposed to be annexed.

The case of Texas is sometimes referred to as a precedent supporting a popular vote, but it is not. Texas was first proposed to be annexed by a treaty negotiated in 1837. After it failed of ratification the same method was followed in 1843. In neither treaty was any vote of the people provided for. In 1844 a bill was introduced into the Senate providing for the annexation of Texas and for the taking of a vote of her people, which bill was defeated. Shortly thereafter a joint resolution was introduced to effect the annexation of Texas, in which no mention was made of a popular vote, but which contemplated the completion of the annexation upon the acceptance of the terms of the joint resolution by the Texan Government. Immediately upon receiving the news of the passage of this resolution the Texan legislature accepted the terms of the resolution and the annexation was complete. Several months thereafter the people of Texas adopted a State constitution, which incidentally ratified the annexation. But such ratification was not necessary, as that had already been completed months before by the legislature.

There is, therefore, no precedent in any of the annexations of the past for taking a popular vote upon the subject. Why, then, is it un-American to annex Hawaii without a popular vote?

There is less reason for taking a popular vote in the case of Hawaii than in any instance in the past, for the reason that there is not now and never has been any Hawaiian law requiring that a treaty of annexation should be submitted to popular vote; but, on the contrary, there is specifically incorporated into the constitution of the Republic an article authorizing and directing the President, by and with the consent of the Senate, to negotiate and conclude a treaty of annexation with the United States.

Again, why in logic is there any more reason for requiring a popular vote on the part of the citizens of Hawaii than by the citizens of the United States? The citizens of the United States, as well as those of Hawaii, assume responsibilities and obligations by reason of annexation. Why should the citizens of Hawaii be individually consulted and those of the United States ignored?

Incidentally, however, as in the case of Texas, there has been a practical vote in Hawaii upon the subject of annexation, for every person who is now a voter in Hawaii has taken the oath to the constitution of Hawaii, thereby ratifying and approving of annexation to the United States.

NO DISFRANCHISEMENT OF HAWAIIAN VOTERS.

Every person who was a voter under the monarchy has the privilege of voting under the Republic, with the sole difference that whereas under the monarchy he took an oath to support it, under the Republic he renounces the monarchy and takes an oath to support the Republic. There has been no disfranchisement of voters in Hawaii. The only persons who could vote under the monarchy and who can not vote now are those who have disfranchised themselves by refusing to accept the Republic.

The situation, then, is—

1. Neither the Constitution nor laws of the United States nor of Hawaii require a popular vote.

2. During fifty years there have been four annexation treaties negotiated by Hawaii with the United States, viz, in 1851, 1854, 1893, and 1897, in which, neither under the Monarchy, Provisional Government, nor the Republic, has any provision been made for a popular vote, either in the United States or Hawaii.

3. Six annexations of inhabited territory by the United States, during the past one hundred years, have been made without a popular vote being taken.

4. The Constitution of the United States, in general terms, and of

Hawaii specifically, authorizes the respective Presidents and Senates to conclude a treaty of annexation.

Under these circumstances, what basis is there for claiming that an annexation treaty can not be legally concluded except by popular vote?

If it is admitted that the legal right exists, and that the objection is based on a sentimental regard for the native Hawaiian, the native Hawaiian may well pray "deliver me from my friends." America has given him a taste of American liberty and civilization. Americawards lies the full freedom and the proud status of republican citizenship. Unless annexation takes place, the only future for the native Hawaiian is retrogression to the status of the Asiatic coolie, who is already crowding him to the wall.

If the theoretical philanthropists of America, who are lifting up their voices against annexation through sympathy for the native Hawaiian, could descend out of the clouds long enough to ascertain the facts, they would learn that every native minister of the gospel; most of the better educated natives; almost without exception, all of the white ministers of the gospel; the representatives of the American Board of Foreign Missions; the Hawaiian Board of Missions; the practical educators; those who have for years contributed their time, their money, and their lives to the Hawaiian people; who feel that their welfare is a sacred trust—all of these are working, hoping, and praying for annexation as the one last hope of the native Hawaiian.

ELEVENTH OBJECTION.

A protectorate will secure to the United States all the advantages which will accrue under annexation, without involving the country in the responsibilities of ownership.

This is one of the problems which has confronted every American statesman who has been compelled to practically consider how best to maintain American control in Hawaii. It was the problem which faced President Pierce and Secretary of State Marcy in 1854; President Harrison and Secretary Foster in 1893, and President McKinley and Secretary Sherman in 1897. In each case the alternative of protectorate or annexation was presented, and in each case, after full deliberation, the decision was against a protectorate and in favor of annexation. The reason is that, under a protectorate, the independent government of Hawaii would still be free to get into troubles with other governments, thereby creating international complications for the settlement of which the United States would be responsible; while under annexation no international complications would arise, except such as might be created by the United States itself. The difference between a protectorate and annexation is that, under a protectorate, the United States would assume all the responsibilities, incident to ownership, without the power of control; while under annexation, it would assume no more responsibilities, and would acquire absolute control. Under a protectorate, Hawaii would still remain an incubator of international friction. Under annexation, it would be removed absolutely from international politics, as much so as is California or Florida.

TWELFTH OBJECTION.

It will be injurious to the beet-sugar industry, as Hawaiian sugar will compete with beet sugar raised in the United States.

The only way in which Hawaiian sugar can injure beet sugar is by being produced in such quantities as to supplant the beet product of the United States, or by cutting the price so as to lower the price of beet sugar to its producers.

Hawaii can never produce enough sugar to supplant the beet or any other sugar in the United States. The sugar consumption of the United States was approximately two millon tons during 1896, which consumption is rapidly increasing year by year. During 1896 Hawaii produced a little over two hundred thousand tons, or approximately one-tenth of the consumption of the United States. This is the highest output ever made by Hawaii, and is the best it has been able to do after twenty years of encouragement under the reciprocity treaty with the United States.

All of the natural cane lands of Hawaii are already under cultivation. The only remaining lands which can possibly be cultivated with sugar cane are those now dry and barren, which can only be cultivated by artificial irrigation, by pumping water to an elevation of from one hundred and fifty to six hundred feet. It goes without saying that such irrigation must be limited in area and problematical in profits.

As to Hawaiian sugar cutting the price, sugar is a world product, and its price is determined by the world's price, which is fixed in New York and London. If the Hawaiian crop were cut off entirely, or doubled, it would not raise or lower the price of sugar in the United States one mill. It is sometimes suggested that Hawaiian sugar may more than equal the consumption of the Pacific coast, and that Hawaiian planters would lower their price rather than send it to New York. The reply to this is that the Pacific coast's consumption is only about seventy-five thousand tons per annum, and long ago the Hawaiian product far exceeded this. About one-third of the Hawaiian product for 1896–97 was sent to New York, and probably more than one-half of the crop of 1897–98 will be sent there.

Again, the Hawaiian cane-sugar planters suffer under many disadvantages which the beet-sugar producers do not. It takes from eighteen to twenty-two months to grow a crop of sugar cane in Hawaii, during the entire period of which it must be irrigated on most of the plantations every week or two. It takes the beet-sugar planter only about six months to make a crop.

The cane-sugar planter has to employ his laborers all the year around; the beet-sugar planter discharges his laborers when the crop is made.

The cane-sugar planter of Hawaii pays now somewhat less wages per month than does the beet-sugar planter, although not as much less as is generally supposed, the average laborer in Hawaii costing the planter from fifteen to eighteen dollars per month. *Under annexation the Asiatic supply of labor will be cut off*, and this slight advantage will be eliminated.

Again, it costs the Hawaiian cane planter approximately ten dollars a ton to get his sugar from the plantation to its market, while the beet-sugar planter has his market at his door.

Taken all in all, the cane-sugar planter of Hawaii stands on no more favorable basis than does the beet-sugar planter of the United States, and there is no reason why their interests should clash any more than do the interests of the corn planter of Kansas clash with those of the corn planter of Nebraska.

THIRTEENTH OBJECTION.

It will excite the jealousy of, and create complications with, foreign governments.

When the annexation treaty of 1893 was negotiated, no protest was made by any foreign country. None has been made now, except by Japan, and the reasons assigned by Japan for her protest are absolutely inconsistent with the traditional policy of the United States, that they shall control Hawaii.

The rapid development of Japanese pretensions in Hawaii since 1893 is a signal illustration of the danger of further postponing that which all American statesmen agree must at some time be done, viz, definitely and finally secure to the United States the control of Hawaii. This can never be done with as little friction as at present, and if it is further delayed the increasing importance of the Pacific and the interests of other nations therein may at an early date cause other nations than Japan to also assume an attitude of hostility toward annexation. There is danger in delay. There can be little danger of foreign complication if immediate action is taken.

FOURTEENTH OBJECTION.

The Government of Hawaii consists of foreign adventurers, who have no authority or jurisdiction over the country.

This was an objection made when the Provisional Government was first formed, and when its members were unknown to the world. The history of the Provisional Government and the Republic of Hawaii and its dealings with the world have refuted this charge. If anything more were needed as proof in the matter, it is furnished by a report from Minister Willis to Secretary Gresham, when he was in the midst of his attempt to restore the ex-Queen, and it was feared that the attempt might be forcibly resisted by the citizens of Honolulu. Mr. Willis wrote:

"Fortunately, the men at the head of the Provisional Government are acknowledged by all sides to be of the highest integrity and public spirit."

It is sufficient to say further, that of the so-called "foreign population," nearly 10,000 were born in and are natives of Hawaii, with as much right to speak for Hawaii as the American-born white man has to speak for the United States;

That the other so-called "foreigners" have made Hawaii the land of their adoption; have acquired property, homes, and political rights; have built up the country and made it what it is, and have as much right to speak for Hawaii as the multitude of European-born American citizens who occupy every official position throughout the land, save that of President, have to legislate and speak for the United States;

That the President, two members of the cabinet, the chief justice, and a very large number of the leading officials of the Government were born and have always resided in Hawaii, and that the other members of the Government are, almost without exception, old residents, while, without exception, the members of the Government are the leading business and professional men of the country, who have temporarily taken on the cares of public office until the Government can be established on a permanent basis, when they will only too willingly hand over its conduct to others. It would seem sufficient to meet the charge that they are adventurers, seeking their own private benefit, to show that they are, by every means within their power, advancing a treaty which by its terms will legislate them out of office.

FIFTEENTH OBJECTION.

Annexation will be beneficial to the sugar trust.

No one has advanced any theory showing how the sugar trust will be benefited by annexation. As a matter of fact, no sugar refiner in the

United States will be benefited by annexation, for the reason that it will place just so much more sugar upon the American market free of duty, to come into competition with the product of the American sugar refiner.   There is no probability that a large quantity, if any, sugar will be refined in Hawaii, but entry to other portions of the United States for high-grade raw sugars will enable the sugar planters of Hawaii to place in the markets of the United States a light-colored, wholesome raw sugar, which can compete with the refined product of the sugar trust.   This Hawaiian sugar will be limited in amount, to be sure, but to the extent to which it goes it will compete with the product of the trust, with no compensating advantage to that organization.

SIXTEENTH OBJECTION.

Under the proposed treaty of annexation the United States assumes the Hawaiian public debt without receiving in return the means or property with which to pay it.

This statement can only be made by one unfamiliar with the property and resources owned by the Hawaiian Government.   The present net debt of the Republic of Hawaii is approximately $3,900,000, and the schedule of its salable property, exclusive of the public streets and roads, upon which not less than a million dollars have been expended, amounts to $7,938,000, leaving a clear net profit to the United States in property acquired of approximately $4,000,000, all of the property owned by Hawaii being transferred by the terms of the annexation treaty to the United States.   This does not include the revenues from customs, rent, post-office, etc., which largely exceed current expenses.

SEVENTEENTH OBJECTION.

There is leprosy in Hawaii.

This is, unfortunately, true.   Nothing in the climatic conditions of Hawaii, however, caused the disease.   It was brought from China about thirty years ago, and has attacked a large number of the natives, it being confined almost exclusively to them.   There are not, however, as many lepers in Hawaii as there are in Norway, nor do there begin to be the numbers that there are in Japan, China, India, and other Eastern countries.   Moreover, Hawaii is the one country in the world dealing with the subject which rigorously segregates the victims of the disease.   No cases are seen at large, and all of the patients are most carefully cared for by the local government.   Moreover, I have yet to learn that the political relations existing between two countries will increase the danger arising from diseases existing in either.   The local government of Hawaii will continue in the future as in the past to care for its own unfortunates, with no more expense nor danger to the people of the United States than there now is.

EIGHTEENTH OBJECTION.

The monarchy was overthrown through the agency of American troops.

This accusation is ancient history.   If it were true, which is not admitted, it would have no more effect to-day upon the status of the Hawaiian Republic than does the fact that French troops assisted Washington to overthrow the British monarchy in America have any effect upon the present status of the American Republic.

Regardless of its origin, the Republic of Hawaii is to-day recognized by every sovereign government of the world as an independent nation, with all the rights and powers of any other sovereign or independent nation, and this with the full knowledge that its constitution contains an article providing explicitly for annexation to the United States.

Concerning the truth of the charge mentioned, we have the positive statements of United States Minister Stevens and Captain Wiltse, of the United States Navy, who were on the ground at the time, that the American troops were not landed for such purpose and did not take any part in the overthrow of the monarchy. There has been a vast amount of controversy upon the subject, and in 1894 the United States Senate appointed a committee for the express purpose of investigating this very point, Senator Morgan, of Alabama, a Democrat, being the chairman of the committee. The committee made an exhaustive examination of the subject, and made a report to the Senate covering over two thousand pages of fine printed matter. The conclusion of the committee upon this point, formulated by Senator Morgan, is as follows:

"The committee, upon the evidence as it appears in their report (which they believe is a full, fair, and impartial statement of the facts attending and precedent to the landing of the troops), agree that the purpose of Captain Wiltse and of Minister Stevens were only those which were legitimate, viz, the preservation of law and order to the extent of preventing a disturbance of the public peace, which might, in the absence of troops, injuriously affect the rights of the American citizens resident in Honolulu."

History will vindicate Minister Stevens and prove, what those who knew him best already know, that the United States never possessed a truer officer or a more patriotic citizen or one who more fearlessly met difficult and unexpected conditions and did his duty to his country.

NINETEENTH OBJECTION.

It is unlikely that the United States will go to war with any other country. But if it does, and it then wants Hawaii, there is time enough to take it.

It is idle to discuss whether the United States will again go to war. It is a matter of opinion. Judging the future by the past, the chances are strongly that it will. Its might is not an insurance against war. Rome ruled the world, but war came. The intervening sea will not prevent it. England, the one isolated nation of Europe, has as many wars as all the rest of Europe put together.

The certainty that the United States would probably conquer in the end is no guarantee against it. Small boys frequently fight big ones, expecting to be whipped. There can be no doubt concerning the ultimate result of a war with Spain; but it seems probable that Spain might welcome war with the United States as the method by which she can get out of Cuba with the least injury to her national dignity and prestige.

There is no certainty that there *will* be war; but on the other hand there is no certainty that there *will not* be. Human nature has developed but has not radically changed. The nations of the world never spent more time or money in preparation for war than they are doing to day.

It is not wise for a man to leave his doors unlocked when burglars are around simply because none have been to his house. They may come when least expected.

Wars come nowadays suddenly and unexpectedly. The nations are in such a state of preparation that they can accomplish in a week what formerly took months.

The Austro-Prussian war was finished and Austria prostrated in six weeks.

No sooner was war declared than Germany overran France and was victorious within four months.

Japan opened the war on China with an attack which destroyed a ship and a thousand men and made formal declaration at her leisure.

Turkey and Greece each began hostilities without notice.

Any nation which attacks the United States by way of the west will, as a military necessity, first occupy Hawaii as a base of operations.

The first intimation of war which the United States will have may be the seizure of Hawaii; and, with its natural defensive possibilities, any strong maritime nation once intrenched in Hawaii can be evicted therefrom, if at all, only by vast expenditure and tremendous effort.

Gibraltar is a century-long lesson of how much easier it is to let a warlike nation *in* than it is to get it *out* of a strong position.

TWENTIETH OBJECTION.

The United States already has enough territory, people, and problems. We want no more of them. Let well enough alone.

It has already been stated above that *the chief reason for the annexation of Hawaii is to secure a vantage ground for the protection of what the United States already owns.* It is not primarily to secure new territory, promote shipping, and increase commerce, but as a measure of precaution to prevent the acquisition by a foreign, and perhaps in the future hostile, power of an acknowledged military stronghold, possessing peculiar strategic relations toward the territory and commerce of this country. In comparison with the benefit and advantage to the country of securing control of this strategic stronghold, what do the disadvantages amount to?

Even if all the people of Hawaii are not up to the highest ideal American standard, how can they harmfully affect the American people or Government? They number 109,000. No more than are sometimes landed in New York in a single month. About one-tenth of one per cent of the present population. Can anyone seriously maintain that this insignificant, fractional addition of people, without the powers appurtenant to Statehood—with only such limited Territorial form of government as Congress pleases to grant—can to any appreciable extent injuriously affect the political life and fortunes of the American people? Can such claim be urged in good faith when the dominant element in Hawaii, politically, socially, and financially, is, and for years has been, so strongly American in its business, financial, and political methods as to have converted an alien land and people into what is universally recognized as being "the most American spot on earth?"

As to problems, what problems that the United States does not now have will it have after annexation?

None arising from the people of Hawaii coming over here. If they wanted to come to America, they could come now. But they have no reason for coming. They are more prosperous now than the people of the United States, and after annexation they will be more prosperous still.

The movement of population is already to, and not from, Hawaii, and annexation will greatly accelerate it.

The people of Hawaii will remain in Hawaii, and will themselves settle locally the local problems arising out of local conditions, with no more effect upon the political life and principles of the General Government than has a town election or local-option agitation in Arizona.

As a Territory Hawaii will have no vote in national affairs; and with the trend of existing feeling against admitting new States, the time for discussing statehood is so far in the future that it is beyond the domain of practical life.

Financially no problem will be created. Hawaii is more than self-supporting.

Internationally no problems will be created. On the contrary, an international problem which has made demands upon the time and attention of American statesmen for two generations—the problem of "how to keep other nations out of Hawaii"—will be solved and written off the books.

From a military standpoint no problems will be created. On the contrary, the military situation will be simplified. Military experts, American and foreign, unite in acknowledging that Hawaii is a strategical point of the first importance, ranking with Gibraltar and the Suez canal.

If it is ever deemed essential to American interests to fortify Hawaii, it will certainly be far easier to do so if it belongs to and is already occupied, by the United States than if it belongs to another, and possibly hostile, government.

This objection is made by those who think that the United States is sufficient unto itself; that it does not need to take a part in affairs beyond its borders, and that danger lies in every direction beyond them.

The day when the United States can, hibernating, live off itself has passed. In this end of the nineteenth century a "hermit nation" is no longer possible. The United States resurrected Japan from that status, but it can not assume the rôle itself.

No man lives unto himself; neither can a nation. No nation can stand still; it must either progress or retrograde.

For a number of years the apparent paradox was seen of the United States growing and developing faster than anything known in history, while paying but slight attention to her international relations, either political or commercial.

The manifest reason was that it possessed a vast undeveloped area which afforded within its borders full scope for all surplus energy and capital that, in the kindred country of England, has spread itself over every quarter of the globe.

That condition no longer exists. The unoccupied territory has been taken up, and, while much remains to be done, the creative energy of the American people can no longer be confined within the borders of the Union. Production has so outrun consumption in both agricultural and manufactured products that foreign markets must be secured or stagnation will ensue.

Foreign trade means foreign interests which must be protected. It means rivalries and jealousies with other exporting nations, in which the American citizen must have the support of his Government.

The day has gone by when the United States can ignore its international relations, privileges, and obligations. Whether it will or no, the logic of events is forcing the American people and their Government to take their place as one of the great "international nations," and incidentally thereto to adopt such means as are necessary to sustain the position.

OPINIONS OF PRESIDENTS OF THE UNITED STATES CONCERNING THE CONTROL OR ANNEXATION OF HAWAII.

JOHN TYLER.

United States opposition to foreign control.

On December 31, 1842, President Tyler sent a special message to the Senate, relating to the Hawaiian Islands, from which the following extracts are made.

After speaking of the development of the Island Government and the importance of the islands to shipping, he continues:

It can not but be in conformity with the interest and wishes of the Government and the people of the United States that this community * * * should be respected and all its rights strictly and conscientiously regarded. * * * Far remote from the dominions of European powers, its growth and prosperity as an independent state may yet be in a high degree useful to all whose trade is extended to those regions, while its near approach to this continent and the intercourse which American vessels have with it—such vessels constituting five-sixths of all which annually visit it—*could not but create dissatisfaction on the part of the United States at any attempt by another power, should such attempt be threatened or feared, to take possession of the islands, colonize them, and subvert the native government.* (Vol. 2, Rep. Sen. Com. on For. Rel., concerning Hawaiian Islands, p. 847.)

MILLARD FILLMORE.

President Fillmore reiterated this sentiment in stronger language in 1850–51. See dispatches of Secretaries Clayton and Webster, quoted below.

FRANKLIN PIERCE.

Approval of annexation.

President Pierce desired the annexation of Hawaii and authorized the negotiation of the treaty of annexation of 1854. See treaty in full, hereunder. (See dispatch of Secretary Marcy to U. S. Minister Gregg, April 4, 1854. Vol. 2, Rep. Sen. Com. on For. Rel., concerning Hawaiian Islands, p. 929.)

First attempt at reciprocity.

A treaty of reciprocity was negotiated between the United States and Hawaii under President Pierce, but was not confirmed by the Senate. (Vol. 2, Rep. Sen. Com. on For. Rel., concerning Hawaiian Islands, p. 944.)

JAMES BUCHANAN.

Foreign control highly injurious to United States.

President Buchanan, in his dispatch as Secretary of State, September 3, 1849, quoted below, stated that English or French control of Hawaii would be "highly injurious" to the interests of the United States.

ANDREW JOHNSON.

Reciprocity advocated as leading to annexation.

The following is an extract from the annual message of President Johnson to the 40th Congress, December 19, 1868:

I am aware that upon the question of further extending our possessions it is apprehended by some that our political system can not successfully be applied to an area more extended than our continent; but *the conviction is rapidly gaining ground in the*

American mind that, with the increased facilities for intercommunication between all portions of the earth, the principles of free government, as embraced in our Constitution, if faithfully maintained and carried out, would prove of sufficient strength and breadth to comprehend within their sphere and influence the civilized nations of the world.

The attention of the Senate and of Congress is again respectfully invited to the treaty for the establishment of commercial reciprocity with the Hawaiian Kingdom, entered into last year, and already ratified by that Government. The attitude of the United States toward these islands is not very different from that in which they stand toward the West Indies. It is known and felt by the Hawaiian Government and people that their institutions are feeble and precarious; that *the United States, being so near a neighbor, would be unwilling to see the islands pass under foreign control.* Their prosperity is continually disturbed by expectations and alarms of unfriendly political proceedings, as well from the United States as from other foreign powers. *A reciprocity treaty, while it could not materially diminish the revenues of the United States, would be a guarantee of the good will and forbearance of all nations until the people of the islands shall of themselves, at no distant day, voluntarily apply for admission into the Union.* (Vol. 2, Rep. Sen. Com. on For. Rel., concerning Hawaiian Islands, p. 954.)

U. S. GRANT.

The annexation of Hawaii was favored by President Grant. (See dispatch Sec'y State Seward to Minister McCook, Sept. 12, 1867, quoted hereunder.)

Question of annexation submitted to Senate.

In February, 1871, *Mr. Pierce*, American Minister to Honolulu, wrote, *recommending the subject of annexation* to the attention of the President. President Grant thereupon sent to the Senate a confidential message, accompanied by Mr. Pierce's statement. The message is as follows:

To the Senate of the United States:

I transmit confidentially, for the information and consideration of the Senate, a copy of a dispatch of the 25th of February last, relative to the annexation of the Hawaiian Islands, addressed to the Department of State by Henry A. Pierce, minister resident of the United States at Honolulu. Although I do not deem it advisable to express any opinion or to make any recommendation in regard to the subject at this juncture, the views of the Senate, if it should be deemed proper to express them, would be very acceptable with reference to any future course which there might be a disposition to adopt.

U. S. GRANT.

WASHINGTON, *April 5, 1871.*

(Vol. 2, Rep. Sen. Com. on For. Rel., concerning Hawaiian Islands, p. 824.)

NOTE.—The dispatch from Mr. Pierce is given hereafter under the heading, "Statements of American Ministers at Honolulu," etc.

CHESTER A. ARTHUR.

President Arthur was in full sympathy with the Americanizing of Hawaii. See Secretary Blaine's dispatches of December 1, 1881, quoted below.

BENJAMIN HARRISON.

Annexation treaty negotiated and advocated.

In February, 1893, President Harrison caused an annexation treaty to be negotiated with Hawaii. The following is the message accompanying the treaty upon its transmission to the Senate for confirmation:

To the Senate:

I transmit herewith, with a view to its ratification, a treaty of annexation concluded on the 14th day of February, 1893, between Hon. John W. Foster, Secretary of State, who was duly empowered to act in that behalf on the part of the United States, and Lorrin A. Thurston, W. R. Castle, W. C. Wilder, C. L. Carter, and Joseph

Marsden, the commissioners on the part of the Provisional Government of the Hawaiian Islands.

The treaty, it will be observed, does not attempt to deal in detail with the questions that grow out of the annexation of the Hawaiian Islands to the United States. The commissioners representing the Hawaiian Government have consented to leave to the future and to the just and benevolent purposes of the United States the adjustment of all such questions.

I do not deem it necessary to discuss at any length the conditions which have resulted in this decisive action.

It has been the policy of the Administration not only to respect, but to encourage, the continuance of an independent government in the Hawaiian Islands so long as it afforded suitable guarantees for the protection of life and property and maintained a stability and strength that gave adequate security against the domination of any other power. The moral support of this Government has continually manifested itself in the most friendly diplomatic relations and in many acts of courtesy to the Hawaiian rulers.

The overthrow of the monarchy was not in any way promoted by this Government, but had its origin in what seems to have been a reactionary and revolutionary policy on the part of Queen Lilioukalani, which put in serious peril not only the large and preponderating interests of the United States in the islands, but all foreign interests, and, indeed, the decent administration of civil affairs and peace of the islands.

It is quite evident that the monarchy had become effete and the Queen's Government so weak and inadequate as to be the prey of designing and unscrupulous persons. The restoration of Queen Lilioukalaui to her throne is undesirable if not impossible, and unless actively supported by the United States would be accompanied by serious disaster and the disorganization of all business interests. *The influence and interest of the United States in the islands must be increased and not diminished.*

Only two courses are now open—one, the establishment of a protectorate by the United States, and the other, annexation full and complete. I think the latter course, which has been adopted in the treaty, will be highly promotive of the best interests of the Hawaiian people and is the only one that will adequately secure the interests of the United States. These interests are not wholly selfish. *It is essential that none of the great powers shall secure these islands. Such a possession would not consist with our safety and with the peace of the world.*

This view of the situation is so apparent and conclusive that no protest has been heard from any Government against proceedings looking to annexation. Every foreign representative at Honolulu promptly acknowledged the Provisional Government, and I think there is a general concurrence in the opinion that the deposed Queen ought not to be restored. Prompt action upon this treaty is very desirable.

If it meets the approval of the Senate, peace and good order will be secured in the islands under existing laws until such time as Congress can provide by legislation a permanent form of government for the islands. This legislation should be, and I do not doubt will be, not only just to the natives and all other residents and citizens of the islands, but should be characterized by great liberality and a high regard to the rights of all the people and of all foreigners domiciled there.

The correspondence which accompanies the treaty will put the Senate in possession of all the facts known to the Executive.

BENJ. HARRISON.

EXECUTIVE MANSION, *February 15, 1893.*

(Vol. 2, Rep. Sen. Com. on For. Rel., concerning Hawaiian Islands, p. 1005.)

The treaty of annexation is hereinafter contained.

WILLIAM M'KINLEY.

Annexation treaty negotiated and advocated.

On June 15, 1897, President McKinley caused an annexation treaty to be negotiated with the Republic of Hawaii.

Message to the Senate.

The following is the message accompanying the treaty upon its transmission to the Senate for confirmation

To the Senate of the United States:

I transmit herewith to the Senate, in order that, after due consideration, the constitutional function of advice and consent may be exercised by that body, a treaty for the annexation of the Republic of Hawaii to the United States, signed in this capital by the plenipotentiaries of the parties on the 16th of June instant.

For better understanding of the subject I transmit in addition a report of the Secretary of State, briefly reviewing the negotiation which has led to this important result.

ANNEXATION NECESSARY SEQUEL OF HISTORICAL EVENTS.

The incorporation of the Hawaiian Islands into the body politic of the United States is the necessary and fitting sequel to the change of events which, from a very early period in our history, has controlled the intercourse and prescribed the association of the United States and the Hawaiian Islands. The predominance of American interest in that neighboring territory was first asserted in 1820, by sending to the islands a representative agent of the United States. It found further expression by the signature of a treaty of friendship, commerce, and navigation with the King in 1826—the first international compact negotiated by Hawaii. It was signally announced in 1843, when the intervention of the United States caused the British Government to disavow the seizure of the Sandwich Islands by a British naval commander, and to recognize them by treaty as an independent State, renouncing forever any purpose of annexing the islands or exerting a protectorate over them.

CESSION OF HAWAII IN 1851.

In 1851 the cession of the Hawaiian Kingdom to the United States was formally offered, and although not then accepted, this Government proclaimed its duty to preserve alike the honor and dignity of the United States and the safety of the Government of the Hawaiian Islands. From this time until the outbreak of the war in 1861 the policy of the United States toward Hawaii and of the Hawaiian sovereignty toward the United States was exemplified by continued negotiations for annexation or for a reserved commercial union.

RECIPROCITY TREATY OF 1875 AND 1884.

The latter alternative was at length accomplished by the reciprocity treaty of 1875, the provisions of which were renewed and expanded by the convention of 1884, embracing the perpetual cession to the United States of the harbor of Pearl River, in the island of Oahu.

REFUSAL OF JOINT ACTION WITH GERMANY AND GREAT BRITAIN IN 1888.

In 1888 a proposal for the joint guaranty of the neutrality of the Hawaiian Islands by the United States, Germany, and Great Britain was declined on the announced ground that the relation of the United States to the islands was sufficient for the end in view.

CONTINUOUS POLICY EXCLUSION OF ALL FOREIGN INFLUENCE.

In brief, from 1820 to 1893 the course of the United States toward the Hawaiian Islands has consistently favored their autonomous welfare, with the exclusion of all foreign influence save our own, to the extent of upholding eventual annexation as the necessary outcome of that policy.

ANNEXATION A CONSUMMATION, NOT A CHANGE.

Not only is the union of the Hawaiian territory to the United States no new scheme, but it is the inevitable consequence of the relation steadfastly maintained with that mid-Pacific domain for three-quarters of a century. Its accomplishment, despite successive denials and postponements, has been merely a question of time. While its failure in 1893 may not be a cause of congratulation, it is certainly a proof of the disinterestedness of the United States, the delay of four years having abundantly sufficed to establish the right and the ability of the Republic of Hawaii to enter, as a sovereign contractant, upon a conventional union with the United States, thus realizing a purpose held by the Hawaiian people and proclaimed by successive Hawaiian governments through some twenty years of their virtual dependence upon the benevolent protection of the United States. *Under such circumstances annexation is not a change. It is a consummation.*

DETAILS OF FORM OF GOVERNMENT LEFT TO CONGRESS.

The report of the Secretary of State explains the character and course of the recent negotiations and the features of the treaty itself. The organic and administrative details of incorporation are necessarily left to the wisdom of the Congress, and I can not doubt, when the function of the constitutional treaty-making power shall have been accomplished, the duty of the national legislature in the case will be performed with the largest regard for the interests of this rich insular domain and for the welfare of the inhabitants thereof.

WILLIAM McKINLEY.

EXECUTIVE MANSION, *Washington, June 16, 1897.*

[Secretary Sherman's report to President McKinley, accompanying the treaty, is hereinafter contained.]

OPINIONS OF SECRETARIES OF STATE OF THE UNITED STATES CONCERNING THE CONTROL OR ANNEXATION OF HAWAII.

DANIEL WEBSTER.

First public statement of superior interest of United States in Hawaii.

Upon application of the Hawaiian Government for recognition by the United States, Secretary of State Webster replied, on December 19, 1842, that the matter had been submitted to the President [Tyler] and—

The President is of opinion that the interests of all the commercial nations require that that Government [Hawaii] shall not be interfered with by foreign powers. * * * *The United States* * * * *are more interested in the fate of the islands and of their government than any other nation can be,* and this consideration induces the President to be quite willing to declare, as the sense of the Government of the United States, that the Government of the Sandwich Islands ought to be respected; that no power ought either to take possession of the islands as a conquest or for the purpose of colonization, and that no power ought to seek for any undue control over the existing Government, or any exclusive privileges or preferences in matters of commerce. (Appendix 2, For. Rel. of the U. S., 1894, p. 44.)

Webster's views were elaborated in 1851, hereafter quoted.

H. S. LEGARE.

Advocated force to keep European powers out.

June 13, 1843, Secretary of State Legare sent a dispatch to Edward Everett, U. S. minister at London, in which the relations of the United States to Hawaii are mentioned, by reason of the then recent seizure of the islands by England. In this connection he says:

It is well known that * * * we have no wish to plant or to acquire colonies abroad. *Yet there is something so entirely peculiar in the relations between this little commonwealth Hawaii and ourselves that we might even feel justified, consistently with our own principles, in interfering by force to prevent its falling into the hands of one of the great powers of Europe.* These relations spring out of the local situation, the history, and the character and institutions of the Hawaiian Islands, as well as out of the declarations formally made by this Government during the course of the last session of Congress, to which I beg leave to call your particular attention.

If the attempts now making by ourselves, as well as other Christian powers, to open the markets of China to a more general commerce be successful, there can be no doubt but that a great part of that commerce will find its way over the Isthmus. In that event *it will be impossible to overrate the importance of the Hawaiian group as a stage in the long voyage between Asia and America.* But without anticipating events which, however, seem inevitable, and even approaching, the actual demands of an immense navigation make the free use of these roadsteads and ports indispensable to us. * * * It seems doubtful whether even the undisputed possession of the Oregon Territory and the use of the Columbia River, or indeed anything short of the acquisition of California (if that were possible), would be sufficient indemnity to us for the loss of these harbors. (Rep. Sen. Com. on For. Rel. concerning Hawaiian Islands, vol. 2, p. 921.)

JAMES BUCHANAN.

Occupation by England or France highly injurious to the United States.

On the 3d of September, 1849, Secretary of State Buchanan sent a dispatch to the U. S. minister resident at Honolulu, Ten Eyck, concerning the relations between Hawaii and the United States, in view of the then threatening conduct of the French against Hawaii, in which the following words are used:

We ardently desire that the Hawaiian Islands may maintain their independence. *It would be highly injurious to our interests if,* tempted by their weakness, *they should be seized by Great Britain or France; more especially so, since our recent acquisitions from Mexico on the Pacific Ocean.* (Vol. 2, Rep. Sen. Com. on For. Rel., concerning Hawaiian Islands, p. 897.)

JOHN M. CLAYTON.

United States could never allow Hawaii to be controlled by any other power.

In a dispatch from Secretary Clayton to U. S. Minister Rives at Paris, July 5, 1850, referring to the differences between the French and Hawaiian Governments, he made the following statement:

The Department will be slow to believe that the French have any intention to adopt, with reference to the Sandwich Islands, the same policy which they have pursued in regard to Tahiti. If, however, in your judgment it should be warranted by circumstances, you may take a proper opportunity to intimate to the minister for foreign affairs of France that *the situation of the Sandwich Islands, in respect to our possessions on the Pacific and the bonds commercial and of other descriptions between them and the United States, are such that we could never, with indifference, allow them to pass under the dominion or exclusive control of any other power.* (Vol. 2, Rep. Sen. Com. on For. Rel., concerning Hawaiian Islands, p. 895.)

DANIEL WEBSTER.

Action by France would seriously disturb friendly relations with United States.

Upon receipt of a communication by Mr. Severance (quoted below, under the heading "Opinions of American Ministers at Honolulu," &c.), Secretary of State Webster, on June 18, 1851, again addressed U. S. Minister Rives at Paris instructing him to immediately inform the French Government that the further enforcement of the French demands against Hawaii—

would be tantamount to a subjugation of the islands to the dominion of France. *A step like this could not fail to be viewed by the Government and people of the United States with a dissatisfaction which would tend seriously to disturb our existing friendly relations with the French Government.*

Reparation requested for Hawaii, indicating claim of United States of right to protect Hawaii.

And he is further instructed to make such representations to France—

as will induce that Government to desist from measures incompatible with the sovereignty and independence of the Hawaiian Islands, *and to make amends for the acts which the French agents have already committed there in contravention of the law of nations and of the treaty between the Hawaiian Government and France.* (Vol. 2, Rep. Sen. Com. on For. Rel., concerning Hawaiian Islands, p. 905-6.)

Declaration of policy—United States can never consent to occupation by, or hostile demands of, European powers.

Secretary of State Webster, replying to U. S. Minister Severance at Honolulu, on July 14, 1851, says, after reciting that the demands of France were improper and "could only end in rendering the islands and their government a prey to the stronger commercial nations of the world:"

It can not be expected that the Government of the United States could look on a course of things leading to such a result with indifference.
The Hawaiian Islands are ten times nearer to the United States than to any of the powers of Europe. Five-sixths of all their commercial intercourse is with the United

States, and these considerations, together with others of a more general character, *have fixed the course which the Government of the United States will pursue in regard to them.* The annunciation of this policy will not surprise the governments of Europe, nor be thought to be unreasonable by the nations of the civilized world, *and that policy is* that while the Government of the United States, itself faithful to its original assurance, scrupulously regards the independence of the Hawaiian Islands, *it can never consent to see those islands taken possession of by either of the great commercial powers of Europe, nor can it consent that demands manifestly unjust and derogatory and inconsistent with a bona fide independence shall be enforced against that Government.* (Vol. 2, Rep. Sen. Com. on For. Rel., concerning Hawaiian Islands, p. 908.)

Copy furnished diplomatic corps at Washington.

A copy of the above letter from Secretary Webster to Minister Severance was, simultaneously with its dispatch, furnished to all the members of the diplomatic corps in Washington, in circular form, which caused offense to the French Government, but they nevertheless acquiesced in its terms, and desisted from the course of aggression which they had been following. (Vol. 2, Rep. Sen. Com. on For. Rel., concerning Hawaiian Islands, p. 913.)

Force advocated to keep France out.

At this time the French were so threatening in Hawaii that the Hawaiian Government requested the American consul, E. H. Allen, to go personally to Washington and represent the state of affairs, which he did. Upon making his statement to Secretary Webster, the latter replied:

I trust the French will not take possession; but if they do, they will be dislodged if my advice is taken, if the whole power of the Government is required to do it.

W. L. MARCY.

Inevitably Hawaii must be controlled by the United States.

Secretary of State W. L. Marcy addressed a communication on December 16, 1853, to Mr. John Mason, U. S. minister to France, in which he states that during the recent disturbances in Hawaii—

the question of transferring the sovereignty of these islands to the United States was much discussed.

He further states that the British and French ministers had both called upon him (Marcy) and tried to induce him to agree—

that this Government would take no measures to acquire the sovereignty of these islands or accept it if voluntarily offered to the United States. * * * Their ministers, particularly the minister of France, labored to impress me with the belief that such a transfer would be forcibly resisted. * * *

ANNEXATION FORESHADOWED.

The object in addressing you at present is to request you to look into this matter and ascertain, if possible, * * * *what would probably be the course of France in case of an attempt on the part of the United States to add these islands to our territorial possessions* by negotiation or other peaceable means.

I do not think the present Hawaiian Government can long remain in the hands of the present rulers or under the control of the native inhabitants of these islands, and both England and France are apprised of our determination not to allow them to be owned by or to fall under the protection of either of these powers or of any other European nation.

It seems to be inevitable that they must come under the control of this Government, and it would be but reasonable and fair that these powers should acquiesce in such a disposition of them, provided the transference was effected by fair means. (Vol. 2, Rep. Sen. Com. on For. Rel., concerning Hawaiian Islands, p. 914.)

Instructions of Marcy to negotiate annexation treaty.

On the 4th of April, 1854, Secretary of State Marcy sent a dispatch to David L. Gregg, U. S. minister at Honolulu, giving special instructions on the subject of annexation, viz:

In your general instructions you were furnished with the views of this Government in regard to any change in the political affairs of the Sandwich Islands. *The President was aware,* when those instructions were prepared, that the question of transferring the sovereignty of those islands to the United States had been raised, and favorably received by many influential individuals residing therein. *It was foreseen that at some period, not far distant, such a change would take place, and that the Hawaiian Islands would come under the protectorate of or be transferred to some foreign power.* You were informed that it was not the policy of the United States to accelerate such a change; but *if, in the course of events, it became unavoidable, this Government would much prefer to acquire the sovereignty of these islands* for the United States rather than to see it transferred to any other power. *If any foreign connection is to be formed, the geographical position of these islands indicates that it should be with us.* Our commerce with them far exceeds that of all other countries; our citizens are embarked in the most important business concerns of that country, and some of them hold important public positions. *In view of the large American interests there established and the intimate commercial relations existing at this time, it might be well regarded as the duty of this Government to prevent these islands from becoming the appendage of any other foreign power.*

It appears by your dispatches lately received at this Department that the ruling authorities of the Hawaiian Government have been convinced of their inability to sustain themselves any longer as an independent State, and are prepared to throw themselves upon our protection or to seek incorporation into our political system. · Fears are entertained by those who favor such a measure that if the United States should manifest a disinclination to receive the proffered sovereignty of this country, the people would seek elsewhere a less desirable connection or be given over to anarchy.

The information contained in your last dispatch, No. 10, dated the 7th of February, renders it highly probable that the ruling powers of that Government will have presented to you, as our diplomatic agent, an offer of the sovereignty of their country to the United States. The President has deemed it proper that you should be furnished with instructions for the guidance of your conduct in such an emergency. *With this dispatch you will be furnished with a full power to treat with the present authorities of the Hawaiian Government for the transfer of the Sandwich Islands to the United States.* This can only be done by a convention or treaty, which will not be valid until it is ratified by the Senate of the United States.

PROTECTORATE DISAPPROVED.

No intimation has ever been given to this Government as to the terms or conditions which will be likely to be annexed to the tender of the sovereignty. It is presumed, however, that something more than a mere protectorate is contemplated. *A protectorate tendered to and accepted by the United States would not change the sovereignty of the country. In that case this Government would take upon itself heavy and responsible duties for which it could hardly expect compensating advantages.*

I understand that the measure proposed by the people, and that in which the present rulers are disposed to concur, is "annexation" as distinguished from protection; and that it is their intention that these islands shall become a part of our territories and be under the control of this Government as fully as any other of its territorial possessions. In any convention you may make it is expected that the rights to be acquired by the United States should be clearly defined.

Should the sovereignty of these islands be transferred to the United States, the present Government would, as a matter of course, be superseded, or, at least, be subjected to the Federal authority of this country.

Annuities to the amount of $100,000 per annum were authorized to be paid to the King and chiefs. (Vol. 2, Rep. Sen. Com. on For. Rel. concerning Hawaii, p. 929.)

Discussion of terms of annexation.

On January 31, 1855, Secretary Marcy wrote to Mr. Gregg that the President did not approve of Hawaii immediately becoming a State, but thought it should come in as a Territory. (Vol. 2, Rep. Sen. Com. on For. Rel. concerning Hawaiian Islands, p. 941.)

S. Doc. 231, pt 7——17

WILLIAM H. SEWARD.

Annexation overtures to be confidentially received.

In reply to a dispatch from U. S. Minister McCook, suggesting the possibility of the annexation of Hawaii, Secretary Seward wrote to him, July 13, 1867:

You are at liberty to sound the proper authority on the large subject mentioned in your note (annexation) and ascertain probable conditions. You may confidentially receive overtures and communicate the same to me.

I will act upon your suggestion in that relation in regard to a party now here. (The Hawaiian Minister at Washington.) (Vol. 2, Rep. Sen. Com. on For. Rel. concerning Hawaiian Islands, p. 948.)

Annexation deemed desirable by U. S. Government.

In a dispatch to U. S. Minister McCook at Honolulu, of September 12, 1867, Secretary Seward says:

Circumstances have transpired here which induce a belief that a strong interest, based upon a desire for annexation of the Sandwich Islands, will be active in opposing a ratification of the reciprocity treaty. It will be argued that the reciprocity will tend to hinder and defeat *an early annexation*, to which the people of the Sandwich Islands are supposed to be now strongly inclined. * * *

Second. You will be governed in all your proceedings by a proper respect and courtesy to the Government and people of the Sandwich Islands; but it is proper that you should know, for your own information, that *a lawful and peaceful annexation of the islands to the United States, with the consent of the people of the Sandwich Islands, is deemed desirable by this Government; and that if the policy of annexation should really conflict with the policy of reciprocity, annexation is in every case to be preferred.* (Vol. 2, Rep. Sen. Com. on For. Rel. concerning Hawaiian Islands, p. 951.)

HAMILTON FISH.

Control of Hawaii discussed.

In a dispatch from Secretary Fish to the American Minister at Honolulu, March 25, 1873, the following occurs:

The position of the Sandwich Islands as an outpost *fronting and commanding the whole of our possessions on the Pacific Ocean,* gives to the future of those islands a peculiar interest to the Government and people of the United States. It is very clear that this Government cannot be expected to assent to their transfer from their present control to that of any powerful maritime or commercial nation.

MILITARY SURVEILLANCE BY BERMUDA MUST NOT BE REPEATED IN THE PACIFIC.

Such transfer to a maritime power would threaten a military surveillance in the Pacific similar to that which Bermuda has afforded in the Atlantic—the latter has been submitted to from necessity, inasmuch as it was congenital with our Government—but we desire no additional similar outposts in the hands of those who may at some future time use them to our disadvantage.

CONSIDERATION OF HAWAII'S FUTURE FORCED ON UNITED STATES.

The condition of the Government of Hawaii and its evident tendency to decay and dissolution *force upon us the earnest consideration of its future—possibly its near future.*

There seems to be a strong desire on the part of many persons in the islands, representing large interest and great wealth, to become annexed to the United States. *And while there are,* as I have already said, *many and influential persons in this country who question the policy of any insular acquisitions, perhaps even of any extension of territorial limits,*

POLICY OF WISE FORESIGHT TO ACQUIRE HAWAII.

there are also those of influence and of wise foresight who see a future that must extend the jurisdiction and the limits of this nation, and that will require a resting spot in mid-ocean, between the Pacific coast and the vast domains of Asia, which are now opening to commerce and Christian civilization. (Vol. 2, Rep. Sen. Com. on For. Rel. concerning Hawaiian Islands, p. 827.)

JAMES G. BLAINE.

Hawaii the key of the American Pacific.

In 1881, the British Government having made certain demands upon the Hawaiian Government, arising out of the reciprocity treaty with the United States, negotiated in 1876, Mr. Blaine, in a dispatch dated December 1, 1881, to U. S. Minister Comly, at Honolulu, used the following language:

This Government firmly believes that *the position of the Hawaiian Islands as the key to the dominion of the American Pacific* demands their benevolent neutrality, to which end it will earnestly cooperate with the native Government. And if, through any cause, the maintenance of such a position of benevolent neutrality should be found by Hawaii to be impracticable,

AN AVOWEDLY AMERICAN SOLUTION.

this Government would then unhesitatingly meet the altered situation by seeking an avowedly American solution for the grave issues presented. (Vol. 2, Rep. Sen. Com. on For. Rel. concerning Hawaiian Islands, p. 831.)

In a further dispatch he said:

The Government of the United States * * * has always avowed and now repeats that under no circumstances will it permit the transfer of the territory or sovereignty of these islands to any of the great European powers. It is needless to restate the reasons upon which that determination rests. It is too obvious for argument that the possession of these islands by a great maritime power would not only be a dangerous diminution of the just and necessary influence of the United States in the waters of the Pacific, but in the case of international difficulty it would be a positive threat to interests too large and important to be lightly risked.

Hawaii's relations to the United States.

In a confidential dispatch to U. S. Minister Comly, at Honolulu, December 1, 1881, Mr. Blaine says:

EARLY EXTINCTION OF NATIVES—TRANSFER OF POWER TO OTHERS.

In my formal instruction of this date I have reviewed the general question of the relationship between the United States and the Hawaiian Islands, and the position of the latter, both as an integral part of the American system and as the key to the commerce of the North Pacific. As that instruction was written for communication to the Hawaiian secretary of state, I touched but lightly on the essential question of the gradual and seemingly inevitable decadence and extinction of the native race and its replacement by another, to which the powers of government would necessarily descend.

A single glance at the census returns of Hawaii for half a generation past exhibits this alarming diminution of the indigenous element, amounting to $1\frac{1}{2}$ per cent per annum of the population. Meanwhile, the industrial and productive development of Hawaii is on the increase, and the native classes, never sufficiently numerous to develop the full resources of the islands, have been supplemented by an adventitious labor element, from China mainly, until the rice and sugar fields are largely tilled by aliens. *The worst of this state of things* is that it must inevitably keep on in increasing ratio, the native classes growing smaller, the insular production larger, and the immigration to supply the want of labor greater every year.

HAWAII COMMERCIALLY A DISTRICT OF CALIFORNIA.

I have shown in a previous instruction how entirely Hawaii is a part of the productive and commercial system of the American States. So far as the staple growths and imports of the islands go, *the reciprocity treaty makes them practically members of an American zollverein, an outlying district of the State of California.* So far as political structure and independence of action are concerned, Hawaii is as remote from our control as China.

PERPETUITY OF NATIVES BASIS OF INDEPENDENCE.

This contradiction is only explicable by assuming what is the fact, that thirty years ago, having the choice between material annexation and commercial assimilation of the islands, the United States chose the less responsible alternative. The soundness of the choice, however, entirely depends on the perpetuity of the rule of the native race as an independent Government, and that imperiled, the whole framework of our relations to Hawaii is changed, if not destroyed.

The decline of the native Hawaiian element in the presence of newer and sturdier growths must he accepted as an inevitable fact, in view of the teachings of ethnological history. And *as retrogression in the development of the islands can not be admitted without serious detriment to American interests in the North Pacific, the problem of a replenishment of the vital forces of Hawaii presents itself for intelligent solution in an American sense—not in an Asiatic or a British sense.*

ANNEXATION WOULD CAUSE AMERICAN COLONIZATION.

There is little doubt that were the Hawaiian Islands, by annexation or district protection, a part of the territory of the Union, their fertile resources for the growth of rice and sugar would not only be controlled by American capital, but so profitable a field of labor would attract intelligent workers thither from the United States.

Throughout the continent, north and south, wherever a foothold is found for American enterprise, it is quickly occupied, and this spirit of adventure, which seeks its outlet in the mines of South America and the railroads of Mexico, would not be slow to avail itself of openings for assured and profitable enterprise even in mid-ocean. (Vol. 2, Rep. Sen. Com. on For. Rel., concerning Hawaiian-Islands, p. 977.):

THOMAS F. BAYARD.

The reciprocity treaty with Hawaii was negotiated in 1875 under Secretary Fish. An extension of the treaty was negotiated by Secretary Frelinghuysen, and finally carried into effect under Thos. F. Bayard, Secretary of State in Mr. Cleveland's first Administration. In an interview published in the Philadelphia Ledger, February 1, 1897, Mr. Bayard discusses the objects and intent of these treaties. Among other things he states that he was "greatly impressed with the special advantages which our exclusive rights in the islands gave us, and would have preferred to extend the period of its duration, so that our commercial interests there would have ample time to develop, and American control of the islands, in a perfectly natural and legitimate way, would be assured by the normal growth of mercantile and political relations." He further states that the British minister requested that the United States join England and Germany in a guaranty of the neutrality of Hawaii, which Mr. Bayard declined to do, February 15, 1888. Continuing, Mr. Bayard says:

I held that there could be no comparison between our rights in the Hawaiian Islands, as secured by the treaties of 1875 and 1887, with those of other nations, and I would not consent that the United States should be put upon an equality with them. * * * *We had an interest in Hawaii that no other country could have. A political union would logically and naturally follow, in course of time, the commercial union and dependence which were thus assured.* * * * *It was my idea that the policy originating in the Fish treaty of the Grant Administration in 1875 should be permitted to work out its proper results. The obvious course was to wait quietly and patiently and let the islands fill up with American planters and American industries until they should be wholly identified in business interests and political sympathies with the United States. It was simply a matter of waiting until the apple should ripen and fall. Unfortunately, nothing was done by Congress in pursuance of this easy, legitimate, and perfectly feasible process of acquisition.* * * *

JOHN W. FOSTER.

Secretary of State Foster made a report accompanying the treaty of annexation negotiated by him February 15, 1893, in which he says:

The policy of the United States has been consistently and constantly declared against any foreign aggression in Hawaii inimical to the necessarily paramount rights and interests of the American people there, and the uniform contemplation of their annexation as a contingent necessity. But beyond that it is shown that annexation has been on more than one occasion avowed as a policy and attempted as a fact. (Ib., vol. 1, p. 136.)

Duty of the United States to annex.

In an address to the National Geographic Society, March 26, 1897, Mr. Foster said:

It is, in my opinion, the plain duty of the United States to annex Hawaii to its territory. And in a matter which involves the interests and destiny of a great nation of 70,000,000 people no mere technical questions of procedure should be allowed to embarrass our action. * * *

ANNEXATION PRESENTS NO DIFFICULTIES—PROTECTORATE IMPRACTICABLE.

To my mind annexation presents no political or administrative difficulties. * * * I do regard the suggestion of a protectorate as practicable. We can not assume it without becoming responsible for the government of the islands and we should not become responsible for the government unless we can * * * control its management. Such a system would bring no end of complications with foreign powers and in domestic affairs.

EITHER ANNEX OR LET ALONE.

We must either annex the islands or leave them free to make such other alliance as they may choose or as destiny may determine.

JOHN SHERMAN.

Report accompanying annexation treaty of 1897.

Secretary of State Sherman made a report to the President accompanying the treaty of annexation negotiated by him June 15, 1897, as follows:

The President:

The undersigned, Secretary of State, has the honor to lay before the President for submission to the Senate, should it be deemed for the public interests to do so, a treaty signed in the city of Washington on the 16th instant by the undersigned and by the duly empowered representatives of the Republic of Hawaii, whereby the islands constituting the said Republic and all their dependencies are fully and absolutely ceded to the United States of America forever.

It does not seem necessary to the present purpose of the undersigned to review the incidents of 1893, when a similar treaty of cession was signed on February 14 and submitted to the Senate, being subsequently withdrawn by the President on the 9th of March following. The negotiation which has culminated in the treaty now submitted has not been a mere resumption of the negotiation of 1893, but was initiated and has been conducted upon independent lines. Then an abrupt revolutionary movement had brought about the dethronement of the queen and set up instead of the heretofore titular monarchy a provisional government for the control and management of public affairs and the protection of the public peace, such government to exist only until terms of union with the United States should have been negotiated and agreed upon. Thus self-constituted, its promoters claimed for it only a de facto existence until the purpose of annexation in which it took rise should be accomplished.

REPUBLIC EVOLVED FROM PROVISIONAL GOVERNMENT.

As time passed and the plan of union with the United States became an uncertain contingency the organization of the Hawaiian commonwealth underwent necessary changes. The temporary character of its first government gave place to a permanent scheme under a constitution framed by the representatives of the electors of the islands, and the government, administered by an executive council, not chosen by suffrage but self appointed, was succeeded by an elective and parliamentary régime, and the ability of the new government to hold—as the Republic of Hawaii—an independent place in the family of sovereign States, preserving order at home and fulfilling international obligations abroad, has been put to the proof.

Recognized by the powers of the earth, sending and receiving envoys, enforcing respect for the law, and maintaining peace within its island borders, Hawaii sends to the United States not a commission representing a successful revolution, but the accredited plenipotentiary of a constituted and firmly established sovereign State. However sufficient may have been the authority of the commissioners with whom the United States Government treated in 1893, and however satisfied the President may then have been of their power to offer the domain of the Hawaiian Islands to the United States, the fact remains that what they then tendered was a territory rather than an established government, a country whose administration had been cast down by a bloodless but complete revolution, and a community in a state of political transition.

HAWAIIAN CONSTITUTION AUTHORIZES ANNEXATION.

Now, however, the Republic of Hawaii approaches the United States as an equal, and points for its authority to that provision of article 32 of the constitution promulgated July 24, 1894, whereby the President, with the approval of the cabinet, is expressly authorized and empowered to make a treaty of political or commercial union between the Republic of Hawaii and the United States of America, subject to the ratification of the Senate.

SIMPLE COMMERCIAL UNION IMPRACTICABLE.

The present negotiation is therefore, as has been said, not a mere renewal of the tender of Hawaiian territory made in 1893, but has responded to the purpose declared in the Hawaiian constitution, and the conferences of the plenipotentiaries have been directed to weighing the advantages of the political and the commercial union alternately proposed and relatively considering the scope and extent thereof.

It soon appeared to the negotiators that a purely commercial union on the lines of the German zollverein could not satisfy the problems of the administration in Hawaii and of the political associations between the islands and the United States. Such a commercial union would on the one hand deprive the Hawaiian Government of its chief source of revenue from customs duties by placing its territory in a relation of free exchange with the territory of the United States, its main market of purchase and supply, while on the other hand it would entail upon Hawaii the maintenance of an internal-revenue system on a par with that of the United States, or else involve the organization of a corresponding branch of our revenue service within a foreign jurisdiction.

We have had with Hawaii since 1875 a treaty of commercial union, which practically assimilates the two territories with regard to many of their most important productions, and excludes other nations from enjoyment of its privileges, yet, although that treaty has outlived other less favored reciprocity schemes, its permanency has at times been gravely imperiled. Under such circumstances, to enter upon the radical experiment of a complete commercial union between Hawaii and the United States as independently sovereign states, without assurances of permanency and with perpetual subjection to the vicissitudes of public sentiment in the two countries, was not to be thought of.

POLITICAL PROTECTORATE IMPRACTICABLE.

Turning then to the various practical forms of the political union, the several phases of a protectorate, an offensive and defensive alliance, and a national guaranty were passed in review. In all of these the independence of the subordinated state is the distinguishing feature, and with it the assumption by the paramount state of responsibility without domain. This disparity of the relative interests and the distance separating the two countries could not fail to render any form of protective association either unduly burdensome or illusory in its benefits, so far as the protecting state is concerned, while any attempt to counteract this by tributary dependence or a measure of suzerain control would be a retrograde movement toward a feudal or colonial establishment alike inexpedient and incompatible with our national policy.

ANNEXATION ONLY SATISFACTORY SOLUTION.

There remained, therefore, the annexation of the islands and their complete absorption into the political system of the United States as the only solution satisfying all the given conditions and promising permanency and mutual benefit. The present treaty has been framed on that basis, thus substantially reverting to the original proposal of 1893, and necessarily adopting many of the features of that arrangement. As to most of these the negotiators have been constrained and limited by the constitutional powers of the Government of the United States.

ORGANIC PROVISIONS OF GOVERNMENT RESERVED FOR ACTION OF CONGRESS.

As in previous instances when the United States has acquired territory by treaty, it has been necessary to preserve all the organic provisions for the action of Congress. If this was requisite in the case of the transfer to the United States of a part of the domain of a titular sovereign, as in the cession of Louisiana by France, of Florida by Spain, or of Alaska by Russia, it is the more requisite when the act is not cession, but union, involving the complete incorporation of an alien sovereignty into the body politic of the United States.

For this the only precedent of our political history is found in the uncompleted treaty concluded during President Grant's Administration, November 29, 1869, for the annexation of the Dominican Republic to the United States.

Following that example, the treaty now signed by the plenipotentiaries of the United States and the Republic of Hawaii reserves to the Congress of the United States the determination of all questions affecting the form of government of the annexed territory, the citizenship and elective franchise of its inhabitants, and the manner in which the laws of the United States are to be extended to the islands.

HAWAIIAN TREATIES ABROGATED.

In order that this independence of the Congress shall be complete and unquestionable, and pursuant to the recognized doctrine of public law, that treaties expire with the independent life of the contracting state, there has been introduced, out of abundant caution, an express proviso for the determination of all treaties heretofore concluded by Hawaii with foreign nations, and the extension to the islands of the treaties of the United States.

This leaves Congress free to deal with such especial regulation of the contract labor system of the islands as circumstances may require. There being no general provision of existing statutes to prescribe the form of government for newly incorporated territory, it was necessary to stipulate, as in the Dominican precedent, for continuing the existing machinery of the government and laws in the Hawaiian Islands until provision shall be made by law for the government, as a territory of the United States, of the domain thus incorporated into the Union; but having in view the peculiar status created in Hawaii by laws enacted in execution of treaties heretofore concluded between Hawaii and other countries, only such Hawaiian laws are thus provisionally continued as shall not be incompatible with the Constitution or the laws of the United States or with the provisions of this treaty.

PROHIBITION OF CHINESE IMMIGRATION.

It will be noticed that express stipulation is made prohibiting the coming of Chinese laborers from the Hawaiian Islands to any other part of our national territory. This provision was proper and necessary in view of the Chinese exclusion acts, and it behooved the negotiators to see to it that this treaty, which in turn is to become, in due constitutional course, a supreme law of the land, shall not alter or amend existing law in this most important regard.

JOHN SHERMAN.

DEPARTMENT OF STATE, *Washington, June 15, 1897.*

OPINIONS OF AMERICAN MINISTERS AT HONOLULU, LONDON, AND PARIS CONCERNING THE CONTROL OR ANNEXATION OF HAWAII.

EDWARD EVERETT.

English seizure of Hawaii prevented French occupation.

Edward Everett, U. S. minister at London, sent a dispatch to the U. S. State Department relating to the seizure of Hawaii by the English and their subsequent restoration thereof. In the course of the dispatch he says:

There is now reason to think that the occupation of the islands by Lord George Paulet was a fortunate event, inasmuch as it prevented them from being taken possession of by a French squadron, which (it is said) was on its way for that purpose. Had France got possession of the islands she would certainly have retained them.

Had intelligence been received here of Lord George Paulet's occupation of them before her promise was given to recognize them, England, I think, would not have given them up. As it is, an understanding between the great European powers, amounting, in effect if not in form, to a guaranty of their independence, is likely to take place. *This is the only state of things with which the United States could be content. As it will be brought about without involving us in any compacts with other powers,* * * * (Vol. 2, Rep. Sen. Com. on For. Rel., concerning Hawaiian Islands, p. 926.)

J. TURRILL.

Protest against French aggression.

On August 18, 1849, the French admiral Tromelin made demand for settlement of certain alleged grievances against the Hawaiian Government, with a threat to use force if not complied with.

Mr. Turrill, U. S. consul at Honolulu, thereupon addressed a communication to him, in which he used the following language:

The demands which have been made upon this Government are, in my judgment, in direct opposition to the plain provisions of the treaty, and the enforcing them in the manner indicated would be a palpable violation of the law of nations.

As the course you have advised me that circumstances may induce you to pursue must of necessity *seriously affect the great American interests* connected with these islands, it becomes my imperative duty, as a representative of the United States, to interpose my solemn protest against it, which I now do, and I shall lose no time in communicating to the President of the United States the facts and circumstances attending this case. (Vol. 2, Rep. Sen. Com. on For. Rel. concerning Hawaiian Islands, p. 884.)

French admiral replies, none of United States' business.

To this Admiral Tromelin replied, expressing surprise at the communication received, saying:

The policy of the American Government made it your duty to not interfere officially in our affairs with the Administration of His Majesty Kamehameha III, for you know as well as I do that the United States of America has made it to themselves a law of not mixing ever in the affairs of other nations, and especially those of France. (*Ibid.*, p. 884.)

French action injurious to American interests.

To this Mr. Turrill replied:

You are right in supposing it not to be the policy of the United States to mix in the affairs of other nations. But when a case like the one under consideration occurs, and I clearly see that the course military power is to take against this weak nation *must greatly injure my countrymen and seriously embarrass the extensive American commerce* connected with these islands, it becomes my duty so far to interfere officially as to interpose my protest; and in doing so I doubt not my course will meet the entire approbation of the President of the United States. (*Ibid.*, p. 885.)

LUTHER SEVERANCE.

Provisional cession of Hawaii to United States.

The French aggressions in Honolulu being renewed in 1851, the King, on the 10th day of March, 1851, executed a document reciting his inability to withstand the aggressions of the French, and placing the country—

under the protection and safeguard of the United States of America until some arrangements can be made to place our said relations with France upon a footing compatible with my rights as an independent sovereign, * * * or, if such arrangements be found impracticable, then it is our wish and pleasure that *the protection aforesaid under the United States of America be perpetual.*

And we further proclaim as aforesaid that from the date of publication hereof the flag of the United States of America shall be hoisted above the national ensign on all our forts and places and vessels navigating with Hawaiian registers.

This was delivered to U. S. Minister Severance. (Vol. 2, Rep. Sen. Com. on For. Rel. concerning Hawaiian Islands, p. 897.)

Annexation desired by Hawaii.

In a dispatch from Mr. Severance to Secretary of State Webster, dated March 11th, 1851, giving at length a statement concerning the situation, Mr. Severance says:

* * * The King, with the approbation of his chiefs, and I believe nearly all the principal officers of the Government, have it in contemplation to take down the Hawaiian flag and run up that of the United States. *They contemplate annexation to our Republic, and have already consulted me about it.* * * *

The popular representative body recently elected by native votes is for the most part composed of natives of the United States, and so is the executive part of the Government, as well as the judiciary, at least in the high courts. * * * *Three-fourths, at least, of the business done here is by Americans, and they already own much of the real estate.* * " * If the action of the French should precipitate a movement here, I shall be called on, perhaps, to protect the American flag. *I was inde d requested to go and see the King on Monday night, and in the presence of the council to give him assurance of protection should he raise the American flag instead of his own;* but I preferred to keep away, so as to avoid all appearance of intrigue to bring about a result which, however desirable, and as many believe ultimately inevitable, must still be attended with difficulties and embarrassments. * * *

After referring to the French and their possible further attack, he continues:

The natives look upon them as enemies, and if they come again on a like errand we shall be again appealed to for protection, and *the subject of annexation will come up again with added force.* (Vol. 2, Rep. Sen. Com. on For. Rel., concerning Hawaiian Islands, pp. 897-8.)

Referring to the document executed by the King, above referred to, Mr. Severance continues that he has not committed himself other than to say—

that if the King cedes the islands to the United States and puts up the American flag, I will do what I can to protect it for the time being, until the pleasure of my Government shall be known. Leaning upon us as they do, and sympathizing with them under aggravated wrongs and repeated insults, I could not tell them we should reject their proffered allegiance, and stand passive while they, with the American flag in their hands, should be trampled under foot by the French.

Distance no objection to annexation.

Continuing, Mr. Severance says that arrangements are being made for steam navigation with San Francisco:

With these steamers and a telegraph from San Francisco to Washington we can communicate with you in about a week; so *I hope you will not object to a political connection on account of distance.* Nor are we so far from the centripetal force of our Republic as to be in danger of being thrown off in a tangent. *We must not take the islands in virtue of the " manifest destiny " principle, but can we not accept their voluntary offer? Who has a right to forbid the bans?* (Vol. 2, Rep. Sen. Com. on For. Rel. concerning Hawaiian Islands, p. 903.)

DAVID L. GREGG.

Treaty of annexation negotiated.

Acting under instructions from Mr. Marcy, U. S. Minister Gregg negotiated a treaty of annexation with the Hawaiian Government.

It was completed ready for signature, August 7, 1854, but before it was signed the King, Kamehameha III, died, and his successor, Kamehameha IV, declined to ratify it.

This treaty of annexation and the dispatches concerning it are to be found in Vol. 2, Rep. Sen. Com. on For. Rel., concerning Hawaiian Islands, p. 935.

It is hereinafter contained.

JAMES M'BRIDE.

English control would be injustice to Americans.

In a dispatch from U. S. Minister McBride, at Honolulu, to Secretary Seward, dated October 9, 1863, he sets forth the growing power of the English and the tendency of the King and Government of Hawaii to Anglicize everything in connection with the Government, and the danger that the country would come under British control.

Upon this subject he says:

It would be a flagrant injustice to American citizens, after they have labored for the good of these islands for the last forty years, after they have brought these people out of barbarism and taught them civilization, science, and religion; in a word, made them an intelligent and Christian nation, and have done all that has been done in the development of the resources of the country, and given it a worldwide popularity, to be either driven out or so treated and harassed as to make it necessary for their interests to sacrifice their property and leave, which is believed would be the case provided the English obtain greater influence with the King than they now have, which influence it is the desire of Americans here and for the interests of the American Government to avert. Some merchants and planters are contracting their business, so that they may not suffer so heavy a loss in the event of the change which seems probable at no very distant day. (Vol. 2, Rep. Sen. Com. on For. Rel., concerning Hawaiian Islands, p. 943.)

EDWARD M'COOK.

Hawaii absolutely necessary to the United States in case of war.

In a dispatch to Secretary Seward, dated September 3, 1866, U. S. Minister McCook, at Honolulu, after giving a general résumé of conditions of the islands, says:

Geographically these islands occupy the same important relative position towards the Pacific that the Bermudas do towards the Atlantic coast of the United States, a position which makes them important to the English, convenient to the French, and, in the event of war with either of those Powers, absolutely necessary to the United States. Destitute of both army and navy, the Hawaiian Government is without the power to resist aggression, to compel belligerents to respect the neutrality of her ports. Equally destitute of financial resources, they are without the means of indemnifying those who may suffer through their weakness.

SPIRIT OF COUNTRY WHOLLY AMERICAN AND FAVORABLE TO ANNEXATION.

The spirit of this whole people is heartily republican and thoroughly American. The King, his half dozen half-civilized nobles, as many cabinet ministers, and the Lord Bishop of Honolulu (Staley) constitute the entire aristocratic element of the country, either in fact or in feeling. And when this dynasty ends, as end it will, probably within the next year, I am sure that if the American Government indicates the slightest desire to test in these islands the last Napoleonic conception in the way of territorial extension you will find the people here with great unanimity demanding by votes, freely expressed, annexation to the United States. (Rep. Sen. Com. on For. Rel., vol. 2, concerning Hawaiian Islands, p. 947.)

Annexation favored.

A reciprocity treaty was in process of negotiation between Hawaii and the United States under President Johnson, in 1867. U. S. Minister McCook, at Honolulu, June 7, 1867, writes to Secretary Seward:

Should the treaty be ratified I will feel that I have possibly accomplished all I can accomplish in my present position, and will probably wish to return to my home in Colorado unless you should favor the absolute acquisition of the Hawaiian Islands, in which event I would like to conduct the negotiations. *I think their sovereignty could be purchased from the present King, and feel sure that the people of the United States would receive such a purchase with universal acclamation.* (Rep. Sen. Com. on For. Rel., Vol. 2, concerning Hawaiian Islands, p. 947.)

HENRY A. PIERCE.

The dispatch concerning annexation which Grant submitted for confidential consideration of the Senate.

On February 25, 1871, Mr. Henry A. Pierce, then U. S. minister at Honolulu, wrote to Secretary of State Hamilton Fish a dispatch concerning annexation, which, upon reference to President Grant, was deemed by him so important that he forwarded it to the Senate, accompanied by a confidential special message recommending it to the consideration of the Senate.

The dispatch from Mr. Pierce is as follows:

Annexation ultimate destiny of Hawaii.

Impressed with the importance of the subject now presented for consideration, I beg leave to suggest the inquiry whether the period has not arrived making it proper, wise, and sagacious for the United States Government to *again consider the project of annexing the Hawaiian Islands* to the territory of the Republic. *That such is to be the political destiny of this archipelago seems a foregone conclusion in the opinion of all who have given attention to the subject in this country, the United States, England, France, and Germany.*

A majority of the aborigines, creoles, and naturalized foreigners of this country, as I am credibly informed, are favorable, even anxious, for the consummation of the measure named.

The event of the decease of the present sovereign of Hawaii, leaving no heirs or successor to the throne, and the consequent election to be made by the legislative assembly of a King, and new stirps for a royal family, will produce a crisis in political affairs which, it is thought, will be availed of as a propitious occasion to inaugurate measures for annexation of the islands to the United States, the same to be effected as the manifest will and choice of the majority of the Hawaiian people, and through means proper, peaceful, and honorable.

It is evident, however, no steps will be taken to accomplish the object named without the proper sanction or approbation of the United States Government in approval thereof.

AMERICAN SENTIMENT IN HAWAII.

The Hawaiian people for fifty years have been under educational instruction of American missionaries and the civilizing influence of New England people, commercial and maritime. Hence they are Puritan and democratic in their ideas and tendencies, modified by a tropical climate. Their favorite songs and airs are American.

The Fifteenth Amendment to the Constitution of the United States has made the project of annexation to our Union more popular than ever, both here and in the United States.

DECREASE OF NATIVES.

The native population is fast disappearing. The number existing is now estimated at 45,000, having decreased about 15,000 since the census of 1866. The number of foreigners in addition is between 5,000 and 6,000, two-thirds of whom are from the United States, and they own more than that proportion of the foreign capital, as represented in the agriculture, commerce, navigation, and whale fisheries of the kingdom.

FOREIGNERS TO SUCCEED. IF NOT AMERICANS, WHO?

This country and sovereignty will soon be left to the possession of foreigners, "to unlineal hands, no sons of theirs succeeding." To what foreign nation shall these islands belong if not to the great Republic? At the present those of foreign nativities hold all the important offices of Government and control legislation, the judiciary, etc. Well disposed as the Government now is toward the United States and its resident citizens here, in course of time it may be otherwise, as was the case during our civil war.

POINTS WHICH SHOULD INFLUENCE U. S. POLICY.

I now proceed to state some points of a mere general character which should influence the United States Government in their decision of the policy of acquiring possession of this archipelago.

NECESSITY AS NAVAL DEPOT.

Their geographical position occupying, as it does, *an important central, strategical point in the North Pacific Ocean, valuable, perhaps necessary, to the United States for a naval depot and coaling station and to shelter and protect our commerce and navigation,* which in this hemisphere is destined to increase enormously from our intercourse with the 500,000,000 population of China, Japan, and Australia. Humboldt predicted that the commerce on the Pacific would, in time, rival that on the Atlantic. A future generation, no doubt, will see the prophecy fulfilled.

The immense injury inflicted on American navigation and commerce by Great Britain in the war of 1812–1814, through her possession of Bermuda and other West India Islands, as also that suffered by the English from French privateers from the Isle of France during the wars between those nations, are instances in proof of the necessity of anticipating and preventing, when we can, similar evils that may issue from these islands if held by other powers.

COMMERCIAL VALUE.

Their proximity to the Pacific States of the Union, fine climate and soil, and tropical productions of sugar, coffee, rice, fruits, hides, goatskins, salt, cotton, fine wool, etc., required by the West, in exchange for flour, grain, lumber, shooks, and manufactures of cotton, wool, iron, and other articles, are evidence of the commercial value of one to the other region.

EUROPEAN POWERS MAY SEIZE IN TIME OF WAR.

Is it probable that any European power who may hereafter be at war with the United States will refrain from taking possession of this weak Kingdom, in view of the great injury that could be done to our commerce through their acquisition of them?

PALMERSTON'S VIEW OF DESTINY OF HAWAII.

Prince Alexander and Lott Kamehameha (the former subsequently became the fourth Hawaiian King and the latter the fifth) and Dr. G. P. Judd, my informant, visited England in 1850 as Hawaiian commissioners.

Lord Palmerston, at their interview with him, said, in substance, "that the British Government desired the Hawaiian people to maintain proper government and preserve national independence. If they were unable to do so he recommended receiving *a protectorate government under the United States* or by becoming an integral part of that nation. Such," he thought, "was the destiny of the Hawaiian Islands, arising from their proximity to the States of California and Oregon and natural dependence on those markets for exports and imports, together with probable extinction of the Hawaiian aboriginal population and its substitution by immigration from the United States." That advice seems sound and prophetic.

HISTORICAL FOREIGN AGGRESSIONS.

The following historical events in relation to these islands are thought worthy of revival in recollection:

February 25, 1843.—Lord George Paulet, of Her Britannic Majesty's ship *Carysfort*, obtained, by forceful measures, cession of the Hawaiian Islands to the Government of Great Britain July 31, 1843. They were restored to their original sovereignty by the British Admiral Thomas.

November 28, 1843.—Joint convention of the English and French Governments, which acknowledged the independence of this archipelago and reciprocally promised never to take possession of any part of same. The United States Government was invited to be a party to the above, but declined.

August, 1849.—Admiral Tromelin, with a French naval force, after making demands on the Hawaiian Government impossible to be complied with, took unresisted possession of the fort and Government buildings in Honolulu and blockaded the harbor. After a few weeks' occupation of the place the French departed, leaving political affairs as they were previous to their arrival.

January, 1851.—A French naval force again appeared at Honolulu and threatened bombardment and destruction of the town.

DEED OF CESSION TO UNITED STATES.

The King, Kamehameha III, with the Government, fearing it would be carried into effect, and in mortal dread of being brought under French rule similar to that placed by the latter over Tahiti, of the Society Islands, executed a deed of cession of all the Hawaiian Islands and their sovereignty forever in favor of the United States of America. * * * (Vol. 2, Rep. Sen. Com. on For. Rel., concerning Hawaiian Islands, p. 825.)

Annexation under discussion in Hawaii.

In a dispatch to Secretary of State Hamilton Fish, February 17, 1873, U. S. Minister Henry A. Pierce, at Honolulu, writes as follows:

Annexation of these islands to the United States and a reciprocity treaty between the two countries are the two important topics of conversation and warm discussion among Government officials and foreign residents.

A large majority of the latter favor the first-named project, while the former advocate reciprocity. All are convinced, however, that some measure should be taken by the Hawaiian Government to effectually stay the decline in the prosperity of the country, evidenced in decreasing exports, revenue, population, whale fishery, and an increasing public debt.

OVERTHROW OF GOVERNMENT, ESTABLISHMENT OF REPUBLIC, AND ANNEXATION FORESHADOWED.

Annexation of the islands to the United States will never, in my opinion, be adopted or presented as a Government measure, however much the people as a whole may desire it. The glitter of the crown, love of power, and emoluments of office have too many attractions to prevent it. *Should the great interests of the country, however, demand that "annexation"* shall be attempted, the planters, merchants, and foreigners generally will induce the people *to overthrow the Government, establish a republic, and then ask the United States for admittance into its Union.* My opinion has recently been frequently asked in regard to probable success of the two measures proposed. I have said that if annexation or a reciprocity treaty is proposed on the part of Hawaii to the United States, that the subject will in either case be profoundly considered and decided upon.

KING WILLING TO SELL OUT.

Those favoring the former measure think it can be carried if the King's consent thereto is first obtained (and endeavors will be made to that end), provided the United States will, for and in consideration of said cession, pension off His Majesty and all the chiefs of royal blood with the aggregate sum per annum of $125,000, and pay off the Hawaiian national debt, now amounting to about $250,000, and bestow upon the cause and for the benefit of education, public schools, and the nation's hospitals (three of the latter in number) the proprietorship and revenues of the crown and public lands. The value of said lands is at present estimated at about $1,000,000. It includes, however, the public buildings, waterworks, wharf property, fish ponds, etc. The income of the crown lands, now inuring to the sovereign, amounts to about $25,000 per annum. The public, or Government, waterworks give about $15,000 per annum, wharf property about the same, notwithstanding the free use of them granted to steamship lines.

U. S. GOVERNMENT SHOULD DECLARE ITS POLICY.

Many persons are lukewarm on the subject of annexation to the United States solely for the reason that they fear repulse by the United States Government. I think the latter should declare its policy and object in regard to this important subject. This nation is bewildered and suffering to some degree, not knowing how to shape its own policy in connection with its hopes and expectations in regard to the United States. (Vol. 2, Rep. Sen. Com. on For. Rel., concerning Hawaiian Islands, p. 961.)

The Kalakaua election riot.

In a dispatch to Secretary of State Hamilton Fish, U. S. Minister Pierce describes the riot in Honolulu at the time of and consequent upon the election of Kalakaua as King, which was suppressed by United States troops.

American war vessels should always be maintained at Honolulu.

He concludes:

Hereafter a United States vessel of war should always be stationed at these islands under a system of reliefs. *A time may arrive when the United States Government will find it necessary, for the interests of our nation and its resident citizens here, to take possession of this country by military occupation.* (Vol. 2, Rep. Sen. Com. on For. Rel., concerning Hawaiian Islands, p. 970.)

Reciprocity urged to bind Hawaii to the United States.

Mr. Pierce, to Secretary Fish, urges the negotiation of a treaty of reciprocity between the two countries, and concludes:

In view of the best interests of the United States in their relations with these islands, I take the liberty to express the hope that a liberal commercial treaty may soon be inaugurated by the two countries, feeling confident that such act would result to the equal benefit of both nations in a pecuniary sense, *and, moreover, be the means of binding this archipelago to the United States by the chains of self-interest, never to be severed.* (Vol. 2, Rep. Sen. Com. on For. Rel., concerning Hawaiian Islands, p. 971.)

JOHN L. STEVENS.

Increase of annexation sentiment in Hawaii.

U. S. Minister John L. Stevens, at Honolulu, on February 8, 1892, says in a dispatch to Secretary of State Blaine, after describing the situation in Honolulu:

There are increasing indications that the annexation sentiment is growing among the business men as well as with the less responsible of the foreign and native population of the island. The present political situation is feverish, and I see no prospect of its being permanently otherwise until these islands become a part of the American Union or a possession of Great Britain. The intelligent and responsible men here, unaided by outside support, are too few in numbers to control in political affairs and to secure good government. There are indications that even the "Liberals," just beaten at the election, though composed of a majority of the popular vote, are about to declare for annexation, at least their leaders, their chief newspaper having already published editorials to this effect.

NEW DEPARTURE NECESSARY—PROTECTORATE IMPRACTICABLE—ANNEXATION ONLY REMEDY.

At a future time, after the proposed treaty shall have been ratified, I shall deem it my official duty to give a more elaborate statement of facts and reasons why a "new departure" by the United States as to Hawaii is rapidly becoming a necessity, that a "protectorate" is impracticable, and that *annexation must be the future remedy, or else Great Britain will be furnished with circumstances and opportunity to get a hold on these islands which will cause future serious embarrassment to the United States.*

At this time there seems to be no immediate prospect of its being safe to have the harbor of Honolulu left without an American vessel of war. Last week a British gunboat arrived here, and it is said will remain here for an indefinite period. (Vol. 2, Rep. Sen. Com. on For. Rel., concerning Hawaiian Islands, p. 989.)

Revolutionary movement for annexation.

On March 8, 1892, U. S. Minister Stevens, in a dispatch to Secretary Blaine, states that there are indications of a revolutionary attempt to overthrow the Queen and establish a republic, with a view of ultimate annexation to the United States, and asks for instructions. (Vol. 2, Rep. Sen. Com. on For. Rel., concerning Hawaiian Islands, p. 990.)

NOTE.—(The revolution indicated was not by the persons who afterwards carried out the revolution of 1893, but was being gotten up by an almost exclusively native combination, under the leadership of a half-white, Wilcox. They were politically hostile to the persons organizing the successful revolution of 1893, and since 1893 have been rabid royalists.)

Superior interests in Hawaii the avowed policy of the United States.

Mr. Stevens sent a dispatch to Secretary of State Foster, November 20, 1892, in which he states:

An intelligent and impartial examination of the facts can hardly fail to lead to the conclusion that the relations and policy of the United States toward Hawaii will soon demand some change, if not the adoption of decisive measures, with the aim to secure American interests and future supremacy by encouraging Hawaiian development and aiding to promote responsible government in these islands. It is unnecessary for me to allude to the deep interest and the settled policy of the United States Government in respect to these islands, from the official days of John Quincy Adams and of Daniel Webster to the present time. In all that period we have avowed the superiority of our interests to those of all other nations, and have always refused to embarrass our freedom of action by any alliance or arrangement with other powers as to the ultimate possession and government of the islands. (Vol. 2, Rep. Sen. Com. on For. Rel., concerning Hawaiian Islands, p. 996.)

Analysis of conditions.

He then proceeds to give an analysis of the situation, referring to the commercial and naval importance of the islands, its government, existing business status, and recommends that—

EITHER ANNEXATION OR CUSTOMS UNION.

One of two courses seems to me absolutely necessary to be followed, *either bold and vigorous measures for annexation, or a "customs union,"* an ocean cable from the California coast to Honolulu, Pearl Harbor perpetually ceded to the United States, with an implied but not necessarily stipulated American protectorate over the islands.

REASONS WHY ANNEXATION PREFERABLE.

I believe the former to be the better, that which will prove much the more advantageous to the islands, and the cheapest and least embarrassing in the end for the United States. If it was wise for the United States, through Secretary Marcy, thirty-eight years ago, to offer to expend $100,000 to secure a treaty of annexation, it certainly can not be chimerical or unwise to expend $100,000 to secure annexation in the near future. *To-day the United States has five times the wealth she possessed in 1854, and the reasons now existing for annexation are much stronger than they were then.* * * * A perpetual customs union and the acquisition of Pearl Harbor, with an implied protectorate, must be regarded as the only allowable alternative. This would require the continual presence in the harbor of Honolulu of a United States vessel of war and the constant watchfulness of the United States minister while the present bungling, unsettled, and expensive political rule would go on, retarding the development of the islands, leaving at the end of twenty-five years more embarrassment to annexation than exists to-day, the property far less valuable, and the population less American than they would be if annexation were soon realized. * * *

OBJECTIONS TO CUSTOMS UNION.

To give Hawaii a highly favorable treaty while she remains outside the American Union would necessarily give the same advantages to hostile foreigners, those who would continue to antagonize our commercial and political interests here as well as those of American blood and sympathies. * * * Besides, *so long as the islands retain their own independent government there remains the possibility that England or the Canadian Dominion might secure one of the Hawaiian harbors for a coaling station. Annexation excludes all dangers of this kind.*

DECISION SHOULD BE MADE AS TO WHICH POLICY TO FOLLOW.

Which of the two lines of policy and action shall be adopted our statesmen and our Government must decide. *Certain it is that the interests of the United States and the welfare of these islands will not permit the continuance of the existing state and tendency of things.* Having for so many years extended a helping hand to the islands and encouraging the American residents and their friends at home to the extent we have, we cannot refrain now from aiding them with vigorous measures, without injury to ourselves and those of our "kith and kin," and without neglecting American opportunities that never seemed so obvious and pressing as they do now. (Vol. 2, Rep. Sen. Com. on For. Rel., concerning Hawaiian Islands, pp. 1002-3.)

OPINIONS OF U. S. MILITARY AND NAVAL OFFICERS CONCERNING THE CONTROL OR ANNEXATION OF HAWAII.

GEN. J. M. SCHOFIELD AND GEN. B. S. ALEXANDER.

Report on defensive capabilities of Hawaii in case of war.

On June 24, 1872, Secretary of War Wm. W. Belknap issued confidential instructions to Generals Schofield and Alexander to go to Honolulu and investigate its defensive capabilities in the event of war between the United States and some other maritime nation.

Their report is lengthy and contains the following:

* * * We ascertained from the officers of the U. S. Navy, from maps, and from seafaring men that Honolulu is the only good commercial harbor in the whole group of the Sandwich Islands.

An enemy could take up his position outside of the entrance to the harbor and command the entire anchorage, as well as the town of Honolulu itself. *This harbor would, therefore, be of no use to us as a harbor of refuge in a war with a powerful maritime nation.*

PEARL RIVER ONLY HARBOR THAT CAN BE PROTECTED IN TIME OF WAR.

With one exception, there is no harbor on the islands that can be made to satisfy all the conditions necessary for a harbor of refuge in time of war. This is the harbor of *Ewa,* or *Pearl River,* situated on the island of Oahu, about 7 miles west of Honolulu.

Pearl River is a fine sheet of deep water extending inland about six miles from its mouth, where it could be completely defended by shore batteries. The depth of water after passing the bar is ample for any vessel.

Pearl River is not a true river; it partakes more of the character of an estuary. It is divided into three portions called "locks"—the east lock, the middle lock, and the west lock, the three together affording some 30 miles of water front, with deep water in the channels. * * *

EASILY DEFENDED—WATER—LAND—PROVISIONS.

If the coral barrier were removed, Pearl River Harbor would seem to have all, or nearly all, the necessary properties to enable it to be converted into a good harbor of refuge. It could be completely defended by inexpensive batteries on either or both shores, firing across a narrow channel of entrance. Its waters are deep enough for the largest vessels of war, and its locks, particularly around Rabbitt Island, are spacious enough for a large number of vessels to ride at anchor in perfect security against all storms. Its shores are suitable for building proper establishments for sheltering the necessary supplies for a naval establishment, such as magazines of ammunition, provisions, coal, spars, rigging, etc., while the island of Oahu, upon which it is situated, could furnish fresh provisions, meats, fruits, and vegetables in large quantities.

IF MADE A NAVAL STATION JURISDICTION SHOULD BE TRANSFERRED TO THE UNITED STATES.

In case it should become the policy of the Government of the United States to obtain the possession of this harbor for naval purposes, jurisdiction over all the waters of

Pearl River, with the adjacent shores to the distance of 4 miles from any anchorage, should be ceded to the United States by the Hawaiian Government.

This would be necessary in order to enable the Government to defend its depots and anchorages in time of war by works located on its own territory. Such a cession of jurisdiction would embrace a parallelogram of about 10 by 12 miles. * * *

ACTION MUST BE IN ADVANCE OF WAR.

It is to be observed that if the United States are ever to have a harbor of refuge and naval station in the Hawaiian Islands in the event of war, *the harbor must be prepared in advance* by the removal of the Pearl River bar.

When war has begun it will be too late to make this harbor available, and there is no other suitable harbor on these islands. (Vol. 2, Rep. Sen. Com. on For. Rel., concerning Hawaiian Islands, pp. 963-6.)

GEO. BROWN.

Hawaiian sentiment in favor of annexation.

Admiral Geo. Brown, September 6, 1892, in a dispatch to Secretary of the Navy Tracy, says:

There is a strong sentiment existing in Hawaii, among the native Hawaiians as well as among the Americans and Germans, in favor of a change in the form of government, looking toward the ultimate annexation of the islands to the United States * * *

It is thought that the Queen will consent to abdicate in favor of a republican form of government if she can be assured that a suitable provision will be made for her in the way of a permanent pecuniary settlement. * * * (Vol. 2, Rep. Sen. Com. on For. Rel., concerning Hawaiian Islands, p. 991.)

G. C. WILTSE.

Growing annexation sentiment.

Capt. G. C. Wiltse, October 12, 1892, in a dispatch to Secretary of the Navy Tracy, says:

There is a large and growing sentiment, particularly among the planters, *in favor of annexation* to the United States, but I am informed that the leaders do not think an opportune moment will arrive for some time to come. *However, everything seems to point toward an eventual request for annexation.* (Vol. 2, Rep. Sen. Com. on For. Rel., concerning Hawaiian Islands, p. 993.)

CAPTAIN A. T. MAHAN.

Favors annexation.

(*Ib.*, vol. 1, p. 113, and the Forum, Mar., 1893:)

The United States finds herself compelled to make a decision. * * * Whether we wish to or no, we *must* make the decision. * * *

To anyone viewing a map that shows the full extent of the Pacific, * * * two circumstances will be strikingly and immediately apparent. He will see at a glance that the Sandwich Islands stand by themselves in a state of comparative isolation, amid a vast expanse of sea; and again, that they form the center of a large circle whose radius is approximately the distance from Honolulu to San Francisco. This is substantially the same distance as from Honolulu to the Gilbert, Marshall, Samoan, and Society islands, all under European control except Samoa, in which we have a part influence. * * *

REMARKABLE STRATEGICAL POSITION OF HAWAII.

To have a central position such as this, and to be alone, having no rival and admitting no rival, * * * are conditions that at once fix the attention of the strategist. * * * But to this striking combination is to be added the remarkable relations borne * * * to the great commercial routes traversing this vast expanse. * * *

Too much stress cannot be laid upon the immense disadvantage to us of any maritime enemy having a coaling station well within 2,500 miles, as this is, of every

S. Doc. 231, pt 7——18

point of our coast line from Puget Sound to Mexico. Were there many others available, we might find it difficult to exclude from all. There is, however, but the one.
Shut out from the Sandwich Islands as a coal base, an enemy is thrown back for
supplies of fuel to distances of 3,500 or 4,000 miles—or between 7,000 and 8,000 going
and coming—an impediment to sustained maritime operations well-nigh prohibitive.
* * * *It is rarely that so important a factor in the attack or defence of a coast line—of
a sea frontier—is concentrated in a single position, and the circumstance renders it doubly
imperative upon us to secure it if we righteously can.*

STATEMENT OF GEN. SCHOFIELD.

FAILURE TO ANNEX WOULD BE A CRIME.

"I went to the Hawaiian Islands 20 years ago. The annexation question was up
then. My business was to look the question over from the military point of view.
I made a report that while I regarded annexation as inevitable, and but a matter of
time, the conditions were not ripe for it then. * * *
"There can be no doubt now about the time for annexation, or that it should be
the outcome of the present negotiations. Annexation may not be the immediate
step; but it is near at hand and is a foregone conclusion, whether it is put off a little
while by a protectorate or until a commission further ascertains the conditions
favorable to it."
In regard to the question of suffrage, the General said there would be no trouble.
If annexed, all those who are citizens now would of course become citizens of the
United States. The Chinese and Japanese, who are not citizens there now, would
be excluded. * * *
One thing is plain enough, the Hawaiian people must have protection from some
quarter. If they cannot get it from the United States, they will have to reach out
for it in some other direction. * * * *To fail those people now would be a crime.*"
(N. Y. *Tribune*, March 15, 1893, p. 2.)

In 1875 General J. M. Schofield, then, commanding the Division of
the Pacific, gave his views to Congress, through Mr. Luttrell, concerning the reciprocity treaty, then pending before Congress, as follows:

The Hawaiian Islands constitute the only natural outpost to the defences of the
Pacific coast. In possession of a foreign naval power, in time of war, as a depot
from which to fit out hostile expeditions against this coast and our commerce on the
Pacific Ocean, they would afford the means of incalculable injury to the United
States. If the absolute neutrality of the islands could always be insured, that
would suffice; but they have not, and never can have, the power to maintain their
own neutrality, and now their necessities force them to seek alliance with some
nation which can relieve their embarrassment. The British Empire * * * stands
ready to enter into such an alliance, and thus complete its chain of naval stations
from Australia to British Columbia. We can not refuse the islands the little aid
they need and at the same time deny their right to seek it elsewhere. The time has
come when we must secure forever the desired control over those islands or let it
pass into other hands. The financial interest to the United States involved in this
treaty is very small, and if it were much greater it would still be insignificant when
compared to the importance of such a military and naval station to the national
security and welfare.

ADMIRAL BELKNAP.

OVERTHROW OF MONARCHY EXPECTED.

The revolution in the Hawaiian Islands, resulting in the deposition of the Queen
and the establishment of a provisional government, is an event not unexpected to
diplomatic, naval, and consular officers who have had any acquaintance or familiarity with the course of affairs in that island Kingdom for the past twenty years.

ANNEXATION OF MOMENTOUS INTEREST AND VITAL IMPORTANCE.

To the people of the United States the present situation is of momentous interest
and of vital importance. Indeed, it would seem that nature had established that
group to be ultimately occupied as an outpost, as it were, of the great Republic on
its western border, and that the time had now come for the fulfillment of such
design.
A glance at a chart of the Pacific will indicate to the most casual observer the
great importance and inestimable value of those islands as a strategic point and

commercial centre. Situated in mid-North Pacific, the group looks out on every hand toward grand opportunities of trade, political aggrandizement, and polyglot intercourse.

*　　　*　　　*　　　*　　　*　　　*　　　*

The group now seeks annexation to the United States. The consummation of such wish would inure to the benefit of both peoples commercially and politically. Annex the islands, constitute them a Territory, and reciprocal trade will double within ten years. Let the islanders feel that they are once and forever under the folds of the American flag, as part and parcel of the great Republic, and a development will take place in the group that will at once surprise its people and the world.

FAILURE TO ANNEX WOULD BE FOLLY.

Not to take the fruit within our grasp and annex the group now begging us to take it in would be folly indeed—a mistake of the gravest character, both for the statesmen of the day and for the men among us of high commercial aims and great enterprises.

Our statesmen should act in this matter in the spirit and resolve that secured to us the vast Louisiana purchase, the annexation of Texas, and the acquisition of California. The Administration that secures to the United States the *"coign of vantage"* in the possession of those beautiful islands will score a great measure of beneficent achievement to the credit side of its account.

*　　　*　　　*　　　*　　　*

SHOULD ANNEX EVEN AT HAZARD OF WAR.

We want no joint protectorate, no occupation there by any European power, no Pacific Egypt. We need the group as part and parcel of the United States, and should take what is offered us, even at the hazard of war.

Westward the star of empire takes its way. Let the Monroe doctrine stay not its hand until it holds Hawaii securely within its grasp.

In this matter the undersigned speaks from personal knowledge, gained through official visits to the islands in 1874 and 1882. * * * (Sen. Com. of F. R. on H., vol. 1, p. 169, and Boston Herald, January 31, 1893.)

ACTS OF THE UNITED STATES CONGRESS CONCERNING THE CONTROL OR ANNEXATION OF HAWAII.

THE GRANT RECIPROCITY TREATY, 1874.

A reciprocity treaty was negotiated by Secretary Fish under President Grant.

THE POLITICAL CLAUSE.

The vital feature of the treaty to the United States is in Article IV, which provides that so long as the treaty exists Hawaii—

will not lease or otherwise dispose of or create any lien upon any port, harbor, or other territory * * * or grant any special privilege or right of use therein to any other government * * *

nor make any reciprocity treaty with any other government.

THE PEARL RIVER CLAUSE.

A renewal of the reciprocity treaty for seven years was concluded November 9, 1887, by President Cleveland.

The extended treaty also gives the United States—

* * * The exclusive right to enter the harbor of Pearl River, in the Island of Oahu, and to establish and maintain there a coaling and repair station for the use of vessels of the United States, and to that end the United States may improve the entrance of said harbor and do all things needful to the purpose aforesaid. (The full treaty is printed in vol. 2, Rep. Sen. Com. on For. Rel., relating to Hawaii, p. 978-9, and hereunder.)

RESOLUTION OF U. S. HOUSE OF REPRESENTATIVES.

[February 7, 1894.]

Resolved, * * * That foreign intervention in the political affairs of the (Hawaiian) Islands will not be regarded with indifference by the Government of the United States. (Cong. Record, 53d Cong., 2d sessn., p. 2001.)

RESOLUTION OF U. S. SENATE.

[May 31, 1894.]

Resolved, That * * * any intervention in the political affairs of these islands (Hawaii) by any other government will be regarded as an act unfriendly to the United States. (Cong. Record, 53d Cong., 2d sessn., p. 5499.)

REPORT OF SENATE COMMITTEE ON FOREIGN RELATIONS CONCERNING HAWAII.

The Senate Committee of Foreign Relations was, by resolution of the Senate, instructed to enquire into and report upon matters arising out of the revolution in Hawaii of January, 1893.

On February 26th, 1894, an elaborate report was filed by the chairman, Senator John T. Morgan, from which the following extracts are made:

HAWAII AN AMERICAN STATE.

Hawaii is an American State, and is embraced in the American commercial and military system.

This fact has been frequently and firmly stated by our Government, and is the ground on which is rested that peculiar and far-reaching declaration, so often and so earnestly made, that the United States will not admit the right of any foreign government to acquire any interest or control in the Hawaiian Islands that is in any way prejudicial, or even threatening, toward the interests of the United States or her people. ˝ * * (Report Sen. Com. on For. Rel. on Hawaii, vol. 1, p. 2.)

WITHIN THE SCOPE OF THE MONROE DOCTRINE.

Observing the spirit of the Monroe doctrine, the United States, in the beginning of our relations with Hawaii, made a firm and distinct declaration of the purpose to preven˙ the absorption of Hawaii or the political control of that country by any foreign power.

Without stating the reasons for this policy, which included very important commercial and military considerations, the attitude of the United States toward Hawaii was, in moral effect, that of a friendly protectorate.

It has been a settled policy of the United States that if it should turn out that Hawaii, for any cause, should not be able to maintain an independent government, that country would be encouraged in its tendency to gravitate toward political union with this country. * * * (*Ib.,* p. 20.)

Annexation is a question of long standing which has been under favorable consideration by the Kings and people of Hawaii and the Government and people of the United States for more than fifty years.

It is well understood, and its importance increases with every new event of any consequence in Hawaii, and with the falling in of every island in the Pacific Ocean that is captured by the great maritime powers of Europe. * * * (*Ib.,* p. 28.)

Senators Sherman, Frye, Dolph, and Davis, of Minnesota, added to this report the following words:

We are in entire accord with the essential findings in the exceedingly able report submitted by the chairman of the Committee on Foreign Relations. But they proceed to set forth certain points wherein they differ from him and elaborate others. In this connection they say:

The question of the rightfulness of the revolution, of the lawfulness of the means by which the deposition and abdication of the Queen were effected, and the right of the Provisional Government to exist and to continue to exist was conclusively settled, as the report so forcibly states, against the Queen and in favor of the Provisional Government, by the act of the Administration of President Harrison recogniẑing such Provisional Government; by the negotiation by that Administration with such Provisional Government of a treaty of annexation to the United States; by accrediting diplomatic representation by such Administration and by the present Administration to such Provisional Government. * * * (*Ib.*, pp. 33, 34.)

Senators Turpie and Butler, of South Carolina, added to the report the following words:

* * * I am heartily in favor of the acquisition of those islands (Hawaii) by the Government of the United States; and in the proper case and on an appropriate occasion I should earnestly advocate the same. ' # * (*Ib.*, p. 36.)

OFFICIAL ACTS OF HAWAII CONCERNING THE CONTROL OR ANNEXATION OF HAWAII TO THE UNITED STATES.

CESSION OF HAWAII TO UNITED STATES.

Kamehameha III executed and delivered to the American minister in Honolulu a provisional cession of Hawaii to the United States on March 10, 1851. (Vol. 2, Rep. Sen. Com. on For. Rel., concerning Hawaii, p. 897.)

RATIFICATION OF CESSION TO UNITED STATES.

June 21, 1851, a joint resolution was passed by the two houses of the Hawaiian Legislature, authorizing the King, in his discretion, to place the Kingdom under the protection of some foreign State. This was in confirmation of the provisional cession of the country to the United States, above quoted, which was dated the 10th of March, 1851. (Vol. 2, Rep. Sen. Com. on For. Rel., concerning Hawaiian Islands, p. 934.)

ANNEXATION TREATY NEGOTIATED.

A formal treaty annexing Hawaii to the United States was negotiated in 1854 by Kamehameha III and U. S. Minister Gregg, under the instructions of Secretary Marcy. The draft was agreed to, but the King died before the final copy was signed. (*Ib.*, pp. 932–5.)

THE RECIPROCITY TREATY.

In 1875 Hawaii made a treaty with the United States never to cede any port or territory to any other government as long as the treaty of reciprocity lasted. (The treaty is hereinafter contained.) (*Ib.*, p. 972.)

THE PEARL RIVER TREATY.

November 9, 1887, Hawaii granted to the United States the exclusive use of Pearl Harbor for a naval and repair station. (The treaty is hereinafter contained.) (*Ib.*, p. 978.)

HAWAIIAN CONSTITUTION PROVIDES FOR ANNEXATION.

The constitution of the Republic of Hawaii, adopted July 4, 1894, provides, article 32, that—

The President, with the approval of the cabinet, is hereby expressly authorized and empowered to make a treaty of political or commercial union between the Republic of Hawaii and the United States of America, subject to the ratification of the Senate. (President's message, Senate Ex. Document No. 156, p. 13, 53d Congress, 2d session.)

Hawaiian Legislature unanimously votes for annexation.

The following joint resolution was unanimously adopted by both the Senate and House of Representatives of the Legislature of the Republic of Hawaii, May 27, 1896:

Whereas it has heretofore been the announced policy both of the Provisional Government and of the Republic of Hawaii to advocate the annexation of the Hawaiian Islands to the United States of America; and

Whereas the Legislature of the Republic of Hawaii is now in regular session assembled, and will soon adjourn for a considerable period; and

Whereas it is fitting that the elected representatives of the people should place themselves on record as to the present state of feeling among themselves and their constituents on this subject;

Be it resolved by the *Senate* and the *House of Representatives*, that the Legislature of the *Republic of Hawaii* continues to be, as heretofore, firmly and steadfastly in favor of the annexation of the Hawaiian Islands to the United States of America, and in advocating such policy they feel assured that they are expressing not only their own sentiments but those of the voters of this Republic.

Approved this 27th day of May, A. D. 1896.

(Laws of the Rep. of Hawaii, 1896, p. 274.)

TREATY OF ANNEXATION OF HAWAII, NEGOTIATED IN 1854, UNDER PRESIDENT PIERCE, SECRETARY OF STATE MARCY.

His Majesty the King of the Hawaiian Islands, being convinced that plans have been, and still are, on foot hostile to his sovereignty and to the peace of his Kingdom, which His Majesty is without power to resist, and against which it is his imperative duty to provide, in order to prevent the evils of anarchy and to secure the rights and prosperity of his subjects, and having in conscientious regard thereto, as well as to the general interests of his Kingdom, present and future, sought to incorporate his Kingdom into the Union of the United States, as the means best calculated to attain these ends and perpetuate the blessings of freedom and equal rights to himself, his chiefs, and his people; and the Government of the United States, being actuated solely by the desire to add to their security and prosperity and to meet the wishes of His Majesty the King of the Hawaiian Islands, and of his Government, have determined to accomplish by treaty objects so important to their mutual and permanent welfare.

ARTICLE I.

His Majesty the King of the Hawaiian Islands, acting in conformity with the power vested in him by the constitution of his Kingdom, and with the wishes of his chiefs and people, and of the heads of every department of his Government, cedes to the United States his Kingdom with all its territories, to be held by them in full sovereignty, subject only to the same constitutional provisions as the other States of the American Union. This cession includes all public lots and squares, Government lands, mines and minerals, salt lakes and springs, fish ponds, public edifices, fortifications, barracks, forts, ports and harbors, reefs, docks, and magazines, arms, armaments and accouterments, public archives, and funds, claims, debts, taxes and dues existing, available, and unpaid at the date of the exchange of the ratifications of this treaty.

ARTICLE II.

The Kingdom of the Hawaiian Islands shall be incorporated into the American Union as a State, enjoying the same degree of sovereignty as other States, and admitted as such as it can be done in consistency with the principles and requirements of the Federal Constitution, to all the rights, privileges, and immunities of a State as aforesaid, on a perfect equality with the other States of the Union.

ARTICLE III.

His Majesty the King of the Hawaiian Islands, his chiefs and subjects of every class, shall continue in the enjoyment of all their existing personal and private rights—civil, political, and religious—to the utmost extent that is possible under the Federal Constitution, and shall possess and forever enjoy all the rights and privileges of citizens of the United States, on terms of perfect equality, in all respects, with other American citizens.

ARTICLE IV.

The decision of the board of land commissioners made and not appealed from at the date of the final ratification of this treaty shall be and remain forever valid and undisturbed, and all titles to real estate which are now or shall have then been declared valid under the laws of the Hawaiian Kingdom, shall be held to be equally valid by the United States, and measures shall be adopted by the United States for the speedy and final adjudication of all unsettled claims to land in conformity with the laws and usages under which they may have originated.

ARTICLE V.

All engagements of whatever kind affecting the rights of corporations or individuals, validly contracted and lawfully incumbent upon the King's Government or the Hawaiian Nation to pay and discharge, shall be respected and fulfilled in as prompt, full, and complete a manner as they would have been respected and fulfilled had no change of sovereignty taken place.

ARTICLE VI.

The public lands hereby ceded shall be subject to the laws regulating the public lands in other parts of the United States, liable, however, to such alterations and changes as Congress may from time to time enact. The grants of land for the promotion of education heretofore made by the Government of the King of the Hawaiian Islands shall be confirmed by the United States, which, in addition thereto, shall grant and set apart for the purposes of common schools, seminaries of learning, and universities so much of the public lands and of the proceeds thereof as may be equal proportionally to the grants for such purposes in any of the States of the Union.

ARTICLE VII.

The laws of the Hawaiian Kingdom, so far as they are compatible with republican institutions and conformable to the Constitution of the United States, shall be and remain in full force and effect until modified, changed, or repealed by the legislative authority of the State contemplated by this treaty.

ARTICLE VIII.

In consideration of the cession made by this treaty, and in compensation to all who may suffer or incur loss consequent thereon, the United States shall pay the aggregate sum of three hundred thousand dollars ($300,000) as annuities to the King, the Queen, the crown prince, those standing next in succession to the throne, the chiefs, and all other persons whom the King may wish to compensate or reward, to be apportioned as may be determined by His Majesty the King and his privy council of state, which amounts, to be apportioned as aforesaid, shall be paid ratably without deduction or offset on any ground or in any shape whatever to the parties severally named in such apportionment at Honolulu on the first day of July of each successive year so long as they may live. It is, however, expressly agreed upon that on the demise of His present Majesty the annuity of the immediate heir to the throne shall then be increased to the same amount before allowed and paid to the King himself.

As a further consideration for the cession herein made, and in order to place within the reach of the inhabitants of the Hawaiian Islands the means of education, present and future, so as to enable them the more perfectly to enjoy and discharge the rights and duties consequent upon a change from monarchical to republican institutions, the United States agree to set apart and pay over for the term of ten years the sum of seventy-five thousand dollars per annum, one-third of which shall be applied to constitute the principal of a fund for the benefit of a college or university, or colleges or universities, as the case may be, and the balance for the support of common schools, to be invested, secured, or applied as may be determined by the legislative authority of the Hawaiian Islands, when admitted as a State into the Union, as aforesaid.

ARTICLE IX.

Immediately after the exchange of the ratifications of this treaty the President of the United States shall appoint a commissioner, who shall receive in due form, in the name of the United States, the transfer of the sovereignty and territories of the Hawaiian Islands; also all public property, archives, and other things hereinbefore stipulated to be conveyed, and who shall exercise all executive authority in said islands necessary to the preservation of peace and order, and to the proper execution of the laws, until the State contemplated in this treaty can be duly organized and admitted as such State; and until the arrival of such commissioner all departments of His Majesty's Government shall continue as now constituted.

ARTICLE X.

This treaty shall be ratified by the respective high contracting parties, and the ratifications exchanged at the city of Honolulu within eight months from the date hereof, or sooner, if possible, but it is agreed that this period may be extended by mutual consent of the two parties.

In witness whereof, we, the undersigned, plenipotentiaries of His Majesty the King of the Hawaiian Islands and of the United States of America, have signed three originals of this treaty of annexation in Hawaiian and three in English, and have hereunto affixed our respective official seals.

Done at Honolulu this ―― day of ――――, in the year of our Lord one thousand eight hundred and fifty-four.

SEPARATE AND SECRET ARTICLE.

Whereas it is desirable to guard against the exigencies declared in the preamble to the foregoing treaty, and to secure the King of the Hawaiian Islands, his chiefs, and all who reside under his jurisdiction from the dangers therein referred to and expressed, it is hereby provided and expressly agreed that at any time before the final exchange of the ratifications of said treaty, if the same shall be duly ratified on the part of His Majesty the King and satisfactory notice thereof given to the commissioner of the United States, it shall be competent for His Majesty, by proclamation, to declare his islands annexed to the American Union, subject to the provisions of such treaty as negotiated; and the commissioner of the United States, for the time being, shall receive and accept the transfer of the jurisdiction of the said islands, in the name of the United States, and protect and defend them by the armed forces of the United States, as a part of the American Union, holding the same for and in behalf of his Government and exercising the jurisdiction provided for in said treaty, with the understanding, however, that in case the said treaty is not finally ratified, or other arrangement made by the free consent and to the mutual satisfaction of the contracting parties, the sovereignty of the islands shall immediately revert, without prejudice, to His Majesty, or his immediate heir, in the same condition as before the transfer thereof; and it is further understood and agreed that this article shall be as binding for all the ends and purposes herein expressed as if it formed a part of the foregoing treaty.

RECIPROCITY TREATY OF 1875.

ARTICLE I.

For and in consideration of the rights and privileges granted by His Majesty the King of the Hawaiian Islands in the next succeeding article of this convention, and as an equivalent therefor, the United States of America hereby agree to admit all the articles named in the following schedule, the same being the growth and manufacture or produce of the Hawaiian Islands, into all the ports of the United States free of duty.

(SCHEDULE.)

*

ARTICLE II.

For and in consideration of the rights and privileges granted by the United States of America in the preceding article of this convention, and as an equivalent therefor, His Majesty the King of the Hawaiian Islands hereby agrees to admit all the articles named in the following schedule, the same being the growth, manufacture, or produce of the United States of America, into all the ports of the Hawaiian Islands free of duty.

(SCHEDULE.)

*　　　　*　　　　*

ARTICLE III.

The evidence that articles proposed to be admitted into the ports of the United States of America, or the ports of the Hawaiian Islands, free of duty, under the first and second articles of this convention, are the growth, manufacture, or produce of the United States of America or of the Hawaiian Islands, respectively, shall be established under such rules and regulations and conditions for the protection of the revenue as the two Governments may from time to time respectively prescribe.

ARTICLE IV.

No export duty or charges shall be imposed in the Hawaiian Islands, or in the United States, upon any of the articles proposed to be admitted into the ports of the United States or the ports of the Hawaiian Islands free of duty under the first and second articles of this convention. *It is agreed, on the part of His Hawaiian Majesty, that so long as this treaty shall remain in force he will not lease or otherwise dispose of or create any lien upon any port, harbor, or other territory in his dominions, or grant any special privilege or rights of use therein, to any other power, state, or government, nor make any treaty by which any other nation shall obtain the same privileges, relative to the admission of any articles free of duty, hereby secured to the United States.*

ARTICLE V.

The present convention shall take effect as soon as it shall have been approved and proclaimed by His Majesty the King of the Hawaiian Islands, and shall have been ratified and duly proclaimed on the part of the Government of the United States, but not until a law to carry it into operation shall have been passed by the Congress of the United States of America. Such assent having been given, and the ratifications of the convention having been exchanged as provided in Article VI, the convention shall remain in force for seven years from the date at which it may come into operation; and further, until the expiration of twelve months after either of the high contracting parties shall give notice to the other of its wish to terminate the same, each of the high contracting parties being at liberty to give such notice to the other at the end of the said term of seven years, or at any time thereafter.

ARTICLE VI.

The present convention shall be duly ratified, and the ratifications exchanged at Washington City, within eighteen months from the date hereof, or earlier if possible.

In faith whereof the respective plenipotentiaries of the high contracting parties have signed this present convention, and have affixed thereto their respective seals.

Done in duplicate, at Washington, the thirtieth day of January, in the year of our Lord one thousand eight hundred and seventy-five.

PEARL RIVER CLAUSE.

(On the 9th of November, 1887, the reciprocity treaty was extended for seven years and the following clause added to it:)

His Majesty the King of the Hawaiian Islands grants to the Government of the United States the exclusive right to enter the harbor of Pearl River, in the Island of Oahu, and to establish and maintain there a coaling and repair station for the use of vessels of the United States, and to that end the United States may improve the entrance to said harbor and do all other things needful to the purpose aforesaid.

TREATY OF ANNEXATION OF HAWAII, NEGOTIATED IN 1893, UNDER PRESIDENT HARRISON, SECRETARY OF STATE FOSTER.

The United States of America and the Provisional Government of the Hawaiian Islands, in view of the natural dependence of those islands upon the United States, of their geographical proximity thereto, of the intimate part taken by the citizens of the United States in their implanting the seeds of Christian civilization, of the long continuance of their exclusive reciprocal commercial relations whereby their mutual interests have been developed, and the preponderant and paramount share thus acquired by the United States and the citizens in their productions, industries, and trade of the said islands, and especially in view of the desire expressed by the said Government of the Hawaiian Islands that those islands shall be incorporated into the United States as an integral part thereof and under their sovereignty, in order to provide for and assure the security and prosperity of the said islands, the high contracting parties have determined to accomplish by treaty an object so important to their mutual and permanent welfare. * * *

ARTICLE I.

The Government of the Hawaiian Islands hereby cedes, from the date of the exchange of the ratifications of this treaty, absolutely and without reserve to the United States forever all rights of sovereignty of whatsoever kind in and over the Hawaiian Islands and their dependencies, renouncing in favor of the United States every sovereign right of which as an independent nation it is now possessed; and henceforth said

Hawaiiau Islands and every island and key thereunto appertaining and each and every portion thereof shall become and be an integral part of the territory of the United States.

ARTICLE II.

The Government of the Hawaiian Islands also cedes and transfers to the United States the absolute fee and ownership of all public, government or crown lands, public buildings or edifices, ports, harbors, fortifications, military or naval equipments and all other public property of every kind and description belonging to the Government of the Hawaiian Islands, together with every right and appurtenance thereunto appertaining. The existing laws of the United States relative to public lands shall not apply to such lands in the Hawaiian Islands, but the Congress of the United States shall enact special laws for their management and disposition: *Provided,* That all revenue from or proceeds of the same except as regards such part thereof as may be used or occupied for the civil, military, or naval purposes of the United States or may be assigned to the use of the local government, shall be used solely for the benefit of the inhabitants of the Hawaiian Islands for educational and other public purposes.

ARTICLE III.

Until Congress shall otherwise provide, the existing government and laws of the Hawaiian Islands are hereby continued, subject to the paramount authority of the United States. The President, by and with the advice and consent of the Senate, shall appoint a commissioner to reside in said Islands who shall have the power to veto any act of said government, and any act disapproved by him shall thereupon be void and of no effect unless approved by the President.

Congress shall, within one year from the exchange of the ratifications of this treaty, enact the necessary legislation to extend to the Hawaiian Islands the laws of the United States respecting duties upon imports, the internal revenue, commerce and navigation; but until Congress shall otherwise provide, the existing commercial relations of the Hawaiian Islands both with the United States and foreign countries shall continue as regards the commerce of said islands with the rest of the United States and with foreign countries, but this shall not be construed as giving to said islands the power to enter into any new stipulation or agreement whatsoever or to have diplomatic intercourse with any foreign government. The consular representatives of foreign powers now resident in the Hawaiian Islands shall be permitted to continue in the exericise of their consular functions until they can receive their exequaturs from the Government of the United States.

ARTICLE IV.

The further immigration of Chinese laborers into the Hawaiian Islands is hereby prohibited until Congress shall otherwise provide. Furthermore, Chinese persons of the classes now or hereafter excluded by law from entering the United States will not be permitted to come from the Hawaiian Islands to other parts of the United States, and if so coming shall be subject to the same penalties as if entering from a foreign country.

ARTICLE V.

The public debt of the Hawaiian Islands, lawfully existing at the date of the exchange of the ratifications of this treaty, including the amounts due to depositors in the Hawaiian Postal Savings Bank, is hereby assumed by the Government of the United States; but the liability of the United States in this regard shall in no case exceed three and one quarter millions of dollars. So long, however, as the existing Government and the present commercial relations of the Hawaiian Islands are continued as hereinbefore provided, said Government shall continue to pay the interest on said debt.

ARTICLE VI.

The Government of the United States agrees to pay to Liliuokalani, the late Queen, within one year from date of the exchange of the ratification of this treaty, the sum of twenty thousand dollars, and annually thereafter a like sum of twenty thousand dollars during the term of her natural life, provided she in good faith submits to the authority of the Government of the United States and the local Government of the islands.

And the Government of the United States further agrees to pay to the Princess Kaiulani, within one year from the date of the exchange of the ratifications of this treaty, the gross sum of one hundred and fifty thousand dollars, provided she in good faith submits to the authority of the Government of the United States and the local Government of the islands.

ARTICLE VII.

The present treaty shall be ratified by the President of the United States, by and with the advice and consent of the Senate, on the one part, and by the Provisional Government of the Hawaiian Islands on the other, and the ratifications thereof shall be exchanged at Honolulu as soon as possible. Such exchange shall be made on the part of the United States by the commissioner hereinbefore provided for, and it shall operate as a complete and final conveyance to the United States of all the rights of sovereignty and property herein ceded to them. Within one month after such exchange of ratifications the Provisional Government shall furnish said commissioner with a full and complete schedule of all the public property herein ceded and transerred.

In witness whereof the respective plenipotentiaries have signed the above articles and have hereunto affixed their seals.

Done in duplicate at the city of Washington this fourteenth day of February, one thousand eight hundred and ninety-three.

TREATY OF ANNEXATION OF HAWAII, NEGOTIATED IN 1897, UNDER PRESIDENT M'KINLEY, SECRETARY OF STATE SHERMAN.

The United States and the Republic of Hawaii, in view of the natural dependence of the Hawaiian Islands upon the United States, of their geographical proximity thereto, of the preponderant share acquired by the United States and its citizens in the industries and trade of said islands, and of the expressed desire of the Government of the Republic of Hawaii that those islands should be incorporated into the United States as an integral part thereof and under its sovereignty, have determined to accomplish by treaty an object so important to their mutual and permanent welfare.

To this end the high contracting parties have conferred full powers and authority upon their respectively appointed plenipotentiaries, to wit:

The President of the United States, John Sherman, Secretary of State of the United States.

The President of the Republic of Hawaii, Francis March Hatch, Lorrin A. Thurston, and William A. Kinney.

ARTICLE I.

The Republic of Hawaii hereby cedes absolutely and without reserve to the United States of America all rights of sovereignty of whatsoever kind in and over the Hawaiian Islands and their dependencies; and it is agreed that all territory of and appertaining to the Republic of Hawaii is hereby annexed to the United States of America under the name of the Territory of Hawaii.

ARTICLE II.

The Republic of Hawaii also cedes and hereby transfers to the United States the absolute fee and ownership of all public, Government, or crown lands, public buildings, or edifices, ports, harbors, military equipments, and all other public property of every kind and description, belonging to the Government of the Hawaiian Islands, together with every right and appurtenance thereunto appertaining.

The existing laws of the United States relative to public lands shall not apply to such lands in the Hawaiian Islands, but the Congress of the United States shall enact special laws for their management and disposition: Provided, That all revenues from or proceeds of the same, except as regards such part thereof as may be used or occupied for the civil, military, or naval purposes of the United States, or may be assigned for the use of the local government, shall be used solely for the benefit of the inhabitants of the Hawaiian Islands for educational and other public purposes.

ARTICLE III.

Until Congress shall provide for the government of such islands, all the civil, judicial, and military powers exercised by the officers of the existing Government in said islands shall be vested in such person or persons and shall be exercised in such manner as the President of the United States shall direct; and the President shall have power to remove said officers and fill the vacancies so occasioned.

The existing treaties of the Hawaiian Islands with foreign nations shall forthwith cease and determine, being replaced by such treaties as may exist or as may be hereafter concluded between the United States and such foreign nations. The municipal legislation of the Hawaiian Islands, not enacted for the fulfillment of the treaties so extinguished, and not inconsistent with this treaty nor contrary to the Constitution of the United States, nor to any existing treaty of the United States, shall remain in force until the Congress of the United States shall otherwise determine.

Until legislation shall be enacted extending the United States customs laws and regulations to the Hawaiian Islands, the existing customs relations of the Hawaiian Islands with the United States and other countries shall remain unchanged.

ARTICLE IV.

The public debt of the Republic of Hawaii, lawfully existing at the date of the exchange of the ratifications of the treaty, including the amounts due to depositors in the Hawaiian Postal Savings Bank, is hereby assumed by the Government of the United States, but the liability of the United States in this regard shall in no case exceed $4,000,000. So long, however, as the existing Government and the present commercial relations of the Hawaiian Islands are continued, as hereinbefore provided, said Government shall continue to pay the interest on said debt.

ARTICLE V.

There shall be no further immigration of Chinese into the Hawaiian Islands, except upon such conditions as are now or may hereafter be allowed by the laws of the United States, and no Chinese, by reason of anything herein contained, shall be allowed to enter the United States from the Hawaiian Islands.

ARTICLE VI.

The President shall appoint five commissioners, at least two of whom shall be residents of the Hawaiian Islands, who shall, as soon as reasonable and practicable, recommend to Congress such legislation for the Territory of Hawaii as they shall deem necessary or proper.

ARTICLE VII.

This treaty shall be ratified by the President of the United States, by and with the advice and consent of the Senate, on the one part; and by the President of the Republic of Hawaii, by and with the advice and consent of the Senate, in accordance with the constitution of said Republic, on the other; and the ratifications hereof shall be exchanged at Washington as soon as possible.

In witness whereof the respective plenipotentiaries have signed the above articles and have hereunto affixed their seals.

Done in duplicate at the city of Washington, this sixteenth day of June, one thousand eight hundred and ninety-seven.

JOHN SHERMAN.	[SEAL.]
FRANCIS MARCH HATCH.	[SEAL.]
LORRIN A. THURSTON.	[SEAL.]
WILLIAM A. KINNEY.	[SEAL.]

APPENDIX 3.

IS HAWAII OF STRATEGIC VALUE TO THE UNITED STATES?—WILL ITS POSSES-
SION STRENGTHEN OR WEAKEN AMERICAN CONTROL OF THE PACIFIC?—
OPINIONS OF CAPTAIN A. T. MAHAN, U. S. N.; GEORGE W. MELVILLE, ENGINEER
IN CHIEF, U. S. N., GENERAL J. M. SCHOFIELD, T. S. A , ADMIRAL BELKNAP,
U. S. N.; ADMIRAL DUPONT, U. S. N.

THE STRATEGIC POSITION OF HAWAII

The main argument in favor of the annexation of Hawaii is that, by
reason of its strategical position, the efficient protection of the Pacific
coast and American commerce necessitates American control of Hawaii.

The reply is made to this that Hawaii has no strategical value to
the United States, and that its possession would weaken instead of
strengthen the latter country.

The main reason why Hawaii is a strategical point of value to the
United States is that the Pacific is so wide that battle ships can not
cross it from any foreign naval station to the Pacific coast without
recoaling, and there is no place to recoal except Hawaii.

Exclusion of foreign countries from Hawaii will therefore practically
protect the Pacific coast from trans-Pacific attack.

The following statements have been made by the leading experts of
the United States Army and Navy directly upon the point at issue.

They are unanimously in support of the proposition that Hawaii will
strengthen the United States, and that control of Hawaii is essential to
the safety of the Pacific coast and American commerce:

[New York Journal, February 10, 1898.]

MAHAN ON HAWAII.

ANNEXATION WILL STRENGTHEN, NOT WEAKEN, THE UNITED STATES.—
GREATER NAVY NEEDED TO PROTECT PACIFIC COAST WITHOUT
THAN WITH THE ISLANDS.

Captain Mahan's views on the importance of Hawaii as a military
and naval stronghold are given in the following correspondence, which
was read in the executive session of the Senate by Senator Teller:

QUESTIONS PUT TO MAHAN BY SENATOR KYLE.

WASHINGTON, D. C., *Feb. 3, 1898.*

Captain A. T. MAHAN, U. S. N.,
160 West Eighty-sixth Street, New York.

DEAR SIR: Recent discussions in the Senate have brought prominently to the
front the question of the strategic features of the Hawaiian Islands, and in this connection many quotations have been made from your valuable and highly interesting
contribution to literature in regard to these islands, and I am led to believe that you
are as well qualified to give information relating to them as any man in the country.

I hand you herewith a list of four questions, and I shall be greatly pleased if you
will kindly answer them. Thanking you in advance, I remain, very truly, yours,

JAMES H. KYLE.

1. Would the possession of Hawaii strengthen or weaken the United States from a military standpoint?

2. In case of war, would it take a larger navy to defend the Pacific coast with or without the possession of Hawaii?

3. Is it practicable for any trans-Pacific country to attack the Pacific coast without occupying Hawaii as a base?

4. Could such attack be made by transporting coal in colliers and transferring coal at sea?

MAHAN'S REPLY.

160 WEST 86TH STREET, *New York, Feb. 4, 1898.*

Hon. JAMES H. KYLE,
    U. S. Senate.

DEAR SIR: Your letter of the third is at hand. You appreciate, doubtless, that to give a categorical reply to questions such as you propose is very like giving a quotation apart from the context in which it stands. I shall try, however, to present such replies and their reasons as summarily as possible.

THE POSSESSION OF HAWAII WILL STRENGTHEN THE UNITED STATES.

1. From a military point of view the possession of Hawaii will strengthen the United States. Of course, as is constantly argued, every addition of territory is an additional exposed point; but Hawaii is now exposed to pass under foreign domination—notably Japan—by a peaceful process of overrunning and assimilation. This will inevitably involve its possession by a foreign power—a grave military danger to us—against which preoccupation by the United States is, in my judgment, the only security.

A LARGER NAVY NECESSARY WITHOUT THAN WITH HAWAII.

2. In replying to the second question, I must guard myself from being understood to think our present Pacific fleet great enough for probable contingencies. With this reservation a greater navy would not be needed for the defence of the Pacific coast than would be required with the islands unannexed. If we have the islands, and in the Pacific a fleet of proper force, the presence of the latter, or of an adequate detachment from it, at the Hawaiian Islands, will materially weaken, if not wholly cripple any attempted invasion of the Pacific coast (except from British Columbia), and consequently will proportionately strengthen us. With a fleet of the same size and Hawaii unoccupied by either party, the enemy would at least be in a better position to attack us; while, if he succeeded in establishing himself in any of our coast anchorages, he would be far better off. For, in the latter case, the islands would not menace his communications with home; which they would if in our possession, because Hawaii flanks the communications.

It is obvious, also, that if we do not hold the islands ourselves we can not expect the neutrals in the war to prevent the other belligerent from occupying them; nor can the inhabitants themselves prevent such occupation. The commercial value is not great enough to provoke neutral interposition. In short, in war we should need a larger navy to defend the Pacific coast, because we should have not only to defend our own coast, but to prevent, by naval force, an enemy from occupying the islands; whereas, if we had preoccupied them, fortifications could preserve them to us.

INVASION OF PACIFIC COAST IMPRACTICABLE WITHOUT HAWAII AS A BASE.

3. In my opinion, it is not practicable for any trans-Pacific country to invade our Pacific coast without occupying Hawaii as a base.

COALING AT SEA IMPRACTICABLE.

4. Coal can be transported in colliers, but as yet it can not be transshipped at sea with either rapidity or certainty. Even if it be occasionally practicable to coal at sea, the process is slow and uncertain. Reliance upon such means only is, in my judgment, impossible. A base must be had, and, except the ports of our own coast, there is none to be named alongside of Hawaii.

With much respect, I am, very truly yours,

A. T. MAHAN.

THE INCREASING NECESSITY OF HAWAIIAN ANNEXATION IN THE LIGHT OF RECENT EVENTS.

[By George W. Melville, Engineer in Chief, U S. N , in New York Tribune, February 13, 1898]

Recent events in the history of lands bordering the Pacific Ocean give added strength to the strategic reasons favoring the annexation of Hawaii, which have existed almost since the United States was a nation, and which have had full force since the conquest and purchase of California.

THE EUROPEANIZING OF CHINA.

To the westward, the acquisition by Germany of a commanding position on the Shan-Tung Promontory and the rumored desire for Hai-Nan by another government, with the occupation since 1842 of Hong-Kong by the British, point to the seemingly inevitable Europeanizing of the long littoral of China. Northward of that empire Russia marches steadily on, pushing her Siberian railway to completion, extending her already vast resources and strength at Vladivostock, wintering her fleet at Port Arthur, and apparently entering into the affairs, domestic and foreign, of the Corean Peninsula.

JAPAN THE ENGLAND OF THE EAST.

The fleet of Japan, too, has had, and still has, phenomenal growth. Japan has made Formosa her territory, and if her new rôle as the England of the East be adequately filled, other island territory may fall to her before the disturbed balance of power in the Orient shall cease to oscillate and shall settle into quiet for a time.

EUROPE FACES AMERICA ON THE WEST AS WELL AS ON THE EAST.

In place, then, of facing China, peaceful, and in war inert, with no force to dispatch far afield by sea or land, and Japan, eager, brilliant, but yet young and weak, there will presently confront the United States on its western as well as its eastern shore the Powers of Europe, with their relatively large fleets and home reserves established, not only in the far East, but in many of the nearer Pacific islands, the acquisition of which in these later years has been not a "blind grab for territory," but in pursuit of definite strategic aims. To these forces on the West there must be added also that of the new Japan, whose navy will soon surpass our own in fighting power.

MODERN WAR LIKE A THIEF IN THE NIGHT.

It is true that we are wholly at peace with these nations, and that since the United States desires no Asiatic territory, but is interested only in the full maintenance of its treaty rights with Eastern peoples, there would seem to be no probable cause for a clash. Yet modern war is sometimes like a "thief in the night," coming swiftly and without warning. Jomini, a master of strategy, has said, "No enemy is so insignificant as to be despised or neglected by any power, however formidable." A wise State should apply the same reasoning to possible foes. Again, he says, "Iron weighs at least as much as gold in the scales of military strength," an answer wholly apt to the argument of those who, calm in the consciousness of present peace, would rely upon the unsurpassed wealth of the United States and our limitless resources to meet the stress of sudden war—remembering the "gold" only, and forgetting the vital "iron" of military strength.

HAWAII BRIDGES A SEA OTHERWISE IMPASSABLE.

And so while at this time we are wholly at peace on the Pacific, and the breadth of that wide ocean lies between us and the arsenals of nations which may some time be hostile to us, yet it must be remembered that in a moment peace may fade and that *Hawaii bridges the stretch of sea which without the island group would be at this stage in the development of marine propulsion impassable to an enemy's fleet.*

PEARL HARBOR THE KEY TO WESTERN DEFENCE.

Pearl Harbor is the sole key to the full defence of our Western shore, and that key should lie in our grasp only. Again, the sudden and wholly unforeshadowed development of Alaska, which the gold discoveries of the Klondike probably presage, adds a new element of commanding importance to the problem of Pacific defence—supremacy, if you will. It seems not unlikely that this territory will repeat the history of California—first, the wild rush for gold; then abnormal growth in tributary industries; then a wholesale and rapid expansion on natural lines.

THE RESOURCES OF ALASKA.

It is true that Alaska has not the sunny vineyards, the teeming fruit gardens, and the broad and fertile fields of California, but of its resources which are known it may be said that in addition to its possibilities, nay surety, of much gold it holds the world's greatest reserve of timber, its lands are full of coal, it has the finest grazing lands for cattle, and its fisheries are unsurpassed.

Disregarding, however, the uncertainties of future development, let us consider solely the necessities, now plainly apparent, of the gold seeker. While a multitude of the latter seem to be preparing for the new Eldorado, many must fail to find it owing to the lack, for the time at least, of transportation facilities. The problem of the carriage of even a fraction of the waiting throng over the miles of sea and river to the Klondike is one involving for the present the gravest difficulties. The distance from Seattle to St. Michaels is 2,500 miles by sea, and after the latter port is reached there are still 2,500 miles of the Yukon to traverse by river steamers, which as yet do not exist.

IMMEDIATE NECESSITIES OF ALASKAN COMMERCE.

With each Alaskan emigrant from Seattle there must go a ton of supplies for clothing and sustenance, a ton of fuel for his warmth during one winter, and a considerable weight of lumber for his housing. To these there must be added materials of construction for the great number of small and light-draft Yukon steamers yet to be transported in sections to and erected upon the banks of that river, and the fuel for the use of this river fleet, which will average not less than two tons for each gold miner and his baggage, stores, lumber, etc. According to a conservative estimate, embracing all of the items noted above, to transport fifty thousand men, with the necessary stores, fuel, and materials, will require an ocean service giving at least one arrival per day at St.

Michaels of large steamers from Seattle during the five months of available summer weather.

One arrival a day means, as well, an average of one departure a day. At fifteen knots' speed steamers will cover the distance of twenty-five hundred miles between the two ports in seven days. Admitting the premises, as above, there will then be always en route during the time noted fourteen large steamers, or their equivalent in a greater number of smaller and slower vessels, steam or sail—those outward bound carrying stores, without which the Yukon settlers will perish and our interests there be destroyed; those returning freighted, it is hoped, like the galleons of old Spain, with much treasure, wrested by herculean toil from a frozen and unyielding soil.

ALASKAN COMMERCE EXPOSED TO HOSTILE FLEETS.

In the event of conflict between the United States and a maritime power this throng of richly laden but helpless vessels will present to the enemy a noble field for attack by the "guerre de course," that "commerce destroying" which first formed a factor of naval war during the reign of Elizabeth of England, which was followed with such deadly effect by the Alabama and her consorts, and which has at this time many strong advocates, notably in the United States and France.

HAWAII COMMANDS ALASKAN ROUTE.

Now, Hawaii commands fully this ocean route, at a distance from it of less than twenty-five hundred miles—not five days' steaming for the cruiser Columbia—and in that flanking position which will give a naval force using it as a base such immense power to harass and destroy.

The Klondike is Canada's; soon she will doubtless lay down railways reaching its limits. Great Britain will then have, not only for the gold lands but for all Alaska, the surpassing strategic advantages of "inner lines" on which to operate in the event of war.

ALASKA AN OVER-SEA PROVINCE.

Alaska is, for us, practically an over-sea province. Our sole means of communication with it would appear now, at least, to be an ocean route. Shall we hazard the safety of Seward's imperial territory for this and for all time by refusing Hawaii, the ocean fortress, which in our hands, with an adequate naval force, would make our Alaskan lines of transit unassailable by any foe?

WHY HAWAII IS A STRATEGIC POINT AND MADEIRA NOT.

Hawaii's unique advantages as a strategic point of prime importance have been set forth so ably and so often as to forbid their citation here. One or two objections raised by not a few nontechnical critics may, however, be considered.

Pearl Harbor is twenty-one hundred miles from our western coast, and Madeira is about the same distance from our eastern shore. The latter has little, if any, military value. Why, then, should Hawaii, parted by the same stretch of sea, exceed it in importance?

PACIFIC SO BROAD WARSHIPS MUST RECOAL AT HAWAII.

The critics forget that the paramount worth of the Hawaiian group in war will lie, first, in the fact that the Pacific is so broad that its passage will exhaust the coal supply of a war vessel, making necessary a renewal at Honolulu; and, second, in the isolation of the group, with the absence of other land between it and our coast. If the Pacific were as narrow as the Atlantic, or if other islands intervened—as with Madeira—between our western shore and Hawaii, the strategic value of the latter would be largely reduced.

PEARL HARBOR IMPREGNABLE.

Again, it has been urged that if we shall take the group we shall but acquire territory to defend—an element not of strength but of weakness in war, and one which will make necessary large additions to our fleet. Pearl Harbor can be made an impregnable ocean fortress. It is true that one does not wage war with fortresses. It is also true, however, that they form vantage points from which a force may sally and under whose wing that force may supply and recruit for fresh attack.

If Hawaii in naval conflict shall have no useful function in this, then it would seem that, through the wars of all time, the eager strife for the possession of fortresses, of guarded ports, of frontier outposts, has been false strategy, an error militarily.

ENEMY ATTACKING WESTERN COAST MUST FIRST CONTROL HAWAII.

As to the dread of the economist or of the altrurian, that annexation will require largely augmented naval strength, it may be said that if an adequate force of the United States be stationed at Hawaii, and its coast communications be properly guarded, an enemy from over sea would violate some of the cardinal principles of naval strategy and invite sure disaster in attacking our western shores without first blockading or defeating the Hawaiian squadron. The force of Pearl Harbor should then form simply but the first line of defense. Then the seagoing ships "fit to lie in a line," with their torpedo auxiliaries, should be gathered to meet the first assault, leaving the coast guard to the reserve of torpedo craft and monitors stationed at fortified ports. The strength of the squadron at this mid-Pacific outpost should be, doubtless, sufficient to meet the enemy, but the force on the coast could be reduced.

OCEAN DISTANCES SHOULD BE MEASURED IN TIME, NOT MILES.

Some misconception as to Hawaii's value in war seems to rise through a lack of appreciation of what steam has done in the reduction of ocean distances, measuring the latter in the time spent in traversing them. A clearer view may be obtained, perhaps, by referring this time to land travel. Admiral Colomb speaks of "the sea considered as territory over which military forces march." Let us extend this expression somewhat and assume the ocean to be not a neutral plain, but a "No Man's Land," on which armies may manœuvre.

NAPOLEON'S SYSTEM OF WAR.

Napoleon gave his system of conducting a war as: "To march twenty-five miles a day, to fight, and then to camp in quiet."

At fifteen knots' speed, a fleet could steam from Pearl Harbor to San Francisco is less than six days. The Emperor, in that time, would have marched his army one hundred and fifty miles.

MEASURED BY NAPOLEON'S MARCHING SPEED, HAWAII ONLY 150 MILES FROM SAN FRANCISCO.

If, then, we assume the sea to be a great land plain, we must locate Pearl Harbor on that plain at about one hundred and fifty miles from San Francisco, and, to complete the parallel, must make it practically impregnable and capable of sheltering one hundred thousand men. From this point of view Hawaii's remoteness would seem to be apparent rather than real.

ANNEXATION WILL SECURE WESTERN SHORE AND PACIFIC COMMERCE.

In the wars which gave our Government birth and which have attended great crises in its history, thousands spent life itself that a nation might be formed and preserved for those who were to follow them. The men of this generation have added not a few stars to the blue field of our flag. As captains of industry or as toilers in its ranks, they have so developed the resources of our wide land that after the wants of the greatest home market in the world are filled there remains of our products a surplus which, in ever-increasing variety and quantity, forces its way into foreign marts. Shall not we, too, serve the greater Republic that is to come, and in accepting the gift of the Hawaiian group, not only make secure our western shore, but give the coming generations a firm grasp on the vast—but for us almost untouched—trade of Pacific shores and islands?

GEORGE W. MELVILLE,
Engineer in Chief, U. S. N.

HAWAIIAN ANNEXATION A PUBLIC NECESSITY.

[By General Schofield.]

ST. AUGUSTINE, FLA., *Jan. 12, '98.*

Hon. JOHN T. MORGAN,
United States Senate, Washington, D. C.

MY DEAR SENATOR: In compliance with the request contained in your letter of January 9, I do not hesitate to write you without reserve in respect to my views upon the pending question of annexation of the Hawaiian Islands.

FOR TWENTY-FIVE YEARS REGARDED ANNEXATION AS A PUBLIC NECESSITY.

From the time, twenty-five years ago, when I made a personal examination for the purpose of ascertaining the value of those islands to this country for military and naval purposes, I have always regarded ultimate annexation of the islands to this country as a public necessity. But the time when this should be accomplished had to depend on natural political development. In the meantime our national interests should be secured by the exclusive right to occupy, improve, and fortify Pearl River Harbor, so as to insure our possession of that harbor in time of war.

PEARL HARBOR MUST BE HELD AT ANY COST.

To illustrate my views on this subject, I have likened that harbor to a commanding position in front of a defensive line which an army in the field is compelled to occupy. The army must occupy that advanced position and hold it at whatever cost, or else the enemy will occupy it with his artillery and thus dominate the main line. If we do not occupy and fortify Pearl River harbor, our enemy will occupy it as a base from which to conduct operations against our Pacific coast and the Isthmean canal, which must, of course, in due time be constructed and controlled by this country. The possession of such a base at a convenient distance from our Pacific coast would be a great temptation to an unfriendly nation to undertake hostile operations against us.

PEARL HARBOR CAN BE DEFENDED WITHOUT A NAVY.

One of the greatest advantages of Pearl River harbor to us consists in the fact that no navy would be required to defend it. It is a deep, landlocked arm of the sea, easily defended by fortifications placed near its mouth, with its anchorage beyond the reach of guns from the ocean.

Cruisers or other war ships which might be overpowered at sea, as well as merchant vessels, would find there, behind the land defenses, absolute security against a naval attack. A moderate garrison of regular troops, with the militia of the island, would give sufficient protection against any landing parties from a hostile fleet. Of course an army on transports, supported by a powerful fleet, could land and capture the place. But that would be an expensive operation; one much less likely to be undertaken than the occupation of an undefended harbor, as a necessary preliminary to an attack on our coast or upon our commerce.

GREATEST NECESSITY IS TO KEEP OTHER NATIONS OUT.

The value of such a place of refuge and of supplies for our merchant marine and our cruisers in time of war can hardly be overestimated, yet the greatest value to us of that wonderful harbor consists in the fact that its position and adequate defense by us prevents the possibility of an enemy using it against us.

So far as I know, the leading statesmen, no less than the military and naval authorities, of this country have always been in accord on this subject.

TIME HAS COME TO CARRY TRADITIONAL POLICY INTO EFFECT.

While it has not been proposed to interfere with the continued occupation by foreign nations of their military strongholds in this hemisphere, it has been publicly and emphatically declared that none of those strongholds should ever be allowed to pass into the possession of any other nation whose interests might be antagonistic to ours.

Now, for the first time, the occasion has arisen to carry into effect our long-declared national policy.

HAWAII CAN NOT STAND ALONE—PROTECTORATE WOULD LEAD TO DISASTER.

A little State like Hawaii can not stand alone among the great nations, all of whom covet her incomparable harbor. She must have the protection of this country or of some other great nation. But *a protectorate without sovereignty is the last thing this country could afford to assume.*

In the absence of authority to regulate and control the intercourse between the islands and other countries, controversies must arise which would lead to war or to the loss of our invaluable military possession in the islands.

No halfway measures will suffice. We must accept the islands and hold and govern them or else let some other great nation do it.

FAILURE TO ANNEX, A BLUNDER WORSE THAN A CRIME.

To fail now to carry into effect our own great national policy upon the first occasion offered to us would, in my judgment, be one of those blunders which are worse than crimes.

DUTY TO AMERICAN RESIDENTS OF HAWAII.

To my mind, what may be regarded, perhaps, as the sentimental aspect of the question is entitled to consideration.

A colony of intelligent, virtuous, and patriotic Americans have rescued a country from barbarism and raised it to a high state of civilization and prosperity, until in the natural course of events the government of that country has fallen entirely into their hands. They now ask the privilege of adding that country to their own native land; of returning with their new possessions to the parental fold. Can they be turned away to seek a home among strangers? Not without violating one of the most sacred laws of nature and incurring the penalty which must, sooner or later, necessarily follow.

I am, dear Senator, with great respect, sincerely, yours,

J. M. SCHOFIELD.

ADMIRAL BELKNAP ON ANNEXATION.

[Boston Herald, January 31, 1893]

OVERTHROW OF MONARCHY EXPECTED.

The revolution in the Hawaiian Islands, resulting in the deposition of the Queen and the establishment of a provisional government, is an event not unexpected to diplomatic, naval, and consular officers who have had any acquaintance or familiarity with the course of affairs in that island Kingdom for the past twenty years.

ANNEXATION OF MOMENTOUS INTEREST AND VITAL IMPORTANCE.

To the people of the United States the present situation is of momentous interest and of vital importance. Indeed, it would seem that nature had established that group to be ultimately occupied as an outpost, as it were, of the great Republic on its western border, and that the time had now come for the fulfillment of such design.

A glance at a chart of the Pacific will indicate to the most casual observer the great importance and inestimable value of those islands as a strategic point and commercial center. Situated in mid-north Pacific, the group looks out on every hand toward grand opportunities of trade, political aggrandizement, and polyglot intercourse. * * *

The group now seeks annexation to the United States; the consummation of such wish would inure to the benefit of both peoples commercially and politically. Annex the islands, constitute them a Territory, and reciprocal trade will double within ten years. Let the islanders feel that they are once and forever under the folds of the American flag as part and parcel of the great Republic, and a development will take place in the group that will at once surprise its people and the world.

FAILURE TO ANNEX WOULD BE FOLLY.

Not to take the fruit within our grasp and annex the group now begging us to take it in would be folly indeed—a mistake of the gravest character, both for the statesmen of the day and for the men among us of high commercial aims and great enterprises.

Our statesmen should act in this matter in the spirit and resolve that secured to us the vast Louisiana purchase, the annexation of Texas, and the acquisition of California. The Administration that secures to the United States the "coign of vantage" in the possession of those beautiful islands will score a great measure of beneficent achievement to the credit side of its account. * * *

SHOULD ANNEX EVEN AT HAZARD OF WAR.

We want no joint protectorate, no occupation there by any European power, no Pacific Egypt. We need the group as part and parcel of the United States, and should take what is offered us, even at the hazard of war.

Westward the star of empire takes its way. Let the Monroe doctrine stay not its hand until it holds Hawaii securely within its grasp.

In this matter the undersigned speaks from personal knowledge, gained through official visits to the islands in 1874 and 1882. * * *

ADMIRAL DUPONT ON THE COAST DEFENSES OF THE UNITED STATES.

In 1851 Congress, by formal resolution, requested the Navy and War Departments to make a report upon the condition and requirements of the coast defenses of the United States. Embodied in the report of the Navy Department is a report from Admiral Dupont, in which he uses the following language:

The position of Halifax, Bermuda, and the West Indies must ever be borne in mind where fleets may wait for a fitting opportunity for incursions. To suppose that there is to be no such thing as a surprise because railroads have been invented and hollow shot cast seems to be taking for granted that human life has changed. Those who indulge in such theoretical securities are preparing themselves for surprises—perilous ones, too. * * *

In the Pacific we already have outposts on our flanks in the hands of first-class powers. * * *

It is impossible to estimate too highly the value and importance of the Sandwich Islands, whether in a commercial or military point of view. Should circumstances ever place them in our hands they would prove the most important acquisition we could make in the whole Pacific Ocean—an acquisition intimately connected with our commercial and naval supremacy in those seas.

APPENDIX 4.

ASSETS.

Summary of inventory and estimated value of property belonging to the Hawaiian Government, as of date September 30, 1897.

JUDICIARY DEPARTMENT.

Furniture, law library, etc.. \$25,000 00

DEPARTMENT FOREIGN AFFAIRS.

Furniture and articles in care of Bishop Museum............................	\$26,500.00	
Military arms and equipments, artillery stores and utensils..................	54,300.00	
		80,800 00

INTERIOR DEPARTMENT.

Furniture, executive building, council hall, etc................................ 11,250 00

Registry of conveyances.

Records and indexes.. 65,000.00

Interior Department, Land Office.

Furniture, records, maps, etc... 166,190.00

Government survey.

Office furniture, maps, records, instruments, etc........................... 260,000.00

Office public lands.

Office furniture, plans, maps, etc..	2,350.00
Government buildings...	940,350.00
Electric lights, dredging, and pile-driving plants.......................	100,850.00
Wharf building, tools and equipment, material, etc.......................	14,000.00
Steam tug *Eleu*...	25,000.00
Wharves and landings..	285,700.00
Buoys..	3,350.00
Marine railway..	50,000.00
Battery, sea wall, etc...	40,000.00
Light-houses..	15,450.00
Bridges...	126,800.00
Sundry material and equipments, other districts.........................	12,700.00

Bureau waterworks.

Value waterworks on net income of \$30,000 (6 per cent)...................	500,000.00
Waterworks, other islands...	26,800.00

Insane asylum.

Sundry property, furniture, crops, live stock, etc 5,000.00

Roads, Honolulu.

Stock, material, equipment, etc..	17,100.00
Stock, district road boards...	12,000.00

Road taxes.

On special deposit.. 54,256.00

Honolulu fire department.

General equipment...	40,000.00
Hilo general equipment..	8,000.00

Sundries

Furniture, crockery, glassware, carriages, harness, etc , in executive building
    stables; jewels and plate in treasury vault, etc $8,766.00
                                                                                                    $2,796,912.00

Board of health.

Office furniture, Lahaina lot, medicines, etc 2,420.00
Buildings, carts, horses, tools, etc.. 4,600.00

Hospitals

Buildings, furniture, medicines, etc 12,000.00
Quarantine stations, buildings, fumigating and electric-light plants 17,500.00
Receiving stations... 7,800.00

Molokai settlement.

Buildings, warehouses, pipe lines, waterworks, live stock, etc................. 77,000.00
                                                                                                    121,320.00

                                                                                                    3,024,032.00

Finance department.

Office furniture and fittings 4,500.00
Stamps (invoice value) 1,500.00
Cash on hand.. 123,149.00
Special deposit.. 21,696.00
Office furniture, auditor's and tax assessor's office............................ 1,300.00

Customs bureau.

Furniture and appurtenances... 3,250.00

Postal Bureau.

Furniture, stamps in stock, stamp dies, etc 34,634.00
Money-order department, capital... 14,611.00
                                                                                                    206,640.00

ATTORNEY-GENERAL'S DEPARTMENT.

Furniture, law library, police arms and equipments, etc........................... 12,500.00

Board of education.

Office furniture $700.00
School books and supplies... 7,500.00
School funds, special deposit... 35,939.00
School lands, buildings, etc.. 272,800.00
                                                                                                    316,989.00

                                                                                                    3,560,161.00

GOVERNMENT LANDS.

Island.	Coffee.	Cane.	Rice.	Grazing.	Forest, etc.	Estimated value.
	Acres.	*Acres.*	*Acres.*	*Acres.*	*Acres.*	
Hawaii	62,890	18,156	140	368,349	749,302	$1,874,900
Maui	8,180	520	110	112,570	58,550	453,800
Oahu	800	2,050	327	71,414	13,778	983,500
Kauai	4,400	4,900	400	80,050	86,650	648,000
Molokai	....	....	....	40,625	....	75,500
Lanai and Kahoolawe ...	....	....	....	77,669	....	70,000
Laysan, etc., Islands	....	....	....	....	....	40,000
Total	76,270	25,626	977	751,177	908,280	....	4,147,700.00

Building lots, Honolulu 521,800
Building lots, Town Hilo.. 160,000

Esplanade and city front.

Leased lots (including esplanade, storage), rent, $27,000 per annum............ 450,000
Old lots, unleased, including fish market, custom-house site, etc................ 250,000
New lots (reclaimed land) 100,000
                                                                                                    1,481,800.00

    Grand total.. 9,189,661.00

The total area of the Government lands may be roughly classified as follows:

	Acres.
Valuable building lots	145
Cane lands	25, 626
Rice lands	977
Coffee lands	76, 270
Homesteads—Government interest in	20, 000
Grazing lands of various quality	451, 200
Forest lands (high)	681, 282
Rugged, inaccessible mountain tracts	227, 000
Barren lands, nominal value	300, 000
	1, 782, 500

NOTE.—The above classification of Government lands is necessarily somewhat arbitrary, and the statement in my report of 1894 to the surveyor-general applies also at this date, "that the lack of positive knowledge of quality and adaptability of the soil in untried sections, and the imperceptible gradation by which the best land merges into indifferent and indifferent into that of nominal value, makes a report of this nature to a considerable extent a matter of personal opinion rather than of scientific certainty."

I would further state that under the head of grazing lands and high forest land is included a large area which, in the future, may be devoted to a class of temperate-climate products, grain, fruits, etc., which area is now practically undeveloped.

The estimate of values of Government lands has been made independently of the leases and rents received from same. In the case of recent leases these rents are fairly representative of the value of the land, but in many of the older leases are much below the present standard of value.

J. F. BROWN,
Agent of Public Lands in Hawaii.

October 17, 1897.

APPENDIX 5.

BEET SUGAR.

The following letter from Mr. James T. Taylor, of Pecos, New Mexico, a member of the American Society of Civil Engineers, and chief engineer of the Pecos Irrigation and Improvement Company, on whose estate the Pecos beet sugar factory is located, gives the following opinion:

LETTER FROM MR. JAMES T. TAYLOR.

DEAR SIR: From personal observation of the beet-sugar industry both in California and New Mexico, extending over a period of several years, I do not believe that annexation will have any injurious effect upon the beet-sugar industry of the United States; and in support of that view I cite the following facts as they exist to-day:

I know from personal knowledge the climatic conditions of the Hawaiian Islands, and the general nature of their soil and products. There is approximately only 80,000 acres of cane land under cultivation, which, under the most favorable circumstances, produce, say, an average of a little over 200,000 tons of sugar annually. The present is practically the limit of area naturally available for the successful growth of sugar cane.

The entire annual crop of sugar exported from the islands is only approximately 10 per cent of the annual amount of sugar consumed in the United States, which amount is mainly imported from foreign countries, and has for the past few years averaged more than two million tons of sugar per annum; consequently the price of Hawaiian sugar can not affect the price of beet sugar of the United States, as the market price of such staples is fixed at the great commercial centers of the world, namely, London and New York.

The consumption of sugar in the United States is rapidly increasing with the settlement and development of our country, so that in the near future the Hawaiian sugar crop will be a still smaller percentage of the annual sugar output of the world.

Of the total amount of sugar consumed annually in the United States only approximately 16 per cent was produced on American soil for the year 1897, making 84 per cent the approximate amount of importations, coming principally from Europe and the East, West, and British Indies.

To produce the amount of sugar now imported from foreign countries (other than Hawaii) would require at least (500) *five hundred beet-sugar factories having an average daily capacity of* (500) five hundred tons of beets, each factory utilizing the product of 3,300 acres of sugar beets.

The five hundred factories would utilize the product of 1,650,000 acres of beets, based on an average of ten tons of sugar beets per acre, or

16,500,000 tons of beets, valued at $58,000,000, as the average price paid to the farmer for beets is four dollars per ton.

The production and handling of this quantity of beets would directly and indirectly give employment to more than a million of people.

The only conclusion that can be drawn is that danger from competition by reason of reduction in the price or overproduction of sugar by the Hawaii sugar planters can not be considered a valid objection to annexation from the standpoint of a sugar-beet grower.

The sugar-beet farmer of the United States stands on a very favorable basis for the production of sugar, as the crop is planted and harvested generally during a period of six to seven months.

Good beet land with water is obtained in the Pecos Valley, New Mexico, at a rental of two dollars per acre per annum. The only other location where beets are grown by irrigation is at Lehi, Utah.

The Hawaiian sugar planter requires sixteen to eighteen months to produce a cane crop, and then only by heavy irrigation. The climatic conditions and nature of the soil require the frequent application of water in generous quantities.

The duty of water is very low and the value correspondingly high, as the irrigation of cane requires at least one cubic foot per second for fifty acres or less, this being in excess of the requirements of the lands of the arid West of America.

The Eddy Sugar Factory, constructed by the Pecos Valley Beet Sugar Company, is the first factory to be erected in the great Southwest and the sixth to be erected in the United States.

The sugar content of the beet root grown in the Pecos Valley exceeds that of all other countries.

The factory has a rated capacity of 200 tons in 24 hours and employs from 75 to 100 men during the campaign.

The results of the past two seasons clearly demonstrate that a first quality of sugar can be produced in the Pecos Valley and that the annexation of Hawaii can not in any way affect the sugar industry of this country.

   Yours, respectfully,   JAMES T. TAYLOR,
                M. A. M. Soc. C. E.

EDDY, NEW MEXICO.

APPENDIX 6.

[From Commercial America, New York, January 7, 1898.]

TRADE WITH HAWAII—COMMERCIAL ARGUMENTS IN FAVOR OF THE POLICY OF ANNEXATION—BUYERS OF AMERICAN GOODS—SEVENTEEN NATIONS WITH WHICH WE TRANSACT LESS BUSINESS—PATRONS OF AMERICAN VESSELS—SUGAR INTERESTS WILL NOT BE INJURED—DANGER TO BE AVOIDED.

Hawaiian annexation should be broadly studied from its commercial standpoint, but this rather seems to be lost sight of in all political discussions. American commercial interests are paramount in the Hawaaiin group. Fully 75 per cent of the business transacted there is in the hands of Americans and fully 75 per cent of the sugar plantations are owned by Americans. Is it good public policy to ignore or to imperil American commercial interests, even though they be situated in a foreign country? Is it not our duty to protect them and endeavor to augment them?

American farms and factories need every available outlet for their products. So rapidly have our industrial and agricultural interests expanded that we need trade in foreign countries in order to be able to dispose of our surplus supplies. And there is no better market for American goods than in the Hawaiian group. Though the bulk of this trade is transacted from the Pacific coast, that is no reason why Eastern merchants and Eastern shippers should ignore its importance. Large quantities of the goods shipped there are supplied from Eastern mills and factories. If these goods, whether from farm or factory, were not sold in Hawaii, they would add to the surplus in our own country, tending to a further cheapening of values in lines that can hardly bear any further strain of cut rates.

The goods we sell to Hawaii comprise almost every article that is seen in our own markets, possibly with the sole exception of heavy winter clothing. The Hawaiians are very free and liberal buyers—none more so in the world for American products. They get practically everything that they eat, wear, and consume from the United States. Their business is our business. Their merchants are nearly all our own kinsmen, and, from a commercial standpoint, we should encourage, protect, and strengthen the ties that bind us together.

Under annexation this liberal channel of business would be largely expanded, because there would be a strong tide of immigration toward these islands of the Pacific, and their present population of some 90,000 souls would be largely increased. There is no reason whatever why a portion of the trade with Hawaii that is now transacted by the merchants of the West should not be diverted to the East. Even if this be not done, there should be sufficient patriotism in the East to enable us to gladly witness a growth of trade in the West which must, directly or indirectly, aid other sections of the United States. An idea of the importance of this trade can be gathered from the following statement of facts:

EXTENT OF OUR HAWAIIAN TRADE.

In the fiscal year ending June 30, 1897, the aggregate trade between the Hawaiian Islands and the United States reached $18,385,000.

This is greater than our total trade with Argentina, which amounted to $17,157,000 in the same year.

It was greater than our total trade with Central America, which amounted to $16,464,000 last year.

It was greater than our total trade with Spain, which amounted only to $14,600,000.

It was greater than our total trade with Switzerland, which amounted only to $13,950,000.

It was greater than our total trade with Venezuela, which amounted only to $12,960,000.

It was greater than our total trade with Austria, which amounted only to $12,200,000.

It was greater than our total trade with Russia, which amounted only to $10,700,000.

It was greater than our total trade with Denmark, which amounted only to $10,500,000.

It was greater than our total trade with Colombia, which amounted only to $8,540,000.

It was greater than our total trade with Norway and Sweden, which amounted only to $7,963,000.

It was greater than our total trade with the Guianas, which only amounted to $6,770,000.

It was greater than our total trade with Chile, which only amounted to $6,370,000.

It was greater than our total trade with Uruguay, which only amounted to $4,729,000.

It was nearly four times greater than our total trade with Portugal, which amounted only to $4,750,000.

It was nearly seven times greater than our total trade with Turkey, which only amounted to $2,821,000.

It was ten times greater than our total trade with Peru, which only amounted to $1,830,000.

It was more than twenty times greater than our total trade with Greece, which only amounted to $850,000 in the last fiscal year.

Here are seventeen countries with which we are constantly transacting business, and yet not one of them is nearly as valuable to us as the Hawaiian Islands. And, what is more, if any commercial interest were threatened in any one of these seventeen countries, there would be an immediate outcry against a disturbance in that trade.

We do 40 per cent more business with Hawaii than with Greece, Portugal, Turkey, Peru, and Uruguay combined.

We do more business with Hawaii than with Sweden, Norway, and Chile combined.

We do more business with Hawaii than with Russia and the three Guianas combined.

Yet in face of these solid facts there are people who would turn the Hawaiian market over to some foreign country!

FROM ANOTHER VIEWPOINT.

Now, glance at the importance of the Hawaiian trade from another standpoint—that of a basis of per capita consumption.

The Hawaiian people buy American products from us at the rate of $53.35 for every inhabitant on the islands.

Our immediate neighbor, Canada, buys our goods only at the rate of $14 per capita of her population.

Our other contiguous neighbor, Mexico, buys from us at the rate of but $1.95 per capita of her population.

The entire Australian continent buys from us only at the rate of $3.67 per capita of its population.

The whole of Europe buys only at the rate of $2.12 per capita of its population.

South America buys from us only on a 90 cents per capita basis.

The continent of Africa buys from us only on a 13 cents per capita basis.

Asia seeks our markets only to the extent of 4 cents per head of her population.

The United Kingdom, popularly supposed to be our best customer, buys from us only what she can not get elsewhere, and on a basis of $13.42 per capita of her population, as compared with the purchases made by the Hawaiians on a basis of $53.35 per capita of their population.

How is this trade conducted? is naturally the next question that arises.

Of America's total commerce with foreign countries, but 11.03 per cent was conducted last year in American ships. Of our total trade with North America, 48.38 per cent was in American ships. Of our trade with Australia, 23.41 per cent was in American ships. Of our trade with South America, 20.77 per cent was carried in American ships. Of our trade with Asia, 13.43 per cent was carried in American ships. Of our trade with Africa, 11.77 per cent was carried in American ships. Of our total trade with Europe, only 3.96 per cent was carried under the American flag. But it remained for Hawaii to transact no less than 80.72 per cent of its business with the United States under the Stars and Stripes.

The Hawaiians patronize our farms, our factories, and our shipyards. They give the preference to the United States in every commercial transaction. There should be no question about fostering and encouraging this friendly business sentiment and taking it under our own protection.

THE SUGAR QUESTION.

One objection made to the acquisition of the Hawaiian Islands as part of American territory is that it will interfere with the production of sugar in the United States. For nearly a quarter of a century Hawaiian sugar has practically had a free market in this country and the American sugar industry has grown in spite of it. Hawaii has reached its limit of sugar production. All the lands there available for this crop are now under cultivation, but it has large possibilities for coffee culture.

The total sugar crops of the world for 1897–98, as given by Willett & Gray, are 7,849,847 tons. The total crop of Hawaii is given by the same authority as 275,000 tons. Yet it is claimed that the little Hawaiian crop, constituting but 3½ per cent of the whole, will affect the market price of sugar to the injury of American producers.

The United States already produces more sugar than Hawaii—321,317 tons, as compared with the islands' crop of 275,000 tons. Under normal conditions Cuba gives a million tons of sugar a year, yet there is a very general sentiment in favor of the annexation of Cuba, and not a word is said about the possibility of its injury to the American sugar interests. We are, next to England, the largest consumers of sugar in in the world, using 64½ pounds per annum per capita of our population. Our total consumption last year was 2,096,263 long tons, of which 336,656 tons were produced in the United States, while 1,066,684 tons of cane sugar and 616,635 tons of beet sugar came from foreign countries. We must buy sugar from abroad, so why not buy the sugar that is grown by those Americans who are the largest buyers in the world of our products?

There is one more commercial argument in favor of the annexation of the Hawaiian Islands that has never yet been referred to in the press or in Congress. It is this:

If the Hawaiian Islands are unable to maintain a responsible form of government, and events during the last fifteen years have certainly shown this to be the case, why should the United States refuse its protection to this American colony and permit its annexation by some foreign country?

What would the acquisition of Hawaii by England, by Germany, or by Japan mean?

It would simply mean this: Within 2,000 miles of our Pacific coast the only available territory in the Pacific Ocean would be transformed into a huge manufacturing depot, supplied with European capital, worked by Asiatic labor, for the supreme control of the trade of every country bordering upon the Pacific, whether in North or South America, in Asia or in Australia.

Can we, as a large manufacturing nation, for one moment permit the possibility of such an occurrence? We have excluded the Chinese from our own shores because of their industrial competition with American labor. Shall we now throw our gates wide open to the labor of the Orient in the shape of goods that would surely be made in Hawaii by Chinese or Japanese labor just as soon as we refused to take those islands under our protection, and afforded an opportunity to some foreign nation to seize them and establish there a commercial policy that would give to that nation the trading supremacy of the world, for which there exists to day such a bitter strife?

These are commercial arguments submitted on behalf of that American commerce for Greater America which Commercial America represents.

APPENDIX 7.

NAVY DEPARTMENT,
Washington, March 7, 1898.

SIR: I have to acknowledge the receipt of your letter of March 3, and in reply to inform you that a vessel has been in Hawaiian waters practically continuously since 1887. The *Vandalia* arrived there August 27, 1887, and remained until the following year, when she was relieved by the *Alert*, which vessel was relieved in 1890 by the *Mohican*. The *Mohican* left in 1891, having been replaced by the *Iroquois, Charleston,* and *Marion.* For a period of about two months of this year the islands were left without a United States man-of-war. The *San Francisco*, which visited those waters early in 1892, was relieved by the *Boston* August 24, the latter vessel remaining until September 15, 1893, at which time the *Philadelphia* took her place, leaving the islands August 12, 1894. The *Charleston* then went to the islands, but for about three months of the latter part of this year they were without a man-of-war. The *Philadelphia* returned in January, 1895, and was relieved by the *Bennington* in June of the same year, the latter being relieved by the *Marion* and the *Adams* March 5, 1896, these vessels remaining the balance of that year. During 1897 the *Marion, Philadelphia,* and *Adams* were there, the *Baltimore* also joining them in October. In addition, many other vessels have been in these waters for short periods.

Very respectfully,

JOHN D. LONG, *Secretary.*

Hon. JOHN T. MORGAN,
United States Senate.

APPENDIX 8.

[Mormon Church v. United States, 136 U. S. Reports, p 1. Decided May 19, 1890]

Mr. Justice BRADLEY delivered the opinion of the court (p. 42).

Mr. Chief Justice FULLER, with whom concurred Mr. Justice Field and Mr. Justice Lamar, dissenting (p. 66).

*   *   *   *   *   *   *

The power of Congress over the Territories of the United States is general and plenary, arising from and incidental to the right to acquire the territory itself, and from the power given by the Constitution to make all needful rules and regulations respecting the territory or other property belonging to the United States. It would be absurd to hold that the United States has power to acquire territory, and no power to govern it when acquired. The power to acquire territory other than the territory northwest of the Ohio River (which belonged to the United States at the adoption of the Constitution) is derived from the treaty-making power and the power to declare and carry on war. The incidents of these powers are those of national sovereignty, and belong to all independent governments. The power to make acquisitions of territory by conquest, by treaty, and by cession is an incident of national sovereignty.

The Territory of Louisiana, when acquired from France, and the Territories west of the Rocky Mountains, when acquired from Mexico, became the absolute property and domain of the United States, subject to such conditions as the Government, in its diplomatic negotiations, had seen fit to accept relating to the rights of the people then inhabiting those Territories. Having rightfully acquired said Territories, the United States Government was the only one which could impose laws upon them, and its sovereignty over them was complete. No State of the Union had any such right of sovereignty over them; no other country or government had any such right. These propositions are so elementary, and so necessarily follow from the condition of things arising upon the acquisition of new territory, that they need no argument to support them. They are self-evident. Chief Justice Marshall, in the case of the American Insurance Company v. Canter (1 Pet., 511), well said:

Perhaps the power of governing a Territory belonging to the United States which has not, by becoming a State, acquired the means of self-government, may result necessarily from the facts that it is not within the jurisdiction of any particular State and is within the power and jurisdiction of the United States. The right to govern may be the inevitable consequence of the right to acquire territory. Whichever may be the source whence the power is derived, the possession of it is unquestioned.

*   *   *

Dissenting opinion: FULLER, *C. J.*   FIELD, LAMAR, *J. J.*

I am constrained to dissent from the opinion and judgment just announced.   Congress possesses such authority over the Territories as the Constitution expressly or by clear implication delegates.   Doubtless territory may be acquired by the direct action of Congress, as in the annexation of Texas; by treaty, as in the case of Louisiana; or, as in the case of California, by conquest and afterwards by treaty; but the power of Congress to legislate over the Territories is granted in so many words by the Constitution.   (Art. 4, sec. 3, clause 2.)

   *   *   *   *   *   *

[See p. 189, and pp. 11, 15, 33, 78, 199, 363, Vol. VI.]

FIFTY-FIFTH CONGRESS, SECOND SESSION.

March 31, 1898.

[Senate Report No. 816.]

Mr. Lodge, from the Committee on Foreign Relations, submitted the following report:

The three islands of the Antilles now in the possession of Denmark are St. Thomas, St. John, and Santa Cruz. St. Thomas lies in 18° 20′ 40″ north latitude and 64° 55′ 38″ west longitude, and St. John about 3 miles to the southeast of it. They both form part of the group known as the Virgin Islands, which lies about 38 miles from the Spanish island of Puerto Rico at the nearest point. This group of about fifty islands, small and large, scattered over an area 24 leagues east and west by 16 north and south, was discovered and named on November 30 by Christopher Columbus during his second voyage to the West Indies, in 1493. At the time of discovery these islands were, when inhabited at all, in the possession of the Caribs, a tribe of warlike cannibals, and it was not until 1550 that they were definitely driven from the archipelago by the Emperor Charles V.

It is not entirely certain when and by whom St. Thomas, the largest of the Virgin group, was first settled. On recent and reliable authority, however, Erik Smidt, who was, it appears, at the head of a trading company which had been formed at Copenhagen at about that time, took possession of the island in behalf of the Danish Crown on the 30th of May, 1666. The Danes, however, seem not to have been the first settlers, but there is no certainty who the first settlers actually were. At all events, in 1671, on the forming of the West India and Guinea Company at Copenhagen, the island of St. Thomas passed definitely under the Danish Crown, and, with the exception of a short period in 1801 and from 1807 to 1815, when on both occasions it was occupied as a war measure, the island has remained under the Danish flag for two hundred and twenty years.

In a letter written by the directors of the Danish West India Company on December 20, 1716, permission was given to 16 of the inhabitants of St. Thomas to cult'vate the island of St. John. The Danes had taken formal possession in 1684, and after the settlement the fate of this little island was bound with that of its larger sister. The events in the history of these two islands are not numerous.

In 1724 St. Thomas was formally declared a port of entrance for all nations, though this had in fact long been the case. In 1733 occurred the great slave insurrection on the island of St. John, which resulted in the death of several whites and which was finally put down by the assistance of some French troops from Santo Domingo.

The history of the island of Santa Cruz, which lies somewhat to the south of the Virgin group, is far more dramatic. Discovered by Columbus in the same month in which he came upon the Virgin group, we first find it inhabited in the year 1643 by two distinct parties of English and Dutch. Two years later, as a result of mutual jealousies and civil war between the two parties, the Dutch were compelled to leave the island. The English, however, were not long allowed to enjoy the fruits of their victory, for in 1650 they were attacked by a force of 1,200 Spaniards and driven from the island. A small company of Spaniards was left to hold the place. After an unsuccessful attempt to regain possession of the island by the Dutch, the 65 Spaniards who had been left to defend it were attacked by a force of 160 Frenchmen from St. Kitts and surrendered to the newcomers without resistance. Thus in the space of seven years English, Dutch, Spanish, and French had in turn sought to gain possession of the island of Santa Cruz.

During the next century its history was also eventful. In 1651 the Knights of Malta bought St. Christopher, St. Martin, St. Bartholomew, Tortuga, and Santa Cruz for 120,000 livres, which were paid down by Commandant de Poincey. He was thus virtual owner of the islands until 1653, when he ceded them to the Knights of Malta, whose dominion was confirmed by a royal concession, made in March, 1683, and signed by Louis XIV. The affairs of the islands were not prosperous, owing to sickness, restriction of their commerce, and consequent hindrance to agriculture. After futile attempts to restore prosperity to the islands, things became so bad that in 1720 the French settlers demolished their forts, abandoned the island, and removed to Santo Domingo. "After this," says Knox, "it was visited by the ships of all nations until 1727, when the French captured seven English merchant vessels, which were lying there, and again took possession of the island. From this time until the year 1753 it continued to be the property of France, from whom it was at length purchased by King Christian VI for 750,000 French livres."

In 1736 the Danish West India Company allied themselves with a body of merchants in Copenhagen, and, by excluding the Dutch from all commerce with the islands, established a monopoly of trade. The result of this restriction was most unfortunate to the islanders, and things went from bad to worse until in 1758 the King took over the colonies, paying the company 2,200,000 pieces of eight ($1,418,000) for them. They have remained ever since in the possession of the Danish Crown.

Santa Cruz, the capital of the Danish Islands, has an area of about 81 English square miles. Its shape is elongated, being about 19 English miles east and west and from 5 to 1 English miles north and south. The northern part of the island is intersected from east to west by a range of hills or low mountains. The southwestern part of the island is level or slightly undulating. The shores are surrounded by coral reefs, except in the northwest, where depths of 1,000 fathoms are found near the shore. There are several small creeks or water courses in the island. The climate is tropical, the temperature high and subject to little variation; the yearly average is 27.2° C., with a little more than three degrees difference between the mean temperature during the warmest month, August, and the coldest month, February.

A trade wind blows during the whole year with the exception of the hurricane months—August, September, and October—when it becomes irregular and sometimes ceases altogether. According to the last census the population of St. Croix numbered 19,683 souls, of which 9,552 are males and 10,251 females. The town of Christiansted contains 5,499 persons and Frederiksted 3,685. The remainder live in the rural districts. Sugar is the staple production. Of the 51,980 acres which the island contains 16,478 acres are in sugar, and of the remainder 29,776 acres are chiefly pasture, while 4,926 acres are unused. There are some 100 sugar estates on the island in cultivation, and in 1896 the export of sugar amounted to about 15,000 tons. There is semiweekly regular communication with St. Thomas, and the Quebec and the Pickford and Black lines of steamers proceed as a rule from St. Thomas to West End or Frederiksted on their outward voyages, the former touching at both ports on the return.

The island of St. Thomas is about 13 miles long by 4 in width, with a population of something like 12,000 souls, of which about 200 enjoy electoral privileges. Owing to its geographical position and fine harbor, which is so easy of access, it long maintained an important position as the entrepôt of the West Indies, headquarters for many lines of steamers, a coaling station, and a port of refuge. In late years business has somewhat fallen away. St. Thomas is the West India headquarters and coaling station of the Hamburg-American Packet Company, and the German, French, and English mail companies also have coaling stations there. The French mail stops once a month from Havre, Bordeaux, and the Spanish port of Santander, with an intercolonial boat from Martinique and Guadeloupe. The German mail from Hamburg direct about every ten days, and the English mail every fourteen days, make connection with the English and French Windward Islands. The New York service is done by the Quebec Line about every three weeks, and by the "Red D" Line once a month. The Pickford and Black steamers call regularly every four weeks from St. Johns, New Brunswick, and Halifax via Bermuda. In addition there is a monthly service by the West India and Pacific Company from Liverpool, proceeding to Colon, Jamaica, etc.

St. John is an island with an area of 42 square miles and a population of 915 souls. The product of the island is sugar.

The first negotiations of the United States for the purchase of the Danish Islands were begun by Mr. Seward, then Secretary of State, in January, 1865, at least so it is supposed. There is mention in contemporary pamphlets of a dinner party at the French embassy, where Mr. Seward first expressed to General Raaslof, the Danish chargé d'affaires, the desire of the United States to buy the Danish Islands in the Antilles. Afterwards other conferences followed of an unofficial character, Mr. Seward urging the Danish minister, who replied that Denmark had no desire to sell the islands. Great secrecy was insisted upon and preserved. This was under the Presidency of Lincoln. General Raaslof, who was himself opposed to the sale, reported these interviews to his Government, who replied that it would be advisable to drop the negotiations, as the Danish Government had no desire to part with these colonies. Mr. Seward's carriage accident, consequent illness, and temporary incapacity for public affairs confirmed this attitude on the part of Denmark.

In April came the assassination of the President, the wounding of Mr. Seward, and the accession of Mr. Johnson to the Chief Executive. Mr. Seward's recovery was slow, and it was not until December, 1865, on the eve of his departure for the South, a journey taken to restore his health, that the Secretary of State again mentioned the matter to General Raaslof. The complexion of affairs was now somewhat altered. A new ministry had come into power at Copenhagen, and it was less opposed to the sale than the former one had been. Hence, a note to Mr. Seward, declaring that although the Government had no desire to sell, still it was not unwilling to entertain the Secretary's propositions. A request was made that the United States declare how much it was willing to give.

Mr. Seward departed, and during his absence visited St. Thomas and convinced himself of the necessity of the purchase. On his return he pressed General Raaslof to name a price, and the Danish minister in turn demanded that, as the United States wished to buy, and not Denmark to sell, an offer should be made by the American Government. Finally, on July 17, 1866, as General Raaslof was leaving for Copenhagen, Mr. Seward delivered to him a note offering, on behalf of the United States, $5,000,000 for the three Danish islands, St. Thomas, St. John, and Santa Cruz. Mr. Seward personally informed General Raaslof that the representative of the United States in Denmark would, for a time, have charge of the affair; also that the United States was not pressed for an answer. A few days after General Raaslof left America, and soon after his arrival at Copenhagen he was appointed minister of war, and, in the work of reorganizing the Danish army, lost sight of affairs in America.

Count Frijs, the Danish minister for foreign affairs, who consequently now had charge of the negotiations, was in favor of the sale, but still the affair dragged until January 19, 1867, when Mr. Yeaman, United States minister at Copenhagen, received the following telegram from Mr. Seward: "Tell Raaslof haste important." However, nothing was done for two months. Denmark felt a good deal of hesitation, owing to the uncertainty of the treaty being ratified by the Senate, but she became more assured by the absence of opposition in the United States to the purchase scheme and by the speedy ratification of the Alaska purchase treaty. Nevertheless, at the end of two months Mr. Seward telegraphed again to Mr. Yeaman, "Want yea or nay now." Mr. Yeaman at once communicated with General Raaslof, but it was not until the 17th of May, 1867, that Count Frijs made a counter proposition to Mr. Seward's note. Through the medium of Mr. Yeaman, he declined on behalf of Denmark the offer of $5,000,000 and offered the islands for $15,000,000, or St. Thomas and St. John for $10,000,000, with the option of taking Santa Cruz for $5,000,000 more.

Count Frijs explained that the ratification of the treaty of cession by the Rigsdag would be necessary, and that the Danish Government would require that the consent of the people of the islands should be freely and formally given. In ten days Mr. Yeaman was in receipt of Mr. Seward's answer to this proposition, which was in substance this: "The United States will pay for the three islands $7,500,000 in gold." Mr. Seward objected, however, to the condition that the consent of the inhabitants of the islands was necessary, and thought it sufficient that they should have the free choice of leaving the islands within two years or remaining and becoming American citizens. Mr. Yeaman immediately communicated these instructions to the Danish minister for foreign

affairs, who promised an early answer. This answer was given in a
month, in an interview between Count Frijs and Mr. Yeaman. Mr.
Seward's second offer was refused and a counter proposition made. This
was that Denmark would cede the islands for $11,250,000, or 20,000,000
Danish rix dollars, or St. Thomas and St. John for $7,500,000, and
Santa Cruz at option for $3,750,000. Count Frijs further declared
that taking a vote of the people of the islands before the cession was
absolutely indispensable.

Mr. Seward's second offer being thus formally rejected by the Danish
Government, Mr. Yeaman now informed Count Frijs that his instructions obliged him to announce that the offer of the United States was
withdrawn and the negotiations ended. Nevertheless, on July 6, 1867,
Mr. Seward telegraphed to Mr. Adams in London: "Tell Yeaman close
with Denmark's offer. St. John, St. Thomas, seven and one-half millions. Report brief by cable. Send treaty ratified immediately."
Still the negotiations lagged. Mr. Seward was strongly opposed to the
vote by the islanders, but the Danish Government was firm on this
point, and he finally cabled to Mr. Yeaman: "Concede question of vote."
On the 24th of October, 1867, the treaty was finally signed by the
Danish minister, and by Mr. Yeaman on behalf of the United States.

There remained the vote of the islanders. Mr. Carstensen was sent
as Danish commissioner to take the vote, and Mr. Seward dispatched
Dr. Hawley to the islands to attend to American interests. He arrived
at St. Thomas on the 12th of November, 1867; on the 18th of November, before the vote was taken, there occurred a terrible earthquake,
which did much damage to the island, and affairs came temporarily to
a standstill. They were resumed on November 26, and on January 9,
1868, the vote was taken in St. Thomas, and on the following day in St.
John. In the larger island there were cast 1,039 votes for the cession
and only 22 against it, and in the smaller 205 votes for and none against.
There were fears in Denmark that the United States would not ratify
even after Denmark was fully committed, but Mr. Seward calmed these
fears with renewed assurances of success, and after some hesitation the
treaty was ratified by the Rigsdag and signed by the King on January
31, 1868. This ratification occurred in the midst of the fierce political
war between President Johnson and Congress. The limit of time
named in the treaty for ratification was February 24, 1868, and this
went by without action by Congress. The time was then extended to
October 14, 1868. All, however, was useless. Denmark made repeated
endeavors, in the person of her minister and through the medium of
other powers, to conclude the negotiations, but in vain. The treaty fell
a victim to the storm of political hatred then raging in this country,
and in the session of 1868, after an adverse report, the United States
Senate dropped it.

In Schuyler's American Diplomacy, page 23, we find the following
comment:

Denmark had no particular desire to sell to the United States, but was persuaded
to do so. The inhabitants of the islands had already voted to accept the United
States as their sovereign. The late Mr. Charles Sumner, then chairman of the Committee on Foreign Relations of the Senate, who was engaged in a personal quarrel
with the Administration, simply refused to report back the treaty to the Senate, and
he was supported by a sufficient number of his committee and of Senators to enable
the matter to be left in this position. It required new negotiations to prolong the
term of ratification, and it was with great difficulty that in a subsequent session the
treaty was finally brought before the Senate and rejected. As may be imagined, our
friendly relations with Denmark were considerably impaired by this method of doing
business.

After a lapse of twenty-four years since the rejection of this treaty, the negotiations were reopened in 1892, while Hon. John W. Foster was Secretary of State. The accompanying papers (Appendix A), which, in response to a request for information, were sent to the chairman of the Committee on Foreign Relations by the Assistant Secretary of State on May 12, 1897, contain a full account of the most recent negotiations, including, in addition to those of Mr. Foster, the correspondence of Mr. Olney on this subject, in 1896, for the purchase of the Danish islands and of the condition and value of the harbor of St. Thomas.

The arguments in favor of the possession of these islands can be briefly stated, and appear to the undersigned to be unanswerable. So long as these islands are in the market there is always the danger that some European power may purchase, or try to purchase, them. This would be an infraction of the Monroe doctrine, and would at once involve the United States in a very serious difficulty with the European power which sought possession of the islands. In the interest of peace, it is of great importance that these islands should pass into the hands of the United States and cease to be a possible source of foreign complications, which might easily lead to war.

From a military point of view the value of these islands to the United States can hardly be overestimated. We have always been anxious to have a good naval and coaling station in the West Indies. Important in time of peace, such a station would be essential to our safety in time of war. Successive Administrations have labored to secure a West Indian naval station. During the war of the rebellion the United States leased the harbor of St. Nicholas from Hayti for this purpose. General Grant endeavored during his Presidency to secure Samana Bay. The effort to obtain the Danish Islands, as has been shown, was begun by Mr. Seward during the Presidency of Abraham Lincoln. The fine harbor of St. Thomas fulfills all the required naval and military conditions.

As has been pointed out by Captain Mahan, it is one of the great strategic points in the West Indies. The population of the three islands is only 33,000, of whom nearly 30,000 are negroes, the others being chiefly of English or Danish extraction. There is no possibility of any material increase in the population, and annexation would never involve at any time the troublesome question of Statehood. The Danish islands could easily be governed as a Territory—could be readily defended from attack, occupy a commanding strategic position, and are of incalculable value to the United States, not only as a part of the national defense, but as removing by their possession a very probable cause of foreign complications.

APPENDIX A.

[Confidential]

LEGATION OF THE UNITED STATES,
Copenhagen, November 28, 1892.

SIR: I am unofficially authorized to inform you that a proposal from the Government of the United States to revive the convention of 1867, by which it was proposed to cede the islands of St. Thomas and St. John to the United States, would now receive favorable consideration from the Danish Government, the meaning of which is that the Danish Government will now, if desired, cede those islands to the United States upon the terms of the convention of 1867. The incidents through which I feel myself authorized to so inform you are as follows:

On Thursday, the 15th instant, I called upon Mr. Estrup, the minister of finance and premier of Denmark, to speak with him in regard to the loan of the Icelandic books, giving an account of the discovery of America by Lief Anderson, so much desired by you for the State Department exhibit at the World's Columbian Exposition. In the course of the conversation we recalled some of the interesting questions which have been considered by the United States and Denmark, and special reference was made to the treaty in question in which Mr. Estrup was specially interested, he having been at the time of its consideration a member of the Danish cabinet, occupying the post of minister of the interior. Reference was also made to his (Mr. Estrup's) conversations with Colonel Arendrup, governor of the Danish West Indies, an account of which I gave in my No. 47 of July 17, 1891.

In the course of the conversation Mr. Estrup said that he would now be willing to cede those islands to the United States, and indicated that he would be willing to do so upon the terms then agreed upon, etc., and it was suggested that the treaty could be revived, etc. I replied that while I had no authority from my Government to make any declaration whatsoever in regard to the matter, I should feel it to be my duty, if informed that the Danish Government were willing to give the matter favorable consideration, to so report to my Government. I then explained the condition of affairs at Washington incident to the coming change of Administration, and said that it was scarcely probable, however the matter might be regarded, that there could be any action at present, etc., but added that there seemed to be a growing feeling in the United States that we require a naval, coaling, and supply station in the West Indies, etc.

The conversation was quite extended, the minister giving me his views at length, the substance of which was that while these islands would be of inestimable value to the United States, it would be better for Denmark to cede them on the terms of the convention of 1867, etc. I left him, substantially agreeing with him in this view of the matter, but declaring that I had no authority to make any proposals, nor even suggestions, and that I should not feel it to be my duty to give the matter attention unless it should appear that the Danish Government was disposed to give the matter favorable consideration, in which case I should feel it to be my duty to inform my Government of such disposition, etc.

On Tuesday, the 22d instant, a week after this conversation, Mr. Estrup called at my house to say that he had been considering the matter since our interview, and had spoken at length concerning it with Baron Reedtz-Thott, the minister of foreign affairs, who was of the same opinion as himself, and that he, Baron Reedtz-Thott, would speak with me about it, etc.

On the same afternoon, upon my calling at the foreign office, the matter was brought up and Baron Reedtz-Thott expressed himself as equally ready to receive with favorable consideration a proposal from our Government to revive the treaty, etc. I repeated to him what I had said to the premier as regarded the present Administration, and that I had no authority to make any proposal nor suggestion, etc., he declaring that he knew this perfectly well, that Mr. Estrup and he had talked this all over, but that they could see no harm in me and my Government being apprised confidentially of their views, etc. I then said that I should feel it to be my duty to communicate these views confidentially to you, etc.

About an hour after I left the minister of foreign affairs, he called upon me at my house and said that be had been reflecting upon the matter and had concluded that it was his duty, before authorizing me to make any statement to my Government, to lay it before His Majesty the King, which he could do in a day or two, to which, I, of course, replied that I would await further information from him.

On Friday afternoon, three days later, the minister of foreign affairs again called upon me at my house and simply said: "You may write to your Government that the matter will receive favorable consideration."

The question will naturally arise as to the motives which prompted the Danish authorities to so express themselves in regard to this matter, and it may possibly be inferred that the Government is in financial embarrassment and that money is needed to tide over some pressing financial difficulties. This is by no means the condition of affairs. There is scarcely a Government of Europe whose financial condition or credit is more sound. The Danes are a prudent, economical, thrifty people, with whom the idea of pay as you go is carried out in public as well as in private affairs. There is no emergency which requires them to so act, and while the authorities express themselves confidentially, as has been stated, in consequence of the failure of the treaty of 1867 in the Senate of the United States, they will never formally propose that it be revived. Whatever may be the views of our people upon the action of the Senate at that time, after the people of those islands, at the suggestion and request of the King of Denmark, had, with almost perfect unanimity, voted for separation, and the Danish Rigsdag had confirmed the treaty, the failure of the Senate of the United States to confirm it was most humiliating to the Danes.

There are, however, certain public improvements which the Danes would like to make, to only one of which I will refer.

In the otherwise beautiful city of Copenhagen, the most conspicuous and unsightly object is the ruined palace of Christiansborg, whose grim and blackened walls have stood since 1884 when the great edifice was burned. It had been the abode of royalty, contained the assembly chambers of their legislative bodies, great galleries of art, and all that went to make up and embellish this magnificent building, which was really the capitol of Denmark. The entrances to the great palace were sentineled by colossal statues, masterpieces. of Thorwaldsen, wonders of art, which fortunately were uninjured and are still standing in all their splendor, in striking contrast with the grim and somber ruin they were created to adorn. From every quarter of the city one may see Christiansborg, which, though in ruins, in grandeur and sublimity still surpasses every other object. Everywhere in Copenhagen, and even in the country, one is reminded of the ruins of the great palace. In several of the galleries of art one sees exquisite pictures, creations of the great masters, which were torn from their frames while the palace was burning. Surrounding the ruined palace, adjoining the courtyard, are the Thorwaldsen Museum, the Old North Museum, the great library containing 600,000 volumes, and the departments of state, all of which were saved from destruction.

It was in one of these buildings, an annex to the ruined palace, the department of finance, where I first spoke with Mr. Estrup on this question, and from this point of view it did not seem strange to me that a finance minister of this Kingdom should be willing and should regard it as the part of wisdom to obtain the means of restoring his capital and to make other public improvements through the cession of territory thousands of miles distant, whose people have voted with almost perfect unanimity and still wish to cast their lot with the people of the hemisphere to which they belong and with whom they are allied in language and in trade relations.

I need not recall the argument upon the treaty of a quarter of a century ago, but it is proper that something be said about the harbor of St. Thomas and the conditions that now present themselves. It is almost circular in form, the entrance to which is by a neck guarded by two heavy forts, and capable of accommodating 500 vessels. The island, 13 miles long by an average of 3 miles wide, has been justly designated as a small Gibraltar. It is asserted by the highest authority that it can at small expense be made impregnable.

Unlike the mole of St. Nicholas, where a large amount would have to be expended to erect suitable wharves and other necessary improvements and to defend them against dangers from a capricious Government, St. Thomas has already, through private enterprise, her great wharves, upon which thousands of tons of coal are deposited, an enormous floating dock capable of receiving vessels of 3,000 tons, marine slips for repairing small vessels, immense cisterns for the storage of water for the supply of vessels, a factory where every kind of ironwork for the repair of vessels can be turned out, including boilers, shafts, etc. The representatives of every industry and trade relating to the building and supply and navigation of ships—ship brokers, ship carpenters and calkers, iron founders, coal dealers, and others—can supply every demand of commerce. There are wharves alongside of which ships drawing 27 feet of water can be moored and coaled, day or night, at the rate of from 60 to 100 tons an hour.

It is asserted and believed that the necessary defenses and the furnishing and equipping any other naval station in the West Indies, which nature and enterprise have already supplied to St. Thomas, if this were possible, would cost much more than the sum fixed upon in 1867 as a consideration for the cession of the islands of St. Thomas and St. John to the United States.

These Danish Islands, with the splendid harbor of St. Thomas, presenting all we can possibly desire for a naval and supply station—location, security, amplitude, development—everything is within our reach upon terms which were regarded as reasonable when far less important or valuable to us. The vast increase of steam navigation necessitating supply stations for coal and machinery, the expansion of our commerce, the building up of our splendid new Navy, the prospect of a ship canal across the isthmus, which will make St. Thomas one of the most important stations upon voyages around and to most of the countries of the world, all these considerations and many more combine to make the possession of this harbor of far more importance to us than when the question of its acquisition was under consideration a quarter of a century ago.

I therefore feel it to be my imperative duty to apprise you of the views of the Danish authorities in regard to this important matter, and at the same time to venture to declare as my deliberate opinion that we should avail ourselves of the opportunity which now presents itself to acquire this haven and stronghold for our commerce and ships of war, and to express the hope that this Administration, if it can do no more, will take measures to open the way to so desirable a consummation.

I have, etc.,

CLARK E. CARR.

Hon. JOHN W. FOSTER,
  Secretary of State, Washington, D. C.

LEGATION OF THE UNITED STATES,
Copenhagen, November 29, 1892.

DEAR MR. SECRETARY: I send you to-day a confidential dispatch, No. 129, on the Danish West Indies, by which you will see that, without committing myself or the Government in the least, I have learned that we can have St. Thomas and St. John on the terms agreed upon in 1867.

I believe that we must have a station in that region, and that it will be found that this is the best one available, and that it will be sought for on our part soon, and that this Administration should take the initiative. This can now be done if desired, but should the President not be inclined to do so, we are not, as you will see, committed in the least.

It seems to me that it would be wise for the President to take up the matter of securing such a station in his message to Congress, but of course I would not presume to advise him. There are certainly many reasons why we had better have such a splendid harbor and own the whole islands inhabited by a people who really desire to cast their lot with us, and who will become loyal, patriotic Americans, than to have a station situated among a people of a different nationality.

Whatever may be thought of the matter, I hope that you will so instruct me that I may be able to show Mr. Estrup and Baron Reedtz-Thott that you are not indifferent to their feelings in the matter, and that you appreciate the suggestions they have confidentially made in our private unofficial interviews. They will not be disappointed if you simply say that the matter can not be taken up so late in the Administration, as I have informed them that this will probably be the case, but you know far better than I what is best. You are only, of course, supposed to be confidentially informed that it will receive favorable consideration. * * *

Gen. JOHN W. FOSTER.   CLARK E. CARR.

[Confidential.]

DEPARTMENT OF STATE,
Washington, December 20, 1892.

SIR: I have to acknowledge the receipt of your confidential dispatch No. 129, of November 28, 1892, with reference to the willingness evinced by the Danish Government to cede to the United States the islands of St. Thomas and St. John on the basis of the convention of 1867.

I take pleasure in commending the skill and tact with which you have received the approach of the Danish Government on the subject, and while ascertaining the disposition of the Danish Government have in no way committed the Government of the United States.

The question of the acquisition of the islands is one of far reaching and national importance, the extent of which is appreciated by no one more than the President. As his Administration is, however, drawing to its close, he considers it inadvisable to express any views or indicate any policy the consummation of which he could not effect.

He directs me to express his cordial appreciation of the friendly attitude of the Danish Government and of the confidence and frankness displayed by Mr. Estrup and Baron Reedtz-Thott in their conversations with you.

You are therefore instructed to convey verbally to these gentlemen the sentiments of the President, and to explain the reasons, if they are not clearly apprehended, why the present consideration of the cession of the islands of St. Thomas and St. John is impracticable.

I am, etc.,   JOHN W. FOSTER.
CLARK E. CARR, Esq., *Copenhagen.*

[Telegram.]

DEPARTMENT OF STATE,
Washington, December 31, 1892.

CARR, Minister, *Copenhagen.*
Take no action on instruction No. 128 for present.

FOSTER.

[Telegram.]

DEPARTMENT OF STATE,
Washington, February 4, 1893.

CARR, Minister, *Copenhagen.*
You can execute instruction No. 128 at convenient opportunity.

FOSTER.

LEGATION OF THE UNITED STATES,
Copenhagen, January 2, 1893.

SIR: On Saturday night, the 31st ultimo, I received from you a telegram as follows: "Carr, minister: Take no action on instruction No. 128 for present. Foster."

On this morning came in the mail your confidential dispatch No. 128.

As I understand the telegram, it is my duty to say nothing more concerning the matter until I receive further advices from the Department. Should it still be under consideration, it is no doubt better to wait, but I hope in the near future to be authorized to make some recognition on the part of our Government of the suggestions of the Danish authorities.

I have, etc.,

CLARK E. CARR.

Hon. JOHN W. FOSTER,
Secretary of State, Washington, D. C.

[Confidential.]

LEGATION OF THE UNITED STATES,
Copenhagen, February 22, 1893.

SIR: Referring to my confidential dispatch No. 129, to your confidential dispatch No. 128, and to your two dispatches 129 and 134, and to my 132, regarding the confidential information that the United States can now, if desired, acquire the islands of St. Thomas and St. John upon the terms designated in the convention of 1867 between the United States and Denmark, I have to say that as soon as opportunity offered after receiving your second telegram I spoke with Mr. Estrup and Baron Reedtz-Thott, giving them the views of the President as you instructed me to do.

They were not surprised at this, as I had previously given them to understand that it was improbable that the President would take the matter up when his Administration was so near its close. Each, however, spoke of the pending negotiations regarding Hawaii, and suggested that perhaps they may have had some influence in the matter, and reference was made to a statement that has appeared in the newspapers that we are looking to the acquisition of Samana Bay, etc., and that this may perhaps influence our Government unfavorably in regard to St. Thomas, etc. Of course I could express no opinion in regard to this, but it seemed to them, as it appears to me, that with a canal across the isthmus the acquisition of Hawaii makes it even more important that we should have a station in the West Indies.

Of course any action will depend upon the views of the incoming Administration. Should it be regarded as worthy of further consideration, while it would be a great satisfaction to me to be permitted to pursue a matter to which I have given some considerable thought, it will be a pleasure to me as well as my duty to aid my successor in office in every way in my power to attain the end that may seem desirable.

It seems to be the opinion of all those who are informed as to the needs of our new Navy and of our growing commerce, that the time has arrived when we require a naval station in the West Indies. For such a station, in location, accessibility, amplitude, and natural strength, the harbor of St. Thomas presents far greater advantages than any other that is available.

With its natural advantages it can be made impregnable, and it is my deliberate opinion that with these advantages, and its wharves and docks and buildings and machinery already established by private enterprise, the acquisition of this splendid harbor upon the terms suggested, and its equipment, would in the end be far less expensive than that of any other in that region.

I have, etc.,

CLARK E. CARR.

Hon. JOHN W. FOSTER,
Secretary of State, Washington, D. C.

LEGATION OF THE UNITED STATES,
Copenhagen, January 14, 1896.

SIR: Several New York newspapers, of dates about the 1st instant, arrived here yesterday and created considerable interest by certain contents to the effect that Denmark was offering through Mr. Henrick Cavling, a newspaper editor of this city, but now in Washington, to sell to the United States the West India Islands, St. Thomas, St. Croix, and St. John; and intimating that if the United States did not buy them, Germany would probably do so. Some newspaper reporters called at this legation and asked to be informed whether any such negotiations were pending. Of course I declined to say anything whatever on the subject.

During the day I had an entirely informal conversation with Mr. Vedel, the director-general of the ministry of foreign affairs, in which he exhibited to me copies of the articles in question, which he said had been sent to him by one of the city news-papers with a request for information, but he said he would say nothing about it to the press; to me he said, however, that Mr. Cavling was a self-appointed agent, and had no authority nor instigation from the foreign office; nor was there any negotia-tion whatever pending between Denmark and Germany for the sale or transfer of the islands.

Thinking that in the changed condition of affairs it might be, or might become desirable for the United States to reopen the negotiation for the purchase of the islands, I said that while I had no instructions whatever on the subject from my Government, I would personally be glad to be informed whether Denmark was inclined to reopen the matter. He replied that certainly Denmark, having met with a disastrous failure in the effort of 1868, could not propose to reopen it; but if the United States should choose to do so, he was of opinion that his Government would be inclined to sell them, though he was personally opposed to it.

I am aware of the action taken by the Department and my predecessor in the early months of 1893, but the subject was dropped then because of the approaching close of the Administration of President Harrison.

It is wholly unnecessary for me to discuss the value of these islands to the United States. It is quite apparent that in certain contingencies they might be very use-ful, but whether on the whole it would be wise to purchase them I do not presume to express an opinion. All I desire to say is that if our Government shall wish to take up the matter I believe it can be brought to a more speedy conclusion and with more secrecy and safety by carrying on the negotiation here rather than in Wash-ington.

I have, etc.,

JOHN E. RISLEY.

Hon. RICHARD OLNEY,
Secretary of State, Washington, D. C.

LEGATION OF THE UNITED STATES,
Copenhagen, January 18, 1896.

SIR: I have the honor to report that early this afternoon Baron Zytphen-Adler, from the Danish foreign office, called at this legation and said the minister would be much obliged if I would call at the ministry at 3.30 o'clock. On complying with the request, the minister told me he had received two cablegrams from Mr. Brun, Danish minister at Washington, in regard to the sale of the Danish West India Islands.

The first, received yesterday, was to the effect that Mr. Brun had a conversation with yourself, which his excellency said he did not clearly understand and had awaited further advices; the second came to-day and was to the effect that a resolu-tion on the subject had been offered in the Senate. There was no explanation of the character of the resolution, nor was the name given of the Senator who offered it.

The minister said he wished me to clearly understand that no one had been author-ized to offer the islands for sale to any power whatever, nor would they be offered for sale. The minister continued, however, to say that if the United States should make an offer for them he could assure me that it would be fairly considered; that the great publicity given to the subject would no doubt increase the difficulties here and make it more difficult to carry the matter through to success; and there might possibly be an objection from France as to the island of St. Croix, from whom it was acquired some two hundred years ago. He thought not, but deemed it right to men-tion the possibility, as it was better to have everything as clearly understood as pos-sible before proceeding further.

The foregoing is the substance of what his excellency said. I replied that I understood the position of the Danish Government to be that they would make no offer, but that if an offer should be made by the Government of the United States it would be considered in a friendly spirit, and I informed him I had already writ-ten to you to that effect, substantially, on the strength of an informal conversation had with Mr. Vedel, the director-general.

The impression made on my mind is that the minister will gladly welcome an offer from the United States. Though not a word was said on the subject in this connec-tion, I think the condition of political parties here would make it rather desirable to the ministry to carry to a speedy success such a negotiation.

Awaiting any instructions you may have to give,

I have, etc.,

JOHN E. RISLEY.

Hon. RICHARD OLNEY,
Secretary of State, Washington, D. C.

AFFAIRS IN CUBA.

AFFAIRS IN CUBA.

[See pp. 13, 40, 143, 187, and pp. 72, 119, 199, 276, Vol. VI.]

FIFTY-FIFTH CONGRESS, SECOND SESSION.

April 13, 1898.

[Senate Report No 885.]

Mr. Davis, from the Committee on Foreign Relations, submitted the following report:

The Committee on Foreign Relations, to which was referred the following Senate resolutions: Joint resolution No. 2, authorizing and requesting the President of the United States to issue a proclamation recognizing the political independence of the Republic of Cuba; Senate resolution No. 40, instructing the Committee on Foreign Relations to inquire what obligations the United States have assumed toward the people of Cuba by asserting and maintaining the right to prevent the acquisition of that island by any European power and compelling its people to remain subject to the dominion of Spain; Senate resolution No. 185, that it is the sense of the Senate that Congress should, with all due and convenient speed, acknowledge by appropriate act the political independence of the Republic of Cuba; joint resolution No. 132, recognizing the political independence of the Republic of Cuba, and for other purposes; joint resolution No. 133, recognizing the independence of the Republic of Cuba and declaring war against the Kingdom of Spain; joint resolution No. 134, recognizing the independence of the Republic of Cuba and providing for intervention by the United States; joint resolution No. 135, directing and empowering the President, in his discretion, to terminate, by intervention, the hostilities between Spain and the people of Cuba, and in favor of the independence of said people; joint resolution No. 142, for the recognition of the independence of the Republic of Cuba, and joint resolution No. 145,

S. Doc. 231, pt 7——21   321

authorizing the President to take such steps as are necessary to put
an end to hostilities in Cuba and to establish a republican form of
government on that island; and the messages of the President of the
United States dated March 28, 1898, and April 11, 1898, having duly
considered the same, report as follows:

The destruction of the United States battle ship *Maine* and of 2 of
her officers and 264 of her crew in the harbor of Havana on the night
of February 15, 1898, excited, to an unprecedented degree, the compassion and resentment of the American people.

Manifestations of that resentment were suspended, although the feeling was not allayed, by the self-restraint of our people, who determined to hold their judgment in suspense concerning their ultimate
action until an official investigation should disclose the cause of that
great disaster and enable them by direct or circumstantial testimony
to impute the responsibility therefor.

That investigation has been made. It was conducted with judicial
thoroughness and deliberation The difficulty of demonstrating by
conclusive proof the efficient personal cause of that sinister event was
the usual one of exposing plotted and mysterious crimes. No such
difficulty, however, obscures its official and responsible cause.

The evidence and findings of the Court of Inquiry were transmitted
to the Senate by the President, and, with the message, were duly
referred to the Committee on Foreign Relations. That committee has
considered them, and also the message of the President of April 11,
1898, with all the careful and anxious deliberation which great duties
and responsibility impose upon the judgment and conscience.

The event itself, though in a certain sense a distinct occurrence, was
linked with a series of precedent transactions which can not in reason
be disconnected from it. It was the catastrophe of a unity of events
extending over more than three years of momentous history. Standing
by itself it would be, perhaps, merely an ominous calamity. Considered,
as it must be, with the events with which reason and common sense
must connect it, and with animus by Spain so plainly apparent that no
one can even plausibly deny its existence, it is merely one reason

for the conclusion to which the investigating mind must come in consid-ering the entire subject of the relations of the United States with that Government. Your committee have also before them several Senate resolutions, which make it their duty to consider all our relations with Spain for the last three years, including the destruction of the *Maine*, as one of the incidents of the history of the war which during that time has devastated the Island of Cuba.

So clearly is the destruction of the *Maine* only a single incident in the relations of this Government with Spain, that if that calamity had never happened the questions between the United States and that Government would press for immediate solution.

It is the opinion of your committee, having considered the testimony submitted to the board of inquiry, in connection with further testimony taken by the committee and with the relevant and estab-lished facts presented by the events of the last three years, that the destruction of the *Maine* was compassed either by the official act of the Spanish authorities or was made possible by a negligence on their part so willing and gross as to be equivalent in culpability to positive criminal action.

The status of the *Maine* while in the harbor of Havana and the duty of Spain toward her are defined in the opinion of Chief Justice Mar-shall in Schooner Exchange *v.* McFadden, 7 Cranch, 116, 141:

"If there be no prohibition, the ports of a friendly nation are considered as open to the public ships of all powers with whom it is at peace, and they are supposed to enter such ports and remain in them, while they are allowed to remain, under the protection of the Government of the place."

It is not contended that this duty of protection to which the public ship is thus entitled while allowed to remain in a port of a friendly nation imposes the obligation of an absolute guaranty of her safety. But it is insisted that the existence of the duty creates the obligation to use due diligence in its performance. When property and life are destroyed by an act which the exercise of due diligence by the person whose duty it is to use it could have prevented, the happening of such an event is sufficient proof that such diligence was not employed.

The system of civil and military police and espionage in Havana is all-pervading to an extent probably unequaled in any city in the world It is not pretended that any employment was made as regards the safety of the *Maine* of this instrumentality for the detection or prevention of any attempt against her by private persons.

It is established that the *Maine* was destroyed by the explosion of a submarine mine, in position under her in a Spanish harbor, at a place where she had been moored to a buoy by the express direction and guidance of the Spanish authorities.

Explosive contrivances of this character are almost exclusively government agencies of warfare. There is no operation of a pacific character for which they can be employed, excepting the removal of wrecks or of harbor obstructions. They are not to be had in any place of private sale. Their destructive contents, excepting, perhaps, gunpowder, which undoubtedly was not employed in this instance, can not be easily obtained and are not easily made. The entire contrivance is a mechanism of a somewhat complicated character, not generally understood except by special manufacturers or by military or naval officers who have been instructed how to operate it.

Such mines, when sunk in harbors, are almost invariably discharged by an electric current, conducted over a wire leading from the engine of destruction to some place on the shore where a battery can be housed, guarded, and attended by trained operators. They are now placed, or are made ready to be placed, in all important harbors; it may fairly be presumed that they had been placed in the harbor of Havana, the history of the last three years being considered.

In complaisance to Spanish aversion no public vessel of the United States had visited that port during that period. The coming of the *Maine* had been announced to the Spanish authorities, and the military and naval portion of these did not receive her with the cordiality which such visits usually produce. Many of them expressed resentment at her presence. Certain newspapers in Madrid and Havana commented upon her visit in hostile terms.

There was, especially in Havana, among the officials who had been adherents of Weyler and who resented his recall, an expressed hatred of the United States. The time of the explosion must have been calculated for the moment when the *Maine* should swing within the destructive radius of the mine.

The report of the Spanish board of inquiry, sedulously promulgated in advance of that of the board of the United States, finding, after a hurried and most superficial investigation, that the catastrophe was from an internal and not from an external cause, was manifestly false, and was intended to induce public opinion to prejudge the question.

The duplicity, perfidy, and cruelty of the Spanish character, as they always have been, are demonstrated still to continue by their manifestations during the present war in Cuba. All these circumstances considered cumulatively, together with other considerations which will exactly accord with and add force to them, undenied and unexplained as they are by any authority excepting the baseless report of the Spanish board of inquiry, warrant the conclusion stated hereinbefore that the destruction of the *Maine* was compassed either by the official act of the Spanish authorities (and the ascertainment of the particular person is not material), or was made possible by a negligence en their part so willing and gross as to be equivalent in culpability to positive criminal action.

Upon due consideration of all of the relevant facts of the relations of this Government with Spain, including the destruction of the *Maine*, and of the history of the rebellion, it is the opinion of your committee that the United States ought at once to recognize the independence of the people of Cuba, and also ought to intervene to the end that the war and its unexampled atrocities shall cease, and that such independence shall become a settled political fact at the earliest possible moment, by the establishment by the free action of the people of Cuba when such action can be had, of a government independent in fact and form.

It is believed that recognition of the belligerency of the insurgents in Cuba, if it had been given seasonably, when it was suggested by concurrent resolutions to that effect passed by Congress, would have insured the speedy termination of the war without involving the United States in the contest. Such recognition was not given, and conditions have changed so materially since it was thus proposed that, if given now, it would fall far short of supplying the just requirements of the present situation in the light solely of the interests of the United States.

The recognition of the independence of the people of Cuba is justified and demanded by the highest considerations of duty, right, and policy.

The insurgents hold the eastern portion of the island, to the practical exclusion of Spain. This possession extends over one body of territory comprising fully one-half of the area of Cuba.

The extermination by Spain of the peaceful inhabitants of the western portion of the island has so affected the balance of population between these moieties of Cuba that the insurgents comprise in the eastern half nearly one-third of the population of the island. That third of the population pays taxes to them, serves in their armies, and in every way supports and is loyal to them. This situation has existed ever since the first few months of the war. The armies of Spain under Campos, Weyler, and Blanco, successively have been repelled in every invasion that they have attempted of the eastern half of the island.

The cause of Spain has continually grown weaker and that of the insurgents has grown stronger. The former is making no substantial effort for the recovery of these lost provinces. Their people are secure from invasion and cruel administration. Spain has never been able to subject them to her unprecedented and murderous policy of concentration and extermination. Her armies have been more than decimated in the attempt to subdue them. Two hundred thousand of her soldiers have failed to reduce the insurgents. The few reinforcements that she is now sending to Cuba do not supply a tithe of her losses caused by battle and disease.

Her control over the western portion of the island is dominance over a desolation which she herself has created. Even there she controls only the territory occupied by her cantonments and camps. Outside these the insurgents are everywhere in presence.

In the population of Cuba the native born preponderate in a very large proportion, probably of 8 to 1. We have been assured by the most unimpeachable authority (we mean Senators Proctor, Gallinger, Thurston, and Money) that the native-born Cubans everywhere, even within the military lines of Spain, are opposed to the parent State, and are in sympathy with the insurgents.

We have also been assured by the same authority that the native Cubans, by superiority in education, are better qualified than the Spaniards, and are thoroughly capable to administer the government of the island.

The preceding observations have assumed a certain control and sovereignty by Spain over the western portion of Cuba. We have indicated its character. It is limited to scattered and fortified areas, and it is not a civil sovereignty. It is merely a military occupation of fortified places. Even this dominion has been made possible and continues only by the infliction of a policy for which the history of no people (excepting possibly that of Spain herself) furnishes any example. The world knows what that policy is and all civilization execrates it. It consists in compelling, under penalty of death, the rural population of the western part of the island to leave their homes, their fields, their stock, and other chattels, and mass themselves between the outskirts of certain designated towns and a military cordon intercepting their return into the country. As they departed from their homes their houses were burned; the growth of their fields was trodden down by cavalry; their agricultural implements, furniture, and domestic utensils were destroyed; their cattle and horses were swept away by Spain. Throughout wide areas of a region of unsurpassed fertility, which had been densely populated for more than two centuries, not one living thing, brute or human, not one habitation, not one productive field is to be seen.

For the miserable condition to which an entire population is reduced Spain has afforded no substantial relief, and the evil and distress have become so huge and her financial debility is so extreme that she is now unable to relieve, even if she could be supposed to have the disposition to do so.

The result has been that over 200,000 of the subjects of Spain have been killed by the action of that Government, and 200,000 more are suffering from famine and disease.

There has been no distinction of sex or age in this protracted and torturing massacre. The children of this generation have been starved to death, and the immolation of womanhood has destroyed the possibility of posterity.

There can be no doubt that the contriver of this unexampled scheme of atrocity intended to depopulate, to the full extent of an ability undeniably great in the conception and perpetration of colossal crime, the island of its native people and to repeople it by natives of Spain.

We can not consent upon any conditions that the depopulated portions of Cuba shall be recolonized by Spain any more than she should be allowed to found a new colony in any other part of this hemisphere or island thereof. Either act is regarded by the United States as dangerous to our peace and safety.

That Government has violated the laws of civilized warfare in the conduct of her military operations. Her troops have slaughtered prisoners after their surrender; and have massacred the sick and wounded insurgent soldiers and their physicians and nurses in their captured hospitals.

When publicists and jurists speak of the right of sovereignty of a parent State over a people or a colony they mean that divinely delegated supremacy in the exercise of which man should show "likest God." They never mean that a usurpation of diabolism shall be sanctified upon the plea that it is sovereignty none the less than that of a well-ordered and humane government. Against such reasoning the

moral laws
Of nature and of nations speak aloud

and declare that the State which thus perverts and abuses its power thereby forfeits its sovereignty. And this principle has been the foundation of the repeated interventions by the States of Europe in the affairs of Turkey, who, abominable and atrocious as her cruelty has been toward her subjects in Greece and in the northern part of her dominions in Europe, and in Armenia, has not approached the eminence at which Spain stands in solitary and unapproachable infamy.

The recognition of the independence of the people of Cuba would not be a justifiable cause of war by Spain against the United States. Upon this principle the best-esteemed authorities are agreed. Among their opinions the following declaration of Mr. Webster in his letter to Mr. Hülsemann stands preeminent:

"If, therefore, the United States had gone so far as formally to acknowledge the independence of Hungary, although, as the result has proved, it would have been a precipitate step, and one from which no benefit would have resulted to either party, it would not nevertheless have been an act against the law of nations, provided they took no part in her contest with Austria."

If not an act against the law of nations, it, of course, could not be a justifiable ground for war.

The recognition of the independence of the people of Cuba entitles the United States to insist that the war shall be conducted in accordance with those humane laws which have been ordained by the common consent of the civilized world, and which have done so much to mitigate the horrors of warfare. So long as this Government abstains from such recognition, Spain is entitled to insist that we agree with her that the insurrection is merely a treasonable riot and not a formal and organized rebellion, and that she is therefore entitled to execute upon the insurgents and upon American citizens, and all persons upon the island, the penalties of a domestic code which is an affront to civilization.

The United States has been in this attitude of concurrence ever since the beginning of the war. It has, as a consequence, in a spirit of forbearance, submitted to many atrocities perpetrated by Spain upon our own citizens which, under recognition, would have

had no warrant in international law and would have afforded just
grounds of procedure by this Government under its acknowledged
principles. Citizens of the United States have been condemned to
death by military tribunals in violation of their treaty rights. The
expostulations of this Government have been in effect merely petitions
for royal clemency. The *Competitor* prisoners, captured under our
flag, were imprisoned nearly seventeen months and were never
brought to trial, though they were subjected to many harsh, illegal,
and degrading preliminary examinations. The entire proceeding
against them was unlawful and in derogation of their rights and of our
honor. But as they were technically, in the attitude which the United
States had assumed and had placed them in refusing recognition of
belligerency or independence, merely ordinary criminals prosecuted
by Spain under her domestic penal code, this Government, it was logically insisted by Spain, had no right to make the question one of
international obligation. It accepted royal clemency and, in the person
of its citizens, received a pardon for a crime instead of demanding
reparation for a violated right.

The United States has been compelled by its attitude of nonrecog-
nition to assist Spain by its execution of our neutrality statutes.
If there is no war, and the insurgents are merely an unlawful confederacy of common insurrectionists, they can have no legitimate commercial dealings with the citizens of the United States.

Nor can the insurgents object to Spain having such dealings of
every character, including the purchase of supplies, which, had recognition been accorded, would be contraband of war, and therefore not
to be furnished except through breach of neutrality. The United
States has therefore been an assistant of Spain. The supplies for
that power have been largely purchased in this country. The unrecognized insurgents have had no right to complain. On the other
hand, they and their adherents have been prohibited from making
such purchases and from exporting any supplies, however acquired.
There has, therefore, been no real neutrality by this Government
throughout the entire business. To the contrary, Spain has been the
customer of the people of the United States, who have sold her, with

technical lawfulness, everything that she has required to repress by such processes as we have indicated a people struggling against tyranny for their liberties. To prevent the insurgents from buying or exporting at all while Spain has bought and exported to the extent of her requirements the Navy and revenue vessels of the United States have been diligently and successfully employed. It has been stated, and we believe with entire correctness, that this vigilance and policing of the seas by the United States in favor of Spain and against the insurgents has cost this Government more than $2,000,000.

The conflict of opinion and definition among the jurists upon the subject of intervention is very great. Some of them deny its existence as a right under any circumstances, excepting of self-defense against an imminent peril, while other writers, of equal authority, maintain the validity of its assertion as a right for causes which may be inconsistent with that great foundation principle of international law, the equal and inviolable sovereignty of States.

The extremes of these opinions are represented by Guizot and Arntz. The former declares that "no State has the right to intervene in the situation or internal government of another State, except only when the interest of its own safety renders such intervention indispensable."

Arntz maintains that the right of intervention exists:

1. "When the institutions of one State violate or threaten to violate the rights of another State, or when such violation is the necessary consequence of its institutions and the impossibility of an orderly coexistence of States results therefrom;

2. "When a government, acting entirely within the limits of its prerogatives of sovereignty, violates the rights of humanity, whether by measures contrary to the interests of other States, or by excess of injustice and cruelty which deeply wounds public morals and civilization.

"The right of intervention is a legitimate one, because, however important may be the rights of sovereignty and independence, there is one thing of still greater importance, and that is the law of humanity and human society, which ought not to be outraged."

Between these extremities of opinion the differences among the publicists are exceedingly various and irreconcilable. Professor Hall, in his work on International Law (3d ed., p. 288, note 1), in considering the opinions of modern international jurists who touch upon humanitarian intervention, says that "the treatment which the subject receives from them is merely fragmentary, notice being taken of some only of its grounds, which are usually approved or disapproved without very clear reference to a general principle.

Vattel (liv. 1, ch. iv, s. 56) considers it permissible to succor a people oppressed by its sovereign, but does not appear to sanction any of the analogous grounds of intervention. Wheaton (Elem., pt. 11, ch. 1, s. 93), Bluntschli (s. 478), Mamiani (p. 86), give the right of aiding an oppressed race.

Heffter (S. 46), while denying the right of intervention to repress tyranny, holds that so soon as a civil war has broken out a foreign state may assist either party engaged in it. Calvo (S. 166) and Fiore (1, 446) think that states can intervene to put an end to slaughter."

Vattel says, Book II, Chap. IV, top p. 157, "As to those monsters who, under the title of sovereigns, render themselves the scourges and horror of the human race, they are savage beasts, whom every brave man may justly exterminate from the face of the earth.

"All antiquity has praised Hercules for delivering the world from Antaeus, a Busiris, and a Diomede."

If these opinions state the correct rule, as we believe they do, the right of intervention by the United States in the present instance is indubitable. They are, however, controverted by other publicists of great eminence. It is possibly correct to say as to this conflict of opinion that this portion of international law is, though operative in certain cases, in that formative and progressive condition of development by which many benign principles, though formerly contested, have at last become firmly established.

The following reflections of Mr. Pomeroy upon this subject (Int. Law, p. 242, et seq.) appear to be well considered:

"How far the right of intervention legitimately extends, under what circumstances it may be invoked, to what extent it may be carried, are questions which have given rise to much discussion—questions that have never been authoritatively settled, and perhaps never will be settled.

"Hardly a writer absolutely denies the existence of the right at all; it would seem to be unsafe to go to this length. On the other hand, it seems almost equally unsafe to admit the right to exist at all, for, as it is utterly impossible to place any exact limits upon it, its very admission may open the door to vast and terrible abuses.

* * * * * * *

"While the fact is as stated that instances of intervention are and have been constantly occurring, I am of opinion that the whole subject does not so much belong to international law as to politics.

* * * * * * -

'In short, I can not think that the subject of intervention has been, or perhaps can be, regulated by the positive international law. It must be relegated to the domain of those high politics, those principles of expediency, which control the conduct, both domestic and foreign, of nations."

The actual conduct and policies of nations give warrant to these observations. To sustain repeated intervention during the present century no law has been invoked. They have been acts of necessity or policy. This statement is corroborated by the creation and existence of two policies, one of Europe, the other of the United States, each of which is based distinctly upon the assertion of an intention to intervene under certain circumstances. We refer to the principle of the balance of power and to the Monroe Doctrine. Each is a distinct and arbitrary policy of intervention, to be effected in certain contingencies in furtherance of national policies, and to justify which no canon of international law was ever invoked. The former has profoundly affected the relations of the European States and the independence of many of those sovereignties.

The latter has kept the powers of Europe out of the American continents ever since it was promulgated. It was a distinct announcement that the United States would intervene, under certain expressed circumstances, in the affairs of every Central American and South American State. The United States did intervene by threat and show

of force in the affairs of Mexico and France, and compelled the evacu-
ation of that Republic by a European power, whose own prior intervention in Mexican affairs had overthrown a republic and established
a monarchy upon its ruins　No publicist has ever asserted that either
of these policies is part of the law of nations.

Justification for intervention is strengthened in such cases as the
present, where the oppressions by a State of its subjects have been
so inveterate, atrocious, and sanguinary as to require intervention by
other nations in the interests of humanity and the peace of the world,
for the purpose of overthrowing that Government and establishing or
recognizing another in its place as the only means of extirpating an
otherwise incurable and dangerous evil.

Th conduct of the European powers respecting Turkey has been
pursuant to the policy which impels one nation to intervene in the
affairs of another State to stop cruelty and massacre, and, if necessary,
to depose it from sovereignty　That State became a member of the
commonwealth of European powers by the treaty of Paris of 1856.
The integrity and sovereignty of the Ottoman Empire were guaranteed. It has stood ever since upon an equality with Spain in all
respects. And yet Turkey has been the subject of repeated interventions since 1856, which have restrained her sovereignty, usurped
her domestic administration, repressed her cruelties, and partially
dismembered her empire.

The people of her several Danubian provinces, oppressed by her
misgovernment, rose in rebellion. A scene of massacre followed, which
stood without precedent until it was made to seem merciful by the
atrocities perpetrated by Spain upon her subjects in Cuba. Europe

protested at the conference of Constantinople and suggested reforms and concessions in favor of the oppressed people, which Turkey promised to grant in part, but vitiated that promise by evasions and subterfuges as to some most material requirements. Upon this Europe ceased to represent, remonstrate, and implore. Russia intervened by force. Her military successes produced the treaty of San Stefano between that power and Turkey, which established the political status of the revolted provinces. But, in the opinion of the other European powers, Russia herself had obtained too much under that treaty.

The consequence was the interposition of the great powers of Europe in the affairs of Russia and Turkey. It was substantially an intervention, though otherwise denominated, which compelled Russia and Turkey to take part in the Congress of Berlin, held in 1878. They did so because they were constrained by the certainty of intervention by force in case they should refuse. The result of that Congress was the partial dismemberment of European Turkey, and the establishment of new States therein, some partially autonomous, others entirely independent. The cause of these great interventions was the cruelty of Turkey toward her own subjects. The result was that the interventions secured their independence.

The cases of the Danubian provinces are so similar to that of Cuba as to be nearly identical. The fact that the wrongs were inflicted by Mohammedans upon Christians does not mitigate the responsibility of Spain or make intervention as to her any less rightful. Surely Christian Spain, from the fact that she is a Christian state, is not given greater warrant to exterminate her subjects than Mohammedan Turkey possessed to extirpate hers.

Great Britain intervened as to Egypt upon financial grounds, and is now administering the revenues and finances of that province.

The recent interventions of the European powers in favor of Turkey and against Greece in her endeavor to assist the Cretan insurgents, is familiar history. So, also, is the intervention of the same powers which checked the advance of the armies of Turkey into Greece.

The attitude of the United States toward the present question has been based upon the right of intervention and the intention to exer-

cise it in certain contingencies. President Cleveland, in his message
of December 7, 1896, declared that—

"Whatever circumstances may arise, our policy and our interests would constrain
us to object to the acquisition of the island or an interference with its control by
any other power.

"It should be added that it can not be reasonably assumed that the hitherto expectant attitude of the United States will be indefinitely maintained. While we are
anxious to accord all due respect to the sovereignty of Spain, we can not view the
pending conflict in all its features, and properly apprehend our inevitably close
relations to it, and its possible results, without considering that by the course
of events we may be drawn into such an unusual and unprecedented condition,
as will fix a limit to our patient waiting for Spain to end the contest, either
alone and in her own way, or with our friendly cooperation.

"When the inability of Spain to deal successfully with the insurrection has become
manifest, and it is demonstrated that her sovereignty is extinct in Cuba for all purposes of its rightful existence, and when a hopeless struggle for its reestablishment
has degenerated into a strife which means nothing more than the useless sacrifice
of human life and the utter destruction of the very subject-matter of the conflict, a
situation will be presented in which our obligations to the sovereignty of Spain will
be superseded by higher obligations, which we can hardly hesitate to recognize and
discharge. Deferring the choice of ways and methods until the time for action
arrives, we should make them depend upon the precise conditions then existing; and
they should not be determined upon without giving careful heed to every consideration involving our honor and interest, or the international duty we owe to Spain.
Until we face the contingencies suggested, or the situation is by other incidents
imperatively changed, we should continue in the line of conduct heretofore pursued,
thus in all circumstances exhibiting our obedience to the requirements of public
law and our regard for the duty enjoined upon us by the position we occupy in the
family of nations.

"A contemplation of emergencies that may arise should plainly lead us to avoid
their creation, either through a careless disregard of present duty or even an undue
stimulation and ill-timed expression of feeling. But I have deemed it not amiss to
remind the Congress that a time may arrive when a correct policy and care for our
interests, as well as a regard for the interests of other nations and their citizens,
joined by considerations of humanity and a desire to see a rich and fertile country,
intimately related to us, saved from complete devastation, will constrain our Government to such action as will subserve the interests thus involved, and at the same
time promise to Cuba and its inhabitants an opportunity to enjoy the blessings of
peace."

President McKinley, in his message of December 6, 1897, said:

"The instructions given to our new Minister to Spain before his departure for his post directed him to impress upon that Government the sincere wish of the United States to lend its aid toward the ending of the war in Cuba by reaching a peaceful and lasting result, just and honorable alike to Spain and to the Cuban people. These instructions recited the character and duration of the contest, the widespread losses it entails, the burdens and restraints it imposes upon us, with constant disturbance of National interests, and the injury resulting from an indefinite continuance of this state of things. It was stated that at this juncture our Government was constrained to seriously inquire if the time was not ripe when Spain of her own volition, moved by her own interests and every sentiment of humanity, should put a stop to this destructive war and make proposals of settlement honorable to herself and just to her Cuban colony. It was urged that as a neighboring nation, with large interests in Cuba, we could be required to wait only a reasonable time for the mother country to establish its authority and restore peace and order within the borders of the Island; that we could not contemplate an indefinite period for the accomplishment of this result.

"No solution was proposed to which the slightest idea of humiliation to Spain could attach, and indeed precise proposals were withheld to avoid embarrassment to that Government. All that was asked or expected was that some safe way might be speedily provided and permanent peace restored.

*   *   *   *   *   *   *

"Sure of the right, keeping free from all offense ourselves, actuated only by upright and patriotic considerations, moved neither by passion nor selfishness, the Government will continue its watchful care over the rights and property of American citizens and will abate none of its efforts to bring about by peaceful agencies a peace which shall be honorable and enduring. If it shall hereafter appear to be a duty imposed by our obligations to ourselves, to civilization and humanity to intervene with force, it shall be without fault on our part and only because the necessity for such action will be so clear as to command the support and approval of the civilized world."

These declarations more than implied that this Government would interpose in the event of failure within a reasonable time to conquer the insurgents or to induce them by concessions of home rule to lay down their arms. They have not been subdued. The autonomy proffered was specious and illusory. It has been rejected by the insurgents not because it was specious and illusory, but because they will accept nothing short of complete national independence. The suggestion of a more complete autonomy has also been rejected by them. They declare to the United States and Spain alike that no terms short of independence, which those powers may attempt to prescribe to them will be accepted. Spain refuses to grant independence.

The war, then, must go on, and the misery which has shocked the civilized world must continue and increase unless it is terminated by the triumph of Cuba or Spain or by the interposition of the United States.

It is the opinion of this committee that the time to interpose has arrived; that intervention which will stop the war and secure the national independence of Cuba should at once take place. If under all the circumstances Spain shall choose to regard such action by this Government as a cause of war, that consequence, however deplorable, will be accepted by the American people with all the fortitude that confidence in the justice of their action can inspire.

Such intervention is justifiable and necessary for the following reasons: The present situation in Cuba has become a menace to the peace of the world, and especially to the peace and safety of the United States. Spain has bid for European intervention, thus far apparently without success, but the conditions which make such intervention possible should be removed at once.

For nearly three years the hostilities in Cuba and the Spanish administration of that island have involved this Government in perilous relations with Spain and raised questions of right and responsibility of which no prospect of settlement is apparent. So long as these conditions are allowed to remain unsettled they will increase an irritation which has already become intolerable, and which will inevitably ultimately require adjustment by measures much more vigorous than now seem adequate to compose existing difficulties.

Spain has failed to perform her treaty obligations and other international duties toward the United States. To give a minute specification of these derelictions would unnecessarily extend this paper. They are the familiar matters of current history. American citizens have been seized and imprisoned without shadow of right, and have been proceeded against by violent and irregular forms in violation of treaty obligations.

The assassination of Ruiz, an American citizen, was the act of the Spanish officials who held him in a custody unwarranted by his treaty rights. No reparation has been made for this act, although it has been demanded by this Government.

A justifiable cause for intervention has been afforded by the barbarity with which Spain has conducted her military operations; by her slaughter of captured insurgent soldiers, and by her extermination of not less than 200,000 of her own noncombatant subjects—men, women, and children—by driving them from their homes into places of concentration and there suffering them to die of starvation and disease.

In 1893 there were $50,000,000 of property in the Island of Cuba belonging to the citizens of the United States. Much of this has been destroyed, and much of that destruction has been by the acts of Spain. The destruction of the remainder she has been unable or unwilling to prevent.

The claims on file in the Department of State against Spain for indemnity for this destroyed property are about $16,000,000 in amount.

Her military officers have levied contributions upon American planters as the price for the preservation of their estates and the continuance of their agricultural operations.

In 1893 the commerce of the United States with Cuba had reached the annual sum of nearly $100,000,000. Since that time it has been substantially annihilated by the methods of Spanish military and civil maladministration. Certain sworn statements made before the committee and other documents are herewith submitted as part of this report.

The committee recommend the adoption of the accompanying resolution:

Whereas the abhorrent conditions which have existed for more than three years in the Island of Cuba, so near our own borders, have shocked the moral sense of the people of the United States, have been a disgrace to Christian civilization, culminating, as they have, in the destruction of a United States battle ship, with two hundred and sixty-six of its officers and crew, while on a friendly visit in the harbor of

Havana, and can not longer be endured, as has been set forth by the President of the United States in his message to Congress of April eleventh, eighteen hundred and ninety-eight, upon which the action of Congress was invited: Therefore,

Resolved by the Senate and House of Representatives of the United States of America in Congress assembled, First. That the people of the Island of Cuba are, and of right ought to be, free and independent.

Second. That it is the duty of the United States to demand, and the Government of the United States does hereby demand, that the Government of Spain at once relinquish its authority and government in the Island of Cuba and withdraw its land and naval forces from Cuba and Cuban waters.

Third. That the President of the United States be, and he hereby is, directed and empowered to use the entire land and naval forces of the United States, and to call into the actual service of the United States the militia of the several States, to such extent as may be necessary to carry these resolutions into effect.

VIEWS OF MINORITY.

The undersigned members of said committee cordially concur in the report made upon the Cuban resolutions, but we favor the immediate recognition of the Republic of Cuba, as organized in that island, as a free, independent, and sovereign power among the nations of the world.

DAVID TURPIE.

R. Q. MILLS.

JNO. W. DANIEL.

J. B. FORAKER.

FIFTY-FOURTH CONGRESS, FIRST SESSION.

[Senate Document No. 166.]

LETTER OF HON. T. ESTRADA PALMA TO HON. RICHARD OLNEY, SECRETARY OF STATE.

· WASHINGTON, *December 7, 1895.*

SIR: I hand you herewith a statement of the facts upon which I, as authorized representative of the Cubans in arms, ask that the rights of belligerency be accorded them by your Government.

If you so desire I can exhibit to you the originals of the documents mentioned or set forth in said statement.

Should it be necessary or desirable for me to point out the arguments, based on the facts submitted, which I deem proof that we are now in condition to ask for belligerency, it will afford me great pleasure to do so.

Begging your earliest and most favorable consideration of this subject, I have the honor to remain, very respectfully, yours,

T. ESTRADA PALMA.

To Hon. RICHARD OLNEY,
Secretary of State of the United States of America,
Washington, D. C.

WASHINGTON, D. C., *December 7, 1895.*

SIR: While admitting that, as a rule, governments do not take cognizance of the justice or injustice of a struggle in which they are called upon to grant the rights of belligerency to one of the contending parties, the revolution for the independence of the Cuban people, initiated on February 24 last, is so similar in its character to that which resulted in the establishment of the foremost Republic in the world, the United States of America, that I feel called upon to point out the causes leading to the present uprising in Cuba.

CAUSES OF THE REVOLUTION.

These causes are substantially the same as those of the former revolution, lasting from 1868 to 1878 and terminating only on the representation of the Spanish Government that Cuba would be granted such reforms as would remove the grounds of complaint on the part of the Cuban people. Unfortunately the hopes thus held out have never been realized. The representation which was to be given the Cubans has proved to be absolutely without character; taxes have been levied anew on everything conceivable; the offices in the island have increased, but the officers are all Spaniards; the native Cubans have been left with no public duties whatsoever to perform, except the payment of taxes to the Government and blackmail to the officials, without privilege even to move from place to place in the island except on the permission of governmental authority.

Spain has framed laws so that the natives have substantially been deprived of the right of suffrage. The taxes levied have been almost

entirely devoted to support the army and navy in Cuba, to pay interest
on the debt that Spain has saddled on the island, and to pay the salaries
of the vast number of Spanish officeholders, devoting only $746,000
for internal improvements out of the $26,000,000 collected by tax. No
public schools are within reach of the masses for their education. All
the principal industries of the island are hampered by excessive imposts. Her commerce with every country but Spain has been crippled
in every possible manner, as can readily be seen by the frequent protests
of shipowners and merchants.

The Cubans have no security of person or property, The judiciary
are instruments of the military authorities. Trial by military tribunals
can be ordered at any time at the will of the Captain-General. There
is, beside, no freedom of speech, press, or religion. In point of fact,
the causes of the Revolution of 1775 in this country were not nearly as
grave as those that have driven the Cuban people to the various insurrections which culminated in the present revolution.

A statement of the facts and circumstances that have forced the
Cubans from peaceful to belligerent measures of obtaining that redress
which they are satisfied can only come with absolute independence and
republican form of government are set forth at large in the pamphlet
hereto annexed, marked "A."

ABSOLUTE INDEPENDENCE OR EXTERMINATION.

Every promise of reform made to procure peace in 1878 having been
broken by the Spanish Government, and subsequent peaceful endeavor
in that direction having proved useless, Cuba is to-day in the condition
described by Vattel (Law of Nations, sec. 291):

If his (the sovereign's) promises are not inviolable, the rebels will have no security
in treating with him; when they have once drawn the sword they must throw away
the scabbard, as one of the ancients expressed it, and the prince destitute of the more
gentle and salutary means of appeasing the revolt will have no other remaining
expedient than of utterly exterminating the insurgents; these will become formidable
through despair; compassion will bestow success on them; their party will increase,
and the state will be in danger.

The only solution of the revolution in Cuba is independence or extermination.

PRELIMINARY ORGANIZATION FOR REVOLT.

Years before the outbreak of the present hostilities the people within
and without the island began to organize, with a view of preparing for
the inevitable revolution, being satisfied, after repeated and patient
endeavors, that peaceful petition was fruitless.

In order that the movement should be strong from the beginning, and
organized both as to civil and military administration, the Cuban Revolutionary party was founded, with José Martí at its head. The principal
objects were by united efforts to obtain the absolute independence of
Cuba, to promote the sympathy of other countries, to collect funds
with these objects in view, and to invest them in munitions of war.
The military organization of this movement was completed by the
election of Maximo Gomez as commander in chief. This election was
made by the principal officers who fought in the last revolution.

THE UPRISING.

The time for the uprising was fixed at the solicitation of the people
in Cuba, who protested that there was no hope of autonomy, and that
their deposits of arms and ammunition were in danger of being discovered and their leaders arrested. A large amount of war material was

then bought by Marti and vessels chartered to transport it to Cuba, where arrangements were made for its reception in the provinces of Santiago, Puerto Principe, and Santa Clara; but at Fernandina, Fla., it was seized by the United States authorities. Efforts were success-fully made for the restitution of this material; nevertheless valuable time and opportunity was thus lost. The people in Cuba clamored for the revolution to proceed immediately, and in consequence the uprising was not further postponed. The date fixed for the uprising was the 24th of February. The people responded in Santiago, Santa Clara, and Matanzas. The provinces of Puerto Principe and Pinar del Rio did not respond, owing to lack of arms. In Puerto Principe rigorous search had previous to the 24th been instituted and all arms and ammunition con-fiscated by the Government. The leaders in the provinces of Matanzas and Santa Clara were imprisoned, and so the movement there was checked for the time being.

On the 27th the Governor-General of the Island of Cuba, Emilio Calleja, issued a proclamation declaring the provinces of Matanzas and Santiago in a state of siege, and fixed a period of eight days within which all those who surrendered were to be pardoned. Under these conditions, on the 3d of March, Juan Gualberto Gomez surrendered, was brought to Havana, and set at liberty, but before he could leave the palace of the Captain-General was rearrested on the ground that he had bought arms for the movement, and was subsequently court-martailed and sent in chains to the Spanish penal colony in Ceuta, Africa.

GROWTH OF THE REVOLUTION.

In the province of Santiago the revolution rapidly increased in strength under the leadership of Bartolome Masso, one of the most influential and respected citizens of Manzanillo; Guillermo Moncada, Jesus Rabi, Pedro Perez, José Miro, and others.

It was characterized by the Spanish Government as a negro and bandit movement, but many of the most distinguished and wealthy white citizens of the district flocked to the insurgent camp.

The Spanish authorities, through some of the Autonomists, attempted to persuade these men to lay down their arms. Gen. Bartolome Masso was twice approached in this behalf, but positively refused to enter-tain any negotiations which were not based on the absolute independ-ence of Cuba.

On the 1st of April, Generals Antonio and José Maceo, Flor Crom-bet, and Agustin Cebreco, all veteran leaders in the former revolt, landed at Duaba, in the province of Santiago, and thousands rose to join them. Antonio Maceo then took command of the troops in that province, and on the 11th of April a detachment received Generals Maximo Gomez, José Marti, Francisco Borrerro, and Angel Guerra.

Captain-General Calleja was, on the 16th of April, succeeded by Gen. Arsenio Martinez Campos, the present commander in chief of the Span-ish forces, who has the reputation of being Spain's greatest living general.

BATTLES AND CAMPAIGN.

Campos's first plan of campaign was to confine the revolution to the province of Santiago, and he then stated that he would crush the insur-gents, establish peace, and return to Spain by the November following.

He asserted that the province of Puerto Principe would never rise in rebellion; and in order to give color to the statement and hope of labor to the unemployed, he projected a line of railway from Santa Cruz to Puerto Principe, planning also another from Manzanillo to Bayamo.

These two projects, as well as the proposed construction of wharves, were never seriously contemplated. From the very beginning of the uprising, conflicts between the Spanish troops and the Cubans were of daily occurrence, and many engagements of importance also took place, forts being captured, towns taken and raided.

It is of course useless to describe every skirmish in this province; the following are among the most important operations:

Los Negros, where General Rabi defeated the Spanish colonels Santoscildes and Zubikoski; Ramon de las Yaguas, where Colonel Garzon suprised and captured Lieutenant Gallego and 50 men, who were disarmed and permitted to leave unmolested—the troops sent to reinforce the Spaniards being also defeated; El Guanabano, where General Masso and Colonel Estrada forced Santoscildes to retreat to Bayamo, with great loss; Jarahuca, where General Maceo defeated General Salcedo, who had more than 3,000 men under him.

Combined operation of Generals Antonio and José Maceo, who captured the town of Cristo and 200 rifles and 40,000 rounds, while Colonel Garzon took the town of Caney, and Colonel Planas attacked a military convoy on the railroad.

The town of Campechuela was attacked by Colonel Guerra and Colonel Estrada, who forced the garrisons of the two forts to surrender.

Juraguanas, where Colonel Estrada, with 1,000 men, met an equal number of Spanish regulars and defeated them.

Colonel Guerra surprised a Spanish guerrilla under Boeras; made many prisoners, whom he set at liberty.

El Cacao, where General Rabi cut to pieces the Spanish forces under Lieut. Col. U. Sanchez and obtained many rifles and ammunition.

El Jobito: This was one of the most important engagements in the east. It took place near Guantanamo, and Lieutenant Colonel Bach was killed and his troops decimated by Generals Maceo and Perez.

About the middle of July Gen. Martinez Campos, urged by the numerous complaints through the press that the Spanish forces in Bayamo were in a deplorable condition, without food or hospitals, and were cut off from Manzanillo, and wishing by a concerted movement of his lieutenants to crush the revolution at one blow, started from Manzanillo on the 12th for the purpose of relieving Bayamo, and intending thence to march west and drive Gomez into the Spanish military line between the province of Santa Clara and Puerto Principe, thus catching the Cubans between two fires. At the same time three Spanish columns were to march against Maceo and his forces from different directions, and surround and exterminate them. Campos, with 4,800 men under the command of Gen. Fidel Santoscildes, met 3,600 Cubans under Generals Maceo and Rabi on the road to Bayamo at Peralejos.

The battle which followed is known as the battle of Bayamo, Valenzuela, or Peralejo. It lasted eleven hours. General Santoscildes fell in the early part of the engagement, and thereupon Campos himself took command. The Spaniards, completely routed, were forced to kill all their mules and horses to form with them a barricade; left their convoy, the wounded, and dead on the field, and fled in disorder to Bayamo. The loss of the Spaniards was 400 killed and a larger number wounded. The Cubans' was 137 in all. Maceo took care of the Spanish wounded, and sent word to Campos to send a detachment to receive them, which was done.

General Campos, on reaching Bayamo, sent for heavy reenforcements, withdrawing a considerable number of troops from the province of Santa Clara.

Generals Roloff, Sanchez, and Rodriguez landed in that province at about this time with a large amount of war material, but not enough, as it proved, to fully arm all those who enthusiastically rushed to join them. Before the Spaniards had extricated Campos from his perilous position, the Cuban forces in the province of Santa Clara had been organized into the Fourth Army Corps, and operations were immediately begun.

Santa Clara is one of the wealthiest provinces in the island, and to protect the interest there large reenforcements were called from Spain, as they could not rely on the Spanish " volunteers." The best proof of this was that 400 Spanish volunteers, under Major Casallas, deserted and joined the Cuban ranks in a body at their first opportunity, taking with them all their arms, ammunitions, and supplies. Here, as in other provinces, skirmishes are of daily occurrence, and many fierce encounters have taken place. Among the most important engagements were the capture of Fort Taguasco by Gen. Serafin Sanchez; Las Varas, where 2,000 Spanish troops under Colonel Rubin were defeated by Generals Roloff and Sanchez; Cantabria, where Colonel Rego took many prisoners and war materials, and the raid and burning of the town of Guinia de Miranda by Colonel Perez, and Cayo Espino, where Colonel Lacret inflicted a severe defeat on the Spaniards under Colonel Molina. A most important part of the work of the forces in Santa Clara, which occupied considerable time and caused many encounters with the enemy, was the destruction of telegraph and telephone communications and railroads, of which there are many lines or branches in this district.

GOMEZ'S CAMPAIGNS.

Immediately on the landing of Generals Martí and Gomez they set out to cross the province of Santiago and enter that of Puerto Principe. It will be remembered that at about this time General Campos arrived in the island with reenforcements of over ten thousand men; the object of Gomez in marching into Puerto Principe was to lead those whom he knew were only expecting his arrival in that province in order to take the field. The citizens of Puerto Principe, or Camaguey, as it is also called, had the reputation of being rather conservative and hence both Spaniards and Cubans waited their determination with great interest.

Gen. Martinez Campos boasted that the inhabitants of Camaguey would never rise in revolt against Spain, but to make assurance doubly sure he placed a cordon of troops numbering about 10,000 on the border between Santiago and Puerto Principe to prevent the entry of Gomez into the latter district. Gomez and Marti started on their westward journey with about 300 men. In trying to pass the first line of troops at Boca de Dos Rios a severe conflict took place May 19, with a greatly superior force in which José Martí was killed. Great joy was manifested by the Spaniards, who claimed that the revolution had received its deathblow in the loss of Martí, but Gomez continued his advance westward, and ordering a feint to be made by Gen. Antonia Maceo at a point in the north of the Spanish cordon, he succeeded in eluding the enemy and entering the southern part of the province of Puerto Principe in the beginning of June. Here he was joined by Salvador Cisneros Betancourt, now the President of the Republic, the most influential Cuban of that province, together with all the young men of the city, and his forces were rapidly swelled to thousands by additions from all parts of the province. These he subsequently organized into the Third Army Corps.

Thus Gomez was successful in this first campaign of the revolution. Immediately on his arrival in Camaguey he proceeded by a series of rapid cavalry movements to increase his supply of arms and ammunition. He captured and burned Alta Gracia and captured the fort of El Mulato; he cut to pieces a Spanish guerrilla near Las Yeguas. The town and fort of San Jeronimo surrendered to him, and he attacked and raided the town of Cascorro; in all of which places many arms and ammunition as well as prisoners were taken; the latter being invariably released.

During the summer the city of Puerto Principe was constantly menaced in order to allow Gomez to complete his organization of the province.

He was much criticised by Gen. Martinez Campos for his inactivity during the summer, but the Spanish troops nevertheless did not interfere with his plans. Early in July he issued the first of the now famous orders relative to the sugar crop, and announced his intention of marching through Santa Clara and into Matanzas in the winter in order to superintend the carrying out of his decrees, increasing his military stores in the meantime, as well as securing the food supply of his army by corralling the cattle of the province in secure places.

As will be shown further on, General Gomez was upon the establishment of the Government confirmed as commander in chief of the Cuban forces.

In order to carry out his winter campaign he placed Maj. Gen. José Maria Rodriguez in command of the Third Army Corps. The Spaniards explained the wonderful progress of the revolution by the fact that it is impossible for their soldiers to operate during the wet season, and stated that as soon as the winter or dry season set in, or, as it has been expressed by one of her diplomatic representatives, after three days of a northern wind, the Cubans would be driven back from the provinces of Santa Clara and Puerto Principe in the province of Santiago, intending then, by a concentration of their entire fleet at the eastern end of the island, to cut off all basis of supplies and starve the Cubans into submission. At the beginning of the dry season Gomez had perfected all the arrangements of his march to the west; he had ordered Gen. Antonio Maceo with about 4,000 men, mostly infantry, to follow and join him at Sancti Spiritus, on the western boundary of Santa Clara, where Generals Roloff, Sanchez, Perez, and Lacret were waiting, under orders, for the advance of the commander in chief.

Between the provinces of Santa Clara and Puerto Principe there is a line of forts extending from the town of Jucaro to the town of Moron, called the Trocha. To prevent the entrance of Gomez into Santa Clara, Gen. Martinez Campos reenforced their garrisons and placed strong columns along the line to fill up the gaps. General Gomez, with a few hundred men, succeeded by a series of maneuvers into getting through this line and falling upon the town of Pelayo, and captured the forts which guarded it, together with the entire garrison and a large amount of arms and ammunition. He then moved north in the province of Santa Clara, into the district of Remedios, moved west, recrossed the Trocha, and there joined forces with Gen. Antonio Maceo. The latter had marched his soldiers through the entire province of Puerto Principe, although four large Spanish columns were sent to interrupt his progress. These he succeeded in eluding, defeating them, however, on several occasions. The combined forces of Maceo and Gomez, by a series of strategic movements, again succeeded in passing the Trocha; their rear guard defeating Colonel Segura, inflicting heavy loss and capturing nearly 200 mules laden with arms, ammunition and supplies.

On the arrival of the combined forces in Santa Clara, Gomez, taking charge of all the forces in the district, divided them, sending flying columns in advance under Generals Suarez, Perez, and Lacret, dispatching others to Sagua, in the north, and toward Trinidad, in the south. Maceo's forces made a demonstration on the city of Santa Clara, which was now Martinez Campos's headquarters, while Gomez threatened Cienfuegos. In all the operations which now followed General Gomez had ample forces in his rear, so that his retreat, if made necessary, would not be cut off.

Immediately on the threatening of Cienfuegos Gen. Martinez Campos removed his headquarters from Santa Clara to Cienfuegos, and thence dispatched a large number of troops to form a line between Cienfuegos, Las Cruces, and Lajas, to impede the westward march of the Cuban army. Still advancing westward, and ordering a concentration of his troops, Gomez outflanked the Spanish command, his rear guard distracting their attention and engaging them severely at Maltiempo, in the western part of the province.

On the border of Matanzas Gomez again radiated his troops, Gen. Quintin Bandera on the north, General Maceo in the center, General Gomez himself to the south, while Generals Suarez, Perez, Lacret, and other officers attracted the attention of the enemy by rapid marches and raids. Martinez Campos had again changed his headquarters, this time moving to Colon, in the province of Matanzas; he hoped that the Spanish forces to the rear of the Cubans would be able to cooperate with him, but every means of communication by railroad, telephone, or telegraph had been completely destroyed by the Cubans in their progress, and no word could be sent nor soldiers transported quickly enough for a combined attack of front and rear of the Cubans. From this time on fighting was very sharp, and, as the order of Gomez concerning the grinding of the sugar crop was evidently being disobeyed in Matanzas and Santa Clara, the torch was applied, and it is estimated that a very insignificant part of the sugar crop will be exported this season.

With calls for the protection of the plantations in Santa Clara and Matanzas to attend to, the cities of Santa Clara, Cienfuegos, Matanzas, Cardenas, and Colon threatened, with all communications to the east, except by water, cut off, with the Cuban forces still advancing in oblique directions to the west, Martinez Campos concentrated as many troops as possible, sending to the most easterly province, that of Santiago, all the troops that could be spared from that district, he himself again changing his headquarters with the advance of Gomez to Jovellanos, thence to Limonar, to Matanzas, and finally to Havana, where, at the present writing, he is actively engaged in fortifying the land approaches to the capital, while he has hurried to the neighborhood of Batabano as many troops as could be spared, withdrawing even a large number of the marines from the fleets, thus assigning them to shore duty. Even the line at Batabano has been broken by the Cuban forces, and all communications to the east have been cut off.

So grave has the situation become that martial law has been proclaimed in the provinces of Havana and Pinar del Rio, so that the entire island from Point Maysi to Cape Antonio is now declared to be in a state of siege. The censorship of the press has been made more rigid than ever, and an order issued for the delivery of all horses in the

island to the Spanish Government at prices ranging from $18 to $35.
It is not intended to pay for these in cash, as only certificates of the
delivery of the horses to the Government with the value of the animal
as fixed by the latter are given to the owners.   Either this is an extreme
war measure taken only because of absolute necessity and of the scarcity of money, or it is another example of the gentle methods of the
Spanish Government in its treatment of the Cuban and his property.

While the westward march of Gomez was in progress Gens. Francisco
Carrillo and José M. Aguirre landed on the eastern end of the island
with a considerable supply of munitions, including some artillery, and
succeeded in marching through the provinces of Santiago and Puerto
Principe into that of Santa Clara, capturing several forts on the way.
General Carrillo has taken command in the Remedios district, where
his personal popularity has caused thousands to join him.   General
Aguirre reported to the commander in chief, and is now assisting in
the operations of Matanzas.

It was not the intention of General Gomez when he planned his winter
campaign to march on and lay siege to the capital, his only object being
to prevent the grinding and export of the sugar crop and the consequent flow of treasure into the Spanish coffers, and to demonstrate to
the world that he could control the provinces and enforce his orders.

While this march of the main bodies of troops westward has been
carried on, the Cuban forces of the other army corps have also succeeded in carrying out the orders concerning sugar cane and preventing the establishment of Spanish lines of communication.   As artillery
has now been introduced into the Cuban army, forts are more easily
taken.   There has been constant communication from the interior to
the coast; vessels of the Spanish navy have frequently been engaged
by the insurgents., and in one case a small armed coast-guard vessel was
captured by them

Supplies are received by the Cubans at convenient points on the coast
and transferred to the interior.   When it is remembered that in the
revolution of 1861 to 1878 there were never more than 10,000 armed
insurgents in the field; that these rarely, if ever, took the offensive,
and yet compelled Spain to maintain an army of 120,000 men in the
field, many of whom were Cuban volunteers in the strict sense of the
term; that this little band caused Spain to spend in the ten years over
$700,000,000 and to lose over 200,000 men, and that when in contrast
we see in this revolution there are already more than 50,000 Cubans in
the field, directed by veterans of the last war, who now are on the offensive, and that now Cuban does not fight against Cuban, the chance of
ultimate success of the Cuban arms must appear to an impartial
observer, especially in the light of Gomez's wonderful western march,
and that in two months more the climate will again militate against
the Spanish troops.

MILITARY ORGANIZATION.

The military organization of the Cubans is ample and complete.

Maj. Gen. Maximo Gomez is the commander in chief, as we have said,
of all the forces, a veteran of the last revolution, as indeed are all the generals almost without exception.   Maj. Gen. Antonio Maceo is second in
command of the army of liberation, and was, until called upon to
cooperate with the commander in chief in the late march to the western province, in command of Santiago.

The army is at present divided into five corps—two in Santiago, one
in Puerto Principe, and two in Santa Clara and Matanzas.   These corps

are divided into divisions, these again into brigades, and finally into regiments; the forces are moreover divided into cavalry and infantry, besides having engineers, and lately artillery and a perfect sanitary corps, which latter is in command of Eugenio Sanchez Agramonte, with the grade of brigadier-general. Maj. Gen. José Maceo commands the First Santiago Corps, while Maj. Gen. Bartolome Masso commands the Second Corps in that province.

Commanding divisions and brigades in these two corps are Brig. Gens. Pedro Perez, Agustin Cebreco, Jesus Rabi, Luis Feria, Bernardo Capote, Higinio Vasquez, and Angel Guerra.

The Third Corps is in command of Maj. Gen. José M. Rodriguez. The Fourth Corps is in command of Maj. Gen. Cartos Roloff, the divisions and brigades being commanded by Maj. Gens. Francisco Carrillo and Serafin Sanchez and Brig. Gens. Tranquilino Perez, Juan B. Zayas, and Rogelio Castillo. The Fifth Corps is in command of Maj. Gen. Manuel Suarez, and the divisions and brigades are commanded by Francisco Perez, José Lacret, and José M. Aguirre.

The first two corps consist of 26,000 men, mostly infantry; the third, of about 4,000 men, mostly cavalry; the Fourth and Fifth Corps consisted before the late invasion of Gomez of over 20,000 men, both infantry and cavalry, which force has been considerably increased in these last days. Of the 50,000 men that there are at least in the field, more than half are fully armed and equipped, the rest carrying miscellaneous weapons or side arms.

The work of fully equipping the army is now proceeding rapidly. The higher grades and commissions are all confirmed by the Government.

Stations for the manufacture of powder and the reloading of cartridges are established, as well as manufacturing of shoes, saddles, and other equipments. The hospitals for the sick and wounded are also provided. Red Cross societies have offered their cooperation, but the Spanish commander in chief has refused to allow them to enter the insurgent lines.

The discipline of the army is strict and marauding is promptly punished, as was done in the case of Lieut. Alberto Castillo, an officer of the Second Corps, who was tried and shot for robbery, and as has been repeatedly done with the "Plateados," men who, taking advantage of the unsettled condition of affairs in the country, have turned bandits. The Cuban Army of Liberation is entirely volunteer, without pay.

CIVIL GOVERNMENT.

As above indicated, José Martí was the head of the preliminary civil organization, and he, immediately upon landing with Gomez in Cuba, issued a call for the selection of representatives of the Cuban people to form a civil government.

His death postponed for a time the selection of these men, but in the beginning of September the call previously issued was complied with.

Representatives from each of the provinces of Santiago, Puerto Principe, Santa Clara, and the western part of the island, comprising the provinces of Matanzas and Havana, making twenty in all, were elected to the constituent assembly, which was to establish a civil government, republican in form.

A complete list of the members of the constituent assembly which met at Jimaguayu, in the province of Puerto Principe, on the 13th of September, 1895, together with an account of its organization and subsequent action, will be found in the document hereto annexed and marked B.

A constitution of the Republic of Cuba was adopted on the 16th of September, and copy of which will be found in document annexed marked B.

On the 18th of September the following officers of the Government were elected by the constituent assembly in accordance with the terms of the constitution:

President, Salvador Cisneros Betancourt, of Puerto Principe; vice-president, Bartolome Masso, of Manzanillo; secretary of war, Carlos Roloff, of Santa Clara; secretary of the treasury, Severo Pina, of Sancti Spiritus; secretary of the interior, Santiago Garcia Canizares, of Remedios; secretary of foreign relations, Rafael M. Portuondo, of Santiago de Cuba; subsecretary of war, Mario Menocal, of Mantanzas; subsecretary of the treasury, Joaquin Castello, of Santiago de Cuba; subsecretary of the interior, Carlos Dubois, of Baracoa; subsecretary of foreign relations, Fermin Valdes Dominguez, of Havana.

The installation of these officers duly followed. The election of the general in chief and the second in command, who is to bear the title of lieutenant-general, was then had, and resulted in the unanimous election of Maximo Gomez and Antonio Maceo, respectively.

On the same day the constituent assembly elected by acclamation as delegate plenipotentiary and general agent abroad of the Cuban Republic, the undersigned, Tomas Estrada Palma. The credentials issued to me are hereto annexed, marked C.

Immediately thereafter the government council proceeded to the headquarters of General Gomez, in Puerto Principe, where the latter took the oath of allegiance to the constitution of the Republic, together with his troops, who there gathered for this purpose, and was installed as commander in chief of the armies of the Republic.

The government council then proceeded to the province of Santiago, where Gen. Antonio Maceo and his forces took the oath of allegiance.

Thence the council proceeded to the province or Santa Clara to inspect and administer the oath to the troops of the Fourth and Fifth Army Corps. They are now on their way to the province of Santiago, where their permanent headquarters will be established.

The divisions of the provinces into prefectures under the supervision of the secretary of the interior and the duties which devolve in this department are fully set forth in Exhibit B, as well as the duties of the secretary of the treasury. The impositions, rate and collection of the taxes, and sources of income of the Government will also be found in Exhibit B.

All moneys collected in accordance with the laws of the Republic, as well as those received through voluntary contributions, are delivered to him or his duly authorized agent and expended under his supervision or that of his agents, to supply the present needs of the Government, which are mainly purchase of arms and ammunition.

The money thus collected has been sufficient to equip the army and keep it supplied with ammunition, although, as it is natural, from the rapid increase of the ranks and the difficulty of bringing supplies into the island, many of the new recruits have not yet been fully armed. The problem of equipping the army is not a financial one, but arises from the caution necessary to blockade running and, above all, the preventive measures taken by foreign Governments, and the notice which is in all cases given to the enemy of the embarkment of munitions. No report of the secretary of the treasury has yet been made, as he has been in office but three months.

For the purpose of properly collecting the imposts the roads to all cities, as well as the coast, are patrolled by the Cubans. The Cuban

Government publishes two newspapers, El Cubano Libre and the Bole- tin de la Guerra.

TREATMENT OF PRISONERS.

From the beginning of this insurrection the conduct of the Cubans as to prisoners has been in strong contrast to that of the Spaniards; prisoners taken by the Cubans have been invariably well treated, cared for, and liberated, officers as well as common soldiers, as soon as it was possible under the circumstances, and word sent to the Spanish officers to call for them on the guaranty that the detachment would be respected.

As instances we may recite those even admitted by the Spaniards, namely: Ramon de las Yaguas, Campechuela, and Peralejos, in Santiago; el Mulato, San Jeronimo, and Las Minas, in Puerto Principe; Taguasco, Pelayo, and Cantabria, in Santa Clara. After the last-mentioned engagement Colonel Rego returned his prisoners to the Spanish lines, obtaining a receipt for their delivery signed by a lieutenant, of which a copy is hereto annexed, marked D.

This action, in accordance with the spirit of the insurrection, which is declared not to be against the Spaniards, of whom many are fighting for the independence of the island, but against the Spanish Government, is echoed by the general order of the commander in chief on this subject, of which the following is a copy:

CIRCULAR OF THE GENERAL IN CHIEF.

GENERAL HEADQUARTERS OF THE ARMY OF LIBERATION,
Camaguey, August 1, 1895.

In order to establish in a clear and precise manner the mode of procedure toward the chiefs, officers, and soldiers of the monarchy captured in action or operations, and toward those who voluntarily surrender to our columns or authorities, I have deemed it convenient to order as follows:

ART. 1. All prisoners captured in action or by the troops of the Republic will be immediately liberated and returned to their ranks, unless they volunteer to join the army of liberation. The abandoned wounded will be gathered and attended to with all care, and the unburied dead interred.

ART. 2. All persons who shall be arrested, charged with committing the misdemeanors in the circular of July 1, by violating or disregarding the said order, will be summarily proceeded against.

ART. 3. Those of the prisoners who are chiefs or officers of the army of the monarchy will be respected and considered according to their rank and treated according to the valor with which they may have resisted, and will all be returned to their ranks if they so desire.

ART. 4. Those who volunteer to join the ranks of the republicans, and appear before our columns and authorities, will have their option in the mode of serving the cause of the Republic, either in arms or by more peaceful occupations, civil or agricultural pursuits.

I communicate this to you for your instruction and for your rigid compliance. Country and liberty.

MAXIMO GOMEZ,
The General in Chief.

On the part of the Spanish, attention is called to the order prohibiting newspaper correspondents from entering insurgent lines to prevent accurate information being given to the world at large; the order to shoot all who supply food or medicines to the insurgents; the order, which in every instance has been carried out, to shoot all officers of the Cuban army who may be captured, under which Domingo Mujica, Gil Gonzalez, Quirina Amezago, and Acebo have been executed. At the recapture of Baire, old men, women, and children were ruthlessly slaughtered by the Spanish soldiery, the hospital at Gran Piedra was captured and over seventy wounded and defenseless Cubans were killed; at Cayo Espino peaceful men and women were butchered by Colonel Molina and the outrages committed by the troops under Garrido and Tejera are legion. The action of convicts, who have been liberated by Spain to fight the Cubans under such leadership as that of the notorious Lola Benitez, who bears the title of colonel, are, as might be expected, a blot on any Christian army.

As to the treatment of Cubans suspected of sympathy with the insurgents, we have but to consider the large number of men who have lately been arrested and on bare suspicion summarily sent to the Spanish penal colonies for life; some foreign citizens have indeed escaped court martial on the interference of their Governments, but it is well known that even civil trials at this time are under the absolute control of the Government.

NOT A NEGRO MOVEMENT.

The Spaniards charge, in order to belittle the insurrection, that it is a movement of negroes. It should be remembered that not more than one-third of the entire population are of the colored race. As a matter of fact, less than one-third of the army are of the colored race. Take, for instance, the generals of corps, divisions, and brigades; there are but three of the colored race, namely, Antonio and José Maceo and Augustin Cebreco, and these are mulattoes whose deeds and victories have placed them far above the generals of those who pretend to despise them. None of the members of the constituent assembly or of the Government are of the colored race. The Cubans and the colored race are as friendly in this war as they were in times of peace, and it would indeed be strange if the colored people were not so, as the whites fought for and with them in the last revolt, the only successful purpose of which was the freedom of the slaves.

If it be true that this is merely a movement of bandits and negroes and adventurers, as the Spaniards assert, why have they not armed the Cuban people to fight against the outlaws, or why have not the Cuban people themselves volunteered to crush this handful? On the contrary, they know that giving those Cubans arms who have them not would be but to increase the number of insurgents, and they have therefore sent more than 125,000 troops from Spain, mostly conscripts; they have sent over forty of their most famous generals; they have increased their navy, and virtually, so far as the Cubans are concerned, blockaded the entire coast. They have been compelled to make many onerous loans to carry on the campaign; they have increased the fortifications of their ports; they have brought torpedoes to protect their harbors, and they have even placed armed troops on their mail steamers to prevent their capture.

Besides this large army, they have between 60,000 and 80,000 volunteers to protect their towns. These volunteers, so called, are native Spaniards and a branch of the regular army, the service being compulsory; that is, instead of serving in the regular army at home, where their entire time must be given up, they volunteer to enter this body on emigration to Cuba, where they may follow to a considerable extent their occupation; in other words, they correspond to our home guards or militia, except that the service is obligatory and that the men can not leave the island without permission.

It is not denied that a large number of what the Spaniards term the lower classes are in this revolution, but this is only a proof of how deep into the mass of the people have been implanted the seeds of discontent and of republicanism. This is a movement not like our last revolution—the result of the agitation of the wealthy and the educated—but one which is the outcome of the popular sentiment of all classes.

Much surprise has been expressed that with the immense army and resources at hand Spain has not been able to crush the insurrection or prevent its rapid growth. Aside from the climate, which is deadly to the raw, ill-fed, ill-clothed, ill-treated, and badly paid Spanish troops, the greater part of whom are mere lads, the Spaniards have to divide their troops into an army of occupation and another of operation. These must necessarily move in considerable numbers, because if compelled to flee without a knowledge of the intricacies of the country they would be decimated.

A Cuban command on dispersion is readily reorganized, as each man is his own guide. This is one of the most valuable of Cuban movements—to disperse as if routed, to rally at a previously agreed point, and then to fall upon and surprise the seemingly victorious enemy. The Cuban, used to the country and the climate, marches and rides much faster than the Spaniard. He can live and thrive, and does so in necessity, on food that is death to the Spanish soldier. Moreover in a friendly country the movements of the enemy are readily ascertained by the Cuban general, who can thus select his own position or evade the engagement, while the Spanish are never so well informed and are at the mercy of their guides.

It must be remembered that the Cuban fights for the noblest principle of man—independence. That he does so without compulsion or pay, but spontaneously and enthusiastically—nay, he fights the battle of despair, knowing it is better to be killed thus than to bear the tortures of a Spanish prison or to trust himself to the tender mercy of a Spanish commander. On the other hand, the Spanish troops fight by compulsion and for pay, which is even now months in arrears; they fight without faith, for their heart is not with their cause. They know that surrender means pardon and good treatment, while fighting may mean death. Hundreds of Spanish soldiers have singly or in groups gone over to the insurgent lines, being satisfied that they would live there under better conditions.

CHARACTER OF THE WAR.

There was also an attempt made by the Spanish to brand the Cubans with carrying on an uncivilized warfare because of their use of dynamite. General Roloff before using this explosive issued a proclamation warning all persons of the danger of traveling by rail. Dynamite has been used freely, but only as a substitute for gunpowder in the destruction of railroad bridges, trestles, and trains which could be used and were used for the transportation of Spanish troops. Of course it is a serious loss to Spain to have these railroads destroyed, but no one can seriously deny that it is a measure justified by the necessities of war. The use of this explosive as a substitute for gunpowder in the operation of mines is simply a proof that the Cubans are keeping pace with the advance of inventions in the art of war.

DESTRUCTION OF PROPERTY.

The subject, however, which has caused probably the most discussion is the order of General Gomez to prevent the grinding of sugar cane and in case of the disobedience of said order the destruction of the crop.

General Gomez issued a preliminary warning dated July 1, of which the following is a copy:

GENERAL HEADQUARTERS OF THE ARMY OF LIBERATION,
Najasa, Camaguey, July 1, 1895.

To the Planters and Owners of Cattle Ranches:

In accord with the great interests of the revolution for the independence of the country and for which we are in arms:

Whereas all exploitations of any product whatsoever are aids and resources to the Government that we are fighting, it is resolved by the general in chief to issue this general order throughout the island that the introduction of articles of commerce, as well as beef and cattle, into the towns occupied by the enemy, is absolutely prohibited. The sugar plantations will stop their labors, and whosoever shall attempt to grind the crop notwithstanding this order, will have their cane burned and their buildings demolished. The person who, disobeying this order, will try to profit from the present situation of affairs, will show by his conduct little respect for the rights of the revolution of redemption and therefore shall be considered as an enemy, treated as a traitor, and tried as such in case of his capture.

MAXIMO GOMEZ,
The General in Chief.

Nevertheless throughout the country preparations were made for the grinding of the crop. A peremptory order, of which the following is a copy, was then issued on November 6:

HEADQUARTERS OF THE ARMY OF LIBERATION,
Territory of Sancti Spiritus, November 6, 1895.

Animated by the spirit of unchangeable resolution in defense of the rights of the revolution of redemption of this country of colonists, humiliated and despised by Spain, and in harmony with what has been decreed concerning the subject in the circular dated the 1st of July, I have ordered the following:

ARTICLE I. That all plantations shall be totally destroyed, their cane and outbuildings burned, and railroad connections destroyed.

ART. II. All laborers who shall aid the sugar factories—these sources of supplies that we must deprive the enemy of—shall be considered as traitors to their country.

ART. III. All who are caught in the act, or whose violation of Article II shall be proven, shall be shot. Let all chiefs of operations of the army of liberty comply with this order, determined to unfurl triumphantly, even over ruin and ashes, the flag of the Republic of Cuba.

In regard to the manner of waging the war, follow the private instructions that I have already given.

For the sake of the honor of our arms and your well-known courage and patriotism, it is expected that you will strictly comply with the above orders.

M. GOMEZ, *General in Chief.*

To the chiefs of operations: Circulate this.

On the 11th of November the following proclamation was issued:

HEADQUARTERS OF THE ARMY OF LIBERATION,
Sancti Spiritus, November 11, 1895.

To honest men, victims of the torch:

The painful measure made necessary by the revolution of redemption drenched in innocent blood from Hatuey to our own times by cruel and merciless Spain will plunge you in misery. As general in chief of the army of liberation it is my duty to lead it to victory, without permitting myself to be restrained or terrified, by any means necessary to place Cuba in the shortest time in possession of her dearest ideal. I therefore place the responsibility for so great a ruin on those who look on impassively and force us to those extreme measures which they then condemn like dolts and hypocrites that they are. After so many years of supplication, humiliations, contumely, banishment, and death, when this people, of its own will, has arisen in arms, there remains no other solution but to triumph, it matters not what means are employed to accomplish it.

This people can not hesitate between the wealth of Spain and the liberty of Cuba. Its greatest crime would be to stain the land with blood without effecting its purposes because of puerile scruples and fears which do not concur with the character of the men who are in the field, challenging the fury of an army which is one of the bravest in the world, but which in this war is without enthusiasm or faith, ill fed and unpaid. The war did not begin February 24; it is about to begin now.

The war had to be organized; it was necessary to calm and lead into the proper channels the revolutionary spirit always exaggerated in the beginning by wild enthusiasm. The struggle ought to begin in obedience to a plan and method more or less studied, as the result of the peculiarities of this war. This has already been done. Let Spain now send her soldiers to rivet the chains of her slaves; the children of this land are in the field, armed with the weapons of liberty. The struggle will be terrible, but success will crown the revolution and efforts of the oppressed.

MAXIMO GOMEZ, *General in Chief.*

The reasons underlying this measure are the same which caused this country to destroy the cotton crop and the baled cotton in the South during the war of the secession.

The sugar crop is a source of large income to the Spanish Government, directly by tax and export duty, as well as indirectly. The action of the insurgents is perfectly justified, because it is simply a blockade, so to speak, on land—a prevention of the gathering, and hence the export, of the commodity with, naturally, a punishment for the violation thereof.

PROTESTS OF ALIENS.

Strenuous protests have, too, been made by and on behalf of aliens residing in or having property in Cuba.

It is admitted in civilized warfare that the property of alien residents, whether they are in sympathy with the enemy or not, when in the track of war, is subject to war's casualties, and that all property which might be of aid and comfort to the enemy may be taken or destroyed, the commander in the field being the judge of the exigency and necessities which dictate such action. This proposition has been laid down by the State Department and the Supreme Court of this country in the matter of the destruction of cotton in the late war.

The provision of the constitution of the Republic of Cuba that the citizens of a country which acknowledges the Cubans as belligerents, shall be exempt from the payment of taxes and contributions to the Republic, naturally implies that the property of such citizens after the granting of belligerency by their country, even though by all the laws of war it is contraband and may be seized or destroyed, will be absolutely respected, and, I have all reason to assert, will be under the special protection of the Cuban Government and its army.

For aliens to ask this protection as a right while their Government denies the existence of the belligerency of the Cubans might well be considered by the latter as allowing aid and comfort to go to their enemy, simply on the expectation that some time in the future the Government of those aliens may, out of gratitude to the Cubans, acknowledge, what is after all but a state of fact, belligerency. In the meantime the aid and comfort thus allowed by the Cubans to flow to the Spaniards must strengthen the latter and thus draw out the struggle or weaken the former. General Gomez explains the importance of this measure in the following letter:

DISTRICT OF REMEDIOS,
Province of Santa Clara, December 8, 1895.

To TOMAS ESTRADA PALMA.

MY DEAR AND ESTEEMED FRIEND: It is not long since I wrote you, but an opportunity offers by which I may send you a few words of encouragement and good cheer. Rest assured I write you whenever I can, which is not often, owing to the great amount of work which at present falls upon my shoulders. I know the pen is mightier than the sword, but my mission at present is with the latter; others must wield the pen.

Eight days ago Gen. Antonio Maceo and myself met and fought the enemy with our forces in conjunction. The Spanish column, including infantry, cavalry, and artillery were our superiors in number, but the arms of the Cuban Republic were again victorious. I have not time at present to go into details of the battle, they will follow later. Suffice it to say, Spanish reports to the contrary notwithstanding, we won the day.

Our advance may be slow, but it will be sure and firm. If you hear of our retreat remember that it will be temporary and for a purpose. Our faces are turned toward the west and nothing will stop us. The result of my observations as we proceed is that the Spaniards are in need of almost everything—money, sympathy, soldiers, and even leaders who have faith and courage in the righteousness of their cause.

If Cuban valor and resolution do not fail us, and if the hearts of Cuba's children do not weaken, I have every reason to believe that the close of the six months' campaign now initiated will find everything satisfactorily settled and Cuba free.

I know that unfavorable comment has been made on some of the methods we have been forced to employ in this revolution, but it will not do to listen to the complaints of the superficial and irresponsible. No sugar crop must be made this winter under any circumstances or for any amount of money. It is the source from which the enemy still hopes and dreams of obtaining its revenue. To prevent that end, for the good of our country, has been and shall be our programme.

We are Cubans and have one great aim in view, one glorious object to obtain—the freedom of our country and liberty. It is of more importance to us than glory, public applause, or anything else. Everything else will follow in time. I have never believed in or advised a sanguinary revolution, but it must be a radical one. First of all we must triumph; toward that end the most effective means, although they may appear harsh, must be employed.

There is nothing so bad, so dishonorable, so inexcusable, in the eyes of the world as failure. Victory is within our reach. To hesitate, to delay it, to endanger it now, would be stupid, would be cowardly, would be criminal. We will succeed first; the applause of the world will follow. To do otherwise would be not to love one's country. I have never felt more confident than at the present moment. You can rest assured that Cuba will soon achieve her absolute independence.

Ever your true friend,   MAXIMO GOMEZ.

As I have through various sources been approached on this subject in behalf of property of American citizens on the island, and as I know the cordial friendship which the Cubans bear to the Government and people of the United States of America, feeling assured that this country, from its very history, must likewise feel a deep sympathy with a people who are treading in their footsteps, I have written to the Government of the Republic of Cuba the following letter:

NEW YORK, *December 23, 1895.*

SALVADOR CISNEROS BETANCOURT,
         President of the Cuban Republic.

MY DISTINGUISHED FELLOW-COUNTRYMAN: There have been many complaints made to me from various sources that the property of citizens of the United States of North America has been destroyed by our army of liberation in Cuba under the order of our distinguished general in chief, Maximo Gomez. I know very well how you and all my countrymen feel toward this Republic, and that you desire to do everything in your power to demonstrate your friendship, and I deem it my duty to communicate the above facts to you so that you may consider the matter carefully and thoroughly; at the same time I know that many Spaniards intend to transfer their property, as some have done already, to American citizens or companies especially organized for their purposes, in case that you should, before or after receiving the rights of belligerents, take active measures for the protection of North American interests.

I say this because I am sure that, at least after the granting of belligerency, you will do your utmost to guard the interests of the citizens of a country which warmly sympathizes with us in our present struggle.

Hoping that you will give this subject your most thoughtful consideration, I remain your devoted friend, for country and liberty,

T. ESTRADA PALMA.

In view of the history of this revolution as herein stated, in view of the causes which led to it, its rapid growth, its successes in arms, the establishment, operation, and resources of the Government of the Cuban Republic, the organization, number, and discipline of its army, the contrast in the treatment of prisoners to that of the enemy, the territory in its control and subject to the carrying out of its decrees, of the futility of the attempts of the Spanish Government to crush the revolution, in spite of the immense increase of its army in Cuba and of its blockade and the many millions spent for that purpose, the cruelties which on the part of the Spanish have especially characterized this sanguinary and fiercely conducted war, and the damage to the interests of the citizens of this country under the present conditions, I, as the duly accredited representative, in the name of the Cuban people in arms who have fought singly and alone against the monarchy of Spain for nearly a year, in the heart of a continent devoted to republican institutions, in the name of justice, in the name of humanity, in the name of liberty, petition you, and through you the Government of the United States of America, to accord the rights of belligerency to a people fighting for their absolute independence.

Very respectfully, yours,

T. ESTRADA PALMA.

The Hon. RICHARD OLNEY,
    Secretary of State of the United States of America.

A

CUBA v. SPAIN.

War is a dire necessity. But when a people has exhausted all human means of persuasion to obtain from an unjust oppressor a remedy for its ills, if it apeals as a last resource to force in order to repel the persistent aggression which constitutes tyranny, this people is justified before its own conscience and before the tribunal of nations.

Such is the case of Cuba in its wars against Spain No metropolis has ever been harsher or more obstinately harassing; none has ever exploited a colony with more greediness and less foresight than Spain. No colony has ever been more prudent, more long-suffering, more cautious, more persevering than Cuba in its purpose of asking for its rights by appealing to the lessons of experience and political wisdom. Only driven by desperation has the people of Cuba taken up arms, and having done so, it displays as much heroism in the hour of danger as it had shown good judgment in the hour of deliberation

The history of Cuba during the present century is a long series of rebellions; but every one of these was preceded by a peaceful struggle for its rights—a fruitless struggle because of the obstinate blindness of Spain.

There were patriots in Cuba from the beginning of this century, such as Presbyter Caballero and Don Francisco Arango, who called the metropolitan Government's attention to the evils of the colony, and pointed to the remedy by pleading for the commercial franchises required by its economical organization, and for the intervention of the natives in its government, not only as a right, but also for political expediency, in view of the long distance between the colony and the home government, and the grave difficulties with which it had to contend. The requirements of the war with the continental colonies, which were tired of Spanish tyranny, compelled the metropolitan Government to grant a certain measure of commercial liberty to the Island of Cuba; a temporary concession which spread prosperity throughout its territory, but which was not sufficient to open the eyes of the Spanish statesmen. On the contrary, prompted by suspicion and mistrust of the Americans, they began by curtailing, and shortly after abrogated the limited administrative powers then possessed by some of the corporations in Cuba, such as the "Junta de Fomento"— (a board for the encouragement of internal improvements).

As if this were not enough, the Cubans were deprived of the little show of political intervention they had in public affairs. By a simple royal decree in 1837 the small representation of Cuba in the Spanish Cortes was suppressed, and all the powers of the Government were concentrated in the hands of the captain-general, on whom authority was conferred to act as the governor of a city in a state of siege. This implied that the captain-general, residing in Habana, was master of the life and property of every inhabitant of the island of Cuba. This meant that Spain declared a permanent state of war against a peaceful and defenseless people.

Cuba saw its most illustrious sons, such as Heredia and Saco, wander in exile throughout the free American Continent. Cuba saw as many of the Cubans as dared to love liberty and declare it by act or word die on the scaffold, such as Joaquin de Aguero and Placido. Cuba saw the product of its people's labor confiscated by iniquitous fiscal laws imposed by its masters from afar. Cuba saw the administration of justice in the hands of foreign magistrates, who acted at the will or the whim of its rulers. Cuba suffered all the outrages that can humiliate a conquered people, in the name and by the work of a Government that sarcastically calls itself paternal. Is it to be wondered, then, that an uninterrupted era of conspiracies and uprisings should have been inaugurated? Cuba in its despair took up arms in 1850 and 1851, conspired again in 1855, waged war in 1868, in 1879, in 1885, and is fighting now since the 24th of February of the present year.

But at the same time Cuba has never ceased to ask for justice and redress. Its people, before shouldering the rifle, pleaded for their rights. Before the pronunciamento of Aguero and the invasions of Lopez, Saco, in exile, exposed the dangers of Cuba to the Spanish statesmen, and pointed to the remedy. Other farsighted men seconded him in the colony. They denounced the cancer of slavery, the horrors of the traffic in slaves, the corruption of the officeholders, the abuses of the Government, the discontent of the people with their forced state of political tutelage. No attention was given to them, and this brought on the first armed conflicts.

Before the formidable insurrection of 1868, which lasted ten years, the reform party, which included the most enlightened, wealthy, and influential Cubans, exhausted all the resources within their reach to induce Spain to initiate a healthy change in her Cuban policy. The party started the publication of periodicals in Madrid and in the island, addressed petitions, maintained a great agitation throughout the country, and having succeeded in leading the Spanish Government to make an inquiry into the economical, political, and social condition of Cuba, they presented a complete plan of government which satisfied public requirements as well as the aspirations of the people. The Spanish Government disdainfully cast aside the proposition as useless, increased taxation, and proceeded to its exaction with extreme severity.

It was then that the ten-year war broke out. Cuba, almost a pigmy compared with Spain, fought like a giant. Blood ran in torrents. Public wealth disappeared in a bottomless abyss. Spain lost 200,000 men. Whole districts of Cuba were left almost entirely without their male population. Seven hundred millions were spent to feed that conflagration—a conflagration that tested Cuban heroism, but which could not touch the hardened heart of Spain. The latter could not subdue the bleeding colony, which had no longer strength to prolong the struggle with any prospect of success. Spain proposed a compact which was a snare and a deceit. She granted to Cuba the liberties of Puerto Rico, which enjoyed none.

On this deceitful ground was laid the new situation, throughout which has run a current of falsehood and hypocrisy. Spain, whose mind had not changed, hastened to change the name of things. The capitan-general was called governor-general. The royal decrees took the name of authorizations. The commercial monopoly of Spain was named coasting trade. The right of banishment was transformed into the law of vagrancy. The brutal attacks of defenseless citizens were called "componte." The abolition of constitutional guarantees became the law of public order. Taxation without the consent or knowledge of the Cuban people was changed into the law of estimates (budget) voted by the representatives of Spain; that is, of European Spain.

The painful lesson of the ten-year war had been entirely lost on Spain. Instead of inaugurating a redeeming policy that would heal the recent wounds, allay public anxiety, and quench the thirst for justice felt by the people, who were desirous to enjoy their natural rights, the metropolis, while lavish in promises of reform, persisted in carrying on unchanged its old and crafty system, the groundwork of which continues to be the same, namely: To exclude every native Cuban from every office that could give him any effective influence and intervention in public affairs; the ungovernable exploitation of the colonists' labor for the benefit of Spanish commerce and Spanish bureaucracy, both civil and military. To carry out the latter purpose it was necessary to maintain the former at any cost.

I.

In order to render the native Cuban powerless in his own country, Spain, legislating for Cuba without restriction as it does, had only to give him an electoral law so artfully framed as to accomplish two objects: First, to reduce the number of voters; second, to give always a majority to the Spaniards; that is, to the European colonists, notwithstanding that the latter represent only 9.3 per cent of the total population of Cuba. To this effect it made the electoral right dependent on the payment of a very high poll tax, which proved the more burdensome as the war had ruined the larger number of Cuban proprietors. In this way it succeeded in restricting the right of suffrage to only 53,000 inhabitants in an island which has a population of 1,600,-000; that is to say, to the derisive proportion of 3 per cent of the total number of inhabitants.

In order to give a decided preponderance to the Spanish European element, the electoral law has ignored the practice generally observed in those countries where the right to vote depends on the payment of a poll tax, and has afforded all the facilities to acquire the electoral privilege to industry, commerce, and public officials, to the detriment of the territorial property (the ownership of real estate). To accomplish this, while the rate of the territorial tax is reduced to 2 per cent, an indispensable measure, in view of the ruinous condition of the landowners, the exorbitant contribution of $25 is required from those who would be electors as freeholders. The law has, moreover, thrown the doors wide open for the perpetration of fraud by providing that the simple declaration of the head of a commercial house is sufficient to consider all its employees as partners, having, therefore, the right to vote. This has given us firms with thirty or more partners. By this simple scheme almost all the Spaniards residing in Cuba are turned into electors, despite the explicit provisions of the law. Thus it comes to pass that the municipal district of Güines, with a population of 13,000 inhabitants, only 500 of which are Spaniards and Canary Islanders, shows on its electoral list the names of 32 native Cubans and of 400 Spaniards—only 0.25 per cent of the Cuban to 80 per cent of the Spanish population.

But, as if this were not enough, a so-called permanent commission of provincial deputations decides every controversy that may arise as to who is to be included in or excluded from the list of electors, and the members of this commission are appointed by the Governor-General. It is unnecessary to say that its majority has always been devoted to the Government. In case any elector considers himself wronged by the decision of the permanent commission he can appeal to the "audiencia" (higher court) of the district, but the "audiencias" are almost entirely made up of European magistrates; they are subject to the authority of the Governor-General, being mere political tools in his hands. As a conclusive instance of the manner in which those tribunals do justice to the claims of the Cuban electors, it will be sufficient to cite a case which occurred in Santa Clara in 1892, where 1,000 fully qualified liberal electors were excluded at one time, for the simple omission to state their names at the end of the act presented by the elector who headed the claim. In more than one case has the same "audiencia" applied two different criterions to identical cases. The "audiencia" of Havana, in 1887, ignoring the explicit provisions of the law, excused the employees from the condition of residence, a condition that the same tribunal exacted before. The same "audiencia" in 1885 declared that the contributions to the State and to the municipality were accumulative, and in 1887 decided the opposite. This inconsistency had for its object to expunge from the lists hundreds of Cuban electors. In this way the Spanish Government and tribunals have endeavored to teach respect for the law and for the practice of wholesome electoral customs to the Cuban colonists.

It will be easily understood now why on some occasions the Cuban representation in the Spanish Parliament has been made up of only three deputies, and in the most favorable epochs the number of Cuban representatives has not exceeded six. Three deputies in a body of four hundred and thirty members! The genuine representation of Cuba has not reached sometimes 0.96 per cent of the total number of members of the Spanish congress. The great majority of the Cuban deputation has always consisted of Spanish peninsulars. In this manner the ministers of "ultramar" (ministers of the colonies), whenever they have thought necessary to give an honest or decent appearance to their legislative acts by an alleged majority of Cuban votes, could always command the latter—that is, the peninsulars.

As regards the representation in the senate, the operation has been more simple still. The qualifications required to be a senator have proved to be an almost absolute prohibition to the Cubans. In fact, to take a seat in the higher house it is necessary to have been president of that body or of congress, or a minister of the crown, or a bishop, or a grandee of Spain, a lieutenant-general, a vice-admiral, ambassador, minister plenipotentiary, counselor of state, judge, or attorney-general of the supreme court, of the court of accounts, etc. No Cuban has ever filled any of the above positions, and scarcely two or three are grandees. The only natives of Cuba who can be senators are those who have been deputies in three different Congresses, or who are professors and have held for four years a university chair, provided that they have an income of $1,500; or those who have a title of nobility, or have been deputies, provincial deputies, or mayors in towns of over 20,000 inhabitants, if they have in addition an income of $4,000, or pay a direct contribution of $800 to the treasury. This will increase in one or two dozen the number of Cubans qualified to be senators.

In this manner has legislative work, so far as Cuba is concerned, turned out to be a farce. The various Governments have legislated for the island as they pleased. The representatives of the peninsular provinces did not even take the trouble of attending the sessions of the Cortes when Cuban affairs were to be dealt with; and there was an instance when the estimates (budget) for the Great Antille were discussed in the presence of less than thirty deputies, and a single one of the ministers, the minister of "ultramar" (session of April 3, 1880).

Through the contrivance of the law, as well as through the irregularities committed and consented in its application, have the Cubans been deprived also of representation in the local corporations to which they were entitled, and in many cases they have been entirely excluded from them. When, despite the legalized obstacles and the partiality of those in power, they have obtained some temporary majority, the Government has always endeavored and succeeded in making their triumph null and void. Only once did the home-rule party obtain a majority in the provincial deputation of Havana, and then the Governor-General appointed from among the Spaniards a majority of the members of the permanent commission. Until that time this commission had been of the same political complexion as the majority of the deputation. By such proceedings have the Cubans been gradually expelled, even from the municipal bodies. Suffice it to say that the law provides that the derramas (assessments) be excluded from the computation of the tributary quotas, notwithstanding that they constitute the heaviest burden upon the municipal taxpayer. And the majorities, consisting of Spaniards, take good care to make this burden fall with heavier weight upon the Cuban proprietor. Thus the latter has to bear a heavier taxation with less representation.

This is the reason why the scandalous case has occurred lately of not a single Cuban having a seat in the "Ayuntamiento" (board of aldermen) of Havana. In 1891 the Spaniards predominated in thirty-one out of thirty-seven "Ayuntamientos" in the province of Havana. In that of Güines, with a population of 12,500 Cuban inhabitants, not a single one of the latter was found among its councilors. In the same epoch there were only three Cuban deputies in the provincial deputation of Havana; two in that of Matanzas, and three in that of Santa Clara. And these are the most populous regions in the Island of Cuba.

As, on the other hand, the government of the metropolis appoints the officials of the colony, all the lucrative, influential, and representative offices are secured to the Spaniards from Europe. The Governor-General, the regional and provincial governors, the "intendentes," comptrollers, auditors, treasurers, chiefs of communications, chiefs of the custom-houses, chiefs of administration, presidents and vice-presidents of the Spanish bank, secretaries of the Government, presiding judges of the "audiencia," presidents of tribunal, magistrates, attorneys-general, archbishops, bishops, canons, pastors of rich parishes—all, with very rare exceptions, are Spaniards from Spain. The Cubans are found only as minor clerks in the Government offices, doing all the work and receiving the smallest salaries.

From 1878 to this date there have been twenty governors in the province of Matanzas. Eighteen were Spaniards and two Cubans. But one of these, Brigadier-General Acosta, was an army officer in the service of Spain, who had fought against his countrymen; and the other, Señor Gonzàlez Muñoz, is a bureaucrat. During the same period there has been only one native Cuban acting as governor in the province of Havana, Señor Rodriguez Batista, who spent all his life in Spain, where he made his administrative career. In the other provinces there has never, probably, been a single governor born in the country.

In 1887 there was created a council, or board of ultramar, under the minister of the colonies. Not a single Cuban has ever been found among its members. On the other hand, such men as Generals Armiñan and Pando have held positions in it.

The predominance of the Government goes further still. It weighs with all its might upon the local corporations. There are deputations in the provinces, and not only are their powers restricted and their resources scanty, but the Governor-General appoints their presidents and all the members of the permanent commissions. There are "ayuntamientos" elected in accordance with the reactionary law of 1877, restricted and curtailed as applied to Cuba by Señor Canovas. But the Governor-General appoints the mayors, who may not belong to the corporation, and the governor of the province appoints the secretaries. The Government reserves, moreover, the right to remove the mayors, of replacing them, and of suspending the councillors and the "ayuntamientos," partly or in a body. It has frequently made use of this right for electoral purposes, to the detriment always of the Cubans.

As may be seen, the crafty policy of Spain has closed every avenue through which redress might be obtained. All the powers are centered in the Government of Madrid and its delegates in the colony; and in order to give her despotism a slight varnish of a representative régime she has contrived with her laws to secure complaisant majorities in the pseudoelective bodies. To accomplish this purpose she has relied upon the European immigrants, who have always supported the Government of the metropolis in exchange for lasting privileges. The existence of a Spanish party, as that of an English party at one time in Canada, has been the foundation of

Spanish rule in Cuba. Thus, through the instrumentality of the laws and the Government, a régime of castes has been enthroned there, with its outcome of monopolies, corruption, immorality, and hatred. The political contest there, far from being the fruitful clash of opposite ideas, or the opposition of men representing different tendencies, but all seeking a social improvement, has been only a struggle between hostile factions—the conflict between infuriated foes which precedes an open war. The Spanish resident has always seen a threat in the most timid protest of the Cuban—an attack upon the privileged position on which his fortune, his influence, and his power are grounded, and he is always willing to stifle it with insult and persecution.

II.

What use the Spanish Government has made of this power is apparent in the threefold spoliation to which it has submitted the Island of Cuba. Spain has not, in fact, a colonial policy. In the distant lands she has subdued by force Spain has sought nothing but immediate riches, and these it has wrung by might from the compulsory labor of the natives. For this reason Spain to-day in Cuba is only a parasite. Spain exploits the Island of Cuba through its fiscal régime, through its commercial régime, and through its bureaucratic régime. These are the three forms of official spoliation, but they are not the only forms of spoliation.

When the war of 1878 came to an end two-thirds of the island were completely ruined. The other third, the population of which had remained peaceful, was abundantly productive; but it had to face the great economical change involved in the impending abolition of slavery. Slavery had received its deathblow at the hands of the insurrection, and Cuban insurrectionists succeeded at the close of the war in securing its eventual abolition. Evidently it would have been a wholesome and provident policy to lighten the fiscal burdens of a country in such a condition. Spain was only bent on making Cuba pay the cost of the war. The metropolis overwhelmed the colony with enormous budgets, reaching as high a figure as $46,000,000, and this only to cover the obligations of the state, or rather to fill the unfathomable gulf left by the wastefulness and plunder of the civil and military administration during the years of war, and to meet the expenses of the military occupation of the country. Here follow a few figures: The budget for the fiscal year of 1878 to 1879 amounted to $46,594,000; that of 1879 to 1880 to an equal sum; that of 1882 to 1883 to $35,860,000; that of 1883 to 1884 to $34,180,000; that of 1884 to 1885 to the same sum; that of 1885 to 1886 to $34,169,000. For the remaining years, to the present time, the amount of the budget has been about $26,000,000, this being the figure for 1893 to 1894, and to be the same by prorogation for the current fiscal year.

The gradual reduction that may be noted was not the result of a desire to reduce the overwhelming burdens that weigh upon the country. It was imposed by necessity. Cuba was not able by far to meet such a monstrous exaction. It was a continuous and threatening deficit that imposed these reductions. In the first of the above-named years the revenue was $8,000,000 short of the budget or appropriations. In the second year the deficit reached the sum of $20,000,000. In 1883 it was nearly $10,000,000. In the following years the deficits averaged nearly $4,500,000. At present the accumulated amount of all these deficits reaches the sum of $100,000,000.

As a consequence of such a reckless and senseless financial course, the debt of Cuba has been increased to a fabulous sum. In 1868 we owed $25,000,000. When the present war broke out our debt, it was calculated, reached the net sum of $190,000,000. On the 31st of July of the current year the Island of Cuba was reckoned to owe $295,707,264 in bulk. Considering its population, the debt of Cuba exceeds that of all the other American countries, including the United States. The interest on this debt imposes a burden of $9.79 on each inhabitant. The French people, the most overburdened in this respect, owe only $6.30 per inhabitant.

This enormous debt, contracted and saddled upon the country without its knowledge; this heavy load that grinds it and does not permit its people to capitalize their income, to foster its improvements, or even to entertain its industries, constitutes one of the most iniquitous forms of spoliation the island has to bear. In it are included a debt of Spain to the United States; the expenses incurred by Spain when she occupied Santo Domingo; those for the invasion of Mexico in alliance with France and England; the expenditures for her hostilities against Peru; the money advanced to the Spanish treasury during its recent Carlist wars; and all that Spain has spent to uphold its domination in Cuba and to cover the lavish expenditures of its administration since 1868. Not a cent of this enormous sum has been spent in Cuba to advance the work of improvement and civilization. It has not contributed to build a single kilometer of highway or of railroad, nor to erect a single light-house or deepen a single port; it has not built one asylum or opened one public school. Such a heavy burden has been left to the future generations without a single compensation or benefit.

But the naked figures of the Cuban budgets and of the Cuban debt tell very little in regard to their true importance and signification as machines to squeeze out the substance of a people's labor. It is necessary to examine closer the details of these accounts and expenditures.

Those of Cuba, according to the last budgets or appropriations, amount to $26,411,-314, distributed as follows:

General obligations... $12,884,549.55
Department of justice (courts, etc.) 1,006,308.51
Department of war... 5,918,598.16
Department of the treasury 727,892.45
Department of the navy.. 1,091,969.65
Government, administration.. 4,035,071.43
Interior improvements (fomento) 746,925.15

There are in Cuba 1,631,687 inhabitants according to the last census, that of 1887. That is to say, that this budget burdens them in the proportion of $16.18 for each inhabitant. The Spaniards in Spain pay only —42.06 pesetas per head. Reducing the Cuban dollars to pesetas at the exchange rate of $95 for 500 pesetas, there results that the Cubans have to pay a tribute of 85.16 pesetas for each inhabitant; more than double the amount a Spaniard has to pay in his European country.

As shown above, most of this excessive burden is to cover entirely unproductive expenditures. The debt consumes 40.89 per cent of the total amount. The defense of the country against its own native inhabitants, the only enemies who threaten Spain, including the cost of the army, the navy, the civil guard, and the guardians of public order, takes 36.59 per cent. There remains for all the other expenditures required by civilized life 22.52 per cent.

And of this percentage the State reserves to us, what a liberality! 2.75 per cent to prepare for the future and develop the resources of the country!

Let us see now what Spain has done to permit at least the development of natural wealth and the industry of a country impoverished by this fiscal régime, the work of cupidity, incompetency, and immorality. Let us see whether that nation has left at least some vitality to Cuba, in order to continue exploiting it with some profit.

The economical organization of Cuba is of the simplest kind. It produces to export, and imports almost everything it consumes. In view of this, it is evident that all that Cuba required from the State was that it should not hamper its work with excessive burdens, nor hinder its commercial relations; so that it could buy cheap where it suited her and sell her products with profit. Spain has done all the contrary. She has treated the tobacco as an enemy; she has loaded the sugar with excessive imposts; she has shackled with excessive and abusive excise duties the cattle-raising industry; and with her legislative doings and undoings she has thrown obstacles in the way of the mining industry. And to cap the climax, she has tightly bound Cuba in the network of a monstrous tariff and a commercial legislation which subjects the colony, at the end of the nineteenth century, to the ruinous monopoly of the producers and merchants of certain regions of Spain, as in the halcyon days of the colonial compact.

The district which produces the best tobacco in the world, the famous Vuelta Abajo, lacks every means of transportation afforded by civilization to foster and increase the value of its products. No roads, no bridges, or even ports, are found there. The state in Cuba collects the taxes, but does not invest them for the benefit of any industry. On the other hand, those foreign countries desirous of acquiring the rich tobacco-raising industry have closed their markets to our privileged product by imposing upon it excessive import duties, while the Spanish Government burdens its exportation from our ports with a duty of $1.80 on every thousand cigars. Is this not a stroke of actual insanity?

Everybody is aware of the tremendous crisis through which the sugar industry has been passing for some years, owing to the rapid development of the production of this article everywhere. Every Government has hastened to protect its own by more or less empirical measures. This is not the place to judge them. What is important is to recall the fact that they have endeavored to place the threatened industry in the best condition to withstand the competition. What has Spain done in order, if not to maintain the strong position held before by Cuba, at least to enable the colony to carry on the competition with its every day more formidable rivals? Spain pays bounties to the sugar produced within its own territory, and closes its markets to the Cuban sugar by imposing upon it an import duty of $6.20 per hundred kilograms. It has been calculated that a hundredweight of Cuban sugar is overburdened when reaching the Barcelona market with 143 per cent of its value. The Spanish Government oppresses the Cuban producer with every kind of exactions; taxes the introduction of the machinery that is indispensable for the production of sugar, obstructs its transportation by imposing heavy taxes on the railroads, and winds up the work by exacting another contribution called "industrial duty," and still another for loading or shipping, which is equivalent to an export duty.

As a last stroke, Spain has reenforced the commercial laws of June 30 and July 20, 1882, virtually closing the ports of Cuba to foreign commerce, and establishing the monopoly of the peninsular producers, without any compensation to the colony. The apparent object of these laws was to establish the "cabotaje" (coasting trade) between Cuba and Spain. By the former all the Cuban products were admitted free of duty in the Spanish Peninsula, excepting, however, the tobacco, rum, sugar, cocoa, and coffee, which remained temporarily burdened. By the latter the duties on the importations from Spain in Cuba were to be gradually reduced through a period of ten years, until, in 1892, they were entirely abolished. The result, however, has been that the temporary duties on the principal, almost the only, Cuban products have remained undisturbed until now, and the duties on the Spanish products have disappeared. The "cabotage" (coasting trade) is carried on from Spain to Cuba, but not from Cuba to Spain. The Spanish products pay no duties in Cuba; the Cuban products pay heavy duties in Spain. As at the same time the differential tariffs which overburdened with excessive duties the foreign products have been retained, the unavoidable consequence has been to give the Cuban market entirely to the Peninsula producers. In order to have an idea as to how far the monopoly of Spain goes, it will be sufficient to point to the fact that the burdens which many of the foreign articles have to bear exceed 2,000 and even 2,300 per cent, as compared with those borne by the Spanish products. One hundred kilograms of cotton prints pay a duty, if Spanish, of $26.65; if foreign, $47.26. One hundred kilograms of knitted goods pay, if from Spain, $10.95; if from a foreign country, $195. One thousand kilograms of bags for sugar, when they are or are represented to be Spanish, pay $4.69; if from other country, $82.50. One hundred kilograms of cassimere, if it is a Spanish product, pay $15.47; if foreign, $300.

Still, if Spain was a flourishing industrial country, and produced the principal articles required by Cuba for the consumption of its people, or for developing and fostering its industries, the evil, although always great, would be a lesser one. But everybody knows the backwardness of the Spanish industries, and the inability of Spain to supply Cuba with the products she requires for her consumption and industries. The Cubans have to consume or use Spanish articles of inferior quality or pay exorbitant prices for foreign goods. The Spanish merchants have found, moreover, a new source of fraud in the application of these antiquated and iniquitous laws; it consists in nationalizing foreign products for importation into Cuba.

As the mainspring of this senseless commercial policy is to support the monopoly of Spanish commerce, when Spain has been compelled to deviate from it to a certain extent by an international treaty, it has done so reluctantly and in the anxious expectation of an opportunity to nullify its own promises. This explains the accidental history of the reciprocity treaty with the United States, which was received with joy by Cuba, obstructed by the Spanish administration, and prematurely abolished by the Spanish Government as soon as it saw an opportunity.

The injury done to Cuba, and the evil effects produced by this commercial legislation, are beyond calculation; its effects have been material losses which have engendered profound discontent. The "Circulo de Hacendados y Agricultores," the wealthiest corporation of the Island, last year passed judgment on these commercial laws in the following severe terms:

"It would be impossible to explain, should the attempt be made, what is the signification of the present commercial laws as regards any economical or political plan or system; because, economically, they aim at the destruction of public wealth, and, politically, they are the cause of inextinguishable discontent, and contain the germs of grave dissensions."

But Spain has not taken heed of this; her only care has been to keep the producers and merchants of such rebellious provinces as Catalonia contented, and to satisfy its military men and bureaucrats.

For the latter is reserved the best part of the booty taken from Cuba. High salaries and the power of extortion for the officeholders sent to the colony; regular tributes for the politicians who uphold them in the metropolis. The Governor-General is paid a salary of $50,000, in addition to a palace, a country house as a summer resort, servants, coaches, and a fund for secret expenses at his disposal. The director-general of the treasury receives a salary of $18,500. The archbishop of Santiago and the bishop of Havana, $18,000 each. The commander-general of the "Apostadero" (naval station), $16,392. The general segundo cabo (second in command of the Island), and the president of the "audiencia," $15,000 each. The governor of Havana and the secretary of the General Government, $8,000 each. The postmaster-general, $5,000. The collector for the Havana custom-house, $4,000. The manager of lotteries, the same salary. The chief clerks of administration of the first class receive $5,000 each; those of the second class, $4,000, and those of the third class, $3,000 each. The major-generals are paid $7,500; the brigadier-generals, $4,500, and when in command, $5,000; the colonels, $3,450, and this salary is increased when they are in command of a regiment. The captains of "navío" (the largest men-of-war) receive $6,300; the captains of frigate, $4,560; the lieutenants of "navío" of the the first class, $3,370. All these functionaries are entitled to free lodgings and domestic servants. Then follows the numberless crowd of minor officials, all well provided for, and with great facilities better to provide for themselves.

At the office of the minister of "ultramar" (of the colonies), who resides in Madrid, and to whom $96,800 a year are assigned from the treasury of Cuba—at that office begins the saturnalia in which the Spanish bureaucrats indulge with the riches of Cuba. Sometimes through incapacity, but more frequently for plunder, the money exacted from the Cuban taxpayers is unscrupulously and irresponsibly squandered. It has been demonstrated that the debt of Cuba has been increased in $50,232,500 through Minister Fabié's incapacity. At the time this minister was in power the Spanish Bank disposed of twenty millions from the Cuban treasury, which were to be carried in account current at the disposal of the minister for the famous operation of withdrawing the paper currency. Cuba paid the interest on these millions, and continued paying it all the time they were utilized by the bank. Minister Romero Robledo took at one time (in 1892) $1,000,000 belonging to the treasury of Cuba from the vaults of the Bank of Spain, and lent it to the Transatlantic Company, of which he was a stockholder. This was done in defiance of law and without any authorization whatever. The minister was threatened with prosecution, but he haughtily replied that, if prosecuted, all his predecessors from every political party would have to accompany him to the court. That threat came to nothing.

In June of 1890 there was a scandalous debate in the Spanish Cortes, in which some of the frauds committed upon the Cuban treasury were, not for the first time, brought to light. It was then made public that $6,500,000 had been abstracted from the "caja de depósitos," notwithstanding that the safe was locked with three keys, and each one was in the possession of a different functionary. Then it was known that, under the pretext of false vouchers for transportation and fictitious bills for provisions, during the previous war, defalcations had been found afterwards amounting to $22,811,516. In the month of March of the same year General Pando affirmed that the robberies committed through the issue of warrants by the "junta de la deuda" (board of public debt) exceeded the sum of $12,000,000.

These are only a few of the most salient facts. The large number of millions mentioned above represent only an insignificant part of what a venal administration, sure of impunity, exacts from Cuban labor. The network of artful schemes to cheat the Cuban taxpayer and defraud the State covers everything. Falsification of documents, embezzlement of revenues, bargains with delinquent debtors, exaction of higher dues from inexperienced peasants, delays in the dispatch of judicial proceedings in order to obtain a more or less considerable gratuity; such are the artful means daily employed to empty the purse of the taxpayer and to divert the public funds into the pockets of the functionaries.

These disgraceful transactions have more than once been brought out to light; more than once have the prevaricators been pointed out. Is there any record of any of them having ever been punished?

In August of 1887 General Marin entered the custom-house of Havana at the head of a military force, besieged and occupied it, investigated the operations carried on there, and discharged every employee. The act caused a great stir, but not a single one of the officials was indicted or suffered a further punishment. There were, in 1891, 350 officials indicted in Cuba for committing fraud; not one of them was punished.

But how could they be punished? Every official who comes to Cuba has an influential patron in the court of Madrid for whose protection he pays with regularity. This is a public secret. General Salamanca gave it out in plain words, and before and after General Salamanca all Spain knew and knows it. The political leaders are well known who draw the highest income from the officeholders of Cuba, who are, as a matter of course, the most fervent advocates of the necessity of Spanish rule in Cuba. But Spanish bureaucracy is moreover so deep-rooted in Spain that it has succeeded in shielding itself even against the action of the courts of justice. There is a royal decree (that of 1882) in force in Cuba, which provides that the ordinary courts can not take cognizance of such offenses as defalcation, abstraction or malversation of public funds, forgery, etc., committed by officials of the administration, if their guilt is not first established by an administrative investigation. The administration is, therefore, its own judge. What further security does the corrupt officeholder need?

III.

We have shown that notwithstanding the promises of Spain and the ostensible changes introduced in the government of Cuba since 1878, the Spaniards from Europe have governed and ruled exclusively in Cuba, and have continued exploiting it until they have ruined the country. Can this tyrannical system be justified by any kind of benefits that might compensate for the deprivation of actual power of which the natives of the colony complain? More than one despotic government has tried to justify itself with the material prosperity it has fostered, or with the safety it has secured to its citizens, or with the liberty it has given to certain manifestations of civilized life. Let us see whether the Cubans are indebted to the iron government of Spain for any of these compensating blessings.

Personal safety is a myth among us. Outlaws, as well as men of law, have disposed at will of the property, the peace, and the life of the inhabitants of Cuba. The civil guard (armed police), far from being the guardians, have been the terror of the Cuban peasants. Wherever they pass they cause an alarm by the brutal ill treatment to which they submit the inhabitants, who in many cases fly from their homes at their approach. Under the most trifling pretext they beat unmercifully the defenseless countrymen, and very frequently they have killed those they were conveying under arrest. These outrages became so notorious that the commander in chief of the civil guard, Brigadier-General Denis, had to issue a circular in which he declared that his subordinates, "under pretext of obtaining confidential information. resorted to violent measures," and that "the cases are very frequent in which individuals arrested by forces of the corps attempt to escape, and the keepers find themselves in the necessity of making use of their weapons." What the above declarations signify is evident, notwithstanding the euphemisms of the official language. The object of this circular was to put a stop to these excesses; it bears the date of 1883. But the state of things continued the same. In 1886 the watering place of Madruga, one of the most frequented summer resorts in the island, witnessed the outrageous attacks of Lieutenant Sainz. In 1887 occurred the stirring trial of the "componte," occasioned by the application of torture to the brothers Aruca, and within a few days were recorded in the neighborhood of Havana the cases of Señor Riveron, who was stabbed in Govea by individuals of the public force; of Don Manuel Martinez Moran and Don Francisco Galañena, who were beaten, the former in Calabazar, and the latter in Yaguajay; of Don José Felipe Canosa, who narrowly escaped being murdered in San Nicolas, and of a resident of Ceiba Mocha, whom the civil guard drove from his home.

This was far from the worst. In the very center of Havana, in the Camp de Marte, a prisoner was killed by his guards, and the shooting at Amarillas and the murders at Puentes Grandes and Alquízar are deeds of woful fame in the country. The administration of General Prendergast has left a sorrowful recollection for the frequency with which prisoners who attempted to escape were shot down.

While the armed police force were beating and murdering peaceful inhabitants, the highwaymen were allowed to escape unscathed to devastate the country at their pleasure. Although three millions are assigned in the budget to the service of public safety, there are districts, such as the Province of Puerto Príncipe, where its inhabitants have had to arm themselves and undertake the pursuit of the bandits. The case has occurred of an army of 5,000 or 6,000 troops being sent to pursue a handful of highwaymen within a small territory without succeeding in capturing them. Meanwhile a special bureau was established in Havana for the prosecution of highwaymen, and fabulous sums were spent by it The best the Government succeeded in doing was to bargain with a bandit, and deceive and kill him afterwards on board the steamer *Baldomero Iglesias* in the bay of Havana.

Nevertheless, the existence of highwaymen has served as a pretext to curtail the jurisdiction of the ordinary courts and submit the Cubans to the jurisdiction of the courts-martial, contrary to the constitution of the state, which had already been proclaimed. In fact, the code of military laws (codigo de justicia militar) provides that the offenses against persons and the means of transportation, as well as arson, when committed in the provinces of ultramar (the colonies) and the possessions of Africa and Oceanica, be tried by court-martial.

It is true, however, than an explicit legal text was not necessary for the Government to nullify the precepts of the constitution. This was promulgated in Cuba, with a preamble providing that the Governor-General and his delegates should retain the same powers they had before its promulgation. The banishment of Cubans have continued after as before said promulgation. In December of 1891 there was a strike of wharf laborers in the Province of Santa Clara. To end it the governor captured the strikers and banished them en masse to the Island of Pinos.

The deportations for political offenses have not been discontinued in Cuba, and although it is stated that no executions for political offenses have taken place since 1878, it is because the Government has resorted to the more simple expedient of assassination. General Polavieja has declared with utmost coolness that in December of 1880 he had 265 persons seized in Cuba, Palma, San Luis, Songo, Guantánamo, and Sagua de Tánamo, and transported the same day and at the same hour to the African Island of Fernando Po. At the close of the insurrection of 1879–80 it was a frequent occurrence for the Government to send to the penal colonies of Africa the Cubans who had capitulated. The treachery of which Gen. José Maceo was a victim carries us to the darkest times of the war of Flanders and the conquest of America.

Cuba recalls with horror the dreadful assassination of Brig. Gen. Arcadio Leyte Vidal, perpetrated in the Bay of Nipe in September of 1879. War had just broken out anew in the eastern department. Brig. Gen. Leyte Vidal resided in Mayari, assured by the solemn promise of the Spanish commander in chief of that zone that he would not be molested. One month had not elapsed since the uprising, however, when having gone to Nipe, he was invited by the commander of the gunboat *Alarma* to take dinner on board. Leyte Vidal went on board the gunboat, but never returned. He was strangled in a boat by three sailors, and his corpse was cast into the sea. This villainous deed was committed in compliance with an order from the Spanish general, Polavieja. Francisco Leyte Vidal, a cousin to Arcadio, miraculously escaped the same tragic fate.

The mysterious deaths of Cubans who had capitulated long before have been frequent in Cuba. To one of these deaths was due the uprising of Tunas de Bayamo in 1879.

If the personal safety of the Cubans, in a period which the Spaniards would depict with brilliant colors, continues at the mercy of their rulers, who are aliens in the country both by birth and in ideas, have the Cubans' honor and property any better safeguard? Is the administration of justice good, or even endurable? The very idea of a lawsuit frightens every honest Cuban. Nobody trusts the honesty or independence of the judges. Despite the provisions of the constitution, without warrant and for indefinite time, imprisonments are most common in Cuba. The magistrates can tighten or loosen the elastic meshes of the judicial proceedings. They know well that if they curry favor with the Government they can do anything without incurring responsibility. They consider themselves, and without thinking it a disgrace, as mere political tools. The presidents and attorneys-general of the "audiencias" receive their instructions at the captain-general's office. Twice have the governors of Cuba aimed at establishing a special tribunal to deal with the offenses of the press, thereby undermining the constitution. Twice has this special tribunal been established. More than once has a straightforward and impartial judge been found to try a case in which the interests of influential people were involved. On such occasions the straightforward judge has been replaced by a special judge.

In a country where money is wastefully spent to support a civil and military bureaucracy the appropriation for the administration of justice does not reach $500,000. On the other hand, the sales of stamped paper constitute a revenue of $750,000. Thus the State derives a pecuniary profit from its administration of justice.

Is it, then, a wonder that the reforms that have been attempted by establishing lower and higher courts to take cognizance of criminal cases, and by introducing oral and public trials should not have contributed in the least to improve the administration of justice? Onerous services have been exacted from people without proper compensation as gratuitous services. The Government, so splendidly liberal when its own expenses are in question, haggles for the last cent when dealing with truly useful and reproductive services.

Is the Cuban compensated for his absolute deprivation of political power, the fiscal extortions, and the monstrous deficiencies of judicial administration by the material prosperity of his country? No man acquainted with the intimate relations which exist between the fiscal régime of a country and its economical system will believe that Cuba, crushed as it is, by unreasonable budgets and an enormous debt, can be rich. The income of Cuba in the most prosperous times has been calculated at $80,-000,000. The state, provincial, and municipal charges take much more than 40 per cent of this amount. This fact explains itself. We need not draw any inferences therefrom. Let us confine ourselves to casting a glance over the aspect presented by the agricultural, industrial, and real estate interests in Cuba at the beginning of the present year.

Despite the prodigious efforts made by private individuals to extend the cultivation of the sugar cane and to raise the sugar-making industry to the plane it has reached, both the colonists and the proprietors of the sugar plantations and the sugar mills (centrales) are on the brink of bankruptcy and ruin. In selling the output they knew that they would not get sufficient means to cover the cost of keeping and repairing their colonies and sugar mills. There is not a single agricultural bank in Cuba. The "hacendado" (planter, landowner) had to recur to usurious loans and to pay 18 and 20 per cent for the sums which they borrowed. Not long ago there existed in Havana the Spanish Bank, the Bank of Commerce, the Industrial Bank, the Bank of St. Joseph, the Bank of the Alliance, the Bank of Maritime Insurances, and the Savings Bank. Of these there remain to-day only the Spanish Bank, which has been converted into a vast State office, and the Bank of Commerce, which owes its existence to the railways and warehouses it possesses. None of these give any aid to the sugar industry.

The cigar-making industry, which was in such flourishing condition a short time ago, has fallen so low that fears are entertained that it may emigrate entirely from Cuba. The weekly El Tabaco came to the conclusion that the exportation of cigars from Cuba would cease entirely within six years. From 1889 to 1894 the exportation from the port of Havana had decreased by 116,200,000 cigars.

City real estate has fallen to one-half and in some cases to one-third the value it had before 1884. A building in Havana which was erected at a cost of $600,000 was sold in 1893 for $120,000.

Stocks and bonds tell the same story. Almost all of them are quoted in Havana with heavy discounts.

The cause of the ruin of Cuba, despite her sugar output of 1,000,000 tons and her vast tobacco fields, can be easily explained. Cuba does not capitalize, and it does not capitalize because the fiscal régime imposed upon the country does not permit it. The money derived from its large exportations does not return either in the form of importations of goods or of cash. It remains abroad to pay the interest of its huge debt, to cover the incessant remittances of funds by the Spaniards who hasten to send their earnings out of the country, to pay from our treasury the pensioners who live in Spain, and to meet the drafts forwarded by every mail from Cuba by the Spaniards as a tribute to their political patrons in the metropolis, and to help their families.

Cuba pays $2,192,795 in pensions to those on the retired list and to superannuated officials not in service. Most of this money is exported. The first chapters of the Cuban budget imply the exportation of over $10,600,000. Cuba pays a subsidy of $471,836.68 to the Transatlantic Company. It would be impossible to calculate the amount of money taken out of Cuba by private individuals; but this constant exportation of capital signifies that nobody is contented in Cuba and that everybody mistrusts its future. The consequence is that notwithstanding the apparently favorable commercial balance exchange is constantly and to a high degree against Cuba.

On the other hand, if Cuba labors and strives to be on the same plane as its most progressive competitors, this is the work of her own people, who do not mind any sacrifices; but the Government cares little or nothing about securing to the country such means of furthering its development as are consigned in the budget under the head of "Fomento."

And now, at the outbreak of the present war, Spain finds that, although the appropriations consigned in our budgets since 1878 amount to nearly $500,000,000, not a single military road has been built, no fortifications, no hospitals, and there is no material of war. The State has not provided even for its own defense. In view of this fact, nobody will be surprised to hear that a country 670 kilometers long, with an area of 118,833 square kilometers, has only 246½ lineal kilometers of high roads, and these almost exclusively in the province of Havana. In that of Santiago de Cuba there are 9 kilometers; in Puerto Principe and Las Villas not a single one. Cuba has 3,506 kilometers of seashore and 54 ports; only 15 of these are open to commerce. In the labyrinth of keys, sand banks, and breakers adjacent to our coasts there are only 19 light-houses of all classes. Many of our ports, some of the best among them, are filling up. The coasting steamers can hardly pass the bars at the entrance of the ports of Nuevitas, Gibara, Baracoa, and Santiago de Cuba. Private parties have sometimes been willing to remedy these evils; but then the central administration has interfered, and after years of red tape things have remained worse than before. In the course of twenty-eight years only 139 kilometers of high-roads were built in Cuba; 2 first-class light-houses were erected, 3 of the second class, and 1 of the fourth class, 3 beacon lights and 2 port lights; 246 meters of wharf were built, and a few ports were superficially cleaned and their shoals marked. This was all. On the other hand, the department of public works consumes unlimited millions in salaries and in repairs.

The neglect of public hygiene in Cuba is proverbial. The technical commission sent by the United States to Havana to study the yellow fever declared that the port of the capital of Cuba, owing to the inconceivable filth, is a permanent source of infection, against which it is necessary to take precautions. There is in Havana, however a "junta de puerto" (board of port wardens) which collects dues and spends them with the same munificence as the other bureaucratic centers.

Does the Government favor us more in the matter of education? It will suffice to state that only $182,000 are assigned to public instruction in our splendid budget. And it may be proved that the University of Havana is a source of pecuniary profit to the State. On the other hand, this institution is without laboratories, instruments, and even without water to carry on experiments. All the countries of America, excepting Bolivia, all of them, including Haiti, Jamaica, Trinidad, and Guadalupe, where the colored race predominates, spend a great deal more than the Cuban Government for the education of the people. On the other hand, only Chile spends as much as Cuba for the support of an army. In view of this it is easily explained why 76 per cent of such an intelligent and wide-awake people as that of Cuba can not read and write. The most necessary instruction among us, the technical and industrial, does not exist. The careers and professions most needed by modern civilization are not cultivated in Cuba. In order to become a topographer, a scientific agriculturist, an electrician, an industrial or mechanical engineer, a railroad or mining engineer, the Cuban has to go to a foreign country. The State in Cuba does not support a single public library.

Are the deficiencies of the Spanish régime compensated by the wisdom of its administration? Every time the Spanish Government has undertaken the solution of any of the gieat problems pending in Cuba it has only confused and made it worse. It has solved it blindly or yielded to the influence of those who were to profit by the change. It will be sufficient to recall the withdrawal from circulation of the bank notes, which proved to be a highly lucrative transaction for a few persons, but which only embarrassed and impaired the monetary circulation of the island. From one day to another the cost of living became 40 per cent dearer. The depreciated Spanish silver entered in circulation to drive out, as was natural, the "centen" (five-dollar gold coin) and make small transactions difficult. To reach these results the Spanish Government had transformed a debt on which it had no interest to pay into a debt bearing a high rate of interest. It is true that, in exchange, all the retail dealers whose votes it was desirable to keep derived very large profits from the operation. These dealers are, of course, Spaniards.

IV.

In exchange for all that Spain withholds from us they say that it has given us liberties. This is a mockery. The liberties are written in the constitution but obliterated in its practical application. Before and after its promulgation the public press has been rigorously persecuted in Cuba. Many journalists, such as Señores Cepeda and Lópes Briñas, have been banished from the country without the formality of a trial. In November of 1891 the writer Don Manuel A. Balmaseda was tried by court-martial for having published an editorial paragraph in El Criterio Popular, of Remedios, relative to the shooting of the medical students. The newspapers have been allowed to discuss public affairs theoretically; but the moment they denounce any abuse or the conduct of any official they feel the hand of their rulers laid upon them. The official organ of the home-rule party, El País, named before El Triunfo, has undergone more than one trial for having pointed in measured terms to some infractions of the law on the part of officials, naming the transgressors. In 1887 that periodical was subjected to criminal proceedings simply because it had stated that a son of the president of the Havana "audiencia" was holding a certain office contrary to law.

They say that in Cuba the people are at liberty to hold public meetings, but every time the inhabitants assemble, previous notification must be given to the authorities, and a functionary is appointed to be present, with power to suspend the meeting whenever he deems such a measure advisable. The meetings of the "Círculo de Trabajadores" (an association of workingmen) were forbidden by the authorities under the pretext that the building where they were to be held was not sufficiently safe. Last year the members of the "Círculo de Hacendados" (association of planters) invited their fellow-members throughout the country to get up a great demonstration to demand a remedy which the critical state of their affairs required. The Government found means to prevent their meeting. One of the most significant events that have occurred in Cuba, and one which throws a flood of light upon its political régime, was the failure of the "Junta Magna" (an extraordinary meeting) projected by the "Circulo de Hacendados." This corporation solicited the cooperation of the "Sociedad Económica" and of the "Junta General de Comercio" to hold a meeting for the purpose of sending to the metropolis the complaints which the precarious situation of the country inspired. The work of preparation was already far advanced when a friend of the Government, Señor Rodriguez Correa, stated that the Governor-General looked with displeasure upon and forbade the holding of the great meeting. This was sufficient to frighten the "Círculo" and to secure the failure of the project. It is then evident that the inhabitants of Cuba can have meetings only when the Government thinks it advisable to permit them.

Against this political régime, which is a sarcasm and in which deception is added to the most absolute contempt for right, the Cubans have unceasingly protested since it was implanted in 1878. It would be difficult to enumerate the representations made in Spain, the protests voiced by the representatives of Cuba, the commissions that have crossed the ocean to try to impress upon the exploiters of Cuba what the fatal consequences of their obstinacy would be. The exasperation prevailing in the country was such that the "junta central" of the home-rule party issued in 1892 a manifesto in which it foreshadowed that the moment might shortly arrive when the country would resort to "extreme measures, the responsibility of which would fall on those who, led by arrogance and priding themselves on their power, hold prudence in contempt, worship force, and shield themselves with their impunity."

This manifesto, which foreboded the mournful hours of the present war, was unheeded by Spain, and not until a division took place in the Spanish party, which threatened to turn into an armed struggle, did the statesmen of Spain think that the moment had arrived to try a new farce, and to make a false show of reform in the administrative régime of Cuba. Then was Minister Maura's plan broached, to be modified before its birth by Minister Abarzuas.

This project, to which the Spaniards have endeavored to give capital importance in order to condemn the revolution as the work of impatience and anarchism, leaves intact the political régime of Cuba. It does not alter the electoral law. It does not curtail the power of the bureaucracy. It increases the power of the general Government. It leaves the same burdens upon the Cuban taxpayer, and does not give him the right to participate in the information of the budgets. The reform is confined to the changing of the council of administration (now in existence in the island, and the members of which are appointed by the Government) into a partially elective body. One-half of its members are to be appointed by the Government and the other half to be elected by the qualified electors—that is, who assessed and pay for a certain amount of taxes. The Governor-General has the right to veto all its resolutions and to suspend at will the elective members. This council is to make up a kind of special budget embracing the items included now in the general budget of Cuba under the head of "Fomento." The State reserves for itself all the rest. Thus the council can dispose of 2.75 per cent of the revenues of Cuba, while the Government distributes, as at present, 97.25 per cent for its expenses, in the form we have explained. The general budget will, as heretofore, be made up in Spain: the tariff laws will be enacted by Spain. The debt, militarism, and bureaucracy will continue to devour Cuba, and the Cubans will continue to be treated as a subjugated people. All power is to continue in the hands of the Spanish Government and its delegates in Cuba, and all the influence with the Spanish residents. This is the self-government which Spain has promised to Cuba, and which it is announcing to the world, in exchange for its colonial system. A far better form of government is enjoyed by the Bahama or the Turks islands.

The Cubans would have been wanting not only in self-respect but even in the instincts of self-preservation if they could have endured such a degrading and destructive régime. Their grievances are of such a nature that no people, no human community capable of valuing its honor and of aspiring to better its condition, could bear them without degrading and condemning itself to utter nullity and annihilation.

Spain denies to the Cubans all effective powers in their own country.

Spain condemns the Cubans to a political inferiority in the land where they are born.

Spain confiscates the product of the Cuban's labor without giving them in return either safety, prosperity, or education.

Spain has shown itself utterly incapable of governing Cuba.

Spain exploits, impoverishes, and demoralizes Cuba.

To maintain by force of arms this monstrous régime, which brings ruin on a country rich by nature and degrades a vigorous and intelligent population, a population filled with noble aspirations, is what Spain calls to defend its honor and preserve the prestige of its social functions as a civilizing power of America.

The Cubans, not in anger but in despair, have appealed to arms in order to defend their rights and to vindicate an eternal principle, a principle without which every community, however robust in appearance, is in danger—the principle of justice. Nobody has the right of oppression. Spain oppresses us. In rebelling against oppression we defend a right. In serving our own cause we serve the cause of mankind.

We have not counted the number of our enemies; we have not measured their strength. We have cast up the account of our grievances; we have weighed the mass of injustice that crushes us, and with uplifted hearts we have risen to seek redress and to uphold our rights. We may find ruin and death a few steps ahead. So be it. We do our duty. If the world is indifferent to our cause, so much the worse for all. A new iniquity shall have been consummated. The principle of human solidarity shall have suffered a defeat. The sum of good existing in the world, and which the world needs to purify its moral atmosphere, shall have been lessened.

The people of Cuba require only liberty and independence to become a factor of prosperity and progress in the community of civilized nations. At present Cuba is a factor of intranquillity, disturbance, and ruin. The fault lies entirely with Spain. Cuba is not the offender; it is the defender of its rights. Let America, let the world decide where rest justice and right.

ENRIQUE JOSÉ VARONA,
Ex-Diputado a Cortes.

NEW YORK, *October 23, 1895.*

S. Doc. 231, pt 7——24

B.

COMPILATION OF THE LAWS, RULES, DECREES, CIRCULARS, AND OTHER ORDERS PASSED BY THE NATIONAL COUNCIL FROM THE 19TH OF SEPTEMBER, 1895, THE DATE ON WHICH IT COMMENCED TO EXERCISE ITS FUNCTIONS.

MANGOS DE BARAGUA.

The National Council, in a meeting held on the 16th of October, 1895, resolved that the publication in book form in an edition of 500 copies of all the laws, rules, decrees, and other orders passed by it be printed after being previously approved by the Council and sanctioned by its president.

JOSÉ CLEMENTE VIVANCO,
The Secretary of the Council.

CONSTITUENT ASSEMBLY, REPUBLIC OF CUBA.

I, José Clemente Vivanco, secretary of the National Council and chancellor of the Republic of Cuba, certify that the representatives of the different army corps, into which the army of liberation is divided, met in constituent assembly on the 13th day of September, 1895, at Jimaguayu, agreed to have a preliminary session where the character of each representative would be accredited by the respective credential of his appointment. There resulted, after the proper examination by the chairman and secretaries, who were temporarily Citizens Salvador Cisneros Betancourt and Secretaries José Clemente Vivanco and Orencio Nodarse, the following distribution:

Representatives of the First Army Corps, Citizens Dr. Joaquin Castillo Duany, Mariano Sanchez Vaillant, Rafael M. Portuondo, and Pedro Aguillera.

For the Second, Citizens Licentiate Rafael Manduley, Enrique Cespedes, Rafael Perez Morales, and Marcos Padilla.

For the Third, Citizens Salvador Cisneros Betancourt, Lopez Recio Loinaz, Enrique Loinaz del Castillo, and Dr. Fermmin Valdes Dominguez.

For the Fourth, Licentiate Severo Pina, Dr. Santiago Garcia Canizares, Raimundo Sanchez Valdivia, and Francisco Lopez Leiba.

For the Fifth, Dr. Pedro Pinan de Villegas, Licentiate José Clemente Vivanco, Francisco Diaz Silveria, and Orencio Nodarse.

They proceeded to the election of officers for the following session and the following appointments were made: Salvador Cisneros Betancourt, president; Rafael Manduley, vice-president; secretaries, Licentiate José Clemente Vivanco, Francisco Lopez Leiba, Licentiate Rafael M. Portuondo, and Orencio Nodarse.

The assembly having been organized as above, and in the presence of the above representatives, they proceeded to hold the sessions to discuss the constitution which is to rule the destinies of the Republic. These sessions took place on September 13, 14, 15, and 16, instant, and in all the articles which were to form the said constitutional charta were discussed. Every article of the projected constitution presented to the assembly by the representatives licentiate, Rafael M. Portuondo, Dr. Joaquin Castillo Duany, Mariano Sanchez Vaillant, and Pedro Aguilera, was well discussed, and, together with amendments, reforms, and additions were also discussed by the proposers. On deliberation, in conformity with the opinion of the assembly, it was unanimously resolved to refer the said constitution, with the resolutions of the said assembly, to a committee of revision of the text, composed of the secretaries and of the representatives, Dr. Santiago Garcia, Canizares and Enrique, Loynaz del Castillo, who, after complying with their mission, returned the final draft of the constitution on the 16th. It was then read, and the signature of each and every representative subscribed.

The president and other members of the assembly, with due solemnity, then swore upon their honor to loyally and strictly observe the fundamental code of the Republic of Cuba, which was greeted by the spontaneous and enthusiastic acclamations of all present; in testimony of which are the minutes in the general archive of the Government.

In compliance with the resolution passed by this council in a meeting held to-day, and for its publication, I issue the following copy, in the Mangos de Baragua on the 18th of October, 1895.

JOSÉ CLEMENTE VIVANCO,
Secretary of the Council.

CONSTITUTION OF THE PROVISIONAL GOVERNMENT OF CUBA.

The revolution for the independence and creation in Cuba of a democratic Republic in its new period of war, initiated on February 24 last, solemnly declares the separation of Cuba from the Spanish monarchy, and its constitution as a free and independent State, with its own Government and supreme authority under the name of the Republic of Cuba and confirms its existence among the political divisions of the world.

The elected representatives of the revolution, in convention assembled, acting in its name and by the delegation which for that purpose has been conferred upon them by the Cubans in arms, and previously declaring before the country the purity of their thoughts, their freedom from violence, anger, or prejudice, and inspired only by the desire of interpreting the popular voice in favor of Cuba, have now formed a compact between Cuba and the world, pledging their honor for the fulfillment of said compact in the following articles of the constitution:

ARTICLE I. The supreme powers of the Republic shall be vested in a government council composed of a president, vice-president, and four secretaries of state, for the dispatch of the business of war, of the interior, of foreign affairs, and of the treasury.

ART. II. Every secretary shall have a subsecretary of state, in order to supply any vacancies.

ART. III. The government council shall have the following powers:

1. To dictate all measures relative to the civil and political life of the revolution.

2. To impose and collect taxes, to contract public loans, to issue paper money, to invest the funds collected in the island, from whatever source, and also those which may be raised abroad by loan.

3. To arm vessels, to raise and maintain troops, to declare reprisals with respect to the enemy, and to ratify treaties.

4. To grant authority, when it is deemed convenient, to order the trial by the judicial power of the president or other members of the council, if he be accused

5. To decide all matters, of whatsoever description, which may be brought before them by any citizen, except those judicial in character.

6. To approve the law of military organization and the ordinances of the army, which may be proposed by the general in chief.

7. To grant military commissions from that of colonel upward, previously hearing and considering the reports of the immediate superior officer and of the general in chief, and to designate the appointment of the latter and of the lieutenant-general in case of the vacancy of either.

8. To order the election of four representatives for each army corps whenever in conformity with this constitution it may be necessary to convene an assembly.

ART. IV. The Government council shall intervene in the direction of military operations only when in their judgment it shall be absolutely necessary to do so to realize high political ends.

ART. V. As a requisite for the validity of the decrees of the council, at least two-thirds of the members of the same must have taken part in the deliberations of the council, and the decrees must have been voted by the majority of those present.

ART. VI. The office of councilor is incompatible with any other of the Republic, and requires the age of twenty-five years.

ART. VII. The executive power is vested in the president, and, in case of disability, in the vice-president.

ART. VIII. The resolutions of the government council shall be sanctioned and promulgated by the president, who shall take all necessary steps for their execution within ten days.

ART. IX. The president may enter into treaties with the ratification of the government council.

ART. X. The president shall receive all diplomatic representatives and issue the respective commissions to the public functionaries.

ART. XI. The treaty of peace with Spain, which must necessarily have for its basis the absolute independence of the Island of Cuba, must be ratified by the government council and by an assembly of representatives convened expressly for this purpose.

ART. XII. The vice-president shall substitute the president in the case of a vacancy.

ART. XIII. In case of the vacancy in the offices of both president and vice-president on account of resignation, deposition, or death of both, or from any other cause, an assembly of representatives for the election to the vacant offices shall be convened, the senior secretaries in the meanwhile occupying the positions.

ART. XIV. The secretaries shall have voice and vote in the deliberations of resolutions of whatever nature.

ART. XV. The secretaries shall have the right to appoint all the employees of their respective offices.

ART. XVI. The subsecretaries in cases of vacancy shall substitute the secretaries of state and shall then have voice and vote in the deliberations.

ART. XVII. All the armed forces of the Republic and the direction of the military operations shall be under the control of the general in chief, who shall have under his orders as second in command a lieutenant-general, who will substitute him in case of vacancy.

ART. XVIII. All public functionaries of whatever class shall aid one another in the execution of the resolutions of the government council.

ART. XIX. All Cubans are bound to serve the revolution with their persons and interests, each one according to his ability.

ART. XX. The plantations and property of whatever description belonging to foreigners are subject to the payment of taxes for the revolution while their respective governments do not recognize the rights of belligerency of Cuba.

ART. XXI. All debts and obligations contracted since the beginning of the present period of war until the promulgation of this constitution by the chiefs of the army corps, for the benefit of the revolution, shall be valid as well as those which henceforth the government council may contract.

ART. XXII. A government council may depose any of its members for cause justifiable in the judgment of two-thirds of the councilors and shall report to the first assembly convening.

ART. XXIII. The judicial power shall act with entire independence of all the others. Its organization and regulation will be provided for by the government council.

ART. XXIV. The present constitution shall be in force in Cuba for two years from the date of its promulgation, unless the war for independence shall terminate before. After the expiration of the two years an assembly of representatives shall be convened which may modify it, and will proceed to the election of a new government council, and which will pass upon the last council. So it has been agreed upon and resolved in the name of the Republic by the constituent assembly in Jimaguayu on the 18th day of September, 1895, and in witness thereof we, the representatives delegated by the Cuban people in arms, signed the present instrument. Salvador Cisneros, president; Rafael Manduley, vice-president; Pedro Pinan de Villegas, Lope Recio, Fermin Valdes Dominguez, Francisco Diaz Silveira, Dr. Santiago Garcia, Rafael Perez, F. Lopez Leyva, Enrique Cespedes, Marcos Padilla, Raimundo Sanchez, J. D. Castillo, Mariano Sanchez, Pedro Aguilera, Rafael M. Pontuondo, Orencio Nodarse, José Clemente Vivanco, Enrique Loynaz Del Castillo, Severo Pina.

ELECTION OF GOVERNMENT.

The constituent assembly met again on the 18th of the said month and year, all the said representatives being present. They proceeded to the election of members who are to occupy the offices of the Government council, the general-in-chief of the army of liberation, the lieutenant-general, and the diplomatic agent abroad. The secret voting commenced, each representative depositing his ballot in the urn placed on the chairman's table, after which the count was proceeded with, the following being the result:

President: Salvador Cisneros, 12; Bartolome Maso, 8.

Vice-president: Bartolome Maso, 12; Salvador Cisneros, 8.

Secretary of war: Carlos Roloff, 18; Lope Recio Loinaz, 1; Rafael Manduley, 1.

Secretary of the treasury: Severo Pina, 19; Rafael Manduley, 1.

Secretary of the interior: Dr. Santiago Garcia Canizares, 19; Carlos Dubois, 1.

Secretary of the foreign relations: Rafael Portuondo, 18; Armando Menocal, 1, blank, 1.

Subsecretary of war: Mario Menocal, 18; Francisco Diaz Silveira, 1; blank, 1.

Subsecretary of the treasury: Dr. Joaquin Castillo, 7; Francisco Diaz Silveira, 5; José C. Vivanco, 3; Armando Menocal, 3; Carlos Dubois, 1; blank, 1.

Subsecretary of the interior: Carlos Dubois, 13; Oreneio Nodarse, 5; Armando Menocal, 1; blank, 1.

Subsecretary of foreign relations: Fermin Valdes Dominguez, 18; Rafael Manduley, 1; blank, 1.

Therefore, the following were elected by a majority of votes:

President, Salvador Cisneros; vice-president, Bartolome Maso; secretary of war, Carlos Roloff; secretary of the treasury, Severo Pina; secretary of the interior, Dr. Santiago Garcia Canizares; secretary of foreign relations, Rafael M. Portuondo; subsecretary of war, Mario Menocal; subsecretary of the treasury, Dr. Joaquin Castillo; subsecretary of the interior, Carlos Dubois; subsecretary of foreign relations, Dr. Fermin Valdes Dominguez.

The vice-president of the assembly immediately installed the president in the office of the government council that had been conferred upon him; the latter in turn installed those of the other members elected, who were present, all entering on the full exercise of their functions after previously taking the oath.

On proceeding to the election of those who were to occupy the positions of general in-chief of the army, lieutenant-general, and diplomatic agent abroad, the following citizens were unanimously elected by the assembly for the respective places: Major-General Maximo Gomez, Major-General Antonio Maceo, and Citizen Tomas Estrada Palma. All these appointments being recognized from that moment.

LAWS FOR THE CIVIL GOVERNMENT AND ADMINISTRATION OF THE REPUBLIC.

CHAPTER I.—TERRITORIAL DIVISION.

ARTICLE I. The Republic of Cuba comprises the territory occupied by the Island of Cuba from Cape San Antonio to Point Maisi and the adjacent islands and keys.

ART. II. This territory shall be divided into four portions, or states, which will be called Oriente, Camaguey, Las Villas or Cabanacan, and Occidente.

ART. III. The State of Oriente includes the territory from the Point Maisi to Port Manati and the river Jobabo in all its course.

ART. IV. The State of Camaguey includes all the territory from the boundary of Oriente to the line which starts in the north from Laguna Blanca through the Esteros to Moron, passing by Ciego de Avila, follows the military trocha to El Jucaro in the southern coast, it being understood that the towns of Moron and Ciego de Avila belong to this State.

ART. V. The State of Las Villas has for boundary on the east Camaguey, on the west the river Palmas, Palmillas, Santa Rosa, Rodas, the Hannabana River, and the bay of Cochinos.

ART. VI. The State of Occidente is bordered on the Las Villas, extending to the west to Cape San Antonio.

ART. VII. The islands and adjacent keys will form part of the states to which they geographically belong.

ART. VIII. The State of Oriente will be divided into ten districts, which shall be as follows: Baracoa, Guantanamo, Sagua de Tanamo, Mayari, Santiago, Jiguani, Manzanillo, Bayamo, and Tunas.

Camaguey comprises two—the eastern district and the western district.

Las Villas comprises seven—Sancti-Espiritus, Trinidad, Remedios, Santa Clara, Sagua, Cienfuegos, and Colon.

That of Occidente comprises sixteen—Cardenas, Matanzas, Union, Jaruco, Guines, Santa Maria del Rosario, Guanabacoa, Habana, Santiago de las Vegas, Bejucal, San Antonio, Bahia Honda, Pina del Rio, and Mantua.

ART. IX. Each of these districts will be divided into prefectures, and these in their turn into as many subprefectures as may be considered necessary.

ART. X. For the vigilance of the coasts there will be inspectors and watchmen appointed in each State according to the extent of the coasts and the number of ports, bays, gulfs, and salt works that there may be.

ART. XI. On establishing the limits of the districts and prefectures, the direction of the coast, rivers, and other natural boundaries shall be kept in mind.

CHAPTER II.—OF THE GOVERNMENT AND ITS ADMINISTRATION.

ART. XII. The civil government, the administration, and the service of communications devolve upon the department of the interior.

ART. XIII. The secretary of the interior is the head of the department; he will appoint the employees and will remove them whenever there will be justifiable cause, and will have a department chief to aid him in the work of the department.

ART. XIV. The department chief will keep the books of the department, take care of the archives, will be the manager of the office, and will furnish certifications when requested to do so.

ART. XV. The department of the interior will compile from the data collected by the civil governors the general statistics of the Republic.

ART. XVI. The civil governor will inform the department of the interior as to the necessities of his state, will order the measures and instructions necessary for compliance with the general laws of the Republic and the orders given by that department, will distribute to the lieutenant-governors the articles of prime necessity which will be delivered to them for that purpose, will communicate to his subordinates the necessary instructions for the compilation of statistics, and will have a subsecretary who will help him in the discharge of his functions.

ART. XVII. The lieutenant-governor will see that the orders of the governors are obeyed in the district, and will have the powers incident to his position as intermediary between the civil governors and the prefects. In case of absolute breach of communication with the civil governors, they will have the same powers as the latter.

ART. XVIII. The prefect shall see that the laws and regulations communicated to him by his superior authorities are complied with. All residents and travelers are under his authority, and, being the highest official in his territory, he in his turn is bound to prevent all abuses and crimes which may be committed.

He will inform the lieutenant-governor as to the necessities of the prefecture; will divide these into as many subprefectures as he may consider necessary for the good conduct of his administration; he will watch the conduct of the subprefects; he will distribute among them with equity the articles delivered to him, and he will have all the other powers incident to him in his character of intermediary between the lieutenant-governor and the subprefects.

ART. XIX. The prefect will also have the following duties: He will harass the enemy whenever possible for him to do so; will hear the preliminary information as to crimes and misdemeanors which may be committed in his territory, passing the said information to the nearest military chief, together with the accused and all that is necessary for the better understanding of the hearing. He will not proceed thus with spies, guides, couriers, and others who are declared by our laws as traitors and considered as such, for these, on account of the difficulty of confining them or conducting them with security, shall be tried as soon as captured by a court consisting of three persons, the most capable in his judgment in the prefecture, one acting as president and the others as members of the court. He will also appoint a prosecuting officer, and the accused may appoint some one to defend him at his pleasure.

After the court is assembled in this form, and after all the formalities are complied with, it will in private judge and give its sentence, which will be final and without appeal; but those who form the said court and who do not proceed according to our laws and to natural reason will be held responsible by the superior government. Nevertheless, if in the immediate territory there be any armed force, the accused shall be sent to it with the facts in order that they shall be properly tried.

The prefects will take the statistics of his prefecture, setting down every person who is found therein, noting if he is the head of a family, the number of the same, his age, his nationality and occupation, if he is a farmer the nature of his farm, and if he has no occupation the prefect will indicate in what he should be employed. He will also keep a book of civil register in which he will set down the births, deaths, and marriages which may occur.

He will establish in the prefecture all the factories that he can or may consider necessary in order to well provide the army, as it is the primary obligation of all employees of the Republic to do all possible so that the hides shall not be lost, and organizing in the best manner, and as quickly as may be, tanneries, factories of shoes, rope, blankets, and carpenter and blacksmith shops.

He will not permit any individual of his district to be without occupation. He will see that everyone works, having the instruments of labor at hand in proportion to the inhabitants of his territory. He will protect and raise bees, he will take care of abandoned farms, and will extend as far as possible the zones of agriculture.

As soon as the prefect learns that the secretary of the interior or any delegate of this authority is in his district he will place himself under the latter's orders. This he will also do on the arrival of armed forces, presenting himself to their chief in order to facilitate the needed supplies and to serve him in every possible manner. He will have a bugle to warn the inhabitants of the enemy's approach; he will inform the nearest armed force when his territory is invaded. He will collect all horses and other animals suitable for the war and lead them to a secure place, so that when the army may need them or they may be required by the civil authorities to whom they may appertain.

He will provide the forces that may be, or pass through his territory with whatever they may need, which may be within his power, and especially shall he provide guides and beeves and vegetables which the chief may require to maintain the said forces. He will also deliver the articles manufactured in the shops under his immediate inspection, demanding always the proper receipts therefor.

He will also provide the necessary means for the maintenance of all the families of the territory, especially those of the soldiers of the army of liberation.

Until otherwise decreed he will celebrate civil marriages and other contracts entered into by the residents of his prefecture; he will act in cases of ordinary complaints and in the execution of powers and wills, registering the same in a clear and definite manner, and issuing to the interested parties the certificates which they may require.

ART. XX. The subprefects will see that the laws and orders communicated to him by his superior authorities are obeyed in territory under his command; he will inform the prefect as to the necessities of the subprefecture and will see to the security and order of the public; arresting and sending to the prefects those who may travel without safe-conduct, seeing that no violation of law whatsoever is perpetrated, and will demand the signed authority of the civil or military chief who has ordered a commission to be executed.

ART. XXI. The subprefects will compile a census in which the number of inhabitants of a subprefecture will be stated and their personal description; he will keep a book of the births and deaths which will occur in his territory, and of all this he will give account at the end of the year. He will invest the means provided by the prefect to pay the public charges, and if the said resources are insufficient he will collect the deficit from the inhabitants; he will not authorize the destruction of abandoned farms, whether they belong to friends or enemies of the Republic, and he will inform the prefect of the farms which are thus abandoned.

ART. XXII. For the organization and better operation of the states manufactories a chief of factories shall be appointed in each district, who will be authorized to establish such factories which he may deem convenient, employing all citizens who, on account of their abilities can serve, and collecting in the prefectures of his district all the instruments he can utilize in his work. These chiefs will be careful to frequently inspect the factories, to report any defects which they may notice, and to provide the superintendents with whatever they may need, that the work may not be interrupted.

Together with the prefect he will send to the department of the interior the names of the individuals he considers most adapted to open new shops, and on the first day of each month he will send to that department a statement of the objects manufactured in each shop of his district, indicating the place of manufacture, what remains on deposit, what has been delivered, with the names of commanders of forces, civil authorities, or individuals to whom they were delivered.

ART. XXIII. The coast inspectors will have under their immediate orders an inspector, who will be his secretary, who will occupy his place in his absence or sickness, and as many auxiliaries as he may deem convenient. He may demand the aid of the prefects and armed forces whenever he may consider it necessary for the better exercise of his functions. The duties of the inspectors will be to watch the coasts and prevent the landing of the enemy, to be always ready to receive disembarkments and place in safety the expeditions which may come from abroad, to establish all the salt works possible, to capture the Spanish vessels which frequent the coasts on his guard, and to attend with special care to the punctual service of communications between his coast and foreign countries.

ART. XXIV. The coast guards will acknowledge the inspector as their superior, will watch the places designated to them, and will execute the orders given.

ART. XXV. The lieutenant-governors, as well as the inspectors of whatever class, will have their residence, wherever the necessity of their office does not prohibit it, in the general headquarters, so that they can move easily, furnish the necessary aid to the army, and carry out the orders of the military chief.

Country and liberty.

OCTOBER 17, 1895.

The secretary of the interior, Dr. Santiago Garcia Canizares, being satisfied with the preceding law, I sanction it in all respects.

Let it be promulgated in the legal form.

SALVADOR CISNEROS BETANCOURT,
The President.

OCTOBER 18, 1895.

LAW OF CIVIL MARRIAGE.

ARTICLE I. Males of 18 years of age and females of 14 can contract marriage.

ART. II. To contract marriage they must go to the notary of their residence, two witnesses being present who will sign the contract with the parties and the notary.

ART. III. The marriage contract may contain any agreement or convention which the contracting parties may agree upon and which is not opposed to the nature of the contract nor to law.

ART. IV. If one of the contracting parties is less than 20 years of age, the marriage can be contracted with notice to the father, the mother, or the guardian, according to the circumstances, and if these oppose the celebration of the marriage, the judge of the district, with knowledge of the facts, will decide the question.

ART. V. The following reason will prevent marriage: Consanguinity in the direct line. In the collateral, brother and sister can not marry; it is null by the relationship in said degrees, or by being contracted by fraud or by force. It is completely dissolved for incompatibility by a chronic and contagious disease, or one which will cause impotency, and by adultery; moral or physical ill treatment of the wife gives to the wife the right to demand from the husband, when they live apart, to bear the expenses of the marriage; if the woman commits adultery she loses this right.

ART. VI. In case of separation, the male children of 14 years of age and upward and female children of 12 and upward may elect between their parents as to residence. Those less than 3 years of age must remain with the mother. Those who have not yet reached the age of puberty, but are older than 3 years, remain with the parent who has not given the motive for the separation. This is in case that the separation is caused by some guilt. If it occurs on account of sickness, the children will remain with the one who did not desire the separation. If the separation is on account of incompatibility, the parents must agree as to this point. On reaching the age of 3 years, the children who until then have been with the mother, the question of their custody will be governed by the other provisions of this article.

When the male reaches the age of 14 and the female of 12, whatever may have been their previous residence, they may alter it.

ART. VII. Marriage being once dissolved, the parties may remarry, but the woman shall not do so until twelve months have elapsed, in order to avoid confusion of paternity.

ART. VIII. Civil marriage is placed on an equal footing, as to duty and effects, with that recognized by our former legislation, and celebrated by the intervention of the church.

ART. IX. The promise of marriage does not have any other result than that of the payment of the penalty, which must be stipulated by the contracting party. If no penalty is stipulated, no duty of payment is incurred.

ART. X. The seduction of a female, whether she be a minor or not, obliges the seductor to marry the seduced or to pay a penalty in proportion to the fortune of both, which the judge of the district must determine.

Country and liberty.

PROVIDENCIA, *September 25, 1895.*

GARCIA CANIZARES.
Secretary of the Interior:

Let the foregoing be promulgated in the legal form, it having my sanction.

Providencia, September 25, 1895.

SALVADOR CISNEROS BETANCOURT,
President.

CIVIL MARRIAGE.

Instructions which must be observed by the prefects of the Republic of Cuba in the celebration of civil marriage, exercising the function which is given them by the provisional law passed by the Government Council on the 25th of September, 1895.

ARTICLE I. The prefect of the residence of the wife, who is the only one competent to celebrate the marriage, will demand of the parties a copy of their certificate of birth, so that they can prove their marriageable age, which of the male is 18 years and of the female 14 years.

ART. II. If either of the contracting parties should not have that document, by the omission, suppression, or burning of the register, or for any other cause, this credential may be substituted by a certificate of the authorities as to the nationality or residence, in which certificate the cause of the absence of the original certificate shall be stated (after previous investigation and on information received as to its omission) the names of the parents, their civil status, and the year and month of the birth of the contracting parties.

ART. III. If it appears that the contracting parties are over 20 years of age the prefect will proceed to the celebration of the civil marriage without further requisite than to give it publicity, for which purpose he shall affix notices in the most frequented places of the prefecture.

ART. IV. But if either of the parties is less than 20 years of age the contract must not only be made public, as previously stated, but notice given to the father, the mother, or the guardian, so that if these oppose the marriage it may be suspended until, with a full knowledge of the facts, the question be decided by the judge, who must investigate, the prefect fixing a time for the opposing parties to establish and justify their position, which must not be longer than eight days.

ART. V. In all cases the prefect will demand from the contracting party their assurance of the consent of each other, or at least that of the bride, and of her ability to enter into the matrimonial contract, which requisite the prefect may omit if he himself possesses knowledge of the circumstances.

ART. VI. If there are no disabilities to the marriage the prefect will register in a book entitled Book of Civil Marriages Contracted in the Prefecture ———, designating on the first page the year and making an index at the end in alphabetical order.

ART. VII. The contract will be formulated in the following terms:

"Formula of the marriage of persons of 20 years and upward:

"In the prefecture of ——— on the ——— day of 189—, before me, the prefect ———, and before me, the undersigned secretary, there appeared ——— and ———, of 20 years and upward, the former born and resident of ———, son of (here the names of parents), and the latter born and resident of the prefecture ———, daughter (here the names of parents), who are known to the prefect and to myself, the secretary, or who, unknown, were presented to M. and P., who act as witnesses, who affirm that that they know them, or at least that they know her, and they so declare and affirm."

"The contracting parties thereupon say, in the presence of these witnesses and those to this instrument, A and B, called for that purpose, that of their own free will, and without any violence, they promised to marry civilly, which marriage they now celebrate, and they agree to live in complete harmony and conjugal union, and never to separate unless because of incompatibility, or for any of the other reasons allowed by law, declaring that this marriage is for the welfare and honor of both, and for their offspring, and as the laws and customs of good government require (here any agreement made between the contracting parties shall be inserted, besides the nuptial contract), and the register will thus end; and in order that this marriage shall be known, and always and in all cases have its legal force, the prefect orders the minutes of this contract to be drawn in the said terms, signing with the contracting parties, and the said witnesses (if they can write, and if they can not others, at their request, may do so), to all of which I, the secretary, certify."

FORMULA FOR THE MARRIAGE OF THOSE LESS THAN TWENTY YEARS OF AGE.

The beginning will be as in the above formula, adding that the contracting parties being minors, the father, mother, or guardian appeared, who declared their assent and signed (if they can write) the register, and if not, a person of their confidence whom they may select. The declaration as to register will be the same as in the preceding formula.

FORMULA OF CIVIL MARRIAGE TO WHICH THERE IS OPPOSITION.

After the preamble similar to the first formula in the register is declared, that the father, mother, or guardian whosoever has interposed before the competent authority, has dissented, declares the contract not to be proper, as he explains in the following declaration. As to the rest, the register will be as in the first formula to its conclusion.

But in case the father, mother, or guardian do not make any opposition, it shall be so declared in the register that the time fixed having passed and the person having the right to exercise this right having failed to do so, the marriage has been consummated.

NOTE.—Of every marriage there will be formed a file consisting of the copy of the register of birth, of the cedula, of the declaration of the opposition of father, mother, or guardian, and of the decree in which it shall be declared proper, or it is ordered that the marriage shall take place because they have not exercised that right, or because the party opposing has not complied with the law. This file shall be kept for future use.

Country and liberty.

GARCIA CANIZARES,
Secretary of the Interior.

PROVIDENCIA, *September 25, 1895.*

Let the foregoing be promulgated in its legal form, as I sanction the foregoing law in all its parts.

SALVADOR CISNEROS BETANCOURT,
President.

PROVIDENCIA, *September 25, 1895.*

———

EXTRACT OF THE SESSIONS.

[Republic of Cuba, Provisional Government, secretary of the council—José Clemente Vivanco, secretary of the Government Council and chancellor of the Republic]

I certify that among the resolutions passed by this council, according to the minute book of the sessions, the following are to be found:

To give two months' time to the chiefs and officers of the last revolution to join the new army of liberation, so as to have their ranks recognized, and four months' time to those in foreign countries to place themselves in communication with the delegates. To allow the Cuban emigrants individual freedom in the nature of their contributions for the revolution. To permit the export of wooden blocks on payment of $5 in gold as tax for each piece. To prohibit absolutely the export of corn and all forage; of cattle, pigs, horses; without allowing anything to enter the towns without the previous payment of taxes.

To prohibit absolutely also the introduction in the towns of all kinds of fruits and articles of commerce which may favor the said towns and indirectly the Government which we are fighting.

San Andres de la Rioja, October 9, 1895.

(Signed)   JOSÉ CLEMENTE VIVANCO,
Secretary of the Council.

REGULATIONS FOR THE SERVICE OF COMMUNICATIONS.

ARTICLE 1. The secretary of the interior will be the postmaster-general of the whole island, and the civil governor the chief of his territory.

ART. 2. The postal service is established between the prefectures of the Republic and between the towns and prefectures near by.

ART. 3. In order to organize the postal service, an inspector will be named for each district; as many chiefs as there are post-offices, and as many couriers and auxiliaries as are necessary for each one.

ART. 4. The inspector is the superior chief in his district of the postal service; under his direction will be the postmasters, couriers, and auxiliaries. He shall organize the service by placing the post-offices in the most convenient places, so that the service shall be carried out with the greatest ease and with the greatest rapidity. He will employ the number of employees that are necessary. He will ask for their resignations whenever there is any justifiable cause for it. He will see that every one shall fulfill his duties, and shall name the hours when the couriers shall depart. He shall correct all defects that come under his notice, propose all modifications which he may think will give a better service, and give an account of all extraordinary services which his subalterns may render in order that they should be registered and rewarded.

ART. 5. The chiefs will reside in the post-office, from which they can not be absent during the appointed hours, and they are to act whenever possible as auxiliaries to the prefect's office. They will receive official and private correspondence, sign receipts for that delivered by mail carriers, setting down the hour of delivery, and they will deliver, under receipt in which they will also put down the time of departure, to the outgoing postman the mail matter in their hands, giving with it a memorandum stating the name of mail carried and the time of departure. They will also see that the post-offices are well attended and have in them the necessary number of horses required for the service, unless in cases where the service is carried on foot. They will report to the inspector the defects they may observe in the service, without forgetting the importance of their position.

ART. 6. The mail carriers will collect daily at the appointed hours, along the route marked out, without delaying on the way nor hurrying their horses except in urgent cases that will be pointed out by the chief. They will have a receipt for the correspondence delivered to them, and will receive in exchange for the receipt a signed memorandum stating what mail they carry; which memorandum they will present to the chief of postal department, so that he may sign it and declare that he has received them, and, after complying with this requisite, change it for a receipt which he will leave in the office of departure.

A great service will be done by the couriers, and for that reason men of known honesty and valor shall be chosen, who are capable of appreciating the service they render their country.

ART. 7. A mail service will be organized in every city occupied by the enemy, and will consist of as many chiefs and carriers as may be considered necessary.

ART. 8. The inspectors of mails will be the immediate superior officer of the service in the town of his residence, and will have under his command the postmasters and mail carriers, and they will exercise their functions in the same manner as the coast inspectors. They will have special care in the selection of employees and in keeping all possible secrecy to elude the vigilance of the enemy.

ART. 9. The postmasters will be considered as the chiefs of mail carriers and will act with the carriers, as the carriers with the drivers, always giving an account of any extra services rendered.

ART. 10. The mail carriers will have charge of receiving from the postmasters the mail matter and carry it out of the cities for delivery to the office of the nearest prefect. They will give and ask for receipts as the drivers and like these must be honest men, sharp and brave enough with courage to overcome the difficulties that may arise in the performance of their important and dangerous mission and worthy to occupy these positions of trust in which they can lend such valuable services to the sacred cause every Cuban is bound to defend.

ART. 11. The inspectors and postmasters will keep a book to record the appointments of employees and the services rendered by them and will make up their archives with this book and circulars, communications, and official documents that they receive on the copies of those they may have to transmit.

Country and liberty, September, 1895.

Dr. SANITAGO GARCIA CANIZARES,
Secretary of the Interior.

In conformity with the preceding regulations I sanction them in every part; and that it may govern and produce its corresponding effects have it published in the legal form.

Country and liberty.

Residence of the Executive in Limones, the 6th day of October, 1895.

SALVADOR CISNEROS, *President.*

LAW FOR THE ORGANIZATION OF THE PUBLIC TREASURY.

ARTICLE I. All property of whatever description situated in the territory of the Republic comes under the jurisdiction of the secretary of the treasury; therefore this department shall take charge of articles of whatever description brought to this island by expeditions from abroad; this department also has the faculty of raising public loans and general taxes.

ART. II. The secretary of the treasury will be the superior chief of his department throughout the Island of Cuba, and through him the subaltern officers will receive the orders given by the council. The duties of the secretary will be to determine, on information of the collectors, the taxes which shall be paid in each state and the form in which they shall be collected, to nominate the employees of his department and to discharge them for justifiable cause. He will deliver to the chiefs of corps and civil governors the articles which he receives from abroad; he will give a receipt for the articles or sums of money which from any source whatever may be collected by the public treasury. He may trade with the merchandise belonging to the Republic; he may lease or sell whatever be convenient and will present an account every three months to the council of the funds belonging to the Republic.

ART. III. To facilitate the work of the treasury a chief of department will be appointed who will act as general comptroller, and in each State a collector and a secretary of the administration of the treasury, and for each district a delegate

ART. IV. The chief of the department, or general comptroller, will have charge of the archives of the department, will keep the books in due form, and will take part in all the collections and disbursements which may occur.

ART. V. The collector will represent in each State the secretary of the treasury, he will give information as to the taxable property in his State, he will dictate the necessary measures to carry out the general orders communicated to him by the secretary of the treasury, he will collect by means of agents the taxes fixed upon, and he will send to the department as soon as possible the funds collected; nevertheless he may deliver the amounts he may deem necessary to the chiefs of the different army corps, who will give a receipt for them and justify their expenditure. The collectors will monthly send to the department a statement of their operation.

ART. VI. The secretary of the administration of the treasury will keep the archives of his respective State, will keep the books in due form, and will take part in the operations of the collector.

ART. VII. The delegates or agents will be the collectors of taxes in each district, and the commissioners will see that the orders of the collectors of the State are carried out. They may appoint auxiliaries whenever necessary, and are authorized to demand the aid of the prefects and armed forces for the better fulfillment of their commissions.

Country and liberty.

Canaster, October 16, 1895.

SEVERO PINA,
Secretary of the Treasury.

In conformity with the previous law, I sanction it in all its parts. Let it be promulgated in legal form.

Country and liberty, October 18, 1885.

MANGOS DE BARAGUA.

SALVADOR CISNEROS BETANCOURT,
President.

INSTRUCTIONS TO THE OFFICERS OF THE DEPARTMENT OF THE TREASURY OF THE REPUBLIC OF CUBA.

ARTICLE I. According to article 18 of the constitution and the decree of the general in chief of the 20th of September last, the military chiefs shall give the necessary aid to the officers of the treasury for the better fulfillment of their duties.

ART. II. With the aid of the armed forces, they will proceed to the destruction of those plantations, whatever be their nationality, which will refuse to pay the taxes decreed by the Government of the Republic.

ART. III. As a basis for the rate of tax, the production of the plantations shall serve as well as the price of their products, taking into consideration the expense of transportation.

ART. IV. The amount of the tax will be paid in advance in gold or in drafts on New York, Paris, or London in the form agreed upon.

ART. V. All kinds of traffic with the enemy is absolutely prohibited, only the following articles and products are allowed to be exported:

Coffee and cocoa, $4 per hundredweight.

Wood in blocks, $8 per thousand feet or $3 apiece, as will best suit the interests of the Republic and the functionary authorizing the exportation.

Guana (a textile palm), $4 per hundredweight.

Wax, $4 per hundredweight.

Fattened steers, $3 per head.

Cheese, $2 per hundredweight.

In regard to mines, tobacco, and plantains for exportation, it is left to the judgment of the collector of the treasury.

ART. VI. The exportation of wood or guana (the latter until December 6) will only be permitted when worked or packed by individuals who are in the confidence of our authorities.

ART. VII. The exportation of cattle will only be allowed when, in the judgment of the authority, they run imminent risk of falling into the hands of the enemy.

ART. VIII. The collector of the treasury of each State may suspend, temporarily, the exportation of the products referred to in Article V, immediately giving an account of it to the secretary of the treasury for final adjudgment.

Sabanilla del Contra Maestre, October 24, 1895.

SEVERO PINA.
Secretary of the Treasury.

In conformity with the previous law, I sanction it in all its parts. Let it be promulgated in legal form.

Sabanilla, October 25, 1895.

SALVADOR CISNEROS BETANCOURT,
President.

EXTRACT OF THE SESSIONS OF THE GOVERNMENT COUNCIL, REPUBLIC OF CUBA.

Secretary of the Government José Clemente Vivanco, secretary of the Government Council and chancellor of the Republic, I certify that in the minute books of the sessions celebrated by this council the following resolutions are found:

SEPTEMBER 19, 1895.

To appoint a secretary of the Government and chancellor of the Republic, José Clemente Vivanco. To send the appointments of general in chief, lieutenant-general, and delegate plenipotentiary abroad to Maj. Gen. Maximo Gomez, Maj. Gen. Antonio Maceo, and Tomas Estrada Palma, respectively.

To appoint as civil governor of Camaguey, Dr. Oscar Primelles, and of Oriente, Rafael Manduley.

To complete the system of the division of the territory of the island into zones, and that the subsecretary of war, in the absence of the secretary, agree with the general in chief as to the organization of the army of liberation.

SEPTEMBER 20, 1895.

To give two months' time to the chief and officers of the past revolution to join the newly organized army of liberation, for the recognition of their grades, and four months' time to those outside of the island. That each secretary of state may name a chief of his department. To appoint as director of the treasury in Oriente Diego Palacios, and in Camaguey, Col. Lope Recio Loynaz. That the secretary communicate with the general in chief so the latter may indorse the authorities, passes, and orders given by the Government and require all the forces of the army of liberation to respect and obey them.

To ask the general in chief for Capts. Francisco Garcia, Manuel Merrero, and Ensign Enrique Boza, as their services are needed by the Government. That the Cuban emigrations shall be at liberty as to the manner of contributing to the revolution.

To ask from abroad a copy of all the decrees passed by the government of the last revolution, and to order that in conformity with the minutes sent from here all documents shall be printed emanating from the Government as well as the constitution passed by the constituent assembly which shall be placed in our archives.

SEPTEMBER 24, 1895.

To publish a circular of the secretary of the interior, addressed to the prefects, subprefects, and other functionaries of civil order, recommending them to fulfill their respective duties.

To approve the order given by the general in chief as to the respect due peaceful families and their interests, excepting in cases of military necessity or on account of manifest or suspected treachery, and that the secretary of the interior address such communication to the civil governors advising them of this resolution.

To appoint chief of postal service for the eastern and western district of Camaguey, Manuel Manero, and Francisco Garcia, respectively, and to confirm the appointments of prefects temporarily made by the general in chief.

To ask the general in chief to order all the chiefs of army corps to send to the secretary of war a detailed account of the chiefs and officers under his orders, their record of service, the positions which they occupy, and their respective abilities.

To communicate to Maj. Gen. Carlos Roloff that his aides, Francisco Diaz Silveira and Orencio Nodarse remain with this Government.

SEPTEMBER 25, 1895.

To permit the export of wood in blocks after the payment of $5 in gold for each block. To absolutely prohibit the sale of corn and all kinds of forage, cows, oxen, and horses, permitting only other animals to be taken within a radius of 6 leagues from the towns on a payment of the tax.

That through the secretary of the treasury a detailed statement of the tax-paying property shall be sent to the prefects and military chiefs.

To approve the provisional law of civil marriage passed June 4, 1869, by the Chamber of Representatives of the past revolution and to put it in force on motion of the secretary of the interior.

To approve and enforce the instructions as to said law, which were passed June 21, 1869, by the said chamber.

To confirm the appointment of inspectors of coasts and coast guards made previously by the general in chief.

OCTOBER 5, 1895.

That each secretary of state shall present to the council such projects of laws and regulations as shall be in force in their respective departments, and that the secretary of foreign relations, together with the subsecretary, the acting secretary of war, shall draw a project of criminal procedure for deliberation and approval by the council.

OCTOBER 6, 1895.

To absolutely prohibit the introduction in the towns of all articles of commerce which, favoring trade indirectly, aid the enemy's Government, and to confirm the appointment of the inspector of shops and prefectures in the district of Tunas to Citizen Luis Marti, provisionally given by the general in chief of the third division José M. Capote, on September 17, 1895.

OCTOBER 16, 1895.

That the secretary of the Government shall collect all the laws, rules, decrees, and all other orders of this council and an extract of the resolutions for publication in book form for an edition of 500 copies.

To approve the project of the law for the organization of the public treasury presented by the secretary of the treasury.

To approve the law for the civil government and administration of the Republic, presented by the secretary of the interior.

OCTOBER 21, 1895.

To send a communication to the chiefs of army corps; to send the secretary of the treasury a detailed account of all the contracts made by them since the beginning of the war, in order that in conformity with article 21 of the constitution they be approved.

To give military consideration to all civil functionaries, appointing for this purpose a commission composed of the secretary of the interior and the subsecretary of war, so that they may present a report as to the rules to be followed in this behalf.

OCTOBER 24, 1895.

To approve the project as to instructions of the officers of the public treasury presented by the secretary of the treasury.

To approve the report as to the military considerations to be enjoyed by the civil functionaries, presented by the secretary of the interior and the subsecretary of war, commissioned for this purpose at the last session, which is as follows:

The president of the Republic, that of general in chief of the army; the vice-president, and the secretaries of state, of major-generals.

The secretary of the council and chancellor, brigadier-general; the chiefs of departments of states, civil governors and collectors of the treasury, colonels; the lieutenant-governor, delegate of the treasury and the secretary of administration, of the treasury, majors; the prefects, the inspectors of shops, of coast and communication, that of captains; the subprefects, and ensigns.

All these considerations shall be enjoyed by them unless they have higher rank.

OCTOBER 25, 1895.

The following decree was approved:

ARTICLE I. No one can be punished by death, or by imprisonment or reprimand, without having been previously judged by court-martial.

ART. II. The factories, barns, houses, fruit trees, and useful wood trees will be respected by all the citizens of the Republic.

ART. III. Housebreaking and unjustifiable raids will be severely punished.

ART. IV. No citizen can be dispossessed from the house he occupies without justifiable motive.

ART. V. The forces on the march, detachments, or commissions will not occupy inhabited houses without the consent of their owners, unless the exigencies of the war require it or in extraordinary cases, when it will be justified by the officer who orders it.

And for the publication thereof in accordance with the resolution of the 16th instant, I publish the present compilation, which is a true copy of the originals, on file in the archives of my secretaryship.

Country and liberty.

Sabanilla, October 25, 1895.

JOSÉ CLEMENTE VIVANCO,
Secretary of the Council.

There will soon be published the laws of organization and military ordinances drafted by the general in chief and approved by the council, which shall be joined to the present compilation, C.

[COAT OF ARMS OF CUBAN REPUBLIC.]

In the name of the Republic of Cuba by delegation of the Cuban people in arms. The constituent assembly resolved by acclamation on this day to confer on Tomas Estrada Palma, the diplomatic representative and agent abroad, the title of delegate plenipotentiary of the Republic of Cuba.

In witness whereof we have affixed our signatures in Jimaguayu on the 18th of September, 1895.

Salvador Cesneros, B., President; Rafael Manduley, Vice-President; Enrique Loinaz del Castillo, Severo Pina, Fermin Valdes Dominguez, Rafael Perez Morales, Raimundo Sanchez, J. D. Castillo, Pedro Pinan de Villegas, Pedro Aguilera, Marcos Padilla, Rafael M. Portuondo, Dr. Santiago Garcia Canizares; Lope Recio, L.; Orencio Nodarse, secretary; Franco Diaz Silveira, Enrique Cespedes, Mariano Sanchez Vaillant, F. Lopez Leiva, secretary; José Clemente Vivanco, secretary.

D.

ARMY HEADQUARTERS AT CUMANAYAGUA.

Mr. ALFREDO REGO.

MY DEAR SIR: I had the pleasure to receive your polite note. I see by it the generosity of your heart, and I thank you, in the name of my superior officers, to whom I will communicate your humanitarian act.

I send the committee desired to bring back the prisoners. It takes this letter to you and is composed of Benito Mesa and Telesforo Ramirez. I beg you to give them the necessary aid, promising you that your men will be respected by this garrison.

Yours, truly,

(Signed.)   JOSÉ BRETONES, *Lieutenant.*

FIFTY-FOURTH CONGRESS, FIRST SESSION.

[Senate Document No 213.]

Message from the President of the United States, in response to resolution of the Senate of March 24, 1896, requesting that the Senate be furnished with the correspondence of the Department of State between November 5, 1875, and the date of the pacification of Cuba in 1878, relating to the subject of mediation or intervention by the United States in the affairs of Cuba, transmitting report from the Secretary of State with such papers as seem to be called for by the resolution.

APRIL 15, 1896.—Referred to the Committee on Foreign Relations and ordered to be printed.

To the Senate of the United States:

In response to the resolution of March 24, 1896, requesting that the Senate be furnished with the correspondence of the Department of State between November 5, 1875, and the date of the pacification of Cuba in 1878, relating to the subject of mediation or intervention by the United States in the affairs of that island, I transmit a report from the Secretary of State, forwarding such papers as seem to be called for by the resolution in question.

GROVER CLEVELAND.

EXECUTIVE MANSION,
Washington, April 15, 1896.

The PRESIDENT:

In response to the resolution of the Senate of the United States dated March 24, 1896, reading as follows—

Resolved, That the President be requested, if in his opinion not incompatible with the public interest, to transmit to the Senate copies of all dispatches, notes, and telegrams in the Department of State, from and after the note from Secretary Fish to Mr. Cushing of November 5, 1875, and including that note, until the pacification of Cuba in 1878, which relate to mediation or intervention by the United States in the affairs of that island, together with all correspondence with foreign Governments relating to the same topic—

the undersigned, Secretary of State, has the honor to submit for transmission to the Senate, if deemed compatible with the public interest, copies of such papers on file in this Department as appear to be called for by the above resolution.

RICHARD OLNEY.

DEPARTMENT OF STATE,
Washington, April 15, 1896.

CORRESPONDENCE.

SPAIN.

Mr. Fish to Mr. Cushing.

No. 266.]   DEPARTMENT OF STATE,
                                        Washington, November 5, 1875.

SIR: Pursuant to the intimation conveyed in my No. 242, I deem it
necessary to recur to the general question of our relations with Spain,
and to consider the progress which has been made in disposing of the
outstanding questions which for some time past have seriously threatened the relations of the two countries.

At the time of your departure for Madrid, apart from the general
question of the unsatisfactory condition of affairs in Cuba and the failure to suppress the revolution, several prominent questions remained
unadjusted, the settlement of which was deemed necessary before any
satisfactory relations with Spain could be established or maintained.
Upon all of these you were instructed.

The most prominent among them were the questions arising from the
embargo and confiscation of estates of American citizens in Cuba; those
relating to the trial of American citizens in that island, in violation of
treaty obligations, and the claims arising out of the capture of the
Virginius, including the trial and punishment of General Burriel.

After the expiration of more than eighteen months, it seems advisable to examine what progress has been made and to consider our present relations with Spain.

In reference to the arbitrary seizure and withholding of the estates and
property of citizens of the United States in Cuba, under proceedings of
confiscation or embargo, so called, a separate instruction was addressed
to you under date of February 6, prior to your departure for your post.

I referred therein to the general facts surrounding these cases, to the
arbitrary action of the authorities, by which the property of American
citizens had been seized in violation of treaty provisions, in the absence
of judicial proceedings, without hearing, and under such circumstances
as to call for vigorous protest and demands on behalf of this Government.

The general facts surrounding these cases are well known.

It is not pretended, so far as I am aware, that any legal justification
for these wrongs has been attempted on the part of the authorities of
Spain, or that these proceedings in Cuba are defended or upheld.

On the contrary, pursuant to the decree issued by the Government
on the 12th of July, 1873, the illegality and indefensible character of
these acts were admitted, and the embargoes were ordered to be
removed and the property to be restored.

This decree was at first received in Cuba with calm indifference, not
even published or adverted to, and the proceedings of the authorities
were in no notable respect changed thereby.

_____

[1] Reprinted from House Ex. Doc. No. 90, Forty-fourth Congress, first session.

At the time of the visit of Señor Soler y Pla, minister of ultramar, the decree was in some instances recognized, and some insignificant steps taken, in individual cases, to comply therewith.

In general, however, it was claimed, either that incumbrances existed, making a compliance therewith impossible, or the delivery was offered burdened by leases or incumbrances, and coupled with unfair conditions or demands, or delivery was avoided, on the ground that particular property was confiscated, not embargoed. In fact, the decree was treated in general with supreme indifference.

You were informed that the President, while not disposed to question the willingness of the authorities in Spain to do justice to this Government and her citizens, expected that means would be found to compel the agents in Cuba to obey the orders of the supreme Government.

Such was the condition of the question at the date of your departure. Numbers of American citizens had at this time been deprived of their property, and were anxiously awaiting the performance of the promises and assurances which had been given by the Spanish Government. In spite of all the efforts which you have made, intelligent and energetic as they have been, no effectual result has been accomplished.

Immediately after you had entered on your duties, in your No. 24, under date of June 2, you reported a conversation with Mr. Ulloa, having reference to this question, and in your No. 39, of June 22, you advise the Department of a note addressed to the minister of state, calling attention to the particular cases of Mr. Criado and Mrs. Farres de Mora, and to the general question.

Although orders of disembargo had been issued, and as early as January, 1873, the then minister of state at Madrid had expressed surprise and regret at the continued delay in these particular cases, Mr. Ulloa informed you, under date of July 7, 1874, that the ministry was in want of information as to these cases, and that the information had been requested through the minister of the colonies. He added, however, that the Spanish Government proposed to adopt, with all possible dispatch, a general system with respect to pending embargoes, and that that important question would be set at rest in conformity with the true interpretation of the treaty of 1795, and with that respect which the Spanish Government had for its obligations.

These assurances were repeated to you by Mr. Ulloa (as reported in your No. 95, under date of September 7, 1874), and in your No. 153, dated November 23, it appears that similar statements were again made.

Nevertheless, with all these cases long since brought to the attention of the Spanish Government, with the case of Mrs. Farres de Mora before the minister of state, in connection with that of Mr. Criado, Mr. Ulloa took occasion to reply in the case of Mr. Criado alone, as reported in your No. 195, to the effect that he was not a bona fide citizen of the United States, and thus to avoid the decision of the issue before him.

So far as this case was concerned, Mr. Criado was but one individual jointly interested with others in the decision of a principle, and because some flaw was supposed to have been found as to his right to claim the benefit of the general principle when decided, opportunity was taken to decline to make any decision on the principle itself. It is ascertained, however, not only that the claim that Mr. Criado is not a citizen is not well founded, but a trial of his claim before the mixed commission is progressing, and this question has not there been raised; but the advocate on the part of Spain is understood to have declared himself satisfied as to Mr. Criado's citizenship. The Spanish Government thus avoiding the issue, you again argued the question in the cases of Mrs. Farres de Mora and Mr. Delgado, as reported in your No. 322.

Subsequent to this date, in several dispatches, viz, in your Nos. 387 442, 452, and 511 (the last being dated September 8 ultimo), and in several telegrams, you have reported the progress of a scheme of settlement, which it was thought was about to be accomplished, when a change in the cabinet suddenly displaced Mr. Castro.

Whether, had Mr. Castro remained in office, a general order or decree would have been issued of the character referred to in your No. 511, it is of course impossible to say, and whether, if issued, it would have received a more respectful obedience than the prior orders on this question, must also remain unanswered.

However, you state that the question has been reopened, and as you inform me with some prospect of an adjustment. But no adjustment has yet been reached, and the general question has been pending for more than six years.

The kindred treaty question in reference to the trial of citizens of the United States in Cuba by court-martial and the arrest and punishment of our citizens without trial in that island in violation of the provisions of the treaty of 1795 is substantially in the same position. This Government, prior to your appointment, had unfortunately been compelled to interfere in behalf of its citizens on several occasions where the authorities in Cuba had entirely disregarded not only provisions of our treaty, but the rules of civilized warfare.

After your arrival at your post, you addressed the Government in reference thereto on various occasions, both in connection with the confiscation and embargo cases and separately.

The authorities of Spain have been loud in their denunciations of acts of cruelty when perpetrated by the Carlists, and while in some quarters martial law has been looked upon as the natural refuge of the mother country or her colonial authorities, when deemed necessary and convenient, still the same difficulty has occurred in inducing any minister of state to fairly meet the question, and either commit himself to a justification of such practices or to frankly admit that they were in violation of treaty obligations and public law and to provide a remedy.

It is true that in isolated cases, where the Spanish Government has been shown that insistance on trial by courts-martial implied a state of war in Cuba, which might lead to logical consequences, the authorities have admitted the justice of our position, as in the orders sent to the Captain-General in 1873, proposing the trial of the sailors of the bark *Union* by the ordinary tribunals, pursuant to the treaty of 1795, as referred to in my No. 246; but, in general, when these questions have been presented, the different ministers of state have contented themselves with expressing their intention to fairly respond, and the intention of Spain to perform all her treaty obligations. Notably among them you state, in your No. 195, that after having addressed Mr. Ulloa upon this question in Dockray's case he promised to meet the issue.

That promise remains unperformed, and although the late negotiations by which it was hoped some solution of these questions might be reached would have applied also to this question the matter remains undisposed of, and the authorities of Cuba are enabled upon convenient occasion, in obedience to supposed necessity, to again resort to such military tribunals or to punish without a trial.

This simple narration of facts as to these two questions, the promises made and repeated, the assurances given from time to time that something should be done, the admission of the justice of the demands of this country, at least to the extent of expressing regret for these wrongs and promising redress, followed as they have been by absolutely no performance and no practical steps whatever toward performance, need no extended comment.

In the cases of embargo and confiscation, not only have wrongs been long since done, but continuing and repeated wrongs are daily inflicted. The authorities of Spain in Cuba, during all this time, have been and are using the revenues of the confiscated or embargoed estates, appropriating much of the property itself, and in some cases executing long leases, or actually making sales, either on the allegation that taxes were due or without any excuse whatever.

In the cases of arrest and punishment, citizens of the United States, in like manner, have undergone punishment because the authorities of Spain do not meet the issue and decide the question.

Turning to the questions which arose from the capture of the *Virginius*, and the executions which followed, no extended reference is required.

The particulars of the delivery of the vessel to this Government, and the payment to both Great Britain and the United States of considerable sums as compensation for the acts of the authorities in ordering the execution of 53 of the passengers and crew under circumstances of peculiar brutality, have passed into history.

So far as a payment of money can atone for the execution of these unprotected prisoners, that has been accomplished.

The higher and more imperative duty which the Government of Spain assumed by the protocol of November 29, 1873, namely, to bring to justice General Burriel and the other principal offenders in this tragedy, has been evaded and entirely neglected.

Having made this neglect the subject of a separate instruction, under this date, I abstain from further reference thereto.

While I have no desire to detract from the settlement which was obtained, or to depreciate the action of Mr. Castro, the minister of state, in the payment of the indemnity, particularly as he seemed from the first presentation of the question to be impressed with the justice of the complaint, and to regard with natural aversion the acts which gave rise to it, it is but just, in considering the general course of the authorities in Spain toward this country, to refer to the long delay in reaching an adjustment, and principally to the fact that a basis of settlement was at last reached only after every delay had apparently been exhausted.

As you are aware, Mr. Ulloa, then minister of state, under date of August 18, 1874, and probably impelled by some pressing necessity, addressed the British chargé d'affaires at Madrid, substantially agreeing to settle the claim of Great Britain for the execution of the British subjects on board that vessel.

The equally strong, if not stronger, claim of the United States continued to be discussed in Madrid after the promise of settlement with Great Britain had been made, and information of this adjustment reached this Government a considerable time after its conclusion, and not through the authorities of Spain. Our settlement was only accomplished in the month of March following.

In doing exact justice it is but proper, however, to give Mr. Castro due credit for the payment of the amount finally agreed upon, without further controversy, and before the time stipulated for payment had expired.

In adverting to these delays and failures to meet our just demands on the part of the authorities, I must express satisfaction with your patience and energy under these adverse circumstances, and particularly in beginning anew with each rapidly succeeding minister of state, and representing again and again these different questions. Progress in these matters has not been delayed from want of information from you, nor from lack of faithful and forcible presentation.

Having touched on these particular questions, which have lately been prominent as disturbing causes with Spain, it is necessary to also refer to the general condition of affairs in Cuba as affecting our relations with the mother country.

In my No. 2, of February 6, 1874 (the first instruction addressed to you on general matters pertaining to your mission), I referred at length to the views entertained by the President and to the position of this Government.

It was then more than five years since an organized insurrection had broken out which the Government of Spain had been entirely unable to suppress. At that time the firm conviction of the President was announced that whatever might be the vicissitudes of the struggle, and whatever efforts might be put forth by the Spanish power in Cuba, no doubt could be entertained that the final issue of the conflict would be to break the bonds which attached Cuba as a colony to Spain.

While remembering and observing the duties which this Government, as one of the family of nations, owes to another member, by public law, treaties, or the particular statutes of the United States, it would be idle to attempt to conceal the interest and sympathy with which Americans in the United States regard any attempt of a numerous people on this continent to be relieved of ties which hold them in the position of colonial subjection to a distant power, and to assume the independence and right of self-control which natural rights and the spirit of the age accord to them.

When, moreover, this struggle, in progress on our very borders, from its commencement has involved the property and interests of citizens of the United States, has disturbed our tranquillity and commerce, has called upon us not infrequently to witness barbarous violations of the rules of civilized warfare, and compelled us for the sake of humanity to raise our voice by way of protest; and when, more than all, we see in the contest the final struggle in this hemisphere between slavery and freedom, it would be strange indeed if the Government and people of this country failed at any time to take peculiar interest in the termination of such contest.

In this early instruction was expressed the sincere and unselfish hope of the President that the Government of Spain would seek some honorable and satisfactory adjustment, based upon emancipation and self-government, which would restore peace and afford a prospect of a return of prosperity to Cuba.

Almost two years have passed since those instructions were issued and those strong hopes expressed, and it would appear that the situation has in no respect improved.

The horrors of war have in no perceptible measure abated; the inconveniences and injuries which we then suffered have remained, and others have been added; the ravages of war have touched new parts of the island, and well nigh ruined its financial and agricultural system and its relations to the commerce of the world. No effective steps have been taken to establish reforms or remedy abuses, and the effort to suppress the insurrection by force alone has been a complete failure.

In the meantime the material interests of trade and of commerce are impaired to a degree which calls for remonstrance, if not for another line of conduct, on the part of all commercial nations.

Whether it be from the severity and inhumanity with which the effort has been made to suppress the insurrection, and from a supposed justification of retaliation for violations of the rules of civilized warfare by other violations and by acts of barbarism, of incendiarism, and outrage, the world is witnessing on the part of the insurgents, whom Spain still claims as subjects, and for whose acts, if subjects, Spain must be held accountable in the judgment of the world, a warfare, not of the legitimate strife of relative force and strength, but of pillage and incendiarism, the burning of estates and of sugar mills, the destruction of the means of production and of the wealth of the island.

The United States purchases more largely than any other people of the productions of the Island of Cuba, and therefore, more than any other for this reason, and still more by reason of its immediate neighborhood, is interested in the arrest of a system of wanton destruction which disgraces the age and affects every commercial people on the face of the globe

Under these circumstances, and in view of the fact that Spain has rejected all suggestions of reform or offers of mediation made by this Government, and has refused all measures looking to a reconciliation, except on terms which make reconciliation an impossibility, the difficulty of the situation becomes increased.

When, however in addition to these general causes of difficulty, we find the Spanish Government neglectful also of the obligations of treaties and solemn compacts and unwilling to afford any redress for long-continued and well-founded wrongs suffered by our citizens, it becomes a serious question how long such a condition of things can or should be allowed to exist, and compels us to inquire whether the point has not been reached where longer endurance ceases to be possible.

During all this time, and under these aggravated circumstances, this Government has not failed to perform her obligations to Spain as scrupulously as toward other nations.

In fact, it might be said that we have not only been long suffering, because of the embarrassments surrounding the Spanish Government, but particularly careful to give no occasion for complaint for the same reason.

I regret to say that the authorities of Spain have not at all times appreciated our intentions or our purposes in these respects, and, while insisting that a state of war does not exist in Cuba and that no rights as belligerents should be accorded to the insurrectionists, have at the same time demanded for themselves all the rights and privileges which flow from actual and acknowledged war.

It will be apparent that such a state of things can not continue. It is absolutely necessary to the maintenance of our relations with Spain, even on their present footing, that our just demands for the return to citizens of the United States of their estates in Cuba, unincumbered, and for securing to them a trial for offenses according to treaty provisions and all other rights guaranteed by treaty and by public law should be complied with.

Whether the Spanish Government, appreciating the forbearance of this country, will speedily and satisfactorily adjust the pending questions, not by the issue of empty orders or decrees without force or effect in Cuba, but by comprehensive and firm measures which shall everywhere be respected, I anxiously await further intelligence.

Moreover, apart from these particular questions, in the opinion of the

President the time has arrived when the interests of this country, the preservation of its commerce, and the instincts of humanity alike demand that some speedy and satisfactory ending be made of the strife that is devastating Cuba.

A disastrous conflict of more than seven years' duration has demonstrated the inability of Spain to maintain peace and order in an island lying at our door. Desolation and destruction of life and property have been the only results of this conflict.

The United States sympathizes in the fact that this inability results in a large degree from the unhappy condition of Spain at home and to some extent from the distractions which are dividing her people. But the fact remains. Added to this are the large expanse of ocean separating the peninsula from the island and the want of harmony and of personal sympathy between the inhabitants of the territory of the home government and those of the colony, the distinction of classes in the latter between rulers and subjects, the want of adaptation of the ancient colonial system of Spain to the present times and to the ideas which the events of the past age have impressed upon the peoples of every reading and thinking country.

Great Britain, wisely, has relaxed the old system of colonial dependence, and is reaping the benefits in the contentedness and peaceful prosecution of the arts of peace and in the channels of commerce and of industry, in colonies which under restraint might have questioned and resisted the power of control from a distant government and might have exhibited, as does Cuba, a chronic condition of insurrection, turbulence, and rebellion.

In addition to all this, it can not be questioned that the continued maintenance, in the face of decrees and enactments to the contrary, of a compulsory system of slave labor is a cause of disquiet and of excitement to a large class in the island, as also in the United States, which the Government of Spain has led us, by very distinct assurances, to expect should be removed, and which the enlightened Christianity of the age condemns.

The contest and disorder in Cuba affect the United States directly and injuriously by the presence in this country of partisans of the revolt who have fled hither (in consequence of the proximity of territory) as to a political asylum, and who, by their plottings, are disturbers of the public peace.

The United States has exerted itself to the utmost, for seven years, to repress unlawful acts on the part of these self-exiled subjects of Spain, relying on the promise of Spain to pacify the island. Seven years of strain on the powers of this Government to fulfill all that the most exacting demands of one Government can make, under any doctrine or claim of international obligation, upon another, have not witnessed the much hoped for pacification. The United States feels itself entitled to be relieved of this strain.

The severe measures, injurious to the United States and often in conflict with public law, which the colonial officers have taken to subdue the insurrection; the indifference, and ofttimes the offensive assaults upon the just susceptibilities of the people of the United States and their Government, which have characterized that portion of the peninsular population of Havana which has sustained and upheld, if it has not controlled, successive governors-general, and which have led to the disregard of orders and decrees which the more enlarged wisdom and the more friendly councils of the home Government had enacted; the cruelty and inhumanity which have characterized the contest, both on the part of the colonial government and of the revolt, for seven years, and the destruction of valuable properties and industries by arson and pillage, which Spain appears unable, however desirous, to prevent and stop, in an island 3,000 miles distant from her shores, but lying within sight of our coast, with which trade and constant intercourse are unavoidable, are causes of annoyance and of injury to the United States, which a people can not be expected to tolerate without the assured prospect of their termination.

The United States has more than once been solicited by the insurgents to extend to them its aid, but has for years hitherto resisted such solicitation, and has endeavored by the tender of its good offices, in the way of mediation, advice, and remonstrance, to bring to an end a great evil, which has pressed sorely upon the interests both of the Government and of the people of the United States, as also upon the commercial interests of other nations.

A sincere friendship for Spain, and for her people, whether peninsular or insular, and an equally sincere reluctance to adopt any measures which might injure or humble the ancient ally of the United States, has characterized the conduct of this Government in every step during these sad and distressing years, and the President is still animated by the same feelings, and desires above all things to aid her and her people to enter once more upon the path of safety and repose.

It will be remembered that the President, in the year 1869, tendered the good offices of the United States for the purpose of bringing to a close the civil war in Cuba. This offer was made delicately, in good faith, and in friendship to both parties to the contest.

General Prim, as the representative of the Spanish Government, while recognizing the good faith and friendship with which this offer was made, replied:

We can better proceed in the present situation of things without even this friendly intervention. A time will come when the good offices of the United States will be not only useful but indispensable in the final arrangements between Spain and Cuba. We will ascertain the form in which they can be employed and confidently count upon your assistance.

The United States replied that its good offices for that object would be at any time at the service of the parties to the conflict. This Government has ever since been ready thus to aid in restoring peace and quiet.

The Government of the United States has heretofore given expression to no policy in reference to the insurrection in Cuba, because it has honestly and sincerely hoped that no declaration of policy on its part would be required.

The President feels that longer reticence would be inconsistent with the interests of both Governments.

Our relations with Spain are in that critical position that another seizure similar to that of the *Virginius*, other executions of citizens of the United States in Cuba, other wrongs of a less objectionable character even than many which have been already suffered by our citizens with simple remonstrance, or possibly even some new act of exceptional severity in Cuba, may suddenly produce a feeling and excitement which might force events which this Government anxiously desires to avoid.

The President hopes that Spain may spontaneously adopt measures looking to a reconciliation and to the speedy restoration of peace and the organization of a stable and satisfactory system of government in the Island of Cuba.

In the absence of any prospect of a termination of the war, or of any change in the manner in which it has been conducted on either side, he feels that the time is at hand when it may be the duty of other Governments to intervene, solely with a view of bringing to an end a disastrous and destructive conflict, and of restoring peace in the island of Cuba. No Government is more deeply interested in the order and peaceful administration of this island than is that of the United States, and none has suffered as has the United States from the condition which has obtained there during the past six or seven years. He will, therefore, feel it his duty at an early day to submit the subject in this light, and accompanied by an expression of the views above presented, for the consideration of Congress.

This conclusion is reached with reluctance and regret.

It is reached after every other expedient has been attempted and proved a failure, and in the firm conviction that the period has at last arrived when no other course remains for this Government.

It is believed to be a just and friendly act to frankly communicate this conclusion to the Spanish Government.

You will therefore take an early occasion thus to inform that Government.

In making the communication, it is the earnest desire of the President to impress upon the authorities of Spain the continued friendly disposition of this Government, and that it has no ulterior or selfish objects in view and no desire to become a party in the conflict, but is moved solely by the imperative necessities of a proper regard to its own protection and its own interests and the interests of humanity, and, as we firmly believe, in the ultimate interest of Spain itself.

In informing the Spanish Government of these conclusions pursuant hereto, you are authorized to read this instruction to the minister of state, or to state the substance and purport thereof, as you may deem most advisable.

You will, of course, keep me advised, by telegraph and by post, of your proceedings pursuant to this instruction.

I am, etc.,

HAMILTON FISH.

————

Mr. Fish to Mr. Cushing.

No. 267.]

DEPARTMENT OF STATE,
Washington, November 5, 1875.

SIR: Herewith you will receive instruction No. 266, being a general review of our relations with Spain, and the announcement of certain conclusions of the President which you are therein instructed to communicate to the Government of Spain.

It has been deemed proper to send confidentially a copy of instruction No. 266 to General Schenck, the minister of the United States at London, with instructions to read the same to Lord Derby, and to suggest to the British Government that it would be agreeable to the United States, and in our opinion tend to the adjustment of the question of the pacification of Cuba, if not to the preservation of general peace, if the British Government would support by its influence the position assumed by this Government.

A copy of this instruction to General Schenck is herewith inclosed.

He has been instructed, as you will perceive, to notify the Department by telegraph of the result of this communication to Lord Derby.

Should it appear probable that the British Government will enforce the position of this Government, it may be wise to defer your interview with the minister of state until joint action can be agreed upon.

Should that Government hesitate or decline, you will be at once instructed to proceed to carry out the instructions contained in No. 266. In case the Government of Great Britain shall determine to support our position by its influence, proper instructions will doubtless be sent to its representative in Madrid to that effect.

As no great delay will be occasioned thereby, it is deemed better to postpone your action in communicating these conclusions until General Schenck shall have communicated the views of the British Government, by telegraph, to the Department, and telegraphic instructions can be sent you based thereon.

A copy of instruction No. 266 will also shortly be sent to all our diplomatic representatives, in confidence, for their information, and the ministers to the principal European courts will be instructed to communicate its purport to the Governments to which they are respectively accredited.

I am, sir, etc., HAMILTON FISH.

Mr. Cushing to Mr. Fish.

[Telegram.]

MADRID, *November 25, 1875.*

Your Nos. 266 and 267 have been just received, but not 265.

You call for my opinion; I give it according to my best lights. If Great Britain cooperates, Spain will succumb, in sullen despair, to whatever terms the two Governments may jointly dictate; but if Great Britain refuses to cooperate, Spain will conclude that she has the sympathy of all European powers; more especially, as she thinks she has now gone, by her note of the 15th, to the ultimate point in satisfaction of each of the particular griefs of the United States.

In other words, there will be war, and a popular though desperate one on the part of Spain, unless she can be convinced that the real and true object of the contemplated measure is to prevent war, as I understand it to be intended. But to ward off war will exact the steady exercise of all my personal influence here (which my colleagues tell me is great), and will require that influence to be efficiently backed by my Government both here and at Washington.

I am here to "obey orders though it break owners," as the shipmasters say.

I earnestly beg you, therefore, in proportion as you desire peace, to address me specific and explicit replies in regard to certain most needful instructions which I shall ask for by telegram, provided a negative answer comes from Great Britain.

CUSHING.

Mr. Cushing to Mr. Fish.

No. 684.] LEGATION OF THE UNITED STATES,
Madrid, November 25, 1875.

SIR: I have received your dispatches Nos. 266 and 267. No. 265 has not yet come to hand.

My telegram of this date, as called for by you, communicates my impression of the probable effects of the contemplated measure.

Although what is most important in the question will reach you by that telegram long before the arrival of this dispatch, yet it may not be amiss to add here explanations on some less important, but closely related, points.

(1) *The military situation.*—Many of the most thoughtful men in Spain really long for a foreign war as the only efficient remedy for the domestic dissensions which now distract the country.

Moreover, the statesmen of the country foresee that on the close of the war in the North, which can not fail to come in the course of the winter or early in the spring, there will be an army of two or three hundred thousand men to dispose of, with its officers, who will be but too much disposed to dominate in public affairs and push the civilians into the background.

In addition to which, there is a multitude of unthoughtful men, proud, angry, resentful, who would gladly rush into a war with the United States.

Finally, there are the mercenary, the ambitious, the déclassés and the bad, to whom war presents the usual attractions. Multis utile bellum, says Sallust.

It is the received opinion in Spain that for the commencing period of a war she has a more efficient navy than ours.

In these circumstances, if Great Britain declines to cooperate with us, Spain will, at the least, despatch to Cuba at once a large fleet, laden with troops, there to await the eventualities of diplomacy; and she may break off relations, with a hostile appeal to the European Powers.

(2) *The diplomatic question.*—I profess that the contents of your No. 266, from page 40 and the words "In my No. 2" to the end, strike me as a most powerful and effective presentation of the general considerations inducing the proposed announcement of intervention.

I must frankly say, however (and the emergency demands frankness), that the previous contents of the dispatch, from page 1 to page 20, inclusive, do not strike me with equal force of themselves, either as to effect on the Spanish mind or on that of Europe, more especially as appearing here (although not written) after the delivery of the Spanish note of the 15th instant.[1] I almost wish it were less specific.

I should have made a practical suggestion in this respect by telegram but for the supposition that the contents will have been already communicated to Great Britain and other Governments of Europe.

I have no wish to exaggerate the results lately attained by me here. I can not but think, however, that the contents of the late Spanish note, if faithfully carried out in detail, as they certainly would be, go far toward satisfying the particular reclamations of the United States.

If, however, the terms of that note, coming in after your dispatch was written, tend to weaken the force of your argument, still it may, nevertheless, be serviceable to aid you in moderating the temper of Congress.

I have, etc.,

C. CUSHING.

---

[1] The Spanish note to Mr. Cushing contained proposals for adjustment of existing differences between the United States and Spain. Its substance was telegraphed to Mr. Fish by Mr. Cushing November 16, 1875. It has no reference to mediation or intervention by the United States in the affairs of Cuba.

Mr. Cushing to Mr. Fish.

[Telegram]

MADRID, *November 26, 1875.*

The response of England lingers. Time passes. I begin with questions for either alternative: First. I can not read your dispatch to the minister; he does not understand English. To state its substance to him orally would be doing extreme injustice to the dispatch.

In just such a case Mr. Canning refused to hear anything without a copy of the document. (Lawrence's Wheaton, seventh edition, p. 388.)

Why not give a copy to the Spanish minister?

Second. Will you authorize me, after the Spanish minister is informed, in whatever way, of the contents of the document, to talk to him as a friend and wellwisher regarding what, in my opinion, Spain ought to do and may honorably do in this emergency?

CUSHING.

Mr. Cushing to Mr. Fish.

No. 686.] LEGATION OF THE UNITED STATES,
Madrid, November 26, 1875.

SIR: My dispatches of yesterday were prepared for the French courier; but as he does not depart until to-day, opportunity is afforded me of adding a supplement to my No. 684.

The finances of Spain are in a very bad condition, simply for want of credit in the stock markets of Europe.

Nevertheless, she is enabled to carry a large floating debt by loans on short time, say six months or a year, and to renew the bonds as they fall due by merely adding the interest to the mass of such floating debt.

But she has considerable resources in reserve for times and occasions of desperation

First. The Bank of Spain possesses a large metallic fund which the Government could and would seize upon in such emergency, in imitation of what Great Britain did in the wars of the French Revolution.

Second. There is really much wealth in the country, and it would be drawn forth in a war with the United States. Patriotic gifts would come in, forced loans would be submitted to, and the domestic capitalists would more freely advance to the Government.

Third. Spain might recur to forms of credit, which all other nations resort to in the last necessity, as we ourselves did in the legal-tender act. The process would begin with indefinite issue of bills of the Bank of Spain in the whole country, instead of, as now, in the province of Madrid alone; and it would extend to the issue of treasury notes or certificates. To be sure, such action would speedily raise the price of gold, but not to a higher point than it reached with us in similar circumstances.

Meanwhile the augmented circulation would serve, as it did with us, to prompt new enterprises, and thus add to the actual productive resources of the country, not only in industries dependent on war, but in mines and in undeveloped agriculture, to the ultimate advantages of Spain.

The Spaniards are a people preeminently sober in food and drink, economical, and enduring under privations and hardships—as you may infer from the wages of labor, which vary according to the quality from 2 to 3 or 4 pesetas a day, where, in the United States, similar labor would be reckoned at the same number of dollars. Hence, armies are contentedly supported here, and always have been, so cheaply as to constitute a real addition to the relative military resources of Spain. The contrast in this respect between Spanish and English soldiers struck the Duke of Wellington.

I note these facts as being material and important in the present question. That is, we must not confide in a deficiency of financial resources standing in the way if Spain be hard pushed and stirred up to make sacrifices in case of a war with the United States.

And the finances of Spain are not in a much worse condition than they were in the time of Charles V and his successors of the Austrian dynasty. Great loans were rarer then than now. Spain relied much on wealthy Jews for anticipations, although Jews and Gentiles, in the matter of money lending, incurred hazards quite in proportion to the profits, as illustrated in the hardships of the Jews in Spain and the case of Jacques Coeur in France. In truth, the Fuggers of Augsburg are among the few houses of that class which remain to this day. Hence the terrible financial straits which the Philips—II, III, and IV—were constantly suffering in Spain. Nevertheless, they sustained great wars all over the world.

I add that, according to telegrams received from Habana, the mission of Mr. Rubi has already produced important results, so that he is able to make assurance of having equalized the revenue and the expenditures and of undertaking to pay regularly all current obligations after the 1st of January.

I have, etc.,   C. CUSHING.

Mr. Fish to Mr. Cushing.

[Telegram]

WASHINGTON, *November 27, 1875.*

CUSHING, *Minister, Madrid:*

Schenck was instructed to delay presentation of 266, in consequence of your telegram of 16th.

The President's message will discountenance recognition of either belligerency or independence; will refer to the injuries to the United States and its citizens from the long-continued struggle and the absence of prospect of termination; will intimate intervention as an ultimate necessity unless satisfactory results be soon reached, but will abstain from advising it at present; will refer to pending proposals not yet received here, with hope that they may afford the relief required and lead to a satisfactory settlement and removal of causes of grief; will intimate that a communication will soon be made to Congress as to the result of the proposals now on their way, and that, if it do not satisfactorily adjust all important questions, he will before long make a recommendation to Congress of the course to be pursued.

The above is for your guidance in your interview with minister; be careful that it be not communicated by minister or otherwise to the press or public in anticipation of what will be done here.

The instruction 266 is not intended as minatory in any sense but in

------

[1] Reprinted from House Ex. Doc. No. 90, Forty-fourth Congress, first session, but omissions supplied.

the spirit of friendship, as a notice of a necessity which may be forced upon the President, but which he hopes to avoid, and desires Spain to aid him in escaping. We are sincerely desirous to preserve peace and to establish all relations with Spain on the most amicable and liberal basis, but we must be relieved and be secure as to the future, and you may give positive assurances to this effect.

You may give copy of 266 to minister, and may speak in the sense indicated in your telegram of yesterday, provided it be not to do away the object of the instruction.

You will make the communication and present copy instruction without waiting for presentation in London.

Schenck will to-day be instructed to read paper as soon as he can.

FISH, *Secretary.*

Mr. Cushing to Mr. Fish.

[Telegram.]

MADRID, *November 30, 1875.*

Dispatch of 5th just delivered to minister of state with verbal explanations as near as foreign idiom would permit in the exact sense of telegram of 27th. Further conference on the subject deferred until after the minister shall have had the dispatch translated, and shall have duly considered its contents. Interview in good spirit.

CUSHING.

Mr. Cushing to Mr. Fish.

No. 692.] LEGATION OF THE UNITED STATES,
Madrid, November 30, 1875.

SIR: I received your telegram of the 27th on the afternoon of Sunday, the 28th, and became informed of its contents just in season to be able to avail myself of the opportunity of meeting the minister of state at the King's dinner in the evening, as recounted in another dispatch, to arrange for an interview with him the ensuing Tuesday.

I repaired to the ministry of state, therefore, to-day, in pursuance of that appointment, for the purpose of communicating to him the contents of your telegram and delivering a copy of your dispatch of the 5th.

Not being willing to trust myself to extemporaneous representation in a foreign language in a matter of so much gravity, I prepared a written statement in Spanish of what I had to say, in form to be read to the minister.

I explained this to Mr. Calderon y Collantes immediately on entering, and without further preface proceeded to read to him the paper, of which copy and translation are annexed.

After listening attentively to the contents of the paper as read, he requested me to leave it with him; to which I saw no objection, as it would thus assume almost the character of a protocol.

I then offered to read to him the dispatch of the 5th, or, if he preferred, to deliver to him a copy. He of course chose the latter alternative.

I then repeated the request already made, that before taking any definite action on the subject he would favor me with another interview. He assented, with the remark that Spain was in no hurry to go to war with the United States; to which I added, that neither were the United States in a hurry to go to war with Spain.

A little to my surprise, he took the whole matter very coolly, notwithstanding that possible "intervention" was expressly mentioned in my oral statement, and said nothing as to the matter of that, except to express satisfaction at learning that the President proposed to discountenance the concession of recognition of independence or even of belligerence to the insurgents of Cuba.

We then conversed a few minutes on indifferent matters not material to the present subject, except in one particular. He said he had heard we were building a fleet of ironclads. I replied that it might be so, but that no such thing was within my knowledge; that, for myself, I had not a very high opinion of the impenetrability or the manageableness of the huge ironclads which had been built in England, France, and Spain.

This remark of mine led us into reflections on the misadventures of the British *Captain*, *Agincourt*, *Vanguard*, and *Iron Duke*, and the comparative value of them and of the Russian *Popoffkas*, with which the interview ended.

    I have, etc.,
                                       C. CUSHING.

———

[Appendix B in No. 692.—Translation of remarks of Mr. Cushing to Mr. Calderon y Collantes, read in the interview of November 30, 1875.]

My Government orders me to give to your excellency frank and detailed explanations with respect to the actual state of the questions pending between the two Governments.

On receiving your note of the 15th of the current month, I sent it to London by a special messenger, in order to insure its prompt transmission to Washington. It ought to arrive in the first days of December; that is to say, a little before the meeting of Congress.

I addressed at the same time an extended telegram to my Government, giving it a résumé of the contents of the note in a favorable sense, and subsequently other telegrams in the same sense.

The effect of the telegrams has been advantageous to the good understanding of the two Governments.

Prior to the delivery of the Spanish note of the 15th and to the reception of my telegrams, my Government had addressed to me a dispatch, dated the 5th of the current month, in which are fully recited the subsisting causes of disagreement, all having relation to the condition of Cuba; and in the case of failure to make an amicable settlement of those disagreements, there would suggest itself the only remedy which, in the opinion of the President, remains for the United States, and which he proposed to present to Congress in his message.

But now, in the hope that the contents of the Spanish note may be satisfactory, the President desists from the concrete purpose expressed in the dispatch of the 5th and substitutes a proposition which is merely expectant.

Meanwhile, I am charged in the first place to explain to you confidentially what will be the actual text of the message.

The President will discountenance the concession of the recognition of either independence or belligerence to the insurgents of Cuba; he will allude to the injuries inflicted upon the United States and on their citizens by the prolonged struggle in Cuba, and the absence as yet of clear indications of its termination; he will intimate, as an ulterior necessity, intervention, unless positive results be soon reached, but he will abstain from advising it at present; he will make reference to proposals awaited, but not yet received, in the prospect that those propositions may lead to a satisfactory settlement of all questions of importance; if not, he will submit in due time a recommendation for the consideration of Congress.

I am charged to express to you the hope that these explanations will be received by the Government of His Majesty in the friendly spirit which animates my Government in giving them, and to beg you to consider this unusual and friendly step of an anticipated communication of the contents of the President's message as absolutely confidential, in order to guard against premature discussions in the press, whether of Europe or of America.

Moreover, I am instructed to deliver to you a copy of the said dispatch of the 5th instant, written before the delivery to me of the Spanish note, and, as is to be supposed, without knowledge of the intentions of the Government of His Majesty.

This dispatch is not conceived in any minatory sense, but on the contrary, in the spirit of friendship, as a notice of a pressing necessity, which may force the hand of the President in given circumstances, from which he desires to save himself, and desires Spain to aid him in escaping them. He sincerely desires to maintain peace and to establish the relations of the United States with Spain upon the most friendly and most liberal bases, provided they contain satisfaction for the present and security for the future; and I am authorized, to this end, to offer the most positive assurances to the Government of His Majesty.

It remains for me to place in your hands the copy of the dispatch of the 5th. It is somewhat long and merits to be read attentively, as well by reason of its contingent importance as for its tone of moderation and of consideration and good will toward Spain.

In conclusion, I beg you, after having read the dispatch and made yourself acquainted with its contents, and before taking any definite resolution in the matter, to do me the favor to grant me another private interview, in order that I may present to you some pertinent observations on my part and on the part of my Government.

Mr. Cushing to Mr. Fish.

No. 698.]   LEGATION OF THE UNITED STATES,
Madrid, December 3, 1875.

SIR: Mr. Layard called on me yesterday to say that he had just received instructions by telegraph from Lord Derby to confer with me on the subject of Cuba.

He proceeded to say that General Schenck had read to Lord Derby your No. 266, and that the matter was under consideration in the British cabinet.

He also spoke of his knowledge of conferences between you and Sir Edward Thornton in this respect, without stating whether that knowledge came to him directly from Sir Edward or indirectly through Lord Derby.

Mr. Layard expressed readiness to back me in the matter of Cuba so soon as our respective Governments should have settled on a line of action, and instructed us to that effect.

He expresses great discontent at the failure of Spain to pay attention to the various claims, thirteen in number, presented by him in behalf of his Government, and says that his situation will be untenable here without some improvement in the conduct of the business of the ministry of state.

He thinks Great Britain has abundant cause of her own to interfere in the affairs of Cuba under her slave-trade treaties with Spain.

Further conference between us was deferred until hearing again from Lord Derby.

I received from General Schenck on the 1st instant a telegram dated the 30th ultimo, in the following words:

CUSHING, *Minister, Madrid:*

Have communicated to Lord Derby your instruction 266. He will give me views of this Government on Thursday.

SCHENCK, *Minister.*

I assume that the telegram thus addressed to you within, and on cover to me, is a duplicate transmitted to me in this form in order to save time and labor of preparing a separate and particular telegram for the legation.

I await information as to the decision to have been taken by Lord Derby yesterday, as stated by General Schenck.

I have, etc.,   C. CUSHING.

Mr. Cushing to Mr. Fish.

No. 699.]   LEGATION OF THE UNITED STATES,
Madrid, December 3, 1875.

SIR: I annex hereto translated extract of an article of last night in the Epoca, which constitutes the preface of that journal to a translation it inserts of a long article of antifilibuster spirit from the New York Herald.

The definite references of the Epoca to my interview with Mr. Calderon y Collantes on the 30th, and to the telegrams received from Mr. Mantilla, sufficiently show that the Epoca received its information from some member of the Government.

I have never mentioned the contents, date, or even existence of your No. 266 to anybody except Mr. Calderon y Collantes, not even to Mr. Layard, until he came to speak to me concerning it, on the 1st instant, by telegraphic direction from Lord Derby, as reported in another dispatch.

Of course all which the Epoca says of the contents of that note must have been derived from the Government.

Four things are, it seems to me, worth noting in that article:

First. In speaking of your No. 266, it undertakes to characterize the first part, devoted to the exposition of particular grievances, but makes no allusion to the second part.

Secondly. It gives quite a novel turn to the question of intervention and the relations of Great Britain to that subject, supposing it to be on the part of some "great continental Power" between the United States and Spain. I have no knowledge, nor any ground of conjecture even, as to what Power is thus intended. Is it Germany? Or France? Or Russia?

Thirdly. The Epoca seems to put forward the article of the Herald by way of insinuating the opposition of Great Britain to any positive action of ours on the side of Cuba.

Fourthly. It is observable that the Epoca, thus inspired by the Government, does not speak excitedly, or otherwise betray signs of irritation on the part of the Government on occasion of the suggestion of our possible intervention, ex nomine, as intimated in your No. 266, and also expressly in the oral statement made by me to Mr. Calderon y Collantes.

I have, etc.,   C. CUSHING.

[Inclosure in No 699 —Appendix A, No. 699.—Translated extract of leading article in the Epoca of December 2, 1875]

We have not been mistaken in asserting time and again that, whatever might be the language of the American papers, and however offensive might appear to us the attitude of that Government, we had such confidence in our own right, in the justice of our cause, and in the equity of the Government of Washington, even though appearances represented it as inclined to political extremes, that we have not for an instant become alarmed in view of the bravado of a few journals, nor even because of the too-spirited notes which, according to the public voice, were being exchanged between the two Cabinets. Our hopes have not been fallacious, and we are sincerely glad of it, although this would not have prevented us from meeting with manly resolution any precipitate resolve of the North Americans, sure of not being alone in the contest, and that, however prostrated we may be deemed to be, we still have the means of inflicting serious injuries upon those who might go so far as to risk an armed struggle.

Our hopes have not been deceptive, we repeat, because at the very time that, according to public report, there was received in Madrid a most lengthy note of the date of the 5th of November, energetically recapitulating the grievances of which President Grant thought he had the right to complain, there were also received important official telegrams wherein, in view of the firm attitude and, at the same time, of the decorous explanations given by our Government, the attitude of the United States essentially changed, the terms of the message were modified, all motive of misunderstanding disappeared, and supposition even went so far as to hint that the Government of the White House would not be averse to admitting the mediation of a great continental Power (y hasta se avanzaba á suponer que el Gobierno de la Casa Blanca no estaría distante de admitir la mediacion de una gran potencia continental).

If these notices are not entirely official, they combine all the traits of likelihood, they circulate and are believed in diplomatic centers, and all the press echoes these and like indications.

The Correspondencia speaks of a friendly conference held by the ad interim minister of state, Mr. Calderon y Collantes, with the Honorable Mr. Caleb Cushing, and gives high praise to the rectitude, the elevated spirit of justice, and the loyalty and conciliatory judgment which the American representative has brought to bear on these questions.

In effect, without omitting in the slightest degree to execute the instructions of his Government; without for a moment neglecting the duties of his difficult position, we have seen the North American minister follow attentively the palpitations of public opinion, study to the bottom the aims and purposes of the Government, transmit faithfully to his own the result of his investigations, and when he became cognizant of the prudent and dignified terms of the note of state, he telegraphed again and again, giving extracts from that document, in order that his Government might not allow itself to be influenced by equivocal impressions.

These telegrams, joined to those which the active representative of Spain would receive and would cause to be known in North American councils; the language of the North American press, which had been modified in a notable manner, and the inconveniences of provoking a rupture which no solid reasons authorize and which would be ill in keeping with the great national solemnity prepared by the United States—all these circumstances combined have doubtless influenced the change of counsel which we logically expected by reason of the knowledge we possess of the springs of politics in the United States.

All this is good, and it is better to prevent adventures than to rush upon them without knowing what their result will be; but the North American men of affairs ought to accustom themselves, in their own interest, to follow a more constant policy, and not to produce continual inquietudes, the consequences of which touch, first of all, their own immense commerce. Let it be left to weak or ambitious governments to cajole and flatter certain passions of the baser sort, and let the United States tranquilly follow the evolutions to which they are invited by domestic difficulties, which it would not cost us much labor to reveal and which demand an efficient remedy.

But we have said that the language of the press had become considerably modified, and it is incumbent upon us to show it. The task is easy, with the article in the New York Herald now before us, and with others which we postpone until to-morrow.

Mr. Cushing to Mr. Fish.

[Telegram.]

MADRID, *December 4, 1875.*

Brief important interview with minister of state. He takes office solely in the hope of settlement with us; has carefully read your 266; admits our grievances; is opposed in principle to sequestration of property of foreigners; condemns the delays of redress; will take up and promptly settle each case; will remove all cause of complaint as to treaty; reprobates conduct of local authorities in Cuba as more injurious to Spain than to the United States.

CUSHING.

Mr. Cushing to Mr. Fish.

No. 703.]   LEGATION OF THE UNITED STATES,
Madrid, December 5, 1875.

SIR: I availed myself of the occasion afforded by Mr. Calderon y Collantes having been appointed proprietary minister of state to call upon him yesterday to congratulate him, and at the same time to repeat

S. Doc. 231, pt 7——26

expressions of hope that the Spanish Government would regard your dispatch No. 266 in the light intended, not of a menace, but of a friendly notice of what might be the enforced consequences of the continuance of the present state of things in Cuba; and to say further that it was our common duty, as it seemed to me, to labor together to remove all causes of difference between the two Governments, to do which depended primarily on the attitude of the Spanish Government itself in the pres ence of subsisting complications.

Mr. Calderon y Collantes replied at once that he concurred with me in this view of the subject; that he should not have consented to leave the post of minister of grace and justice, which best suited him as a lawyer and a magistrate, and to take that of state, which was out of the line of his lifetime pursuits, save only in the hope of being able to cooperate with me in healing all differences, in order to do which he counted much on our long-standing personal friendship and mutual confidence; that he had carefully read and considered the contents of your No. 266, and must confess that the United States had good reason to complain, not only of unjustifiable acts on the part of the local authorities of Cuba, but of the delays and half measures of the Spanish Government to accord redress; that the local administration of Cuba, civil and military alike, had, in his conception, been greatly injurious to the interests of Spain herself, even more than to the United States; that, as a jurist, he repudiated on principle the sequestration of the property of foreigners in Cuba; that if the Spanish note of the 15th ultimo should prove acceptable to the President as a basis, he should be prepared to take up each individual grief as presented, and consider it with me in good faith as if we were associate judges on the bench, and decide it promptly; that while not able conscientiously to admit that by the letter of the treaty civil courts were stipulated for to the exclusion of military, yet he was ready so to arrange the ground of controversy in that relation as to put an end to all reasonable complaint in the premises on the part of the United States.

I could but declare the high gratification it afforded me to receive from his lips the communication of these just and elevated sentiments, which it would be my pleasure to transmit immediately to my Government.

You will have received already by telegram a summary report of the interview; which, however, does not relieve me of the duty of now reporting it in extenso.

I have, etc.,

C. CUSHING.

Mr. Fish to Mr. Cushing.[1]

[Telegram.]

WASHINGTON, *December 6, 1875.*

CUSHING, *Minister, Madrid:*

Your 658[2] received this day, on which Congress meets. Note is being carefully considered. Its tone is recognized as friendly; and such is that of message, which is ready for transmission. The note of 15th suggests no occasion for any alteration. It will be as indicated in my

---

[1] Reprinted from House Ex. Doc. No. 90, Forty-fourth Congress, first session, but omissions supplied.

[2] No. 658 is the dispatch inclosing Spanish note, already referred to, containing pro-posals for adjustment of pending differences between the United States and Spain.

telegram of 27th November—will condemn recognition of independence and belligerency in strong terms; will refer to mediation and intervention by other Powers as a contingent possibility if contest be protracted; will intimate readiness to mediate if desired; will in terms abstain from present recommendation of intervention. The text is too long to telegraph, but no just susceptibility should be excited by its purport, statements, or language, which are extremely friendly and conciliatory, but firm.

FISH, *Secretary.*

Mr. Cushing to Mr. Fish.

No. 705.]   LEGATION OF THE UNITED STATES,
Madrid, December 6, 1875.

SIR: I received on the afternoon of Saturday the 4th a telegram from General Schenck, purporting to be the duplicate of one sent to you on the 2d instant. It seems proper, however, that you should see a copy of it as deciphered here, and it will accordingly be transmitted, but as a separate dispatch.

Your dispatch No. 267 instructs me to communicate with Mr. Layard on the matter of its contents. I conferred with him fully last evening. He is prepared to cooperate with me now, if there should be any occasion, toward keeping the peace; but my interview with the minister of state on the 4th, as reported by telegram of that day, and more fully by my No. 703 of yesterday, satisfies me that all is going well on the side of the Spanish Government, and that there is no present occasion for the friendly interposition of Mr. Layard. He concurs in opinion of the inexpediency of taking any further step until the arrival of more definite instructions from Lord Derby and yourself.

Mr. Layard expresses opinion, founded partly on personal observation and partly on information received from the British consul-general in Havana, that the present is a very unfavorable moment for attempting intervention, friendly or other, between Spain and the insurgent Cubans. People in Spain are now animated and hopeful as to both civil wars, in view of the large reenforcements recently sent to Cuba, of the pacification of Valencia and Cataluna, and of the extensive military preparations for moving on the positions of the Vasco-Navarrese. Spain needs, he thinks, to be left to try the experiment of the operations of this winter They are not likely to succeed, at least not in Cuba; and if interfered with now, she will attribute the failure which is to come, not to her own weakness or the strength of the insurgents, but to the disturbing action of the United States. But, left to herself, and thus failing, she will then feel discouraged in proportion as she now feels exalted, and will be in the mood to listen to judicious counsels, whether coming from the United States or from Great Britain.

These remarks of Mr. Layard could not fail to impress me, and so much the more, in consonance as they were with the views expressed in my No. 636 of the 30th of October.

The impression which Lord Derby's observations to General Schenck make on my mind is that of a disposition on the part of the British Government to aid us in a mediatory form rather than as a cooperator in the exercise of forcible pressure on Spain.

Our advance to Great Britain in the present question insures good offices at least, and may go further.

And she might, if she would, powerfully contribute to the solution

. of the slavery question, not only as impelled by the same considerations of humanity which actuate the United States, but likewise in virtue of treaties under which she may rightfully assert the freedom of nearly all the bozal negroes—that is, of half the actual slaves in Cuba.

It was a bold step on the part of the President, and it seems to me a wise one, thus to invite the cooperation of Great Britain.

It opens a wide perspective. It looks like breaking down the last barrier of distrust between the two great branches of the British race in Europe and America.

It would seem that now at length, after the lapse of a century of heartburning, the old jealousy of the emancipated colonies toward the mother country, and the rancors of the Sovereign toward rebel subjects become an independent State, had wholly died out, to give place to mutual confidence advantageous to us, but not less so to Great Britain.

The treaty of Washington was, in fact, not merely a settlement of a transitory modern question growing out of our secession war, but a clearing up also of long-standing frets dating back to the war of Independence.

I have, etc.,   C. CUSHING.

Mr. Fish to Mr. Cushing.

[Telegram.]

WASHINGTON, *December 13*, 1875.

CUSHING, *Minister, Madrid:*

Instruction 266 read to Von Bülow at Berlin on 7th, suggesting good effect if representations made by Germany of importance of ending contest. He expressed desire of Germany for peace and promised to consult Emperor and Prince Bismarck. Read also in same way to Duke Decazes in Paris. He desired to consult English Government. Thought Madrid Government too weak to settle question. Have instructed representatives at St. Petersburg and Vienna to follow same course.

.FISH, *Secretary.*

Mr. Fish to Mr. Cushing.

No. 278.]   DEPARTMENT OF STATE,
           Washington, December 17, 1875.

SIR: I inclose herewith, for your information, a copy of an instruction under date of the 15th November, 1875, to the ministers of the United States at Paris, Berlin, Vienna, Rome, Lisbon, and St. Petersburg, transmitting to them a copy of an instruction to you of the 5th of the same month (No. 266) referring to the relations between this Government and that of Spain.

I also inclose copies of telegram forwarded to and received from those ministers in reference to their proceedings pursuant to such instructions up to and including this date. No telegram has been sent to the legation at Lisbon, and no directions have been given to Mr. Moran since the instruction referred to was addressed to him.

Referring to an instruction No. 805, addressed to General Schenck, of which a copy was transmitted with my No. 267, I also inclose herewith copies of all telegrams addressed to him or by him to the Department in reference thereto.

I am, sir, etc.,   HAMILTON FISH.

[Inclosures.]

Mr. Fish to United States ministers at Paris, Berlin, Vienna, Rome, Lisbon, and St. Petersburg.
Mr. Fish to Mr. Schenck, November 19, 1875.
Same to same, November 29, 1875.
Mr. Schenck to Mr. Fish, November 29, 1875.
Same to same, November 30, 1875.
Same to same, December 2, 1875.
Mr. Fish to Mr. Schenck, December 6, 1875.
Mr. Fish to Mr. Washburne, December 6, 1875.
Mr. Fish to Mr. Davis, December 6, 1875.
Mr. N. Fish to Mr. Fish, December 7, 1875.
Mr. Hitt to Mr. Fish, December 9, 1875.
Mr. Marsh to Mr. Fish, December 14, 1875.
Mr. N. Fish to Mr. Fish, December 15, 1875.
Mr. Boker to Mr. Fish, December 16, 1875.
Mr. Stevens to Mr. Fish, December 16, 1875.

Mr. Cushing to Mr. Fish.

[Telegram]

MADRID, *December 19, 1875.*

Spanish Government hears to-day from Austria of circular addressed by you to European Governments, suggesting intervention in Cuba. Your 266 evidently intended. If I am interrogated on the subject by minister of state what answer shall I make?

CUSHING.

Mr. Fish to Mr. Cushing.

[Telegram.]

WASHINGTON, *December 20, 1875.*

Two sixty-six communicated also to Russia, Italy, and Austria. Gortchakoff promised if Emperor consent to make representations to Spain toward preservation of good relations, but doubts Russian influence. Italy will instruct minister to urge expediency of fulfilling duties to the United States, and pacifying Cuba, without specifying measures. Austria promises answer this week probably unsatisfactory Copy all telegrams and circular instruction mailed 17th.

Intervention of foreign Powers was neither asked or suggested at present, but expression of their views desired to impress on Spain necessity of terminating contest, and to avoid necessity of intervention. This course adopted in the direction of friendship and of peace and to exhaust every effort, and avoid all possible suspicion of selfish, unfriendly, or ulterior purposes. You may so reply if interrogated.

FISH, *Secretary.*

Mr. Cushing to Mr. Fish.[1]

No. 730.]   LEGATION OF THE UNITED STATES,
Madrid, December 22, 1875. (Received Jan. 17, 1876.)

SIR: You will doubtless have noticed in the London Times of the 9th instant an editorial article of some interest respecting the relations between the United States and Spain.

----

[1] Reprinted from House Ex. Doc. No. 90, 44th Cong., 1st sess.

Portions of this article have been translated and published in several of the newspapers of Madrid, with more or less pertinent observations.

I annex translation of the observations of the Cronista, of Madrid (a journal in close affinity with the Government), calling your attention especially to the concluding paragraph, in which is accepted without protest the remarkable phrase of the Times concerning the rule of Spain over Cuba, to the effect that "the limits of her power are the limits of her right."

I have the honor, etc.,

C. CUSHING.

———

[Appendix A.—No. 730 —Translation of editorial article from El Cronista, Madrid, December 20, 1875.]

THE QUESTION OF THE UNITED STATES.

The Times of the 9th instant, referring to the message of General Grant, and after devoting some little space to the religious question, which is commencing to arise in the United States, and threatens to perturb their interior peace, if not with armed struggles, at least with those moral combats which cause so much injury to civil societies, passes on to analyze very especially that portion of the message which treats of the Cuban question.

The English journal qualifies it as the most important part of the message, and calls observance to the confession of the President that the rebels do not constitute a civil organization which could be recognized as an independent government capable of fulfilling international obligations and worthy of being treated as a power; from which Grant himself draws the inference that to recognize the insurgents as a government would be an act inconsistent with the reality.

And the Times adds:

"Any other conclusion would have come strangely indeed from the Chief Magistrate of a nation which was angry with this country for recognizing the belligerency of the Southern States, although they had a regular government, a fixed capital, agents abroad, a formidable navy, and an elaborately organized army. The Cuban insurgents are as yet little better than splinters of revolt."

The President concludes, and the Times applauds him for it, by saying that it would be imprudent, premature, and indefensible as a measure of right to treat the rebels as belligerents.

But at the same time that the English journal notes these satisfactory statements it observes that in the next line the President lays it down as his opinion that, the indefinite continuance of the war being prejudicial to the subjects of the Republic, it will be necessary for the Spanish Government to do everything possible to conclude it, under penalty of that Republic being obliged to adopt such measures as may be deemed necessary.

And the journal adds:

"It is exceedingly difficult for English observers to do justice to the claims on which President Grant's threats are founded. We are apt to think that they are merely a veil for a determination to seize one of the richest islands in the world. America has long had her eye on Cuba, and it may not uncharitably be thought that she is unwilling to let slip this chance of seizing the prize. But it would be well for us to suspend our judgment till we see a specific statement of the injury which the Cuban rebellion has inflicted upon the United States. It certainly injures trade, and does great harm to many of the President's countrymen. The mischief thus done may be insufficient to warrant more than a remonstrance, or it may call for a less gentle style of treatment."

The periodical then goes on to make reflections upon the possibility of Spain's overcoming the insurrection, and terminates with these notable words:

"Were Cuba as near to Cornwall as it is to Florida, we should certainly look more sharply to matters of fact than to the niceties of international law. But everything, we repeat, depends on those matters of fact. If Spain can suppress the insurrection and prevent Cuba from becoming a permanent source of mischief to neighboring countries, she has the fullest right to keep it. But she is on her trial, and that trial can not be long. When she is made to clearly understand that the tenure of her rule over Cuba depends on her ability to make that rule a reality, she will not be slow to show what she can do, and the limits of her power will be the limits of her right."

Thus ends the article, which, from more than one point of view, deserves to attract the attention of our Government and serve as a stimulus and a spur to it, in order to accelerate on the one hand the final campaign against the Carlists, and on the other the preparations for another and likewise decisive campaign in Cuba.

It is indispensable—it is demanded by our interest and our honor, pledged before the civilized world—it is indispensable to make a supreme effort and triumph, and triumph speedily, over both insurrections. Neither of the two has succeeded in placing itself in condition to be recognized as a belligerent; both of them are daughters of the disconcertedness in which we have lived, of the debility which the principle of authority contracted among us in a lamentable period of political insanity; both of them are decaying in proportion as authority regains its place and the nation restores itself.

One effort more and we will end it: and let us at every moment think that, in this matter as in many others, it is a melancholy truth that "the limits of our power must be the limits of our right."

Mr. Cushing to Mr. Fish.

No. 748.]   LEGATION OF THE UNITED STATES,
                                       Madrid, January 4, 1876.

SIR: Recent publications in New York, London, and Paris, passed around by the telegraph, are drawing attention to the communications made by the United States to European Governments on the subject of intervention in Cuba.

Most, if not all of these publications, will probably have passed under your eye.

I annex, nevertheless, in appendix, several such, which are the subject of particular comment at Madrid.

When questioned in this relation, my answer has been, conformably to the tenor of your telegram of the 20th ultimo, that intervention had neither been asked nor suggested at present, but only expression of views desired to impress on Spain the necessity of terminating the contest and to avoid necessity of intervention, and in the intention of peace and friendship, and to preclude all possible suspicion of selfish or unfriendly or ulterior purposes on the part of the United States.

I think that such is the understanding of the matter in every well-disposed quarter, as evidenced by the state of mind of the minister of state, as reported in my No. 745 of the 2d instant.

The concluding sentences of the communication made by the Marquis de Molins to Galignani's Messenger, and reproduced to day in Madrid by the Havas Agency, seem intended to imply that some of the European Governments at least have interchanged views on the subject, and in a sense acceptable to Spain, which may be the substance of the information communicated to the Marquis de Molins by the Duc Decazes

In Madrid there is a dispute on the question whether or not the Spanish Government has taken any action in the premises. But, as we now know, the minister of state is preparing a communication in behalf of Spain.

Speculation is active also as to the ultimate question of what the United States will do if left alone by other powers—whether the President will intervene by force, and if so, whether in armed alliance with Spain, or whether in arms against her and in aid of the insurgents, which it is assumed would be war. Observation of what is going on at the present time in Constantinople respecting Bosnia and Herzegovina, and what occurred there formerly in the matter of Greece, leads many persons to anticipate the development of a similar series of incidents at Madrid as respects Cuba.

Hence, Count Greppi's "Question d'Orient" is read here with interest, as affording a key to the enigma of coming events, both in Europe and America.

History, it is said, repeats itself, but unfortunately with such variations that we misapply the lesson quite as often as we apply it rightfully, as in the case of the rejuvenated old man of the "Si jeunesse savait, si vieillesse pouvait," by Soulié. And all experience on the bench and at the bar demonstrate that it is much easier to find precedents than it is to adapt them to new facts.

Meantime, while steering as prudently as possible amid the shoals and breakers of these larger questions, I am awaiting patiently the instructions which are to govern me in the pending particular negotiations.

Apropos of which, a letter, purporting to be addressed from Madrid to the New York Herald of the 15th ultimo, puzzles me. Supposing that the pretense of interview with Mr. Cánovas del Castillo and Mr. Ruiz Gomez, two of the Spanish gentlemen plainly alluded to, is fictitious, yet the fact remains that although the Herald has a correspondent here, yet he did not arrive until after the date of this letter; and no American has been here capable of entering so minutely or intelligently into the questions at issue. On the other hand, it is not easy to suppose (although it is possible) that with the aid of some Spaniard of considerable political and juridical experience, such as are continually passing between Spain and Cuba, the letter may have been got up in New York.

On the whole, although the letter contains errors of fact and of language which a Spaniard of the instruction of Mr. Ruiz Gomez, for instance, would not have committed, still the matter of the letter may have been prepared here by some Spaniard of intelligence desirous of thus making his views known to the people of the United States, and sent to New York to be worked into its present shape in the office.

I have, etc.,

C. CUSHING.

[Appendix A in No. 748.—Sundry newspaper extracts in relation to the Cuban question and the attitude of the United States and Spain with respect to foreign powers]

(A) From the New York Times, December 16, 1875:
"The published report that the United States have submitted proposals to Great Britain, France, and Germany, looking to an intervention in the Cuban question, is contradicted by the language of the President in his recent annual message. In addition, it may positively be asserted that even if this Government should in future be inclined to such intervention, it would do so without asking or desiring the coopcration of foreign powers."

(B) From the London Times, December 30, 1875:

LATEST INTELLIGENCE—SPAIN AND THE UNITED STATES.

[By cable from our American correspondent.]

"PHILADELPHIA, *December 29.*
"The Secretary of State recently addressed a circular to the leading European Governments, including Spain, upon Cuban affairs, suggesting mediation or intervention to restore peace, and asking them if they approved of joining in an international effort for this object."

(C) From the London Times, December 31, 1875:
"WASHINGTON, *December 30.*
"The American minister in London has, in the name of this Government, addressed himself to the English Government for the purpose of learning its views with respect to a collective intervention of the European powers with the object of stopping the bloodshed in Cuba. The English Government has, however, deferred giving a definite answer at present."

(D) From Galignani's Messenger, Paris, December 31, 1875:

"NEW YORK, 30*th.*

"The American Government addressed recently to the European Powers, Spain included, a circular in which it proposed a mediation or an intervention to restore peace in Cuba, and asked them if they would associate in an international proceeding with that object. On that subject the New York Herald publishes a telegraphic message from Vienna stating that all the Powers, comprising England, have given their adhesion to the proposal."

(E) From Galignani's Messenger, Paris, January 1, 1876:

"We have received the following communication from the Spanish embassy:

"'The New York Herald, according to a telegram from that city, asserts that the Government of the United States had invited the great Powers to join with it in an intervention in Cuba, and that they had consented. That news is erroneous from several points of view. * * * The American note which is already several weeks old, although it was only read to the European cabinet a fortnight ago, does not propose intervention. After having rendered justice to the honorable efforts made by Spain to put an end to the insurrection, it affirms that she is powerless to master it, and exhorts the Powers to make friendly remonstrances to her on the state of things. That conclusion has been coolly received by the European Governments, which have postponed all reply to these overtures. The American ministers have not insisted, nor even left a copy with the Governments to which they are accredited.'"

Mr. Fish to Mr. Cushing.

[Telegram]

WASHINGTON, *January 4, 1876.*

CUSHING, *Minister, Madrid:*

Would inconvenience result from publication of 266 and attendant correspondence in case Congress call for it?

FISH, *Secretary.*

Mr. Cushing to Mr. Fish

[Telegram]

MADRID, *January 5, 1876.*

I think not, seeing that the Spanish Government already has copy of dispatch, and the public generally will consider it in connection with the President's friendly message.

CUSHING.

Mr. Cushing to Mr. Fish.

No. 754.] LEGATION OF THE UNITED STATES,
Madrid, January 7, 1876.

SIR: The ministerial journals continue to publish short paragraphs founded on the communication made to Galignani's Messenger by the Spanish ambassador at Paris, all belonging to the class which the physicians denominate soothing medicines, of which the following, in the Correspondencia, may serve as example, namely:

Various colleagues give account of a note which the Government of the United States passed some weeks since to the cabinets of Europe, in which, after doing justice to the bona fide efforts of Spain to terminate the insurrection in Cuba, the United

States pretends that she is impotent to subdue it, and exhorts other Governments to make friendly representations to that of Spain on the subject.

This vague conclusion has been coldly received by the European Governments, which have deferred making reply to the indications of the United States.

The American ministers have not insisted nor left a copy with the Governments to which they are respectfully accredited.

Such is the truth regarding this incident.

Our own information is to the same effect.

Thus for the Correspondencia.

I add that rumors are afloat of a telegram received by the Spanish Government from London, purporting that Great Britain is proposing to assert her treaty rights to the freedom of the loyal blacks in Cuba.

I have the honor, etc.,

C. CUSHING.

Mr. Cushing to Mr. Fish.

No. 755.] LEGATION OF THE UNITED STATES,
Madrid, January 8, 1876.

SIR: The ministerial journals of last evening continue to rejoice over the tenor of the communiqué of the Marquis de Molins, reported in my No. 748, of the 4th instant.

They now publish a variation by way of New York and London, as follows:

The [American] Government admits having sent to the European Powers a circular respecting the affairs of Cuba.

It denies having proposed a confederation of Cuba and Puerto Rico under a Spanish governor, but it does not publish the text of the circular.

All this, pursue the journals in question, is nothing but the document so coldly received by the Powers to which it was read by the representatives of the United States.

But, nevertheless, in the very same journals appears the following telegraphic item, which seems likely to put a new face on things, namely:

BERLIN, *January 7.*

It is positively asserted that the German Government shows itself favorable to the American circular relative to Cuba, in consequence of the injuries which the present situation of the island involves to the commerce of Germany.

I hear nothing further as to the alleged intentions of Great Britain.

I have, etc.,

C. CUSHING.

P. S.—Since the above dispatch was written the London Times has come to hand, containing a telegram from Vienna, which is annexed. It is confused, illogical, and incorrect, like all such telegraphic reports.

If "Cuba" is a European question of "incalculable consequences," as the telegram asserts, then you had good cause to consult Europe, and Europe has good cause to act in the premises.

It was not in the middle of December, but the 30th of November, that the Spanish Government received copy of your No. 266. See my No. 692 of the 30th November. But intelligence of No. 266 being communicated to European Powers did come here about the middle of December, as reported to you in my telegram on the 19th of December.

C. C.

VIENNA, *January 4.*

The cabinet of Madrid learned in the middle of December from a confidential quarter the contents of the circular note of the United States Government to the European powers relative to Cuba. It thereupon instructed its representatives abroad to explain to the Governments to which they are accredited that the Cuban question was one not only of American, but of European, interest. Complications between America and Spain might have incalculable consequences for Europe. In the first place, they would encourage the Carlists to make a prolonged resistance and revive the hopes of the Federalist Republicans and Socialists in Spain. The Austrian Government received these declarations in a friendly manner, and will not reply to the long American dispatch, which was only read to the Austrian minister for foreign affairs, and which, moreover, not only repudiates any intention of annexing Cuba, but in reality contains no definite conclusion.

Mr. Cushing to Mr. Fish.

No. 759.]
LEGATION OF THE UNITED STATES,
Madrid, January 10, 1876.

SIR: I annex translation of an article from the Cronista, a serious ministerial paper, containing a very formal semiofficial denial of the alleged concurrence of Germany in the suggestion by the United States of intervention in Cuba.

There is report here of the capture of a German vessel charged with supplying arms to rebels in the Filipinas Count Hatzfeldt informs me that he has no information respecting the affair, but apprehends it will be the occasion of unpleasant controversy

I annex translation of an article on the subject from a ministerial journal of respectability, the Tiempo.

I have the honor, etc.,
C. CUSHING.

[Appendix A, No. 759.—Translation of article from El Cronista of January 8, 1876]

A dispatch of the Agencia Fabra from Berlin, which we published yesterday, as did our contemporaries, give news, which would be grave if true, that the German Government showed itself favorable toward the American circular referring to Cuba, because of the damage brought upon German commerce by the condition of the island.

Duly informed, we are able to assert that the statement referred to is not true, and that the cabinet of Berlin continues to express the greatest sympathies for our country.

The circular of the Government of the United States has not met with a favorable reception from any European power.

[Appendix B, No. 759 —Translation of article from El Tiempo of January 8, 1876]

We again call the attention of the Government toward our possessions in the Philippine Archipelago. We know that the enemies of Spanish integrity rest not, although their affairs in London have recently assumed a bad aspect, and that the English Government looks upon them with suspicion.

Upon that immense network of islands of Oceanica belonging to Spain they have fixed their vision. They do not overlook that these offer excellent positions, and they will take advantage of every opportunity to snatch some one of the rich pearls of so precious a jewel.

There, more than anywhere, will they direct their efforts, because elsewhere they will find immediate opposition from first-class powers. If there be vigilance, more than sufficient is Spanish patriotism against all conspiracies, native or foreign; and not for a moment do we doubt that there will be such (conspiracies) as is proved by the news which gives rise to these lines.

Mr. Fish to Mr. Cushing.

No. 286.]   DEPARTMENT OF STATE,
                                  Washington, January 11, 1876.

SIR: Referring to previous correspondence on the Spanish question,
I now inclose herewith, for your confidential information, a copy of two
dispatches, numbered 220 and 222, dated, respectively, the 8th and 14th
December, 1875, upon the subject from Mr. Nicholas Fish, chargé d'
affaires ad interim, of the United States at Berlin, Prussia.

I am, etc.,

                                            HAMILTON FISH.

———

Mr. Fish to Mr. Cushing.

No. 288.]   DEPARTMENT OF STATE,
                                  Washington, January 11, 1876.

SIR: Referring to my No. 266 and to the various telegrams which
have passed in relation thereto, I have to acknowledge the receipt of
your Nos. 692, 698, 703, and 705.

With your 692 you inclose a copy of the remarks made by you to the
minister of state in your interview of November 30, on presenting a
copy of No. 266.

It is perceived that you state that No. 266, dated the 5th November,
was written before the delivery to you of the Spanish note of November 15, and "as is to be supposed, without knowledge of the intentions
of the Government of His Majesty." In this you are quite correct, as
No. 266 bore a date anterior to that of the Spanish note, and was prepared without knowledge of its contents. At the same time, the
substance of the Spanish note of November 15 had reached this Government by means of your telegrams of November 16, 18, and 19, prior
to my telegram to you of the 27th of November, directing the presentation of the instruction of the 5th of November, and after a careful
consideration, a conclusion was reached that it raised no occasion for a
change in the instructions which had been sent.

At the conclusion of your memorandum read to the minister of state
you requested a further interview before any definite resolution was
adopted by the Government of Spain; and in your No. 703 you report
an interview with him upon December 4, in which incidental reference
is made to instruction No. 266, and in which he appears to have frankly
spoken of some of the grievances of which we had complained; but it
is not stated whether this is the interview which you had requested
should be held prior to any decision being reached on the part of the
Spanish Government.

In your No. 698 you report an interview with Mr. Layard, and his
willingness to back you in the matter of Cuba, as soon as some joint
course of action should be determined on by the two Governments; and
in your No. 705 you say that while Mr. Layard is prepared to cooperate
with you if there should be any occasion, "toward keeping the peace,"
your interview with the minister of state upon the 4th had been so satisfactory that there seemed no present occasion for his friendly interposition, and that he concurred in the opinion as to the inexpediency
of any further steps, until the arrival of more definite instructions from
Lord Derby.

In your interview of December 4, reference to instruction No. 266
appears to have been confined to our particular griefs, no allusion being

made to the general question of the condition of Cuba as distinguished therefrom.

A telegram from General Schenck, dated December 2, says that Lord Derby had received a telegram from Mr. Layard stating that you had requested no definite action on instruction No. 266, in the expectation that the Spanish note might induce the President to modify the views in his message, and that therefore Lord Derby hesitated to act.

I have as yet no written dispatch from General Schenck on the subject of his interview with Lord Derby, and am in hopes, when fuller information is received, that it will show that Lord Derby misapprehended Mr. Layard as to a request being made by you to the Spanish minister that he take no definite action on the communication addressed to the Government at Madrid. It would be unfortunate if such impression had delayed instructions from London to Mr. Layard, or had induced him to postpone the presentation of the views of the British cabinet, which General Schenck represented as willing, in the interests of humanity and friendship, to cooperate in any way short of putting pressure on Spain that promises to bring about a settlement of troubles in Cuba.

General Schenck has not informed the Department as to any late interviews with Lord Derby, and information has not reached me whether any particular instructions have been sent to Mr. Layard. General Schenck's attention has been called thereto.

As several of the other Governments of Europe are understood to have instructed their representatives at Madrid to make representations to the Spanish Government, and as it is presumed that some such representations may have already been made, it is highly advisable that all of these, to be effective, should be as simultaneous as possible.

Early information was given to the Government of Great Britain concerning the course which this Government intended to adopt on this question, in order to secure the effect of any representations which that Government might be inclined to authorize its representative at Madrid to make, so that the effect and purpose of instruction No. 266, in its relation to the general question of the condition of Cuba, should have its full force. The President indulges the hope that you will, by vigorous but prudent and wise insistence, be enabled to secure the position which this Government has taken its full force. He looks confidently to a friendly and satisfactory termination of all pending questions with Spain, including the important one of the termination of the conflict in Cuba.

I am, etc., HAMILTON FISH.

Mr. Cushing to Mr. Fish.

No. 762.] LEGATION OF THE UNITED STATES,
Madrid, January 11, 1876.

SIR: Political circles at Madrid continue to occupy themselves with the question of intervention in Cuba, interest in which is kept excited by the now frequent references to the subject in the journals of England, Germany, and Austria, reproduced by those of Madrid.

Articles heretofore transmitted to you afford pabulum to persistent discussion.

To-day there is a new crop, founded on articles of the Gazette of Cologne and the Press of Vienna.

I annex translation of the article of the Press, with comments of the Epoca, and shall transmit to-morrow translation of the article of the Gazette of Cologne.

Late news from Cuba by private letters narrates the destruction of "Jaquey Grande" and of several ingenios by the insurgents, the capture by them of a railway train between Cienfuegos and Villa Clara, near to the headquarters of Valmaseda at Las Cruces; their operations in the neighborhood of Sagua, and the extreme distress presenting in the departments of Puerto Principe and in Cinco Villas, all of which gives much solicitude to the Government.

I have, etc., C. CUSHING.

———

[Appendix A, No. 762 —Translation of article from La Epoca of January 10, 1876]

The more important German journals, the semiofficial ones especially, have expressed the surprise caused to them by the note of the United States Government consulting in regard to the opportuneness of an intervention for the sake of reestablishing peace in Cuba. The Gazette, of Cologne, has published an article well worthy of attracting attention, which we shall reproduce to-morrow; and another from one of the most authoritative Austrian dailies expresses itself in the following no less significant terms:

"The threats against Spain contained in the articles of the New York press and in the last message of President Grant not having produced any results, the news is propagated from New York that the American Government has approached the European Powers, including Spain, with intent of sounding them as to their views respecting the opportuneness of obtaining, by means of united action, the reestablishment of peace in the island of Cuba.

"Should this news be confirmed, it would not be difficult to foresee the reply which would be given by the cabinets.

"Spain, for her part, has nothing to do but to refer to the large reenforcements she has lately sent, and to General Jovellar, as an energetic chief and one well acquainted with the Island of Cuba, whereby a speedy pacification of the insurrection there may be expected. And however much the filibusters and insurgents may attempt to sustain it through the organs of the New York press and the declarations of President Grant, they can only delay the end."

We had anticipated the advice of the Austrian journal. We have in Cuba 70,000 men, excellent soldiers, and 100,000 volunteers, a number more than sufficient to suppress the rebellion should it come out from its fastnesses.

———

Mr. Cushing to Mr. Fish.

No. 764.] LEGATION OF THE UNITED STATES,
Madrid, January 12, 1876.

SIR: I transmit hereto annexed a translation of the article of the Gazette, of Cologne, respecting intervention in Cuba, referred to in my No. 762 of the 11th instant, with remarks of the Epoca thereon, which article is assumed here to be an expression of the public opinion of Germany on the subject.

I have, etc., C. CUSHING.

———

[Appendix A, No. 764.—Translation of article from the Gazette, of Cologne, from La Epoca, Madrid, January 11, 1876.]

The article from the Cologne Gazette, to which we referred yesterday, an article the spirit of which is opposed to any Americo-European intervention in the question of Cuba, runs thus:

"The President of the United States could not have found a more unfavorable moment for inviting the European powers to take common measures with the object of restoring order in the confused state of things in the Island of Cuba. Our part of the world is at present very much occupied in disentangling itself from another analogous question, or at least postponing it for the longest time possible. So long as there is a conflagration in our neighbor, Turkey, and the diplomatic fire-engines are laboring to put it out, Europe has neither time nor room for giving attention to the little fire in the far-off Antilla. But President Ulysses Grant deems it opportune to make his voice heard in the diplomatic concert of the world, so that on this side of the ocean his existence may not pass into the state of oblivion. For this reason, he has caused course to be given to his circular note by his ministry of foreign affairs, of which the papers have spoken for the last few days, and of which we now give a long extract sent to us by our London correspondent."

(Here follows a long extract from the note in question, which is already known.)

"The introduction of this note was already known (at least its principal contents) by means of the message which President Grant addressed a few weeks ago to the Congress assembled for the new session."

(Here the Gazette inserts that part of the message which speaks of the insurrection of Cuba and of the necessity of ending it.)

"To whomsoever reads these complaints, even superficially, it must occur that nothing is needed save to change the proper names to have an exact picture of that civil war which devastated the United States a little more than ten years ago. Not merely destruction and pillage, but also the contempt of the modern laws of warfare, offered in the Southern States a spectacle as moving as that of to day in Cuba, even though we may be forced to recognize that acts as horrible as those of shooting innocent prisoners of war, whose only crime consisted in having taken part in the insurrection, may be excused as measures of reprisal on the part of the Northern States.

"Scenes as fearful as those which passed in the prison of Andersonville, in contempt of the lightest demands of humanity and under the superior vigilance of Captain Wirz, of the Southern States, have had no equal in Cuba. And, in spite of that, the United States opposed by every means any European interference in a civil war, and not [sic] with full right, as was recognized at least in Germany, where the state of things was then judged with more coolness than in France and England. As apart from this the statistical data prove conclusively that the commerce of Cuba has developed itself in spite of the insurrection, Spain, in rejecting all foreign interference, can simply refer to the precedent set by the United States.

"In a letter from Madrid of official origin, which one of our Parisian correspondents recently mentioned, it is said that the insurrection mainly has its focus in those interior parts of the island which, by reason of being covered with impenetrable woods and morasses, are uninhabitable for Europeans; that it does not possess a single town of importance, and that it never has been able to attain the point of conducting even a moderately regularized warfare. President Grant has recognized this fact when he declares in his message that the real facts do not properly permit of recognizing the insurgents as possessing the character of belligerents.

"In our opinion the European powers have still far less motives for intermixing in the Cuban disturbances. Much to the contrary. If Europe has an interest in the affairs of Spain, it is to avoid all that might lead that country out of the pathway of order upon which it now seems to have entered. This question has no more sensitive point than Cuba, and the sovereign who, as the result of foreign pressure, might find himself forced to dissolve or even weaken the ties which united the colony to the mother country, would feel the ground slipping from under his feet.

"Now then, to shake the throne of Alfonso XII might eventually please the trans-Atlantic Republic, but assuredly would not please the states of the Old World. It appears, moreover, as if President Grant finds no support in his own country for his designs, because it is only too generally suspected that he touches on foreign questions and treats largely of them for the purpose of finding himself, in the moments of serious complications, as an experienced general, the sole master of the situation. He himself seems to have a firmer conviction that he personally is absolutely necessary, than the people of the United States appear to have. The negative replies he will in all probability get from all the foreign cabinets may make mention of the present greatly improved situation of the Government of Madrid with respect to the Carlist insurrection. There are hopes that the Peninsula will soon be freed from the pest of civil war, and then the moment will have come for putting an end, with redoubled energies, to the insurrection in Cuba. As Europe has played for so many years the part of a tranquil looker-on, she may well wait, in all conscience, a few months yet, before taking into consideration the question whether there is room for intervening."

This language, friendly toward Spain and prudent in what relates to the relations of Europe with our country, is the more significant as the significance attributed to the Gazette of Cologne is great. It should be borne in mind, however, that this article has been republished by the North German Gazette, as though seeking to make it appear that these are the opinions of Germany, already officially known by the silence with which was received the note of the Government of the United States, which Government, for its part, can not withdraw from the positions set forth in the Presidential message.

Mr. Cushing to Mr. Fish.

No. 771.]   LEGATION OF THE UNITED STATES,
                                  Madrid, January 11, 1876.

SIR: In turning over the leaves of one of the bound, but unindexed, volumes of dispatches in the legation, in search of a particular paper, my sight fell on a dispatch of Mr. Seward, addressed to the diplomatic representatives of the Governments abroad, on the subject of foreign intervention in the United States between the Union and the Southern Confederates.

It is a printed circular, dated August 18, 1862.

This document may not have fallen under your observation; and if not, it may be worthy of perusal, as presenting the obvious arguments against intervention common on both sides to all questions.

It is an apt illustration of the rhetorical theorem of commonplaces—arguments pro and contra on a question—with which college studies rendered us all familiar in the pages of Cicero's Topica.

There is no instruction in this dispatch to communicate it or its contents to other Governments, and it does not otherwise appear to have been communicated to that of Spain.

But the document acquired general publicity by being communicated to Congress annexed to the next annual message of the President (Ex. Doc., 1862–63, vol. 1, p. 176), and may, therefore, have become known to the Spanish Government.

The minister of state at the time was D. Saturnino Calderon y Collantes, in the second administration of General O'Donnell. It was not until his third administration that D. Fernando Calderon y Collantes, the present minister of state, entered the cabinet as minister of grace and justice.

Whether or not the present ministers have knowledge of this document does not appear. Probably not, for such has been the political anarchy and ministerial shiftiness of the recent years in Spain—such the wild contention of parties—and so complete the absence of authentic history, amid the immense mass of polemical publications and of extravagant party diatribes, absurdly dignified with the name of history, in the presence of which the tragedy of cruel wars and ever-recurring rebellions and the comedy of transitory quarrels of mere personal ambition and partisanship, serve to crowd out of sight all things of serious importance that this document is not likely to be remembered, if it was ever within the knowledge of the public men of Spain.

Thus, while there is no end here of books of literary criticism, romance, poetry, and plays, and especially the rubbish of party disquisitions, more or less elaborate, which the future historian of the country will have to toil through with disgust and shame; all my efforts thus far have failed to obtain any, even the most superficial, account of the six great acts of the reign of Queen Isabel, namely: the successive military adventures in Rome, in Santo Domingo, in Morocco, in Mexico, on the coast of Chile and Peru, and in Cochin-China.

While, therefore, it is quite improbable that the ministers of to-day have any recollection, if they had any knowledge of Mr. Seward's circular, yet certain it is that the arguments contained in its second, third, and fourth commencing paragraphs and in its four penultimate paragraphs, are such as continually meet my eye in the newspapers, and my ear in conversation, at Madrid.

I have, etc., C. CUSHING.

Mr. Cushing to Mr. Fish.

No. 776.] LEGATION OF THE UNITED STATES,
Madrid, January 15, 1876.

SIR: In continuation of noticeable articles concerning Cuba, please find annexed translation of two short editorials of the Cronista and the Epoca, both ministerial journals, the former commenting on language attributed to the President

The Politica prints in translation an article of the New York Herald of the 28th ultimo, purporting to report an interview of its correspondent with yourself, and makes prefatory and concluding comments thereon, which are also annexed in translation.

I have, etc., C. CUSHING.

P. S.—Permit me to call your attention to an editorial on Spain, with incidental reference to intervention in Cuba, of the London Times of the 10th instant.

[Appendix A, No. 776 —Translation.—Editorial paragraph from La Epoca, Madrid, January 14, 1876.]

The effort continues to cause the belief that the relations between Spain and the United States are not good, when the exact opposite is the case.

A telegram has gone the rounds announcing that in the roads of Port Royal, S. C., the American squadron would be concentrated, but it needs one to be denuded of all political common sense to suppose that when the Exposition is in full blast, conflicts are to be provoked, and as the desire of the North Americans is to have the Cuban war ended, we trust to be able to satisfy their desires shortly, if, indeed, the name of a war can be applied to the rebellion, sustained in the shelter of the impenetrable woods, without having mastered a single important town and without having organized a government.

The only thing we know for certain is that the religion of the insurgents is idolatry, which must be very gratifying for the traitors, who, in order to escape merited chastisement, go to swell the ranks of the rebels.

[Appendix B, No. 776.—Translation.—Editorial article on Cuba, from El Cronista, Madrid, January 14, 1876.]

The right which is on the side of Spain in the affairs of Cuba is so clear and so patent that it could not fail to have been recognized, even though shamefacedly and in private circles, by the President of the United States, General Grant. We were right in asserting, as we have repeatedly done, that the parliamentary curvets (excarceos) of the Government of the American Republic with respect to the question of Cuba obeyed, rather than its own opinions, electoral machinations, and the pressure of the filibuster element, so numerous in the United States.

We say this à propos of an important piece of news which we receive to-day by the Cuban mail. A Habana paper publishes correspondence from New York, in which it is positively said that the President of the United States has declared in private circles that he considers the independence of the Island of Cuba as impossible, and that its annexation to the United States would cause immense injuries to the country.

If General Grant has said so, he has spoken like a book, even though he has required some seven years to convince himself of that which was seen and said from the beginning by those who well knew the especial circumstances of the Great Antilla.

Perfectly do we agree with the President of the United States that the Island of Cuba can not be independent, because it does not possess the indispensable elements to constitute a state capable of governing itself in peace, with preservation of even a portion of the culture and prosperity it has acquired under the Spanish flag; and the reasons which he alleges for pronouncing against its annexation appear to us to be very well founded.

All this is logical and natural; but as the Eco de Cuba very rightfully remarks, President Grant has not duly considered the deduction he draws, that "a friendly intervention is the only thing which can restore peace in the island, obtaining from the mother country the concession of autonomy under the protectorate of Spain."

The Island of Cuba not being able to govern itself well as an independent and sovereign State could still less do so as an autonomic semi-State, and in such circumstances it were in every way impossible for Spain to reserve to herself a protectorate which, without positive benefit to Cuba, would drag the mother country into the most serious complications within and without this territory.

To prove this absolute impossibility so many considerations throng to the subject that it is no small task to select the prominent ones.

In the Island of Cuba there exists an immense majority which does not desire separation, which does not desire annexation, which does not desire autonomy, which wishes to keep on in the same conditions as those in which they have lived with respect to the mother country. In the Island of Cuba there exists a slender minority which is split up into "independents," "annexationists," and "autonomists." The immense majority reject autonomy, which would weaken their ties with the mother country. The independents and the annexationists are not content with autonomy, which does not satisfy their aspirations. The autonomists would be the only ones left satisfied, but they are so few in number that they would lack moral and material strength.

The Eco de Cuba, then, is right: the Great Antilla is not fitted to be anything save what it has been hitherto. Thus it is that the right of Spain is supported by every kind of reason based on expedience. Therefore, in spite of all the efforts of the ambitious ojalateros (sans culottes) of New York, and in spite of the misdeeds of the criminals of the manigua, the Island of Cuba will continue to be a Spanish province.

———

[Appendix C in No. 776.—Translation.—Extracts from an editorial article from La Política, Madrid, January 14, 1876.]

In the New York Herald of the 28th (ultimo) we find a conversation which took place between a reporter of that paper and the Secretary of State, Mr. Fish. That conversation demonstrates to what extent the news published by the North American press concerning complications between the United States and Spain are fantastical and of pure caprice. Our readers will also thereby see confirmed the opinion which we have always expressed, that the relations between the two Governments maintain themselves on a cordial and friendly footing.

This is what the Herald relates:

"As the press and public men on this side of the water, in Spain, and out of Spain are given to discoursing of combats, conflicts, and disasters growing out of the Cuban question, we hope that the positive language of the North American Minister of State will serve to calm impressionable minds and restore the truth of the facts."

———

Mr. Cushing to Mr. Fish.

No. 777.]   LEGATION OF THE UNITED STATES,
                                     Madrid, January 16, 1876.

SIR: I called on the minister of state yesterday, in conformity with previous request of his, to relieve his solicitude regarding the non-arrival of your instruction on the subject of his note of the 15th of November.

I told him that my dispatch, covering that note, only reached you on the 6th of December; that my last dates from you were on the 22d of December; that no more time had elapsed than might naturally be required for the due consideration of the points of detail involved; and that therefore there was no delay to give cause of solicitude.

He said it had occurred to him that you might have concluded not to act until after hearing from the European Governments whose opinion you had asked in the matter; and that in this view he had resolved to defer writing the contemplated responsive circular of Spain to those Governments until after hearing from you, as he was anxious to avoid saying or doing anything which might infer offense to the United States.

I expressed gratification at his taking this view of the subject, and said that his conjecture might be correct, but that I had no information on which either to contradict or confirm it.

He then proceeded to say that he wished you were seated by his side, as I was, that he might say to you in the unreserve of friendship and outside of diplomatic forms that the United States could desire nothing in the sense of peace, good government, or liberty in Cuba which the Government of Don Alfonso does not desire still more earnestly; that his Government freely admitted the political expediency and necessity of abandoning the old colonial system and of promptly consummating the emancipation of the slaves; that the predatory bands of runaway blacks, headed by foreigners from Dominica and Venezuela, engaged in the work of incendiarism and devastation, in face of which all the social forces of the island were devoted to self-defense, were the only obstacle to the introduction of radical reforms in Cuba; that if the slaves were now emancipated at once many of them would betake themselves to the mountains as maroons and become additional agents of disorder and bloodshed; that he did not admit as possible the idea that the President contemplates acts of naval or military hostility on the side of those incendiary bands in order to obstruct or possibly defeat the efforts of Spain to restore order, to do which would of course be simply the commencement of war of aggression against Spain; and that if it were in his power to speak to you directly he would embrace the privilege to beg you to tell him explicitly—as a friend, if you would permit, and if not, as a statesman and a man of honor—what is the precise thing which you would advise or wish Spain to do under the mediation of the United States, with the assurance that if the thing proposed were just and practicable—and he could not conceive that you would propose anything unjust or impracticable—Spain would be but too glad to do it, as well in her own interest as in good will toward the United States, and in the consciousness that the United States and Spain are by commercial ties inseparably associated in the question of the tranquillity and prosperity of Cuba.

I confess these remarks of Mr Calderon y Collantes made an impression on my mind which he may or may not have intended, but which, nevertheless, seems to me to be the inner thought behind the words uttered, namely:

If what the United States contemplates is, whether by the use of their naval squadron or by landing troops, to intervene by force to prevent Spain from subduing the insurrection in Cuba, that is war, and Spain must, of necessity, fight, at whatever cost and ultimate loss, or cease to hold up her head as an independent nation either in Europe or America.

But if the view of the United States is to act by mediation in behalf of the insurgents, to induce them to lay down their arms, to make acceptable terms for them, to secure the execution of these terms, to provide for the introduction of good government and the abolition of slavery in officious concert or in formal treaty with Spain, then Spain is ready to meet the United States halfway in such action, to receive, and even invite, their interposition in the affairs of Cuba.

The impression on my mind to this effect was so strong as to half tempt

me to say, Will you then accept our mediation? But I restrained
myself, in the doubt whether my present instructions would justify me
in thus committing the United States.

I limited myself, therefore, to thanking him cordially for the frankness and friendliness which seemed to inspire what he said, and to assure
him that I would lose no time in communicating the same to you, as
nearly as possible in his own words, and regretting that no mere written report could do justice to the impressiveness of oral representation.

He then referred briefly to the mere robber character of what there
is now of insurrection in Cuba, composed of scattered parties of negroes
and mulattoes, without the slightest pretension to any government—
directed, so far as they had any general direction, by foreigners, mere
desperado adventurers, without right or stake in the country [I interrupted him here to say there were no citizens of the United States among
them, to which he assented, and then continued], engaged in mere plunder and incendiarism, not in war—the worst form of that tendency to
guerrilla hostilities in the place of regular warfare which the Spaniards
had inherited from their remote Celtiberian progenitors, and which, if
one of the glories, was not the less one of the national calamities, of
Spain.

But of all this, he said, the President's message showed that we in
the United States had a clear conception; and he added that neither
such bad foreigners as Maximo Gomez in the Managua, nor worse Spaniards, like Miguel Aldama in New York, could ever make of Cuba any
better republic than Haiti; and that appeared to be their only purpose—to ruin where they could not rule.

It was impossible for me conscientiously to contradict these appreciations, and therefore I could but listen attentively, and, when he
had concluded, take leave, assuring him that he would be informed at
once when my expected instructions should arrive from Washington.

The concluding remarks of Mr. Calderon y Collantes suggest to me
some considerations, which you will permit me to subjoin by way of
commentary.

The Spaniards have great qualities, as many a page in their history
demonstrates, but they have also the defects of those qualities; and
my dispatches have not been sparing in the exhibition of those defects,
such as intolerance of opinion, exaggerated individualism, ill-regulated
ambitions, disposition to pronunciamentos, insurrection, civil war, and
especially guerrilla warfare.

The Spanish emigrants to America carried all their national qualities
and defects with them, as did our own English, Scottish, Irish, and
Dutch ancestors; and hence the difference between the colonial career
and the political position of British America and those of Spanish
America.

And of all Spanish America that which has presented the least balance of good condition is Cuba.

It is curious to read in the ample history of Cuba by Pezuela how
at the outset the island was plagued with swarms of mere adventurers
in the vain search after gold, the best of whom followed Cortez to
Mexico, leaving the worst behind; how it was that in Cuba, as in Santo
Domingo, by these adventurers the aboriginal inhabitants were exterminated, while in the rest of Spanish America these have increased in
numbers; how for several generations afterwards the most profitable
occupation of the settlers was contraband trade, with all its corrupting
effects; how the colonial administration presented the spectacle of
a chronic three-sided quarrel between the military, the civil, and the

judicial authorities; how. when the insurrection in French Santo Domingo put an end to the cultivation of sugar and coffee there, that cultivation passed to Cuba; how it flourished there, with the conse-quent development of slavery and the slave trade; how overflowing wealth ensued. and with it came ill-directed education, unwholesome ambitions, and traitorous plots of annexation to the United States, not for the promotion of liberty, but for the security of slavery; how there-upon and therefore came acts and measures of angry repression on the part of Spain, culminating in the present state of hostility between the peninsular Spaniards and the Cuban Spaniards.

If the Cuban emigrants in the United States are a proper sample, as they possibly may be, of the better Cuban Spaniards, what are we to think of those of average or inferior degree?

While those emigrants have made themselves ridiculous in spending their time in quarreling with one another in the newspapers and in public meetings, instead of fighting the common enemy in the field, they have rendered themselves odious by their systematic violation of the law of the land of their asylum, and the acts of fraud and perjury which that implies, and by their frantic hostility to the Government of the United States.

Meanwhile, we see what the insurgents at home are after six years' experience—incapable, as the President so clearly shows, of independ-ence, unworthy even of the concession of belligerence.

If the emigrants in the United States were now in Cuba, if the insur-gents in arms were to lay down their arms, could they and the rich sugar planters and merchants of the seaports and of the western part of the island, with or without anterior solution of the slavery question, live in peace together as a republic based on free popular suffrage, which is the only intelligible conception of a republic? To me it seems impos-sible. To say nothing of Santo Domingo, we may look to the case of Jamaica, where, without any civil war to embitter men against one another, with generously regulated emancipation, with a colonial policy just, nay amicable and even kind, it has been found impossible to main-tain the existence of well-ordered society except by the constant exer-cise of paternal authority on the part of the metropolis.

All which leads me to the conclusion that the United States would have an immense task on their hands in undertaking the pacification of Cuba alone and by hostile force, inferring the necessity not only of a fleet and an army of operations, but also of occupation to keep the peace, but might well contribute efficiently to the result in cooperation with Spain.

I have the honor, etc.,   C. CUSHING.

Mr. Cushing to Mr. Fish.

No. 779.]   LEGATION OF THE UNITED STATES,
Madrid, January 17, 1876.

SIR: The observations imputed to the President and yourself, as reported in my No. 776 of the 15th inst., continue to be the subject of a dropping fire of commentary in the public journals of Madrid, the most notable of which is annexed from the Epoca.

I have the honor to be, etc.,   C. CUSHING.

[Appendix A, No. 779.—Translation.—Article from La Epoca of January 15, 1876.]

The New York Herald of the 28th attributes to the Secretary of State, Mr. Fish, the following words upon the relations between Spain and the United States:

"There is not a word of truth in the stories relative to difficulties between the United States and Spain; the two countries maintain the best relations, and the slight difficulty originated by the reclamations in Cuba is on the best road toward amicable settlement."

The opinion is also attributed to the President that he considers the independence of the Island of Cuba impossible, and that its annexation to the United States would cause great harm to the country.

We are of the same opinion. The Island of Cuba, independent, would be worth no more than Haiti or Santo Domingo, and its rich products would cease to sustain the market of the United States. Mr. Grant is mistaken, for the adventurers in the manigua no longer obey political ideas of any kind, nor would they accept any form of government save that which exempts them from the penalties which they have merited by the ordinary crimes which led them to mingle in the forces of the rebellion. And as an autonomic state the Island of Cuba can not sustain itself, since should it cease to belong to Spain it would become the patrimony of the negro race. But as no one desires this, the Government of the United States will do better by allowing us to conquer the insurrection, as we shall finally overcome it, raising the production of the Island of Cuba to amounts never before known and instituting there the reforms which may be compatible with justice.

Mr. Fish to Mr. Cushing.

No. 298.]   DEPARTMENT OF STATE,
                            Washington, January 19, 1876.

SIR: Referring to previous correspondence on the Spanish question, I now inclose herewith, for your information, a copy of a dispatch under date of the 18th instant (No. 36)[1] upon the subject from Mr. Boker, the minister of the United States at St. Petersburg.

I am, etc.,   HAMILTON FISH.

Mr. Fish to Mr. Cushing.

No. 299.]   DEPARTMENT OF STATE,
                            Washington, January 21, 1876.

SIR: Referring to my No. 298 of the 19th instant, transmitting a copy of a dispatch on the Spanish question from Mr. Boker, the minister of the United States at St. Petersburg, I have now to inclose herewith for your further information a copy of another dispatch under date of the 23d ultimo from that gentleman, stating that the Russian Government has consented to make representations to that of Spain upon the question, and that the Russian minister at Madrid has been instructed accordingly.

I am, etc.,   HAMILTON FISH.

Mr. Cushing to Mr. Fish.

No. 786.]   LEGATION OF THE UNITED STATES,
                            Madrid, January 21, 1876.

SIR: I continue to make for your information such extracts from newspapers as appear to me most worthy of attention.

(1) I remark, first, that whatever inconvenience may be involved in communicating the correspondence to Congress will be fully compen-

¹ See p. 132.

sated by putting an end to the false rumors which fill the newspapers and lead to misconstruction both in the United States and Europe.

(2) The report of a late interview with the minister of state will have served to show you how accessible this Government is to good influences on the part of the United States.

If we make ourselves the instrument, morally or by force, either of the maroon incendiaries in Cuba or of the false Cubans, who, instead of staying at home and taking up arms for their pretended country, run away from it to parade their desertion and their shame in New York, we shall, in my opinion, encounter serious trouble, while otherwise we shall have our own way in all things.

(3) I was impatient at first in view of the nonarrival of ultimate instructions, but have now become reconciled to this in the supposition that before acting definitely you will have desired ·to feel the pulse not only of the European Governments, but also of Congress.

(4) Don Alfonso's Government will be all-powerful in the Cortes, which is to assemble on the 15th of February; but that circumstance will not, in my opinion, produce any change of policy as regards the United States.

Indeed, the stronger the Government in the Cortes, the better for us; for according to constant experience in Spain, in every previous Cortes, while the Government has been disposed to calmness and conciliation, the opposition breaks out but too frequently into transports of hostility against the United States.

(5) Some of the French and German newspapers, you will see, misled by those of the United States, attribute the policy of our Government to electoral purposes; while the Spaniards, more candid or more keen-sighted, think they find the key to it in the interested clamors of the filibuster party in and out of Congress.

(6) At the same time, in spite of excitations to the contrary, the respectable journals of Madrid are constant in the expression of belief in the peaceful and just professions of the President and the Government of the United States.

I have, etc., C. CUSHING.

[Appendix A, No. 786.—Translation.—Editorial article from La Epoca, Madrid, January 19, 1876.]

The New York papers lately received publish extracts from several journals of Madrid which have commented upon the message of General Grant, manifesting their surprise that these should attribute to him a spirit of hostility against Spain which, in their judgment, he is very far from holding. The desire of the first magistrate of the great American Republic and of his Cabinet is, on the contrary, to maintain the cordial relations which happily exist between the two peoples, avoiding whatever difficulties might compromise those relations for the future. In Madrid, say the New York journals, the signification of the message has not been well understood, for its general tone is conciliatory and friendly.

In this sense we ourselves construed it on examination, and the facts have since come to show the exactness of our appreciations. President Grant has to satisfy the exigencies of a certain group, not very numerous, but excitable in the extreme, which sympathizes with the Cuban insurgents, and whose opposition might run counter to his aspirations to the third Presidency of the Republic; and, nevertheless, on examining that document with due attention, not a single phrase of encouragement for them can be found in it. The hopes of obtaining the declaration of belligerence in favor of the rebels of the Managua are completely dispelled; there is nothing in the message which can be construed as a menace nor inspire fears of the most remote danger, and the idea of European intervention in the affairs of Cuba, vaguely formulated, has had no other object than to silence to a certain extent the exigencies we have mentioned, without the Government of Washington showing much zeal in sustaining the idea. Such a project may be regarded as a failure. It is so, assuredly, after receiving from the Governments of Europe communications wherein they refer to it with marked indifference and do not show themselves disposed to second it.

The change of attitude which is observable in the North American press reveals the tendency which dominates in the country, openly contrary, not merely to war, but to any solution which would make of independent Cuba a new Santo Domingo. It is very well known there that upon the separation of the Great Antilla from the mother country, it would fall under the brutal dominion of that crowd of bandits and incendiaries who mark their raids by leaving behind them heaps of ruins; and the United States, which keep up such important mercantile transactions with that Spanish province, would be the first to suffer the evil consequences of the separation. The interest of commerce, which prevails in all the acts of the American Government, demands that Cuba should be what it was before the present destructive insurrection, and that its wealth, which has been such a source of profit to the Great Republic, should increase. This can not be obtained without restoring tranquillity under the shadow of the Spanish flag, and it will be obtained, cost what it may, by the patriotic effort of the whole nation, resolved to maintain its integrity and regain its greatness..

Thus, doubtless, is the matter understood by the North American Government and people, whose attitude is day by day more strongly marked in favor of our country. The communications of the minister of foreign affairs in Washington, and the friendly spirit which reigns in the conferences of his representatives in Madrid, remove all fear of future complications, which can only have existed in the imagination of the laborantes and their sympathizers.

———

[Appendix B, No. 786.—Translation.—Editorial paragraph from La Epoca, Madrid, January 2C, 1876

We are informed from Paris, on the 15th, that the correspondence from New York in the English and German press is occupied with the American note addressed to the Powers concerning the question of Cuba.

All are unanimous in roundly denying that the United States entertains any intention, even remote, of intervening directly in Cuba.

The correspondent of the Times supposes that the note has for its cause the impatience to which the prolongation of a struggle which causes serious injuries to commerce gives rise in the United States.

The correspondent of the Frankfort Gazette asserts that the American Chambers will in no case give their approbation to an intervention in Cuba, and conjectures that nothing more than a fresh maneuver of the Grant party is to be seen in this note.

The Paris Journal sums up these comments in a paragraph of its bulletin, deducting as a consequence that the note is contrary to all diplomatic traditions of the Union, since it consults the powers about a question which only interests Spain, Mexico, and England. It adds that the only thing to be seen in it is an attempt on the part of Grant to make profit of this question in favor of his third reelection.

We have already said yesterday that our own news was entirely tranquilizing; that in the Cabinet of the United States the best disposition prevails, and that to this result have contributed the loyal, and at the same time dignified explanations of our Government, as well as the knowledge that the commerce of the United States has much more to gain under the possession of Cuba by Spain than by means of reckless schemes otherwise arising. To such a point does one of our friends in New York carry his assurances that, in a recent letter, he announced to us the possibility that the American Cabinet itself would take upon itself the responsibility of guaranteeing to Spain the possession of her Antillas, joining to this new commercial ties.

———

Mr. Fish to Mr. Cushing.

No. 301.]   DEPARTMENT OF STATE,
                    Washington, January 25, 1876.

SIR: The German minister, Mr. Schlözer, called to-day, and I give the substance of the conversation which took place between him and myself.

He said that he was instructed by the minister of foreign affairs to express thanks for the friendly communication which was made to the

German Government of the instruction to Mr. Cushing, referring to that of November 5, 1875, No. 266, and to state that they feel the justice of our complaint and appreciate the moderation of our conduct; that German interests suffer in the interruption of commerce resulting from the condition of affairs in Cuba, and that her citizens have also sustained wrongs, but that she does not feel disposed at present to take any decided steps.

I remarked that Mr. von Bülow had given our chargé d'affaires to understand that their minister in Madrid would be instructed to represent to the Spanish Government that in the opinion of Germany the United States was justified in her complaint and in the wish for an early termination of the conflict in Cuba.

Mr. Schlözer's reply was equivocal. He answered: "Oh, yes; but you know in these matters the Governments of Europe like to act in concert."

I answered that this was the object which induced us to communicate with the great powers simultaneously, believing that they would feel, as we understood Mr. von Bülow to have expressed himself, the fairness of our position, and believing that a simultaneous expression to that effect could not fail to exercise a powerful influence in inducing Spain to appreciate the necessity of bringing to a termination a war which had lasted for more than seven years, without any apparent approach to a result, and which was now threatening the destruction of the producing capacity of the island.

He inquired whether I could tell him the course which Great Britain proposed to take.

I answered that I supposed that Great Britain would communicate with Germany if she wished to know the views she had of the matter; that I did not undertake to express them for her, but I believed that she recognized the justice and moderation of our position, and the importance of an early termination of the conflict.

I called attention to the fact that we neither sought nor desired any physical force or pressure, but simply the moral influence of concurrence of opinion as to the protraction of the contest.

He assured me his Government agreed with us, but I could obtain from him no intimation that it was intended to inform Spain that such was the fact.

As this seems to place Germany in a different attitude from that indicated in Mr. Bülow's conversation with Mr. Fish (as communicated to you in my No. 286), it seems proper to make known to you the substance of the interview.

I am, etc., HAMILTON FISH.

Mr. Cushing to Mr. Fish.

No. 794.]   LEGATION OF THE UNITED STATES,
Madrid, January 28, 1876.

SIR: I annex four or five items which appear in the Correspondencia, numbered 1 to 4.

I am not sure what the exact meaning is of Nos. 1 and 2, but transmit them as they stand.

I have, etc., C. CUSHING.

[Appendix A, No 794.—Translation.—Sundry items from La Correspondencia.]

No. 1.

A telegram from Washington was received last night at the ministry of state denying that the note had been addressed to the Spanish Government, of which the newspapers have spoken, and which was supposed to have been communicated to the
other European powers.

No. 2.

[Telegram.]

VIENNA, *January 26.*

The ministry of state has asked confidentially of the American minister at this
court a copy of Mr. Fish's circular referring to the affairs of Cuba. The representative of the United States, after reflection, has refused, for which reason it is believed
possible, later on, that a new American note will be presented.

No. 3.

From January 1, 1875, up to January 21, 1876, there have been embarked for the
army of the island of Cuba 28,445 soldiers in 43 expeditions. This cipher proves all
we have said on different occasions with respect to the zeal and activity displayed by
the respective departments of the ministry of war, in order to endow the army of
Cuba with the forces needed to put down the insurrection.

No. 5.

The Times of the 24th instant, referring to the note of the American minister, Mr.
Fish, says:
" We are sure that Lord Derby and the ministers of the other powers, will reply
courteously to the invitation of Mr. Fish; but the question of knowing whether we
ought to intervene between Spain and her rebellious colony is much less evident.
It is not probable we shall do more than give a simple counsel, in case we go so far
as to give any, unless it be that our honor and our interests would suffer; for the
complaints which have any real foundation are the business of Spain alone.
"Nevertheless, it is possible that the powers may take part in a convention, which,
guarding the honor of Spain, shall terminate the question of Cuba."

Mr. Cushing to Mr. Fish.

No. 799.] LEGATION OF THE UNITED STATES,
Madrid, January 31, 1876.

SIR: In continuance of the purpose of transmitting to you from time
to time newspaper paragraphs indicative of public opinion respecting,
especially, the question of intervention, translation is annexed of an
article of La Patria, which is supposed to express views of the minister
of gobernacion, Mr. Romero y Robledo, lately married to a daughter of
D. Julian Zulueta.

The journals of Madrid abound with discussions of the supposed electoral prominence of the religious question in the United States.

Several of them also are occupied with examination of the condition
and fortunes of our Indians, with appreciations to our prejudice, drawn
from the book of Mr. Pumpelly.

I have, etc., C. CUSHING.

[Appendix A, No. 799.—Translation.—Extract from La Patria of January 29, 1876.]

* * * * * *

The English journal (the Times) doubts whether its Government will go so far as
to interfere in our affairs in the way the Cabinet of Washington seeks, but at the
same time it says that the powers may aid in forming a compromise which may save
the honor of Spain while terminating the Cuban question.

This, after all, is no other than a friendly intervention, which reveals the good spirit wherewith the English people is animated with respect to Spain, but we do not know to what extent our Government would conform to the intervention of the powers, provoked by that of Washington, in order to bring about the settlement of the affairs of our country in Cuba—a settlement which pertains solely and exclusively to ourselves.

At any rate, it is needful that the exaggerated pretensions of the North Americans should receive a corrective on the part of our Government, and we doubt not that it will receive it, within the bounds of dignity and decorum befitting a nation which, in the settlement of affairs which are its own, and exclusively its own, can not permit interferences founded in strange captiousnesses and in imaginary dangers and prejudices.

Mr. Cushing to Mr. Fish.

No. 804.]   LEGATION OF THE UNITED STATES,
Madrid, February 5, 1876.

SIR: I annex, in translation, extracts of a notable editorial article of the Política respecting the present relations of the United States and Spain.

I have, etc.,   C. CUSHING.

[Appendix A, No. 804 —Extracts translated.—Leading editorial from La Política, Madrid, February 4, 1876]

AMERICAN AFFAIRS.

The notices which the transatlantic cable has brought to us with respect to the political spirit which reigns in the United States with reference to the question of Cuba are too serious to permit of their not being taken up by the Spanish press, the duty of which is to watch over and defend our interests on the other side of the ocean. The field of politics is a vast chess board, where, from the king to the pawn, not a move can be made without affecting in a greater or less degree the situation of all the other pieces. Thus it is that the agitation aroused in the United States with respect to the political affairs of Cuba, which, it would seem, ought merely to be confined to the United States and to Spain, has taken such a turn that to-day all the principal powers of Europe are playing a part in this affair. Can the Spanish press, therefore, remain meanwhile indifferent and silent? We think not.

What is the matter?

The matter is that the Government of the United States, whose President, Mr. Grant, had already announced in his last message another special one on the Cuban policy, has passed to its representatives in Europe a note, to the end that, without leaving a copy of it, it may be read to the European ministers of foreign affairs. The object of the note has doubtless been to enable the Cabinet of Washington to discover indirectly the impression which would be produced by its interference, direct or indirect, in the relations of Spain with her Antillean province; but even though this note may have merely been a pilot balloon to get the drift of European sentiment it has for that reason none the less attracted the attention of political men.

We do not know whether this reserved communication to the European nations will receive anything else than a purely polite and diplomatic welcome, but what is very probable, in our opinion, is that none of them is disposed to accept an active part in an enterprise having for its object to exert upon Spain a pressure which could be interpreted as a minatory act.

We do not doubt that the sensible party of the United States would see with satisfaction the termination of the Cuban conflict, out of respect for the laws of humanity; but who better than that same North American Republic could have prevented the duration of that sanguinary war by simply complying with and causing its subordinates to comply with the laws which prohibit the sending of resources, arms, and munitions to an insurrection born in the bosom of a friendly power? For, if the custom-houses of New York, of Charleston, of Savannah, Mobile, and New Orleans, in fulfillment of existing laws, had detained the filibuster ships laden with arms and munitions for the insurgents and thus aiding in warfare against a friendly power—if they had prevented these violations of international right—then but a brief time would have passed before the insurrection, which had its origin on the banks of the Yara, had succumbed, without having so much prolonged its existence, or having caused such disasters, or having counted so many victims. And, if this be an evident and palpable fact, how is it that the United States to-day recall the name of humanity, and to what result do the judgments of humanity lead when invoked by the nation which might have arrested the career of the evils which it to-day recognizes?

Nearly eight years have passed by, and the mother country has had not merely to meet the serious difficulties which follow in the train of a reckless insurrection, but it has also had to sustain a hand-to-hand struggle because of the conflicts excited against Spain by permanent elements in the American Union which sympathize with the Cuban insurrection. And when all the combustibles have been accumulated for a conflagration, and the blaze has been kept knowingly stirred up, it is a rare sight to see those who have done all this lamenting the ravages of that fire, shrinking appalled from its horrors, and clamoring before Europe for the rights of humanity.

It is not that we ourselves fail to lament the horrors which, there as elsewhere, are involved in civil war. We have valiantly condemned acts which have taken place in the island, but of which acts we everywhere find like examples, even in the civil war of the United States. We appeal to the families of the Confederate States during the titanic contest between the States of the North and of the South of the American Union to tell us whether we are, or are not, right?

And if, from the point of view of humanity, we do not recognize that the United States have either the right or the opportunity to take the initiative which they have taken in the Cuban question, still less could we concede it to them if they appeal to the resource of supposing that the Cuban war affects their commerce. The North Americans are intelligent men in questions of figures and statistical calculations, and they know that the commercial relations between the United States and Cuba have increased during these last eight years in spite of the war; and, therefore, the excuse that the war affects their commercial interests can not serve for their intervention. There is no need of our reproducing the statistical data which demonstrate the increase of commerce between the Island of Cuba and the United States during the Cuban war, because they are data known to all the world, and which will easily be found by the North American dailies.

What remains besides that which has been set forth to serve as a support to the United States in order to pretend to the direct or indirect intervention which they propose? In our conception, it has for its basis no other thing than the eternal tendency which, from beginning of the century and from one motive or another, has been ever manifested by the partisans of the Monroe doctrine—a policy which served to rend from Mexico the greater part of her territory; a policy which has ever sought to deprive Spain of the brightest jewel of her crown, of the jewel which symbolizes a world of memories for the nation which discovered America.

*   *   *   *   *   *   *

The notes of Mr. Henry Clay to Mr. Everett in 1825, to the end that Spain should conclude the wars of Mexico and Colombia for the sake of humanity; subsequently those of Mr. Buchanan to Mr. Saunders, minister in Madrid, for the purchase of Cuba for one hundred millions of dollars, recommending him to get it as cheap as possible; the mission of Mr. Soulé; the Ostende conference; the refusal of the United States to subscribe the compromise with England and France to guarantee to Spain the possession of the Island of Cuba, and a thousand other antecedents which we might evoke, if the scope of this article permitted us to do so, are the key to explain this stroke of humanity with which the United States present themselves before Europe, soliciting its moral cooperation to end the war in Cuba.

The Government must understand it thus, as will Mr. Canovas del Costillo and Mr. Calderon y Collantes, both eminent statesmen of Spain, and profoundly acquainted with the North American policy, and they will doubtless have presented before the courts of Europe the true aspect of the Cuban question; and we do not entertain the least doubt of the support which our Government will receive, sustaining its dignity and its rights.

But, at any rate, what is undoubtedly indispensable as a measure of salvation is that this insensate insurrection in Cuba, which gives rise to so many conflicts, be terminated as soon as possible. The Carlist war is already dominated, and if the 30,000 soldiers who have recently crossed the Atlantic be not enough to pacify the island let there be speedily sent as many more as may be necessary in order to obtain that object, and let the reforms be made which ought to be introduced for the purpose of bettering the financial state of the island and rendering the operations of the campaign more effective.

Mr. Fish to Mr. Cushing.

No. 311.]
DEPARTMENT OF STATE,
Washington, February 9, 1876.

SIR: Your dispatch No. 779, of the 17th ultimo, has been received. It relates to the continued comments of the public journals in reference to certain observations on Cuba imputed to the President and Secretary of State, and incloses an article from La Epoca in regard thereto.

In reply I have to state that while the remarks attributed to the President and Secretary of State in the article from La Epoca above referred to may not be very far from what they might be inclined to have said, newspaper reports of interviews or of attributed opinions or speeches are not to be relied upon. In this country their general value, or rather want of value, is understood.

I am, etc.,
HAMILTON FISH.

Mr. Cushing to Mr. Fish.

No. 828.]
LEGATION OF THE UNITED STATES,
Madrid, February 14, 1876.

SIR: In my interview with the minister of state of the 12th, the conversation passed at length naturally to the question of our intervention in Cuba.

I observe, by way of preface, that the intervention of the great powers in Turkey is, of course, the subject of universal interest in Madrid, the more so as the Spaniards regard it in the light of its analogies with the suggested possible intervention of the United States in the affairs of Cuba.

I said to Mr. Calderon y Collantes that, approaching, as now, the conclusion of the various special questions at issue between the two Governments, it might be my duty at an early day to communicate with him on the larger and more purely political question of the general state of Cuba.

He replied that he had already addressed to Mr. Mantilla a "memorandum" setting forth the views of the King's Government on the subject, in opposition to the suggested intervention, with instructions to read the same to you, or, if you desired, to deliver to you a copy; that the ministers of Spain at other courts had received copies for the purpose of reading the same to the respective Governments, as in the case of your note to me of the 5th of November, and that he trusted this document would satisfy you of the inconvenience of the idea of intervention.

Parenthetically, let me note that in the newspapers of to-day appears a telegram from Paris in the following terms:

The Spanish memorandum on the subject of Cuba has been received in several courts of Europe. Various periodicals give extracts therefrom. It is written skillfully, and has produced an excellent impression.

Returning to Mr. Calderon y Collantes, he said there was no difficulty on the part of the Spanish Government in the introduction of all practicable reforms in the organization or administration of Cuba, including emancipation, which it was resolved to do, with or without any friendly suggestion on the part of the United States; that, on the contrary, the whole difficulty lies with the rebels and the impracticable Cuban emigrants in Paris and New York, who obstinately repel even the idea of autonomic institutions in Cuba like those of Canada and other colonies of Great Britain, and thus leave to Spain no possible means of action but force.

He concluded from these premises that it was not Spain to whom pressure needed to be applied in order to put an end to the present calamatous state of things, but the rebels in arms and their sympathizers and pretended directors abroad; that while in the matter of Turkey the mediating allies in taking the step of suggesting reforms in the administration of Bosnia and Herzegovina admitted the consequent duty of taking a second step, that of exerting their influence to induce the rebels to cease from rebellion, the United States appeared to stop at the first step, that of assuming a menacing attitude toward Spain.

I replied that he might rest assured of the truth and sincerity of the repeated assurances of my Government, repelling all suggestion of hostile purpose, avowing, on the contrary, the most friendly ones, and anxious only to see the end of a warfare of desolation and bloodshed in a possession contiguous to our shores, and socially and commercially in the closest relation with us, so as to render the actual state of things intolerable to us, and that the subject would be reverted to by me again at an early day in a more deliberate manner.

I may here observe in passing that the concentration of our ships of war at Port Royal impresses the Spaniards as a menace against Spain. They say: We have not made any naval demonstrations in the waters of the Antilles; we have done nothing to call for defensive preparations on the part of the United States, and we are unable to account for these naval preparations of theirs, unless intended for the invasion of Cuba in aid of the insurgents, in imitation of the action of Navarino.

Their suspicions in this respect stand greatly in the way of mere friendly diplomatic negotiation in the sense of mediation.

Now, as to the naked question of intervention or mediation in Cuba, the only foreign minister here who speaks to me in a helpful spirit is Mr. Layard. We have an appointment for some day this week to consider and determine how far his instructions enable him to support me; in other words, up to what point in this direction the United States may count on the support of Great Britain.

I have no information on this point later than General Schenck's report by telegraph of December 2, on the subject of his interview of that date with Lord Derby, wherein reservations of moment are made by the latter, not only as to the object and aim of intercession, but also as to the definite conclusions of the British Government.

I may remark that we stand in no need of the good offices of other Governments in the matter of our private griefs; on the contrary, my colleagues think that in this respect we are more favored than they by this Government.

The critical question is, How far any of them will go with us in the direction of intervention, if that be repelled by Spain.

As to this, it will be in my power to write to you in the course of a few days.

  I have, etc.,   C. CUSHING.

Mr. Fish to Mr. Cushing.

No. 315.]   DEPARTMENT OF STATE,
                              Washington, February 16, 1876.

SIR: Referring to previous correspondence on the subject, I have now to inclose herewith, for your information, an extract of a dispatch from General Schenck, at London, a copy of two dispatches from Mr. Davis, at Berlin, and of one from Mr. Hitt, the chargé d'affaires ad interim, at Paris, all of which relate to the Spanish question.

I am, etc.,

HAMILTON FISH.

Inclosures: Mr. Schenck to Mr. Fish, January 28, 1876, No. 862 (extract); Mr. Davis to Mr. Fish, January 22, 1876 (No. 249); Same to same, January 26, 1876 (No. 254); Mr. Hitt to Mr. Fish, January 23, 1876, No. 1279.

Mr. Cushing to Mr. Fish.

[Telegram.]

                                   MADRID, *February 18, 1876,*

FISH, *Secretary, Washington:*

Two more of the three remaining claims settled.

Question of judicial procedure goes on without controversy.

I begin to think mediatory arrangements between the two Governments by themselves, without aid from others, may not be impossible.

I need indication of bases.

CUSHING.

Mr. Cushing to Mr. Fish.

No. 835.]   LEGATION OF THE UNITED STATES,
                              Madrid, February 18, 1876.

SIR: Mr. Layard has made me acquainted with the negotiations for the pacification of Cuba in 1870, undertaken by him at the instance of Mr. Moret, in Madrid, and continued in concert with the United States, at Washington, on the basis of the submission of the insurgents, emancipation, radical reforms of colonial administration, and general amnesty, with exception of such compromised insurgent chiefs as should elect to leave the island in ships of war provided by the United States.

He seems to think this plan a feasible one in itself, but that neither that nor any other project of mediation would be seasonable now, nor until the Spanish Government shall have gone through with its present experimental winter campaign in Cuba.

Taking as a point of departure the conclusive exhibition in the President's message of the present unfitness of the insurgents in Cuba for independence, or even for a concession of belligerence, and also the explicit disavowal on the part of our Government of any wish or purpose to acquire Cuba—on these premises, the point, which most labors in the minds of the Spaniards, is the question as to the precise form of intervention contemplated by the United States.

In this connection there is much comment on the line of action pursued by the intervening powers in the matter of Bosnia and Herzegovina, as being the reverse of that pursued by the same powers in the matter of Greece. Seeing that in the latter case the demonstration of force was against Turkey and in favor of her rebels; while in the former, it is against the rebels and in favor of Turkey, as manifested by the concentration of Austrian troops in Croatia and of a fleet of the allies off Ragusa, in the avowed purpose of compelling the impenitent and persistent insurgents to accept the terms of reform arranged at Constantinople.

I have, etc.,
C. CUSHING.

Mr. Cushing to Mr. Fish.

No. 841.] LEGATION OF THE UNITED STATES,
Madrid, February 19, 1876.

SIR: I have received from the minister of state a copy of the memorandum addressed by him to the representatives of Spain in other countries, including the United States, on the subject of Cuba.

Copies have also been sent by him to the other foreign ministers in Madrid.

He informs me that Mr. Mantilla has been instructed to deliver to you a copy of the memorandum, which relieves me of the necessity of sending to you the copy in the possession of the legation.

I have, etc.
C. CUSHING.

Memorandum by Sr. Ferndo. Calderon y Collantes given by Antonio Mantilla to Mr. Fish, Secretary of State.

MINISTRY OF STATE, POLITICAL SECTION,
Madrid, February 3, 1876.

MOST EXCELLENT SIR: The great interest which Spain feels in the suppression of the insurrection which broke out years ago in the Island of Cuba renders it the imperative duty of Spain to rectify all the errors to which the rebels have undertaken to give currency, by rendering perfectly evident, by means of irrecusable facts, the real animus of that insurrection to-day, laying aside the consideration of its origin; by showing, moreover, what would be the consequences of any settlement of the question other than the complete triumph (which will be gained) of Spain over the insurgents; the real effect which that state of things has had and continues to have upon the wealth of the island, the commerce of the world, and, finally, the resources upon which Spain relies for the complete suppression of the insurrection, as, notwithstanding the civil war which has unfortunately raged on its soil for years, and the notorious contretemps which have been experienced of late years, and which have so greatly weakened the action of the Governments, it has not only succeeded in repressing it, but also in constantly diminishing its importance.

The first cry of insurrection was raised at Yara, an unimportant town situated in the eastern department of the island, on the 11th day of October, 1868, immediately after the receipt of the news of the revolution begun at Cadiz on the 17th of September, and consummated at Madrid on the 29th of the same month. The leaders of the rebellion availed themselves of the preparations which they had doubtless previously made, and of the favorable circumstance that the Government had not more than 7,500 troops all told on the island at the time, and that, too, for a territory peopled by 1,400,000 inhabitants, and having an area of 12,000 square miles, including the keys and the adjacent islands. The flag of the independence of the island was not raised at the outset, much less that of annexation to any other State. The only cries were, "Hurrah for Prim!" that general being there regarded as the leader of the Spanish revolution, and "Hurrah for the revolution!" Thus it was that many joined in the insurrection who, while really loving Spain, thought that the only object had in view was a political change, and, subsequently repenting when they became aware of the tendency which the enemies of the country were seeking to give to the movement, voluntarily took up arms against it. It may be admitted, however, in examining this question with the constant good faith and sincerity with which the Government of Her Majesty proposes to treat it in this memorandum, very soon after the outbreak of the revolution, it assumed a character of opposition to the domination of Spain, because such was the purpose of all who obtained control of the rebel forces and who directed their movements as leaders.

It can not be denied that the movement for secession subsequently carried away a part—certainly not the greater or the more important—of the white population of the island, especially the unreflecting and rash youth, who, misled by their own inexperience, imagined that it was possible to establish an independent and republican government in a country in which the African race formed by far the major portion of the population, and was still in a state of slavery. This secessionistic tendency was disguised under the apparent desire of securing reforms in the government of the island. It soon became apparent, however, that this was only a pretext. Reforms and franchises were granted which have never been excelled or even equaled by any nation, and the rights were introduced there which are proclaimed by the democracy of both Europe and America, which rights had never been enjoyed even by the Spaniards themselves. Far from showing any gratitude for such ample and important concessions, the rebels took advantage of them to foment the insurrection, which, far from diminishing, increased in extent and intensity. The struggle was still carried on, however, with a certain kind of regularity, and both parties respected the property which has since been so barbarously destroyed by the new insurgent leaders and soldiers.

All this is now changed, and of the leaders of the secession movement, Cespedes, the Agramontes, Cavada, Donato, Marmol, Castilla, Mola, the Betancourts, the Agüeros, Jesus del Sol, Bembeta, Salomé Hernandez, Marcono, Inclan, Goicuria, Rosas, and others, all of whom were Cubans, and really opposed to Spain, not one is now living. Of those who have succeeded them in the command not a single one is a Cuban. Máximo Gómez, the principal one, and Modesto Diaz, the next in importance, are Dominicans; Rulof is a Pole; the person known by the nickname of "el Inglesito" is an Englishman; and the rest, who are now few in number on account of the great diminution of the insurgent forces, are adventurers from various countries, without antecedents, and having no interest in the island. The same may be said of almost all the insurgents. Their forces now consist of negroes, mulattoes, Chinese, deserters from the battalions which were formed provisionally in Santo Domingo during our brief rule there, and a few independent bodies which were formed in Spain during the most disorderly period of the revolution, and which were largely composed of the most turbulent elements of the country, and it may be confidently asserted that there are to-day not more than eight hundred white natives of Cuba with arms in their hands in the insurgent ranks.

The consequence of this radical change in the elements of the insurrection is that what could be considered in the beginning as a struggle for independence has now assumed a character of ferocity and become a war of races and of devastation, which it was not before. Wherever a band of insurgents make their appearance, they steal and plunder everything that they can lay their hands on and set fire to the crops and buildings. The acts of this kind which have been committed there are all their work; not a single instance can be pointed to in which such a deed has been committed by our troops. The reason is that the insurgents carry on a savage warfare, without feeling any affection for the soil on which they tread, while our troops defend it as a possession of the mother country. It is easy to estimate what would be the consequences, not only for Spain but for the world at large, of the triumph (which is fortunately quite impossible) of such an insurrection. If such a triumph were once gained through the efforts of the negroes, mulattoes, and adventurers, the power would be in their hands; they would establish such a government as their capacity would permit, and, far from being the commencement of an era of peace for the island and of security for the interests of Europe and America, it would be the utter ruin of them all and the end of all civilization.

It would be a very great error to suppose that the Cuban emigrants in the United States, who only send good wishes and advice to the insurgents, taking good care to keep out of harm's way themselves, would be able to constitute a government. Those among them who were brave enough to face death on the battlefield have almost all either fallen or surrendered; and in every civil contest the party which triumphs through its own efforts, and by shedding its own blood, has a right to the chief authority, takes possession of it, and does not give it up to or divide it with those who have done nothing. It is evidently therefore to the interests of all Europe and America, and even of the white race in Cuba, not to encourage, either directly or indirectly, as they might sometimes do, against their own will, the insurrection in Cuba; it is to their interest that the insurrection should result in the triumph of Spain, which will be at once the triumph of law and civilization, and the only one that can offer solid guarantees to all interests and preserve the regular relations which should be maintained by civilized nations with all countries. Any other solution would be not only ineffective, but contrary to the true and well-understood interests of humanity and civilization. Even if the Government of Spain could, with a proper regard for its own dignity, enter into any other kind of arrangement, it would have no one to treat with, for no one could expect it to do so with the half-savage negroes and mulattoes, or with the Chinese, Dominicans, deserters, and adventurers, who are the only ones who hold the real power of the insurrection. The triumph of Spain would soon be followed by the judicious but total abolition

S. Doc. 231, pt 7——28

of slavery, which still exists in Cuba in spite of the sincere wishes of His Majesty's Government; it would insure the administrative reforms which have been offered to the island; it would open the door to the representation of the inhabitants in the Congress of Deputies; and finally, it would speedily bring to pass what will in vain be sought by other means.

Guaranties of the sincerity of these assertions, and of the firmness and resolution with which Spain would make them good, are to be found not only in the measures which have already been carried out in Puerto Rico, but also in those which, notwithstanding the insurrection, have been adopted for Cuba, by virtue of which more than one-third of those persons who were held as slaves have obtained their freedom. In Puerto Rico, which has remained faithful to the mother country, and where perfect order has prevailed, slavery ceased to exist several years ago. Those who were slaves are now freemen, and as such they make contracts with their former masters, and the most perfect harmony prevails between the two classes. That island will send its freely-elected senators and deputies to the next Cortes to represent it and to defend the rights and interests of that important province, which now differs in no respect from the other provinces of Spain. All this would have been accomplished in Cuba had it not been for this unjustifiable insurrection, which is a disgrace to civilization, and all will be established there when peace shall have been reestablished. The Government of His Majesty has made every effort to bring about this result, and there is no sacrifice that it has not made and is not willing to make in order to secure it.

In the midst of a formidable civil war, in which liberty and the conquests of modern civilization are hazarded, it has sent since the accession of His Majesty to the throne—that is to say, in one year—28,445 soldiers of all kinds, who would have been very serviceable to it could they have been used against the Carlist forces. When General Jovellar was asked for by public opinion as governor-general of the great Antilla, on account of the excellent record which he had left there before, His Majesty's Government did not hesitate to let him go, although it had for some time been intending to give him another important command in the peninsula; and if, as there is every reason to expect, the civil war is soon brought to an end in Spain, a new army will at once be sent to Cuba, which will speedily give the deathblow to the already expiring insurrection. Even without this His Majesty's Government has sufficient forces in the island to secure this result, although of course not so speedily. We have the following land and naval forces there, and I do not fear that the correctness of this list will be disputed:

Forty-five vessels of all classes, with a nominal force of 4,770 horses, 135 cannon, and 2,426 seamen; 55 battalions, 6 regiments of cavalry, 2 of artillery, 1 of light field troops, 1 company of naval mechanics, 3 regiments of civil guardsmen, 1 sanitary brigade, 1 battalion of engineers, 33 companies of skirmishers, 2 squadrons of dragoons, and 1 transport brigade, making altogether a total of 273 chiefs, 3,054 officers, 68,115 soldiers, 8,478 horses, 462 mules, and 42 pieces. Since the foregoing enumeration was made, moreover, 10,370 men have embarked for the island.

There are also the volunteer bodies, consisting of natives of the Peninsula and Cubans, amounting to upward of fifty thousand men. These last figures are official and irrecusable, and show what is the true spirit of the island and its adhesion to the mother country; for while the Cubans who are fighting for the insurrection are less than one thousand in number, those who have voluntarily taken up arms against it number more than forty thousand. There is one fact which may seem incomprehensible to those who have not carefully considered the matter and who are not familiar with the nature of the war in Cuba and the topographical characteristics of the territory in which it is carried on. I refer to the duration of the contest in spite of the disparity existing between the forces of the contending parties; and yet this fact is susceptible of an easy explanation, and numerous analogous instances in the history of nations may be adduced. For the very reason that the Cuban rebels are, for the most part, negroes and mulattoes, they do not experience the ordinary necessities of civilization. They are able to live in the jungles and deserts of the island, and thence fall upon estates and other property like birds of prey, pillaging and applying the torch of the incendiary. They live on the fruits of the country, such as the plaintain and others which grow spontaneously in that fertile soil. Salt, and hogs and other animals are so numerous that they are everywhere met with, and serve as food.

A single fact will suffice to convince anyone of the strength of this element as an aid to the insurrection. The Baracoa district, having an extent of 90 miles, had but 42 inhabitants, while there was about the same number in Las Tunas and the territory which separates the Mayari district from Guantánamo. The average number of inhabitants to the square geographical league throughout the island is 350. It is not, therefore, to be be wondered at that the insurgents should be able to sustain themselves as nomadic tribes in a country of such a character—uncultivated, almost a wilderness, extremely broken and mountainous, and covered with immense forests which can not even be set on fire by reason of their constant and extraordinary humidity. Thus it is that they have never been able to establish even the shadow of a government. If the insurgents were regular troops and carried on a civilized warfare, the contest would long since have been ended by two or three battles. The matter, however, becomes one of much greater difficulty when they avoid all fighting save from an ambuscade, and run and hide when they see our troops, in order to meet again in their lurking places when the danger is past.

It is thus seen why it has never been possible to entirely destroy the so-called palenques, or bands of fugitive negroes, who have fled from the estates, and who seek refuge in the aforesaid Baracoa district. Even when the island was in a state of profound peace, neither the battues of the inhabitants of the towns nor the pursuit of our troops could accomplish this.

Instances of the long duration of wars of this kind are neither new nor rare. To causes similar to those mentioned was due the fact that the United States, notwithstanding their immense resources and the enormous disparity which existed between the forces of the combatants, required more than double the time that the insurrection has lasted in Cuba to suppress the one in Florida. France too, with all her power, was many years in subduing the rebel tribes of Algeria; and scarcely is there a nation in the world that does not furnish similar instances. The effects of the insurrection, although deplorable, as the effects of an insurrection always are, have not sensibly diminished the wealth of the island; this is due to the fact that the insurgents have not been able to burn the many and rich estates of the western department, which is the most wealthy of all, both in point of population and production, as may be readily seen by glancing at the map of Cuba which accompanies this memorandum, and as is proved beyond all doubt by the following official and irrecusable data:

In the western department there were and still are—for, far from diminishing, their number has increased during the war—1,070 sugar estates, while in the central department there were but 102, and in the eastern 200. The quantity of sugar produced in the first-named department amounted to 500,000,000 kilograms, which quantity has also been increased, while that of the second only amounted to 17,000,000, and that of the third to 35,250,000 kilograms. The quantity of tobacco produced in the western department is 44,000 quintals, in the central department only 5,500, and in the eastern 252,000. It must be remembered that in the territory comprised between Pinar del Rio and Guanajay, in the first of those departments, the exquisite tobacco known as that of La Vuelta de Abajo is exclusively produced. The price of this tobacco is constantly increasing, and is much higher than that produced in the eastern department, which is a second-class article. The quantity of coffee produced in the western department amounts to 3,750,000 kilograms, that of the central department to 3,750, and that of the eastern to 5,000,000. Finally, the value of the cattle of all kinds in the western department is 2,000,000 pesetas, or $4,000,000; in the central and eastern departments, $1,000,000 each.

It is therefore seen that the real wealth and the bulk of the population of the Island of Cuba are in the western department, which has scarcely suffered at all from the insurrection, and which for the most part, has remained perfectly tranquil. But it is to be observed that the majority of the estates in the eastern department, situated near Santiago de Cuba and other towns, still remain unharmed, because, having been protected by our troops, it was impossible for the rebels to burn them, and the exportation of their products still goes on with the utmost regularity, because the railroad by which they are sent is held by our army, as is likewise the railway which connects Puerto Principe with the port of Nuevitas.

For these reasons and because the insurgents do not hold a single port in the whole island, foreign commerce, instead of suffering any diminution, has greatly increased since the outbreak of the insurrection, as is shown by the following statistical data, also official. This fact is due to the much greater production of the western department and to the increase in the value of its products. The amount of the receipts from customs in Cuba during the years stated is here given as follows:

Years.	Import duties.	Export duties	Other duties.	Total receipts.
				Reals.
1865				240,881,160
1866				225,185,180
1867				155,426,850
1868				146,697,190
1869				196,776,400
1870				264,066,090
1871				338,175,260
1872				377,330,140
1873	205,835,210	83,457,660	179,082,700	468,375,570
1874	200,792,830	75,930,660	166,825,220	443,548,710
1875	78,502,160	70,220,490	58,241,860	206,964,510

NOTE.—The receipts for 1875 are only for the first six months.

These figures furnish the best evidence that the general commerce of the world with the Island of Cuba has in no wise suffered, but that it has, on the contrary, increased since the insurrection began and during its prevalence. The greatest increase is observed in the trade of the island with the United States, with which country its commercial transactions are much more extensive than with any other. According to newspapers published in the United States, which keep aloof from politics and busy themselves exclusively with watching the progress and development of industry and commerce in all parts of the world, the commerce between the two countries has increased by more than one-third since the outbreak of the Cuban insurrection. Such testimony can be regarded with suspicion by no one.

It is true that while commerce in general has not suffered, some foreigners residing in Cuba have sustained serious losses. His Majesty's Government, however, which deeply laments this, has always done justice to all claims that have been presented to it, amply indemnifying the losers for the injuries suffered by them; and this is acknowledged by all foreign Governments in their high impartiality. The Government of Spain, with equal good faith, admits that the taxes which it has been necessary to impose in consequence of the insurrection are burdensome. Even in this respect, however, the Government of His Majesty will not only scrupulously observe its treaties with other nations, but it is conscientiously seeking the best means of lightening these burdens. In consequence of the insurrection, moreover, the property of various foreigners, real estate owners, and manufacturers in the island was embargoed, but these measures, which have never been approved by the present Government, will be immediately annulled, and all the embargoes which have been ordered as a war measure will be raised. To this effect the most positive instructions have been given to General Jovellar, the new Governor-General, which he will carry out with the good faith and energy which are characteristic of him in the cases of those who are really citizens of foreign countries.

With this statement of facts, your excellency will be able, in view of your experience and well-known talent, to enlighten the opinion of the country to whose Government you are accredited on the interesting subject which I have been discussing, and successfully to refute the misstatements which the filibusters have sought to circulate everywhere. Although this memorandum is designed only for your own information and guidance, you may read it to the minister of foreign affairs of the United States, and give him a copy of it, confidentially, if he desires it.

God guard, etc.

FERNDO. CALDERON Y COLLANTES.

Mr. Cushing to Mr. Fish.

[Telegram.]

MADRID, *February 21, 1876.*

FISH, *Secretary, Washington:*

My last telegram seems not to have been understood. I repeat, in different words.

I see prospect of possibility of mediatory arrangements if you can answer for the desperate men of the Cuban Junta, enemies of Spain, but worse enemies of the United States.

I need instructions as to reasonable bases of such possible arrangement. See private letter of this date.

CUSHING, *Minister.*

Mr. Cushing to Mr. Fish.

No. 849.]
LEGATION OF THE UNITED STATES,
Madrid, February 21, 1876.

SIR: It surprised me exceedingly to learn by your No. 288 that the idea had been conceived in London and transmitted thence to Washington of any delay on my part of action on your No. 266.

What occurred in this respect of erroneously supposed delay will be apparent on comparing my two dispatches, Nos. 692 and 703, in the light of the following explanations:

On the day of receiving your telegraphic instructions of November

27—that is, November 28—Mr. Calderon y Collantes and myself met at dinner at the palace.

I availed myself of that opportunity to request an interview at the earliest possible opportunity, which was fixed by Mr. Calderon y Collantes for the 30th, when copy of your note was delivered to him.

It was impossible for us to discuss your note then, because he is not sufficiently acquainted with English to have read it intelligently; nor, if he had been, was it desirable that he should have spoken on the hasty impressions of the moment.

My apprehension was lest some such hasty and ill-considered appreciation of your note should elicit expressions fatal to the continuance of peaceful relations. On reading or hearing read that note a minister might, if forced to pronounce on the moment, repel intervention; none certainly would invite or accept it, without consulting his colleagues and the King.

I therefore requested him to receive me again so soon as he should be able to have the note translated and to read and reflect upon it, and not to come to any conclusion on the subject until after such second interview, which was fixed for the 4th of December.

I regarded this arrangement as the best possible for us, nay, as the only one involving any probability of advantage.

Now, that necessary pause of three days is the delay of which Lord Derby speaks.

I think the use, or abuse, rather, made of it in London is very suggestive and significant.

Lord Derby, as reported by General Schenck, began by suggesting postponement of definite action in express words. He then proceeds to repel, in various forms of expression, the idea of any pressure—that is, intervention. He concluded with vague expression of "good offices."

Has he ever communicated to you the definite purpose, communication—and even conception—of which he expressly postponed?

I do not know. I presume not; or that if he has, it is not of a nature to serve us here, for if it were, you would have instructed me on the subject.

I do know that he has instructed Mr. Layard that it would be unseasonable and premature to think even of mediation until after Spain shall have made further efforts unsuccessfully to suppress by her own force the insurrection in Cuba.

I have great esteem and respect for Mr. Layard. We work together very well on specific questions of common concernment, such as Burriel and the procedure question. But he has his own official cares, which are sufficiently grave; more private claims than we, and two troublesome treaty questions, while we have but one. It is quite natural and proper that he should look primarily to the interests of his own Government.

You suggest further, in your No. 288, that the interview of the 4th of December "appears to have been confined to our particular griefs, and no allusion being made to the general question of the condition of Cuba as distinguished therefrom."

I do not so understand it. On recurring to the full report of that interview, in my No. 703, you will perceive that every word uttered by me was on that "general question" and the consequent complication. I said nothing of our "private griefs." It was Mr. Calderon y Collantes who introduced and dwelt upon that point, evidently evading the general question.

Was it convenient for me then and there to push him on the question of intervention? I thought not. The first great object of diplomatic tactics had been attained—that of avoiding rupture and preparing the ground for the continuance of negotiation.

Next, as to intervention. I supposed, erroneously it may be, that no pressure in that direction was to be undertaken by me in the first instance until it should be known whether we were to be supported or opposed by the powers. Why else invoke their moral support?

I knew on the 4th of December what Lord Derby had said, and to my mind it was anything but encouraging; and the result has justified that impression.

But the other powers had not then spoken, nor have they to this day spoken at Madrid in any sense of encouragement to us.

For instance, the Austrian minister is instructed against us; the German minister, from which quarter something might have been expected, declares that he has received no instructions on the general question (he is careful to remind me of this when we converse on the procedure question); and the British minister, as we have seen, is instructed that it is not yet time to mention even mediation to Spain.

Of course, it is impossible to force any of my colleagues to speak on the general subject; and they are all reserved and reticent regarding it, except when they are adverse.

It is my duty to tell you the truth in this respect, and the truth is that no foreign minister here is prepared to back us in saying to Spain: You must close up the war in Cuba immediately, or we will intervene to force a conclusion in our own way.

The question of intercession or mediation is different. Lord Derby despairs on that point; I do not.

The essential premises of mediation are reciprocal confidence and good will, with mutual interests.

The interests of Spain and of the United States in Cuba are identical. At present we derive great net benefits from it; she, none. The imminent destruction of its productiveness would be alike disastrous to her and to us.

. She is willing enough to confide in us if we will let her. The proof of that is to be found not in profession (although that we have), but in the analysis of the diplomatic relations of Spain with other powers, contained in previous dispatches. In fine, whatever causes of grief or jealousy she has against us, she has greater against others. Nevertheless, she is now anxious and suspicious with regard to the United States. She knows that thousands of bad Spaniards (called Cubans), having a holy horror of the smell of gunpowder, have fled to "snug harbor" in New York, Key West, and New Orleans, have been dedicating themselves there for years, by distribution of bonds, by speeches, newspapers, solicitations, exaggerated claims, violations of law, and in every other possible way, to the task of embroiling the two Governments in war, and are the efficient authors of all our troubles with her, directly or indirectly, including the tragedy of the *Virginius.*

I dread emigrant rebels. How fatal were the French emigrés to Prussia in the early years of the French Revolution! How frequently the Jacobites involved France in fruitless hostility with England! How the refugee Poles lured Napoleon I to his destruction by Russia, and refugee Mexicans Napoleon III to the commencement of his destruction in America! I do not yet forget the picture of the disastrous intrigues of the rebel emigrants of the Greek Republics, more prejudicial to their friends than to their enemies, as drawn by the masterly hand of Thucydides, or of those of the Italian Republics, so graphically described by Guicciardini and Machiavelli.

God forbid that these dishonored men, who prate of the independence of Cuba, without manliness or courage to fight for it, preferring the safer occupation of trading in bogus bonds and calumniating the President and yourself, should succeed in making our country the instrument of their rancorous hatred of their own country, Spain.

In this connection, be it remembered that the President's message asserts the absolute nonexistence in Cuba at the present time of the essential elements of an independent state, and thus proclaims this fact to the world.

Then, Spain is told every day, by leading newspapers of the United States, that the objects of our naval preparations is to force the hand of Congress and of the people by producing some casus belli for electoral purposes; and although nobody really believes what newspapers say, yet they have their effect in the propagation of mischievous irritations and dangerous suspicions, as so well exposed in the late remarkable speech of Prince Bismarck in the German Reichsrath.

I meet all these things as well as I may by pointing to the kindly assurances contained in your note of November 5, in the President's message, and in sundry special dispatches, such as your No. 281, notwithstanding their being dispatches of complaint against acts or omissions of the Spanish Government.

But the obstacles which thus far it has been impossible for me to get over are in the insolent assumption of the knots of Spanish traitors in New York and Paris, who presume not only to dictate to Spain, but also to the United States, and in the impracticable character of the Dominican chiefs of the insurgents in Cuba.

If you can answer for them, there is hope for peaceful and harmonious action between the two nations, to the end of peace, emancipation, and good government in Cuba, by the mediation of the United States, with or without the aid of Great Britain or Germany.

As for these European powers, suffer me to say, " Timeo Danaos et dona ferentes."

I have, etc.,

C. CUSHING.

Mr. Cushing to Mr. Fish.

No. 855.]

LEGATION OF THE UNITED STATES,
Madrid, February 28, 1876.

SIR: My No. 853, as being written for the special purpose of replying to the inquiry propounded in your No. 301 on the subject of the course followed here by Germany in the matter of our relations to Cuba, touched but incidentally on that of Russia.

On reflection, it seems to me convenient to be more explicit on this point.

The Russian minister here, Mr. Koudriaffsky, is in very infirm health and goes but little into society. I rarely have opportunity of meeting him except in special calls, given or received. On such occasions we talk together very cordially and freely. His intelligence and other qualities entitle him to much consideration. His relations to men and things you may infer from the fact that, for so many years, Russia has kept aloof from Spain, even under Queen Isabel, that she paid a pension to Don Carlos, and that she only changed her line of policy in these respects on the accession of Don Alfonso.

Your dispatch No. 298 of the 19th of January, communicating the tenor of the interview between Mr. Boker and Prince Gortchakoff, arrived here on the 9th instant.

The first time of my meeting the Russian minister thereafter was at the ministry of state, when he was suffering so much that, so far from attempting to speak to him on business, I could but voluntarily yield to him my turn, in order that he might be able as soon as possible to return to his own house, suggesting my intention to call on him at an early day when he should be in condition for conversation.

Subsequently he left his card with intimation that he should be glad to see me, and I called accordingly.

I found him very feeble, dozing in his armchair by the fire.

After a little miscellaneous conversation, I introduced the subject of our difficulties with Spain.

He said that he had supposed that the Spanish Government had satisfied all our claims, but that it seemed we had since presented some new ones.

I replied that we had not presented any claims, old or new, other than such as were comprehended in principle in previous general reclamations; but that a much more serious question remained pending, that of the unsuppressed insurrection in Cuba, which imposed on us embarrassments of the same nature as those which Russia and Austria suffered from the troubles in Turkey; and that I had hoped his Government would deem it advisable to make such representations to the Spanish Government as might hasten the peaceful settlement which the United States had in view (purposely employing, as near as possible, the introductory language of Mr. Boker in his interview with Prince Gortchakoff).

Mr. Koudriaffsky replied that he had not received instructions to that effect; that he had information of the interview of Mr. Boker with Prince Gortchakoff, and understood it had for its subject the reclamations of the United States, and no more; that he had heard of your note of November 5, but had never seen it, nor, so far as he knew, had his Government.

I then explained to him that the note consisted of two parts, one enumerating our unsatisfied reclamations, and the other setting forth the exigency of a speedy conclusion of the existing hostilities in Cuba, so prejudicial alike to Cuba, to Spain, and to the United States.

He repeated that, having no instructions on the subject, he therefore had not taken any interest in it.

I could not with propriety urge the matter any further, and proceeded to converse with him on other topics of secondary political interest, especially to answer particular inquiries of his concerning Alaska and its metallic productions, and concerning the condition of our Indians.

Let me now revert to the remarks of Prince Gortchakoff to Mr. Boker, and collate them with what was said to me by Mr. Koudriaffsky.

It is true, as Prince Gortchakoff says, that there is little relation of interests or intercourse of any kind between Russia and Spain, except of a dynastic or nobiliary character.

It is not true, as he says, that the past alienation of Russia from Spain deprives the former of present influence at Madrid, as you may judge from the efforts of the Spanish Government to conciliate that of Russia, of which you have been informed by me from time to time.

He does not encourage the United States to proceed to "serious measures" in the present condition of Spain, but the contrary.

He spontaneously offered good offices and friendly advice, "if this course should be in accordance with the wishes of the Emperor;" not a very satisfactory reservation.

He is profuse in the utterance of courtier expressions, and in profes sions of sympathy with the United States; all which results in his advising Mr. Koudriaffsky that we are but pushing private claims here, with which Russia has no concernment.

There, in my opinion, crops out a reminiscence of the Perkins claim and of Mr. Catacazy.

Permit me, before leaving this unwelcome subject, to submit some relative suggestions.

All the flattering and sympathetic utterances of Prince Gortchakoff sound hollow to my ear. Russia can have no ties of sympathy with us, political, religious, or commercial. She had very close ties to attach her to us until twenty-five years ago, down to which time we were her best customers, and almost her sole channel of supply for the commodities of the West Indies, but our prohibitory duties on iron and hemp have cut off that connection, so profitable to both of us, and our chief commercial relation now is one of repulsion, that of rivals in the production of wheat for the consumption of Europe.

Moreover, she doubts now, since the extension of her power in the seas of Japan, whether she did wisely in ceding to us the mainland, and especially the islands, of Alaska.

In my judgment, therefore, the best that we can hope from Russia in the present question is indifference, and we have cause to fear, in the last resort, tendencies of rapprochement to Spain rather than to the United States.

I observe in your circular to Mr. Boker (as well as to others) that the idea of the spontaneous abandonment by Spain of the contest in Cuba is presented in more distinct terms than it is in the note of November or in the message.

Now, it is self-evident that Spain will not spontaneously abandon Cuba.

The other alternatives presented are, agreement between the parties in the contest, or leaving Spain to terminate the contest by force.

I can not judge from the report of Mr. Boker's interview with Prince Gortchakoff whether these three alternative suppositions were each distinctly represented to him by Mr. Boker; but certainly nothing appears in the remarks of Prince Gortchakoff to show that, if Spain refuses to spontaneously abandon the contest (as she certainly will), and if she is unable (however willing she may be) to end the contest by any agreement with the insurgents or their professed chiefs in New York—and if nothing remains for her but to continue to endeavor to exterminate the contest by force, and if the United States intervene to defeat her endeavors in that respect, which is war—I say, nothing appears in the report to show that Russia would countenance such extreme action on the part of the United States.

One thing more. All the great powers are preoccupied with the question of Turkey. France looks on with angry consciousness of her incapacity to act a first part in the question, and while dissatisfied with the substitution of the influence of Great Britain in Egypt for her own, yet feels inclined, nevertheless, for want of other resources, to lean on Great Britain, while anxiously deferring to Russia. Meanwhile the three Emperors have undertaken the task of nominal intervention, reduced almost to mere intercession, in the internal affairs of Turkey, in which Great Britain, after securing control of the Suez Canal without so much as saying "by your leave" to the other powers, acquiesces in the present initiatory step, reserving to herself perfect freedom of action respecting all further incidents in the East.

Now, what is the present step, in which alone all the powers are of accord?

The brief but significant response of the Porte is, it seems to me, a remarkable exhibition of statemanship. It says, in effect, to the allies: "You advise us, in the interest of peace, to introduce certain specified reforms of administration in our discontented provinces. We had already determined to do not only so much, but even much more; we cheerfully take your advice therefore, but we do so in the express understanding that you, Russia; that you, Austria, are to cease to allow your subjects or protégés to aid our rebels in Bosnia and Herzegovina; that you are to use all your moral authority at least to induce those rebels to lay down their arms and accept the measures of reform graciously granted by the Sultan."

Such are the conditions of a practical friendly intervention which are now present to everybody's mind in Madrid, to wit, an agreement between the Porte and its rebel subjects by means of the mediation and moral influence of the allies on condition of certain administrative reforms conceded by the Porte.

The sympathies, the sentimental emotions, the reminiscences of frontier disturbances, the contingent ambitions of Russia and Austria with respect to the rebel subjects of the Porte are far stronger than ours on the side of Cuba. And yet those powers recognize the duty of applying pressure in the sense of peace equally to the rebels as to the Porte.

It is the third of the alternatives suggested in your circular instruction, namely, agreement between the parties to the contest in Cuba. In such a plan, if promoted by us, the great powers would go with us, while if we undertake to force Spain to abandon Cuba, which is hostilities at least, if not formal war, we shall have all the powers exerting their moral authority (if not more) in behalf of Spain.

I have, etc.,

C. CUSHING.

Mr. Fish to Mr. Cushing.

No. 323.]   DEPARTMENT OF STATE,
Washington, March 1, 1876.

SIR: I have laid before the President your No. 777, under date of the 16th of January, and he received with sincere gratification the expressions of Mr. Calderon y Collantes of the earnest desire of the Government of Don Alfonso in the sense of peace, good government, and liberty in Cuba, and that his Government freely admitted the political expediency and necessity of abandoning the old colonial system and of promptly consummating the emancipation of the slaves in that island.

The President feels that these expressions bring the two Governments in accord in their views and wishes on these points.

He accepts, also, the earnest expression of consciousness on the part of Spain that the United States and Spain are by commercial ties inseparably associated in the question of the tranquillity and prosperity of Cuba.

Nature has placed that island in our immediate neighborhood, and has established the foundations of the relations of business, commerce, and material interest, which Spain thus recognizes.

Discovery and long occupation have made the island a possession of Spain, and the United States has no desire to disturb the relations which result therefrom. These positions being reciprocally recognized, there should be no cause for serious disagreement, or for any mistrust between the two powers with regard to the future of the island, or in reference to the measures to be adopted to bring about a return of peace and prosperity.

Part of the territory of the one power, it is the seat of immense trade for the other. The interests of both in its welfare, its peace, and its good government are equal but not identical. The people of both Governments resort thither, associate together, and, with the natives of the island, invest their means, and are alike anxious for its best interests. It behooves the two Governments, therefore, each in the direction and in the proportion of its respective but different relations, to seek its peace, to advance its welfare, and to assist toward its prosperity.

Having a common desire, with similar interests to protect and equivalent advantages to gain from an improvement in its condition, the Government of the United States has been ready to effectually cooperate with or aid the government of His Majesty in securing these results, and the earnest efforts of the President in that direction are still ready to be called into exercise.

In considering the means to this end he desires to propose none but those of friendly suggestion and, if it be practicable, of friendly advice to those who are in resistance in Cuba.

He finds in the statement reported by you as made by Mr. Calderon y Collantes that his Government freely admits the political expediency and necessity of abandoning the old colonial system of administration in Cuba, an agreement with the opinion expressed in a recent instruction to you (No. 266, under date of 5th of November, 1875), which avoids any necessity of reference to the causes which have led to the insurrection of Yara, and which have prevented its suppression.

The admission that the old colonial system is inadequate to the government of a people of a million and a half, in the present age, imposes upon the parent Government the urgent necessity of the early formation of another system to take the place of that which has outlived its capacity and adaptation to the happiness and welfare of those for whose happiness and welfare government alone exists. In the present case the President is of opinion that it belongs to the enlightened wisdom of the Government of Spain without delay to inaugurate this new system, suited to the more advanced opinions of modern civilization and more consonant with the prevailing opinion of enlarged powers of local self-government.

But Mr. Calderon y Collantes, as you inform me, was pleased to invite a frank statement concerning the precise thing which the United States would advise or wish Spain to do, adding that he could not conceive that anything unjust or impracticable would be proposed. In this last expression he does no more than justice to the desire and the wishes of the United States. In response therefore to the suggestion of the distinguished minister of state and in full accord with the feelings and frankness which led him to invite expression on the part of this Government, I venture to submit some views which the President desires to bring to his consideration.

In so doing, it would be unjust both to the minister of state and to the United States if what is to be said were other than a plain and frank statement of the views of the President. At the same time, if in the reference which may be herein made to any relations or incidents there be found ought to excite any sensibilities, he desires in advance to assure His Majesty's Government that it will be deeply regretted, and that no word will be said other than with the view to a full consideration of the real and actual condition of the question, with which he believes His Majesty's Government as well as himself is endeavoring to deal, in the interests of both nations, and for the peace, prosperity, and development of the wealth and industry of the Island of Cuba.

In the first place, the President desires emphatically to disabuse the mind of the Government and people of Spain of the existence of any desire on the part of the Government of the United States for the acquisition of Cuba or for its annexation, directly or indirectly, to the possessions of this country. Whatever suspicions of such desire may heretofore have been entertained should be rejected to enable Spain to do justice to the motives, policy, and feelings of the United States. Whatever grounds may be supposed to have existed in the past evincing such desire, there are at this time no considerations, moral, social, political, or financial, which are regarded by the President as making the acquisition of Cuba by the United States either desirable or convenient.

The President, moreover, desires in an equally emphatic manner to express the desire of the United States to maintain a firm, solid, and enduring peace with Spain, and to remove every disturbing question which embarrasses or which can threaten the relations of the two countries.

With these premises, I proceed to respond to Mr. Calderon y Collantes's request for a frank statement of what the United States would advise or wish Spain to do with regard to Cuba. You will, in the name of the President, state that his earnest wish is:

First. The mutual and reciprocal observance of treaty obligations, and a full, friendly, and liberal understanding and interpretation of all doubtful treaty provisions, wherever doubt or question may exist.

Second. Peace, order, and good government in Cuba, which involves prompt and effective measures to restore peace, and the establishment of a government suited to the spirit and necessities of the age; liberal in its provisions, wherein justice can be meted out to all alike, according to defined and well-established provisions.

Third. Gradual but effectual emancipation of the slaves.

Fourth. Improvement of commercial facilities and the removal of the obstructions now existing in the way of trade and commerce.

Concerning the first point the President at this time does not desire to make particular reference to questions which alone concern individual grievances of the United States or its citizens.

These have already been placed fully before the minister of state, and it is hoped that negotiations now in progress will dispose of all such questions in a manner satisfactory and beneficial to both parties.

He therefore contents himself with the expression of this hope, and is of opinion, if irreconcilable constructions be found, or if the provisions of existing treaties be too indefinite or not sufficiently comprehensive, that these difficulties may hereafter be removed by a new and more explicit convention.

Concerning the second point, providing for the return of peace, the establishment of order and good government in Cuba, the President recognizes that the successive governments which have existed in Spain since the breaking out of the insurrection and the different ministers who have, from time to time, directed the affairs of state have been unanimous in their expression of desire to restore peace and create reforms in Cuba.

That the system under which Cuba has been governed has become antiquated, unsuited to her condition, calculated to excite opposition and hostility, and attended by acts of oppression and wrong to her people and of injury to all having relations with her appears to be fully admitted, and is commented upon and proclaimed continually both in Spain and Cuba.

Upon many occasions when these matters have been discussed, the facts have been frankly admitted, and the assurance given that when the rebellion had been crushed out by force, then wise and just reforms would be introduced.

But it has been found up to the present time impossible to conquer a peace by force of arms, and every suggestion that amnesty, reform, and the certainty of good government might be effective where force has failed has been repelled.

More than six years ago such was the condition of affairs, and it remains the same to-day. Assurances were then given that reforms and concessions would be inaugurated as soon as the insurrection should be subdued, but that they would not be allowed while armed opposition remained. Since then, and under the policy of making that last which should be first, of making that the result which should be the means, the insurrectionary forces have year by year prosecuted their operations over more extensive regions, and their torch is devastating farther and father.

Experience has shown, upon this continent at least, the difficulty, if not the impossibility, of subduing by mere force any serious uprising of a people against a distant government where grave causes of discontent and injury exist, and where the parent government persistently refuses to remove the causes of complaint or to remedy the evils until the insurrection shall have been effectually crushed.

In the last century Great Britain refused to concede to her colonies which now are embraced within the United States privileges and rights which, if then conceded, would have left those colonies part of the possession of Great Britain. Separation ensued.

In the present century when Canada complained of wrongs and of the maladministration of government, Great Britain, with the experience of the past, wisely made concessions and introduced reforms. Resistance disappeared, and Canada is a loyal, happy, and quiet dependence of Great Britain.

The earlier part of the present century presents instances of colonies on this continent dropping off from the parent country for want of timely concession

Puerto Rico is a contented possession of Spain, having received concessions withheld from Cuba, which has been the scene of war for seven years.

The President believes and desires most earnestly, in the way of friendly consultation and fraternal advice, to impress upon His Majesty and his Government that in order to allay the existing strife in Cuba the olive branch is more potent than the sword.

If, in addition, the measures adopted to repress the insurrection are harsh and ill-directed, each new effort gives foundation for a new dissatisfaction and new cause for rebellion.

The President therefore amicably, sincerely, and earnestly suggests the immediate adoption of measures founded on a declaration of complete and entire amnesty, with an invitation to all Cubans to return at will, and to all those in arms to return to peaceful occupation, guaranteeing to all immunity in person and property for acts of rebellion, such declaration to be accompanied by the adoption and proclamation of the necessary measures to provide a just and liberal government, with large powers of local and self control, under proper municipal organizations, suited to the colonial possessions of an enlightened distant power at the present day.

He places these requirements together and dependent each upon the other, because experience has demonstrated that no other course can be effective.

The President is of opinion that the administration of law in Spain has been demonstrated to be prompt, searching, and decisive when the Government so desires; that impositions by way of taxation or contribution to the support of the Government have not there generally been excessive or unequally distributed; that justice is meted out to individuals with impartiality and fairness; that positions of trust and honor are held by men worthy of distinction, and that the opportunities for education and cultivation are ample to all who desire to avail themselves thereof.

It is believed, however, that in Cuba no such advantages or immunities have been provided or enjoyed, and that abuses and wrongs which would not be tolerated in the peninsula have been allowed and are perpetuated in this island.

The administration of law has been substantially subordinate to military force; offenses against the Government, whether really committed or only suspected, have been punished at the will of military officers or under the forms of military courts, and the island has been, in fact, governed, even in times of peace, by martial law.

Exactions by way of taxes, imposts, and contributions have been onerous and oppressive, so much so, in fact, as to make it often questionable whether the possession of property, with the risks attendant upon its cultivation, would not result in loss. These exactions have been governed by no fixed rule, are enforced by an arbitrary power in the island, and large proportions fail to reach the public treasury, or to contribute in any manner to the support of the Government, but are diverted to private purposes. The existence of such a system actually tends to prolong the war, and to make those who profit by such transactions unwilling to change the condition of affairs.

Public positions are held by persons sent by Spain to the island, who are wanting in interest in the welfare of Cuba, and who resort thither for the mere purpose of pecuniary profit, intending to return to Spain so soon as their avarice is satisfied.

General report and belief speak loudly of corruption, and a large number of public officers are charged with securing profit from their positions. As a consequence, the whole administration of the island suffers in public estimation and is believed to be wanting in the qualities which alone can satisfy an enlightened public opinion.

Oppressive commercial regulations, injurious to trade, discriminating directly against Cuba, enhance the price of commodities. Fines imposed upon vessels for trivial offenses and large exactions by way of consular fees for clearances of vessels destined for her ports discourage trade and commerce and tend to place the island at a serious disadvantage.

All these evils are matters of public notoriety, discussion, and comment, and are as loudly condemned in Spain as in the United States.

Spain can not desire to continue such a system, or to permit it to exist, and at the same time she stands before the world as perpetuating the system and as responsible directly for all the results which legitimately flow therefrom.

The absence of just rights and protection and the perpetuation of these wrongs has been the cause of the discontent in Cuba; the further continuance of this condition of things will protract the strife.

Upon the third point it seems necessary only to point to recent events in this country and in Europe, which have demonstrated that the day has passed when the enlightened sentiment of the world will tolerate the holding of a race of human beings in a condition of slavery.

It is true that private rights, organized methods of labor, which can not be rudely changed, and public considerations growing out of the enfranchisement of a large body of slaves may make it necessary that the steps to this end should be carefully adopted. At the same time, the point to be gained is the fact of the emancipation attended by well-devised measures to render it effectual.

Upon the last point, concerning the improvement of commercial facilities and the removal of the obstructions to trade, it can not be questioned that, with peace established and liberal government introduced in Cuba, the existing commercial regulations will prove entirely inadequate, whether regarded in the light of the interests of the inhabitants and owners of property in Cuba or in that of the interests of commercial nations trading with the island.

The obstructions which hamper and burden commerce at the present day with Cuba, to a large extent closing the trade of the island to many of the productions of the United States and of other countries, are part and parcel of a system which should be removed in the interest and for the welfare of the people of Cuba and for the promotion of free commercial intercourse between that productive island and the rest of the world.

Establish peace, good order, and good government; allow full opportunity for the development of the resources of the island and the introduction into it upon terms favorable to its interests of the productions of other countries and Spain will certainly convert the island, now in a state of discontent, distrust, and rebellion, into a prosperous and happy people.

If the views of the Government of the King are in accord with those of the President (as herein expressed on the invitation of the minister of state) as to the means to be adopted to restore peace and tranquillity to Cuba, and if that Government request his good offices to that end, he will cheerfully and readily use every proper effort in his power to secure this much-desired result.

These views are given in response to the invitation of Mr. Calderon y Collantes, as communicated by you, and are expressed in sincerity and with the frankness due to a grave and important question.

Should the Government of Spain agree in these suggestions and earnestly and firmly pursue such policy as is herein referred to, little doubt exists in the opinion of the President that such measures will prove effective. In any event, such a course would, in his opinion, immediately draw to the Spanish Government the moral support of the nations of the earth, and remove from the insurrection any sympathy which now attaches to it.

The alternative of the course of conciliation and of reform which the President has suggested, in response to the invitation for the expression of advice, would involve Spain in the illogical position of a continued maintenance of a system which she admits to be wrong until greater sacrifices of life than have yet been made be incurred in sustaining and in enforcing such wrong, and other lives be sacrificed in the effort to obtain what Spain declares herself willing to accord.

The President concludes with the renewed expression of his earnest hope that peace and order may soon be reestablished, and that the course of peaceful trade and intercourse may be soon restored to the peoples of both nations, with Cuba and its inhabitants undisturbed by the derangements which have attended upon the strife which has prevailed in the island for the past seven years.

You are authorized to read this to the minister of state.

I am, etc.,

HAMILTON FISH.

Mr. Cushing to Mr. Fish.

No. 862.] LEGATION OF THE UNITED STATES,
Madrid, March 2, 1876.

SIR: The President's message has had the salutary effect of modifying and mollifying to a very sensible degree the opinions and feelings, as well of the Cuban Spaniards as of the Peninsula Spaniards.

As to the former, it has awakened them from the dream of immediate independence. Moreover, they desire to put a stop to the incendiary operations of the insurgents in Cuba, which they see tend to render the island as useless to them as to Spain and the United States.

Such is now the state of mind of influential Cuban Spaniards in Europe, as manifested by late important publications of theirs, and as it also appears to be with the Cuban Spaniards in New York.

Spain herself, while determined not to abandon Cuba (no Spanish Government, however constituted, could do that spontaneously and live a month), has been made more pliant by the confidence she finds in the message of the disinterestedness of our Government and in our recognition of the nonexistence in Cuba at the present time of the necessary elements of independence; and she longs to have peace, to be relieved from further sacrifice of men and money, and to stand well with the world, and especially with the United States, in the administration of Cuba.

The complete overthrow of Don Carlos, with the domestic questions and difficulties, political and financial, which the Government has now to encounter, augments rather than diminishes its anxiety for a real pacification of Cuba.

And the problem, as regarded here, is whether the Dominicans who conduct the so-called military operations in Cuba, bred up as they have been in the traditions of mere devastation, which have converted Santo Domingo, once the richest of the great West India Islands, into the poorest, and kept it for three-quarters of a century in a state of semi-barbarism, can be reached by any pacific influences, either of Spain or of the United States.

I have, etc.,

C. CUSHING.

Mr. Fish to Mr. Cushing.

No. 324.] DEPARTMENT OF STATE,
Washington, March 3, 1876.

SIR: Referring to your No. 777 under date of January 16, and in particular to the statement that in your interview of the preceding day the minister of state had informed you that as it had occurred to him that this Government might have concluded not to act on his note of November 15 without hearing from the European Governments in relation thereto, and that in this view he had resolved to defer writing the contemplated responsive circular of Spain to those Governments until after hearing from the United States, I have to state that on several occasions, and in various quarters, information has reached this Government of some circular having been issued by the Spanish Government as to affairs in Cuba and in Spain.

With these expressions of the minister of state before me, and as no copy of any such circular has directly or indirectly reached this Department, it is not considered likely that any response to instruction No. 266, addressed to you and read to the minister of state, has been issued, as has been stated, nor that any general circular has been issued bearing on affairs in Cuba.

I shall be glad, however, to be informed to what paper these statements refer, and to be promptly furnished with copies of any paper or circular which may have been issued by the Spanish Government bearing on events in Cuba or in reference to Spanish affairs.

If any such paper exists, you will appreciate that the reasons which have prevented the Department from making direct inquiries here concerning it render it inadvisable for you to make formal application therefor.

I am, etc.,   HAMILTON FISH.

Mr. Cushing to Mr. Fish.

No. 865.]   LEGATION OF THE UNITED STATES,
                                    Madrid, March 7, 1876.

SIR: Your note of November 5 has been printed in a Spanish translation without abridgment in several of the newspapers of Madrid, and is the subject of prolonged discussion by them, as well as of commentary in political circles

It is not in my power to send you translation of these articles without neglecting other things of more importance, nor does there seem to be need of it.

I content myself with indicating some of the more salient points of criticism in this relation. which appear in print or in conversation.

I.—THE REBELLION IN CUBA.

1. It is alleged, while admitting acts of censurable violence on the part of officers or troops of the Government, that such acts were forced upon them by still worse acts of the rebels, beginning with the foreign adventurer Quesada, and continued by other foreign adventurers, Dominicans, Venezuelans, Mexicans, North Americans, and others, having no real interest in Cuba.

2. It is alleged that the rebellion is really abandoned by most of the Spanish Cubans, who now are serving in the ranks of the loyal volunteers, or hiding their shame and their sorrow as voluntary exiles in various countries of Europe and America.

3. Much is said of the discreditable character and acts of the pretended directors of the rebellion in New York, who, it is charged, are mainly occupied in criminal intrigues against the peace of the United States.

4. It is alleged that in its persistent efforts, at any cost of treasure and blood, to suppress the insurrection in Cuba, the Spanish Government does but follow in the footsteps of the United States in their recent determined stand for the maintenance of their national integrity.

5. It is alleged that the commerce of the United States has not suf-

fered prejudice by the rebellion in Cuba; and that, in addition to the ordinary commerce, we now possess that of the supply of arms, provisions, and other military and naval supplies greatly to our advantage.

Nearly all the small arms used in Spain and Cuba, on both sides, are, it seems, manufactured in the United States.

In this connection attention is called to the very great prejudice which our civil war inflicted on Great Britain and other countries by raising the price or cutting off the supply of the cotton of the United States.

6. It is alleged that the intervention proposed by the United States appears to imply pressure on Spain rather than on the rebels, and that such intervention must necessarily be repelled by Spain for the same considerations, self-respect, and sovereign right which induced the United States to repel foreign intervention during the secession rebellion of our Southern States.

7. Finally, it is alleged that all the European Governments, preoccupied with cares of their own, regard with indifference the intimations on the subject of Cuba which have been made by the United States.

I think what is said in this respect is based in part on informal conversation between members of the diplomatic body and some of the members of the King's Government.

II.—As to Reclamations.

1. It is alleged that most of the reclamations put forward by the United States are for slave property, to the discredit of our emancipation professions.

In this relation attention is called by the newspapers to the pertinent clause of the President's message, and more especially to your recent letter to Mr. Swann, translation of which has made its appearance here in Spanish.

The point is much dwelt upon, with citations from our newspapers.

2. It is alleged that Spain has acted with great promptitude in agreeing to a claims commission earlier than any other Government ever did; while, on the contrary, we, the United States, have not to this day made provision for civil war claims of Germans, Frenchmen, and especially Spaniards.

3. Much is alleged as to the dishonest character of the citizenship of the claimants; most of them Spaniards of recent naturalization, few of whom, it is said, ever had bona fide residence in the United States.

The minister of state has more than once alluded to this point in terms the more disagreeable for being founded on truth.

He says it can be proved that most of these new-born North Americans were domiciled in Cuba, with their city residences and their country plantations there, and in the public exercise of all the rights of Spaniards, during the very time of their pretended residence in the United States, to which at most they had paid but transitory summer visits, and that some of them have founded on their being at school in the United States when boys, although after that they had lived in Cuba, engaged in business, and claiming and exercising all the rights of Spaniards.

He concedes, however, that questions of this class ought to have been raised at an early day, and says the King's Government submits to the burden in this respect imposed upon it by the negligences and procrastinations of its predecessors, and therefore now acquiesces in the claims of all Spaniards who at the time of the imputed wrong were certified citizens of the United States.

To conclude, the above notes are a faithful but greatly abridged abstract of the comments referred to, and appear to me to be as full as is required for information.

I have, etc., C. CUSHING.

Mr. Fish to Mr. Cushing.

No. 329.]
DEPARTMENT OF STATE,
Washington, March 11, 1876.

SIR: Referring to previous correspondence on the subject, I inclose herewith for your further information, a copy of a dispatch, No. 56, under date of the 10th ultimo, from Mr. Boker, the minister of the United States at St. Petersburg, relating to the Cuban difficulty with Spain.

I am, sir, etc., HAMILTON FISH.

Mr. Fish to Mr. Cushing.

No. 331.]
DEPARTMENT OF STATE,
Washington, March 15, 1876.

SIR: Referring to your No. 841, under date of the 19th ultimo, relating to the memorandum addressed by the minister of state at Madrid to the representatives of Spain in foreign countries on the subject of Cuba, I have to state that Mr. Mantilla left a copy of the memorandum at the Department on the 8th instant.

I am, etc., HAMILTON FISH.

Mr. Fish to Mr. Cushing.

No. 332.]
DEPARTMENT OF STATE,
Washington, March 15, 1876.

SIR: Recurring to my No. 315 of the 16th ultimo, transmitting a copy of two dispatches from Mr. Davis at Berlin, relating to Cuban affairs, I have to state that Mr. Davis has since requested that the following correction may be made in his No. 249.

In the last paragraph but one, after "Petersburg," insert "wrote the Government there," so that the passage may read: "Lord Odo also added that the British ambassador at Petersburg wrote that the Government there manifested," etc.

I will thank you to make the above correction in the copy transmitted to you.

I am, etc., HAMILTON FISH.

Mr. Fish to Mr. Cushing.

No. 333.]
DEPARTMENT OF STATE,
Washington, March 15, 1876.

SIR: Referring to previous correspondence on the subject, I inclose herewith, for your further information, a copy of a dispatch under date of the 15th ultimo, No. 1288, from Mr. Washburne at Paris, relating to Spanish-Cuban affairs.

I am, etc., HAMILTON FISH.

Mr. Cushing to Mr. Fish.

No. 868.]   LEGATION OF THE UNITED STATES,
                        Madrid, March 16, 1876.

SIR: My No. 834,[1] of the 16th ultimo, reported to you the opening of the colegislative chambers of the Spanish Cortes.

During their sessions of the first fortnight they were chiefly occupied with consideration and determination of the comparatively few cases of contested returns of members, either of the Senate or of the Congress.

Since then the subject of debate has been the proposed message of response to the opening address of the King.

In this debate leading men of the diverse factions of the opposition, such as the Marquis de Sardoal, Mr. Pidal, Mr. Romero Ortiz, Mr. Moyano, and Mr. Sagasta, have respectively said their say with more or less of zeal or ability, and have been answered chiefly by four of the ministers, Messrs. Canovas del Castillo, Martin Herrera, Calderon y Collantes, and Romero Robledo—the president of the council and the minister of state especially distinguishing themselves in defense of the acts, plans, and purposes of the Government.

With but here and there a trivial exception, the debate has been dignified in form, although most unprofitable in substance, for it has mainly consisted of easy exhibition of the inconsistencies, the errors and the crimes, the tergiversations, pronunciamientos, treasons, and insurrections of which all parties have heretofore been guilty, as, one after the other, they attained the giddy heights of political power, or sank into the depths of angry, impatient, and factious opposition.

In these mutual recriminations of parties, in this general settlement of political account between successive governments and administrations—which has only served to show that all of them, as they rose, ascended on the ruins of their country, and, as they fell, left behind a deplorable deficit of wisdom and usefulness to the debit of each—there is little which would interest you sufficiently to justify the labor of translation.

I annex, however, an extract from the speech of Mr. Sagasta touching the United States, both because of its matter and of the political importance of the speaker, who undoubtedly, apart from the special weight of his position as the parliamentary leader of the Constitutional party, deserves to be ranked among the most practical and the most influential of the statesmen of Spain.

I have, etc.,   C. CUSHING.

[Appendix A with No. 868.—Extract translated.—Remarks of Mr. Sagasta in the Cortes, March 15, 1876, touching the United States.—From the Gaceta de Madrid, March 16, 1876]

  *   *   *   *   *   *   *

As does the committee, so does the Constitutional party, desire that a frank and elevated policy be adopted, resting on the principle of strict neutrality, our nation invoking an equal right with respect to the other nations. The Government ought to be resolute in this, and it will then count upon the support of the Constitutional party in this course, provided it do not interfere in the affairs of other nations and do not permit other nations to interfere in ours, without, however, thereby ceasing to strive for the recuperation of her ancient splendor; not by means of force, but in common accord with other nations interested in this subject.

It is to be hoped that, in pursuance of this policy, the settlement of our differences with the United States may be speedily reached. If in the Island of Cuba such atrocious crimes are committed as that of fixing a price for the assassination of our soldiers and volunteers, still those horrible deeds of which other civilized countries have given us examples have never been witnessed there.

---

[1] Not printed.

The United States well know how difficult it is to subject to determinate rules a fratricidal struggle, because not long ago they themselves had such a struggle, with a great advantage compared with ours, since they were not forced to cross the seas in order to fight. Our war in the Island of Cuba has not assumed the character of a genuine war, but of savage brigandage (bandolerismo), and it is to be hoped that the United States, instead of taunting us, will try to show us their good will.

And now that I am treating of the United States, I touch the confines of the colonial question, and I would speak of the colonial question; but I do not wish to do so so long as the rebellion exists there; so long as there remains one to cry, "Death to Spain;" and I will therefore confine myself to saying that the Government should have no other thought than that of saving, cost what it may, the national integrity, sending out to that end not only all the necessary forces, but also whatever resources may be demanded by the state of the island, and adopting severe measures against those who, forgetting that it is not allowed to them to attack the integrity of their country, are aiding the rebels who slay our volunteers and soldiers.

Having made these brief observations, which I merely do in outline, I shall now enter upon the examination of our domestic policy.

*   *   *   *   *   —   —

Mr. Cushing to Mr. Fish.

No. 869.]   LEGATION OF THE UNITED STATES,
                    Madrid, March 17, 1876.   (Received April 5.)

Sir: I continue to receive expressions of good will from Mr. Layard in reference to the special questions connected with Cuba, in which our respective Governments have a common interest, but with complete silence on the general question of intervention or mediation in Cuba.

The truth is that the European relations of Great Britain and Spain outweigh the matter of their relations in America.

The general relations of the two Governments stand on the most equivocal premises, prolific in difficult and vexatious questions, to wit, old treaties dating back as far as the reign of James I, modified from time to time, and, what is worse, annulled by successive wars, and then renewed at the conclusion of peace by broad stipulations of revivor, covering in terms many commercial provisions which are of difficult, if not impossible, application in the present state of Europe.

I annex a copy of extracts from several of these treaties on a single point, the "favored-nation" stipulation, by which you may see clearly the vague and loose condition of the existing treaty relations of the two Governments.

If these stipulations are to be liberally observed, it is plain to see that the revenue system of Spain becomes totally and perpetually dependent on that of Great Britain.

I think we in the United States have at all times been scrupulous on that point, especially avoiding to concede perpetuity of stipulations affecting revenue.

My own opinion has always been adverse to such stipulations, except in specific cases, where they involve special equivalents of reciprocal value. (See Attorney-General's Opinions, Vol. VI, p. 149.)

Indeed, if these "favored nation" clauses were of definite and effective application, it would be superfluous to enter into extended treaty after extended treaty, for it would suffice to make every new treaty consist merely of a general "favored nation" stipulation. Happily for us, who have spread ourselves out so much in several of our treaties, especially those with the petty States of Central America and some others, the stipulations of that nature are of limited application, just in proportion to their indefiniteness and their generality of expression.

Meanwhile, in these loose and, many of them, obsolete stipulations, finally revived en bloc by the treaty of August 25, 1814 (see Cantillo, p. 733), questions are continually springing up between Great Britain and Spain which lead to prolonged discussion, not always in amiable spirit.

Thus, what is the forum for the trial of British subjects in Spain? A special juez conservador says, in effect, the treaty of 1667, which gives to England all the privileges enjoyed by the Hanse Towns, among which was a juez conservador. And yet the recent laws of Spain long since abolished that forum, with the apparent acquiescence of Great Britain.

Again, to what taxes are British subjects liable in Spain? The royal order of June 18, 1875, transmitted with my No. 630, carefully distinguished, you remember, between treaty rights in this respect and comity rights outside of treaty, and refuses to place Great Britain in the first-named class in virtue of the "favored nation" stipulation, although in virtue of such a stipulation it places Belgium on the footing of the exemptions accorded by express treaty to Germany.

You will readily perceive what a crop of treaty questions between Great Britain and Spain is produced by the equivocal nature of their treaty relations, which apparently cover everything, but are so vague as to afford to either Government opportunity to deny their application to any specific thing in controversy.

Spain is particularly discontented on two points: One, the heavy differential duty imposed by Great Britain on Spanish wines; and the other, the systematic prosecution of contraband from Gibraltar, the efforts of Spain to protect her commerce in this respect giving rise to frequent collisions in the bay of Algeciras, a recent example of which is the capture and recapture of the smuggling schooner *Amalia*.

I annex a statement of the case as understood by the Spaniards.

I might enlarge on these various points, but what has been said will serve to explain further my belief, heretofore expressed, that the British Government has too many questions of its own to discuss here to be ready to follow or accompany us at present in any official act for the pacification of Cuba.

My conclusion in this respect, let me say, was founded on considerations which assume all possible friendliness of spirit on the part of the British Government, although Spaniards are not wanting who suggest to me that Great Britain is secretly impelled in this particular question toward a state of sympathy with Spain rather than the United States, in view of the magnitude of her own great insular or continental dependencies in America.

I have, etc.,

C. CUSHING.

[Appendix A, No. 869.—Extracts from treaties between Spain and Great Britain.]

Thirty-eighth article of treaty of 1667.

It is agreed and concluded that the people and subjects of the King of Great Britain and of the King of Spain shall have and enjoy in the respective lands, seas, ports, havens, roads, and territories of the one or the other, and in all places whatsoever, the same privileges, securities, liberties, and immunities, whether they concern their persons or trade, with all the beneficial clauses and circumstances which have been granted or shall be hereafter granted by either of the said Kings to the Most Christian King, the States General of the United Provinces, the Hanse Towns, or any other Kingdom or State whatsoever, in as full, ample, and beneficial manner as if the same were particularly mentioned and inserted in this treaty.

Second article of treaty of Utrecht, 1713, November 28–December 9.

And as it has been agreed, as is above mentioned, concerning the rates of duties, so it is ordained as a general rule between their Majesties that all and every one of their subjects shall, in all lands and places subject to the command of their respective Majesties, use and enjoy at least the same privileges, liberties, and immunities concerning all imposts and duties whatsoever which relate to persons, wares, merchandise, ships, freighting, mariners, navigation, and commerce, and enjoy the same favor in all things (as well in the courts of justice as in all those things which relate to trade, or any other trade whatsoever) as the most-favored nation uses and enjoys, or may use or enjoy for the future, as is explained more at large in the thirty-eighth article of the treaty of 1667, which is specially inserted in the foregoing article.

Ninth article of the treaty of 1713, July 9–13.

It is further agreed and concluded as a general rule that all and singular the subjects of each Kingdom shall in all countries and places on both sides have and enjoy at least the same privileges and immunities as to all duties, impositions, or customs whatsoever relating to persons, goods, and merchandise, ships, freights, seamen, navigation, and commerce, and shall have the like favor in all things as the subjects of France, or any other foreign nation, the most favored, have, possess, and enjoy, or at any time hereafter may have, possess, or enjoy.

Third article of treaty of 1715.

After referring to duties on wool and other merchandise, the article concludes

"*   *   *   And all the rights, privileges, franchises, and immunities which shall be granted or permitted to any nation whatever shall likewise be granted and permitted to the said subjects (of His Britannic Majesty); the same shall be granted, observed, and permitted to the subjects of Spain in the Kingdom of His Britannic Majesty."

By the treaty of 1814 (August 25) all these previous treaties between Great Britain and Spain are "ratified, confirmed."

[Appendix B, No. 869.—Translation.—Extract in reference to smuggling at Gibraltar, from **La** Politica, March 16, 1876.]

From Algeciras we receive the following:

"The commandant of the coast-guard station at Algeciras having received confidential intelligence that the schooner *Amalia* was about to sail from Gibraltar under the English flag for the purpose of clandestinely landing her cargo on the Mediterranean coast, as she has done many times before, eluding the vigilance of the coast guards, he gave instructions to the cutter *Invincible* to take up a convenient position, and, in effect, on the 27th of February when the schooner sailed from Gibraltar, she was seized by the *Invincible* outside of British waters, and the captain embarked four seamen on her, setting sail toward the anchorage of Algeciras, the schooner being escorted by the cutter (escampavía), which is a Spanish vessel of war (the same as though she was a frigate); but the weather being bad, with a heavy wind, her mast gave way and she was not able to keep on escorting the captured schooner, whereupon the crew of the latter being superior in numbers, the four seamen charged with navigating her were overpowered by the Spanish smugglers (revolver in hand), and she made sail for Gibraltar, anchoring at the arsenal, and the English authorities took charge of the vessel, sending to jail the four seamen of the Spanish ship of war which had captured her. The cutter, having repaired her damages, anchored at Algeciras, and reported to the commandant of the coast guard, who immediately sent a telegram of what had occurred to the captain-general of the department of Cadiz, and went to Gibraltar to confer with our consul there, protesting energetically, and forthwith ordered the preparation of the corresponding sumario, in order to clear up and ascertain the facts. Our consul endeavored to procure the release of the four seamen detained in jail, mixed up there with brigands, and was only able to do so on making a deposit of 500 reals for each of them."

Mr. Fish to Mr. Cushing.

No. 342.]

DEPARTMENT OF STATE,
Washington, March 22, 1876.

SIR: I have to acknowledge your dispatch, No. 853, marked "Confidential," relating to the attitude of the German minister at Madrid on the question of intervention of the United States in Cuba, with comments by yourself.

I appreciate fully the difficulty and the delicacy of your position and your duties at Madrid, and am glad to recognize the ability with which you meet those duties; and after reading with interest (as I read all your dispatches) the larger part of the dispatch, but with increasing anxiety as I proceeded in its perusal, lest some grave mistake had been made in the instructions from this Department or some series of wrongs had been committed or permitted by this Government, I was very much gratified in reading the concluding part of the dispatch, from the paragraph beginning with "I add that the communication of the note of November to other powers" to find that the instruction of November 5 (No. 266), has in your judgment had the very effect which it had in view.

In these concluding sentences you have condensed, with a force and power peculiar to yourself, and for which I return you my acknowledgment, the main object, so far as effect with other powers was in contemplation, of the instruction. I need not here repeat what you have heretofore been told, that there was neither desire on the part of the Government of war with Spain nor expectation that war was imminent. That war might be the eventual result of a continuance of the condition in which Spain was allowing the relations with this Government to drift was a contingency not to be ignored; and the fact to which you have more than once alluded as one of the causes of alarm and of supposed menace, of the collecting of a naval force at Port Royal, was, in the first instance, for the wintering of the fleet; and secondly, as that harbor was at the same time commodious, convenient, and healthful, to have the force together. The possibility that Spain might protract negotiations for the settlement of the questions which you have been gradually bringing to a close, and the possibility of other events which the President's message sought to prevent, and which in your concluding paragraphs you think (as I do) that he has prevented, were not overlooked, and may have had a remote and incidental influence in the selection of a single harbor for the united winter quarters of the fleet; but in this the inducements of thé Government were precautionary, not minatory.

The fact that it has attracted the attention which you report may possibly indicate that it has not been without influence in hastening some of the conclusions which seem to be happily in progress of attainment, and may have contributed to an appreciation of the serious earnestness of the President and of the sincerity of his expressions with regard to belligerence or independence, which, as you justly remarked, have "prepared the way to confidence." It was time that Spain should recognize the sincerity and long endurance of this Government under unfulfilled promises and repeated assaults on the rights of our citizens, and it was time that Spain should earnestly undertake the work of repressing an insurrection which was becoming—which had become—a public nuisance.

In the instruction, No. 266, sent to you, and communicated to other powers, the President had gravely and deliberately considered the course which he believed tended to the best interests of the country, and in the exercise of his constitutional powers and duty he declared it solemnly and earnestly. Had he contemplated or apprehended a hostile movement toward Spain he would not have left it to vague speculation, and you would have been advised of any, however ultimate or remote, intention in that direction.

It is a source of gratification to learn from the concluding part of the dispatch now acknowledged that the instruction of November 5 is appreciated in the sense in which it was intended, and that it meets your approval, as I am confident it will receive your cooperation.

I have also to acknowledge your dispatch No. 855, of the 28th of February, also relating to intervention with especial reference to the attitude of Russia.

I am, etc.,
HAMILTON FISH.

Mr. Cushing to Mr. Fish.

No. 877.]
LEGATION OF THE UNITED STATES,
Madrid, March 23, 1876. (Received April 10.)

SIR: My Nos. 835, 849, 853, 855, and 869 will have communicated the impression received by me from intercourse with my principal colleagues of the diplomatic body in reference to the possibility of our being backed in any way by other powers in the idea of intervention or mediation with Spain on the subject of Cuba.

I reported in detail whatever could be gathered by me in this relation from the ministers respectively of Great Britain, Germany, Austria, and Russia.

The contents of your No. 315 have now come to more than confirm the convictions, previously formed by me, as to the indifference, if not opposition, to be expected by us from all the European powers.

1. *Great Britain.*—The Earl of Derby, in a carefully meditated argumentative paper under his own hand, concludes "that if nothing were contemplated (by the United States) beyond an amicable interposition having peace for its object, the time was ill chosen and the move premature."

These expressions, it seems to me, do not merely involve absolute determination of refusal to support us, but even rather positive, if not rude, condemnation of the proposition. Among his premises, two are to be specially noted, namely: (1) Refusal to cooperate, notwithstanding his doubts of the speedy success of the Spanish Government against the Carlists, and (2) citation of the corroborative opinions of Mr. Layard, seemingly done for the purpose of expressly contradicting the suggestion on my part of the favorable disposition of Mr. Layard.

Whatever hopes may have been entertained by me in this respect, based on general expressions of Mr. Layard, you are well aware have been long since dissipated.

I note also that Lord Derby is silent on the subject of the special treaty rights or duties of Great Britain in the matter of the emancipation in Cuba.

And the hint of a favorable disposition on the part of France is met by the declaration of Lord Derby that, in the opinion of the time for interposition being "ill chosen" and the "move premature," the view of the British Government was also that of the French and German Governments.

The observations of Lord Odo Russell to Mr. Davis are curious and suggestive. Was Lord Odo Russell ignorant on the 21st of January of the actual views of his own Government? That seems impossible. Or was he endeavoring to sound Mr. Davis on the hypothesis of joint action on the part of the British and American Governments?

2. *Germany.*—Mr. Davis's report of his interview with Mr. von Bülow edifies and almost amuses me, as offering an example of skillful fence

on the part of the latter to uphold the Spanish side of the question without giving umbrage to the United States, driving Mr. Davis to the necessity of arguing the very premises of the question on our side, without his having been able to extract from Mr. von Bülow explicit information "whether any counsel had been given to Spain, and if any, what it was." I should have preferred the plain rebuff of the Earl of Derby, or even some exhibition of the famous "brutal frankness" of Prince Bismarck.

For the rest, my study of the Count von Hatzfeldt enables me perfectly to understand what there is behind these studied, reticences of Mr. von Bülow.

3. *Russia.*—Lord Odo Russell, on information of the British ambassador at St. Petersburg, states that "all was going on very well for the United States there."

What is the meaning of this statement? Are the two British ambassadors ignorant of the true state of the question at St. Petersburg as well as at London? Or are they in concert to deceive us?

The Russian minister's statement to me was explicit that he was informed (which means, of course, instructed) that your note of November 5 and the consultation of other Governments thereupon were intended only as means of enforcing the settlement of our personal reclamations at Madrid, which shows unmistakably how the question stands at St. Petersburg.

4. *France.*—All that Mr. Hitt could extract from the Duc Decazes consisted of evasive generalities, but in avowed opposition, however, to any intervention in Cuba.

I say evasive generalities, for while the Duc Decazes explicitly states, on the 22d of January, that the action of France will depend on the decision of Great Britain, but excuses his indefiniteness of explanations by pretended ignorance of the intentions of the Earl of Derby, the latter, on the 25th of January, declares in effect that France had already signified concurrence of view with Great Britain in her definite determination.

In conclusion, permit me to express the hope that you will regard this dispatch and the previous dispatches on the same subject in the light in which they are intended—that is, the execution of plain duty in this important relation.

I stand behind the players here and see the cards they are playing. It is not our game. We can do much with Spain, but it will have to be done on our own ground. We have no cause, in my belief, to expect aid from the European powers, not even from Great Britain. The problem rather is to work out our own policy in such way as to avoid obstructions on the part of those powers.

I have, etc.,   C. CUSHING.

Mr. Cushing to Mr. Fish.

[Telegram.]

MADRID, *March 29, 1876.*

FISH, *Secretary, Washington:*

I have explained to Calderon the nature of your 323, and prepared him to receive it in the right spirit. It can not be read to him in English. I might explain it to him in Spanish, but with risk of loss of effect for you as well as for him.

May I give him copy?

CUSHING.

Mr. Fish to Mr. Cushing.

[Telegram]

WASHINGTON, *March 29, 1876.*

CUSHING, *Minister, Madrid:*

If requested, you may give copy.

FISH, *Secretary.*

Mr. Cushing to Mr. Fish.

No. 886.] LEGATION OF THE UNITED STATES,
Madrid, March 31, 1876. (Received April 18.)

SIR: On receiving your dispatch No. 323 and reflecting on its contents, my first conclusion was to seek to prepare the minister of state for the communication and to ascertain in what spirit it was likely to be received.

To this end it seemed to me convenient to preface by telling him what had been the inducement of your dispatch.

I accordingly sought and obtained a special interview, which took place by appointment at the private residence of Mr. Calderon y Collantes on the morning of the 29th instant.

I began by stating the reception of an important message from you to communicate to him, which had been drawn forth by what he had said to me on the 15th of January last, my report of which I should be glad to make him acquainted with in order to ascertain whether it was correct.

He assented, and I then placed in his hands a Spanish translation of so much of my dispatch No. 777 as relates to the subject (beginning at p. 3 and ending at p. 10), begging him to read it aloud and to deny or qualify if he found occasion.

He took the paper and read it aloud deliberately, saying repeatedly as he went along, "Exacto, exacto," and when he had finished, adding that it was a true and accurate account of what he had said at that interview and commending the fidelity of the report.

He subjoined, in passing, that all such of my reports of conversation at the ministry as had appeared in print had been scrutinized and found to be correct by the respective ministers.

I then said that you would be glad to sit by his side in person, as supposed in that interview, and respond to his friendly suggestion in the same spirit of friendship in which it was made, communicating to him your views of what, as "a statesman and a man of honor," you conceived to be fit to be done in Cuba in the common interest of the United States and Spain; and, as you could not do this in person, you desired to do it in writing, if it would be agreeable to him to receive a communication of considerable advice and kindly intentioned counsel.

He promptly replied that it would be entirely agreeable to him.

I said that the communication was of considerable length which my instructions permitted me to read to him, and that this involved the necessity of making a translation, in which something of the delicacy as well as the force of expression might disappear in passing from one idiom to the other, and that with dependence on the ear only for means of appreciation.

He then begged me to obtain leave to deliver to him a copy, which was the occasion of my telegram of the 30th on the subject, to which you have replied assenting thereto.

He mentioned the fact of a copy of his memorandum having been delivered to you by Mr. Mantilla, and said that the King's Government was meditating to do all which that memorandum indicated, and even more, in the direction of good government in Cuba.

Some reference was made to the apparent difference of opinion growing up among the Cubans in Europe as to the policy of mere devastation in Cuba pursued under the advice of the Cubans in New York.

Conversation then passed to the late bad news from Mexico, and thence to recent similar events in Ecuador, Colombia, Peru, the Argentine Confederation, and other countries of Spanish America, their frequent revolutions, pronunciamentos, and civil wars, and the apparent incapacity of the Spanish-American Republics to manage republican institutions or to maintain domestic peace, and to the question whether Cuba was capable of self-government, it being agreed between us that the Spanish Americans inherit all the vices, but not all the virtues, of their parent race in Europe.

But these points, incidental only to the matter in hand, it is unnecessary for me to report at length.

I am now having a copy made of your dispatch, to be delivered to the minister of state at an expected interview on the 1st of April.

I have, etc.,

C. CUSHING.

Mr. Cushing to Mr. Fish.

No. 911.]   LEGATION OF THE UNITED STATES,
                                Madrid, April 19, 1876.

SIR: On the 12th instant the minister of state invited me to a special interview for the express purpose of conversing with me on the subject of your note of the 1st of March.

He said that he had prepared and should speedily send to me a note in reply, in the same cordial and friendly spirit in which your note was written; but that he desired by anticipation to communicate to me orally the substance of what he proposed to say in more deliberate manner.

He then took up your note and commented on its several suggestions seriatim substantially as in the written note annexed.

In addition to which, some practical points were touched upon, which it seems to me convenient to communicate in a separate and confidential dispatch, which will go by this or by the next mail.

I have, etc.,

C. CUSHING.

[Appendix B with No. 911.—Translation.]

Mr. Calderon y Collantes to Mr. Cushing.

MINISTRY OF STATE,
The Palace, April 16, 1876.

EXCELLENCY: I have read and meditated upon, with the profound interest which its importance merits, the note which under date of the 1st of March of the present year your excellency was pleased to communicate to me, and to which I have the honor of replying.

Before all I beg your excellency to be pleased to express to the Government, which you so worthily represent at this court, the satisfaction and gratefulness of that of His Majesty by reason of the tone, not merely benevolent but friendly, in which the instructions addressed to your excellency by Mr. Fish are conceived. This noble conduct on the part of the President constrains the Government of His Majesty to respond in all sincerity to the same sentiments of friendship and benevolence.

Passing now to examine the kindly suggestions of Mr. Fish relative to the actual situation of Cuba and to the means most adequate for putting a speedy and satisfactory end to it, I shall endeavor to give the solution in the same order as that in which the suggestions are presented.

First. The Government of His Majesty is in entire conformity as regards complying for its part with all the stipulations of the existing treaties, and giving to them a perfect, friendly, and liberal interpretation in all that which may be the subject of doubt or question.

Second. The Government of the King likewise proposes, because it believes it necessary, to change in a liberal sense the régime hitherto followed in the Island of Cuba, not only in its administrative but also in its political part.

Third. Not merely gradual and genuine, but rapid emancipation of the slaves, because the Government of His Majesty recognizes and unreservedly proclaims that slavery neither can nor ought to be maintained in any of its dominions, by reason of its being an anti-Christian institution and opposed to present civilization.

Fourth. The Government of the King finds itself in complete accord not only as to increasing but as to extending to the furthest possible limit all commercial facilities, and causing the disappearance of all the obstacles which to-day exist, and which hinder the rapid and free course of commercial negotiations.

The Government of the King ardently desires to see in the Spanish Senate and in the Congress of Deputies the representatives of the Island of Cuba, as those of Puerto Rico already are in both the colegislative bodies, enjoying in all respects equal rights and privileges with those elected by the Spanish Provinces.

Even effecting the pacification of Cuba exclusively by force of arms, it would not be in any way inexorable toward the conquered, nor does it propose to apply to them the rigor of the law of victory. It will endeavor, on the contrary, to attract the good will of all, to unite all the good sons of Cuba, to grant them rights which they did not enjoy before, and to join them to the common fatherland by the gentle yet strong ties of gratitude and affection.

Such, Mr. Minister, are the sentiments and the purposes of the Government of His Majesty, in perfect consonance with those which are expressed in the note of your excellency to which I have the honor of replying.

But, coming to the practical point and the development of those (sentiments and purposes), the impartiality and uprightness of your excellency and of your Government, of which such striking proofs have been and are now being given, will doubtless admit that not all of them can be realized at the present moment, as the Government of His Majesty would sincerely desire.

In so far as concerns the amnesty and the consequent restoration of property of all kinds embargoed from the insurgents and the refugees, no serious inconvenience stands in the way of its being conceded forthwith, provided they previously submit themselves to the Government of the King.

It is materially impossible to hold elections for senators and deputies in the actual state of insurrection, as it has been so in Spain itself in the provinces wherein the civil war raged; but the Government of His Majesty contracts from henceforth the solemn engagement to command that they take place so soon as the island be pacified, or the insurrection be at least reduced to insignificant proportions.

Without fear that anyone will deny it with proper grounds therefor, I am able to assure you that, but for the insurrection, there would not now have been for some time a single slave in the Island of Cuba; but at the present time, the negroes and mulattoes constituting one of the principal elements of the insurrection, their freedom would be, even in the judgment of those most opposed to slavery, a very grave peril, not only for Spanish rule and for all the Spaniards and Cubans faithful to the metropolis, but also for the whole white race of the island.

The Government of His Majesty, cherishing the well-grounded hope of accomplishing within a brief period the pacification of Cuba, or reducing the insurrection to unimportant limits, is now engaged in preparing the means of replacing, without injury to agriculture, slave labor by free labor, whereby all the nations which maintain commerce with the Island of Cuba will be the gainers, because that commerce would be but poorly nourished did the soil cease to produce through lack of cultivation.

I have set forth with perfect sincerity the desires and the views of the Government of His Majesty, thus reciprocating, as I should, the friendship of the Government of the Union and its loyal purposes. I desire to know the opinion of the latter respecting the solutions and the occasion of realizing them, which I have just indicated; and I conclude by reiterating to your excellency my earnest wish to go on in perfect accord with the Government of the Great Republic in a matter wherein, when examined with true elevation and without prejudice, there is a common and legitimate interest; that is to say, the peace of Cuba, and a government prudent, generous, and liberal in all its proceedings.

I avail, etc.,

FERNDO. CALDERON Y COLLANTES.

Mr. Cushing to Mr. Fish.

No. 914.]   LEGATION OF THE UNITED STATES,
                                        Madrid, April 19, 1876.

SIR: What I have to add to the contents of my No. 911, of this date,
consists of a few points of practical suggestion, arising out of my
interview with the minister of state.

You speak in your note of modification of existing treaties. Mr.
Calderon y Collantes says he is perfectly ready to act on any modification you may propose. Spain will receive in the best disposition any
proposal for the amendment of the treaty of 1795 which may be presented by the United States.

COMMERCIAL ARRANGEMENTS.

Mr. Calderon y Collantes says Spain would be but· too glad, either
by treaty or by concerted legislative arrangements, to enlarge the scope
or facilitate the prosecution of the commercial intercourse of the two
nations. The great solicitude of Spain at this time is to cultivate her
material interests. She invites negotiation on the subject with the
United States.

AMNESTY.

Mr. Calderon y Collantes says the King's Government would cheerfully grant amnesty to the rebels in Cuba. It is not actuated by the
slightest vengefulness of spirit. Indeed, in its dealing with the Carlists, its mercifulness of temper is the subject of vehement reproach on
the part of the opposition. But how, he says, can the Government
force an amnesty on the negro incendiaries and assassins in Cuba?
Can the Government restore his property unconditionally, to be used
by him from his refuge in New York in procuring the conflagration of
the property and the assassination of the persons of the innocent and
helpless noncombatants of the Island of Cuba?

Such is the dilemma he propounds to me in this relation.

Now, what shall I say to the minister of state on these three critical
points?

As to the question of modification of existing treaties, or negotiating for commercial advantages, my hands are tied by the peremptory
tenor of your dispatches on this point, repelling all idea of treaty
negotiation with Spain.

But, how shall we proceed in the beneficial modification of treaties,
or the acquisition of new commercial advantages, without a mutual
understanding; in a word, without either treaties or agreed legislative
enactments in the nature of treaty?

It occurs to me that, now that the two Governments have at length
for the first time frankly and definitely considered the text of the treaty
of 1795, and that the question of its application has been reduced to
its due proportions by your No. 281 of December 27, 1875, and that all
controversy on that point is in the way of being satisfactorily terminated, you may possibly be less disinclined to enter into new treaty
negotiations with Spain. May not that be inferred from these heads of
your note of March 1? I hesitate, however, to act in this direction
without specific instructions, and therefore can not take up these intimations on the part of Mr. Calderon y Collantes.

Be it remembered that Spain has never failed to treat in the most friendly spirit with or in behalf of the United States, as witness the treaties of 1779, 1783, 1795, 1802, 1819, 1834, and 1870. She thinks the treaties of 1795, 1819, and 1870 were eminently of this amiable character.

Be it remembered also that all our troubles with Spain have been incidents of the delirium tremens of anarchy and revolution which seized upon her in 1868, involving civil war in Cuba, in the northern provinces, indeed all over the peninsula. With recovery from that craze has come a steady course of reparation as regards the United States. Why should we not avail ourselves of such inviting circumstances?

In like manner my hands are tied and my lips are closed on the subject of amnesty, which so far as concerns us involves the single question whether the United States, while so constantly striving to influence Spain, can and will do anything to influence the rebels of Spain.

All Madrid believes that, faulty as has been the administration of Spain in Cuba, most of the maladministration has been the logical effect of the factious, ungovernable, and traitorous spirit and conduct of the Cubans themselves, rebellious, as all Spaniards are prone to be, by their hereditary national character.

Thus it is alleged that no repressive measures would ever have been adopted in Cuba but for the frequent rebellions or attempted rebellions there in times of complete order, tranquillity, and prosperity, as in 1823, 1829, 1837, and 1854, including the infamous acts of Narciso Lopez in twice recruiting armed foreign adventurers to invade the island, the worst of all forms of treason.

In fine, as every American bears witness after seeing both, the Cubans are Spaniards, with all the faults of Spaniards in aggravated degree, and whereas discontent is the habit in Spain, and violence the ordinary manifestation of discontent—whereas in Spain opposition parties systematically pursue the practice of quarreling with any and all Governments, however well-intentioned these may be, and deliberately provoking measures of repression in order to have pretext to declaim against oppression and tyranny—so the Spaniards say it always has been in Cuba.

However this may be, it certainly makes the blood run cold to read letters like that of the American lady, Mrs. Julia M. Garcia, narrating the sack and burning of her plantation and the murder of her servants by one of the negro bands of ———. Assuredly, indiscriminate incendiarism and assassination, applied to the property and persons of innocent and peaceful persons, noncombatants, is not war.

So, in reading the manifestations of ——— in the Revolucion, the Independencia, and the Sun, and contemplating their base calumniation of the President, yourself, and the Government of their asylum, and the cowardly malignity and cold-blooded atrocity of the policy of systematic incendiarism and assassination which constitutes their theory of independence in Cuba, one is prone to ask whether these men are not mere wild beasts, fit only to be shot down at sight to rid the world of such loathsome and hateful monsters.

Indeed, the conduct of the Cubans and of their directors in New York has had the mark of infamy indelibly stamped upon it by the expressions contained in the last annual message of the President.

Oftentimes, it is true, in the history of rebellions, especially as they become prostrated or hopeless, the worst traits of human wickedness appear to become developed, as in the plan for burning or poisoning

New York conceived by some of the Confederates, and as in the horrors perpetrated by the Communists of Paris.

Spaniards, also, are among the worst of rebels. They do not stop to draw the line between political opposition and rebellious conspiracy, to estimate the morality of the means employed to gratify their feverish thirst for office, or to calculate the dynamic relation of the means to the proposed end.

We in the United States would think it strange enough to see a disappointed candidate for a ministerial portfolio or a foreign mission undertake to get up a rebellion against the Government, or to invade it in arms at the head of a gang of foreign miscreants and ruffians recruited in Canada or Cuba. Yet that is the way they do things in Spain.

In short, these men are Spaniards, in whose character the most flagitious sentiments are seen to be most prominent, while behind is a fund of generosity and honor.

Their present line of action is abominable as to morality, while it is stupid suicide as to politics. It is abominable to burn the property and murder the persons of peaceful planters in Cuba in order to weaken Spain; it is suicide to pursue the policy of systematically endeavoring ing to destroy Cuba in order to spite Spain.

That destruction involves irreparable loss to the United States as well as Spain.

But are —— and —— so bad as they seem, and as their acts indicate? On the face of things it is hard to see in what respect Thomassen or Keith, he of the infernal machine, is a worse man than —— or ——.

Still, it seems impossible to believe that they can be wholly insensible to influences of honor and of reason. In their case, as in other analogous cases, it would seem that a sort of mental alienation supervenes to blind men to the true character of their acts.

Are these men, then, or are they not, amenable to influences of reason and humanity, addressed to them by the United States?

Surely, if they are not, Spain may well think it is of no use for her to seek to influence them by acts of gratuitous generosity, even to oblige the United States.

These considerations are of the very essence of the question of amnesty as between the United States and Spain.

You have touched on this point once or twice, but so lightly as to leave me in doubt whether it is right or proper for me to enter into the question with the minister of state; which compels me to be silent at the very point where explicitness of conversation might efficiently promote the desires of the United States for the pacification of Cuba.

Submitting these views to your better judgment,

  I have, etc.,   C. CUSHING.

Mr. Fish to Mr. Cushing.

No. 383.]   DEPARTMENT OF STATE,
           Washington, June 16, 1876.

SIR: Upon reading your No. 956[1] of the 20th of May, inclosing an extract from the Independencia, of New York, professing to contain a "programme" of the revolutionists in Cuba, with your comments as to the extremities to which the insurgents have proceeded, I am reminded

---

[1] Mr. Cushing's No. 956 incloses a programme of the revolutionist junta in New York, and comments upon its effects in Spain. It does not seem to be responsive to the resolution.

of your two dispatches, Nos. 911 and 914, both dated April 19, 1876, informing me of the communication to the minister of state of instruction No. 323 of the 1st of March.

You will remember that this instruction was addressed to you because the minister of state was pleased to invite a frank statement concerning the precise thing which this Government would advise or wish Spain to do, pursuant to which intimation I frankly informed you of the views of this Government as to what course might be adopted with a view to the restoration of peace in Cuba.

On almost every occasion heretofore, when complaints have been made of the damage to this country and to all countries having relations with Cuba, growing out of the insurrection, or when friendly suggestion has been made, as in this case, substantially the same answer has been returned, namely, that the insurrection was about to be suppressed; and when that had happened, then, but not before, reforms which were admitted to be required would be inaugurated and measures necessary to the peace and prosperity of the island adopted. The insurrectionists, on the other hand, have been unwilling to rely on these assurances or to lay down their arms. Thus things have proceeded, and the insurrection is no nearer to suppression now than years ago, and the needed reforms as distant as some years since.

It has been averred that certain high authorities in Spain did not at first object to a show of revolution or revolt in Cuba, as such a condition of affairs gave ready excuse for increased taxation and new burdens. Of this I say nothing and express no opinion; but it seems to be indisputable that the determination of Spain to do nothing by way of reforms, nor to aid in any improvement in affairs until the insurrection had been suppressed, has prevented its suppression and virtually prevented the introduction of any better state of affairs in the island.

With, therefore, a continuation of the same policy on the part of the authorities of Spain as is foreshadowed by the minister of state in his communications to you touching my instruction of the 1st of March, and in other quarters, and with the determination of the insurgents, if such can be said to be foreshadowed in this extract from the Independencia, or if the same be genuine, with the extreme views of the two parties, neither willing or intending to yield to the other, and with the want of power or ability of either to coerce the other, there seems little hope that anything is soon to be expected in the interest either of good government in Cuba or that will lead to peace and prosperity in the island.

I am, etc.,

HAMILTON FISH.

Mr. Cushing to Mr. Fish.

No. 1027.]   LEGATION OF THE UNITED STATES,
Madrid, July 10, 1876.

SIR: I received some time ago a letter from the American Peace Union, inclosing an address to the King to propose a board of international arbitrators to settle the little misunderstanding between the "nation" of Spain and the "nation" of Cuba, to which I have just now snatched a moment to make response. A copy of the correspondence is annexed.

I have, etc.,   C. CUSHING.

S. Doc. 231, pt 7——30

[Inclosure 1 with No. 1027.]

Mr. Love to Mr. Cushing.

PHILADELPHIA, *January 19, 1876.*

RESPECTED FRIEND: The Peace Society of America has passed the resolution inclosed and has to request that you favor us by presenting or forwarding it to the court of Spain, that the proposed matter may be considered there as well as at our capital and in Cuba, as we have forwarded duplicates to both places—and I believe President Grant favors the proposition.

We have had this written in Spanish for Spain and Cuba, and we trust it will receive proper attention.

We are well convinced that this course will be popular and profitable, and with the highest appreciation of your services, and thanking you in advance for the favor asked,

I am, etc., ALFRED H. LOVE,
President of the Universal Peace Union, American Branch.

[Inclosure 2 with No. 1027.—Translation.]

PROPOSED ADDRESS OF THE PEACE SOCIETY TO THE KING OF SPAIN.

At the ninth anniversary of the Society of Peace of Pennsylvania, branch of the Universal Peace Union, celebrated in the city of Philadelphia the 30th of November, 1875, the following conviction was unanimously adopted, and it was ordered that it be sent to the King of Spain, to the President of the United States, and to the powers of Cuba, with the hope of its adoption by all:

"We are convinced that the principle of national and international arbitration may be made popular and appropriate for terminating all differences between nations, and that if the motives of disturbance between Spain and Cuba were submitted to a tribunal of wise and conscientious arbitrators they would be adjusted with comparatively small cost and delay, to the mutual satisfaction and great benefit of both countries."

ALFRED H. LOVE,
President of the Universal Peace Union,
No. 215 Chestnut Street, Philadelphia, United States.

PHILADELPHIA, *January 1, 1876.*

[Inclosure 3 with No. 1027.]

Mr. Cushing to Mr. Love.

MADRID, *July 7, 1876.*

RESPECTED FRIEND: I have had under consideration your esteemed favor; and, cordially concurring as I do in appreciation of the laudable object you have in view—that is, the pacification of Cuba—and earnestly as I have myself labored in the same spirit on various occasions, I regret that it is not in my power to deliver to the King of Spain the address which you inclose, suggesting a board of international arbitration for the settlement of the contest between him and his insurgent subjects in Cuba.

In the first place, I have no right, as envoy and minister of the United States, to make any political communication to the King. That is a privilege reserved exclusively to ambassadors. To overstep the line of diplomatic rule and usage in that respect would not only expose me to censure, but would be prejudicial to the contemplated object.

In the second place, I have no right to make official communications of this nature to the minister of state, with whom alone it is competent for me to treat, except on instructions from my Government.

Meanwhile, the object of your proposed address to the King, as appears by documents communicated to Congress, with which you are probably acquainted, has been the subject of continual correspondence here, in obedience to specific instructions of the Department of State, which define and limit my rights and duties in this respect.

For these reasons I have felt myself constrained to adopt in your case the rule of conduct observed in all new matters presented to me—that is, to refer the subject of our correspondence to the Secretary of State of the United States.

Permit me, in conclusion, to make a single observation respecting the tenor of your proposed address to the King of Spain, and this not in the sense of criticism, but of explanation.

This address starts from the premises of the general utility of international arbitration. You will see, by glancing at the third chapter of the volume which accompanies this letter, that my own advocacy of international arbitration is as earnest as that of the Peace Union.

But your address proceeds to assume that Spain and the insurgent Cubans are in the relation of foreign nations one to another. To the contrary of this, as the last annual message of the President of the United States conclusively demonstrates, such is not either in fact or in right the present condition of the Cubans. A secession insurrection exists in Cuba, but not in a state to be recognized by the United States (or by other Powers) as an independent, or even belligerent, nationality.

Moreover, the question which shall yield to the other, and on what terms—insurgent subjects or their sovereign—the issues of a war of independence—is one of the questions on which arbitration is impossible.

Could President Lincoln have entered into international arbitration with the persons in arms in the Southern States on the question of the dissolution of the Union? Clearly not; nor, I think, did the "Peace Union" or any other friends of peace advise such a course on the part of our Government. We did not regard the Southern States as a nation, although they had been recognized as belligerents by foreign powers and had infinitely higher pretensions to be considered a nation than the comparatively handful of insurgents in Cuba. Nor has Spain yet consented to regard the insurgents in Cuba as a "nation." Of course she is not likely to enter into an agreement with them to arbitrate the question of the secession of Cuba from Spain.

Let me ask, on the other hand, what is the relation of the "Peace Union" to the insurgents in Cuba? Have they listened to your suggestion of an arbitration? If you, the friends of peace, can exert any influence in that quarter, you will be performing a great and glorious work, in the interest alike of Spain and of Cuba.

I remain, etc.,

C. CUSHING.

Mr. Cushing to Mr. Fish.

No. 1029.]   LEGATION OF THE UNITED STATES,
Madrid, July 11, 1876.

SIR: Will you permit me to make some observations of a consolatory tendency in reference to the nonsuccess of your earnest efforts to meliorate the condition of things in Cuba?

1. You encounter, in the first place, the indisposition of either party to the contest in Cuba to listen to the counsels of wisdom and friendship. It is the very predicament described by a late writer in the following words:

There are conjunctures in history in which reasoning and the attempt at persuasion fail. Where opposition is irreconcilable, where each party is striving heart and soul for an object, which the other looks upon as ruin and ignominy to himself, there can be no arbitrament but force. The ruler must show his power to rule, the subject must show his power to win independence.

Is not this true? Is there any example in history in which rebellions have yielded to reason—when either the sovereign or the rebellious subjects could be persuaded to cease from strife, until after the one or the other party had been vanquished?

We in the United States have possessed parliamentary institutions for more than three centuries—not one only, as might be inferred from the rejoicings of the late Fourth of July. We think we are—we are—imbued with all the instincts of order, peace, and good government.

Now, would we of the North have listened to any suggestion from abroad to desist from the effort to put down secession by force of arms? Would our insurgent fellow-citizens in the South have been persuaded to lay down their arms by any promises, assurances, or even concrete acts on the part of the Government of the Union?

Again, going back to our own insurrection against Great Britain, would any proposition of hers, or even enacted measures for better administration of the colonies have influenced us to make peace? Or could Great Britain yield to us until defeated in all quarters, and completely disheartened, by the combined forces of the United States, France, Spain, and the Netherlands?

With enlightened zeal you have labored thanklessly for the peace and welfare of Cuba and of Spain herself, and if you have not been able to effect all the good you desire, it is only because you have had to encounter impediments of moral impossibility in the nature of things.

2. In the second place, my residence in Spain has enabled me to appreciate the true cause and character of maladministration in Cuba. It is that the governors are incapable of conducting and the governed equally incapable of receiving good government. They are all Spaniards alike, as General Prim so often said, whether you call them Peninsulars or Cubans. And (to say nothing of the colored population) it is not the best of the Spaniards, Creole or Peninsular, which constitutes the population of Cuba.

Now, has there been maladministration in Cuba? So there has been in Spain herself. Have there been rebellions in Cuba, guerrilla warfare, burnings, sacking of towns, military executions, deportations, embargo of private property, banishments, suspension of suffrage, arbitrary domination of captains-general? So all these things have been occurring in Spain. She has had naught else for more than sixty years but alternations betwixt anarchy and despotism. The few periods of comparative, but transient, tranquillity she has enjoyed during the reign of Queen Isabel were due to the mere usurpation of two great generals, Narvaez and O'Donnell, to whose administrations of the sword men look back now as to the halcyon days of Spain. Since the dethronement of Queen Isabel—that is, during the very period of the civil war in Cuba—there has not only been civil war in Spain, but, simultaneous therewith, a rapid succession of provisional and experimental governments, each destitute of inherent stability, and every one of which subsisted only by means of irresponsible dictatorships, except that of King Amadeo alone, who fell simply, as men say, because he was the only man in Spain scrupulously faithful to his oath and obstinately adhesive to the constitution of the country.

And yet, constitutionally honest as he was, his ministers betrayed him and assassins (not yet punished) fired on him on a bright moonlit evening in one of the most frequented and brilliantly lighted streets of Madrid. Possibly if Prim had not been assassinated in the street (by men, they also not yet punished), Spain might have been saved from her extremest days of misery, the cantonal insurrection, but that is doubtful, since the misfortunes of Spain and of Cuba are conditions of the national character, as manifested alike in Spain and in all Spanish America.

For, let me repeat, the governors and the governed, all the same in race, and with defects aggravated in the latter by tropical life and by association with slaves, are at least equally to blame for the calamities of Cuba.

In fine, looking at the subject from the point of view of the interests of the United States, which alone is of account in the face of a civil contest where both parties are deaf to the counsels of friendship and to considerations of sympathy and humanity, it seems to me that we have much to lose and nothing to gain by compromising ourselves in the matter of Cuba, it being superabundantly evident that, whether as to

Lopez and his companions laboring professedly to betray their country to a foreign nation for the promotion of slavery, or in the case of Aldama and his associates, laboring to betray it to the same nation for the gratification of personal resentment and ambition, they all have but one thought as respects us, namely, to make a cat's-paw of our Government, while ready to emulate, on the earliest possible opportunity, the "sublime ingratitude" of Schwartzenberg.

I have, etc., C. CUSHING.

Mr. Fish to Mr. Cushing.

No. 401.] DEPARTMENT OF STATE,
Washington, August 1, 1876.

SIR: Your dispatches Nos. 1025,[1] 1026,[1] 1027, 1028,[1] 1029, 1030,[1] 1031,[1] 1032,[1] 1033,[1] and 1034[1] have been received.

With reference to No. 1027, inclosing a copy of the correspondence between the American Peace Union and yourself on the subject of a board of arbitration between Spain and the insurgent Cubans, I have to state that your course as therein set forth is approved.

I am, etc.,

HAMILTON FISH.

AUSTRIA.

Mr. Fish to Mr. Orth.

No. 38, of November 15, 1875, and telegram of December 13, 1875. (Same as No. 756, of November 15, 1875, and telegram of December 6, 1875, to Mr. Washburne, pp. 480, 481.)

Mr. Orth to Mr. Fish.

No. 75.] LEGATION OF THE UNITED STATES,
Vienna, December 14, 1875.

SIR: This morning I received the following telegram, dated Washington, December 13, 1875:

Proceed as instructed in No. 38.

Accordingly, I repaired to the office of the imperial royal ministry for foreign affairs to seek an interview with Count Andrássy, but learned from Baron Hofmann, "sections chef," or assistant secretary of foreign affairs, that Count Andrássy was somewhat indisposed; that he is now in Budapest, but is expected to return to-morrow. I informed Baron Hofmann that I was instructed by the President to make a confidential communication to the minister of foreign affairs, and he replied that I could, if it suited my convenience, have an interview for such purpose on Thursday, at 12 o'clock, with Count Andrássy, or, should the Count still be indisposed, then with Baron Hofmann. I shall, therefore, on next Thursday, as instructed, communicate "instruction No. 266 to Mr. Cushing, United States minister at Madrid," contained in your dispatch No. 38, of date November 15, 1875.

I have, etc., GODLOVE S. ORTH.

---

[1] Not printed.

Mr. Orth to Mr. Fish.

[Telegram]

VIENNA, *December 16, 1875.*

Instruction communicated. Answer next week. Probably unsatisfactory.

ORTH.

Mr. Orth to Mr. Fish.

No. 78.]   LEGATION OF THE UNITED STATES,
Vienna, December 16, 1875.

SIR: In my dispatch No. 75 of day before yesterday I stated that
my interview with the Imperial Royal minister of foreign affairs was
arranged for this day at 12 o'clock. I accordingly repaired to the
foreign office, where I met Baron Hofmann, who informed me that Count
Andrássy had returned from Budapest still somewhat indisposed, but
that he was, by previous arrangement, having a consultation with the
ambassadors from Germany and Russia with reference to the proposed
action of the three powers in the matters connected with the insurrection in Bosnia and Herzegovina; that these matters, in which the
Austro-Hungarian Government had such direct and immediate interest,
would probably occupy the entire attention of Count Andrássy for several days; that for these reasons the Count regretted very much that
he could not receive in person the communication I was instructed by
the President to make to his Government, and that, in order to avoid
further delay in receiving such communication, he had authorized Baron
Hofmann to receive the same for him. Thereupon I informed Baron
Hofmann that the communication I was instructed by the President to
make to the Austro-Hungarian Government had reference to the unfortunate condition of affairs now, and for several years past, existing
between the Government of the United States and that of Spain, growing out of the insurrection in the island of Cuba.

That such contest had now continued between Spain and her colony
for the period of about seven years, characterized by violations of the
rules of civilized warfare, by pillage, by wanton destruction of property, and was threatening the desolation of a large and most fertile
island, in close proximity to our own shores, and in whose peace, prosperity, and commerce the people of the United States had a most
direct and immediate interest.

That the unhappy contest thus long waged between Spain and the
insurrectionary forces in Cuba still continues unabated and with no
present prospect of a termination.

That during the years of this conflict citizens of the United States
had frequently suffered in person and estate from the lawless acts of
the parties engaged therein, and that the Spanish Government, after
frequent representations on the part of the Government of the United
States, had not been able, or willing, to compensate such citizens for
losses incurred and damages sustained, nor could the Spanish Government give any reliable assurance of immunity from such acts in the
future.

That the Government of the United States has no ulterior or selfish
motives in this matter, and no desire to take advantage of the distracted internal condition of Spain, but, on the contrary, it is the earnest desire of the President that there should be "a termination of the

disastrous conflict in Cuba by the spontaneous action of Spain, or by the agreement of the parties thereto."

After this preliminary statement to Baron Hofmann, I proceeded to read to him the instruction No. 266, of date November 5, 1875, addressed by the Secretary of State to Mr. Cushing, United States minister at Madrid. The Baron listened with marked attention to the statement and "instruction," taking notes of the principal points contained in each.

He then remarked that, personally, he takes a lively interest in everything pertaining to the Government and people of the United States, and desired me to say to the President that the Austro-Hungarian Government felt a continuing friendship for that of the United States, and everything pertaining to its honor and prosperity, and that I should convey to the President the thanks of this Government for the frank manner in which he had caused to be brought to its attention the delicate and critical relations now existing between the Government of the United States and that of Spain, and expressing a sincere hope on the part of his Government that the friendship between the United States and Spain might not suffer even temporary interruption in consequence of the causes arising from the present unhappy state of affairs existing between Spain and her ancient colony.

I thereupon ventured to suggest that it might be consistent with the views of the Austro Hungarian Government, in the interest of humanity and of peace, and in the spirit of that good-fellowship so long existing between Austria and Spain, to bring to the attention of the latter Government the importance to her of the termination, of her own volition, or with the concurrence of her insurgent subjects, of a contest already waged for seven long years, and thus far without any reasonable prospect of being ended by the further effusion of blood or waste of treasure.

The Baron replied that from the communication I had made he felt that he fully comprehended the present position of the Government of the United States in this matter; that he should make a full brief of the case for the consideration of Count Andrássy and the Imperial and Royal ministerial council, but should Count Andrássy desire fuller information he would not hesitate to apprise me and request a future interview for that purpose, to which I rejoined that it would afford me pleasure at any time to comply with Count Andrássy's wish in this respect.

That, occupying a subordinate position himself, he could not undertake to say what might be the view of the Austro-Hungarian Government in reference to my suggestion, but he might be permitted to add that inasmuch as the position of the Government of the United States, as set forth in the instruction No. 266, had been brought to the attention of the Spanish Government by Mr. Cushing, it was not improbable that the Spanish Government, through its minister at Vienna, would also bring the matter to the attention of the Austro-Hungarian Government, and using as he said, "a common expression," there are generally "two sides to a question." That he meant, however, by this expression only to say that his Government might, out of deference at least to the Government of Spain, desire to hear from its representative before forming any judgment or expressing any opinion upon a matter so gravely affecting the future peace of both countries.

He added further, that it was at all times a most delicate matter for one government to volunteer suggestions to another regarding its action, with reference to which the "suggesting Government" had no immediate interest. That, as I was well aware, the Austro-Hungarian Government "had its hands full" in the present troubles on her southern border (alluding to Bosnia and Herzegovina), and that she might deem it the part of wisdom to refrain from even a suggestion in which she had only an interest in common with other Governments.

That these were to be taken by me only as his own ideas, and not as indicating what might be the views of his Government after a more thorough examination of the question in all its phases, but he desired especially to impress me with the fact that the Austro-Hungarian Government entertained for the Government of the United States the utmost respect and friendship, with best wishes for her continued peace with the other nations of the world, and a continuance in that career of prosperity that has thus far distinguished her history, and that I should, at as early a day as practicable, be informed in writing as to the conclusion to which his Government should arrive in the premises.

I have, etc.,

GODLOVE S. ORTH.

Mr. Orth to Mr. Fish.

[Telegram.]

VIENNA, *January 12, 1876.*

Andrássy requests copy of Cuban dispatch. Shall I comply?

ORTH.

Mr. Orth to Mr. Fish.

No. 90.]   LEGATION OF THE UNITED STATES,
                            Vienna, January 13, 1876.

SIR: I have been waiting patiently for the reply of the Austro-Hungarian Government to the note on the Cuban question, which I was instructed to bring to its notice, and which reply in writing was promised at an early day, as I advised you in my No. 78.

On the 8th instant I received a copy of the Daily (London) Telegraph, in which I found a telegram sent from this city on the 4th instant, relating to this subject, which is attached hereto.

This telegram speaks in a tone of official inspiration, and mentions facts which its author could hardly have divined. My first impulse was to bring it to the attention of the ministry of foreign affairs, and learn whether it be true as stated that "the Austrian Government * * * will not reply to the long American dispatch, which was only read to the Austrian minister for foreign affairs," etc.

Upon reflection, however, I deemed it the wiser course to await the further action of the ministry.

In this connection I desire to state that Count Andrássy is still at Budapest in conference with the ministries of the two Governments of Austria and Hungary, as advised in my No. 88, and will probably remain there two or three weeks. as there is at present no immediate prospect of a settlement of the difficulties now engaging their attention. And in addition to this, the "Eastern question" is so constantly engrossing his attention that it is very doubtful whether I can soon obtain a personal interview with Count Andréssy upon this subject.

Hearing nothing from the Imperial and Royal ministry on the subject of the Cuban note, I repaired yesterday to the foreign office and had a somewhat lengthy interview with Baron Hofmann. I commenced the interview by stating that for certain sufficient reasons the President would be pleased to receive an answer as promised from this (the Baron's) Government, with reference to the note I had the honor of reading to him at our last interview. The Baron replied by stating that the attention of Count Andrássy had been, and still is, so thoroughly engrossed with important matters—the Eastern question and differences in Hungary—immediately affecting his own Government that he had not been able as yet to consider the matter I had brought to his attention. That the Count was very desirous of having a copy of the Cuban note so that he could carefully examine it before giving any answer. To which I responded that my instructions merely authorized me to read it to him. The Baron then proceeded, stating that after our last interview he had an interview with the Spanish envoy, the Duke de Tetuan, on the subject, who informed him that the Spanish Government was exceedingly anxious to suppress the revolt in Cuba, and was only awaiting the final overthrow of the Carlist insurrection to send an armament of sufficient strength to Cuba to restore tranquillity to the island.

The Baron further stated that whatever might be the views of his Government on this question, they were not prepared to take the initiative, and hence had soon after my last interview entered into correspondence with the Governments of Great Britain, France, Germany, and Russia for the purpose of ascertaining their views and intentions, and had also fully communicated their action in the premises to their envoy at Washington. That thus far they had not received any response from either of the Governments of Great Britain, France, or Russia, letting me infer that the German Government had made a response, although he (the Baron) did not expressly say so.

At this point I called his attention to the telegram in the London Telegraph which seems to state with the positiveness of authority that no answer would be given by the Austrian Government. After examining the telegram very attentively, the Baron with some warmth replied that it was untrue that such was the position of his Government. He reiterated that his Government would not take the initiative, and especially did they desire to know the views of Great Britain, which, of all European Governments (with the exception of Spain), was most directly and immediately interested in the Cuban question.

Again he expressed the desire of Count Andrássy to have a copy of the Cuban note, when I replied that I would advise you by telegram, as I did soon after leaving the foreign office, of such desire, and be governed by your direction in the premises.

I have, etc., GODLOVE ORTH.

———

[Inclosure 1 in No. 90.—Extract from the Daily (London) Telegraph, January 5, 1876.]

VIENNA, January 4.

The cabinet of Madrid learned in the middle of December, from a confidential quarter, the contents of the circular note of the United States Government to the European Powers relative to Cuba. It thereupon instructed its representatives abroad to explain to the Governments to which they are accredited that the Cuban question was not one only of American but of European interest. Complications between America and Spain might have incalculable consequences for Europe. In the first place, they would encourage the Carlists to make a prolonged resistance, and revive the hopes of the Federalist Republicans and Socialists in Spain. The Austrian Government received these declarations in a friendly manner, and will not reply to the long American dispatch, which was only read to the Austrian minister for foreign affairs, and which, moreover, not only repudiates any intention of annexing Cuba, but in reality contains no definite conclusions.

Mr. Fish to Mr. Orth.

[Telegram]

WASHINGTON, *January 14, 1876.*

ORTH, *Minister, Vienna:*

Copies two sixty-six not furnished other Governments, nor communicated here. Vienna papers first published purport after your interview. Give information on any point, but prefer at present not to give copy.

FISH, *Secretary.*

Mr. Orth to Mr. Fish.

No. 91.]   LEGATION OF THE UNITED STATES,
                              Vienna, January 17, 1876.

SIR: On Saturday morning, the 15th instant, I received from you the following cable telegram, which I have translated as follows:

Copies two sixty-six not furnished other Governments nor communicated here. Vienna papers first published purport after your interview. Give information on any point, but prefer at present not to give copy.

This afternoon I called at the foreign office, and finding Count Andrássy still absent at Budapest, I informed Baron Hofmann that I had received an answer from you and that you "preferred at present not to give copy" of No. 266. The Baron made no special remark further than to say the copy was desired by Count Andrássy rather than by himself.

With reference to that portion of your telegram which says, "Vienna papers first published purport after your interview," I will state that some of the papers of this city during the first week in this month published extracts from some Parisian paper indicating that our Government had addressed a note to the several Powers in Europe on the subject of Cuba without giving any very distinct idea of the contents of such note; that on the morning of the 5th instant the Presse, of this city, which is understood to be in the confidence of the ministry here, published the following telegram from London, dated January 4—

Reuter's Agency reports from New York that in the note of the Government of the United States addressed to the Powers relative to Cuba, the union of Cuba and Puerto Rico under one Spanish Governor-General is proposed—

and on the same day it had a leading editorial, based apparently upon the foregoing telegram, in which, however, it alludes, at least incidentally, to the note—doubtless meaning No. 266—and gives its views at length upon the Cuban question.

This editorial assumes more importance than it otherwise would from the fact, as stated above, that it is said to enjoy the confidence, and hence may be regarded as somewhat reflecting the views, of the ministry.

I attach hereto the original, as well as translations of said editorial and also of said telegram.

I have, etc.,

GODLOVE S. ORTH.

[Inclosure 1 in No. 91.—Translation from the Presse of Wednesday, January 5, 1876.]

NORTH AMERICA AND CUBA.

North America labors vigorously and incessantly to make the Cuban question an international one, and to elevate it to the position of a burning one before the Spanish arms can succeed in making it disappear from the world To-day it is announced by telegram from New York that the note of the Government of the United States to the Powers relative to Cuba proposed the union of Cuba and Puerto Rico under one Spanish governor-general. The European diplomacy, which was enlightened with the hearing of the extraordinarily long American document—a copy of the same was not left—might be not disagreeably astonished to learn what actually might be the small meaning of the long discourse. The omission of every conclusion in the document of Mr. Secretary Fish was until now everywhere remarked; he had hitherto excused the European Governments from the duty of giving an answer to the Washington Government, and the Madrid Government did not this time require, as with the message of President Grant, to answer with a formal memorandum. Substantially, the long and short of the American note was to the effect that the insurrection in Cuba must come to an end. It was careful to represent, in constantly recurring phrases, that no individual interest of any kind had actuated the United States, who positively had not the least thought of appropriating the Pearl of the Antilles.

Here and there the idea is brought forward that the creation of a certain autonomy for Cuba was to be recommended, but as to a formal proposition to the Powers to unite Cuba and Puerto Rico under one Spanish governor-general, it is, to the best of our knowledge, not mentioned. Such a proposition would not have the slightest prospect of success either with Spain herself or with the Powers. In the first place, it does not appear how such a union of the two Antilles would solve the question for which alone the Washington Government is desirous of interesting the Powers, nor how it could produce an end to the insurrection in the Island of Cuba. Then all European powers, without exception, would reflect twice before they would with such a proposition so deeply interfere in the internal affairs of a foreign nation But as regards Spain herself, it is exclusively the affair of her army, in the first place, fully to suppress the insurrection in Cuba, and the affair of the future Cortes to durably regulate the relations between the colonies and the mother country. Still less than any one of the former Governments would that of King Alphonso permit laws to be dictated to it from abroad in an affair so eminently national.

The European Powers are at the present time accurately informed what standpoint the Spanish Government occupies in opposition to the arguments of the American Government. It was easy for the representatives of Spain abroad to reply to the pretense of the Washington Government that the Spanish war force would find it impossible to subdue the insurgents in Cuba, by producing the declarations in Grant's message that these insurgents were without everything which could entitle them to recognition as belligerents. When the insurgents to-day, after six years' efforts, were unable to occupy any other territory other than forests without roads, and unfruitful and unhealthy swamps, and not a single locality having more than 200 inhabitants, thus it becomes manifest—and herein the Spanish diplomacy accredited to the foreign Powers successfully weakens the chief argument of the Government at Washington—why, according to the statistical proofs, could both the State revenue of Spain from Cuba, as well as the commerce of America with the Island, constantly and very largely increase in spite of the insurrection? On the other hand, Spain raises the simple question why just now as order is being firmly restored in the mother country, and the prospect of an early end of the Carlist war presents itself, and thereby the possibility is apparent of concentrating all her forces for suppressing the Cuban insurrection—why now the Washington Government preaches to the world that the insurrection in Cuba must come to an end, and why this was not then done when the revolution in Andalusia, the Canton insurrection in Carthagena, and the civil war in the north, seemed really to deprive the Madrid Government of the possibility of terminating the contest with Cuba.

Moreover, the representatives of Spain abroad successfully, and in accordance with the instructions of their Government, called attention to the fact that in this affair not only a question of American but one of decidedly European interest was affected. Persons may estimate as they will the argument that Spain represents in Cuba European interests and culture; it could not be a matter of indifference to the European powers if the attack of America against Spain should bring a moral and material assistance to the Carlists and if the Spanish republicans in the undoubted renewal of their agitation should render it evident that the starry banner of the United States had been raised in hostility against Spain, not under the republic, but only under the monarchy. And, finally, whosoever has some historical remembrance does not require any proof that a serious complication between America and Spain (and the latter would not hesitate at the most extreme proceedings in order to retain her possession) might have for Europe incalculable consequences.

Mr. Fish to Mr. Orth.

[Telegram]

WASHINGTON, *January 20, 1876.*

ORTH, *Minister, Vienna:*

May give copy two sixty-six to minister if desired.

FISH, *Secretary.*

Mr. Orth to Mr. Fish.

No. 92.] LEGATION OF THE UNITED STATES,
Vienna, January 21, 1876.

SIR: I hereby acknowledge the receipt of the following telegram, which I translate as follows:

May give copy two sixty-six to minister if desired.

As Count Andrássy desires a copy of said note, I shall, as thus directed, give him a copy as soon as the same can be prepared.

I have the honor, etc.,

GODLOVE S. ORTH.

Mr. Orth to Mr. Fish.

No. 94.] LEGATION OF THE UNITED STATES,
Vienna, January 24, 1876.

SIR: Pursuant to your cable telegram of the 20th instant, I to-day transmitted to the Imperial and Royal minister of foreign affairs a copy of instruction No. 266 to Mr. Cushing.

Herewith inclosed is a copy of my communication to Count Andrássy accompanying such transmission.

I have the honor, etc., GODLOVE S. ORTH.

[Inclosure in No. 94.]

Mr. Orth to Count Andrássy.

The undersigned, envoy extraordinary and minister plenipotentiary of the United States of America, begs leave to remind His Excellency the Count Andrássy, minister of the imperial house and Imperial Royal minister for foreign affairs, that on the 16th day of December, 1875, in pursuance of the instructions of the President of the United States, the undersigned had the honor to bring to the notice of the imperial and royal minister of foreign affairs, by reading to His Excellency the Baron von Hofmann, in the absence from this city of His Excellency the Count Andrássy, a copy of the instructions of the President to his envoy extraordinary and minister plenipotentiary at Madrid on the subject of the relations then and still existing between the United States and Spain growing out of the unfortunate situation of affairs in the island of Cuba.

At a subsequent interview with Baron von Hofmann on this subject he informed the undersigned of the desire of His Excellency the Count Andrássy, to be furnished with a copy of said instructions, with which desire the undersigned was not at liberty to comply, and so informed the Baron von Hofmann; but the undersigned at the same time remarked that he would communicate with his Government and advise the President of the desire of His Excellency the Count Andrássy in this respect.

The undersigned has now the honor to inform his excellency that he has had such communication with his Government, and he is instructed by the President to furnish to his excellency a copy of the said instructions, which copy the undersigned has now the honor of herewith inclosing.

In making this communication to his excellency the undersigned is instructed by the President to assure his excellency that it is the sincere and earnest desire of the President for the termination of the disastrous conflict in Cuba, by the spontaneous action of Spain, or by the agreement of the parties to said conflict. And the undersigned is further instructed to say to his excellency that, should the Government of His Imperial and Royal Majesty find it consistent with its views to urge upon Spain the importance and necessity of either terminating or abandoning this contest, which now, after a continuance of seven years, has not advanced toward a prospect of success on either side, but which is characterized by cruelties, by violations of the rules of civilized modern warfare, by pillage, desolation, and wanton incendiarism, threatening the industry, capacity, and production of an extended and fertile country, the President believes that the friendly expression of such views to Spain by the Government of His Imperial and Royal Majesty might lead that Government to a dispassionate consideration of the hopelessness of the contest, and tend to the earlier restoration of peace and happiness to Cuba, if not to the preservation of the peace of the world.

The undersigned need hardly add that such a course on the part of the Government of His Imperial and Royal Majesty would be exceedingly gratifying to the United States, and, in the opinion of the President, conducive to the interests of every commercial nation and of humanity itself.

The undersigned is further instructed distinctly to assure His Excellency the Count Andrássy that the Government of the United States is not actuated by any ulterior or selfish motives in this matter, nor has it any desire to take advantage of the distracted condition of Spain, but rather to induce her of her own accord to seek an adjustment of the contest now existing between her and her colony.

The undersigned embraces this opportunity, etc.,

GODLOVE S. ORTH.

LEGATION OF THE UNITED STATES,
Vienna, January 24, 1876.

Mr. Orth to Mr. Fish.

No. 95.]   LEGATION OF THE UNITED STATES,
Vienna, January 29, 1876.

SIR: I was somewhat surprised this morning while reading the London Telegraph of the 27th instant to find in it what purported to be a telegram from this city of date January 26, and which I herewith inclose.

The matter is probably not of sufficient importance to bring to the attention of the Imperial and Royal ministry for foreign affairs, yet I deem it proper to apprise you of it and to add the remark that it seems somewhat strange that the Imperial and Royal ministry for foreign affairs should not be more reticent with reference to interviews between it and foreign Governments, for I feel sure that it is only through some-one connected with the foreign office here that these matters are thus paraded in the public press.

I have the honor, etc.,   GODLOVE S. ORTH.

[Inclosure in No. 95.—Extract from the London Telegraph of January 27, 1876.]

UNITED STATES AND SPAIN.

[Reuter's telegram]

VIENNA, *January 26 (evening).*

The United States minister here having been confidentially asked by the Austrian foreign office to leave with it a copy of Mr. Fish's note concerning Cuba, in order that an answer might eventually be returned, he telegraphed to Washington for instructions and received a reply declining the request. It is understood that another note may possibly be sent at a future period.

No. 49.]   DEPARTMENT OF STATE,
                                         Washington, February 9, 1876.

SIR: I have to acknowledge the receipt of your No. 90, under date of January 13, and which reached the Department on the 4th instant.

You inclose a copy of a telegram which appeared in the London Daily Telegraph, sent from Vienna on the 4th ultimo, stating that the cabinet in Madrid had instructed its representatives abroad to make certain explanations to the Governments to which they were accredited, and that the Austrian Government would not reply to the American dispatch, which had only been read to the minister for foreign affairs.

You state that on January 12 you repaired to the ministry of foreign affairs and commenced the interview by stating that for certain sufficient reasons the President would be pleased to receive an answer, as promised, from the Austrian Government, and that later in the interview you called Baron Hofmann's attention to the telegram referred to, stating that no answer would be given.

While you were instructed to promptly advise the Department of the result of your interview with the minister for foreign affairs, it was not intended that a pressure should be brought upon the minister to furnish you with a reply, especially when it was intimated that the Austrian Government was not disposed to make representations at Madrid.

It may also be said that the language employed by you might have led the minister to suppose that some new instruction addressed to you, or some exigency made it advisable to obtain an answer.

You were instructed to read 266, and to make certain verbal representations in so doing, and it was not contemplated that the reply to be given to such a communication would be in writing.

It was quite competent, however, for the Austrian Government to reply in that form if deemed more advisable—but it does not seem advantageous at the present time and in view of the present situation of the question to press for any formal reply.

I am, etc.,   HAMILTON FISH.

Mr. Fish to Mr. Orth.

[Telegram.]

                                         WASHINGTON, *February 14, 1876.*

ORTH, *Minister, Vienna:*

Your ninety-four received. Your instructions did not contemplate a written communication from you to minister, nor to press for a formal answer.

                                         FISH, *Secretary.*

Mr. Fish to Mr. Orth.

No. 50.]   DEPARTMENT OF STATE,
                                         Washington, February 14, 1876.

SIR: Referring to your dispatches relating to instruction No. 266, addressed to Mr. Cushing, and to your proceedings pursuant to instruction No. 38, the Department is now in receipt of your No. 94, with which you forward a copy of a note addressed to the foreign office under date of January 24, inclosing a copy of No. 266 to the minister for foreign affairs.

By instruction No. 38 you were directed to make certain oral statements in person to the minister for foreign affairs on reading 266, and it is now perceived that in transmitting a copy thereof you have formally repeated in the note the oral statement which you had once made to Baron Hofmann.

On receipt of your telegram that a copy of 266 was desired by the foreign office, a reply was sent to the effect that as it had not been given to other Governments, it was preferred not to give a copy at that time, particularly so, as very shortly after your interview of December 16 the purport thereof was telegraphed from Vienna and given to the public.

Congress having called upon the President for the correspondence, and in response thereto No. 266 being about to be communicated, you were then authorized to give a copy to Count Andrássy, if still desired.

It was expected that you would await a renewal of the expression by the foreign office for a copy before giving it, and it was not anticipated that in delivering such copy any departure should be made from the personal and oral mode of communication prescribed in the original instruction.

I have already suggested, under date of February 9 and in my telegram of this date, that it is not deemed advisable to ask from the foreign office a formal reply.

I am, etc.,   HAMILTON FISH.

Mr. Orth to Mr. Fish.

No. 99.]   LEGATION OF THE UNITED STATES,
                                              Vienna, February 16, 1876.

SIR: I am in receipt of telegram. I shall, of course, not "press for formal answer."

I have the honor, etc.,

                                         GODLOVE S. ORTH.

Mr. Fish to Mr. Orth.

No. 54.]   DEPARTMENT OF STATE,
                                       Washington, February 28, 1876.

SIR: I have to acknowledge the receipt of your No. 95 under date of January 29, with which you inclose a copy of a telegram which appeared in the London Telegraph of the 27th of January, to the effect that upon being asked by the Austrian foreign office for a copy of dispatch 266 in reference to Cuba, you had requested instructions, and a reply had been received declining the request.

You state your surprise that such matters should be communicated by the foreign office at Vienna, from whence you are assured the information has come. I have to say in reply that nearly every step in this matter taken by you at Vienna has in like manner appeared in the public prints in the form of telegrams, appearing to come from Vienna, to the London papers or to those in this country.

At your first interview the facts with particularity immediately appeared in the papers, and I am quite satisfied that a telegram appeared, at the time a copy of 266 was asked for, stating that you had asked for instructions.

This last telegram seems to complete the information.

It would be quite proper to call the attention of the foreign office, at some convenient season, to the surprise which such publications have occasioned in this country.

In my telegram of the 14th of January last, declining to give a copy of 266 at that time, and in the statement that the facts concerning the reading of that dispatch had been given to the public, I referred to the telegram concerning your first interview.

  I am, etc.,　　　　　　　　　　　HAMILTON FISH.

Mr. Orth to Mr. Fish.

No. 104.]　　　　　　LEGATION OF THE UNITED STATES,
　　　　　　　　　　　　　　　Vienna, February 29, 1876.

SIR: While at the office of the imperial and royal ministry of foreign affairs on yesterday, Count Andrássy remarked to me that he had read with much interest the copy of the Spanish note (referring to No. 266) which I had furnished in pursuance to instructions and inquired whether it was expected that he should, on behalf of his Government, present any reply.

I told him the object of presenting the note to the Government of His Imperial and Royal Majesty was merely for information, and that my Government did not expect any reply thereto.

  I have the honor, etc.,

         GODLOVE S. ORTH.

FRANCE.

Mr. Fish to Mr. Washburne.[1]

No. 756.]　　　　　　　DEPARTMENT OF STATE,
　　　　　　　　　　　　　　Washington, November 15, 1875.

SIR: Herewith you will receive a copy of an instruction, No. 266, dated the 5th day of November instant, addressed to Mr. Cushing, the minister of the United States at Madrid, which sets forth at length the considerations which have led this Government to the adoption of the views therein expressed concerning the condition of affairs in Cuba. It is believed that other powers, as well for the interests of their own subjects or citizens as for the sake of humanity at large, will recognize the justice thereof, and the necessity of the course which the President feels it his duty to pursue.

You will read this instruction 266, or state orally the substance thereof, to the minister of foreign affairs confidentially (but will not give a copy thereof), and will assure him of the sincere and earnest desire of the President for a termination of the disastrous conflict in Cuba by the spontaneous action of Spain, or by the agreement of the parties thereto.

You will further state that the President is of opinion that should the Government to which you are accredited find it consistent with its views to urge upon Spain the importance and necessity of either

---

[1] Same to legations of the United States at Berlin, St. Petersburg, Vienna, Rome, and Lisbon.

terminating or abandoning this contest, which now, after a continuance of seven years, has not advanced toward a prospect of success on either side, but which is characterized by cruelties, by violations of the rules of civilized modern warfare, by pillage, desolation, and wanton incendiarism, threatening the industry, capacity, and production of an extended and fertile country, the friendly expression of such views to Spain might lead that Government to a dispassionate consideration of the hopelessness of the contest, and tend to the earlier restoration of peace and prosperity to Cuba, if not to the preservation of the peace of the world.

Such a course on the part of the Government to which you are accredited would be exceedingly satisfactory to the United States, and in the opinion of the President conducive to the interests of every commercial nation, and of humanity itself.

You will at the same time distinctly state that this Government is actuated by no ulterior or selfish motives, and has no desire to take advantage of the distracted condition of Spain, but rather to induce her to spontaneously seek an adjustment of this contest.

I need not impress upon you the confidential nature of these instructions, nor the delicate duty which is imposed upon you.

Similar instructions have been issued to the representatives of the United States accredited to the principal European powers.

You will seek an early interview with the minister of foreign affairs, and promptly advise me by telegraph, in cipher, of the result thereof.

I am, etc.,

HAMILTON FISH.

P. S.—Since the above instruction was prepared, a telegram[1] has been received from Mr. Cushing, which renders it advisable that no steps be taken by you to communicate instructions No. 266, as directed, until further instructions be sent you by telegraph.

H. F.

Mr. Fish to Mr. Washburne.[2]

[Telegram.]

WASHINGTON, *December 6, 1875.*

WASHBURNE, *Minister, Paris:*

Proceed as instructed in No. 756; message will discountenance recognition of belligerence or independence; will refer to continuance of struggle, and intimate that mediation or intervention by other powers will be an ultimate necessity unless adjustment reached; will express willingness to mediate; will be friendly and conciliatory in tone.

FISH, *Secretary.*

---

[1] Mr. Cushing's telegram, dated November 16, here referred to, brought satisfactory assurances from the Spanish Government upon the points in dispute. It is printed in House Ex. Doc. No. 90, Forty-fourth Congress, first session.

[2] Reprinted from House Ex. Doc. No. 90, Forty-fourth Congress, first session. Same to legation of the United States at Berlin, and, under date of December 13, to the legations at St. Petersburg, Vienna, and Rome.

Mr. Hitt to Mr. Fish.

[Telegram]

PARIS, *December 9, 1875.*

Duke Decazes wishes to consult with English Government before answering. Thinks Madrid Government so weak it dares not settle Cuban question.

HITT, *Chargé.*

———

Mr. Hitt to Mr. Fish.

No. 1263.]   LEGATION OF THE UNITED STATES,
                                      Paris, December 10, 1875.

SIR: On the morning of Tuesday the 7th instant I had the honor to receive your cipher telegram, addressed to Mr. Washburne, of date the 6th, to "proceed as directed in dispatch No. 756."

Immediately after deciphering the telegram, I went o the foreign office, but the Duke Decazes had gone to Versailles, being engaged in the debate on the Egyptian judiciary reform bill. It was expected that the debate would close that day, and that I could have an interview the next. The debate continued, however, and the Duke having to make his speech the next day closing the debate, which had excited a good deal of public interest, he desired to devote his whole attention to that subject. Wednesday he was therefore at Versailles, but sent me word that he would hurry back after the session and see me at half past 5 Thursday, when I accordingly had an interview with him. This will explain the delay.

In this interview I stated orally the substance of your dispatch to Mr. Cushing accompanying your No. 756: the long-continued and unsatisfactory correspondence between our Government and that of Spain in relation to the questions growing out of the strife in Cuba; the embargo and confiscation of estates in Cuba belonging to our citizens and the failure to comply with the stipulations of the treaty of 1795; the delays for now over six years to remedy this admitted injustice, the tardy orders of the home Government being disregarded by the colonial authorities; the trial by courts-martial of American citizens and their summary punishment, the equally unsatisfactory result, in fact, of correspondence with successive ministries; the failure to try General Burriel, who had received promotion instead of punishment; the nature of the war in Cuba, involving so much injury to our interests and entailing a constant strain upon our Government in maintaining all its obligations, of which it has been scrupulously careful; the utter hopelessness of the war on the part of Spain, the friendly feeling of our Government, and its earnest and unselfish desire to see an end to this ruinous struggle.

At this point I stated the substance of that part of the President's message which relates to this subject, as given by the cable, and then communicated to him the opinion of the President that if France, in her situation specially favorable for such an office, should see fit to urge in a friendly spirit upon Spain the necessity of an immediate solution of this seven years' trouble, by either abandoning the useless struggle or in some way adjusting the differences with the Cubans, it might be received in a dispassionate spirit and lead to results which would obviate the increasing danger of further complications and tend to the preservation of peace; and that our Government would view such an act on the part of our ancient ally with great satisfaction. This is, briefly, what I stated with more detail and precision.

The Duke Decazes replied, that while cordially desiring the end of the strife in Cuba, there were many embarrassments surrounding the proposition, and reason to apprehend that such a suggestion to Spain would be fruitless. He had been informed that a similar presentation of the case had been made to Lord Derby, and asked me if it had not been made in the same terms.

I answered that I did not know that the proposition had been made in the same terms precisely, but I presumed so.

The Duke proceeded: "Lord Derby, I am advised, asked for time before giving a categorical answer. I wish to have further communication with the London cabinet, that there may be an understanding between us on the subject; and therefore I will defer any formal answer for the present. The question is one of a very delicate nature, and whatever we might wish to see done at Madrid, or that Government might be disposed to do, the great obstacle to any result lies in the weakness (impuissance) of the Government of the young Alphonso. That weakness as regards this particular question arises from a general condition (ensemble) of affairs in Spain. Many circumstances together have produced such a situation that, although the Spanish Government might wish to take such steps as were proposed—tending to self-government and emancipation in Cuba—it dare not do it. It would fall if it attempted a policy which could be used against it with the Spanish people. The northern provinces, disturbed by the Carlists, and Cuba with its insurrection, are both held with difficulty. The young King's Government must move with exceeding care. Besides, there is doubt of the power of the home Government to enforce its will. Have you not just told me of one of its decrees in regard to embargoed estates that was disregarded?"

I replied: "That is true; but the Spanish Government is the only power responsible for what is done in Cuba. They do not admit that war exists. The question, however, is not merely what will suit the special interests of any one, but it concerns the preservation of the general peace. The United States have endured the condition of things I have described for seven years. Would France have been more patient? Is it not well for you, situated so favorably, to try in the interest of mankind to end a state of things, so threatening as it might become in the event of another *Virginius* affair, if you can do it by a friendly word?"

The Duke resumed: "I appreciate the situation. I listened to your statement with the deepest attention; but the question is grave and surrounded with difficulties. The young King dare not commence his reign with a failure (defaillance). We have suffered from the strife in Cuba in our interests, though less than you, and we wish it were ended. But if the Spanish Government allowed the Carlists a pretext to assume to be the champions of the preservation of the colony to Spain, it would increase its embarrassments. There is the recent letter of Don Carlos, proposing to subdue the rebellion in Cuba; the Spanish people (ces pauvres diables espagnols) take it for serious, and do not see the ridiculous side of it."

The Duke asked if I was at liberty to give him a copy of your dispatch. I informed him that my instructions were to read or state orally the contents to him. He said he would reduce our conversation to writing from memory, and send me a copy by his chef du cabinet for correction. He asked if there was not news of recent accommodation having been effected. I told him that the newspaper dispatch referred to from Madrid only professed to give the substance of a dispatch from the Spanish minister, assenting to our claim for a trial before civil tribunals, and defenders for Americans arrested in Cuba, in conformity with the treaty of 1795; but that twice before the Spanish Government had, in particular cases, promised to carry out that treaty and redress such wrongs; that it only concerned one of the several questions pending, and not the general question.

He resumed, describing the situation of Spanish politics, but I have given above all that fell in direct response or reference to the proposition I had presented.

I have, etc.,   R. R. HITT.

Mr. Fish to Mr. Hitt.

No. 775.]   DEPARTMENT OF STATE,
                             Washington, January 7, 1876.

SIR: Your No. 1263, giving the statement of your interview with the Duke Decazes, pursuant to the instructions contained in my No. 756, has been received.

Your statements in bringing to the notice of the minister of foreign affairs No. 266 to Mr. Cushing were judicious and apposite, and your proceedings as reported are approved.

No definite conclusion seems to have been reached by the minister of foreign affairs, as you report that information having reached the French Government in reference to the communication made to Lord Derby on the same question, the Duke Decazes stated that he desired an opportunity to consult with the English Government as to the course which should be pursued.

It is not known what communication, if any, has taken place between Duke Decazes and Lord Derby. General Schenck, however, stated in a telegram under date of December 2 that Lord Derby had informed him that while his Government was not then prepared to give a categorical answer as to what steps would be taken, at the same time he was willing to say that his Government was ready to cooperate with the United States in such way as might bring about a settlement of the troubles in Cuba, without bringing pressure to bear upon Spain or putting forward such proposals as would certainly be rejected.

I deem it proper to inform you as to the condition of the question, and you will forward to the Department any information which may be obtained in reference thereto, and in case the minister of foreign affairs has communicated to you no conclusion on the part of his Government, you will take a suitable occasion again to delicately call his attention to the matter.

I am, etc.,   HAMILTON FISH.

Mr. Hitt to Mr. Fish.

No. 1279.]   LEGATION OF THE UNITED STATES,
                             Paris, January 23, 1876.

SIR: Last evening I saw the Duke Decazes a second time in regard to the Cuban question. I had received your dispatch No. 775 in the morning, and during the course of the day took occasion to ask his chef du cabinet when I might see the minister. The answer came at once that he would see me at 5 o'clock.

In this interview I recalled his attention to the subject of our conversation a month ago, and said that I did not come to ask for an answer to what I had then presented nor to urge it upon him again; but he had remarked that he desired to have an understanding with Lord Derby before giving a full response; I had been informed that Lord Derby, while not answering categorically, had signified the readiness of the English Government to cooperate with the United States to bring about a settlement of the Cuban troubles without bringing pressure to bear upon Spain, or making proposals certain to be rejected. I had therefore called, remembering the friendly spirit in which he had treated the subject before, to hear any suggestions or information he might choose to communicate.

The Duke Decazes replied that since our former conversation he had given the question very serious attention. He had made note of the substance of my statement at that time, had ascertained that the statement presented to Lord Derby was substantially the same; had made similar inquiry at Vienna; also at St. Petersburg, though he had not as yet received an answer from the Russian minister. He had ascertained that Lord Derby was disposed to agree to any step toward a solution, provided it could be seen that it would produce a practical result, but Lord Derby feared that in the present position of affairs in Spain, such proposals as were suggested by the United States, if addressed to Spain, would be useless. Lord Lyons had recently called upon him (Decazes) on this subject, and there was an exchange of views in regard to the condition of Spain and this question of Cuba and the way in which it was regarded by the English Government.

"I told him," said the Duke, "that I thought we might say some word to Spain which would lead to something, if it was done with due regard to the susceptibilities of that Government, if it was managed properly and with care and preceded by a manifestation of the friendly spirit of those offering it."

"It is true," he continued, "the opportunity for such a suggestion is not striking just now. They are occupied over there in Spain with the elections and with the Carlist war. They have been making a greater effort than before to end that Carlist war. They are all in uncertainty about themselves, and are thinking of the elections and their results. How can one ask them to attempt the settlement of such a grave and difficult question as their relations with Cuba, and that long contest there, when they are uncertain whether they will be the ministers twenty-five days from this time? They are looking ahead with anxiety, and do not care to broach such a business now. Still, I think it might be well to make some representation in regard to this Cuban trouble in the way I have mentioned, say some word which would not be unacceptable, and would accord with the wishes of your Government; and I wish to act in an understanding with Lord Derby. It is now two weeks since I offered the suggestion which I have just recited to you, and I have not yet received a response; but at that I am not surprised, for Lord Derby has been out of town and only returned the other day for a council, and probably has been so occupied otherwise as would account for the delay."

I thanked him for the cordiality and frankness with which he discussed the question, which was one of profound interest to the United States and just now engaged the attention of Congress, having been, as he was aware, the subject of a part of the President's message. The

English Government had had occasion to accord with our own repeatedly in the discussions growing out of affairs in Cuba, and the Government of France had so long been friendly to the United States that we had no hesitation in approaching it in regard to a case which we deemed so manifestly just.

He remarked: "Be assured that we have not neglected this matter. Although a month has passed, the considerations you offered have received much attention, and we recognize the character of the question. In all this, however, you know you have a special interest, and you look at the struggle in Cuba in view of the facts that urgently affect you. Our interests are also touched, but not so largely as yours, by that insurrection. European Governments do not feel so pressingly the need of instant action. We must consider all the circumstances, the condition of the Spanish Government, and the probability of a result if we said anything just now. I wish your Government to know that we are sincerely interested in the matter you have presented, and anxious to be able to give you such an answer as will be pleasing to your Government."

I have, etc.,

R. R. HITT.

Mr. Washburne to Mr. Fish.

No. 1288.] LEGATION OF THE UNITED STATES,
Paris, February 15, 1876.

SIR: Learning that the Duke Decazes had returned to Paris, I took occasion on Friday last to make an official call upon him, in order to pay my respects upon my return to Paris and to speak to him in relation to several pending questions.

I first called his attention (and this for the third time) to the subject of your circular letter in regard to diplomatic intercourse in China.

He excused the long delay in answering, and promised to send a note on the subject in a few days.

I then had a conversation with him touching the proposition which I had made for a telegraphic treaty, and particularly in regard to a late communication I had received from him on the subject. I shall probably be able to make a separate dispatch in regard to this matter before a long time.

But the important part of the interview was in relation to Spanish affairs and to your circular, which in my absence Mr. Hitt had submitted to him. I asked him how far he had considered the subject, and what I could write to my Government in reply. With great frankness he answered, in substance, as follows:

I have thought of it, and am still thinking of it. This Cuban question touches us also very closely—it affects our interests as it does yours. Our commerce with the island is now paralyzed, and the continuance of the state of things which exists there has been to us a source of many kinds of annoyance. We suffer from that state of things like you, and we would desire very much to see an end put to it. Unfortunately, it is difficult to suggest anything practicable in this respect. What could be said to Spain at this moment which would be of any use to you and to her? She is actually under so many embarrassments, and she has so many things that are the subjects naturally of her gravest attention that we would fear to hurt her susceptibilities unnecessarily and render the situation more embarrassing to both Governments than it is, should we just now approach her directly on this question. I have, however, said a word in the matter—a discreet word. I have communicated to the Marquis de Molins the analysis of the conversation I had with Mr. Hitt. I made him that communication confidentially, and I told him:

"I don't ask of you any answer. but think of this. There is here a grave situation which calls for your attention. There is something to do; reflect upon it. I will have probably to speak again of this to you, and if you yourself bring the subject up, so much the better."

Winding up his statement, the Duke resumed:

In short, I beg you to bear two things in mind: Firstly, that we are sincerely desirous to assist you and Spain in this affair; secondly, that the situation of Cuba affects our own interests, and that we would be quite willing to cooperate with you in bringing it to an end if we thought the opportunity was favorable for that. Il faut attendie.

The Duke Decazes is very much occupied at present in his canvass, being a candidate for deputy in the new assembly. He is running in the eighth arrondissement of Paris, in which this legation is situated; also in the department of Aveyron, in the southern part of France. He did not seem to be entirely confident of an election in either district. You will have the result, however, by Monday next, by telegraph.

I have, etc.,

E. B. WASHBURNE.

Mr. Fish to Mr. Washburne.

No. 783.]
DEPARTMENT OF STATE,
Washington, February 17, 1876.

SIR: I have received and read with attention Mr. Hitt's dispatch, No. 1279, under date of January 23 last, in reference to his interview with the Duke Decazes concerning the substance of instruction No. 266, addressed to Mr. Cushing.

The dispatch is a clear and concise statement, and his proceedings, as detailed therein, are approved.

I am, etc.,
HAMILTON FISH.

GERMANY.

Mr. Fish to Mr. Davis.

No. 148 of November 15, 1875. (Same as No. 756 of same date to Mr. Washburne, p. 480.) Telegram of December 6, 1875. (Same as that of same date to Mr. Washburne, p. 481.)

Mr. Nicholas Fish, Chargé, to Mr. Fish.

[Telegram]

BERLIN, *December 7, 1875.*

Telegram of 6th received. Inclosure of 148 read to Mr. von Bülow. He thanked for information. Said he would lay it at an early day before Emperor and Prince Bismarck. That in the interest of peace and commerce Germany desired question settled, but he could only take the matter ad referendum.

FISH, *Chargé.*

Mr. Nicholas Fish, Chargé, to Mr. Fish.

No. 220.]   LEGATION OF THE UNITED STATES,
                         Berlin, December 8, 1875.

SIR: I had the honor to receive your telegraphic instruction of December 6 at 10.30 a. m. yesterday, directing me to proceed as instructed in No. 148.

As soon as the telegram could be deciphered, I called at the foreign office and explained to Mr. von Bülow the object of my visit, and in order that he might more perfectly understand the views of the President, I took with me instruction No. 148, and refreshed my memory therefrom.

I was careful to inform him that it was believed that other powers would recognize, for the interests of their own citizens as well as for the sake of humanity, the necessity of the course which the President feels it his duty to pursue. I stated to him the opinion of the President that should this Government find it consistent with its views to urge upon Spain the necessity and importance of either terminating or abandoning the contest in Cuba, the friendly expression of such views to Spain might lead to the earlier restoration of peace and prosperity to Cuba, if not to the preservation of the peace of the world.

I told him that such a course on the part of Germany would be exceedingly satisfactory to the United States, and, in the opinion of the President, conducive to the interests of every commercial nation, and of humanity.

I distinctly stated that the Government of the United States is actuated by no ulterior or selfish motives, and has no desire to take advantage of the distracted condition of Spain, but rather to induce her to spontaneously seek an adjustment of this contest.

In order to impress this upon him, I read from instruction 148 the paragraph relating thereto.

I then read to him confidentially your instruction to Mr. Cushing, No. 266.

As I began he checked me to inquire what the date of it was, and then listened attentively to the whole reading.

At its close he thanked me for the information and said that he would take an early occasion to lay the matter before the Emperor and Prince Bismarck, and that he could only say that in the interest of peace and commerce Germany desired the question settled, but that he could only take the matter "ad referendum."

He also told me that they had some questions of unjust treatment of German subjects in Cuba, to which attention had been called in the Reichstag, and that while their treaty with Spain was ambiguous, they would seek to protect the rights of their citizens there.

With this my interview closed, and on leaving the room I found the Spanish minister waiting in the antechamber; he had been announced while I was reading the first portion of your instruction to Mr. Cushing.

I inclose an account cut from the Post of the 25th November (with translation of the same) of the interpellation in the Reichstag, to which Mr. von Bülow referred.

I have the honor to be, sir, etc.,

                                        NICHOLAS FISH.

[Inclosure in No 220.—Translation. Extract from German Parliamentary proceedings, the Post. November 25, 1875]

The title "Consulate at Havana" being called, Deputy Mosle expresses the wish that the prayers for protection against contributions addressed by the German merchants resident there to the foreign office might be responded to.

Federal Commissioner von Phillipsborn declared that the possibility of intervention might be judged of differently according to different interpretations of the treaty; the foreign office was, however, in connection with the representatives of other Governments, occupying itself with the question.

Mr. Nicholas Fish, Chargé, to Mr. Fish.

No. 222.]
LEGATION OF THE UNITED STATES,
Berlin, December 14, 1875.

SIR: Since my No. 220, I have called twice at the foreign office to see if Mr. von Bülow had any information to give me in regard to the restoration of peace in Cuba. It was not until to-day that I succeeded in finding him.

He stated to me that he had communicated the substance of your instruction 266 to Mr. Cushing to Prince Bismarck, as well as the length of the instruction would enable him to do so, and that the Prince had laid it before the Emperor.

I thanked him for the information, and said that I would communicate it to you, and that I felt sure that the President would be pleased to know of the manner in which his views had been received.

I have, etc.,
NICHQLAS FISH.

Mr. Nicholas Fish to Mr. Fish.

No. 224.]
LEGATION OF THE UNITED STATES,
Berlin, December 17, 1875.

SIR: Referring to my Nos. 220 and 222, I have the honor to inclose herewith translation of a telegram I sent you at 2 p. m. on the 15th instant.

I have the honor to acknowledge the receipt of your telegram of the 16th instant, which was received at 2 a. m. to-day.

I inclose a copy and translation of the account given in the Neue Preussische Zeitung of the interpellation in the Reichstag, which appears to be fuller than the one given in the Post, though not essentially different.

The interpellation occurred in the session of November 23.

I have been unable to find any newspaper comments upon the subject of the interpellation, and it does not appear to have attracted much attention at the time.

I have the honor, etc.,
NICHOLAS FISH.

Mr. Fish, Chargé, to Mr. Fish.

[Inclosure 1 to No. 224.—Telegram of December 15, 1875—2 p m.]

Two sixty-six to Cushing in substance laid before Emperor by Bismarck. Germany desires peace, and will continue to urge necessity of tranquillity with view of adjustment of German grievances.

FISH, *Chargé.*

[Inclosure 2 in No. 224 —Interpellation in regard to the consulate at Havana in German Parliament November 23, 1875, from the Neue Preussische Zeitung]

In regard to title 45 (consulate at Havana) Deputy Mosle remarks: The German merchants in Havana, as well as in every part of Cuba which is in the possession of the Spanish Government, are subjected to the war contributions, which the Spanish Government has imposed in consequence of the revolution, in the most exorbitant and insupportable manner. Now, it is clear that in times such as exist in Cuba, in which the revolution demands great sacrifices on the part of the Government, those also should contribute who have long enjoyed the advantages of peace. The German merchants in Havana, however, believe that these demands have been excessive and that they are entitled to exemption from these war contributions under the treaty with Spain, and for the reason that Cuba is no longer a colony but has become a Spanish province. They have in consequence, if I am not in error, addressed themselves to the imperial chancellor for relief from this evil. I desire on my part to ask the representatives of the Government if steps have been taken to relieve these complaints of the merchants. I should be much obliged if information could be given me on this subject.

The Federal Plenipotentiary von Philipsborn: The complaints of Germans concerning these contributions have long since come to the knowledge of the foreign office. The latter at once made a close investigation of the subject, with the result that there arose for consideration a number of treaty provisions which are otherwise interpreted by the other side than by us. We could take no action alone, but only in conjunction with other friendly Governments concerned in like manner. To this is added the necessary consideration not to cause more difficulties to the Spanish Government at this moment than the position of things absolutely requires. The foreign office is, however, continually endeavoring to further the matter in the interests of the Germans at Havana.

Deputy Mosle: I thank the representative of the Federal Government for the information, and shall hope that it may succeed in mastering these difficulties at a very early day.

Deputy Kapp inquired how it happened that so important a consulate as that at Havana should have been unoccupied for half a year.

Federal Plenipotentiary von Philipsborn: As is known, the last consul at Havana was lost on the steamship *Schiller*, and it has not yet been possible to definitely fill this consulate. The representation of the consulate for the time being is, however, in good hands, and the interests of the Germans at Havana are now preserved and protected in every direction.

The position is approved.

Mr. Fish to Mr. Nicholas Fish.

No. 165.]

DEPARTMENT OF STATE,
Washington, January 7, 1876.

SIR: I have to acknowledge the receipt of your 220 and 222, dated, respectively, December 8 and December 14, ultimo.

Your proceedings in communicating to Mr. von Bülow instruction 266, addressed to Mr. Cushing, as reported in your 220, and in your further interview, as reported in your 222, are approved.

No information has reached the Department of any representations having been made by the German representative at Madrid in the sense indicated by Mr. von Bülow, and you will report to the Department any information which you may be able to obtain on that subject, and with reference to the exact instructions which have been issued, and as to any steps which have been taken at Berlin, bearing on the question.

You will take an early occasion to express to the minister of foreign affairs the satisfaction of the President that the views expressed in instruction 266 are in some measure at least concurred in by the Government of Germany, and that, appreciating the purpose in view, that Government was ready to instruct its representative at Madrid, as referred to by Mr. von Bülow.

I am, sir, etc., HAMILTON FISH.

Mr. Nicholas Fish to Mr. Fish.

No. 242.]　　　　　　　LEGATION OF THE UNITED STATES,
　　　　　　　　　　　　Berlin, January 10, 1876.

SIR: In the interview which I had with Mr. von Bülow to-day, and which I have reported to you in my No. 241,[1] I asked him if he had anything to communicate to me, in hope that he would state more definitely what this Government intends doing in regard to Spain. He said, without referring to the subject by name, that he had nothing new to communicate.

While paying a visit at the house of the Spanish minister on Friday, he took occasion to turn the conversation to the affairs of his own country, and stated that all their efforts were being urged and strained for the purpose of suppressing the Carlists; that they would very shortly have 380,000 men in the field, and that their army would move to the north as soon as the winter would permit; he said that he felt sure of success, and that then it was the desire of his Government to turn all its energies to the restoration of peace in Cuba; and that then it desired to perform all its obligations to the United States in a spirit of justice, equity, and friendship.

I answered that I knew very little of the condition of affairs in Spain, but that in the United States, where the duration of the insurrection in Cuba gave rise to many causes of vexation, we would be greatly pleased at seeing peace restored in Cuba, but that officially I could not say anything on the subject.

I report the conversation, as the minister, Mr. Merry y Colom, seems to be on intimate terms with the Spanish minister of foreign affairs, and purported to express his views.

　　　　I have, etc.,　　　　　　　　　　　　NICHOLAS FISH.

Mr. Davis to Mr. Fish.

No. 254.]　　　　　　　LEGATION OF THE UNITED STATES,
　　　　　　　　　　　　Berlin, January 26, 1876.

SIR: At the interview with Mr. von Bülow to-day, reported in my No. 255,[1] we also spoke of Cuba. I asked him if he could say to me what answer had been made to the German representation about the duration of the war. He replied that the Spanish Government had assured Count Hatzfeldt that the insurrection would be shortly suppressed—as soon as the Carlists should be put down—and that as soon as the rebellion was crushed liberal reforms would be given to Cuba. I told him that I had frequently before heard of such promises, and I asked him whether it was proposed to withhold all advances to the insurgents until the rebellion should be crushed. He said he believed it was. I said that I was very sorry to hear it, for judging from the past there seemed to be little probability of the speedy suppression of the rebellion. He said that the Spanish Government represented that the insurrection was confined to insignificant numbers of negroes and mulattoes; that no or few Cuban white persons were engaged in it, and that none of the white population of the island sympathized with it.

I replied that I had no instructions on the subject, and that in what I was about to say I spoke my individual opinion and in no sense the

---

[1] Not printed.

views of my Government. Speaking thus individually, I would say that I believed such representations to be incorrect. I believed almost the whole creole population of the island was dissatisfied with the violent and arbitrary measures of Spain, and that if the Spanish troops were withdrawn from the island, and the persons known as peninsulars were left alone to deal with the insurrection, the world would soon see that the opposition to Spain was not confined to a few negroes and mulattoes. He said that the subject was full of difficulties for Germany—that their traders and merchants have large interests in Cuba which are suffering, and that they would be glad to see peace restored. I learn from other sources that this is the case, that the tobacco merchants of Bremen and Hamburg have been much injured, and that they are pressing the Government to do something in their behalf with more zeal than is agreeable to the Government.

I have, etc.,

J. C. BANCROFT DAVIS.

GREAT BRITAIN.

Mr. Fish to Mr. Schenck.

No. 803.]

DEPARTMENT OF STATE,
Washington, November 5, 1875.

SIR: Herewith you will receive a confidential copy of an instruction this day addressed to Mr. Cushing, the minister of the United States in Madrid. Such part as relates to our particular causes of complaint against the Spanish authorities concerns the United States alone. Such part of the instruction, however, as announces to Mr. Cushing the conclusions to which the President has arrived in reference to the strife now raging in Cuba, and as instructs him to communicate these conclusions to the Spanish Government, is believed to be not only of interest to the Government of Great Britain, but such as it is supposed will be regarded by that Government as just and necessary.

The instruction sets forth the considerations which have led this Government to the conclusions which have been reached, and it is hoped that the Government of Great Britain, having similar interests to protect, and regarding this strife from a similar point of view, as well for the interests of its own subjects as of humanity at large, will not be unwilling at least to support our position by its approval and influence. This being the case, the President is of opinion that it is just to the Government of Great Britain to communicate in confidence these conclusions, and to suggest that, in his opinion, the expression by Great Britain to Spain of its approval of the view of this Government, and its influence to induce a settlement, will tend to a more speedy adjustment and will more surely induce the Government of Spain, by some wise and conclusive measures, to render all thought or necessity of intervention from any quarter unnecessary.

The Government of Great Britain may possibly, of its own accord, think proper, in view of its own interests, to cooperate with the United States in this effort to arrest a cruel war of devastation. This, however, is a question to be raised by Her Majesty's Government. Humanity, its own great interests, and a regard for the preservation of the peace of the world, it is believed, will, without doubt, lead it to support the position which this Government has at length been forced to assume, and to address its representative in Madrid to that end.

Mr. Cushing has further been instructed to defer his interview with the minister of state until you shall have communicated to this Department the result of your interview with Lord Derby. You will read to Lord Derby, in confidence, the copy of the instruction to Mr. Cushing (No. 266), inclosed herewith, and will distinctly state that this Government has no selfish or ulterior objects in view, and no desire to take advantage of the difficulties which have surrounded the Spanish Government.

You will take the earliest occasion practicable to comply with this instruction, and will promptly communicate with the Department by telegraph, and in cipher, the result thereof.

I also inclose for your information and for such use as may be advisable in this interview, a copy of an instruction addressed to Mr. Cushing (No. 267), by which he is instructed to await further instructions from the Department before communicating with the minister of state, in order that the disposition of the British Government may be ascertained.

I need not impress upon you the confidential nature of all of these instructions, and the delicate duty which is imposed upon you.

You may say to Lord Derby, without reading to him the instruction last mentioned, that Mr. Cushing is instructed to withhold the presentation to the Spanish Government of the decision of the President until after it shall have been made known to Her Majesty's Government.

I inclose also for your information a copy of an instruction to Mr. Cushing (No. 265, of the date of November 5, instant) on the subject of General Burriel. * * *

I am, etc., HAMILTON FISH.

Mr. Fish to Mr. Schenck.

[Telegram.]

WASHINGTON, *November 19, 1875.*

SCHENCK, *Minister, London:*

Advices from Cushing suggest delay in reading inclosure to eight hundred and five. You will await further instructions.

FISH, *Secretary.*

Mr. Schenck to Mr. Fish.

No. 830.]   LEGATION OF THE UNITED STATES,
            London, November 20, 1875. (Received December 6.)

SIR: I received last evening your telegram of yesterday.

Your No. 805 referred to in your telegram reached me early this morning, and would have been read to Lord Derby to-day had not your telegram delayed my action.

I have, etc., ROBT. C. SCHENCK.

Mr. Fish to Mr. Schenck.[1]

[Telegram.]

WASHINGTON, *November 27, 1875.*

SCHENCK, *Minister, London:*

Read inclosure to eight hundred five as soon as opportunity will admit. You will explain that intervention is not contemplated as an

---

[1] Reprinted from House Ex. Doc. No. 90, Forty-fourth Congress, first session, but omissions supplied.

immediate resort, but as a contingent necessity in case the contest be prosecuted and satisfactory adjustment of existing griefs be not reached, and that we sincerely desire to avoid any rupture, and are anxious to maintain peace and establish our relations with Spain on a permanent basis of friendship. I now state further, for your own information and for your guidance in your interview with minister, that message will discountenance recognition of belligerency or independence; will allude to intervention as a possible necessity, but will not advise its present adoption. Cushing is instructed to communicate to minister without waiting result of your interview, but you will communicate with him in cipher after your interview.

Take precaution that the purport of instruction or of information above be not given through minister to press or public.

FISH, *Secretary.*

Mr. Schenck to Mr. Fish.

[Telegram.]

LONDON, *November 30, 1875.*

FISH, *Secretary, Washington:*

Have communicated confidentially and fully with Lord Derby and read instruction to Cushing.

He will give me views of this Government Thursday.

SCHENCK, *Minister.*

Mr. Schenck to Mr. Fish.

[Telegram

LONDON, *December 2, 1875.*

FISH, *Secretary, Washington:*

Had interview again with Lord Derby. He received telegram yesterday from Layard saying Cushing had delivered to Spanish Government your note of 5th, but requested no definite action upon it until he could communicate with you. He expected you would receive yesterday or to-day a communication from the Spanish Government, and if that affords basis for settlement of grievances the President might modify views in message.

Lord Derby prefers in this state of circumstances not to discuss the matter until the President has had opportunity of considering last communication from Spain. He has no objection, however, to say his Government would be willing, in the interest of humanity and friendship, to cooperate in any way that promises to bring about a settlement of troubles in Cuba, but is not prepared to put any pressure on the Spanish Government or to put forward proposals which he has reason to think it would not be inclined to accede to. Thinks Spain, as a saving of her dignity, might be willing to accept some interposition, in which case Great Britain would not object to use good offices, but not if Spain stands off and declines any interference. Believes Spain will certainly reject any proposal for her giving up Cuba, and would never yield that except to force, but might be induced to agree on a basis of self-government of the island.

SCHENCK.

Mr. Fish to Mr. Schenck.[1]

[Telegram.]

WASHINGTON, *December 6, 1875.*

SCHENCK, *Minister, London:*

Communication from Spanish Government, referred to in your telegram of 2d, received to-day. It is friendly in tone and is hoped will afford basis of adjustment of our particular grievances.

It suggests no alteration in message upon general questions of the condition of Cuba and continuance of struggle.

As indicated in my telegram of 27th, message will discountenance recognition of belligerence or independence; will intimate that mediation or intervention by other powers will be an ultimate necessity unless adjustment soon reached; will express our readiness to mediate; will be friendly and conciliatory in tone.

FISH, *Secretary.*

Mr. Schenck to Mr. Fish.

No. 860.]   LEGATION OF THE UNITED STATES,
London, January 27, 1876. (Received February 11.)

SIR: The text of your note of the 5th November to Mr. Cushing was considered of so much interest here that it was telegraphed in full by the cable immediately after it was communicated to Congress. It was printed in the London Times and in one or two other metropolitan newspapers on the morning of the 24th instant, with leading articles commenting on the exposition thus authentically conveyed to the public of the actual diplomatic position and relations between the United States and Spain.

I inclose of these articles three or four which may help to give you some idea of the outside English feeling and temper always exercising no little influence on the views of Her Majesty's Government.

The Morning Post and the Pall Mall Gazette are not to be much regarded, for they represent that sort of Toryism which is given to carping at almost everything done by our Government. But the articles in the Times, which are much fairer, reflect, I think, a good deal of what may be taken as the general tendency of British sentiment, or I may even say of British judgment, in relation to our complaints against Spain.

I would attract your attention more particularly to what appeared in the columns of the Times yesterday. The writer could not forbear a flippant fling at what he characterizes as your "rhetoric," but otherwise the spirit in which that article is conceived and the views it presents so nearly shadow the disposition of this Government that I am inclined to believe it has been in some sense officially inspired. It followed the next morning after an interview I had with Lord Derby; and in the suggestion that the representatives of friendly States might, without the formality of intervention, show Spanish ministers at Madrid it would be no discredit to grant reasonable demands, I think I see something of the idea which is in the mind of his lordship.

It was my intention to give you by to-day's mail an account of what passed between Lord Derby and myself in the interview referred to, which took place on the 24th instant—two days ago. But he promised

---

[1] Reprinted from House Ex. Doc. No. 90, Forty-fourth Congress, first session.

at parting to send mo an informal memorandum of the views he expressed, so that I might report his words with perfect accuracy; and he has not yet furnished me with that memorandum.

I shall communicate the substance of the conversation by the mail of Saturday.

I have, etc.,

ROBT. C. SCHENCK.

[Inclosure 1 in No. 860.]

Editorial, London Times of January 24, 1876.

A long and severe criticism of Spanish policy in Cuba, contained in the American note of November last, was laid before the House of Representatives at Washington on Friday. Our readers are enabled to peruse these interesting documents in full, by the aid of the Atlantic cable, this morning, though they were only published in the United States on Saturday. Mr. Fish's dispatches to Mr. Caleb Cushing are unsparing in their condemnation of Spain, and are weighted with menaces directed against Spanish misdoing. But the indignation and reproaches of Mr. Fish have not been provoked only by the Madrid Government, and do not fall upon that Government alone. If it were merely administrative recklessness or political blundering that had been assailed the danger would be less, and some way out of the difficulty would at least be visible. But we know that the least justifiable acts of the Madrid Government, those most likely to provoke a collision with the United States, have fallen short of rather than gone beyond the arrogance of the national spirit. Spain is arraigned on as many charges as were solemnly paraded against George III in the Declaration of Independence, and each charge is pressed home with a vigor of rhetoric to which few parallels can be found in diplomatic history.

Yet, on the whole it must be allowed that Mr. Fish's able argument has a solid basis of justice, and that his conclusion is tempered with unexpected moderation. Summing up the general and special grievances relating to Cuba that the United States have alleged against Spain, Mr. Fish raises questions so serious as these: "How long this condition of things can or should be allowed to exist," and "whether a point has not been reached where longer endurance ceases to be possible." This ominous estimate of the relations between Spain and the United States is fortunately modified by the remedy to which, as it seems, the Washington Government are ready, at all events in the first instance, to resort. A copy of the American note was simultaneously transmitted to the capitals of the six European powers, and General Schenck was instructed to make a special communication to Lord Derby, suggesting a conjoint or, at least, a concurrent remonstrance and, as a "contingent necessity," a conjoint intervention for the restoration of peace in Cuba.

This remarkable correspondence can hardly fail to excite American politicians, not because there is likely to be any difference of opinion in the United States as to the iniquities of Spain, but because the policy of inviting the cooperation of the European powers is a bold departure from the political traditions of the United States. The invitation has not been addressed to Great Britain alone, but also to the Governments of France and Italy, and to the three Empires. This is manifestly an abandonment of the "Monroe doctrine" which has so long controlled American policy, and has disconnected it, at all events in theory, from the general web of political interests throughout the civilized world. To exclude from the American continent not only every advance by annexation or colonization of the monarchical powers of Europe, but every direct influence of those Governments for good or evil, was in substance the political dogma which takes its name from President Monroe. This monstrous pretension at the time when the Democratic party and the slave power were in close alliance had nearly assumed an aggressive form, and if events had not checked and rebuked it, would probably have tempted the Union into a ruinous filibustering policy.

The civil war prevented the United States from actively asserting the Monroe doctrine, though the intervention of France, England, and Spain in the affairs of Mexico excited vehement protests on the other side of the Atlantic. But Mr. Fish's invitation to the European powers, recognizing, as it does, the fact that the nations of Europe have interests to watch and defend on the American continent, mark very distinctly the progress of the people of the United States in political good sense. It is sheer folly for any country, however powerful and however confident in its destiny, to take upon itself to wall off half the world, and say to the commonwealth of nations, "You have nothing to do with all on this side." The claim is as inadmissible as that of the Holy See to partition the unknown lands of the East and the West between Spain and Portugal. The premises of the argument on which the

Monroe doctrine is based are unsound. It is not true that the nations of Europe, whom that doctrine would restrain from any interference in American affairs, have not a great deal to do directly with America. England and Spain, France and Holland, have their colonies on the mainland or in the Central Archipelago.

But, setting aside the fact that many of them are really thus American as well as European powers, they are all of them closely interested in the prosperity of the American communities through their commerce. But commerce even is only one of many bonds which are continually multiplying the relations of human societies. It is vain to think that any part of the work of the world can be isolated, as some American politicians labored to isolate the development of their continent. If it were possible to effect this, the injury to human progress would be incalculable, but a man might as well measure a square mile of the ocean and protest that it was his private property and that none of the unappropriated waves should presume to trespass upon it.

While, however, we can not refrain from expressing our satisfaction at the improvement of political thought in the United States upon this subject, and while we are sure that Mr. Fish's invitation will be courteously answered by Lord Derby and by the foreign ministers of the other European powers, it is not obvious that it is incumbent upon us to interfere in the dispute between Spain and her revolted colonists. If we choose to take the risks and responsibilities, we should, no doubt, be justified in intervening for the sake of humanity; but it is not the business of this country, nor, for that matter, any other, to play the knight-errant among nations. It is unlikely that we shall go beyond advice, if we go so far, unless we have suffered a wrong so serious as to touch the national honor or interests, and have been denied redress. We must confess it is for the American people to decide whether they have been injured and insulted so that "endurance is no longer possible."

The catalogue of offenses committed by Spain which Mr. Fish has elaborated in his dispatch is formidable in its appearance, and no doubt most of its particular charges can be proved. Some of them, as the delay in executing the stipulations of the Virginius treaty, the embargo and confiscation of property of American citizens, and their irregular and unjust treatment by Spanish military tribunals in Cuba, are apparently admitted by the Spanish Government. Others, as, for instance, the injury to American commerce, are open to question, and have, indeed, been keenly questioned in the United States. Others again, such as the cruelty and inhumanity of the war are no doubt to be deplored, but if repressed by foreign intervention must show some distinct menace of danger to the intervening power. On the whole, the grounds of complaint, so far as they are well founded, have exclusive reference to the United States and Spain, and third parties can not with any prospect of international advantage take part in the negotiations. The aggrieved and the offending powers must patch up their differences for themselves; for though Spain may be vexed at being rated and the United States may use harsh threats, the risk or loss if the disputants should try to settle the quarrel by force is too serious to be rashly incurred.

It is possible, however, that the European powers might help to promote a compromise which, while saving the honor of Spain, would put an end to the Cuban difficulty. The Anti-Slavery Society about a fortnight ago addressed a memorial to Lord Derby, in which it was asserted that the Spanish Government was willing to make great changes in the position of Cuba, giving the island the right of a self-governing colony, such as Canada or New Zealand, in the British Empire, but on condition that slavery might be retained. The Anti-Slavery Society protested against any sanction being given by the British Government to the latter stipulation, which, it was alleged, the United States Government had determined to reject.

It is noticeable that in Mr. Fish's note the example of the relation between Great Britain and her colonies is held up for approval and contrasted with the old despotic colonial system of Spain. If, then, the two Governments are agreed as to the end, there ought to be little difficulty in devising the means of execution. The theoretical question of slavery need occasion little controversy. Cuba with a practically independent legislature would soon find itself obliged to abolish the "peculiar institution." The island in all probability would be badly governed, but, at any rate, a hopeless, purposeless, fruitless war would be ended, Spain would be freed from a heavy burden without loss of honor, and the Pearl of the Antilles would be able to develop in peace her magnificent natural resources.

[Inclosure 2, in No. 860.]

Editorial London Morning Post, January 24, 1876.

The precise attitude of the American Government towards Spain in regard to the Hispano-Cuban affair is shown in the correspondence published at Washington

It appears that on the 5th of November Mr. Fish sent a note to the United States minister at Madrid setting forth the views and demands of the Government on the subject. There are reiterated protestations of friendliness toward Spain in both the note and observations of the minister in presenting it. If the action of America is friendly in this matter, Spain may well exclaim, "Defend me from my friends." Certainly the American idea of friendliness is sufficiently strange. Under any circumstances it would have been curious friendliness to have sent a communication of the kind; but to choose the moment of Spain's greatest trial and difficulty to send it was alike unusual and indefensible.

Let us see, however, what it is that America complains of and demands. Mr. Fish starts by making an admission that might have suggested to him the propriety of doing nothing to embarrass Spain; says that "the war on the part of the insurgents is one of pillage and destruction, which the United States are most interested in stopping." Is not Spain far more interested than America in stopping such a war? The "pillage and destruction," spoken of are much more injurious to Spain than to the United States, and as it is the insurgents that are giving this character to the war, it would be more fitting to seek to discourage and embarrass them than the Spaniards. The complaint is then preferred that Spain has "rejected all suggestions for reform, mediation, or reconciliation." What would America have said if Spain or any other country had offered to intervene between her and her own revolted provinces? Would she not have rejected the suggestion as lowering to her dignity and detrimental to her interests and authority? No one knowing America could doubt as to the answer that would have been given in such a case; yet here is America making formal complaints of her proffered interference having been neglected.

As usual, it is one law for America and another for the rest of the world. Mr. Fish then remarks that "the violation of treaty obligations" by Spain and "her unwillingness to afford redress" leads the American Government to ask if Spain's conduct is "any longer to be endured." Here, it will be observed, the American Government makes no distinction between a failure to carry on the due administration of a country, owing to sad misfortunes and crushing difficulties, and a willful "violation of treaty obligations" and an "unwillingness to afford redress." But, of course, the American Government is perfectly well aware that the Cuban difficulty is nothing as compared to the difficulty in Spain itself, and that the Cuban difficulty has existed so long solely on account of that other. America is aware, also, of the immense exertions and sacrifices made by Spain to overcome her various difficulties; and yet, just as Spain is on the point of directing all her force, so painfully accumulated, against the root of the whole evil, in steps the United States to distract her attention and compel a division of her force and resources in respect to a minor matter that would have been settled, and to much better effect, in its turn.

This is President Grant's idea of judicious and friendly action. Mr. Fish then goes on to tell Spain that while she insists that there is no war, she claims the rights of war, and that this can not continue. Even if this were strictly correct, would it lie in America's mouth to bring the charge? "Mutato nomine de te fabula narratur," is a proverb that applies exactly to this case. Mr. Fish then alludes to the precise claims that his Government has to make in the shape of the restoration of embargoed estates and the trial of American citizens; and as Spain at once agreed to do all that she could in the matter, America may have had some cause for complaint. But even so, would it not have been in better taste and equally effective if America had proceeded gently and really kindly in the matter, and had avoided a bullying tone and attitude toward a Government almost at its wit's end from a concatenation of trials and troubles? The United States foreign minister then proceeds to lecture Spain on "the interests of humanity," the treatment of her colonies, and slavery.

He seems to forget that probably America would to this day be exhibiting herself as of old the inhumanity of slavery but for the accident of the revolt of the Southern provinces. The way in which slavery came to be abolished in America must be looked to as well as the mere fact of the abolition. America is hardly the country to lecture another on the subject of slavery. Anyhow, America might have waited until after the suppression of the pillaging and destructive insurrection, until the civil war in Spain had been ended, and until the King and Government of Spain had had a fair opportunity of dealing with the question of the colonies, before lecturing and advising on the matter. The note winds up with the hope on the part of the President that "Spain may secure peace, otherwise he feels that it may become the duty of other Governments to interfere." On this point, Spain can reply that she is straining every nerve to secure peace; that foreign intervention does but encourage the rebels; that the action of the American Government has driven her to divert forces and resources to Cuba that ought to have been employed in crushing the Carlists, and that America has no commission to speak for "other Governments."

Such being the character of the note from the American to the Spanish Government, what are we to think of the injunction to Mr. Cushing to "assure Spain of the friendly disposition of the United States, which have no selfish object in view, and are moved solely by the necessity for self-preservation and the interests not only of humanity but of Spain herself." This is the friendship of the wolf to the lamb.

Luckily the wolf has got no teeth; America has neither army nor navy worth mentioning, and she can not even deal with her red Indians, who afford her a field for the practicing of the "humanity" that she would preach to others. America is good enough to inform Spain that she has no selfish motive, but "qui s'excuse s'accuse," why speak of the matter? Lastly, America tells Spain that intervention is not contemplated as an "immediate result, but only as a contingent on failure of other efforts." This is very kind of America; but people, interpreting for themselves her pettifogging selfishness, will be apt to reflect that without the permission and aid of "other Governments," America could not intervene at all, and that the "other Governments" will avoid hampering the hands and weakening the efforts of Spain at the very moment when she is in all sincerity, honesty, and diligence striving by every means to reestablish peace and order in her dominions both at home and abroad.

[Inclosure 3 in No. 860]

Editorial from London Pall Mall Gazette, January 25, 1876.

THE UNITED STATES AND CUBA.

The note sent by Mr. Fish to Mr. Cushing for presentation to the Spanish Government is a singular combination of reasonable complaint and unreasonable declamation. The Government of the United States are entirely within their right in pointing out to Spain the inconvenience caused to American citizens by the civil war in Cuba and in warning her that unless redress can be obtained for the past injuries and some security provided against their recurrence they may be obliged to redress their own grievances by their own hands No power can be expected to endure the unprovoked seizure of property legally possessed by its subjects, or the banishment of them without trial There is no need in this case to consider whether the charges are well founded, because the Spanish Government admits that they are substantially true. In his telegram of the 4th of December last Mr. Cushing reports that the minister of state admits the American grievances, "is opposed on principle to the sequestration of the property of foreigners, condemns the delay of redress, and will take up and promptly settle each case."

If Mr. Cushing's remonstrances had gone no further than the ground covered by this reply, the question might be regarded as disposed of. That Spain can insure the United States from the annoyances which war necessarily inflicts upon mutual neighbors is impossible; but if she is in earnest in reducing these annoyances to a minimum she can greatly soften the legitimate irritation which now exists in America. But Mr. Fish's dispatch is much more comprehensive than the minister of state's reply. The sufferings of American citizens are thrown into comparative insignificance by the side of those higher considerations which Mr. Fish invokes. When the civil war broke out in the United States the Federal Government treated the belief expressed by individual Englishmen that the seceding States would eventually establish their independence as something not far short of an insult, for which the British Government ought to be held responsible The Executive of the United States sees no harm in doing officially what it blamed Englishmen for doing in their private capacity. "More than five years since," writes Mr. Fish, "the firm conviction of the President was announced that whatever might be the vicissitudes of the struggle, and whatever efforts might be put forth by the Spanish power in Cuba, no doubt could be entertained that the final issue of the conflict would be to break the bonds which attached Cuba as a colony to Spain."

General Grant's convictions are his own property, and if he had expressed them as General Grant Spain would at most have had to complain of a violation of international decorum. But when the President of the United States convictions on the issue of a civil war are announced in formal dispatches they assume in some respects the character of active forces. If Spain had been strong enough she would have been perfectly justified in warning the United States that they must take their choice between active intervention or complete abstention. Nothing short of active intervention can be more unlike complete abstention than the attitude of a Government which cheers the Cuban insurgents with predictions that they must certainly succeed. Great powers do not love to see themselves proved false prophets; and it can hardly be questioned that one at least of the causes which have made the suppression of this insurrection so difficult has been the belief of its authors that in the last extremity President Grant would make good his words and help the Cuban rebels "to assume independence and a right of self-control which natural rights and the spirit of the age accord to them."

Of course, Spain had abundant reason for not taking up the quarrel; but what can be said of the diplomacy which revives the recollection of an insult offered in a dispatch the ostensible object of which is to obtain redress for injuries sustained? Either Mr. Fish is a singularly blundering workman, or at the time of writing his note of the 5th of November he had some other end in view than the mere redress of grievances, which is all that he explicitly demands. When it is remembered that the substance of the dispatch was communicated to the American newspapers on the eve of the November elections, and that the subject thus suddenly brought to the front has since been allowed to drop out of notice, it is not an unnatural inference that the effect of the note on the American electors was more in Mr. Fish's thoughts than its effect on the Spanish Government.

The result has been that the American electors have shown themselves wiser than their guides. Whatever force there may prove to be in the plea that General Grant must be elected President a third time in order to carry on a war with the Vatican, there is seemingly no popular conviction that it is worth while to provoke a war with Spain in order to overcome the prejudice against a third term. It does not indeed require any keen political acumen to detect the difficulties which surround both the alternatives suggested in Mr. Fish's dispatch. It is a cheap exercise of international officiousness to hope that Spain may spontaneously adopt measures for the organization of a stable and satisfactory system of government in Cuba, but if Mr. Fish had to state in words what the measures in question should be, the impossibility of framing them would be at once apparent. If Spain succeeds in putting down the insurrection, a stable government of a certain kind may be established. If the United States go to war and annex Cuba, a stable government of a certain kind may be established.

But to talk of a stable government in an island in which the passions excited by quarrels of race, of color, of social position, have raged with scarcely any restriction for more than five years, while proclaiming in the same breath the impropriety of these passions being subdued by the hand of any external power, is to use words which have no meaning. The concession of independence to Cuba might mean peace as between the mother country and her emancipated colony, but it would not mean peace in Cuba itself. On the contrary, it would only mean war, renewed with greater determination, and conducted with greater fierceness, between the insurgents and that part of the population which, as Mr. Fish very truly puts it, "has sustained and upheld, if it has not controlled, successive governors-general." How this conflict would end we do not pretend to say, but it is safe to predict that while it lasted it would be characterized by yet greater atrocities, and inflict yet greater annoyances on foreign residents than the war which has gone on so long.

After a time the exhaustion of resources and the partial extermination of the fighting population would bring active hostilities to an end; but the experience of West Indian and South American independence does not make their subsequent resumption at all unlikely. It is to create this sort of wilderness within sight of the United States that the American people were invited to run the risk of a war with Spain. For that a war with Spain involves very grave risk to the United States is undoubted. At the outset of a contest which can only be carried on at sea the comparative wealth, numbers, and resources of the combatants go for little, except so far as they are embodied in actual ships.

The power of Spain, such as it is, is so embodied; the power of the United States is not; and it is at least possible that the first act of a war between the two countries might be the bombardment of every American seaport. It does credit to the good sense of the American people that they have not cared to run this risk for the doubtful benefits of annexing an island which they do not want and being ruled for four years longer by General Grant.

————

[Inclosure 4 in No. 860.]

Editorial from the London Times, January 26, 1876.

In Europe at least there will be a tendency to do injustice to Mr. Fish's indictment of Spain, precisely for the reason which may render it effective among his own countrymen. When American diplomacy states a complaint, it usually makes a large call on those general terms of invective which please half-educated readers, but shock the taste and rouse the suspicions of the more fastidious students.

Critical minds are apt to fancy that the rhetoric has been framed for the purpose of touching the Americans themselves, and when they mentally translate it into scholarly English they tend to cut away much of the truth as well as to improve the style. We speak the more frankly because Mr. Fish seeks to obtain the moral support of European countries in his contest with the Spanish minister of foreign affairs respecting the civil war in Cuba. He would, we assure him, have been much more effective if he had given specific examples of the wrongs or hardships suffered by his countrymen and left his readers to supply general phrases of indictment. Nevertheless, there need be no doubt that his charges are substantially just, and the truth itself is so grave as to need little ornament from rhetoric.

In Cuba Spain owns one of the fairest and most fertile islands in the world, and it has been detestably misgoverned. While we have allowed our colonies to rule themselves in their own way, Spain has persisted in keeping Cuba in the same state of tutelage as when she herself was the greatest power in the world, and when the very idea of colonial rights had scarcely arisen. The island has been dependent on the will of a Government changed every few years by a pronunciamiento or a popular revolution. It has been used as a place of honorable banishment for unruly soldiers. The dangerous spirits of the army have been sent to Cuba to be kept out of mischief, and they have let loose in the colony the temper which had been found perilous at home. Freed from responsibility, they have often displayed a repetition of that domineering spirit, that contempt of the rights of others, and that cruelty which once added dark chapters to the history of the Spanish conquest. The slaughter of the crew of the *Virginius* was an act which would have been quite natural three centuries ago, but which, when committed in our time, seems wonderful on account of its folly as well as of its atrocity. If the author of such a deed had been an Englishman, he would assuredly have been hung, yet he is still at liberty, and we believe he has still some kind of command

We can not wonder that Mr. Fish. who speaks for a people as proud in their own way as the Spaniards and immeasurably more powerful, should peremptorily demand the trial of General Burriel. America has also many other causes of complaint. Her citizens owned much property in Cuba and a great deal of it has been confiscated by the Spanish Government Restitution has been promised and evaded. Americans, Mr. Fish thinks, have been wrongfully condemned by the insular courts, and they have failed to obtain redress The Spanish Government has violated its treaty obligations. Still more serious is the injury which it has done to Cuba, and indirectly to America, by the savagery of its warfare It is laying great part of the island absolutely waste, and thus injuring the interests of the United States in order to maintain slavery and Spanish rule. Nor does Mr. Fish believe that the rebels can be put down, and therefore he calls upon the Government at Madrid to give Cuba at least those privileges of self-rule which have had an admirable effect in the colonies of this country.

It will be very difficult to answer an indictment so formidable in itself and ending in so mild a demand The purists of international law may at once be warned off the field of discussion. They may say that the United States has no more right to dictate how Spain shall govern Cuba than Spain has to order the reorganization of the South They may say that the American citizens who live in Cuba went there at their own risk, and must bear the inevitable penalties of civil war. Much the same fate, it may be pleaded, would have come to any Spaniards who had owned property in Virginia during the war between the North and the South, and yet they would have received no redress. Nor, it might be added, were either the Confederate or the Federal cruisers particularly respectful of foreign rights in their efforts to destroy each other. But these arguments are fit merely for lecture rooms. The practical answer is that the general rules of international usage, conveniently called international law, can be applied only to ordinary cases of warfare. Since there is no international parliament, each nation is justified in defending its interests by exceptional measures when they are attacked in an exceptional manner.

Mr. Fish may plead that international law presupposes the power or the readiness of States to be guided by the ordinary rules of civilized morality, and that in her relations with Cuba Spain has systematically set those rules at defiance. The case of the *Virginius* was such an outrage on the usual laws of warfare as to debar her from afterwards invoking them on her own behalf. The duty, therefore, of the United States must be determined, not by the letter of international law, but by general considerations of policy. We find, then, that Spain has driven one of the finest islands in the world into revolt; that she is trying to suppress the revolt by systematic savagery; that she refuses to promise the colonists any form of self-government, and that the restoration of peace by mere force is all but hopeless. The Spanish minister of foreign affairs has promised, it is true, that justice shall be done to those American citizens who have been wronged, but he does not offer to remove the real cause of strife by abolishing slavery or allowing the colonists to rule themselves. We can scarcely expect Mr. Fish to be satisfied with the repetition of a pledge which has already been broken, or with less than the pacification of the island itself. Nor can we blame him for insisting that if Spain will not set Cuba free, she is bound to make it orderly; but at the same time we can not admit that there is any need for war.

America is acting with at least as much moderation as this country would display if Cuba were as near to Cornwall as it is to Florida. In such a case we should require Spain to protect the property of our countrymen and to take the obvious means of restoring her colony to a state of peace. The rhetoric of an English dispatch would be more measured and precise than that used by Mr. Fish, but it would lead to demands at least as keen. On the other hand, the dispute is one of those which may be arranged without war, or even without the formal intervention solicited by America. The representatives of foreign States at Madrid will, of course, discuss the quarrel with the Spanish ministers, and they can not fail to point out with friendly politeness the folly of the outrages inflicted on American citizens. They will also be able, we should hope, to show the necessity of granting reparation.

In the course of the negotiations with America, the Spanish ministers may likewise be brought to see that they must grant some form of self-government to the revolted colony. The representatives of friendly States can easily show the Spanish ministers, without the formality of intervention, that it would be no discredit to grant reasonable demands, especially when they have been put forward by a State which would in the long run be a match for Spain, even if she were as powerful as she was in her imperial days. It ought to be the more easy to give and take advice, because the United States is manifestly eager to avoid extremities, and would be glad of any reasonable compromise.

On the other hand, the Spanish people are as ignorant as they are proud, and it will need more courage than their ministers usually display to tell the Cortes what is the real state of Cuba and what is the sole remedy for misrule.

Mr. Schenck to Mr. Fish.

No. 862.]
Legation of the United States,
London, January 28, 1876. (Received February 12.)

SIR: In a dispatch sent yesterday I informed you that I had had another conversation with Lord Derby on the subject of our relations with Spain and the condition of affairs in Cuba.

The interview took place three days ago (25th), but I have waited until I could report his lordship's language in his own words, and it was only last evening that I received from him a memorandum which he had promised, enabling me to do so.

* * * * * * *

I began by reading to his lordship a copy of the cable telegram I sent you on the 2d of December, reporting what he had said to me at that time. He remarked that "nothing could be more accurate" than my statement of his own language, and at once added that he "still remained in the same view as to any intervention."

We had then a conversation of some length. I called his attention to the fact that the text of the President's message, as he must have observed, corresponded strictly and in all points with the assurances and explanations which I had been instructed to give him in advance of its delivery; that the President had discountenanced any present recognition of the independence of Cuba, or recognition of belligerent rights to the insurgents; that the United States desired no rupture with Spain, nor any but the most friendly relations; that any earnest movement on the part of the Government at Madrid to satisfy the just demands of the United States and to put an end by some effective plan of pacification to the deplorable condition of affairs in the island would be gladly hailed and met by us in the most cordial spirit, and that mediation or intervention by other powers was only contemplated as an ultimate necessity. His lordship admitted that such was the tenor and spirit of the message. I told him that the later note from the Spanish Government, to which Mr. Layard had referred as likely to afford a basis for adjustment, had failed to furnish any reason to the President for a modification of the views which he had resolved to express and did put forth in his message; and that indeed the communication, while it afforded hope of a settlement of the particular grievances of the United States, appeared to leave the general question where it was.

Our special causes of complaint and reclamation against Spain for the wrongs done to our citizens and their property I said was, of course, our own concern, and would be taken care of by ourselves, but the interests of humanity, national friendship, and the peaceful security of commerce were all involved in the question of the pacification of the island.

Incidentally I ventured to allude to the opportunity which might, in this connection, be afforded to Her Majesty's Government to manifest their known desire to cooperate by their influence in putting an end everywhere to the institution of slavery.

I referred to the disposition, as learned from Mr. Cushing, of the British minister at Madrid to back him in the matter of Cuba, if a line of action could be agreed on between our two Governments; and I desired to know whether any definite instructions had been given, or would be sent to Mr. Layard tending in that direction.

I was enabled also—having reference to Mr. Hitt's dispatch communicated to me with your No. 833—to say that I had reason to know that France was favorably disposed toward some form of friendly mediation, but that her decision was, to a degree at least, dependent on the course which the Government of Great Britain might adopt.

Lord Derby said in reply, and I give in what follows the succinct statement of his views, as furnished by his own memorandum, that—

The questions with which the United States Government were dealing—the redress of the grievances of American citizens, and the proposal to put an end to the war by mediation—seemed to him to stand on an entirely different footing. In regard to the first, the United States Government had put forward claims which, assuming them to be just in substance, they were entitled to press as a matter of right. In regard to mediation, though everyone could understand the inconvenience and damage to American interests produced by the continuance of the war, yet, strictly speaking, it was not easy to see how any foreign power could claim a right of interference.

They could give friendly advice, but it would rest with the Government of Spain whether to take or to reject it. Lord Derby could only repeat what he had said at a former interview—that, in the interest of humanity and in view of the injury produced by the war, he would be glad to offer the good offices of England to bring about a reconciliation between Spain and Cuba.

But Her Majesty's Government were not prepared to bring pressure to bear on that of Spain, in the event of their overtures being rejected; and that being so, he was unwilling to take any step without having, he would not say a certainty, but a reasonable probability, that some good result would follow After his former interview with General Schenck, he had consulted Mr. Layard, Her Majesty's minister at Madrid, and that gentleman in reply had expressed a strong opinion that no attempt at mediation by a foreign power was likely to succeed at the present time. Lord Derby agreed with Mr. Layard in this view. He knew, as did also General Schenck, the extreme pride and sensitiveness of the Spanish character, and he was aware that the mere suggestion of foreign interference had produced an outbreak of indignation at Madrid. He was convinced that at this moment Spain would listen to no proposal of mediation.

The Spanish Government hoped to finish the Carlist war in the spring, and would then be free to put forth their whole military strength for the reduction of the island, in which they confidently hoped to succeed. They might be disappointed in both expectations, and Lord Derby thought it not unlikely that they would be so, but they certainly would not abandon the idea of crushing the insurrection without further trial.

Lord Derby thought therefore that if nothing were contemplated beyond an amicable interposition, having peace for its object, the time was ill chosen and the move premature:

He had some reason to think that this was also the view of the French and German Governments.

* * * * * * *

I will only add that the general tone and manner of Lord Derby was obviously in sympathy with the idea that it was incumbent on Spain to take as early as possible some decided step in the direction of a reform of her policy toward Cuba. The practical difficulty in opening the subject to her, and in any action to be taken by her Government, lay in the pride and ignorance of her people. He evidently thought that, without any direct offer of mediation, some wholesome influence might perhaps be exercised over the counsels of her ministers by the representatives of friendly powers at Madrid.

I have, etc.,

ROBT. C. SCHENCK.

Mr. Schenck to Mr. Fish.

No. 863.]   LEGATION OF THE UNITED STATES,
          London, January 31, 1876. (Received February 16.)

SIR: With my No. 860 I sent you among other articles of the English press commenting on your dispatch of the 5th of November to Mr. Cushing on the subject of Cuba, one extracted from the London Times of the 26th instant, to which I directed your particular attention. It may interest you to read the comment of the Pall Mall Gazette on that Times article, which I now inclose. · This reply sets up a question about the obligations of international law, for disregard of which it would take the Times to task. I still think the views of the Times are those which are most in harmony with those entertained at the foreign office.

I inclose at the same time a short article on Cuba, taken from the Evening Standard, which is a high Tory paper; and also a scrap from the Spectator, a weekly paper which is considered liberal.

I have, etc.,

ROBT. C. SCHENCK.

[Inclosure 1 in No. 863.]

Article from the Evening Standard, London, January 29, 1876.

The Cuban insurrection is as long lived as the Carlist revolt. There is no calculating the amount of blood and treasure which have been drawn from the mother country to restore quiet to the island within the past few years. Reenforcements of troops have been sent periodically from Cadiz and Santander, not a tithe of whom will ever see Spain again; captain-general succeeds captain-general with the regularity of clockwork, and notwithstanding the end never is, but always to be. The insurgents are beaten on the average twice a month, yet somehow they always turn up in excellent health and spirits as if they thrived on repeated defeat. It is very difficult to get at the truth about Cuba; but one prediction may be made with safety: As long as Don Carlos parades Navarre and the Vascongadas, the pacification of Cuba will be adjourned. No Spaniard with the spirit of a true hidalgo will allow for a moment in public controversy that his country can part with the island, and yet there is scarcely one traveled and educated Spaniard, we venture to affirm, who will not admit in the intimacy of private conversation that his country can not hold the island. If we are to credit a statement of the grievances of the Cubans published in the Paris Temps yesterday evening, Spain deserves to lose the rich possession which she has held and misgoverned since 1511.

According to this document, the island contains nearly a million and a half of people, a quarter of them European Spaniards, birds of passage, desiring to make a fortune and then return home: another quarter negroes, and the other half natives— the offspring of creoles, colonists, or foreigners. Cuba returned deputies to the Cortes till 1837, when it was deprived of its representation and subjected to special laws. This course was instigated by the then Governor-General Tacon, influenced by the Catalans, who carried on the slave trade and were afraid the deputies would denounce their trade, and the monopoly of the resources of the island by Spanish adventurers. The colonists vainly protested; their hopes of a separate constitution were disappointed, and in 1851 there was a rising, aided by American filibusters, which was easily suppressed. In 1865 Marshal Serrano assured the Cubans that they would soon be again represented in the Cortes; but the reactionaries and slave

PORTUGAL.

Mr. Fish to Mr. Moran.

No. 21 of November 15, 1875. (Same as No. 756 of same date to Mr. Washburne, p. 480.)

Mr. Moran to Mr. Fish.

No. 47.] LEGATION OF THE UNITED STATES,
Lisbon, December 9, 1875.

SIR: I received your Nos. 21 and 22, with inclosures, on the 6th instant, and have made myself thoroughly familiar with their contents. In compliance with the instructions in the postscript to No. 21, I have not communicated the substance of your No. 266 to Mr. Cushing to Mr. Corvo; but should you direct me by telegraph or otherwise to do so your orders shall be promptly attended to.

At present I can not form a reliable opinion as to the steps Portugal may be disposed to take in her intercourse with Spain touching this painful conflict in Cuba, but I think that her anxiety to be on good terms with that Government will cause her to hesitate to urge upon the Spanish cabinet at this time the importance and necessity of either abandoning or terminating the contest, however much she may desire to see it brought to an end.

I have, etc., BENJAMIN MORAN.

Mr. Moran to Mr. Fish.

No. 51.] LEGATION OF THE UNITED STATES,
Lisbon, December 31, 1875.

SIR: Señor Alexander de Castro, who was recently appointed ambassador extraordinary and minister plenipotentiary from Spain near this court, arrived in Lisbon on the 21st instant, had an audience with and presented his letter of credence to the King on the 28th, and yesterday and to-day received by invitation his colleagues of the corps diplomatique at the palace of the Marquis de Penafiel, which he has taken for his residence during his stay in Lisbon.

I called upon his excellency this afternoon and was cordially received. He is a person of good presence, is tall and courtly, and would be called distingué in any society. Our conversation was brief, but we did not in any way touch upon politics. As neither he nor I had anything to say to each other about the relations between the United States and Spain, we prudently avoided any reference to that subject; but I was struck with the conviction that I shall find him at least a courteous colleague.

Why Spain has sent an ambassador here to replace an envoy extraordinary is not very well understood, especially as Portugal can not return the honor. It is generally believed, however, in well-informed circles in Lisbon, that it is more a personal compliment to Señor de Castro on the part of his sovereign than a mark of admiration for Portugal, although his speech to the King, a copy and translation of which I inclose, with the King's reply, would lead the world to a different conclusion. He is a man of considerable influence in Spain under the present Government, and it is well known that he has no intention of remaining here for more than five or six months. You will observe that he cautiously insinuates disapprobation of an Iberian union; but this Government is very anxious on that point, and it is not sure that Spain will not overrun Portugal in the event of the independence of Cuba as compensation for the loss of her greatest colony. And yet, although Spain undoubtedly longs for the unification of the peninsula—although such unification would be quite as beneficial to Portugal as to Spain—although England and Scotland hated one another worse than Spain and Portugal do, and yet eventually came together to their common advantage—although the tendency toward unification is the general fact in modern times, as evinced in the cases of Sweden and Norway, of Italy, and of Germany, and can not fail to come sooner or later as respects Spain and Portugal—yet, I believe that no sensible Spaniard contemplates this union by means of war or of any force other than that of circumstances, which it is certain, sooner or later, will induce Portugal to desire it equally with Spain, however strong the opposition to such an end may now be in this Kingdom.

The underlying fear, however, on the part of this Government and people that Spain will seek an early pretext to imperil the independence of Portugal in the event of her losing Cuba, is so apparent to me that I am satisfied that Portugal will under no circumstances at present venture to urge upon the Spanish Government the importance of a speedy termination of the conflict in Cuba, although I am satisfied that this Government ardently desires such a result. I hope, however, that I may be mistaken in this, and that when the time arrives for action Portugal will not be found wanting in her duty to the cause of humanity, justice, and mercy.

I have, etc.,

BENJAMIN MORAN.

[Inclosure 1 in No. 51.—Translation of speech of Señor de Castro to the King, December 28, 1875.]

SIR: The King, Alfonso XII, of Spain sends me to Your Majesty as ambassador extraordinary and minister plenipotentiary. I have now the high honor to place in Your Majesty's hands the royal letter which accredits me.

Sir, the personal representation with which my august Sovereign has deigned to invest me is a demonstration of the high esteem in which Your Majesty is held and of my Sovereign's ardent desire to cement more and more the friendship with the august person of Your Majesty, with the royal family, as well as the intimate and cordial alliance between two people who mutually respect each other and hold fraternal relations.

To obey the desire of my august Sovereign is my principal duty. To fulfill this is my ardent wish. One and the other will be easy for me to accomplish if Your Majesty concedes me his good will and his Government the cooperation which is necessary.

Portugal and Spain are as two good and old friends, who in the recollection of their respective and similar glorious actions can and ought to live together without other rivalries than an honorable incentive to add to such actions, while being both supported by the constitutional monarchies by which they are governed.

May Your Majesty deign to accept the homage of my profound respect.

[Inclosure 2 in No. 51.—Translation of the King's speech in reply to Señor de Castro, December 28, 1875.]

Señor AMBASSADOR: Having received the letter of His Majesty the King of Spain, which accredits you as ambassador extraordinary and minister plenipotentiary at my court, I have heard with sincere pleasure all that you have just expressed to me in the name of His Majesty; both what relates to myself, the royal family, and to the nation over whose destinies I preside, as also concerning the honorable and important mission to represent him personally which your august sovereign has designed to entrust you with.

Deeply sensible of this act of courtesy on the part of His Majesty the King Alfonso XII, I shall always hold it as an agreeable duty to reciprocate his beneficent wishes. I shall, moreover, not cease to employ every means within my reach to preserve the good harmony, and cement more and more the relations of sincere friendship which happily subsist between the two people, united by identity of political institutions, by the record of their glorious deeds in the forefront of civilization and human progress.

As to yourself, Señor Ambassador, I have much pleasure in assuring you that I hold in high esteem your celebrity and the distinguished qualities which adorn you; with such honorable precedents already known to me, no doubt need rest in your mind but that you have obtained already the right of my good will and to the esteem and loyal cooperation of my Government.

Mr. Fish to Mr. Moran.

No. 26.]   DEPARTMENT OF STATE,
                                        Washington, January 4, 1876.

SIR: Your dispatches numbered 46 and 47 have been received. With reference to the last-mentioned dispatch, I have to state that, although a copy of the instruction addressed to Mr. Cushing (No. 266) was transmitted to you, the Department, upon considering the question of which it treats, reached the same conclusions as to the course which would likely be taken by the Government of Portugal as are expressed by you; hence it did not instruct you to make any communication in regard thereto to that Government, nor is it at this time deemed advisable to so instruct you.

I am, etc.,   HAMILTON FISH.

RUSSIA.

Mr. Fish to Mr. Boker.

No. 13 of November 15, 1875, and telegram of December 13, 1875.
(Same as No. 756 of November 15, 1875, and telegram of December 6, 1875, to Mr. Washburne, pp. 480, 481.)

Mr. Boker to Mr. Fish.

[Telegram.

ST. PETERSBURG, *December 16 1875.*

Gortchakoff promises, if Emperor consent, representations shall be made to Spanish Government freely, agreeing to do all in his power for the preservation of good relations. He, however, doubts influence of Russia at Madrid, but sympathetically appreciates our difficulty.

BOKER.

Mr. Boker to Mr. Fish.

No. 35.]   LEGATION OF THE UNITED STATES,
                                       St. Petersburg, December 16, 1875.

SIR: I have the honor to inform you that on the morning of the 14th instant I received from you a cipher telegram. As this was not written

S. Doc. 231, pt 7——33

with the key I had sent to you, nor with that which I had at first received from you, it was impossible to decipher it. I therefore telegraphed to you, "Cipher unintelligible; send keyword or use scythe."

That evening Mr. Schuyler succeeded in deciphering your telegram, making it read, "Proceed as instructed in number thirteen," thus getting your keyword, and this interpretation was confirmed by your telegram received yesterday morning.

I immediately acted upon your instructions and saw Prince Gortchakoff. The details of this interview I shall give you in another dispatch. As a summary of its result, I sent you a cipher telegram, a copy of which I inclose.

I have, etc., GEO. H. BOKER.

Mr. Boker to Mr. Fish.

No. 36.] LEGATION OF THE UNITED STATES,
St. Petersburg, December 18, 1875.

SIR: I have the honor to say that in accordance with your instructions, already referred to in my dispatch No. 35, I called on Prince Gortchakoff for the purpose of laying before him the state of the relations existing between the United States and Spain, as set forth in the inclosures to your dispatch No. 13, and of suggesting to him whether, in the present uncertain condition of the negotiations, it might not be deemed advisable by the Government of Russia to make such representations to the Spanish Government as may hasten the peaceful settlement which the Government of the United States has in view.

On laying before Prince Gortchakoff a condensed statement of the facts, and the arguments contained in your dispatches to Mr. Cushing, I found that the chancellor not only took a deep interest in the questions before him, but he spontaneously offered, if that course should be in accordance with the wishes of the Emperor, to employ the good offices and the friendly advice of the Russian Government with that of Spain, with the intention of effecting an equitable adjustment of the difficulties. At the same time Prince Gortchakoff cautioned me not to expect too much from the intervention of Russia in Spanish affairs, as the influence of the Imperial Government with that of Spain could not be very great at the present time, owing to the long-existing diplomatic rupture between the two countries, the memory of which had scarcely died away at Madrid, the little intercourse between the peoples, and the almost complete separation in which each power exists in relation to the interests of the other.

When I recounted to Prince Gortchakoff a narrative of the events which had led to the complication between the United States and Spain, he expressed the warmest sympathy with the United States. He seemed to be surprised at the patience and the forbearance with which our Government had acted, not only toward the Government of Spain, but toward the more easily approached provincial authorities of Cuba. He said, significantly, that history does not show us that this has been the usual conduct of strong powers toward weaker ones. He commended the reluctance which the Government of the United States seemed to feel in proceeding to serious measures with a country in the distracted condition of Spain, and he said that this last act, the laying of the question before the great powers for their consideration and possible action, was a display of candor and of magnanimity on our part that was almost without precedent in international affairs, and that it must forever set at rest the report that the United States had views of territorial extension in the direction of Cuba.

In commenting on the possible results of a rupture between the United States and Spain, Prince Gortchakoff observed that the earliest and the most inevitable consequence of hostilities would be the loss of Cuba to the Spanish Crown. This event, in his opinion, would be fatal to the prospects of the yet unsettled King of Spain; as it would be a humiliation to Spanish pride which none of the many political parties of the Kingdom could venture to forgive for the sake of upholding the insecure throne of the young King. That consideration seemed to Prince Gortchakoff to be the most important and pressing one to Spanish interests, and should the Emperor agree that representations be made to the Spanish Government, as to the questions at issue between Spain and the United States, I have little doubt that the argument addressed to that Government will be most strongly urged from the point of view just stated.

I shall take care to acquaint myself with any steps that may be taken by the Government of Russia in the direction above proposed, and I shall give to the Department the earliest intelligence of the result of the movement.

I have, etc., GEO. H. BOKER.

Mr. Boker to Mr. Fish.

[Telegram.]

ST. PETERSBURG, *December 23, 1875.*

Russian envoy at Madrid instructed to make representations to Spanish Government. Gortchakoff thinks everything will depend on action of England.

BOKER.

Mr. Boker to Mr. Fish.

No. 38.] LEGATION OF THE UNITED STATES,
St. Petersburg, December 23, 1875.

SIR: I have the honor to say that this morning I had an interview with Prince Gortchakoff in regard to the diplomatic representations which it was proposed should be made by Russia to the Spanish Government touching the precarious relations at present existing between the latter Government and that of the United States, the substance of which interview I this day transmitted to you in a cipher dispatch, a copy of which is herein inclosed.

Prince Gortchakoff informed me that the Emperor had acquiesced in the design, and that instructions had been forwarded to the Russian minister at Madrid to lay before the Spanish Government the views of the chancellor as expressed in my dispatch No. 36, of December 18, 1875, and to proffer friendly and serious advice to that Government in accordance with the spirit of those views.

While Prince Gortchakoff assured me of the pleasure which it gave the Emperor and himself to act in the interest of peace and of good understanding between friendly nations, he once more requested me to remember that which he had previously said as to the moderate influence which Russia must be supposed to exercise in Spanish affairs.

He also reiterated the opinion—as though it were the summing up of his judgment as to the question—that the course of Spain would depend altogether upon the action of the British Government, and the repre-sentations which might be made by it at the court of Madrid, regard-ing the unsatisfactory relations between the United States and Spain. He said that the combined influence of all the other powers was not equal to that of Great Britain with the Spanish Government; and he supposed that as the United States and Great Britain had a common interest and a like grievance in the questions which grew out of the affair of the *Virginius*, the policy and the action of the two nations would be in harmony.

I have, etc., GEO. H. BOKER.

Mr. Fish to Mr. Boker.

No. 25.] DEPARTMENT OF STATE,
Washington, January 13, 1876.

SIR: Your No. 36, reporting the result of your interview with Prince Gortchakoff on communicating to him No. 266 to Mr. Cushing, pursuant to instruction No. 13, has been read with interest and attention, and it is a source of satisfaction to learn that the chancellor should have been impressed with the views of the President contained therein and the patience and forbearance manifested by the United States toward Spain.

It was because the President was satisfied that such conclusions must be reached by an unbiased friendly power to whom the facts might be communicated, that you were instructed to bring the instruction and the views of this Government to the notice of the minister for foreign affairs.

I await with interest further intelligence as to the course pursued by Russia and as to any instructions which may be issued to the repre-sentative of that Government at Madrid.

While appreciating the frankness of the chancellor and the friendly disposition manifested by him, there are certain expressions in your dispatch which suggest the possibility of some misapprehension of the purpose of this Government in making the communication in question.

You state that on laying before the chancellor a condensed statement of the facts and arguments, he spontaneously offered, if in accordance with the wishes of the Emperor, to employ the good offices and friendly advice of the Russian Government with that of Spain with the inten-tion of effecting an equitable adjustment of the difficulties, and in the latter portion of the dispatch that the chancellor stated that the act of this Government in laying the question before the great powers for consideration and possible action was a display of candor and magna-nimity almost without precedent in international affairs.

Instruction No. 266 having been presented to the Government of Spain by Mr. Cushing at Madrid on November 30, you were instructed on the 13th day of December to read the same to the minister for for-eign affairs at St. Petersburg, and to assure him of the sincere desire of the President for a termination of the conflict in Cuba by the spon-taneous action of Spain, or the agreement of the parties, and to state that should the Government to which you are accredited find it consist-ent with its views to urge upon Spain the necessity of terminating or abandoning this contest, it was believed that the friendly expression of such views might tend to the earlier restoration of peace and prosperity to Cuba.

It was intended to bring to the notice of Spain the friendly expression of the unbiased and disinterested views of a member of the great family of nations in reference to the necessity of a termination of the conflict in Cuba, but it was not the intention of this Government to go further, nor was it expected that the Russian Government should take any steps toward effecting an adjustment of the individual griefs of the United States, nor that it should lend any material assistance under any circumstances. The course adopted by this Government was deemed a just and manly one toward Spain, beneficial to humanity at large, and calculated to put at rest any question of ulterior motives on the part of the United States.

I refer to this question by way of greater caution, because on such delicate subjects a shade of misapprehension or a slight change of meaning may at times lead to erroneous impressions, and while therefore conveying to the chancellor the thanks of this Government for his declarations, and with an appreciation of his friendly disposition, it may be well to make it certain that no misapprehension exists in reference to the subject.

I am, etc., HAMILTON FISH.

Mr. Boker to Mr. Fish.

No. 55.] LEGATION OF THE UNITED STATES,
St. Petersburg, February 9, 1876.

SIR: Referring to your dispatch No. 25, under date of January 13, 1876, I have the honor to say that I am confident no misapprehension exists or ever existed in the mind of Prince Gortchakoff as to the purpose of the Government of the United States in orally communicating to the Government of Russia dispatch No. 226, addressed to Mr. Cushing, in accordance with your instruction No. 13.

After having carefully considered the three concluding paragraphs of your dispatch No. 25, I feel justified in saying that Prince Gortchakoff understood my communication in the sense in which the purpose of the Government is therein expressed, and in no other sense of which I am at present aware. He distinctly understood from me that the only remedy that could be applied to the many difficulties which have grown out of the civil war in Cuba, as set forth in the dispatch to Mr. Cushing, No. 266, was, in the opinion of the Government of the United States, a speedy pacification of the island. That is to say, the main question which concerned the powers friendly to Spain was the general condition of things in Cuba, while the particular questions between the United States and Spain which had arisen from the situation were exposed to the Government of Russia by way of furnishing argument and illustration of the direction in which matters were drifting.

Prince Gortchakoff did not understand from me that any kind of intervention between the United States and Spain was suggested or desired on the part of my Government; nor could he have inferred from my language that the Government of the United States did not consider itself to be capable, without foreign aid, of settling its affairs with Spain.

The suggestion which I made to Prince Gortchakoff, and upon which I believe he acted, was, that if, after considering the state of things in Cuba, the Imperial Government should, in the interests of Spain, and with a view to the preservation of the peace of the world, make such

friendly representations as it saw fit to the Government of that country, such a course would be satisfactory to the Government of the United States. I did not attempt to prescribe the character of the representations to be made; but as all the difficuities had arisen from the distracted state of the Island of Cuba, it could not but be inferred that the only feasible advice that could be given must have for its object the pacification of that island.

From the first I saw how delicate were the issues involved in the business which I had undertaken, and how readily Prince Gortchakoff might decline to act, on the principle of noninterference with the domestic affairs of a friendly nation. On the other hand, I desired to succeed in the negotiation, and to bring about the end which my Government had in view, without placing the United States under the burden of an obligation to Russia. I therefore kept prominently in sight the ulterior interests of Spain, which were to be served by an induced change in her policy, and I thought that I had met with a fair measure of success when I perceived that Prince Gortchakoff's views took the same direction.

I take it for granted that it was hardly supposed by the Government of the United States that the exposition of the facts and the arguments employed in dispatch No. 226, although communicated confidentially to Prince Gortchakoff, would not be used substantially by him in any representations which he might instruct the minister of Russia at Madrid to make to the Government of Spain, since without that information, according to Prince Gortchakoff's statement as to his slight knowledge of the subject, he would have had no grounds upon which to base the proposed representations.

On reading over my two dispatches Nos. 36 and 38, from the stress which I have laid upon the then exciting topic, the precarious relations existing between the United States and Spain, and the rumors of an impending war, which indeed greatly influenced the direction of the conversation between Prince Gortchakoff and myself, I can easily understand how I, in writing my dispatches, was led away from the main subject, the present condition of Cuba, and confined myself almost wholly to Prince Gortchakoff's views of the threatening aspect of affairs between the two countries.

I believe, however, that neither Prince Gortchakoff nor I lost sight of the fact that the cause of the perilous aspect of affairs lay in the state of things in Cuba, and that the only remedy for the difficulty would be found in a change of the policy of Spain toward her colony. I now observe, however, that in the two dispatches above referred to I rather reported Prince Gortchakoff's words than my own, and by thus giving a too one-sided view of the matter I conveyed an erroneous impression as to the attitude which I assumed on the part of the United States.

I have, etc.,

GEO. H. BOKER.

Mr. Boker to Mr. Fish.

No. 56.]   LEGATION OF THE UNITED STATES,
St. Petersburg, February 10, 1876.

SIR: In order to satisfy the Government of the United States fully as to the understanding of Prince Gortchakoff of the communication made to him by me, which forms the subject of my dispatch No. 55,

under date of the 9th of February, I, to-day, had an interview with that gentleman.

On communicating to him the substance of the three concluding paragraphs of your dispatch No. 25, he assured me that he had not had any misapprehension of the object sought to be accomplished by the Government of the United States, nor any misunderstanding of the language which I had used to him on the occasion of my first interview, and that instructions to the Russian minister at Madrid to use his good offices with the Spanish Government for the proposed object had been written in accordance with the spirit of the words contained in your dispatch No. 25.

When I communicated to Prince Gortchakoff that part of your dispatch No. 25 in which the thanks of the Government of the United States are conveyed to him for his opinions and course regarding our complications with Spain, the chancellor seemed to be deeply touched, and he warmly returned his acknowledgments for the courtesy extended to him.

I have, etc.,   GEO. H. BOKER.

CUBA.

PAPER SUBMITTED BY MR. MORGAN, PRINTED FOR THE USE OF THE
COMMITTEE ON FOREIGN RELATIONS.

The Congress of the United States, deeply regretting the unhappy state of hostilities existing in Cuba, which has again been the result of the demand of a large number of the native population of that island for its independence, in a spirit of respect and regard for the welfare of both countries, earnestly desires that the security of life and property and the establishment of permanent peace and of a government that is satisfactory to the people of Cuba should be accomplished with the consent of Spain.

And to the extent that the people of Cuba are seeking the rights of local self-government for domestic purposes, the Congress of the United States expresses its earnest sympathy with them. The Congress would also welcome with satisfaction the concession, by Spain, of complete sovereignty to the people of that island, and would cheerfully give to such a voluntary concession the cordial support of the United States. The near proximity of Cuba to the frontier of the United States, and the fact that it is universally regarded as a part of the continental system of America, identifies that island so closely with the political and commercial welfare of our people, that Congress can not be indifferent to the fact that civil war is flagrant among the people of Cuba.

Nor can we longer overlook the fact that the destructive character of this war is doing serious harm to the rights and interests of our people on the island, and to our lawful commerce, the protection and freedom of which is safeguarded by treaty obligations. In the recent past and in former years, when internal wars have been waged for long periods and with results that were disastrous to Cuba and injurious to Spain, the Government of the United States has always observed, with perfect faith, all of its duties toward the belligerents.

It was a difficult task thus forced upon the United States, but it was performed with vigor, impartiality, and justice, in the hope that Spain would so ameliorate the condition of the Cuban people as to give them peace, contentment, and prosperity. This desirable result has not been accomplished. Its failure has not resulted from any interference on the part of our people or Government with the people or government of Cuba.

The hospitality which our treaties, the laws of nations, and the laws of Christianity has extended to Cuban refugees in the United States has caused distrust on the part of the Spanish Government as to the fidelity of our Government to its obligations of neutrality in the frequent insurrections of the people of Cuba against Spanish authority. This distrust has often become a source of serious annoyance to our people, and has led to a spirit of retaliation toward Spanish authority in Cuba, thus giving rise to frequent controversies between the two countries. The absence of responsible government in Cuba, with powers adequate to deal directly with questions between the people of

the United States and the people and political authorities of the island, has been a frequently recurring cause of delay, protracted imprisonment, confiscations of property, and the detention of our people and their ships, often upon groundless charges, which has been a serious grievance.

When insurrections have occurred on the Island of Cuba the temptation to unlawful invasion by reckless persons has given to our Government anxiety, trouble, and much expense in the enforcement of our laws and treaty obligations of neutrality, and these occasions have been so frequent as to make these duties unreasonably onerous upon the Government of the United States.

The devastation of Cuba in the war that is now being waged, both with fire and sword, is an anxious and disturbing cause of unrest among the people of the United States, which creates strong grounds of protest against the continuance of the struggle for power between Cuba and Spain, which is rapidly changing the issue to one of existence on the part of a great number of the native population.

It is neither just to the relations that exist between Cuba and the United States, nor is it in keeping with the spirit of the age or the rights of humanity that this struggle should be protracted until one party or the other should become exhausted in the resources of men and money, thereby weakening both until they may fall a prey to some stronger power, or until the stress of human sympathy or the resentments engendered by long and bloody conflict should draw into the strife the unruly elements of neighboring countries.

This civil war, though it is great in its proportions and is conducted by armies that are in complete organization and directed and controlled by supreme military authority, has not the safeguard of a cartel for the treatment of wounded soldiers or prisoners of war.

In this feature of the warfare it becomes a duty of humanity that the civilized powers should insist upon the application of the laws of war recognized among civilized nations to both armies. As our own people are drawn into this struggle on both sides, and enter either army without the consent of our Government and in violation of our laws, their treatment when they may be wounded or captured, although it is not regulated by treaty and ceases to be a positive care of our Government, should not be left to the revengeful retaliations which expose them to the fate of pirates or other felons.

The inability of Spain to subdue her internecine enemies by the measures and within the time that would be reasonable when applied to occasions of ordinary civil disturbance is a misfortune that can not be justly visited upon citizens of the United States, nor can it be considered that a state of open civil war does not exist, but that the movement is a mere insurrection and its supporters a mob of criminal violators of the law, when it is seen that it requires an army of 100,000 men and all the naval and military power of a great kingdom even to hold the alleged rebellion in check.

It is due to the situation of affairs in Cuba that Spain should recognize the existence of a state of war in the island, and should voluntarily accord to the armies opposed to her authority the rights of belligerents under the laws of nations.

The Congress of the United States, recognizing the fact that the matters herein referred to are properly within the control of the Chief Executive until, within the principles of our Constitution, it becomes the duty of Congress to define the final attitude of the Government of the United States toward Spain, presents these considerations to the President in support of the following resolution:

Resolved by the Senate (the House of Representatives concurring), That the present deplorable war in the Island of Cuba has reached a magnitude that concerns all civilized nations to the extent that it should be conducted, if unhappily it is longer to continue, on those principles and laws of warfare that are acknowledged to be obligatory upon civilized nations when engaged in open hostilities; including the treatment of captives who are enlisted in either army; and due respect to cartels for exchange of prisoners and for other military purposes; truces and flags of truce, and the provision of proper hospitals and hospital supplies and services to the sick and wounded of either army: And therefore it is

Resolved, That this representation of the views and opinions of Congress be sent to the President; and if he concurs therein that he will, in a friendly spirit, use the good offices of this Government to the end that Spain shall be requested to accord to the armies with which it is engaged in war the rights of belligerents, as the same are recognized under the laws of nations.

FIFTY-FOURTH CONGRESS. FIRST SESSION.

[Senate Document No 278]

Message from the President of the United States, transmitting, in response to resolution of the Senate of May 16, 1896, relative to the rights of the United States, under our treaty with Spain, as to the trial of our citizens arrested in Cuba and under condemnation and sentenced to death by the Spanish military tribunals for alleged offenses of a political or other character against the Spanish laws or Government, a report of the Secretary of State, with accompanying papers.

MAY 23, 1896.—Referred to the Committee on Foreign Relations and ordered to be printed.

To the Senate of the United States :

I transmit herewith, in response to a resolution of the Senate of the 16th instant, a report of the Secretary of State, to which are attached copies in English and Spanish of the original text of a protocol executed January 12, 1877, between the minister plenipotentiary of the United States of America to the Court of Spain and the minister of state of His Majesty the King of Spain.

It being in my judgment incompatible with the public service, I am constrained to refrain from communicating to the Senate at this time copies of the correspondence described in the third paragraph of said resolution.

GROVER CLEVELAND.

EXECUTIVE MANSION,
Washington, May 23, 1896.

The PRESIDENT :

The undersigned, Secretary of State, to whom was referred certain resolutions passed by the Senate of the United States on the 16th instant, in the following terms:

Resolved, That the Committee on Foreign Relations is directed to inquire and report to the Senate what are the rights of the United States, under our treaties with Spain, as to the trial of our citizens arrested in Cuba and now under condemnation and sentenced to death by the Spanish military tribunals for alleged offenses of a political or other character against the Spanish laws or Government, and to report on that subject by bill or otherwise.

2. That the Secretary of State is directed to send to the Senate literal copies of the original text of a protocol of conference and declarations concerning judicial procedure signed by Caleb Cushing, as minister of the United States, and Señor Don Fernando y Collantes, minister of the King of Spain, on January twelfth, eighteen hundred and seventy-seven, as the same was executed and interchanged, both in the English and Spanish languages; and that he will inform the Senate whether the established or agreed original text of said protocol is in the English or the Spanish language.

3. That the President is requested, if it is not incompatible with the public service, to communicate to the Senate copies of any correspondence that has taken place between the Governments of Spain and the United States respecting the said protocol and its bearing or effect upon the trial and condemnation of citizens of the United States who were recently captured on or near the vessel called the *Competitor*, which was seized under Spanish authority in Cuban waters or near to that island—

has the honor to annex herewith literal copies, in English and Spanish, of the original text of the protocol referred to in the second paragraph of said resolutions, and to report that the original of said protocol is in both the English and Spanish languages.

Respectfully submitted.

RICHARD OLNEY.

DEPARTMENT OF STATE,
Washington, May 23, 1896.

———

Protocol of a Conference held at Madrid on the 12th of January, 1877, between the Honorable Caleb Cushing, Minister Plenipotentiary of the United States of America, and His Excellency Señor Don Fernando Calderon y Collantes, Minister of State of His Majesty the King of Spain.

The respective parties, mutually desiring to terminate amicably all controversy as to the effect of existing treaties in certain matters of judicial procedure, and for the reasons set forth and representations exchanged in various notes and previous conferences, proceeded to make declaration on both sides as to the understanding of the two Governments in the premises and respecting the true application of said treaties.

Señor Calderon y Collantes declared as follows:

1. No citizen of the United States residing in Spain, her adjacent islands or her ultramarine possessions, charged with acts of sedition, treason or conspiracy against the institutions, the public security, the integrity of the territory or against the Supreme Government, or any other crime whatsoever, shall be subject to trial by any exceptional tribunal, but exclusively by the ordinary jurisdiction, except in the case of being captured with arms in hand.

2. Those who, not coming within this last case, may be arrested or imprisoned, shall be deemed to have been so arrested or imprisoned by order of the civil authority for the effects of the Law of April 17, 1821, even though the arrest or imprisonment shall have been effected by armed force.

3. Those who may be taken with arms in hand, and who are therefore comprehended in the exception of the first article, shall be tried by ordinary council of war, in conformity with the second article of the hereinbefore-mentioned Law; but even in this case the accused shall enjoy for their defense the guaranties embodied in the aforesaid Law of April 17, 1821.

4. In consequence whereof, as well in the cases mentioned in the third paragraph as in those of the second, the parties accused are allowed to name attorneys and advocates, who shall have access to them at suit-

able times; they shall be furnished in due season with copy of the accu-sation and a list of witnesses for the prosecution, which latter shall be examined before the presumed criminal, his attorney and advocate, in conformity with the provisions of Articles twenty to thirty-one of the said Law; they shall have right to compel the witnesses of whom they desire to avail themselves to appear and give testimony or to do it by means of depositions; they shall present such evidence as they may judge proper; and they shall be permitted to be present and to make their defense, in public trial. orally or in writing, by themselves or by means of their counsel.

5. The sentence pronounced shall be referred to the Audiencia of the Judicial District, or to the Captain General, according as the trial may have taken place before the ordinary Judge or before the council of war, in conformity also with what is prescribed in the above-mentioned Law.

Mr. Cushing declared as follows:

1. The Constitution of the United States provides that the trial of all crimes except in cases of impeachment shall be by jury, and such trial shall be held in the State where said crimes shall have been com-mitted, or when not committed within any State the trial will proceed in such place as Congress may direct (Art. III, Sec. 2); that no person shall be held to answer for a capital or otherwise infamous crime unless on presentment of a grand jury except in cases arising in the land and naval forces or in the militia when in actual service (Amendments to the Constitution, Art. V); and that in all criminal prosecutions the accused shall enjoy the right to a speedy and public trial, by an impartial jury of the State and district wherein the crime shall have been committed, and to be informed of the nature and cause of the accusation; to be confronted with the witnesses against him; to have compulsory process for obtaining witnesses in his favor; and to have counsel for his defense. (Amendments to the Constitution, Art. VI.)

2. The Act of Congress of April 30, 1790, chap. 9, sec. 29, re-enacted in the Revised Statutes, provides that every person accused of treason shall have a copy of the indictment and a list of the jury, and of the witnesses to be produced at the trial, delivered to him three days before the same, and in all other capital cases two days before that takes place; that in all such cases the accused shall be allowed to make his full defense by counsel learned in the law, who shall have free access to him at all seasonable hours; that he shall be allowed in his defense to make any proof which he can produce by lawful witnesses, and he shall have due power to compel his witnesses to appear in Court.

3. All these provisions of the Constitution and of Acts of Congress are of constant and permanent force, except on occasion of the tempo-rary suspension of the writ of habeas corpus.

4. The provisions herein set forth apply in terms to all persons accused of the commission of treason or other capital crimes in the United States, and therefore, as well by the letter of the law as in virtue of existing treaties, the said provisions extend to and comprehend all Spaniards residing or being in the United States.

Señor Calderon y Collantes then declared as follows:

In view of the satisfactory adjustment of this question in a manner so proper for the preservation of the friendly relations between the respective Governments, and in order to afford to the Government of the United States the completest security of the sincerity and good faith of His Majesty's Government in the premises, command will be given by Royal order for the strict observance of the terms of the present Protocol in all the dominions of Spain and specifically in the island of Cuba.

In testimony of which we have interchangeably signed this Protocol.

CALEB CUSHING.
FERNDO. CALDERON Y COLLANTES.

MINISTERIO DE ESTADO.

Protocolo de una conferencia celebrada en Madrid el dia 12 de Enero de 1877, entre el Exmo. Sor. Don Fernando Calderon y Collantes, Minis- tro de Estado de Su Magestad el Rey de España, y el Honorable Caleb Cushing, Ministro Plenipotenciario de los Estados Unidos de América.

Las dos partes respectivas mutuamente deseosas de terminar amisto- samente toda controversia sobre el efecto de los Tratados vigentes en determinados casos de jurisdiccion y procedimientos judiciales, y a consecuencia de las razones espuestas y las observaciones cambiadas en varias notas y conferencias anteriores, hicieron por ambas Partes declaracion de la inteligencia de los dos Gobiernos en la materia y acerca de la recta aplicacion de dichos Tratados.

El Señor Calderon y Collantes declaró lo siguiente:

1º. Ningun ciudadano de los Estados Unidos residente en España, sus Islas adyacentes ó sus posesiones de Ultramar, acusado de actos de sedicion, infidencia ó conspiracion contra las instituciones, la seguridad pública, la integridad del territorio ó contra el Gobierno supremo, ó de cualquier otro crímen, podrá ser sometido á ningun tribunal escepcional, sino exclusivamente á la jurisdiccion ordinaria, fuera del caso en que sea cogido con las armas en la mano.

2º. Los que, fuera de este último caso, sean arrestados ó presos, se considerará que lo han sido de órden de la Autoridad civil para los efectos de la Ley de 17 de Abril de 1821, aun cuando el arresto ó la prision se haya ejecutado por fuerza armada.

3º. Los que sean cogidos con las armas en la mano, y por tanto estén comprendidos en la escepcion del artículo primero serán juzgados en consejo de guerra ordinario, con arreglo al artículo segundo de la citada Ley; pero aun en este caso, disfrutarán para su defensa los acusados de las garantias consignadas en la citada Ley de 17 de Abril de 1821.

4º. En su consecuencia, asi en los casos mencionados en el párrafo tercero como en los del segundo, se les permitirá á los acusados nombrar procurador y abogado, que podrá comunicar con ellos á cualquiera hora propia, se les dará oportunamente copia de la acusacion y una lista de los testigos de cargo, los cuales serán examinados ante el presunto reo, su procurador y abogado, segun se establece en los artículos veinte al treinta y uno de dicha Ley; tendrán derecho para compeler á los testi- gos de que intenten valerse á que comparezcan á prestar su declaracion ó á que la presten por medio de exhorto; presentarán las pruebas que les convengan y podrán estar presentes y hacer en el juicio público su defensa de palabra ó por escrito, por si mismos ó por medio de su abo- gado.

5º. La sentencia que recaiga se consultará con la Audiencia del terri- torio ó con el Capitan General del distrito, segun el jucio haya sido ante el Juez ordinario or ante el Consejo de guerra, con arreglo tambien á lo que en la citada Ley se determina.

El Señor Cushing declaró lo que sigue:

1º. La Constitucion de los Estados Unidos consigna que el enjuiciamiento para todos los delitos, escepto aquellos de que sean acusados altos funcionarios, será por el jurado, y tal enjuiciamiento ha de veri-ficarse en el Estado donde se hayan cometido dichos delitos ó crímenes, y si estos no fueren cometidos dentro de un Estado, se seguirá el juicio en el lugar que designe el Congreso, (Art. III, Parragrafo 2º); que nadie será obligado á responder por un crímen capital ó de otro modo infamante, sino en virtud de informe del gran jurado, con escepcion de los casos que ocurran en las fuerzas de tierra ó de mar, ó en la milicia, cuando esté actualmente de servicio (Enmiendas á la Constitucion, Art. V); y que en toda formacion de causa criminal disfrutará el acusado del derecho á juicio pronto y público por un jurado imparcial del Estado y distrito donde se haya cometido el crímen, y á que se le dé conocimiento de la naturaleza y motivo de la acusacion; á ser careado con lost estigos de cargo, á valerse de mandamiento ú orden imperativa del tribunal para obligar á los testigos de que intente valerse á que presten su declaracion, y á tener abogado y procurador para su defensa. (Enmienda á la Constitucion, Art. VI.)

2º. El acto del Congreso de 30 de Abril de 1790, capº. 9, sec. 29, sancionado de nuevo en los Estatutos Revisados, consigna que á toda persona acusada de infidencia le será facilitada copia de la acusacion, con una lista del jurado y de los testigos que han de presentarse en el juicio, tres dias antes que este se celebre, y en todos los demás casos capitales, dos dias antes del mismo; que en todos los casos de tal clase podrá el acusado hacer su amplia defensa por medio de Abogado, quien tendrá libre comunicacion con él á toda hora propia; que podrá en su defensa hacer cualquier prueba que pueda presentar por testigos hábiles y tendrá derecho para compeler á sus testigos á que comparezcan ante el Tribunal.

3º. Todas estas disposiciones de la Constitucion y de los actos del Congreso están constante y permanentemente vigentes, con escepcion del caso de la suspension temporal del Auto de "Habeas Corpus."

4º. Las disposiciones aquí consignadas se aplican espresamente á todas las personas acusadas de infidencia ú otros crímenes capitales en los Estados Unidos, y por lo tanto, asi segun la letra de la Ley como tambien en virtud de los Tratados vigentes, las espresadas disposiciones alcanzan y comprenden á todos los Españoles residentes ó estantes dentro del territorio de los Estados Unidos.

El Señor Calderon y Collantes entonces declaró lo que sigue: En vista del satisfactorio arreglo de esta cuestion de una manera tan propia para la conservacion de las relaciones amistosas entre los respectivos Gobiernos y á fin de dar al Gobierno de los Estados Unidos la mas completa seguridad de la sinceridad y buena fé del Gobierno de Su Magestad en la materia, se mandará por Real Orden la estricta obser-vancia del presente Protocolo en todos los dominios de España y par-ticularmente en la Isla de Cuba. En testimonio de lo cual hemos firmado alternativamente este Protocolo.

FERNᵈᵒ CALDERON Y COLLANTES.
CALEB CUSHING.

FIFTY-FOURTH CONGRESS, SECOND SESSION.

[Senate Document No 39]

Message from the President of the United States, transmitting, in response to a resolution of the Senate of December 22, 1896, a report from the Secretary of State, accompanied by copies of correspondence, concerning the death of Charles Govin, a citizen of the United States, in the island of Cuba.

JANUARY 5, 1897.—Referred to the Committee on Foreign Relations and ordered to be printed.

To the Senate:

I transmit herewith, in response to a resolution of the Senate of the 22d ultimo, a report from the Secretary of State, accompanied by copies of correspondence, concerning the death of Charles Govin, a citizen of the United States, in the Island of Cuba.

GROVER CLEVELAND.

EXECUTIVE MANSION,
Washington, January 5, 1897.

The PRESIDENT:

The Secretary of State, to whom was referred the resolution of the Senate of December 22, 1896, requesting the President, "if not incompatible with the public interest, to transmit to the Senate such information as the State Department has relating to the death of Charles Govin, a citizen of the United States and a newspaper correspondent, from violence by the Spanish forces at Corredana, in the Island of Cuba," has the honor to lay before the President copies of the correspondence called for.

RICHARD OLNEY.

DEPARTMENT OF STATE,
Washington, January 4, 1897.

[Telegram]

Mr. Rockhill to Mr. Lee.

DEPARTMENT OF STATE,
August 18, 1896.

Newspaper advices from Key West of 16th state that Charles Govin. an American citizen and correspondent, was captured near Jaruco by Spanish troops and put to death. Investigate and report by cable.

ROCKHILL.

[Telegram.]

Mr. Lee to Mr. Rockhill.

HABANA, *August 19, 1896.*

Charles Govin landed from the *Three Friends* July 6th; joined insurgents; captured in a skirmish on the 9th with Arturo Adrian and Adolfo Mijares. They were bound and taken off. Nothing heard of them since. They are not in the fort nor prisoners.

[Telegram.]

Mr. Rockhill to Mr. Lee.

DEPARTMENT OF STATE,
August 20, 1896.

Replying your cable of yesterday in reference Charles Govin you are instructed to demand of Captain-General full information. In case Govin still alive insist on his enjoying full treaty rights under paragraph 2 or 3 of protocol of 77, as case may be.

Mr. Lee to the Governor-General of Cuba.

UNITED STATES CONSULATE-GENERAL,
Habana, August 26, 1896.

EXCELLENCY: Having been informed in a communication dated the 21st August by the Secretary-General that you have referred a previous communication concerning the American citizen, Mr. Charles Govin, to the Captain-General, who will remit to you the data requested, and in order to aid your efforts in this direction, I beg to inform your excellency that I have information which may or may not be correct, but if correct, should be followed up in order to secure the necessary information as to the fate of Charles Govin. It is certain that the American public now believes that Govin was captured, tied, and afterwards killed. It seems to me to be the duty of both of us to remove that impression if the information upon which it is based is false.

I hear that Govin was captured in a skirmish on the 9th of July between the Spanish troops under General Ochoa and the insurgents under Valencia, at a point north of Jaruco and near the coast; that the Spanish General Ochoa, having in charge the captured Govin and

S. Doc. 231, pt 7——34

other prisoners, encamped that night, namely, the 9th July, at San Matias. I am further told that next morning, the 10th July, Govin, bound to two men, named, respectively, Arturo Adrian and Adolfo Miyares, was taken off by the infantry portion of Ochoa's command. The commanding officer of that detachment is responsible for the prisoners of war committed to his care and should be required to produce or account for Govin if living, or if not, report the mode and manner of his death.

I take this opportunity to reiterate to your excellency the assurances of my most distinguished consideration.

FITZHUGH LEE.

Mr. Adee to Mr. Lee.

DEPARTMENT OF STATE,
Washington, August 27, 1896.

SIR: Your dispatch No. 93, of the 20th instant, relative to the fate of Charles Govin, who belonged to the *Three Friends* expedition, has been received, and in reply you are informed that your proposal to make a peremptory demand for information concerning him is approved by the Department. No effort should be spared by you to have this case thoroughly investigated.

I am, etc.,

ALVEY A. ADEE,
Acting Secretary.

Mr. Rockhill to Mr. Lee.

WASHINGTON, *September 5, 1896.*

SIR: The Department has received your dispatch, No. 106, of the 29th ultimo, with inclosures, relative to the fate of Charles Govin, a citizen of the United States, and in reply you are instructed to press unremittingly for a full investigation and a report in this matter.

I am, etc.,

W. W. ROCKHILL,
Acting Secretary.

Mr. Lee to Mr. Rockhill.

UNITED STATES CONSULATE-GENERAL,
Habana, September 10, 1896.

SIR: I beg to acknowledge the receipt of your instruction, No. 76, directing me to press unremittingly for a full investigation and report as to the fate of Charles Govin, a citizen of the United States. It is to be remembered that the Captain-General, in a communication dated August 24, stated that said Govin had been wounded in a skirmish and had died from said wounds. To that communication I replied under date of the 29th of said month to the effect that I was constrained to believe that the information furnished to the Captain-General was not correct, and requesting that Govin's matter be referred back to the commanding officer of the troops engaged, as it is possible that he may have confounded the case of some other person with that of Charles Govin. ' Since that I have heard nothing further, but if no response is made within the next few days I will again call the attention of the Captain-General to the subject.

* * * *

I am, etc.,

FITZHUGH LEE.

Mr. Lee to Mr. Rockhill.

UNITED STATES CONSULATE-GENERAL,
Habana, September 10, 1896.

SIR: I beg to acknowledge receipt of your instruction, No. 73, of the 3d instant, transmitting a letter * * * inclosing the affidavit of ———, stating that he was an eye witness of the murder of Mr. Charles Govin by Spanish troops.

The statements contained in the affidavit do not agree with those given to my representative, and tend to confuse the manner and mode of Govin's death. I am inclined to believe ———, for he had no object in making any such statements and did not volunteer to do so.

I am, etc.,

FITZHUGH LEE.

[Telegram.]

Mr. Rockhill to Mr. Lee.

DEPARTMENT OF STATE,
September 15, 1896.

Your No. 123 received. Is answer you expected received? If not, press for immediate and satisfactory one.

ROCKHILL.

Mr. Lee to Governor-General of Cuba.

[Translation.]

UNITED STATES CONSULATE-GENERAL,
Habana, September 15, 1896.

To His Excellency, the Governor-General of the Island of Cuba:

EXCELLENCY: On the 29th of August last I had the honor to address a communication to your excellency in reference to the American citizen, Charles Govin. To the communication of the date designated no reply has been received.

I am instructed by the Department of State at Washington to press for a full investigation and a report on this matter.

I write, therefore, to ask whether any further investigation and report will be made, or whether it is proposed to rest the case, so far as your Government is concerned, upon your letter to me of the 24th August, in which it was stated that "it appears that in the several exchanges of shot had with the rebels at the mountains of San Martin some prisoners were made, among whom appeared, wounded, Charles Govin, who died in consequence of his wounds."

I take this occasion, etc., FITZHUGH LEE.

Mr. Lee to Mr. Rockhill.

UNITED STATES CONSULATE-GENERAL,
Habana, September 18, 1896.

SIR: I have the honor to submit herewith the translation of an official communication from the Spanish Government on this island embody-ing a report as to the fate of Mr. Charles Govin, an American citizen, from an officer of the Spanish army to Captain-General Weyler, who in turn reported it to Governor-General Weyler. The name of the officer making the report is not given nor the place where Govin is said to have died in consequence of wounds.

It will be observed that this is a communication in reply to one from me to General Weyler dated the 29th of August, a copy of which has been duly forwarded to the Department. In that communication I had the honor to say that the account of Govin's death was not satisfactory and did not conform to the information in my possession. It will be seen that the inclosed report of the Captain-General to the Governor-General is a reiteration of his former communication.

   *   *   *   *   *   *   *

I respectfully submit this matter to the consideration of the Department.

I am, etc.,   FITZHUGH LEE.

[Inclosure in No. 138.—Translation.]

Governor-General of Cuba to Mr. Lee.

GENERAL GOVERNMENT OF THE ISLAND OF CUBA,
OFFICE OF THE SECRETARY-GENERAL,
Habana, September 15, 1896.

To the Consul-General of the United States, Present.

SIR: His excellency, the Captain-General, reported yesterday to the Governor-General, as follows:

"EXCELLENCY: His excellency, the general in command of the third brigade of the second division of the third corps of the army of this island, under date of the 25th ultimo, reports to me as follows:

"'EXCELLENCY: In answer to the two respectable communications of your excel-lency of the 23d instant, relative to the information requested by the consul-general of the United States regarding the American citizen, Mr. Charles Govin, I have the honor to inform your excellency that the said person was made a prisoner after hav-ing been seriously wounded in the engagement on the 9th of July, which took place in the mountains of San Martin, and that he died in consequence of his wounds on the following day upon being taken to this place, as I had the honor to inform your excellency in the report of said engagement dated July 11, No. 197, in the list of prisoners made that day, and consequently the private information furnished to said consul is without foundation, or perhaps it has been maliciously furnished by persons disaffected to the good name of the Spanish army.'"

By order of his excellency, I transmit to you the above in answer to your com-munication of the 29th ultimo relative to the matter.

God guard you many years.   •

EL MARQUES DE PALMEROLA.

Mr. Lee to Governor-General of Cuba.

[Translation.]

CONSULATE-GENERAL OF THE UNITED STATES,
Habana, October 2, 1896.

EXCELLENCY: I duly received your communication of the 18th of September, transmitting the report of the chief of the brigade, second division, third corps of your army, and I am now directed to say to you that in view of the facts in my Government's possession tending to show the killing of Govin after he was taken prisoner, it does not consider the report of your subordinate a satisfactory account of his death. I will have also to request the name of the officer making the report in question as well as the name of the place at which it was written, this last seeming to be important because in the said report the commander of the brigade states that Govin died in consequence of his wounds on the following day after being taken to this place, but nowhere is the name of said place stated.

I take, etc.,

FITZHUGH LEE.

* * *

Mr. Rockhill to Mr. Lee.

DEPARTMENT OF STATE,
Washington, October 8, 1896.

SIR: The Department has received your dispatch, No. 160, of the 3d instant, with inclosure, relative to the fate of Charles Govin, and in reply you are informed that your action in demanding of the Governor and Captain General of Cuba the name of the subordinate general who made the report of the death of Mr. Govin and the name of the place at which it was written, is approved by the Department.

*   *   *   *   *   *   *

I am, etc., W. W. ROCKHILL.

* * *

Mr. Lee to Mr. Rockhill.

UNITED STATES CONSULATE-GENERAL,
Habana, October 17, 1896.

SIR: With further reference to my dispatch, No. 160, of the 3d instant, and instruction, No. 119, of 8th instant, relative to the case of Charles Govin, I have the honor to transmit copy translation of a communication from the Governor-General, in which he states the name of the officer who reported Govin's death to have been Brig. Gen. Eduardo Lopez Ochoa, and the place where said official report was written was Jaruco.

I have, etc., FITZHUGH LEE.

* * *

[Inclosure in No. 184 —Translation.]

Captain-General of Cuba to Mr. Lee.

ARMY OF THE ISLAND OF CUBA, CAPTAINCY-GENERAL,
OFFICE OF THE GENERAL STAFF,
Habana, October 16, 1896.

In answer to your communication of the 2d instant, I have to inform you that the report relative to the death of the citizen of the United States, Mr. Charles Govin, which in due season was communicated to you, is dated at Jaruco, and signed by the general of Brigade D, Eduardo Lopez Ochoa.

As the report referred to is official, to which I give full credit, I regret that the Government of your nation does not consider it satisfactory, undoubtedly because it takes into consideration private reports which, deprived of an official character, and perhaps furnished indirectly by enemies of Spain, I understand, should not be taken into consideration by a friendly nation.

God guard you many years. VALERIANO WEYLER.

FIFTY-FOURTH CONGRESS, SECOND SESSION.

[Senate Document No. 79.]

Message from the President of the United States, transmitting, in response to Senate resolution of December 15, 1896, report from the Secretary of State, submitting a list of claims filed in the Department of State by citizens of the United States against Spain, arising out of the insurrection existing in the island of Cuba, and the accompanying papers relating to the vessel called "Competitor" and the persons claiming American citizenship captured thereon.

JANUARY 22, 1897.—Referred to the Committee on Foreign Relations and ordered to be printed.

To the Senate of the United States:

In response to the resolution of the Senate of December 15, 1896, relating to Cuban affairs, I transmit a report from the Secretary of State, submitting a list of the claims filed in the Department of State by citizens of the United States against Spain, arising out of the insurrection existing in the Island of Cuba, and the accompanying correspondence relating to the vessel called the "*Competitor*" and the persons claiming American citizenship captured thereon, which I deem it not incompatible with the public interests to communicate.

GROVER CLEVELAND.

EXECUTIVE MANSION,
Washington, January 22, 1897.

The PRESIDENT:

In response to the resolution of the Senate of the United States of December 15, 1896, reading as follows—   -

Resolved, That the President is requested, if it is not in his opinion incompatible with the public service, to send to the Senate copies of the papers relating to the condition of affairs in the Island of Cuba, which are referred to in the report of the Secretary of State that accompanies his last annual message as papers collected in the annual volume entitled Foreign Relations of the United States. And also a statement of the several amounts of the claims lodged in the Department of State by citizens of the United States against Spain, growing out of the alleged insurrection now existing in the Island of Cuba.

And also all correspondence with the Spanish Government relating to the vessel called the *Competitor* and the persons captured with or near that vessel, with a statement of the charges pending in any court in Spain or Cuba against said persons, and the proceedings of such court in those cases, and the place of their imprisonment, the character of their treatment while in prison, and the condition of their health; whether said prisoners have had the privilege of counsel of their own selection on any trial that has taken place on such charges, or were represented by any consul, attorney, or other agent of the United States—

the undersigned, Secretary of State, has the honor to submit a list of claims filed in the Department of State by citizens of the United States against Spain, arising out of the existing insurrection in the Island of Cuba, and correspondence relating to the vessel known as the *Competitor* and the persons claiming American citizenship captured thereon, with a view to its transmission to the Senate if deemed not incompatible with the public interests.

The preparation of the copies of correspondence called for in the first part of the resolution requiring more time than has been found necessary in the case of those herewith transmitted, it has been thought proper not to delay longer in submitting to you the documents now ready.

Respectfully submitted.

RICHARD OLNEY.

DEPARTMENT OF STATE,
Washington, January 22, 1897.

I.

List of claims against Spain, growing out of the insurrection in Cuba, filed in the Department of State.

Name of claimant	Ground of claim	Amount claimed.
August Bolten	Arrest and imprisonment	$10,000.00
John D Ferrer	....do	25,000.00
Mrs. C. J Diaz de Clarke	Property losses	116,335.00
John F Java	....do	90,585.00
Jose Ygnacio Toscano	....do	15,000.00
Pedro Plutarco Ortiz	....do	84,000.00
F. J. Cazanas	....do	39,843.00
Jose G and Jose M. Delgado	....do	178,534.00
Jose Antonio Yrnaga	....do	156,500.00
Ricardo Machado	....do	64,900.00
Francisco Seiglie	....do	778,510.00
Jose Rafael de les Reyes y Garcia and wife.	.... do	729,161.00
Frederick P Montes	....do	160,000.00
George L Lay	....do	(a)
Andres L Terry	....do	334,905.00
John A. Sowers	Arrest, imprisonment, and expulsion	200,000.00
Perfecto Lacosti	Property losses	652,900.00
Wm. A and Louis M Glean	Imprisonment	150,000.00
Wm A Glean	Property losses	4,668.00
Louis M Glean	....do	7,547.00
Whiting & Co	....do	60,240.00
Mrs. A. L. Whiting	....do	17,000.00
J. B Carrillo de Albornoz	....do	36,000.00
Ignacio Larrondo	....do	129,472.38
Cristobal N. Madan	Property losses and personal injuries	88,000.00
Antonio A. Martinez	Property losses	35,000.00
Joaquin P. Cruz and wife	....do	70,000.00
George W. Hyatt	....do	285,400.54
Manuel A R Morales	....do	275,000.00
Peter Dominguez	Expulsion	10,000.00
Teresa Joerg	Property losses	2,500.00

a Value of horse.

List of claims against Spain, etc.—Continued.

Name of claimant.	Ground of claim.	Amount claimed.
James A. Glean	Property losses	$28,425.00
Peter S. Rodriguez	....do	40,796.00
Antonio M Jimenez	....do	19,158.45
Pedro C. Casanova	....do	40,400.00
Do	Personal injuries	40,000.00
Walter G. Dygert	Arrest and imprisonment	100,000.00
Frederick A Libbey	Property losses	23,166.00
Jose M Caraballo	....do	90,470.00
Do	Arrest, imprisonment, etc	60,000.00
Angel Gronlier	Property losses	34,779.00
Albert V. de Goicouria	....do	130,000.00
Rosa A. Maragliano	....do	30,000.00
Juana M. C do Maragliano	....do	25,000.00
J de Armas y Armas	....do	69,525.00
Maximo M Diaz	....do	10,000.00
Wm W. Gay	Expulsion	25,000.00
Thomas R Dawley	Arrest imprisonment, etc	100,000.00
George Fortier	Property losses	32,450.00
L F Marejon y Marquez	....do	15,000.00
Wm G. Thorne	....do	25,000.00
M D J Garcia y Pino, executrix, etc	....do	200,000.00
Manuel Prieto	....do	58,850.00
Gustave Richelieu	Imprisonment	(a)
Miguel de la Vega y Gener	Property losses	71,683.00
J Sanchez y Coba	....do	16,200.00
F J Terry y Dorticas	....do	202,952 50
J. C de Albornoz O Farrill	....do	106,105.49
A C de Albornoz O Farrill	....do	130,703.12
Heine Safety Boiler Co	....do	27,316.80
R M y de la Cruz	....do	(b)
Francisco Rionda (Central Tuinucu Sugar Cane Manufacturing Co).	....do	527,480.20
Charles Rosa	....do	882,840.00
Rabel & Co	....do	75,785.00
Joseph M Duenos	....do	15,000.00
P P. de Leon	....do	379,000.00
J. F. de Cossio	....do	20,000.00
Peter E Rivery	Personal injuries	(c)
Samuel T. Tolon	....do	50,000.00
Do	Property losses	100,000.00
Adolphus Torres	Imprisonment	25,000.00
A L Terry y Dorticos and A. E Terry	Property losses	81,888.00
A. E. Terry	....do	110,500.00
Frederick L Craycraft	Personal injuries	25,000.00
Thomas E. Rodriguez	Property losses, banishment, etc	61,000.00
Oscar Giguel	Property losses	100,000.00
Jose Tur	....do	251,500.00
Adolfo Santa Maria	....do	120,803.32
Enrequita Santa Maria	....do	94,953.32
Joseph M. Fernandez	....do	61,115.61
George Becket	....do	75,000.00
Manuel F Lopez	Killing of son, S N Lopez	100,000.00
Adolfo Torres	Arrest and imprisonment	25,000.00

a A fair indemnity.   *b* Not stated.   *c* Suitable indemnity.

II.

CORRESPONDENCE RELATIVE TO THE COMPETITOR.

List of papers relative to the "Competitor" and the persons claiming American citizenship captured thereon.

Mr. Williams to Mr. Rockhill, April 30, 1896.
Mr. Williams to Mr. Olney, May 1, 1896.
Mr. Olney to Mr. Taylor, May 1, 1896.
Mr. Williams to Mr. Rockhill, May 1, 1896.
Mr. Rockhill to Mr. Williams, May 1, 1896.
Mr. Williams to Mr. Rockhill, May 2, 1896.
Mr. Olney to Mr. Williams, May 2, 1896.
Mr. Williams to Mr. Olney, May 2, 1896.
Mr. Olney to Mr. Williams, May 2, 1896.
Mr. Williams to Mr. Rockhill, No. 2940, May 2, 1896.

Mr. Taylor to Mr. Olney, May 4, 1896.
Mr. Williams to Mr. Rockhill, No. 2946, May 5, 1896.
Mr. Olney to Mr. Williams, May 6, 1896.
Mr. Williams to Mr. Olney, May 6, 1896.
Mr. Williams to Mr. Olney, May 7, 1896.
Mr. Olney to Mr. Williams, May 7, 1896.
Mr. Olney to Mr. Williams, May 8, 1896.
Mr. Williams to Mr. Olney, May 8, 1896.
Mr. Williams to Mr. Olney, May 8, 1896.
Mr. Williams to Mr. Olney, May 8, 1896.
Mr. Olney to Mr. Williams, May 9, 1896.
Mr. Williams to Mr. Olney, May 9, 1896.
Mr. Olney to Mr. Williams, May 9, 1896.
Mr. Rockhill to Mr. Williams, No. 1362, May 11, 1896.
Mr. Williams to Mr. Olney, May 11, 1896.
Mr. Williams to Mr. Rockhill, No. 2968, May 11, 1896.
Mr. Williams to Mr. Olney, May 11, 1896.
Mr. Taylor to Mr. Olney, No. 510, May 11, 1896.
Mr. Olney to Mr. Williams, May 11, 1896.
Mr. Williams to Mr. Olney, May 12, 1896.
Mr. Williams to Mr. Olney, May 13, 1896.
Mr. Williams to Mr. Olney, May 16, 1896.
Mr. Williams to Mr. Rockhill, No. 2987, May 21, 1896.
Mr. Williams to Mr. Rockhill, No. 2988, May 21, 1896.
Mr. Williams to Mr. Rockhill, No. 2996, May 23, 1896.
Mr. Taylor to Mr. Olney, June 16, 1896.
Mr. Olney to Mr. Taylor, June 30, 1896.
Mr. Lee to Mr. Rockhill, No. 50, July 14, 1896.
Mr. Lee to Mr. Rockhill, No. 79, August 11, 1896.
Mr. Lee to Mr. Rockhill, No. 90, August 19, 1896.
Mr. Olney to Mr. Taylor, September 3, 1896.
Mr. Taylor to Mr. Olney, September 4, 1896.
Mr. Taylor to Mr. Olney, September 8, 1896.
Mr. Lee to Mr. Rockhill, No. 118, September 9, 1896.
Mr. Lee to Mr. Rockhill, No. 190, October 21, 1896.
Mr. Rockhill to Mr. Lee, No. 152, October 28, 1896.
Mr. Springer to Mr. Rockhill, No. 211, November 12, 1896.
Mr. Springer to Mr. Rockhill, No. 212, November 14, 1896.
Mr. Springer to Mr. Rockhill, No. 220, November 18, 1896.
Mr. Rockhill to Mr. Springer, No. 165, November 19, 1896.
Mr. Springer to Mr. Rockhill, No. 223, November 20, 1896.
Mr. Springer to Mr. Rockhill, No. 226, November 23, 1896.
Mr. Springer to Mr. Rockhill, November 26, 1896.
Mr. Springer to Mr. Rockhill, No. 231, November 26, 1896.
Mr. Springer to Mr. Rockhill, No. 246, December 3, 1896.
Mr. Springer to Mr. Rockhill, No. 251, December 5, 1896.
Mr. Springer to Mr. Rockhill, No. 260, December 15, 1896.

[Telegram.]

Mr. Williams to Mr. Rockhill.

HABANA, *April 30, 1896.*

The American schooner *Competitor*, from Key West, with part of the crew, was captured near San Cayetano, to the westward, while, it is alleged, landing arms for the insurgents, and towed here yesterday. The case subject to marine jurisdiction. I have seen admiral, who tells me it is now under examination of the judge of instruction. I have verbally asked for observance, as heretofore, of the protocol in the trial of the Americans among them, and I shall confirm it in writing.

[Telegram.]

Mr. Williams to Mr. Olney.

HABANA, *May 1, 1896.* (Received 3 p. m.)

Urgent. Please instruct the United States minister at Madrid to request Madrid Government to instruct Captain-General to observe strictly the protocol in the trial of American citizens found on board *Competitor.*

[Telegram]

Mr. Olney to Mr. Taylor.

DEPARTMENT OF STATE,
Washington, May 1, 1896.

Urge Spanish foreign office to at once instruct Captain-General Cuba to strictly observe protocol applicable to trial of American citizens found on board *Competitor.* This cable sent at instance of Consul-General Williams. Cable result.

[Telegram.]

Mr. Williams to Mr. Rockhill.

HABANA, *May 1, 1896*—11 p. m.

Urgent. As the marine jurisdiction has cognizance of the *Competitor* and persons captured on board, I have delivered to-day personally a communication to the admiral, asking that the case be tried under seventh article, 1795, and the protocol therein, protesting against trial by summary court-martial or any form of procedure not adjusted to the treaties. Admiral received me most courteously, but seemed to hold the opinion that the case does not come under any treaty of Spain with the United States, because first article of the protocol says "citizens of the United States residing in Spanish dominions," and these men do not reside therein. I replied that the protocol is contained in the seventh article of the treaty of 1795, and there is nothing therein making residence of American citizens within Spanish dominions or Spanish subjects in the United States a condition necessary to entitle either of them to the enjoyment of all its guaranties.

Please to instruct by cable.

[Telegram.]

Mr. Rockhill to Mr. Williams.

WASHINGTON, *May 1, 1896.*

Was Ambrose Urbach, of Key West, among prisoners captured on schooner *Competitor?*

[Telegram.]

Mr. Williams to Mr. Rockhill.

HABANA, *May 2, 1896.*

Can not say if Urbach was on board *Competitor,* my request to see prisoners and their names being yet refused.

[Telegram]

Mr. Olney to Mr. Williams.

WASHINGTON, *May 2, 1896.*
Yours of yesterday respecting *Competitor* passengers received and
acted upon. What is situation to-day? Cable.

[Telegram]

Mr. Williams to Mr. Olney.

HABANA, *May 2, 1896.*
No change in situation *Competitor* passengers. I have received answer
to my communication from acting admiral saying chief admiral cruising,
but has been informed by him of the case and is expected to return
immediately, when my communication will be answered. Meanwhile no
procedure will be taken in prejudice to the rights of the American
citizens.

[Telegram.]

Mr. Olney to Mr. Williams.

WASHINGTON, *May 2, 1896.*
If your position is that *Competitor* passengers must be tried by the
regular marine tribunal having jurisdiction in the like cases, and not by
special court-martial, your position is approved and you are instructed
to insist upon it.

Mr. Williams to Mr. Rockhill.

No. 2940.]   HABANA, *May 2, 1896.*
SIR: Referring to my dispatches Nos. 2933 of the 30th ultimo and
2934 and 2938 of the 1st and 2d instant, respectively, relating to the
capture of the American schooner *Competitor*, with several persons on
board, while, as is alleged, landing arms and ammunition for the insurgents, near San Cayetano, on the north coast of Cuba, to the westward
of Habana, I have now the honor to inclose copy, with translation,
of the communication dated the 30th ultimo, which, as I cabled on
the same day and yesterday evening, I delivered into the hands of the
admiral of the Spanish West Indian naval station, asking that the
American citizens found on board be tried in accordance with the terms
of the seventh article of the treaty of 1795, and protesting, in the name
of the Government of the United States, against their trial by summary
court-martial or by any other form of procedure not adjusted to the
terms of the treaty.
As mentioned in my cablegram of last evening, the admiral expressed
himself conversationally as holding the opinion that as these men were
not residents of the Spanish dominions they did not come. therefore,
under the treaty engagements between Spain and the United States.
I answered this, in substance, that article 7 of the treaty of 1795 embraced
American citizens and Spanish subjects in general and excluded none,

and that no one of its parts could be annulled by the protocol, such as excluding from the enjoyment of its guaranties American citizens not residing, in the sense of domiciliation, within the Spanish dominions, nor Spanish subjects not residing within those of the United States. In this understanding of the treaty I shall continue to act unless otherwise instructed by the Department.

I beg to inclose a copy (with translation) of a communication received * to-day from the admiral acknowledging receipt of mine of the 30th ultimo.

I am, sir, very respectfully, your obedient servant,

RAMON O. WILLIAMS,
Consul-General.

[Inclosure No. 1, with dispatch No. 2940, Habana, May 2, 1896.]

UNITED STATES CONSULATE-GENERAL,
Habana, April 30, 1896.

EXCELLENCY: The fact of the seizure and bringing into this port of the American schooner *Competitor*, of Key West, Fla., with several persons on board, by a Spanish man-of-war, and of the subjection of the vessel and persons for trial to the tribunals of the marine jurisdiction of this island, having reached the knowledge of this consulate-general, and it being natural to suppose that these persons are either all or in part citizens of the United States, and having no exact information of the causes and the charges justifying their subjection to the said tribunals; therefore and in conformity with instructions, I have to ask your excellency to please inform me at your earliest convenience of the specific charges against this American vessel, as likewise against the persons, with names of the latter, that I may at once transmit the information to my Government.

Also, in compliance with the same instructions, I have to cite as strictly applying to the trial of these persons the terms of article 7 of the treaty of October 27, 1795, between the United States and Spain, which says

"The citizens and subjects of both parties shall be allowed to employ such advocates, solicitors, notaries, agents, and factors as they may judge proper in all their affairs and in all their trials at law in which they may be concerned before the tribunals of the other party ; and such agents shall have free access to the proceedings in such cases, and at the taking of all examinations and evidence which may be exhibited in the said trials "

In consequence, I have to ask your excellency for the strict observance of these stipulations in the trial of the said persons, as was confirmed and agreed upon between the two Governments in the protocol of the 12th of January, 1877, for the amicable termination of all controversy as to the effect of existing treaties in certain matters of judicial procedure, and with respect to the application of the said treaties in the trial of citizens of the United States within the dominion of Spain, which reads as follows

"1. No citizen of the United States residing in Spain, her adjacent islands, or her ultramarine possessions, charged with acts of sedition, treason, or conspiracy against the institutions, the public security, the integrity of the territory, or against the supreme Government, or any other crime whatsoever, shall be subject to trial by any exceptional tribunal, but exclusively by the ordinary jurisdiction, except in the case of being captured with arms in hand.

"2. Those who, not coming within this last case, may be arrested or imprisoned, shall be deemed to have been so arrested or imprisoned by order of the civil authority for the effects of the law of April·17, 1821, even though the arrest or imprisonment shall have been effected by armed force.

"3. Those who may be taken with arms in hand, and who are therefore comprehended in the exception of the first article, shall be tried by ordinary council of war, in conformity with the second article of the hereinbefore-mentioned law; but even in this case the accused shall enjoy for their defense the guaranties embodied in the aforesaid law of April 17, 1821.

"4. In consequence whereof, as well in the cases mentioned in the third paragraph as in those of the second, the parties accused are allowed to name attorneys and advocates, who shall have access to them at suitable times; they shall be furnished in due season with copy of the accusation and a list of witnesses for the prosecution, which latter shall be examined before the presumed criminal, his attorney and advocate, in conformity with the provisions of articles 20 to 31 of the said law;

they shall have the right to compel the witnesses of whom they desire to avail themselves to appear and give testimony or to do it by means of depositions: they shall present such evidence as they may judge proper, and they shall be permitted to present and to make their defense, in public trial, orally or in writing, by themselves or by means of their counsel.

"5. The sentence pronounced shall be referred to the audiencia of the judicial district, or to the Captain-General, according as the trial may have taken place before the ordinary judge or before the council of war, in conformity also with what is prescribed in the above-mentioned law."

For the reasons above expressed, and in view of the jurisprudence already established by the civil and military courts of this island since the 12th of January, 1877, date of the mutual understanding between the two Governments as to the application of their treaties in cases of this nature, I can not less than expect that the marine courts will also strictly observe the said article 7 and the protocol, granting to the persons now accused the enjoyment of all the means of defense therein stipulated.

And it being agreed between the two Governments under article 3 of the above inserted protocol that those American citizens who may be taken with arms in hand shall be tried by ordinary council of war, I must, therefore, protest in the name of my Government against the trial of these American citizens by summary court-martial, because of this method being excluded from the protocol, as I also protest against every form of procedure not adjusted to the treaty.

I am, etc.,

RAMON O. WILLIAMS,
Consul-General.

The ADMIRAL OF THE SPANISH WEST INDIAN SQUADRON, ETC.

[Inclosure No. 2 with dispatch No. 2940, Habana, May 2, 1896 —Translation]

OFFICE OF THE ADMIRAL OF THE SPANISH WEST INDIAN SQUADRON,
Habana, May 1, 1896.

SIR: I have the honor to acknowledge the receipt of your courteous communication of yesterday's date, personally delivered by you to-day at 2 p. m., and to inform you that the case of the seizure of the schooner *Competitor* being under indictment proceedings (en sumario), it is not possible to answer at present your said communication nor your note relating to same; but I promise to do so at the earliest convenience.

I am, etc.,

P. A. JOSE GOMEZ IMAZ.

The CONSUL-GENERAL OF THE UNITED STATES.

[Telegram.]

Mr. Taylor to Mr. Olney.

MADRID, *May 4, 1896.*

Telegraphic orders sent Cuba suspending all executive action until examination can be made as to all taken upon *Competitor* who may prove to be American citizens.

Mr. Williams to Mr. Rockhill.

No. 2946.]   HABANA, *May 5, 1896.*

SIR: In continuation of my dispatches Nos. 2933, 2934, and 2938. of the 30th ultimo and 1st and 2d instaut, in relation to the capture of the American schooner *Competitor*, with several persons on board. near San Cayetano, on the north coast of this island, to the westward of Habana, I now have the honor to inclose for the information of the Department a copy, with translation, of the answer of the acting admiral of this naval station to my communication addressed him on the 30th instant in relation to this affair.

It will be noticed that the acting admiral informs me that the admiral in chief is absent from Habana on a cruise, and that as soon as he returns he will take under consideration and decide upon the several particulars presented in my said communication of the 30th ultimo, with the assurance that no essential determination will be taken in the meantime to the detriment of the rights of the American citizens engaged in this affair.

I am, sir, very respectfully, your obedient servant,

RAMON O. WILLIAMS,
Consul-General.

[Inclosure No 1, with dispatch No. 2946, Habana, May 5, 1896.—Translation.]

COMMANDANCY-GENERAL OF MARINE AND OF THE SPANISH NAVAL
STATION OF THE WEST INDIES, OFFICE OF THE GENERAL STAFF,
Habana, May 2, 1896.

SIR: His excellency the commanding general of this station and squadron, to whom the exercise of the marine jurisdiction belongs in this island and that of Puerto Rico, being absent from the seat of government, there is no legal medium present through which to reply, in view of their judicial character, to any of the points to which your respectable official note of the 30th of April last refers.

The said authority having been informed by me of the capture of the schooner said to be called the *Competitor,* I am expecting his immediate return, and as soon as this occurs he will decide upon all the particulars treated of by you, my powers being limited to the inspection of the proceedings which are being carried on, in conformity with the provisions of the law of organization and attributions of the marine courts, and to assure you that in the meantime no essential determination will be taken in detriment to the rights of any citizen of the nation which you so worthily represent.

I have the honor to communicate the above to you in amplification of my communication to you of yesterday.

God guard you many years.

JOSE GOMEZ IMAS,
Second in Command of this Naval Station.

The CONSUL-GENERAL OF THE UNITED STATES OF AMERICA.

[Telegram.]

Mr. Olney to Mr. Williams.

WASHINGTON, *May 6, 1896.*

Report by cable upon present status of *Competitor* case. Give names of prisoners claiming to be American citizens.

[Telegram.]

Mr. Williams to Mr. Olney.

HABANA, *May 6, 1896.*

Your telegram received. I have seen acting admiral, who tells me the examination of *Competitor* proceedings will be finished to-day and that admiral commanding is expected to arrive to-night, when my communication of the 30th ultimo in which I have asked the names of American citizens and permission to see them will be answered.

[Telegram]

Mr. Williams to Mr. Olney.

HABANA, *May 7, 1896.*

I have received 5 o'clock p. m. from admiral commanding the answer to my communication of the 30th in regard to the American citizens captured on *Competitor*. He replies seventh article of the treaty 1795 and the protocol do not apply to them as they are not residents in accordance with law relating to foreigners and they are to be tried by summary court martial. I am preparing answer and protest in accordance with your telegram 2d instant.

[Telegram]

Mr. Olney to Mr. Williams.

WASHINGTON, *May 7, 1896.*

Competitor case. Informed officially that only one American citizen was taken and is now under arrest. If possible, report by cable, who and where he is, on what charges held and how treated.

[Telegram]

Mr. Olney to Mr. Williams.

WASHINGTON, *May 8, 1896.*

Competitor case. Did American citizens have fair trial, with opportunity to summon and examine witnesses, and to be defended by counsel of their own selection, and with all other legal guarantees.

[Telegram.]

Mr. Williams to Mr. Olney.

HABANA, *May 8, 1896.*

I have seen prisoners this morning. Laborde, captain *Competitor*, tells me was born New Orleans and formerly was deputy sheriff Tampa. Was going Lemon City with twenty-four passengers when they seized the vessel by force, putting pistol to his breast, and took command. Off Cape Sable took on board twenty-three men more. William Gildea, mate, born Liverpool, England; Ona Milton, born Kansas.

[Telegram.]

Mr. Williams to Mr. Olney.

HABANA, *May 8, 1896.*

In case of *Competitor*, trial terminated. Prosecuting officer asks penalty death for all, giving precedence to the local law relating to foreigners over the treaty and the protocol in this case. As the court and authorities here agree on this point, I inform you for such diplomatic action you may deem proper. I am preparing remonstrance Captain-General as the superior delegate of Spain in this island.

[Telegram]

Mr. Williams to Mr. Olney.

HABANA, *May 8, 1896.*

Competitor American citizens have not had opportunity to summon and examine witnesses and to be defended by counsel of their own selection. For their defense their only counsel at the trial was a Spanish naval officer. Captain-general and admiral both contend that they are not embraced in the treaty because not residents Spanish territory, therefore outlaws, and have been tried for piracy and rebellion, consequently have not had fair trials under the treaty.

[Telegram.]

Mr. Olney to Mr. Williams.

WASHINGTON, *May 9, 1896.*

Has death sentence been imposed? When is it to be executed? Dupuy claims Milton is the only American citizen. How is it as to Laborde and Gildea?

[Telegram.]

Mr. Williams to Mr. Olney.

HABANA, *May 9, 1896.*

Milton undoubtedly is a native-born citizen. Laborde says he was born in New Orleans; Gildea, in England. However, one being master and the other mate of an American vessel entitles them to protection of the United States under paragraph 171 Consular Regulations, based on statutes, and were, therefore, entitled to be tried under seventh article of the treaty and in accordance with fourth article of the protocol, allowing them to name attorneys and advocates with all other mentioned guarantees, instead of which they have only had a naval officer for their defense. Death sentence asked for by prosecutor not yet imposed, but executions twelve hours afterwards is customary.

[Telegram.]

Mr. Olney to Mr. Williams.

WASHINGTON, *May 9, 1896.*

Have urged upon Spanish Government, through Dupuy and our minister at Madrid, that recent Havana court-martial sentences upon American citizens should not be executed until this Government is satisfied that it ought not to interpose, for which purpose it needs and asks record of proceedings of court, charges, evidence, and should be officially informed what opportunities of defense defendants had through counsel of their own choice, examination and summoning of witnesses, and otherwise. Make same representations and request to governor-general, urging that request of United States, which would be proper in any case, is specially so in view of the extremely questionable juris· diction of the court-martial, which can be justified only by a new, strained, technical construction of treaty stipulations and which is con· trary to their spirit, to their fair interpretation, and to the intent of the parties at the time they were entered into, as clearly shown by their correspondence.

Mr. Rockhill to Mr. Williams.

No. 1362.]   WASHINGTON, *May 11, 1896.*

SIR: The Department has received your dispatch No. 2940, of the 2d instant, with inclosures, relative to the capture of the American schooner *Competitor.*

I am, etc.,   W. W. ROCKHILL.

[Telegram.]

Mr. Williams to Mr. Olney.

HABANA, *May 11, 1896.*

Admiral has advised consul-general of Great Britain that Madrid Government has ordered suspension of effects of the *Competitor* pro· ceedings and their transmission to supreme council, Madrid.

Mr. Williams to Mr. Rockhill.

No. 2968.]   UNITED STATES CONSULATE-GENERAL,
                                         Habana, May 11, 1896.

SIR: I beg to acknowledge the receipt of the Department's telegram of the 9th instant.   *   *   *

In consequence I addressed a communication to the governor and captain-general in the same sense almost word for word.

I am, etc.,
                                         RAMON O. WILLIAMS.

[Telegram.]

Mr. Williams to Mr. Olney.

HABANA, *May 11, 1896.*

Admiral having adhered to opinion of the judge-advocate making treaty subordinate local law for trial *Competitor* men and having twice rejected my protests against the procedure, I addressed captain-gen· eral, on the 8th instant, declining in him, as the superior delegate of the authority of the King of Spain, the responsibility of the conse· quences, and he has advised me that he has informed Government of His Majesty of my protests; but meantime I learn from good source that the men have been sentenced to death, notwithstanding the pro· ceedings show they were captured without arms in hand.

S. Doc. 231, pt 7——35

Mr. Taylor to Mr. Olney.

No. 510.]   LEGATION OF THE UNITED STATES,
                                        Madrid, May 11, 1896.

SIR: I have the honor to acknowledge the receipt of your telegram of the 9th instant, as follows:

Make immediate representations to Spanish Government that United States conceives it to be its right and duty to insist that court-martial sentences just imposed at Habana upon American citizens shall not be executed until this Government has opportunity to become satisfied that its interposition is not warranted. To enable it to reach a conclusion in the matter, it should have and now asks record of proceedings of court, charges and evidence, and should know what opportunity defendants had to defend themselves by counsel, of their own choice, and by examination and summoning of witnesses. United States would be entitled to insist upon such request, with the necessary reasonable delay in any case, but is especially so entitled in the present case, where the jurisdiction of the court-martial is extremely doubtful and can be justified only by a new strained technical construction of treaty stipulations, such being contrary to their spirit, to their fair interpretation, and to the intent of the parties at the time they were entered into, as clearly shown by their correspondence. Call particular attention to the words in article 4 of the protocol, "all Spaniards being in the United States," as well as "residing" there. It is inconceivable that residence as a condition to advantages of protocol was required in one case and not in the other. Ask for an immediate answer to request that execution of court-martial sentences be postponed for reasons and with purposes stated.

I at once obtained an interview with the minister of state, in which I presented to him your telegram, together with the following observations in the way of argument:

In my opinion it is certain that the protocol of 1877 is not limited, upon a reasonable construction, to citizens of the United States residing in Spanish territory, for the conclusive reason that the benefits of American law are extended to all Spaniards "being" in the United States, although they may not be residents there. To dispute that construction is to deny to the protocol mutuality. That point settled, it is certain that, even conceding for the sake of argument that the American citizens in question were taken with arms in their hands, and for that reason triable by a council of war, they are nevertheless entitled to all the benefits of section 4 of the protocol, which reads as follows:

"In consequence whereof, as well in the cases mentioned in the third paragraph as in those of the second, the parties accused are allowed to name attorneys and advocates, who shall have access to them at suitable times. They shall be furnished in due season with copy of the accusation and a list of witnesses for the prosecution, which latter shall be examined before the presumed criminal, his attorney and advocate, in conformity with the provisions of articles twenty to thirty-one of the said law; they shall have right to compel the witnesses of whom they desire to avail themselves to appear and give testimony or to do it by means of depositions; they shall present such evidence as they may judge proper, and they shall be permitted to be present and to make their defense in public trial, orally or in writing, by themselves or by means of their counsel."

My Government has therefore in any case the right to demand an inspection of the record of the proceedings of the council of war in order to determine whether or no the accused have been given all the benefits of section 4 of the protocol.

The minister promptly gave a favorable response to your request, which I reported to you in the following telegram:

Presented your request, with argument, based on terms protocol. Minister of state promptly replied all executive action suspended by order given under promise made me 3d instant. Entire record will be ordered Madrid for review by supreme council war and marine. When there, Government can control record, copy of which will be furnished you for inspection prior to execution in the event supreme council should hold proceedings to have been regular.

The newspapers of this morning say that the review of this case by the supreme council of war and marine will involve a delay of at least two months.

I am, etc.,   HANNIS TAYLOR.

[Telegram]

Mr. Olney to Mr. Williams.

WASHINGTON, *May 11, 1896.*

Competitor case. Execution of death sentences upon American citizens suspended pending diplomatic consideration of their rights under treaty and protocol.

[Telegram]

Mr. Williams to Mr. Olney.

HABANA, *May 12, 1896.*

Urgent. The afternoon newspapers report that two American citizens,. Charles Barnett and William Leavitt, captured on land, forming part of the *Competitor* expedition, are to be tried by ordinary court-martial of the marine jurisdiction. I beg that immediate instruction be given to our legation, Madrid, to ask suspension of the effects of the trial until our Government can be satisfied it is in conformity with the treaty, for I apprehend the condition of the treaty will not be observed.

[Telegram.]

Mr. Williams to Mr. Olney.

HABANA, *May 13, 1896.*

In reply to my yesterday's communication, asking for the application of the treaty and protocol to the trial, two Americans, *Competitor* crew, and suspension of execution in case of death sentence until I could inform you, Captain-General advises me officially that American citizens are tried according to the treaty between Spain and the United States, and further that no death sentence will be executed without approval of His Majesty's Government.

[Telegram.]

Mr. Williams to Mr. Olney.

HABANA, *May 16, 1896.*

I am preparing correspondence relating to the *Competitor* case which is voluminous and important, mostly in Spanish, which I am translating. Can not be transmitted before next week.

Mr. Williams to Mr. Rockhill.

No. 2987.] UNITED STATES CONSULATE-GENERAL,
Habana, May 21, 1896.

SIR: In continuation of my dispatches in relation to Alfred Laborde, William Gildea, and Ona Melton, captured by a Spanish gunboat on board the American schooner *Competitor* and tried at 8.30 o'clock of the morning of the 8th instant, at the arsenal of this port by the naval authorities, under the form of procedure known here as the most summary process (juicio sumarisimo), I now have the honor to accompany translations of the correspondence had since the 7th instant between the authorities and this consulate-general on the subject.

The first communication forming part of this correspondence in the order of reference and consideration is that addressed to me on the 7th instant by the admiral of the station. It is made up wholly of the opinion, adverse to my remonstrance, of the judge-advocate to whom my two communications of the 30th ultimo were referred in consultation. It will be seen that the admiral adheres to and approves of this opinion. In it the judge-advocate assumes:

First. That the specification of the charges against these men, that I had asked for in my first communication of the 30th, could be furnished me in reference to the friendly relations existing between the two countries. I must observe, however, that the trial of these men took place within the short time of fifteen hours after this offer, with the night intervening; and, that notwithstanding the men have been tried and condemned to death, that the specific charges have not yet been furnished me for transmission to you.

Second. That with respect to the list of the names of the men, the judge-advocate tells the admiral that there was reason to suppose that Melton was the only American citizen on board. But I must here observe, too, that, as there was reason to believe that Laborde was the master, and Gildea the mate, according to paragraph 171 of the Consular Regulations, based on statute, and the fact of the vessel being American, the flag covered them. In consequence, it became my duty and right to interpose in their favor.

Third. The judge-advocate assumes that neither article 7 of the treaty of the 27th of October, 1795, nor the protocol of 1877, invoked by me, apply to the case in question. Because, as he further assumes, foreigners must be tried by the same courts having cognizance in all affairs of Spanish subjects, in accordance with the local law relating to foreigners of the 4th of July, 1870. And at this point I beg to remark that the judge-advocate subordinates the treaty to the local law instead of giving precedence to the treaty as a part of the supreme law of Spain.

Fourth. He also assumes that whatever interpretation and scope may be given to the treaty and the protocol construing it, that the latter from the beginning embraces only resident American citizens. But against this assumption I beg to state that article 7 of the treaty of 1795 imposes no condition of residence either on Spanish subjects in the United States nor American citizens in the dominions of Spain; for, were it so, then the status of Spanish subject and of American citizen would be taken away from thousands of Spaniards and Americans who visit both countries every year either on business or pleasure, as merchants, manufacturers, tradesmen, travelers, and tourists.

Besides, the protocol can not detract any force from the treaty as understood by the President and Senate of the United States, who have sanctioned it; and not being yet revoked it continues in force as the matrix of the protocol. It is clear, therefore, that the protocol must conform to the treaty and not the treaty to the protocol. But even then, the protocol explicitly mentions, in the declaration of Mr. Cushing, all Spaniards residing or being in the United States, and conversely, in the sense of article 7, should embrace all Americans either residing or being in the Spanish dominions.

Fifth. The assumption that foreigners must be inscribed at the provincial governments and at their respective consulates in accordance with article 7 of the local law relating to them can not be maintained, for it would be equivalent to depriving them of their rights of nationality and of the protection of their respective Governments, a doctrine that no Government will admit, not even that of the judge-advocate, to whose opinion on these several points the admiral adheres and approves.

Sixth. It is also erroneously assumed by the judge-advocate that the law of the 17th of April, 1821, is derogated by Spanish laws of subsequent enactment—that is to say, that a treaty as an international contract can be derogated by either party at pleasure by local legislation or decretal action—a most dangerous doctrine indeed for the friendly intercourse and peace of nations.

Seventh. The judge-advocate also contends that the jurisprudence established here under the treaty and protocol since 1877, in such cases as that of Rosell, at Santiago de Cuba, Mayolin, at Santa Clara, Sanguily, Aguirre, Carrillo, and Cepero, at Havana, forms no precedent in these cases of Melton, Laborde, and Gildea—that is, that the naval jurisdiction has a distinct and exceptional authority in cases coming under its jurisdiction to that possessed by the military and civil powers by which those other cases were tried.

In reference to the passage on page 2 of the admiral's communication to me of the 9th instant, wherein the judge-advocate calls attention in the sense of amplitude, to the term of ten days having been employed in substantiating and trying this case, I have to say: That the time thus gained for the defense was accidental and not intentional, and was owed entirely to the temporary absence of the admiral in command who was then on a cruise at the eastern end of the island, and that had he been present at the time of the bringing of the men to this port, there are reasons to believe that they would have been tried and sentenced within the next twenty-four hours.

I beg also to observe that during the civil war in the United States it was a very common thing for vessels loaded with arms and munitions of war to leave the ports of Habana and Nassau and land their cargoes in the Southern States; but I know of no case in which parties intercepted and arrested by the Federal authorities were ever deprived of the right to name counsel of their own choice and to be sentenced to death by most summary process, as has been done in this case with the men captured on board the American schooner *Competitor*.

In conclusion, I beg to say that copies are also accompanied of my answer dated the 7th instant, of his reply of the 9th to my said communication; of my communication to the captain general, dated the 8th, and also that of the 9th, to the admiral, in answer to his of the same date; the admiral's reply, also a note from the governor-general acknowledging receipt of my communication of the 8th, above referred to; Likewise, copies of correspondence had with the British consul-general relative to William Gildea; Mr. Laborde's statement signed besides by Melton and Gildea; letter dated the 2d, received on the 7th from Ona Melton; another one of same date from William Gildea, and a third letter signed jointly by the three prisoners under date of the 7th instant.

I am, &c.,

RAMON O. WILLIAMS,
Consul-General.

[Inclosure 1 with No 2987.—Translation.]

COMMANDER-GENERAL OF MARINE OF THE NAVAL STATION
AND SQUADRON OF THE WEST INDIES,
Habana, May 7, 1896.

SIR: Your official letter and note of the 30th ultimo having been referred in con- .sultation to the judge-advocate of this naval station, this counsellor reports as follows:

"EXCELLENCY: Under date of the 30th of April last the consul-general of the United States in this capital addressed your excellency the two preceding communications passed to me for examination and report accompanied with the proceedings of the case. In the first of those communications, starting from the supposition that the schooner *Competitor* and the persons captured on board might be Americans, and not having exact information respecting the charges and accusations justifying their submission to the naval courts of this island, and in accord, as he alleges, with the instructions of his Government, he asks your excellency to have the goodness to inform him as soon as may be possible of the specific charges brought against the said schooner and citizens, with the names of the latter, for the purpose of transmitting them at once to his Government.

"Respecting the first part of this consular petition it is the opinion of the undersigned, in view of the good desires always animating and inspiring your excellency when treating of matters that may in some manner directly or indirectly affect a friendly nation with which the best relations are maintained, that your excellency can at once manifest to the consul-general of the United States that, in effect, this naval jurisdiction is now occupied in trying the case of the capture of a schooner hailing from the port of Key West, whose certificate of inscription and sailing license agree as to her name being that of *Competitor*, or the same one which, refusing to show any flag, made armed resistance to a vessel of war of our nation and landed a cargo of arms, ammunition, explosives, and other effects belonging to a filibuster expedition, under command of the so-called Colonel Monzon; the same that he conveyed from the coast of Florida to Berracos Cove, where the schooner was discharging when discovered. It is evident that the accusations and charges springing from this fact will be formulated according to regular rules and within the time fixed by our code of criminal procedure, it being, therefore, impossible to anticipate the specification desired by the consul. But if agreeable to your excellency he could be assured that at the proper time he will be informed of all the details he desires to know of the case.

"With respect to the list of the names of the men captured that might be supposed to be American citizens, there appears no reason up to the present to suppose there is any other than Olna Milton of that nationality, who declares he is a native of Kansas, 23 years of age, single, newspaper reporter, son of Daniel and Nancy, and resident of Key West. On reaching this point I am pleased to call the attention of your excellency to the contradiction in which the consul appears to incur when, after giving the assurance in the first cited paragraph of his estimable communication to the effect that he had no exact information regarding the case, on continuing he asks that the men who might perhaps appear to be American citizens be tried in strict accord to Article VII of the treaty of the 27th of October, 1795, but of whose names and circumstances he then knew nothing.

"Neither the Article VII invoked by the consul nor the interpretation given it by the protocol signed at Madrid the 12th of January, 1877, apply to this case, because of the following reasons:

"First. Because foreigners without distinction of nationality are subject to the laws and courts of Spain for crimes committed within Spanish territory, and as such foreigners do not enjoy any special right or privilege, being subject to the same courts that have cognizance of the affairs of Spaniards in conformity of articles 41 to 47 of the law relating to foreigners in the ultramarine provinces of the 4th of July, 1870.

"Second. Because whatever may be the interpretation and scope that may be given to the treaty and its meaning given by the protocol, this from its beginning declares it only embraces resident American citizens, and these only in the case of not being arrested with arms in hand, circumstances that do not concur in the present case.

"Article VII of the said law relating to foreigners exacts, among other requisites for a foreigner to be considered a resident in the colonies (ultramar), that he must be inscribed in the register which to that effect is kept in the superior civil governments and in the consulates of his nation.

"And lastly, because the law of the 7th of April, 1821, mentioned in the protocol and invoked by the consul in its relation to the procedure that was fixed in the articles 20 to 31 of the said law and in the fourth and fifth declarations of the protocol are totally derogated under the final enactment of the present law governing crimi. nal procedure, by article 750 of the code of military justice and by article 472 of the law of military marine procedure.

"The jurisprudence to which the consul refers in his communication and alleges to be established by the civil and military courts of this island has been limited to the competency of the courts and not the rules, forms, requisites, and solemnities of the methods of procedure observed by them.

"Finally, excellency, you should not receive nor accept in any form the protest addressed to you by the consul of the United States in the name of his Government against the application of most summary proceedings (juicio sumarisimo) to those who in the case might be American citizens because he considers that form of pro- cedure excluded from the protocol and, because in his opinion, it is not the ordinary council of war mentioned in Article III of the protocol.

"This is an error of law in which the consul incurs, the correction of which he will find if, in his recognized ability2he will revise the latest organic law relating to the procedure of marine courts.

"In conclusion I am going to refer to the second communication of the consul- general of the United States, referring to his desire to communicate with the pris- oners. The prohibition of outside intercourse to which they were subjected having . been removed, your excellency can grant the petition.

"In the above sense it is understood by the undersigned that your excellency can be pleased to reply to the consul-general of the United States should you not esteem it better to decide otherwise. Moreover, I have to say, that the official correspond- ence that had given rise to this consultation, as also the superior decree your excel- lency may have given it, should be passed to the judge of instruction encharged with the examination of the case for their attachment to the proceedings. Your excellency will decide."

And having accepted the preceding report I have the honor to so inform you in reply to your above-cited esteemed communication.

I am, etc.,

JOSE NAVARRO Y FERNANDEZ.

The CONSUL-GENERAL OF THE UNITED STATES.

[Inclosure 2 with No. 2987.]

UNITED STATES CONSULATE-GENERAL,
Habana, May 7, 1896.

His Excellency the Admiral in Command of this Naval Station and Squadron.

EXCELLENCY: I have the honor to reply to your attentive communication of this date, received at this 5 p. m., and to protest at once against the narrow and antag- onistic sense with which it considers the treaties and conventions existing between the United States and Spain. And being especially instructed by my Government in the present case, I must insist to the point of obtainment—that the citizens of the United States are to be judged by the courts of this country, in conformity with the treaty, notwithstanding the opinion of the judge-advocate of this naval station, and to which your excellency has officially adhered with transmission of a copy of it to me.

I can never, as the representative of the United States in this island, lend assent to the trial of my countrymen by the exceptional tribunal called by the name of the *most summary process* (juicio sumarisimo), because such form of trial is contrary to what has been agreed and ratified in the treaty of 1795 and the protocol of 1877 between our respective nations, and its application would constitute a most flagrant violation. Therefore I trust to be able to convince your excellency of the error in which his honor the judge-advocate has incurred on submitting his opinion to your excellency, for the point in dispute is of the clearest nature.

Your excellency, by accepting the opinion of the judge-advocate, affirms that article 7 of the treaty of 1795, as likewise this protocol of 1877, for several stated reasons, do not apply to the present case, and which I will now proceed to refute, interpreting in the following manner, with all fidelity, the intent of my Government. which has been duly communicated to me.

First. It is not absolutely exact with respect to citizens of the United States, the affirmation of your excellency that they, in their character of foreigners, must be subject for crimes of which they are accused within Spanish territory to all the laws and tribunals of Spain, neither that they are not exempt from the tribunals which in certain cases have cognizance in the affairs of Spaniards, notwithstanding the prescriptions of articles 41 and 47 of the said law relating to foreigners, which your excellency mentions. And it is not exact because there are exceptions guaranteed by existing treaties to American citizens. And, indeed, the present case is a typical example of this statement, treating as it does of citizens of the United States accused of acts against the integrity of Spanish territory; for article 7 of the treaty of 1795 provides that the detention or arrest for offenses committed by citizens of the United States within the jurisdiction of Spain shall be "made and prosecuted by order and authority of law only and according to ordinary proceedings in such cases" (segun los tramites ordinarios en tales casos).

But notwithstanding the clearness of the object, doubts arose as to the preciseness of its meaning, and the Governments of the United States and Spain agreed upon an interpretation and reduced it to a formal understanding under what is now known as the protocol of 1877, the third article of which textually says:

"Those who may be taken with arms in hand, and who are therefore comprehended in the exception of the first article, shall be tried by ordinary council of war, in conformity with the second article of the hereinbefore-mentioned law; but even in this case the accused shall enjoy for their defense the guaranties embodied in the aforesaid law of 1821."

And article 4 confirms article 3 in all its parts. And it will therefore be seen how the opinion, approved by your excellency, of the judge-advocate is mistaken. For Spanish subjects trial by most summary process may be in order under certain circumstances, but never for citizens of the United States. Exceptional tribunals may try the first, but never the second. Neither the laws nor the judges of exceptional councils of war have application within the dominions of Spain to citizens of the United States.

If American citizens are captured in those dominions with arms in hand, they are to be judged solely in accordance with article 3 of the protocol, which in that sense interprets authentically the treaty of 1795, and as that article refers to the second of the law of the 17th of April, 1821, this last article is therefore the one of immediate application. That second article of the law of the 21st of April, 1821, says:

"The accused will be tried militarily in ordinary council of war, as prescribed in the law 8, title 17, book 12, of the last recompilation."

There exists, therefore, an absolute conformity between the treaty of 1795, the protocol of 1877, and the law of 1821, for they all agree that the citizens of the United States captured with arms in hand in Spanish territory can not ever be tried by *most summary process* but by ordinary council of war.

My Government can not, therefore, consent that its citizens be tried under any other form of procedure than that expressed in the treaty, and to which it strictly adheres.

The second manifest error contained in the communication of your excellency is that which approves the part of the opinion of his honor the judge-advocate by which he affirms that the stipulations of the treaty of 1795 and protocol of 1877 embrace only American citizens residents of Spanish territory. But this error disappears at once when it is shown that the treaty does not distinguish between American citizens residing or being in Spanish territory. Article 7 embraces all American citizens without difference of any kind. Again, if there was any doubt on this point it would be dispelled by the protocol of 1877, for it is not to be supposed that in a treaty between two nations the one would put its citizens or subjects in a disadvantageous position with respect to those of the other; to the contrary both themselves on an equal footing. For article 4 of the protocol, on referring to Spanish subjects in the United States, reads as follows:

"The said provisions extend to and comprehend all Spaniards residing or being in the United States."

Therefore, if the protocol comprehends all Spanish subjects residing or being in the United States, it must equally comprehend all American citizens residing or being in the dominions of Spain; the Spanish equivalent of the English word being is estante, as used in the translation, and signifies in this case the temporary occupation by a person of a place or spot regardless of permanent residence in the sense of domiciliation. These American citizens are in a Spanish dominion, where they are to be subjected to judicial trial, and necessarily this must be done in accordance with the form of procedure solemnly agreed upon in treaties between Spain and the United States. The theory advanced by the judge-advocate, and admitted by your excellency, places these American citizens on an inferior plane of justice to Spanish subjects in the United States, and the words used in the protocol by the minister of Spain for foreign affairs, Mr. Calderon Collantes, that "the said provisions extend to and comprehend all Spaniards residing or being in the United States," are limited solely to Spanish subjects, the protocol would then favor one of the contracting parties to the prejudice of the other, and this is impossible to suppose since article 7 of the treaty of 1795, interpreted by the protocol, makes no distinction between those American citizens who reside and those being within the dominion of Spain, but comprehend all alike, and where the law makes no distinction the judicial authorities can not create them.

Third. According to your excellency only such foreigners as are inscribed in the registers determined by the Spanish law relating to foreigners can be considered as entitled to treaty stipulations. My Government does not admit any such interpre. tation, for, above all, it is the only one competent to qualify its citizens and to rec. ognize or reject them, as every Government with its own, for the law mentioned by your excellency as relating to foreigners is merely a local police regulation of inte. rior application and can not derogate a treaty of Spain with another nation. Other. wise the nationality of foreigners entering the territories of Spain would depend upon its laws relating to foreigners; and to convince your excellency that my Gov. ernment does not recognize this assumption, I have the honor to copy, in continuation, the following words in which in a like case it instructed me, and to which I must adhere:

"That while it may be expected that citizens of the United States sojourning in a foreign State shall comply with reasonable local requirements of registration, omis. sion to do so can not vitiate their right to protection as citizens of their own Gov. ernment in case of need. That citizenship is a fact of which the citizen's country is the authoritative judge under its own laws regarding naturalization and nationality; and that its certification of that fact by passport imparts a verity which the foreign Governments are bound prima facie to admit in executing any treaty obligations with regard to such citizens."

Having acquainted your excellency with this view of my Government, it does not become me to add a word more on this point, leaving the rest to the consideration of your excellency.

Fourth. The communication of your excellency which I have the honor to answer maintains, besides, another point which in the name of my Government I must absolutely reject, and which point is expressed in the said communication under exaggerated proportions, and is that the law of the 17th of April, 1821, which fixes the form of procedure, and that the fourth and fifth articles of the protocol are now totally abrogated by the Spanish law regulating criminal procedure, by the code of military justice and that of naval procedure, to which your excellency adds that the jurisprudence established by the civil and military courts of this island in similar cases since 1877 is limited solely to questions of competency between those courts, without respect to the rules, requisites, and solemnities of procedure.

The first thing that contradicts these observations of your excellency is the pro. tocol itself, which in its preamble says:

"The respective parties, mutually desiring to terminate amicably all controversy as to the effect of existing treaties in certain matters of judicial procedure, etc."

It is patent, therefore, that the purpose of the protocol is to interpret and fix the form of procedure, as also to determine the jurisdiction of the courts. And it is not abrogated, neither is the law of April, 1821, in its application to the treaty relations between the United States and Spain, for it is a principal of international law which from universal consent has acquired axiomatic force, that treaties subsist so long as they are not denounced and revoked by the contracting parties, and if one of them violates them the other has the right to exact their strict fulfillment.

Therefore, the treaty of 1795 interpreted in its doubts by the protocol of 1877, is in force and constitutes the international law voluntarily agreed upon by the United States and Spain. Both nations recognize and invoke it as the supreme law that obligates them unto each other in the regulation of their intercourse and in the set. tlement of their differences. For that treaty and its protocol agree upon the only form of procedure to be applied in the trial of American citizens either being or residing in the dominions of Spain, and the form incorporated in the protocol is the same as that above cited, of April, 1821, and provides that such citizens as are captured with arms in hand are to be tried by ordinary council of war.

The treaty still existing, the protocol must naturally be contained in it. There. fore, as a logical consequence, your excellency must admit that neither article 7 of the treaty, the protocol, nor the law of 1821 are abrogated, but subsist and must last so long as the treaty is not abolished by the consent of both contracting parties.

The local special laws cited by your excellency only refer to Spanish subjects within Spanish territory, and can not be applied under the treaty to American citizens. To that end the consent of the Government of the United States would be necessary, and, without previous denunciation and revocation of the treaty, it continues in force, and local laws passed since its date by either Government can only affect the citizens or subjects of such Government and not those of the other, since a treaty forms a part of the supreme law of every country. These, without the common assent of the contract. ing parties, prevail at all times without in any manner being affected by the laws made by any one of the contracting parties without the knowledge of the other or others.

The treaty subject of this note is an international law, and those cited by your excellency are solely national or local; that is, exclusively obligatory on Spanish subjects, but in no way applicable to foreigners when opposed to the treaties existing between their Governments and Spain.

Fifth. Hence the form of trial called *most summary process* (juicio sumarisimo) which your excellency has decided to apply to these American citizens completely violates the treaty in force between the United States and Spain, for it provides for a form diametrically opposed.

Sixth. And with respect to the rejection by your excellency of the protest I have presented you in the name of my Government against the violation of the treaty, it suffices for me to say that notwithstanding its rejection and the adherence of your excellency to the contrary opinion of the judge-advocate, still this can not deprive it of its legal effects, since I have presented it in due season.

Seventh. And, finally, as in support of the *most summary process*, which, as your excellency informs me, is to be applied to the trial of these American citizens, you cite certain laws that are of merely national or local enactment, I have, in consequence, to again remind your excellency that the case in question is governed by the treaty, and, therefore, not by the local law of Spain, which should conform to the treaty as a part of the supreme law of Spain. Consequently, the trial of these American citizens under the form of *most summary process* is a violation of article 7 of the treaty of 1795 between the United States and Spain.

Therefore, and in the name of my Government, I have to ratify my previous protest presented to your excellency against the violation of trial to which those American citizens have been subjected, and hereby solemnly renew it, protesting against this form of trial as a manifest violation of the said treaty between the United States and Spain.

I avail myself of this occasion to reiterate to your exellency the assurances of my most distinguished consideration.

RAMON O. WILLIAMS,
Consul-General.

[Inclosure 3 in No. 2987.—Translation.]

COMMANDANCY-GENERAL OF MARINE OF THE NAVAL STATION
AND SQUADRON OF THE WEST INDIES,
Habana, May 9, 1896.

SIR: Your esteemed communication of the 7th instant, in which you answer mine of the same date, having been received, I have now the honor to inform you that having referred it in consultation to the judge-advocate of this naval station, he reports upon it as follows:

"EXCELLENCY: In obedience to your above superior decree, the undersigned has studied with the greatest care the esteemed communication addressed you by the consul-general of the United States of America in this capital, on the margin of which your decree is placed.

"The latest communication of the consul is a petition against the answer given him by your excellency to his remonstrance of the 30th of April last. The consul has strengthened his first arguments with the skillful resource of better diction and without mention of legal provision. I comply, on my part, by duplicating the reasons and arguments of my previous report, which, with the greatest respect, are now reproduced. If the present case, as the consul-general of the United States affirms, is typical of Article VII of the treaty of 1795, it is not possible, without incurring in a grave misconception of fact and of law, to maintain that the American citizen, Ona Melton, who is the only one that could in any manner profit by the efforts of the consul, has not been prosecuted by order and authority of law only, and according to the regular course of proceeding. Such is the estimation given to the proceeding had within the unquestionable competency of the marine courts in a case in which no precept of law of procedure of this Department has been omitted, and in the substantiation of which a period of ten days has been employed, notwithstanding the method of *most summary process* (juicio sumarisimo) has been utilized, which is not the exception tribunal capriciously believed, and to which the consular communication now the object of my attention alludes.

"I repeat, there is a remarkable misconception of law in considering that the form of most summary process excludes the ordinary council of war and is opposed to the employment of the most ample and efficient means of defense by the parties accused, the sole object of the most summary process being to gain time (conseguir la mayor brevidad) in the different stages of procedure, simplifying some labors or proceedings of little importance. On a former occasion, when treating of the same case, I was enabled to convince your excellency that charges for certain kinds of crimes are triable by the ordinary most summary process, whose proceedings are equally applicable to natives and foreigners, and, of course, to citizens of the United States, as much in those cases coming under the military, naval, or civil jurisdictions. It is therefore beyond all doubt Melton and his companions have been tried in the ordinary way in such cases as come under the cognizance of the most summary process.

"It is not necessary to insist on the point of residence or stay as determinative of the competency, which neither the accused, the consul, nor directly the Government of the United States has discussed, because not being the only cause of it.

"To the argument presented on that point, it suffices to say that the declarations of the protocol of 1877 were in no manner reciprocal, but, to the contrary, each one of the signers made his own separately and upon distinct subjects as could not less than incur in view of the nature of the matters treated about and the special legis. lation of the respective countries. The protocol of the 12th of January, 1877, is not a treaty negotiated between two nations, nor even an addition nor complement of any preexisting treaty. It is only and exclusively what its preamble says: the result of a conference held with the desire to terminate amicably all controversy as to the effect of existing treaties in certain matters of judicial procedure, and communicated for its observance by a royal order. Therefore, the citation of international law about the revocation and denunciation of treaties is needless. Consequently, there being no violation in any shape or manner of the treaty solemnly agreed upon between Spain and the United States of the 27th of October of 1795, it is plain that within the terms of the most exquisite courtesy it is impossible for your excellency to accept any of the protests of the consul of that friendly nation in this city."

And with the approval of the above report I have the honor to transmit you a copy of the same, and avail myself of the opportunity to reiterate to you the assurances of my most distinguished consideration.

JOSE NAVARRO FERNANDEZ.

The CONSUL-GENERAL OF THE UNITED STATES.

[Inclosure 4 in No. 2987.]

URGENT.]   CONSULATE-GENERAL OF THE UNITED STATES,
                                             Habana, May 8, 1896.
His Excellency the Governor and Captain-General of the Island of Cuba.

EXCELLENCY: Yesterday, at 5 p. m., his excellency the admiral of the naval station has replied to a communication addressed him on the 30th ultimo by this consulate-general in which, by reason of the capture of the American schooner *Competitor*, with several persons on board, I reminded him of the treaty obligations which absolutely prohibit, without exception in any case, the trial of American citizens within Spanish territory by exceptional military tribunals, such as are here called by the name of most summary process.

I explicitly informed his excellency the admiral that on addressing him I did so in obedience to the orders of my Government, which exacts the strict fulfillment of its treaties with Spain; and at the end of seven days and at 5 o'clock in the afternoon of yesterday I received his answer, denying my affirmation and maintaining that the provisions of the treaty of 1795 between the United States and Spain have been abrogated by national or local laws subsequently enacted to the date of that treaty by the Government of Spain.

And I am just informed by the morning newspapers that the trial is to take place this same morning at 8 o'clock under the form of procedure known here as the most summary process, or fifteen hours after the receipt of the admiral's communication in reply to the one which, in the name of my Government, I personally delivered to the second in command on the 30th ultimo.

But, excellency, notwithstanding his excellency the admiral denies it, still the fact exists that the only criminal procedure under which citizens of the United States can be tried in the dominions of Spain is that designated in the treaty of 1795 and the protocol of 1877 construing it, under conformity to the procedure established by the law of the 17th of April, 1821.

All the existing treaty obligations between the United States and Spain having application to the case in question prohibit absolutely the trial of American citizens within the Spanish dominions under the procedure known as most summary process. The treaty from which these obligations emanate has never been revoked, and therefore still exists.

In the same afternoon (of yesterday) I replied to the erroneous communication of his excellency the admiral, protesting, in the name of my Government, against the trial by the form of most summary process in case it should be carried out, against the existing treaty.

My Government can not consent to any other form of trial for its citizens within the Spanish dominions than those so clearly established in the treaty of 1795. They may by force be tried by the most summary process; but, then on my part, I must decline all the responsibility that may in consequence accrue from such flagrant violation of the treaty. My last communication to his excellency the admiral refutes and destroys all the errors in which his is inspired.

But as the persons accused, Ona Melton, Alfred Laborde are, as they inform me, American citizens, Laborde a native of New Orleans, Melton of Kansas; and Gildea, though of British nativity, the mate of an American vessel; and as article 5 of the protocol textually says "the sentence pronounced shall be referred to the audiencia of the judicial district, or to the captain-general, according as the trial may have taken place before the ordinary judge or before the council of war," I have therefore, within the instructions of my Government, yet in time, to address myself to your excellency, as you have to pass on the sentence of this most summary process, to see that justice is done to these American citizens, and to annul the whole proceedings because having been practiced throughout in manner contrary to the treaty between the United States and Spain.

Your excellency being the superior representative in this island of the Government of His Majesty, and my legal and just demand having been rejected by the admiral, and as the sentence in the case, whatever it may be, has in last instance to be submitted to the approval or disapproval of your excellency, I have therefore to beg your excellency to order the delivery to you of my communication of the 30th ultimo and 7th instant, addressed to his excellency the admiral with the view that your excellency may personally examine the reasons and arguments therein stated.

Should your excellency refuse to accede to my petition addressed to you in the preceding paragraph, in the name of my Government, I then most solemnly protest in its name before your excellency against the violation of the treaty on the part of the Government of Spain, which your excellency so worthily represents in this island, giving account of the act to my Government and of my remonstrance and protests presented to the naval authorities and to the superior authority of your excellency, before which in last instance the sentence must come, from a court incompetent under the treaty to take judicial cognizance in the affairs of American citizens in this island.

I have the honor to subscribe myself, with the greatest respect and consideration, your excellency's most obedient servant,

RAMON O. WILLIAMS,
Consul-General.

[Inclosure No. 5 in No. 2987.]

CONSULATE-GENERAL OF THE UNITED STATES,
Habana, May 9, 1896.

His Excellency, the Admiral of this Naval Station and Squadron.

EXCELLENCY: In reply to your attentive communication of this date I have to say:

First. That the officers and crew of an American vessel enjoy, under the laws of any country, regardless of their nativity, the protection due to American citizens, and Laborde and Gildea, having assured me that they are master and mate, respectively, of the American schooner *Competitor*, it is therefore clear that they are embraced in the clauses of the treaties between the United States and Spain, and as to Melton, he being a native-born American, there can not be any doubt about his status and rights.

Second. The accused have been deprived of their right to name advocate and solicitor of their own choice for their defense and to freely communicate with them; neither have they been furnished with a copy of the accusation and with a list of the witnesses of the prosecution, or allowed to examine them in the presence of themselves and attorney and advocate, nor to summon witnesses in their favor; in a word, none of the provisions of article 4 of the protocol have been practiced in their behalf, and instead of a professional lawyer of their own choice a naval officer, as I understand, has been designated for their defense.

Third. The protocol of 1877 not only confirms the treaty of 1795, but is its most authentic interpretation.

Fourth. The difference between the form of procedure known as *most summary process* and the stipulated ordinary council of war, constitutes an exceptional tribunal of the kind expressly excluded by the protocol, the ordinary council of war admitted in the protocol being that which is defined in article 2 of the law of the 17th of April, 1821.

Fifth. The statement that the signers of the protocol only expressed their private opinions therein is not correct; to the contrary, they together, and in common, and in the representation of the two countries, agreed upon that plan for the removal of all doubts and obscurities that had until then existed as to the methods of judicial procedure to be observed in the prosecution of American citizens within the dominions of Spain.

Consequently I ratify my previous protests, and, in the name of my Government, decline in your excellency and in his excellency the captain-general of this island, all the responsibility that may supervene from the trial of these men by *most summary process* and denial of their right to be tried in the manner expressed by the treaty of the 27th of October, 1795, and the protocol construing it of the 12th of January, 1877, between the United States and Spain.

I am, etc.,
RAMON O. WILLIAMS,
Consul-General.

[Inclosure No 6 in No. 2987—Translation.]

COMMANDANCY-GENERAL OF MARINE OF THE NAVAL STATION
AND SQUADRON OF THE WEST INDIES,
Habana, 9 May, 1896.

DEAR SIR: Having received your attentive communication of this date insisting on the points treated in your two previous ones and ratifying your protests, I have the honor to inform you that I passed it in consultation to the judge-advocate of this station, and he has reported thereon in the following terms:

"Information having been given to the Government of His Majesty in everything concerning the proceedings had by reason of the capture of the schooner *Competitor*, and being subject to its decision, it is not possible for your excellency to take any resolution in this affair, or to accept protests from the consul-general of the United States of America in this capital, nor enter in new disquisitions about a question already so much debated, and consequently it is my opinion that your excellency should be pleased to reply in this sense to the said consular functionary, leaving his action open for the fulfillment of the instructions of his Goverment in the manner and way he may esteem most convenient."

With my approval of the above report, I have the honor to send it to you in reply to your said communication, and to reiterate to you the testimony of my most distinguished consideration.

JOSE NAVARRO Y FERNANDEZ.
The CONSUL-GENERAL OF THE UNITED STATES.

[Inclosure 7 in No. 2987.—Translation.]

GENERAL GOVERNMENT OF THE ISLAND OF CUBA,
OFFICE OF THE SECRETARY,
Habana, May 9, 1896.

SIR: In reply to your attentive communication of yesterday, protesting in the name of the Government of your nation against the court-martial being held by the commandancy-general of the navy for the trial of the prisoners of the schooner *Competitor*, Laborde, Melton, and another, I have the honor to inform you, by order of his excellency the Governor-General, that knowledge of the said protest has been given to the Government of His Majesty.

I am, etc.,

EL MARQUES DE PALMEROLA.
The CONSUL-GENERAL OF THE UNITED STATES.

[Inclosure 8 in No. 2987.]

BRITISH CONSULATE-GENERAL,
Habana, May 8, 1896.

MY DEAR COLLEAGUE: I have just heard that one of the *Competitor's* crew (who are to be tried to-day) is a British subject named Gildea. Now, I am not at all sure that, in a case of this kind, consular interference will be of any avail; but at all events, as I understand the *Competitor* is an American vessel, it appears to me that you alone are competent to intervene. If, therefore, you find yourself in a position to give any assistance to your own people, might I beg of you to extend the same valuable aid to my poor countryman?

Believe me, dear Mr. Williams, yours, very sincerely,

AJEX. GOLLAN.
RAMON O. WILLIAMS, Esq.,
United States Consul-General.

[Inclosure 9 in No. 2987.]

UNITED STATES CONSULATE-GENERAL,
Habana, May 8, 1896.

MY DEAR COLLEAGUE: In reply to your note of this morning, I am pleased to inform you that 1 included William Gildea, a native of Liverpool, England, but the mate of the American schooner *Competitor*, in my petitions to the captain-general and admiral, that the American prisoners of the *Competitor* be tried in accordance with article 7 of the treaty between the United States and Spain of 1795, and the protocol of January 12, 1877, construing it.

I am, etc.,

RAMON O. WILLIAMS.

ALEX. GOLLAN, Esq.,
Her Britannic Majesty's Consul-General, Habana.

[Inclosure 10 in No. 2987.]

BRITISH CONSULATE-GENERAL,
Habana, May 11, 1896.

MY DEAR COLLEAGUE: I have to thank you for your note of the 8th instant. I felt quite sure in writing to you on behalf of my countryman, William Gildea, that I could count upon all the assistance in your power.

It will probably be of interest to you to know what action I myself took in regard to the matter. On Friday, the 8th instant, as soon as I heard that the public prosecutor had demanded that the extreme penalty of death should be applied to the prisoners, and was likely to be enforced forthwith, I addressed official communications both to the Governor-General and admiral requesting that if this was the decision arrived at, its execution should be suspended until I had the opportunity of communicating the facts by telegraph to Her Britannic Majesty's secretary of state for foreign affairs. On the following morning, on the 9th, the admiral sent me a courteous reply stating that it was true the "consejo" had agreed to a death sentence, but that in deference to my wishes he had telegraphed to his Government at Madrid. Last night I received a further communication from the admiral in which he states:

"El Gobierno de S. M. la Reina Regente (q. D. g.) ha dispuesto suspender los efectos del consejo de guerra celebrado en el arsenal con motivo del apresamiento de la goleta filibustera *Competitor* y la remision de la causa al consejo supremo."

Believe me, etc.,

ALEX. GOLLAN.

RAMON O. WILLIAMS, Esq.

[Inclosure 11 in No. 2987.]

UNITED STATES CONSULATE-GENERAL,
Habana, May 11, 1896.

MY DEAR COLLEAGUE: I have to acknowledge the receipt of your note of to-day, with many thanks for the interesting information therein conveyed.

Sincerely, yours,

RAMON O. WILLIAMS.

ALEX. GOLLAN, Esq.,
Her Britannic Majesty's Consul-General, Habana.

[Inclosure No. 12 in No. 2987.]

BRITISH CONSULATE-GENERAL,
Habana, May 11, 1896.

MY DEAR COLLEAGUE: In a telegram which I received last evening from our foreign office regarding Gildea, I am informed that the newspapers had reported the man to have become a naturalized American citizen. Will you kindly inform me if such is the case?

Yours, etc.,

ALEX GOLLAN.

RAMON O. WILLIAMS, Esq.,
United States Consul-General.

[Inclosure 13 in No 2987.]

UNITED STATES CONSULATE-GENERAL,
Habana, May 12, 1896.

My DEAR COLLEAGUE: In reply to your note of the 11th instant, just received, I have to state that I have no information whatever as to the report that William Gildea is a naturalized citizen of the United States. He told me at the prison that he was an Englishman and a native of Liverpool. He did not claim American citizenship, but as one of the crew (he had engaged as mate) of the American schooner *Competitor* it became my consular duty to defend him under paragraph 171 of Consular Regulations, based on statutes, which states:

"That the circumstance that the vessel is American is evidence that the crew on board are such, and that in every regularly documented vessel the crew will find their protection in the flag that covers them."

And as the *Competitor* was such a regularly documented vessel, Gildea was entitled to the protection of the United States Government, regardless of whatever rights he may have as a native-born British subject.

I am, etc.,

RAMON O. WILLIAMS.

ALEX. GOLLAN, Esq.,
Her Britannic Majesty's Consul-General, Habana.

[Inclosure 14 with No 2987]

ARSENAL OR NAVY-YARD, *Habana, May 8, 1896.*

My name is Alfredo Laborde; I am 38 years of age; I am a native of New Orleans, La.; I was the captain or master of the American schooner *Competitor*, belonging to Mr. Joseph Well, of Key West. This vessel had a license, a wrecking license, and I cleared her at the Key West custom-house, with four others besides myself as crew; five all told. I took on board twenty-four men as passengers for Lemon City, Fla., at $2 each, and sailed from Key West at 2 o'clock in the morning. When in the neighborhood of Cape Sable, on the 22d ultimo, the passengers took charge of the ship, seized her, and six of them came into my cabin to make me surrender the ship. One of them, named Taboada, held a pistol to my breast and I gave up the command. They then took the schooner to Cape Sable and here took on board twenty-three men with arms and munitions. They then informed me that from Cape Sable to Rebecca Light they expected to meet a steamer with more men and arms for Cuba, but when we arrived off Rebecca Light I told them that the schooner could not go into the Gulf on account of her bad condition, but Taboada, who acted as pilot, told me to shut up, and overpowered my objections.

We reached Cuba, near Berracos, San Cayetano, on Saturday, the 25th April, and immediately landed. They forced me to go in the first boat with one of the crew and 19 men; all landed and escaped. I went back on board with the boat and another lot landed. We were sighted by a Spanish tug or steam launch. I ordered the American flag to be set; but the mate, Mr. William Gildea, who tried to set it, found the halliards foul, and as he was shot at twice he threw it down. I held the flag against the rigging so that it should be seen. Not a shot was fired from the schooner, for we had no arms; the passengers had arms and, we understood, also dynamite. We made no efforts to escape with the passengers, because we had been forced, and therefore we determined to stay by the ship; then we were seized or captured by the Spanish launch.

They put me into what is called a Spanish windlass, by tying my writs together and then drawing the rope tight by a stick thrust through, which caused me great torture and made my wrists swell.

I know nothing of a proclamation signed Laborde; there was another Laborde among the passengers, taller than I and about 32 years old, who spoke French well. All our papers, letters, etc., were taken away by our captors and we have none to show.

ALFREDO LABORDE.

We have heard the foregoing statement read, and do also subscribe and depose to the same, Ona Melton declaring further that as a newspaper correspondent he ought not to be considered as part of the crew.

ONA MELTON.
WM. GILDEA.

Witness:
JOSEPH A. SPRINGER, *Vice-Consul-General.*

Subscribed and sworn to before me at the arsenal, Habana, at 7.30 a. m. this 8th May, 1896.
Witness my hand and official seal.

RAMON O. WILLIAMS, *Consul-General.*

[Inclosure 15 in No. 2987.]

HABANA NAVAL PRISON,
May 2, 1896. (Received May 7.)

DEAR SIR: I wish to know if you are aware that three American citizens have been imprisoned here for some time. If so, please inform me immediately.

Relying on your wisdom and integrity, as well as the high esteem with which you are held in the United States, I await your advice.

Most respectfully,

ONA MELTON.

Mr. WILLIAMS.

[Inclosure No. 16 in No. 2987.]

SATURDAY, *May 2, 1896.*

SIR: I belong to the schooner *Competitor*, captured last Saturday by the man-of-war launch *Mensagera*, and I am accused of landing men and arms in Berracos opening. I would request you to see if anything could be done to help me out of the fix we are in. I can't say more, but would explain fully if I could see you.

Yours, etc.,

WM. GILDEA.

The UNITED STATES CONSUL, *Habana.*

[Inclosure 17 in No. 2987.]

HABANA, *May 7, 1896.*

DEAR SIR: We, the undersigned, the captain and the mate of the schooner *Competitor*, of Key West, and a correspondent of the Times-Union, of Jacksonville, Fla., citizens of the United States, who have been imprisoned here for some time, as you are probably aware, are to be tried at some hour to-morrow before the "Consejo de guerra."

Being informed this evening that we might write to you, we approve of the opportunity to respectfully urge that you attend our court-martial in person, or, if it is not possible, that you exert your best efforts in our behalf to the end that we may receive justice.

Respectfully, yours,

CAPTAIN ALFREDO LABORDE.
WILLIAM GILDEA.
ONA MELTON.

CONSUL OF THE UNITED STATES.

Mr. Williams to Mr. Rockhill.

No. 2988.]   UNITED STATES CONSULATE-GENERAL,
Habana, May 21, 1896.

SIR: I beg to inform you that having sent Mr. Sanchez Dotz, the deputy consul-general, this morning to visit Laborde, Gildea, Melton, Barnet, and Leavitt, of the *Competitor* expedition, and now held in custody at Fortress Cabanas, he reports to me that he found all the men well; that they stated they were well treated and have no complaint on this score. William Leavitt, a seaman, says that he is a native of Bangor, Me., and Charles Barnet, steward, that he is a native of Staffordshire, England.

From their report it appears that these two were captured while asleep on a farm about 8 miles from "La Palma," a village near San Cayetano, on the northwest coast of Cuba.

I am, etc.,   RAMON O. WILLIAMS.

Mr. Williams to Mr. Rockhill.

No. 2996.]   UNITED STATES CONSULATE-GENERAL,
Habana, May 23, 1896.

SIR: With reference to my dispatch, No. 2988, of the 21st instant, relative to Charles Barnet and William Leavitt, seamen supposed to belong to the crew of the American schooner *Competitor* and who were captured on land, I now beg to inclose the copies of the correspondence had with the Governor-General and the admiral of the naval station regarding same.

I am, etc.,   RAMON O. WILLIAMS.

[Inclosure in No. 2996.]

Mr. Williams to Governor-General of Cuba.

CONSULATE-GENERAL OF THE UNITED STATES,
Habana, May 12, 1896.

EXCELLENCY: Being informed by the newspapers of this afternoon that two American citizens, named Charles Barnet and William Leavitt, who are supposed to belong to the expedition of the American schooner *Competitor*, have been captured on land, and that they are to be tried by the marine jurisdiction, I have to apply to your excellency, as the superior representative and delegate of the Government of His Majesty the King of Spain, to ask in the name of my Government—

First. For the strict observance of article 7 of the treaty of 1795, interpreted by both Governments in articles 1, 2, 3, 4, and 5 of the protocol of 1877, respecting American citizens accused of seditious acts in Spanish territory against the Supreme Government of Spain; and—

Second. That if the sentence should be that of death its execution be suspended to give time to communicate by telegraph to his excellency the Minister of State at Washington.

I am, etc.,   RAMON O. WILLIAMS.

[Inclosure 2 in No. 2996.]

Mr. Williams to admiral of naval station.

UNITED STATES CONSULATE-GENERAL,
Habana, May 12, 1896.

EXCELLENCY: Having read in the papers of this afternoon that two American citizens named Charles Barnet and William Leavit, who are supposed to belong to the expedition of the American schooner *Competitor*, have been captured on land, and that it is intended to try them by the marine jurisdiction, I have to ask your excellency, in the name of my Government:

First. The strict observance of article 7 of the treaty of 1795, as interpreted by both Governments in articles 1, 2, 3, 4, and 5 of the protocol of 1877, concerning citizens of the United States in the Spanish dominions accused of acts of sedition against the supreme Government of Spain; and

Second. That if the sentence pronounced should be that of death its execution be suspended to give me time to communicate by telegraph with his excellency the Minister of State at Washington.

I am, etc.,   RAMON O. WILLIAMS.

[Inclosure 3 in No. 2996.]

Mr. Williams to Governor-General of Cuba.

UNITED STATES CONSULATE-GENERAL,
Habana, May 13, 1896.

EXCELLENCY: Having been informed that the two American citizens recently arrested, to whom I referred in the communication I had the honor to address yesterday afternoon to your excellency as belonging to the expedition of the American schooner *Competitor*, are simply sailors belonging to the crew of that vessel, I have

S. Doc. 231, pt 7——36

to beg your excellency that if this is the fact to please order through the proper authorities that the trial of these American citizens be conducted with adherence to the terms of the existing treaty between the United States and Spain, according to which only those captured with arms in hand are to be tried by ordinary council of war, circumstances which can hardly concur in mere sailors of a merchant vessel of the United States.

I have the honor to reiterate to your excellency the testimony of my most distinguished consideration, signifying at the same time that in the same sense I have addressed the marine authority.

RAMON O. WILLIAMS.

[Inclosure 4 in No. 2996.]

Mr. Williams to admiral of the West Indies naval station.

UNITED STATES CONSULATE-GENERAL,
Habana, May 13, 1896.

EXCELLENCY: Having been informed that the two American citizens recently arrested, to whom I referred in the communication I had the honor to address yesterday afternoon to your excellency as belonging to the expedition of the American schooner *Competitor*, are simply sailors belonging to the crew of that vessel, I have to beg your excellency that if this is the fact to please order through the proper authorities that the trial of these American citizens be conducted with adherence to the terms of the existing treaty between the United States and Spain, according to which only those captured with arms in hand are to be tried by ordinary council of war, circumstances which can hardly concur in mere sailors of a merchant vessel of the United States.

I am, etc.,   RAMON O. WILLIAMS.

[Inclosure 5 in No. 2996.]

El Marques de Palmerola to Mr. Williams.

GENERAL GOVERNMENT OF THE ISLAND OF CUBA,
OFFICE OF THE SECRETARY,
Habana, May 13, 1896.

SIR: Replying to your attentive communications of yesterday and to-day, referring to two American citizens named Charles Barnet and William Leavit, who are supposed to belong to the expedition of the schooner *Competitor* and which you understand have been made prisoners, I have the honor to inform you, by order of the Governor-General, that citizens of the United States are judged in accordance with the treaties existing between Spain and the United States, and that the sentences of death are not executed unless they are approved by the Government of His Majesty.

I am, etc.,
EL MARQUEZ DE PALMEROLA.

[Telegram.]

Mr. Taylor to Mr. Olney.

MADRID, *June 16, 1896.*

Resume duties to-day. Referring to your cablegram, received Paris, please indicate what you would consider just decision *Competitor* case as basis for my efforts.

[Telegram.]

Mr. Olney to Mr. Taylor.

DEPARTMENT OF STATE,
Washington, June 30, 1896.

Inquire and report when decision appellate tribunal *Competitor* case is expected.

Mr. Lee to Mr. Rockhill.

No. 50.]   UNITED STATES CONSULATE-GENERAL,
                                        Habana, July 14, 1896.

SIR: I herewith transmit copy translation of a communication received from the father of Alfredo Laborde, the captain of the schooner
Competitor, and signed "The families of the *Competitor's* prisoners," in
which a request is made of me to intercede with the honorable Secretary of State that our Government may ask for the pardon of the
Competitor's prisoners.

I forward the same for such action as the honorable Secretary of
State shall deem best to take in the matter.

I am, etc.,   FITZHUGH LEE.

[Inclosure in No. 50.]

                                              HABANA, *July 13, 1896.*

THE CONSUL-GENERAL OF THE UNITED STATES,
                Habana:

The consul-general is requested to intercede with the honorable Secretary of
State, that he in turn may appeal to the Spanish Government, in order to obtain the
pardon of the captain and crew of the schooner *Competitor.*

Should the consul-general decide to do so by cable, there would be an opportunity
by said pardon to solemnize the birthday of Her Majesty the Queen Regent, which
is celebrated the 21st of this month.

It is unquestionable that the Spanish Government must thank the United States
Government for the attitude it has observed during this civil war, always favorable
to the former, notwithstanding the popular manifestations against it, which has
been expressed by all the organs of public opinion in the United States.

Therefore, if in the strict ground of law there are no terms wherein to request
what is hereby petitioned of the consul-general, yet on the ground of grace and
mercy there is room enough without counting also that every occasion is fit to perform a good action.

The high illustration and intelligence of the consul-general will add to this petition such other considerations as may give it more strength and greater probabilities
of a favorable result.

                THE FAMILIES OF THE COMPETITOR'S PRISONERS.

Mr. Lee to Mr. Rockhill.

No. 79.]   UNITED STATES CONSULATE-GENERAL,
                                        Habana, August 11, 1896.

SIR: With reference to an unofficial letter received from Mr. Rockhill, accompanying copy of a letter from a citizen of Key West, Fla.,
respecting the food furnished to the American prisoners of the *Competitor* under confinement in the fortresses and jail of this city, I have to
inform the Department that on the 5th instant I again called the attention of the Governor and Captain-General to the subject, and have
received his reply, of which I accompany herewith a copy translation.

I am, sir, very respectfully, your obedient servant,

                                              FITZHUGH LEE,
                                                Consul-General.

[Translation.]

                GENERAL GOVERNMENT OF THE ISLAND OF CUBA,
                                Habana, August 7, 1896.

SIR: I have the honor to acknowledge the receipt of your courteous communication of the 5th instant, in which, in compliance with a special instruction of your
Government, you request that a change be made in the food furnished to the American

citizens imprisoned in the fortresses and jail of this capital; or otherwise, to be informed if there is any objection to authorize subscriptions in the United States for the purpose of purchasing, with the proceeds thereof, food for the prisoners referred to, in order that they may be supplied with the same after 4 o'clock in the afternoon and 12 noon, the only hours in which the meals are served in those establishments.

With respect to the first part of your said official letter, it becomes the duty of this government to make known that the food supplied to the prisoners of all kinds in the fortresses and jail of this city, besides being healthy, of superior quality, and well seasoned, is provided in abundance and in a varied form, the same for all prisoners, without distinction of race or nationality.

That the good condition of such food is evidently justified in the fact, very noticeable, that, notwithstanding there are other prisoners, national as well as foreigners of other nations besides that of which you are a most worthy representative in this island, none of them, with the exception of the American citizens, complain of the quality or quantity of food.

The hours during which this is distributed are in conformity with the provisions of the regulations which are indispensable to the discipline and interior order of this kind of establishment, such hours being fixed after a complete preliminary study of the climatological exigencies and customs of the country, it not being possible to make any special distinction in favor of a certain class of prisoners; having further to add that, besides the daily food, or properly speaking meals, supplied in the prisons referred to, they are provided daily with coffee, resulting thereby that there is not such a long interval as you have been erroneously informed between the time during which the prisoners receive food; and that, notwithstanding their condition of prisoners, they are supported in the same manner and hours the generality of the inhabitants of this capital, in accordance with the customs of the country.

These considerations, derived from real and positive facts, will, undoubtedly, bring to your upright and impartial attention the conviction that these complaints made to you and to the respectable Government which you represent are unfounded, and will persuade you that it is not prudent nor possible that this Government should conform itself to the proceeding referred to in the consultation contained in the second part of your respectable communication; to which is opposed, besides the serious considerations of prestige and national dignity, foundations of strict justice, connected with the interior order of penal establishments, that in no case, nor in any country, can there be allowed privileges or concessions in favor of certain classes, which is always irritating and the cause of conflicts which the international harmony and mutual friendly relations between the Government of Spain and that of the Republic which you represent with so much prestige, should advise their avoidance.

God guard you many years.   WEYLER.

The CONSUL-GENERAL OF THE UNITED STATES.

Mr. Lee to Mr. Rockhill.

No. 90.]   UNITED STATES CONSULATE-GENERAL,
Habana, August 19, 1896.

SIR: With reference to my dispatch, No. 79, of the 11th instant, in which I communicated to the Department the answer of the Governor-General to the inquiry if funds subscribed in the United States to ameliorate the condition of the American prisoners of the *Competitor*, in confinement at the Cabaña fortress, might be forwarded them to provide them better food and accommodations, I have now the honor to transmit a copy translation of another communication from General Weyler, to the effect that the governor of the fort has been asked to report on the condition of said prisoners; and with respect to their food, which is the same as that supplied to all prisoners by the municipal authorities, they might obtain it at their own expense and of better quality.

I therefore infer from said communication that the friends of the prisoners will be allowed to transmit them funds, either through this office, to be delivered to them direct, or to purchase food to be sent them.

I am, etc.,

FITZHUGH LEE.

[Inclosure in No. 90 —Translation]

Captain-General Weyler to Mr. Lee.

CAPTAINCY-GENERAL OF THE ISLAND OF CUBA,
Habana, August 14, 1896.

SIR: In answer to your courteous official letter of the 10th ultimo, relative to the American prisoners of the *Competitor* imprisoned at the Cabaña fortress, I have the honor to state that the general-governor of said fortress has been asked to report whether if it is possible to better the condition of said prisoners; and in regard to the food supplied to them I have to say, that it is the same given to all prisoners supplied by the municipality, but as it is not obligatory on the prisoners to take it, they can try to acquire it in better condition.

God guard you many years.

VALERIANO WEYLER.

[Telegram]

Mr. Olney to Mr. Taylor.

WASHINGTON, *September 3, 1896.*

Delay of Spanish Government in deciding *Competitor* and Delgado cases absolutely unreasonable. Call for prompt action and reasons justifying past delay or additional delay, if such is asked for.

[Telegram.]

Mr. Taylor to Mr. Olney.

SPAIN, *September 4, 1896.*

Understood here *Competitor* case already decided annulling judgment and ordering new trial before ordinary tribunal. Decision expected shortly.

[Telegram]

Mr. Taylor to Mr. Olney.

SAN SEBASTIAN, *September 8, 1896.*

Minister of foreign affairs told me last night confidentially *Competitor* case actually decided as indicated in my last telegram. Will be made public soon. Cortes adjourned yesterday.

Mr. Lee to Mr. Rockhill.

No. 118.]   UNITED STATES CONSULATE-GENERAL,
Habana, September 9, 1896.

SIR: I transmit herewith copy translation of a note from Captain-General Weyler relative to the quarters in the Cabaña fortress occupied by the *Competitor* prisoners.

I am, etc.,

FITZHUGH LEE.

[Inclosure in No. 118.]

Captain-General Valeriano Weyler to Mr. Lee.

ARMY OF THE ISLAND OF CUBA,
OFFICE OF THE CAPTAIN-GENERAL, CHIEF OF STAFF,
Habana, September 5, 1896.

SIR: In continuation of my official note of the 14th August last, I have the honor to state that, as I am informed by the general governor of the Cabaña fortress, the American citizens that belonged to the schooner *Competitor* occupy the casemates (calabozos) Nos. 41 and 42 of said fortress, which are the ones that are best conditioned among those in the fort.

God guard you many years.

VALERIANO WEYLER.

Mr. Lee to Mr. Rockhill.

No. 190.] UNITED STATES CONSULATE-GENERAL,
Habana, October 21, 1896.

SIR: I have the honor to transmit herewith copies of two letters I have received from Ona Melton, one of the prisoners of the *Competitor*. I have replied by quoting for his information, and for the information of the officers taking the preliminary depositions at La Cabaña, articles 171 and 172 of the regulations prescribed for the use of the consular service of the United States.

It is held there "that the circumstance that the vessel is American is evidence that the seamen on board are such, and that in every regularly documented merchant vessel the crew will find their protection in the flag that covers it."

I am, etc., FITZHUGH LEE.

[Inclosure 1 in No. 190.]

Mr. Ona Melton to Mr. Lee.

FORT CABAÑAS, CALABOZA 41,
Habana, October 18, 1896.

DEAR SIR: Yesterday I was taken to the "cuarto de banderas" (guardroom) to make a preliminary deposition, preparatory for a "consejo de guerra ordinario" (ordinary court martial) to "ver y faller" (try) the case against the men of the *Competitor*, charged with the crimes of "pirateria y rebelion" (piracy and rebellion).

I had hardly expected that we were to be tried again under the accusation of piracy and rebellion. From an American standpoint the charge of piracy seems absurd, but according to the interpretation that was placed on certain parts of the "diccionario de Puerto Rico y Cuba" (code of criminal procedure existing in Cuba and Puerto Rico) at our recent trial by a "consejo de guerra sumarisimo" (summary court-martial) we might come under the classification of pirates.

In my declaration they insisted on my stating that I would furnish proof of my American citizenship. They seemed to doubt my citizenship because I talked Spanish somewhat fluently. They then wanted to know what kind of proof I could furnish. I had never thought of my citizenship being brought into question, and I was somewhat perplexed. I replied that I did not know, but that I would ask your advice.

I do not know what I ought to do. They said I ought to have a certificate of my birth or baptism. Such a request seems to be absurd. It would require months of time to get either, if, which is very unlikely, either is still in existence.

I was born at Vinland, Kans. In fact, I do not know if births are registered in Kansas, although I suppose they are.

I registered and voted in the Arkansas State election two years ago at my home in Aurora, Ark. If it is positively necessary, I could write to my father and get a deposition made to show my citizenship, but it will require, at the very least time possible, twenty days, and perhaps thirty, to write and receive returns.

I was also asked concerning my papers as a correspondent of the Times-Union of Jacksonville, Fla. At the other trial my credentials were taken from me and never returned, and apparently have been made away with. Gildea read them, and I think

Laborde also. If necessary, William L. Delaney, of Key West, Fla., can produce evidence concerning my credentials.

The naval officer who took the deposition seemed very badly informed. He asked: "Do you see Consul-General Lee every day?" "Certainly not," said I. He seemed surprised, and said: "How often do you see him?"

I do not think that the depositions of any of the *Competitor* men were taken, except of Captain Laborde and I. I shall await your advice.

Yours, most respectfully, ONA MELTON.

[Inclosure 2 in No. 190]

Mr. Ona Melton to Mr. Lee.

FORT CABAÑA, CALABOZO (CELL) 41,
October 20, 1896.

DEAR SIR: I have not yet received an answer to my letter of the 18th instant, but write this to inform you of the further proceedings in our case.

Yesterday I was again taken to the "cuarto de banderas" to make declaration. I was again asked what proofs I could produce to show that I was an American citizen. I replied that I did not know what would be considered as sufficient proof, but I explained, as I explained to you in my letter of the 18th instant, that to constitute positive proof it would probably be necessary to have a deposition made before a justice of the peace at my home, but that I considered that after the other "consejo de guerra" the United States Government and the courts of Madrid had accepted me as an American citizen; that it was now late to raise such a question. Then the "juez instructor" asked if you would vouch for my citizenship. I replied that I did not know. Then he asked me if Consul Lee knew me. Again I hardly knew what to answer, and replied that I did not know that you had seen me one time.

He then asked if you had any documents showing that I was an American citizen. At first I replied "No," but on second thought I said that you perhaps had documents from Secretary Olney recognizing me as an American citizen. He asked if I had any protest to make, and I replied that I protested against being tried without being given an opportunity to consult with my consul, and that I did not consider that a trial held inside of Fort Cabaña would be legal, because no representative of the United States consulate was allowed inside of the fort, and that such representative ought to be present at the trial. I said that I protested against being tried by consejo de guerra ordinario (ordinary court-martial), because according to the treaties with the United States an American citizen should be tried in the civil courts. My protest was entered, and the judge instructor announced that these claims would be investigated. As I passed Captain Laborde's cell he called out, "I protested," so I suppose that he entered a protest similar to mine. It was stated that the depositions of the other *Competitor* prisoners would be taken to-day. It is said that if we are tried by the civil court we will have to wait at least eighteen months for our return on the docket. I shall anxiously await your instructions.

Yours, respectfully,

ONA MELTON.

Mr. Rockhill to Mr. Lee.

No. 152.] WASHINGTON, *October 28, 1896.*

SIR: The Department has received your dispatch No. 190 of the 21st instant, relative to the case of Ona Melton, one of the crew of the captured schooner *Competitor.*

As of possible use to the prisoner in establishing his character of newspaper correspondent to the satisfaction of the Cuban courts, I inclose a certified copy of two affidavits relative to Melton's appointment as correspondent of The Florida Times-Union, of Jacksonville.

I also inclose for your information a copy of a letter on the subject from the general manager of the Times-Union. Copies of these papers were sent on August 5 last to our minister at Madrid for such use as he might be able to make of them in the interest of Melton.

These are the only documents which the Department has received bearing on the matter. It is presumed that Melton has an attorney looking after his case, but you will of course assist him as far as you can to establish his claim of American citizenship, which, it seems from his note to you, inclosed in your dispatch under acknowledgment, he has so far experienced some difficulty in doing to the satisfaction of the Spanish authorities.

I also inclose a copy of a letter from Mrs. Emmie Laborde, wife of Alfredo Laborde, master of the schooner *Competitor*, this being the only information which the Department has bearing on his citizenship.

I am, etc.,

W. W. ROCKHILL.

Mr. Springer to Mr. Rockhill.

No. 211.]   ·   UNITED STATES CONSULATE-GENERAL,
Habana, November 12, 1896.

SIR: I have been informed by the sister of Laborde, one of the *Competitor* prisoners, that he was yesterday afternoon, at the time of her weekly visit to him, seized with cerebral congestion and removed to the old military hospital of this city.

Charles Leavitt, another of the prisoners, was removed several days ago to the same hospital, supposed to be ill with yellow fever, but it seems to be a sort of prison fever, induced by confinement and insufficient food.

Ona Melton, it is stated, is greatly reduced for the same reasons.

I am, etc.,

J. A. SPRINGER.

Mr. Springer to Mr. Rockhill.

·   No. 212.]   UNITED STATES CONSULATE-GENERAL,
Habana, November 14, 1896.

SIR: I have the honor to acknowledge the receipt of your instruction No. 152, of 28th ultimo, covering certified copies of affidavits relative to the appointment of Ona Melton, one of the *Competitor* prisoners, as correspondent of the Florida Times-Union, of Jacksonville.

These documents, after having been translated and a certificate of same affixed, I transmitted on the 11th instant to the Governor and Captain-General, with the request that they be forwarded to the court having cognizance of Melton's case, as they had been furnished by the Department of State, to be of use to him to establish before the court his character of a newspaper correspondent.

I have received a note from the Secretary of the General Government that the documents were transmitted the same day to the commandant general of marine, admiral commanding this naval station, being the authority having cognizance of the case of the seizure of the schooner *Competitor*.

I am, sir, your obedient servant,

JOSEPH A. SPRINGER.

Mr. Springer to Mr. Rockhill.

No. 220.]   UNITED STATES CONSULATE-GENERAL,
Habana, November 18, 1896.

SIR: With reference to the case of the *Competitor* prisoners, I herewith transmit a copy of a letter received this morning from Ona

Melton respecting the continuation of the trial of himself and the other prisoners and the information given him by the judge that the case would be settled very soon.

I am, etc., JOSEPH A. SPRINGER.

[Enclosure in No. 220.]

Mr. Ona Melton to Mr. Springer.

FORT CABANA, CELL 41, *November 16, 1896.*

DEAR SIR: The trial of the *Competitor* prisoners by ordinary naval court-martial in the "cuarto de bandera" in Fort Cabana was continued yesterday before the Naval Judge Instructor Fernandez Lopez Saul and the full depositions of Dr. Vedia, Jorge Ferran, Teodoro Maza, and myself were taken. As far as I know, nothing new or different was developed by these depositions from those made in the previous court-martial of May.

The "juez instructor" told me personally that the case would be settled very soon.

I take the first opportunity to inform you of this, as I was requested to write to the consulate whenever anything new occurred, to keep the consulate informed. This was before General Lee left.

I protested against the method of procedure when the trial began a few weeks ago, but really I suppose it makes but little difference about the method of trial, as I fancy that the Spaniards have decided beforehand what they intend doing with us, and the trial will be a mere form.

I am, etc., ONA MELTON.

Mr. Rockhill to Mr. Springer.

No. 165.] WASHINGTON, *November 19, 1896.*

SIR: I inclose for your information and such action as the exigency of the case demands, a copy of a letter from Mrs. Emmie Laborde, transmitting a communication from Alfred Laborde, master of the *Competitor*, relative to a new trial of the men of the *Competitor*.

I am, etc.,

W. W. ROCKHILL.

Mr. Springer to Mr. Rockhill.

No. 223.] UNITED STATES CONSULATE-GENERAL,
Habana, November 20, 1896.

SIR: I have the honor to inform the Department that on the 14th instant I received from Mrs. Emma Laborde, of Key West, a copy, certified by the collector of customs of that port, of the oath and appointment of her husband as master of the American schooner *Competitor.*

I returned this certificate to the collector, with the request that he procure the authentication of his signature by the Spanish consul, believing that the document would be more valid before the court here, and also forestall any objection that might be offered for the want of such formality.

The certificate has been returned duly indorsed, and I have transmitted it to the Governor-General, with the request that it be forwarded to the court having cognizance of Mr. Laborde's case.

In her letter, Mrs. Laborde states that she had been informed by the collector that the Spanish consul had also obtained a certificate regarding her husband, and the port he had cleared for, Miami.

I am, etc.,

JOSEPH A. SPRINGER.

Mr. Springer to Mr. Rockhill.

No. 226.]   UNITED STATES CONSULATE-GENERAL,
Habana, November 23, 1896.

SIR: Referring to dispatch No. 223, of the 19th instant, I have to inform the Department that the copy of the oath and appointment of Alfred Laborde as master of the schooner *Competitor*, transmitted by this office to the General Government, has been forwarded to the commandant-general of marine, the admiral commanding this naval station, which authority has cognizance of the case of the capture of the said vessel.

I am, etc.,   JOSEPH A. SPRINGER.

P. S.—Mr. Laborde sent me a message, that he had been well treated while recently in the hospital (as reported in No. 211, November 12), and had been returned to the "Cabaña" at his own request.

J. A. S.

[Telegram.]

Mr. Springer to Mr. Rockhill.

HABANA, *November 26, 1896.*

Am informed that the declarations of *Competitor* prisoners are being taken again by ordinary marine court-martial. Confrontation of the master of the *Competitor* with witnesses day before yesterday lasting five hours. Shall I enter a protest even against preliminary proceedings by the naval authorities or the military authorities?

Mr. Springer to Mr. Rockhill.

No. 234.]   UNITED STATES CONSULATE-GENERAL,
Habana, November 26, 1896.

SIR: I have the honor to confirm the following telegram, transmitted this morning.[1]

I understand that these preliminary proceedings are intended as investigatory, the case being in "sumario" (the nearest equivalent of which is taking declarations for a grand-jury indictment). But in the case of Sanguily, the United States declined to recognize the validity of the military jurisdiction in preliminary or at any stage of the proceedings.

I am, etc.,   JOSEPH A. SPRINGER.

---

[1] See telegram of November 26, 1896.

Mr. Springer to Mr. Rockhill.

No. 246.]   UNITED STATES CONSULATE-GENERAL,
Habana, December 3, 1896.

SIR: I have the honor to acknowledge the receipt of your cablegram, reading: .   ·

WASHINGTON, D. C., *November 28.*

I do not believe that protest at this preliminary stage of proceedings against *"Competitor"* prisoners can be of any avail. Obtain conclusions of preliminary inquest as soon as they are reached and cable Department. Watch all proceedings carefully.

ROCKHILL.

With respect to the prisoners, after the usual formalities a clerk from this office was allowed to visit them yesterday morning. He reports that Laborde returned from the hospital on November 26. All the prisoners had again made declarations before the military judge of instruction, Laborde having declared four times and Melton three times. Nothing is yet known respecting the conclusions of the preliminary examination. Their treatment and food continue the same.
I am, etc.,

JOSEPH A. SPRINGER.

Mr. Springer to Mr. Rockhill.

No. 251.]   UNITED STATES CONSULATE-GENERAL,
Habana, December 5, 1896.

SIR: I have the honor to inform the Department that I received from Mr. William L. Delaney, of Key West, an affidavit, made at Aurora, Ark., respecting the American citizenship of D. W. Melton, and birth of Ona Melton, one of the *Competitor* prisoners. which I sent to the Governor-General to be transmitted to the court having cognizance of the case of said *Competitor* prisoners.
I am, etc.,   JOSEPH A. SPRINGER.

Mr. Springer to Mr. Rockhill.

No. 260.]   UNITED STATES CONSULATE-GENERAL,
Habana, December 15, 1896.

SIR: I have the honor to transmit herewith copy of a letter received from Alfred Laborde, one of the *Competitor* prisoners, respecting certain phases of his examination by the authorities in the prosecution of the case against him.
I am, etc.,

JOSEPH A. SPRINGER.

[Inclosure in No. 260.]
Mr. Laborde to Mr. Springer.

FORT CABAÑA, *December 11, 1896.*

SIR: I beg to inform you that yesterday afternoon I was ordered by the actual military judge of the prosecution of the *Competitor's* crew to dress a military's suit, with the purpose of being recognized by some one. Of course I formally protested of such act and refused to be disguised that way. He answered immediately that he was going to compel me by force, and fearing to become the victim of his brutality, I obeyed. As he did not allow my protest to be considered, I hurry to let you know this, and afford a proof in the way justice is dealt with me.
I am, sir, your humble servant,

ALFRED LABORDE, *Master.*

FIFTY-FOURTH CONGRESS, SECOND SESSION.

[Senate Document No. 146.]

Message from the President of the United States, transmitting, in response to resolution of the Senate of February 6, 1897, a report from the Secretary of State in regard to the persons claiming American citizenship captured on board of the Competitor.

FEBRUARY 29, 1897.—Referred to the Committee on Foreign Relations and ordered to be printed.

To the Senate:

I transmit herewith, in response to the resolution of the Senate of February 6, 1897, a report from the Secretary of State in regard to the persons claiming American citizenship captured on board of the *Competitor.*

GROVER CLEVELAND.

EXECUTIVE MANSION,
Washington, February 23, 1897.

The PRESIDENT:

Referring to the resolution of the Senate of the 6th instant of the tenor and terms following:

Resolved, That the Senate, being informed by common rumor and by testimony taken by the Committee on Foreign Relations, that a vessel of the United States called the *Competitor* has been captured by a Spanish ship of war, and that one or more citizens of the United States were captured on board said vessel and have been tried and condemned to death by a military tribunal in Cuba, and are now in prison at Habana awaiting the execution of the sentences; and the Senate having instructed said committee to inquire into and make report respecting the rights of said citizens under the treaties existing between the United States and Spain and under the laws of nations, the President is requested, in conformity with section two thousand and one of the Revised Statutes, to inform the Senate whether any such capture has been made by a Spanish war ship, and whether any citizen of the United States has been captured on or near such vessel, and "has been unjustly deprived of his liberty by or under the authority of" the Government of Spain, and whether the President forthwith demanded of Spain the reason of such imprisonment, and, if such imprisonment is unlawful, and if such sentence to death violates the laws of nations or the treaties with Spain, whether the President has demanded the release of such citizens.

And that the President communicate to the Senate all the facts and proceedings relative to such capture, sentence and imprisonment of such citizens as soon as practicable, in accordance with the statute in such cases made and provided, as follows:

"SEC. 2000. All naturalized citizens of the United States while in foreign countries are entitled to and shall receive from the Government the same protection of persons and property which is accorded to native-born citizens.

"SEC. 2001. Whenever it is made known to the President that any citizen of the United States has been unjustly deprived of his liberty by or under the authority of any foreign Government it shall be the duty of the President forthwith to demand of that Government the reasons of such imprisonment; and if it appears to be wrongful and in violation of the rights of American citizenship, the President shall forthwith demand the release of such citizen, and if the release so demanded is unreasonably delayed or refused the President shall use such means, not amounting to acts of war, as he may think necessary and proper to obtain or effectuate the release; and all the facts and proceedings relative thereto shall, as soon as practicable, be communicated by the President to Congress."

I have the honor to state that practically all the information called for by the resolution has been submitted to the President, and was by the President transmitted to the Senate January 22, 1897, as will appear by reference to Senate Document No. 79, Fifty-fourth Congress, second session, and that since that date nothing has taken place of consequence either in the way of information received or correspondence exchanged.

Respectfully,

RICHARD OLNEY.

DEPARTMENT OF STATE,
February 20, 1897.

FIFTY-FIFTH CONGRESS, FIRST SESSION.

July 14, 1897.

[Senate Report No. 377.]

Mr. Davis, from the Committee on Foreign Relations, submitted the following report:

The Committee on Foreign Relations, to whom was referred Senate resolution No. 149, presented by Mr. Berry, submit the following report:

On the 25th day of April, 1896, the schooner *Competitor*, a regularly documented American vessel, was captured by a Spanish gunboat at a place alleged to be within the territorial waters of Spain, a few miles west of Habana. The following persons, being then on board of her, were taken prisoners, viz, Alfredo Laborde, Ona Melton, and William Gildea. Laborde claims to be a native of New Orleans, La. He was the regularly licensed master of the vessel, and to be such must have been a citizen of the United States. William Gildea acted as mate, but was born in Liverpool, England. Ona Melton was born at Vinland, in the State of Kansas, and he voted at Aurora, in the State of Arkansas, in 1894.

The circumstances preceding and attending the capture of the vessel and these men are stated in the affidavit of Laborde, Melton, and Gildea, made May 8, 1896, to be as follows:

The vessel belonged to Mr. Joseph Well, of Key West, and had a regular license. Laborde cleared her at the Key West custom-house, with 4 others besides himself as crew, 5 in all, and took on board 24 men as passengers for Lemon City, Fla., at $2 each. When in the neighborhood of Cape Sable, on the 22d of April, 1896, these passengers forcibly took charge of the ship, and 6 of them came into the cabin to make him surrender the vessel. This he did at the muzzle of a pistol presented at his breast by one of them named Taboada. They ran the schooner to Cape Sable and there took on board 25 men with arms and munitions, and informed Laborde that between Cape Sable and Rebecca Light they expected to meet a steamer with more men and arms for Cuba.

When they arrived off Rebecca Light, Laborde told them that the schooner could not go into the Gulf on account of her bad condition, but Taboada, who acted as pilot, told him to shut up, and overpowered

his objections. The vessel reached Cuba, near Berracos, San Caye
tano, on the 25th of April, and immediately landed her cargo and
passengers by boats. The passengers forced Laborde to go in the first
boat, with one of the crew and 19 men, all of whom landed and escaped.
He went back on board and another lot landed. At this time they
were sighted by a Spanish tug or steam launch. He ordered the
American flag to be set. While William Gildea, the mate, tried to set
it, he found the halyards foul, and being shot at twice, he threw the flag
down. Laborde then held the flag against the rigging so it could be
seen.

No shot was fired from the schooner, for they had no arms, although
the passengers who had gone ashore had arms, and, as Laborde also
understood, dynamite. No effort was made by Laborde or the others
to escape with the passengers, because they had been forced into their
existing situation. The captors put Laborde into what is called a
Spanish windlass by tying his wrists together and then drawing the
rope tight by a stick thrust through, which caused great torture and
made his wrists swell. The *Competitor* and the captives were immedi.
ately taken to Habana, and the latter were placed in prison, where they
have ever since remained.

These affidavits are not contradicted by any statements in the mes.
sage and accompanying documents transmitted by the President to the
Senate, nor do these papers present any evidence as to whether the
Competitor, when seized, was within 1 marine league of the coast of Cuba.

The case was considered by the Spanish authority to be one of admi.
ralty jurisdiction, and accordingly, upon the 1st day of May, 1896, a
summary naval court-martial was constituted for their trial for crimes
designated, by reference and allusion in the copies of official documents
which are in the possession of this committee, as piracy and rebellion.
No copy of the charges has, so far as your committee can ascertain,
ever been furnished to this Government, though frequently requested.

Against the jurisdiction and competency of this tribunal and method
of procedure the American consular representative at Habana, under
instructions from the Department of State, most earnestly protested on
the same day, insisting that the case should be tried under the seventh
article of the treaty with Spain, concluded in the year 1795, and under
the protocol to said treaty of 1877, and that it should not be tried by a
summary court-martial, or by any other form'of procedure not adjusted
to the terms of the treaty. He also insisted that Laborde, being the
master, and Gildea, the mate of the vessel, were, according to paragraph 171 of the Consular Regulations, entitled to the protection of the
United States.

The admiral to whom this protest was made, and who was the official
in whom the Spanish jurisdiction in the premises seems to have rested,
while expressing a willingness to furnish a copy of the charges against
the men to the American consul as had been demanded, seems never to
have done so. Their trial took place within fifteen hours after he made
this offer. The admiral, acting under the advice of the Spanish judge-
advocate, denied the validity of these objections and protest upon the
ground that neither Article VII, of the treaty of the 27th of October,
1795, nor the protocol of 1877 applied to the case, for the reason, as he
asserted, that foreigners must be tried by the same courts having cognizance of Spanish subjects, according to the local law relating to
foreigners, of the 4th of July, 1870, and because that, whatever interpretation and scope may be given to the treaty and the protocol construing it, the latter, from the beginning, embraces only resident
American citizens.

To this last contention as to the protocol the American consul very properly replied that Article VII of the treaty of 1795 imposes no condition of residence either on Spanish subjects in the United States or on American subjects resident in the dominions of Spain; for were it so the status of American citizens could be taken away from thousands of Spaniards in the United States, who visit both countries every year as merchants, manufacturers, traders, and tourists. He also interposed to this contention of the Spanish admiral the very decisive objection that the protocol can not detract from the treaty, and that the protocol must be construed to conform to the treaty, and not the treaty to the protocol.

The foregoing is a compendium of demands, protests, objections, and refusals which began before the trial of these men, and which were continued for some time after such trial had been completed by their sentence to death.

They were tried by a naval court-martial of the most summary character, on the 8th day of May, 1896, the trial lasting but a few hours. They had no opportunity to summon or examine witnesses, or to be defended by counsel of their own selection. They were not tried separately but together, and, it seems, with several other persons. The evidence against them consisted solely of the testimony of Captain Butron and the other officers of the *Mensajerra*, the Spanish gunboat which had taken them prisoners. A lieutenant of the Spanish navy was assigned to their defense, who asked no questions upon the trial and who produced no witnesses. His summing up consisted of a plea for mercy to the prisoners, although it is said that he stated they were American citizens. There was an interpreter present, but he did not make his presence known to the prisoners until they were asked if they had anything to say in their own defense. This was after the summing up of the prosecution, and of course was after the evidence, both of which were given in Spanish and were not translated to the prisoners.

The naval officer who was appointed to defend them did not communicate to them the substance of the evidence or of the summing up of the prosecutor. It is very evident that this naval officer could not speak English. It appears to the satisfaction of your committee that he did not utter a single word to his clients during the trial, and that he did not say or do anything in behalf of the prisoners, except to ask mercy.

After this mockery of a trial the presiding officer of the court-martial asked Laborde in Spanish what he had to say in his defense. Laborde understood that language. He said a few words. So it went on until the last man was reached, William Gildea, and the presiding officer spoke to him in Spanish. He did not understand, and then the interpreter said, "Do you wish to say anything?" and Gildea then arose and said, "All I have to say is, I do not understand one word which has been said to-day, either for me or against me, and, at any rate, I appeal to both the British and American consuls." Melton said, truly, that he came aboard the schooner as the correspondent of the Jacksonville Times-Union. The trial terminated immediately after these statements were made. The prosecutor moved for a sentence of death and it was straightway pronounced.

The Department of State requested, or demanded, that Spain should not execute the sentence until a copy of the charges and evidence could be furnished to this Government and an opportunity given to investigate the case. The execution of the sentence seems to have been stayed, pending an appeal to the superior tribunals of Spain at Madrid, and the result was that after long delay the judgment of the court-martial was annulled about September 8, 1896, and a new trial ordered before the ordinary tribunals.

It will be observed that this judgment of reversal proceeds upon the theory that these captives are justiciable in the Spanish courts for crimes alleged to have been committed by them against Spanish laws, and it decided nothing more than that the naval court-martial was not a proper or competent tribunal for their trial. The appellate court merely held that Spain had mistaken her own forum.

Shortly after this decision, Melton, on the 17th of October, 1896, was taken to the guardroom in the prison to make a preliminary deposition, preparatory, as he says, for trial by an ordinary court-martial upon the charge of piracy and rebellion. The first trial had been by a summary naval court-martial. On the 19th of October this procedure was continued, and he was asked, as he had been on the previous day, what proofs he could produce to show he was an American citizen, notwithstanding the fact that it seems to have been conceded throughout the first trial that he was an American citizen.

This mode of examination continued until December 11, 1896, and probably thereafter, for upon that day Mr. Laborde wrote to Mr. Springer, informing him that he had been ordered on the day before by the military judge of the prosecution of the *Competitor* crew to dress himself in a military suit for the purpose of being recognized by someone. Against this requirement Laborde protested, and refused to disguise himself. The military judge immediately answered that he would compel Laborde by force to comply, and, fearing brutality, he obeyed. Since that time no proceedings by way of trial have been had. From the 30th of April or the 1st of May, 1896, down to the present time, a period of more than fourteen months, Melton, Laborde, and Gildea have been in close confinement in the Cabanas prison or fort at Habana.

The portions of the treaty, protocol, Consular Regulations, and statutes having reference to the foregoing statements are as follows:

ARTICLE VII.

And it is agreed that the subject or citizens of each of the contracting parties, their vessels or effects, shall not be liable to any embargo or detention on the part of the other, for any military expedition or other public or private purpose whatever; and in all cases of seizures, detention, or arrest for debts contracted, or offenses committed by any citizen or subject of the one party within the jurisdiction of the other, the same shall be made and prosecuted by order and authority of law only, and according to the regular form of proceedings usual in such cases. The citizens and subjects of both parties shall be allowed to employ such advocates, solicitors, notaries, agents, and factors, as they may judge proper, in all their affairs and in all their trials at law in which they may be concerned, before the tribunals of the other party; and such agents shall have free access to be present at the proceedings in such causes, and at the taking of all examinations and evidence which may be exhibited in the said trials. (Treaty with Spain, 1795.)

1. No citizen of the United States residing in Spain, her adjacent islands, or her ultramarine possessions, charged with acts of sedition, treason, or conspiracy against the institutions, the public security, the integrity of the territory, or against the supreme Government, or any other crime whatsoever, shall be subject to trial by any exceptional tribunal, but exclusively by the ordinary jurisdiction, except in the case of being captured with arms in hand.

2. Those who, not coming within this last case, may be arrested or imprisoned, shall be deemed to have been so arrested or imprisoned by order of the civil authority for the effects of the law of April 17, 1821, even though the arrest or imprisonment shall have been effected by armed force.

3. Those who may be taken with arms in hand, and who are therefore comprehended in the exception of the first article, shall be tried by ordinary council of war, in conformity with the second article of the hereinbefore-mentioned law; but

even in this case the accused shall enjoy for their defense the guaranties embodied in the aforesaid law of April 17, 1821.

4. In consequence whereof, as well in the cases mentioned in the third paragraph as in those of the second, the parties accused are allowed to name attorneys and advocates, who shall have access to them at suitable times; they shall be furnished in due season with copy of the accusation and a list of witnesses for the prosecution, which latter shall be examined before the presumed criminal, his attorney, and advocate, in conformity with the provisions of articles 20 to 31 of the said law; they shall have the right to compel the witnesses of whom they desire to avail themselves to appear and give testimony or to do it by means of depositions; they shall present such evidence as they may judge proper, and they shall be permitted to present and to make their defense, in public trial, orally or in writing, by themselves or by means of their counsel.

5. The sentence pronounced shall be referred to the audiencia of the judicial dis-.trict, or to the Captain-General, according as the trial may have taken place before the ordinary judge or before the council of war, in conformity also with what is prescribed in the above-mentioned law. (Protocol of 1877.)

171. If the consul is satisfied that an applicant for protection has a right to his intervention he should interest himself in his behalf, examining carefully his griev-ances. If he finds that the complaints are well founded he should interpose firmly, but with courtesy and moderation in his behalf. If redress can not be obtained from the local authorities the consul will apply to the legation of the United States, if there be one in the country where he resides, and will in all cases transmit to the Department copies of his correspondence, accompanied by his report. (United States Consular Regulations.)

Officers of vessels of the United States shall in all cases be citizens of the United States. (Rev. Stat., sec. 4131, p. 795.)

'   If the uncontradicted affidavits of Melton, Laborde, and Gildea are to be taken as true, and if it is conceded that the vessel was seized and that they were arrested, within 1 marine league of the coast of Cuba, it is equally well established that they were coerce.' to that point by supe-rior force.   Under such circumstances these captives can not be made amenable to the laws of Spain.   It is a well-settled principle of inter-national law that the ships and subjects of a neutral nation, which are driven by superior force into prohibited ports or waters of a belligerent, draw upon themselves no penal consequences therefor, but must be allowed freely to depart therefrom; and the carrying of these three men into Cuban waters was as involuntary on their part as if they had been driven thither by storm or stress of weather.

Under the facts and circumstances of this case, it is not competent for Spain to try these prisoners by any military tribunal whatever.   Two of the men, Gildea and Laborde, were officers of an American vessel driven under duress into Cuban waters; Melton, a passenger, was an American native citizen before he took passage—a friendly neutral, a noncombatant, not armed in any way, and his character was not changed by the forcible diversion of the vessel from its voyage to Lemon City to the Cuban coast.

They are not amenable to the jurisdiction of any Spanish courts for piracy, for the reason that it plainly appears that they had never com-mitted or could have intended to do any act of robbery or depredation upon the high seas, which acts are the essentials of piracy, and it is clear that no such acts were ever intended by either of these prisoners.

Piracy is an assault upon vessels navigated on the high seas, committed animo furandi, whether the robbery or forcible depredation be effected or not, and whether or not it be accompanied by murder or personal injury. (1 Phill., Sec. CCCLVI.)

Piracy, by the law of nations, is defined with reasonable certainty to be robbery upon the seas. (U. S. v. Smith, 5 Wheat., 153.)

By the law of nations, robbery or forcible depredation upon the sea, animo furandi, is piracy. (Story Const., S. 1159.)

It is not competent for Spain, by declaring that to be piracy which is not piracy under the definitions of international law, to extend the pen-alties of that crime, or the jurisdiction of its courts as to piracy, to the subjects of other nations, or to incorporate in any way its own municipal definition of the crime of piracy into the law of nations to any degree beyond the definition established by international law.

Nor are these prisoners amenable to any Spanish court for the crime of rebellion by reason of any acts committed by them, even if such acts are subjected to the most strict and adverse construction. Allegiance either as a subject or as an alien amenable by residence or presence to the laws of a foreign state is an indispensable element to constitute the crime of treason or rebellion. It is the opinion of your committee that these men never became amenable to the laws of Spain to that intent.

Irrespective of any of the foregoing considerations, the conduct of Spain, as hereinbefore detailed, constitutes such delay and denial of justice and such an actual infliction of injustice upon these men as to make it the duty of this Government to demand reparation therefor, irrespective of any act which these prisoners may have committed up to the date of their capture. Among the acts of reparation which ought to be demanded should be the release of these captives.

The principles which govern the trial of such cases as this were correctly expressed by Mr. Evarts, while Secretary of State, as follows:

It has, from the very foundation of this Government, been its aim that its citizens abroad should be assured of the guarantees of law; that accused persons should be apprised of the specific offense with which they might be charged; that they should be confronted with the witnesses against them; that they should have the right to be heard in their own defense, either by themselves or such counsel as they might choose to employ to represent them; in short, that they should have a fair and impartial trial, with the presumption of innocence surrounding them as a shield at all stages of the proceedings, until their guilt should be established by competent and sufficient evidence. (2 Wharton Dig., p. 623.)

The rights thus defined have been violated in the persons of these prisoners. They have been tried and sentenced to death by a summary naval court-martial in a proceeding which has been annulled by the appellate courts of Spain at Madrid, upon the ground that such a court-martial had no jurisdiction whatever over them. Ten months have elapsed since this death sentence was annulled, and they have not again been brought to trial. In the mean time they have been subjected to protracted preliminary examinations preparatory to their trial by another court-martial, which differs from the first one only in the fact that it is less summary and more formal in its character than the first.

At the first trial they were not allowed to be defended by counsel of their own selection; opportunity or time to produce witnesses was denied to them by the celerity with which that trial was instituted and conducted. They were only defended by a Spanish naval officer, assigned to that duty by the court, who could not or did not speak English, who never spoke to them during the trial, who did not introduce or attempt to introduce any evidence in their behalf, who asked for no delay of the trial, and whose only exertion in their defense was a plea for mercy, which admitted their guilt. Although an interpreter was present, neither the evidence for the prosecution nor the summing up of the prosecutor was translated to them. His presence was not disclosed until after the prosecution had closed its testimony and argument. The only translation made to them was just before the close of these sanguinary proceedings, when they were asked if they had anything to say. Necessarily they had or could have little to say, although one of them, Gildea, protested that he had not understood a word of the proceedings against him by which his life was to be adjudged forfeited. With these protests the trial ended, and the defendants were immediately sentenced to death.

It is now fourteen months since they were arrested, during all of which time they have been held in the Cabañas fortress as prisoners.

Melton and Laborde are unquestionably citizens of the United States. Gildea is a British subject, but he was a sailor upon an American vessel when taken; was acting as its mate, and it is the opinion of your committee that he is entitled to be protected by this Government. He was serving under the flag and he is entitled to be protected by it.

In our opinion these acts of delay and denial of justice, and of the infliction of injustice, vitiate and make void any right which Spain had at the beginning of this transaction to proceed criminally against any of these men. This Government should demand that they be set at liberty and that the *Competitor* be restored to her owner, as there is no evidence that the owner knew anything about the divergence of the vessel from its regular voyage to Lemon City, Fla.

The committee report the accompanying joint resolution as a substitute for the aforesaid Resolution 149 and recommend its adoption.

FIFTY-FOURTH CONGRESS, SECOND SESSION.

[Senate Document No. 84.]

Message from the President of the United States, transmitting, in response to Senate resolution of December 21, 1896, a report of the Secretary of State covering a list of persons claiming to be citizens of the United States who have been arrested on the island of Cuba since February 24, 1895, to the present time.

JANUARY 25, 1897.—Referred to the Committee on Foreign Relations and ordered to be printed.

To the Senate of the United States:

I transmit, herewith, in response to the Senate resolution of December 21, 1896, addressed to the Secretary of State, a report of that officer covering a list of persons claiming to be citizens of the United States who have been arrested on the Island of Cuba since February 24, 1895, to the present time.

GROVER CLEVELAND.

EXECUTIVE MANSION,
Washington, January 25, 1897.

The PRESIDENT:

The undersigned, Secretary of State, having received a resolution passed in the Senate of the United States on December 21, 1896, in the following words—

That the Secretary of State be, and he is hereby, directed to send to the Senate a report of all naturalized citizens of the United States of whose arrest and imprisonment, trial, or conviction, or sentence, either to imprisonment at the penal colony of Ceutro or elsewhere, he has any information, and that he shall inform the Senate in such report of the persons now held in confinement at Ceutro and of the charges, briefly stated, on which they were condemned and the nature of the evidence, so far as the same appears on the files of the State Department.

has the honor to lay before the President a list of persons claiming to be citizens of the United States who have been arrested in Cuba since February 24, 1895, to the present date, to the end that, if in the President's judgment not incompatible with the public interest, the same be transmitted to the Senate in response to the foregoing resolution.

Since the breaking out of the insurrection in Cuba, on February 24, 1895, to the present time, 74 persons, citizens of the United States, or claiming to be such, have been arrested by the Spanish authorities of the island.

Passports, certificates of naturalization, registration in the consulates of this Government on the Island of Cuba, and service on ships sailing under the flag of the United States, having been alike accepted by our consular officers and the Spanish authorities as prima facie evidence of citizenship establishing the rights of the claimants to the treatment secured to our citizens under our treaties and protocols with Spain, it has been deemed advisable to include in the subjoined list all persons of the classes referred to who have been arrested.

Of the 74 persons arrested, 7 have been tried, namely: Nos. 1, 36, 70, 71, 72, 73, and 74. In the cases of 2 of these (Nos. 1 and 36) appeals have been taken, and in the cases of the other 5, the *Competitor* prisoners, a new trial has been ordered.

Thirty-six persons arrested have been released after the charges against them had been investigated and found to be baseless.

Eighteen have been expelled from the island, after periods of confinement lasting from a few days to nearly a year in the case of José Aguirre (No. 2); while 17 cases are still pending. The charges against 14 of the 17 are as follows:

Nos. 31 and 55, sedition and rebellion.

No. 38, rebellion.

Nos. 37, 40, 61 and 62, rebellion with arms in hand.

No. 43, purchase and concealment of arms and ammunition.

No. 53, disorderly conduct and insults to Spain.

Nos. 70, 71, 72, 73, and 74, landing arms from *Competitor* for insurgents.

In the remaining three cases (Nos. 35, 47, and 52), the nature of the charges having not yet been ascertained, demand has been made both at Habana and Madrid that they be at once formulated and communicated or that prisoners be released.

Mr. Delgado (No. 54) died in hospital at Habana on the 19th instant.

Besides the above 74 cases, 9 correspondents of various newspapers in the United States have been expelled from Cuba by the Spanish authorities, after temporary detention by the military.

No American citizen has been sentenced or is confined at Ceutro.

Demands have been made upon the Spanish Government in every case where trial seems to be unreasonably delayed that it go forward at once or prisoner be released.

Respectfully submitted.

RICHARD OLNEY.

DEPARTMENT OF STATE,
Washington, January 22, 1897.

List of American citizens, native and naturalized, arrested and imprisoned in Cuba since February 24, 1895, to date, stating also cause of arrest, charges, place of confinement, whether tried, released, deported, or cases pending.

1. JULIO SANGUILY, 49 years; native of Cuba; naturalized 1878; arrested February 24, 1895; charge of rebellion; tried November 28, 1895; found guilty and sentenced to life imprisonment; case appealed to supreme court, Madrid. Was also tried on charge of participation in the kidnapping of the sugar planter Fernandez de Castro, in 1894, by the late bandit, Manuel Garcia, and acquitted. Tried for the second time December 21, 1896, for rebellion, the case remanded from Spain, and again sentenced December 28 to life imprisonment; an appeal taken. Has been imprisoned in the Cabana fort.

2. JOSE MARIE TIMOTEO AGUIRRE, 52 years; native of Cuba; naturalized 1881; arrested February 24, 1895; charge of rebellion; confined in Cabana fort; acquitted and deported September 6, 1895; went to the United States.

FRANCISCO PERAZA, arrested at Sagua March 2, 1895; charge of participation in the robbery of some cattle; released March 4, 1895.

4. FRANCISCO CARRILLO, 45 years; native of Cuba; naturalized 1891; arrested at Remedios on February 24, 1895, upon a gubernative order for not having inscribed himself in the register of foreigners in any province of the island; confined in Cab. anas fort; released and deported to United States May 29, 1895.

5. JUAN RODRIGUEZ VALDES, native of Cuba; naturalized 1876; arrested at Puerto Principe April 5, 1895; released April 6.

6. JUSTO GENER, 68 years; native of Cuba; naturalized; arrested at Matanzas April 6; released April 9, 1895.

7. JOSE MARIA CARABALLO, 42 years; native of Cuba; naturalized 1877; arrested at Matanzas April 6; released April 9, 1885.

8. MANUEL FUENTES, 33 years; native of Cuba; naturalized 1889; correspondent New York World; arrested at Caimanera April 30, 1895; released May 4, 1895, on condition that he return to United States.

9. MANUEL VARGAS, arrested at Remedios July 3, 1895; released and expelled July 13, 1895; charged with being an agent of the insurgents, etc.; naturalized.

10. DOMINGO GONZALEZ Y ALFONSO, 42 years; native of Cuba; naturalized 1876; arrested at Quivican July 3, 1895; expelled September 3, 1895, for the reason that his presence in the island is a source of danger to the Government.

11. VICTORIANO BULIT PEREZ, 33 years; native of Cuba, of American parents; arrested at Sagua July 12, 1895; accused of "proposing treasonable acts;" released November 8, 1895.

12. JOSEPH A. ANSLEY, 56 years; born in Habana, of American parents; arrested at Sagua August 26, 1895; charge, "presence prejudicial to peace of island;" deported to United States September 21, 1895.

13. AURELIO ANSLEY, 34 years; son of Joseph A. Ansley. Same as above.

14. LUIS ANSLEY, 30 years; son of Joseph Ansley. Same as above.

15. JOHN A. SOWERS, 65 years; native of Virginia. Same as above.

16. CARLOS M. GARCIA Y RUIZ, 28 years; born in the United States; arrested at Sagua September 7, 1895; accused of attempting to join the insurrectionists; released October 7, 1895.

17. JOSE MARTINEZ GONZALEZ, 45 years; native of Cuba: naturalized 1873; arrested at Sagua September 12, 1895; charge of riding on railroad without paying fare; no evidence against him; released September 19, 1895.

18. MARIANO RODRIGUEZ ZAYAS, native of Cuba; arrested Habana September 17; released September 19, 1895; naturalized; no charges.

19. JOSE MARTINEZ MFSA, 41 years; native of Cuba; naturalized 1878; arrested at Habana September 17, 1895; released September 19, 1895; no charges.

20. EUGENE PELLETIER, 42 years; native of Cuba; naturalized 1877; arrested at Cienfuegos December 5, 1895; charged with recruiting for the insurrection; released, under surveillance, May 17, 1896.

21. JOSEPH J. TRELLES, native of Cuba; naturalized; arrested at Matanzas December 24, 1895; released December 26, 1895; no charges.

22. MANUEL M. (or W.) AMIEVA, 39 years; native of Cuba; naturalized 1878; arrested at Matanzas December 24, 1895, as a suspect; released December 31, 1895; no charges.

23. SOLOMON, CHAS. S., native of the United States, arrested and released.

24. MARCOS E. RODRIGUEZ, 57 years; native of Cuba; naturalized 1875; arrested January 17, 1896, on board American steamship Olivette; charge, aiding the rebellion, sedition, etc.; released April 1, 1896.

25. LOUIS SOMEILLAN, sr., 58 years; born in Cuba; naturalized Key West 1878; arrested January 17, 1896, at Habana; released April 1, 1896; charge, aiding rebellion, sedition, etc

26. LOUIS SOMEILLAN, jr., 36 years; born in Habana, son of above; arrested January 17 at Habana; released April 1, 1896; charge, aiding rebellion, sedition, etc.

27. LADISLAO QUINTERO, born in Key West; made a prisoner of war February 22, 1896, at Guatao, where he had been wounded by Spanish troops; released April 11, 1896.

28. WALTER GRANT DYGERT, 25 years; born in the United States; arrested February 23, 1896; imprisoned at Guines; supposed to be insurgent leader El Inglesito; finally released and sent to United States April 24, 1896.

29. Rev. ALBERT J. DIAZ, native of Cuba; naturalized; arrested at Habana April 16, 1896, charged with forwarding rebel correspondence; confined at police headquarters; expelled April 16, 1896; accused of abetting insurrection.

30. ALFRED DIAZ; brother of above; arrested, same charge; both of the Diazes were released April 22, 1896, on condition of leaving the country; went to Key West.

31. JOSEPH L. CEPERO, native of Cuba; naturalized 1881; arrested prior to January 20, 1896, on board steamer from Cienfuegos to Batabano; case now pending before civil court Santa Clara; confined in Santa Clara prison; charge, sedition, rebellion, etc.

32. LUIS MARTINEZ, arrested about March 1, 1896; charged with treasonable correspondence; released April 13, 1896, on $400 bail; naturalized 1873.

33. WILLIAM A. GLEAN, native of Cuba, of American parents; arrested at Sagua April, 1896; charge, rebellion; military jurisdiction inhibited in favor of civil July 28, 1896; released and returned to the United States.

34. LOUIS M. GLEAN, brother of the above; same as above.

35. FRANK J. LARRIEU, native of Cuba; naturalized; arrested at Cardenas May 15, 1896; case pending; charges not made known.

36. LOUIS SOMEILLAN, 58 years; native of Cuba; naturalized; arrested July 7, 1896, for second time; charge, aiding rebellion; turned over to civil court, is confined in city prison; trial held January 8, 1897; sentenced January 13 to imprisonment in chains for life; appeal taken.

37. MANUEL FERNANDEZ CHAQUEILO, 19 years; native of Key West; captured July 9, 1896; was the companion of Charles Govin; is in Cabana fort; case pending, under military jurisdiction; charge, "rebellion with arms in hand."

38. GEORGE W. AGUIRRE, 25 years; born in the United States; captured by a Spanish gunboat July 10, 1896; case pending before civil court of Jaruco; confined in Cabana fort; charge of rebellion.

39. SAMUEL T. TOLON, 45 years; native of Cuba; naturalized 1878; arrested on board American steamer *Seneca* September 3, 1896; incomunicado twenty-two days; charged with being a delegate to the Cuban Junta; released and deported September 30, 1896; went to New York.

40. OSCAR CESPEDES, 20 years; native of Key West; captured without arms in insurgent hospital near Zapata swamp about September 5, 1896, imprisoned at San Severino fort, Matanzas; question of competency between military and civil jurisdiction decided in favor of military; case pending.

41. FRANCISCO E. CAZANAS, arrested as suspect at Matanzas October 14, 1896; released October 16, 1896.

42. ALFREDO HERNANDEZ, 44 years; native of Matanzas; naturalized 1876; arrested at his house at Habana September 6, 1896; suspicion of being concerned in the insurrection; expelled September 23, 1896; went to Key West.

43. ANTONIO SUAREZ DEL VILLAR, native of Cuba; naturalized; arrested at Cienfuegos September 5, 1896; charged with purchase and concealing of arms and ammunition; case sent to civil jurisdiction December 23, 1896; in prison at Cienfuegos; case pending.

44. JOSE CURBINO, native of Cuba; naturalized; arrested at Rincon, September 18, 1896; surrendered to military authorities without arms; released and is residing at Santiago de las Vegas.

45. JOSEPH AUSTIN MUNOZ, native of New Orleans; arrested at Matanzas September 18, 1896; released September 19; claimed that arrest was by mistake.

46. RAMON RODRIGUEZ, native of Cuba; naturalized; arrested September 20, 1896, upon requisition from governor of Matanzas; had been in insurrection; surrendered and failed to report regularly; sent to Cardena and released.

47. ESTEBEN VENERO, 22 years; native of Cuba; naturalized 1895; arrested at Los Palos (Habana province) about September 22, 1896; charges not stated; Captain-General asked for evidence of American citizenship on December 9, which was sent him; case pending cognizance of military or civil jurisdiction.

48. ADOLFO TORRES, native of Cuba; naturalized; arrested October 4 at Sagua; charges not stated; release ordered November 23, 1896, question of competency not established; released November 26, officer remarking "we have no charges against you."

49. ESTEBEN CESPEDES (colored), born in Cuba; naturalized Key West, 1891; arrested October 13, 1896, charged with naniguismo (voodoo); expelled November 7, and went to Key West.

50. RAMON CRUCET, 48 years; born in Cuba; naturalized 1873; arrested in Colon November 1, 1896; charges, public censure of acts of Spanish Government; released December 18, 1896; no grounds of complaint.

51. LOUIS LAY, 18 years; native of Cuba, of American parents; arrested November 9, 1896, during a raid upon a social club in Regla; confined in Cabana fort; case ordered to be transferred to civil court at Guanabacoa, December 23; charges, aiding rebellion. Released January 15, 1897.

52. JOSE GONZALEZ, 63 years; native of Bejucal, Cuba; naturalized 1882; arrested at Las Mangas November 10, 1896, taken to prison at Pinar del Rio; charges not yet made known to consulate-general, Habana.

53. THEODORE L. VIVES, native of Cienfuegos; naturalized 1891; arrested November 19, 1896; charges, first disorderly conduct and then insults to Spain; case pending cognizance of military or civil jurisdiction; is confined in jail.

54. HENRY J. DELGADO, native of the United States; captured about December 10, 1896, at an insurgent hospital in Pinar del Rio province, after having been ten weeks in a hut sick; sent to Havana to Cabana fort; removed to hospital December 28, 1896, where, our consul-general reports, he received best medical attention; died in hospital January 19, 1897.

55. GASPAR A. BETANCOURT, 63 years; native of Cuba; naturalized 1877; arrested December 26, 1896, confined at police headquarters incommunicado, charged with sedition.

56. FERNANDO PINO HERNANDEZ, 19 years (colored); native of Key West; charged with naniguismo (voodoo); ordered to be expelled December 30. 1896; will be sent to Key West.

57. AMADO PINO HERNANDEZ, 21 years; brother of the above; same as above.

58. JOSE ANTONIO IZNAGA, native of Cuba; naturalized; expelled in August, 1896; no report.

59. AUGUST BOLTON, naturalized 1893.

60. GUSTAVE RICHELIEU, naturalized 1870; taken in a boat near Santiago de Cuba about February 23, 1896; released from prison about March 1, 1896; subsequently rearrested and recommitted for leaving Guantanamo without permission; consul considers second arrest an excuse for detention; release granted shortly after.

61. FRANK AGRAMONT, and 62, THOS. JULIO SAINZ, arrested with arms in their hands, May, 1895; charge, rebellion; to be tried for armed insurrection against the Government; Santiago de Cuba.

63. JOHN D. FERRER, no evidence against him; released March 23, 1896; naturalized at New York, 1878.

64. PEDRO DUARTE; 65, JORGE CALVAR, and 66, RAMON ROMAGOSA, arrested at Manzanillo for alleged conspiracy in insurrection; expelled August 11, 1896.

67. DONALD B. DODGE or F. M. BOYLE, arrested at Santiago de Cuba August 2, 1895; charge rebellion; (consul thinks his mind unbalanced;) released August 31, 1895, and sailed for the United States; native of New York.

68. BERT S. SKILLER, arrested at La Caleta, in open boat, April 28, 1896; released at Baracoa September 3, 1896.

69. MANUEL COMAS, arrested October 25, 1895, and released.

70. ALFRED LABORDE, native; arrested on steamer *Competitor* April 25, 1896; charge, landing arms for insurgents; confined in Cabana fortress; condemned to death May 8; order suspended; new trial opened May 11, 1896.

71. WILLIAM GILDEA, naturalized; same as above.

72. ONA MELTON, native; same as above.

73. CHARLES BARNETT, native; supposed to be one of *Competitor* crew; captured on land; same as above.

74. WILLIAM LEAVITT, British subject; supposed to be one of *Competitor* crew; captured on land; same as above.

List of newspaper war correspondents who have been expelled from the island.

WILLIAM MANNIX, native of United States; expelled as a dangerous alien, etc., February 11, 1896.

SYLVESTER SCOVEL, World, native of United States; reported that he had arrived from insurgent lines, and it was intended to deport him in January; reported January 20 that he had returned to insurgent lines.

CHARLES MICHELSON and LORENZO BETANCOURT, correspondent and interpreter of New York Journal; arrested February 25; confined in Morro Castle; released February 27, 1896; charged with having communicated with insurgents by passing through Spanish lines at Marianco, etc.

ELBERT RAPPLEYE, Mail and Express; expelled March 26, 1896, for sending news to his paper which was false and disparaging to the authorities in the island.

JAMES CREELMAN, World, born in Canada; expelled May 5, 1896, for sending to paper false reports touching the insurrection.

F. W. LAWRENCE, Journal, born in the United States; expelled May 5, 1896, same cause as above.

WILLIAM G. GAY, World; native of New York. Expelled June 27; went to New York.

THOMAS J. DAWLEY, war correspondent; native of New York. Arrested several times between March 24, 1896, and July 3, on suspicion; charges, "taking views of forts and conspiring to blow up same with dynamite;" confined thirteen days in Morro; released.

FIFTY-FOURTH CONGRESS, SECOND SESSION.

[Senate Document No 119]

Message from the President of the United States, transmitting, in response to Senate resolution of February 4, 1897, a report of the Secretary of State, submitting correspondence relative to the arrest and detention of Gaspar A. Betancourt, a citizen of the United States, by the Spanish authorities in Cuba.

FEBRUARY 11, 1897.—Referred to the Committee on Foreign Relations and ordered to be printed.

To the Senate of the United States:

In response to the resolution of the Senate of February 4, 1897, I transmit a report from the Secretary of State, submitting copies of correspondence relative to the arrest and detention of Gaspar A. Betancourt, a citizen of the United States, by the Spanish authorities in Cuba.

GROVER CLEVELAND.

EXECUTIVE MANSION,
Washington, February 11, 1897.

The PRESIDENT:

In response to the resolution of the Senate of the United States of February 4, 1897, reading as follows:

Resolved, That the President is requested, if it is not in his opinion incompatible with the public interest, to inform the Senate whether Gaspar Betancourt, a citizen of the United States, is held in prison by the Spanish authorities in Cuba, and the grounds of the arrest and detention; and that he will also inform the Senate whether the release of said Betancourt has been demanded, and when and how often such demand has been repeated, and what answer has been made to the same—

the Secretary of State has the honor to submit copies of correspondence relating to the subject, with a view to its transmission to the Senate if deemed not incompatible with the public interests.

Respectfully submitted.

RICHARD OLNEY.

DEPARTMENT OF STATE,
Washington, February 10, 1897.

Mr. Lee to Mr. Rockhill.

[Telegram]

HABANA, *December 28, 1896.*

Gaspar A. Betancourt, American citizen, arrested and incomunicado. Charges unknown.

LEE.

Mr. Lee to Mr. Rockhill.

No. 276.]　　　　　UNITED STATES CONSULATE-GENERAL,
Habana, December 30, 1896.

SIR: I have the honor to confirm my telegram to the Department of the 28th instant. * * * Under the same date I asked the Acting Governor-General to give me the reasons for the arrest of Mr. Betancourt.

I am, etc.,　　　　　　　　　FITZHUGH LEE,
Consul-General.

Mr. Rockhill to Mr. Lee.

[Telegram]

DEPARTMENT OF STATE,
Washington, January 2, 1897.

See that Betancourt well treated and case speedily investigated. His age entitles him to consideration. Cable result.

ROCKHILL.

Mr. Rockhill to Mr. Lee.

No. 196.]　　　　　　DEPARTMENT OF STATE,
Washington, January 2, 1897.

SIR: I append for confirmation a copy of a telegram received from you on the 28th ultimo. You are instructed to take, on behalf of Gaspar A. Betancourt, the usual steps in cases of arrest of American citizens.

I am, etc.,

W. W. ROCKHILL.

Mr. Lee to Mr. Rockhill.

[Telegram.]

HABANA, *January 4, 1897.*

Had already taken steps Betancourt case. Hope to arrange release
and departure from island in few days.

LEE.

Mr. Lee to Mr. Rockhill.

No. 286.]   UNITED STATES CONSULATE-GENERAL,
Habana, January 6, 1897.

SIR: With reference to my dispatch No. 276, of the 30th December,
last, relative to the arrest of the American citizen, Dr. Gaspar A.
Betancourt, I have the honor to inclose a copy translation of a communication received from the Captain and Governor-General of this
island in answer to mine invoking in behalf of Dr. Betancourt the
rights to which he is entitled under the treaty of 1795 and protocol of
12th January, 1877, between the United States and Spain, and also
that the question be solved by expelling from·this island the said
American citizen. It will be observed that the Captain-General states
that there being sufficient reasons for the proper courts to take cogui-
zance of Betancourt's case, the proceedings have been referred to the
ordinary civil courts of justice, considering his condition of an American
citizen.

I am, etc.,   FITZHUGH LEE,
Consul-General.

[Inclosure 1 with No. 286.—Translation.]

GENERAL GOVERNMENT OF THE ISLAND OF CUBA.

In answer to your courteous notes of the 28th and 31st ultimo and 4th instant,
relative to the American citizen Mr. Gaspar A. Betancourt, I have the honor to inform
you, that in view of the reports received by this Government and of gubernative proceedings having been initiated against him and others on the charge of sedition,
and resulting from the said proceedings that there are sufficient reasons for the proper
courts to take cognizance of the same, said proceedings have been referred, as regards
Betancourt, to the ordinary courts of justice, considering his condition of a citizen
of the United States.

God guard you many years.

VALERIANO WEYLER.

HABANA, *January 5, 1897.*
The CONSUL-GENERAL OF THE UNITED STATES.

Mr. Rockhill to Mr. Lee.

[Telegram.]

DEPARTMENT OF STATE,
Washington, January 15, 1897.

In the case Gaspar A. Betancourt insist that charges be immediately
communicated to you or man released.

ROCKHILL.

Mr. Lee to Mr. Rockhill.

No. 306.]

HABANA, *January 16, 1897.*

I have the honor to confirm the following telegram from you reading: [See telegram of January 15].

In compliance therewith I addressed at once a communication to the Governor and Captain-General, and as soon as an answer is received I will transmit it to you.

I am, etc.,

FITZHUGH LEE.

Mr. Rockhill to Mr. Lee.

[Telegram.]

DEPARTMENT OF STATE,
Washington, January 19, 1897.

Cable reply to Department's cable instruction 15th January.

ROCKHILL.

Mr. Lee to Mr. Rockhill.

[Telegram.]

Asked for information from the Captain-General on 15th to reply to dispatch of that date. I have received no response to communication. Captain-General left this morning with column troops to proceed easterly direction Matanzas. Will demand to-day from the Acting Captain-General reply to unanswered communication. If I do not promptly receive answer, will notify Department.

LEE.

Mr. Lee to Mr. Rockhill.

[Telegram.]

HABANA, *January 22, 1897.*

Have not succeeded in getting any reply from Captain or Acting Captain-General in reference to the charges against the person named in your dispatch of 15th. Shall I demand his release?

LEE.

Mr. Lee to Mr. Rockhill.

No. 329.]

HABANA, *January 30, 1897.*

I have the honor to report that yesterday I visited the jail in this city and found there Dr. Gaspar A. Betancourt, who has now been in confinement about thirty-three days. As reported, this gentleman was kept in solitary confinement, or *incomunicado*, as is called, for two hundred and eighty-eight hours, when first imprisoned, contrary to the treaty between Spain and the United States, which prescribes seventy-two hours as the limit.

I have duly made protests in this case, as in that of others, but no attention has been paid to such protests by the authorities here. This is the person referred to in your telegram of the 15th instant, in which you direct me to insist that the charges against him be made known or release be demanded. In compliance therewith I addressed at once a communication to the Governor and Captain-General, to which no reply has yet been received, notwithstanding my having again called the attention of the Acting Captain-General to said communication.

On the 22d instant I telegraphed to the Department, reporting that no reply to my communication asking for said charges had been received, and asking if I should proceed in demanding release. I have obtained no answer from the Department to date.

I am, etc.,   FITZHUGH LEE.

Mr. Rockhill to Mr. Lee.

[Telegram.]

DEPARTMENT OF STATE,
Washington, February 2, 1897.

Understand Betancourt's case plainly one mistaken identity. Can nothing be done?

ROCKHILL.

Mr. Lee to Mr. Rockhill.

[Telegram]

HABANA, *February 5, 1897.*

Betancourt and Eva Adan will be released. Previous order for latter's release said to have miscarried.

Mr. Rockhill to Mr. Lee.

[Telegram]

DEPARTMENT OF STATE,
Washington, February 9, 1897.

Referring your cablegram 5th instant, are Betancourt and Eva Adan released?

ROCKHILL.

Mr. Lee to Mr. Rockhill.

[Telegram.]

HABANA, *February 9, 1897.*

Both Betancourt and Eva Adan at liberty.

LEE.

FIFTY-FOURTH CONGRESS, SECOND SESSION.

[Senate Document No. 120]

Message from the President of the United States, transmitting, in response to Senate resolution of February 2, 1897, report from the Secretary of State relative to the killing of Segundo N. Lopez, son of M. F. Lopez, at Sagua La Grande, in Cuba.

FEBRUARY 11, 1897.—Referred to the Committee on Foreign Relations and ordered to be printed.

To the Senate of the United States:

In response to the resolution of the Senate of February 2, 1897, I transmit a report from the Secretary of State relative to the killing of Segundo N. Lopez, son of M. F. Lopez, at Sagua la Grande, in Cuba.

GROVER CLEVELAND.

EXECUTIVE MANSION,
Washington, February 11, 1897.

The PRESIDENT.

Referring to a resolution of the Senate of the United States of February 2, 1897, in the terms following—

Resolved, That the Secretary of State be requested to send to the Senate any information that he may have in regard to the killing, by Spanish soldiers, of the son of M. F. Lopez, an American citizen, at Sagua la Grande, in Cuba, and any report or letter from the American consul at that point relating to the subject—

I have the honor to make the following report, with a view to its transmission to the Senate if deemed not incompatible with the public interests.

It is claimed that Segundo N. Lopez, son of M. F. Lopez and a native of Cuba, was an American citizen—a claim which is supported by the fact that he was registered as such by the United States consul at Cienfuegos. On the other hand, his name is not to be found in the register of American citizens kept by the consul-general at Habana. The ex parte evidence in the possession of the Department tends to show that Lopez, in the middle of April last, was visiting relatives in a district of Cuba which he had been accustomed to frequent as an agent and interpreter of American buyers of tobacco for export; that he was not connected with the insurrection; that on the 11th of said April he was arrested by Spanish troops, being at the time wholly unarmed; that on being asked who he was by the officer in command, he at first replied that he was a "pacifico," and presently declared that he was an American citizen and produced papers which the officers looked at and returned to him; and that within a short time thereafter he was killed by the troops either by or without orders on the part of the officer in command, but so far as known without charges, process, or trial of any sort.

The above brief summary of evidence on file in the Department is submitted because the same was communicated in strict confidence and on the express understanding that no clew should be given to the identity of the witness.

Upon the receipt of the evidence above referred to the consul-general of the United States at Habana was instructed, August 21, 1896, to call upon the Captain-General of Cuba for an investigation of the facts respecting the death of Lopez, and for due punishment of all persons criminally connected therewith. The Captain-General promptly acceded to the request for an examination, and stated that the results when reached would be reported to this Government. Thus far, however, no report on the subject has been received, the last communication from the office of the Captain-General being to the effect that the inquiry was still pending, so that no definite conclusion could be given.

Notice of a demand by the father of Lopez for indemnity for the injuries sustained by him through the death of his son has been duly presented to the Spanish Government through our minister at Madrid.

Respectfully submitted.

RICHARD OLNEY.

DEPARTMENT OF STATE,
Washington, February 11, 1897.

FIFTY-FOURTH CONGRESS, SECOND SESSION.

[Senate Document No. 172]

Message from the President of the United States, transmitting, in response to Senate resolution of February 24, 1897, a report from the Secretary of State, covering copies of the correspondence and reports of the consul-general of the United States at Habana relating to all American citizens now in prison in the island of Cuba not previously reported on.

MARCH 1, 1897.—Referred to the Committee on Foreign Relations and ordered to be printed.

To the Senate:

In response to the resolution of the Senate of the 24th ultimo, I transmit herewith a report from the Secretary of State covering copies of the correspondence and reports of the consul-general of the United States at Habana relating to all American citizens now in prison in the Island of Cuba not previously reported on.

GROVER CLEVELAND.

EXECUTIVE MANSION,
Washington, March 1, 1897.

The PRESIDENT:

The undersigned Secretary of State, having received a resolution passed in the Senate of the United States on the 24th ultimo, in the following words—

Resolved, That the Secretary of State be, and he is hereby, requested to transmit to the Senate either in open or secret session as he may prefer, all the correspondence and reports of the consul-general of the United States at Habana relating to all American citizens now in prison in the Island of Cuba not previously reported on,

has the honor to lay before the President a report covering the correspondence requested in said resolution, to the end that, if in the President's judgment not incompatible with the public interest, the same be transmitted to the Senate in response to the foregoing resolution.

Respectfully submitted.

RICHARD OLNEY.

DEPARTMENT OF STATE,
Washington, March 1, 1897.

S. Doc. 231, pt 7——38

CORRESPONDENCE.

ARREST OF SYLVESTER SCOVEL.

1. Telegram, Mr. Lee to Mr. Rockhill, February 6, 1897.
2. Telegram, Mr. Olney to Mr. Lee, February 7, 1897.
3. Telegram, Mr. Rockhill to Mr. Lee, February 7, 1897.
4. Telegram, Mr. Lee to Mr. Olney, February 7, 1897.
5. Telegram, Mr. Lee to Mr. Rockhill, February 8, 1897.
6. Telegram, Mr. Lee to Mr. Rockhill, February 8, 1897.
7. Telegram, Mr. Lee to Mr. Rockhill, February 9, 1897.
8. No. 339, Mr. Lee to Mr. Rockhill, February 10, 1897.
9. Telegram, Mr. Lee to Mr. Rockhill, February 11, 1897.
10. No. 349, Mr. Lee to Mr. Rockhill, February 13, 1897.
11. Telegram, Mr. Lee to Mr. Rockhill, February 16, 1897.
12. No. 354, Mr. Lee to Mr. Rockhill, February 16, 1897.
13. Telegram, Mr. Lee to Mr. Rockhill, February 19, 1897.

ARREST OF CHARLES SCOTT.

1. Telegram, Mr. Lee to Mr. Rockhill, February 9, 1897.
2. Telegram, Mr. Lee to Mr. Rockhill, February 20, 1897.
3. Telegram, Mr. Lee to Mr. Olney, February 23, 1897.
4. Telegram, Mr. Lee to Mr. Olney, February 23, 1897.
5. Telegram, Mr. Lee to Mr. Olney, February 23, 1897.

ARREST OF F. J. CAZAÑAS.

1. Telegram, Mr. Lee to Mr. Olney, February 17, 1897.
2. Telegram, Mr. Rockhill to Mr. Lee, February 23, 1897.
3. Telegram, Mr. Lee to Mr. Rockhill, February 24, 1897.
4. Telegram, Mr. Rockhill to Mr. Lee, February 25, 1897.
5. Telegram, Mr. Lee to Mr. Rockhill, February 25, 1897.
6. Telegram, Mr. Rockhill to Mr. Lee, February 26, 1897.
7. Telegram, Mr. Lee to Mr. Rockhill, February 26, 1897.
8. Telegram, Mr. Lee to Mr. Rockhill, February 27, 1897.

ARREST OF SYLVESTER SCOVEL.

Mr. Lee to Mr. Rockhill.

[Telegram.]

HABANA, *February 6, 1897.*

Sylvester Scovel, World correspondent, arrested yesterday, Tunas, Santa Clara province.

LEE.

Mr. Olney to Mr. Lee.

[Telegram.]

DEPARTMENT OF STATE,
Washington, February 7, 1897.

See that all Scovel's rights as American citizen are protected. Report facts.

Mr. Rockhill to Mr. Lee.

[Telegram.]

DEPARTMENT OF STATE,
Washington, February 7, 1897.

In case Scovel use every exertion; no summary action taken. Great fear is entertained by friends on account previous expulsion from island. Endeavor to have prisoner brought Habana or nearest United States consulate.

Mr. Lee to Mr. Olney.

[Telegram]

HABANA, *February 7, 1897.*

Scovel will be sent here; think he was returning from an interview insurgent commander in chief. He is a splendid scout.

LEE.

Mr. Lee to Mr. Rockhill.

[Telegram.]

HABANA, *February 8, 1897.*

Expect Scovel here on Friday; do not anticipate serious trouble in his case.

LEE.

Mr. Lee to Mr. Rockhill.

[Telegram.]

HABANA, *February 8, 1897.*

Just seen acting captain-general. Scovel arrested on railroad between Sancti Spiritus and Tunas, Santa Clara Province, coming from insurgent camp. It is supposed he had criminating papers, which gives case more serious aspect. May have to be tried Sancti Spiritus. Am trying to get him sent here. Acting captain-general promises to do what he can in that direction.

LEE.

Mr. Lee to Mr. Rockhill.

[Telegram.]

HABANA, *February 9, 1897.*

Scovel's case has passed to civil jurisdiction Sancti Spiritus. Acting captain-general says he no longer has authority over it. Will send special messenger there, and will arrange to see that Article IV protocol be strictly complied with.

LEE.

Mr. Lee to Mr. Rockhill.

No. 339.]   UNITED STATES CONSULATE-GENERAL,
Habana, February 10, 1897.

SIR: As supplementary to my previous dispatch numbered 338, of yesterday's date, confirming, among others, six telegrams relative to the arrest of Sylvester Scovel, an American correspondent, near Tunas, I now have the honor to inclose copies of my communication to the acting captain-general asking that Scovel be brought to Habana, in compliance with the telegraphic instruction of the Department, and his answer thereto to the effect that Scovel's case had been referred to the civil courts in conformity with the treaty and protocol. Consequently I have addressed a note to the judge of Sancti Spiritus having cognizance of the case, asking that article 4 of the protocol of 1877 be strictly complied with.   I have made the same request to the acting captain-general.

To-morrow morning a delegate from me will leave for Sancti Spiritus, accompanied by a competent lawyer, to prepare Scovel's defense and see that his rights are protected.   I will advise the Department as soon as any further step is taken in the case.

I am, etc.,   FITZHUGH LEE.

———

[Inclosure 1 in No. 338.]

Mr. Lee to Acting Captain-General of Cuba.

UNITED STATES CONSULATE-GENERAL,
Habana, February 8, 1897.

EXCELLENCY: I have the honor to inform you that Mr. Sylvester Scovel, an American correspondent, has been arrested at Tunas, province of Santa Clara. In compliance with instructions from my Government, I beg your excellency will please instruct the military commandant of said place, or General Luque at Sancti Spiritus, or whatever officer it may correspond, to the end that Mr. Scovel be brought to this capital at the earliest convenience.

I am, etc.,   FITZHUGH LEE.

———

[Inclosure 2 in No. 338.]

Acting Captain-General to Mr. Lee.

[Translation.]

ARMY OF THE ISLAND OF CUBA,
Captaincy-General, Staff.

General Luque informs me by cablegram of the 5th instant that an American citizen, who said his name was Scovel, had been placed at the disposal of the civil jurisdiction; that the said person was arrested on the railroad track coming from the insurgent camp, and is supposed to be the same one referred to by you in your communication of to-day. Consequently, he is now beyond my authority.

I am, etc.,
                                    El Marques de AHUMADA.
HABANA, 8 February, 1897.

———

Mr. Lee to Mr. Rockhill.

[Telegram.]

HABANA, *February 11, 1897.*

Scovel in well-ventilated cell, good food, and bed at Sancti Spiritus. Treaty rights have been respected. Is in hands civil jurisdiction. I have sent messenger to report case.

LEE.

Mr. Lee to Mr. Rockhill.

No. 349.]   UNITED STATES CONSULATE-GENERAL,
                                    Habana, February 13, 1897.

SIR: I have the honor to inclose herewith a copy of a letter received from Mr. Sylvester Scovel, a correspondent of the New York World, recently arrested, and now in prison of Sancti Spiritus.

I am, etc.,

FITZHUGH LEE.

[Inclosure in No. 349.]

Mr. Sylvester Scovel to Mr. Lee.

                                    CARCEL OF SANCTI SPIRITUS,
                               Santa Clara, Cuba, February 8, 1897.

DEAR GENERAL: I have had the misfortune to be without a military pass and was apprehended and am now in prison for that reason. I wished to return to Habana and boarded the train for Tunas at the way station of Zaza. The lieutenant of the guardia civil guarding the train had been instructed by General Luque to look out for an "Ingles" without papers. He saw me, and as I unfortunately came under that category he took me into custody and later into jail. I cabled you the same night on arriving at Tunas (February 6) by permission of the very gentlemanly commandante of the port, but have received no answer.

Rafael Madrigal, the United States representative here, has also cabled and has done everything possible for my comfort. He should receive his credentials as soon as possible. He is a good man. All speak well of him.

I have been well treated and have now a well-ventilated cell, a bed, and good food. Who could want more—in prison?

As I don't see just how I have violated Spanish civil law, and as my case has been handed over to civil jurisdiction, I can't quite "figure out" what crime I have committed.

I made my declaration to the "judge of the first instance" yesterday afternoon, and he courteously immediately put me "in communication," so my rights have so far been respected, I fancy.

I frankly told the judge that I had gone into the field without let nor hindrance from any authority in the performance of my legitimate duties as war correspondent, and that I had never comported myself in any other manner.

I feel sure of your help. Remember me most kindly to your family, and believe me,

Yours, respectfully,   SYLVESTER SCOVEL.

Kindly acknowledge receipt.

                                                              SCOVEL.

Mr. Lee to Mr. Rockhill.

[Telegram.]

                                    HABANA, *February 16, 1897.*

Scovel's cell Sancti Spiritus large, clean; is provided with all comforts; more comfortable there than would be here; do not recommend his transfer now. Charged, first, rebellion for travelling in the country without military pass; second, possessing false pass; third, obtaining same; fourth, making use of same. Preliminary proceedings closed; date trial not fixed; no papers found on him, except notes eulogistic Spanish soldier.

LEE.

Mr. Lee to Mr. Rockhill.

No. 354.]   UNITED STATES CONSULATE-GENERAL,
                              Habana, February 16, 1897.

SIR: I have the honor to transmit herewith a copy of a teleg.am received from Tunas de Zaza, the cable station of Sancti Spiritus, referring to the case of Scovel.

I am, etc.,   FITZHUGH LEE,
                                          Consul-General.

[Inclosure No. 354.]

[Telegram.—Translation.]

TUNAS DE ZAZA. (Received Habana, February 15, 1897.)

LEE, *Consul-General, Habana:*

Scovel treated like a king; his cell in jail ample and clean; consular agent Madrigal providing him with all comforts; authorities courteous; preliminary proceedings concluded; charges: First, rebellion, for traveling in the country without a military pass; he attempted no act of rebellion; second, possessing a false cedula; third, obtaining same; fourth, making use of same. First charge preferred in the bando, declaring state of war. Preliminary proceedings. Leave Friday for Santa Clara. Scovel will remain here until date of trial is designated. I will arrive at Santa Clara to-morrow to activate matter, and thence by train to Habana. Only notes eulogizing the Spanish soldier were found on Scovel. I forward reports and documents, through Madrigal, by steamer leaving to-night.

Mr. Lee to Mr. Rockhill.

[Telegram.]

HABANA, *February 19, 1897.*

Competent lawyer obtained of Santa Clara to defend Scovel, who will remain at Sancti Spiritus until trial Santa Clara. Date not yet fixed.

LEE.

ARREST OF CHARLES SCOTT.

Mr. Lee to Mr. Rockhill.

[Telegram.]

HABANA, *February 9, 1897.*

Charles Scott, American citizen, arrested Regla this morning; charges not yet known.

Mr. Lee to Mr. Rockhill.

[Telegram.]

HABANA, *February 20, 1897.*

Charles Scott, a citizen of the United States, arrested Regla; no charge given. Been without communication, jail, Habana, two hundred and sixty-four hours. Can not stand another Ruiz murder and have demanded his release. How many war vessels Key West or within reach, and will they be ordered here at once if necessary to sustain demand?

LEE.

Mr. Lee to Mr. Olney.

[Telegram.]

HABANA, *February 23, 1897.*

Situation simple; experience at Guanabacoa made it my duty to demand before too late that another American who had been incomunicado two hundred and sixty-four hours, be released from said incomunicado, and did so in courteous terms. If you support it and Scott is so released the trouble will terminate. If you do not I must depart. All others arrested with Scott have been put in communication. . Why should only American in lot not be? He has been incomunicado now three hundred and thirty-eight hours.

LEE.

Mr. Lee to Mr. Olney.

[Telegram.]

HABANA, *February 23, 1897.*

Demand complied with. Scott is released from incomunicado.

LEE.

Mr. Lee to Mr. Olney.

[Telegram.]

HABANA, *February 23, 1897.*

Scott released from incomunicado to-day on demand, after fourteen days' solitary confinement in cell 5 feet by 11; damp; water on bottom cell. Not allowed anything to sleep on or chair; discharges of the body removed once five days. Was charged with having Cuban postage stamps in the house. Scott says went always twelve hours without water; once two days. He was employee American gas company.

LEE.

ARREST OF F. J. CAZAÑAS

Mr. Lee to Mr. Olney.

[Telegram.]

HABANA, *February 17, 1897.*

F. J. Cazañas, a citizen of the United States, arrested Sagua 13th. Report from consul forwarded by mail to-day. Proceedings a great outrage. Similar cases here and elsewhere on island. Redress can be obtained here.

LEE.

Mr. Rockhill to Mr. Lee.

[Telegram.]

WASHINGTON, *February 23, 1897.*

Barker dispatch, relative to Cazañas case, just received. Report upon whole case, facts as to naturalization and citizenship, and what you have done or are preparing to do.

ROCKHILL.

Mr. Lee to Mr. Rockhill.

[Telegram.]

HABANA, *February 24, 1897.*

Francis Cazañas registered here already; insisted his treaty rights should be respected. Captain-General replied two days ago. Facts in case are being ascertained. Sagua will report result.

LEE.

Mr. Rockhill to Mr. Lee.

[Telegram.]

DEPARTMENT OF STATE,
Washington, February 25, 1897.

In Cazañas case you must ascertain and report facts as to residence.

ROCKHILL.

Mr. Lee to Mr. Rockhill.

[Telegram.]

HABANA, *February 25, 1897.*

Cazañas resides Sagua since registration here 1872. See my cable yesterday.

LEE.

Mr. Rockhill to Mr. Lee.

[Telegram]

DEPARTMENT OF STATE,
February 26, 1897.

Cable copy entry in your registration book concerning Francis Cazañas. Give number of his passport.

ROCKHILL.

Mr. Lee to Mr. Rockhill.

[Telegram]

HABANA, *February 26, 1897.*

Copy entry October, 1872; number 414; Francis J. Cazañas; age 31; single; planter; domiciled Sagua; passport number, 18766; cedula issued November 5; number 5441.

LEE.

Mr. Lee to Mr. Rockhill.

[Telegram.]

HABANA, *February 27, 1897.*

Cazañas resided on plantation in Santa Clara Province until May last; since then resided in Sagua; owns property in New York.

LEE.

FIFTY-FIFTH CONGRESS, FIRST SESSION.

[Senate Document No. 47.]

Message from the President of the United States, transmitting, in response to Senate resolution of March 26, 1897, a report from the Secretary of State, with accompanying papers, relating to the arrest and imprisonment, at Santiago de Cuba, of the American citizens Gustave Richelieu and August Bolten.

April 20, 1897.—Referred to the Committee on Foreign Relations and ordered to be printed.

To the Senate of the United States:

In response to the resolution of the Senate of March 26, 1897, I transmit a report from the Secretary of State and accompanying papers relating to the arrest and imprisonment, at Santiago de Cuba, of the American citizens Gustave Richelieu and August Bolten.

WILLIAM McKINLEY.

EXECUTIVE MANSION,
 Washington, April 19, 1897.

The PRESIDENT:

The undersigned Secretary of State, in response to the resolution of the Senate of March 26, 1897, reading as follows:

That the President be, and is hereby, requested to furnish, if not incompatible with the public interests, for the use of the Senate, copies of all papers, correspondence, diplomatic or otherwise, on file in the Department of State, relating to and in connection with the arrest and imprisonment at Santiago de Cuba of the American citizens and sailors Richelieu and Bolton, excepting so much of the correspondence as is contained in House of Representatives Document No. 224, Fifty-fourth Congress, first session,

has the honor to submit for transmission to the Senate, if not deemed incompatible with the public interests, the correspondence on file in this Department relating to the arrest and imprisonment of Gustave Richelieu and August Bolten.

Respectfully submitted.

JOHN SHERMAN.

DEPARTMENT OF STATE,
 Washington, April 15, 1897.

List of papers.

Mr. Gordon to Mr. Olney, June 13, 1895.
Mr. Olney to Mr. Gordon, June 18, 1895.
Mr. Richelieu to Mr. Olney, September 26, 1895.
Mr. Gordon to Mr Olney, October 2, 1895.
Mr. Richelieu to Mr. Olney, October 3, 1895.
Mr. Olney to Mr. Gordon, November 1, 1895.
Mr. Olney to Mr. Richelieu, November 1, 1895.
Mr. Morse to Mr. Olney, November 8, 1895.
Mr. Gordon to Mr. Olney, December 27, 1895.
Mr. Adee to Mr. Morse, February 24, 1896.
Mr. Morse to Mr. Olney, March 11, 1896.
Mr. Olney to Mr. Gordon, March 18, 1896.
Mr. Olney to Mr. Taylor, No. 483, March 18, 1896.
Mr. Gordon to Mr. Olney, March 19, 1896.
Mr. Taylor to Mr. Olney, No. 499, April 4, 1896.
Mr. Morse to Mr. Olney, July 23, 1896.
Mr. Morse to Mr. Olney, August 18, 1896.
Mr. Adee to Mr. Morse, August 21, 1896.
Mr. Rockhill to Mr. Morse, August 31, 1896.
Mr. Rockhill to Mr. Taylor, No. 556, August 31, 1896.
Mr. Gordon to Mr. Olney, September 12, 1896.
Mr. Rockhill to Mr. Gordon, September 15, 1896.
Mr. Rockhill to Mr. Morse, September 29, 1896.
Mr. Taylor to Mr. Olney, No. 594, November 4, 1896.
Mr. Olney to Mr. Taylor, No. 603, November 10, 1896.
Mr. Olney to Mr. Morse, November 19, 1896.
Mr. Taylor to Mr. Olney, No. 608, November 21, 1896.
Mr. Morse to Mr. Olney, December 2, 1896.
Mr. Rockhill to Mr. Morse, December 3, 1896.
Mr. Olney to Mr. Morse, December 4, 1896.
Mr. Morse to Mr. Olney, December 19, 1896.
Mr. Olney to Mr. Taylor, No. 634, January 5, 1897.
Mr. Olney to Mr. Taylor, No. 637, January 6, 1897.
Mr. Coakley to Mr. Olney, January 27, 1897.
Mr. Morse to Mr. Olney, March 1, 1897.
Mr. Lodge to Mr. Sherman, March 8, 1897.
Mr. Taylor to Mr. Sherman, No. 660, March 9, 1897.
Mr. Rockhill to Mr. Morse, March 10, 1897.
Mr. Rockhill to Mr. Lodge, March 10, 1897.
Mr. Rockhill to Mr. Coakley, March 26, 1897.
Mr. Morse to Mr. Sherman, April 10, 1897.
Mr. Morse to Mr. Sherman, April 12, 1897.
Mr. Rockhill to Mr. Morse, April 14, 1897.

Mr. Gordon to Mr. Olney.

NEW YORK, *June 13, 1895.*

DEAR SIR: I inclose herewith and ask your careful consideration of the statement of facts of August Bolten, an American citizen, who was unlawfully and unjustly imprisoned for about two months in Santiago de Cuba. Annexed to the statement is Captain Bolten's certificate of naturalization.

I have talked with Bolten very fully, and believe him to be a man of excellent character. I am convinced that his statements are not in any way exaggerated.

Yours, very respectfully,   DAVID GORDON.

STATE OF NEW YORK, *City and County of New York, ss:*
August Bolten, being duly sworn, deposes and says:
I am a native of Sweden, but emigrated to the United States in the year 1874, being then under 18 years of age. I was duly naturalized a citizen of the United

States of America on the 6th day of March, 1893, by the court of common pleas for the city and county of New York. My occupation is that of seafaring man, and I have followed that occupation for over twenty years.

In the month of October, 1894, I left New York City as mate on the brigantine *Kathleen,* commanded by Capt. De La Croix, carrying a general cargo of merchandise and bound for Port au Prince, Haiti. We reached that port about the middle of November, 1894. My services ended there, and I was paid off at the British consulate, the brigantine having sailed under the British flag.

I then got work in Port au Prince as a painter, being somewhat familiar with that work by occasional experience, and kept at that until I saved sufficient money to buy a fishing boat, and on or about January 20, 1895, I purchased a 15-foot open boat. I intended to sail up to Cape Haitien and fish for green turtles. I engaged Gustave Richelieu, likewise a United States citizen, whom I met in Port au Prince, to go with me. I obtained from the United States consul at that port a certificate or passport for Cape Haitien, and on February 5, 1895, with said Richelieu, I left Port au Prince in my boat, heading for Cape Haitien. We sailed along the coast and had been out about three days (February 8) when a heavy gale struck us, tore our sail to shreds, and so otherwise damaged our boat that we made for the nearest shore, and so managed to reach the Haitien coast at a small place called Cape de la Bay. We landed, and were both immediately arrested by several soldiers and taken before an officer, apparently in command, who, after examining our papers, discharged us. We staid at that place—Cape de la Bay—about twenty-four hours, repaired our boat as best we could, got some provisions, and set out for St. Nicholas Mole, Haiti.

We arrived at the Mole on February 12, 1895. Our papers being for Cape Haitien, we were allowed to remain there (the Mole) long enough to get some provisions, and on the following day (February 13) we started for Cape Haitien. The wind and the current, both very strong, were against us, and we were carried out to sea. We drifted about three days, the last two days of which we had no food and but little drinking water. The Cuban coast was in sight and we made for the nearest port, which was Caimanera (known also as Alligator Bay), reaching there February 16. The captain of the port inspected our papers, looked over our boat, and, being satisfied that there was nothing against us, let us go about our business. We told him of our plight—that we had no provisions or money. He (the captain of the port) sent me to the United States consul at Guantanamo, about 15 miles inland. The consul kindly gave me $2, told me there was no work to be found there, and advised us to go to Santiago de Cuba as a place where we could more likely get work. And so on Wednesday, February 19, we set sail for that place and arrived on February 23.

We at once reported to the captain of the port. He examined our papers and questioned us through an interpreter fully as to our movements and as to who we were. We answered fully and freely, and explained to him the distressing circumstances which brought us to Cuba. Some conversation in Spanish, which we do not understand, followed between the captain and some other officers. They then searched our boat and our valises, but we had nothing of a suspicious nature. We asked to be directed to the United States consul. The captain sent along with us two guards, who, instead of accompanying us to the consul, as we requested and expected, took us to a prison. Here, against our urgent protests, we were immediately locked up. We had word sent to the United States consul, Dr. Pulaski F. Hyatt, who came to us soon thereafter and succeeded in getting our release. He took us to his office and gave us some supper. While there an officer called and informed the consul that it would be necessary to detain us in prison until news arrived from Port au Prince respecting us. After supper a servant of the consul escorted us to the prison, where we were again locked up.

The following day (Sunday, February 24), we had an examination before a military court, and were told that we would have to remain in prison until the last of March. The United States consul, Dr. Hyatt, was not present—we could not get word to him, and officers refused to notify him of the examination. We were then taken back to prison and separately confined. The room in which I was put was about 50 feet long by 30 feet broad; it was very filthy; it contained about twenty prisoners besides myself; they were men of the lowest description—thieves, ruffians, and murderers. For three weeks I was thus confined, never being let out for one minute during that time, although the other men in my room were allowed to exercise in the jail yard twice a week, and I afterwards learned that prisoners in the other cells were allowed to exercise daily in the jail yard. As a result of my close confinement, I was, at the end of the third week thereof, taken sick with fever and rheumatism. I was transferred to the prison hospital, which was some distance from the jail, and kept under medical care for about ten days. I was then declared to be well, and ordered back to prison. My arms were tied with a rope around my back, and although very weak and barely able to stand I was marched back to prison under a hot, blazing sun, escorted by two soldiers with drawn swords. I begged the jail officers to put me in some less unwholesome quarters than I was before, and they yielded to the extent of putting me in the same occupied by Richelieu, and I was allowed thereafter to exercise in the jail yard every day. While in the hospital I was informed that my case was transferred from the military court to a civil court. I was kept in jail till April 25, when I was released on condition that I should not leave town, and should report weekly to the judge. On May 3 I was told I could go where I liked.

While we were confined in prison, Dr. Hyatt came to see us about once a week, bringing us newspapers to read and food, and telling us that he was engaged all the time in efforts to secure our liberty.

On May 3, Dr. Hyatt got me a job on the schooner *Eliza Pendleton*, bound for New York, where I arrived on May 29.

I solemnly swear and declare that at no time during the times above mentioned, nor at any other time or place whatsoever, was I engaged in what is called a filibustering expedition against the Spanish Government, or any other government, nor did I ever in my life in any way take part in any revolutionary movement in Cuba or elsewhere.

I am still suffering physically from the effects of my prison experience in Santiago de Cuba. I have not recovered from the attack of rheumatism, which I fear has become chronic.

I learn to-day that Gustave Richelieu has just arrived at New York from the South. My certificate of naturalization is hereto annexed.

Wherefore deponent respectfully petitions for such relief as the facts above set forth shall be found to warrant.

AUGUST BOLTEN.

Subscribed and sworn to before me this 13th day of June, 1895.
[SEAL.]   HARRY E. STAM,
                                        Notary Public, Kings County.
(Certificate filed in New York County.)

DAVID GORDON,
Attorney for Bolten, 60 Wall Street, New York.

UNITED STATES OF AMERICA,
    State of New York, City and County of New York, ss:

Be it remembered that on the 6th day of March, in the year of our Lord 1893, August Bolten appeared in the court of common pleas for the city and county of New York (a court of record having common-law jurisdiction, a clerk, and seal) and applied to the said court to be admitted to become a citizen of the United States of America, pursuant to the provisions of the several acts of the Congress of the United States of America for that purpose made and provided; and the said applicant having produced to the said court such evidence, having made such declaration and renunciation, and having taken such oaths as are by the said acts required,

Thereupon it was ordered by the court that the said applicant be admitted, and he was accordingly admitted to be a citizen of the United States of America.

In testimony whereof the seal of the said court is hereunto affixed this 6th day of March, 1893, and in the one hundred and seventeenth year of the Independence of the United States.

Per curiam.
[SEAL.]   ALBERT WAGSTAFF, *Clerk.*

Mr. Olney to Mr. Gordon.

DEPARTMENT OF STATE,
Washington, June 18, 1895.

SIR: I have received your letter of the 13th instant inclosing the affidavit of Mr. August Bolten, a naturalized American citizen, who claims damages of Spain for unlawful imprisonment, lasting two months, imposed on him by the authorities at Santiago de Cuba.

I inclose a copy of the Department's circular relating to claims against foreign governments. If you will have the statement prepared in accordance therewith, it will be presented to the Spanish Government.

The Department, however, thinks it well to remind you that the revolutionary disturbances existing in the part of Cuba where Mr. Bolten and his companion landed and the not unreasonable suspicion of the authorities that 'they were in some way connected with a filibustering expedition or the landing of parties to aid the insurgents may render it difficult to procure pecuniary indemnity for him from the Spanish Government.

His naturalization paper is herewith returned.

I am, etc., RICHARD OLNEY.

[Translation.]

Mr. Richelieu to Mr. Olney.

WASHINGTON, D. C., *September 26, 1895.*

Mr. MINISTER: On the 8th February, 1895, I and my companion, August Bolten, left the port of Port au Prince, Haiti, for Cape Haitien, with our papers in order and a bill of lading, signed by the American legation. We stopped at St. Marc, where I had a duplicate passport viséd, about the 10th or 11th February. From there we sailed for our destination. We were caught in bad weather, and anchored in a small harbor, the name of which I have forgotten. The next evening we sailed again, and in bad weather arrived at St. P. Moole, where we had a very cold reception from the commandant of the port, who ordered us to take in our provisions and be off. We remained there, however, twenty-four hours. His telegraphic operators supplied us with provisions, and, thanks to them, we sailed on the 13th or 14th. The bad weather threw us on the Cuban coast, where we landed at Alligator Bay. It was a Saturday; the date may be found from an almanac. My friend, August Bolten, went up to Guantanamo with one of the officers of the port to see the American consul, who told him that we had better go to Santiago de Cuba, where we could find work or sell the boat. Bolten came back on Monday morning. We sailed immediately and reached that port on the 23d February. The navy commandant immediately had us arrested.

We appealed to the kindness of the American consul, who immediately protested on seeing that our papers were in order and on our telling him what had happened to us at Alligator Bay, which information was given to the Spanish authorities. This did not satisfy them, and the energetic protests of the consul had no effect. We consequently underwent, from the 23d February to the 25th April, sixty-two days of unhealthy imprisonment. Thanks to the kindness of Mr. George Eugene Brisson, the reporter of the New York Herald, we were protected from hunger My friend Bolten having succeeded in getting on board the American vessel *Templeton* (or *Pemberton*), I was left alone. Mr. Brisson, on the morning of the 11th May, told me to go on board the steamer *Niagara;* that he would come at 2 p. m. to deliver his mail and pay my passage. The Spanish authorities must have prevented him from coming, and as I sailed without a ticket, the mean captain landed me at Nassau, where Mr. Thomas J. McLain, the United States consul at Nassau, was so kind as to have me transported to Key West, paying $16.50 for my passage. From there I succeeded in reaching New York by the help of a friend. I am now, owing to the rheumatism which I contracted in the prison at Santiago, unable to resume my regular profession.

I have made America my adopted country. I have been a citizen since 1871. I have passed my life in this country. I have served the United States under the first present Administration. What I want is only a fair indemnity for sixty-two days of imprisonment and for the confiscation of our vessel.

Hoping, Mr. Minister, that you will kindly grant my petition, I am, your respectful servant,

GUSTAVE RICHELIEU,

(Care of John M. Perreard, 506 Fourteenth street NW.)

Mr. Gordon to Mr. Olney.

60 WALL STREET, NEW YORK,
October 2, 1895.

DEAR SIR: I have been in due receipt of your favor of June 18, 1895, acknowledging receipt of petition of Captain Bolten, making claim against the Spanish Government for unlawful imprisonment in Cuba. With your letter you inclosed a circular of instructions for filing claims against foreign governments, and you kindly advised the preparation of the petition or memorial in accordance with such instructions. This I have endeavored to do, and I inclose herewith the memorial so drawn, duly signed and verified.

Yours, very respectfully,   DAVID GORDON.

Memorial of August Bolten making claim against Government of Spain.

[David Gordon, attorney for August Bolten, 60 Wall street, New York City.]

NEW YORK, *September 30, 1895.*

His Excellency the Honorable GROVER CLEVELAND,
President of the United States of America:

I, August Bolten, memorializing and petitioning your excellency, respectfully show: I am a native of Sweden, but emigrated to the United States in the year 1874, being then under 18 years of age. I am now over 37 years of age. I was duly naturalized a citizen of the United States of America on the 6th day of March, 1893, by the court of common pleas for the city and county of New York. My occupation is that of seafaring man, and I have followed that occupation for over twenty years. I have remained such citizen of the United States ever since, having never transferred my allegiance to any other sovereignty. I now reside at No. 2 Ninth street in the city of Brooklyn, N. Y.

In the month of October, 1894, I left New York City as mate on the brigantine *Kathleen*, commanded by Captain De La Croix, carrying a general cargo of merchandise, and bound for Port au Prince, Haiti. We reached that port about the middle of November, 1894. My services ended there, and I was paid off at the British consulate, the brigantine having sailed under the British flag.

I then got work in Port au Prince as a painter (being somewhat familiar with that work by occasional experience) and kept at that until I saved sufficient money to buy a fishing boat; and on or about January 20, 1895, I purchased a 15-foot open boat. I intended to sail up to Cape Haitien and fish for green turtles. I engaged Gustave Richelieu, likewise a United States citizen, whom I met at Port au Prince, to go with me. I obtained from the United States consul at that port a certificate or passport for Cape Haitien, and on February 5, 1895, with said Richelieu, I left Port au Prince in my boat, heading for Cape Haitien. We sailed along the coast and had been out about three days (February 8), when a heavy gale struck us, tore our sails to shreds, and so otherwise damaged our boat that we made for the nearest shore and so managed to reach the Haitian coast at a small place called Cape de la Bay. We landed, and were both immediately arrested by several soldiers and taken before an officer apparently in command, who, after examining our papers, discharged us. We stayed at that place (Cape de la Bay) about twenty-four hours, repaired our boat as best we could, got some provisions, and set out for St. Nicholas Mole, Haiti.

We arrived at the Mole on February 12, 1895. Our papers being for Cape Haitien, we were allowed to remain there (the Mole) long enough to get some provisions, and on the following day (February 13) we started for Cape Haitien. The wind and the current, both very strong, were against us and we were carried out to sea. We drifted about three days, the last two days of which we had no food and but little drinking water. The Cuban coast was in sight, and we made for the nearest port, which was Caimanera (known also as Alligator Bay), reaching there February 16. The captain of the port inspected our papers, looked over our boat, and being satisfied that there was nothing against us, let us go about our business. We told him of our plight, that we had no provisions or money. He (captain of the port) sent me to the United States consulate at Guantanamo—about 15 miles inland. The consul kindly gave me $2, told me there was no work to be found there, and advised us to go to Santiago de Cuba as a place where we could more likely get work. And so, on Wednesday, February 19, we set sail for that place and arrived on February 23.

We at once reported to the captain of the port. He examined our papers and questioned us through an interpreter fully as to our movements, and as to who we were. We answered fully and freely, and explained to him the distressing circumstances which brought us to Cuba. Some conversation in Spanish, which we do not understand, followed between the captain and some other officers. They then searched our boat and our valises, but we had nothing of a suspicious nature. We asked to be directed to the United States consul. The captain sent along with us two guards, who, instead of accompanying us to the consul, as we requested and expected, took us to prison, where, against our urgent protests, we were immediately locked up. We had word sent to the United States consul, Dr. Pulaski F. Hyatt, who came to us soon thereafter and succeeded in getting our release. He took us to his office and gave us some supper. While there an officer called and informed the consul that it would be necessary to detain us in prison until the news arrived from Port au Prince respecting us. After supper a servant of the consul escorted us to prison, where we were again locked up. The following day (Sunday), February 24, we had an examination before a military court and were told we would have to remain in prison until the last of March.

The United States consul, Dr. Hyatt, was not present. We could not get word to him and officers refused to notify him of the examination. We were then taken back to prison and separately confined. The room in which I was put was about 50 feet long by 30 feet broad. It was very filthy. It contained about 20 prisoners beside myself. They were men of the lowest description—thieves, ruffians, and murderers. For three weeks I was thus confined, never being let out for one minute during that time, although the other men in my room were allowed to exercise in the jail yard twice a week, and I afterwards learned that prisoners in the other cells were allowed to exercise daily in the jail yard. As a result of my close confinement I was, at the end of the third week thereof, taken sick with fever and rheumatism. I was transferred to the prison hospital, which was some distance from the jail, and kept under medical care for about ten days. I was then declared to be well and ordered back to prison. My arms were tied with a rope around my back and, although very weak and barely able to stand, I was marched back to prison under a hot, blazing sun, escorted by two soldiers with drawn swords. I begged the jail officers to put me in some less unwholesome quarters than I was in, and they yielded to the extent of putting me in the same cell occupied by Richelieu, and I was allowed thereafter to exercise in the jail yard every day. While in the hospital I was informed that my case was transferred from the military court to a civil court. I was kept in jail till April 25, when I was released on condition that I should not leave town and should report weekly to the judge. On May 3 I was told I could go where I liked.

While we were confined in prison Dr. Hyatt came to see us about once a week, bringing us newspapers to read and food, and telling us that he was engaged all the time in efforts to secure our liberty

On May 3 Dr. Hyatt got me a job on the schooner *Eliza Pendleton*, bound for New York, where I arrived on May 29.

I solemnly swear and declare that at no time during the times above mentioned, nor at any other time or place whatsoever, was I engaged in what is called a filibustering expedition against the Spanish Government, or any other Government, nor did I ever in my life in any way take part in any revolutionary movement in Cuba or elsewhere.

I am still suffering physically from the effects of my prison experience in Santiago de Cuba. I have not recovered from the attack of rheumatism, which I fear has become chronic.

I learned lately that Gustave Richelieu arrived at New York from the South. Your petitioner verily believes he has been damaged to the extent of $10,000. Wherefore your petitioner prays for the interposition of the United States Government with the Government of Spain to the end that his claim aforesaid shall be presented to and paid by said Government of Spain. And your petitioner will ever pray.

AUGUST BOLTEN, *Petitioner.*

DAVID GORDON,

Attorney for August Bolten, 60 Wall street, New York.

NEW YORK, *September 30, 1895.*

STATE OF NEW YORK, *City and County of New York, ss:*

August Bolten, being duly sworn, deposes and says that he is the petitioner or memorialist named in the foregoing memorial or petition subscribed by him; that he has read the same and knows the contents thereof, and that the same is true of his own knowledge, except as to the matters therein stated to be alleged on information and belief, and that as to those matters he believes it to be true.

AUGUST BOLTEN.

Subscribed and sworn to before me this 30th day of September, 1895.

[SEAL.]   HARRY E. STAM,
                                          Notary Public, Kings County.

(Certificate filed in New York County.)

I, Harry E. Stam, the notary public who administered the oath to August Bolten, the petitioner above named, hereby certify and declare that I have no interest whatever in or to the claim above set forth, or any part thereof, and that I am not, nor have I ever been, the agent or attorney of said Bolten; and I believe said Bolten to be an honest and conscientious man and his statements to be worthy of faith and credit.

New York September 30, 1895.

[SEAL.]   HARRY E. STAM,
                                          Notary Public, Kings County.

(Certificate filed in New York County.)

Mr. Richelieu to Mr. Olney.

[Translation.]

WASHINGTON, *October 3, 1895.*

Mr. MINISTER OF STATE: The declaration which I wrote last week is the truth. I have not related the inward sufferings to which we were subjected in the prison; they are indescribable. We suffered from hunger; we slept on the floor without any covering; we were eaten by lice, fleas, and scorpions. I was compelled to exchange for bread the articles which I possessed. My friend August Bolten caught the yellow fever, and the doctor sent him to the hospital. As we were separated, I only learned it through an employee of the prison. The consul himself had not been informed of it. It was I that told him on Sunday when he came to see us, which he did at every mail that he received from Washington. We gave him a great deal of trouble, and he had warm discussions with the Spanish authorities, which you can read for yourself in his reports to the Department. I did not have the yellow fever myself, but I had fevers caught by the cold in sleeping on the floor. When I awoke I had chills, accompanied by fever, and from those sufferings I have caught rheumatism for the rest of my life. At times I am whole days without being able to move a limb. I am in that condition whenever the temperature changes.

I wish, therefore, to have a prompt and satisfactory settlement. If I had been a person of importance they would perhaps have been less cruel to me. When we left the prison they told us to go wherever we chose. That is why the consul advised us not to complain; that the Department at Washington would have our case settled.

When we arrived at Alligator Bay the consul at Guantanamo advised us to go to Santiago de Cuba, where it would be much easier for us to find a position. If we had done anything we would have been arrested. They would not have thought that we were going to Cuba, as we could have gone to Jamaica, which is only six hours' passage.

On the 25th April, when we left the prison, I went to see the judge of instruction to get my citizenship papers, which he had. He told me that as the record was in his court I would have to wait ten or fifteen days. The consul advised me not to wait; that he would give me a passport which would protect me and which would be entirely sufficient on presenting it at the ministry.

I desire the Minister of State to obtain a pecuniary indemnity for me from the Spanish authorities for all the outrages which I have undergone.

With this expectation I am, with the deepest respect,
Your very humble servant,
GUSTAVE RICHELIEU,
(Care of Mr. Alexander Porter Morse, 1505 Pennsylvania avenue.)

Sworn to and subscribed before me, a notary public, on this 3d day of October, A. D. 1895.
[SEAL.]
JESSE W. RAWLINGS,
Notary Public, District of Columbia.

Mr. Olney to Mr. Gordon.

DEPARTMENT OF STATE,
Washington, November 1, 1895.

SIR: I have received your letter of the 2d ultimo, transmitting the memorial of August Bolten, making claim against the Spanish Government for alleged unlawful imprisonment in Cuba.

The same will be given due consideration.
I am, etc.,
RICHARD OLNEY.

Mr. Olney to Mr. Richelieu.

DEPARTMENT OF STATE,
Washington, November 1, 1895.

SIR: Your communications of the 25th of September and 3d ultimo have been received, wherein you complain of unlawful imprisonment by the Cuban authorities and ask this Government to obtain an indemnity for you from the Spanish Government.

The matter will receive due consideration.
I am, sir, your obedient servant,
RICHARD OLNEY.

Mr. Morse to Mr. Olney.

NOVEMBER 8, 1895.

SIR: I have the honor to transmit herewith power of attorney from Gustave Richelieu in favor of John W. Douglass and Alexander Porter Morse, in prosecution of a claim by the said Richelieu for pecuniary indemnity against Spain for arbitrary arrest and false imprisonment, etc., by authorities of Spain at Santiago de Cuba, during a period of sixty-two days.

. Memorials on behalf of said Richelieu have heretofore been filed at the Department.
I am, etc.,
ALEXANDER PORTER MORSE.

S. Doc. 231, pt 7——39

Power of attorney.

Know all men by these presents:

That I, Gustave Richelieu, a native of France and a citizen of the United States by naturalization, resident in the city of Philadelphia, State of Pennsylvania, have made, constituted, and appointed, and by these presents do constitute and appoint John W. Douglass and Alexander Porter Morse my true and lawful attorneys, irrevocable, for me and in my name, place, and stead, hereby annulling and revoking all former powers of attorney or authorizations whatever in the premises, to present my claim against Spain for arrest and imprisonment by authorities of Spain at Santiago de Cuba, and for the seizure and appropriation of the sloop *Yankee Doodle* on the 23d of February, 1895, and to, from time to time, furnish any further evidence necessary or that may be demanded, giving and granting to my said attorneys full power and authority to do and perform all and every act and thing whatsoever requisite and necessary to be done in and about the premises as fully to all intents and purposes as I might or could do if personally present at the doing thereof, with full power of substitution and revocation, and to receipt and sign all vouchers, hereby ratifying and confirming all that my said attorneys or their substitute may or shall lawfully do or cause to be done by virtue hereof. And I hereby request that any certificates or drafts in payment thereof be sent to me, in care of my said attorneys.

In witness whereof I hereunto set my hand and seal this 23d day of September, 1895.

[SEAL.]   GUSTAVE RICHELIEU.

In presence of—
  G. M. PERREARD,
      506 and 508 Fourteenth street NW.

☞ Signature of claimant *must* be attested by two witnesses.

DISTRICT OF COLUMBIA, *ss:*

Be it known, that on this 23d day of September, in the year eighteen hundred and eighty-five, before me, the undersigned, a notary public in and for said District, personally appeared Gustave Richelieu, to me well known to be the identical person who executed the foregoing letter of attorney, and the same having been first fully read over to him and the contents thereof duly explained, acknowledged the same to be his act and deed, and that I have no interest, present or prospective, in the claim.

In testimony whereof I have hereunto set my hand and affixed my seal of office the day and year last above written.

[SEAL.]   THOS. B. HUYCK, *Notary Public.*

☞ If not acknowledged before the clerk of a court of record of the proper county under his seal of office, then clerk must certify to the official character and signature of the officer before whom this is executed.

Mr. Gordon to Mr. Olney.

60. WALL STREET, NEW YORK, *December 27, 1895.*

Will you kindly inform me what, if any, action has been taken by the State Department in the matter of the memorial of August Bolten, stating the fact of his arbitrary arrest and imprisonment in Cuba and praying for the interposition of our Government with the Government of Spain in his behalf?

Captain Bolten's affidavit was mailed to you June 13, 1895, and I had the honor of a response from you, acknowledging its receipt and suggesting that, if I embodied the affidavit in the shape of a memorial, in accordance with the rules of your Department, such memorial would be presented to the Spanish Government. This I did, and mailed a memorial to you on October 2, 1895, and had the like honor of a response acknowledging its receipt and assuring its being given due consideration.

I reiterate my belief in the merit of Captain Bolten's claim and in the truthfulness of his statements,

I should be pleased and thankful to learn what the present situation is.

Yours, very respectfully,   DAVID GORDON.

Mr. Adee to Mr. Morse.

DEPARTMENT OF STATE,
Washington, February 24, 1896.

SIR: I do not find, among the papers in the claim of Gustave Richelieu against the Government of Spain for imprisonment in Cuba, any evidence of the claimant's citizenship. In his power of attorney to you, which was filed in the Department under date of November 8, 1895, Mr. Richelieu claims to be a native of France and a citizen of the United States by naturalization. Our consul at Santiago de Cuba, in his report concerning Richelieu's imprisonment, speaks of him as a citizen of the United States, but before presenting the claim to the Imperial Government of Spain it will be necessary for Mr. Richelieu to file a certified copy of the record of his naturalization.

I am, etc.,

ALVEY A. ADEE,
Second Assistant Secretary.

Mr. Morse to Mr. Olney.

MARCH 11, 1896.

SIR: I am in receipt of a communication from the Department of State, informing me that the record of naturalization of Gustave Richelieu has not been filed, and asking that the same should be forwarded at once, so that the Department may proceed to take such steps on behalf of his associate (Bolten) and himself as it may deem proper. I have called upon Mr. Richelieu to forward this record, but up to this time it has not been received. Whatever is the cause of this delay, it seems to me that the presentation of the case of Mr. Bolten, whose papers are complete, should not longer be postponed.

The arbitrary arrest and long and harsh imprisonment of these individuals by the Spanish authorities at Santiago de Cuba seems to have been without cause or justification. The statement of the circumstances of their arrest and cruel treatment show a wanton outrage on the part of the Spanish authorities, which is fully confirmed by the dispatches of the United States consul at Santiago. These individuals appear to have been within the protection of the rule of international law which was laid down by Mr. Webster in the case of the *Creole*, and which was maintained by the umpire, Mr. Bates, in the decision before the Commission of Claims under the convention of February 8, 1853, between the United States and Great Britain.

Stress of weather and overruling necessity drove them into a Cuban port for shelter under circumstances which entitle them to the treatment which the comity, the courtesy, and the common sense of justice of all civilized states approves. So far as I am informed or the record discloses there was no probable cause for their arrest.

As Mr. Richelieu is moving from place to place, it is impossible to say when I will again hear from him; but so soon as he produces a copy of his record of naturalization, it will be forwarded to the Department.

I am, sir, your obedient servant,

ALEXANDER PORTER MORSE.

Mr. Olney to Mr. Gordon.

DEPARTMENT OF STATE,
Washington, March 18, 1896.

SIR: I have to acknowledge the receipt of your letter of December 27 last, and to say that the claim of Capt. August Bolten has been held to await the perfection of the claim of his companion and fellow sufferer, Gustave Richelieu, in the hope of presenting both claims together. As there appears, however, no immediate prospect of the complete establishment of Richelieu's right to the intervention of this Government, the claim of the former will now be forwarded alone, without further delay, to the United States minister at Madrid, for presentation to the Spanish Government.

I am, etc.,   RICHARD OLNEY.

———

Mr. Olney to Mr. Taylor.

No. 483.]   DEPARTMENT OF STATE,
Washington, March 18, 1896.

SIR: I inclose a copy of the memorial of August Bolten, a citizen of the United States, against the Government of Spain.   This memorial was filed in the Department by Mr. David Gordon, attorney for Bolten, October 2, 1895.   For your further information, I inclose you a copy of Executive Document No. 224, House of Representatives, Fifty-fourth Congress, first session, being a message from the President to the House of Representatives transmitting correspondence relative to affairs in Cuba.   Pages 111 to 133 of this pamphlet relate to the cause of Mr. Bolten's complaint, and contain the reports of our consular officers in Cuba in regard to the injury done him by the authorities in Cuba.

The facts as alleged by Mr. Bolten are, in brief, that in an endeavor to pass in a small open boat from one Haitian port to another around the northwestern point of that island, he was swept by the wind and current to the coast of Cuba.   Notwithstanding the facts that he was driven upon the coast of Cuba by stress of weather, and that he landed in a small open boat, a seaman in distress, with a single companion and no arms, papers, or other thing to excite suspicion of unlawful intent, he was seized by the military authorities February 23, 1895, and was not released from prison until May 3 following.   During, and it is believed as a result of, his imprisonment he contracted yellow fever and suffered much distress and injury to health in other respects, all growing out of the treatment received during his apparently unjust and uncalled for confinement.

Mr. Bolten asks for an indemnity of $10,000 from the Spanish Government for the injury inflicted upon him by the Spanish authorities in Cuba.

The seizure is believed to have been in violation of article 8 of the treaty of 1795, which provides for the hospitable reception of American citizens who through stress of weather are driven upon Spanish territory.   His arrest and the proceedings inaugurated against him by the military authorities are believed also to have been in violation of the protocol of January 12, 1877, which provides that citizens of the United States taken without arms in hand shall be tried by the ordinary civil tribunals, to the exclusion of any special tribunal, and when arrested and imprisoned shall be deemed to have been arrested or imprisoned by order of the civil authority. Mr. Bolten was held in arrest by the military authorities from February 23rd until the 21st of March, when by the action of the superior authorities of the island he was turned over, without being released, to the civil tribunal of the Province of Santiago. This tardy compliance with the treaty provisions seems not to have in any way benefited Mr. Bolten, as he was detained in the same prison without knowledge of the charges pending against him until his release, without trial, on May 3 following.

The correspondence with the consul at Santiago de Cuba indicates that there was a secret judicial inquiry or search for evidence against Mr. Bolten, and that he was released in consequence of a failure to obtain any evidence whatever to justify his arrest and imprisonment. You are directed to present this claim to the Spanish minister for foreign affairs, and ask that it may receive his early attention.

I am, etc.,

RICHARD OLNEY.

___

Mr. Gordon to Mr. Olney.

60 WALL STREET, NEW YORK, *March 19, 1896.*

DEAR SIR: I have to acknowledge the receipt of your favor of 18th instant conveying the intelligence of the prospective presentation of Capt. August Bolten's claim to the Spanish Government.

I thank you sincerely for the same.

Yours, very respectfully, DAVID GORDON.

___

Mr. Taylor to Mr. Olney.

No. 499.] LEGATION OF THE UNITED STATES,
Madrid, April 4, 1896.

SIR: I have the honor to acknowledge the receipt of your No. 483 of the 18th ultimo with inclosures relative to the case of Mr. August Bolten. According to your instructions, I have presented the case to the Spanish minister of state and asked that it may receive his early attention.

I am, etc., HANNIS TAYLOR.

___

Mr. Morse to Mr. Olney.

JULY 23, 1896.

SIR: I inclose herewith certificate of the declaration to become a citizen of the United States of Gustave Laymet, otherwise "Gustave Richelieu," together with explanatory affidavit of Gustave Richelieu, who heretofore, namely, on the 26th day of September and the 3d day of October, 1895, transmitted to the Department of State memorials setting forth his arbitrary arrest and imprisonment by authorities of Spain at Santiago de Cuba, and praying the intervention of the United States in securing from Spain pecuniary indemnity on account of such unlawful arrest and imprisonment.

I request that the inclosed papers be attached to the memorials filed,

with a view to their use in making a demand upon Spain for pecuniary
indemnity in favor of said Richelieu by reason of said unlawful arrest
and imprisonment by authorities of Spain in violation of international
law and treaty stipulations between Spain and the United States.
   I am, etc.,
                               ALEXANDER PORTER MORSE,
                                     Attorney for Gustave Richelieu.

   Personally appeared before me, Frank H. Mason, clerk of the United States district court within and for the district of Massachusetts, Gustave Richelieu, residing
at 109 D street, Boston, in said district, who, being duly sworn, deposes and says
that affiant is the identical individual who on the 26th day of September and the 3d
day of October, 1895, transmitted to the Department of State of the United States
of North America memorials setting forth his arbitrary arrest and imprisonment by
the authorities of Spain at Santiago de Cuba, at the dates and under the circumstances stated, and praying the intervention of the United States in securing pecuniary indemnity from Spain in redress and vindication of affiant's rights as a citizen
of the United States by naturalization; affiant reiterates the charges against Spain
on account of such arbitrary arrest without cause, and the cruel treatment inflicted
by Spain; and affiant further says that affiant declared his intention to become a
citizen of the United States before the United States district court at Portland, in
the State of Oregon, the 30th day of May, A. D. 1872, under the name and description of Gustave Laymet, and says that affiant is the identical individual whose certificate of such declaration is hereunto annexed and made part of this affidavit;
and affiant further says that "Laymet" was his father's name, and by that name he
was called and known until October, 1884, when affiant adopted the name of Gustave
Richelieu, "Richelieu" being the name of affiant's mother; affiant further says that
affiant has for more than *three* years been a seaman on board merchant vessels of the
United States and is entitled to protection as a citizen of the United States, and at
the time of the arbitrary arrest hereinbefore mentioned was pursuing affiant's occu-
pation as a seafaring man.
                                                     GUSTAVE RICHELIEU.
   Subscribed and sworn to by the above-named Gustave Richelieu before me, at
Boston, in said district of Massachusetts, this 22d day of July, A. D. 1896.
   [SEAL.]   FRANK H. MASON,
                 Clerk of United States District Court, District of Massachusetts,

----

                              Copy of declaration.

                          United States district court.

UNITED STATES OF AMERICA, *District of Oregon, ss:*
   I, Gustave Laymet, being first duly sworn, declare and say that it is bona fide my
intention to become a citizen of the United States of America, and to absolutely
and entirely renounce and abjure forever all allegiance and fidelity to every and any
foreign prince, potentate, State, or sovereignty whatever, and particularly to the
Government of France, of whom I am a subject.
                                                     GUSTAVE LAYMET.
   Subscribed and sworn to before me this 30th day of May, A. D. 1872.
                                             RALPH WILCOX, *Clerk.*

UNITED STATES OF AMERICA, *District of Oregon, ss:*
   I, E. D. McKee, clerk of the district court of the United States for the district of
Oregon, do hereby certify that the foregoing is a full, true, and correct copy of the
original declaration and oath of intention on file and remaining of record in my office.
   In testimony whereof I have hereunto subscribed my name and affixed the seal
of the said district court, at Portland, in said district, this 2d July, 1896.
   [SEAL.]   E. D. McKEE,
          Clerk of the District Court of the United States for the District of Oregon.

Mr. Morse to Mr. Olney.

WASHINGTON, D. C., *August 18, 1896.*

SIR: I have the honor to transmit herewith brief in support of the claim of Gustave Richelieu, seaman, against Spain for pecuniary indemnity on account of arbitrary arrest and imprisonment for sixty-two days by the administrative authorities at Santiago de Cuba. I also transmit an additional affidavit of the complainant, which has been forwarded to the undersigned to be filed with the papers heretofore submitted to the Department.

The official correspondence relating to the case of Richelieu and his companion, August Bolten, appears in Ex. Doc. No. 224, Fifty-fourth Congress, first session, pages 111–134, and discloses a case of cruel treatment of two suffering seamen, who, at the time of the occurrences complained of, were entitled to the protection of the United States, and were by the law of nations and treaty stipulations exempt from apprehension by Spain.

On behalf of complainants the intervention of the Government is solicited, in order that such redress may be obtained as the ends of justice and the exigency of the case demand.

I am, sir, your obedient servant,

ALEXANDER PORTER MORSE.

Affidavit.

During the first week in October, 1893, I left Philadelphia for the purpose of shipping at Wilmington, N. C., on board of the schooner *Orlando*, belonging to the firm of Green & Co., of Boston, bound to Port au Prince, Haiti, * * * at St. Marc, a small town situated at a distance of 25 miles,· * * * where the vessel loaded with logwood for New York. Being somewhat unwell, I applied for my discharge. I had contracted an intermittent fever at Wilmington. After landing I called on Mr. Miot, the American consular agent. I next proceeded to Port au Prince, where I established a modern restaurant at No. 15 rue Americaine, Port au Prince, the capital of the Republic. I gave up the restaurant in the month of July, 1894, and Dr. Terrestre (Terres?), the consul, settled up my affairs for me.

Minister Smythe was then on leave of absence, and during his leave lost his wife. From that time until the month of February, 1895, I had charge of the business of Raphael Agramonte, Nos. 9 and 11 rue des Cesars, Port au Prince. There I made the acquaintance of August Bolten, who had landed from the brig *Katheline*. He worked for the minister in charge of the Episcopal church, and that minister made us a present of the boat. We fixed it up and repaired it, and made a new sail for it. That minister, moreover, wrote to the consul at Santiago, who came to see while we were in prison at Santiago and told us that that letter had stupefied the Spanish authorities, and that their whole intrigue was broken up. I think that that letter must be at the Department.

When we left Port au Prince we had our clearance from the legation, countersigned by the commandant of the place, for the Cape. This proves that we had no dealings with the insurgents as we have been suspected of having.

We wished to engage in turtle catching, each turtle-shell being worth $11, undressed, and we were encouraged to do so by a merchant, who told us that he would take all that we could get.

If the wind had not driven us onto the coast of Cuba we should still be at the Cape, and I should, I dare say, be in a better pecuniary situation than I now am.

We had no arms and had lost our mast, sail, and ropes, our boat having capsized. We were, moreover, entirely out of provisions when we reached Alligator Bay. That was the third day that we had been without food.

The examining judge having telegraphed to Mole St. Nicholas, became convinced that we had left without any other person with us and without any arms. When we were arrested I told the commandant that if he would telegraph at once he would be convinced; he paid no attention to this, however, but, after we had been turned over to the civil authorities, the examining magistrate, who is a perfect gentleman, had the kindness to listen to us, telegraphed, and was convinced in forty-eight hours that we were innocent. The others might have become convinced of our innocence, but they were not willing to take time to do so, notwithstanding the energetic protests of the consul. They kept us in confinement for sixty-two days. I trust that the record kept by the consul gives more specific details of all the trouble that the Department had to get us out of that prison.

I contracted pains in that prison which I shall have for the rest of my life, and am troubled with a great lack of energy. If I had been a British or a German subject I should certainly have had redress. John Bull is prouder than Uncle Sam.

Now, I came to America in 1865, and made a declaration of my intention to become an American citizen in 1872 at Portland, Oreg. I worked for the American Government in 1884 as a steward on board of the survey schooner *Eagle*.

The first American vessel on which I shipped was the bark *Roswell*, Captain Sawyer, of Boston, Mass. I shipped on board of this vessel at Portland, Oreg., in 1872. We lost eight men off Cape Horn, who were washed overboard by a heavy sea. We afterwards put into Valparaiso, Chile. I there shipped on board of the *Governor Langdon*, of Boston, bound to Iquique, Peru, where she was to take in a cargo of nitrate for Hamburg. In 1876 I shipped on board of the *G. B. Boland*, of New York, Captain Baker, which was bound to Cadiz, Spain, to get a cargo of salt for Gloucester, Mass. Since then I have always remained on shore or made voyages to the West Indies to get sugar and molasses. I made these voyages on board of the following vessels: .

Brig *Rocky Glen*, Captain Bray; schooner *Jennie Logwood* (*Lockwood?*), Captain Thomas; schooner *Sarah Lawrence*, Captain Faro; schooner *Raymond T. Maul*, Captain Smith; schooner *Lizzie Young*, Captain Pierce; brig *Daisy Boyton*, Captain Harding.

In 1892 or 1893 I shipped on board of the barkentine *Francis*, of Baltimore, for Brazil. I have also been employed on board of several vessels, the names of whose captains I have forgotten. I have been employed on board of American vessels for twenty years. The year that I was on board of the United States schooner *Eagle* was the year when Mr. Cleveland was first elected. The name of Gustave Laymet will be easily found among the records of the administrative surveys. During that same year I lost my family and took the name of Gustave Richelieu.

GUSTAVE RICHELIEU.

UNITED STATES DISTRICT COURT, *District of Massachusetts, ss:*

.   BOSTON, *July 30, 1896.*

Then appeared the above-named Gustave Richelieu and made oath before me that the foregoing statements by him subscribed by him are true.

[SEAL.]   FRANK H. MASON, *Clerk.*

———

Before the Department of State. In the matter of the claim of Gustave Richelieu against Spain on account of arbitrary arrest and imprisonment.

Brief on behalf of complainant.

STATEMENT OF CASE.

The complainant, a citizen by birth of France, came to the United States in 1865, and has resided in the United States since that date. On the 30th day of May, 1872, in the city of Portland, State of Oregon, and under the name of Gustave Laymet, he declared his intention to become a citizen of the United States. (Certificate of the clerk of the United States district court; affidavit of complainant.)

Subsequent to such declaration he has served as seaman or steward on American merchant vessels for more than twenty years. A portion of this service was as steward on the Government survey schooner *Eagre.* (Additional affidavit of complainant.) In 1893 he embarked at the port of Wilmington, N. C., on the schooner *Orlando*, belonging to the American firm of Green & Co., of Boston, destined for Port au Prince, Haiti, where she went to take a cargo of Campeachy wood for New York. Having been taken ill with fever at Port au Prince, he secured his discharge, and for some time remained at the last-mentioned port engaged in keeping a restaurant. Here he made the acquaintance of August Bolten, a citizen by naturalization of the United States, who had been discharged from the brig *Katheline.* Having concluded to enter together upon the adventure of turtle fishing, they, with the assistance of the minister of the English Episcopal Church, secured a small fishing smack and started upon their voyage in search of turtles. On the 8th of February, 1895, they sailed from the port of Port au Prince for Cape Haitien with regular papers issued from the American consulate, identifying them and recognizing their

American citizenship. (Memorials of Bolten and Richelieu, Ex. Doc. 224, Fifty-fourth Congress. first session, pp. 112, 113, 118, 119.)

Stress of weather disabled their boat so seriously that they put into a small port called Cape de la Bay. Here they were arrested by soldiers, who carried them before an officer, who, after examining their papers, released them. At this port they remained twenty-four hours, repaired the boat as best they could, and proceeded to St. Nicholas Mole, Haiti, where they remained one day. On the 13th of February, 1895, they set sail for Cape Haitien, but wind and current being against them, and very strong, they were driven out to sea. After drifting about for three days. two of which they were without food and with but little drinking water, they came within sight of the Cuban coast and made for the nearest port, which proved to be Caimanera, known as Alligator Bay, which they reached on the 16th of February. Here their papers were inspected by the captain of the port and by the United States consul at Guantanamo, who gave them some aid and advised them to sail for Santiago de Cuba. Accordingly, on the 19th of February, they set sail for that port and arrived on the 23d of February, when they at once reported to the captain of the port, who instituted an examination of boat and baggage. They asked to be conducted to the office of the United States consul, but instead of being directed there they were sent under guard to prison, notwithstanding their earnest protest. Here they were confined in a loathsome prison, in company of the lowest description of criminals, for sixty-two days, under circumstances of indignity and outrage on the part of the Spanish authorities, which are detailed in the memorials on file in the Department of State. The United States consul made earnest and repeated efforts to secure their release, but his efforts were of no avail until after the lapse of the long imprisonment mentioned. The complainants have consistently protested that neither during the times mentioned, nor at any other time or place, have they engaged in what is called a filibustering expedition against the Spanish Government, nor have they in any way taken part in any revolutionary movement in Cuba or elsewhere; and no testimony or proof was produced by Spain during their long imprisonment showing or tending to show that they had at any time or place engaged in such unlawful acts.

The case in brief is this: A fishing smack, bound from one Haytien port to another, bearing two half-starved seamen entitled to the protection of the United States, is forced by stress of weather and lack of food into a Cuban port. They at once report to the captain of the port, produce their papers for inspection, explain their distressing situation, and request to be directed to the United States consul. Instead of complying with this request their boat was seized and, without arraignment or service of judicial process, they were placed under guard, conveyed to prison, and locked up. (Memorials of Bolten and Richelieu, pp. 1 and 2. Ex. Doc. No. 224, Fifty-fourth Congress, first session, p. 113.) The boat carried no cargo or passengers—indeed, there was no accommodation for either, and there was no mystery or concealment in their movements. Upon being informed of their arrest, the United States consul promptly went to the prison, interviewed them, and being satisfied with the truth of their representations, secured their release. The next day, while at the United States consulate. they were rearrested upon a fictitious charge, which was equally flimsy and groundless as that upon which they were first apprehended. (Ex. Doc. No. 224, Fifty-fourth Congress, first session, p. 113.) They were then conveyed to a loathsome prison, where they were subject to cruel treatment, and held for sixty-two days, notwithstanding the earnest and repeated remonstrances of the accredited representatives of the United States. (Ib., pp. 113–133.—Memorials of Bolten and Richelieu.)

One of these, Bolten, was a naturalized citizen of the United States; and a demand for pecuniary indemnity in the sum of $10,000 on account of arrest and false imprisonment has been submitted to Spain. The present brief is submitted in behalf of his associate, Richelieu.

I.

The preliminary question which arises upon this state of facts is:

Is the complainant Richelieu entitled to the protection of the United States as against Spain?

On behalf of the complainant it is respectfully submitted that he is, upon two grounds: First, by reason of his declaration to become a citizen of the United States, and the acquisition of domicile therein; and, second, by reason of his service for more than twenty years as seaman on board merchant vessels of the United States after his declaration to become a citizen.

1. As against a third power, complainant has "a quasi-right to protection" after he has declared his intention to become a citizen.

(Secretary of State Frelinghuysen to Mr. Wallace, Foreign Relations of the United

States, pp. 552, 560; Secretary Bayard's Instructions to Diplomatic Agents of the United States, 1885; Wharton, Int. Dig., sec. 198.) A question as to status or citizenship arising in the United States is determinable by our law.

The questions: Who are citizens, on what conditions are persons admitted to citizenship, are questions of constitutional law which each State determines for itself. And so as to protection and allegiance. (Opinions of Attorney-General, vol. 12, p. 319.)

By act of Congress, March 3, 1863 (12 Stat. L., p. 731), aliens who had made a declaration of intention to become citizens were made subject to the military draft.

If the status of alien-born residents in respect to the country of adoption warrants their being drafted into the service of the State, after declaration of intention, consistency and justice would seem to require that while in this inchoate state of citizenship they should receive protection from outrage and indignity at the hands of an offending State, particularly if such State is not the State of origin.

It is not, however, necessary to claim that the mere declaration to become a citizen changed the nationality of complainant; but such declaration, together with an established domicile extending over a long period of years, did entitle him to demand the protection of the United States.

A person domiciled in the United States is entitled "to our care and consideration, and in most circumstances may be regarded as under our protection." (Mr. Marcy, Secretary of State, to Mr. Buchanan, March 17, 1854. MSS. Inst., Gr. Brit., Wharton, Dig., sec. 198.) By the personal instructions of the Department of State, issued by Mr. Bayard, Secretary of State, in 1885, in section 118 it is provided that "nothing herein contained is to be construed as in any way abridging the right of persons domiciled in the United States, but not naturalized therein, to maintain internationally their status of domicile, and to claim protection from this Government in the maintenance of such status." (Wharton, Int. Dig., sec. 198.)

"The rights which spring from domicile in the United States, especially when coupled with a declaration of intention to become a citizen, are worthy of definition by statute. The stranger coming hither with intent to remain, establishing his residence in our midst, contributing to the general welfare, and by his voluntary act declaring his purpose to assume the responsibilities of citizenship, thereby gains an inchoate status which legislation may properly define." (President Cleveland, First Annual Message, 1885.)

It will be observed that in the opinion of President Cleveland the right exists, and it is desirable that it should be defined by appropriate legislation.

2. By reason of his service as seaman on board a vessel of the United States, forced by stress of weather into a Spanish port, complainant is entitled to the protection of the United States against Spain.

Whatever difference of opinion there may be as to the extent of the protection which an alien who has declared his intention to become a citizen of the United States, and has established a domicile therein, may properly claim from the United States, it would seem to be clear that an alien who has declared his intention to become a citizen, and has served as seaman on board merchant vessels of the United States for more than twenty years, and who, being forced into a Spanish port on a vessel of the United States, and is arbitrarily arrested and imprisoned by Spanish administrative authorities, is in a situation to appeal to the United States for redress.

Such a case seems to be covered by the express provisions of section 29, act of June, 1872 (Stat. L., vol. 17, p. 268), and of the treaty of 1795 between Spain and the United States, Articles VI, VII, and VIII.

Section 29 of the act of June 7, 1872, is carried into the Revised Statutes of the United States under the title "Naturalization," section 2174, although it is not in a strict sense a "naturalization" statute. But it is a provision "for the further protection of seamen." The act of June 7, 1872, was entitled "An act to authorize the appointment of shipping commissioners by the several circuit courts of the United States, to superintend the shipping and discharge of seamen engaged in merchant ships belonging to the United States, and for the further protection of seamen."

This legislation was the result of a comprehensive scheme for the orderly regulation of American shipping interests and for the betterment and protection of seamen engaged on American ships. It had in view the very condition and circumstances developed in this case; and the concluding clause of the section applies exactly to the case in hand.*

---

* "Every seaman, being a foreigner, who declares his intention of becoming a citizen of the United States in any competent court, and shall have served three years on board of a merchant vessel of the United States subsequent to the date of such declaration, may, on his application to any competent court, and the production of his certificate of his declaration, discharge, and good conduct during that time, together with the certificate of his declaration to become a citizen, be admitted

It is a matter of general knowledge that a large proportion of the seamen on American vessels are foreign born, and it was to encourage them to become citizens that exceptional and attractive provisions were enacted which facilitated the acquisition of American citizenship and extended the protection of the flag over them from the first step taken to change their national character.

A wise policy and the commercial character of the nation has naturally made the United States jealous in the protection of its seamen and prompt in the vindication of their rights wherever and by whomsoever assailed. "Trade follows the flag" is a maxim of commerce; but there can be no commerce without freedom alike for ships and crew. "Free trade and sailor's rights" was the rallying cry of an eventful political campaign. And the war, which is sometimes said to have supplemented the American Revolution, was waged to assure protection to those who, on the high seas as elsewhere, were under the protecting folds of the American flag.

The first clause of the section admits the foreigner who shall have declared his intention and shall have served three years on board a merchant vessel of the United States to citizenship The second clause provides that the foreigner, after such declaration and such service, shall be deemed a citizen for the purpose of manning and serving on board any merchant vessel of the United States, anything to the contrary in any act of Congress notwithstanding. And the third clause—with the interpretation of which we are immediately concerned—provides that "such seaman shall, for all purposes of protection as an American citizen, be deemed such, after the filing of his declaration of intention to become such citizen."

The language of the third clause is so plain and explicit that it does not need interpretation And the only question for determination here is: Does the complainant bring himself within its provisions? It is respectfully submitted that he does; and that for all purposes of protection and redress he is to be deemed an American citizen at the time of the injuries complained of. It can not be difficult to determine to what extent the Government should go in demanding redress from a foreign Government in the case of an American citizen who has been the victim of similar treatment under corresponding circumstances. Assuming that Richelieu has made out his right to invoke the aid of the United States in obtaining pecuniary indemnity from Spain on account of the grievances complained of, we proceed to a consideration of the merits of the case as established by the record.

II.

Neither at the time of their first apprehension nor on the occasion of their rearrest were complainants amenable to the jurisdiction of the authorities of Spain.*

The apprehension and confinement of complainants and the seizure of their smack was in direct violation of the guaranties contained in Article VIII of the treaty of 1795 (Treaties and Conventions between the United States and other Powers, pp. 1008, 1009). By the express language of this article the jurisdiction of the local sovereign was waived and suspended in respect of storm or distress driven vessels, subjects, and inhabitants; and the United States consul was entirely justified in his statement that the complainants were "subject to the provisions contained in Article VIII of the treaty." (Ex. Doc. 224, Fifty-fourth Congress, first session, p. 116.)

When first apprehended they were on their way to the United States consulate to report their situation, in compliance with custom, the law of nations, treaty stipulations, and the laws of the United States; and when rearrested they were actually within the consulate. (Memorial of Bolten, p. 3; Ex. Doc. No. 224, Fifty-fourth

a citizen of the United States; and every seaman, being a foreigner, shall, after his declaration to become a citizen of the United States. and after he shall have served such three years, be deemed a citizen of the United States for the purpose of manning and serving on board any merchant vessel of the United States, anything to the contrary in any act of Congress notwithstanding; but such seaman shall, for all purposes of protection as an American citizen, be deemed such, after the filing of his declaration of intention to become such citizen."

* "In case the subjects and inhabitants of either party, with their shipping, whether public or of war, or private or of merchants, be forced, through stress of weather, pursuit of pirates or enemies, or any other urgent necessity, for seeking of shelter and harbor, to retreat and enter into any of the rivers, bays, roads, or ports belonging to the other party, they shall be received and treated with all humanity, and enjoy all favor and protection and help, and they shall be permitted to refresh and provide themselves. at reasonable rates, with victuals and all things needful for the sustenance of their persons or reparation of their ships and prosecution of their voyage; and they shall in no way be hindered from returning out of said ports or roads, but may depart when and whither they please, without any let or hindrance." (Art. VIII, treaty 1795.)

Congress, first session, p. 113; act of Congress, 28th May, 1796, sec 4.) The section here referred to requires the master of every vessel of the United States, any of the crew whereof shall have been impressed or detained by any foreign power, to report at the first port at which such vessel arrives, if such impressment or detention happened on the high seas or if the same happened within any foreign port, then in the port in which the same happened, and immediately make protest, stating the manner of such impressment or detention, by whom made, together with the name and place of residence of the person impressed or detained; distinguishing also whether he was an American citizen; and if not, to what nation he belonged. (Rev. Stats. U. S., p. 889, sec. 4589.) Persons in this situation are within the express conditions of Article VIII of the treaty of 1795, and as such were exempt from the civil or military jurisdiction of the local authorities. A representation of the facts which brought complainants within these conditions was made to the captain of the port immediately on landing, and was repeated to the civil and military authorities of Spain. (Memorial of Bolten, p. 3; Ex. Doc. 224, Fifty-fourth Congress, first session, p. 113 et seq.)

The truth and accuracy of the statements of complainants have not been impeached in any material respect. But the Spanish authorities in Cuba wantonly disregarded the law of nations, the treaty stipulations, and the protests of the Department of State, communicated through the consul-general and the consul. It is clear that it was not ignorance of the obligations which the law of nations and the treaty stipulations imposed upon Spain in respect of individuals situated as were the complainants, but it was a vindictive purpose on the part of the authorities to torture these unfortunate and destitute seamen as long as it was possible to do so in defiance of the United States.

Article XIX of the treaty of 1795 provides that "consuls shall be reciprocally established, with the privileges and powers which those of the most favored nations enjoy, in the ports where their consuls reside or are permitted to be." And the consular convention of February 22, 1870, between Spain and the North German Confederation contains articles exempting storm-driven vessels from local jurisdiction, and specifies the functions and privileges of consuls, vice-consuls, and consular agents. (Martens, Receuil General de Traites et autres actes relatives aux rapports de droit international, Tome XIX, p. 21, et seq.) Under the most-favored-nation clause United States consuls in Spain exercise corresponding functions, and are entitled to like jurisdiction.

The outrage which the administrative authorities of Spain at Santiago de Cuba inflicted upon complainants in violation of the law of nations, treaty stipulations, and the laws of humanity, constitutes an offense against the United States and is an indignity to the flag which covered them. The arrest of complainants seems to have been made without any sufficient ground or proof that can excuse or palliate the arbitrary action of the authorities, while their subjection to unusual cruel treatment and long imprisonment, notwithstanding the evidences of their innocent occupation furnished almost immediately after arrest by the United States consul and others, indicates a studied purpose to inflict punishment upon two American seamen whom misfortune had placed in their power, regardless of guilt or innocence. All the circumstances of arrest and imprisonment on the part of the authorities, subaltern and superior, point to a lack of good faith and honest action. Two days after arrest the United States consul advised the comandancia that complainants were entitled to protection as citizens of the United States; that their papers were in regular form; and that their presence in Santiago was due to stress of weather and misfortune. And in a few days abundant proof of the truth of their story was forthcoming. (Ex. Doc. No. 224, Fifty-fourth Congress, first session, pp. 113, 116 128, and 129.)

On the 13th of April, 1895, the United States consul advised the Department of State as follows: "There have been no definite charges, no release, and the men have been imprisoned seven weeks to-day, and I can see no reasonable ground to expect a speedy trial." (Ib., p. 123.)

The excuse given for the rearrest of complainants was stated to be that "the comandancia had received word that the men had left Guantanamo without a permit." This reason for arrest appears to have been an afterthought of the authorities. If it were true, the omission was not an offense which justified the harsh treatment to which they were subjected. Guantanamo, like Santiago, was a harbor of refuge, and not a port of destination or departure. "This charge," wrote the United States consul, "is admitted to be no more than a pretext for continued imprisonment." (Ex. Doc. No. 224, Fifty-fourth Congress, first session, p. 112.) Subsequent events proved the correctness of this declaration of the consul. (Ib., pp. 112 and 133.) At a date not stated, but which was prior to May 4, 1895, General Salcedo, civil governor, announced to the correspondent of the United Press, "that the Government found the men absolutely innocent." (Ib., ib., p. 130.)

The papers in their possession fully substantiated their story and were sufficient to entitle them to full protection. (Ex. Doc. No. 224, Fifty-fourth Congress, first session, pp. 111-120.)

Whether or not complainants had a sufficient or regular clearance from Port au Prince was no concern of the Spanish authorities at Santiago de Cuba. Both the port of departure (Port au Prince) and the port of destination (Cape Haytien) were outside the jurisdiction of Spain. As the United States consul has pointed out, this was a mere pretext by which it was sought to excuse arbitrary acts and to justify procrastination on the part of the local authorities. The voyage contemplated did not even include any Cuban port as a port of call. It was stress of weather and lack of food that carried complainants against their will into Cuban harbors.

In view of the whole record it is impossible to resist the conclusion that the shifting charges were gotten up by the authorities to meet recurrent emergencies, were fictitious, and were known to be so when made. The holding of the complainants by the "military officials" for more than a month and their subsequent transfer to the "civil authorities" under the circumstances has all the appearance of a scheme to harry and persecute these unfortunate seamen. The fact that they were recognized as citizens of the United States seemed to militate against them and not in their favor. These authorities were fertile in originating charges, for it appears that the supposed act of the United States consul in furnishing complainants with American newspapers containing a picture of José Marti, a Cuban revolutionist, constituted an offense which was to be imputed to the men under arrest. But treatment of this character of American citizens and American interests in the island of Cuba has been going on for forty years, and, as the archives of the Department abundantly testify, the forbearance of the Government of the United States has been met by the persistent and continuous spoliation and outrage of its citizens. (Mr. Fish, Secretary of State, to Mr. Lopez Roberts, December 28, 1870, cited in Wharton's Int. Dig., vol. 3, p. 3402; Proceedings of the United States and Spanish Claims Commission, under agreement February 12, 1871; Ex. Doc. 224, Fifty-fourth Congress, first session.)

The sole subject of inquiry to which the authorities might have properly or rightfully addressed themselves was, Did the apparent facts bring complainants within the conditions of Article VIII, treaty of 1795?

That they did the local authorities had the evidence of their own eyes, the uncontradicted statement of complainants, and the assurance of the United States consul, which was almost immediately confirmed, and which, in default of proof to the contrary, should have been accepted as conclusive.

III.

Having been forced through stress of weather and urgent necessity into a Cuban port while navigating an American fishing smack, complainant and his associate, August Bolten, were exempted from officious and arbitrary interference of the local Spanish authorities by the law of nations and by stipulations of the treaty of 1795 between Spain and the United States.

THE LAW OF NATIONS.

This immunity from local jurisdiction of vessels, crew, and passengers, driven into a foreign port through stress of weather or urgent necessity, was forcibly stated by Mr. Webster in the correspondence with Lord Ashburton in the case of the *Creole*; and the rule of law and the comity and practice of nations is well established by authority.

"A vessel driven by stress of weather has a right to enter, even by force, into a foreign port." (Vattel, Book 2, ch. 9, sec. 123; Puffendorf, Book 3, ch. 3, sec. 8.)

A vessel compelled by stress of weather or other unavoidable necessity has a right to seek shelter in any harbor, as incident to her right to navigate the ocean, until the danger is past, and she can proceed again in safety.

The effect of stress of weather in exempting vessels from liability to local law, when they are driven by it within the ordinary jurisdiction of a foreign state, is well settled by authority in various classes of cases, viz, in reference to the blockade of harbors and coasts; of prohibited intercourse of vessels between certain ports that are subject to quarantine regulations; intercourse between certain countries or sections of countries which is interdicted from motives of mercantile policy; and in cases of liability to general custom duties. (The *Frederick Molkel*, Rob. Rep., 87; The *Columbia*, ib., 156; The *Juffrow Maria Schroeder*, 3 Rob., 153; The *Hoffnung*, 6 ib., 116; The *Mary*, 1 Gall., 206; Prince *v.* U. S., 2 Gall., 204; Peisch *v.* Ware, 4 Crauch, 347; Lord Raymond, 388, 501; Reeves's Law of Shipping, 203; The *Francis and Eliza*, 8 Wheat, 398; Sea Laws, arts. 29, 30, and 31; The *Gertrude*, 3 Story Rep., 68.)

"It can only be a people who have made but little progress in civilization that would not permit foreign vessels to seek safety in their ports, when driven there by stress of weather, except under the charge of paying impost duties on their cargoes or on penalty of confiscation, where the cargo consisted of prohibited goods." (The *Gertrude*, 3 Story Rep., 68.)

Mr. Webster, Secretary of State, in his diplomatic letter of August 1, 1842, to Lord Ashburton, British minister at Washington, contended that if a vessel be driven by stress of weather or other necessity, or carried by unlawful force into a British port, even if it be a prohibited or blockaded port, that necessity exempted the vessel from all penalty and hazard. These immunities were presumed to exist as a part of civilization and to be allowed until expressly retracted. This presumption is deemed to be part of the voluntary and adopted law of nations. There has been occasional criticism of some of the propositions advanced by Mr. Webster in this correspondence,* but no authoritative or judicial dissent can be produced. Although advanced arguendo, there has not been in modern times any respectable dissent from so much of Mr. Webster's propositions as related to exemption from local jurisdiction of storm-driven or refuge-seeking vessels, their passengers, crew, and cargo. A distinction has, however, been drawn between the status of merchant vessels voluntarily entering foreign ports for purposes of trade and such as have entered or been driven in by stress of weather or other necessity. And the propositions of Mr. Webster, which have been sometimes questioned, are those which relate to the former.

But even in respect to the former, the practice under the influence of the law of nations, and by the comity of civilized modern States, as Mr. Webster well insists, is for the sovereign of the port to waive in favor of the sovereign of the flag the exercise of jurisdiction in relation to all matters except those which concern police regulation, or affect the peace and quiet of the port. (The *Exchange*, 7 Cranch, 140; Wildenhus's Case, 120 U. S., p. 1; decision of the supreme court of Grenada, Nicaragua, in re Captain McCrea, of the P. M. S. S. *Honduras*, Foreign Relations of U. S., 1892, pp. 45–49; Dana's Wheaton, Int. Law, No. 95, note 58; Halleck, Int. Law, p.; Albany Law Journal, Nov. 1, 1890, Vol. XLII, p. 345 et seq., where the authorities are collated; Mr. Gresham, Secretary of State, to Mr. Huntington, Foreign Relations of the United States, 1894, pp. 296, 297.)

In the cases of the *Creole*, the brig *Enterprize*, and the *Hermosa*, which were before the Commission of Claims, under the convention of February 8, 1853, between Great Britain and the United States, there was full discussion of these propositions in direct application to the peculiar occurrences which had given rise to this correspondence. The advocate of the United States had laid down on behalf of the claimants several contentions, which set out in substance the position announced by Mr. Webster. These were resisted arguendo by the advocate of Great Britain. Upon submission, Mr. Bates, the umpire, took the following positions, and made awards in favor of the claimants: "The *Creole* was on a voyage, sanctioned and protected by the laws of the United States and by the law of nations. Her right to navigate the ocean could not be questioned, and, as growing out of that right, the right to seek shelter or enter the ports of a friendly power in case of distress or of unavoidable necessity. * * * These rights, sanctioned by the law of nations, viz, the right to navigate the ocean and to seek shelter in case of distress or other unavoidable circumstances, and to retain over the ship, her cargo and passengers the laws of her country, must be respected by all nations, for no independent nation would submit to their violation." (Report of the Commission on British and American Claims, Convention, February 8, 1853, pp. 244, 245.)

It was well said by the United States commissioner, with whose conclusions on this branch of the case the umpire agreed, that "The right of a State bordering on the ocean to a given extent over the waters immediately adjoining attaches for certain fiscal purposes and purposes for protection. But the jurisdiction thus obtained is by no means exclusive. Sovereignty does not necessarily imply all power, or that there can not coexist with it within its own dominions other independent and coequal rights. Indeed, the exception taken furnishes a strong argument in favor of the principle contended for, because the same rule of justice that gives for certain purposes jurisdiction over the waters, as incident to the use of the land, extends, for like reasons, a right over the land for temporary use and shelter, as incident to the use of the ocean. The rule operates with equal validity and justice both ways, and its application in the one case sustains and justifies it in the other. If neither right must give way there seems to be no good reason why the older and better right of the nations to the free navigation of the ocean, with its incidents, should be surrendered to the exclusive claims of any single nation." (Ib., 214, 215.)

When a vessel, engaged in a lawful voyage by the law of nations, is compelled, by stress of weather or other inevitable cause, to enter the harbor of a friendly nation for temporary shelter, the enjoyment of such shelter being incident to the right to

---

* Hall, International Law, p. 168, note. See reply to Hall's criticism in Albany Law Journal, November 1, 1890, pp. 346–350.

navigate the ocean; carries with it, over the vessel and personal relations of those on board, the rights of the ocean, so far as to extend over it, for the time being, the protection of the laws of its country. (Opinion of Umpire Bates in re brig *Enterprize;* Report of British and American Commission, under Convention of February 8, 1853, p. 187.)

The principles of law, stated in the diplomatic correspondence of the American Secretary of State, were judicially recognized by the supreme court of Louisiana in the case of McCargo *v.* New Orleans Insurance Company (10 Rob. La., 202, 316).

In 1845 Mr. Wheaton, in an article upon this subject in the Revue Francaise et Etrangere, lx, 345 (Dana's Wheaton, sec. 103, note), sustained the position of Mr. Webster as to the rule of international law in regard to immunity and exemption from local jurisdiction of distress vessels, cargo, and crews.

The Attorney-General of the United States concurred in the view announced by the American Secretary of State. (The *Creole*, 40, p. 98.)

In his speech on the case of the brigs *Comet, Emporium,* and *Enterprize,* March 3, 1840, in the Senate, Mr. Calhoun had stated the principle in substantially the same terms. (3 Calhoun's Works by Crallé, 465.)

But even if it could be questioned that the exemption from local jurisdiction of storm or distress-driven vessels, crew and passengers exists as a rule of the law of nations, it is clearly sanctioned by the treaty between Spain and the United States

THE TREATY OF 1795

Article VI provides for the protection of the vessels and other effects of citizens or subjects of one nation in the jurisdiction of the other. Article VII relieves from embargo or detention the vessels or effects of subjects or citizens and secures regular and orderly judicial processes for the trial in case of the seizure of subjects or citizens for debts or crimes. Article VIII is little more than declaratory of the law of nations in this regard, but it consecrates the guarantee of immunity from apprehension or detention by proclaiming it solemnly as a part of the law for the observance of the two parties.

Counsel for complainants does not dwell upon the guarantees contained in the protocol of January 12, 1877, because in our view of the case the complainants were at no time answerable to either the military or civil jurisdiction of Spain. They were not "residing in Spain, her adjacent islands, or her ultramarine possessions," but were cast upon her territorial waters by accident and distress. But had they been actually resident in Cuba their treatment would still have been unusual, unwarranted, and harsh.

The circumstance that it was on a small fishing smack that the complainants entered the port of refuge, in no way affects the character or extent of the protection to which they were entitled under the law of nations and the treaty stipulations. They would have been equally entitled to exemption from arbitrary arrest and cruel treatment had they been carried in on a floating spar or on the deck of a clipper ship flying the American flag. (Wharton, Int. Dig., Vol. 3., sec. 410.) Article VIII of the treaty of 1795 between Spain and the United States was declaratory of the law of nations, and is conformable to the comity and practice of modern civilized States. Just one year after the ratification of this treaty the assaults of Great Britain upon the rights of seamen on board American vessels resulted in the passage of the act of May 28, 1796 (1 Stat. L., p. 477), entitled "An act for the relief and protection of American seamen," the substantive provisions of which are carried into the Revised Statutes of the United States. (Secs. 4588 and 4589.)

IV.

Vessels owned by citizens of the United States may carry the flag of the United States on the high seas, and are entitled to the protection of the United States Government, though from being foreign built or from other causes they are not and can not be registered as vessels of the United States.

Ownership is the basis on which nationality rests; ownership is evidenced by bill of sale and guaranteed by the flag she carries; foreign nations will not look into the question of title nor examine how far municipal laws have been complied with, so as to enable the ship, for municipal purposes, to carry the flag; a certificate or passport from the sovereign of the flag, or a certificate from one of his consuls, that the vessel is owned by one of his citizens or subjects, will be a sufficient assurance that the flag, for international purposes, is rightfully carried. (Wharton Int. Law Dig., Vol. III, sec. 410.)

IN CONCLUSION.

The law of nations, treaty stipulations, and the laws of humanity seem equally and persistently disregarded by Spain when it is question of the personal freedom or property interests of American citizens. Within a few days past the counsel who signs this brief filed a protest on behalf of Mr. Libbey, a citizen of the United States, whose extensive properties in the Island of Cuba have been subject to persistent plunder and spoliation, and which have finally been abandoned by his manager, whose personal safety was repeatedly threatened. It seems to counsel that much more is involved in these cases than the mere personal interests—important and serious as they are—of individual sufferers. They involve consideration of the extent and measure of protection which American citizens may expect in Cuba under the guarantees of the law of nations and treaty stipulations; and they present the question whether the United States will continue to submit to the habitual violation by Spain of the law of nations, treaty stipulations, and the laws of humanity in respect of the persons and property of American citizens temporarily or accidentally within Spanish territory.

So far as the record discloses there was neither ground for suspicion nor probable cause for the exceptionally harsh treatment of complainants. There was nothing in their movements or surroundings that was so unusual or extraordinary as to justify their original apprehension without warrant or judicial process, nor for their protracted imprisonment. There appears no excuse for the wanton violation of their natural and treaty rights. On the contrary, all the real evidence was in their favor and corresponded with and corroborated a story that was consistent throughout. Adverse winds and currents, an empty and dismantled fishing smack, and a starving crew, seeking refuge in a port of a nation presumed to be civilized and friendly, presented strong evidence of the literal truth of their narrative. In the long train of events which succeeded their apprehension and cruel captivity there does not appear a single feature or element to warrant suspicion of hostile act or intent. Their physical condition negatived the possibility. The case needs no embellishment. A plain recital of the facts is sufficient to expose the circumstances of aggravation that attended their apprehension and imprisonment. And it is difficult to refrain from the use of language that may not sound diplomatic when contemplating the calm indifference to law, justice, and humanity manifested on the part of the Spanish authorities, even after the facts had been brought to their attention by the repeated remonstrances of the accredited representatives of the United States.

What a pretense and travesty of justice the whole proceeding on the part of the Spanish authorities was clearly appears from the record furnished by themselves. The individual who forwards an official communication to Mr. Hyatt, United States consul at Santiago, and subscribes the same "God guard your honor many years, Sebastian Kindelau," is presumably the governor-general. And it seems from the language of this remarkable production that "the American citizens, August Bolton and Gustav Richelieu" were charged with "the crime of rebellion," and "that a greater part of the charges and discharges have to be proven in a foreign country, as is Hayti." It remains for a Spanish governor-general to explain how American citizens can be guilty of the crime of rebellion against Spain while in Haytien territory. There is a freshness and flavor about the communication of "his excellency, the president of the territorial audiencia," which will repay careful perusal, and it has been fortunately preserved in English, where it no doubt loses some of the suavity of expression that is found in the original. It may be consulted by the student of international jurisprudence in search of a specimen of Spanish diplomatico-judicial utterance. The cuttle-fish has heretofore borne a reputation for his facility in muddying the waters, however lucid, in which he moves; but for clouding and confusing a plain case the Spanish fiscal, governor-general, or president of a territorial audiencia has no competitor. (Ex. Doc., Fifty-fourth Congress, first session, No. 224, p. 123.)

One of the excuses for holding complainants after their release had been formally and repeatedly demanded by the United States is set out in the communication just referred to, wherein it is attempted to justify further delay on the ground "that the state of the sumario (preliminary proceedings) in which is found the cause followed for the crime of rebellion against Bolten and Richelieu holds him from disclosing to the honorable consul the charges that exist in the proceedings against Bolten and Richelieu, as always, according to our law, the sumario (preliminary proceedings) are completely secret, but it can be said for the satisfaction of such a worthy representative that there exists sufficient reason to indict and decree the provisional imprisonment of said individuals. This court has seen itself in the necessity of prolonging the imprisonment decreed by the marine jurisdiction."

The communication in which this curious excerpt occurs was dated April 10, 1895, forty-four days after the arrest, and is significant in the admission, which was no doubt inadvertent, that the civil court was executing a punishment inflicted by "the marine jurisdiction," which the superior authorities had reluctantly conceded had no jurisdiction. But the truth is, as is apparent from the whole record, that this was another subterfuge and evasion couched in diplomatic phraseology equally destitute of honesty and veracity. The temptation to invoke "sumario" and "incommunicado," much as nurses utilize the "bogie" to frighten children from entering prohibited places, may not be resisted by the average Spanish official when every other expedient has failed. The hollowness of this pretense is apparent. Against the sufficiency and integrity of this reply the Secretary of State and the United States consul promptly protested. (Ex. Doc. No. 224, Fifty-fourth Congress, first session, pp. 123, 124.) Forty-four days is a long time to consume in ascertaining the patent fact that complainants were within the conditions of Article VIII of the treaty.

An illustration may here serve a useful purpose. Suppose—if such a case is imaginable in this year of grace 1896—that two Spanish seamen under corresponding circumstances should seek refuge in the harbor of New York, and immediately upon landing should be arrested by the authorities when on their way to the office of the Spanish consul, and should, without arraignment, without formal charges or judicial process, be incarcerated in a loathsome prison; and suppose the representatives of Spain, after proper examination, should satisfy themselves that they were within the conditions of Article VIII, and should demand formal charges, prompt trial, or their release. How long would it be before their freedom would be assured? Would it be an answer which would satisfy any self-respecting State that the grand jury was not in session or that the accused must be held and subjected to harsh treatment for two or three months, or until the authorities could communicate, as to the regularity of the vessel's clearance, with the Government of Mexico, from one of whose ports the dismantled vessel had sailed?

If it be admitted that shipwrecked seamen cast upon the territorial waters of the United States, and apprehended and thrown into prison, would be restored to their freedom within twelve or twenty-four hours, either by Executive order or by the issue of the writ of habeas corpus, and it be added in extenuation of Spanish procrastination that this is practicable by reason of existing municipal law or statute in the United States, but that Spanish procedure furnishes no correspondent or equivalent summary processes, the reply is that it is no answer to a demand founded on international law or treaty stipulation that the municipal law furnishes no procedure for the execution of discharge of such an international obligation. If the obligation exists under the law of nations or treaty stipulation, it is the duty of the nation to supply it. It was maintained in the American case before the Geneva Tribunal that the liability of Great Britain should be measured by the rules of international law, and that it could not be escaped by reason of any alleged deficiencies in any internal legislation. The award says the Government of Her Britannic Majesty can not justify itself for a failure of due diligence on the insufficiencies of the legal means of action which it possessed.

If a more stringent law is wanted to enable a nation to fulfill its international duties, then it is its duty to have a more stringent law. (Wharton's Int. Law Digest, Vol. III, p. 645.) But the truth is, there exists in Cuba process and procedure competent to deal in a summary way where the ends of justice and international law or treaty stipulations require action, and the decision of the examining judge of the 5th of May, 1895, which operated to release complainants, could have been and should have been reached in February had good faith characterized the action of the authorities in respect of the discharge of international obligations. (Ex. Doc. No. 224, first session Fifty-fourth Congress, p. 131.) And the same result could and should have been accomplished at an early day by Executive order. In this case no judicial procedure recognizable by civilized communities was followed; punishment was substituted for charge, arraignment, and judicial process. The whole proceeding was shocking to the sense of justice and humanity. Whatever may have been the real motive, nothing appears to excuse the action of the authorities toward the complainants.

The falsity of each successive and shifting charge brought against complainants has been promptly exposed, and no extenuating circumstances appear to palliate the cruel treatment to which complainants were subjected.

The acts of the administrative authorities at Santiago imperatively call for disavowal by Spain of the indignity to the flag and the payment of a substantial pecuniary indemnity to the United States on account of the arbitrary arrest and long and cruel imprisonment of complainants.

Early in the history of the nation the American doctrine found emphatic expression in the declaration that "the colors that float from the masthead should be the credentials of our seaman;" and its observance has been fearlessly enforced, even to the extreme of war.

It seems to counsel that this is a case which demands summary redress and reparation, and complainant claims damages from Spain in the sum $10,000.

It is respectfully submitted that, for the purposes of arrest and imprisonment, the complainants were not subject to the jurisdiction of the administrative authorities of Spain, but were, at the time of arrest and seizure of their boat, for purposes of protection, within the exclusive protection of the law of nations and the treaty stipulations; and their arrest and imprisonment was arbitrary and unwarranted.

(Treaty of 1795, Articles VIII and XIX; Consular Regulations, pars. 170. 171, 172, 175, 177; Commission between U. S. and Great Britain, Feb. 8, Report, pages 241–245; Wheaton, 153; Dana's Wheaton, 103, note.)

S. Doc. 231, pt 7——40

As a result of the cruel treatment of the authorities at Santiago, one of the complainants barely survived the imprisonment and the other is crippled with infirmity and disease that will probably carry him to an early grave

As both the administrative, military, and civil authorities of Spain at Santiago de Cuba must be held to a knowledge of the law of nations and the treaty stipulations in this regard, the gravamen of the offense consists in the willful and perverse violation by Spain of her obligations in respect of the rights and immunities guaranteed to these complainants.

The euphuistic palaver and the circumambient correspondence of the Spanish authorities thinly veils a deliberate purpose to advisedly disregard these obligations. They may not plead ignorance, for the United States consul immediately protested and continued to protest against the action of the authorities as unwarranted and arbitrary. (Ex. Doc. No. 224, Fifty-fourth Congress, first session, pp. 111-117.)

A nation which persistently insists not only upon the vigorous observance, but upon a latitudinarian extension, of neutral obligations on the part of the United States, ought to be required to faithfully fulfill the duties she has assumed under treaty stipulations in respect of American citizens.

It is submitted that the following propositions have been established:

First. That the complainant Richelieu is entitled to invoke the aid of the United States in enforcing against Spain his demand for pecuniary indemnity on account of arbitrary arrest and false imprisonment.

Second. That the complainants Bolten and Richelieu were never, from the time of their first apprehension to the last minute of their incarceration, amenable to the jurisdiction of Spain for the purposes of arrest, imprisonment, or punishment.

Third. That the apprehension, rearrest, and imprisonment of the complainants and the seizure and appropriation of their fishing smack and outfit by the Spanish administrative authorities at Santiago de Cuba was in violation of the law of nations, the comity and practice of modern civilized States, and the provisions of Articles VI, VII, and VIII of the treaty of 1795.

Fourth. That there was neither justification nor probable cause for the arrest or imprisonment of complainants.

Fifth. That the innocence of complainants of the suggested offenses was indicated by the patent facts.

Sixth. That the acts of the Spanish administrative authorities at Santiago de Cuba clearly indicate bad faith and duplicity toward complainants and the representatives of the United States.

Seventh. That the circumstances of aggravation which characterized the acts of the Spanish administrative authorities present no extenuating feature, and that they call for an apology from Spain to the United States and a liberal pecuniary indemnity to complainants.

Respectfully submitted.

ALEXANDER PORTER MORSE,
Of Counsel.

JOHN W. DOUGLASS,
ALEXANDER PORTER MORSE,
Attorneys for Complainant.

WASHINGTON, *August 18, 1896.*

Mr. Adee to Mr. Morse.

DEPARTMENT OF STATE,
Washington, August 21, 1896.

SIR: I have to acknowledge the receipt of your letter of the 18th instant, inclosing a brief and additional affidavit of Gustave Richelieu in support of his claim against the Government of Spain.

I am, etc.,

ALVEY A. ADEE, *Acting Secretary.*

Mr. Rockhill to Mr. Morse.

DEPARTMENT OF STATE,
Washington, August 31, 1896.

SIR: Referring to my letter of the 21st instant, in acknowledgment of your brief filed in behalf of Gustave Richelieu against the Govern-

ment of Spain, I have to inform you that the memorial of said Richelieu has been sent to our minister at Madrid, with instructions to present
the claim for the consideration of the Spanish Government, along with
the claim of August Bolten, who was Richelieu's companion in the maltreatment for which indemnity is sought.

I am, etc.,   W. W. ROCKHILL,
                                            Acting Secretary.

Mr. Rockhill to Mr. Taylor.

No. 556.]   DEPARTMENT OF STATE,
                                    Washington, August 31, 1896.

SIR: In the Department's No. 483 of March 18, 1896, you were
instructed to present the claim of August Bolten against the Government of Spain for indemnity. Mr. Bolten and his companion, Richelieu, were cast upon the shores of Cuba by stress of weather in a small
fishing smack. Instead of receiving the hospitality of the Cuban
authorities to which they were entitled under our treaty of 1795 with
Spain, they were imprisoned and detained, as related in instruction
No. 483, under the pretense that they were connected with the Cuban
insurrection. All that was said in relation to Bolten's claim applies
equally to Richelieu's. The two men were cast together upon the
Cuban shore, they suffered the same treatment at the hands of the
Spanish authorities, and were released at the same time. Their cases
are precisely similar. That of Richelieu was not presented when Bolten's was, because his right to the protection of the United States was
not at that time fully established. That defect in his case has been
cured, and you are directed to demand the consideration of his claim
by the Spanish Government along with the claim of Bolten, and to
solicit an early settlement of both.

I am, etc.,   W. W. ROCKHILL,
                                            Acting Secretary.

Mr. Gordon to Mr. Olney.

280 BROADWAY, NEW YORK, *September 12, 1896.*

MY DEAR SIR: I have to acknowledge the receipt of your letter of
March 18, 1896, wherein you kindly inform me that the claim of August
Bolten against the Spanish Government for indemnity for false impris-
onment in Cuba would be forwarded to the United States minister at
Madrid for presentation to that Government.

I have heard nothing since from your Department as to the progress
and outcome, if any, in this matter, and I write now to inquire for
such information as you may be in a position to give herein. I shall
thank you exceedingly for the same.

Yours, very respectfully,   DAVID GORDON,

Mr. Rockhill to Mr. Gordon.

DEPARTMENT OF STATE,
Washington, September 15, 1896.

SIR: In reply to your letter of the 12th instant, I have to say that in
a recent instruction to our minister at Madrid, in regard to the case of

Gustave Richelieu, he was again directed to ask an early settlement of the claim of August Bolten.

I am, etc.,   W. W. ROCKHILL,
                                                  Acting Secretary.

———

Mr. Rockhill to Mr. Morse.

DEPARTMENT OF STATE,
Washington, September 29, 1896.

SIR: Referring to previous correspondence, I have to state that I am advised by our minister to Spain that he has presented the claim of Gustave Richelieu to the Spanish Government.

I am, etc.,
                                              W. W. ROCKHILL,
                                                  Acting Secretary.

———

Mr. Taylor to Mr. Olney.

No. 594.]   LEGATION OF THE UNITED STATES,
                                          Madrid, November 4, 1896.

SIR: Replying to your numbers 483 of March 18 and 556 of August 31 last, I have the honor to transmit to you herewith the reply of the minister of state refusing to consider the claim of Mr. August Bolten, and likewise of Mr. Gustave Richelieu, on the grounds set forth in the evidence accompanying this note, with translation.

I am, etc.,
                                              HANNIS TAYLOR.

———

[Inclosure.—Translation.]

MINISTRY OF STATE,
San Sebastian, September 29, 1896.

EXCELLENCY:

MY DEAR SIR: I had the honor in due course of time to state to your excellency in the note dated April 8, of the current year, that I asked my colleague, the minister for the colonies, data concerning the American citizen, Mr. August Bolten, referred to in your excellency's courteous note, dated the 1st of the same month. The Cuban authorities having been consulted, I have just received a certified copy of the "expediente" instituted against the above-mentioned North American citizen and his companion, Richelieu, in consequence of their presenting themselves in the port of Santiago de Cuba, manning a boat without clearance papers or any document proving the nationality of the vessel and the object of the voyage. The length of said "expediente" deprives me of the pleasure of sending to your excellency a literal copy of the same, which, however, I place at your disposal in case you should desire to read it, confining myself to communicate to you the inclosed 11 copies, which, in my opinion, are sufficient to give a just idea of the same.

Your excellency may be convinced by said copies that there was a reasonable ground to arrest and institute proceedings against the two American citizens, Bolten and Richelieu, and also that the action of the court was the shortest and most expeditious permitted by the laws of procedure, which both Spaniards and foreigners are equally submitted to.

The depositions of Felix Tahureaux, accusing the North American prisoners of having shipped from Haiti insurgents and ammunitions; the numerous contradictions indulged in by Bolten and Richelieu, which are evidenced in their having been made to give evidence face to face, to which they were submitted on May 5, 1895, there having both agreed, as shown in the confrontation, to falsify and exaggerate the facts; the strange plans of both, which have not, indeed, been fully justified, and the most important circumstance that their anomalous voyage coincided with the first filibuster expeditions and insurrectional uprising, fully justify the suspicions which they inspired from the beginning and the proceedings instituted by the marine jurisdiction.

As soon as the North American nationality of the prisoners could be verified, the marine jurisdiction, in conformity with the international compacts, and most especially with the procotol of January 12, 1877, did not go on with the case, which came under the cognizance of the ordinary courts.

The report of the marine attorney of Santiago de Cuba, the written opinion of the auditor of the Apostadero of Habana, and the resolution of the commander-general of the Apostadero and of the squadron of the Antilles show how strictly the international compacts in force between both countries are carried out in the island of Cuba.

When the suit came under the action of the ordinary jurisdiction the proceedings were diligently pursued, and as the assertions of the consul of the United States at Santiago de Cuba were favorable to the prisoners, as were likewise later on those of a Protestant clergyman established in Haiti and those of a Spaniard who had resided for some time in Puerto Principe, the charges proffered by the deponent Thaureaux not having been proved, the instructing judge issued an order setting the prisoners free, and later on the superior court, owing to a lack of evidence, issued an order provisionally suspending the suit.

On February 23, 1895, they were arrested; on the following April they were set free; on June 22 the suspension was ordered, so that they had been arrested only during two months, and within four months all the procedure was ended, notwithstanding the fact that letters rogatory had to be issued, the difficulty of communications and the condition of rebellion of the country having to be contended with.

Anyone who will impartially examine the case will acknowledge, as I hope the friendly Government of the United States shall have to acknowledge, that on the part of the Spanish authorities there was no abuse of power whatever, and that the case, in view of the circumstances in which the country was involved, gave rise to the suspicion which the authorities had and forced them to proceed in the form and manner in which they acted.

It is true that Bolten, during his imprisonment, was ill; but it is also true that he was transferred to the hospital and attended to as required by his condition.

It is to be remarked that Bolten claims the considerable sum of $10,000, a quantity which, even if the imprisonment had not been justified, would have been considered absurd, as it is exorbitant.

In view of the above statements, which your excellency and the Government of the United States will appreciate in their high sense of justice, His Majesty's Government finds itself obliged to reject in an absolute manner the demand for an indemnity, considering this case finally and irrevocably ended.

With this motive, and reiterating to the Government and people of the United States the assurances of friendship in which the Spanish Government and people have always been inspired, it is very gratifying to me, Mr. Minister, to renew to your excellency the assurances of my most distinguished consideration.

THE DUKE OF TETUAN.

The MINISTER PLENIPOTENTIARY OF THE UNITED STATES.

[Inclosure.]

Deposition of Felix Thaureaux.

At Santiago de Cuba, in the justice hall of the prison of this city, on March 3, 1895, appeared the individual mentioned in the margin, who, being sworn according to the ordinance, promised to tell the truth on every question put to him, and the general questions having been put to him, said: That his name was as already stated; that he was 49 years old, a native of Guantanamo, a country laborer, and is undergoing a four-months' sentence as receiver of stolen goods.

Asked whether he knows the American citizens, Gustave Richelieu and August Bolten, and, in the affirmative case, state all he knows with regard to them, said: That he knows both of them; that he has spoken little with the latter, because he knows very little the English language, but that he makes himself perfectly understood by the former, who speaks French; that, according to what he said to him, they left Puerto Principe (Haiti) at the beginning of February; that in a place of the coast between Santo Domingo and Haiti they took on board two men, one white and the other colored; that the former said his name was Marcial Figueredo or Figuerola; that they shipped with them three boxes of regular dimensions, one of them containing revolvers, another machetes, and he does not know what the other contained.

That they sailed for the Cuban coast, landing the men and the boxes at the mouth of a river situated between Guantanamo and Punta Maisi, near some wharves which are situated in the coast; that they brought a small map of those coasts, by means of which they expected to find out their landing place; that when they left Guantanamo, and near the mouth of the first river to be found going to Cuba, they saw on the coast certain caves in which he assured him there were arms and ammunitions of war, and that if he was well paid he would run the risk to bring them; that he saw there two armed individuals whom he supposed were rebels; that they left Puerto Principe in understanding with the Protestant clergyman, and for this reason they say they ask him for references of their good behavior; that the clergyman's name is John; that it was also spoken of telegraph operators with whom they dined and drank in a place on the coast; that higher up the Cape Haitiano they took on board the two men and the ammunitions; that Richelieu was staying in an hotel of Puerto Principe in which the Cuban insurgents had meetings, among them Maceo, Marcano, and Mancebo; that Maceo made frequent trips to Santo Domingo and Jamaica; that he saw Richelieu destroy newspaper clippings which contained portraits of prominent insurgents, and that amongst them he took one which contained that of Marti, which clippings the guard José Baro delivered to him.

That when the two individuals came on board with the three boxes they also carried with them a package with papers which seemed dangerous for them to keep, because a big piece of iron was tied to it in order to throw it deep into the water in case of emergency; that they intended to return to Haiti to bring more people, but that owing to the bad condition of the boat they did not dare to undertake the journey, and decided to come to Cuba in order to go from here in a steamer; that they have not yet given him money for the commission, which money they would deliver to him on coming back to Haiti; that he has nothing else to say. After this deposition was read to him, on being asked if he had anything further to say or anything to correct, he said no, and affirms and ratified his statement, signing with the attorney and present secretary, to which I certify.

FELIX THAUREAUX.
GONZALO DE LA PUERTA.

Sworn before me.

MANUEL BRIOSO.

A true copy.

Confrontation of August Bolten and Gustave Richelieu as witnesses.

In the hall of justice of the prison of this city on May 5, 1895, appeared the individuals mentioned in the margin, who on being duly asked, as set forth in their depositions, replied as in the following:

August Bolten on being asked, after his deposition contained on the tenth sheet and supplemented on the overleaf of sheet 22, whether he has anything further to say or rectify and whether he confirms and ratifies his deposition, said that he confirms and ratifies the statements made.

On being asked whether he knows Gustave Richelieu; whether he knows that he (Gustave Richelieu) bears him any hatred or ill will, or whether he considers him suspicious, says that he knows him; that he believes Gustave Richelieu bears him no hatred or ill will, and that he does not consider him as suspicious.

On being asked how it is that he states in his deposition that the only implements they carried were nets and seines, whereas Richelieu refers in his deposition to two fishing nets 30 fathoms long, said that he never saw such seines on board, and that they only had the implements mentioned in his deposition.

On Gustave Richelieu's being asked, after having read to him his deposition on the 19th leaf, and amplification of leaves 19 and 54, whether he has anything further to say or rectify, and whether he confirms and ratifies his statement, said that he has nothing further to say nor to rectify, and that he confirms and ratifies his statements.

On being asked whether he knows August Bolten and is aware that he (August Bolten) bears him any ill will, and whether he considers him suspicious, said that he knows him, and that he does not believe that August Bolten bears him any ill will, nor does he consider him as suspicious.

Asked how it is that he says in his deposition of the overleaf of leaf 15 that besides the fishing nets they carried two seines about 30 fathoms long, whereas Bolten assures that they only carried a small seine, he said that he saw them in the boat the day before leaving Puerto Principe, and he does not know whether Bolten had given them back because he had not paid for them.

Asked how he states this about Bolten, whereas he declares that said nets, which were the most important fishing implements carried by them, were lost by them by leaving them outside of the boat while fishing, said that he has made this deposition because he was told so by Bolten, without being able to say whether it was a truth, because it was nighttime when they lost them, he could not see them.

Asked how he says,that the planks which were given to them at Puerto Principe to be placed in the floor of the boat were used by him in the fishing tackle, said it is true that he has deposed this and that he procured the planks for that purpose before leaving that port.

Asked how it is that he declares in the overleaf of sheet 15 that the hooks and lines were all well rolled up in the floor of the boat and were covered by his companion's waterproof coat, he said that as they were covered by the waterproof he could not see what was under it, nor could he be sure whether they were there, judging only by the size of the parcel.

Asked whether he neither saw them on some of the occasions when he slept on the floor of the boat, nor when Bolten threw them into the water in order to fish, said that he did not see them on any occasion.

On August Bolten being asked whether he has anything to say against all the statement made by Richelieu, said that all the statements made by Richelieu in regard to the nets were not true, but that it had been arranged by them when they wanted to come to the island to excite pity for themselves.

On Richelieu being asked to state the truth about the statement just made by Bolten, he (Richelieu) said that it is true they had so arranged.

On Richelieu being asked how he said in his deposition on the overleaf of the 15th sheet that he placed the implements in the bottom of the boat, covered with the waterproof of his companion, while the latter said in his deposition on sheet 12 that he kept the implements in a box, said that Bolten has told him so many lies that he does not now know what is the truth.

On Bolten being asked whether he had to say anything against Richelieu's statement, replied that if Richelieu would only tell the truth, setting aside the lies which they had agreed to tell, the depositions would better agree.

Being asked what was their purpose in stating what was not true, said that it was in order to move the pity of the people whom they would meet, but that the very moment they were arrested he recommended him to tell only the truth.

Upon Richelieu being asked whether the statement Bolten had just made is true, the latter said that the first part is true, but that he did not recollect having been recommended to tell the truth.

Upon Bolten being asked why they thought it necessary to invent losses which they had not sustained in order to appeal to compassion, if they did not consider sufficient their condition of shipwreck and nineteen days' voyage, said that it was Richelieu's invention, which he agreed to tell because he found nothing out of the way in it; that Richelieu also proposed to him to say that a ship had met them which had given them something to eat, but that he (Bolten) objected to so much invention.

Upon Richelieu's being asked whether there is any truth in Bolten's statement, he (Richelieu) said that he did not remember.

At this state of the proceedings the attorney ordered the suspension of the confrontation and ruled that the deponents had agreed upon the nonexistence of the nets.

Signed by the attorney, interpreter, and me, the secretary.

AUGUST BOLTEN.
GONZALEZ DE LA PUENTE.
GUSTAVE RICHELIEU.
I. AGOSTINO, *Interpreter.*

Before me.

MANUEL BRIOSO.

A true copy.

Report of the marine attorney.

On the 23d day of February last a boat reached this port in a rather bad condition, 4½ meters long, and provided with sails, manned by two men, who turned out to be Swedish, one of them, and French the other, but both citizens of the United States. The boat has neither name nor documents, and her crew, Bolten and Richelieu, only carry the following documents: The former a passport issued on February 4 by the consul-general of the United States of America at Puerto Principe (Haiti) to enable Bolten to go to Cape Haitien to attend to his private business, and the latter a certificate issued on the 7th of the same month by the consular agency of the same nation at San Marcos, showing that Richelieu landed in accordance with the law of November 29, 1893, from the American schooner *Orlando.* From their depositions, which are the only data upon which an opinion can be formed, they left with the boat without any clearance papers on February 4 to go to the Haitien Cape to fish tortoises and without any agreement, either written or even conventional, containing the conditions under which each one went. After touching at various ports of the coast, among them San Marcos, where Richelieu received his certificate, they reached the "Mole de San Nicolas" on the 12th. With westerly winds, they left on the 13th without being able on that day to round the cape, for which reason they cast anchor at sunset.

On the following days they had easterly winds, which accounts for their not being able, in view of the boat's condition, to go to "Cabo Haitiano;" but there is nothing to justify the voyage undertaken then by them to the Cuban coast, as, although Bolten says that he did not desire to return to Puerto Principe, they might have stayed at "La Mole" to wait for favorable winds, which would enable them to continue to Cabo Haitiano, where they went, attracted by the abundance of tortoise on that coast and the facility of its being fished, according to their representation. They arrived at Caimanera on the 17th, and after seeing at Guantanamo the consular agent of the United States, they left on the 20th without clearance papers and verbally cleared, as reported by said agent. It seems natural that since they did not wish to return to Haiti and desired to look for work in this island, they should have tried to find it at Guantanamo. However, in spite of the bad condition of the boat, they preferred to come to this port and look for work here. Taking into account all the above statements and the special present condition of the island, particularly this region, and likewise that their arrival at Caimanera took place immediately before the uprising of the insurgent forces at Guantanamo.

Resulting, that said individuals have no document whatever showing the place where the boat comes from.

Resulting, that they left Caimanera without clearance papers, knowing that they ought not to do it.

Considering the facts set forth in his deposition by Felipe Thaureaux from Richelieu's confidences and also the different newspaper clippings with portraits of insurgents carried by them, among which is that of Marti;

Considering the chart which Thaureaux said they had in their clothes and which was actually found on them; although a small one, it can give a knowledge of the distance from Cuba with respect to any place of the Haitien coast;

Considering the contradictions which appear in their first depositions and the facts which, being untrue, they agreed to state,

Everything tends to show in a suspicious light the American citizens Bolten and Richelieu. Taking into account the protocol signed at Madrid on January 12, 1877, the carrying out of which was ordered on April 8 of the same year, my opinion is, subject to your own superior judgment, that the present proceedings should come under the ordinary jurisdiction, or that they may be continued by the marine jurisdiction owing to the present circumstances, or that the case may be abandoned, for which reasons, if you deem it advisable, I have naturally refrained from ordering them to be set free.

Santiago de Cuba, March 9, 1896.

GONZALO DE LA PUERTA.

A true copy.

———

Report of the auditor of the naval station of Havana, and decision of the commander-general relinquishing the case on behalf of the ordinary jurisdiction.

EXCELLENCY: In view of the proceedings instituted in the court of admiralty of Santiago de Cuba on the occasion of the arrival at that port of a boat without clearance papers, manned by two individuals named Gustave Richelieu and August Bolten, American citizens, as shown by the documents of folios 4, 5, and 6 of said proceedings, taking into account the provisions of protocol of January 12, 1877, which was ordered to be carried out by Royal order dated 19th May, of the same year, it is my opinion, entirely in accord with the previous decision of the attorney of the naval station, in considering that no citizen of the United States accused of acts of sedition, disloyalty, or conspiration against the institutions, public safety, integrity of the territory, or against the supreme government, or of any other offense, may be submitted to any exceptional tribunal, but exclusively to the ordinary jurisdiction except in the case when he is taken with arms in hand, which does not occur in the present case as it is inferred from the examination of these proceedings, that according to the law it seems right that your excellency should be pleased to provide for the reference of the case to the ordinary jurisdiction, leaving at its disposal the two individuals imprisoned in the prison of Santiago de Cuba; and these proceedings, the luggage, and boat referred to in said proceedings, to the court of instruction of the corresponding district of said capital, and making this decision known to the consul of the United States in the same city.

Notwithstanding, your excellency will decide.

Habana, May 20, 1895.

JOSÉ VALCARCEL.

HABANA, *May 21, 1895.*

Agreeing entirely with the above advice, let it pass to the commander of marine to Santiago de Cuba in order that he may carry it out in all its parts all that is proposed therein.

ALEJANDRO ARIAS SALGADO.

A true copy.

Communication of the commander of marine of Santiago de Cuba to the judge of instruction, delivering him the papers relating to the case.

COURT OF ADMIRALTY AND OFFICE OF THE CAPTAIN OF THE PORT,
Attorney's Office.

In view of the decree of the general commander of the naval station approved by the auditor, providing that the ordinary jurisdiction shall take cognizance of the case and ordering that the two individuals imprisoned in the prison of this city mentioned in the second sheet, and also the delivery of these proceedings, of the luggage and boat referred to in the judicial proceedings to the judge of instruction of the corresponding district, I have the honor to inclose herewith the papers above referred to, and also to inform you that the luggage was handed to said prisoners as shown in sheets 75 and 76, and that the boat is in this court of admiralty at your disposal. I hope that you will be pleased to acknowledge receipt of said papers to this attorney's office.

May God preserve you many years.

Cuba, March 28, 1895.

GONZALO DE LA PUERTA.

The Judge of Instruction of the South District of this City.

Decree of the ordinary judge on taking charge of the case.

CUBA, *March 31, 1895.*

The receipt of this case is acknowledged. Let it be delivered to the clerk of the court, Isidro de Tapia, he being one of the clerks who has less cases in course of process. Let the usual reports of its initiation be given.

And pending the decision with regard to further proceedings, let the examination of August Bolten and Gustave Richelieu be amplified, and for that purpose the court shall be transferred to the hospital and prison and the Government interpreter.

Ordered and signed by the judge before me, to which I certify.

ARISTIDES MARAGLIANO.
ISIDRO DE TAPIA.

A true copy.

[Translation.]

Communication of the United States consul at Santiago de Cuba to the judge of instruction.

UNITED STATES CONSULATE,
Santiago de Cuba, April 1, 1895.

His Excellency Don ARISTIDES MARAGLIANO,
Judge of Instruction of the South District of Santiago de Cuba.

SIR: I acknowledge receipt of your courteous communication of to-day's date, and in answer to the interrogatories therein contained I have to say the following:

First. With the jailer's permission, this consulate has given now and then to the prisoners Bolten and Richelieu, American citizens, newspapers to read, generally the New York Herald, World, and Philadelphia Record, because they complained at not being able to speak Spanish, and time seemed too long to them.

As said papers were taken from piles of old numbers at random and without looking at the dates nor the contents, I do not know whether the portrait referred to of José Marti was printed in some of them. Judging, however, by the publicity given to the present movement and by the tendency to the illustrations noted in the American press, it is very possible that the portrait of said individual may have been printed in one of the newspapers.

(2) August Bolten, born in Sweden, was naturalized in the court of first instance of the city and county of New York, on March 6, 1893. The document of naturalization, together with letters which recommend Bolten's credit, which were given me

a little after his imprisonment, I have in my keeping, and I shall have pleasure in placing them at your disposal for their examination.

Gustave Richelieu, born in France, was, I am informed, naturalized at Boston in 1870 or 1871. The latter, at the moment of his arrest, had a landing certificate from the American pailebot *Orlando*, duly signed and sealed by Charles Miot, consular agent of the United States at St. Marc, Haiti, which document gives him all the rights of an American sailor.

The document also certifies that Richelieu is an American citizen.

The original document was seized by the attorney, commander of marine. I have, however, kept a copy of it.

(3) The consulate identifies the prisoners by their documents, which at first sight is a strong proof unless there is a positive evidence to the contrary. Private intelligence also corroborates the question of identity. I assure you that I am gratified to know that the case of the prisoners, in accordance with the protocol of 1877, has been placed under the jurisdiction of the court so worthily presided over by you, and I am confident that the prisoners will be treated in accordance with law and justice. You will pardon me if I state that this consulate has been disposed to believe the men above referred to to be free from any intention to violate the law or public peace, and that it is inclined to the opinion that they come under section 8 of the solemn treaty between Spain and the United States relating to shipwrecked. As these men have been imprisoned for more than five weeks I shall be gratified if you will expedite their trial.

I have the honor to be, sir, your obedient servant,

PULASKI F. HYATT.

A true copy.

Letter from the missionary, Mr. Westmase, to the consul of the United States at Santiago de Cuba.

The AMERICAN CONSUL,
Santiago de Cuba.

SIR: I have just received a letter from my friend, Captain Bolten, who is in prison because he is suspected to have stolen a boat and has arrived at the port of Santiago de Cuba without passport.

I wish to state that I know the Captain well and I may verify the fact that the boat in which he made the voyage from Mole to Cuba was his exclusive property, as he bought her when he was in my house.

I know him to be a good and honest man, and I trust that you will use your authority to obtain his liberty.

Believe me, very truly, yours,

WESTMASE S. SMITH,
Wesleyan Missionary.

A true copy.

Decree ordering the liberty.

CUBA, *April 25, 1895.*

Mr. Judge of Instruction of the South District of this City.

Whereas by a decree dated the 1st instant proceedings were instituted against Messrs. August Bolten and Gustave Richelieu, and their imprisonment was decreed without bail.

Whereas although the investigation which the Spanish consul may have made at Port au Prince has not been received, yet, owing to the deposition made by the Spanish citizen, Don Manuel Barnuevo, and the other data contained in the procedure, there is no doubt that the motives which led to said imprisonment do not exist now, for which reason the provisions of article 528 of the law of criminal procedure have to be carried out. Let the above-mentioned August Bolton and Gustave Richelieu be set free, causing them to constitute a bond for their presentation every eight days before the court of tribunal which has cognizance of the case, and let the proper order be issued to the jailer.

Ordered by the judge and signed by him, which I certify to.

ARISTIDES MARAGLIANO.
ISIDRO DE TAPIA.

A true copy.

Order for the conclusion of the proceedings.

SANTIAGO DE CUBA, *April 26, 1895.*

Whereas this procedure was begun on February 23, on a charge of rebellion, against the American citizens Messrs. August Bolten and Gustave Richelieu, all the proceedings having been officially instituted;

Whereas the fact has been duly investigated and also its circumstances and authors; the conclusion of the summary is to be lawfully declared in the opinion of the signer of this order;

In view of articles 622 and 623 of the law of criminal procedure, the summary is delivered to be ended and let it pass to the superior court in the respectful form of style, after the prisoners have been summoned, and let the present order be communicated to the illustrious attorney of His Majesty.

A true copy.

———

Suspension.

TERRITORIAL COURT, SANTIAGO DE CUBA, *Secretaryship of the Island:*

In the criminal suit proceeding from that court instituted against August Bolten and Gustave Richelieu for the offense of rebellion and order for temporary suspension of the same, has been issued by the court of justice on June 22 of the present year, returning the papers of the case to you.

Which I communicate to you that you may take action upon them, duly acknowledging their receipt.

God guard you for many years.

Cuba, July 30, 1895.

A true copy.   Dr. RAMON MARTINEZ, *Secretary.*

———

[Translation.]

MINISTRY OF STATE,
San Sebastian, September 30, 1896.

EXCELLENCY.

MY DEAR SIR: After the note which I had the honor to send to you yesterday, relative to the claim of Mr. August Bolten, was written and approved, and while the documents accompanying it were being copied, I received your No. 174, of the 15th instant, making a similar claim in behalf of Richelieu, the other individual involved in the same case.

As the case is identical for Bolten and for Richelieu, since both were arrested on the same grounds, and since only one set of proceedings was instituted, I pray your excellency to consider as repeated, in answer to your said note No. 174, all I stated to your excellency in mine of yesterday also referred to.

I avail myself of this opportunity to renew to your excellency the assurances of my most distinguished consideration,

THE DUKE OF TETUAN.

The MINISTER PLENIPOTENTIARY OF THE UNITED STATES.

———

Mr. Olney to Mr. Taylor.

No. 603.]   DEPARTMENT OF STATE,
Washington, November 10, 1896.

SIR: Referring to the Department's No. 483 of March 18 and No. 556 of August 31 last, I have to say that the Department desires to know the status of the claims of Bolten and Richelieu against the Government of Spain.

I am, etc.,   RICHARD OLNEY.

Mr. Olney to Mr. Morse.

DEPARTMENT OF STATE,
Washington, November 19, 1896.

SIR: Referring to your letter of August 18 last, I have to say that the Department is advised by our minister at Madrid that the Spanish Government rejects the claim of Gustave Richelieu on the ground (1) that there was reasonable ground to arrest him and institute proceedings against him, and (2) that the judicial proceedings which resulted in his release were the shortest and most expeditious permitted by the laws of procedure to which both Spaniards and foreigners are subject.

I am, etc.,   RICHARD OLNEY.

———

Mr. Taylor to Mr. Olney.

No. 608.]   UNITED STATES LEGATION,
Madrid, November 21, 1896.

SIR: I have the honor to acknowledge the receipt of your No. 603, relative to the claims of Bolten and Richelieu, and in reply thereto to refer you to my No. 594, of the 4th instant, with inclosures, in which your inquiry is answered.

I am, etc.,   HANNIS TAYLOR.

———

Mr. Morse to Mr. Olney.

WASHINGTON, D. C., *December 2, 1896.*

SIR: I have the honor to acknowledge receipt of communication from the Department dated November 19, 1896, advising " that the Spanish Government rejects the claim of Gustave Richelieu on the ground (1) that there was reasonable ground to arrest him and institute proceedings against him, and (2) that the judicial proceedings which resulted in his release were the shortest and most expeditious permitted by the laws of procedure to which both Spaniards and foreigners are subject."

The answer of Spain as above abbreviated makes it clear to my mind that Spain has purposely or ignorantly misstated or mistaken the ground upon which the claim of Richelieu is rested. The claim rests upon a charge against Spain of the violation of stipulations of the treaty of 1795 in respect to Richelieu and Bolten, which are set out in terms in the brief filed by the undersigned. The law of nations is also relied upon to sustain the claim to a pecuniary indemnity.

However, as the undersigned proposes to reply at length to the answer of Spain rejecting the claim, I request that a copy of the expediente or other papers which have been transmitted to the (?) may be forwarded to the undersigned for consideration and reference when comparing such reply.

I am, sir, your obedient servant,

ALEXANDER PORTER MORSE,
Counsel for Richelieu.

Mr. Rockhill to Mr. Morse.

DEPARTMENT OF STATE,
Washington, December 3, 1896.

SIR: In reply to your letter of the 28th ultimo to Mr. Faison, I inclose herewith a copy of a dispatch from the United States minister at Madrid. No. 594, of the 4th ultimo, with its accompaniments, in regard to the rejection of the Richelieu-Bolten claim for indemnity.

I am, etc.,

W. W. ROCKHILL,
Assistant Secretary.

Mr. Olney to Mr. Morse.

DEPARTMENT OF STATE,
Washington, December 4, 1896.

SIR: In reply to your letter of the 2d instant, I have to say that on the 3d I promised to give you a copy of the dispatch from the United States minister at Madrid, showing the grounds for the rejection of the claim of Gustave Richelieu.

The papers are now being copied and will be sent to you without unnecessary delay.

I am, etc.,

RICHARD OLNEY.

Mr. Morse to Mr. Olney.

DECEMBER 19, 1896.

SIR: I have to acknowledge in due course the receipt of a communication from the Department of State, dated December 3, 1896, transmitting copy of a dispatch from the United States minister at Madrid, No. 594, of the 4th ultimo, with its accompaniments in regard to the rejection of the Richelieu-Bolten claim for indemnity.

Under date November 19, 1896, I had been informed by the Department that "the Spanish Government rejects the claim of Gustave Richelieu on the ground (1) that there was reasonable ground to arrest him and institute proceedings against him; and (2) that the judicial proceedings which resulted in his release were the shortest and most expeditious permitted by the laws of procedure to which both Spaniards and foreigners are subject."

Acknowledging the receipt of the last-mentioned communication I advised the Department that I proposed to reply at length to the answer of Spain rejecting the claim, and requested that a copy of the expediente or other papers which had been transmitted to the Department by the United States minister at Madrid should be forwarded to the undersigned for consideration and reference when preparing such reply.

I have just examined the portions of the expediente which were transmitted by the ministry of state, San Sebastian, September 29, 1896, to the United States minister at Madrid, and by the latter forwarded to Washington, and I have reached the conclusion that these papers, which are supposed to justify the rejection of these claims by Spain, do not require any lengthy reply, for the reasons following:

First. Because the objections to the entertainment by Spain of these claims have been anticipated, and have been, it seems to the under-signed, fully met and answered by a brief filed by the undersigned in the Department on the 20th day of August, 1896.

Second. Because the substantive matter contained in the expediente does not deny or contradict material allegations contained in the record and insisted upon by this Government in the diplomatic correspondence touching these claims. On the contrary, the official reports set out at length of the Spanish administrative authorities fully sustain the position taken on behalf of claimants. As to the first proposition, I am not informed whether or not the brief which I had the honor to transmit to the Department meets its approval; and there is nothing in the letter of transmittal of the United States minister at Madrid to indicate that he rested the claim on the ground taken in my brief. But if the Secretary of State will turn to page 11 of the brief he will observe that the claim against Spain was grounded from a violation by her administrative authorities in Cuba of plain and explicit guaranties of exemption from arrest and arbitrary interference by either Govern-ment in respect of the citizens or subjects of the other under circum-stances analogous to those which surrounded claimants. If I am cor-rect in my reading of the treaty provisions referred to, the claimants were not at the time of their first apprehension nor on occasion of their second arrest amenable to the jurisdiction of the authorities of Spain. And this was the view of the actual situation officially expressed by the United States consul at Santiago de Cuba as early as the 28th of March, 1895. (House Doc. No. 224, Fifty-fourth Congress, first session, p. 116.)

As to the second proposition, the attempt to justify the imprison-ment of Richelieu and Bolton, notwithstanding the evidence which was produced by the United States consul indicating the truth of their entire story, upon the deposition of a prisoner "undergoing a four months' sentence as receiver of stolen goods," which appears to have been the only ground for suspicion, was in keeping with the character of evidence upon which Spain has rested her defense in these cases. The depositions of the convict accused "the North American prisoners of having shipped from Haiti insurgents and ammunition;" and the communication of the ministry of state admits that the charges proffered by the deponent were not proved. That in the nature of things such a charge was without any basis whatever appears from the description of the boat contained in the report of the marine attorney. (See also House Doc. No. 224, Fifty-fourth Congress, first session, pp. 111–131.)

The charge that these American citizens had entered Cuban ports in a small craft without regularly documented clearance papers, if true, did not constitute a crime punishable by arbitrary arrest and cruel imprisonment for sixty-two days; and the failure to produce the same, if not accounted for, was at most a civil offense, subjecting the boat to seizure or detention in default of the payment of fine on the part of the officers or owners. And the personal papers which they carried, estab-lishing their identity and recognizing them as citizens of the United States, entitled them to the protection of the guarantees contained in the treaty of 1795. But, as has been asserted in our brief, neither the port of departure or destination was Cuban, but Haitian; and if the papers satisfied the authorities of the latter State, it was no concern of the Spanish officials. Storm driven and nearly shipwrecked, these unfortunate individuals were entitled to hospitality under the law of nations and the treaty provisions.

The charge that while in Haiti these individuals were plotting the crime of rebellion against Spain finds no basis for indulgence in the record, which, on the contrary contains evidence which exposes the frivolous character of this accusation, which appears to have been an afterthought of the administrative authorities.

In the absence of any criminating proof whatever, the circumstance that Richelieu and Bolten entered Cuban ports in open day at a time "immediately before the uprising of the insurgent forces at Guantanamo," furnished no sufficient ground or excuse for the cruel treatment and long imprisonment to which they were subjected. There is nothing in the record, which has been made up almost in its entirety by Spain, that connects these individuals or their disastrous voyage with the insurgents in Cuba or elsewhere. On the contrary, all the evidence corroborates, as the administrative authorities reluctantly admit, the accuracy in all essential particulars of the story of the storm-tossed seamen. The character and dimensions of the boat negative the possibility of its use as a transport for munitions or men. It was, what it was claimed by the seamen to be, a fishing craft. And the fact of its purchase at Port au Prince and the good character of Bolten is testified to by the Wesleyan missionary at that port.

In conclusion, I invite attention to the circumstance that, as appears from the communication of the ministry of state, San Sebastian, September 30, 1896, to the United States minister at Madrid, the conclusion to reject the claim of Bolten was reached after examination of the record in that case, and before the Richelieu record was considered. So far as the undersigned is informed, the former record was not supported by brief on the part of counsel nor was the claim for pecuniary indemnity placed upon the grounds upon which the claim in the Richelieu case was rested. In the Richelieu case a printed brief containing 30 pages was filed in the Department of State, which rested the claim for pecuniary indemnity upon the law of nations and provisions of the treaty of 1795. As this record was not examined or pressed upon Spain, it seems to me we are justified in asking the Government to again bring this claim to the attention of Spain for a determination of the issue fairly raised in the Richelieu record. I have, therefore, to ask consideration of the points suggested in this communication and to the printed argument on file in the Department, with a view to such action as to the honorable Secretary may seem just and proper under the circumstances.

The claimant, Richelieu, is in a desperate condition physically and financially, the result in great measure, as alleged, of cruel treatment by Spanish authorities in Cuba; and an appeal is made to his Government to secure for him and his associate in suffering, Bolten, some measure of pecuniary redress before the end comes.

But apart from considerations of a merely personal nature, I can not but believe that a high state purpose may well influence the action of the Government in demanding reparation for violations of treaty stipulations by Spain under the circumstances disclosed by the record in these cases.

I am, etc., ALEXANDER PORTER MORSE,
Of Counsel.

Mr. Olney to Mr. Taylor.

No. 634.]   DEPARTMENT OF STATE,
Washington, January 5, 1897.

SIR: Referring to your No. 594 of November 4 last, inclosing the reply made by the Spanish Government in the cases of Richelieu and Bolten, I now transmit copy of a recent letter from Mr. Alexander Porter Morse, counsel for Richelieu, which, together with the printed brief sent along with the memorial in behalf of the claimant, he desires to be placed in the hands of the Spanish Government.

I am, etc.,
RICHARD OLNEY.

Mr. Olney to Mr. Taylor.

No. 637.]   DEPARTMENT OF STATE,
Washington, January 6, 1897.

SIR: Referring to the Department's instruction to you of yesterday in regard to the case of Gustave Richelieu, I have to say that as a part of Mr. Morse's printed brief relates to matters which were for the consideration of this Department alone, you may use the arguments contained in it, with the exception of the reference to the citizenship of Richelieu, in making your reply to the last note of the Spanish Government on the subject.

As the case of Bolten is based upon precisely the same facts and is upon the same footing in all essentials with that of Richelieu, you will make your reply cover both cases. The two cases stand together, and the treatment of them should be joint.

I am, etc.,
RICHARD OLNEY.

[Telegram.]

Mr. Olney to Mr. Taylor.

DEPARTMENT OF STATE,
Washington, January 6, 1897.

AMERICAN MINISTER, *Madrid:*
Suspend action on No. 634.

Mr. Coakley to Mr. Olney.

BOSTON, *January 27, 1897.*

DEAR SIR: A gentleman, Pierre Gustave Laymet Richelieu, who claims to be an American citizen, and that he was unjustly imprisoned in Cuba by the Spaniards, has requested me to write you, asking how his case before the Spanish court stands at present. He has shown me communications from his attorney at Washington, Mr. A. P. Morse, in which that gentleman informs him that his claim for indemnity from the Spanish Government because of his imprisonment has been marked "Special" by the State Department, and that it was to be pressed with all possible speed.

It is some time now since he has heard anything, and he would like to hear from you just how his case stood, and when, if ever, there was a likelihood of its being settled. He is in very straitened circumstances and suffering keenly from poverty.

Hoping for an early reply, yours, very respectfully,

JOHN J. COAKLEY.

(Care of Boston Traveler, Boston, Mass.)

Mr. Morse to Mr. Olney.

WASHINGTON, D. C., *March 1, 1897.*

SIR: My attention has been called to the statement of the case of Gustave Richelieu in the list of American citizens, native and naturalized, who were arrested and imprisoned in Cuba since February 24, 1895, and which was transmitted to the Senate by the President on the 25th of January, 1897, in response to Senate resolution of December 21, 1896.

This statement, as printed in Document No. 84, Fifty-fourth Congress, second session, page 3, understates the case, and is misleading in particulars which it is desirable should be corrected as soon as an opportunity to do so occurs.

The fact is, that Richelieu and his companion, August Bolten, also a citizen of the United States, were not "taken in a boat near 'Santiago,'" as stated, but were arrested after they had landed, and when they were on their way to the United States consulate to report in accordance with their duty and treaty rights; and so far from being released "shortly after" were held in a loathsome prison with criminals and convicts for sixty-two days, notwithstanding the most earnest and repeated demands for their release which were made by the United States consul, under instructions from the Department.

As these cases have received the special consideration of the Department, and as the American minister at Madrid has been instructed to urge their settlement, it is important that no other than a correct statement should appear in a public document issued by the United States. It seems to the undersigned, further, that it should appear that neither Richelieu nor Bolten were natives of Spain, the former being native of France and the latter of Sweden.

I am, sir, your obedient servant,

ALEXANDER PORTER MORSE,
Counsel for Richelieu.

Senator Lodge to Mr. Sherman.

WASHINGTON, D. C., *March 8, 1897.*

SIR: I inclose herewith a letter which explains itself. I bespeak for this case your attention and consideration, and I trust it may be taken up and acted upon.

Very respectfully, yours,   H. C. LODGE.

BOSTON, *March 3, 1897.*

DEAR SIR: I have been requested to write you by a man in Boston here who has a claim against the Spanish Government, and who would like to have you see what has been done or is likely to be done with it.

S. Doc. 231, pt 7——41

His name is Gustave Richelieu; he is a Frenchman, but a naturalized American citizen.   On January 23, 1895, he and a companion named August Bolten were taken prisoners at Santiago de Cuba by the Spaniards, on suspicion of being Cuban spies. After some time they were liberated, and returned to the United States.   They each made a claim for $10,000 indemnity from Spain, and the State Department, after looking their claim up, instructed the American minister at Madrid to push the claims.   Richelieu's attorney is Alexander P. Morse, 505 Pennsylvania avenue, Washington.

Richelieu has not heard anything for some time concerning his claim, and he is anxious to know just where it stands.   He is old and crippled, and lost his all when taken prisoner in Cuba.   He has not a cent in the world, and subsists on what is given him.   Under the circumstances, if you could do anything to hasten a settlement of his claim you would be doing an act of great charity.

Hoping to hear from you,

Yours, very respectfully,

JOHN J. COAKLEY,
307 Washington street, Boston.
(Care of Boston Traveler.)

Senator HENRY CABOT LODGE.

Mr. Taylor to Mr. Sherman.

No. 660.]   LEGATION OF THE UNITED STATES,
Madrid, March 9, 1897.

SIR: I have the honor to inclose, with translation, the last communication of the Spanish Government touching the case of Bolten-Richelieu, and to await your further instructions, if any.

I am, etc.,

HANNIS TAYLOR.

[Translation.]

MINISTRY OF STATE, *Palace, March 1, 1897.*

EXCELLENCY.

MY DEAR SIR: As inclosures to your note of the 29th of January last you sent to me an argument presented in support of the claim of the sailor Gustave Richelieu by his attorney, and a letter from the same lawyer written after having read the answer which I had the honor to address to your excellency on the 29th of September last.

Having examined both documents, I can not find in them any reason to modify the conclusions arrived at in that date.

The whole argument of the lawyer, Mr. Morse, rests upon a supposed violation of Articles VI, VII, and VIII of the treaty of 1795 committed by our authorities in detaining two citizens of the United States for the simple fact of having landed in the coasts of Cuba.

The briefest examination of the true facts discloses a grave mistake in that hypothesis.

Richelieu and his companion, Bolten, were not detained for having landed in Spanish territory, as I have already had occasion to demonstrate to your excellency.

Their arrest took place when the island of Cuba was at the beginning of a formidable insurrection.   In every point of the coast landed large and small expeditions—arrived from several ports and shores of the Mexican Gulf.   Many of those who afterwards took a part in the rebellion as chiefs, rank soldiers, and scouts, came precisely from Haiti, as is well known, using small crafts similar to that of the claimants.   In no other manner did the well-known chief Antonio Maceo join the insurgent bands, and so great was the number of those who used this means of coming to and going from the island that I do not consider it venturesome to say that at a certain time there was a regular communication by means of small crafts and open boats between Cuba and the Antilles and the nearest keys.

Under these circumstances, and when it was necessary to check such infiltration or entering of rebels by means of a close watch upon even the apparently most humble and harmless, the claimants arrived at the port of Guantanamo, without any documents whatever to prove their nationality or that of their vessel, and afterwards, without authorization, they went to Santiago de Cuba.

What charge can be made against the proper marine authority for having detained them, not for the imaginary offense of having landed in Spanish territory, but as suspicious persons—that is to say, only until it could be ascertained whether or not they were entitled to enjoy the benefits of the above-mentioned treaty?   Indeed, who will maintain that those benefits are absolutely unconditional, and that they extend even to those who bear hostile intentions for the integrity or for the sovereignty of Spain? Despite the perspicacity which may naturally be attributed to such an experienced lawyer, Mr. Morse has failed to make a distinction essential for the proper appreciation of the present case, viz, that in practice the time of the application of a legal text may vary when there are sufficient reasons for it. In fact, the application of the treaty of 1795 did not suffer any alteration, but only a justified delay, which was followed by the full and immediate application of the treaty as soon as it was possible to do so.

After obtaining the proofs—which, by the way, were negative—of the innocence of the claimants, they were placed in liberty, and your excellency is well aware, by my previous communications, of the very just causes which delayed the taking of this decision, such as the change of jurisdiction requested by a consul of your nation and the necessity of issuing letters rogatory in the interests of the claimants themselves; therefore no complaint should be based upon that inevitable delay.

It is therefore evident that the agreement of 1795 was perfectly complied with in the case of Bolten-Richelieu, and that all the consequences which it was pretended to draw from the basis of its violation, and with them the whole contents of Mr. Morse's argument, have lost their value.

Only for the purpose of defining more clearly still the true significance and importance of the detention imposed upon the claimants, I will rebate a secondary statement contained in said document. The attorney of Richelieu imagines to have discovered an irregularity in the administration of justice which, according to him, consists of the fact that the civil tribunal confirmed the penalty imposed by that of marine without considering that where there is no sentence there can be no confirmation. One jurisdiction having inhibited the case in favor of the other, and the latter having maintained the detention of the two claimants, it is seen, without doubts of any kind, that that detention was only preventive and not penal, and this essential difference compels that Government of His Majesty to deny the right of the claimants to an indemnity.

I will not answer here to the charges of cruelty made by Mr. Morse against our authorities, nor to the absurd supposition that Bolton and Richelieu had been accused of having rebelled against Spain while in Haiti. I have already rebutted and cleared those charges in my above-mentioned note.

As regards the letter of Mr. Morse, your occupations and mine do not allow me to discuss in detail a writing which is limited to confirming in general terms the contents of the brief. The latter having been answered, the former is also answered, and I believe that your excellency will agree with me in this, although I do not fail to understand the motive of your having sent me a document in which the statements of the former are confirmed.

It only remains for me to observe that the Government of His Majesty finds the conduct of its delegates as regards the case of Bolten-Richelieu to be above all censure and perfectly reasonable and correct, and that it must support and uphold them against the arguments of Mr. Morse with all decision, inasmuch as it has recently shown its purpose to rigorously exact from the Cuban authorities the fulfillment of the interior laws and of the international agreements. The deference which in all occasions the Government of his Majesty observes toward that of the United States has induced this Government, in spite of the decision previously communicated to your excellency, to again take up the subject; but I deem it my duty to inform you that, despite our best wishes to please your Government, it will not be possible for us to discuss any further the present claim which, by the above, I consider to be definitely ended.

I gladly avail myself of this opportunity to renew to your excellency the assurances of my highest consideration.

THE DUKE OF TETUAN.

Mr. Rockhill to Mr. Morse.

DEPARTMENT OF STATE,
Washington, March 10, 1897.

SIR: Your letter of the 1st instant, relating to the arrest and imprisonment in Cuba of Gustave Richelieu, has been received.

Your suggestion regarding a correction of the statement that Richelieu and Bolten were captured in a boat near Santiago has been noted in the dispatch containing this report.

Respectfully, yours,   W. W. ROCKHILL,
Assistant Secretary.

Mr. Rockhill to Senator H. C. Lodge.

DEPARTMENT OF STATE,
Washington, March 10, 1897.

SIR: In reply to your letter of the 8th instant, in regard to the claim of Gustave Richelieu against the Government of Spain, I have the honor to say, by direction of the Secretary, that the claim has been presented to the Spanish Government. That Government denies its obligation to indemnify Mr. Richelieu. The Department has instructed our minister at Madrid to again present the claim with additional arguments. Mr. Alexander Porter Morse, Mr. Richelieu's attorney, is kept fully advised of the progress of the case.

Respectfully, yours,   W. W. ROCKHILL,
Assistant Secretary.

Mr. Rockhill to Mr. Coakley.

DEPARTMENT OF STATE,
Washington, March 26, 1897.

SIR: I have to acknowledge the receipt of your letter of the 22d instant in regard to the claim of Gustave Richelieu against Spain.

In reply I have to say that Mr. Richelieu's attorney, Mr. Alexander Porter Morse, of 1505 Pennsylvania avenue, Washington, D. C., has been kept fully informed in regard to the case, and will no doubt keep his client advised. The claim has been urged with vigor and persistency, but Spain has not conceded the right to indemnity.

Respectfully, yours,   W. W. ROCKHILL,
Assistant Secretary.

Mr. Morse to Mr. Sherman.

WASHINGTON, D. C., *April 10, 1897.*

SIR: I transmit an additional affidavit of complainant in the matter of the claim of Gustave Richelieu against Spain on account of arbitrary arrest and false imprisonment at Santiago de Cuba, setting forth the place and date of complainant's naturalization as a citizen of the United States, with the request that it be filed with and annexed to the papers in this case now on file in the Department.

I am, sir, your obedient servant,

ALEXANDER PORTER MORSE,
Of Counsel for Complainant.

Know all men by these presents:

That I, Gustave Richelieu, of Boston, county of Suffolk and Commonwealth of Massachusetts, do hereby make oath, depose, and swear that on or about the 10th day of September, A. D. 1871, I took out my first papers declaring my intention of being a citizen of the United States, at Portland, Oreg., and that on or about the 12th day of April, A. D. 1876, I took out my final papers which made me a citizen of the United States in Boston, State of Massachusetts, said final papers being made out and recorded in the district court of the United States for the district of Massachusetts. That for some reason unknown to me there is no record of my final naturalization.

Witness my hand and seal this 26th day of December, 1895.

GUSTAVE RICHELIEU.

COMMONWEALTH OF MASSACHUSETTS, *Suffolk, ss:*

BOSTON, *December 26, 1895.*

There personally appeared the above-named Gustave Richelieu and made oath to the truth of the above subscribed by him.

Before me,

CORNELIUS P. SULLIVAN,
Justice of the Peace.

Superior court for the transaction of criminal business within and for said county.

COMMONWEALTH OF MASSACHUSETTS, *Suffolk, ss:*

I, John P. Manning, of Boston, in said county, duly elected, qualified, and sworn as clerk of the said superior court, within and for said county and Commonwealth, said court being a court of record with a seal, which is hereto affixed, do hereby certify that Cornelius P. Sullivan, by and before whom the foregoing acknowledgment or proof was taken, was, at the time of taking the same, a justice of the peace, authorized to act in said Commonwealth, and was duly authorized by the laws of said Commonwealth to take and certify acknowledgments or proofs of deeds of land in said Commonwealth, and, further, that I am well acquainted with the handwriting of said Cornelius P. Sullivan, and that I verily believe that the signature to said certificate of acknowledgment or proof is genuine.

In testimony whereof I have hereunto set my hand and affixed the seal of said court this 27th day of December, 1895.

[SEAL.]

JOHN P. MANNING,
Clerk of said Court.

Mr. Morse to Mr. Sherman.

WASHINGTON, D. C., *April 12, 1897.*

SIR: I transmit herewith certificate of Dr. P. W. Heffern, the attending physician of the Boston Emergency Hospital, dated April 2, 1897, as to the condition and treatment of Gustave Richelieu, claimant for pecuniary indemnity against Spain on account of his arbitrary arrest, false imprisonment, and cruel treatment by the administrative authorities at Santiago de Cuba, with the request that said certificate be filed with and attached to the papers in the claim of said Richelieu.

I am, sir, your obedient servant,

ALEXANDER PORTER MORSE.

BOSTON EMERGENCY HOSPITAL,
Boston, April 2, 1897.

To whom it may concern:

This is to certify that Gustave Pichelieu has been treated by me since December, 1896, for muscular and articular rheumatism, the attacks being so serious at times as to occasion the joints to swell up and rendering him unfit to work.

P. W. HEFFERN, M. D.

Mr. Rockhill to Mr. Morse.

DEPARTMENT OF STATE,
Washington, April 14, 1897.

SIR: The Department has received your letter of the 12th instant, inclosing a certificate of Dr. P. W. Heffern, of the Boston Emergency Hospital, relative to the condition and treatment of Gustave Richelieu, a claimant for indemnity against the Spanish Government.

Respectfully, yours,

W. W. ROCKHILL,
Assistant Secretary.

FIFTY-FIFTH CONGRESS, FIRST SESSION.

July 7, 1897.

[Senate Report No. 371.]

Mr. Lodge, from the Committee on Foreign Relations, submitted the following report:

The facts in connection with this case are fully recited in Document No. 47, Fifty-fifth Congress, first session, and in House Document No. 224, Fifty-fourth Congress, first session, pages 111 to 134.

An examination of these documents discloses, in brief, that August Bolten and Gustave Richelieu, two naturalized American citizens, the former a native of Sweden and the latter of France, set out in a small, open boat about 15 feet long from Port au Prince on February 5, 1895. Their object was to fish for green turtles, and, with this in view, they intended to sail up as far as Cape Haitien. Both men were sailors who had drifted to Haiti from New York during the years 1893 and 1894. It appears that Bolten had managed to save a little money by doing some painting at Port au Prince, and that the small fishing boat was his property. Before leaving port the men secured the usual papers issued from the American consulate, which identified them and established their American citizenship. This attempt to go in a small, open boat from one Haitien port to another did not succeed, and they were finally driven, by stress of weather, to the coast of Cuba. Temporary landings were effected at one or two points along the Haitien and Cuban coasts, and finally, almost destitute of food and water, and after drifting about for several days, they reached Santiago de Cuba. The testimony discloses that they at once produced their papers for inspection to the captain of the port, explained their distress, and asked to be directed to the United States consul. Notwithstanding these admitted facts, they were seized by the military authorities on February 23, 1895, and thrown into a prison, from which they were not released until May 3 following. During this imprisonment both men were kept in close confinement much of the time, and both suffered great injury to health thereby. Bolten contracted yellow fever.

The seizure of these men is believed by the committee to have been in violation of article 8 of the treaty of 1795, which (in the language of Secretary Olney) "provides for the hospitable reception of American citizens who, through stress of weather, are driven upon Spanish territory." It is further evident to the committee that the proceedings inaugurated by the military authorities against Bolten and Richelieu are a violation of the protocol of January 12, 1877, which (again quoting Secretary Olney) "provides that citizens of the United States taken without arms in hand shall be tried by the ordinary civil tribunals, to the exclusion of any special tribunal, and when arrested and imprisoned shall be deemed to be arrested or imprisoned by order of the civil authority." Both men were held by the military authorities from the 23d of February to the 21st of March, when they were turned over to the civil tribunal of the province of Santiago. It ought further to be observed that a most rigid search at the time of their seizure by the Spanish authorities failed to disclose any arms or papers or other evidences of unlawful intent.

Bolten and Richelieu have each asked for an indemnity of $10,000 from the Spanish Government for the injuries resulting from their sixty-two days of confinement and also for the confiscation of the fishing boat. A settlement of this claim has been pressed upon Spain through the proper diplomatic channels of our Government. This effort has been unavailing, and the Spanish Government has distinctly declined "to discuss any further the present claims" and consider the incident "to be definitely ended."

In view of the above, the committee is of the opinion that it is the manifest duty of the United States to take such prompt measures as shall be adequate to obtain an indemnity for all wrongs and injuries suffered by the two American sailors, Bolten and Richelieu.

The committee accordingly reports the following joint resolution, and recommends its adoption:

JOINT RESOLUTION for the relief of August Bolten and Gustave Richelieu. '

Whereas it appears from the correspondence transmitted to the Senate by the message of the President of the nineteenth day of April, eighteen hundred and ninety-seven (Executive Document Numbered Forty-seven, first session Fifty-fifth Congress), that an indemnity has been demanded by the executive department of the United States from the Spanish Government, for, without avail, for the wrongful arrest and imprisonment of August Bolten and Gustave Richelieu, two naturalized citizens of the United States, under circumstances that render the Kingdom of Spain justly responsible therefor; and

Whereas it further appears, from the correspondence aforesaid, that all the diplomatic efforts of the Government of the United States exerted for an amicable adjustment and payment of the just indemnity due to the aforesaid citizens of the United States, upon whose persons the aforesaid wrongs were inflicted, have proved entirely unavailing: Therefore,

Resolved by the Senate and House of Representatives of the United States of America in Congress assembled, That the President of the United States be, and he is hereby, empowered to take such measures as in his judgment may be necessary to obtain the indemnity from the Spanish Government for the wrongs and injuries suffered by August Bolten and Gustave Richelieu, by reason of their wrongful arrest and imprisonment by Spanish authorities at Santiago de Cuba in the year eighteen hundred and ninety-five: and to secure this end he is authorized and requested to employ such means or exercise such power as may be necessary.

FIFTY-FIFTH CONGRESS, SPECIAL SESSION.

[Senate Executive A.]

Message from the President of the United States, in answer to the resolution of the Senate of February 26, 1897, transmitting a report from the Secretary of State and copies of correspondence in regard to the case of George Washington Aguirre, in Cuba.

MARCH 4, 1897.—Read the first time and referred to the Committee on Foreign Relations, and, together with the message and accompanying papers, ordered to be printed in confidence for the use of the Senate.

To the Senate :

I transmit herewith, in answer to the resolution of the Senate of the 26th ultimo, a report from the Secretary of State, accompanied by copies of correspondence, in regard to the case of George Washington Aguirre in Cuba.

As two of these letters, marked "Confidential," contain statements that might, if made public, prove prejudicial to Mr. Aguirre's interests, I suggest that they be regarded as confidential.

                                    GROVER CLEVELAND.

EXECUTIVE MANSION,
    Washington, March 3, 1897.

The PRESIDENT:

The Secretary of State, to whom was referred the resolution of the Senate of the 26th ultimo, wherein the President is requested, "if it is not, in his opinion, incompatible with the public interests, to communicate to the Senate such information as has been furnished to or obtained by the Executive or the Department of State relating to the arrest and imprisonment of, and any proceedings against, George Washington Aguirre, a youth of 19 years of age, and an alleged citizen of the United States, who to obtain the benefit of a general amnesty proclaimed by the Captain-General of Cuba, is alleged to have surrendered to the Spanish authorities in Cuba on the 4th day of July, 1896," has the honor to transmit the accompanying copies of correspondence exchanged between this Department and the consul-general of the United States at Havana upon the subject.

Respectfully submitted.

RICHARD OLNEY.

DEPARTMENT OF STATE,
Washington, March 3, 1897.

List of papers.

Mr. Rockhill to Mr. Lee, telegram, July 14, 1896.
Mr. Lee to Mr. Rockhill, No. 52, July 15, 1896.
Mr. Rockhill to Mr. Lee, *confidential*, July 21, 1896.
Mr. Rockhill to Mr. Lee, telegram, July 24, 1896.
Mr. Lee to Mr. Rockhill, telegram, July 25, 1896.
Mr. Lee to Mr. Rockhill, *confidential*, about July 30, 1896.
Mr. Lee to Mr. Rockhill, No. 72, July 30, 1896.
Mr. Lee to Mr. Rockhill, No. 87, August 18, 1896.
Mr. Taylor to Mr. Olney, No. 636, January 29, 1897.
Mr. Olney to Mr. Taylor, telegram, March 1, 1897.
Mr. Taylor to Mr. Olney, telegram, March 2, 1897.

Mr. Rockhill to Mr. Lee.

[Telegram]

DEPARTMENT OF STATE
Washington, July 14, 1896.

George Aguirre, claiming American citizenship, reported captured by Spanish gunboat and imprisoned at Havana. Investigate and report by cable.

ROCKHILL.

Mr. Lee to Mr. Rockhill.

No. 52.]   UNITED STATES CONSULATE-GENERAL,
Havana, July 15, 1896.

SIR: I have the honor to acknowledge the receipt of your telegram, dated 14th instant. (See preceding.)

I had already addressed the Admiral commanding this naval station with respect to this case, as Aguirre was captured by the marine authorities, and I also sent a communication to the Governor-General of the same tenor, both dated 13th instant. I claimed Aguirre as an American, a native of New York, certifying to his inscription as such in the register of citizens of this consulate-general, and asked for his release should there be no charges against him; otherwise that he be tried by civil jurisdiction, in conformity with the treaty between the United States and Spain of 1795 and the protocol of January 12, 1877.

I have received a communication from the Admiral dated 14th instant, in which he states that the question of jurisdiction is pending and being examined, and that my communication had been referred to the fiscal or prosecuting officer for his opinion thereon, according to law.

I have, in consequence, transmitted the following telegram, which I confirm:

Had already claimed Aguirre American. Informed by Admiral question jurisdiction now pending.

I am, etc.,

FITZHUGH LEE.

Mr. Rockhill to Mr. Lee.

[Personal.—Confidential.]

WASHINGTON, *July 21, 1896.*

DEAR GENERAL LEE: I have been approached here by several friends of young George Washington Aguirre, now in prison in Havana, and about whom I cabled on the 14th instant, asking if his release from prison could not be promptly secured. I told them that you had already asked the Captain-General for his release in case there were no charges against him, and that I entertained no doubt that you would be able to promptly secure it in that case. I added, however, that had he actually taken an active part in the military operations of the insurgents, notwithstanding his American citizenship, there would probably be considerable delay, and he might have to undergo a term of imprisonment.

The boy is represented to me as delicate and under age, and the case would seem to be an exceptionally hard one, although he has flown into the lion's mouth of his own free will.

I trust in view of these facts that the Spanish authorities may be found willing to be especially lenient in his case.

Very truly, yours,

W. W. ROCKHILL.

———

Mr. Rockhill to Mr. Lee.

[Telegram]

WASHINGTON, *July 24, 1896.*

It is reported that George Aguirre has been turned over to the military authorities His American citizenship being shown to your satisfaction, and all known facts disproving capture with arms in hand, you will, if reported delivery to military court be true, renew demand for civil proceedings, pursuant to treaty and protocol.

———

Mr. Lee to Mr. Rockhill.

[Telegram.]

HAVANA, *July 25, 1896.*

Admiral informed me on 23d date previous that he had inhibited marine jurisdiction in case George Aguirre in favor of military jurisdiction. I immediately claimed of Governor-General his trial by civil court under treaty or release. No reply yet received.

LEE.

———

Mr. Lee to Mr. Rockhill.

[Personal.—Confidential.]

CONSULATE-GENERAL OF THE UNITED STATES,
Havana, July —, 1896. (Received about July 30 or 31.)

MY DEAR MR. ROCKHILL: Replying to your personal letter of 21st July, in reference to George Washington Aguirre, I write to say I am informed he has been in the insurgent army, and that he left it, went to the seashore, and with four companions compelled two Spanish fishermen to put him in a boat for the purpose of reaching Havana.

His four companions returned to the interior. Aguirre then gave each fisherman gold to carry him to Havana, and was captured en route. Seeing that he could not avoid capture, he threw his only weapon—his pistol—overboard, with some letters and papers he had on his person, and when taken stated he was on his way to Havana to " present himself," which means, I suppose, to surrender. The impression is that he was on his way to New York.

The poor fishermen have been tried and sentenced to be shot, but the sentence was afterwards commuted to imprisonment for life in the African fortress.

I have protested against Aguirre's trial by military court, but as yet nothing has been done. His case was removed from the marine to the military jurisdiction.

I shall insist, if he is tried, that the trial take place before the civil courts, and shall watch his case closely.

Very truly, yours,

FITZHUGH LEE.

Mr. Lee to Mr. Rockhill.

No. 72.]   UNITED STATES CONSULATE-GENERAL,
Havana, July 30, 1896.

SIR: With reference to my dispatch No. 68, of the 27th instant, relative to the case of the American citizen, Mr. George W. Aguirre, captured, as I am informed, without arms in hand, in a boat while coming to this port, I beg to state that I addressed communications on the 11th instant both to the Captain-General and to the admiral of this naval station asking for Aguirre's release should there be no charges against him; otherwise that he be tried by the civil jurisdiction, in conformity with the treaty between the United States and Spain of 1795, and the protocol of January 12, 1877.

On the 23d of July I received a note from the admiral stating that he had inhibited the marine jurisdiction in favor of the military, and I therefore again addressed another communication to the Captain-General confirming my former request of the 11th to the effect that Mr. Aguirre be released or tried by the civil jurisdiction. I received yesterday, in response to the above, a note from the Governor-General, copy translation of which I beg to submit herewith to the Department.

I am, etc.,

FITZHUGH LEE.

[Inclosure in No. 72.—Translation.]

The Governor-General of the Island of Cuba presents his respects to the consul-general of the United States, and has the pleasure to inform him, in answer to his courteous note of to-day, that the case of the American citizen, Mr. George W. Aguirre, is now pending resolution as to what jurisdiction shall have cognizance thereof, and that the judge-advocate acting as prosecutor having reported thereon, the case is now referred to the judge-advocate-general, who will soon resolve if the war jurisdiction shall inhibit the cognizance of the case in favor of the ordinary.

The Lieutenant-General Weyler, marquis of Tenerife, avails himself of the occasion to reiterate to Mr. Fitzhugh Lee the assurances of his esteem and distinguished consideration.

HAVANA, *July 29, 1896.*

Mr. Lee to Mr. Rockhill.

No. 87.]

UNITED STATES CONSULATE-GENERAL,
Havana, August 18, 1896.

SIR: With reference to my dispatches Nos. 52, 68, and 72, dated, respectively, the 15th, 27th, and 30th ultimo, relative to the case of the American citizen Mr. George W. Aguirre, I now beg to inclose a copy translation of a communication received yesterday from the Captain-General, informing me of the transfer of Mr. Aguirre's case to the civil jurisdiction for trial.

I am, sir, etc.,

FITZHUGH LEE.

[Inclosure in No. 87.—Translation.]

CAPTAINCY-GENERAL OF THE ISLAND OF CUBA,
Havana, August 17, 1896.

The CONSUL-GENERAL OF THE UNITED STATES,
Present.

SIR: In accord with my judge-advocate, I have, under this date, waived the cognizance of the cause which had been instituted on the charge of rebellion against the American citizen, Mr. George W. Aguirre, Santiuste, in favor of the court of instruction of Jaruco, to which in due season will be forwarded the proceedings for their continuation.

I beg to inform you the above for your knowledge.

God guard you many years.

VALERIANO WEYLER.

Mr. Taylor to Mr. Olney.

No. 636.]

UNITED STATES LEGATION,
Madrid, Januarg 29, 1897.

SIR: On the 22d instant I had the honor to receive from you the following cablegram in cipher:

Three United States citizens have been under arrest in Cuba without charges: Frank T. Larrieu, Cardenas jail since May, 1896; Esteben Venero, Havana, since November, 1896; José Gonzales, since September, 1896. Demand that charges be immediately formulated and made known to accused, or that they be released. The following persons have been in Cuban prisons awaiting trial: Joseph L. Cespero, since January, 1896; Theodore Vives, since November, 1896; George W. Aguirre, since July, 1896; *Competitor* prisoners since April. Delay in all these cases unreasonable. Demand immediate trial or release.

* * * * * * *

On the 27th instant I had the honor to receive from you the following in cipher:

Your cable 26th received. Press demands in mine of 22d with all reasonable discretion, of course. Nevertheless, rights and liberty of American citizens are paramount objects of care of this Government.

Thereupon I immediately asked an interview of the minister for foreign affairs, whose result I reported to you as follows on the 28th instant:

Interview with minister for foreign affairs to-day. Following answer given to your cipher telegram of 22d. Proceedings now going on according to protocol against Francis T. Larrieu and *Competitor* prisoners. As to all the rest, whose cases have never before been presented to him, he says he has already requested ministers for war and colonies to order Cuban authorities to take proper proceedings immediately.

I am, sir, etc.,

HANNIS TAYLOR.

Mr. Olney to Mr. Taylor.

[Telegram.]

DEPARTMENT OF STATE,
Washington, March 1, 1897.

Referring my cable January 22 and yours of 28th, am constrained to say no progress apparent in any of said cases. Ask immediate attention to all of them.

OLNEY.

Mr. Taylor to Mr. Olney.

[Telegram.]

MADRID, *March 2, 1897.*

Interview with minister for foreign affairs, read your last cablegram and insisted upon exact answer to each demand contained in your cablegram of January 22. He said that he cabled immediately for reports in each case, which are now arriving by mail. From data in hand, says charges have been made in the three cases of which you complained on that account; in every case says proceedings are going on according to law and protocol, and will do all possible to hasten them. Cuban authorities say José Gonzales has not claimed to be American citizen. Witnesses now being examined in case of Larrieu.

TAYLOR.

CONDITION OF AFFAIRS IN CUBA.

CONDITION OF AFFAIRS IN CUBA.

IN THE SENATE OF THE UNITED STATES,
May 16, 1896.

Resolved, That the Committee on Foreign Relations is directed to inquire and report to the Senate what are the rights of the United States, under our treaties with Spain, as to the trial of our citizens arrested in Cuba and now under condemnation and sentenced to death by the Spanish military tribunals, for alleged offenses of a political or other character against the Spanish laws or Government, and to report on that subject by bill or otherwise.

2. That the Secretary of State is directed to send to the Senate literal copies of the original text of a protocol of conference and declarations concerning judicial procedure, signed by Caleb Cushing, as minister of the United States, and Señor Don Fernando Y. Collantes, minister of the King of Spain, on January twelfth, eighteen hundred and seventy-seven, as the same was executed and interchanged, both in the English and Spanish languages; and that he will inform the Senate whether the established or agreed original text of said protocol is in the English or the Spanish language.

3. That the President is requested, if it is not incompatible with the public service, to communicate to the Senate copies of any correspondence that has taken place between the Governments of Spain and the United States respecting the said protocol and its bearing or effect upon the trial and condemnation of citizens of the United States who were recently captured on or near the vessel called the *Competitor,* which was seized under Spanish authority in Cuban waters, or near to that island.

Attest

WM. R. COX, *Secretary.*

May 20, 1896.

STATEMENT OF FREDERICK W. LAWRENCE.

FREDERICK W. LAWRENCE was duly sworn.

By Senator DAVIS:

. What is your full name?—A. Frederick W. Lawrence.

Q. Where do you live?—A. In New York City at present.

Q. What is your employment?—A. Correspondent of the New York Journal.

. How long have you been so employed?—A. Since December.

. Are you a citizen of the United States?—A. Yes, sir.

. Have you visited the Island of Cuba recently?—A. Yes, sir.

. When did you arrive there?—A. Nine weeks ago last Saturday.

. Until when did you remain?—A. A week ago last Sunday.

Q. In what capacity?—A. As correspondent to the Journal.

Q. In what place in Cuba did you remain?—A. At Habana.

Q. Were you during your stay in Cuba at any time within the lines of the insurgent troops?—A. No, sir; I made no effort to disobey the laws of the Government of Cuba.

Q. Did you make any excursions from Habana?—A. Yes, sir.

Q. How many?—A. Three.

Q. State to what places and the distance to each place.—A. To Guines, a distance of about 40 miles; Guanabacoa, a distance of about 7 miles, and to Marinoa, a distance of about 9 miles.

Q. Were all of these places within the Spanish line?—A. Every one of them; yes, sir; that is to say, the Spanish claimed them, and at the time I went to them they were; but recently the insurgents have gone to at least one of them, that is Marinoa.

Q. Do you mean permanently advanced their line?—A. No, sir; they have no lines; that is, their columns have gone in and got out again; they have broken the Spanish lines.

Q. Under what circumstances did you leave the Island of Cuba?—A. I was expelled by order of the Captain-General.

Q. Was that order verbal or in writing?—A. In writing.

Q. Have you a copy of it?—A. I have it in New York.

Q. Will you furnish a copy to the committee?—A. With pleasure.

Q. When was that order delivered to you?—A. It was delivered to me on Thursday before I left Habana.

Q. Does the order allege for what reason it was given?—A. Yes, sir.

Q. What reason was given?—A. It is alleged that both James Creelman and myself, he being named in the same order, were expelled from the Island of Cuba for sending to our papers false notices of cruelties by the Spanish troops, and inventing news of insurgent victories.

Q. Were those statements true?—A. Not a single statement made in the order of deportation is true, except the words that we are the correspondents. I so informed the Captain-General in writing before I left there.

Q. Did you receive any response?—A. No, sir.

Q. When you arrived in Habana, which I understand you to say was March 20, 1896, did you place yourself in communication with the Spanish authorities?—A. Yes, sir.

Q. For what purpose did you place yourself in communication with them?—A. For the purpose of gathering information concerning the situation of affairs there and gathering news that would be of interest to the people of this country or to my paper.

Q. Did you state your purpose to them?—A. I made no statement to them, but made no attempt to conceal from them my purpose, and openly and avowedly stated I was there for the purpose of obtaining information.

Q. Did you desire to obtain information from the Spanish authorities as to the condition of affairs in Cuba?—A. Yes, sir.

Q. With what success?—A. Very little; absolutely none as far as the true condition of affairs was concerned.

Q. Did they give you at all their version of current events?—A. Yes, sir.

Q. Did you ascertain whether such information was reliable or unreliable?—A. At the time, having no other information at hand, I was compelled to accept it as reliable, and so sent it, but found afterwards that statements given to me were untrue.

Q. From what source did you find those statements were untrue?—A. From gentlemen who came into Habana and also gentlemen in Habana.

Q. From gentlemen who came from where?—A. From gentlemen who came into Habana from where the scene of action was laid.

Q. From territory occupied by the insurgents?—A. Yes, sir.

Q. In what respects, stating generally, did you find this information to be unreliable?—A. As to battles fought.

Q. Well, in what respect as to them?—A. The military censor is the man who gives out the Government reports of engagements between the Spanish and insurgents. He has hours for doing it and at those hours all the newspaper men in Habana are supposed to be present. He edits them, and the Habana newspapers are compelled to print them. Before they are written up they are compelled to be submitted to the censor, who arranges them as to what he wishes the public to know, and if the published news is changed in the smallest particular from the way it is handed in, the papers are subject to fine and the editors are subject to imprisonment. I found that in the reports of skirmishes the military censor invariably reported that the Spanish had killed from three to a dozen, or perhaps more, men, and had captured so many horses or had killed so many horses and had wounded so many, while communication from the ranks of the insurgents to their friends in Habana would be entirely the reverse. The news I received, then, would be entirely different from that given out from the Spanish censor. That was invariably the case.

Q. The result, then, was you could not know which was nearest the truth?—A. Personally I have no knowledge of it. I did not go outside the lines and did not count the dead and dying or anything of that kind; but the gentlemen who would bring me information—and I did not have to seek for it, they were only too willing to give it to me—were men of the very highest character. They were men whose word is certain to be believed, at least on an equality with that of any man who walks the earth. I found that those gentlemen who brought me such information were conservative; that sometimes they would give the Spanish a victory and sometimes they would give the insurgent side a victory in these little skirmishes, while the news given us by the Spanish censor invariably gave the Spanish a victory.

Q. Were these gentlemen on the side of the insurgents?—A. Yes, sir.

Q. So for that reason you were inclined to give their account greater credit than that of the censor?—A. Yes, sir; and for this reason I found the sympathizers with the insurgents were more conservative than the other; that is, they were willing to concede a battle now and then to the other side, while the Spanish side of the news was that of a Spanish victory.

Q. Was there anything in the Spanish account about the capture of Pinar del Rio?—A. The censor did not report the capture of Pinar del Rio, and in fact when it was reported that it was captured it was vehemently denied by the authorities.

Q. Did the censor give out that Maceo had attacked that town and been repulsed?—A. No, sir.

Q. I see in your report to Secretary Olney you say that "the Government gave out the announcement that Maceo had attacked the town and been repulsed in short order and with great loss, the Spanish loss not being stated."—A. That statement is made upon the statement of William Shaw Bowen, as ardent an admirer of Cuba as ever stepped foot in Habana. He told me that within a week after the account of the capture of Pinar del Rio was printed Weyler had informed him personally that the Cubans had not only attacked Pinar del Rio, but had been repulsed.

Q. Did you report that?—A. Yes, sir.

Q. Did you afterwards state that was untrue?—A. From all the information I could gather from people who came in from Pinar del Rio—Cuban sympathizers, it is true, but honorable men—the city of Pinar del Rio was held for nearly two hours, and they created great destruction and were not driven off, but vacated the town of their own accord.

Q. Do you know anything of your own knowledge in regard to the treatment of American citizens by the Spanish authorities during your stay?—A. Do you mean by that was I personally present when ill treatment was inflicted upon them or have I the knowledge from the men themselves?

Q. Just answer that. Did you personally see or know of ill treatment of American citizens?—A. Yes, sir. I found Mr. Walter Grant Dygert, a citizen of the United States, from the State of Illinois, imprisoned at the prison at Guines, in a little cell, probably not half as large as this room, in which there were 22 other men and in which there were no sanitary arrangements worth speaking of.

Q. That would be a room about 16 by 18 feet. How many people were there with him?—A. Twenty-two; he made 23.

Q. Closely confined there all the while?—A. Yes, sir.

Q. What was the condition of the room as to cleanliness?—A. It was simply filthy. The people with him were the dirtiest men I ever looked on in my life, and I have been in a great many American prisons.

Q. How long had he been there?—A. About three months.

Q. How long did he remain there after you discovered him?—A. About two weeks.

Q. What was the charge made against him?—A. The charge made against him was that he was outside the territory designated as that proper to travel in by General Weyler. He was found on the outskirts of the city of Guines. That was one charge against him, and the other charge made against him was that he was William Gold, otherwise known as "Inglesito."

Q. Had there been any investigation made by the Spanish authorities?—Yes, sir.

Q. Any investigation at which he was present?—A. Yes, sir; and testimony taken; and Marquis Palmerola told me the Government was thoroughly satisfied of his innocence for two weeks. I saw the Marquis on a Saturday, and he told me they would have released him the day before or the day before that but for the fact that they were holy days— Holy Thursday and Holy Friday—and the Spanish do nothing on those days.

Q. Did you know anything about the kind of food furnished him?— A. Only what Mr. Dygert told me.

Q. What did he say?—A. He told me the food was execrable. He told me that but for the fact that the commandant of the prison, whose name I forget, but it is in my papers, was a pretty decent sort of a fellow, he would have committed suicide long before he saw me.

Q. Did these prisoners take any exercise?—A. I did not ask about that. They were in a cell with iron bars on the side; that is, they could get air, but not sufficient in that cell.

Q. Was it a stone cell?—A. Yes, sir; with the iron bars on one side.

Q. What kind of a floor?—A. Stone floor. Mr. Dygert told me at the time I was conversing with him that at that very moment he was crawling with vermin, and his scratching and conduct generally was pretty good evidence that he was.

By Senator MORGAN:

Q. What were the sleeping arrangements?—A. None. They had to sleep on the floor.

Q. They furnished him blankets, I suppose?—A. No, sir; that was perhaps unnecessary, for I suppose blankets would have been too warm.

By Senator DAVIS:

Q. Did he speak of being allowed a change of clothing?—A. He had not been allowed a change of clothing during his imprisonment.

Q. How long before his release was it that Marquis Palmerola told you that the Government had known his innocence?—A. He told me the Government had known it two weeks absolutely.

Q. That was three weeks before his discharge?—A. The Marquis Palmerola told me that the Government had been absolutely sure of his innocence two weeks prior to the day I saw the Marquis.

Q. Then that makes about four weeks after they knew or confessed they knew he was innocent?—A. Yes, sir; and the testimony had been in the possession of Marquis Palmerola over two months.

Q. Did he tell you why he had not examined that testimony until after it had been two months in his hands?—A. It was not his business to examine it.

Q. Do you give that to me as his answer or your reason?—A. My reason——

Q. No; answer my question. Did he tell you why he had not examined that testimony for two months after it had been in his hands?—A. He did not.

Q. State any other instances of maltreatment of American citizens by the Spanish authorities there.—A. If you will permit me to state what the American citizens told me——

Q. I will cover that by a subsequent question.—A. I saw no other ill treatment, unless you consider the expulsion of American citizens from Habana ill treatment.

Q. Did you see any expulsion of American citizens?—A. Yes, sir. Mr. Rapley, correspondent of the New York Mail and Express, was resting in his bed——

Q. Did you see this?—A. No; I did not.

Q. Well, during your stay in Habana did you learn from sources you considered reliable of other instances of ill treatment of citizens of the United States by the Spanish authorities? If so, go on and state them, and give your sources of information.—A. Mr. Rapley, the correspondent of the New York Mail and Express, came to me one day about two or three weeks after I arrived at Habana and told me that upon the night before, between 2 and 3 o'clock in the morning, he had been aroused in his bed by the chief of police and three or four commissioners—police inspectors—and had been served with a notice of deportation. He showed me the notice, but it was in Spanish and I could only guess at its contents. He applied to Consul-General Williams to have his time extended. He was to leave on the first steamer, and the first steamer sailed on the following day and he could not get ready to go on it, so he applied to Consul-General Williams for permission to prolong his stay until the following steamer, and Mr. Williams secured him that permission. He left on the following steamer.

Q. What was the alleged cause?—A. Sending false information to his paper. That has been the reason that General Weyler has alleged for the expulsion of all the correspondents whom he has expelled. There were four of us expelled.

Q. Go on and give the next instance.—A. The case of Mr. Darling, an artist for Harper's Weekly, who has been arrested in territory that is not included in the Captain-General's edict, released each time, but detained from one hour to several hours—by several hours I mean eight or ten. I am not certain about the American citizenship of Mr. O'Leary, so I will not state his case. Mr. Creelman, of the New York Herald, was expelled at the same time I was; forbidden to remain longer on the island.

Q. Upon what charge?—A. Upon the charge of sending false information as to the state of affairs in Cuba. I was expelled for the same reason at the same time.

Q. Now, these cases are those of newspaper correspondents. I apply my main question to ill treatment of other American citizens, resident or temporary, of the island.—A. The cases of Alfred Laborde and Milton.

Q. Citizens of the United States?—A. Citizens of the United States.

Q. Is your information derived from what they told you?—A. No, sir.

Q. Who did you get it from?—A. From the testimony produced at the court-martial and from Vice-Consul Joseph Springer.

Q. With what were these two men charged?—A. They were charged with bringing a filibustering expedition into the Island of Cuba.

Q. Is that the case of the *Competitor?*—A. Yes, sir. Those two men, American citizens, were arrested, and, so far as the testimony of the men who captured them goes, had no arms upon their persons. They were brought to Habana, tried by general court-martial against the energetic protest of the United States consul-general there, condemned to death, and, as I am informed, their sentence delayed by the Madrid government at the request of the Secretary of State, and still held in jail.

Q. Do you know whether they were assisted by counsel at their trial?—A. From the American point of view, they were not assisted by counsel at their trial; from the Spanish military point of view, they were.

Q. In what way?—A. They had a lieutenant in the navy, who asked no questions, who cross-examined no witnesses. There were none produced, except Captain Butron and the other officers of the *Mensajerra.*

Q. Did this lieutenant advance by way of plea that these men were American citizens?—A. He stated in his plea that they were American citizens.

Q. Upon what grounds did he rest their defense?—A. He asked for mercy for Laborde, for the illustrious place his name had borne in the Spanish navy, and on account of the things his people had done for the Spanish Government.

Q. And the other man?—A. He asked for mercy for him, stating that he was not there for the purpose of fighting, but merely in his business as a newspaper correspondent.

Q. Do you know whether it appeared on that trial how far the *Competitor* was from the shore of Cuba when she was captured?—A. I do not remember.

Q. Do you know whether there was any evidence of that given on the trial?—A. At the trial there was no evidence given whatever.

Q. I mean as to the distance?—A. As to the distance or anything else.

Q. Have you any information as to the distance she was from the shore?—A. As to the exact distance, I do not know whether she was within the 3-mile limit or not.

Q. Was this trial secret or public?—A. Public.

Q. Did you attend it?—A. Yes, sir.

Q. Were the men in irons when tried?—A. No, sir.

Q. How long did it last?—A. From a little after 8 o'clock in the morning until afternoon.

Q. How many were tried?—A. Five, at once.

Q. How long was this after their arrest?—A. It was in the neighborhood of a week, more or less.

Q. Was any application made at the trial for postponement until they could communicate with their Government?—A. No, sir. Mr. Williams, however, saw them before the trial commenced and asked the judge-advocate in my presence what sort of a trial it was to be, and the judge-advocate replied, "A summary trial." Mr. Williams then replied, "I refuse to lend any official recognition to this trial. I protest against it;" and left.

Q. So that no officer of the consular service of the United States was present at that trial?—A. No, sir.

Q. In what manner was this lieutenant appointed?—A. I do not know. If you care for presumption, I presume the judge-advocate appointed him.

Q. Was he appointed as deputy judge-advocate?—A. No; he was appointed as what they call "defensor." There was a prosecutor also

He made his plea in about the same way as one of our district attorneys would make a plea in this country.

Q. Well, this person was an officer in the Spanish navy, was he?—A. Oh, yes. He asked no questions, however. Neither the prosecutor nor the counsel for defense asked a single question of anybody. There was not a particle of testimony offered except the officers of the *Mensajerra.*

Q. Was there any interpreter present?—A. There was an interpreter present, but he did not make his presence known to the prisoners until they were asked whether they had anything to say in their own defense. These long statements were read by the judge-advocate in Spanish.

Q. These long statements of the prosecuting officer, you mean, was the evidence given in Spanish and translated in their hearing?—A. No, sir.

Q. Did their defender communicate to them the substance of it?—A. He did not utter one single word to them.

Q. Can he speak English?—A. I did not hear him.

Q. Have you any reason to think he could speak the English language?—A. No, sir; I have every reason to think he could not.

Q. So that all this long harangue was delivered in Spanish?—A. Yes, sir.

Q. And then they were asked what they had to say?—A. Yes, sir; what they had to say in defense.

Q. Did he ask that in English?—A. He did not even do that. The presiding officer of the court-martial—there were ten of them, what we might call the jury—the presiding officer of that body said to Laborde in Spanish, "What have you to say?" He said a few words, and so it went until the last man was reached—William Gilday—and the presiding officer spoke to him and he did not understand him, and then the interpreter got up and said, "Do you wish to say anything?" Gilday arose and said, "All I have got to say is I do not understand one word that has been said to-day, for me or against me, and at any rate I appeal to both the British and American consuls."

Q. Now, how many of these prisoners could not speak or understand Spanish?—A. I believe there were two who could not speak and understand Spanish.

Q. Which two?—A. Milton and Gilday. Laborde understood Spanish.

Q. Milton was the American and Gilday the naturalized American subject?—A. Yes, sir; I believe there is some question whether Gilday is a British subject or American. The British consul claims that he is a naturalized American, but he himself says he never renounced his allegiance to Great Britain.

Q. How long was it after they were asked whether they had anything to say before the trial terminated?—A. The trial terminated immediately upon the last man having made his statement.

Q. And when was it the defense summed up in their behalf, if at all?—A. Immediately after the prosecution.

Q. How long did it take him to conclude that summing up?—A. It took probably fifteen minutes.

By Senator MORGAN:

Q. But his appeal, as I understand you, was entirely for mercy and not for justification.—A. All for mercy, except you can call his plea for Milton that he was not there as a filibuster, but merely as a newspaper correspondent.

By Senator DAVIS:

Q. Did Milton undertake to give any account of why he was there?—A. Yes, sir.

Q. What account did he give?—A. He stated he came aboard the schooner as the correspondent of the Jacksonville Times-Union.

Q. Did he state he knew anything of the mission of the schooner?—A. He did not say. That is the statement that was made by him several days before the trial.

Q. What did Gilday have to say for himself?—A. He said he was a poor sailor earning his living, and he went aboard thinking the schooner was bound from Key West—I think it was for Sable Keys, going fishing; that he knew nothing of the nature of the business until after it started. Laborde claimed that his ship had been hired by some person for the purpose of going to Sable Keys for the purpose of fishing there, and he was simply held up by a revolver and told to go to Cuba.

Q. Laborde was the owner of the schooner?—A. No; he was the captain.

By Senator MORGAN:

Q. What did you ascertain to be the general feeling of the native Cubans you saw as to this rebellion or war?—A. The Cubans, all the natives of Cuba that I have seen who in the past have possessed any wealth at all, told me they had wrecked themselves to help along the war.

Q. I have seen statements in the papers about volunteer companies and regiments and perhaps brigades of native Cubans under the Spanish flag. Did you see anything of that sort there?—A. Yes, sir.

Q. To what extent, probably, were those enlistments?—A. Well, just giving a rough estimate—I never looked into the official records—but giving a rough guess, judging by the numbers of volunteers I saw in the streets, I should judge there were 3,000 volunteers.

Q. Were they volunteers for service in the field or for particular duty?—A. No, sir; they were volunteers for service in and around the outskirts of the city of Habana, guarding the banks, public buildings, theaters, and the like.

By Senator DAVIS:

Q. A sort of gendarmes?—A. That is it.

By Senator MORGAN:

Q. Sort of home guards?—A. Yes, sir. In fact they were not required to go into the field at all. Several of the volunteers who are now disgusted with the step they have taken would willingly join the insurgents.

Q. Have any of these volunteer organizations been sent to the trocha?—A. I could not find out. I tried to find out, but the Government authorities would give me no information on the subject at all.

Q. What impression did the Spanish make upon you as to the character of the troops—the people employed in the army—as to whether they were substantial men, and men of intelligence and physical vigor, and so on?—A. They impressed me as being very patriotic and very courageous men—the Spanish themselves—but with one drawback, and that was lack of patriotism, caused, as they told me—that is, the privates, not the officers—caused by the fact that they are illy fed, illy clad, compelled to do the most menial service, and have not been paid for nearly five months. You go into the streets of Habana any hour of the night and if you look like a man of any means at all you will be asked for alms by Spanish soldiers. I used to go along there and give them 10 cents or a nickel or a quarter, whatever I might happen to have in my pocket when they asked me, and at the same time say "Americano," knowing that there was no knowing how long it might be before I would be in the hands of those men, and wished to be friendly with them. So whenever I gave them anything, I always said "Americano."

By Senator DAVIS:

Q. In the course of that trial, were any attacks made by the prosecuting officer upon the United States Government?—A. No, sir.

By Senator MORGAN:

Q. While in Cuba did you visit any places around Habana?—A. Only the places I have named.

Q. How far out?—A. Forty miles.

Q. Did you leave the railroad track?—A. I did not leave the railroad track. I got off the train at the town of Guines and went about my business, which was to see Walter Dygert.

Q. Did you observe, or could you observe, the condition of the people in the country?—A. Yes, sir.

Q. What was it?—A. Wretched. Take a few coppers from your pocket and throw them in the street and half the population would scramble for them. I remember now where I went down one morning to the club, and a little child playing around there attracted my attention. I gave it a few coppers and soon a dozen people came out and begged, saying they had no food. I went out on the drive one morning and went into a grocery store and was besieged by people who wanted me to buy groceries for them.

Q. What is the currency about Habana?—A. Copper, silver, and gold.

Q. No paper money?—A. No; no paper money, except now and then an American greenback.

Q. They have no national paper currency?—A. No, sir; not in Habana, at least.

By Senator DAVIS:

Q. Is there anything else of detail you would like to state that we have not interrogated you about?—A. I can not think of anything that would be of interest. Before leaving there I wrote to the Captain-General offering to prove to him every line I had written.

By Senator MORGAN:

Q. What, in your judgment, derived from what you ascertained while in the Island of Cuba, is the prospect of success of the insurgent government?—A. A very long fight and the ultimate success of the insurgent government if left alone—if left in the condition they are now The insurgents are in a position, in my judgment, to fight for fifty years in the way they are fighting now.

Q. Did you derive any impression from Spanish sources while you were there as to their hopes for subjection of the insurgents?—A. Yes, sir.

Q. What was it?—A. Captain-General Weyler told me himself, within a week after I landed there, that he would have it suppressed within three months, and every Spanish officer I spoke to was very sanguine of it.

Q. I understand that the forces of Maceo and Gomez are divided now by what is called the trocha?—A. Well, they are divided by the trocha and quite a good deal of territory east of the trocha.

Q. In the military arrangements of that country Maceo has been assigned to the district called Pinar del Rio?—A. That is true.

Q. And other generals to two other different provinces and Gomez is commander in chief of the whole army?—A. Of the entire army; and if Antonio Maceo obeys his orders that he has received from his chief, he will remain in Pinar del Rio.

By Senator DAVIS:

Q. Mr. Lawrence, I hold in my hand the New York Journal of May 19, containing your statement to the Secretary of State, signed by you, dated May 18, 1896. Is that statement true?—A. Every word of it.

The statement is as follows   :

Hon. RICHARD OLNEY,
          Secretary of State:

In accordance with the understanding between yourself and Mr. Edward Marshall, of the New York Journal, I herewith submit to you a statement embracing such of my observations of the condition of affairs in Cuba as it seems likely may be of interest to yourself and the State Department. These were gained during my sojourn in Habana as the correspondent of the New York Journal. It is as much the duty of a 'newspaper man as it is the duty of a diplomatic agent to sift rumors and ascertain exact facts. This is what I endeavored to do.

I went to Cuba entirely unprejudiced, and with instructions from Mr. W. R. Hearst, the proprietor of the New York Journal, to exercise the utmost care in preparing my telegrams and letters, and to especially avoid giving favor to one side at the expense of the other. At that time the impression generally prevailed that the wrongs which had led to the insurrection and the strength of the rebels had been somewhat exaggerated by the correspondents of American newspapers. I was one of those who believed that to be true.

On my arrival in Habana (March 20) I immediately placed myself in communication with the recognized Spanish authorities. It was my first effort to gain an impartial and complete view of the condition of affairs in Cuba as it then existed. I found that it was most difficult to obtain information from the Spanish authorities. Such information as they chose to give out—even of military movements long passed—was not announced in the form in which it had been communicated to the authorities by the commanders in the field, but was revised and changed in Habana. This became immediately evident.

SPANIARDS DISTORTED FACTS.

Even after the correspondents had made up their news dispatches from these revised Government reports the dispatches were subjected to the most rigid scrutiny by the press censor, who often changed facts so that they were in complete conflict with the statements which the Government had a few hours previously issued as truths. This was, it was noticeable, only done when the strength and operations of the insurgents could be belittled thereby, or the successful operations of the Spanish troops magnified.

For example, I will instance the capture of the city of Pinar del Rio, a Spanish fortress and stronghold in the Province of Pinar del Rio, in two hours by the army of the Cuban Republic under the command of Gen. Antonio Maceo. This occurred during my first week on the island. The Government gave out the announcement that Maceo had attacked the town and been repulsed in short order and with great loss, the Spanish loss not being stated.

I accepted the Government's statement as true, and cabled it to the

Journal. A few days later reliable information was received from Gen eral Maceo that the battle had resulted in a victory for the army of the Cuban Republic, the Spanish garrison having been driven from the town in a demoralized condition, after which the Cuban soldiers destroyed over 200 houses. The Cuban loss did not exceed 50 men, while 300 Spaniards were killed. This news I telegraphed to my paper after having verified it absolutely.

After its publication the Spaniards in Cuba vehemently denied its truth, reiterating their previous statements. Later the truth of the Cuban story was verified by cable dispatches from Madrid, the verification being based upon Captain-General Weyler's own report to the home Government. I may say that my second dispatch announcing the Cuban victory did not pass through the hands of the press censor. It was sent by means of a private messenger, via Key West, Fla. This is a fair sample of the methods which the Spanish authorities in Habana follow in giving out news to all parties.

FOREIGN POWERS DECEIVED.

The representatives of all the foreign Governments in Habana receive their information through the same unreliable channels through which information is passed to the newspaper correspondents. It is invariably scrutinized and altered to suit the Spanish authorities before it is made public. On the other hand, it is quite as true that unreliable information and exaggerated reports are constantly being offered to correspondents and others by the insurgents and their sympathizers. This false news from the insurgent side, however, is without the official stamp. Such news as goes to the correspondents or others through the Cuban headquarters there, under the sanction of the authorities of the Cuban Republic, is, my experience teaches me, invariably reliable. It is almost always ultimately verified by the Spaniards themselves, either in Habana or Madrid.

These statements, I think, dispose of any question which may arise concerning the reliability of the announcements made by American newspaper correspondents in Habana which have been denied by the Spanish authorities.

TREATMENT OF AMERICANS.

A matter which should, I think, be especially called to the attention of yourself and the State Department concerns the treatment of American citizens by the Spanish authorities in Habana. I will first refer to the case of Walter Grant Dygert, of Illinois. While taking a morning walk on the outskirts of the town of Guines, in the Province of Habana, within 20 miles of the Spanish capital of Cuba, he was arrested by Spanish soldiers under the supposition that he was William Gold, otherwise known as "Inglesito," a noted Cuban officer. He was placed in the military jail at Guines.

Evidence was found in his possession which proved conclusively that he had arrived in Cuba only three days prior to his arrest, and therefore could not have been "Inglesito," who had been fighting with the army of the Cuban Republic for almost a year past. Still, he was placed "incommunicado," which means that he could neither send nor receive communications to or from any living human being except the Spanish authorities. He asserted his American citizenship and his complete innocence of any offense against the Spanish laws, but the authorities even refused to notify the United States consul-general at Habana of the fact that Dygert had been arrested.

Through Cuban sympathizers who had learned of his predicament Mr. Charles Michelson, who was then the Journal correspondent at Habana, was informed of Dygert's arrest. He immediately laid the facts before United States Consul-General Williams. I am informed that Consul-General Williams made every effort to communicate with Dygert, but that he could not gain from the Spanish authorities even an admission that Dygert was under arrest until the fact became so publicly known that further equivocation was useless.

INNOCENT MAN IN PRISON.

In the end the authorities admitted the innocence of Dygert—admitted it even to the American consul-general—but still held him in jail for over two months, in spite of the protests of Consul-General Williams. The reason that he was not released sooner was because he refused to sign a waiver of any claims for damages that he might have against the Spanish Government.

Another case is that of Frank Agramonte, a citizen of New York State and a member of the militia of that Commonwealth. He was arrested and confined in the military jail in the Province of Santiago de Cuba. What has become of him no man except those who have been concerned in his disappearance can tell. The American consular office at Habana informed me that it has never been notified of the arrest of Agramonte, and that inquiries made at the palace of the Captain-General have been met with the reply that they knew nothing about the case.

Personally I made inquiry concerning him, but was not able to learn from the Spanish authorities whether he was in prison or at liberty, alive or dead. That he was arrested there is not the slightest doubt. I have come in personal contact with four men who saw him in the custody of the Spanish soldiers.

You are probably better informed than myself regarding the cases of the Americans arrested in connection with the so-called *Competitor* expedition, but I may add to your information the facts that upon learning of their capture the Captain General issued orders for a court-martial to convene immediately upon their arrival, and personally expressed the hope that they would be executed within twenty-four hours, as a warning to others who might accompany or seek to accompany insurgent expeditions to Cuba. This was before the Captain-General knew that the prisoners had been taken on the water, and were, therefore, subject to the jurisdiction of the naval and not the land authorities.

SPAIN VIOLATED THE PROTOCOL.

You know that in the trial of these men the Government of Spain violated both the letter and spirit of the protocol of 1877, known as the Cushing protocol. I was personally present when Consul-General Williams and Vice-Consul Springer protested against such procedure in the cases of American citizens. The protest was made in the name of the United States Government, and, as Mr. Williams stated, by order of the State Department. The officer who received the protest was the judge-advocate of the court-martial, and the time was one hour before the beginning of the trial.

I may state, however, that Mr. Williams had made the same protest in writing, several days previously, and that his letter was read at the court-martial. The judge-advocate consulted with the prosecuting officer, who decided that the trial must proceed, notwithstanding the objections raised by the American Government. The fact that the trial was held and that the prisoners were found guilty and sentenced to death are matters on which you have already been informed by Consul-General Williams. Even though the Madrid authorities have ordered a suspension of sentence, at the request of Minister Taylor, the prisoners are still subject to the sentence, which may be carried out at any time at the will of the Spanish Government.

WEYLER'S QUEER IDEAS.

It should also be called to the attention of the State Department that Captain-General Weyler does not openly recognize the treaty rights of the United States in this matter, but that he describes concessions which are evidently made under treaty provisions as favors to the United States, thus placing this Government in the attitude of being under obligations to Spain. This may be illustrated by citing the cases of Charles Michaelson and Lorenzo Betancourt, correspondents of the Journal, who were arrested in Habana and confined in Morro Castle.

Messrs. Michaelson and Betancourt were arrested on the charge that they had passed the Spanish lines without the permission of the authorities. It immediately became evident that it was a case of mistaken identity, as neither of the men arrested had, in reality, passed the Spanish lines or had attempted to do so. Shortly after their arrest, and after the consul-general of the United States had made a formal demand upon the Spanish authorities for the release of the men, the *Bermuda* expedition was stopped by the United States Government officials as it was leaving New York Harbor.

Captain-General Weyler then released Michaelson and Betancourt, with the statement that he did it as a favor to the United States in recognition of the prompt action of your Department in stopping the *Bermuda*. Thus, instead of admitting the treaty rights of the United States and according a civil trial to all American citizens arrested in Cuba not actually "with arms in hand," he places this Government in the humiliating position of suing for and accepting favors at the hands of the Spanish Government. I was informed shortly before I left Habana that the cases of Messrs. Michaelson and Betancourt had not been closed, but were still open. The two men are, then, merely on parole. The Spanish Government may take their cases up at any time. Michaelson has left Cuba, but Betancourt is still in Habana.

RECOGNIZES NO TREATY RIGHTS.

In not a single instance has Captain-General Weyler officially recognized the treaty rights of United States citizens in such matters. Invariably when he has ordered a civil trial he has announced that he did it as a favor to the United States. In the case of the *Competitor* Americans he absolutely refused to concede their rights to other than summary trial by court-martial. He insisted, without any foundation in fact for the assumption, that these men were captured with "arms in hand." His own witnesses, Captain Butron, the engineer, and other officers of the war launch *Mensajerra*, which captured the *Competitor*, testified that the men made no resistance whatever; that they yielded to the demands of the officers of the *Mensajerra* without a struggle, and that they had no arms upon their persons.

Nevertheless, the Captain-General would have carried out the sentence of death imposed had not the activity of your Department compelled an order from the home Government at Madrid ordering the sentences to be suspended. It is the general belief in Habana that dozens of Americans occupy cells in the military prisons in the eastern part of the island, and have been there for months past, without a hearing of any kind. In this contemptuous manner does Captain-General Weyler regard and treat Americans generally.

My statements of outrages perpetrated on the peasantry of Cuba by the officers of the Spanish army, and Colonel Melquizo in particular, are susceptible of the clearest and most conclusive proof, while on the other hand they are, I am convinced, only the merest hints of the dreadful state of affairs which really exists in Cuba. Were it possible to relieve some of the most important and highly respected men in the Island of Cuba from the fear of revengeful punishment by the Spaniards, I would give the names of the men of the highest standing and wealth, who have witnessed every one of the horrors to which I have referred in my press dispatches.

VICTIMS OF THE "BUTCHER."

Some of the cases to which I have referred are as follows:

These men were shot without the slightest pretense at a trial near Campo Florida, near Habana: Domingo Lumones, Ramon Castellinos, Manuel Martinez, Jose Cejas, Jesus Ochoa Rodriguez, Joaquin Merina, Bargarito Zarzas, Eleno Guerra, Marguerito Verole, Basilio Rubiro, M. V. Collina, Florencio Rabelli, Benigno Galloso and son, Pedro Cardenas, his wife, Julia, and another woman named Maria Luiz; Apolo Camaronas, Inocento Rabell, Eduardo Sardenes, Cruse Ferrer, Abelardo Cartaya, Martin Diaz and son, Francisco Ferrer, Leonardo Llerena, Caridad Roys, Luz Guitierrez and son, and many others.

I might cite by name a list of men and women which would cover many pages of this statement, all of whom were murdered by the Spanish troops without the slightest excuse, other than the unproved belief that they were Cuban sympathizers. It should be remembered that all these to whom I refer were noncombatants—peaceful white citizens engaged in following their daily callings when ruthlessly assassinated by the heartless men under Captain-General Weyler. Such murders are occurring daily, almost hourly, throughout the island. Weyler absolutely denies that these men are murdered, and asserts that they are killed in battle.

OFFERED TO PROVE HIS STORIES.

I personally offered to prove to the Captain-General that if his officers report that these deaths are the regular casualties of battle their reports are false. I offered to take him or any reliable man whom he might designate and who should not be known as a Spanish official to the districts where these brutal killings occurred and bring him in contact with men who saw the executions, who knew that the victims were not soldiers in the army of the Cuban Republic, had never borne arms, and were not intending to bear arms; that they were peaceful farmers and farm laborers who, at the time they were murdered, were pursuing the peaceful callings of their inoffensive lives.

It was also called to my attention and proved that Captain-General Weyler was at the time I left Habana engaged in equipping his men with brass-tipped bullets, contrary to the convention signed at Geneva by Spain and all other civilized nations.   Thus, he violates the law of nations in the conduct of his warfare.   After this bullet enters the body the brass tip spreads, mutilating flesh, tissues, and bones, and being likely to cause blood poisoning.   These bullets I have myself seen.

Forty-eight hours before leaving Habana I wrote a farewell letter to Captain-General Weyler, in which I informed him of the monstrous conduct of his officers in the field and concluded with this language:

You still have time to order my arrest.   I invite you to do so, and guarantee that an investigation shall be made, the result of which will prove you to be the most barbarous military savage the world has ever known.

The Captain-General ignored such a vigorously worded challenge as that.   In the letter I described to him the conduct of Colonel Melquizo's command while on the march from Jiquiabo to Minas.   The soldiers were in town of Jiquiabo.

CONDUCT OF SPANISH TROOPS.

From an eyewitness, a man of the highest standing in Cuba, who was present that night, I gathered the following information:

There was not a morsel of food in the town that had not been confiscated by Melquizo's men.   Every food animal and fowl had been killed and the people were compelled to appeal to the soldiers for sufficient food to drive away hunger.   The women of Jiquiabo were in a state of terror bordering upon insanity because of the infamous conduct of the soldiers toward them.   This conduct aroused the indignation of the men of the town and they appealed to Melquizo in person for protection for the women.

His reply was that no loyal Spanish woman would refuse a Spanish soldier anything, and he presumed the women of Jiquiabo were loyal Spanish subjects.   An instance was related by my informant of two soldiers entering a hut where they found a woman alone.   They first spoke to her in such language as no good woman would listen to. Finally they attacked her.   She secured a knife and fought them off as best she could until, when her strength was almost exhausted, she broke away from them and ran into the field.   The men followed her and, realizing that the thought of escape was hopeless, the poor woman drove a knife into her breast and within a few minutes was a corpse. The name of this woman was Maria Garmuza.

This is only one of dozens of similar cases that have been reported to me.   My information is of the most reliable kind and, were a proper investigation made, I could prove it beyond a shadow of a doubt.

THE MILITARY SITUATION.

As to the military situation on the island: Enough people in this country to command respect believe that the Spaniards represent the only real army in Cuba from a soldier's point of view, and that the army of the Cuban Republic is composed of mere wandering bands of destroying outlaws led by men who respect and are subject to no law whatever. This is untrue.   The Spaniards are in point of numbers superior to their opponents, but the leaders of the army of the Republic have exhibited superior brains, courage, and military genius.

Landing on the island with only a small following a year ago last February Generals Gomez and Maceo have now under their command in the neighborhood of 100,000 men, whose numbers would be very largely increased if the men who desire to join them could pass through the Spanish lines. The Republic is in possession of almost the whole of the interior of the island. There is scarcely a town that they have not attacked and occupied.

To do this they have been compelled to drive the Spanish garrisons out of the cities, and they have done it most successfully whenever it has been attempted. The only portions of Cuba which the Spaniards have managed to hold are the capital, Habana, and other towns on the seacoast, where they have been favored with the protection of the Spanish gunboats. With their men as well armed as are the Spaniards the Cubans could unquestionably overcome that advantage and hold the entire island against any force Spain might send against them. Even as it is the Cubans now menace the capital. General Gomez, with nearly 30,000 men, is marching westward and has reached a point in Mantanzas close enough to the city of Habana to cause the authorities great trepidation.

HABANA CAN BE TAKEN.

The capital is in almost a defenseless condition against a land attack, the Captain-General having sent nearly all of his available forces to the Province of Pinar del Rio to reinforce the trocha which he has established from the northern to the southern coast of the island. The fortress at Cabanas and the fortress of Santa Clara, which is situated in the city of Habana to the west of the harbor, might prove quite effectual against an attack by sea, but would, in the opinion of military men whom I have interviewed in Habana, prove totally inadequate to defend the city from an invasion on the land side. The only protection the capital has from an attack by land are a few insignificant stockade forts erected around the outskirts and garrisoned by poorly equipped, undrilled, half starved volunteers, who, during the hours when they are off duty, may be seen in the streets of Habana asking alms of citizens like ordinary beggars.

It seems incredible that such men would succeed in holding Habana against an attack by such fighters as the Cubans under General Gomez have on more than one occasion proven themselves to be. In a march of over 500 miles, which the commander in chief of the Cuban army has made since he left Puerto Principe on his second invasion, he has not had a battle nor even a skirmish with the Spaniards, who have persistently avoided a trial of strength. The march has been made without the loss of a single man on either side and, incidentally, hundreds of peasants have swelled the ranks of the Cuban army by enlisting under General Gomez.

In Pinar del Rio Province General Maceo is commander of the situation. He has a comparatively small force, consisting, I have been told, of not over 5,000 men, who, however, are well-trained fighters and splendidly equipped with arms and ammunition. On the trocha, it was reported to me, there are over 40,000 Spanish soldiers, against which body of men flying columns of Spaniards, consisting of from 1,500 to 5,000 soldiers each, are attempting to drive Maceo's troops.

GENERAL MACEO'S VICTORIES.

They find it impossible, however, to get Maceo into a position from which he can not escape, and whenever he has met a force of Spaniards in battle he has invariably succeeded in defeating his enemies. For proof of this, his battles with Alphonso XIII Battalion and with the force under General Suarez Inclan at the battle of Cacarajicara may be cited. After ten hours of fighting Maceo drove Colonel Dubos and the Alphonso XIII Battalion back to the seacoast, where they were compelled to take refuge on board the gunboat *Alerta.* The Spanish loss at this engagement was nearly 1,000, while General Maceo suffered a loss of not more than 200.

At Cacarajicara, Maceo led Inclan into a trap and drove him back to Bahia Honda with great loss. This appears to be the fate of the flying columns that are sent after Maceo, while on the other hand hundreds of Spaniards on the trocha are being exterminated daily by yellow fever and other diseases.

The death rate is so high on the trocha that the supply of Spanish soldiers to take the places of those who have succumbed to disease is exhausted, and General Weyler has been driven to the extremity of calling upon the volunteers from Habana to reinforce the line. At the time I left Habana the Captain-General had attempted to make a draft on the volunteers to go to the trocha, and these young men (who correspond to the State militia in this country) were in open rebellion against his order. The position they assumed was that it was their duty to guard the banks and public buildings of Habana in addition to doing guard duty generally around the city and its outskirts, and that neither General Weyler nor any other commander had authority to order them into the field.

CUBANS IN GOOD CONDITION.

The Cubans are in a position to maintain the present state of affairs for the next twenty years if Spain can find resources to keep up her end of the war for that length of time. Up in the mountains the leaders of the army of the Republic have established ranches, where men are engaged in breeding and raising cattle for food purposes. The raising of vegetables is also encouraged by the Cuban commanders, and in addition to this means of subsistence they have the native food plants that grow in wild profusion all over the island.

From this it will be readily understood that no matter how long the war should last, or how much privation they should suffer in other directions, the Republican army will never suffer dangerously from lack of food. As the Cubans are in a position to stop all farming except such as they indulge in themselves, the Spaniards will presently find that their own shortage of food is a great drawback to their campaign, and they will be compelled to resort to importing their rations from the United States, Spain, or some other country.

The Cubans have been accused of incendiarism in a criminal sense because they have destroyed sugar cane, tobacco, mills, and plantations. They insist that they should not be regarded as criminals, but that the orders which the commanders issued for the destruction of the island were justifiable war measures.

DESTROYED WITH OWNERS' CONSENT.

I have personal knowledge that in a great many cases the plantations have been destroyed with the consent of the owners. In fact, a great number of owners of plantations that have been destroyed informed me personally that they had invited the Cubans to do so because they did not want to grind their cane and thereby supply revenues to the Spanish Government. The fact that wealthy men cherish such hostility to Spain and are ready to help the Cubans in their fight should be sufficient refutation of the charge that the war for Cuban freedom is only backed by the ignorant classes and negroes.

I found that nearly three-fifths of the population of the island were either actively engaged in the war on the Cuban side or that the revolution enjoyed their active sympathy and support. Of course, these men dare not utter their sentiments openly, but they have willingly ruined themselves to aid the cause, and to those whom they can trust not to betray them they are not in the least backward in expresing their views.

Respectfully submitted.

FREDERICK W. LAWRENCE.

MAY 18, 1896.

STATEMENT OF REV. A. J. DIAZ.

A. J. DIAZ was duly sworn.

By Senator MORGAN:

Q. What is your name?—A. A. J. Diaz.

Q. What is your age? A. Forty years.

Q. Where were you born?—A. I was born in the city of Guanabacoa.

Q. How far is that from Habana?—A. About 2 or 3 miles.

Q. Where were you educated?—A. I was educated partly in the Island of Cuba and partly in the United States.

Q. At what school?—A. First I was at the institute, as we call it, in Habana, then went to the university in Habana.

Q. When you came here where did you go?—A. When I came here I was educated by Dr. Alexander Hunter, of New York, a private teacher.

Q. Educated in your profession as a doctor of medicine?—A. No, sir; as a minister.

Q. Well, were you ever educated as a doctor of medicine?—A. Yes, sir; I was educated in Habana.

Q. Did you get your degree?—A. Yes, sir; I got my degree there, and my diploma as a doctor has been registered here in the State of Georgia, too.

Q. Did you commence practicing your profession in Cuba?—A. Very little. At that time I was quite young, and the last revolution was started, and then I joined myself in that revolutionary army.

Q. Who did you serve under?—A. I served with the Cuban party.

Q. Under whose command?—A. Under the command of Julio Funes.

Q. How long did you serve in that army?—A. I served in that army for nearly two years.

Q. Did you have any rank?—A. Yes, sir.

Q. What was it?—A. I was appointed by them as a captain.

Q. Did you have a company under your command?—A. Yes, sir.

Q. When that war closed, what became of you?—A. Before the war closed I was appointed to find some place for our people. We knew very well if they got hold of the Cubans they would kill them. Knowing that, I threw myself into the sea, drifting on a log, in the hope of reaching some place of security, but the current was strong and drove us away. That was in the nighttime, and the next day we found ourselves in a vessel which picked us up.

Q. Where did they take you to?—A. They transferred us to a schooner that was bound to New York, and I went to the city of New York.

Q. How long did you remain in New York?—A. I remained in New York for nearly five or six years.

Q. What were you doing while you were there?—A. At first I was employed in the cigar business. Then I commenced to read to the factories there, employed as a reader, and then I commenced to do some missionary work.

Q. You became a minister?—A. Yes, sir.

Q. What church did you join?—A. The Baptist Church.

Q. Did you join that church in New York?—A. No, sir.

By Senator DAVIS:

Q. Are you now an ordained minister of the Baptist Church?—A. Yes, sir.

Q. How long have you been so?—A. For nearly six years.

By Senator MORGAN:

Q. Where were you ordained?—A. I was ordained in the city of Key West, Fla.

Q. You belong, then, to the Southern Baptist Church?—A. Yes, sir.

Q. After you were ordained did you return to Cuba?—A. Yes, sir; I returned for that purpose to the city of Key West. I was called by the council to the city of Key West, and was ordained there and returned the next week.

Q. Then I suppose you became a missionary of the Southern Baptist Board to Cuba?—A. Yes, sir.

Q. Well, when you got to Cuba did you establish a church there?—A. The church had been already established.

Q. And you were appointed to it?—A. Yes, sir.

Q. What progress have you made in your denominational growth there?—A. Very good.

Q. About how many communicants have you there?—A. I have about 2,700 who have been baptized in the last eight years.

Q. In the city of Habana?—A. Yes; and I organized a Baptist hospital for the poor. I organized seven free schools, where we have over 1,500 children; we educate them; and also have a cemetery. We can not bury our Protestant people in the Catholic cemetery. They do not allow us to bury them there.

By Senator DAVIS:

Q. In whose name is the title to all this property?—A. In the name of Dr. Tichenor, the corresponding secretary of the Home Mission Board.

Q. He holds it as trustee for the mission board?—A. Yes, sir.

By Senator MORGAN:

Q. Where does Dr. Tichenor belong?—A. In Atlanta, Ga.

Q. What would be about the value of that property you have in Habana?—A. The church itself is worth about $140,000. It is a very nice piece of property. The hospital we have is worth about $20,000, and the cemetery—well, we can not say what it is worth, but it brings to the board an income of $6,000 or $7,000 a year.

Q. You have property, then, in San Miguel, also belonging to the church?—A. Yes, sir.

Q. What is the value of that?—A. About $2,000.

Q. How many churches have you organized outside of San Miguel and outside of Habana in the country?—A. We have different missions, but never organized different churches. We have missions at different places. A preacher will go to one for one or two months for a meeting and then move away to another.

S. Doc. 231, pt 7——43

Q. How many ministers are employed in the Baptist denomination?—A. About 24 missionaries.

Q. Are there any of those remaining in Cuba now, or have they left?—A. None remain except the women missionaries.

Q. The men have all had to leave?—A. Yes, sir.

Q. Why have they had to leave?—A. Well, they have been persecuted in one way or another by the Government, and have had to leave.

Q. They have all left?—A. They have all left and come to the United States.

Q. You speak of free schools you have established there; are there any free schools within your knowledge in Cuba sustained by the Spanish Government?—A. Yes, there are some.

Q. How many?—A. A great many, but kept in a very bad condition; they do not teach anything.

Q. Are they under ecclesiastical control?—A. Yes, sir.

Q. The Catholic Church?—A. Yes, sir.

Q. Who supplies the funds?—A. The Government.

Q. I was reading the other day, from a Spanish author, a statement to the effect that the annual taxes upon the people for the support of the Catholic Church in Cuba amounted to about $600,000. Is that correct?—A. I think it is more than that. I think it is about $1,500,000 or $2,000,000.

Q. This book I was reading from was written ten or fifteen years ago?—A. The bishop of Habana gets about $18,000 a year.

Q. And the archbishop how much?—A. He gets about the same.

Q. The archbishop of Cuba and the bishop of Habana get about $18,000 each?—A. Yes, sir.

Q. Well, have you been much over the country in Cuba?—A. Yes, sir; I have been in a great number of places.

Q. When did this war that is existing now in Cuba commence?—A. It broke out about the 29th of February, 1895.

Q. After that war broke out were you visiting over the Island of Cuba in different places?—A. Yes, sir; in behalf of the missions. When the war broke out I did not know exactly what to do. As a captain of the army on one side, and as a minister of the gospel on the other side, I was a little troubled myself, but I concluded to take no part in the insurrection, but just to help both parties, and then I organized what we call a White Cross Society. It is a society based on the Red Cross Society of Geneva, for the purpose of treating both sides.

Q. You mean, to assist them medically and charitably?—A. Yes, sir; and at the same time I sent a letter to President Cleveland to notify him that we were going to do that kind of work, and Mr. Gresham answered the letter saying that they had nothing to do with the matter, but were very much pleased with that thought and encouraged us, but they said they had nothing to do with the Geneva Cross. So our Government was notified that we were going to take part in that movement for a sanitary purpose.

Q. Well, the Spanish Government, then, became one of the parties to the Red Cross Society; that is, to the treaty by which they had certain rights?—A. Yes, sir.

Q. And you were not violating any public law by organizing that society?—A. No, sir; nor private either.

Q. And you say you had determined not to take part with either party in the political struggle that was going on there?—A. Yes, sir.

Q. Have you kept to that resolution faithfully?—A. Yes, sir.

Q. And you have not taken part?—A. I have not taken part on either side.

Q. In any way?—A. In any way; just helping the wounded and sick, that is all.

Q. Well, did you visit the United States recently before you were expelled?—A. Well, I generally visit the United States once or twice a year. I must come to the Southern Baptist Convention when they have a meeting, and give my report, and then they have some association or State convention, and then they call me. So I came to the United States last year twice or three times, to the Southern Baptist Convention which met in Washington, to the Florida State convention, and to the Home Mission Board's meeting.

Q. Well, both visits you made were for the purpose of attending Baptist conventions?—A. Yes, sir; that is all.

Q. You did not come here on a political mission?—A. No, sir.

Q. And had nothing to do with politics or with the war?—A. Nothing to do with it.

Q. What did you do as a member of this sanitary corps, as a physician, in treating the sick and wounded of both parties?—A. We made a by-law and we gave that by-law to the Government of Spain in order that they might approve it, and so they did. They approved it, and the second article says we have the right to constitute neutral camps in order to just take care of the sick and wounded; and while Mr. Campos was there everything was all right, because Mr. Campos conducted the warfare in a civilized way, and we had no trouble about it. We organized about forty delegations to take care of all sick and wounded. We have treated there about 2,000 Spanish soldiers, but as soon as Mr. Weyler came he ordered us to stop—not to take care of the insurgents by any means, only take Spanish troops, who were the only ones we had any right to take care of.

Q. Then did you cease to take care of the insurgents?—A. Yes, sir; I did not want to break any law, right or wrong. I did not want to interfere with any of them.

Q. Now, as a White Cross director, did you have a right to go into the ranks of the enemy?—A. Yes, cross the lines any time I pleased.

Q. You went out to the camp of the rebels?—A. Yes, sir.

Q. Did you make frequent visits to them?—A. Not frequent visits, but when I went to inspect a delegation sometimes I found them in my way. Sometimes, as military operations required, they stopped me and kept me for two or three or four days, and then I stopped there; and if they had something to do in the medical line I did it—made surgical operations.

Q. You are a surgeon?—A. I am a surgeon; yes, sir.

Q. Now, these delegations you speak of, I suppose they were scattered about through Cuba?—A. Yes, sir; in the Province of Pinar del Rio, the Province of Habana, and provinces of Matanzas and Santa Clara.

Q. How many delegations did you have in all?—A. Nearly 40.

Q. And how many people would be engaged in each delegation?—A. About two or three directors and several nurses. Sometimes they have women.

Q. Who supported these delegations?—A. We supported them.

Q. Do you mean the White Cross?—A. Yes, sir; the White Cross Society.

Q. Where did you get the money to do it with?—A. Part I collected from the members of the church and part we got from contributions of the people.

Q. Did the Spanish Government contribute anything to it?—A. No, sir; never contributed a cent.

Q. Now, then, it was in visiting these delegations about through the different parts of Cuba that you had the opportunity to see what was going on in both armies?—A. Yes, sir.

Q. Now, you visited the rebel army—I call it that—the Cuban army in Pinar del Rio?—A. Yes, sir.

Q. When did you go there the last time?—A. The last time I was in Pinar del Rio was on the 13th of March. [Reading from paper.]

I went to the town of Caimito for the purpose of leaving medicines, bandages, etc. On arriving there I was informed that there were two wounded children at the farm known as Saladriga. I went to their assistance.

Q. Now, just stop right there, because I am going to read that paper over to you presently. I am getting at preliminary facts. When you were at Pinar del Rio did you see Maceo?—A. I saw Valdespino, and Maceo also.

Q. About how many troops did Maceo have with him?—A. Well, really, I could not tell you because of the way they appeared; the way they came was an immense crowd of people all riding on horseback. It was a large crowd. I could not exactly tell how many.

Q. You had no statement of the number?—A. No, sir.

Q. Well, would you say it was a strong army?—A. Very strong.

Q. Did he have any artillery with him?—A. I did not see any.

Q. How were they armed?—A. A great many of them were well armed and the balance of them all had the machete.

By Senator DAVIS:

Q. Would you say he had some thousands of men under his command or only a few hundreds? Give some idea.—A. Oh, I think he had some seven or eight thousand men.

Q. You saw them?—A. Yes, sir; I saw them.

By Senator MORGAN:

Q. Did he have a permanent camp there?—A. Well, they were moving around. Sometimes they stay in one place fifteen or twenty days and then move to another.

Q. Well, when you saw him had he made the attack on the city of Pinar del Rio?—A. No, sir; he was just going in the direction.

Q. And that fight occurred afterwards?—A. Afterwards; yes, sir.

· Q. What did you gather to be the result of the fight he had in Pinar del Rio; what did you find out or gather to be the result of it?—A. Well, I asked them, you know, what they intended to do in Pinar del Rio, and they said they were just going on, take possession of the principal towns, and Maceo was appointed as commander of that Province.

Q. He was assigned in command of the Province of Pinar del Rio and is there now?—A. Yes; he is there.

Q. Well, after that was over they had other battles—that of Bahiahonda?—A. Yes, sir.

Q. Do you know anything about that battle?—A. It was the one where the Alphonse XII Regiment was destroyed. It is reported the whole regiment, about 1,000 soldiers, were destroyed, and but 14 or 15 were left. They threw themselves into the water and got a small boat and went out in the bay, and the current brought them to the city of Habana, which is about 60 miles from that place.

Q. Do you think your information about that is correct, that the whole Spanish battalion was destroyed?—A. Yes, sir.

By Senator DAVIS:

Q. Was it a battalion?—A. Yes, sir; a battalion.

By Senator MORGAN:

Q. Did Maceo capture Pinar del Rio?—A. I do not know; I heard that.

Q. How long did he hold it?—A. I presume he held it about two or three days.

Q. Was this fight you tell about before or after the capture?—A. I think it was before the capture. I know that is true because of this: There was published in the paper that the colonel will be tried by court-martial because he did not go to the point where the regiment was.

Q. That is another column?—A. That is another column; yes, sir.

Q. Did you see Gomez when you were out there? When did you see him last?—A. About two months ago.

Q. Where did you see him?—A. I saw him in the Province of Habana.

Q. How far from the city of Habana?—A. I saw him in Bainoa.

Q. How far from Habana?—A. About 35 miles.

Q. Did he have his forces with him?—A. Yes, sir; an immense force.

Q. How many thousands do you suppose?—A. I think he had about 10,000 men.

Q. What was the condition of his health?—A. Pretty good. He had only a little abscess on one of his legs from an old wound, but he has recovered from that and is all right.

Q. He is an old man, is he?—A. He is an old man, about 72 years of age.

Q. Did you talk with him?—A. Yes, sir; he asked me several questions and I answered.

Q. Did you tell him about the condition of the Spanish forces and all that?—A. No, sir; he knew he had no right to ask such questions as that.

Q. What did you think of the appearance of his army; did they look as if they were strong?—A. Very strong.

Q. Well armed?—A. Well armed and in good health.

Q. Have you been personally with any other army in Cuba?—A. Yes, sir; Mr. Aguirre's.

By Senator DAVIS:

Q. When?—A. Just two weeks before they put me in prison.

Q. When did you leave Cuba? Give me the date.—A. I think it was before the 1st of May.

Q. How long before?—A. Just a day or two.

Q. Now, how long was it before you were arrested that you saw the force of Aguirre you mentioned?—A. Fifteen days.

By Senator MORGAN:

Q. Where did you find Aguirre?—A. They found me. I was down there attending a man. While I was amputating his arm the insurgent forces came around the little tent I had for that purpose, and while I was operating I found myself among the insurgents, and he came there and just looked at what I had been doing, and kept everybody away and did not molest us at all.

A. You were not in his camp, then?—A. No, sir.

Q. Did you talk with Aguirre?—A. After I got through with the operation; yes, sir.

Q. Did he speak of his affairs?—A. Yes, sir; and I knew partially of them down there.

Q. You knew the people?—A. Very well; a great many of them had been in my congregation.

Q. Now, what class of people did that army consist of?—A. The best class of young men in Habana, generally.

Q. Do you mean the Province of Habana?—A. No; the city.

Q. Aguirre's command consists mostly of city boys, does it?—A. Yes, sir.

Q. How many were there?—A. He had at that time about 2,000; that was his escort.

Q. He had others?—A. Oh, yes. He had in the province 10,000 or 15,000 men, scattered all over the Province of Habana in different camps.

Q. Now, what kind of people did the army of Maceo appear to be?—A. Very fine people, too; white people; doctors, lawyers, druggists.

Q. Intelligent people?—A. Intelligent people.

By Senator DAVIS:

Q. What kind of people were the private soldiers in Maceo's army?—A. Well, they have some colored people, too—many—and they have some of these intelligent people as private soldiers, a great many of them people who do not want any rank; just wanted to be soldiers, just to do that in the democratic line to encourage others.

By Senator MORGAN:

Q. Now, these people you saw in Gomez's army, did they appear to be men who were farmers and persons living in the country—respectable people?—A. Yes, sir.

Q. White people?—A. Yes, sir; as well as negroes.

Q. Was that the case in Aguirre's army, too?—A. Well, Aguirre had more white people.

By Senator DAVIS:

Q. What proportion of negroes and white in Maceo's army?—A. Well, one third negroes.

Q. Are the negroes and whites in separate companies and regiments, or are they all mixed up together?—A. Well, I do not know very well, but, as I say, they mingled.

Q. In the same organization?—A. The same organization.

By Senator MORGAN:

Q. Now, in traveling there, did you go to Cubitos?—A. No, sir; my organization did not reach as far as that.

Q. How far is that from Habana?—A. Cubitos is in the central part of the island. It is in the Province of Camaguay.

Q. It is up in the mountains, is it?—A. Yes, sir.

Q. Do you know Mr. Cisneros?—A. Yes, sir.

Q. Do you know where he was?—A. Yes, sir; I know where he was. Cisneros has about 20 of the principal men of the city of Habana with him. I inquired for him, and was told he was at that place, Cubitos.

Q. That is his capital?—A. That is his capital.

Q. Is that a place of difficult access?—A. Very difficult. Bartolo Masso is the general up there, with about 10,000 men to protect the government.

Q. Now, I understand that the military arrangement among the Cubans is that a general is assigned to certain provinces?—A. Yes, sir.

Q. Maceo to Pinar del Rio?—A. Yes, sir. Aguirre to Habana, Sanchez to Santa Clara, Roloff to Santo Espiritu, and Calisto in Camaguay; and then in the eastern part of the island is José Maceo.

Q. So that is the military disposition?—A. Yes, sir; men command generally in the province, and then they have subdivisions. They have, for instance, brigades in each province.

By Senator DAVIS:

Q. Gomez is commander in chief over all?—A. Yes, sir.

By Senator MORGAN:

Q. And that is the military organization?—A. Yes, sir.

Q. Let us know something about the civil organization. Did you meet any civil officers?—A. Yes, sir; Mr. Portuondo.

Q. What is his office?—A. He is secretary of the interior.

Q. He belongs to the general government of the Cuban Republic?—A. Yes, sir.

Q. I want you to speak of the local officers—the prefects and subprefects. Do you know anything about them?—A. Yes, sir.

Q. What is a prefect?—A. He is the man in charge to find supplies for the families of insurgents in every place there.

Q. Sort of a commissary?—A. Yes, sir; if the families need something to eat, for instance, he brings food, cattle, etc.

Q. Takes care of the families of the men in the army?—A. Yes, sir; and if the men are sick or wounded the prefects take care of them.

Q. They take care of the sick and wounded, and subprefects have smaller districts?—A. They have smaller districts.

Q. Now, who are the tax collectors there?—A. There are tax collectors, too; I know, personally, Mr. Menocal.

Q. A cousin of our Menocal here?—A. A brother, I think.

Q. Is he a tax collector?—A. Yes; they divide themselves into different places and collect all the revenue.

Q. Do they collect revenue from the people?—A. Oh, yes. Sometimes they have no place to put the money. Sometimes Gomez has mules loaded with money—going from one place to another with money.

By Senator DAVIS:

Q. Do they collect supplies in kind?—A. The prefects do, but these are the tax collectors.

By Senator MORGAN:

Q. Do the people of Cuba voluntarily and freely pay taxes to the Cuban government, or are they forced to do it?—A. No, sir; they freely do it. They pay taxes where the Cubans have no control over it.

By Senator DAVIS:

Q. Now, over this territory, have the Spanish any tax collectors?—A. Not one.

By Senator MORGAN:

Q. Have they any judges?—A. Not one.

By Senator DAVIS:

Q. Any civil officers at all?—A. No. In the larger towns is the only place. In the smaller places they have nothing of the kind—no mayors, no aldermen.

By Senator MORGAN:

Q. Do these various civil officers have offices in any one place, or are they roving around?—A. No; they are roving around.

Q. Have they established headquarters?—A. Well, sometimes they do for one, two, or three months, and then they move around. That depends on the persecution of the Spanish.

By Senator DAVIS:

Q. Do they keep records or written accounts?—A. Yes, sir.

By Senator MORGAN:

Q. Now, how are the mass of the Cuban army received by the popu-lation living in the towns in the country? Are they received cordially or as enemies?—A. Every time they approach any town all the people come out with flags and welcome them. That is natural. The majority of those boys belong in those cities. They can not be received in any other way.

Q. How do they receive the Spanish, on the other hand?—A. Well, there is great excitement when the Spanish troops approach the cities. The people are afraid, and they do not feel safe, because they know the Spanish come in and sack the towns and break the houses and take possession of them, and violate women, and do horrible things. Of course, the people are scared. The soldiers take possession. I saw this case in Managua; soldiers took possession of a house; the ladies screamed out, and the soldiers commenced to search the bureaus and everything there, and the men came and reported that there were some soldiers sacking that house, and the men said, "I can not say a word about it, because they are all officers."

Q. Did you see this yourself?—A. I saw that myself; I was there.

Q. Did they offer any violence to women?—A. Well, the women ran away. I do not know what became of them. I was sitting there with my brother in the drug store when these things occurred.

Q. Now, you have described how the armies of both contending par-ties are received by the people of the country.—A. Yes, sir.

Q. Is your description of that true, as far as you know? Without any specification, is it true generally?—A. Yes, sir.

Q. It is generally true?—A. Yes, sir.

Q. Do you know of a town or village in Cuba where you could say that the people were hostile to the Cuban cause?—A. Natives?

Q. Yes.—A. Not one. The whole country has risen up in arms—men, women, and children.

Q. So you regard the attitude or situation with the Cuban people as being one of general hostility to Spain?—A. Yes, sir.

Q. And is that hostility intense?—A. Past expression. One day I heard General Rui say, "Everything here is against us. The air we breathe is against the Spanish people in Cuba."

Q. How do these Cuban armies maintain themselves; upon what do they subsist, and how do they get it?—A. Well, they use goats and chickens and all the tropical fruits, and yams and sweet potatoes, and things that grow wild, and in some places farmers plant for the insurgents; so they never trouble themselves about what to eat.

Q. They have an abundance?—A. Yes, sir.

Q. How long do you think the country can stand that? Will it wear out, and after a while the people starve?—A. No; people who live in the country are all right. They can stay there for twenty years if they want to, with plenty to eat. Now, the misery is among the people of the cities.

Q. Why?—A. Because they have no resources. They have no money or anything, and insurgents are not allowed to grow anything in cities where the Spanish troops are, and they have nothing to eat.

Q. They are in a starving condition?—A. Yes, sir.

Q. About the destruction of the crops there; has it been very exten-sive—that is, the sugar cane?—A. Very.

Q. Is the Cuban army alone responsible for that destruction?—A. Not the Cuban army alone. The Spaniards do that, too. They set on fire the sugar plantations of Mr. Delgado and others. Part of the city of Managua has been destroyed by the Cubans and the other part has been destroyed by the Spanish troops.

Q. What for?—A. Well, the mayor of that town, Mr. Christo, is a lawyer. They had a battle, and 75 houses were burned, and in a month or two Mr. Christo, the mayor, joined the rebels; and he is a wealthy man, for he has different houses and plantations, and so forth, down there. As soon as he went with the rebel army the Spanish troops set on fire all the houses owned by him. So that part is destroyed by the Spaniards and part by the Cubans.

Q. Is sugar cane an element of subsistence among the Cubans and their horses?—A. Yes, sir.

Q. Now, I want to ask you something about the condition of this Spanish army and Cuban army as to diseases. You have yellow fever in Cuba?—A. Yes, sir.

Q. Does it attack the Cubans?—A. No, sir; not a bit.

Q. Why not?—A. Because they are acclimated.

Q. Does it attack the Spaniards?—A. Oh, yes; fearfully.

Q. Now, take a body of 1,000 soldiers in the season, how many would you expect to find sick out of that number?—A. Nearly all of them.

Q. As much as that?—A. Yes; nearly all of them. Nearly all get sick and about 50 or 60 per cent will die.

Q. You do not mean they all get yellow fever?—A. Yes; that is the principal thing, and dysentery.

Q. And what else?—A. Ulcers.

Q. I wish you would describe those ulcers. Are they syphilitic?—A. Yes, sir; in many cases they are syphilitic.

Q. How is the large majority of cases; is that so?—A. Yes, sir.

Q. State what is the extent of that disease among the Spanish soldiers.—A. Well, about 60 or 70 per cent.

Q. They get sick in that way?—A. Yes, sir.

By Senator DAVIS:

Q. Infected with syphilis?—A. Yes, sir; but they are corrupt people, you know.

Q. Do they bring it with them from Spain or acquire it in the island?—A. Well, they bring it from Spain and acquire it in the island, too, because this is the custom they have; they do not do it now. As soon as they landed they put their guns to one side to have a good time and hunt for women, and of course with that kind of women you know in what condition they are generally.

By Senator MORGAN:

Q. What is your opinion as to the number of Spanish troops now in Cuba?—A. I think they have in Cuba only about 70,000 or 80,000 soldiers. I do not think they have more than that.

Q. How many have come there since this war broke out?—A. Nearly 150,000 to 180,000.

Q. What has become of the balance of them?—A. Well, a great many of them have been killed, and many of them have joined the rebels.

Q. Joined the rebels?—A. A great many them; yes, sir.

Q. Well, how about those who have died in the hospitals from disease?—A. Yes; some have died of disease.

Q. What proportion of the people who have been lost—would you say that half or more than half have died of disease or battles?—A. Well, not many in battles; more of disease than of battles. The difficulty with the Spanish soldiers is that when they are brought from Spain and reach Cuba they are not allowed to speak to anybody. They have a guard, and as soon as soldiers are landed they are sent to the interior in order that they shall not speak to anyone. The Spanish people in Spain deceive these young men—tell them they are going to fight negroes, etc. The officers are not real officers, but sergeants made captains and corporals and privates made lieutenants. That is the kind of soldiers they have in Cuba, showing they do not know what kind of men they are to meet. They are told that all the Cuban army is negroes, and here they find them white and hear hurrahing for freedom and for republicanism, and say, "Well, I am a republican myself. If I had known that I would not fight against them."

By Senator DAVIS:

Q. Were you expelled from the island of Cuba?—A. Yes, sir.

Q. Why?—A. By the Spanish authorities, Mr. Weyler.

Q. When?—A. On the 30th day of last April.

Q. What reason did he give for expelling you?—A. I do not know yet.

Q. Did any of your fellow-missionaries leave about the same time?—A. They left before me.

Q. How many of them?—A. Three ministers.

Q. How many from all the missions?—A. The others, about six or seven.

Q. Now, after you and the other missionaries and the ministers left what became of the church and hospital property?—A. All has been abandoned.

Q. Do you know who has taken possession of it?—A. Yes; some of the members have taken possession of it.

Q. Have the Spanish authorities taken possession of the church?—A. Not that I know of.

Q. Have the other churches and denominations got hospitals in Cuba?—A. Yes; the Episcopalians have them.

Q. Have they been disturbed?—A. Yes, sir.

Q. Has the Episcopalian minister been disturbed?—A. I do not know.

Q. He left?—A. Oh, yes; he left. The general agent of the American Bible Society, Dr. McKean, left the Island of Cuba, too.

Q. Was he expelled?—A. I do not know. They disappear; that is all we know.

Q. What is said to be called the capital of the insurgents?—A. Cubitos.

Q. Is that the seat of government of the insurgents?—A. Yes, sir.

Q. Who is the president?—A. Cisneros.

Q. Where does he hold his office—perform his duties?—A. Right there, in Cubitos.

Q. For how long a time has he performed those duties at that place?—A. Well, I think for ten months.

Q. Has he ever been disturbed or fled from the city since that time?—A. No, sir.

Q. Has he a cabinet?—A. Yes, sir.

Q. Who is the minister of foreign relations?—A. Mr. Palma, I think.

Q. Who is the minister of the interior?—A. Mr. Portuondo.

Q. Who is the minister of justice?—A. Well, I may know the name but do not recall it.

Q. Well, is there a minister of justice there?—A. Oh, yes; I know they have a cabinet there.

Q. Any more ministers?—A. Yes; they have two or three more.

Q. Now, do those gentlemen, except Palma, live in Cubitos?—A. All there.

Q. Performing their duties?—A. Yes, sir.

Q. Have they ever been disturbed?—A. No, sir.

Q. Have they a legislative assembly?—A. Well, they had one about a year ago when they appointed Cisneros.

Q. Has there been any session since?—A. I do not know whether they have had any session recently.

Q. Have they a printing press?—A. Yes; they have a printing press there. I say they have, because I saw a paper that was published up there. The name of the paper was Cuba.

Q. Is it an organ of the insurgents?—A. Yes; it is an organ of the insurgents.

Q. Is it printed regularly?—A. I do not know. I only saw a copy.

By Senator MORGAN:

Q. Have they a post-office department?—A. Yes; a postmaster-general.

Q. And postage stamps?—A. And postage stamps.

By Senator DAVIS:

Q. How do they carry the mail over the island?—A. Well, they have their own means to carry letters.

Q. In cases of battles do the Spanish troops give quarter or do they take prisoners?—A. In a great many cases they do not give quarter.

Q. How about the insurgents; do they give quarter or take prisoners?—A. Yes; they give quarter and take prisoners and give them an invitation to join the rebel army. If they do not accept it they give them parole.

Q. What do the Spaniards do with the prisoners they take?—A. Kill them.

Q. Is that a universal practice?—A. Yes, sir; universal practice.

Q. Do you mean to say the Spanish butcher their prisoners?—A. Yes, sir.

Q. Universally?—A. Universally; yes, sir.

Q. Are any women fighting in the insurgent ranks?—A. No; they do not fight, but they are with the soldiers, because they are wives or relatives or something, and join the ranks.

Q. What do the Spaniards do with the women when they catch them?—A. Kill them.

Q. Do you mean to say they kill them the same as men?—A. They kill them; yes, sir.

Q. What do they do with the children?—A. Kill them.

Q. Do you mean that to the full extent of what you say, that they kill men, women, and children?—A. Yes, sir.

Q. How do soldiers treat women when they catch them?—A. Oh, insult them.

Q. Do you mean by insult them they ravish them; do you know anything of that kind?—A. Yes, sir.

Q. Now, these statements you have made impress me very seriously and I want to be certain. Am I to understand that in case of an engagement the Spanish troops give no quarter, and that either then or after the engagement they kill every insurgent, man, woman, and child?—A. Well, not the insurgents, because they never have that chance and could not.

Q. No, not the insurgents, but I ask if the Spanish troops do that?—

A. They do not do that to the insurgents, because the insurgents never allow them to do that; but the general rule is when they have a battle the insurgents retire and the Spanish troops come in, and any person they find in the neighborhood they kill—men, women, and children, non-combatants.

By Senator MORGAN:

Q. When you were taken as a prisoner you were taken by General Weyler's order, were you—you and your brother?—A. Yes, sir.

Q. You were confined in a house?—A. Yes, sir; we were isolated.

Q. I know; but you were confined in a house?—A. Yes, sir.

Q. How long?—A. Eight days.

Q. During that time were any charges at all presented against you?—A. No, sir; not one.

Q. Did you demand charges?—A. Yes, sir.

Q. Well, are you an American citizen?—A. Yes, sir.

Q. Fully naturalized?—A. Yes, sir.

Q. Got your papers and all?—A. Yes, sir.

Q. How long ago did that take place?—A. About thirteen years.

Q. And you have been known as an American citizen since you have been in Cuba?—A. Oh, yes.

Q. Did Weyler allow you to have any communication with the American consul?—A. No, sir.

Q. He refused it?—A. Yes, sir.

Q. You desired it and he refused?—A. Yes, sir.

Q. And no charges were made against you?—A. No, sir.

Q. Were you required to make a declaration?—A. Yes, sir; they asked me two or three different questions.

Q. And after that, did they release you?—A. Yes, sir.

Q. How long after that?—A. Twenty-four hours, I think.

Q. Then you were ordered to leave?—A. Yes, sir.

Q. Leaving on the next steamer?—A. Yes, sir.

Q. And you brought your wife and family with you?—A. Yes, sir.

Q. How many children have you?—A. Two children.

Q. Do the Cubans get any arms and ammunition from the villages or people?—A. Yes; they get them from Habana.

Q. How do they get them?—A. Exactly, I do not know the way they manage it, but I know they get all they need. I heard the people talk about that.

Q. The people supply them, of course?—A. Yes, sir.

Q. Do you know whether there is any order of the Spanish Government to prevent the landing of arms or munitions of war?—A. They do not allow any sale of arms in the city of Habana. You do not find in any store any rifles or any of those hunting guns. You do not find anything of that kind in the city of Habana.

Q. The sale of them is prohibited?—A. Yes; as contraband of war. And now I hear the later report is they consider corn as a contraband of war, too.

Q. Well, you raise corn in plenty in the interior of Cuba, do you not?—A. Yes, sir.

Q. How many crops of corn can you raise in a year in the interior of Cuba?—A. Well, horses are contraband of war, too, and the people of Cuba can not have horses. They have to give all the horses to the Government as contraband of war; and now corn is a contraband of war, too. The trade of Habana has been wretched. They have no trade. All grocery stores are empty; nobody spends a single cent in any store. They have no money, and the Spanish people have been going away from the Island of Cuba.

Q. Do you have any paper money at all in Cuba?—A. No, sir; they have silver and copper and gold. I believe the Spanish people in Cuba—those in business—are all in favor of the rebellion, because if the Spanish Government takes possession of the island again they will have to pay the last debt and this additional debt. They have to pay about $35,000 a day, and this is the interest of the debt; but they do not know how much the debt is. They call it $35,000 a day, and every day. They get it from the custom-house.

Senator MORGAN. Now I will read this paper to you.

Senator Morgan read the paper, as follows:

To the Honorable Chairman of the Foreign Relations Committee, United States Senate.

DEAR SIR: On the 12th day of September, 1895, I received authority from the inspector-general to organize and maintain sanitary delegations at different points throughout the island of Cuba. I have now in my possession the original copy of said certificate of permission, signed officially.

The by-laws were approved on November 18, 1895, copy of which I hand you herewith. I would call special attention to article 2 of chapter 1, by which it will be seen I was permitted to constitute neutral camps.

I, with some other doctors and Christian people, some of whom were American citizens, organized the White Cross, in conformity with said by-laws.

While General Campos was in command the rules of civilized warfare were strictly enforced by his orders.

After General Weyler assumed command we were summoned before him and instructed not to treat or otherwise care for sick and wounded among the soldiers of the insurgents, as we had been permitted to do under the administration of General Campos.

Since the time General Weyler has been in command we have treated about 700 Spanish soldiers, each case being reported to him, at a cost to us of about $5,000, and before he assumed command we had treated about 1,300 Spanish soldiers.

During the time General Campos was in command our delegations treated the sick and wounded of both the insurgents and the Spanish alike.

During the prosecution of this work I have been a great deal out on the fields and have had good opportunities of making observations of the practices and character of the warfare of both armies.

I have seen the general order issued by Gen. Maximo Gomez, directing that all prisoners captured from the Spanish army should be treated with proper consideration. That first they should be disarmed, then offered an opportunity to join the insurgent ranks. If they declined to do this voluntarily then they must be released without parole and escorted to some point of safety. The same order further directed that Spanish prisoners who were either sick or wounded should be nursed and carefully treated until well when, if they do not desire, voluntarily, to join the insurgent ranks, they must be released and conveyed under military escort to a point of safety. It was also ordered by General Gomez that no women should be molested or interfered with by any insurgent soldiers under penalty of death.

Those entire general orders are now in force and have been since the beginning of the insurrection. They are very positive, and severe penalties are provided for their violation.

From my personal observation I know these orders have been strictly enforced. I know of one instance where, in the town of Jamaica, an insurgent soldier violated these orders by laying his hands upon a woman with criminal intent. For this offense he was ordered to be shot, and I saw his body after he had been executed.

I have personal knowledge of this order in regard to the release of prisoners having been complied with.

At Peralego I saw General Macco return to General Campos, at Ballamo, about 150 prisoners, and at Camaguani I saw Rego return to the Spanish authorities 100 prisoners.

I have also had opportunities for observing the methods of warfare and cruelties practiced by General Weyler. It is well known to the residents of Cuba that his record is one of cruelty and blood. I can substantiate the following incidents which have come under my own observation.

At Menocol farm, near Managua, on the 3d day of February, 1896, I was called to attend a woman who had been shot, the bullet entering her shoulder and ranging down her spinal column. I saw her at 4 p. m. The circumstances as related to me by her husband were as follows:

He was engaged plowing near his own home and the woman, his wife, was in the field with him dropping the seed. As soon as the Spanish soldiers, under command of General Ruiz, approached in view, they (the Spanish soldiers) commenced firing. Both the husband and wife lay down on the ground, and in that position she was shot. As the husband was lying down he held a small limb of a tree; this was struck with one of the shots. I treated the wound. They were non-combatants, unarmed, and pursuing their legitimate vocation in their own field; their only offense was that they were Cubans. There were at the time no insurgents within 20 miles of them.

On February 22, 1896, I was present at the city of Punta Braba where a battle was fought between the insurgents and the Spanish under command of Captain Calvo. The insurgents retreated. The Spanish troops then went to Guatao, a suburb about 2 miles distant. The insurgents were not there and had not been there. The Spanish soldiers at once commenced to shoot private citizens indiscriminately on the streets or in their houses, wherever they found them, until they had killed six or seven men (noncombatants).

The soldiers then went into different homes and gathered together 17 men; they tied these together two and two, binding their hands and arms together. Among the number was Mr. Ladislao Quintero, an American citizen, who they found in his own home, sick in bed. He informed the captain that he was an American citizen and protested against being molested. Captain Calvo said he wanted him, too, and forced him to go, bound with the others. When they were all tied they were taken out together on the street and commanded to kneel down. After they had done so, then the whole company fired on them by command of the captain. The whole of the 17 were killed, except Mr. Quintero. He was wounded in the left arm and the man to whom he was tied was killed with all the others. This all occurred at 7.30 p. m., on February 22, in the immediate presence of the wives and children of the unfortunate men. Mr. Quintero was about 21 years of age, born in Key West, Fla. The man to whom he was tied, Mr. Pedro Amador, was 17 years of age.

Mr. Pedro Amador was not killed by the gunshot wound he received, but one of the Spanish soldiers stepped forward to his prostrate body and beat him to death with the butt end of his gun while he was still tied to Mr. Quintero, the American citizen. I was present and saw this entire proceeding. When I returned to Habana I learned that Mr. Quintero was in Morro Castle, a prisoner, where he remained until April 11 without having his wound dressed. On April 11 he was released.

I am informed by persons in Habana, who have been prisoners in Morro Castle, that there are in this prison as many as 100 prisoners confined in one small room. That in the morning they are furnished with only three pails of water. This is generally used up by 11 o'clock a. m. and they are not allowed any more until the following morning.

In the case of Mr. Edward Delgado, from Banao, an American citizen who has a claim against the Spanish Government, his papers being on file in the Department of State at Washington, you will find by reference thereto that I was the physician who certified to his wounds. I am familiar with this case, and it is a very aggravated case of extreme cruelty to a private American citizen at his own home without provocation.

The following is only a few of the many cruel incidents that have occurred while I was present:

When the military courts inflicted the sentence of perpetual imprisonment in the cases of Messrs. Sabourin, Garcia, and others, the Captain-General protested against their leniency and asked for the infliction of the death penalty.

On the 12th of March I was called by the sanitary delegation of our society in the town of Calvario for the purpose of attending to the case of a young man of 19 years, who was wounded in the peaceful pursuit of his business—that of a milk dealer. He was driving into the town in his milk cart when two soldiers fired on him from an ambush without any warning, breaking his right leg.

I assisted in carrying the man to his home, and then made an examination of his wound and found that the bones of his leg had been fractured in such a manner that amputation was necessary. I found that the bullet used was an explosive one made as follows: An outside covering of copper filled with lead, which results in the copper covering flattening against the lead and scattering it in such a manner as to destroy all surrounding tissues and compound the fractures of the bones.

On the 13th of March, at the corner of Reina and Aguila streets, Habana, I found a crowd collected around a prostrate man, and, as a member of the White Cross Society, I proceeded to render him whatever aid was necessary. I found the man dead, and counted and made an examination of his wounds. He had 71 bayonets wounds, 7 of which were through the heart and several though the eyes. He also had 4 cuts with the machete on the head, the skull being fractured into small pieces. The ferocity of the soldiers was also shown by the marks in the sidewalk made by the point of the bayonet after having passed through the prostrate form of the man. The cause of the killing was as follows: The murdered man was in a dry goods store purchasing cloth when the two soldiers entered and, after insulting the proprietor, took this man out and killed him in the manner related, saying he was an insurgent. The man had no arms whatever on his person, and could not, therefore, defend himself in any way. I wrote out a statement of his wounds and gave it to the judge in the case, who holds a position similar to that of coroner in this country.

On the 14th of the same month I, as vice-president of the White

Cross Society, received a report from the town of Artemisa, telling me that the Spanish troops under Gen. Suarez Inclan had bombarded an insurgent hospital, killing over 50 wounded men who were receiving treatment there, and that the surgeon had been compelled to flee to Habana hidden in a cart. Upon his arrival at Habana he confirmed the report made to me. In Artemisa the ladies of our society had two hospitals, one for wounded Spaniards and one for wounded Cubans, the latter being the one bombarded, as told. The insurgent forces have entered the town of Artemisa several times, but have never disturbed the Spanish hospital, although they could have easily done so if they wished.

Another insurgent hospital in the town of Paso Real, Province of Pinar Del Rio, was also destroyed by the Spaniards, killing all the wounded inmates. It is reported that at the time of destruction there were about 200 wounded Cubans in it.

The same thing was done with another hospital in Siguanea, Province of Santa Clara.

Notwithstanding the proclamation of the Captain-General that all those surrendering would be pardoned, Mr. Aleman, who surrendered, and who also had a wound in the hand, was shot a few days later on the plea that his wound showed that he had been fighting.

In the woman's jail in Habana there is a lady who has been imprisoned for the last six months solely because she is suspected of being in sympathy with the insurgents' cause and because she has two brothers in the insurgent army. There are imprisoned, as rebel sympathizers, several children, the age of the youngest being 11 years.

When an armed force approaches any of the interior towns there is great excitement and consternation until it is ascertained whether they are Spanish troops or insurgent forces. If insurgent forces there is immediate tranquillity, as they do not destroy anything unless there are Spanish forces located there. But if the approaching troops turn out to be Spanish forces there is great confusion and fear, as the Spaniards not only sack the town but steal all they desire and also take all detachable woodwork to be used in building their huts. They destroy everything that comes in their way, take complete possession of the houses, violate women in many cases, and commit nuisances in the middle of the streets. They claim to go into the towns for the purpose of defending them against the insurgents, but on the approach of the latter they take refuge in the houses and do not come out until the town is set fire to by the insurgents for the purpose of driving them out. I have personally seen all this in more than ten cases.

On the 13th of March I went to the town of Caimito for the purpose of leaving medicines, bandages, etc. On arriving there I was informed that there were two wounded children at the farm known as "Saladriga." I went to their assistance, but found they had already received medical treatment. The eldest of these was 1 year and 6 months old, and had suffered a fracture of the right arm caused by a bullet wound. The other was 3 months old and had suffered a fracture of the lower jaw from a similar cause. I was informed that 2 miles from this place the insurgents had attacked a troop-laden train without success. The Spanish troops left the train to reconnoiter and took the road on which the insurgents had passed. On this road lived the mother of these two children. Fearing that some harm might befall them, she decided to seek shelter elsewhere. Upon her appearance at the door with two children in her arms, she was fired at with the above results. These Spanish troops were under Commander Calixto Ruiz.

On the 19th of March I went with my brother, Alfred, to the town of Bainoa for the purpose of attending to Mr. Venancio Pino, 70 years of age, who was wounded at the same time as Mr. Delgado. I found that he had several slight bullet wounds in the head, but his right arm had been horribly fractured, necessitating amputation at the shoulder joint. The bone had been fractured into many pieces, and was caused by a bullet similar to the one in the case of the milk dealer spoken of before.

On the 8th of April, at the farms near the town of Campo Florida, the Spanish troop under Commander Fondevilla assassinated Mr. Ramon Castellanos, 19 years of age; Joaquin Medina, 14 years old; Jose J. Ochoa, 30 years, and a schoolmaster 35 years of age; Domingo Luzans, 36 years; Margarito Zarza, 50 years; Camilo Cejas, 40 years old; Jose Valdes, 14 years old; Manuel Martinez, 40 years old. These were buried at a point between the sugar estate of Tivo Tivo and the town, the Spaniards forcing the victims to dig their own graves before murdering them.

For the purpose of brevity, I will give the number of noncombatants assassinated each day. I have their names and can furnish them if required.

On the 9th of April, 4.

On the 15th, between Campo Florida and the sugar estate of Felicia, 10, whose corpses were left without interment.

On the same day, on the road between Guanabacoa and Bacuranao, 5 persons, 2 of whom were cousins of mine.

Over 100 persons were shot within a radius of 10 miles and not distant more than 6 miles from Habana, and within a period of fifteen days.

All of these were noncombatants.

The case against Julio Sanguilly, the imprisoned American citizen, is purposely delayed so as to keep him incarcerated.

In the case of my brother and myself, we were persecuted for the reason that we were American citizens and had charge of American church institutions in Habana.

During the excitement attending the passage of the belligerency resolutions in Congress two dynamite bombs were placed in the church and exploded while we were holding service, but only resulted in the breaking of glass and causing a panic in the congregation. Our house was searched, but nothing incriminating was found, but we were arrested and imprisoned eight days, being released on the condition that we leave Cuba immediately. I would say that no charges were made against us. We immediately left Cuba.

Mr. Toledo, an American citizen employed as a Bible distributer by the American Bible Society, was imprisoned in the town of Jaruco, and has mysteriously disappeared, and it is believed that he has been murdered.

My brother and I are here for the purpose of laying these facts before your committee and to urge the honorable Senate to either recognize the belligerency of the Cubans or to have the United States intervene or the sake of humanity and civilization. These are the only methods of putting a stop to these frightful barbarities.

Yours, respectfully,　　　　　　　　　　　　　　　A. J. DIAZ.

Senator MORGAN. Do you swear to all that?
A. Yes, sir.
Senator MORGAN. Then please sign it.
The witness then signed the paper.

S. Doc. 231, pt 7——44

STATEMENT OF MR. WILLIAM D. SMITH, ON THE 3D DAY OF JUNE, 1897.

Mr. SMITH was sworn by Mr. Davis, chairman of the committee. Senators Clark and Morgan subcommittee.

By Mr. MORGAN:

Q. Will you tell us your name and age?—A. William D. Smith; I am in my forty-third year; I was born on the 29th day of February, so I have had but ten birthdays.

Q. Did you ever belong to the Army of the United States?—A. Yes, sir.

Q. Did you hold any office? If so, what?—A. I went into the Army of the United States, in the first place, as an enlisted man, April 1, 1879, and rose to the rank of first sergeant, and then passed an examination for a commission, under a request from my company commander. I was appointed.

Q. When did you resign, if you did resign?—A. In 1884, at Fort Lowell, Ariz.

Q. In what occupation have you been since that time?—A. I practiced law to the time I went to Cuba. I graduated at Harvard Law School, and read law under Senator Edmunds. I was in Troop F, Fourth Cavalry, Capt. Wirt Davis, stationed now in Texas.

Q. Where did you practice law?—A. In Ohio.

Q. When did you go to Cuba?—A. I went to Cuba in 1896. Do you mean when I arrived there, or when I left here? I arrived in Havana in April, 1896.

Q. Did you go to Cuba on private business, or for the purpose of enlisting in the Cuban army?—A. I was sent there by some Cubans. I went there to join the insurgents for that purpose.

Q. What body of insurgents did you first join and where?—A. General Swarra, in the Province of Camaguey.

Q. How long did you remain with him?—A. I joined General Swarra on the 15th day of April; was with him just two months, nearly, to a day.

Q. Did you hold an office in the army under him?—A. Yes, sir. I will make an explanation of that. I held an office under him; that is, afterwards it developed that way. General Gomez gave me my diploma, dating it from the hour I arrived on the island—that is, he did not then date it, but gave me my rank from the hour I arrived. The Cubans do not use the word commission; they use the word diploma. I have with me my diploma, and that is it, dated the 18th of October last. It is in Spanish, of course.

Q. Was the commission authorized by the civil government?—A. Yes, sir.

(Witness here produced his commission as captain in the Cuban army, signed by Gomez, and dated the 18th of October, 1896.)

A. (Continued.) I will explain about that as to who gives the commissions. The general in chief of the Cuban army, according to their laws, has the authority to give a man a rank as high as comandante, corresponding to a major with us. I was made a comandante two days before I left camp; but the government had not acted on it, and I do not claim the rank until they do. He can appoint officers up to the rank of captain; but when he goes above that he recommends a man and the civil government acts upon his recommendation.

Q. The civil government?—A. Yes, sir; you will see that the general's seal is on there.

Q. Did you receive any further promotion in that army?—A. Only as I tell you. When I left, when I came on this commission, I was recommended for comandante.

Q. Equivalent to major in the United States Army?—A. Yes, sir.

Q. That rank you now hold?—A. Yes, sir; the government had no time to act on it—they were in Camaguey and we were in La Villos.

Q. You do not have your diploma as comandante?—A. No, sir.

Q. When did you join General Gomez?—A. The 15th day of June, 1896, at the battle of Saratoga.

Q. Under whose orders?—A. I was ordered to report to him (I had three generals to report to) by the Cuban government. I had my choice as between Antonio Maceo, Calixta Garcia, or Gomez, and Gomez happened to be the nearest officer after I got into Camaguey. Swarra and Gomez were in one end of the Province, and when they came together I left Swarra and went to Gomez.

Q. Where was he when you joined?—A. At Saratoga. It was during that fight.

Q. He was in the midst of the battle when you joined?—A. Yes, sir.

Q. Did you win that fight?—A. He gave General Catalanio a thorough thrashing. The Spanish acknowledged they were defeated. It was one of the battles in which they never denied they were whipped.

Q. In what Province?—A. At Camaguey, 7 leagues from Puerto Principe—21 miles. They fought two days, and General Gomez drove them off the field and fired at their troops as they entered into Puerto Principe, and then camped on the ground three days.

Q. What were their relative losses, killed and wounded?—A. The Cubans lost 68—that is their official report—killed, and 110 wounded. The Spanish loss we do not know exactly, although I witnessed some 180 dug up and counted by the general's order. The only way the Cubans have of ascertaining the loss of the Spanish is by digging them up. They bury their dead and Cubans dig them up and count them. Then they are reburied at once, without other disturbance.

Q. Where are they buried?—A. Just where they fall.

Q. During that fight?—A. Yes, sir. You have to bury a dead man about as quick as he drops; if you don't there will be no staying there.

Q. Have you been constantly with Gomez from that time until the time you left Cuba?—A. Yes, sir; with the exception, of course, of being sent from time to time in charge of commissions, I have been constantly under his orders until the 2d day of last month.

Q. What was the longest time you were absent from his command?—A. Twenty days was the longest time I was ever absent. He sent me on a commission to a sugar plantation to see about the permits.

Q. Was that before Gomez had been down to the west of Pinar del Rio, or after?—A. Before; I joined after he went down there.

Q. Did you go with him through Pinar del Rio?—A. No, sir.

Q. You were, then, with him on his great march?—A. Oh, no; that is a mistake; I was not. This great march of his was before I joined him. That march from one end of the island to the other was previous. When he came back from Pinar del Rio, then I joined him. After the fight at Saratoga, ten or fifteen days, allowing sufficient time to rest his troops, he made a trip down to the Orient to visit Calixta Garcia, whom he had not seen since the ten-year war, and we found him near Santiago. There was no fight on the way, although we had several battles after we got there and he had met his old comrade.

Q. After that, did he go to Pinar del Rio?—A. No, sir; not since I have been with him.

Q. Have you been in other important engagements in which Gomez was in command?—A. I have been in every engagement he has been in. I have a record of them, but do not have it here. There were 42 engagements I have been in with General Gomez, besides little skirmishes I did not count. It is a dash and a few shots and get out of the way where they outnumber you. There were 242 engagements where he stood his ground and camped on the ground of the Spaniards, the last engagement just a few days before I left, when General Gomez and General Weyler met for the first time.

Q. Where was that?—A. At La Reforma.

Q. A sugar estate?—A. No, sir; not a sugar estate; it is a cattle range; the most beautiful place, I think, in La Villias. It is General Gomez's favorite camping ground, because his son was born there.

Q. How did the last battle wind up?—A. General Weyler withdrew the troops and went to Puerto Principe and Gomez camped on the ground.

Q. How many troops were engaged?—A. Gomez had 1,500, or possibly 2,000—I am trying to get this as near right as possible—I do not want to overestimate. The Spanish had 20,000 men—General Weyler had 20,000 troops with him.

Q. 20,000 in bodies within reach of each other?—A. No, sir; 20,000 men right in the fight at one time; not in a mass, in any one body, but he had 20,000 in columns. The fighting down there requires explanation. It seems ridiculous that 1,500 men would stand and fight 20,000, but the Spaniards always march in a column of 1,000 men and 1 piece of artillery—1 cannon. They came into Reforma in twenty different directions. The trap was being laid by General Weyler to capture General Gomez. The General was cognizant of it for two weeks, and waited for them to come. The way he fought those 20,000, he would have 100 men fight one column, and 50 men fight another column, and 100 men fight another, and 75 still another column, and so on, and he stood them off like that. I have known 10 Cubans to hold a Spanish column of 1,000 men until General Gomez could get together his impedimenta and get out—hold them at a dead standstill. I account for it by the reason that the Spaniards thought that there was a trap, an ambuscade, and they would not run into it. That is General Gomez's tactics; he has done it several times.

Q. What is the area of that estate?—A. Between ten and twelve thousand acres.

Q. What were the losses in the battle of La Reforma?—A. The last one?

Q. Yes, sir.—A. The Cuban losses were 26, I think, killed, during the two days' fighting.

Q. How many days?—A. Two days.

Q. How many wounded?—A. The wounded it is hard to estimate. We never know the exact number wounded, because so many are wounded who do not pay any attention to it. I saw one man wounded who was shot with a Mauser bullet, which passed right through him, and we never knew anything about it for two days. That seems almost miraculous, but it is true. I suppose you have seen that Mauser bullet. The lead is covered by some metal. I can show you a wound that you would have said, if it had happened with any other cartridge, that I would have had to have an amputation. One went right through my ankle, and I was only in the hospital two hours—long enough to have it done up. The bullet does not make any fracture. I have never seen a case of amputation since I have been on the island, and it does not cause septicæmia. There is the wound [exhibiting]. The bullet entered here [pointing to his ankle] and came out there. I was never laid up a minute. The doctor in camp simply dressed it with iodoform and a little antiseptic. That is why I say it is almost impossible to give an exact account of the wounded.

Q. About how many?—A. I should should say 50 or 75.

Q. What was the loss to the Spaniards?—A. Their loss was 180 or 185 killed, and the wounded we never know, although in getting here after leaving camp I ran across a practico—that is, a guide—and he told us he had guided General Weyler's forces across the Rio Sassa, and he got it from the soldiers that they had 300 or 400 wounded.

Q. Weyler was in personal command on the one side and Gomez on the other at that time?—A. Yes, sir; the first time they had ever met. The New York Sun gave an account of it.

Q. Where did Gomez's troops camp after that battle?—A. At Reforma, on the battlefield. He has always marched over the battlefield since I have been with him.

Q. General Gomez is commander in chief of the Cuban army?—A. He calls himself the general in chief. The commander in chief is Cisneros Betancourt.

Q. Under whom does he hold his commission?—A. Under the Cuban Government. He has a diploma, the same as I have—I have seen it—only, of course, with different names and grades.

Q. Do all the officers hold their commissions from the civil government?—A. Everything above a captain.

Q. Does Gomez make report to the civil government?—A. Daily. They may not get them daily, but there is a daily report made by Gomez to the civil government. He makes them up, and every two or three days they are sent by couriers. Of course, there may be a jump of a day or two.

Q. Does he report for his own command or entire army?—A. For the entire army.

Q. The army, then, is divided into—— —A. Into six army corps.

Q. And six generals?—A. Yes. Those army corps are divided into divisions, and those divisions into regiments, and those regiments into companies. It is a facsimile of our Army in that respect.

Q. He receives his reports, then, from the six army corps commanders?—A. Yes, sir; he is the only man that reports to the government; the others all report to him.

Q. How are the communications maintained between Gomez at his headquarters and these other five corps?—A. By the couriers—by dispatch.

Q. Are the communications free, certain, and rapid?—A. They have

there what they call—that is, under the control of the civil government, they have what they call—their mail service, which reaches all
over the island. They have their post office and houses, and they call
it la casa posta. A courier rides up to one of these post-offices——

By Mr. CLARK:

Q. This post-office system is under the Cuban civil government?—A.
Yes, sir; under the civil government. Gomez has only to do with the
army; the post-office is exclusively under the civil government.

By Mr. MORGAN:

Q. What are those Spanish names?—A. La casa posta, that is a
house post-office, a depository for letters, a post-house. General Gomez
wishes to send a communication to General Garcia, we will say. The
mail is delivered to these couriers, who do not do anything but handle
this mail. They are called la casa posta hombres, the post-house men.
He takes these packages from Gomez and signs his receipt to Gomez.
He carries that—the distance varies from 5 to 6 leagues, a league is a
trifle over 3 American miles—he carries it, mounted and in his saddlebags, to the post-house. There he turns it over to another man,
who receipts to him, counts the different packages and letters, and
receipts the number he receives from the courier. He jumps on a pony
and goes right on. No matter what time of day or night, he is compelled to go with it, and so it goes on from hand to hand until it
reaches its destination.

Q. And that is the method by which communication is kept between
the different corps?—A. Yes, sir.

Q. Have they any local telegraph offices?—A. No, sir; the Cubans
do not allow any telegraph offices. Of course, when the war started
they were all over the island, but the wires have all been cut down.

By Mr. CLARK:

Q. It would seem that communication, even mail service, is maintained by the civil government and not by the army?—A. Gomez has
nothing to do with that, not the management.

By Mr. MORGAN:

Q. Where are these six army corps located?—A. The first army corps
is under command of Calixta Garcia. That commences at Baracoa, and
runs to the Province of Camaguey. Then another one is in Camaguey,
commanded by—General Viga is in command of this army corps, called
the second army corps. The third is under command of General
Riviera, who has been recently taken prisoner and is now in Moro
Castle. This is in the extreme west. The fourth is under General
Vegas; the fifth, in Havana Province, under command of General Rosa,
a Colombian, and the sixth is through here, these two Provinces [point-
ing on the map], in command of General Maria Roderigues, in the Province of Matanzas, in Santa Clara.

Q. What is the estimated numerical strength of these six army
corps?—A. The strength of the six army corps at the last report was
40,216 armed men—I will give the exact figures—it will be more now.
Three expeditions have landed on the island since I left General Gomez,
and the strength will be more instead of less. Every expedition that
lands with arms makes the strength of the army greater.

Q. Are the troops waiting for arms?—A. Always. You can find in
Gomez's army all the way from 500 to 1,000 men waiting; that is, in the
vicinity. He does not, of course, allow them in the immediate camp.

Q. If Gomez could get arms, to what extent could he recruit and maintain his army?—A. A little over 60,000.

Q. How are these army corps maintained?—A. What do you mean by that—living?

Q. Yes.—A. That is managed by—so far as the beef is concerned, they manage that themselves, but the vegetables and other food—everything with the exception of beef—is handled by the civil government. It supplies them to the army. To make an explanation, the civil government has under them prefectos and subprefectos in each Province. In each of the Provinces there is a governor and three lieutenant-governors. This governor and these three lieutenant-governors have under them prefectos and subprefectos. The prefectos act the same and are the facsimile of our justices of the peace. They collect the government revenue and report to the lieutenant-governor of the district they are in; the lieutenant governor makes his report to the governor, and the governor makes his report to the government. They have to have a system of that kind. The Cubans are collecting the tax all the length of this island, and have been until Gomez objected to any grinding on the Island of Cuba. Gomez is opposed to having any grinding. He thinks, whether a foreigner or anybody else owns the property, the property should be destroyed if Spain derives any revenue from it, and if the Cubans are successful they can settle with the foreigner, and if not it devolves on the Spanish Government to settle. The government has held him down, and he has held his point so far. There have been a few ready to grind, especially in the Trinidad Valley.

Q. Grind sugar?—A. Yes, sir.

Q. Is there a tax system outside of this license for grinding?—A. Not at present, because there is no one from whom to collect a tax. All the good Cubans are in the army. There may be a few in the cities. I know nothing about that, but there is not a Cuban in the island in the interior who is not either fighting or working ten hours a day to support those who are fighting.

Q. Working how?—A. Tilling the soil, or making shoes or saddles, or something of the kind. In this Province—Puerto Principe—there is a shop where there are 300 mechanics, and they are mechanics. If you could see some of the work, you would agree with me. They have almost every kind of machinery conceivable pertaining to the work in that shop. These 300 men are making shoes. The hides of the beeves killed the entire length of the island are collected as fast as they are taken off the animals, and they are taken to the place for tanning, up in the mountains, and then the leather taken to a shop. Every Province has its shop. I mention this one in Puerto Principe particularly because it is the best, I think. You can go there with a horse and come away with a new saddle and bridle and your horse well shod.

Q. Who pays them?—A. The men?

Q. Yes, sir.—A. They are Cubans; they are supposed to do this for nothing. They have their choice to enter the army or contribute to its support. These shops are all under the management of the civil government. Every Cuban on the Island of Cuba, unless he has run away and got under the protection of the Spanish Government, is supposed to have a gun in his hand or be working for those who have a gun; and they do it with a royal good will. These men work ten hours a day; the pacificos go to the mountains and till the soil. I saw in Trinidad, where there were 15 or 20 acres on the slope of the mountains where they have cut the timber down and planted sweet potatoes, and you can kick out sweet potatoes as large as that cuspidor. I have not eaten a meal on the island without having all I wanted, and the finest honey and beef and sweet potatoes. Gomez is husbanding the beef, and I think he has enough to last time immemorial. They are only allowed to kill what is actually consumed. The same can be said of the horses; all under the control of the Cubans are in depositos. He does not allow a soldier to ride a mare, only geldings; that is in case the war is prolonged, so that they may have their horses. They systematically propagate horses, mules, and cattle.

Q. From your knowledge of resources of Cuba and its power to produce animal life, how long do you think that the Cuban government could sustain an army of fifty or sixty thousand men?—A. Under the plan or system they are working now, I do not know why they should not support it for ages. I know that the cattle are apparently just as many as when I went there a year ago, and more vegetables, because they have been accumulating them all the time. The civil government works at that all the time, and there are more of them than a year ago.

By Mr. CLARK:

Q. How are the women and children provided for?—A. Those in the interior—their husbands, the pacificos—the rule is this: The civil government allows one man to provide food for every five women and children. These can be five women, or one woman and four children, but it allows one man to stay away from the army—or a portion of the time—one man for five women and children. That is the civil law. And they have their houses in these mountains, and they raise their pork and vegetables, and a great many of the women work in the shops where they are making clothes for the soldiers. In one portion of this shop there was a great number—I never counted them—daughters of the Cubans in the field and their wives, in there making clothes. I have seen 10,000 suits of clothes at one time, piled out there. That includes a pair of pants, a coat, and shoes.

Q. Is the Cuban army well fed?—A. The best I ever saw in any army. I have not had a meal—and that applies to the army, when I say myself I mean all—I have not had five meals on the island——

Q. What?—A. There have not been five meals on the island when I have not had my coffee and sugar I say sugar; sometimes we had honey in place of the sugar——

Q. Where is the coffee raised?—A. Certain kinds of coffee grow wild in this province of Santa Clara. In these Trinidad hills there is one vast forest of coffee, where I have seen coffee on the ground 2 inches thick—on the ground rotting.

Q. Is it good coffee?—A. It is fair coffee. It is not the best coffee. Their best coffee is not the very best grade of coffee——

Q. It makes a good, wholesome beverage?—A. Yes, sir; it is good enough, so that when the soldiers don't get it they growl considerably.

Q. You would say the army is well fed?—A. Yes, sir; I hardly think that expresses it; they have luxuries. Now, a soldier who gets a piece of meat, a piece of bacon, and hard tack and coffee is well fed. I consider it for a soldier in the army it is good enough to fight on, but they have a good deal better than that; it is far above the average.

Q. This beef, is it a good quality?—A. It is the best I ever set eyes on, and I have done soldiering on our frontier.

Q. On our Western frontier?—A. Yes, sir; and there is nothing on our Western ranges that can touch it.

Q. You were speaking of the Western country. How many years' experience had you there?—A. I had nearly nine years.

Q. On our Western frontier as a soldier?—A. Yes, sir.

Q. Among the Indians?—A. Yes, sir; in Troop F, Fourth Cavalry. Fred Grant, son of General Grant, was the first lieutenant of the troop when I was in it.

Q. How are the people, the inhabitants who live within the Cuban line—how are they supported—well supported?—A. The same as the soldiers are. They raise all this food for the soldiers, and they take enough for their families. It is they who bring in these vegetables and honey and cheese. I have seen four hundred cheeses lying in Gomez's camp. When a soldier has cheese and honey to eat he is not starving.

Q. Is it a good grazing country?—A. In some parts of Puerto Principe it is a great grazing country, the finest part of the island. They have a great deal of milk there. In certain portions of the Province it is the finest grazing country I ever saw. The great advantage it has over our country is that they never have drought there. The water is exceptionally good. All the streams are mountain streams, virtually springs.

Q. Then you would say, if I understand your statement, that the Cuban Republic, occupying the ground it does now, could sustain an army of 50,000 men for an indefinite period, and that during that period the people would be in comfortable circumstances as to living?—A. Yes, sir; I want this committee to understand one thing about this. I do not have any knowledge regarding the Cubans or anyone else within the cities. I know nothing about that. If there is a Cuban in a city he ought to starve to death. He has no business to be there, and if he would get out and go to work, as a good Cuban ought to do, for his country, he could have all he wanted to eat for himself and family.

Q. What is the condition of health, and what has it been, since you have been there, in the Cuban army?—A. I have not seen a single case of smallpox or fever, and, as for myself, I have not seen a sick man.

Q. Is that true of the rural population?—A. Yes, sir; the Cubans never have smallpox or yellow fever in the country. Those are confined to the cities, where there is dirt and filth, and they do not take care of themselves. That is what they tell me, and I know from my own experience. I have never seen a case of yellow fever or smallpox.

Q. Is it a pleasant country to live in, the rural portions?--A. Delightful. The climate is perfect. There are a few hours in the day, during the months of July and August, from 11 until 1 o'clock, when a man is more comfortable in the shade than where the sun strikes him, considerably more comfortable; but when it comes night—I have not seen a night when I did not want a blanket over me. The Cubans all have blankets, very much like our army blankets, and their hammocks.

Q. You were speaking of these manufactures and shops. Are they scattered throughout the island in different locations?—A. Yes, sir. Suppose General Gomez wishes to supply a few men in his escort or the Victoria regiment, which are always with him. If he wishes to supply 5 or 6 or 10 men, he puts in a written requisition to the civil government. It goes to the government, to President Cisneros Betancourt, and he acts upon their requisition. Of course, all Gomez's requisitions are granted, and it is sent to the nearest factory or shop to General Gomez, to the governor of that Province, and he takes it and gives it to his lieutenant governor, telling him that Gomez is within his jurisdiction, and orders him to supply that requisition. General Gomez himself can not ride up to one of those shops and even get a horseshoe nail without an order from the governor. The only thing Gomez has exclusive command of is matters pertaining to the army. Now I mean by that, in the case of depositories of arms it is a little different. The civil government does not have anything to do with the distribution of the arms, although the arms and ammunition when they first come to Cuba are first turned over to the civil government. These expeditions never account to General Gomez, but to the civil government, and then the civil government turns them over to Gomez and he makes his own distribution.

Q. They have repair shops for arms?—A. Yes, sir. Do you know the Cuban government has made several guns, and made one cannon and molded it? That was done in the Province of Santa Clara.

Q. Have they any manufacturers of explosives or powder?—A. They have a great deal of dynamite.

Q. Do they make it?—A. Oh, no; but they make powder. All the cartridge shells used by the Cubans are preserved. After the fight all the shells are gathered together and sent to these shops. And there are men who reload them and make powder. What they make their powder of I do not know, but I have tested their cartridges and they will work well. They do that constantly.

Q. Is there a general arsenal?—A. No, sir; every province has its own shops.

Q. Its own shop?—A. Yes, sir.

Q. I will ask you about hospitals; have they hospitals established?—A. Yes, sir; some very fine ones. I mentioned Puerto Principe principally because I know that from A to Z; that is where most of my soldiering was done until we came to Santa Clara. There are good hospitals there. The lieutenant-governor has a large hospital under his immediate control. Then there are several smaller hospitals where a man, if he gets a little indisposed, can have a place to go to. They will send him to one of these little hospitals and let him recuperate, and then report back. These hospitals for the wounded are well supplied and well ventilated under the management of a doctor. That is a thing the Cubans are well supplied with; they have some very fine doctors. They are men who have graduated from our colleges and schools, among others from Rush Medical College. The doctor of President Cisneros is a graduate of Hahnemann College, a homeopathist. General Gomez's doctor graduated from Rush Medical College, the old school, then went to New York and took a special course in surgery in Bellevue, and the director—the medical director—with a rank of brigadier, Agramonte, who is the chief medical director of the island, graduated from both schools, homeopathy and allopathy, and speaks English as well as I do.

Q. I wish to ask, Have you visited any of the Cuban hospitals or been about any of the hospitals after they have fallen under the hands of the Spaniards?—A. Yes, sir; about two months. The exact date I do not know. I saw the only one that has come under my personal knowledge, but I heard of several. In the Province of Las Vegas they had a temporary affair put up after a fight at Mahaugh, only a short distance from a royal road, and the Spanish column in marching by there discovered the hospital by some hook or crook. We have always supposed it was discovered by some Cuban, a traitor to the cause and a practico for the Spaniards. They went in there. In that hospital there were 20 wounded, 3 lady nurses, and 1 doctor with the rank of lieutenant, and a guard of 8 men. That column went in and surprised the outfit and killed every one of them. I was on the ground about an hour and a half after, or I should judge about an hour and a half, for their bodies were still warm. They were cut up into pieces by machetes.

By Mr. CLARK:

Q. That includes the nurses?—A. Yes, sir.

By Mr. MORGAN:

Q. How did you happen to be there?—A. We were right after these troops; we knew they were in the field; we had an engagement with them and were following this column.

Q. To what point were they marching?—A. Sancti Espiritus.

Q. On the retreat?—A. Yes, sir.

Q. You were following?—A. Yes, sir.

Q. And in that way you happened to be at that point where they killed these people?—A. It did not happen so; we were bound to reach there. We saw the smoke and we hurried, but when we reached there they were gone and the bodies were not cold.

Q. Were the women dismembered?—A. Yes, sir; the bodies were cut to pieces. I got from a physician—this is something I do not know anything about, it is not in my line, but General Gomez's doctor informed me that these three women had been outraged previous to being killed. That I do not know, and do not state it as knowledge. That is why I did not mention it when I first gave an account of it.

Q. You saw their bodies?—A. Yes, sir; it was the worst sight I ever did see. I never want to have a repetition of that, for a man who once sees it never gets it out of his mind.

Q. Were all destroyed?—A. Yes, sir. You all know what a machete is. They run their machete through one man, and rip him right up the stomach, disemboweling him. That is the only case I ever saw, although I have heard of a great many others.

Q. You think you are safe in saying that no person, whether a soldier, doctor, woman, or patient escaped being killed?—A. I do not think even the dog escaped. Nothing that breathes the breath of life escaped that slaughter.

Q. About what time was that?—A. They must have struck the place about 11 o'clock in the morning, because we were close on them. We had a fight with them that morning at daybreak, and they pulled out and left us, and we followed them up, and when we got on the ground it was between 1 and 2 o'clock in the afternoon. This must have happened about 11.

Q. What month?—A. This was about two months ago, possibly two months and a half; I have no date. I never expected any examination of this kind, and kept no record.

Q. At what place had you fought with them that morning?—A. At Mahawaugh.

Q. During the operations you witnessed in Cuba, by General Gomez and the army under him, have you ever known any ill treatment to be bestowed upon a prisoner or a hospital?—A. No, sir; I want to illustrate that by something I know, that came under my own observation, regarding General Gomez. Three days after we received the information that his son had been assassinated—in one sense he was assassinated, because he was only wounded, and refused to leave his chieftain and was macheted; Captain Gordon told me that Poncho Gomez was only wounded, and after he was wounded he refused to leave the body of Maceo, and the Spaniards came and killed him with their machetes—three days after General Gomez received the news of his son's death there were 10 Spaniards brought in who had been captured by the Cubans, who had been on a foraging expedition; not exactly foraging, but letting their horses graze near the main camp, thinking they were near enough to be safe, but who were gobbled up by a small party of Cubans. I saw Gomez look at them when they were brought in, and he said, in Spanish, of course, " I suppose if this thing should happen under your Government that you men would not stand much show of living. I have no place to keep you"—they had no place in which to keep them, although they have in Camaguey— "all I ask of you, gentlemen, is to get out of my sight," and he let them go, keeping their arms and ammunition. That was three days after the death of his son.

Q. About how many prisoners taken from the Spanish troops or armies have you known Gomez to release without any conditions?—A. I suppose 500 of them. I don't think that an exaggeration.

Q. Have you ever known one of them to be executed?—A. I have known one man that was shot. Of course Gomez did not do that or order it to be done. At the surrender of Wymaro, in Puerto, there were about 200 prisoners, and they were allowed the freedom of the camp, but were told they were prisoners, and if they tried to escape they would be killed, and after that order there was one private soldier tried to run the lines and the guard shot him. That was the only case I knew.

Q. You have never known of any prisoners or soldiers being executed?—A. No, sir; I have not only known of it, but there has not been any. I would not fight with an army that would kill a man without a trial, and if they did I would not help them down there.

Q. I wish to ask you something about the composition of that army. First, as to the races; what is the proportion as to the negroes?—A. The actual proportion, they have got that exact—the Government has; but President Cisneros told me that the white Cubans predominated by a little over three-quarters, one-quarter blacks and mulattoes; it is a little over three-quarters white.

Q. Are the negroes good soldiers?—A. Yes, sir; if they have white men with them. I do not think the negroes will fight well unless they have white troops with them. I know in our army we do not think the negroes—those of Ninth and Tenth Cavalry or the Twenty-fifth— would fight well unless they had white troops with them.

Q. Take the body of the Cuban army, the white people in it, are they as intelligent as the average of people in the rural districts here—what we call backwoods of the United States?—A. Yes, sir.

Q. Are they patriotic?—A. As much so as any class of people I ever saw. So much so that I not only heard General Gomez and the government and the officers, but I have heard private soldiers talk. I will say that there is not a man in the escort or in the Victoria regiment that I have not heard an expression from similar to this: That before they would lay down their arms they would let every Spaniard in Spain walk over their dead bodies, and they would not accept anything but absolute independence. If you want to make them angry, talk autonomy to them. They say they have been caught once, but they will never be the fish to be caught again with the same bait. And I have heard Gomez say that they should be glad to have the United States recognize them, but that they will keep up the war until they secure independence if it takes twenty years to do it.

Q. Is there any considerable proportion of native Americans in the Cuban army?—A. I do not think there is over 20 in the army, unless they have come with these recent expeditions. The Americans in the army are very brave men and a good deal of help to the Cuban cause.

Q. Not over 20?—A. Not over 20 or 25. You have heard of the

Texas cowboys, calling themselves the Lone Star Riflemen, etc. That is not so. I could not tell where these stories originate, but they have been exaggerated. I think I know and could name every American in the Cuban army; and, with the exception of Colonel Gordon and myself, they were all with Gen. Calixta Garcia. The Cubans could not handle the artillery, and the Americans are with the artillery. They have a bodyguard of about 500 men—Cubans—the general has given to them to back them up when they are laying siege to a place. Colonel Gordon was with Maceo and I am with Gomez, and we are the only ones separated from the main body. There is a little fellow named Funston, who made a trip through Alaska, a son of a Representative from Kansas, who is chief of the Cuban artillery force of the island. I saw him at Wymaro. He belonged to Topeka, Kans., to a little volunteer artillery force. He is about 24 or 25. I saw him at Wymaro make 112 shots under the direction of General Garcia, who was telling him where to aim, and out of the 112 shots he only missed one. General Gomez gave it that way in his report.

Q. What would you say was the type of the controlling men in Cuba, as to the character, as to the behavior, as to the education and general social worth?—A. Well, you take the people in the Island of Cuba, and I can not see there is much difference between them and our own Republic except in this respect: The Spanish people have controlled the island and there has not been much opportunity for education, or to amount to anything, except in the large cities. In the rural districts the education they have secured has been by hard knocks; they have picked it up. The Cuban people as a race are peace-loving people. They do not want this war, and do not like it. They are generous, free-hearted people, giving their last dollar or anything to a man in distress or want. I know they do not want the war; they see their island destroyed; every day it is growing less in value. Now, aside from the rural districts, I could take you into General Gomez's camp and introduce you (and I would not jump, I would take all the officials) to as fine a lot of gentlemen as you would want to meet; refined gentlemen, educated gentlemen, some even classically educated. In their different professions and walks of life they have acquired a great deal of knowledge—outside knowledge, of course. A great many of them were educated in the United States. But the country people, a great many of them, can not read nor write; a great many of the negroes can not read nor write; a great many can. I have a servant, a white Cuban, who is the most ambitious fellow I ever saw to learn. He could read and write. I also had a negro, the cook, who was the same way—wanted to learn, anxious to learn, but never had an opportunity.

Q. Are there any private quarrels, or strife, or bickerings, among those people?—A. As far as this point of national freedom is concerned, they are all of one mind. Of course, take an army of soldiers, and little quarrels arise among the men, and are settled. Of course, if Gomez hears of it, they are punished, and put in the guardhouse, and tried by court-martial. General Gomez, after he has once issued a diploma to a second lieutenant or any other officer, can not break that officer or reduce him to the ranks except they are tried by court-martial. Gomez acts on the fine of the court-martial, and it is sent to the civil government, and they either approve or disapprove of findings of the court-martial.

Q. Are the private soldiers, in camp or on the march, protected by the right of the court-martial when accused?—A. Yes, sir; Gomez has no authority to punish a man; he does not pretend to punish without a court-martial. I saw General Gomez shoot a comandante, kill him on the spot (rank of major), and the incident that brought that about would have caused the same in any army. I would have killed him myself, and I am an American. At the siege of Cascorra, Gomez had quite an army, about 3,000 cavalry and 6,000 or 8,000 infantry. The Spanish were out in force. Gomez had decided to annihilate the army, so far as Camaguey was concerned. He had intrusted a very important mission to a comandante, by the name of Meander, to carry his dispatches to the cavalry, about 5,000 cavalry, under different comandantes. It rested with him whether the cavalry should come into that engagement. He was to carry the dispatch. He started with it, but never delivered it. It developed afterwards that he was a sympathizer with the Spanish army, although a Cuban and holding a commission in the Cuban army. The result was that Gomez's cavalry never got into the fight, and the Spaniards got away into Puerto Principe. And when they met, Gomez asked him if he delivered the order, and he said he did not, and the general drew his revolver and shot the man, killing him, and sat down and wrote to the civil government.

By Mr. CLARK:

Q. Does there seem to be a lack of unanimity and authority in the different corps commanders?—A. Not as much jealous feeling as I have seen in my own corps in the United States Army. The more ignorant a man is generally the more that will creep in, but I never saw anything of it with the Cubans. Take it in the case of myself. I was appointed a captain in Gomez's escort, where they are all officers, appointed over the heads of old Cubans who have been in the service for years—some of them with him in the ten-year war—appointed second in command, jumping over all the others, and there is no jealousy of me.

Q. About what is the strength of that escort?—A. From 70 to 90.

Q. All officers?—A. Yes, sir. With the exception of myself. there is no man in it who has got in except through some special act of bravery. They are General Gomez's bodyguard. He goes into an engagement, and they are first into the fight and the last to leave, and, by reason of that, I know they have from 10 to 15 or 20 in the hospital, and they have nearly all been wounded more than once. I have never been wounded except the once.

Q. What is the strength of this Victoria Regiment?—A. When it came into Las Vegas it was 142; when I left there, the other day, they were all, with the exception of 38, in the hospital, wounded.

Q. In the hospital from wounds?—A. Yes, sir.

Q. Not from sickness?—A. No, sir. A Cuban soldier seldom goes to the hospital from being sick. I have never seen one in the hospital from sickness since I have been on the island.

Q. Have you seen Cisneros and the members of the civil government since you have been there?—A. Yes, sir; a great many times. The president is very much a friend of mine, as is also the assistant secretary of war, Portuando, although the secretary himself is there now.

Q. Have they any permanent headquarters?—A. At what they call Nahassa, but Cisneros Batoncourt, the president—you can not keep him anywhere. If they would allow it he would be in the fight, and he wants to be near where the fighting is anyway. He is an old man—about 80 years old. Their headquarters is at Nahassa.

Q. The same place you call Cubitos?—A. It is in the vicinity. Nahassa is a very level piece of country, a beautiful river running through it, and fine grass for the horses. Cubitos is a little back of it, and is a place supposed to be used by the government in case of an emergency, because it is deemed impregnable.

Q. A retreat for the government?—A. Yes, sir.

Q. Does he move over the island whenever business calls him?—A. Yes, sir. He has a bodyguard of about 200 men, used as the body-guard at night and as an advance guard in the daytime. When the Cubans went across the trocha he went along with General Gomez, and stayed there until Gomez told him he wanted them to go back. Gomez would not do any fighting while the government was there, for this reason, because he says I am afraid to fight while you are here. I do not want any of the government killed or captured, and I am nervous when you are around me, and can not fight, and Cisneros pulled up stakes and recrossed the troacha.

Q. Does the cabinet travel with him?—A. His entire cabinet and corps of clerks. A record of everything is kept that transpires on the island, of the civil government, the troops, everything. The impedi-menta is something immense. That is why Gomez does not want them with him. Gomez does not have any impedimenta; he is strictly a cav-alry officer, will not allow his officers even a pack mule, and does not have anything of the kind himself.

Q. I understand there are not many roads in Cuba on which large bodies of men can move.—A. There is El Rey, called the royal roads, on which Spaniards move, but they never leave them. The Cuban army goes everywhere. The only time General Gomez travels these royal roads is when he wants to fight the Spaniards. But the Spaniards never leave these roads, except at night, to go into a savannah—level piece of land near the road—to go into camp.

Q. Are there many of these royal roads?—A. Yes; two or three extend the whole length of the island. There is a picture—some of the Cuban soldiers and myself; you can see that they are not naked.

Q. Describe the killing of Gordon.—A. When I got to Cienfuegos I heard that there was an American who had been killed. I was in dis-guise, or at least traveling under a fictitious name, and had got through at Trinidad. I knew Gordon was in that vicinity, and I was afraid it was him. He was from New Jersey, and we had been great friends. He had been in Gomez's camp a great deal, when he was wounded with Maceo. I hung around there and went up to the barracks where the soldiers were, and I saw a detail coming in. There was another Amer-ican with me by the name of McCurtney, a boiler maker. I saw a Spanish sergeant get off his horse and he swung over his shoulder a saddle blanket, tied at the corners. There was a broad sidewalk run-ning by the barracks, and he kept hold of one end and threw the others out with a jerk, and there were either eight or nine pieces of a man's body. The head was cut from the body, and some one had run a machete into him and disemboweled him. I recognized his head at once; he had a very prominent scar on it. The Spanish officers were laughing and joking about it, and kicked this limb and that piece, and at last, after ten or fifteen minutes, the comandante told the sergeant to pick it up and bury it, and they gathered up the pieces in the blanket and went to the rear of the barracks and buried them; covered it with earth to the extent of 6 inches, perhaps.

Q. Do you know whether Gordon was killed in a fight?—A. All I know is from hearsay. A pacifico who claimed that he witnessed it told me that they had wounded him, and that he fell off his horse—they had laid an ambuscade for him—and as they came up to him he said to them, "Take me a prisoner. I am an American, but in the

Cuban army; take me a prisoner." But they simply laughed at him and killed him with their machetes.

Q. Was that in regular fight?—A. No, sir.

Q. How many were they?—A. There was but one with him, I presume his servant.

Q. You say this was in Las Villas, Cienfuegos?—A. Yes, sir.

Q. On the present journey?—A. Yes, sir.

Q. Coming back to the roads of Cuba and the fact that Cubans pass across the country in any direction they please. I presume you mean that they can and do pass across the country, having an intimate knowledge of it, without reference to roads?—A. The entire island is one network of what we would call in this country trails.

Q. They know these trails and travel anywhere?—A. Yes, sir.

Q. The Spaniards do not?—A. No, sir; they dare not. If they had, this war would have been ended long ago.

Q. They are obliged to move that way?—A. I do not say they are obliged to, but they do.

Q. Outside of the large cities is there any permanent occupation?—A. No, sir. The situation on the Island of Cuba is simply this: The Spaniards control the large fortified town; the Cubans control the country entirely from one end of the island to the other. Without exception that is a fact.

Q. I wish to get some information; I am not certain we ought to publish it. You have been speaking about the postal system, and couriers that pass from one of these posthouses to another. Is there such a thing in Cuba as a coast guard?—A. I do not know but that I am saying something that may hurt them. There is a continuous guard of armed men around that island, called the coast guard. They are fully armed with plenty of ammunition.

Q. About how many men?—A. I presume in that coast guard, about 5,000 men. They fight if necessary, but it is a complete chain of guards. Now, there are several reasons for that guard. The Cuban government has a perfect line of communication, as I say, all through the island. They also have a perfect line of communication with the United States, and that coast guard is for that purpose; one thing also is to watch the water for expeditions. Another thing is, our salt all comes from this portion of the coast, where they have their salt depositories, where it is manufactured. Nearly all the salt is secured by boiling down the salt water of the ocean, and from the manufactories is taken to the interior on pack mules.

Q. Does that coast guard keep up communication, each with the other?—A. Yes, sir; they are around the entire island. In speaking about the guard, I do not mean that they are right close together, just a few rods apart, but a coast guard has two or three or four leagues to march, when he meets another coast guard, and they march back and forth and patrol the coast, on the same system that the English Government has up here in Manitoba a mounted police.

Q. I suppose this mounted police or coast guard gives notice of the approach of expeditions?—A. Yes, sir. The moment an expedition approaches the land, or anywhere near it, notice is immediately sent to the nearest force in the interior, and they send a force down to help get it up into the interior.

Q. Where are the Spanish depots of supplies?—A. Santa Clara, Havana, Santiago de Cuba, Pinar del Rio, Cienfuegos, Matanzas, all seaport towns, and Cardenas. Nuevitas is the seaport town for Puerto Principe.

Q. Have they any principal depots of supplies in the interior?—A. No, sir; none in the island. We wish there were.

Q. You have been speaking about the civil government passing through this trocha. Point out on the map where this trocha is.—A. Here is the trocha [pointing on the map].

Q. Why is it not connected with the sea?—A. This map is all wrong. There is no such thing as that [indicating point near the north end of the eastern trocha]. This trocha should run here to this point [indicating point on the coast touching the water]. The Spanish Government—there is an island here that for a long time was secretly used by the Cubans; this island right here (Island of Taringueano), 7 leagues long. The Cuban government established a prefecto on that island, and we used to come around here after we crossed the trocha. Gomez has three or four places on this trocha he can cross any time, that he is keeping, in case of emergency. We used for a long time to come around water. If the General wanted to send a man to the United States we had boats that we used to send them across to Nassau, until the English Government got to arresting them. Now the Spanish Government has built three fortines in the water and one large fort on the island. Those trochas do not amount to anything; they are a total failure from a strictly military standpoint. The Spaniards are cranks on trochas and always have been for ages. You take this trocha clear across the island—the western part of the island—there are 18,000 men on that trocha. If Maceo wanted to cross any time he could have done so, for the reason that they could not have concentrated their men at one given point. These 18,000 men are taken away from the army in the interior, and are lying idle. Maceo used to say he had 18,000 men in prison. I have crossed this trocha myself six times, on commissions.

By Mr. CLARK:

Q. Are they forts or simply guards?—A. I will give you a description. In the first place there is a clearing 1 American mile wide right across the island of all the shrubbery, trees, and everything taken down. Right in the center of that, half mile from each side, they have built a line of forts, varying in distances from a quarter of a mile or less. In each one they will put 20 or 25 men, or possibly 50. So far, so good. Then they have dug a ditch between these forts, 6 feet wide and 6 feet deep. Then they have gone to work and put in stakes, slantingly, about 6 or 8 inches apart, on the out edge of each side of that ditch. Then they have run American barbed wire in very close together, about 2 inches apart, perhaps 15 of them. Then right on each side of this outer stake they have driven a line of stakes slanting in, and they have run the same kind of wire, and crossed it again, and virtually made a basket network of it. That is their protection to the fort. When the Cubans want to cross that trocha they send ahead a detail of men at night with sharp pinchers and they cut that wire and make a path for the soldiers.

Q. In this clearing are the logs piled up on each side?—A. They are in certain portions.

Q. I read that a railroad extended from seacoast to seacoast along this clearing?—A. That is not so. There is a railroad along this eastern trocha that runs from Moron down a little bit of ways, but it is not used. The track is there, but the Cubans would not allow a railroad to be operated there.

By Mr. MORGAN:

Q. The Spaniards must have spent a great deal of money in building

S. Doc. 231, pt 7——45

these trochas?—A. They have not spent much money. They make their soldiers build them, and they don't pay the soldiers.

Q. I was trying to get at the question of military transportation on those trails and royal highways. The Spaniards keep their main depots of commissary stores and quartermaster stores in these large central points on the seaboard. Do they have any in the interior?—A. No, sir; we wish there were. There are certain places through the island where the Spaniards have established forts. The rations of the soldiers of these forts are taken by convoys, but these forts are all established on the royal roads; I never saw one away from the royal road.

Q. Those commissary depots and quartermaster depots are supplied by railways that run between these different points on the coast?—A. Yes, sir.

Q. When an expedition leaves one of these large fortified towns to hunt up Gomez and his forces, do they take supply trains with them?—A. No, sir; I have never seen a Spanish column come out and stay more than five or six days. They only have supplies as they can take in their saddlebags.

Q. Then they go back?—A. Yes, sir.

Q. Can they depend on the country for forage?—A. No, sir; they never get anything from the country. Well, they do cut down palm trees and use their tops, but we can not help that. But they don't get any vegetables or beef   Just the moment Gomez gets news that a column has left Sancti Spiritus or any other fort he marches toward that column and they meet   I have never known Gomez to lie idle when there was a Spanish column out; when they meet there is a fight right off. At night the Spaniards halt and Gomez retires a mile or so. The Spaniards dare not put out a picket at night; their only guard is in their camps. Just as quick as dark comes Gomez details an officer with 15 or 20 men to keep that camp awake, firing into them all night, and then at daybreak Gomez attacks the camp, and so on, and they are fighting all day and night, and so on. Whenever they go into camp there are 15 or 20 men more keeping them awake all night, and the result is that the Spanish troops are exhausted and obliged to return to the town for rations or from fatigue.

Q. The Spanish commanders are obliged to go back for provisions?—A. Yes, sir

Q. Is the Island of Cuba, in the places where not cultivated, heavily timbered?—A. Yes, sir.

Q. Forests dense?—A. Yes, sir; some of the finest forests the eye ever saw; thousands upon thousands of acres of the finest mahogany, stretching as far as the eye can see.

Q. Are the forests dense, thick?—A. Portions are, but no portion where the Cubans have not trails through them

Q. Those forests furnish excellent protection for what we call guerrilla fighting?—A. Yes, sir; if you are going to order a piece of land made especially for guerrilla fighting, you could not do better.

Q. In the mountainous country are the mountains very high?—A. In some places they are very high. They resemble the foothills of our Rocky Mountains very much.

Q. There are many places where it is easy to fortify and protect a small force against a very large one?—A. There are places in that island they could go into and hold the entire Spanish army at bay, a very few of them.

Q. You speak of Garcia having the entire artillery strength of the Cuban army. What is the artillery strength?—A. I think 14 cannon.

That includes those two dynamite guns, that kill at both ends. That is about all the strength in artillery. They have not a great deal of cannon ammunition; it is hard to get. You can get it there all right, but often these expeditions do not come near to the shore by a league, and you have to take it ashore by a rowboat, and it is heavy and hard to get ashore. The shells come six to a box, and of these boxes you can not put more than two in a rowboat.

Q. How do they take the ammunition into the interior?—A. On mules.

Q. How is it done?—A. The guns are taken off the carriage and packed on mules. Three mules carry the outfit.

Q. The caissons are carried the same way?—A. Yes, sir.

Q. Can you make time that way?—A. Garcia's army will make about 6 or 7 leagues a day.

Q. Leagues?—A. Yes, sir; 18 to 21 miles. Garcia has the finest equipped army on the island. His chief of staff is General Menocal, a very good engineer, who speaks very good English. He has organized an engineer corps; he has got a signal corps; he has got his cavalry and his artillery, and his engineer corps is pretty fine, too. It is right up to date. Anyone who ever told me before I went down there that the Cubans had a good engineer corps I would have laughed at him, but it is true.

Q. Has Gomez a good map of the island?—A. Yes, sir; nothing like this map; this is entirely wrong. He has maps with each Province separate, giving all the little towns and roads and trails.

Q. His people being natives, he has as many guides as he wants?—A. Yes, sir; we have no trouble there with practicos.

Q. That is a guide?—A. Yes, sir.

By Mr. CLARK:

Q. What is the relative strength of the Cuban army as regards infantry and cavalry?—A. About three-quarters of it is infantry. Gomez is strictly a cavalry officer; infantry moves too slow for him. He is a good deal such a person as General Custer was, although I did not know General Custer. Infantry and artillery he can not march with fast enough.

Q. How is his health?—A. He has not seen a sick day since I have been there. To illustrate, General Gomez called me the morning I left there, and said "I want to speak to you. There have been false reports, and some may say to you that I have been sick." Gomez is a man over 70 years old. He put his hand on the pommel of his saddle and vaulted right over, and put his other hand on and vaulted right back again. He said to me, "You do that," and I told him that I had business elsewhere. "A sick man can not do that," he said. The army numbered a little over 40,000, and they can put in the field a little over 60,000 men. Of course every expedition landed there would increase the numerical strength.

Q. When you speak of 40,000 men armed, are they well armed?—A. We consider the Remington a pretty good arm, and that is what they have, except General Gomez's escort, who are armed with repeating rifles, nearly all armed with Mauser rifles, captured from soldiers who have come in or been captured. There is hardly a day that Spanish soldiers do not come in and surrender. When I was on my way here I met 14 soldiers who were on their way to surrender. The Spanish soldiers fight as though they had been lassoed and brought there and forced to fight against their will. The soldier does not fight with any energy or vim. They say "What do we care for this Island of Cuba; it never does us any good, or never will." But they are forced to fight, and they are mostly boys from 16 to 21 years of age.

By Mr. MORGAN:

Q. Do those boys do that butchery?—A. Under command of their officers. They are well disciplined. I will say that much for the Spanish soldiery. They are the best disciplined soldiers I ever saw. I have seen a Spanish officer kick a man and throw him down and jump on him with both feet, and he never say a word or growl or grumble.

Q. I will ask you one question as to General Gomez's character. What do you think of him as a man of talent, energy, honor, humanity, and courage?—A. He is well educated, has done a great deal of study-ing and reading in his life, a man that is firm, stanch, true friend, a bad enemy, but a just man at all times and on all occasions. I think that is General Gomez's character to a letter. I would not want him for an enemy.

After examining and correcting my deposition as above, I sign the same under oath.

WM. D. SMITH.

STATEMENT OF GEORGE BRONSON REA ON THE 11TH DAY OF JUNE, 1897.

Mr. REA was sworn by Mr. Davis, chairman of the committee.

In the absence of Senator Clark, Senator Davis acted as a member of the subcommittee.

By Mr. MORGAN:

Q. Please state your name, age, and place of birth.—A. George Bronson Rea; 28 years old; born in Brooklyn, N. Y.

Q. What is your occupation?—A. Newspaper correspondent; also electrical engineer.

Q. Have you ever been in the Island of Cuba?—A. Yes, sir.

Q. When did you go there, and for what purpose?—A. I went there first in 1890, to take charge of the Matanzas electric light plant; was on the island about four and a half years, until the breaking out of the war, engaged in putting up electric-light plants and machinery.

Q. When did you leave there?—A. About two months ago, finally. On the 18th of January last year I went to the field as correspondent of the New York Herald and joined General Gomez.

Q. Where did you find Gomez?—A. I found Gomez at the sugar estate of San Antonio de Pulido at Alquizar.

Q. What province?—A. Havana.

Q. Have you been with him continuously until you left the island?—A. No, sir; was with him about one month, then joined the forces of Antonio Maceo. I joined after the first campaign in Pinar del Rio, stayed with him some time (six months), and then returned to Havana, and, watching my chance, managed to slip through the Spanish lines, and came home in October last.

Q. Where did you embark?—A. At Havana. I went back in January of this year as war correspondent of the New York Herald, and came home about the middle of April.

Q. At what do you estimate the force of Gomez—I mean all the forces of the insurgents in Cuba—at the time you left the lines?—A. It is a rather difficult thing to figure accurately, but with a little compilation a very fair estimate could be made. At the time I left Gomez he had about 150 men under his personal command.

Q. His escort?—A. Yes, sir; his escort and the Victoria regiment. They each comprised about 80 men. The escort has about 80, and the Victoria regiment also about 80, approximately.

In the Province of Santa Clara his forces are divided into two divisions and various regiments—in one minute I can give the total accu rately. This recent campaign of Gomez in the eastern part of La Villas has been carried out by the first division of what they call the fourth army corps, divided into three brigades: The brigade of Remedios, about 800 men; the brigade of Saucti Spiritus, about 600 men; and the brigade of Trinidad, about 400 men. There are three more brigades, composing the second division: That of Cienfuegos, about 500 men; the brigade of Sagua, about 400; and the brigade of Villa Clara, probably 500 more. That is all in that province. In the province of Matanzas there are very few insurgents; indeed, I think they could be safely estimated at about 400 or 500 men in the whole province. In the province of Havana, probably at the present time there are 2,000 insurgents. Last November—or October, I meant to say—I was down in the province of Havana about one month or a month and a half, and then there were about that number, and the force has not augmented. Contrary to all stories as to their number, the force has not increased. I left Maceo in Pinar del Rio with 6,000 men. The number of men in the eastern part of the island is—what I have said already in regard to the western part can be relied on, but in the eastern part of the island I would not like to give any testimony to be depended upon as accurate—as to my opinion as to the number of men, there are, I should judge, probably about 4,000 or 5,000 men in the two eastern provinces.

Q. What provinces?—A. Santiago de Cuba and Camaguey. The total I• have not figured, but in my estimation they do not exceed 25,000 armed men on the island.

Q. Under whose command is the eastern army?—A. The department of the east is under command of Calixto Garcia, divided into three corps, and subdivided into brigades and regiments.

Q. You have never been with Garcia?—A. No, sir. I never have been in the eastern provinces. I have been all through Pinar del Rio, Matanzas, and Havana——

Q. As a soldier?—A. No, sir; as a correspondent of the New York Herald.

Q. You were not engaged in fighting?—A. No, sir; but I have witnessed some eighty fights, not to mention skirmishes, and have had two bullets through me. I was with Maceo during that second western campaign, and joined Gomez after the invasion.

Q. You was not with Maceo when he was killed?—A. No, sir; I was in New York, but I have seen those who crossed the trocha with him and witnessed his death—Gordon, who was killed, Pedro Diaz, and the servant of Maceo—all who knew most of the details.

Q. How did you get through the trocha?—A. By way of the swamp. I was just showing a picture to Senator Davis—as I saw you were interested in Mr. Bonsal's description of the torcha—I wrote an article last year in regard to it. We were two days in the swamp waiting to cross, and finally, under cover of darkness, we managed to elude the vigilance of the sentries and sneak across. There is a great deal written about that trocha in Pinar del Rio, but there is not one man in a dozen who has ever seen it.

(Mr. Rea here exhibited to the subcommittee a drawing showing a portion of the southern part of the trocha.)

That is the part of the trocha that goes through the Majana swamp. Here is a map I drew of that country down there from actual experience. The trocha runs from Mariel south to this swamp, across the narrowest part of the island, about 21 miles, or 7 Cuban leagues. From Mariel to Guanajay the trocha runs along the macadamized road, which they have taken. as a basis from which to operate and on which to build. From Guanajay to Artimisa it also runs along the macadamized way, and they have these forts scattered all along, and in front of the road to the trocha (the vanguard, as the Spanish say) there is barbed wire fence, and still farther in front they have sown cactus and other thorny plants to prevent cavalry crossing. From Artemisa south, which is probably the strongest part of the line, the trocha leaves the macadamized road. The road passes through Mangas and continues to Candelaria. The trocha runs south through the sugar estates of Waterloo, Sn. Leon, Neptuno, and Maravilla. Neptuno is the head-quarters of the southern division. Here is where it enters the Majana swamp. This is the only place where the insurgents have ever crossed that trocha. I can say, in this part of the trocha——

By Mr. DAVIS:

Q. Which part, south part or north part?—A. From Mariel to Neptuno—the entire part on dry ground—there has never been an insurgent force or party known to cross, except two who made a dash and crossed it. In this part (the southern) the crossing is made in the swamp through the mud and water. I was in mud and slush up to my neck, and Maceo crossed the trocha in this little bay (of Mariel) in boats, the same as Sylvester Scovel did when he crossed westward.

By Mr. MORGAN:

Q. Going east or west?—A. Going east. (Here I referred to my own trip.)

Q. Where was Maceo when you joined?—A. In Havana.

Q. When?—A. In February, 1896.

B. Did you cross the trocha with him to Pinar del Rio?—A. The trocha was not made when we crossed into Pinar del Rio.

Q. Was it in process of construction?—A. No, sir; they started to construct it after Maceo was in the province, with the idea of catching him in a trap, so that he could not get out.

Q. How many men did Maceo take?—A. About 5,000 men when he entered Pinar del Rio.

Q. Where are those men now, or when you left the island?—A. I suppose most of them are there.

Q. In Pinar del Rio?—A. Yes, sir; perhaps some of them crossed the trocha and got back. I suppose there may be 5,000 of them there now, of the 6,000 he had with him.

(NOTE.—There was probably 1,000 there under Bermudez, Sotomayor, and others when he entered.)

Q. You say they got across the trocha through the swamp?—A. Yes, sir; I know they couldn't get through any other way.

Q. Did you cross that trocha?—A. Yes, sir; I crossed that trocha.

Q. Through the swamp?—A. When we entered Pinar del Rio we did not cross through the swamp. There was no necessity of doing so. The trocha was not established at that time.

Q. How many men were with you when you crossed?—A. About 19.

Q. Who were you going to report to?—A. I was trying to get home.

Q. After you got through, you did go home?—A. Yes, sir.

Q. By what route?—A. I came through the southern part of the Province of Havana to San Jose de las Lajas. I was a month and a half in the Province of Havana before I saw my opportunity to get to Havana.

Q. Your opportunity to get through the Spanish lines or the Cuban lines?—A. Through the Spanish lines.

Q. You witnessed some battles after you got back?—A. Yes, sir.

Q. Who was in command?—A. General Aguirre.

Q. Where is he now; was he killed?—A. He is dead.   He died a natural death in December.

Q. How near did he approach Havana while you were in his company?—A. About 20 miles.

Q. What place?—A. At Tivo-Tivo; between San Miguel and Campo Florida.

Q. About what time was it when you left Aguirre and came on home?—A. About the 1st of October.

Q. When did you go back to Cuba?—A. In January of this year; left here on the 13th of January.

Q. Have you seen Gomez since you went back?—A. Yes. sir.

Q. Where did you meet him?—A. When he was besieging the town of Arroyo Blanco, on the 28th of January.

Q. How long did you stay?—A. I stayed with Gomez one day; wrote my dispatches, and got them off, and was back there again in about two weeks, and was with him three different times afterwards.

Q. How did you get through the Spanish lines on these different occasions?—A. The first time I started for the field I left Havana with the credentials of the New York Herald in my pocket, and also a military pass signed by General Arderius, which I have in my pocket now, giving me permission to go with the Spanish columns.   It did not say which columns, but only said the columns in operation in the field. The last time it was simply a question of luck in evading Spanish vigilance, because the Spanish spies were after me very hot.   I managed to shake them off at Trinidad, under pretext of going to a sugar estate.

Q. Were the Cuban spies ever after you when you left their command to go into Havana?—A. Not that I know of.

Q. You came and went, so far as they are concerned, with freedom?— A. Yes, sir; so far as I know.

Q. As far as the Spanish were concerned, you were watched?—A. Yes, sir; I suppose, if caught, I should have suffered the fate of Govin.

Q. What did they do with him?—A. They chopped him up.

Q. Have you any knowledge of that?—A. Yes, sir; no personal knowledge, but I saw his grave four days after he was killed—no, it was in the neighborhood of two weeks after.

Q. Where is your information derived?—A. I derived my information from two persons who were with him; one Lieutenant-Colonel Mirabal and the other Colonel Gordon—both dead now.   They were in a fight between Major Valencia, who had 60 or 80 men, and the Spaniards under General Ochoa from Jaruco.   It took place near the sugar estate of Jiquiabo, and, as generally the case in a little fight, the Cubans, after firing a few volleys, got out of the way, and Govin, never having been in a fight before, found himself alone and the Spaniards very close to him.   They told me that Govin, when he saw he was to be captured, walked forward to meet the Spanish column to surrender, hoping his American .citizenship would help him in this case; but it seems that his papers—parties told me who said they were watching and saw it done (but I do not attach much importance to the statement myself, because I never saw a Cuban that would stay near a Spanish column long enough to watch much)—but they said the papers were torn up and thrown in his face, and he was tied to another man and taken to San Mateo and kept there all night, and the next morning as they were lead out to march to Jaruco he was untied from the other prisoner and fastened to a tree and chopped up with machetes, and two days after, his body being left there, Lieutenant-Colonel Mirabal and Valencia who were looking, as they generally do, for anything left on the ground, or for dead people, found the body and carried and buried it at the end of a potato field, which spot they showed me. I have no doubt Govin was foully dealt with, and I have no doubt the cause was that he was an American.

Q. What was Govin—a correspondent?—A. This is information I have heard—I never met Govin, and while I am in sympathy with him, I understand he came with this expedition, and while he had these papers as correspondent of the Jacksonville Equator-Democrat, he was nominally an insurgent, and from what I can understand he carried a revolver.

Q. Did you carry a revolver while there?—A. No, sir; excuse me, I did carry a revolver for about two weeks, but never used it. I obtained it for one of my servants, and when I had carried it a couple of weeks I gave it to him.

Q. Where were you?—A. In Pinar del Rio.

Q. Did you carry it for protection against the Spaniards or against the Cubans?—A. I never carried it for protection. So far as that goes, or far as the Cubans were concerned, I was treated very well, and as far as the Spaniards were concerned, I could get out of the way when they came by following or keeping up with the Cubans.

Q. You never engaged in hostilities at all?—A. I never engaged in hostilities; no, sir. I directed Gomez once how to burn out a locomotive, and that is all. I took no actual hand in it; I told the old man how they could do it, and men—Cubans—went to work and did it. That is as far as my experience in helping the insurgents has ever gone.

Q. What do you mean by burning out a locomotive—destroying it?—A. Yes, sir. If the water gets low and the fire is kept going, it will burn out the tubes and then it will not stand the pressure.

Q. He had captured the locomotive, and wanted to destroy it?—A. Yes, sir. He asked me how to do it—he knew I was an electrical engineer—and I gave him the benefit of my experience.

Q. Did you give him the benefit of your experience in firing dynamite shells?—A. No, sir.

Q. You knew how to do it?—A. Yes, sir.

Q. Did he ever ask for your assistance?—A. Maceo intimated as much to me once or twice, but I thought I was not there to do that; I was there as a neutral, and it was not my business. They have had a few foreigners come there to show them how to blow up railroad trains and use dynamite cartridges, and they have treated them badly, in such a way as to disgust them and drive them away.

Q. I understand from your statement that both Gomez and Maceo inspected your neutrality.—A. Yes, sir.

Q. Did not compel you to do anything you did not wish to?—A. No, sir.

Q. Who were these men who were badly treated?—A. I remember the powder maker—I do not know anything of him myself; this is hearsay. A powder maker came to Gomez. He may have been an adventurer, but he was well versed in explosives and could have been of great benefit to the Cubans. I know nothing of what was done, but he was disgusted and had to get away. There was also a Frenchman from Havana, who came out to manufacture dynamite, and finally he did make a couple of bombs and wanted to blow up a railway train, but they were jealous because he was going to get some glory and only sent a small force of 18 men to assist him. He exploded the bombs, and when the engine went off the track they had a couple of hand bombs which they were to throw into the train, but when the engine was derailed and the Spanish soldiers poured out of the cars the Cubans got scared and ran away and left the Frenchman alone. He got away safe, but was disgusted, and left them.

Q. That was the bad treatment?—A. Yes, sir.

Q. There was no personal bad treatment?—A No, sir.

Q. Twenty men were not expected to capture any considerable force, were they?—A. No, sir; but they had two big hand bombs prepared—it was in a cut in the railway—and as the first bomb was exploded and the train went off the track and the soldiers began to come out they were to throw these bombs and blow the soldiers to pieces.

Q. You said that the Frenchman was not captured.—A. No, sir; he got away.

Q. A while ago you stated, if I understood you, that if these men, the Spaniards, had caught you while you were slipping through the lines they would have treated you as they did Govin.—A. Yes, sir; if they had caught me in the field, I believe they would. I was virtually an insurgent, as I had violated their military laws. Most any army would have treated a man in that way. They might not have killed me, but might have sent me to Morro Castle. When General Weyler came to the island as Captain General, he issued an order that all correspondents should be prohibited from going into the field. I was in the field already, but he had such a bad reputation that one would feel a little bit uneasy about it after getting into his hands. I rode into Havana on the stage coach, and as luck would have it nobody said anything to me.

Q. You road into Havana on a stage coach?—A. That was the first time—last October. I got on the stage coach that runs to San Jose de las Lajas, about 20 miles out—I should say 20 kilometers.

Q. Was that in the Spanish lines?—A. It is called the Spanish lines, but the highway runs through the open country. I got on the coach at the home of a friend of mine——

Q. Where are the Spanish lines?—A. The Spaniards do not have any force in the open country. They have their garrisons in the town——

Q. You mean at the fortified towns?—A. There are no unfortified towns.

Q. The trocha is in the Spanish lines?—A. Yes, sir. What is understood as the Spanish lines. The Spaniards have the forts and the fortified towns. All the towns not fortified have been burned and destroyed either by the Cubans or by the Spaniards. Cubans started the ball rolling by burning several towns, and the Spaniards evacuated many of the small towns that they considered were no value to them to hold and burned them.

Q. You only know that definition of the Spanish lines?—A. The only definition is in the fortified towns and along the trocha.

Q. Along the trocha?—A. Yes, sir.

Q. Outside the fortified towns the country would be denominated as in the Cuban lines?—A. Hardly, as the Cubans have no lines. The Cuban lines depend entirely on the close proximity of the Spanish column. The Cuban is here to-day and there to-morrow. The Cuban is in this place, and if they hear of a Spanish force coming they cut it and get out.

Q. That applies also to the Sanish?—A. Yes, sir; it applies equally to one as to the other.

Q. The country is disputed ground?—A. Yes, sir; neither one is able to hold it.

Q. You would say that the provinces in the east of Cuba are in the Cuban lines?—A. Yes, sir; in this way: In the campaign of General Weyler last year he paid all his attention to Antonio Maceo, and continued to do so until recently, or up to January. He started in to annihilate Antonio Maceo, and it took up the best part of his time and attention. When he got through there (he did not pacify the country, the insurgents are there to a large extent yet), then he took up Gomez in the province of La Villas. That left the province of Santiago de Cuba and Camaguey to one side, but if Weyler starts to operate in those provinces the conditions there will be the same as in the west.

Q. Until he does they are not the same?—A. He has recently started. I picked up a paper the other morning stating he had issued the recon centration order for the eastern provinces. There is one thing, the provinces of Matanzas, Pinar del Rio, and Havana are largely under the Spanish control, because they are aided by the railroads. They have means of transportation and communication, and little towns are scattered all through this country. Every little black spot on this map represents a fort. In the provinces of Santiago de Cuba and Camaguey there are no such towns. Even before the war it was a very sparsely settled country. There are no railroads, practically. A small railroad runs from Puerto Principe to Nuevitas, and one runs up to Sancti Spiritus from Tunas, and there are but a few small towns scattered through these provinces. The large towns of importance have been fortified and successfully held by the Spaniards, but there was no necessity of expending a large amount of money in places where it was not worth the expense.

By Mr. DAVIS:

Q. Why do they not do it in one part of the island as well as in another?—A. That is because they have the railroads to help them in the west.

Q. In one place they can and in another place they can not?—A. They owe their superiority to the fact that they can readily communicate in the western provinces. At every other town or so there is stationed a Spanish operating column that goes into the field looking up the insurgents. These operating columns are established about 10 or 12 miles apart, and they operate each in its own zone, and when they find an insurgent force, by the sound of the firing the other columns are attracted to the scene, and the Cubans can not stay and fight, because they would be annihilated if they did. In the eastern provinces the Spanish can not do that, because the towns are small and few and far between. Where Gomez is operating at present there is no town except Arroyo Blanco, 14 leagues from Sancti Spiritus, and the Spaniards are compelled to come out in force because they have no place to rest until they reach another large town, and the Cubans have a chance to harass them by bushwhacking and constantly harassing them.

By Mr. MORGAN:

Q. How many fights have you been in, did you say?—A. More or less, about 80; not counting little shooting scraps.

Q. How many?—A. About 80, not counting shooting scraps.

Q. In how many battles have the Cubans held the ground?—A. I have only seen the Cubans advance twice.

Q. I only speak of holding the ground.—A. They may hold the ground temporarily—for one minute or ten minutes or fifteen.

Q. I mean after the battle is over.—A. They generally come back after the Spaniards give up the pursuit.

Q. After the pursuit?—A. Yes, sir. I was with Antonio Maceo in those fights around Tapia, and we had about a dozen of them, hot and heavy. He would wait until the Spaniards came up, and from one hilltop he would hold them back until they grew too strong for him and then retreat to the next hilltop, going back and back until the Spaniards would give it up after a while and retire, getting tired of the conflict.

Q. When they got tired, Maceo would come back?—A. Yes, sir.

Q. Who would win the battle?—A. I would call it a draw. There is one strange thing about it; I rarely saw a Cuban killed. The largest loss suffered by the Cubans was 15 killed and 84 wounded.

Q. When was that?—A. At the night attack on La Palma, in Pinar del Rio, March 31 of last year.

Q. What was the loss of Spaniards in these same fights?—A. In the ordinary fighting, very little difference.

Q. In the heavy fighting?—A. I think the heaviest loss of the Spaniards was in the battle of Cacarajicara, in Pinar del Rio.

Q. Well?—A. Their loss was variously estimated at from four to five hundred killed and wounded.

Q. What has been the comparative loss?—A. About equal. Probably the Spaniards have suffered a little more loss, owing to a certain reason in regard to the bullets. The Cubans are armed almost entirely with the Remington or these little sporting rifles, using the old leaden bullet, which, when it strikes a bone, "mushrooms" and causes a fracture, and with the Spaniards when sent to the hospital it is a grave case. With the Cubans it is different, as far as their wounds are concerned. The Spaniards use the Mauser rifle, and these bullets when they go through do not break or injure the bone. I had a wound where the bullet just scraped the bone.

Q. Did you go to the hospital?—A. No, sir. I have seen a man shot through the temple, and he is living, but lost his sight. It does not shatter the bone as the other bullet does. I think that will explain to a great extent why the Cubans have had so very few killed. And then the Spaniards shoot very wild. The Cubans are very bad shots and the Spaniards are worse, if anything. The Spaniards fire entirely by volley and at the word of command, the Cubans at will. The Spaniard goes into the fight with 150 rounds of ammunition, and the Cubans are lucky if they have ten I have seen them with but two, and that in one of the largest fights they had. The Cubans claim they had but 1,200 rounds among 1,500 men, and yet the Spaniards counted it as one of the biggest fights of the war. The Captain-General was in command. Gen. Sabas Marin was Captain-General in the interim when Campos went to Spain and before Weyler reached the island. At the present time the Cubans are fairly well supplied with ammunition.

Q. What is your estimate of the number of troops Spain has put into this war?—A. I had no means of knowing, except the statement of the Spanish that they number about 125,000 men.

Q. That is, troops imported from Spain?—A. Yes, sir.

Q. They had other troops there?—A. Yes, sir; the guerrillas, or volunteers, and the guarda civil.

Q. What is their strength?—A. I don't know.

Q. What is their reputed strength?—A. I could not tell.

Q. Five thousand, or 10,000, or 20,000?—A. The guerrillas alone, probably 10,000.

Q. That would make 135,000. Now about the guard?—A. They are included in the army.

Q. There have been 135,000 men put in there, then?—A. Yes, sir.

Q. Well armed?—A. Yes, sir.

Q. All the artillery they can take care of?—A. Yes, sir; there are very few columns that do not have artillery with them, especially mountain artillery; but my experience has been that the artillery was of no account. I have been with Maceo when they have shelled us for hours and nobody hurt. I have only seen two men killed by the explosion of shells during my experience.

Q. They sheltered themselves behind trees, elevations of the ground, etc.?—A. No, sir; I think it is because the gunners are at fault and the explosive power of the bursting charge is deficient. The radius of explosion is small, probably not over 25 feet.

Q. Do they use shell or shrapnel?—A. Both. We had about a hundred from the train that was captured at Pozo Redondo by Pedro Diaz, and they were shrapnel with percussion fuses.

Q. Can you account—this war has been going on for two years and a half or more?—A. Yes, sir.

Q. Have you any way of accounting for the fact that the Cubans—according to your estimate being only 25,000 strong—have been able to prevent the 135,000 Spaniards from running over and destroying them?—A. You can not lick a man if he will not let you, or if he runs away from you all the time.

Q. It is bounded by the sea on every side, and that is patrolled by the navy of Spain?—A. There are a great many hills and woods, etc. A body of 1,000 men does not take up much space. That is the reason Gomez has divided his men into bodies of about 150 men, so he can get into the woods.

Q. If his force does not shrink considerably, how long can he protract this struggle?—A. As long as he has anything to eat.

Q. What are his resources for feeding his forces?—A. When I left the Province of La Villas, two months ago, the eastern part, where Gomez is, had quite a large number of cattle, owing to the reason that it is a grazing country, quite the reverse to the western provinces, which are devoted to the culture of cane and tobacco. The eastern provinces of La Villas and Camaguey are devoted to cattle and grazing, the eastern part of La Villas especially. While he had plenty of cattle to last him, economically, for about a year, he had no potatoes, no vegetables, of any account.

Q. At what place had he none?—A. At Los Hoyos and Los Barracones.

Q. That is west of the trocha, in the eastern part of La Villas?—A. La Villas is not a province. When I speak of La Villas I mean the province of Santa Clara; it is commonly called La Villas by the Cubans.

Q. I am speaking of the resources of the provinces under Gomez's and Garcia's commands. What supply of provisions have they?—A. I must give you that information just as I have it from people in the field—people who have come from there. In the province of Santiago de Cuba the cattle have almost entirely disappeared; in fact, I learned that before I left Cuba last year the cattle were almost gone. They never had many cattle there. It is a hilly and mountainous country, almost all coffee plantations, and the insurgents are living on yucca, malanga, and other roots. We find the reverse in the province of Camaguey or Puerto Principe. There they have plenty of cattle, owing to the fact that before the war it was a grazing country, and cattle was the principal support of the people. There are plenty of cattle still that could be made, with economy, to last a long time.

Q. Under whose control?—A. Under both Spanish and Cuban; that is, the Spanish around Puerto Principe have a large number corralled, but the majority are in the hands of the Cubans.

Q. Now, east?—A. In the eastern part of the province of Santa Clara there are still quite a number of cattle and a few vegetables.

Q. Farther east?—A. Farther west?

Q. No; farther east.—A. Farther east? You mean west. I have taken the two eastern provinces. First comes Santiago de Cuba, Puerto Principe, Santa Clara, and then Matanzas.

Q. Santa Clara, then.—A. In the eastern portion there are plenty of cattle, but no vegetables. There is a dividing line about the town of Sancti Spiritus. To the west of that we find a range of mountains called the Trinidad Hills. These hills have always been supposed to be a stronghold for the insurgents, and that they had a large quantity of vegetables planted there. I was under that impression until I traveled through these hills. But, owing to the fact that Gomez had taken all the men out of the district, the Spaniards had invaded them and marched around at their pleasure, and when I made my last trip through the hills I could get nothing to eat—practically nothing to eat—just beef, and that had to be taken from the corrals near the Spanish forts. This statement is borne out by Captain Smith in his statement to me that in the camp of Rodriguez at Polavieja, situated near Trinidad, he had to eat mule steak, which shows that the cattle has practically given out. In the northern part of this province, near Sagua la Grande, there are very few cattle, and their chief subsistence is vegetables.

Q. Let us go to the west.—A. The province of Matanzas. I have very good authority in stating—I have it from the last man who made that trip across the province in February, Maj. Charles Gordon, an American, on whose word I place every reliance. He told me that in the province of Matanzas there are practically no insurgents. There are very few and they have taken refuge in the swamps, and subsist chiefly on a species of jutia or raccoon, and crocodile-tail steaks; have no vegetables and no cattle. Whenever they wanted any cattle they had to go to the nearest Spanish town and take them from the Spaniards, and the same with vegetables. I have every reason to believe this, because in the province of Matanzas the insurgents have been very negligent in looking after their commissaries. They have been very wasteful, and besides they can not establish prefectos.

Q. Why?—A. Because the country is very open. They have a few in the swamps, but in the provinces of Havana and Matanzas it is practically impossible to hold a prefectora.

Q. You say it is open?—A. It is the open country of that island.

Q. Because the Spaniards hold the towns?—A. Because the towns are close together and the Spanish columns are continually on the move and there are no hills and nooks where they can hide themselves in any force, except along the southern coast in these swamps, which are terrible places to live in. The insurgents can not hold out in the province of Matanzas a day.

Q. Is it not a fact that they are holding out?—A. Well, if you want to immerse yourself in the swamp and stay there you are holding out, but you are not doing anything.

Q. But they are still there?—A. Yes, sir.

Q. The Spanish have not driven them out?—A. They have driven them off the open country where they ought to be.

Q. Why ought they to be there?—A. In order to subsist.

Q. They do not die, do they?—A. They are pretty sick; some of them with fever.

Q. They are sick with fever?—A. Yes, sir; in those swamps, the best acclimated man will get pretty sick.

Q. Was you sick?—A. Yes, sir; after being there awhile; that was what kept me back a time.

Q. You say you had to go to the cultivated zones to get vegetables?—A. Yes, sir; in the province of Matanzas.

Q. Did they get them?—A. Yes, sir; sometimes. Whenever they get hungry some of them go after them.

Q. It would be difficult to get the vegetables if the people did not have them?—A. Yes, sir.

Q. Is it not in those towns and around those zones that the people are stated by various authorities to be starving to death?—A. Yes, sir; I believe so.

Q. How do the Cubans get the provisions, then?—A. Because, I think, the starvation business has been exaggerated and overestimated.

Q. Who do you think has exaggerated it?—A. I think they have taken two or three small towns as an example of all the stations. The boniato, or sweet potato, will, if thrust into the ground, grow by itself. I have seen a field of them trampled into the ground by the Spanish cavalry, and in two or three months they have been there again just as plenty. Like the sweet potato——

Q. You think on account of the great propagating power of the sweet potato you can not believe the statements of those other men—— —A. Oh, no.

Q. You think it has been exaggerated, then?—A. Yes, sir.

Q. Have you been in these stations?—A. Yes; I have been at Trinidad, Cienfuegos, Santa Clara, Colon, Jovellanos, and Matanzas on my trip to Gomez last January.

Q. Why do you think it is exaggerated if you have not seen them?—A. Because of my knowledge of the country.

Q. If the people are hemmed in in the towns, and the order authorizing these zones of cultivation has been revoked, and they are ordered to be shot if they attempt it, you would not suppose the people would get much by going after them, even if the potatoes were plenty?—A. No, sir; I don't suppose they would.

Q. Suppose the worst for the Cubans, can not they plant boniatos; and when not assailed by the Spaniards can not they live?—A. Yes, sir; they can, and to a certain extent they do, but in the province of La Villas they have shown a wasteful spirit by eating all they have to-day and never giving a thought to to-morrow.

Q. Maybe they want to prevent Weyler from getting it?—A. The Cubans recognize, too, that they must have enough to eat if they want to wait until the United States intervenes and recognizes them.

Q. That is a pretty safe reliance?—A. I should think so.

Q. Pinar del Rio—how did you subsist there with 6,000 men?—A. I left Pinar del Rio last year, last October. The northern part of the province, from Mariel to a point called La Mulata, cattle had about disappeared. There were a few corralled in the hills by the Cubans. Vegetables had completely disappeared, except those planted around the Spanish forts. The cane fields had been burnt; there was not a stalk of cane standing. It was a devastated country in every sense of the word. This was not done by the Cubans, but by the Spaniards, to take away the fodder for the Cuban cavalry, and the fire spread in all directions; to the thickets, and palm groves, and everywhere else. Antonio Maceo sent every three nights an armed force of men with the impedimenta (two or three hundred unarmed men) down near Cabanas to bring the beniatos out, or, in lieu of that, they went to the zones of cultivation near the large fortified sugar factories La Linza and Bramales, between Cabanas and Bahia Honda, where there were also a few vegetables. In through the hills, at that time, Antonio Maceo had quite a large number of vegetables planted. He was a very practical man, who saw ahead more than any of the rest, and he took all the impedimenta, probably 1,500 men, and he set them to work planting sweet potatoes, so he must have had quite a sufficient supply to last him that campaign in the hills. Along the southern coast, or the part of Pinar del Rio lying south of the Cordillera, there was quite a supply of cattle, and, in fact, all south of the railway was grazing ground, and large cattle ranches were scattered throughout the country, but I should not think there was many cattle left at the present time, because the policy of Weyler, when he found that he could not corner the Cubans, was to destroy their means of subsistence; and all cattle found in the hills and on the plains have been killed.

Q. About how many troops had Weyler?—A. About 40,000.

Q. And Maceo about 6,000?—A. Yes, sir.

Q. It appears the Spaniards, then, were engaged in raising potatoes to feed Maceo's command, principally?—A. Yes, sir; in this case.

Q. Whenever they got out of potatoes they sent out and got them from under the fort?—A. That is right.

Q. If I understood you correctly, there was never a battle ground that Maceo's command did not return to after the battle was over?—A. No, sir; there were several occasions where he came back, especially in that country of Pinar del Rio, where the hills are. In the open country he never came back. I was with Antonio Maceo when he returned after the first invasion of Pinar del Rio and had so many big fights in Havana Province. There was where I joined him, and during the month or more I was with him in this section there was a constant succession of fights, one after the other, and we could not come back and camp where we were the day before. It was simply one continuous skirmish, day after day, moving from place to place.

Q. Take the country 30 miles around Havana, in every direction, is that much devastated?—A. I can only speak of the country lying to the east of Havana; I do not know much about that to the west.

Q. How is that?—A. Because I have not been near enough to Havana on the western side to appreciate the condition of the country. In the country to the east of Havana—I do not think there is any value to this testimony at present, because it covers my experience last October, and that is a little too old. At that time it was not devastated in any sense of the word, or if we compare it to Pinar del Rio. Fine houses were there yet, large sugar estates were still standing, and the majority of the people were well-to-do farmers, raising crops and sending their products to market; in fact, I came into Havana from the house of a friend who has a plantation near San Jose de las Lajas, an American citizen. I can not say that country was greatly devastated then, and, at present, I do not know the real condition.

Q. How far is Matanzas from Havana?—A. About 60 miles.

Q. How far is Guanabacoa?—A. I should judge it was not more than 3 miles, as it is within sight of Havana, and you can see the church towers.

Q. What important towns between Havana and Matanzas?—A. On

the line of the railroad is Minas (the first town where there is a military operating station), then the town of Jaruco, burnt by Antonio Maceo (another operating point), then the next important towns are Agucate and Madruga, and the one next to Matanzas is Ceiba Mocha. Then there are two or three other small towns in between.

Q. We have been informed by other persons who have been there that the concentration of the rural population has taken place at many, if not all, of these towns you have mentioned.—A. Yes; that is, to a certain extent. The Cubans initiated it. There was a partial concentration first, but it was on the part of the Cubans.

Q. How could the Cubans concentrate on the towns unless they had the occupation of the towns?—A. I mean they forced them into the towns. When the invasion reached the provinces of Havana and Pinar del Rio (I was in the island from the time the revolution broke out), when the Cubans reached these provinces, they found a large majority of the people living there were Spanish storekeepers, clerks, etc., many belonging to the volunteer corps (all Spaniards coming to Cuba have to belong to the volunteer corps). If they have not served in Spain, they join the volunteers to free themselves from the enforced military service which all have to suffer in Spain. Also in Pinar del Rio the large bulk of the population are Canary Islanders, not Cubans, and all staunch supporters of the Crown, and belong to the volunteer corps. A large majority of the tobacco planters are also Canary Islanders, as are also many of the sugar planters in Havana and Matanzas. The Cubans commenced their career of—well, they really commenced the atrocities themselves then. The Spaniards of the volunteer corps were taken and hung, and the trail of Bermudez could be followed by the bodies of those who were hung on the trees.

Q. Did you ever see an instance of that kind?—A. Yes, sir; two of them—three of them.

Q. Where?—A. The first was on the sugar estate of Santa Teresa, in the Province of Havana. The second—hold on, he was not a Spaniard, he was a Cuban—I believe, near Rio Bayamos, also in the Province of Havana. In the Province of Pinar del Rio, while I did not see them, I know of the case where Bermudez hung 21—everybody spoke of it—21 to one tree, of these Spanish volunteers.

Q. Who was Bermudez?—A. Bermudez led the vanguard of Maceo's army during the invasion. Bermudez was a bandit before the war, and is called, among the people who lived in the fields, the Weyler of the Cubans.

Q. What has become of him?—A. He is still there, if he did not die of his wound, received just before Maceo crossed the trocha. I do not mean to say that this was approved by Maceo, for when Maceo found that so many people had been killed, he deprived Bermudez of his command.

Q. It was done by a bandit?—A. An ex-bandit; but he was a colonel in the Cuban army.

Q. He was deprived of his command by Maceo?—A. Yes, sir.

Q. Because of these outrages?—A. Yes, sir. Antonio Maceo and all the rest of these Cuban chiefs, when they got this invasion finished, or had carried their revolution to the far western part of the province, started to organize their various zones and appointed local chiefs. One of the first steps of these local chiefs was to eliminate from the country people all those who had Spanish tendencies. All who lived in the country who were in any way suspected of Spanish sympathy and all who belonged to the volunteer corps, were ordered to the towns and their houses were burned over their heads. That started the concentration business. When Weyler began his concentration, there was not a man living in the open fields who was not at least morally, if not openly, a Cuban insurgent. A man to live in the fields has to work for the Cuban government and plant vegetables for them, and he is, technically, an insurgent, living under the laws of the Cuban prefecto, and he has to acknowledge their authority or go to the town. They give no choice.

Q. They do not kill him, but send him to town?—A. They do not kill them. They have hung several for various little offenses.

Q. What kind of offenses?—A. One fellow in the province of Havana, a Cuban colonel—Col. Raul Arango—invited me once to a double hanging. One man he had ordered to town, and had been seen outside afterwards, and he was going to catch him and hang him——

Q. Treat him as a spy?—A. I suppose so. The other man was to be hung because he had taken cattle into town without permission.

Q. Treated him as a spy also?—A. The cattle were his own. If they catch anyone who is giving help to the Spaniards, they string him up.

Q. The Cubans treat those who are not with them as the enemies of the Republic?—A. Yes, sir. It was only recently, in the province of Villa Clara, that I called Gomez's attention to it, and asked him what he meant and if it was his policy. Around the small town of Fomento the Spaniards had not operated for a long time. It was about the beginning of Weyler's campaign, in the month of January or February. There were probably 100 families, or 800 individuals, living within a radius of, say, 3 leagues of this town—all little farmers, most of them Cubans and insurgent sympathizers working for the cause. Many were families of the insurgents where the men were out fighting. To show that Gomez is bound to force this concentration business himself, these people were ordered several times to vacate their homes and either go to the towns or to the hills. They did not obey. I believe the order was given twice, and still they did not notice it. Major Herrera—a Cuban major—was given orders by Brigadier Bravo, of Trinidad, to burn the houses of everyone and thus force them to move. The orders were carried out, and the houses of these people were looted and burned and their money and valuables taken away by their own countrymen. These people left destitute, and a great many enraged at the treatment they received, went to the town and joined the local guerrillas. I reported it to Gomez, and asked if that was his policy, as he was always decrying the Spaniards for employing these methods. He said, "Those people would not get out of there, and I did it as a humane measure. The humanity consists in forcing them to go away, because if they stay there the Spaniards will come along and kill them." The idea is to get the people out of the country. It is just as much to Gomez's ends as to those of the Spaniards not to have too many people around. It is only because he is at present in a country where there are no people, or where there are no pacificos living, that he is able to elude the vigilance of the Spaniards. This policy was not started recently, but long ago, and Weyler has taken the same precaution as Gomez had done previously.

Q. Around what town was this?—A. Fomento.

Q. After they had their houses burnt, they joined the guerrillas?—A. A great many, as they were enraged at the treatment they received at the hands of those they thought their friends. A few poor devils who had no money and no prospects went to the hills and built huts, and had to start life over again.

Q. Most of them went to the guerrillas?—A. Yes, sir; enraged at the treatment they had received. They had been strict pacificos, but they had given their support to the Cuban government; had acted as spies; given vegetables, potatoes, etc., and many of them were connected with the families of those who were then in the Cuban army. In this, I meant they were relatives.

Q. The family, then, would be divided; some on one side——A. No, sir; those who were the families of men fighting went to the hills where they could be with their husbands. I mean women and children; no men.

Q. In these battles, I suppose there have been captures of Spanish troops?—A. I think only one or two is the highest number captured in any one fight. I have probably seen a dozen of them captured in all the time I was with them.

Q. Only about a dozen?—A. Yes, sir; that is all.

Q. What was done with them?—A. One was killed, the rest set free.

Q. Which was killed?—A. That was an incident in the fight at Palma. The prisoner was a guerrillero, caught in this town. The insurgents had their heaviest loss at this fight, and they captured the fellow and accused him of firing on them from a house. Maceo had him brought up and cross-examined, and then ordered his escort to take him to one side. He did not order him killed, but I saw the flash of a machete a minute after, a hoarse groan, and when I went over there a few minutes after they told me they had cut his head off and rolled the body down the hill.

Q. How many captured by the Spaniards?—A. I don't know of any.

Q. The whole number was about a dozen?—A. I know of cases where the Cubans captured forts, etc., but I mean by this dozen those captured in the field.

Q. Take the prisoners captured in any way, what has been their fate?—A. Gomez and Maceo generally set them at liberty, offering them the privilege of joining the Cuban forces. If they did not accept, they let them go free.

Q. Take them back to their lines, sending an escort with them to protect them from the Cuban pickets?—A. No, sir. I wrote an article speaking of the captives of Guaimaro. That was the town the Cubans captured in Camaguey. Captain Smith told me on the field that he had heard that half of the prisoners were butchered on their way to Santiago de Cuba. He denies it since coming here, but I wrote it on the field, giving him as my authority, which he was willing I should do at the time.

Q. Who was the commander?—A. I do not know.

Q. Have you ever seen the articles of surrender?—A. I think I have read them; I don't remember now.

Q. Did you notice the receipt the Spanish officer gave for his troops?—A. That was for the sick.

Q. For the prisoners?—A. I understood the prisoners were sent to the East to plant potatoes; I may be in error in that; I don't make any special point of that.

Q. Do you know—you have had good opportunity for observing—have you known any case where Gomez or Maceo, or any other Cuban general, has caused prisoners captured either in battle or out of battle to be shot?—A. I once had occasion to write about the conduct of Lieut. Col. Frederico Nunez, in the province of Pinar del Rio. He captured five Spanish soldiers on the estate Susi, near Cayajabos, and strung them up.

Q. Did Maceo know of that?—A. No; he was very indignant about it when he heard of it.

Q. What did he do about it?—A. Reprimanded him, I guess.

Q. What was the excuse for doing it?—A. I forget the excuse. There was quite a little talk about it. He had some trouble with General Arolas at the time, and there was something behind it; I could not explain.

Q. Did he do it as an act of retaliation upon some Spanish general?—A. No.

Q. Because they were spies?—A. No.

Q. Well?—A. He might have done it because they were spies. He captured them near the trocha, as Cayajabos was the first town outside the trocha.

Q. How did Maceo know about them?—A. Nunez made the report himself.

Q. Made the report that he captured them and hung them?—A. Yes, sir. You asked me did I know anything. I have a copy of an official document of one of these executions, committed by a Cuban subchief without the knowledge of his superiors. Here is a letter from Juan Ducasse, commanding the southern brigade of the province of Pinar del Rio.

Q. No, sir.—A. "I have notice that you have verified some executions in the district under my command without my previous knowledge"——

Q. Who was that from?—A. Ducasse to his subordinate. "I direct this present letter to you so that in the future you will abstain from doing this without filling all the legal requirements that are necessary in such cases. Please acknowledge the receipt of the present letter." This was, as I say, sent by Ducasse to one of his subalterns (Maj. Tomas Murgado) who had caused a couple of pacificos to be executed.

Q. In every case the act, when it came to the knowledge of the commander, was disapproved and rebuked—the man sometimes deprived of his rank?—A. Yes, sir. In another case I had the confession of a man who did it. Dr. Rojas Sanchez was a commander in Zayas's force. He boasted of having been given eight prisoners to deliver to the Spanish authorities, and openly bragged that only four got there.

Q. Did he say he reported that fact to his commanding officer?—A. No, sir.

Q. He kept that concealed?—A. Yes, sir; to show that Zayas was acting in good faith, when he made a big raid into the town of Esperanza, near Santa Clara city, this same major openly boasted that he refused to go into the town unless given permission to use his machete on all pacificos, and Zayas would not allow him to go in, but ordered him to stay outside the town. A story comes to my mind——

Q. A story I don't care about.—A. It is not a story; it was told to me by two soldiers——

Q. I don't care about putting in this record the stories—

A. I am perfectly convinced of it.

Q. Why so?—A. Because I threatened to have these men before their commanding officers.

Q. Why didn't you do it?—A. Because I had no time.

Q. Why not?—A. I had to get my dispatches to Trinidad.

Q. You got the confessions from two soldiers that they had committed some outrage?—A. No, sir; that when the town of San Pedro was attacked the whole force was given orders to use the machete on all male inhabitants, but to respect women and children, and to burn and loot everything. These were two wounded men in a hospital of a prefecto. They were talking among themselves and with my servant.

I understand Spanish perfectly. I got up out of my hammock and said to them, "Why do you men talk all that stuff, when you know you did not have such orders?" They said, yes they did. I said, "That is against all precedent, and General Diaz never gave you any orders to cut down all male inhabitants. Pedro Diaz is a great friend of mine"—which he was—"and I will have you taken before him;" and they never flinched.

Q. Did you see Diaz again?—A. No, sir.

Q. Did you ever use that conversation?—A. No, sir; I just give it as it comes to my mind.

Q. Do you know Diaz?—A. Perfectly.

Q. Did you believe that?—A. It seems improbable, and I did not like to believe it. That is the reason I raised such a row about it. The order was to burn and loot everything, to kill the men, but to respect women and children. They are very severe on any lack of respect to women. I have seen three cases of men hung for rape.

Q. How do you know any orders were given by any Cuban officer to loot and burn, to machete the men, but respect the women? Do you know that order was ever given?—A. I have heard it at La Palma. I have been at attacks on towns, and I have heard the order to loot and burn the town, but to respect women and children. The reason Maceo suffered such a defeat at Palma was because he put in all his unarmed men to assist in looting, they were so anxious to get clothing. His men were nearly naked.

Q. You went as an electrical engineer when you first went to Cuba?—A. Yes, sir.

Q. How long did you work at that?—A. Until the year after the war began.

Q. Establishing telegraph lines?—A. No, sir; putting up electric-light plants.

Q. What company?—A. Spanish-American Electric Light and Power Company.

Q. Where located?—A. The head office at New York. I was employed by the company to be stationed at Matanzas.

Q. Did you have any plants elsewhere through the island?—A. Myself, personally?

Q. No; this company?—A. One in Havana, at Matanzas, and also at Cienfuegos; one small one also at Regla and Guanabacoa indirectly.

Q. Did they have a good deal of money invested?—A. Yes, sir; it is a pretty rich company.

Q. About how much?—A. I have no idea.

Q. Can't you give us some idea?—A. No, sir; on account of their gas works they probably had more money invested there than any other American company.

Q. Do they control the gas in those cities?—A. Yes, sir; the gas and electric light in Havana and Matanzas.

Q. Controls the telegraph lines?—A. No, sir.

Q. Who controls them?—A. The Government.

Q. Who built them?—A. I don't know who built them.

Q. Could not you give some approximation to the amount of money this company you represented has invested in Cuba?—A. It would be rather hard, for the detail of that company is—it is a big stock company, and I could not give any information; that was not my business.

Q. How many men employed?—A. A couple of hundred altogether.

Q. Americans, usually?—A. No; Cubans. I, myself was the only American in Matanzas, not only in the electric-light works, but in the

city. I think there were only two native Americans in the city of
Matanzas while I was there.

Q. Perhaps you could approach to within $50,000 or $100,000 of the
amount?—A. No, sir; I would not like to make any statement; I am
ignorant of their affairs.

Q. It is very large?—A. Very large. Judging from the size of their
plant, it is very much.

Q. Have they suffered from the war?—A. In this way: I don't think
Spain is paying their gas bills, and they can't get their money from the
town councils.

Q. I suppose they want it pretty bad?—A. Yes, sir.

Q. It cuts you out of a job?—A. Yes, sir.

Q. A good one?—A. I was not employed by them when the war
broke out; I was in business for myself.

Q. What business?—A. I was in with Mr. Schlesinger, who represented Mr. Oscar Stillman, of Boston.

Q. Did you put up many of those plants?—A. Quite a few.

Q. How many?—A. large electric-light plant in the city of Colon,
for a French company of Paris, and also five smaller plants throughout
the island.

Q. Are they still in operation?—A. No, sir; because the smaller ones
were in sugar factories, and the majority are burned.

Q. The war found you in that employment?—A. Yes, sir.

Q. And cut you off from all opportunity of getting along in that
business, and it was then you became a correspondent of the New York
Herald?—A. Yes, sir; I am not a newspaper man by profession.

Q. Were you employed while in Havana, or did you come here and
secure your employment?—A. While in Havana, the first time, by letter from the home office. The second time, I was ordered by letter
from James Gordon Bennett, from Paris, to go there.

Q. Bennett has no interest in the island?—A. None that I know of.
My instructions were to be impartial, to give both sides a hearing, and
I have tried to follow them.

Q. Were your dispatches examined by the Spanish?—A. No, sir;
they never got near the Spanish.

Q. You were not representing both sides then?—A. Well, no; the
fact is that the Spaniards have prohibited the correspondents from
going into the field, and we break their laws by doing so.

Q. You can not give an account of what you see?—A. They would
not let you out into the country.

Q. You could from Havana?—A. Yes, sir; but they would not let
you out with their columns of operation. That system was inaugurated
by Weyler. While Martinez Campos was in Cuba they allowed correspondents to go with the columns, and I had a pass at that time. I
have a pass from the second captain-general, the same position that
Ahumada holds at present.

By Mr. DAVIS:

Q. Did you know William G. Smith, of Gomez's bodyguard?—A.
Yes, sir; he was once with me a month away from Gomez.

Q. How long did you know him?—A. Just that month.

Q. What month was that?—A. It was the month he left Gomez's
camp, on the 14th of February.

Q. This year?—A. Yes, sir.

Q. Was that when he was going home?—A. No, sir; I offered to take
him with me, but Gomez would not let him.

Q. What was his rank?—A. He had the rank of captain in Gomez's escort.

Q. How long has he been with him?—A. About a year, I think. A year last May he joined Gomez, if I am not mistaken—April or May.

Q. What were you and he off a month together for?—A. Smith was greatly interested in the case of Scovil, arrested and put in jail, and we wanted to go down to notify the American consul. We thought word had not been sent up to him about it, and, as I was going to notify the consul, he went as my companion.

Q. Anybody else with you?—A. My two servants.

Q. Where did you go?—A. All through that region, from Reforma to Trinidad.

Q. Did you obtain access to the American consul?—A. Yes, sir.

Q. Notified him?—A. Yes, sir.

Q. And then went back to Gomez?—A. Yes, sir; we saw our consular agent at Trinidad. The consul-general, Lee, we found had been already notified.

By Mr. MORGAN:

Q. On that excursion, when you were with Smith, were you under the orders of anybody?—A. No, sir.

Q. Was he?—A. Only under my orders, to go where we wanted to.

Q. He was on leave of absence?—A. Yes, sir.

Q. Gomez knew what your mission was?—A. Yes, sir; to get my dispatches through, and see about Scovil.

Q. What became of Scovil?—A. He got out.

By Mr. DAVIS:

Q. A great deal has been said, Mr. Rea, about the massacre of the sick and wounded and nurses in the hospitals of the insurgents. Did you ever witness anything of that kind?—A. No, sir; I did not, but I do not doubt that they may have captured a few hospitals.

Q. Irrespective of the number, have you any doubt that when the Spaniards captured the hospital they killed the inmates?—A. No, sir.

Q. That is a well-understood fact?—A. A well-understood fact.

Q. They have captured a great many?—A. No, sir.

Q. But they have killed all when they did capture one?—A. Yes, sir. A Cuban hospital is a difficult place of access, and I was only allowed, as a special favor, to see one of them. The Cubans themselves do not know where they are. They are established in the most inaccessible places.

Q. I suppose for the reason that they know that the inmates will be butchered if captured?—A. Their policy has been to put the hospitals in secure places. As a general rule, they would not allow a trail within a half a mile or mile of the place.

Q. Did you know of any manufactory of clothing on the part of the insurgents?—A. Only of shoes.

Q. To what extent do they manufacture shoes?—A. Quite a little. They make a bad attempt of tanning the hide and make quite a fair shoe for people who have never done anything of the kind before. They also make saddles.

Q. Make no clothing?—A. All the clothing worn by the rebels has to be brought out from the Spanish towns or lines, except when they raid a town. These attacks on the towns, as a rule, are not made with any view except to get clothing or stores. I know that when Maceo attacked towns on three occasions he did it for the purpose of getting clothing for his infantry.

Q. Are there any manufacturing establishments for the repair of arms?—A. Yes, sir; they have armories, and have a few mechanics to repair arms, who do very nice work.

Q. Any manufacturing establishment for powder?—A. None that I know of.

Q. You do not know that there is none?—A. 1 never heard of it. I heard of a powder maker going down there, but he came away dissatisfied. They also made a couple of brass cannon, but they never used them, and they never did them any good.

By Mr. MORGAN:

Q. Did they make any small arms—guns?—A. They do not make any guns; a few machetes are all. It is commonly understood in the United States that they have plenty of men on the Island of Cuba to take up arms, but all that is lacking are the arms themselves. My experience in La Villas goes to prove entirely the contrary, because when Gomez crossed the trochas he brought with him several hundred extra arms from the eastern provinces, and had to force men to take them. He had to take men out of the country to shoulder those arms by what we call a forced draft.

Q. What became of those superfluous men you spoke of around Maceo's camp?—A. I suppose they are there yet. Just before I left the Cubans landed two expeditions, and the junta claim they sent a couple of thousand rifles. That would account for these arms. Maceo had a large number of "impedimenta;" Gomez has none of them at all.

By Mr. DAVIS:

Q. "Impedimenta" means baggage, etc. You used it as meaning unarmed men?—A. Yes, sir.

By Mr. MORGAN:

Q. You spoke of a number of unarmed men who were with Maceo and in his way?—A. Yes, sir; about 1,500.

Q. What became of them?—A. I suppose they are armed now.

Q. Do you think that that tends to show there are no Cubans wanting arms?—A. What I mean is, there are no men leaving the towns for the army.

Q. I am talking about people in the country.—A. In La Villas there are no men in the country.

By Mr. DAVIS:

Q. Do you not understand that those concentrados are mostly women and children and old men?—A. I do not understand that at all.

Q. Have you ever witnessed one of those places?—A. I saw just as many young men as there are old men.

Q. When?—A. Just before I came home—a few months ago.

Q. Men that have come in from the country—Cubans?—A. I saw just as many young men as old men. The Cuban who has his country at heart—who was a patriot—went out during the first year. Those who have joined during the last year have been forced out by various circumstances—by lack of food, by persecutions of the Spaniards, etc. All the Cubans who had money when this war broke out came to the United States, and are carrying on the war from here. Leaving out those who rose up against Spain during the first year of the outbreak, the men carrying on this war in the island are those who could not help themselves or had no money to get away. This insurrection was going on for a year in the provinces of Camaguey and Santa Clara, and those in the west did not have the nerve to take up arms.

Q. Did you ever have any difficulty with Gomez?—A. Yes, sir.

Q. What was it?—A. It is quite a long story. General Gomez and I were very good friends until—I do not say he is a bad friend of mine now, but he treated me very badly. He did not treat me as he had others. He treated Scovil much better. He offered him twenty men to help him get through, and did not offer me any.

Q. What do you mean by impartial manner?—A. He showed partiality to the others.

Q. In what month or in what year did this partiality begin?—A. When I first met the old man.

Q. What other correspondents were in the camp?—A. Sylvester Scovil, correspondent of the World.

Q. He treated him better than you?—A. Yes, sir.

Q. That continued until you ceased all relations with him?—A. Yes, sir.

Q. Now you can go on and make any statement you want to.—A. I had been away from him to Trinidad. I saw things that astonished me—that ought not to have taken place in the Cuban Government, I saw many things that would work against them if printed and prove detrimental to their character. Among other things Smith and I witnessed—not exactly witnessed, but we were within half a mile of the town of Paredes. At 1 o'clock at night the Cubans attacked the town. There were 16 Spanish soldiers in the garrison—in one fort 5, in another 9, in another 2. They attacked the town and captured two forts, and there were but 5 Spaniards to deal with, when someone raised the cry, "Here comes the Spaniards," and they ran out of the town, leaving their dead and wounded. The Cuban commander made a report to Gomez, saying he had gained a big victory, while exactly the opposite was the case. He left his dead and wounded in the streets and ran away. Also, Smith and I had experience with the "majas" or unarmed men, who live in the hills and steal the food from the pacificos and respect no one's authority. We also had seen several cases on the part of the Government prefectos, who would not attend to their business. When I got to Gomez's camp, the old man asked me, very honestly, "How about your trip?" I said, "I have not enjoyed it very much;" and I went on to explain what I had seen. I told the old man, for his benefit, what I had seen, and Smith did also, and the old man was quite interested until finally he got mad and walked away; and I talked some with the other officers and made some criticisms on what had passed and that they did not know anything about. Gomez came to me after supper when I was passing through the camp and said, "What do you mean, Mr. Rea, by telling me all these things that you saw on that trip?" In the afternoon before that he came to me and said, "You have told me these things, I suppose, because you sympathize with me and want them corrected." Afterwards he called to me and asked what I meant by it, and I told him again what I had said before. He said it was not true, and I told him it was not my habit to lie.

Q. Was Smith in the camp?—A. Yes, sir.

Q. Did you call on him to corroborate you?—A. No, sir; Smith is afraid of the old man. Gomez said, "What did you mean by saying my brigadier made a false report?" and I said that he did make a false report if he had said that he won a victory, after he had run away and left his dead and wounded. He said, "What do you think of it, and what are you going to write about it?" I said "I am to write the truth," and he said that I had no business to write the truth.

Q. Did he make any point that you had made the same statements that you made to him to the various men in his command?—A. No, sir; the various men in his command have made these statements to him.

He got very mad about it, and said that if I wrote these stories he would shoot me. I looked at him in surprise. I thought perhaps the old man might take it into his head to do it then. I said that it was a pretty serious thing to shoot a man, especially an American, and he answered that as the United States or nobody else had recognized him as a belligerent, and his status was that of a bandit, he would shoot me, and that he could not be held responsible. After awhile he calmed down and we parted very comfortably. In the morning Gomez, in the front of all his forces, started again on the American Congress, the New York Herald, the American public, Grover Cleveland, and everybody else, and I told him I could not stand it any longer. He said all we cared about it was what we could get out of it or the money we might make.

Q. What did you say about that?—A. I said he was way off—that is not exactly what I said.

Q. Give us exactly.—A. I said "General Gomez, you are very unjust. You very well know that if the United States should set its foot down, and cut off your chance of getting arms and ammunition your revolution could not last."

Q. Was that between you and Gomez alone?—A. No, sir; the whole army was there—that is, the whole of the army he had, 150 men and staff.

Q. They heard it all?—A. Yes, sir. After it was all over they came to me and tried to smooth it over. I said they could not smooth it over until the old man apologized. Smith was there and was very mad. He went up to Gomez and told him that he must stop abusing Americans or he would resign.

Q. Did he give a reason for this?—A. Because he had insulted the nation and Americans.

Q. Smith did not show he was very much afraid of the old man, then?—A. No, sir.

Q. He didn't like it?—A. Yes, sir.

Q. Did you leave Gomez after this incident?—A. About an hour afterwards.

Q. Did you leave his camp then?—A. About an hour afterwards.

Q. Did you report these facts to your paper?—A. To the paper, yes, sir; I did not publish them. I did not know whether I was right in publishing them or not. The old man made these remarks to me, and raised the dickens for no cause whatever. He was quite put out because, I suppose, the old fellow thought we ought to have been arrested and put in prison by the Spanish Government, so as to raise an issue between that Government and our own.

Q. Did you say anything about the partiality he had shown to other correspondents?—A. No, sir; I never said a word about it. He was comparing me with the other correspondents. He had said that it would be a very good thing if Scovil or I were arrested, and then the United States Government would get into trouble with Spain in regard to it, and he made the same remark that morning, and he made a comparison between Scovil and myself, and I said: "General, the day I get arrested by the Spaniards, I don't think it will cause a war that it will redound to your benefit."

Having read and corrected the above statement, I hereby sign the same.

GEO. BRONSON REA,
355 Sixth avenue, Brooklyn, N. Y.

BROOKLYN, N. Y., *June* ——, *1897.*

STATEMENT MADE BY MR. STEPHEN BONSAL ON THE 11TH DAY OF JUNE, 1897.

Mr. BONSAL was first sworn by Mr. Davis, chairman of the committee:

In the absence of Mr. Clark, one of its members, Mr. Davis acted as a member of the subcommittee.

By Mr. MORGAN:

Q. Please state your age, name, and the country of your nativity.—A. Stephen Bonsal; born in the State of Maryland 32 years ago, in 1865.

Q. What is your occupation?—A. Journalist.

Q. What is your acquaintance with the Spanish people, both in Cuba and in Spain?—A. I have been in Spain several times, as correspondent of the New York Herald, a good many years ago; and in 1893 I was appointed secretary of legation in Madrid, and remained about two years, until 1895. During that time I became acquainted with a great many Spaniards, and am very fond of Spain and of the Spaniards in many ways. I have written a great deal about the country, or rather of old Spain, and always in the most complimentary way, until I went to Cuba, and came on the new phase of Spanish character; not new, but new to me.

Q. When did you go to Cuba, and how long did you remain?—A. 1st of January, 1897, and I got back before the middle of April. I have been back more than six weeks.

Q. In what capacity did you go to Cuba?—A. As a special correspondent of the New York Herald.

Q. While there, did you visit the interior of the island?—A. Yes, sir.

Q. At what places?—A. I was, you might say, everywhere in the four western provinces. I was not in the two eastern provinces, generally called Puerto Principe and Santiago de Cuba—I was not in "free Cuba." I was not with Gomez's army; I was not where they control. I was generally within the Spanish lines.

Q. Those two eastern provinces are called La Villas?—A. No. Las Villas—that is very confusing. There are two ways of describing these divisions, by names of certain provinces, and then by certain expressions that have grown up among the Cubans. Las Villas describes the five towns. The real meaning of the expression is the five towns.

By Mr. DAVIS:

Q. It has no value as description?—A. No, sir; it is very confusing. It is like other expressions they have. The Cubans always use the terms, the upturn and the downturn of the island. That is the way the Cubans describe it; that it goes up one way and down the other. There are all sorts of descriptions, but I think the best way is the names of the provinces.

Q. In your visit were you limited to the railways, or did you travel by the ordinary country roads?—A. I traveled some by the ordinary country roads, but on my journey from Havana to what they call the front, the front of operations against insurgents, I traveled principally by train with military convoy. I traveled a good deal in Pinar del Rio by horseback, and also in Santa Clara; but the longest journey, from Havana to the city of Santa Clara, was by train with convoy, which took three or four days.

Q. Taking the country within the lines of the Spaniards as you found it on your first visit to the interior, what was the condition of the rural population outside the towns and cities at that time as to homes and subsistence and general prosperity?—A. When I reached Cuba, the so-called policy of concentration had been already put in force almost completely. There were some places where I still saw them driving in the country people. These orders of concentration were issued by the Captain-General of the island in October, 1896. They were issued on different dates, but began in October, 1896. One of these proclamations I published in the Review of Reviews. I got it from one of the general staff in Havana. I have seen the others, and they are identical, with the exception of different dates for different provinces. Between October and December, 1896, this policy of concentration was perfected and carried out. Every peasant and every person living in the four western provinces outside the garrison towns were driven into stations of concentration, their houses were all burnt, their crops and the palm trees destroyed, all the roots that grew—yams, etc.—were dug up, with the idea, many of the officers told me, to rob insurgent bands in these so-called "pacified" provinces of the means of subsistence.

Q. You mean the houses of all the ordinary rural population?—A. Yes, sir.

Q. There were still places protected in the interior?—A. There were about, I should say, in those four western provinces, 20 centrales, as they call them—sugar estates—protected.

Q. Were troops stationed on those sugar estates?—A. Yes, sir.

Q. In every instance?—A. Yes, sir.

Q. Spanish troops?—A. Yes, sir; of the regular army, and then irregular troops, raised for the purpose of the defense of the estates for which the proprietors had to pay.

Q. The proprietors had to pay the irregulars?—A. Yes, sir; and the regulars too.

Q. Had to pay all?—A. Yes, sir; but the irregulars more.

Q. Was that rule applied indiscriminately to proprietors residing in the United States and those residing in Cuba?—A. The rule as to the defense?

Q. And payment?—A. I do not know exactly to what rule you refer.

Q. I mean the practice as to payment for protection.—A. I do not know whether any man was forced to defend his place. Before the war, where there are now 20 large sugar estates, there were over 200. You go along through those western provinces and you can see the standing chimneys. All the great machinery, the buildings, barns, etc., were burned—the great majority of these estates have been burned. There were many of the American estates protected in the way I have described, and several I have visited.

Q. Your information, derived from the officers of Spanish army, as I understand you, is that the troops that were upon these estates were paid for by the proprietors?—A. Yes, sir; absolutely; paid for openly. It was a bargain. It was arranged at the palace at Havana, and they had to pay extra there. It was a written contract. They had to pay extra to keep the *comandante* sweet. It cost them a pretty penny to have this garrison. Every man had to—the way they did this, they would have these places declared strategic points. That was the way the Spaniards would excuse the fact that they were having large bodies of troops in places where they were absolutely of no use. So Mr. Atkins or the sugar planters would go to Havana and have breakfast with the Marquis Palmerola and have a talk, and have their places declared a strategic point, and the Captain-General would order a certain number of troops there until further orders, with the understanding that the proprietor would pay so much bounty. I visited one estate where there were a thousand men.

By Mr. DAVIS:

Q. What estate?—A. Azpeztequia, on the southern coast, belonging to the Marquis, now in Madrid. and who belongs to the constitutional or tory party in Cuba. It had eighty forts defending it.

Q. Eighty forts?—A. Fortines. They look like forts in Sebastapol, a game we used to play when I was a boy——

By Mr. MORGAN:

Q. Did you learn whether this destruction of sugar plantations was the work of one side exclusively or both?—A. I think it was both sides. It is a rather difficult question, because they have each changed their policy. The Spanish idea the first year of war, the last campaign, as announced over his own signature by Mr. Dupuy de Lome, was to make the sugar crop. That was to show that the revolution was merely local and of little importance. This letter was published in the New York Herald, being the ideas of the representative of the Spanish Government in the United States, and at that time they took steps to protect the sugar estates to the best of their ability. Azpeztequia was the first man to fortify his estate. As soon as they found out, as they did a year and a half ago, while the first sugar crop was making, that even the most loyal Spaniard, being a business man, was perfectly willing to pay 50 cents a bag for the sugar he made to the insurgents, or to the Cuban prefecto—when they found out that the people they were protecting were paying taxes into the patriot treasury they concluded it would be a good thing to destroy all the sugar.

By Mr. DAVIS:

Q. By "them" you mean the Spanish?—A. Yes, sir. This year they have done nothing for the sugar people, because they knew all the sugar people, whether American, French, German, or the most loyal Spaniard, were paying tribute on their prospective crop to the insurgent local representatives. It is so easy to burn cane. One man can burn cane, and 4,000 can not stop it. So the policy of the Spanish Government in Cuba on the sugar question changed entirely. Last year it was to make the crop; this year they think to hurt the Cubans more by destroying it.

Q. It was changed because the Cuban revolutionists could collect the revenue from the Spaniards?—A. Yes, sir.

Q. Was that revenue willingly paid?—A. I think there was no unwillingness. I have talked with many of the Spaniards and they looked on it as a fair business proposition. They would rather pay 50 cents a bag than lose their sugar. Sometimes they refuse. Sometimes a man, because he had a thousand soldiers on his estate, thought that he could refuse and would not pay, but the crop was always burned. That happened to an American.

Q. What was his name?—A. Stillman. He was somewhat sluggish and his crop was burned.

By Mr. MORGAN:

Q. After this policy of concentration had been accomplished, or nearly so, when you arrived there, what was the condition of the small home-steads throughout the portion of the island you visited?—A. They were all either burned or thrown down.

Q. Crops destroyed?—A. Yes, sir; absolutely.

Q. What was the situation of the country as to cattle, hogs, etc.?—A. The cattle that had belonged to these guajiros, or peasant class, had been principally driven into the stations of concentration, as these people understood, to save them the trouble, and that they were to be given back to them when they got to the stations which had been designated for them to reside in, but they never saw the cattle again. They were swept into the commissariat department of the Spanish army and disappeared from view.

Q. Are there any cattle left?—A. Very few.

Q. It was desolation, then?—A. I have been in many countries where there was devastation, but I have never seen such a picture of abso-lute desolation as those provinces presented in the early springtime of this year.

Q. You saw parties of the rural population being driven into these point of concentration?—A. I did.

Q. Were they going willingly?—A. Most unwillingly, but not resist-ing. There had been many cases where they did resist.

Q. What became of them then?—A. They were shot.

Q. Did you see those same people later in your tour in Cuba, these concentrados?—A. I have been to every important station of concen-tration in the four western provinces.

Q. Did you identify any of the people?—A. No, sir.

Q. Did you see them at those stations?—A. Yes, sir.

By Mr. DAVIS:

Q. Are those stations many?—A. I saw every one—I mean every considerable one. There are fifteen or twenty stations of importance.

By Mr. MORGAN:

Q. What was their condition when you last saw them?—A. They were absolutely without food. The last station I saw was at Matan-zas before I left the island. I saw the least suffering there. I have spoken more about that since I have been back because there were so many foreigners there who saw what I saw, and because in the stations in the interior, the purely military points, it is very difficult to have anything to say with the pacificos. You are followed by the soldiers, and they are told to keep their mouths shut.

Q. What was the physical appearance of those people as to starva-tion and condition of health?—A. In many instances they could not walk, could not get up from the seats on which they were sit.ing. This demonstration, made on or about the 22d of March, of the starving people of Matanzas, was the most affecting sight I have ever seen. Of the 8,000 or 9,000, or possibly 10,000, people on this Cascorra hill——

By Mr. DAVIS:

Q. I understand that at Matanzas those people who had been driven in were taken onto a hillside and located?—A. Yes, sir; these people, being absolutely at the end of ther resources, having no resources whatever, being so reduced they could not go any farther, walked down to the palace in Matanzas, as many as could walk—many of them were so weak that they could not even walk—there were about 1,800 or 2,000 of the 9,000 or 10,000 that could walk.

Q. When they got there the men did not dare to talk, and the women did the talking?—A. Yes, sir; the women and children. There were children there 15 years of age without a single stitch of clothing.

Q. Tell us about that officer you mentioned—did you see that?— A. Yes, sir.

Q. Tell us about that.—A. One of the young adjutants came out and wanted to know what was the matter. They were very much frightened before they got near the palace, but one of the women spoke up and said they meant no disrespect, but they wanted his excellency the governor to know their condition. This young fellow went into the house and told the governor, and after quite a while the governor sent ·word to them to go around to the new artillery barracks and he would do what he could for them. An hour or two later he sent out a quantity of potatoes, which was sufficient to give each person that walked down one potato, and then they walked home, the weaker leaning on the more able-bodied, and they got back in various ways to the place where they are dying.

By Mr. MORGAN:

Q. Did you learn while there, in this particular locality of which you are speaking, whether there had been an extensive mortality or fatality, in consequence of their starvation?—A. Yes, sir; in consequence of the starvation and in consequence of the plagues and epidemics raging among them. The yellow fever has been all winter unusually severe, owing to the bad sanitary condition in which they are living and the lack of food. The smallpox has also raged terrifically. There have been weeks in Matanzas where, in a population of 48,000 to 50,000, there have been 350 deaths a week from smallpox, and the death wagons are going all the time to the settlement of these starving people. Accurate and absolute statistics would be difficult to give, but I think I am now quoting correctly. Why, a comparatively short time ago in Matanzas—I have in mind many things that our consul told me, Mr. Brinkerhoff, the Danish consul, and sugar merchants whom I met, say there have been over 3,000 who have died out of the 8,000 or 10,000 concentrated there since the order went into effect.

Q. Within your own observation or knowledge, has there been any effort at a systematic supply of food for these starving people by the Spanish Government?—A. There has been no effort, whether systematic or sporadic, of any kind. While it was not published in the same proclamation, it was stated, when this new system of what is really extermination was introduced, that they would have zones of cultivation when they were driven to the various places where it was good for them to reside, from a Spanish military standpoint; that each head of family would be allotted a place in which to plant and cultivate a garden, and in Cuba it could have been easily done; and while the people would not have lived very well, still they would have survived if such an arrangement had been made, but in no single instance has the zone of cultivation been handed over to the people. In several places they have said: "That is going to be the zone of cultivation." Matanzas was one, I remember, but it has never been done—never had been proposed to give it to them, in my opinion. It was merely a blind to the rest of the world, in my opinion.

Q. If their promise had been kept and these zones of cultivation reserved for the people to give to them, they still would have been without tools or the assistance of animals to cultivate those crops?— A. Yes, sir; but they live on so little, these people. The climate is such that they can live on vegetable diet almost entirely—on potatoes cooked in various ways—and nobody would have died of starvation, in my opinion. They never cultivate much, anyhow; they never plow; things simply grow. But, being compelled to stay in these stations and stay in their huts, with sentries around who would shoot them down if they crossed the line to dig for potatoes or roots, there is nothing left for them but to starve.

Q. We hear a great deal of digging for roots. Can you name the roots on which these people can subsist?—A. I think there is a great deal of exaggeration in it. I do not know the names of any edible roots, and did not eat any myself while in Cuba; but I have been a great deal in the East Indies as well as in the West Indies, and I do not believe any European can live long on roots or leaves or edible palms.

Q. There are edible palms by which considerable subsistence can be received?—A. Yes, sir; but I do not think Europeans can live on them.

Q. The native Cubans can live on such diet?—A. By Europeans I mean the Cubans; I do not mean to refer to the aboriginal Indians. I mean, of course, in Java, Sumatra, etc., the natives live on air and a little rice once a year or so, but I do not think the natives in Cuba can do that. They are very fond of meat when they can get it. They can live very easily, but if, as has been proposed, they turn those people back, send them back to their ruined homes, to dig up roots and live on them, I think a great majority would starve.

Q. If they were driven out now?—A. Yes; of course the country has been entirely destroyed behind them.

Q. Their safety from starvation depends entirely on the people who are wealthy and the Spanish Government?—A. Entirely. They might be assisted back, and kept going for a month or so, until they could plant something. Judge Day asked me two or three days ago, I do not suppose confidentially, what would happen if the Spanish Government should change its policy and drive these people back to the places whence they came. I said that many would die on the way; that many more would die of starvation after they arrived.

Q. And very few would survive?—A. Yes, sir.

Q. So it is death to stay, and death to go back to their homes?—A. Yes, sir.

Q. Were the observations you made at Matanzas—I mean the results you reached at Matanzas—true, in your opinion, as to the other points of concentration?—A. Yes, sir; only at the other points, so far as I could see, each phase of suffering was more severe, because in Matanzas there was a large population, some foreigners, and some people who had had means before the war; and there was such a thing there as a man who would send money to these people to aid them; and there was some effort, though generally ineffectual, to assist them. Take a place like Jaruco, between Matanzas and Havana, simply a little station on the railroad, in the swamp, where 8,000 or 9,000 people have been concentrated, where the ordinary population, if any, was under 100—there death was absolutely sure. I visited this station, and there were continual rows with the Spaniards. I could not see much, but I could see that the conditions were worse, and the troops guarding them, being under no surveillance at all, were treating them in a much more outrageous way.

Q. Speaking of the treatment of the troops toward those poor people, was it immoral?—A. I have never seen that, but I believe it was so. As you know, these reconcentrados are principally women, children, and old men. I have had a great many people tell me that, and I believe it absolutely.

Q. That they were the subjects of violence?—A. Yes, sir.

Q. Did they have any appearance of cheerfulness or resignation to their fate?—A. No; they were perfectly listless; they were hopeless.

Q. What sort of shelter did they have at these places of concentration?—A. A palm-leaf house that they built with wonderful skill. I have seen many of them, and have pictures of many in process of erection. They reach the place where they are told they are to live, and they are told to build the houses—all lie on the ground. They get the dry palm leaves and a few sapling poles for the four corners of the hut, and within an hour they have a very decent hut, all thatched with palm leaves down the side.

Q. Is that any protection against the heavy rains?—A. None at all; they all leak. They have no beds, all lie on the ground, which is death itself in that climate. If a man has a hammock, a soldier comes along and if he wants a hammock he takes it.

Q. How do these huts where these people live in this confinement compare with the houses they lived in while at home?—A. Their houses were very comfortable; many of them frame houses. These people lived in great comfort; they lived easily, and in great comfort. One of these little peasant farmers, with 3 or 4 acres of ground, would have every necessary of life, and even the principal luxuries. These they would grow themselves, such as coffee and tobacco, with very little effort.

Q. Is Cuba an abundant country in the production of coffee?—A. It does not produce a great coffee crop, but you might say it is a great country for the production of coffee. They can produce, perhaps, more coffee to the acre in Cuba than anywhere else. In the last twenty-five or thirty years they have gone almost exclusively to planting sugar cane.

Q. For commercial purposes?—A. Yes, sir.

Q. Do the common peasantry raise coffee?—A. He has; the little farmer has his coffee bushes covering a quarter of an acre, perhaps, and his little tobacco field.

Q. Do they have sugar cane?—A. No, sir.

Q. He depends on the market?—A. Yes, sir; sugar cane itself has no value. If a man wants a little cane, he goes and cuts it in the next field; it has no value before it is ground.

Q. It is a rather indigenous product?—A. Yes, sir.

Q. These concentrados lived well at home and were supplied with coffee and tobacco raised in their own little patches and gardens?—A. Yes, sir.

Q. They had other comforts?—A. Yes, sir.

S. Doc. 231, pt 7——47

Q. They had fruits, oranges, lemons, etc.?—A. Yes, sir; they have a great many fruits peculiar to Cuba that you never see anywhere else.

Q. Are they nice, rich food—pleasant?—A. Yes, sir; they lived extremely well, particularly the country people of the Cubans. They are a well-fed and well-grown people.

Q. Did you see among these concentrados any distribution of fruits, coffee, etc.?—A. No, sir; I have heard, and I know it to be a fact, that in one or two places like Cienfuegos and Jucaro the city council, or ayuntamiento, having on it either Spaniards who had lived a long time in Cuba and sympathized with their neighbors, or other charitable men, have voted to give these people a feed for one or two days. That has been done in one or two instances, but it only accentuates the starving condition of the people. If the people here in Washington should be starving and the city council should feed them for one day, it would only prolong the suffering, and that is the condition of these people. The city councils are very poor and can not do much, but that has been done in one or two instances, but nothing more than voting soup or dinner, or something of that kind.

Q. A casual supply?—A. Yes, sir; I simply mention it as a recognition of the fact by the people on the spot that these people were starving.

Q. Was it or not your conclusion from what you saw, looking over all the facts of the situation, that the policy of the Spanish Government with these people was to exterminate them by starvation?—A. Yes, sir; that was my conclusion, and it was not a conclusion that the Spanish high officials resented you imputing to them at all. Many I have talked with admitted it openly, many of them, and then they go on to say—if this is interesting to you—they tell their experiences in the last war. They say in the last war we finally made an arrangement with the insurgents and the thing was over, and we gave Garcia, who now commands the army in the east, a good place in the treasury, and we provided for various leaders who had surrendered, and then all the time they were drawing money from the Spanish treasury they were arranging for another uprising. They say that the policy of what they call "kindness" has failed, and that now they have quite made up their minds that the only thing is extermination; that there will never be peace on the island as long as there are any of these Cubans left, or any considerable number of them.

Q. The policy is then to exterminate?—A. Yes, sir; and they are not at all squeamish about admitting it.

Q. They propose to destroy the present population?—A. Yes, sir.

Q. And then to repopulate with Spanish?—A. Yes, sir. They have already exterminated one race, and Las Casas tells how they did it. They will probably follow the same methods with the creole race.

Q. None of the Indians are living?—A. No, sir; within forty years of taking possession by the Spaniards the Caribbean or Giboney race quite disappeared, although they had numbered 400,000 or 500,000 in a generation and a half.

Q. Did you observe many Chinamen there?—A. Not as many as I thought would be from the Miaco coolie trade the Spanish had going some years ago; a good many had left. They are very prosperous; generally keep hotels in the small towns; a few are laborers. They are provident and make money.

Q. Are they engaged in the army of either Spain or Cuba, any of them?—A. Some few in the insurgent army; none in the Spanish army. There are a great many negroes in the Spanish army; a great many more, proportionately and absolutely, than in the insurgent army. Almost all the irregular troops in the Spanish army are negroes.

Q. Troops that are called guerrillas here?—A. Yes, sir.

Q. These appear, from the accounts we have had, to be a very desperate and reckless set of marauders?—A. When you look at their antecedents you will see it is only natural they should be. Those coming from Europe are liberated from Ceuta to fight in this war, having been under sentence for murder or other offense so serious as to make them liable to imprisonment in this penal settlement. No man goes there except under sentence of at least twenty years. In this war these jail birds are let loose to do what harm they can.

Q. They form the guerrilla troops?—A. Yes, sir; and they are added to by the local scoundrels.

Q. Did you observe, personally, any of the alleged cruelties and barbarities perpetrated by the guerrillas or by the Spanish army on the Cuban hospitals?—A. No; I was not in a Cuban hospital when they murdered people, fortunately; but I have heard of many of these instances. I have talked with Spanish officers, and they have not denied it. They are only obeying orders, actual orders; not, understand me, acting on their own responsibility. Under the military laws prevailing in the four western provinces they have not only the right, but it is their duty, to shoot any man, woman, or child found outside the Spanish lines.

Q. It amounts to this, that any man, woman, or child outside the Spanish lines in Cuba is outlawed?—A They have told me myself in different places where I went——

Q. The policy then is to exterminate the rural population by starvation, and those who do not come in are to be shot?—A. Their orders are to shoot on sight. They say, " If we see a man on the road we shoot." They are perfectly justified so far as their orders are concerned. They are carrying out exactly the orders of the captain-general.

By Mr. DAVIS:

Q. What justification do they give for shooting women and children?—A. The women might breed and the children may grow up.

Q. Do they talk that way—say the women might breed and the children grow up?—A. Yes, sir; they are not averse, as you might imagine, to going on and describing fully what they mean and what they desire, and General Weyler is not unpopular among what you might call the most powerful section of the Spaniards in the Island of Cuba. On the contrary, he is quite popular. He is just the man they want. They believe with him in command this policy of extermination will be carried out to its logical conclusion. I remember, in Santa Clara, in the Club of Merchants, in the town of Santa Clara—it was at the time when it was proposed that Gen. Martinez Campos should come to Cuba—they said to me, these men of influence, unanimously, that "if Martinez Campos comes to the Island of Cuba and makes any proposition of compromise as he had before we will shoot him in the streets of Havana. We do not want General Weyler removed, because he is our man. He is bloodthirsty, and he is the man we want. We do not know whether he will be successful, but he is going about it the right way."

Q. Do you believe these sentiments to which you refer can be justly attributed to the party in Cuba called "Autonomists"?—A. The Autonomists have been placed in a very awkward position. What they say—I know Montero very well; I knew him in Madrid. I never could tell when he was talking to me, whether he was talking what he thought was the truth or for the gallery. They were evidently deceived by the measure of administrative reform published last February. A different draft of it had been given out to Montero and different leaders of the Autonomist party, with which they were delighted, because it embodied all their platform, for which they had been fighting the last ten years, and they gave their unqualified adhesion to this document of reform. When the official scheme was finally published in the Official Gazette, they found they had been duped, and that Canovas had not given any such reforms as they had been promised, and some of them, like Dr. Lorin, left the country. He feared he could not stay there without expressing his opinion and going to one of the penal settlements like Fernando Po. Montero stayed. I do not know whether he was a party to the trickery or not. He is a very poor man, and I do not think he could go. I really think he was duped himself, but the Autonomists are exceedingly few now. The reform measures, if they did nothing else, certainly served to reduce considerably the numbers of the Autonomist party, who believed that even a good measure such as that of the Dominion of Canada would be a satisfactory solution of the Cuban trouble. It was never considered seriously for a moment even by the Government before this proposed reform became known, but since it has been known nobody refers to it even, least of all General Weyler. He has no illusions as to it. It was simply conceived for effect on the civilized world, and especially on the United States.

Q. Have you seen parties of these guerrillas?—A. Many of them.

Q. Do they act independently or with the regular army?—A. They act quite independently. They are generally in better physical condition than the regular army soldiers, so they are more active, get around more.

Q. Are they mounted men?—A. Generally; some on foot, but generally mounted on these little Cuban ponies.

Q. Are they enlisted in the army of Spain?—A. Yes; it is very difficult to say exactly—their legal status has not been decided down there. They are generally local corps, very much as our national guardsmen, enlisted as soldiers, and then, by their own request, they are mobilized into the regular army under the orders of the military commander of the district in which they are stationed.

Q. They report to him?—A. To him. They are directly under his command; like our militia companies if mustered in. In their activity they are not under him, but have their own officers and maraud the country.

Q. Corresponding to the parties of rangers in the Confederate service?—A. Yes, sir; only they are mercenaries; they enlist for the pay.

Q. Have you collected, to your own satisfaction, the figures in reference to the strength of the Spanish army; or, speaking in terms I prefer, the number of Spanish soldiers, including released prisoners from the African and other prisons, who have been carried to Cuba for the purpose of this war?—A. It is very easy to find out the numbers. They are variously estimated at between 220,000 and 230,000 men that have been brought over since the outbreak.

Q. There were then soldiers on the island?—A. Yes, sir; there was then an army of 15,000 on the island when the outbreak occurred.

Q. The regular standing army in Cuba?—A. Yes, sir.

Q. They have never been free from that standing army?—A. No; never free from them.

Q. That standing army was about 15,000?—A. Yes, sir.

Q. Not for the purpose of protection, but for the purpose of an establishment?—A. They are a part of the Government.

Q. A part of the establishment?—A. Yes, sir.

Q. Had it occurred to you that there was a large excess of troops brought over from Spain to Cuba?—A. Yes, sir; that had occurred to me. I thought the Spaniards could do better if they had fewer men.

Q. Could take better care?—A. Yes, sir; the exposed area would be less. Their chief losses have been from sickness. If they had 50,000 or 60,000 men, grown men, not little boys; they have kept their best troops in Spain, and as the new conscripts came up each year they sent them out to Cuba.

Q. I suppose that accounts for the remark generally made in regard to the Spanish army in Cuba, that it is an army of boys?—A. They are very young.

Q. As a rule that is a fact?—A. Yes, sir.

Q. They are not seasoned soldiers?—A. No, sir; you remarked that in the corporals, sergeants, and noncommissioned officers; they are just boys, too; have seen no service and are not steady.

Q. Spain has a disciplined, matured, and experienced army at her command, I suppose?—A. They have 60,000 to 80,000 very good troops in Spain now.

Q. They are kept in Spain?—A. They keep their best troops in Spain; yes, sir.

Q. For the purpose of conducting the Government there?—A. Yes, sir; to be prepared for emergencies; they have kept their best troops and their best officers.

Q. Do you know anything of any company that has the monopoly or the entire work of bringing over those troops and supplies from Spain to Cuba and carrying them back?—A. They are all brought in the steamers of the Company Trans-Atlantica, but I do not think it is a monopoly; I think they would be glad to turn it over to somebody else. They are carrying it from patriotic motives entirely. The Marquis Cornillas is a very patriotic man. He turned his ships over to the Government at the beginning of the war for this purpose and said they would keep a running account; it is still running.

Q. You think the Government has not paid for this transportation?—A. Yes, sir.

Q. That the account is still running up, unliquidated?—A. Yes, sir.

Q. These trochas seem to require the presence of very large numbers of troops?—A. Certainly, very large numbers of troops are stationed along them.

Q. Could you form an idea as to the number?—A. I have never been to the eastern trocha, but along the Mariel-Majana trocha there were about 15,000 men, supposed to be keeping the insurgents in Pinar del Rio that had gone to the west end of the island.

Q. Have you known of any instance in which there were important military advantages gained over the insurgents by means of these trochas?—A. No; they always seem to me very senseless, very mediæval. I could not understand why they were built. They served no purpose, except to put thousands of men on their backs with fever from the turning up of this low, decaying soil. All along the trocha, the Mariel-Majana, or western trocha, the soldiers are buried in great numbers. I was told by one of the head surgeons in San Ambrosio hospital that they had reached Havana—they don't often send men there—that they had at least 12,000 fever cases from that trocha.

Q. The western trocha?—Yes, sir.

Q. We have had several descriptions of these trochas. I would like you to describe the one you saw.—A. Of course, the trocha is not uniform like a wall. In different places it is different. It has varied architecture with the nature of the ground. It is a sort of ditch—a cut. They dig this ditch and throw up the ground on one side. Every quarter of a mile or so they have a little fortin, according to the nature of the ground; sometimes two; where there is a gulch they have two forts, and in many places they have the barbed-wire fence to keep back cavalry.

Q. What is about the width of the clearing through which it is constructed?—A. The open space, with no trees?

Q. Yes, sir.—A. It varies. Sometimes you go across a vega, and you would not see a tree for 3 or 4 miles.

Q. Where they pass through the wooded districts?—A. It varies. Sometimes the trees come right up to the trocha and furnish protection. So far as I know I have never been with an insurgent band when they crossed the trocha, but it has never presented any obstacle to any of the insurgents that wanted to go in or out.

Q. You would regard it as a failure in a military sense?—A. Yes, sir.

Q. But it requires the protection and attention of a great many men?—A. Yes, sir; and has cost a great many lives.

Q. I wish you would describe the means of transportation the Spanish army employs when it leaves the central depot or commissary station to make an examination or incursion against the enemy.—A. When they go from Havana, they do not make any preparation at all, apparently. I am only speaking from personal knowledge. I spent three days with Spanish troops going from Havana to the town or city of Santa Clara, and they had what I had—only sugar cane we cut along the line of railroad. They made no preparation. When they go out, as they did from Santa Clara after Gomez, the three columns Weyler had converging on Santa Clara started out to drive Gomez across the eastern trocha or make him fight; they had no commissary arrangement. They had little bags in which they put what they had, but they had to go back within twenty-four or thirty-six hours for provisions.

Q. No pack train?—A. No, sir; no mountain gun or train or anything.

Q. They go with what supplies they can carry in their knapsacks or haversacks?—A. Yes, sir.

Q. And must go back when their supply gives out?—A. Yes, sir; it necessarily makes the campaign a short one.

Q. You speak of Weyler going after Gomez. At what point did they meet?—A. I do not think they met. I saw General Weyler in Santa Clara, at the high-water mark of this campaign, and he then told me that it would result in the capture of Gomez or his retreat across the eastern trocha into the Cuban or free Cuba. But it did not. Within ten days Gomez gave news of himself, and he was in General Weyler's rear at that time. Weyler had marched all the way from Havana, and he had three columns that came into Santa Clara. He must have had 40,000 men if he had one.

Q. How many?—A. 40,000 men, and he had the best men that were left.

Q. Was it in that campaign that Weyler attacked Gomez at the estate called La Reforma?—A. I do not know anything about that; I am told it was.

Q. What was your observation, or your reliable information, as to the condition of the Spanish army during the period you were there as to health?—A. They were in wretched health. Hardly a man there that should have been with the colors. The hospitals were simply crowded. They had begun with this one military hospital of San Ambrosio, and they now have eight in Havana alone, and the people were crowded together, and half the men in camp were totally unfit for service—never should have been there—were doing more harm than good, not properly fed, not properly clothed, and, to begin with, were not proper men to send out. They were merely half-grown boys.

Q. Is the Spanish army in Cuba fed by distribution of rations at stated times or by the purchase of rations by the soldiery?—A. Sometimes one is the case and sometimes the other.

Q. The system is not regular?—A. I do not know. I suppose it depends on circumstances, and sometimes it depends on the wishes of the soldiers. Sometimes they have said they would rather have a certain amount of money per day and take care of themselves.

Q. In which case they could buy from the commissariat?—A. Yes, sir.

Q. Is the country capable, in its present condition, of furnishing supplies for the army of Spain?—A. No, sir; they are getting all their supplies, with the exception of the cattle, from outside of the Island of Cuba.

Q. Have you any knowledge of the points from which they chiefly obtain their supplies for the army?—A. I have seen supplies that came from the United States and supplies that came from Cuba. I have seen bales of hay that came from New Orleans, coming for their cavalry in Pinar del Rio, that came to Havana on the New Orleans steamers.

Q. Where do they get their coal for the steamers?—A. I do not know about that. I think there is coal on the Island of Cuba.

Q. You speak of getting their cattle from the island. Do you mean that there are large herds of cattle now there on which the army can subsist?—A. They have a certain amount of cattle there, and outside their garrison towns you see a lot of cattle.

Q. Do you know whether they are native cattle or imported?—A. Native cattle; they belong to the commissariat at those places. You can see them browsing, with a guard over them.

Q. Plenty of green forage? Plenty of grazing for cattle in Cuba?—A. I do not know that; I should say there is plenty. They are not great big cattle like our cattle, and probably do not eat so much. They are more hardy, more like goats. I could not say there was any great amount of fodder; it is not a grass country.

By Mr. DAVIS:

Q. You speak of the portion of the country where you were?—A. Yes, sir.

By Mr. MORGAN:

Q. You have not been in the mountains?—A. No, sir.

Q. Did the Spanish army impress you as being one full of spirit and life?—A. No; they struck me as being very depressed and disheartened, and sick of the whole business; wanting to go home very much.

Q. I believe you say you were not, at any time, in the Cuban lines, in the lines of the insurgents?—A. Not to my knowledge.

Q. You were not with the Cuban forces?—A. No, sir.

Q. Do you know anything of the fate of the correspondent—I think of the New York World—whose name was Govin?—A. Yes, sir.

Q. I wish you would tell what you know or what information you have as to him.

By Mr. DAVIS:

Q. What was his name?—A. Charles Govin.

Q. Where was he born?—A. I do not know anything about that except from information. He was born, as I understand, in the United States; in some State——

Q. Do you know what State?—A. I have it down somewhere, but I do not now remember.

Q. Did you know him personally?—A. I did not.

By Mr. MORGAN:

Q. What account has been given of his death, and to what extent do you credit it as being true?—A. I will have to go back a little to answer that. When I went to Cuba Govin had been dead many months, and it was one of the old stories to which I, naturally having to write, did not pay much attention; but one day I received permission to go to see the American prisoners in the castle. I do not believe they had been seen then by any American except the consul-general.

Q. You obtained information which, in your opinion and judgment, you have a right to rely upon, from an eyewitness?—A. Not of his death. I talked with all these prisoners. One of these men was born in Key West and he went to Cuba in the same expedition with which Govin went as a newspaper correspondent, and when they were captured the Spanish tied them two by two, and this man was tied to Govin. You may remember that when the consul-general in Havana called the attention of the State Department to the fact that there was a rumor that this man had been murdered or killed the Spanish statement of the case was very circumstantial, and various general officers gave their personal word that such was the case—that Govin was killed in a skirmish on a certain day. This man stated that he was tied to Govin and slept by his side two days after the Spanish officers gave their word as to the date of his being killed in a fight. This man stated that he, too, was an American citizen, but was clever enough not to claim American citizenship, and that is the reason he escaped with his life, while Govin claimed American citizenship and, according to this man's story, was cut to pieces with matchetes. The falsity of the Spanish story demonstrates the truth of his.

By Mr. DAVIS:

Q. What paper did he represent?—A. I do not know about that. I am told the Jacksonville Times-Democrat. I think he was born in Ohio.

By Mr. MORGAN:

Q. You visited the prison?—A. Yes, sir.

Q. Did you see the *Competitor* prisoners?—A. Yes, sir.

Q. I suppose you have no knowledge of the circumstances of their alleged offense? That was committed long before you got there?—A. None from being on the spot; nothing except what they told me in my talk with them in their prison.

Q. How were they treated in prison?—A. Very badly, in my opinion.

Q. In what respects?—A. Their food was perfectly disgusting. When I saw Melton three months ago I telegraphed that I did not think the man would live six weeks. He is still alive. He was emaciated to an awful degree and in a terrible condition. He is not a rugged, hardy sailor man like the others.

Q. A young man?—A. Yes, sir.

Q. About how old, do you think?—A. Not over 22 or 23.

Q. Did he appear to be an intelligent man?—A. A very fine fellow in every way, I should say. He stands his imprisonment in the most plucky way; does not complain at all. He said he had written home to his people in Arkansas, and that they had received assurance from the Congressman of his district that everything was being done that could be done in Washington, and he was perfectly satisfied with that, that they were doing what they could, and he never complained. He said the food was very bad, and he could not eat. The captain of the *Competitor* told me that he never could eat; that he did not eat anything to amount to anything from the first. The man looks like a walking skeleton. He is a great big fellow—big framed and I do not suppose he weighs now over 90 pounds. He did not when I saw him.

Q. Do you recollect the other names?—A. The captain's name was Laborde. I have the other names, but do not remember them all now. There is one supposed to be an Englishman, born in Liverpool.

Q. Are they all in one cell?—A. No, sir; separated. They live in what they call galleries, thirty to forty in a dormitory. Melton and Laborde were in one and three or four in the other. When I went to see these men, I did not see them in their gallery; they were brought out. All I saw of the gallery was through the window. They do not allow you to see the cells.

Q. While in Cuba did you have any personal knowledge of the treatment of the Cubans by the Spaniards when they captured them?—A. I saw a great many shot by due process of martial law who were said to have been in the insurgent ranks or broken the military rules. I saw them led out and shot.

Q. Prisoners of war captured in action?—A. Very rarely; I think it was very rare they captured them in action. I think they were mostly captured under the terms to which the proclamation applied, and that therefore whoever found them had the legal right to shoot them down. They were brought in for the purpose of extracting information, and tried by summary court-martial, and then shot.

Q. Did you see the man whose case you recited in the Review of Reviews?—A. Fidel Fundora. He was a cattleman living in the province of Matanzas, a native Cuban. I saw him after he had been tortured.

Q. What was his condition?—A. Both his hands had been tortured by the thumb string, by tying his two thumbs together and increasing the pressure until the string cuts the thumbs off. Gangrene set in, and to save the man's life, which they wanted to save very much at that time, because they thought he had valuable information, they had to amputate both hands, which they did. I saw the stumps.

Q. They tortured him to extract information?—A. Yes, sir; they thought he was acting for the Junta in Matanzas in making this shipment; they wanted to know who he was acting for in making it.

Q. What was the charge against him, or the facts that led to this torture?—A. The charge was—I do not imagine any specific charge was ever made; they do not do that—but the charge they might have made was sending ammunition or supplies to the enemy, or sending food or supplies of any kind, which is forbidden by the bando, or proclamation.

By Mr. DAVIS:

Q. I understand that he was charged with shipping a package purporting to contain hides outside the lines, and they got hold of it and found it contained medicines and antiseptics, etc., and seized it?—A. Yes, sir.

By Mr. MORGAN:

Q. That was the state of facts that led to his torture?—A. Yes, sir.

Q. Where did you see him?—A. I saw him going out of the head-quarters of the civil guard at Matanzas, where he had been under examination of some kind.

Q. He refused to disclose any information?—A. Yes, sir. He had been under examination for many weeks. This day he was coming out from some hearing that had been going on, where he had been brought from his prison. That was the first I had heard of this case.

By Mr. MORGAN:

Q. His hands had been then amputated?—A. Yes, sir.

Q. What was his ultimate fate?—A. I do not know; since I left the island I have not heard.

By Mr. DAVIS:

Q. You understand he refused to disclose anything?—A. He did. At least once, and I believe twice, he had been led out into the yard with the belief that he was to be shot, and they led him out to the court-yard where they shoot men. The priest had given the last sacrament and the order had been given to fire and they had either fired blank or over the man's head. I did not see that; I believe Mr. Consul Bryce saw it.

By Mr. MORGAN:

Q. Their purpose was to get some supposed important information from him?—A. Yes, sir; they believed he was acting for the junta in Matanzas, and they would get 10 or 12 more people to kill if he would betray them.

Q. Do you know the general estimate in the part of Cuba where you were as to the strength of Gomez's forces?—A. It varies even with the people who have been with Gomez, whether Americans, English, or Cubans. Each time it is a different statement. I think from what I have heard that at times his forces are larger than at others, very often owing to the exigencies of his military positions. He divides into smaller bodies, then brings them together if he wants them for military operations. I believe it is a compact body of men generally.

Q. What is the estimate in Havana generally of the general strength of the insurrectionary forces?—A. All through the island?

Q. Yes, sir.—A. I have heard Spanish officers of the general staff say they had at least 40,000 armed men, armed in a modern way with rifles, altogether throughout the island. I think the Spanish have good information on that point.

Q. Is it your opinion, from all you saw there, that it is possible for the Spanish army to conquer, subdue, or pacify the Cuban people?—A. It is not.

Q. Do you think it possible, under existing circumstances, for the Cubans to drive the Spaniards from the island?—A. I do not; but the existing circumstances can not continue very long. If the Spaniards were able to keep their present state of finances and military effective-ness, and that sort of thing, for a long time, I think it would be impossible for the Cubans to drive them out, if they did not receive a large increase of force. But the Spaniard is in the position of a man who is undergoing a severe illness and who does not know when his vitality will give way. The strain is such that he is being weakened every day.

Q. What is the condition of local finances in Cuba?—A. Do you refer to the money?

Q. Yes, sir; to the money in circulation and the sorts of money and its value as compared with gold and silver?—A. They have all sorts of money in Cuba. They have gold and silver, and then they have notes, which compared to gold are depreciated very much.

Q. About how much?—A. $4.80 in gold is worth $15 in paper.

Q. How much in silver?—A. About $8 or $9 in coin. These things have changed very much since I left Havana; it is worse. The depreciation of the note is going on steadily.

Q. Are the Spanish soldiers paid in gold, silver, or paper?—A. They are paid in paper for one month. You see, they are paying them now for last fall; they are in arrears four or five months with the pay. Within the last two months they did pay a portion of one month in silver—in metallic, as they call it—in metal. As a general thing they pay in paper.

Q. Do they complain of it—the officers and soldiers?—A. Yes, sir; the civil guard—that division of the army numbers about 25,000 men—have raised a big row, and threatened mutiny almost, because, under some statutes under which they were organized, it was promised that they should be paid in gold.

Q. What is the civil guard?—A. The corps of élite, you might call it. The officers are all army officers, have the same education, and are chosen for their higher abilities, and the men are all men who have served with credit in the regular army and then reenlisted in the civil guard. In old Spain they are mounted constabulary, who patrol from one end to another. They go by pairs up and down on the Spanish roads.

Q. Are the civil guard enlisted for general service in Cuba or for local service?—A. For general service.

Q. In addition to that, have they any home guard or local guard?—A. They have what they call The Volunteers; it is a sort of national guard for the Island of Cuba, composed entirely of Spaniards. It is a guard for affairs in the island, the volunteers, as they are called. It is a body of men—you have heard of the massacre of the students in 1870 committed by them. They are very powerful; it is an influence. Every Captain-General has to take them into his calculations. One or two Captain-Generals—among them General Dulce—were sent back to Spain by them. They took him down and put him on the steamer, and sent him back to Spain. I only mention this to show their influence.

Q. They are called volunteers?—A. Yes, sir.

Q. They belong to the army?—A. No, sir.

Q. An independent force?—A. Yes, sir.

Q. But loyal to the Spanish crown?—A. Yes, sir; they are mostly officeholders, men in the different Government bureaus, shopkeepers, planters, men who are only in Cuba for a few years.

Q. Are these men required to go to any part of the island that the captain-general may order them to, or are they organized and enlisted for home guard or local purposes?—A. I think they are under their own organization and regulation, but they would have to obey the Captain-General's orders; the Captain-General is their commander in chief, and they would have to obey his orders, but he has never given them any orders for this war.

Q. From your description, I am led to suppose that pretty nearly the whole adult male Spanish population belongs to the army in some form or another?—A. They are in the army or in the volunteers. Since the beginning of the war the volunteers have done nothing but serenade various generals or victorious chiefs, or meet them at the railway station. They have not been under fire much.

Q. In one way or another the adult male Spanish population is nearly all connected with the army?—A. Yes, sir.

Q. In the army in some form or another?—A. Yes, sir.

Q. And the insurgent population was supposed to be in the army of the Republic?—A. Yes, sir.

Q. Then there is a class called pacificos, as I understand, who do not belong to either?—A. In my opinion, the pacificos are the members of the patriot families—the women and children and old men—who are not capable of bearing arms.

Q. Then, in the Island of Cuba, almost every man who owes allegiance to Spain is in one or the other army in some form or another?—A. Yes, sir.

Q. The whole population engaged in war in one way or another?—A. Yes, sir.

Q. No neutrals, if I understand, except the foreigners?—A. Yes, sir.

Q. And the women and children?—A. Yes, sir; they may be neutrals so far as active taking up of arms are concerned, but they are very few. All the Spaniards, with the exception of a few tobacco buyers and planters, and so on, are in the employ of their Government; they are officeholders in some way.

Q. The same is true of the parts of the country occupied by the Cubans?—A. Yes, sir.

Q. So it is an internecine war?—A. Yes, sir.

Q. And extends through all classes of society, in one way or the other?—A. Yes, sir.

By Mr. DAVIS:

Q. Did you meet any of these chiefs of the Spanish irregulars?—A. I knew Fondaviela, the Guanabacoa man.

Q. What was his business?—A. He was in the regular Spanish army, an officer detailed for the military command of the town of Guanabacoa; he is in the regular army.

Q. Did you, in the course of your investigations in the island, discover any American citizens among those who have been driven into the Spanish stations of concentration?—A. No, sir.

Q. You saw none at Matanzas?—A. There were at least 20 Americans who were living in the house of our consul of Matanzas, Mr. Bryce. He was supporting them very charitably. They were people whose means of livelihood had been swept away by the war, and who had been living in Matanzas. They were not of the country population, but were absolutely destitute.

Q. What area on that hillside do these nine or ten thousand people occupy—what space does it cover?—A. Perhaps 20 acres.

Q. Are the houses laid out in any order, in the way of streets?—A. Oh, no; only in lines.

Q. How much space between the houses?—A. About 20 feet. They were huts made of palms.

Q. Was the filth removed, or suffered to accumulate?—A. Suffered to accumulate; but they were in an advantageous position, as they were on the hillside, and the filth washed down; nothing like the condition of those living in the swamps.

Q. Those concentrados were mostly women and children and old men?—A. Yes, sir.

Q. Where did you understand the able-bodied men were gone?—A. I understood—it was a question I never spoke about, but I understood they were with the patriot forces of the Island of Cuba.

Q. Have you made any estimate of the forces of these concentrados driven in?—A. Yes, sir; not from statistics——

Q. From the best information you have?—A. I believe, in the four western provinces, there has been concentrated at least 400,000 people.

Q. Living in the conditions you have detailed?—A. Yes, sir.

Q. That implies total depopulation of the other parts of both provinces?—A. Yes, sir.

Q. Did you visibly see that result as to the country outside those Spanish stations?—A. Yes, sir.

Q. It means depopulation?—A. Yes, sir; absolutely. It is proclaimed officially that nobody is allowed to live there, and anybody living there is an insurgent, and to be shot on sight.

Q. Please state what your information and knowledge is in regard to the Ruiz matter.—A. The day that this man was found dead in his cell, in February last, I met General Lee in Havana, and he told me that he had heard of an American citizen who had been found dead, or, as he understood it, murdered, in his cell in the Guanabacoa prison, and as Mr. Springer, the vice-consul, who was the only man attached to the legation who spoke Spanish, was in Washington, he asked me to go with him as his interpreter.

Q. You speak Spanish fluently?—A. Yes, sir.

Q. Did you go as a representative of the Government?—A. No; he wanted me to go as a citizen, but I had recently been in the United States diplomatic service, and possibly that was the reason he asked me. He got Dr. Burgess, the American doctor in Havana, and we reached Guanabacoa a little before noon. We went first to the palace and saw General Ahumada, who was second in command, General Weyler being out in the country. General Lee demanded the body for the purpose of an autopsy, and Ahumada telegraphed to Guanabacoa, granting this permission. When we reached the jail, Fondaviela, the military governor, Maruru, the civil alcalde, and various other people, the doctor who was supposed to have attended this man, the jailer, and various officials of the jail were present.

The man was lying in a large cell, almost as large as this room, but the doctor told me that when he was called the night before to see this man that he was in another cell, a cell which I did not fully see, but which I will describe as well as I can later. This man, after he had been killed—or driven mad by his treatment, which I consider equally murder, had killed himself—had been removed from that cell to the larger one. All the cells, with the exception of three, one of which I afterwards found out was the cell in which Ruiz had been imprisoned during his lifetime, opened onto the court. These three little cells were down a passageway off the courtyard. We went in and examined the body of the man, and while waiting for the Spanish physicians to be present while Dr. Burgess performed the autopsy, I talked with many of the prisoners in these cells. The bars were opened. They were men, many of these fellows, prisoners for ordinary offenses. Some twenty were men imprisoned under the same suspicion as was the pretext for locking up Ruiz, that he and they had something to do with the capture of the train at Guanabacoa, when Aranguren captured a train with ten officers, took them off and hung two of them, Cubans by birth—traitors, as he considered them—and sent back the Spaniards to their lines. These men all stated that Ruiz had been horribly treated; that his cries had been piteous; that night after night men would go to his cell, and one of these men stated that the night before, what they supposed was the night of Ruiz's death, for they never heard his voice again, that Fondaviela, the military governor, and Marury, the alcalde—the jailer—had come about 10 o'clock. These men had a big cell on the courtyard, and could see about everybody who came along the narrow passageway on which were these cells, in one of which Ruiz was imprisoned. They described that cell and I went and looked at it. It was located—you could not measure it. They had a little aperture where they could pass in food, and looking through there I should say it was about 5 feet 6 by 3 feet 6, about 7 feet high. It may have been a few inches longer, as I say it was impossible to measure it, and it was almost dark there, and I could only look through this ventilator or peeping place. Dr. Burgess and Mr. Lee also saw it.

Q. What did these other prisoners think was being done to Ruiz while he was uttering those cries?—A. That he was being beaten for the purpose of getting him either to confess what he might know, or what he did not know.

Q. Did they profess to hear the sounds of the beating?—A. Yes, sir; they said they could hear the sounds of blows distinctly.

They then carried Ruiz's body from the prison to the city hall, and finally the two Spanish surgeons turned up and the autopsy began. I was present and saw this. I helped carry the body myself and put it on the slab. Dr. Burgess stripped him of all his clothes and the regular medical autopsy was performed. In the first place, it was evident—according to the Spanish story this man had only been dead about five hours when we got there, but the state of decay in which he was would lead you to believe that he had been dead for at least thirty hours, although, of course, decay sets in very rapidly there. His whole right hand was crunched up and mashed as if the componte, or at least a very crushing torture, had been used.

Q. That is a mode of torture used?—A. Yes, sir; I have never seen it.

Q. You say the hand was crushed. In what way?—A. The hand was out of shape. I have seen a man very badly hurt at football or crushed by a horse, and it was something like that, crushed up together [illustrating], but it was hard to get at its condition exactly, owing to the state of mortification; but it was not all mortification, because the other hand was perfect. The forearm of the right arm, the arm with which a man would naturally defend himself from blows, was all marked with welts. They were bruises like those received in single stick without a basket, the same kind of welts that would be received from blows made from a hickory stick. Dr. Burgess examined his head very carefully. Ruiz was a man of long black hair. Right at the top——

Q. What we call the crown?—A. Yes, sir. Dr. Burgess shaved the hair away, and there was disclosed a wound about an inch and a half long and about three-quarters of an inch across. This wound was a severe one, but had not fractured the skull.

Q. Did it cut the scalp?—A. Yes, sir; the bone was laid bare, but the bone was not fractured.. The investigation showed that he had died from concussion of the brain, caused by the impact of this blow.

Q. Did Dr. Burgess make a declaration to this effect in the presence of the Spanish officials?—A. I do not think that he made any statement whatever. They brought out a long written statement they wanted Dr. Burgess to sign (Dr. Burgess and Mr. Lee), and they would not sign it.

Q. To what did that statement attribute his death?—A. To accident; that he had died; met death at his own hands, or something of that kind. Neither Dr. Burgess nor General Lee would sign any statement at all, and the Spanish officials were very much displeased with that. We went to see the widow, General Lee and myself and various other people, including the brother-in-law, to get all the information we could as to the circumstances of the case. There were a great many stories, some of which reached General Lee entirely through Spanish sources. This man had married into a Spanish family. His wife was a Catalan, and all her relatives were Spanish, and there were various stories from them describing how this man had been murdered in his cell, I do not know whether true or not; but it seems to me that the stand taken by General Lee on the matter was a proper one, and that stand was that whether the man met his death at the hands of one of his jailors or, after being subjected to this treatment for fifteen days, he went mad and killed himself, it was all murder.

Q. What was this governor's name?—A. Fondaviela.

Q. These prisoners fixed the hour, the time of Ruiz's death, by the cessation of his cries?—A. Yes, sir.

Q. Did they say anything to you as to whether, on the night before his cries ceased, these Spanish officers went to his cell?—A. Yes, sir.

Q. Who were with him?—A. Fondaviela, and the alcalde, Marury, and several jailers.

Q. What did they say to you, if anything, as to hearing the sound of blows or cries from Ruiz after these men went to his cell?—A. They stated that they did hear cries which lasted up to 11 o'clock, and they said that he was evidently being tortured in a terrible way.

Q. Did they say whether the cries ceased gradually or suddenly?—A. They did not say.

Q. Did they see these Spanish officials come out that night?—A. They were not able to see them either go in or come out of the cell; they saw them go down the passageway and come out of that passageway about 11 o'clock at night; they could not see them enter the cell itself.

Q. Did they overhear any conversation?—A. They did not.

By Mr. MORGAN:

Q. You did not have an opportunity of seeing the cell in which Ruiz died?—A. I saw it through an opening.

Q. You did not see it distinctly?—A. I could not see as to the exact measurements; I could see that the floor of the cell was covered with human excrement, and it was in the same condition when he spent fifteen days in it.

Q. When you saw the body, it was in one of the larger cells, and was carried from there to the city hall?—A. Yes, sir; to the city hall building.

Q. Was the body dressed for burial when you saw it in the larger cell?—A. Yes, sir.

Q. Do you know who did that?—A. His wife sent around a suit of clothes for her husband, but, as she met a man walking on the streets the next day wearing this suit of clothes, she concluded that her husband was not buried in them.

Q. Was Madam Ruiz at the autopsy?—A. No, sir.

Q. Did you see anything of the piece of furniture spoken of, which she sent to him—a chair?—A. Yes, sir.

Q. Did you examine it?—A. Yes, sir; very carefully.

Q. Did you see an inscription on it?—A. Yes, sir.

Q. What was it?—A. It was a long inscription, about eight or nine lines long. It was about this: "Good by, Rita," that is the name of his wife. He then mentioned the names of his five children, good-bye to each one of those. He said: "Be obedient to your mother," and then there was a very curious expression nobody understood. "If they take me to Havana, tell all." Then the last word: "Me maten"—they are killing me. That was the last word of one of the last sentences. It was a long inscription. It was on the seat of something like a summer chair, that had a soft, thick varnish, and all around this and the arm the man had cut it with his finger nails. It began on the right side and ran all around the rim. I understand it is at the State Department now. I saw it in the consulate-general at Havana.

Q. Where did you first see it?—A. At the consulate-general's.

Q. You did not see it on the day of the autopsy?—A. No, sir; the jailer had a very kind hearted wife, and she had taken pity on the condition of this prisoner, who could not sit down or lie down except in his own filth, and who was so patient in it all. Mrs. Ruiz had come to see her husband several times, but was never allowed to see him, and one day she asked her to slip a chair in to him, and this was the way this chair was got in, on the thirteenth day of his imprisonment, and probably in the intervals of his torture he had written these words with his fingers.

Q. Any question raised in the autopsy, in the presence of the Spanish officials, as to whether he had been incommunicado during all the time of his imprisonment?—A. It was never denied; it was admitted. Fondavielas said so, Marury said so, the jailer said so. They did not begin to deny that that morning; they had not well schooled Dr. Vidal when he came in. He was over at the military hospital when he was sent for, and when he came into the large, well-lighted, spacious hall he said: "You have brought him in here, have you?" He had not then been well instructed that the Spanish contention was to be that he had been in that cell during all the course of his imprisonment.

Q. Are the executions of the prisoners at Morro Castle and elsewhere frequent?—A. The shootings?

Q. Yes, sir.—A. They are very frequent; I have seen many at the fortress of San Severino, at Matanzas, from a distance; I went to one, was as close as to you, at Havana; I felt it my duty to go and see one of the poor boys shot in the laurel ditches there at Havana; the others I saw were from a distance, and because I could not help seeing them; the lists are kept in the fortresses publicly, and anybody can go—thousands do go. In Havana, all through the early spring, certainly the average of executions was more than a man a day. Many of the mornings four or more were killed. This morning that I went a man told me a Spaniard said there would certainly be either a shooting or a garroting, both or either of which he thought would be interesting, and so I went.

Q. Is there anything further you wish to add?—A. No, sir.

The foregoing is a correct transcript of my testimony, given before the subcommittee of the Senate Foreign Relations Committee on June 11, 1897.

STEPHEN BONSAL.

NEW YORK, *June 22.*

STATEMENT OF DR. F. R. WINN ON THE 21ST DAY OF JUNE, 1897.

Dr. WINN was sworn by Senator MORGAN.

By Mr. MORGAN:

Q. What is your name, age, and place of residence?—A. F. R. Winn; residence, Sherman, Tex.

Q. What is your profession?—A. Doctor—physician.

Q. Have you been in Cuba recently?—A. Yes, sir.

Q. When did you return from there?—A. I returned on last Wednesday.

Q. Are you a surgeon in the Cuban army?—A. Yes, sir.

Q. What is your rank?—A. Captain.

Q. When were you made a captain in the Cuban army?—A. The 18th of April.

Q. Of the present year?—A. Yes, sir.

Q. Had you been with that army before that time?—A. No, sir.

Q. From what point did you go to join the army?—A. Havana.

Q. Havana?—A. Yes, sir.

Q. Where is your place of residence?—A. Sherman, Tex.

Q. When you first went to the army, with whom did you connect yourself as surgeon?—A. General Castillo.

Q. Where was he?—A. At the time he was near Managua.

Q. In what province?—A. Havana.

Q. Since that time with whom have you served in that capacity?—A. With——

Q. Sir?—A. I was head of the capitan de sanidad, chief of the sanitary corps. I was made chief of the sanitary corps.

Q. A place in independent command of the sanitary corps?—A. Yes, sir.

Q. Of the entire army?—A. Oh, no; of that province.

Q. To whom do you report as chief of the sanitary corps?—A. No one.

Q. From whom do you take orders?—A. From the chief of province.

Q. The chief medical director?—A. No, sir; the chief of the army.

Q. Of the province?—A. Yes, sir.

Q. Since you have been in the army as surgeon, have you been with General Gomez?—A. No, sir.

Q. Have you seen him?—A. No, sir.

Q. You were only with General Castillo?—A. I was with the sanitary corps; I did not go with the general at all unless it was on some commission or at his request. I would go with him to some part of the province in anticipation of a fight, to be close to where he expected wounded men. He would ask me to go to the field, but otherwise I would spend my time visiting the hospitals.

Q. In what province have you been since you have been in Cuba?— A. Havana province all the time, except three days when I crossed the trocha into Pinar del Rio.

Q. What arrangements have the Cuban insurgents in respect to hospital service?—A. The Cuban hospital is a patch of brush—which in that country is very scarce; there is no uncultivated country—and their wounded men are carried after the battle, or a man who is unable to mount his horse from sickness, is carried into this brush, and for each man unable to use himself we must have two nurses, two men to carry him, in case of an invasion by the Spanish army. I had six of these hospitals under my personal supervision, and I moved them about fifteen times in about twenty days, making an average of about a day and a half for each position for hospital. The Spaniards would come to a hospital and they would machete everybody they caught, nurses, wounded, sick, doctors, or anybody else, and on that account they would have to break up and get out of there, and they would get into the brush and hide until night, and then sneak away to another brush hospital, and remain there until the Spanish invaded that brush, and then go back to the other brush, and so on.

Q. How did you get any hospital supplies to provide for these establishments there?—A. In every way possible. They send some supplies on expedition, but it was very little. I do not remember having seen any quinine among the medicines sent on expeditions, but I did receive some disinfectants, bichloride of mercury, and some bandages. I bought most of my supplies from the town, my chloroform, instruments, and everything of that sort.

Q. How did you get access to the town to make these purchases?— A. I would have a man in commission near the town, and the concentrados would come out after sweet potatoes, and the insurgents regard the sweet potatoes as belonging to them and do not allow them to be carried into the town without the tax being paid. Those we could trust we allowed to carry sweet potatoes in and had them in our service, and furnished them money to buy medicine.

Q. They would smuggle it out to you?—A. Yes, sir.

Q. Is there any prohibition against furnishing you medicine on the part of the Spanish?—A. Yes, sir; it is much more difficult to get medicine than it is to get ammunition or arms. You can buy a rifle or ammunition at any time, the soldiers sell them, but the medicine is sold in the drug store, and no one is allowed to buy medicine without a doctor's prescription, and the doctors are usually in the Spanish Government in the towns.

Q. What about the strength of the insurgent forces in the part of the territory you have been in?—A. Some time early in May the Herald correspondent at Havana sent a question to that effect to General Castillo, which he asked me to answer to the Herald correspondent. The general sent his chief of staff with the records to my hospital at Menocal, and at the same time furnished me with an escort and placed an officer at my disposal to visit all the offices in the province and get their records, and I copied from them, and with all the reports from the offices I sent to I summed up 4,700 men armed and in operation, and we estimated the recruits from all sources were equal to the losses from all sources, and in that report I had then there were 4,700 men armed and present.

Q. In that department?—A. Yes, sir. That excluded those in hospitals and those in commissions, collecting taxes, etc.

Q. Are those troops well provided with subsistence and clothes?—A. Well provided with subsistence—that is, healthy, plain nourishment, sweet potatoes, beef chicken, salt—but very poorly clothed, because they are a people that had never been in the habit of wearing much clothing, usually only an undershirt and a pair of trousers; in fact, I was well treated with a shirt and pair of trousers myself, but it is possible for a man to dress as well as he likes to if he has money.

Q. What arrangements, in the province you have been in—Havana, I believe you say—if any, for the manufacturs of shoes or clothing by the Cubans?—A. None at all. The province is so small and the country so open there is no place to hide, and to establish any factory of that kind it would be necessary to put the whole force around it to guard it, and Spain is able to send 10,000 men to any point at any time. The towns are only a mile apart, or 2 miles at the most, and it is much easier to buy from the towns, and we do that altogether.

Q. Have you seen any factories or establishments of any kind in Cuba for the manufacture of shoes or clothing in any part of the island you have been to?—A. No, sir.

Q. Do you know, by common reputation, whether such establishments exist?—A. Yes, sir; in the eastern part of the island, and down as near as Santa Clara, the Cubans manufacture saddles and these pouches in which they carry ammunition, etc., and secretaries' pouches, shoes, and most anything they want.

Q. Havana Province, then, is one that is open and has a number of towns in it?—A. Yes, sir; it is the smallest Province in the island. You can ride across it either way in a day, easily.

Q. Has it a heavy rural population outside of the towns?—A. It has had before the war, but not now.

Q. Why?—A. They have concentrated in the towns until the radius of concentration in the little towns out there is not more than—well, in the largest towns outside of Havana the radius of concentration is not more than a mile.

Q. How much?—A. A mile. They have concentrated, outside of the city of Havana, about 80,000 paisanos—farmers.

By Mr. CLARK:

Q. About how many?—A. Eighty thousand.

By Mr. MORGAN:

Q. Does that cover the whole province, or one locality?—A. The whole province.

Q. In the province of Havana the concentrados number about 80,000?—A. Yes, sir; outside of the city.

Q. What class of people constitute these concentrados?—A. Small farmers, renters, what we would call in this country, I suppose, tenant farmers; a good many storekeepers. Out there they have these small stores scattered all over the country. It is a very old country, and near the sugar plantations or in the thickly settled community they would have five or six of these small grocery stores to sell groceries, small articles, and drinks, etc.—to sell everything; and those people have been scattered and their stores burned. They are loyal; but the greater part of the concentrados are little farmers who were unable to get out of the island, and did not care to join the insurgents, and wanted to get to town; lived in bad houses, which the Spaniards burned. The Spaniards burned all these houses, all the wooden houses.

Q. Was that generally through the Province of Havana, the burning of houses of the common people?—A. Complete; all burnt; none left standing.

Q. None at all?—A. None at all; not a house left standing outside of the fortification.

Q. Have you been about these concentration settlements after the people had been concentrated?—A. No, sir; but I have seen them. They come out for sweet potatoes.

Q. You have not been among them?—A. Yes, sir; about twelve hours, while coming into Havana.

Q. Describe them as to health, means of subsistence, shelter, clothing, etc.—A. They have no way of earning a living. If they care to take the fruits which grow inside the concentrated lines to town to sell they must pay the Spanish officers half they receive; if they take the sweet potatoes in the field they must pay a tax on them and then sell them and pay the Spanish officers half; and, consequently, they are not able to earn a livelihood. They are lucky if they get enough to eat, and very few of them do get enough to eat. Those who are in better circumstances, who have enough money and are not in sympathy with the insurrection, who carried in the cattle with them, live along, kill one of the cattle once in a while, and sometimes a hog, and live better than the Cubans, and manage to get along. The Cubans who are concentrated are not able to earn anything. They left their cattle in the fields and were not able to bring in anything. They were ordered to town immediately, their house was burnt, and they lost everything. You can build a house in any part of the island—you can build it in fifteen or twenty minutes.

Q. What sort of a house is that?—A. It amounts to about as much as a tent in America. It is a palm-leaf hut; it is dry—keeps out the water. Concentrated line will be strung out about these towns under the command of one general. Another general will come to town and say, "This line is too big; you have too much communication with the insurgents; come in here; make the lines smaller" Then they burn the houses again and move them in closer. In a month or so another general will come to town, and he will say, "The people are too many here; the lines are too close; there is too much disease," and he will move them out. In another month or so another general will come to town, and he will move them in again, and consequently they are kept constantly moving. Disease is very rife; they die fast, are killed by the soldiers, exposed to all sorts of indignities, have very little to eat, and no clothes, and consequently are in very bad condition.

Q. You speak of sweet potatoes. Do they cultivate them themselves or are they native growth?—A. No; the potatoes in the province have been planted by people who lived there before the concentration, but the crops continue. The rainy season has come now, and it will rot the crop; but as soon as the rain is over they will spring up again, almost as good as the other crop.

Q. Does that continue without intermission?—A. Yes, sir. The yucca does not rot; that continues to grow, anyhow.

Q. Is that about what these people have to subsist on, what they get out of the earth?—A. Yes, sir; and fruits.

Q. What is the effect (you are a physician and you saw the people—you say you came through their lines) on their health and general condition?—A. It is terrible.

Q. In what regard?—A. They are without food, without any means of earning a livelihood, and they have absolutely nothing to do but to stay inside the lines and sleep about like so many cattle concentrated in the pens; consequently when disease strikes a household they go, one after another, until all are dead.

Q. The mortality is great?—A. Yes, sir.

Q. Can you identify, from personal knowledge any of that mortality as from starvation?—A. I do not know that I could say that any had actually starved to death, but I have seen, in a house the size of this room, twenty sick people.

Q. What disease?—A. Fever, malaria, and what they call peludica and chagres—I do not think it exists in this country—and the other diseases to which the Cubans are subject, smallpox—no yellow fever; Cubans do not have yellow fever. You might say smallpox, dysentery, and malaria.

Q. Do you mean a native Cuban does not have yellow fever?—A. Well, take a Cuban out of the mountains and bring him down into the bottoms, to a settlement where malaria and yellow fever are rank, and it is possible he may have it, but as a general thing native Cubans are inured to yellow fever; they do not have it.

Q. Are these other diseases largely fatal?—A. Yes, sir; malaria is one of the most fatal diseases where it is allowed to run its course, as they do where they have no money to buy quinine. It is not if it is checked by the use of quinine.

Q. Are these little palm-leaf huts furnished with any furniture or conveniences for living?—A. No, sir. Some have a chair—you can get a chair pretty near any place in the island. I could camp any place in the Province and have a chair to sit down on in five minutes. The whole island is strewn with chairs, sewing machines, tables, and household articles, etc.

Q. Broken out of the houses?—A. Yes, sir. These concentrados can not come out for them, and they make their chairs and provide the houses pretty well.

Q. By whom has this wreck of the houses been conducted and carried on?—A. The large stone houses, of which there were a good many in that Province—the wealthy people's houses—were destroyed by the insurgents, as they regarded them as possible fortifications for the Spanish army. The little wooden houses, the small houses, were destroyed by the Spaniards.

Q. You speak about the hospitals in Cuba having been invaded by the Spaniards—the Cuban hospitals. Have you any personal knowledge of such raids?—A. Yes, sir; a good deal of it.

Q. Proceed to tell the instances, as near as you can the dates, of these different cases?—A. The first invasion I remember, that I had anything to do with, was about the 1st of May. I had established an emergency hospital in a place called El Ojo de Agua, near Managua.

Q. One of these brush hospitals?—A. Yes, sir; alongside the mountain——

Q. You mean you had constructed your hospital house out of the palm you have just been mentioning. Is that the way you constructed these brush hospitals?—A. Usually we just get into the brush and lie on the ground. When the Spanish invade hospitals you have not the time to carry away hammocks and fixtures, and it takes two or three days to get out and get the leaves and bring them into the brush. You must let the leaves fall, for you can not climb the tree, and before you have time to construct your house you must move.

By Mr. CLARK:

Q. Your hospital is simply a location in a brush?—A. Yes, sir. If we are allowed to stay forty-eight hours, we will have some houses; if we have to move earlier than that, we will not.

This first place I thought was a very safe place. I do not think I would have gone in there at the head of an army myself. I only had an emergency hospital there. It was close to where the forces were operating, and the other hospitals were rife with infectious disease, and I wanted an acute surgical hospital, and to avoid infection and get better results I established this hospital, and had received about fifteen patients and about twenty-five visiting patients—men wounded in the arm, leg, or anywhere, and unable to fight. Men will not go to the hospital as long as they are able to walk. Coming quite often, they made big trails, and one morning I got up—I slept in the brush out in the wood; I never slept in the open—I came down and I saw about ten or fifteen wounded men on the floor, and I asked where there had been a battle. They said the hospital at Menocal had been invaded and these men had come from there. I dressed the people—they had old and suppurating wounds that had never been dressed, any of them, but I dressed all their wounds and attended to them and my people, and about 12 o'clock had them very comfortably located. About 12 o'clock there began to come in more patients, and they told me they came from Lastre; the hospital had been invaded the day before. That was established about 7 or 8 miles from there. By night they began to come in from a place called La Lona de Santa Barbara. I had about that time sixty-five patients, wounded men unable to walk. I did not like it much, and I sent out word to the other hospitals to stay away from me, as I did not want to get that hospital full of infection, and I would visit at their places. The next morning at daybreak the soldiers were in the hospital. I did not have any armed men; I had arms myself which I proposed to use to protect my own life on any man I had to deal with. About 4 o'clock the soldiers from Managua, about a quarter of a mile or perhaps half a mile, came right on this place. We could see them from the woods, and the men began to pick up their patients and carry them out. They got them all hid in safe places in the brush, but the soldiers went through and destroyed everything they found, hammocks, etc., but did not catch anybody to kill. By night I had them back again, and worked on them to get them in shape once more, but the next morning the soldiers were on us again, and they surprised us this time, as we did not expect the second invasion on the same day, and they caught four men and killed them. I had the men scattered around then, had them there hid, and told them I would have men carry out sweet potatoes to them at night and I would dress their wounds in the daytime and try to make the rounds. I started out the next day and got around to see nearly all my patients. The next day I started back, and I would find an empty hammock and a dead man macheted, and where I left the patient alive and wounds dressed, I would find a dead man, some from the effects of their wounds or some from typhoid fever— I had four cases of typhoid fever. I was about eight days making my rounds, with very little to eat myself, as I could not make a fire in the daytime. I had one patient, a man over at La Loma de Santa Barbar, of which I was very fond, and I went over to see him. I got over about dark and found him macheted. I hung up my hammock near where he was killed and told the men to bury him; and they started to bury him, and up came a little boy, and he said that if we were burying people his father and mother had been killed, too, and to bury them; and he took us over and showed the father and mother and another young man, and I told the men to bury them, and the boy said there were others, and if we were burying them we might as well bury them, too, and I told the men to stop their burying then. I got up in the morning and found they had killed my patient and twelve pacificos, among them three women and two children—I would say babes—about this long [indicating], if the pieces were properly put together. They had been held up by the legs this way, and split down with the machete. They looked to be about 25 or 30 inches long, about a year old. I had them all buried and took the little boy with us—took him away from there. The boy told us about it, but he could not make a clean explanation to me, as I could not speak Spanish well enough to understand, and my men could not speak English. A day or two later my interpreter, who had been on a commission with General Castillo, came and I had the boy tell his story. He said Pizarao's men had seen the smoke from their fire and gone in to investigate, and had come upon the wounded man who was alone, and they told the wounded man they were going to take him to town. They rolled the hammock up and were going to make him go to town by using a crutch, and seemed kindly disposed—seemed to want to take the man to town by killing him. About the time they were ready to start, up came the pacificos with these two men—and the two men had a cup of coffee they had been to make for the wounded man—and the man in command stepped up to take the coffee which they had brought, but they handed it past him to the patient, and as they did that he threw out his sword and killed the patient; and by this time the soldiers had killed the two men and then they killed the others.

Q. Was this work done by guerrillas or regular Spanish troops?—A. By a detachment from Pizarao's regiment. Pizarao's cavalry is the regiment Spain expected to crush the revolution.

Q. An old organization?—A. Yes, sir; and the best regiment on the island in every respect.

Q. Have you seen prisoners taken by the troops of the officers with whose command you have been serving—Spanish prisoners?—A. Yes, sir.

Q. Tell what treatment they received at the hands of the Cubans?—A. All the Spanish prisoners I saw with the exception of two were wounded men, and they were turned over to me and received the same treatment the Cubans did.

Q. You speak of two who were exceptions; what was done with them?—A. They enlisted in the Cuban army and made brave fighters, but before I left were both disabled for life, wounded. They were also from Pizarao's regiment.

Q. Has there been much desertion from the Spanish army to the Cuban forces?—A. Yes, sir; and always propositions to desert, which the Cubans reject, as these men do not make good fighters ordinarily. They must know something of the man, about his record and the regiment to which he belongs, before they will take him.

Q. When deserters come in not diposed to take arms on the Cuban side, what becomes of them?—A. If they bring arms with them, they are allowed to remain; their arms given to the soldiers. If without arms, they are sent back to town.

Q. Is there any considerable number of Cubans in the Province of Havana, where you have been chiefly, that are ready to take up arms in behalf of Cuba—in behalf of the Republic—when they can get the proper equipment, guns, etc.?—A. I would say I know personally that

jt is so. In my visits around there, I found that there were concentrated round about the hospitals about 1,200 or 1,400 men who had
promised to take arms when they are furnished with them, and
expressed a willingness to do so; but whether or not they would, must
be decided when the arms come.

Q. Are the Cubans attempting to raise any crops in the province of
Havana?—A. No, sir.

Q. Where do they get their supplies from?—A. From the crops
already planted. They have never been out of provisions, yuccas, yams,
etc.

Q. They are not cultivating now?—A. There is too much cultivated
now.

Q. You are getting supplies from the places where the houses were
burnt and the crops left standing?—A. Yes, sir.

Q. An abundant supply?—A. Yes, sir.

Q. How about the cattle; plenty of it?—A. Yes, sir; plenty of cattle;
but at the present rate I think they will use up the cattle outside the
lines in the next seven or eight months, when they will have to go
inside the lines and drive out those there.

Q. What do you call the "lines?" You mean in the towns where the
troops are stationed, or is there a dividing line?—A. We call the line
of concentration around the towns the lines.

Q. How are these men armed, the forces you have been operating
with?—A. With Remington rifles, machetes, revolvers, and some
Mausers.

Q. Mounted, usually?—A. Yes, sir; all the force I saw was mounted.
There was a force of infantry in the province, where I never saw them.

Q. Have you witnessed any operations of what is called, or is, the
civil government in Cuba under the Republic?—A. No; with the exception of the collection of taxes under the management of prefecturas.

Q. By whom are the taxes collected?—A. The first of each month
each regiment is ordered to place so many men in commission to collect
taxes in his territory. That force is changed each month; they relieve
the men the first day of each month.

Q. Do they collect the taxes?—A. Yes, sir.

Q. From whom?—A. From the railroad companies, from the plantations still running, and from charging a tariff on everything that goes
into the town.

Q. They charge export duty?—A. Yes, sir.

Q. They permit food to go into the towns if they will pay the
tariff?—A. Yes, sir. If they have plenty of fruit in that province.
In some places they are not allowed to accept a tariff on fruit, because
the fruit is scarce in that territory. In others they can sell as much as
they please.

Q. Are they allowed to carry in poultry, etc.?—A. No, sir.

Q. Just fruits and vegetables?—A. Yes, sir.

Q. Tell us about the spirit of the soldiery down there on the Cuban
side; whether coerced to fight, or whether they fight willingly?—A. The
men who live in Cuba libre are men who fight for the country. They
say they will fight until they die, or live always in Cuba libre; they
do not propose to live under the Spanish Government. The Spaniards
talk of autonomy, and the soldiers wonder what they mean. They say
"What do we want with autonomy? We have autonomy here; we live
in Cuba libre. If the Spaniards want autonomy, they might autonomize their own army." They read in the papers sometimes that there
is talk of Spain selling Cuba to the Junta, or that the Junta wants to

buy the island from Spain. They are not men who want to surrender or pay a cent for their independence, and they protest that the Junta has no right to pay for independence. They say: "We have fought for independence and Spain must necessarily, sooner or later, leave the island. They are afraid to send their soldiers down to fight us; let them autonomize their own forces, but we will live in Cuba libre."

Q. That is the spirit with which they meet these propositions?—A. There is not a man in the army—fighting men—who wants to surrender; there are some who are not soldiers and never will be soldiers in any army—presentados.

By Mr. CLARK:

Q. What do you call them?—A. Presentados, surrendered people. You can pick up a paper and see a list of surrendered men who have come into the Spanish forces and surrendered. They are people who came to America, ran away from Cuba to America, and came to the Junta and were a charge on the Junta, and to get them off their hands they sent them back to the insurgent lines. For the most part they were young men who lived in Havana; dudes, as we would call them here; some bachelors, with a diploma from a college. They would come back to Cuba with their diplomas and call themselves captains, majors, and colonels, and they would come up and represent themselves to the men who have been fighting in the field for two years, and they would say, "We come from the Junta, and you get us a horse and a negro and we want commands in the army," and the officers would say, "You get yourself a horse and a negro, if you want them, and get to fighting," and they would fight for a day or two, and then slip into the brush and wait their chance to come into the Spanish lines. There is another class of presentados called maja, who are in the woods. They took to the woods when the orders of concentration came. They are supposed to be there to fight when arms are sent to them. When arms are furnished them, they are ordered to the force to fight. About 40 per cent of them sneak into the first town and surrender. They will not surrender until they have a gun, but when they have a gun it is a sort of guaranty for them. That is another kind of presentados.

Q. The men in the ranks—you have seen them in battle?—A. Yes, sir.

Q. Often?—A. Every day.

Q. They were fighting every day?—A. Yes, sir.

Q. You mean that the Cuban army in Havana Province is actively engaged in carrying on the war?—A. There was not a day, between daylight and dark, when I could not hear the guns going, or if I was out marching, going to my hospitals, that I could not see more or less fighting.

Q. Do they fight with courage and spirit?—A. I will have to explain something of the situation there. You know each man, each colonel of a regiment, is given a territory to keep, and he must keep that territory at all cost, at any expense stay in it and keep the Spanish soldiers out of it. The Spanish soldiers never operate unless in a column, about 1,200 men, and most of the time a combination of other columns. For instance, there will be a column·spread out from a town here and another town here, and a town here and another town here, all in sight of each other. Here, now, is the colonel's territory, an insurgent colonel, and he is supposed to keep that. In every one of those towns is a volunteer guard and guerillas, and every night they will camp the column of soldiers who have been operating in the hospitals in one of these towns. Every time when they decide to prosecute a vigorous campaign they will try to catch this colonel. If he has 400 men he will have them divided into squads, one here, another here, and another there, and so on, and they have it arranged that if a column comes out and starts a fight another column can come out quickly and capture the insurgents, and when these columns are operating the insurgents march around and try to avoid wasting any ammunition—they march around and try to evade the soldiers. They will chase them around for two or three days and then let up. Maybe another leader will adopt different tactics, and he will send out a column here and another there, and they will split up into columns of 300 or 400 men each. Every morning we know what they are going to do. We have commissions in the town, and every night they send out word from these different towns. If word comes that small groups are coming to catch us, for instance, when these small columns come in sight the colonel will move off, leaving a small guard to attack this column and another guard to attack this column, and another guard for another column, and we will chase them around until we get them into different places, and then the force will reconcentrate and give them the machete, and so we can, in two or three hours, catch the whole batch and machete them.

Q. The first point is to break up the organization of the Spaniards by attacking in different directions?—A. Yes, sir.

Q. When that is done, the Cubans reconcentrate and attack the small parties?—A. Yes, sir; it would be folly to stop and make a pitched battle; it would be suicide.

Q. Does this general with whom you are serving have any artillery?—A. No, sir.

Q. Nearly all mounted?—A. Alexander Rodriguez, chief of the province, had artillery. General Castillo was brigadier-general and commanded the central and western divisions of the province.

Q. Rodriguez had artillery?—A. Yes, sir.

Q. Were you with him at all?—A. I met him twice.

Q. What was about the strength of Rodriguez's command altogether?—A. Rodriguez's command was the whole province.

Q. And you have already stated that?—A. Yes, sir; he operates, himself, with a personal escort of a regiment, between 350 and 400 men.

Q. The real point in the tactics of the Cubans was to avoid general engagements and harass the enemy when they could get to him?—A. Yes, sir; to fight cavalry always, but infantry it is hard to fight without making a pitched battle. They fight cavalry always.

Q. Wherever they meet it?—A. Yes, sir; but when the soldiers come out they are not very troublesome. For instance, they will come out of a town and march in sight of the insurgents and open fire. They are not in a distance to hurt and the insurgents do not care much, and they stay there. The Spaniards stand there half a day and shoot away and then go back to town. It is only occasionally they get troublesome.

Q. When the Spaniards are out on these forays or strategic movements, do they carry any provision trains with them?—A. No, sir; always go back to town to camp.

Q. How is the Spanish army subsisting; do they have depots of provisions?—A. I don't know much about that; I am not able to say, as I was on the other side. I never saw them in the field with anything to eat. They always go to the nearest town at 5 o'clock to camp, and if they do not like their food they throw it away and send word to us to let them come out and fight, if they will feed them, and the insurgents tell them to go back and starve to death and then Spain will take them home.

Q. How did you get away from there when you left to come here?—A. Through Havana.

Q. In disguise, I suppose?—A. No, sir; dressed like I am now; just the same.

Q. Anybody arrest you, or attempt it?—A. No, sir.

Q. Why did they not? They had opportunities, I suppose?—A. They thought I was dead, in the first place, and did not know me, anyway. They knew me at the palace, but I didn't go to the palace.

Q. Had you contrived to leave the impression that you were dead?—A. No, sir; it was accidental that they thought I was dead. They had all my papers at the palace; have them yet, and reported so from the palace. Those who were on the inside got the news of my death from the palace and sent it to the States. A friend of mine knew I was not dead, but he was afraid to correct the impression, for fear it might injure me, and also him.

Q. Have you ever been engaged in any military operations, except as a surgeon, with arms in your hands?—A. I always carried arms.

Q. Have you ever engaged in battle?—A. Only when necessary to cut my way through.

Q. Never been regarded as a soldier?—A. No, sir.

Q. You were not a regularly enlisted man?—A. No, sir; a volunteer.

Q. Volunteered as a surgeon?—A. Yes, sir.

Q. From your rank as a surgeon and the fact that you were only employed in that benevolent work, would the Spaniards have killed you if caught?—A. They sent me word to that effect; in fact, the same colonel that took my clothes and papers to the palace and reported me dead had sent word that I was a rebel, and his policy was to kill all rebels, and if I ever fell into his hands he would kill me, and for me not to attempt to bribe him with a cup of chocolate. I had sent him a cup of chocolate, of which I had some, into the town by a pacifico woman.

Q. How did you get that chocolate?—A. Bought it.

Q. Do they raise anything of the kind in the island?—A. No, sir; I bought it in the town.

Q. Is it the product of the cocoa bean?—A. I do not know; in fact, I never paid much attention to chocolate or cared for it until I went there.

Q. Does coffee grow there?—A. Yes, sir.

Q. Abundantly?—A. No, sir.

Q. Cultivated or wild?—A. Wild.

Q. Is it a good berry for food?—A. Very good. It is about all used up when I got there. I never saw any of it growing, but I stopped one night at a prefectura and the men were all cleaning coffee, and that night I had some, and they gave me 2 or 3 pounds of it, and I carried it in my pocket and used it.

Q. The Cuban army is all supplied from the country?—A. They do not have much coffee, and what they usually have is bad.

Q. The coffee is grown in the country?—A. No, sir; I do not think it is. There would be no necessity to buy it if grown in the country.

Q. Are there any districts where the coffee grows wild, or are there coffee plantations?—A. There are coffee plantations in the other parts of the island—in the other provinces, but not in Havana.

Q. Do you get your supply from the other parts of the island, or from Havana, or from the towns?—A. We buy it in the towns. The chiefs only have coffee; it is very seldom soldiers have any.

Q. In Havana province?—A. Yes, sir. Sometimes the friends will send some out from the town.

Q. It is a sugar district?—A. Yes, sir; the finest plantations, I reckon, on the island.

Q. Is the cane destroyed?—A. The Spaniards destroyed a great deal of cane, but they do not know how to destroy cane, and consequently it grows up again. You can get plenty of cane to eat, if you want to cut it down.

Q. Do they give it to their horses?—A. Horses will eat it, but I don't think it is very good for a horse.

Q. Is forage abundant to support the horses of the Cubans?—A. Oh, yes.

Q. What kind?—A. We have had plenty of corn until now, and I think the corn will last, maybe, the rest of this month, until the rainy season comes; after a rainy season the corn will grow up again in two or three months, and until then they will eat the grass.

Q. There is plenty of that?—A. Yes, sir.

Q. A good grass country?—A. Yes, sir.

Q. Do they make hay of it?—A. Yes, sir.

Q. Is it very abundant?—A. Yes, sir; and as good as it is here; it will grow as high as on the prairie; the grass will grow there in the trails or anywhere else.

Q. Are these engagements you have been speaking about, and which you saw the troops at war with each other, in the vicinity of towns and villages?—A. Yes, sir; very hard to be away from the vicinities of towns and villages in Havana Province; always in sight of a town.

Q. Always?—A. Yes, sir; I could see a town any time I was in the war by walking to any little elevation, and it was never more than a mile to some town.

Q. Take the great body of the Cuban people of all classes—I mean, now, those in the country you have visited and see yourself—are they in favor of fighting for their liberty, or are they opposed to it or indifferent to it?—A. In favor of fighting for it.

Q. Is that a determined spirit, as you understand it—a determined and well-settled purpose on their part?—A. Yes, sir.

Q. You spoke about the collection of taxes, and said something, also, about the civil government. In what other respect besides the collection of taxes does the civil government operate among the Cuban insurgents?—A. The Cuban government really has no operation except in the prefecturas, and the captain of the prefecturas is the chief. The laws of the civil government are executed there, but there is no law necessary. The military government is all that is necessary, as there are no families living there, no farms in operation; everything must be under military command. But the taxes are turned in to the civil governor of the province.

Q. Are they judicial officers or merely executive officers?—A. Both.

Q. Are there any exclusively judicial offices?—A. No, sir.

Q. You speak of the taxes?—A. That goes to the civil government—that is, what is not paid to the soldiers. On the 1st day of May and the 1st day of June each soldier got a gold centime.

Q. How much is that?—A. $5.30.

Q. Paid the 1st of June and the 1st of May?—A. Yes, sir.

Q. Paid for wages?—A. No, sir; it was given to them; they are not fighting for wages.

Q. That was a present?—A. Yes, sir; it was given them to buy whatever they wanted—cigarettes, hat, pair of shoes, or anything they wanted.

Q. Are rations served to them?—A. No, sir; each man provides his own rations. They eat together in messes, and one man provides beef, and another salt, and another sweet potatoes; each whatever they have.

Q. They make up a fund and buy it?—A. They don't have to buy it; they dig it up.

Q. How about the beef?—A. When they kill a beef, the chief stands there and the beef is cut up and divided among them, and he superintends the division of the beef.

Q. Isn't that a ration?—A. Yes, sir.

Q. The Cuban government really supplies everything except what is dug up by the messes?—A. Yes, sir.

Q. What is the system of communication between the different parts of the island?—A. What they call a commission. One chief wants to communicate with another, and he gives a man an escort and puts him in commission, and sends him to the other.

Q. Is there any postal system in Havana Province?—A. The commission when he goes carries letters, but they don't care much about writing.

Q. Suppose he wants those letters taken to a far-distant point, to the eastern or western part of the island, is there any postal system for that?—A. There is always a commission between the east and the west.

Q. Really a mail service?—A. The reports from the subchiefs to the chiefs and the general chief, and the return orders from the general to the chiefs and the subchiefs are sent in that way.

Q. You spoke of being in Pinar del Rio—how far did you penetrate in that province?—A. I do not know how far it was, because it is hard to estimate distances, traveling the way we did. We could not go in direct lines, as we had to avoid the town. At the time we were on commission and rode three days into Pinar del Rio, but it is hard to say how far we went.

Q. Were you executing commission then?—A. Yes, sir.

Q. What command was with you?—A. General Castillo's.

Q. The whole army?—A. No, sir. Castillo went over after some arms to arm some other people in Havana.

Q. Did he get them?—A. Yes, sir.

Q. Bring them back?—A. Yes, sir.

Q. Did he cross the trocha?—A. Yes, sir; near Mariel.

Q. Near where?—A. Mariel. That trocha is practically abandoned now.

Q. The Mariel trocha?—A. Yes, sir.

Q. That is the western trocha?—A. Yes, sir.

Q. They still keep up the other trocha?—A. Yes, sir.

Q. What is that called?—A. The Jucaro-Maron trocha.

Q. Did you meet any Spanish troops on your way over or back?—A. We went three times before we could cross the trocha and reach the arms.

Q. Driven back by the Spanish?—A. Yes, sir; but we finally went across.

Q. And got successfully back with the arms and ammunition?—A. Yes, sir. On that trip we never encountered a Spanish soldier; had no trouble whatever.

Q. How did you transport them?—A. Gave each man so many guns, and gave each man so much ammunition to carry.

Q. Each man took so many guns and so much ammunition?—A. Yes, sir.

Q. Were you at any landing of an expedition?—A. I never was at a landing, or saw an expedition.

Q. What is the general health of the Cuban population, living in Cuba Libre, as you call it?—A. Good.

Q. What is the general health of the Cuban army?—A. Good.

Q. Have any epidemics visited that army since you have been there?—A. No, sir; the only disease we have is typhoid fever. They have had some occasionally, about four cases, and they all died—all that I had. All the other cases I have had since I have been with them have been malaria. I diagnosed these four as typhoid fever, but they said they never had typhoid fever in Cuba, but that it was some kind of——

Q. Are these Cubans in the army strong, healthy fellows, or thin and weak?—A. They are pretty husky fellows. The Cubans are not a large race. There are no such men as Mr. Decker, but they are strong and healthy.

Q. How do they compare with the Spanish soldiers?—A. The men in the Spanish army are good, strong fellows. But a man is very scarce in the Spanish army; it is mostly composed of boys.

Q. How do you account for that?—A. They have had to send so many soldiers to the island that they did not have enough men.

Q. Have you had any chance of personal observation as to the ravages of disease among the Spanish army?—A. Yes, sir; some.

Q. What have you to say about that?—A. Disease is the greatest enemy the Spanish army has and they die very rapidly—very fast. For instance, crossing the trocha to come to Havana—the Havana trocha—at night, as soon as I crossed I stopped with some pacificos camped there, and they told me that three or four Spaniards were dying each day in those forts in that neighborhood, and when I got into town I found it was true. I was two or three days hiding in Havana, waiting for a chance to come away from there through America, and I spent that time in the outskirts of the city, where the hospitals are located, and in the low coffee houses where the Spanish soldiers are, and, we might say, put in my time visiting the Spanish soldiers, talking about the war, their condition, etc., buying them cigarettes and fruit—those who did not have any money—helping them out a little.

Q. What American newspaper correspondents were in the army where you were operating?—A. None.

Q. How many hospitals—regular hospitals—did you have under your charge?—A. Some days they would amount to a hundred, and the next day maybe only five or six. I had six regularly named hospitals that I tried to keep up all the time in spite of the soldiers, and where, if the soldiers came, I would offer armed resistance, and hold them off until I could get my men out.

Q. When the soldiers came out to attack, all you could do was to make resistance until such time as you could carry your sick and wounded away?—A. Well, the first resistance I made I stood off a column all day long with four men, and that night got the men out.

Q. Were you in the thick woods?—A. Very thick.

Q. They were afraid—afraid to approach in the woods?—A. Yes, sir.

Q. I suppose the advance of an attacking party or column through those thick woods would be very much embarrassed by the surroundings—the trees, vines, brush, and all that?—A. Yes, sir; I at one time got out of the woods before the soldiers got in, and sat on a hill 300 or 400 yards away and watched them go into the woods. The chief stopped about 300 yards from where they entered the brush, and the infantry marched up and all the officers stood back, and the sergeant or lieutenant or small officers ordered the men in. The men marched up to the brush and then they would hesitate, and these officers would draw their canes—they nearly all carry canes—or some of them machetes, and they would whip them in. They would grab a man by the arm and strike him with a cane and drag and push him in. By the time a man got a little ways in he would cry "Viva Espagnol," and then the others would follow, and they would all rush in and set the houses afire, and yell and raise the mischief generally, and those on the outside would run up and try to set the brush afire, try to set the whole army afire, as it looked to me. If it had been dry brush, like American undergrowth, they would have burnt the entire army up.

Q. By brush, do you mean trees and bushes that have been cut down?—A. No, sir; it is short growth that has not been cut down. The ground is not fit for cultivation, it is rocky, and the bushes grow right out of the rocks, and we have to pick out the trail very carefully. They are sharp and jagged rocks that stick up there; you can not walk across them, you have to pick your way, and it makes a very narrow trail to get in.

Q. Has General Castillo kept practically the same ground all the time you have been with him?—A. Yes, sir; practically the same ground since he first went in there since the invasion.

Q. He really has not been driven out?—A. No, sir.

Q. Took his position and stayed there?—A. Yes, sir.

Q. He has shifted his position?—A. He would avoid a fight with a superior force. General Castillo himself is marching his force from one position to another, always looking for a fight. He does not rest himself. Every territory, you might say the whole territory, is occupied by a force that has occupied it since the invasion, and their business is to stay there.

Q. They are never driven out?—A. No, sir; General Castillo and Alex. Rodriguez have a large territory; General Castillo has the western part of the province, operating all through it, and at the same time there are smaller forces operating in different parts of the province, who stay each in its own territory.

Q. If I understand you correctly, the Cuban generals who have been operating in the province of Havana have been operating there since the insurrection broke out?—A. Since the invasion.

Q. Since Gomez invaded the west from the east?—A. Yes, sir.

Q. And have not been driven out?—A. Yes, sir; the army has grown continually and the territories spread daily.

Q. So far as military operations are concerned, they are in the occupation of the country and have been so?—A. Yes, sir.

Q. I suppose many efforts have been made to drive them out?—A. They are fighting every day.

Q. There is constant pressure to overcome and drive them out?—A. Yes, sir; the guerrillas and volunteers made the hardest fight, but they have been practically killed out and whipped, and they are afraid to fight any more.

Q. Who?—A. The guerrillas. The last guerrillas were those of Salug. There were 36 of them, and they killed the whole 36 about a week ago.

Q. The guerrillas are very severe?—A. Yes, sir.

Q. Very severe on the Cubans; cruel?—A. Yes, sir.

Q. You say they are practically driven out of the province?—A. Not driven out, but afraid to operate there; afraid to go out without the escort of a column of soldiers.

Q. Got enough of it?—A. Yes, sir; they have been whipped, and that gives the insurgents more territory, because these guerrillas were stationed in the towns, and were supposed to protect the pacificated zone and to carry the pacificos out to get food in the country.

Q. The important question I wish to ask you, based upon your observation since you have been in Cuba and associated with these fighting forces, is whether the Cubans have gained ground or lost ground as to strength and equipment and fighting ability generally since you have been there?—A. I would say they have gained ground and gained strength and gained knowledge in war.

Q. You intend to return to them?—A. Yes, sir.

. Q. In the same capacity you are now?—A. In the same capacity.

Q. As a surgeon?—A. Yes, sir.

Q. Did you have many assistants, surgeons?—A. No, sir; none.

Q. Had none at all, had to perform the work yourself?—A. Yes, sir I had practicantes, medical students.

Q. Medical students?—A. Yes, sir.

Q. They were your only assistants?—A. Yes, sir.

Q. No regular practitioner associated with you in your work?—A. No, sir.

Q. With whom did you leave the hospitals when you came away?—A. With the practicantes. Unless I can get supplies, surgical supplies, the practicantes can do as well as I could.

Q. That is what you came to this country for?—A. Yes, sir.

Q. To get surgical supplies?—A. Yes, sir; to try to make arrangements for regular supplies for the hospitals.

Q. I believe you mention Spanish soldiers have been in your charge?—A. Yes, sir.

Q. Spanish soldiers?—A. Yes, sir.

Q. Did you treat them with equal care as the Cubans?—A. Yes, sir.

Q. You felt bound by professional courtesy?—A. Yes, sir.

Q. Is there any order of any Cuban general to do contrary to that?—A. No, sir; that is the order to the army in the military regulation, and each chief is provided with a copy, that each Spanish soldier shall be returned to the towns or held as prisoners; no soldiers killed except when captured as spies.

Q. Have the Spanish any permanent camps outside the towns?—A. None that I ever saw or knew of.

Q. Never heard of any?—A. No, sir.

Q. When you speak of a town you mean a town garrisoned by Spanish troops?—A. Yes, sir.

Q. Fortified?—A. In every little town there was a string of forts.

Q. What kind of forts; any strength?—A. Yes, sir; strong enough to resist the arms the Cubans have.

Q. Small arms?—A. Yes, sir. I do not think they could resist artillery—any heavy artillery—or even 4 or 5 pounders.

Q. What are they made of?—A. Stone.

Q. Is there plenty of stone?—A. Yes, sir; the whole island, you might say, is a great big rock.

Q. The whole island?—A. Yes, sir.

Q. From what place did General Castillo get his supply of salt?—A. Any town he would happen to be near he would send in for it.

Q. In order to get salt he would have to capture a town; fight for it?—A. No, sir; he would give a man a centen and tell him to go in and get salt. He would buy it.

Q. He kept up a trafic with the towns?—A. Yes, sir.

Q. How could he manage that where there was a concentration of pacificos and Spanish garrison?—A. The pacificos came out after sweet potatoes—each man can bring something in his sack (cigarettes, a hat, blankets) which do not take up much space. I bought a big blanket, a hat, pair of shoes, and suit of clothes, all brought in one cargo—one man brought it. He brought that right past the fort and sentries; the next day brought out three Mausers.

Q. He had no permit to do it?—A. No, sir.

Q. He smuggled it out; he would have lost his life if caught at it?—A. Yes, sir. They usually make four or five trips, and then the next trip they will be caught and shot.

Q. They catch up with them finally, and then they are done for?—A. Yes, sir.

Q. Is there any other matter you wish to state that you think would be of importance?—A. I do not know of anything else; it seems to me we have gone over about the whole ground.

After examining and correcting my deposition as above, I sign the same under oath.

FOSTER R. WINN, M. D.

WASHINGTON, D. C., *June 28, 1897.*

S. Doc. 231, pt 7——49

STATEMENT OF DR. H. W. DANFORTH.

In the absence of Senator Morgan, Mr. Lodge acted as a member of the subcommittee.

Mr. Danforth was sworn by Senator Clark.

By Mr. CLARK:

Q. What is your name, profession or occupation, and present place of residence?—A. H. W. Danforth; physician and surgeon; Milwaukee, Wis.

Q. You may state whether or not you have been engaged in professional work recently on the Island of Cuba; and if so, in what capacity and with whom?—A. I have been engaged in Cuba as a physician to the President of Cuba, Salvador Cisneros.

Q. How long have you been in that position?—A. One year.

Q. During that time have you been near by the person of the President?—A. All the time.

Q. Now, the committee is very anxious to learn a particular thing that probably comes within your knowledge, and that is, as definitely as possible, as to the civil government carried on by the Cuban insurgents, so called. We would be glad if you will give, at large and in detail, whatever knowledge you may have.

By Mr. LODGE:

Q. Let me ask, before that question is answered: President Cisneros is the head of the civil government?—A. He is, sir.

Q. You have not been attached to the army in a military capacity?—A. I have not. I will now answer the first question. The civil government, as far as my observation extends, has power over the country. They have that power through the governors of the various States who are appointed by the President or elected by the people. They also have power through the prefects and through the subprefects appointed by the President or by the Secretary of the Interior, Dr. Canasarius. Their duty, of course, is—the subprefects' duty is—to attend the mails, see that they are diligently forwarded, and, in so far as possible, contribute to the relief of the military authorities that chance to be in their neighborhood, by giving them rations and treating them in that way. They are also delegated or appointed to power by the President to celebrate all marriages which may occur among the insurgents. They have the power from the cabinet of celebrating those marriages.

By Mr. LODGE:

Q. How is this civil government organized?—A. It is organized by—pardon me, I do not understand.

Q. I mean when was it organized?—A. It was organized in—well, I do not know exactly when it was organized; I can tell when the President was elected, if that will do. It was two years ago the 22d of February; that is, he was installed in office two years ago the 22d of February.

Q. Do you understand that a popular election was held?—A. An election of the army only. Of course, it is simply here, gentlemen—the island is, at the present time, in revolution, and a great many people have gone to the towns—a great many of the pacificos—and the result is that it is almost an impossibility for them to secure a free and independent—I can not exactly express it.

Q. It is impossible to get a full vote?—A. That is it.

Q. This government adopted a constitution, which, of course, has been published. Was there a convention held of representative delegates?—A. Oh, yes.

Q. And a civil government was organized?—A. Yes, sir. There were—I have forgotten the number of delegates, although I have seen it; I have read of the number that were present; but there were a number of delegates chosen from the army from the various Provinces of Cuba, and those delegates met at Jimagua, or some such named place, and elected the President and Vice-President, and his secretaries. The secretaries were all elected in place of being appointed, as in this country.

Q. Does that civil government, organized in this way—does it operate and have power?—A. Indeed it does so, sir.

Q. The military forces hold their commissions from it?—A. They hold their commissions from the civil government.

Q. What has been the capital—what has been the seat of government?—A. They have had no capital until about the 1st of February of this year, and then they put up a number of houses at Aguira, about 3 leagues to west of the city of Wymero, in Puerto Principe, and they established that as the seat of government.

Q. Were they not at Cubitos?—A. No, sir.

Q. Have they ever been driven out of their seat of government by the Spaniards?—A. Not up to the time I left; but I will tell you in candor that all the Spaniards have to do, if they want to, is to march 100 men down there and drive the Cubans out. I was there on the 29th of April and they had but 8 men in the capital. The President was in one place, the Vice-President here, and the secretaries there, and so on; they were distributed according to the business relations they had, and were seeing, too, about the country.

Q. They have never been disturbed by the enemy?—A. No, sir.

Q. They have been able to carry on all the functions of civil government?—A. They have.

Q. You understand why I asked these questions?—A. No, sir.

Q. The charge is made here that the Cuban government is purely military; that Gomez is all there is to it.—A. That is all nonsense. Gomez and Garcia and Maceo were under the entire control of the government.

Q. Never questioned it?—A. Never so much as raised the question as to the source of their power.

Q. President Cisneros has taken an active part in carrying on the government?—A. Of course he has; he is with the government all the time.

Q. Over how large a part of Cuba is that government recognized?—
A. All over Cuba, except in the towns, and there the Spanish have
authority and control.

Q. What do the Spanish hold control of?—A. The towns and where
they are camped.

Q. Only where they have garrisons or where they encamp?—A. Yes,
sir; the balance of the island is in the hands of the Cubans.

Q. All the rest?—A. Yes, sir; save where the Spaniards are encamped.

Q. The insurgents move freely all through the country?—A. I have
gone from Moron down to Banos, a distance of about two weeks' ride,
and hard riding, too, on horseback, entirely alone except for my assistant, and never experienced the slightest trouble.

Q. Through all these country districts the power of the civil government of President Cisneros is recognized?—A. Yes, sir; you will find
that the President has prefects established at about every 3 to 6 leagues
all over the island, from east to west and from north to south; whichever way you go prefects are established every 3 to 6 leagues. At their
houses all officers or travelers on commissions to or from the government are expected to stop if they can. Those prefects are bound by
law to furnish those men with care, protection, comfort, and shelter,
and of course they supply them with food and other things in proportion as they can.

Q. They carry on the usual functions of civil government, such as
you alluded to, solemnizing marriages, etc.?—A. Certainly, except as it
may be in this direction. We will say a murder has been committed.
They have no judges in Cuba at all, though I think they are just as fair
there as the Spaniards. The Spaniards have plenty of judges, but
they are not as fair as they might be. The Cubans have no judges,
but the prefect will arrest the man, examine him and send him to the
nearest general in command of the forces, and he will treat him as he
deserves; if innocent, free him; if guilty, doubtless shoot him.

Q. Has there been more than one election of delegates in the
island?—A. More than one election of delegates?

Q. Has there been more than one? I had heard that there was more
than one convention.—A. I do not know that there had been up to the
time I left the island, which was on the 29th of April. Up to that
time there had not been, although very shortly the election was to be
held, and the delegates were to assemble at the capital for this coming
election. The president's term of office expires September 22, I think.

Q. And they intend to hold another election, and choose delegates
again?—A. They intend to hold another election during the summer,
and have the new officer, whoever it be—Cisneros or any other—ready
to be installed on the 22d of September, when the President's term is
out. That is the fact with reference to the Vice-President, and the
fact with reference to all the secretaries of his cabinet—they are all to
be elected, and will take their offices accordingly.

Q. And you say these delegates were chosen largely by the insurgents in arms? I suppose others, who were not in arms, had the right
to vote if they wished?—A. Certainly; all the Cubans in the country
districts—all not under the control of the Spanish in the islands—have
the entire right to vote.

Q. And are not prevented?—A. And are not prevented. On the contrary, the prefects are speaking, or were speaking when I was there, to
the inhabitants all through their various districts, telling them the
election was about to occur soon and they wanted to be there to vote.
I did not know at the time, and do not know now, exactly when the election is to occur, but I have heard the prefects stating to the various

people that an election was to be held and that they (the people) wanted to be there and cast their votes for whom they wanted to have serve them.

By Mr. CLARK:

Q. I would like to make some inquiry as to the postal service of the island, if you know about it.—A. I know a little.

Q. Is there any regular postal service?—A. Yes, sir.

Q. In what manner is it conducted?—A. On this plan: They have the prefects of these districts, and they act as distributing officers in the postal service, I believe.

Q. They are from 3 to 6 leagues apart?—A. Yes, sir. All the people in their districts are coming and going to and from their place. They usually visit the prefects at least once every week or two to get mail and see if there are any orders for provisions or to get provisions. They are usually coming and going there every week or two.

Q. About how is the mail transported?—A. On horseback entirely.

Q. Is that a regular service?—A. There is no regular service in Cuba.

Q. How frequent or general is it, for instance?—A. I do not exactly get the question.

Q. Suppose I am living at one station, and I want to forward a letter 100 miles to the west, to another station?—A. It will go within twenty-four hours.

Q. What means of communication—you say the army is entirely subject to the civil government—what means has the president of communication with Gomez or Garcia or other divisions of the army? Is that done through the regular mail service?—A. It is done by special couriers and through the regular mail service.

Q. I would like to know how frequently, whether generally or only upon special occasions, the military authorities communicate with the civil, and receive orders from them?—A. There you have me. I am sorry to say I do not know, not having been thrown into such very intimate and close relations.

Q. You do not know whether regular reports are made to the civil government from the military?—A. I do not.

Q. You speak of various secretaries. What others are there besides the secretary of the interior?—A. There are those of foreign relations, Mr. Portuando, who is a very, very pleasant man; the secretary of the interior, Dr. Canasious; and the secretary of the treasury, Mr. Pina. I believe that to be all, and the vice-president, General Masso.

Q. These various secretaries or heads of the departments; are they regularly and constantly engaged in the duties of their various offices, or merely figureheads for the purpose of making up a government?—A. They and their secretaries are regularly and constantly engaged in attending to the duties of their offices. I have seen—I will not say how many times, because I do not know, but it is a great many times, when we have pitched camp, usually about 1 o'clock in the afternoon, and about half past 2, after we have finished breakfast—I have seen the secretaries busy dictating to their secretaries, and their secretaries busy in writing.

Q. If you have had opportunity to judge, I would like to know as to the confidence which this civil government has in the ultimate success of the independence of Cuba?—A. If I have had the opportunity to judge?

Q. Yes, sir.—A. I will tell you this. The civil government of Cuba will—all, each, and every one of them—go down to destruction unless their independence is attained.

Q. And still that does not——A. I have heard the president of Cuba make that same remark.

Q. We very often find men who are willing to die for the cause they maintain, and yet who have not so much confidence in the success of their cause as in the certainty of their own death. What I want to get at is their confidence whether Cuban freedom will be achieved.— A. It is my opinion that it is the opinion of every one in the insurgent ranks that liberty will eventually be obtained.

Q. I will ask you, from your experience and your intimate association with public affairs there, what would be your judgment?—A. My judgment is the same. I will give you my reasons, and then you can judge for yourself as well as I can. At the last war Spain had on the island 250,000 soldiers. There were but two provinces in insurrection, Orient and Camaguey, or Puerto Principe and Santiago de Cuba. The revolutionists had from 6,000 to 7,000 armed men, and yet the revolutionists prolonged the struggle for ten long years before Spain could subdue them. This year every section of the island is in insurrection. Spain has but 300,000 men, but 50,000 more than they had before, and the revolutionists have about 30,000 to 35,000 well-armed men, and it is my opinion that Cuba will eventually win her freedom, I do not care whether Spain is willing or not.

By Mr. LODGE:

Q. You say Spain has 300,000 men. That is the whole body of men Spain has been able to send to the island—you do not mean she has 300,000 effectives there now?—A. Certainly. She had on the 1st of January 153,000 regular soldiers from Spain.

Q. They have sent out more than that?—A. Yes, sir; but I am not counting anything——

Q. By and by I would like your estimate of Spanish losses.—A. The guerrillas number between 50,000 and 60,000—the Spanish guerrillas. They are Cubans, or should be Cubans in reality, who have adopted the cause of Spain.

Q. You mean the voluntarios?—A. Yes, sir; then they have the guarda civil and they have all the firemen in the island, and they have armed them all and are using them as soldiers.

Q. The guarda civil, were they brought from Spain or is it a native body?—A. A native body of men, but under the ruling of the power of Spain. All in all, I think the number is fully 300,000 men. The Cubans, on the contrary, have but 30,000 to 35,000 well-armed men, about 1 to every 10. Is it anything very wonderful, therefore, that you do not hear of some immense battle? I do not think it to be so at all. I think the Cubans are conducting the campaign as they should.

Q. Spain is said, and I am told all authorities seem to agree, she is said to have sent out more than 150,000 men?—A. She has.

Q. Have not her losses from disease and these various little engagements been very severe?—A. Very; it is simply—why, in this morning's paper I was noting the return of some steamship to Spain from Havana, and was noting that it stated that the Spanish had shipped some 793 invalided soldiers on that ship. Every ship that leaves Havana carries, as a rule, from 200 to 500 men, so you can imagine Spain must lose pretty heavily.

Q. Only the invalided and wounded; the dead are buried there?—A. The dead are always buried there, and there are a great many who die, especially of fevers. The Spanish troops are young, nothing but boys in many instances, and being unacclimated and unfit practically for any experience in the rough warfare of Cuba, the climate goes very hard with them.

By Mr. CLARK:

Q. Right in that connection I would like to ask as to the physique and health of the Cubans actively engaged under arms, their means of subsistence, and how well they are cared for.—A. The Cubans are, in every way in good health, save for an occasional fever. You have the yellow fever and you have the malarial fever, which I had an experience with last December, anything but pleasant—where no quinine was to be obtained—you can imagine. They are good physique; a trifle lighter than I am. I suppose I was as light as they in April or May of this year, when I was there. With reference to their food, they have the best that can be obtained.

Q. When you say "the best that can be obtained," do you mean under the circumstances?—A. Yes, sir.

Q. That is what I want to find out, how well they are subsisted.—A. In Camaguey, where I was, they have boniato, or sweet potatoes. Sometimes they will have yucca, sometimes plantains, sometimes conchanchilla, a mixture of honey and hot water. Sometimes they will have coffee, sometimes they will not have anything except, perhaps, meat.

Q. How about their supply of meat?—A. It is ample.

Q. Where is that obtained?—A. Everywhere, anywhere. By the laws of the Cubans, by the law of the land, it is a fact that the Cuban rulers declared, when this war first started, that all horses and all cattle in the island, wherever found, were to be regarded as public property. The result is you can find cattle everywhere in Camaguey. I do not believe I have ever ridden 3 miles without seeing more or less cattle.

By Mr. LODGE:

Q. Do they take good care of them?—A. Yes, sir.

Q. So that they have an indefinite supply?—A. Yes, sir. Their horses are kept in bortraros, very large spaces, from half a league long to a quarter of a league in width.

By Mr. CLARK:

Q. Corrals, or pastures?—A. Pastures, protected by barbed-wire fences, and horses are kept grazing within. Anyone passing there with his horse very much fatigued, with the permission of the man in charge, can change him for another. It is a very good idea.

Q. As to the food question, what is your opinion as to the amount necessary to sustain the war?—A. I am a specimen of it. I have been there a year and a quarter and I have done very well, indeed, and I have lived on meat for almost five months, and nothing but meat, and I believe that my looks are reasonably good for a meat diet.

By Mr. LODGE:

Q. What would be your judgment as to the general feeling of the great mass of the native Cubans?—A. Animosity to the Spaniards and a desire to be free.

Q. The insurgent government and army represent the wishes of the great body of the people?—A. They do, I believe.

Q. What do you think would be the effect of any action on the part of this country?—A. Is that to be taken——

Q. Suppose this country should intervene?—A. I can not but think it would terminate the war.

Q. Is it your impression that the Spanish campaign have got there weaker and weaker; that they are in process of exhaustion; that money is more difficult to obtain?—A. My idea is that the money is growing more and more scarce and harder for the Spanish to get hold of, but, with reference to their campaigns, they are just as well conducted as ever.

Q. Were they ever well conducted?—A. That is the point. Of course it is susceptible of two answers, yes or no.

Q. Have they won any very serious victories there?—A. No, sir. I desire while I am about it—I was looking over some papers last evening—I desire to most positively and emphatically deny the statements of Mr. Olney or President Cleveland, that the government is a military usurpation. I deny that most emphatically. I claim that there is a civil government and that that government is exercising its functions, and is in force to-day just as much as the civil government in the United States. I just happened to think of that in the course of your remarks. You hit on something that reminded me of it.

Q. Have they any workshops?—A. Yes, sir; and a great many of them. They are irregularly situated, but, for instance, they will kill a cow or kill a dozen cattle at this encampment to-night at 7 o'clock. The hides are taken off and hung on the branches of a near by tree, and at 8 o'clock in the morning they are taken to the prefect, and he will send them by a messenger to the tannery, which they have in every district, or one tanner to so many prefects within a certain distance—within easy riding distance, at least—and those hides are there tanned by the tannery. After that is over with, after the hides are tanned, they are sent to the manufactory, where they manufacture shoes or saddles—the manufactory of saddles and bridles—or anything that one can want. I got there last summer a pair of boots and a pair of leggings made. I had saddlebags also, and one thing and another of a similar kind, a saddle and bridle, made as well, and those things I used and wore until I left the island. Well, I had them made last July, and I wore them until this May, and they were all in just as good condition when I gave them up as when I got them, so you can imagine they are made well.

Q. How about clothing?—A. They are deficient in supplies of clothing. It is very hard to get clothing there. You can not buy it, and the result is I have seen men in Cuba have their cartridge belts across their chests and their rifles across their shoulders and a little piece of cloth about 6 inches in width across the middle; and that is all they had. They came to the president and petitioned him for more clothes—about seven or eight of them. It looks funny to see them—those fellows, well-built, strong, and muscular men—without a dud of clothes on; but they all got clothing. They have clothing of one kind or another. Sometimes it is rather rough and ragged and a good many patches—a good many patches on the seat of the pantaloons, but I do not know but it answers all their purposes as well as the clothing we have here.

By Mr. MORGAN:

Q. They would not be able to wear any heavy clothing?—A. No, sir; very light, all linen cloth. The cost of pantaloons in Cuba varies from $1.75 to $2.50.

Q. Linen pantaloons?—A. Yes, sir.

Q. White or colored?—A. White.

Q. By using cotton cloth they could still further reduce the price?—A. Yes, sir.

Q. Do you know anything about the repair shops of guns?—A. They have, at various of these factories, men whose sole and only duty it is to attend to and repair guns in so far as possible and fix the munitions of war in proper shape. They also have, in various places, cartridge factories—not cartridge factories, because they could not manufacture the whole cartridge, but the soldiers will save the shells after they have been discharged and these men will recap and recharge them.

Q. Do they make any powder?—A. I do not know, but I think they must, because they do a very large amount of reloading cartridges, and I have seen the bills of lading of two or three expeditions that have arrived, and I have never seen any loose powder mentioned on these bills; so they must have them, but where they are I do not know. They have printing presses (paper) established in various sections of the island. I think they have—I would not like to say how many, but I think four or five papers.

Q. Weekly papers?—A. Weekly or monthly.

Q. Do they circulate freely among the people?—A. Yes, sir; indeed they do, and are found in the cities as well.

Q. I suppose the government has been able to keep up a constant flow of information in regard to the movements of the Spaniards.—A. Oh, yes; that is very readily done. It is simply here. They have, we will say—take Puerto Principe for sample. They have before that city a small detachment of men, all on duty all the time, riding around the city, back and forth, here and there and elsewhere. Their sole and only purpose is to see when a detachment comes out, and when a detachment appears they will immediately notify the nearest commander as to the probable course of the Spainards, and they will then follow that column and see where they go and what course they take, and will notify him or all the commanders in that district, and again when the column returns they will notify them that they are back in the town.

Q. So that they are in constant observation of the enemy?—A. Yes, sir; they have every city in the country guarded that way.

Q. Do the Spaniards attempt any such system of espionage?—A. No, sir; they can not do it, unless it be by series of spies, which I doubt very much the capacity of the Spaniards to obtain. I believe the men would be detected, and if a man is detected in the capacity of a spy his fate is pretty sure and pretty sudden; at least it would be there.

Q. Have they flour or corn mills in Cuba, or do they rely on the pestle and mortar?—A. They have no mills that I saw anything of. The reason simply is that the Spanish would, if they had any such thing, only be too glad to come out and destroy it from the towns. They rely on pestles and mortars and grind the corn in their coffee mills.

Q. Corn mills?—A. They grind the corn in the coffee mills.

Q. How many crops of corn are raised in Cuba?—A. I asked that question myself about six months ago, and you want me to give the answer I received?

Q. Yes, sir.—A. The answer as given me was three crops, and I was surprised.

Q. So it is substantially a continual supply of corn?—A. Yes, sir.

Q. And they also have the advantage of roasting ears?—A. Yes, sir; and they have sweet potatoes. You can plant them and they will grow without any cultivation.

Q. Without cultivation?—A. Yes, sir. All you have to do is to scratch the ground and drop in the seed, and it will grow of itself.

Q. Do they grow of a fine size?—A. Yes, sir.

Q. It is a good potato?—A. Yes, sir.

Q. Sweet?—A. Sweet and very palatable. The yucca grows in the same way, without any care at all. They have also a great many bananas, or plantains, as they are termed, growing in Cubitos at the present time. They have a great many of those, and they send over from the rest of the province every once in a while to secure several mule loads of the yucca and plantain, or boniato—the sweet potato.

Q. I do not understand about that plant yucca. Is that a plant which grows in moist soil, like a radish?—A. No, sir; it belongs to the family of tubers, I believe. It is the root, and the root will increase in size, and will weigh anywhere from 5 to 100 pounds. They are very large.

Q. Is it palatable and nutritious?—A. Indeed it is. It is just about like our Irish potato; just about the same thing.

Q. Do they cook it in the same way as Irish potatoes?—A. Yes, sir; they cut it up and put it in water and allow it to boil just about as with Irish potatoes.

Q. It comes out mealy?—A. No, sir; it comes out in the original pieces, very nicely done—mealy and nice to the taste.

Q. They eat it with salt, just as you would an Irish potato?—A. Yes, sir.

Q. That food does not require cultivation?—A. No, sir.

Q. Grows indigenous?—A. Yes, sir; wherever you chance to put it.

Q. I have been interested, too, in another thing, and that is, what is the production of hogs in the island of Cuba?—A. They have an immense number. Contrary to the custom in the United States, they allow them to run wild, and they eat whatever they find. I do not know exactly what they do live on, but they live very well. They have what they call hog dogs, and if you want a hog you call the dogs, and they will take after the hogs, and after chasing them around, the dogs will seize them by the ears and maintain their hold until the man comes up, and then they tie their legs together and sling him across the saddle and take him to the house and kill him.

Q. They are in good condition?—A. Always. I do not know what they live on; it is absolutely impossible for me to say that; but it is impossible to say that they are otherwise than in good condition.

Q. They make good meat?—A. I think the flesh of a hog in Cuba is far better and more palatable than the flesh of the hog grown in the United States.

Q. Owing to the character of the food?—A. Yes, sir; I suppose so.

Q. I have heard the same observation made about the beef in Cuba. Do you justify the statement that the beef is excellent?—A. Yes, sir. I do not believe, however, that the beef in Cuba is better than the beef found in the United States, for the reason that you can not secure a cut of beef there as you can here.

Q. The cattle are smaller?—A. Yes, sir; and again, in cutting the meat up they do not use the same care.

Q. Is it native wild stock or improved?—A. I do not know how that is.

Q. Are they broad-horned?—A. Some; but the major portion are short-horned or no horns at all.

Q. As a rule, are they good milch cattle?—A. Yes, sir; very good, indeed. You know how they milk there? It struck me as being one of the funniest things I ever saw. I do not believe I ever saw it done that way in this country. They will have a square inclosure with a high fence around it, and they will drive the cow in, and they will loosen her calf, and the calf will come and smell around and begin sucking, and the man will wait until it has taken two or three sucks, and then he will take a rope and slip it over the calf's head and tie it in such a way as to keep the calf's head about a foot or a foot and a half from the teats, and the cow will then stand still and the man will commence his milking. When he is through he will take the rope off, and the calf will then go back to sucking. It is the first place I ever saw it done.

Q. Some witnesses have stated that there is rather an abundant production of butter and cheese.—A. There is an abundant production of cheese; but butter, I never saw a particle while I was in Cuba; but of cheese there is plenty, and of honey.

Q. Take the food resources of the Island of Cuba in the part of it under the control of the Cubans. Do you think they are able to keep up their belligerent operations and supply their army of, say, 30,000 to 50,000 men for a considerable length of time against the Spanish?—A. I do, sir.

Q. And at the same time afford to the rural population a comfortable subsistence?—A. Yes, sir; they are able to do that, and do it very easily.

Q. How about Cubitos and the town near there which is the capital?— A. The capital is at Aguira; that is in Camaguey. Cubitos is in Camaguey, but it is a province, and Aguara is in Puerto Principe, 3 leagues west of Wymero, which was captured by the Cubans last November.

Q. Is that a town?—A. Yes, sir—no, it is not a town—it is a collection of houses that the President has put up for the capital.

Q. Have the Spanish ever attempted to drive them out of there?— A. Never as yet, up to the time I left Cuba, although one day there was word sent that a Spanish column of 4,000 men was only a league and a half off, and we had orders to get our horses up and saddled, and everything on them, ready to start at a moment's notice. However, it proved to be a false rumor, and we turned the horses out and allowed them to feed. If the Spaniards so desire, there will be nothing under Heaven to prevent them from destroying it.

Q. It is not surrounded by a cordon of troops?—A. No, sir.

Q. How is it with the fortress at Cubitos; is there a fortified place there?—A. Not a thing.

Q. Is that as at Aguira?—A. Cubitos is a province, and the Spaniards have not in this war invaded the province of Cubitos, and the result is that all the rest of the province of Camaguey sends to Cubitos for provisions. They grow everything in Cubitos.

Q. What advantage would the Cubans have in defending Cubitos over any other province?—A. None at all.

Q. Can you count on the Spaniards not disturbing it?—A. No, sir.

Q. Is it elevated?—A. It is an elevated place by one or two roads, but approached by all the others it is level and plain. I have no idea why the Spaniards do not invade it. I should think they would, but apparently they seem to hesitate and balk.

Q. How far is it from the nearest railroad?—A. The line Nuevitas is here, and Puerto Principe is here [indicating]. There is a line between Nuevitas and Principe, and Cubitos is just this side of the railroad track.

Q. Right on the line with the railroad?—A. Yes, sir; right on the line, but of course the railroad only passes along the line, and the line extends back here several leagues.

Q. I am speaking about the collection of houses you call the seat of government.—A. At Aguira?

Q. Yes, sir; how far is that from the railroad?—A. About 16 or 17 leagues.

Q. From the railroad?—A. Yes, sir.

Q. How far from the coast?—A. It could not be more than 3 or 4 leagues.

Q. Is there any fort near it?—A. Yes, sir; there is a fort; but what the name of that fort is I have forgotten—Guayamo. There is a port near it, however; that is, within a day's ride.

Q. How far from Banos?—A. Way, way to the west of Banos; that is, in Orienta, near the eastern part. This is about 17 or 18 leagues—possibly 20—from Puerto Principe.

Q. Since you have been in Cuba has there been any invasion of that part of the country you speak of?—A. No, sir; there were of course several columns at previous times, and last November, when the Spaniards held Wymero and Cascorra and some other towns up there, there were several columns during the year visited those places with supply trains. Every so often they would send a train load of provisions to the various towns, and every train of provisions sent the Spanish and Cubans used to have a picnic; in other words, to have a tussle—a fight.

Q. Do the Spaniards supply themselves from the country around the towns where they are located?—A. They do not.

Q. They have to import from the seaboard towns?—A. Entirely. If they had supplied themselves from the country 'round about, which they might readily have done, the course of the war would be different altogether, but they could not do it now.

Q. Heretofore they have been afraid to attempt it?—A. Yes, sir.

Q. I would like for you to state in your own way your observations upon the condition of the Spanish soldiers in Cuba as to health and strength.—A. You will have to excuse me, but allow me to inform you that I have been on the revolutionist side, and I have no idea of my own personal knowledge as to the food or other supplies of the Spanish army, nor of their health.

Q. You have seen Spanish prisoners?—A. No, sir; I have seen the prisoners captured at Wymero and one or two other little skirmishes, but those only at a distance. I have not cared to have anything to do with them.

Q. From the reputation, or the facts detailed by the Cuban soldiers, what is your idea of the condition of health of those Spanish soldiers?—A. My opinion is that their health is not as good as it might be. The Spanish soldiers, in the first place, are exceedingly careless—exceedingly so. They have no sanitary regulations whatever, not in the least, and the result is that they die of yellow fever or dysentery, or other fevers, and they die like sheep.

Q. Do the reports as to their mortality show that the losses are very heavy from that source?—A. They do. Now, at—I have forgotten the name of the point; it is a point on the Moron trocha—there is one street that is the principal street of the town, and all along that street is the camp of the Spanish soldiers. They must have a thousand men camping in that street, and if you try to cross that street you will have to keep your eyes very wide open, and look where you are stepping with the utmost care, because of the filth on the ground; and yet those soldiers sleep right there, eat, and have their being right there; and how it is possible for those men to exist is more than I can say.

Q. Do you know anything about the civil government crossing the trocha?—A. Yes, sir.

Q. Have they done that?—A. Yes, sir.

Q. How often have you been across the Moron trocha?—A. Twice—once in December and once in February.

Q. How did you get over?—A. Passed through the line very easily.

Q. At night or in the day?—A. Night.

Q. No attack on you?—A. No; there was some firing, however—some firing at us. One of the cooks on the way back got a bullet through the back in his right lung, but it never bothered him at all; he kept right on his horse, and kept right on with his business of cooking; it never bothered him, as I could see.

Q. How do you account for that?—A. As I account for all wounds made by the Mauser rifle bullet. It is the most harmless and most humane rifle, and I am intensely surprised by Spain's using it; the most barbarous nation in their treatment of the Cubans according to the stories, and yet the most humane in the use of firearms. The Mauser bullet is a steel-clad bullet of .31 and a fraction caliber. That bullet will penetrate anywhere, and will go through you as a flash of sunlight will go through glass, but it leaves no disabling effect, and unless it hit in a vital spot, as, for instance, the heart, which is the only spot where you can kill a person instantly—and even there I have seen a person live. Unless hit in a vital spot you will not die. I have seen a man shot through here, in the head, and seen him alive and perfectly well, except for paralysis, a year after. I saw another man, Major Osgood, of the artillery, shot through the center of the forehead, and he lived for three hours; but if you take an ordinary bullet, what chance has a man shot there to live three seconds? I saw a man shot only an eighth of an inch over the heart, and I could not tell for three hours whether the heart was touched or not. He was put in the hospital, and in seven days he was discharged from the hospital. In case a Winchester ball had gone there, only an eighth of an inch from the heart, where would that man be? Dead, without a question. Another man was shot through the thigh, and it came out on the inner side of the leg, traversing the femur all the way down. The man wanted to remain on his horse and continue fighting, and I slit up his pants and put a piece of plaster on the wound, above and below, and in ten minutes he was engaged in a machete charge. If that had been a Winchester ball his leg would have been amputated.

Q. When the civil government passed through the trocha on the occasion you speak of, did you have any considerable guard of men?—A. Going to the west, yes; Gomez and all his forces were with them. Coming to the east, no; they did not have to exceed 20.

Q. In what way do you transport their government archives?—A. I have spoken of the mail.

Q. By what means does the government preserve the papers—the archives of the Republic?—A. They have those all indexed, and they are kept in boxes, and the boxes divided into compartments and indexed, and any or all communications for the government are put in those boxes or compartments, and when the government gets time they are weeded out, and the boxes are, every morning, on the march, placed on the backs of mules and bound there with ropes and carried in that way. The archives of the government always travel with the government.

Q. But the government does not always travel with the army?—A. It very, very rarely travels with the army—very rarely. Last October, when we were before Wymero, we must have traveled about 10 leagues with a portion of the army, and that is the only time I can recollect, save in December, when the president crossed the trocha with General Gomez, that the army was with them.

Q. And where is the treasury of the government kept?—A. That is somewhat complex. The treasurer of the government is Mr. Pina, and he receives and disburses all moneys, and as fast as he will get on hand any considerable store of money that money is sent, I believe, to New York, in some one way or another, to the junta, and there is used for the purposes that are best calculated to help the revolutionists.

Q. In the meantime where does he keep his money; where does he have it for safe-keeping?—A. In the chests.

Q. Carried with the government?—A. Yes, sir; with the President's escort.

Q. Carried along with the archives?—A. Yes, sir.

Q. Is there any hostility you have ever discovered among the native population?—A. The Cuban army?

Q. Yes, sir.—A. Oh, no; only the kindliest of feeling prevails between the army and the people. I have never been able to discern the least trace of feeling between anyone in the army and any of the people.

Q. State your impression as to the affection or want of regard on the part of the Cuban rural population for the cause of freedom and independence for the Cubans.—A. There is nothing in the rural population existing excepting the kindliest sentiment and the warmest feeling for the ultimate freedom of Cuba.

Q. Are they willing to make sacrifices?—A. They are doing it every day. Is it no sacrifice for a man to have his house destroyed, his property all gone up in smoke, to be compelled to go to the woods and put up another house? That has been done by almost every Cuban.

Q. And still they adhere to their demand for liberty?—A. Yes, sir; and adhere to that demand in stronger terms than ever.

Q. You do not find the feeling for liberty and independence decreasing, but, on the contrary, increasing?—A. It is increasing, and it is my impression it will increase, for among all the people they know in general terms the taxation to which they are liable, and they know how much heavier that taxation must be to pay the interest on the increased debt.

Q. Has the paper currency now being circulated in Cuba, what we call " Weyler currency," any circulation among the rural people?—A. None at all.

Q. Not considered of any value?—A. None at all.

Q. Their currency consists of gold and silver coin?—A. Entirely.

Q. The Cuban government has not issued any currency?—A. No, sir; no bills of any kind. It has no currency.

Q. How are the soldiers of the Cuban army paid?—A. They are not paid; i is all free, voluntary service by everybody in the Cuban army or rank.

Q. They expect to get pay?—A. When freedom is declared, but not until then.

Q. The pay, then, consists in support of life, being provided with arms and a horse to ride?—A. Yes, sir.

Q. And such clothes as can be had?—A. As can be obtained; yes, sir. The president will endeavor to see, of course, that every man is clad as he should be.

Q. Are there regular muster rolls kept of the Cuban republic?—A. I believe there are.

Q. At the headquarters of the government?—A. No, sir; I think not;

but yet I do not positively know about that. I know they are kept by the regimental commanders, but whether they make returns to the civil government is more than I can say. I know this, that is, that the government has a list of every officer serving on the island. I only know that through my desire to see when I enlisted in the service, Manola Betancourt, the president's secretary, undertook to look it up for me, and he got this list and hunted until he found the index, when he speedily got the day of my enlistment; and I asked him then if he had a list of every officer in the island, and he said of every officer, from a second lieutenant up, is in this list.

Q. In going about with the government, have you visited and examined the hospitals in Cuba?—A. Several times.

Q. Have they sufficient hospitals and hospital supplies for their army?—A. No, sir. In hospital buildings they have an abundance, or they could secure abundance, but in hospital supplies they are very, very deficient, and they have no bandages. This, of course, is to be taken as my last experience in Cuba. They have no bandages, they have no antiseptics, they have no chloroform or ether, they have no surgical instruments. But I would do as I have always done heretofore, in case of necessity, borrow the surgical instruments of the surgeon nearest to me until I was through with them, and then return them.

Q. Speaking of this want of material, instruments, etc., you speak of the hospitals. The surgeons in the field have surgical instruments and some supplies?—A. Many times they do and many times they do not. I know that in several engagements, two in special, late last fall, there were no surgical instruments and no supplies of any kind, and the wounded had to be removed a number of leagues distant to be cared for, and when they got there they had nothing, not even a bandage, not a yard of bandaging, to care for them with.

Q. How are the wounded transported from one place to another?—A. Carried in hammocks.

Q. By men?—A. Yes, sir.

Q. On foot or horseback?—A. Either way. Many times on foot by carriers, and other times they have the hammocks suspended between two horses, and carried in that way.

Q. Under these very unfavorable conditions, can you say that the service of the Cuban soldier is cheerful and active?—A. I can say I have never seen any service rendered by any men more cheerfully than the service rendered by the Cuban soldiers; and I believe they will have that cause still more at heart before they get through.

Q. They must have their cause very much at heart?—A. I believe they have, and I believe they will have that cause still more at heart before they get through.

Q. By which you mean that they do not intend to yield?—A. Yes, sir; they will not yield. In the conversation I had with President Cisneros, he said to me that the revolutionists or patriots who were in the field would not accept autonomy, or anything which could be offered by the Spanish Government, save or unless it was freedom.

Q. This was in response to a question you asked him as to what he thought the Cubans would accept?—A. Yes, sir.

Q. Do the Spaniards ever go about singly or in small parties in the country in Cuba?—A. No, sir.

Q. Why not?—A. The Spanish soldier is too careful of himself. He is very fearful of being injured. The smallest party going out is about 3,000 men, from 2,000 to 4,000 usually.

Q. They carry with them no transportation for provision?—A. Usually they have a few horses and carry their provisions on their backs.

Q. So that their campaigns away from their base of supplies must necessarily be short?—A. Yes, sir.

Q. Then the interior of the country, except when these columns are moving, is practically free from Spaniards?—A. Yes, sir.

Q. They are not found there?—A. They are never found at all. You will never find one or two, or a little cluster of five or ten here and there. You will find the guards thrown out around their camp and the Spaniard within that camp, and outside none at all.

Q. How far out are those guards?—A. It depends on the location. If it be hilly, half or three-quarters of a mile.

Q. But they do not picket very far from the camp?—A. Oh, no; very close to it, as a rule.

Q. About what proportion of the Cuban army is negroes?—A. Well, I should say less than 50 per cent. I do not know how much less, but less than 50 per cent.

Q. As a rule, are the negroes under white officers, white Cuban officers?—A. Yes, sir.

Q. Are they good soldiers?—A. Yes, sir; very good, indeed; and splendid fighters, too.

Q. Are they volunteers in the proper sense, or are they driven into it?—A. Nobody is driven. You can not drive a Cuban to do a thing and force him to do it continually.

Q. The whole Cuban army you would call a volunteer organization?—A. Yes, sir; from beginning to end. There is nothing in the army to force a soldier to remain if he does not want to.

Q. You mean there is no effort at coercion?—A. None at all. I have seen General Garcia in Oriente with only 20 men encamped in the field, and that was his whole force.

Q. Where was the balance of the army?—A. Gone; scattered to their homes on leaves of absence for two weeks. The General stayed around, traveling to and fro to while away the time for those two weeks, waiting for the army to come together. At the end of the two weeks the army began assembling and at the end of three weeks it was all there and Garcia started operations.

Q. Showing it was purely a volunteer army?—A. Yes, sir.

Q. Does that indulgence to the soldiers destroy discipline?—A. Not a particle.

Q. Take it at large, I suppose you would say these operations of the Cubans and these military organizations are not only volunteer, but all the men regard it as their cause and their fight?—A. Every last man in Cuba regards it as his fight and his cause, without regard to his neighbor, and he fights, and fights as though it was his own cause. He does as much damage to the Spaniard as he possibly knows how.

Q. Does that individually and also in the collective army?—A. Yes, sir.

Q. I suppose, from the account I have heard, that there is a large area of the eastern provinces in which the Spaniards have never penetrated.—A. Yes, sir.

Q. That is devoted to agriculture?—A. To agriculture entirely.

Q. Any stock growing?—A. Not only stock growing, but vegetables for the use of the army; plantains, yucca, sweet potatoes, etc.

Q. Coffee?—A. In the eastern part of Santiago de Cuba coffee is grown in large quantities; in Camaguey none whatever; I mean no considerable amount. Of course you may find in the rear of some of the houses from 10 to 100 coffee trees, and they are bearing, but no considerable amount of coffee is grown in Camaguey.

Q. In a general way, is the Cuban army supplied with coffee?—A. It is not.

Q. Supplied with tobacco?—A. Supplied? No, sir; it is not. The individual members of the army get tobacco occasionally.

Q. They get coffee also?—A. No, sir; they could not, as a rule. I could not get a particle of coffee for four months that I was with the army. I could not get a drop; could not buy a grain.

Q. Some persons speak of wild coffee trees in certain portions of Cuba. Have you ever come across them?—A. No, sir; I never came across any of them. I have had corn coffee—coffee made from corn—but that is quite a rarity to some of us. There is not such a very great difference in the taste.

Q. Have the Cubans, the rural population, any way of reducing the sugar cane to molasses or treacle? Do they boil it down and make molasses?—A. No, sir; there is no cane growing in Cuba.

Q. Not in Cuba?—A. In the part of Cuba I have been in.

Q. They do not grow it there?—A. No, sir.

Q. There are some portions devoted to sugar and some to tobacco and coffee?—A. Yes, sir; that is it exactly; and they also have gardens devoted to the use of the household.

Q. Are there any considerable number of deserters or prisoners taken from the Spaniards engaged in the eastern provinces in stock growing or stock herding?—A. Yes, sir; I believe Garcia took the prisoners from Wymero and sent them to the eastern part of Oriente, and had them engaged in tilling the crops, and for all I know they are there still, tilling the crops, but it is the only instance I know of. I know it to be a fact that the Cuban government pays every deserter so much for his rifle. When he deserts, he brings his rifle and ammunition over to the Cubans usually, and I know his rifle is taken, and he is paid so much in gold for it.

Q. And then released?—A. Yes, sir; he can do as he desires; he can enter any branch of the service of the government that he desires, without a question.

Q. So he can become a Cuban volunteer or not, according to his own fancy as to what he wants to do after he gets with them?—A. Yes, sir.

Q. Would you say, from your own observation, that there had been much of this desertion from the Spanish lines?—A. I have had very little chance of seeing the deserters, but from—I have had no knowledge of that personally.

Q. What is your information?—A. From my information from other channels I should say there was considerable desertion. The greatest number of deserters I ever saw was nine or ten, I think, come in at once, and they all got somewhere between $14 and $15 apiece.

Q. I gather from what you say that it is not the policy of the Cuban generals to keep their troops in camp unless there is some demonstration about to be made by the enemy?—A. That is a fact.

Q. When that takes place they are quickly summoned and put to work?—A. Instanter.

Q. But that this dispersion of troops does not at all disorganize the army nor have a bad effect on its capacity for fighting when its services are needed?—A. Not at all.

Q. And in the interim these Cubans are permitted to visit their families?—A. Yes, sir; to grow their crops and look after them.

Q. They are very much in the situation the rebels were during the early stage of the revolution, when they were not fighting they were allowed to go home and look after their families?—A. Very much.

S. Doc. 231, pt 7——50

Q. And they would come back on the information of an officer to come with their guns and form a line of battle and go to work?—A. Yes, sir; except the Cubans are not called upon to form a line of battle at all. The Spanish, in traversing the country, usually traverse it with a powerful column and the Cubans want no line of battle at all.

Q. They want to fight from cover?—A. They want to ambush the Spanish. The Cubans never will fight an open fight, for the reason that the Spanish so very greatly outnumber them. Why, in our escape from Cuba, in rounding Puerto Principe, there was a column of 5,000 Spaniards out, and they were confronted by all the force they had in that vicinity—all the men they could get together. All the men had gone to General Garcia in Oriente, and they could only raise 60 men to confront 5,000. Of course, they did not confront them. They had several little tussles, but the Cubans were concealed, and I do not blame them for being concealed.

Q. You do not intimate that General Garcia, if he had any intention of a campaign, could summon only 60 men?—A. Oh, no. General Garcia could summon—I will not say how many, but a great number of men.

Q. Several thousand?—A. Yes, sir; several thousand; and have them well armed and equipped with plenty of ammunition.

Q. When these men go to their homes in this interim, do they take their guns and ammunition with them?—A. Yes, sir; all the soldier has in the field he takes to his home. He takes them with care, and looks after them, oils them, cleans them, and is observing them every day. Takes them down during the rainy season, oils them, and goes over them thoroughly once or twice a week, and usually works the lock or trigger to see that all is right. They are very careful with their arms. They have to be during the rainy season, or they would be so clogged with rust as to be unusable.

Q. The rainy season is on now?—A. Yes, sir; it begins the latter part of May and extends to the latter part of October or first of November.

Q. You have been clear through one of these seasons?—A. Yes, sir.

Q. What effect does that season have on the roads?—A. They are horrible.

Q. Makes them impassable?—A. Almost impassable. In places the horses will go in up to their knees and above. I have gone out for two hours on horseback, and the horse was walking, and it was the hardest kind of walking at the slowest pace possible. We would be over a little divide, and then we would go in away up to above his thighs, and the poor beast was obliged to stop and rest occasionally; could not go on.

Q. The Spaniards, as I understand it, in their movements or forays, confine themselves to the main roads?—A. Yes, sir.

Q. They do not undertake to go by the trails, as the Cubans do?—A. Very rarely. The Cubans have a perfect knowledge of the country. They can go from place to place without ever once touching on the public road. The Spaniards have not that perfect knowledge of the country. In case of a dispersion of a little cluster of Cubans, say thirty or forty, they can disperse immediately, agreeing to rally at a given point, and be at the appointed place at the time set. In case the Spaniards are dispersed, they can not do so; they have not that knowledge of the country; they are lost and done for.

Q. In this rainy season are the trails available?—A. Yes, sir.

Q. They are not cut up?—A. They are cut up, but still passable.

Q. In the dry season how are these great national roads you

speak of?—A. The great national roads in Camaguey are moderately good; but I have seen the high road of Cuba—I have seen points in that where you might just as well try to fly as to get a wagon (a two-wheel wagon, I mean) over. A four-wheel wagon is simply out of the question. You could not do it. The royal high road of Cuba is supposed to be calculated to enable one to pass at any time.

Q. That reaches from Havana to —— —A. From Havana to Cape Maisi, the eastern end of the island.

Q. From one end to the other?—A. Yes, sir.

Q. One single road?—A. Yes, sir.

Q. The royal high road?—A. Yes, sir.

Q. That is the road you say, even in dry weather, is simply impassable at times?—A. Yes, sir. I do not know whether the places are due to the storms that have washed the road out or whether they have always been there, but I have seen places in the road where I had to dismount and let my horse pick his way alone. I was afraid to stay on his back for fear he should fall.

Q. Is Cuba a very stony country?—A. No, sir; it is not. It is only in these one or two spots that there are any considerable number of stones. In fact, all the fields—looking back and thinking of it, I do not recollect passing a 5-acre field of stone or stony country while I was in Cuba.

Q. Are their fields or farms inclosed with fencing—A. Yes, sir; usually barbed wire; but the barbed wire has mostly been destroyed—has been cut.

Q. So that cattle now are all loose and roam at large throughout the country?—A. Yes, sir; the horses did the same until they were finally gathered in portreros and retained there for the use of the Cubans.

Q. Take it by and large, what kind of a grazing country is Cuba?—A. A magnificent grazing country. The grass is nutritious and grows very, very high, and the country affords grazing ground for an enormous number of cattle.

Q. That is one great resource of the Cubans?- A. Yes, sir.

Q. They do not have to go far to get forage?—A. It is a godsend to the Cubans; but late last fall prairie fires began to start here and there and elsewhere, and by and by there was no grass at all. For leagues along the way we could not find a particle of grass. The ground is as black as your hat and as smooth for the want of grass as that table. But now the grass has sprung up again, and now you can obtain pasturage for your horse in any part of the country; but then you had to push on for 5 or 6 leagues at least to get where grass was to be found.

Q. Do the Cubans feed their horses on grain at all?—A. No; grass entirely. In La Villas they feed their horses sugar cane.

Q. Good feed?—A. Splendid. They give them sugar cane and grass in Camaguey, and in Oriente they give grass only.

Q. The cattle are never fed anything?—A. Never at all, or watered, except in the case of a man who has a well and a pump on the well or a bucket, and no water or river of water near. He, of course, will fill the water trough with water, and the cattle will come in and drink from it.

Q. Take the country generally, is it well watered?—A. Yes, sir.

Q. Good water?—A. Very good, indeed.

Q. What is the effect on the rural population of this rainy season; do they appear to have worse health in the rainy season?—A. Not a particle. Their health appears to be about the same at any season, without reference to the season.

Q. Is it good?—A. Yes, sir; very good, indeed. The Cubans are careful not to expose themselves, very careful; they do not expose themselves any more than they are absolutely compelled to do to these rains.

Q. Are the rains warm or cold?—A. Usually warm, but last August there was one day I recollect that I was on the march, and I got about three-fourths of a league from where I was going when a furious storm broke. I was in the midst of a deep, heavy woods; could not see any sky at all until I got to the edge of the clearing. When the storm broke, wasn't that water cold? I thought I was in Iceland. I almost froze before I got to a house a half a league from there, on cleared ground. I was wet through to the skin in about a second. I had on very light clothing, but as soon as I got there I changed and put on a little heavier clothing, and I was not warm even then. My teeth chattered and I shivered and shook for two or three hours, and I finally took my blanket from my hammock and wrapped that about my shoulders to try and keep warm.

Q. That is only an occasional thing?—A. Yes, sir; that was the only time during the entire year. I simply cited that to show that they do have such things.

Q. A man who is not acclimated and did not know how to protect himself under those circumstances would be very apt to be very sick?—A. Not if he took care of himself; but if he went out and about he might have the fever.

Q. What is the result of those rains on an unacclimated person?—A. If they have no hammock and no house to shelter in it is bad; they will, as sure as fate, get the fever.

Q. Is most of the fever in Cuba yellow fever?—A. Yellow fever is the principal fever that is fatal, but I have never seen a case among the rural Cubans.

Q. Have you seen smallpox?—A. Two or three cases only.

Q. Do they take precautions against smallpox? Are they vaccinated?—A. No, sir; because they have no vaccine matter, but they take precautions by isolating the patient and nurse and keeping them isolated.

Q. They are careful about it?—A. They are as careful as they can be, and immediately following the recovery or death of the person from the smallpox the house and its contents are burned.

Q. The habitations of the rural portion of Cuba, of what are they constructed?—A. Of the palm leaf almost entirely. They take several poles, or sticks, if you will, and plant them in the ground at regular intervals, and over these they lash other poles with thongs taken from the trees and from wild vines, and on those poles they place palm leaves for the roof.

Q. Thatch them?—A. Yes, sir.

Q. Does that make a good protection?—A. Yes, sir; splendid. In fact, I do not recollect being in a house in Cuba that leaked, unless it had a hole in the roof such as you put your head through or something of that kind.

Q. They have no chimneys?—A. No, sir.

Q. Do their cooking outdoors?—A. Yes, sir; or else—we will say here is the house [indicating]—they will leave this part, have a little partition across the center, and this part is entirely open; no walls.

Q. A shed?—A. Yes, sir; and in that corner they will have a fire, or in case it is a large place and has several of these houses, this portion is inclosed with a roof and has sides. In case they have several, they have a little place beside it that they will use for a cook house, with a fireplace constructed in the center, but with no chimney or anything of the kind.

Q. You speak of the sides of an inclosed house. Is that composed of palm leaves?—A. Entirely.

Q. That is the chief material for the construction of houses?—A. Yes, sir.

Q. Does it grow abundantly?—A. Yes, sir; they have hundreds of thousands of palm trees.

Q. Are these palm leaves cut and dried for this purpose?—A. They are cut and allowed to remain in the sun to dry for a number of days before they are used.

Q. It makes them tough?—A. I do not know how it makes them, but they make a good roof—a very good roof.

Q. Do you suppose, in times of peace, that the rural population of Cuba live with any degree of comfort?—A. I think they did, in times of peace. From what I have seen of them in times of war, and comparing the life they now lead, I should say they must lead better lives in times of peace.

Q. An abundant supply of food?—A. Yes, sir; some of them have an abundant supply now.

Q. Fruits abound?—A. Very, very many.

Q. In great varieties?—A. Yes, sir. The mango was becoming ripe when I left Cuba, and I have no doubt everybody there is now eating them.

Q. Are they very nutritious?—A. Very. It is a fact that during the last war the entire army was given 40 mangoes a day and nothing else.

Q. For rations?—A. Yes, sir.

Q. How long does that crop last?—A. Four or five months.

Q. In the wet or dry season?—A. In the wet.

Q. It comes in the wet season particularly?—A. Yes, sir.

Q. Is the principal cropping done during the wet or dry season?—A. I do not know how that is; I have never seen them during a time of peace. I should say, as a rule, in the wet season the crops grow best.

Q. And ripen at the end of it?—A. Yes, sir; by the end of it they are thoroughly ripe, and harvested.

Q. I should suppose it does not require much physical labor to secure a living.—A. No, sir; if you merely disturb the ground and drop a little seed that seed will grow if you never touch the ground again. It is not necessary to pay any attention to the ground, plowing it, and going over it continually with the harrow, as in the north.

Q. Taking it all together, in its animal life, its vegetable productions, its fruits, and its grasses, you would say Cuba is an unusually abundant country?—A. Cuba is a paradise; Cuba is a paradise in times of peace.

Q. Is it a pretty country?—A. Indeed it is. Riding along the road, to the right side or to the left, you will see the elevations looming in the distance, and they are covered with forests, light or dark green, and it is one of the most beautiful sights or outlooks one can see. Again, without hesitancy, you are between rows of trees and in a dense, dark shade, terribly warm in the sun, and yet in the shade very nice and cool, and you have good herba or grass for your horse, and the scenery on some of the lakes is most beautiful.

Q. Taking the climate of Cuba, during the wet and dry seasons, should you say it was agreeable?—A. Very agreeable, taking the year round. Of course, during the rainy season it is too wet, and during the hot season too dry.

Q. Too dry and too wet?—A. Yes, sir; I should say the climate is all that could be desired of any climate.

Q. I do not know whether you have thought about it or not, but how do you account for the fact that the Spanish navy has made so few captures of expeditions?—A. I can not account for it. The only expedition they have captured is that of the *Competitor*, and that was merely a little sailing boat, that could not do anything in the nature of getting out of the way. They surely have the gunboats, but, I believe, one trouble is, or has been heretofore, that they have not cleaned the bottom of their gunboats for several years' time, and the result is they have got barnacles and one thing and another on the bottoms of their boats until they can hardly see them.

Q. When you escaped from Cuba you came off in a common boat?—A. Not in a gunboat; a 16-foot, small sailboat.

Q. How many days were you out?—A. Four days. We landed at Nassau.

Q. Did you come across any war ships?—A. Not a one. Did not have a sight of a Spaniard or a Spanish ship, and I thank the Lord we didn't. I had no desire that we should see them. I was praying, on the contrary, that they would remain out of sight.

Q. I suppose, therefore, that communication between Cuba and the outside world—the different islands of the Caribbean Sea and the United States—is practically open?—A. Well, it is open, and yet at the same time it is closed, for the reason that you will not find a man willing to make that trip from choice. If he is ordered to go, that is different, but he will not take it from choice. In that direction I can say I wrote home, on an average, about once every second week all the time I was in Cuba, and I thought my mother wrote to me. I did not know anything about it, but she had said in one of her letters that she would write to me. But I looked in vain for a letter from August until February, and then I received two, one announcing my brother's death and calling me home. I got home and found that just about the time I ceased hearing from home they had not heard from me, and they had not heard anything from last August until they received a telegram announcing that I was in this country, and saw an interview published in the paper.

Q. Through what channels did you receive these letters that you did receive?—A. I do not know; they were all addressed to the junta in New York to be forwarded.

Q. They were addressed to you?—A. Yes, sir; and I received them until last August, when everything stopped.

Q. When you sent the letters did you send them through the Spanish post-offices?—A. At times. Sometimes I sent them that way and they went through without trouble, and at other times they were never heard from. Sometimes they were sent to neighboring islands in small boats, such as we escaped on.

Q. What is the distance from Puerto Rico to Cuba?—A. I do not know, nor do I know what the distance is from Nassau to Cuba.

Q. Since you have been in Cuba have you either known or heard of any cruelty being practiced by the Cubans upon Spanish prisoners?—A. No, sir; I have not.

Q. Neither know nor heard of it?—A. No, sir; neither have I known or heard of any cruelty by any Cuban toward any Spanish, or Cuban either.

Q. If such thing had occurred you would have known of it?—A. Yes, sir; I would have heard it. It would have been heralded and blazoned over the camp as publicly as if in the newspaper. Everybody would have been literally filled with talk of that cruelty toward a prisoner. But that is not so on the other side. I have heard of many, many stories of cruelty on the part of the Spaniards, although I have seen none. At the siege of Wymero, which was taken by Garcia by storm last November, at the siege of that town, there was the commandant of the town and 15 or 18 soldiers wounded, some very seriously, some comparatively slightly. What did Garcia do? He sent word to the nearest Spanish fort that he had such a number of wounded men, and that they were at liberty to send for them an unarmed force, to get those wounded men, and in time the unarmed men showed up at the camp. Garcia promised they would be respected, and they were respected, and not only so, but those men and their wounded compauions were escorted back to their camp by two companies of Cubans, to see that no wandering band of Cubans inflicted any damage on them. What would have been the result if the Spanish had captured that number of wounded men? Would they have sent them into the Cuban camp? Not by several degrees. They would have bayoneted them all or hammered all semblance of humanity out of their faces with the butts of their muskets.

After having read and corrected the foregoing statement I sign the same, under oath.

HARRY W. DANFORTH, M. D.

WASHINGTON, D. C., *July 2, 1897.*

STATEMENT OF MR. C. F. KOOP, FEBRUARY 21, 1898.

Examination by Senator MORGAN:

Q. Please state your name, age, and place of residence.—A. C. F. Koop, 39 years of age, and resident of Boston, Mass.

Q. How long have you resided in Boston?—A. Fifteen years.

Q. What has been your occupation there?—A. I am in the tobacco business.

Q. Buying and selling tobacco, or manufacturing it?—A. Buying and selling the raw material.

Q. Have you had trade in Cuba?—A. Yes; all the time, more or less.

Q. Has it been at any time extensive?—A. Quite extensive.

Q. Had you ever been to Cuba before your last visit?—A. Yes; two or three times.

Q. Do you speak Spanish fluently?—A. I speak Spanish; I can not say that I speak it fluently.

Q. What are the principal tobacco districts in Cuba?—A. Vuelta, Abija, and Santa Clara.

Q. Did you ever travel over this district before your last visit?—A. Once before, but not as extensively as I did this time.

Q. When did you make your last visit to Cuba?—A. I got there on the 6th of January.

Q. When did you leave?—A. I left on the 12th of February, a week ago last Saturday.

Q. How did you occupy your time while you were in Cuba?—A. Largely, of course, looking after my business, and in traveling through the island from one point to another.

Q. Did you travel on passes?—A. No, sir; on money.

Q. I didn't mean that. Did you have a permit?—A. Yes; I had my passport, having been told that it was absolutely unnecessary for an American to have any special pass.

Q. Could you, with the passports, have had access to the lines of the insurgents?—A. No, I could not; not without some difficulty.

Q. Would the Spanish troops allow you to pass out?—A. No, the Spanish troops would not allow you to pass out.

Q. Would the insurgents have been willing to receive you?—A. Yes. I have met the insurgents in various districts. If I went to the lines of the insurgents, outside of the military lines of the Spanish army, I would have had to do it through a great deal of maneuvering and difficulty.

Q. Can you give us a statement of your itinerary through the different provinces?—A. Well, I left Havana the very day after I arrived from New York, and the first stop I made at that time was at Cardenas, which is not a tobacco-growing place or situated in a tobacco-growing district. I went there to consult with the man from whom I bought some property. I stayed there two days.

Q. Now, how far is Cardenas from Havana?—A. About 160 miles.

Q. Did you find the country in cultivation?—A. Absolutely none, except around military towns.

Q. What was the condition of the population at Cardenas?—A. Something horrible; something beyond all description.

Q. Do you apply that to the reconcentrados as well as to the people who are not affected by that order?—A. I apply that strictly to the reconcentrados, because the condition of the other class of the population is altogether different. They have something on which to live; they have their homes, too. The number of recoucentrados forced into Cardenas amounts to 35,000, out of which about 26,000 have died.

Q. What you saw, then, was a people in a very pitiable and starving condition?—A. Yes. At one time I saw a woman lying in a doorway in Cardenas with two dead children lying in her arms, and herself absolutely unable to speak, or even make a motion. She was in the last stages of starvation.

Q. What doorway was that?—A. I don't know exactly; but it was on one of the leading streets there. I can not exactly describe the doorway. Then again, I saw four or five crazy men—lunatics—who were chattering, laughing, crying, cursing—horrible beyond description. And inquiring what brought them to that crazy state from an individual in the Hotel Union there, I was told that it was brought on them by starvation, mainly. With one of them it was the result of finding his whole family starved, and he not able to help them.

Q. Do you know whether any of the benevolent offerings of the United States had reached Cardenas yet while you were there?—A. No, they had not.

Q. Can you state any fact which will show that they had not?—A. I was informed by prominent American officers that they did not have even enough to reach over the city of Havana. Nothing came outside of the city of Havana while I was there.

Q. In what kind of habitations do these people at Cardenas dwell?—A. They live in straw huts, as you might call them, built up from the ground about 7 feet high, and covered with straw. They are built like an "A" tent and are called *bojios*.

Q. While in Cardenas did you note what was called "the zone of cultivation"?—A. I noticed it very distinctly in going into the city on the railroad and in walking about the country. It is on the other side of a military line and is called zone of cultivation, and no one is allowed to go outside.

Q. Inside of that zone was there any cultivation?—A. It was filled with huts, and not much room for cultivation.

Q. Were there any crops growing?—A. No. There was no room. There were a few gardens, and little ones at that.

Q. Did you see any vegetables growing?—A. Yes; something of that kind, but very meager; not even enough for a population of 2,000, much less a population of 60,000 or 70,000.

Q. From its appearance would you suppose or would you judge that that agricultural zone around Cardenas would, if cultivated to its fullest extent, enable the reconcentrados who are upon it to live?—A. Simply impossible.

Q. I suppose Cardenas is a fortified town.—A. It is. It is a seaport town and is also fortified with blockhouses in the rear, and has also one or two small forts there.

Q. You spent two days, I believe you said, in Cardenas?—A. Yes.

Q. During that time did you observe that there was any business being carried on from the outside?—A. Very little indeed. Every man whom I interviewed, from the hotel men to the ship brokers, said that business was absolutely at a standstill.

Q. Was the gentleman you went there to see one of your customers or correspondents?—A. He was. He was the man from whom I bought property.

Q. Did you know him before?—A. I did.

Q. What was his condition as regards business?—A. He was a man who was at one time very well off, and even now has some property and manages to get along rather well.

Q. If I get a correct idea of your statements, the land between Havana and Cardenas was a waste, and the country around Cardenas a waste?—A. Yes. I will give you a fuller description. On my journey I passed through the following towns: The first one of any importance was Jocoro, and the condition around there was pitiable, the children and women gathering around the depot and asking for pennies and for bread and crying with hunger. It was too horrible to describe. The next town of any importance was Bainda, and the condition there was the same. The next town was Aggucata, of seven or eight thousand population, and into this town were forced 10,000 reconcentrados. The condition in this town was something terrible, and I understood from the conductor of the train that in this town out of 10,000 population only about 2,000 lived.

The next town was a small one—Empline—which was in the same condition as the others, the women and children running around the depot begging. The next one was Mocha. This is a very large town, and into it had been forced from eight to ten thousand reconcentrados, and very few of them lived. I remember we had to lay over there for half an hour, and I got out and examined some of the huts. They were all scattered along the railroad track, hundreds of them in a row. I went through a great many rows, and looked into a great many of the huts. They were empty, their occupants having died. About one-fourth of the huts were occupied and the rest unoccupied. The next town was Matanzas.

Q. As you have mentioned Matanzas, please to describe on your visits there what you saw.—A. Matanzas is one of the worst towns on the whole island. It has a population of 70,000.

Q. Is it a fortified town?—A. Yes; it has a very large harbor, and in ordinary times does a good business—sugar business especially.

Q. What was the state of business as you observed at the time of your visit?—A. Absolutely at a standstill. Everything in the way of manufacturing is at a standstill, and the condition of the reconcentrados in Matanzas, what there is left of them, is about as bad as you will find anywhere on the island.

Q. How many had been assembled there?—A. Somewhere between 35,000 and 40,000.

Q. How many were left when you were there?—A. About 8,000 or 9,000.

Q. You saw them?—A. I did. As I have said, at every railroad station crowds of women and children gathered around and begged for money and for bread. It is an everyday experience.

Q. What they live upon, I suppose, is alms?—A. Alms, yes; which they get from strangers passing through the towns. The Government is not making any attempt to feed them, and the local people there are in such a condition that there are few of them who are able to give anything; and those who would have been able to give them something have left the country. In fact, that is the same story of a great many towns. The people who live there and belong there are poor themselves, and are not able to help these people even if they wanted to.

Q. Now, about the "zone of cultivation" around Matanzas?—A. The "zone of cultivation" around Matanzas is, of course, considerably larger than around the other towns, but in proportion to the population there is in Matanzas to the proportion of reconcentrados who have been forced in there it is even smaller, I presume, than in some of the other towns. Into that town of 70,000 population were forced 35,000 or 40,000, and that is quite an addition to a town, and for that reason the line of cultivation, while it is larger than in other towns, is simply insufficient for such a population as there is there.

Q. Could you see from appearances that the population of reconcentrados were really deriving any support from these cultivation zones?—A. It is hard to tell who receives the benefit from these cultivation zones. I am under the impression that most of the products from these cultivation zones were supplied to the city markets. They had not much of a chance to cultivate anything. What they do cultivate is done practically in the street. Between every row of huts there is a road about twenty feet wide, and along in that road, in what you might really call the street, I have seen them try to plant potatoes, etc. I have at various times tried to find out where the vegetables, etc., which were raised inside the military zone went, but was never able to find out. I was always told that they were sent to the markets.

Q. Was that supply of any real consequence toward the support of the population?—A. It was absolutely insufficient. In all my experiences with the living expenses in the interior of Cuba, I will say that it is something phenomenal, and altogether beyond the reach of ordinary individuals. I have paid at various times 25 cents for a little piece of bread which weighed not more than two ounces. For two eggs and rice I have paid anywhere from 50 to 75 cents; and for a small piece of ice, such as you would want for your glass of water, I have paid 25 cents. Beef and other meats, if they have any, is enormously high in price and absolutely unfit to eat. The only thing they have there on which you could really live is rice and eggs, and occasionally some potatoes; but they are all very expensive.

Q. Are there any other incidents attending your visit at Matanzas that will throw any light on the condition of the people there?—A. Well, I did not stay so very long at Matanzas, although I was there three different times—merely stopping off to take the next train—and I did not look around so very much; not so much as I did at other towns.

Q. Proceed.—A. Guanbama is a town of 8,000 or 10,000 population. This is another miserable town, and the affairs there are in a very bad state. A great many were driven in there, but I have not the exact figures, having given it to a party in Havana, and kept no copy.

Q. Now, is that in the sugar district?—A. Yes.

Q. Did you find any business going on in Guanbama?—A. Absolutely none; and the condition there was the same as in the other towns; women and children gathering around, all in a starving condition, begging for bread. The next place was Limonar. That was another place in which the condition was very bad. I passed lots of small places of which I made no note. Next place was Coliso, which also was in a very bad state. The next place was Jovejouna, a railroad center where you change cars for Santa Clara, Cardenas, and other places; and I have passed through that place seven or eight times on my travels on the island, and during these visits I have had several times a lay over of half an hour, and during that time would go and investigate the huts.

I found them to be in horrible shape there. The town has a population of, I think, 10,000, and the amount of concentrados, I was told, amounted to as many as the population. I was informed that very few of them lived, the death rate being phenomenal. And there, also, you could see half-naked women and children in a starving condition, their

feet and stomachs swollen. After studying the disease one could calculate about how long they would live in that condition. I recall another
incident. In getting into Jovejouna there was, as usual, a crowd of
women and children begging; and four or five little girls came through
the train begging. They ranged from three to six years of age. In the
car was a Spanish officer, and as the little girls went by one of them
brushed against him, and he immediately turned and kicked her in the
stomach, knocking her over, and in falling she knocked over the one
next to her, and so on until all five of the little girls fell down in the
aisle.

It was so brutal that I felt like throwing him out of the window, but
of course had to restrain myself. Quintana was another town about
which about the same story is to be told. It is not so large as some of
the other towns. The next town is Precio. I went through it also.
The next town Reta Mal. The next one Aguica. The next is Magagua,
and the next Alvarez. At the last-named place the condition was poor—
a large amount of concentration to a small population, and nothing left
of them. The next town is Modoza. The next Santo Domingo, a railroad center, where you change cars, and which is in very poor condition.
You have all read the story of it sent here by Mr. Pepper. That is the
true story, and I indorse Pepper's story of that and of other places in
Cuba as being correct. Esperanza is a very bad place. Before the war
it was a thriving place, but now there is nothing going on whatever.
The next place is Santa Clara, which is the capital of Santa Clara Province, and military headquarters for that province also. It is a town of,
ordinarily, a population of fifteen to eighteen thousand, and into that
city were driven something like 12,000 concentrados.

Q. How many were there when you visited it?—A. How many reconcentrados? I have the exact figures. Out of that number 7,829 have
died.

Q. From whom did you get this information?—A. Right from the
judge of the civil court. He has to issue certificates for burial for everyone who dies.

Q. The account you got was of those who had been buried according
to law?—A. According to law, yes; entirely.

Q. For everyone of them a certificate of burial has been issued, and
doubtless very many not included?—A. Yes; a great many not included,
they being carted off and buried, and we never see or hear of them.

Q. Nobody ever knows who they are?—A. No; they are gone and
that's all. In the State of Santa Clara I saw so much suffering and so
many horrible sights that I do not know whether there is any use in
relating any of them.

Q. You can state some of the instances which impressed you as being
characteristic of the situation.—A. One of the saddest, if not the saddest, sight I saw was the case of a woman who stood in front of a
hotel in Santa Clara, and who dropped dead when I handed her a piece
of bread. That was the saddest sight I saw on the whole trip.

Q. Did she undertake to eat it?—A. She dropped the baby which
she had in her arms, grabbed the piece of bread which I handed her,
drove her teeth into it and fell over dead. She had a baby in her arms
and two little children hanging on to her skirts.

Q. What became of the baby she let drop?—A. The baby died that
night or the next morning. I found out in the morning that it had
died; and the other two children died a day or two afterwards.

Q. Died of starvation?—A. Yes; starvation.

Q. What is the condition, or the apparent condition, of the persons in Santa Clara who are not concentrado?—A. Fairly good. That is due to the fact of Santa Clara being a railroad town and a good many rich persons living there. It is a town that has the support of the military as well as the civil government, who have their headquarters there; and all courts are held there, more or less. Of course, as I have said, I noticed that in every town the wholesale houses and shipping houses, and a great many retail houses, about one-half, are closed, but in Santa Clara there was more going on than in any other of the interior towns. You can, however, go on the principal thoroughfares and find shutters closed and doors locked. Nevertheless, the condition of the concentrados in Santa Clara is something beyond description.

I traveled around on horseback a great deal and investigated the huts of these people, and all the persons I saw in them were in the last stages of starvation. There was absolutely no food. They were in such a state that even professional nursing would not have saved them. Having stayed in that city for a longer period, and at various times, I, perhaps, investigated it a little closer than I did the other towns, due probably to the fact that I wanted to get out and see something different from what I had been witnessing. I wanted to relieve my mind, if possible. Wherever I had been there was death and starvation staring me in the face. There has not one spot inside the military line where there was a condition that would relieve one's mind, and I was sorely tempted to leave the town with my business unfinished.

Q. Were you out in the zone at Santa Clara?—A. Yes; and the story is the same as it is of every other interior town. In interior towns the zone is drawn much closer and stricter than in seaport towns. Especially is that the case with Santa Clara, Alvarez, and Cruces, because they are somewhat in the line of ranges of mountains that are not very far off, and for that reason the insurgents have more or 'ess access to those places, and they draw their cultivation zone almost within 200 yards of the last house on the street.

Q. Let me ask you whether these reconcentrados are permitted to go outside of this zone to cultivate?—A. No.

Q. Have you seen any evidences tending to show that they are not allowed to go outside of the zone?—A. I have seen at Cruces a little boy, perhaps 9 or 10 years of age, trying to go outside, and who, not complying with the order to halt, was shot at. I myself have been stopped at various times in trying to get across.

Q. What is the condition of the Spanish soldiery in these various places as to food and clothing?—A. The ordinary Spanish soldier is in very bad shape. Of course, the officers seem to have plenty, but the ordinary soldier is in a very bad way. You see them begging in the streets in the interior towns quite often. Their clothing is very poor, and they are a sickly looking lot of men.

Q. Young men or old men?—A. Young men, 15 to 20 years old.

Q. Well, proceed.—A. Ranchuelo is another town that I visited, and found it in a very bad condition. Cruces is also a town in bad condition. Ranchuelo, Cruces, and Santa Clara are in a state that nobody would imagine. You can not imagine it. It is simply terrible. Cienfuegos is about the only town in which I can say I saw any business. Of course, it always has been a business center. All the sugar business goes there, and still the merchants complain that there is absolutely no business there. And the condition, as far as the reconcentrados are concerned, is not quite as bad as it is in other localities. Batabano, which is a seaport town and railroad center, is connected with the boats of the Southern Steamship Company from the eastern part of the

island, and to Havana. From Batabano to Havana I passed through
several towns, but made no enumeration, because I was told to stop
writing notes on the train.

Q. You were prevented from making notes on the train?—A. Yes.

Q. By whom prevented?—A. Officers of the Spanish army. And
that same state of affairs existed several other times during my travels
in Santa Clara district. In some of those travels, whenever I had a
pencil in my hand and was trying to write down notes, a Spanish officer always came up and wanted to know what I had written down. I
usually told them that I had simply written down the name of the town.
In traveling on any road from Havana to Santa Clara, or in any direction east of Havana, the travel is very light. In fact, many times I was
the only passenger on the train. Every train is guarded by a strong
military force and the cars are ironclad. The road from Batabano to
Havana has an immense amount of military guards around it. Every
mile you will find a whole column of Spanish cavalry, guerrillas, marching along up and down the track.

Q. What is the distance from Batabano to Havana?—A. I do not
know exactly, but presume it is about 20 miles; and in that distance
there were in the neighborhood of 3,000 soldiers—men on horseback
guarding the road.

Q. Were your visits to the large cities mainly for business?—A. Yes;
altogether on business.

Q. Now, is Cuba a fertile country—the parts you saw?—A. The most
fertile country I ever saw.

Q. Suppose those reconcentrados had just been allowed to go out
into the country, could they have made a subsistence on the native
productions?—A. Yes; they could have lived alone on the articles which
grow in the district of Santa Clara or any other part of the island.

Q. That you saw.—A. Yes. There is an abundance of sweet potatoes, bananas, and other fruits which are very nourishing, and which
the natives, to a large extent, use in their daily existence.

Q. In passing through the country did you see any herds of cattle?—
A. Absolutely none. All the cattle I saw were strongly guarded by
military forces along the railroad, and they were very few at that.

Q. The country had been stripped of its cattle absolutely?—A. Yes.
The price of cattle has increased 200 per cent, and as I have said before,
all the cattle I saw were under a strong guard of Spanish soldiers; and
there is no cultivation going on in any part of the island that is not
under the guard of the Spanish army, or, rather, Spanish arms.

Q. According to your observations, how do the Spanish get their
provisions?—A. Provisions are sent in from seaport cities somewhat.
My observation has been that the Spanish troops suffer almost as
much as the native population for the want of food. They are not
properly fed. There is no question about that. They themselves
acknowledge that they beg for bread. Of course the officers do not
come under that category.

Q. From what you saw, and from what you have learned while you
have been in Cuba, will you say that there had been any relaxation of
the military regulations in respect of those reconcentrados, of this population, since Blanco has gone into power?—A. None. Whenever I had
an opportunity I made inquiries as regards that point, and was told
invariably that the agricultural zone existed just the same as it did
before.

Q. Did they say that was because the soldiers would not obey Weyler's
orders, or because they were not required to do it?—A. They did not

receive any orders. I have not understood that at any time there were any orders in any of the interior towns to relax any of the agricultural zones. The people who are there just have to starve to death.

Q. Did you, at any place you visited in Cuba, ascertain or learn that the Spanish Government was making any provision for the reconcentrados?—A. Never. I have not, in all the thirty-odd towns in which I have been, I have not heard that the Spanish Government has supplied or helped to supply any starving individual with bread or anything else.

Q. Did you meet with any of our consuls in the interior of Cuba?—A. Yes.

Q. Did you have opportunity to know whether they had been contributing out of their private resources to the support of these poor people?—A. All the consuls whom I have met have done a great deal toward the betterment of the starving individuals there out of their private means.

Q. Would you give it as your opinion that they had expended all their salaries beyond their living in this effort?—A. I would not hesitate to say that they have gone beyond it. I know that as a fact.

Q. Did they manifest a spirit of charity and generosity toward these people?—A. Yes.

Q. I will ask you generally whether, from your observation, our consuls have interested themselves earnestly in the effort to relieve the unfortunate condition of the people in Cuba?—A. I can say right here, that in all my observations I have felt proud of General Lee and of every consul in whose province I have been; proud of the way they have treated and helped some of the starving individuals at their own expense.

Q. From what you could gather while you were in the interior of Cuba, would you say, and is it your belief and opinion, that our consuls in the interior have used all of the means that came under their control, public or private, to save these poor people from starving?—A. There is absolutely no doubt on that point. They have not only used the means given to them publicly, but have used also their private means, working day and night, to further the interests of those poor individuals.

Q. For what purpose did you visit Washington, and what was your method in coming here?—A. In the first place, being in Cuba all this time, and seeing all the suffering, day in and day out, and night and morning, it was absolutely impressed on my mind that the suffering there was not the fault of those people. It was not men who were suffering, it was women and children. They were driven from their own homes and forced into these military lines. When I came home, and on my way over, I could hardly sleep at night. I brooded over the matter, and at length decided to come to Washington and free my mind to some person in authority here, or to the Senate, the House of Representatives, or wherever I could find someone who would try to do something. It was not because I wanted any political changes on the island, or that I cared what government they had. My only point in coming here was simply to try and save these 400,000 who are still left from starving, although there is quite a number of them beyond help.

Q. Do you believe that if the Congress of the United States would vote an adequate sum to buy provisions for these people it would reach them?—A. No; I do not.

Q. Why?—A. Simply because it would be impossible for the American authorities to get the property into the interior of the island; and even if it did get there, there would be only about one-third of it, as the rest would be absorbed by the Spanish Government and soldiers, and distributed among the Spanish people rather than among the Cubans.

Q. Do the Spanish treat the Cubans with repugnance?—A. They feel that a Cuban is worse than a dog.

Q. You think, then, that the purpose of the regulation was really to starve these people to death?—A. Yes; the sole purpose. It is well known that 900,000 of those natives were forced in from their homes, and out of that number 500,000 have died already. Therefore the results have proved the motive.

Q. What was the apparent relation between the soldiers and these reconcentrados, or did the soldiers seem to have any sort of human regard for them?—A. Many of the soldiers are low spirited and absolutely incapable of having such resentment, because, in the majority of cases, they were mere boys and in such a condition as to be hardly able to take care of themselves. The repugnance was largely among the officers and the Spanish guards, which is the flower of the army. They are in better condition than the common soldiers. The Home Guard, picked men, are also in better condition.

Q. What is the feeling of this class that are in better condition—what is their feeling toward these poor reconcentrados, as you saw it?—A. There was a sort of a feeling between them that they would eat at one another's table, if they could. If one had anything, they would give it to the other. There was no animosity among the ordinary soldiery of the Spanish army. I am not speaking of the volunteers, nor of the Home Guard, nor of the officers, but the ordinary soldier. I never noticed any particular hatred between them and the natives.

Q. How is it with the officers of the Home Guard?—A. They consider the Cubans like so many brutes.

Q. With contempt?—A. Yes; absolutely.

Q. I suppose these reconcentrados of whom you have been speaking are natives?—A. Absolutely all natives.

Q. All natives of Cuba?—A. The majority are white. They are of Spanish, French, and other nationalities, but largely Spanish, with some colored people among them.

Q. If I comprehend your description of the interior of Cuba, it is a country that is almost entirely wasted and destroyed?—A. Absolutely. There is nothing at all going on in the interior of Cuba. No houses standing. Ruined sugar estates wherever you look. Wherever there is any sugar growing you will see a force of soldiers guarding it, these soldiers being kept there by the sugar owners, and are therefore able to exist.

Q. It is already then a country laid to waste?—A. The whole country is a waste.

Q. In the present condition of these people, would it be possible in their weak state that they could survive by the assistance of the fruits of the earth?—A. A great many of them now, if let loose, would recover at once—women especially, although a great many of them are absolutely too feeble to move much.

Q. What per cent of them, as you saw them, would you say would be able and capable, if they were turned loose, of going back to their places where they formerly lived, or to any other place, and get an existence out of the wild fruits, potatoes, etc., which grow in the interior?—A. Seventy per cent would be able to go back.

Q. If they were let loose?—A. Yes.

Q. So that retaining them is starving them in the face of opportunity to live?—A. Yes, it is.

Q. Then, you think—it is your opinion—if I understand you, that the failure to relax the orders of Weyler in regard to the reconcentrados of this people to hold them, is still the actual and direct cause of their present starvation?—A. The only cause.

Q. While you were in Cuba, were you in control of any large amount of means for the purpose of assisting your former customers?—A. I was in position to buy merchandise to quite a large extent, if I had been able to find it.

Q. To what extent?—A. $25,000.

Q. You could not find the merchandise?—A. No; absolutely none. The kind of merchandise for which I was looking (tobacco) was not to be had.

Q. Are owners of real estate in Cuba, as far as you observed, anxious to dispose of it?—A. There is a large amount of property which has been absorbed by the American citizens in Cuba; a very large amount of it.

Q. Well, is there an anxiety on the part of those landholders to dispose of their estates?—A. There is. Some of the Spanish landholders are selling off all they have.

Q. What did you learn about the emigration?—A. About 400,000 to various American cities from Cuba.

Q. Were they a class of people who had means of emigrating?—A. They were the people who could get away.

Q. A very large part, then, of that class must have left the island?—A. Yes.

Q. Those who remained were the poor people and the soldiers?—A. Yes.

Q. Did you make any computation of the number of lives that have been sacrificed in Cuba through war, starvation, and disease all put together?—A. Yes; I have at various times asked that question of officers, and learned that the amount of people who have died from sickness and starvation is somewhere in the vicinity of 600,000. Of course that does not include Spanish soldiers.

Q. Does it include the insurgents?—A. It does. It includes the death rate in the Island of Cuba, excluding Spanish soldiers.

Q. You think rather above it than below it?—A. Rather.

Q. You have made careful examination on that subject, and have consulted with men who had opportunity to ascertain as to the statistics?—A. Statistics have been collected carefully, and are obtainable by the American Government if it wants them.

Q. And are obtainable by the authorities?—A. Yes.

Q. Did you ascertain, or did you observe while you were in Cuba, from what country the Spanish Government obtains its supplies for its army—all the coal and provisions and other necessities?—A. In that respect, I have not made a great many inquiries. I heard in Havana from an English shipping house that the Spanish Government tried to force all their merchants to buy whatever they had to from the Spanish merchants, instead of allowing them to buy from Americans.

Q. Is the coal which is brought into the island from the United States or from a foreign country?—A. I judge it is from a foreign country.

Q. What was your judgment, from all that you saw, as to the state of feeling of the Spanish people and the pro-Spanish people toward the people of the United States in the Island of Cuba?—A. Well, the Spanish business men would all like that the island be annexed to the United States in preference to its being continued under Spanish rule. There are, of course, two or three different parties there. For instance, the Independents and the Annexationists.

S. Doc. 231, pt 7——51

Q. Among the native Cubans, or those persons who have been a long time residents of the island, did you find any hostility toward the United States?—A. Absolutely none. Whenever I met any Cubans they were always anxious to do everything they could for me.

Q. In going through Cuba did you meet up with acquaintances of former years?—A. Yes.

Q. Were they numerous?—A. No; not very.

Q. Did you have consultation and conversation with men of character and influence?—A. I did. I have met some of the leading members of the autonomy government, and also some of the present Spanish administration.

Q. Now, without stating with whom these consultations were, what conclusion did you reach as to the popularity of the autonomy movement in the interior towns?—A. One that any man would come to after having visited the island for even a short while, and that is that autonomy is a matter of indifference there, and it is only believed in by a very few persons, and those are largely concentrated in the city of Havana. When you come outside the city of Havana you find no autonomy party

Q. You think, then, that the probability of that form of government being accepted in Cuba is small?—A. It will never be accepted. It will never be accepted by the Spanish people.

Q. As I understand you, you are not speaking of the insurgents?. A. No; speaking of the Spanish people themselves.

Q. Were these consultations and conversations with men of such character as to lead you to satisfactory conclusions as to the opinions you have just expressed?—A. They are, in fact, men of very high standing and leaders of the autonomy movement in the city of Havana.

Q. Your acquaintance with Cubans grew chiefly out of business relations?—A. Chiefly with the Spanish and Cuban merchants.

Q. And have been of sufficient years' standing?—A. Oh, yes; a number of years.

Q. Did you ascertain in Cuba whether or not the leading men engaged in business pursuits had any confidence in the good faith of the Spanish Government?—A. There is only one answer to that: Nothing. They have no confidence in the autonomy plan the Spanish Government has so far offered.

Q. Was the subject of an American protectorate in connection with autonomy discussed?—A. It was generally discussed by merchants and business men that if they could get an American protectorate with autonomy they might have some confidence.

Q. Their willingness was, after all, upon the intervention or protection of the American Government?—A. Yes; absolutely.

Q. Under the most favorable of circumstances, if Spanish authority was fully reinstated in Cuba by the subjugation of the insurgents, would you expect Cuba to be able to regain its former conditions within a number of years?—A. Not within a number of years.

Q. How do you believe it would be in the event of the success of the insurgent army, accompanied by close and friendly relations with the United States; what do you believe it would be then?—A. I believe that the Island of Cuba would be in a flourishing condition inside of two or three years. There are hundreds of thousands of Cubans who have emigrated. They would return to business on the island, and citizens from other countries would also go there.

Q. And invest money?—A. Yes, and invest money.

Having examined and corrected the foregoing statements made under oath to John T. Morgan, a member of the Committee on Foreign Relations of the Senate, and having stricken out some passages that are true, but may affect the interest of myself and others unnecessarily and dangerously, I make oath that the statement as revised is true to the best of my knowledge, information, and belief.

C. F. KOOP.

FEBRUARY 21, 1898.

DISTRICT OF COLUMBIA, CITY OF WASHINGTON:

Subscribed and sworn to before me this 21st day of February, A. D. 1898.

[SEAL.]   R. B. NIXON, *Notary Public.*

STATEMENT OF COMMANDER R. B. BRADFORD, U. S. N., March 30, 1898.

Commander R. B. BRADFORD, U. S. N., sworn by the chairman. •

Examination by Senator FRYE

Q. Please state your name and profession.—A. R. B. Bradford; naval officer, at present Chief of the Bureau of Equipment, Navy Department.

Q. What experience, if any, have you had with torpedoes?—A. I have been on duty at the torpedo station at Newport, R. I., when it was a school of instruction, as instructor and lecturer in torpedo warfare, altogether for a period of about six and a half years, and during that time I conducted a great many experiments with torpedoes and saw a great many explosions and the effect of torpedo explosions on small vessels and various kinds of materials; probably have had more experience than the average naval officer in that direction.

Q. Suppose you state to the committee the several kinds of torpedoes.—A. At the present day torpedoes are largely employed, under the name of mines, for harbor defense. They were formerly called torpedoes exclusively—during the war of the rebellion they were known as such. Since that time they have received various names in accordance with their usage. Those used for harbor defense are placed under the army and received an army name, and are recognized as such, and are now known as mines or submarine mines. They are the most powerful, because the amount of explosive used for submarine mines is practically unlimited, depending upon the size of the case, which can be made almost any dimensions. It is only limited by methods of handling, such as derricks, etc.

The kind of torpedoes used mostly in the Navy are known as electro-motive torpedoes, sometimes termed fish torpedoes, and now they are generally or frequently spoken of by the names of the inventors—the Whitehead, the Scwartzkoff, etc. They are all of the movable type, ejected from a tube, and contain, you may say briefly, all the mechanism of a complete steam vessel, provided with engines and motive power, means of steering, and carry in their forward ends an amount of explosive which is limited to about 100 pounds, gun cotton usually, and exploded on contact with any object. They have been very carefully designed and improved for a period of thirty years, so that they are now very perfect pieces of mechanism, mostly used from torpedo boats and torpedo destroyers and torpedo cruisers. They were formerly used in all naval vessels, but with the advent of rapid-firing guns, etc., they have been largely discarded for use in tubes above water, except the small vessels which I mention, such as torpedo boats and destroyers.

The reason is they are liable to be hit by small projectiles and exploded on board. They are still retained for use in larger ships for tubes under water, where they are protected by the water from shot or by armor.

Our cruisers formerly fitted with them are now discarding them for the reasons I have given. Then, of course, there are a great many improvised torpedoes, and a kind that is frequently carried on ships of a small size, and sufficient to destroy or disable larger vessels, carrying from 50 to 100 pounds of explosive, known as electro mechanical torpedoes, carrying a small battery inside with an arrangement that when it strikes the circuit of this battery is completed on an explosive, and they are discharged. They are for the general purpose of fencing in ships that are disabled, or of being planted in narrow passages where enemy's vessels may pass. They are mobile affairs that are carried like any destructive material on board ships of war. Those three are the chief kinds used to-day, but any kind of torpedo can be improvised from almost any water-tight vessel, and are depended upon more or less, but the three kinds which I have mentioned are the perfected kinds.

Q. What is the difference between a torpedo boat and a torpedo-boat destroyer?—A. Only in size. The destroyer is larger. It has the advantage over a torpedo boat of being more seaworthy and stronger. It is a steamer designed to destroy torpedo boats, being a larger and more powerful vessel. The name indicates the idea of the design. They are capable of being used in rougher water, and they have a larger radius of effective use, carrying more supplies, and more coal, and more men. They carry also more guns and heavier guns. Torpedo boats of about a hundred tons' displacement carry only small guns and are in every way inferior, but the destroyers are practically only torpedo boats.

Q. And attack a ship in the same way?—A. Yes, sir.

By Mr. MILLS:

Q. Do they attack with torpedoes or guns?—A. They are chiefly designed to use torpedoes; the guns are mostly auxiliary or incidental.

Q. How far can they send those torpedoes?—A. They are limited to about 600 yards—the mobile or Whitehead torpedoes, such as I have described.

By Mr. FORAKER:

Q. Will they go straight?—A. They are so perfected that if in perfect order they will go straight. They are subject to deviation from very slight derangement. They are handled very much as though made of glass. They require the greatest care, and will perform a great deal of work if everything is nicely adjusted. Even with the greatest care on board ship we sometimes find in our experiments that they deviate from some unnoticed or unknown cause that we can not ascertain—probably, in handling, the vertical rudder has been bent somewhat, so slightly we can not detect it. They go under water some 13 feet, so they can not be interfered with by shot after once discharged. They are also liable to be deflected by currents to some extent.

Q. How rapidly do they go?—A. They go at the rate of from 25 to 30 knots per hour.

By Mr. MORGAN:

Q. What is the impelling power?—A. Two propellers. The motive power is compressed air in tubes. When they are ejected from their tubes, the valve communicating between the air reservoir and the engines is opened, so that they act precisely, you may say, as any steam vessel—automatically.

By Mr. FRYE

Q. Have their own machinery?—A. Yes, sir; the most perfect that can be built, of the most perfect and best material. They cost from $2,000 to $2,500 apiece, so you may know they are very perfect.

By Mr. MORGAN:

Q. Can they be sent from the shore without the assistance of a torpedo tube?—A. No, sir; they could not be pointed. They could be started with the aid of the trigger. The tube from which they are shot is worked very much like a gun; it is on a pivot, and is carefully adjusted, and allowance is made in firing for the speed of the ship at which they are fired.

Q. I would like to know, briefly, the danger from this Spanish flotilla of torpedo boats and torpedo destroyers?—A. I am not impressed as much as many naval officers with the dangerous character of torpedo boats and torpedo destroyers. They are frail craft, because everything is sacrificed to speed, and weights are kept down for that reason, and very thin plates used in their construction, very slight frames, and they are easily deranged. I may say that they are boats of possibilities rather than of probabilities.

Under certain conditions they are no doubt very formidable. Their chief value in my opinon is in preventing blockades, if in ports that are attempted to be blockaded. They choose their own time of attack, and of course the most favorable time. They are previously groomed up for the occasion, everything in readiness, and they slip out to a vessel outside, and try to get in their work. At sea with a squadron they are so liable to accident and so often deranged that the chances of being effective, in my opinion, are slight. I understand that the present flotilla, crossing from Spain, have been dismantled. That is to say, the torpedo tubes and guns carried on the upper deck have been taken off and are being brought over by the convoying steamer, which is a converted cruiser. That adds to their seaworthiness and stability. With those off they are completely helpless, shorn of any power

The destroyers are supposed to be capable of ramming the small boats and destroying them that way. If within the destroying radius of a fleet, of course they can be used in the same way I described in a blockade. For instance, the port of Havana is about 90 miles from Key West or Tortugas. They have high speed. They can slip out at night, get in their work, and return under cover of darkness, and, vice versa, our own could do the same work. We happen to have no destroyers, and our torpedo boats have found it rather rough work crossing the Gulf Stream between those ports.

Q. How long a voyage, on the average, between the Canaries and Puerto Rico?—A. That depends entirely on speed and the water. It is very difficult to form an estimate. They are coming, no doubt, in a latitude where the weather is very good. The route from Las Palmas, where they left the Canaries, to Puerto Rico is through the trade-wind belt, and there is rarely any bad weather there. I presume they would make somewhere—their speed would be governed largely by the accompanying steamer—say from 10 to 12 knots. I think the distance is about 2,800 miles. Say 10 knots—240 miles a day—that would be about 12 days.

Q. Have you read the testimony taken by the naval board of inquiry?—A. Only sketches of it in the newspapers. I have not seen the full report as published.

Q. Have you read the accounts of the witnesses who testified as to two explosions?—A. Yes, I have; and previously in the newspapers.

Q. What do these accounts indicate to your mind was the cause of the explosion?—A. If you have noticed, the accounts are conflicting as to there being two explosions; some officers state they heard but one. In all torpedo explosions there always, apparently, are two explosions or two shocks. That is universally the case, and it is markedly so with a torpedo or mine on the bottom. The first appears to be transmitted by the land or by the water, and then the next appears to be the emission of this great quantity of highly heated gas into the open air, and in the same manner we have thunder after a stroke of lightning. But that is very well known to people who have exploded torpedoes, that there are always two shocks, and I have been of the opinion generally that those who thought there were two explosions confounded that fact with the idea that there was a second explosion.

It seemed to me that it was quite possible that the explosion of a mine broke the ship in the neighborhood of the magazines—we know the explosion was in the neighborhood of some of the magazines—broke some of the powder cases and dispersed this powder and at the same time ignited it, and this in a measure accounted for the flame about the ship. The result of the divers' work would seem to favor that theory. They found many powder cases broken open and battered up more or less. I do not think myself there was any serious explosion of the magazine from what I have read.

Q. What, in your opinion, did cause the trouble?—A. A mine—a submarine mine.

Q. Have you any doubt about it, after reading the testimony?—A. No, sir; I have not.

Q. In your opinion, what kind of a mine must that have been to have the effect shown there?—A. It must have been a mine of what is termed "high explosives," I think.

By Mr. GRAY:

Q. Dynamite?—A. Dynamite or gun cotton, or any of the modern high explosives. It is possible to do the same with gunpowder.

By Mr. FRYE:

Q. What would be the size and weight and general character of that mine?—A. I am at a disadvantage in answering that question, because I have not seen the wreck and have not read fully the testimony, but there are cases on record where ships—not as strong as the *Maine*, but metal ships—have been destroyed by the explosion of torpedoes alongside and not in contact, and varying in size from 250 to 300 pounds. In the Chilean war two ships were sunk by an explosion in this manner.

By Mr. GRAY:

Q. Were they in contact?—A. No, sir; not in contact, but a couple of feet at the side and at the surface. They did not have the advantage of the tamping of the water. Of course, the destruction is caused by the release of an immense volume of highly heated gas that escapes to the atmosphere through the path of least resistance. Water being incompressible, and if it is under the ship the path of least resistance is through the ship, and everything must give way to it. It is rather difficult to estimate the amount of explosive, but I would say 300 pounds of modern explosive, in my opinion, would do all the damage that was done to the *Maine*, and very possibly a less amount.

By Mr. MORGAN:

Q. Do you mean dynamite or gun cotton?—A. Yes, sir; they are included as modern explosives. I notice—I think the opinion was given by Commander Converse, who is a very excellent expert, and who has had almost all his duty on shore in connection with torpedoes—either he or someone else stated they thought the work was done by a slower burning explosive, and I take it to mean—I understand that he meant gunpowder. Gunpowder has a slower action; it is simply combustion as wood burns, while modern explosives, by their fuse, are turned instantly from a solid to an immense volume of highly heated gas, called detonation. The effect of detonation is to rend everything in the immediate neighborhood. Even tamping is sufficient for that, but gunpowder is slower acting.

By Mr. MILLS:

Q. How would it be ignited?—A. By electricity.

Q. Either on shore or on some other vessel?—A. Yes, sir; it is very simple to do that; it is well understood.

By Mr. GRAY:

Q. Do you think it possible for a mine to have been placed there after the ship was anchored with the discipline probably on board?—A. Oh, yes; I think it was possible.

Q. How?—A. There are various ways. One, for instance: It could be attached to a line run forward the ship, ahead of it so far it could not be seen, to some point beyond, and then taken back. For instance, here is the bow of the ship [indicating]. Start from a point here. There is the shore line, and suppose we carry a line to that point, run it across, and come down here. As you haul in the slack you would have a line taking that direction. If you knew the distance of the ship from the shore you would know exactly when the torpedo was under the bows of the ship, and you would haul on the line until you reached the proper mark, and the torpedo would be here. [Indicating under the forward part of the ship.] I do not think it would be possible to prevent it.

By Mr. DAVIS:

Q. How would you anchor it, then?—A. Either haul the line taut or allow the torpedo to sink by its own weight.

Q. Can you haul an electric wire so?—A. Yes, sir; they offer very little resistance; it could be very small, not larger than my pencil.

By Mr. CULLOM:

Q. Was that in the mud?—A. It is not known. In all probability it was resting on the bottom, and in my opinion it was placed there before the vessel was sent there.

Q. When that was placed there, why, no matter how, or when, how was it to be exploded?—A. How could it have been exploded?

Q. How must it have been exploded?—A. It was possible to explode it by a trigger line and something somewhat similar to what is known as a friction fuse. The first ship destroyed during the war of the rebellion was destroyed by a torpedo of that kind. It was at Cairo, and was commanded by Captain, at present Commodore, Selfridge. That was by a trigger concealed in a rifle pit, and the operator judged by the eye when the vessel was over it, and simply pulled the trigger as you would the lock of a gun. The use of explosives for so many purposes—blasting, mining, everything—is so common that probably anyone who designed to do that work would resort to it. I think it is improbable anything else was used.

Q. Could that have been used without the knowledge of any of the officials at Havana?—A. Possibly, but not probably.

Q. You have read the descriptions of the vessel given by the divers; did it leave in your mind any doubt as to its destruction .having been caused by a mine?—A. No; I think I have no doubt on that subject; I think it was done by a mine.

By Mr. MORGAN:

Q. In the case of a torpedo that works automatically, or by a torpedo localized by itself, would the explosion take place by the impact of the ship?—A. Yes, sir; electricity is not used in these movable, automatic torpedoes. Fulminate is used, and the explosion caused by the impact of a plunger which is driven back into the case of fulminate.

Q. So that when the vessel struck it——A. No; this torpedo I am describing progresses until it strikes something and then this plunger is driven back.

Q. Are mines ever used of this kind?—A. Yes; contact mines; they are both mechanical. I mean the operation of exploding it is not connected with the of operation of electricty. They are electro-mechanical where both forces are brought in play, applying to torpedoes which must be tipped over by the object striking it. The electric torpedo or mine is one where the operator must close the circuit by a key.

Q. I notice in the examination by the judge advocate that questions were asked of the witnesses, particularly the officers aboard the ship, as to whether she had the same bearing or heading at the moment of explosion as she had been accustomed to having at the same hour of the day on preceding days, and they said there was a difference?—A. This question was asked because if the torpedo had been placed at a certain point—the ship was riding to a buoy--in order that the torpedo should do the utmost damage, it would be necessary for the ship to be over it, and as she swung about it was possible to explode it without doing much damage, but if a time was selected when she swung exactly over it, it would destroy her. Of course, a very little distance makes a great difference in the amount of damage done. The radius of effective damage is not very large, not nearly so large as the radius a ship would describe in swinging around a buoy.

By Mr. DAVIS:

Q. Was it moored by the stem or stern?—A. Stem.

Q. Did she swing with the wind and tide?—A. Yes, sir.

Q. What would be the arc?—A. That would depend on the chain. They probably had a small amount of chain out. If she was riding to an anchor, of course the arc would be quite large.

Q. Taking into account that she was riding to a buoy, and that this accident happened a hundred feet from the stem, what would be the arc of swing?—A. She might have had out 12 to 18 feet of chain, and if the torpedo was a hundred feet from the buoy, and she swung 180 degrees from that point, her bow would then be 112 to 118 feet from the torpedo.

Q. Where would this hundred feet point be—how much play had that point of 100 feet on an arc——A. Your question, I think, placed the torpedo, supposing there was one for the sake of the argument, 100 feet from the buoy, and if she headed a certain direction she would be directly over it. If she headed 180 degrees away, the distance would be 100 feet plus the length of the chain, which would be about 112 to 118 feet.

By Mr. GRAY:

Q. Feet or fathoms?—A. Feet. You would have just enough chain out to swing clear of the buoy. Is that plain?

Q. Here is the ship. [Indicating.] Here is the buoy. Here is the point of 100 feet where we suppose the torpedo to be. This ship swings how far? Can she swing from one side to another over the torpedo?—A. It would be the distance from the buoy plus the length of the chain, which would be 112 to 118 feet.

Q. That would be the amount of the swing?—A. Yes, sir.

By Mr. FORAKER:

Q. She swings that way?—A. In any way.

By Mr. MILLS:

Q. In your study of this question, have you ever known of private individuals putting torpedoes in harbors to destroy ships?—A. I never heard of it.

Q. It costs a great deal of money?—A. Yes, sir; and it can not be carried on without attracting attention.

By Mr. MORGAN:

Q. What would be the weight of a torpedo to work the amount of damage done on this ship?—A. That can not be answered definitely. It is usual for ground mines, those placed on the bottom, to use very heavy cases, so that the case may serve as an anchor. They are frequently made of cast iron, very thick walls. Buoyant mines, placed where the water is very deep, to bring them to near the bottom of the ship, are made of comparatively light material, such as steel plate. So there is an opportunity for very wide speculation as regards weight. I have given you the amount of explosive, and the case would, roughly estimated, probably weigh 500 pounds.

By Mr. CULLOM:

Q. What would be probably the length of a submarine mine with 300 pounds of explosive material in it?—A. They are very frequently made the shape of a sphere. Those placed on the bottom are commonly flat, while the buoyant are spherical.

Q. One man could not handle it?—A. No, sir; only with derrick and tackles.

By Mr. DAVIS:

Q. What do I understand you to say might be the total weight of this, case and all?—A. Five hundred to a thousand pounds.

Q. Could that kind of a contrivance be drawn under that ship by a line as you described?—A. No, sir; I was describing the ordinary mines used for service. You can put dynamite or gun cotton in a rubber bag with air space enough to float it.

Q. How large are the conducting wires by which these explosions are made?—A. That is very variable. Cables laid down prepared for use with permanent systems are armored.

Q. Insulated?—A. Not only insulated, but armored like a submarine cable in order to resist abrasion, etc. Yet, for ordinary use you can use a small wire like my pencil.

Q. Do those contrivances generally have either one or two wires?—A. Either. In salt water you can use either a reel service or two wires without the reel service.

By Mr. LODGE:

Q. Would the ordinary torpedo be sufficiently powerful to produce the result produced in the *Maine?*—A. In my opinion it would not. I so stated immediately after the report of the damage done to the *Maine.*

By Mr. DAVIS:

Q. Why do you think the torpedo was sunk before the arrival of the *Maine?*—A. Because of the difficulty of placing it without detection—without its being known—after the arrival of the *Maine.*

By Mr. GRAY:

Q. That was the purport of my question, as to how that could be done, with proper discipline?—A. You can tell how difficult it is to detect work going on at night, and you know something about the intelligence of men who do sentry duty in army and navy. You probably know many instances where sentries and lookouts, particularly in the Army and in important places, have been surprised and overcome in hand-to-hand conflict. I do not think myself that any such thing as that occurred. I believe the torpedo was placed there before the *Maine* went there, but there is a possibility of it.

Q. Even with good discipline?—A. There was no question the ship had good discipline.

By Mr. DAVIS:

Q. Considering the swing of the vessel, must it not have been a matter of very nice calculation when to spring that mine?—A. Yes, sir. Not in the sense of nicety of practice in adjusting instruments, not such a degree of nicety. It was a comparatively easy job to judge by the eye.

Q. Would it have to be done by bearings?—A. No, sir. ·

Q. How would you do it?—A. Because the shore was so near—only 500 or 600 yards off. Besides, anyone doing that work had the buoy as a guide, and if he knew the distance of the torpedo from the buoy, and knew the ship, when headed in a certain direction would be over the mine, it would be not difficult.

By Mr. GRAY:

Q. That observation would be very difficult at night?—A. I do not think it would, because you would only have to see what direction the ship was heading, and it is not difficult to do that. If you know that when a ship heads or tails in a certain direction she must be over a torpedo, there is only to know what direction she is heading.

Q. The lights would indicate that?—A. Certainly.

By Mr. LODGE: ·

Q. Was there not opportunity to determine the exact hour on previous nights when it would be over the torpedo?—A. The winds at Havana are generally north to east; those are the prevailing winds. The currents are small. I have read, though I do not know that it is true, that the ship had never headed before in the direction she did at the time of the explosion.

By Mr. FORAKER:

Q. A submarine mine is only a torpedo?—A. Yes, sir, under another name.

Q. As I have understood, while you have described the way it could be put under the ship, yet in your judgment it would be very difficult to do that without it being discovered?—A. Yes, sir.

By Mr. CULLOM:

Q. I have heard it said that boats were running in and out that harbor almost within shaking hands distance from the battle ship, and that, on a night for instance, a boat could go in there and slip something under it without the call of the sentry?—A. Perhaps I have not made myself clear in one respect. I discussed and described regular submarine mines for harbor defense. I think I also mentioned that modern explosives do not require a strong envelope or inclosure to be effective——

By Mr. MORGAN:

Q. You also said that dynamite or modern explosives might be conveyed in a rubber bag?—A. Yes, sir, and I want to enlarge on that now. It does not follow of necessity that that damage could not be done in any other way than by the use of a submarine mine. That explosion which destroyed two Chilean ships, there the explosive was placed loosely in a boat with a false bottom, and did so much damage that both ships sunk almost immediately, one while the boat was being hoisted and the other while the boat was being cleared of some tempting provisions on the false deck.

By Mr. FRYE:

Q. In the one case you deal with probabilities and in the other with possibilities?—A. Yes, sir.

By Mr. FORAKER:

Q. Your belief is that it was destroyed by a mine under the vessel?—A. Yes, sir.

Q. And exploded from the shore?—A. Yes, sir.

By Mr. MILLS:

Q. How far was the ship from the shore?—A. I have seen it stated that it was about 500 yards, but that is susceptible of exact determination. I think the buoy she was using, No. 4, is given on the charts.

By Mr. FORAKER:

Q. Do you know of any regulations of Havana for the use or sale of explosives?—A. I do not.

Q. These are not ordinarily found in stores or toy shops for sale?—A. By no means; particularly in a place like Havana to-day, where fighting is going on more or less all the time in the neighborhood.

By Mr. MILLS:

Q. You think that mine could not be placed there without the consent of the authorities?—A. I do—I will change that; I do not think it was probable.

By Mr. FORAKER:

Q. The probability is that it was put there by Government authority, and known to be there by the Government officials?—A. Yes, sir.

By Mr. LODGE:

Q. If that flotilla of torpedo destroyers and torpedo boats now on its way from the Canaries could be brought to Havana and placed in the harbor, would it not then become formidable and an increased danger in the naval situation to us?—A. An increased danger?

Q. Yes, sir.—A. Yes, sir; I think it would.

By Mr. DAVIS:

Q. I ask the same question as to Puerto Rico?—A. In a less degree. They would be formidable anywhere in the case of war and operations of a campaign were conducted against both islands at the same time, and that would be advisable, in order to deprive the Spaniards of a base. To attack Cuba and leave Puerto Rico would simply leave them a base to work from.

By Mr. FORAKER:

Q. I suppose, in a harbor like Havana, when mined at all there is more than one such mine, as a rule?—A. Oh, yes.

Q. And the electric wires are taken to the shore to the same place, as a rule?—A. As a rule, in harbor defense the cables are laid to a gallery under water connected with a fort or some secret place. This gallery is always kept secret as far as possible, never given out. For instance, our own forts, fitted with cables and galleries, the precise location is always kept secret. I know our forts are planted and have these galleries, but I do not know where they are; that is very confidential.

Q. Confided only to Government officials—army or navy?—A. Army exclusively.

By Mr. FRYE:

Q. Why should not those cables leading to the torpedoes have been destroyed after the explosion?—A. It was a very simple matter to haul them in.

Q. They are made to haul in?—A. Certainly. Not necessarily, but that could be done. After the torpedo is exploded the wires have done their work.

By Mr. TURPIE:

Q. Hauled in by machinery, and payed out?—A. Not torpedoes; cables.

By Mr. FORAKER:

Q. Do you think the ship could have been blown up by dynamite carried in a rubber bag, or anything of that kind?—A. I think the probability is against it.

Q. If carried in that way there would have been somebody about there?—A. Yes, sir; in that vicinity.

Q. It would have to be done in a small boat, and fired at the time used?—A. It has just occurred to me that one theory might be advanced that I have not explained. I spoke of a buoyant mine which is attached to a cable and also to an anchor. Suppose this box to represent the mine, and my pencil a cable attached to an anchor, that is made to explode automatically, so that when a ship, say, swings against it and inclines it a certain amount—a favorite mechanical arrangement is to have a ball inside which rolls down an inclined plane and completes the circuit.

This arrangement can be made harmless by disconnecting the battery on shore, and the ship may bump and it will not be exploded, because there is no electric current—it has been switched off on shore. When it is desired these mines shall watch, as it is termed, the current is then put on on shore, and they will not then be exploded until struck by some object, and in this instance heeled over. It is not impossible that the *Maine* might have been destroyed by a mine of that description.

By Mr. DAVIS:

Q. What is the weight of 1,500 feet of this conducting wire, should you think?—A. I can not give you an estimate on that. In the first place, as I stated, the wire varies so very much.

Q. The smallest kind you know? What does a foot of that kind of wire weigh?—A. Wire that could do the work might, that length, weigh perhaps only ten or fifteen pounds; you could carry the coil on your arm, and it might run up to ten or fifteen hundred pounds. I would not want to go on record as giving an estimate for that—it is capable of such a wide range.

By Mr. MILLS:

Q. What would be our method of protecting our fleet if we wanted to blockade Havana—shoot at it at a distance—the torpedo boats, destroy them?—A. We suppose the flotilla to be in Havana and our ships outside endeavoring to blockade, and they came out to attack.

Q. Yes, or we wanted to prevent them from attacking their way—what is our plan of attack to prevent them or destroy them?—A. I do not know that we have any plan, but if we approached near enough the port to bombard it, of course the ships would be subject to bombardment. The most efficacious, and at the same time the most hazardous way, would be to send vessels in to ram them—light draft vessels that probably would not strike any obstruction.

By Mr. FORAKER:

Q. Ram these torpedo boats?—A. Yes, sir, surprise them and ram them. Of course if they get near enough the ship they are subject to a very severe fire from the secondary batteries, small quick-firing guns, and onslaughts from the vidette boats—picket boats. We have no cases on record in experiment where, in the daytime, torpedo boats have succeeded in getting within striking distance of well-armed ships.

By Mr. DAVIS:

Q. Please explain the torpedo nettings.—A. Formerly many vessels—we never had any in our Navy—were supplied with nettings to catch these electromotive torpedoes, but they have been found so serious a detriment to the mobility of the vessels that they have been discarded. Now torpedoes also have a crescent-shaped knife for cutting, and their speed is so great and there is so much danger of the nets fouling the screws of the vessels and disabling them that they have been done away with.

By Mr. CULLOM:

Q. So that the fact that the nettings were not let down makes no case against the captain of the *Maine?*—A. The *Maine* had no nets; they never had any in our Navy.

By Mr. MILLS:

Q. How many torpedo boats have we?—A. We have six at Key West; three more ready to go in a few days down there; all small though.

By Mr. CULLOM:

Q. Are you familiar with this flotilla that is coming over?—A. Only in a general way. Of course I could get access to any information at any time. I believe the squadron that has started is composed of three destroyers and three torpedo boats, and a converted cruiser accompanying them. I do not know the name of the steamer.

Q. I understand that another squadron has started?—A. Yes; I saw that. I believe it is composed of the *Maria Theresa*, a sister boat to the *Vizcaya*; the *Colon*, and a torpedo destroyer named the *Destructor*.

By Mr. DAVIS:

Q. Where is the *Pelaya?*—A. At Ferrol.

By Mr. LODGE:

Q. Have they not three more armored ships in dock now?—A. I do not know. The latest information——

Q. I was told they were still in dock, and would be out between the 15th of April and the 1st of May.—A. I do not know.

By Mr. FORAKER:

Q. I saw a cable that the *Pelaya* had started for Toulon.—A. She has been opposite Toulon, and has been repaired there, at La Seyne.

Q. How do we compare with Spain as to first-class battle ships or first-class armored cruisers?—A. We have more battle ships; we have not quite as many armored cruisers.

By Mr. LODGE:

Q. Ours are heavier ships?—A. Yes, sir; the *Brooklyn* and *New York*——

Q. In battle ships we are much more powerful?—A. Very much.

Q. Should you not think it very important in case war was coming to dispose of that flotilla before it reached Havana?—A. It would be an important advantage. Much depends upon the proposed campaign— what we are going to do; whether it is to be strictly a naval war— whether we are to confine ourselves to marine operations, or whether we are to land troops on the islands of Cuba and Puerto Rico, and what the purpose of the Government is. That ought to be decided first, in my opinion, and then we could decide what to do.

By Mr. MILLS:

Q. Could we land troops with this flotilla at Havana?—A. I would not advocate it. Warfare can not be carried on now as it used to be, where a fleet could go in under the guns of a fort and land troops and bombard the fort and town and take possession. The lesson of the *Maine* proves that such forts must be taken by attack on shore, with such aid as the ships can give, and some place not mined must be selected to land. The object of the Navy now is to destroy what it can by bombardment and destroy ships. The capture of territory must be left to the Army.

By Mr. FORAKER:

Q. How are our ships supplied with ammunition?—A. Very well.

By Mr. MORGAN:

Q. How is the *Oregon*, compared with others?—A. She is the same caliber as others in our Navy.

Q. What would happen if she were ordered around from Callao? What length of time would she require to make the voyage?—A. I have not the distances at my finger ends—she is not due at Callao——

By Mr. LODGE:

Q. They call it sixty days from San Francisco?—A. That is a better statement than I can make without working out the distance.

You all understand the geographical situation of these islands. In the west the islands of Key West and Dry Tortugas, where we hope to keep coal enough, are only 90 miles from Havana, and ships operating around the west end of Cuba can coal there, but it is about 600 miles to the east end of Cuba, Cape Maysi on the Windward Channel, and on that route the navigation is difficult and the navigable waters are narrow and confined. The coast of Cuba presents many advantages for small vessels to dodge out from the shore and do a good deal of harm to passing ships. So, it would be dangerous to pass to and fro in order to get coal at Key West, and, also, it is too far to go, it takes too much time to go and come. If you are on the south coast of Cuba the distance is about 900 miles.

It is very important to have a coaling station at the east end of Cuba, and right across the Windward Channel is the very excellent harbor of St. Nicholas Mole, which belongs to Haiti. We used that as a coaling station in the war of the rebellion, and it did not then require any very urgent defense. I have urged on the Secretary, and I believe it has been communicated to the President, that that port be hired or leased, or obtained in some way, as a coaling station.

And also, as I should certainly recommend if operations were conducted at the same time about Puerto Rico, which is still farther to the eastward some considerable distance, it would be necessary to have a coaling station near by, and I would recommend St. Thomas, a very good port and capable of defense, good anchorage there, smooth water, and I understand that the islands of the Danish West Indies can be purchased for a few millions, probably five or under, I have on good authority, and I should think the purchase of those islands would be cheap at five millions, simply to get the islands, as you would buy a cruiser or anything else.

Q. Do you not think we ought to have those Danish islands anyway?—A. Yes, sir. If we are going to go ahead ourselves in the West Indies, we must have coaling stations there.

Q. For our own protection?—A. Yes, sir.

In response to a letter addressed to him by Senator Frye, asking for his opinion as to the tenability of the statement made in the report of the Spanish board of inquiry on the destruction of the *Maine*, that one of the grounds for considering the explosion to have occurred on the inside of the vessel, was that no dead fish were found on the following morning, the following letter from Commander Bradford was received by Senator Frye:

WASHINGTON, D. C., *March 31, 1898.*

MY DEAR SENATOR: In reference to your note concerning dead fish about the *Maine*, I beg to state that they always disappear very soon after an explosion. Many of the fish that appear to be dead after a submarine explosion are only stunned, and after a time recover and disappear. I have noticed this a great many times during experiments at Newport. The explosion of the *Maine* occurred at 9.40 p. m.; I consider that there was ample time for the fish to have disappeared before daylight. I have seen it stated in newspapers that there are very few fish in Havana Harbor on account of its being very foul. I do not personally know this to be a fact, but I do know that the harbor is very foul.

The men at Newport who frequently gathered in the fish after a torpedo explosion so well understood the fact that they must be quick that they were always ready in their boats with their nets, and were the first on the ground in order to scoop up the fish. On one occasion I saw a sturgeon weighing at least 100 pounds apparently dead after a torpedo explosion, and men went alongside to gather him in, when he suddenly righted, disappeared, and was never seen afterwards.

Yours, very truly,   R. B. BRADFORD.

STATEMENT OF CAPT. CHARLES DWIGHT SIGSBEE, U. S. N., March 31, 1898.

Capt. CHARLES DWIGHT SIGSBEE sworn by the chairman.

Examination by Senator FRYE:

Q. What is your full name and profession?—A. Charles Dwight Sigsbee, captain, United States Navy, late commanding the United States steamer *Maine*. I transferred the command at Havana. I held it until I left; the flag was still flying.

Q. What, in your opinion, caused the explosion which destroyed the *Maine?*—A. It is, of course, merely matter of opinion. My opinion is that a mine destroyed the *Maine*, either permanent or temporary.

Q. Please describe what you mean by a mine?—A. I mean a large vessel or receptacle filled with explosive matter and submerged at a low depth, so that a vessel can swing over or against it.

Q. How large a mine—of course I am not asking for exact figures—how large and heavy a mine in your opinion would be required to have the effect which was had upon your ship?—A. The effect on the ship is not known with sufficient accuracy to permit me to state, and, moreover, I think that question is one for an expert, what we would consider in the Navy an expert in matters of that kind.

It would, however, undoubtedly take a very large one, but in my opinion no larger than could be planted near the vessel at any time in broad daylight and under direct vision with the means available in Havana for that purpose. This assumes that about 12 men, having mutual confidence and preserving secrecy, would be necessary to plant such a mine.

Q. And that could be done while your ship was preserving the ordinary discipline and watchfulness of a ship in the harbor of an enemy?—A. Absolutely, in my opinion. I could dilate a little on that if you would like to have it. That [indicating] represents a ship lying at a buoy, that being the buoy. That ship will swing around there.

If a mine is planted anywhere in that area, she will swing over that mine in time, it is obvious. Let a vessel come to Havana. She proceeds here and drops a mine there. In time the vessel will swing over it. It could not immediately produce the destruction of the vessel, but in time that vessel will swing over that buoy, and at that time it could be exploded. Let that be a scow with a between decks. There there is a tube coming above the water line; there is another. There is the water line. Outside this is a section. There is a bar with two trips on it working with a crank fastened on standards; slings are down there, and a mine can be slung there right under the boat, the slings passing up through two tubes there.

From here the wires pass through another tube and are fastened to a reel. That mine can be weighted so the specific gravity is very little more than water. Tugs and lighters are passing and repassing constantly, and all that such a vessel—a lighter, say—has to do is to drop that buoy. It is entirely submerged and makes no wave, has very little specific gravity more than water, hence very little pull on the boat. Now, they have a number of hoys in Havana with derricks on the deck, very slow and very noisy, and they are passing and repassing all the time until late in the evening. A vessel of that kind can go past there every day. and she can go to a wharf or anchor in the stream, and when you swing over that buoy that vessel can strike the wires and sink you, and she can cut the wires and steam away, or she can drop the wires wherever she pleases.

There was a lot of idle army officers there; I do not charge them with anything, but speak of the possibilities of the case. In this case I have spoken of more than need be. I showed a similar sketch to Captain Sampson, who has also commanded a torpedo station, and is besides an ordnance officer, and I asked, pointing to a vessel, "Could that vessel drop that instantly?" and they said undoubtedly she could, it could be done. I then said, "Can I make report to the Navy Department; will you permit me to say this could be done undoubtedly?" The only qualification was that it would take about twelve men to do it. That is the real reason I asked to have the *Montgomery* taken away. If they were going to do anything to blow us up I wanted to have it done with a smaller vessel. They had no vigilance whatever and no guard over us or our vessels. Their vigilance was great wherever their own vessels were concerned.

By Mr. GRAY:

Q. No vigilance as regards you?—A. No; once or twice they played a searchlight on us, but the boats were coming and going all the time, and we would hail them, and they must have heard our hail, but they would refuse to answer the first time and commonly the second time, and then they would finally answer in a rather impudent manner when they did answer. It was a very peculiar thing; they seemed to have no experience of other nations' vessels.

By Mr. FRYE:

Q. Suppose that had happened as you suggest. I am only asking your opinion. In your opinion could that be done without the knowledge of any Spanish official?—A. I think it is possible it could have been done without the knowledge of the high officials—the higher officials.

By Mr. MORGAN:

Q. How would they get hold of the torpedo?—A. I assume they could make that out of a section of old hogshead, or even a wine pipe. For the short time it was to be down an immense wine pipe, or even two of them, might have been taken, and stealing up to a boat it could have been taken from one boat to another and then dropped in shallow water.

Q. What, in your judgment, was the probability?—A. I am not certain in my mind whether to attribute it to a temporary mine like that or a permanent one. It is a curious fact that the officers of the deck say we never swung in that particular direction before. The *Maine* is lying now in about the position she would have taken to play on the Spanish batteries—the Morro and Cabanas. That is to say, if the *Maine* had taken a notion to play on the batteries, she would be in that position. Now, I give this merely as a fact; I do not draw any special inference. Here is the mooring point; here is the Spanish admiral's house. The *Maine* was swinging about in that direction.

Now, if a mine had been planted there, where the *Maine* could play on the batteries, I assume it would have been planted in just that place where the *Maine* was blown up. If only one had been planted, it would have been just there. If a mine were planted in range from that residence to the buoy, of course, when the *Maine* swung to that buoy, it would show the mine was under the ship's keel. It was my business to note all these things, but, as for connecting it absolutely with the blowing up of the ship, I can not do any further than I have stated.

Q. If that ship had swung into position to fire on the castle and a torpedo had been placed, or mine placed, under water so as to blow the ship up in case she did fire, then it would have been placed exactly where you were blown up?—A. I would have placed it there.

Q. That suggests the possibility of its having been placed there before you were located there?—A. It does.

Q. Has it not occurred to you that very likely it was done so?—A. I think if we had owned the port and had suspected a possible aggressive spirit, I think we would have done the same thing.

Q. You would have put it right there?—A. If we only had one mine I should have put it right there.

Q. If that mine had been placed so, how would it have been exploded?—A. I infer they never would have put a contact mine there that would have been exploded by contact with the bottom of the vessel, because other vessels were coming and going all the time, but an electric mine, having wires leading ashore or elsewhere.

By Mr. CULLOM:

Q. To have the explosion at a time when they could have control of it?—A. Yes; the time and opportunity to control it.

By Mr. FRYE:

Q. If that was the condition, who would be likely to have charge of the electric battery which exploded the mine?—A. I am unable to say that; I infer the Navy.

Q. An official?—A. I have a certain reason for believing this, which perhaps it would be injudicious to disclose.

By Mr. MORGAN:

Q. Taking the lights on the ship, which had not been extinguished at the time of the explosion, I understand they would furnish the observer on the shore the position of the ship. Would such an observer be able at night to ascertain that that ship was at that moment in such bearing as she could fire on the batteries?—A. We have a forward and after light showing, and even without a light he could have seen it by the smokestacks, which are large.

By Mr. DAVIS:

Q. Could have seen at night?—A. Yes, sir.

By Mr. FRYE:

Q. No difficulty in determining whether it was over a submarine mine?—A. No, sir; if there was one there. I have no knowledge whatever that the Spanish authorities blew the ship up; I am merely giving the possibilities of the case.

Q. The Spaniards, in their report of the destruction of the *Maine*, make a very strong point of the fact that no dead fish were found the next day. What is your judgment about that proposition?—A. The ship was blown up at 9.40 p. m., and even though there were dead fish, no one knows where they might have gone the next morning. In the next place, I fancy, if any dead fish were available, the reconcentrados would be glad to get them. Again, they say the fish leave the harbor and go to sea at night. I have seen an occasional fish jump in the daytime, but the water is very foul and nasty, and I fancy it is a bad water for fish.

By Mr. MORGAN:

Q. The walls amidships on both sides, to nearly amidships, were broken down?—A. Especially so; very much disintegrated. It is all gone on the port side.

Q. So that if that was done by an internal explosion the force of the explosion would have gone out through the water?—A. That is a question, if there was an internal explosion.

Q. If there was, the force of that explosion must have gone through the water?—A. Yes, sir.

Q. Why would not that have killed the fish?—A. I think it would. Perhaps not so much, but I think it would have killed them. We regarded that excuse as rather peculiarly Spanish and all that about the wave, etc. They were groping for results and reasons.

By Mr. FRYE:

Q. I suppose there had been an outward tide from the time they were hunting for the fish until the morning.

By Mr. GRAY:

Q. Is there much tide?—A. Very little tidal flow. There is an ebb and flow, of course. If there were permanent wires ashore to the points established by the Government, it is conceivable that somebody may have dragged for those wires at some intermediate point between the station and mine, and having them, may have blown the ship up, or they may have gotten control of the switchboard on shore. They did not like us; that was very plain.

Q. What examination did those Spanish boards make of the accident?—A. They had not done anything for a week; had not been down at all. Our people laughed at them. Our people kept going down steadily, and they a little at a time, and there sat a correspondent of a great American journal in their boat, humbugging them all the time; passing out cigars to them and making fun of them, and they did not know him. They thought he was a great American engineer who did not care much for Americans. When the boatswain came to them with the other boat he transferred to that, and they did not know him. They did very little work on the wreck. It was absurd as compared with our work.

Q. Did you make the examination as thorough as possible?—A. The examination was made very much under the wishes of the board of inquiry; whatever they wanted they got. We had over the divers all the time commissioned officers. They had part of the time, not all the time, a boatswain. The greatest point on our side was that we had Ensign Powelson. He went to Glasgow to study naval architecture for a year; then he preferred to be a line officer. Of course, the ship was very much disrupted. Whenever any diver would come out Mr. Powelson would take him and have him give, in the first place, exact measurements for the length and breadth and thickness.

He would take his statement, draw a diagram of what he had seen, take it to the detailed diagrams of the ship, and reduce it to a certainty. He would know that a certain beam, forward of a certain place would be, for instance, 3 feet, and abaft it would be 4 feet, and it would be a certain distance from one of the longitudinals, and so on, until he had proved conclusively this was that plate or beam and no other. When the military and naval men come to look at our report and compare it with their report, with the fish story and all that sort of thing, I think a military smile will go around the world.

By Mr. FORAKER:

Q. Was the ship in the habit of swinging all the way around that circle, around that buoy?—A. The trade wind—the prevailing wind—is east, and as the sun comes up it blows stiffer and varies less, but during the time we were there it was not so steady in direction, but we commonly tailed to the east with the stern to the Admiral's house.

By Mr CULLOM:

Q. That night did your boat swing to the location of the house?—A. She swung away from the Admiral's house that night.

By Mr. FRYE:

Q. Was that the first time that vessel swung that way?—A. Some of the officers said that. I did not notice it. I have not seen the *Fern* swing once in the direction the *Maine* swung.

Q. The report of the officers was to that effect?—A. I think the court reports to that effect.

By Mr. MORGAN:

Q. What point of the compass is that ship now?—A. Her bow is twisted to a right angle and shot down in the mud. The general direction is to the northward and westward. The trade winds are to the eastward.

By Mr. MILLS:

Q. Are they in the habit of docking vessels at the same place as the *Maine?*—A. It was riding to a buoy. When a man-of-war comes in, she makes fast to one of these buoys and swings to a pivot. Captain Stephens, of the *City of Washington*, that night or the next day said in all his experience he never knew a vessel to be buoyed in just that place, and I think some others said that.

By Mr. FORAKER:

Q. Do you know what other ships preceded you?—A. The captain of the *City of Washington* said he never saw any vessel moored there before. It was almost in the same position as one of the regular plotted buoys, No. 4, and there was nothing to make anyone suspicious.

Q. Were there any torpedo boats in port while you were there?—A. All the Spanish vessels carry torpedo tubes. The vessel blew up on the port side, and the starboard side was to the Spanish vessel.

Q. I saw a statement in a paper that a Spanish vessel was the last one before you anchored at that buoy?—A. The *La Gasca* came out and anchored the day before or the second day before we went in. She has torpedo tubes. I was informed several days after the explosion by a Cuban who said his father was an American citizen that the *La Gasca* was General Weyler's dispatch boat, the one used by him in any tour about the waters of the island. The captain of that vessel never called on me. I do not know why. Perhaps he thought his was too small a vessel. I permitted myself to suspect him, but I must say I never had anything in the nature of proof.

By Mr. MORGAN:

Q. Had you any intimation of danger?—A. Never, except one day when I was going to a bullfight I received a placard, handed to me in the street, and I took it and put it in my waistcoat pocket and went on to the bullfight.

Q. Was there any writing on it?—A. That was another, which was sent through the mails, and on the bottom was written, "Look out for your ship." These cards are sent by these people—General Lee gets them periodically. When someone complained of it, he asked if there was any date on it. He said the people generally fixed a date for his assassination.

Q. The placard was handed to you while you were going to a bullfight?—A. Yes, sir; and another was sent me through the mails.

By Mr. GRAY:

Q. Was it printed?—A. Yes, sir.

Q. What was printed on it?—A. A lot of stuff: Viva Weyler and viva Spain, and down with the United States of America, etc. Are we going to submit to this vessel coming here from their rotten old fleet, etc.

By Mr. CULLOM:

Q. With these lines written?—A. That came through the mails. People handed them to me on the street. I could not help thinking some of the American colony got them up themselves for a joke.

By Mr. FRYE:

Q. Have you examined the testimony sent to Congress?—A. I heard a great deal of the testimony, but have not read it all, because I have not a copy. I know most of the important testimony. When I found things were going very, very carefully and scientifically in the court, I did not take the trouble to attend all the time. I preferred to be measured by the judgment of other people.

By Mr. TURPIE:

Q. Before they commenced the examination, did the Spanish Government make any offer of reward for the detection or discovery of persons concerned in the destruction of the *Maine*?—A. They decided at once, and so stated to me, that it was an accident, and must have been an accident. For a few minutes, say fifteen or twenty minutes, after the explosion, on the *City of Washington*, they were very anxious to know the cause, and I replied that I must await an investigation; it was perhaps all natural.

By Mr. FRYE:

Q. They insisted it was an accident?—A. The Spanish admiral said first it was the dynamo boiler. I said we have no dynamo. He then said it was the boilers, and then I said the aftermost boilers only were used, and the forward boilers had not been lighted for three months. As for the coal bunker alongside the 10-inch magazine, that was in use that day; we were using it. There was a full bunker on the port side next the 6-inch reserve magazine that had been filled for three months, the coal in particularly stable condition, bunkers inspected, and all right. It was the most exposed bunker in the ship with radiating surface, so that it is inconceivable that bunker should have been heated without being noticed.

By Mr. GRAY:

Q. There was a special examination made?—A. Yes, sir; and the magazine temperature is taken daily and recorded and sent to the Navy Department for every day in the month.

Q. Do you remember the temperature?—A. No, sir; for it would not come to me unless it were abnormal. To show you the kind of a man who took the temperature, made the inspection—he was a three-medal man. The gunner was under suspension for insubordination. The gunner's mate, who was a much better man and had three good-conduct medals—that meant that for three enlistments he had good-conduct medals. He had been two years under his present enlistment, and every mark under every heading was the maximum, and no punishments recorded against him.

By Mr. CULLOM:

Q. This suspended man had nothing to do with taking the temperature?—A. No, sir.

By Mr. GRAY:

Q. Did this man escape with his life?—A. No, sir; he was killed.

By Mr. FRYE:

Q. It takes, if I am correct, 600 degrees Fahrenheit to blow up powder.—A. It takes a very high temperature. We had the brown prismatic powder. I should rather trust the temperature to an expert. The forward magazine was normal; the after magazine, which is near a number of steam tanks and pipes, etc., was often above the normal, the temperature there often being 112, but that gave no concern, for that was well within the safety limit. It might be, on a hot day, 103 or 104, or even 112, and no concern felt.

Q. Do you think it would have been possible to reach that high degree of heat without discovering it?—A. It is inconceivable. All those compartments are electrically connected with annunciators outside my door. These annunciators are very sensitive, and often ring even when there is nothing there.

By Mr. MORGAN:

Q. In what part of the ship was Lieutenant Jenkins's body found?—A. The wardroom messroom. Just forward of that is a large compartment. On one side are the torpedo tubes. His body was found opposite that. The ship is very high there, higher than that brass railing. Everything was buoyant and everything rose to the top, and all the loose articles and rubbish was up there, and that shows why it was difficult to get down there to clear away by a single diver.

Q. I ask the question because it is stated he was found in one of the magazines.—A. No, sir; it was a particularly wide open, beautiful compartment. He was sitting at the mess table——

By Mr. CULLOM:

Q. When the explosion occurred?—A. Yes, sir. If he had been in the shell room—none of the shell rooms exploded. The after part was not torn or hurt. The plates were torn 10 or 12 feet above the amidship section. Forward of that all the damage occurred. Consequently no damage was attributable to anything aft, for there was no explosion there. The Spanish said the war heads exploded. They were all aft. There was but one thing to be taken under suspicion in the *Maine*. That was the mere fact that there was a bunker alongside a magazine; but there is not the slightest suspicion of that bunker besides its existence there.

By Mr. GRAY:

Q. That bunker had been examined that day?—A. Yes, sir; and I had my hands on it the day before. You had to go in a passage right around three sides of it, and it was the loafing place of the men, where they made their little ships and models and did their playing, so it would have roasted them out if there had been anything of that heat there.

By Mr. FORAKER:

Q. There was an annunciator at your door, anyhow?—A. Yes, sir.

By Mr. GRAY:

Q. Is the officer, commissioned or petty, who took the temperature of that bunker that day alive?—A. Yes, sir; he was examined.

By Mr. DAVIS:

Q. What time of the day was the examination made?—A. I do not remember the exact time.

Q. What was the custom?—A. Saturday afternoon was the usual

time. There was no rigid time to examine; one time was as good as another.

By Mr. FRYE:

Q. Did you have soft or anthracite coal?—A. Both kinds. We had soft coal which had been examined at Newport News, and which had been in the ship three months and was very stable. Commonly, we used all the coal from the forward bunkers first, because that brought the ship down in the head. At Key West they made us take in anthracite coal which had been there a long time and they wanted to get rid of it. We were quite as anxious, having got it aboard, to use it as they were, and I wanted to keep all my soft coal, as it was so stable, and that is the reason for retaining the coal in the forward bunkers.

By Mr. CULLOM:

Q. What was your special reason for using the anthracite coal?—A. It was old, and consequently we could not use it to the best advantage. And the soft coal is better for steam purposes. Besides, the anthracite had been lying in the air for a long time.

By Mr. GRAY:

Q. Have you ever made any examinations as to spontaneous combustion?—A. No, sir; but the English have gone into it with a great deal of particularity. Their tests, I believe, show that the gas works along through the layers of coal and through the coal dust, and works along until it strikes a draft of air, which fed it and ignited it, and in their experiments they found in that way, from a great number of cases, what to expect of it. Captain Wainwright, of the *Maine*, and formerly head of the office, said he never knew of spontaneous combustion without heat in the first instance.

By Mr. CLARK:

Q. Do you treat coal with water or anything of that kind when not using it?—A. No, sir.

By Mr. FORAKER:

Q. State briefly the effect of the explosion upon the keel plates.—A. The keel plate was driven upward decidedly in one respect. That is given so clearly in the report that I regret to go into it. I left that to the court. It was suggested to me to make the drawing, and I declined because I did not wish to be in it any way.

Q. Can you indicate in those drawings the one showing its existence above the deck?—A. That is supposed to represent there the keel plate. It is thrown up like that, I think just a few feet below the water line of the vessel. I do not like to go too far in this myself, because I might misjudge something of what the court said. I believe that was one of the strongest reasons for the assumption that that thing could not have been caused by an internal explosion.

By Mr. DAVIS:

Q. How many feet was it blown up from its normal place?—A. About 30, I think, from where it would have rested in the mud in a normal condition.

By Mr. FORAKER:

Q. What is that drawing showing the vertical keel broken?—A. Take this and pile it up like that. This edge and that edge come together. That also shows the rise where it is blown up.

Q. Showing the force came from below?—A. I think that was the inference of the court, and would be of anybody.

Q. Is that the bottom of the ship?—A. Yes, sir; that is called the keel plate. Instead of having a keel outside it is inside and perfectly flat.

By Mr. CULLOM:

Q. Outside of what you have mentioned, were there any indications of a mine?—A. Not so far as I know, except indentations of the plate.

Q. A hole in the mud?—A. Yes, sir; there was that.

Q. No pieces of material in which that mine, if there was one, was incased?—A. Captain Converse says that would have been destroyed by the explosion.

By Mr. MORGAN:

Q. I saw a statement that some concrete or plaster had been thrown on the awnings or the upper deck of a steamer?—A. A large piece was thrown on the *City of Washington*, a large piece 2 or 3 feet in thickness. That might have come from the blower engines on the berth deck below the upper deck. That was screwed down in a bed of cement in the men's washroom.

Q. Was there any cement in the bottom of the ship?—A. Yes, sir; all through the bilging there was cement, but my recollection is it was not demonstrated—there was no evidence to show conclusively that cement came from the bottom of the ship.

Q. It might have come from either place?—A. Yes, sir. I only heard the chief engineer's statement, or rather the constructor, who thought that it came from the bottom of the ship.

By Mr. FRYE:

Q. There was a double bottom?—A. Yes, sir.

By Mr. LODGE:

Q. In the report there is a telegram addressed to Forsythe, Key West, etc.: "Many killed and wounded. Do not send war vessels if others available." Why, if I may ask, did you say that last?—A. In the first place, there was a great deal of excitement and I wanted to work along without men-of-war and to allay the excitement in the city; and in the next place, if there were any more mines I did not want any more war vessels blown up.

Up to that time I had strongly recommended that the *Indiana* be sent there, just to show them that the *Maine* was not the only vessel in the Navy or the most powerful. After that time I had no more confidence in the people. Treachery had been shown us, and there was no special care for us; they had not attempted to protect us as we did with the *Vizcaya* in New York.

By Mr. MORGAN:

Q. You spoke of the reconcentrados getting the fish, etc. Did you see any of that class of people in Havana?—A. Oh, yes, a great many. I was invited to go to see them, but in my position as naval officer I did not care to take part in any political affairs. I desired to have things as peaceful and friendly as possible. I received and entertained out of my own pocket I suppose three or four hundred people on board the ship, but I never accepted any invitations.

By Mr. FORAKER:

Q. Did you occupy this same position all the while you were in Havana?—A. Yes, sir.

Q. Who stationed you at this place?—A. When I came into Havana I struck well to the westward, so as to show myself well to the people. I hoisted the American ensign at the peak and the jack at the fore. That showed I was an American vessel and wanted to enter. They sent off a man—he was an official pilot—and I complimented him on his skill in entering, and I saw him at the office of the captain of the port, and I know he was the official pilot.

Q. Was there any position from which you could have shelled Havana or Moro Castle as advantageously as this?—A. We could have shelled the town from any position. That is the position from which we could have brought our batteries to bear on the castle; one broadside brought to bear on one, and the other broadside on the other.

By Mr. CLARK:

Q. The committee was yesterday trying to get information as to the rules, or laws, or regulations governing the keeping or disposal of high explosives in the city of Havana. Do you know anything of that?
A. Not strictly, except just before I left there was an arrest made, or rather dynamite was seized opposite General Lee's consular office—so the Spanish papers stated—seized by the authorities; but I fancy that thing must be regulated very carefully where there is an insurrection, and where the custom-house laws are so very strict. General Lee could give you an opinion immediately on that point, but I take it for granted nothing could get in without permission of the authorities.

By Mr. MORGAN:

Q. Some witnesses testified there was an explosion some time after, supposed to be fixed ammunition.—A. I did not notice the separate phenomena of explosion.

Q. I mean an explosion after the first.—A. I know there were various explosions. We had some rockets in the signal room, etc., and there were some shooting stars and signals, and the pilot house was directly above the center of the explosion.

Q. Was there any explosion from shells?—A. I have not heard of any instance where heavy shell exploded. A piece of shell—a piece of 6-inch shell was found on the *City of Washington*. I have not heard of any instance where 10-inch shell exploded in the air. In the pilot house, directly above the explosion, there were some 6-pounder and 1-pounder ammunition. That began to explode before we left the ship, and exploded until two o'clock that night.

Q. Why was that?—A. Because the ship was afire. It also continued after we left the ship.

Q. If any magazine had exploded, would not that have caused the explosion of the detached ammunition?—A. It ought to have done so. There is much ammunition there now.

Q. Unexploded?—A. Yes, sir; there was some ammunition in the handling room, in the loading room—10-inch shell. We can not find any of these shells were hurled anywhere; we have no information of that.

Q. Suppose the explosion had taken place in the magazine, everything in that magazine would have exploded?—A. I should think so.

Q. The force would have been confined, and the effect of the gases would have exploded everything?—A. Of course very curious things happen——

Q. It would have been very curious if that had not exploded?—A. Yes, sir.

By Mr. FORAKER:

Q. You have no doubt your ship was destroyed by an explosion from the outside?—A. I have none whatever—none from the first minute.

STATEMENT OF CAPT. ALBERT S. BARKER, U. S. N., MARCH 31, 1898.

Capt. ALBERT S. BARKER, U. S. N., sworn by the chairman.

Examination by Senator FRYE:

Q. What is your name and profession?—A. Albert S. Barker, captain, United States Navy.

Q. Are you familiar with the testimony in the *Maine* case as disclosed?—A. I have not read it, except portions that I have seen in the newspapers.

Q. You have read all that has appeared in the papers?—A. I have read it, but not carefully.

Q. Have you formed any opinion as to what caused the explosion?—A. I think from the report of the board, if they state the truth, as I have no doubt they do, that there was a mine under the keel of the *Maine*.

Q. And a mine of great power or small?—A. Certainly of considerable power, and if it was a small mine it must have been placed in the very best position to produce the best results that flames from the mine might have communicated with the forward magazines to assist in the explosion.

Q. Have you formed an opinion as to whether or not that mine was placed there before the *Maine* was buoyed?—A. On no good evidence.

Q. Have you an opinion?—A. My own opinion is that Havana Harbor has been mined, but I have nothing to base it upon.

Q. You have an opinion that Havana has been mined?—A. Yes, sir.

Q. If the mine was located there before the *Maine* was attached to the buoy, from what source would it necessarily have been exploded?—A. Ordinarily, if the mines were put down by the Government, they would have been exploded by Government officials.

Q. It would have been exploded from the shore from an electric battery?—A. Presumably.

Q. Are such things in all these forts and fortifications in charge of officials?—A. So far as I know. In our own country they are.

Q. Are you an expert in explosives?—A. Well, I do not know that I would care to call myself an expert in explosives. I was the first one who ever fired dynamite in shells in this country.

Q. In your judgment, what kind of a mine would it be, if mine it was? How many men would it take to handle it, etc.?—A. It would be impossible to say. As Captain Sigsbee said, a mine could be towed out, as he explained, very easily. Again, if they were permanent mines, the chances are it would be a heavier mine, and would take a greater force to place it.

Q. Commander Bradford testified they would run to from 500 to 1,000 pounds to do such work as was done by this?—A. If the whole damage was caused by the mine, it certainly would.

Q. In your opinion, was that mine located there before the ship moored, or are the probabilities that it was dropped there, as Captain Sigsbee testified it might have been, by some of these vessels?—A. It would be entirely guesswork, but I would suppose myself they would mine Havana Harbor.

Q. Have you any doubt they have mined it?—A. I have nothing to base an opinion upon except on general principles—what we would do ourselves.

Q. On general principles?—A. I suppose they would mine the place.

Q. Are you familiar with Havana Harbor?—A. I have been in there once only, twenty years ago.

Q. The Spanish naval inquiry, as one strong reason why an accident from the inside caused the explosion, declared there were no dead fish. What is your judgment about that?—A. I should not think that of much value. I agree perfectly with that letter you read from Captain Bradford. Only a few fish are killed in comparison with the number stunned, provided there are a number around, and those fish stunned very soon recover their wits and swim off.

Q. So you would not regard that as of any value?—A. No, sir.

Q. Have you read the findings of the Spanish naval board?—A. No, sir; have not seen them.

By Mr GRAY:

Q. Do you consider any hypothesis to account for this catastrophe more reasonable than that it was caused by a mine that had been placed there in conformity to a general system of mining, or at least placed there before the arrival of the *Maine*, and exploded by an electric current as in such cases is usual, either officially or by some person in his enthusiasm who got control of the place where it was?—A. I can conceive of no cause other than that you mention more reasonable than that, particularly as it is stated in the testimony, as I understand it, that the war heads of our own torpedoes were not shipped. That was the only thing I ever had any fear about.

Q. What are those war heads?—A. They are of gun cotton, and are stowed down in the ship. When you prepare a torpedo, not for practice but for actual work, these war heads are taken up and secured on the forward part of the torpedo.

By Mr. MORGAN:

Q. The other part of the torpedo is harmless until the war head is on?—A. Yes, sir.

By Mr. FORAKER:

Q. The testimony shows they were not on?—A. Yes, sir.

By Mr. TURPIE:

Q. They are a sort of percussion cap?—A. Yes, sir.

By Mr. MORGAN:

Q. It is the explosive in the war head which causes the damage?—A. Yes, sir.

By Mr. MILLS:

Q. What are the elements of gun cotton?—A. It is the action of nitro glycerine on cotton, on the fiber.

By Mr. DAVIS:

Q. Does it dissolve the fiber, or merely soak it?—A. Dissolves it.

By Mr. FORAKER:

Q. I understand you to state, from all the circumstances, it is according to your best judgment that it was exploded by a mine planted there before the *Maine* was anchored or buoyed there, and in the usual way such mines are operated, by an electric current, the battery for which was somewhere on the shore?—A. That is what I infer.

Q. That is your better judgment, gathered from all the circumstances?—A. Yes, sir.

By Mr. GRAY:

Q. That is the most reasonable hypothesis?—A. To my mind.

Q. Where are you stationed now?—A. At the Navy Department.

By Mr. MILLS:

Q. How were these torpedoes to be used on the *Maine?*—A. Fired from tubes.

Q. How far can you send them?—A. At the rate of 20 or 30 miles for 400 yards, and then 600 or 800 yards farther.

Q. And then if they do not hit anything they are lost?—A. Yes, sir; they lose their speed and fall into the sea.

Q. Are our war vessels fitted so?—A. Yes, sir; most of the larger vessels, the cruisers.

Q. In close quarters they are pretty dangerous?—A. Yes, sir; you do not want to get within 400 yards.

STATEMENT OF ADMIRAL JOHN IRWIN U. S. N., APRIL 2, 1898.

Admiral JOHN IRWIN, U. S. N., sworn by Senator Frye:

Examination by Senator FRYE:

Q. What is your full name and profession?—A. John Irwin; admiral, United States Navy.

Q. Have you had considerable experience with torpedoes?—A. I have.

Q. Have you at any time been in the harbor of Havana?—A. I am a pilot in the harbor of Havana. I have been there hundreds of times, I should say; was there a great deal while I was employed in assisting in laying the West India cable system, and before that I was there in the times of Fulton, in the old filibustering days, when those expeditions were fitting out for Nicaragua. During a period of four years, from 1867 to 1871, I never took on a pilot there. The ship I commanded was the only American war vessel allowed to go in, night or day, ad libitum. That was because we were in the cable business.

Q. Were you there during the last rebellion?—A. Three years of the last rebellion, from when it began in 1868 to 1871.

Q. With your ship?—A. Yes, sir; with two different ships.

Q. Were you attached to this same buoy to which the *Maine* was?— A. I was anchored at the buoy No. 4, off the Machina Navy-Yard, and from the description of the position assumed by the *Maine* shown me on the chart, and from the middle grounds on the shoals just beyond it, I take it that buoy was in the same position of my buoy.

Q. What was the disposition of the people on shore toward your ship at that time—the Spaniards?—A. Bitterly hostile at all times.

Q. Did they exhibit that hostility actively on shore at that time?— A. They exhibited it actively, constantly. Going in and out, when we would pass the slopes leading down from the Cabanas fortress and the Morro Castle, and the battery on the port hand coming out, the Spanish soldiers and volunteers at different times, sometimes the volunteers and at others the regulars were the sole garrison, would come down and use the most indecent gestures to us and curse us in Spanish, and taunt us in every conceivable way.

By Mr. MORGAN:

Q. That was during the former war?—A. In 1868, 1869, and 1870.

By Mr. FRYE:

Q. Did they fire at you any time on shore?—A. I was on shore on Christmas night, 1868, with Gen. William F. Smith, president of the cable company I was aiding; Sir Charles Bright, the great electrician, who had the contract for laying this cable, and Mr. John Nininger, the rich European banker, vice-president of the company. We had taken dinner at the cafe right opposite the opera house, and had left the cafe and adjourned to our rooms near the Machina on account of the unusually severe cold of that night, the thermometer going down to 50, something unknown in Havana.

On the night we left one of my officers who had been in the cafe reported to me the volunteers had fired two volleys, one into the lower part, the other into the billiard room above, at one of the tables of which Lieutenant (now Commander) Clover was playing billiards. A number of persons were killed and wounded, among others Mr. Charles Kohler; and I was told he was laughing, telling a funny yarn, and he was shot dead, his head falling in his plate. That cafe was the resort of Americans very largely, Havana being then a health and winter resort, and thousands of Americans going every winter. We could conceive of the animosity being intended for any other parties, as no other foreigners were ever insulted to our knowledge, and the impression conveyed was that these volleys were fired with the deliberate intention of assaulting Americans.

Q. Have you read the testimony taken with regard to the destruction of the *Maine?*—A. I have read all the expert testimony.

Q. You have read the testimony?—A. Yes; the testimony of the subordinates before the court I simply glanced at, but the expert testimony I studied very carefully.

Q. Have you formed an opinion?—A. I have a very positive opinion.

Q. What is it?—A. The destruction of the *Maine* was caused by the explosion of a submarine mine.

Q. What do you mean by "a submarine mine?"—A. Submarine mines are of two characters, mines being of various shapes, some of them mushrooms. One is a mine that is anchored, and to the anchor a buoy would be attached. They are attached mushroom shape; that is, the insulated wire attachment communicating with some safe magazine located within view of it, so that it could be exploded at the will of the operator by an electric instrument.

Q. Either on shore or on board a Spanish ship?—A. Yes, sir. If it nad been originally laid to communicate with a magazine on shore, and then they had changed their minds, and wished to use it from a ship, say the *Alfonso*, it would be a very simple operation to detach the cable from the shore magazine and convey the end surreptitiously or any way to the *Alfonso* or any other ship. Anyone versed in handling, and knowing the ground, would have no difficulty. Or the cable might have been tapped from any ship and the splice made. It could have been made in the space of half an hour under cover of darkness without anyone having any knowledge of it except the parties implicated.

Q. If it appeared by the testimony that this ship had been swinging as ships always do at the buoy, and that, for the first time since her arrival, she had reached the position where she was blown up, what would be your judgment, that the torpedo was placed there in advance?—A. Decidedly so.

Q. Would it be difficult for people on shore at that time of night to know the exact location of that ship, and that she was over the mine?—A. None at all: The torpedo mines are planted at exactly known points, and those points determined by the most accurate triangulation. The operator whose duty it was to explode the mine would have to be an expert, have his map before him, and be able by his observations to locate the position of the ship within a few feet, or else the mine would be of no value, if it was simply guesswork.

I know that in the mapped-out preparation for the defense of our own harbors the positions of our own mines are determined by triangulation within two or three feet, and very possibly exactly determined. It is a very simple problem in surveying to do so.

Q. You having been in Havana in times of serious trouble, in the conditions existing in Havana now, in your judgment would it be possible for any private individuals to obtain the necessary combustible materials for this mine?—A. In my judgment it would be impossible. The military power is absolute; the people are held in a grip of iron; they have their military force, their police force, and everyone known to have been there—if a Cuban ventures outside his house he takes his life in his hand.

Q. Would not the surveillance be exceedingly careful when the fact was known that there must have been in Havana many Cubans who would have delighted to have blown up the Spanish ships?—A. Unquestionably so: there is no doubt about that. We know from various accounts received from Havana that, on a small scale, the Cubans have repeatedly exploded what are known as dynamite bombs in various locations around Havana, and are blowing up railway bridges and obstructing the Spaniards constantly, but that is a different matter from having access to the harbor and being able to plant a mine of that character

Q. What experience have you had with torpedoes yourself?—A. Commencing the 13th of April, 1865, when the news was received in Mobile of General Lee's surrender, hostilities ceased, and it was necessary for our fleet to enter the harbor of Mobile itself, we being in the outer harbor below Dog River Bar. Rear-Admiral Thatcher placed me in command of a division and instructed me to remove all the torpedoes in Mobile Bay and to blow up the obstructions to Dog River Bar, and after that was done I piloted the fleet through, carried them in safety to Mobile. In doing that work I raised some 400 torpedoes at very great risks in shallow water. During the operations we lost altogether some seven vessels, and I became very familiar with those torpedoes.

At first we used to destroy them by boring auger holes through and sousing them with water, but afterwards, having found in the naval arsenal at Mobile a number of safety caps that screwed on the head and rendered them innocuous, I saved those torpedoes and used them in blowing up obstructions, using the electric fuse. We also procured from the same naval arsenal in Mobile a number of submarine mines that had been prepared for use, all of which I employed in blowing up the main obstruction. This obstruction was about 240 feet in length, 40 feet beam, and 24 feet deep, built of 24-inch timber, and filled in with brick and stone, all of which we blew up.

In conducting those operations I had abundant opportunity to observe the effect of submarine mines and torpedoes, and I had also closely observed the effect of these torpedoes on our vessels that were blown up. That work lasted some three or four weeks, and after that, having become interested in the subject and being a part of my profession, I have naturally been a close student ever since.

Q. I call your attention to what was testified to by the people on the *City of Washington*, that there were two explosions. What have you to say to that?—A. It struck me, and Admiral Matthews, who was our first officer in charge of the torpedo school at Newport, also, that it was somewhat strange that it was not generally known that the explosion of a torpedo or submarine mine is always a double explosion. There are two reports; the first report, I take it, from the earth shock or earth sound wave, if I may so describe it, which is followed by the blast, which makes the latter explosion on the gases reaching the open air, as of the powder coming from the muzzle of a gun.

When you are near any such explosion the difference in sound could hardly be measured by time, but it is palpable to the trained ear. It is about like the sound in firing a gun that strikes the ear of the officer firing, the sound of the explosion of the cap, followed almost instantaneously by the explosion from the muzzle. I give that as an illustration to show you how short a space there is, but that space is patent to the sensitive drum of the ear; you know it instinctively. Admiral Matthews, having been in charge of a torpedo school, said that was his experience lasting over a series of years.

Q. So, from a submarine mine, you would expect the report to be as in this case?—A. Precisely.

Q. Captain Sigsbee does not mention it?—A. I can readily understand that. Captain Sigsbee was in his cabin writing home. This thing was so sudden and a terrific shock, taking him exceedingly by surprise, and the vibration on board the ship from this terrible upheaval would probably blend the sounds so together that he would not notice the difference. There was a rupture and tearing of the whole fabric, and together with the shock of surprise and the uplifting of the ship and the general crash of the whole fabric, I do not wonder that Captain Sigsbee was unable to distinguish the double report.

Q. I suppose it does not surprise you that the people on the *City of Washington* were able to distinguish them?—A. Not at all. They were in a different case; they were farther away. Captain Sigsbee was so exceedingly close to the explosion that the double sound probably merged into one; that is, the conveyance of the sound wave in the air and the ground shock were to his ear, together with the other sounds, simultaneous.

Q. If the ship was blown up from the shore or from the Spanish ship, must it not have been done by some Spanish official?—A. Unquestionably.

Q. Would anybody else, any ordinary people around the city, have access to the instrument from which a submarine mine would be discharged?—A. I should think that common prudence would impel the Spanish to guard a magazine containing an instrument used for exploding a mine very carefully in their own selfish interests. It might be possible that one of their own ships would drift over it, and if it had been in the power of a hostile Cuban to touch it off he would certainly do so.

Q. So that, if discharged from ship or shore, it was discharged by a Spanish official?—A. Unquestionably.

Q. In the case of that ship lying over that submarine mine with her full magazines, state whether or not it would have been a reasonable supposition on the part of whoever exploded the mine that there would be no one left to tell the story at all?—A. It would be quite reasonable to expect that, supposing, as we have a right to suppose in our assumption, that this mine was touched off by a Spanish official, that this official would be an expert, naval or military—and the various bureaus of military and naval intelligence have, to my knowledge, complete plans of all great structures afloat. We have, I know, because I have been furnished them myself.

The Spanish have had their naval attaché here, who has, no doubt, been supplied with the same information. We have an attaché at the Court of Madrid, endeavoring to get all the information there—Lieutenant Dyer. Assuming that the person who touched off that mine was either a naval or military officer, he would want to place his mine and cause the explosion where it would do the utmost amount of damage, and from the testimony adduced that explosion occurred in the vicinity of the forward magazines in the vessel. They could not cover the whole ground with one mine. The after and forward magazines being so far apart, they could not cover both with one mine.

This mine was exploded very near one of the magazines, and the force of that explosion passed directly through some of those magazines. The effect of such a blast, destroying a vast amount of steel bulkheads and frames and beams and other structures of steel, would send this hurtling mass grinding through a magazine, through the powder, the fragments impinging one upon another; and anyone who has seen the foot of a horse striking sparks from a piece of Belgian pavement at night can imagine the number of sparks and can also imagine the heat evolved by these steel fragments driven through a mass of powder, a sufficient amount of heat to explode powder. In my judgment that is the way it was done, and that is the way and result I would expect to follow if I intended to blow up the magazine of a ship. I would intend to blow not only the bottom of the ship but the magazine.

Q. Suppose the main magazine had blown up?—A. If the main magazine had blown up, as we have the right to suppose would be the case, there would be no one to tell the story.

By Mr. MORGAN:

Q. You mean the forward magazine?—A. I am satisfied the heavy charges did not explode.

By Mr. FRYE:

Q. If they had exploded, they would have blown up everyone on board?—A. Yes, sir.

By Mr. MORGAN:

Q. You speak of the forward magazines?—A. If they could have located the mine under the after magazine, the ship would have been utterly destroyed. There were stored the gun cotton and the war heads for the torpedoes, and the heavy ammunition—everything was stored there. But they were 120 feet away from the scene of the explosion and are intact—were not disturbed.

By Mr. FRYE:

Q. You have read the testimony and examined the plates?—A. I have.

Q. Does that reading leave any doubt in your mind as to the fact that the ship was blown up by an external submarine mine?—A. It leaves no doubt, and removes any doubt I might have entertained, as being absolutely impossible. Assuming we would like to go to work to prove that there was an internal explosion, this evidence of the testimony and these drawings refute that absolutely and decidedly, for the reason—we will go back to our schoolboy days, to Marryat's law—gases and fluids have the property of expanding equally in all directions. The force would be lateral, upward, and downward. and equally strong, the bottom, sides, and decks blown out and uplifted, a general clearance of everything.

The drawings accompanying this report show conclusively the tremendous effect caused by an explosion underneath, which lifted the body of the ship and plunged the bow and ram down in the mud, and it was such a tremendous power that it has left that portion of the ship in the same position now, with a portion of the bottom plating showing the germicide paint—the green paint—not used anywhere else except for antifouling purpose, 4 feet above the water.

By Mr. DAVIS:

Q. How far above its normal position?—A. Thirty-six feet. Now, I suppose—at least I am quite sure—there is not a naval expert in the world who would view those drawings who would give any other testimony; I can not imagine anyone who has had any experience at all giving any other.

By Mr. MORGAN:

Q. Is that green paint used on any other portion of the ship?—A. It is used nowhere else.

Q. It is a green paint?—A. Yes, sir; it is a germicide paint, and is poisonous.

By Mr. DAVIS:

Q. Is it used anywhere except on the bottom?—A. Nowhere else.

By Mr. TURPIE:

Q. The outside of the bottom?—A. Yes, sir; nowhere else.

By Mr. FRYE:

Q. That Spanish naval board which made a report in regard to this explosion and found it was caused by an accident inside could not have made any reasonable examination?—A. It is quite possible the Spanish divers, and also the Spanish officials in charge of those divers, may have made what they consider an examination. It is also quite possible that not one of them was an expert; had ever handled an explosive, or knew anything whatever about the action of high explosive mines.

Q. They find this, as they say, one important fact, that there were no dead fish next day.—A. That does not surprise me. A boy can explode a little dynamite on the surface of the water and stir up quite a number of dead fish if there are any fish there; and again, during my work in Mobile Bay, and it is a fine fish-producing water, in three or four weeks' work I never saw one dead fish. I was expecting to see them, but I did not. I have myself, as president of the board of inspection, in California, inspecting ships fitting out and returning from a cruise for several years, and the Mare Island Straits abounds in fish, and one of our drills is to fire our bomb torpedoes somewhat below the surface of the water to see whether the men were proficient in that sort of work, and I have had occasion to fire a great many torpedoes in those waters, and I never saw a dead fish in those waters while I was there.

S. Doc. 231, pt 7——53

By Mr. MORGAN:

Q. About how many torpedoes and mines did you explode in Mobile Bay?—A. We were sending down these mines and exploding them as rapidly as we could fill and plant them; I suppose averaged one in every half hour, and that extended over a period of three weeks.

By Mr. DAVIS:

Q. Over a large area?—A. No; we were blowing up the main obstruction.

By Mr. FRYE:

Q. You are familiar with the waters of Havana Harbor and have been there a long time. Are there many fish there?—A. I saw very few there. I saw a few surface fish. The fishing to supply Havana is all done outside the harbor. Boats go outside in the morning and return in the evening for the fish market. I have seen what I took to be the small fish that had been brought in, spawned there probably.

Q. Is the water very foul?—A. The water is very foul. The accumulated bilgewater of sugar ships for a century or so, like molasses, and the outflow of the scouring of Havana gutters all pours into the harbor, all the filth and offal from the fish markets and the beef market, and so on—all refuse is dumped there.

Q. What is the tide there?—A. It is what is known as a swelling and ebbing tide. There is a tidal rise and fall, with a light surface current which runs in in moderate force and reflows.

Q. Every six hours?—A. Ebb and flow enough to swing ships that would swing at the buoys.

Q. Do you know the difference between the high and low-water?—A. Two or three feet; enough to make quite a surface current.

Q. If this explosion had taken place at 9.30 in the evening and the waters not been inspected until the next day, even if there had been any fish killed by the explosion would you have expected to find them?—A. There was abundant time for the fish to flow from the harbor, or up and be left stranded by the falling tide. That is a great harbor for saluting with very heavy guns, and sometimes if a poor unfortunate fish happens to be below the muzzle of a gun he will turn up. They are saluting there all the time, and I never saw any dead fish lying around.

Q. You think there is nothing in that dead fish Spanish evidence?—A. I do not. I saw the departure of a Captain-General from the port of Havana early in 1869 or late in 1868, and they had quite a large Spanish fleet there. He was quite a popular man, and from the fleet and from the forts began a system of saluting which was equivalent to a bombardment in volume of explosion, to do honor to this big man of theirs. The concussion of that saluting was something terrific. We joined in as a matter of course, and there were no dead fish in that case, at least none ever noticed.

By Mr. MORGAN:

Q. Have you been to Puerto Rico?—A. I have.

Q. I wish you would describe the bay there, at San Juan, I believe?—A. It is a second Havana, on a smaller scale, with powerful fortifications of the old type defending it. It is a walled city and it has a deep harbor that would afford refuge for the largest battle ships in the world.

Q. How is the anchorage in the bay?—A. Very good and perfectly secure. It is considered a capital hurricane harbor, to use a West

Indian term. That is, that ships with three or four anchors down could ride out a hurricane there.

Q. Is the bay commodious?—A. It is not as large as Havana, but it is large enough for quite a fleet, and being landlocked the ships could anchor with a small scope of chain, giving room for a large navy.

Q. Can the bay be shelled?—A. Yes, sir; from the entrance and over the town. Those old fortifications were magnificent in their day, and cost so much that there is an old story of the King of Spain with his telescope. On one occasion one of the Spanish kings was looking from his palace with a large telescope. The captains-general and the officials of those days were about as now, exceedingly corrupt.

They had charged a great many millions for the building of the defenses of St. Johns, Puerto Rico, while the work was all done by Carib labor under the lash and did not cost anything. One of the courtiers asked him, "Your Majesty, what interests you so much?" He said, "I am looking to see the golden walls of St. Johns. They have charged a hundred millions for them, and I thought they must be in sight from here." These golden walls were magnificent pieces of masonry, and against the 12 and 18 pounders and powder of that day they were impregnable, but as against the 12 and 13 inch guns of the *Indiana* and the *Massachusetts* they are of no more value than a wooden fence.

By Mr. FRYE:

Q. Do you know whether they have recently put in any guns there?—A. I do not know, except from report, but I am quite sure that our military bureau, or naval bureau, of intelligence has positive information in regard to every gun there.

By Mr. MORGAN:

Q. I want to ask you about the Bay of St. Thomas?—A. That is another magnificent harbor.

Q. Protected by defenses?—A. Very small defense. The Danes have had no war, except their little war when Moltke overwhelmed them and took Holstein. They have some small, old-fashioned forts, but with batteries that could be readily constructed, as Beauregard did, building them of sand, the best of all forts could be put up very readily.

Q. Plenty of sand there?—A. Plenty of material. General Gilmore said as a result of his operations, beginning with Pulaski and ending with Morris Island, that if he were ordered to build a fort in New Hampshire, if there were no sand there and none within 200 miles, he would haul it there in wagons, as being the only material which can stand pounding, as shown by the terrific pounding that Morris Island was submitted to and withstood until the crest of the parapet was used up. It was marvelous. What few little holes were made during the day were filled up with sand bags during the night, and they were as good as ever the next day.

Q. How wide is the bar exit into the sea?—A. There is no bar. There is no river outflow. It is a very open, deep-water harbor. Any ship can go in day or night. There is no river to cause a bar. The anchorage is good, and in the harbor they have a floating dock, and there are sites for good docks if anyone chose to put them up, perfectly secure. It could be made a Gibraltar, the facilities for defending it are so great.

Q. What is the important command of that situation as a place of military or naval strategy?—A. If it belonged to a country having command of the sea it completes its control of the whole West India system, including the Isthmus. It is on the direct route of communication. The French, English, and German lines of commerce all pass there, and it was the steamship depot for a number of years, being a free port, having great facilities for coaling and all that.

Q. What is your opinion of its importance as a location for a coaling station ?—A. It is unsurpassed. I was very much interested in knowing the harbor and the people so well at the time we were negotiating for the purchase of the islands originally, St. John, St. Thomas, and Santa Cruz, and I made a close study of it. Of course from my ideas as a military man I considered it a military necessity that we should have it. I was looking forward to the possibility of an Isthmian canal at some time in the future. There is always a great stock of the best kind of coal, Cardiff coal, English coal, there.

Q. In times of peace do you consider that a coaling station there would be of great advantage to commerce as well as in times of war to war ships?—A. Unquestionably.

Q. If you were in command of a fleet and required to be stationed off or near the Dry Tortugas or Key West, to what points would you look for your supply of coal?—A. I would look, as long as it remained in our control—we get our supplies from the northern ports, Mobile and the Mississippi Valley

Q. In time of war would not your coal fleet be very much exposed coming down the coast to find a war fleet at Key West or Dry Tortugas?—A. They would be very much exposed if you were at war with a nation having a superior naval force. As General Grant well expressed it, the objective point of an enemy is its main army. In a naval war our objective point would be the naval fleet of Spain, which is now concentrated at St. Johns, Puerto Rico If you strike that fleet and strike it successfully, Spain is dead so far as naval operations are concerned, and Spain being dead the coal fleet is safe You deal her such a blow and she can never recover from it. If she selects Havana, very well; we will strike her there, and if she occupies Puerto Rico, strike her there and take it away.

Q. In that event, how far would you be from your coal supply at Key West or Tortugas?—A. If I strike for Puerto Rico I have my secondary supply of coal at St. Thomas.

Q. In the absence of that supply, if coal were contraband of war, where would be your base of supply, at Key West or Tortugas?—A. If I had any doubt of being able to procure coal in the friendly harbor of St. Thomas I would carry my coal with me, steam colliers accompanying the fleet I would take St. Johns and coal comfortably inside the harbor I am giving what I firmly believe to be in our power to do if our fleet assembles and if we concentrate and strike such a blow. It is feasible and entirely practicable. I could take the *Vesuvius*, and after silencing the guns of the fort send half a dozen of those terrible projectiles from her guns into the harbor, and she would blow up every ship in that harbor.

Q. How far is it by a proper sailing line for a fleet from Key West to St. Johns. Porto Rico?—A. I have not a chart, but I think about 900 miles.

Q. So that if you had possession of St. Thomas you would have a great advantage in coaling your fleet over the situation in case you had to get your supply from Key West?—A. You are so near to Porto Rico from St. Thomas that from the elevation above St. Thomas you can view the eastward end of the island.

By Mr. FORAKER:

Q. Assuming that at the time of the explosion of the *Maine* the electric lights on shore in the city of Havana were extinguished, to what would you attribute that result, judging from your knowledge of how submarine mines are arranged for explosion, and basing your opinion on all the knowledge you have of such matters and the circumstances attending this particular explosion?—A. In order that this mine should have any effect on the Havana electric-light system, it must have been connected with one of its switch boards. The explosion of the mine disrupting the cable and making ground connection would release the full electric current, taking it to earth. In the system connected with that, all the lights would immediately go out.

Q. Would you, or would you not, then be of the opinion that the fact that the electric lights on shore were extinguished simultaneously with the explosion indicate that there was a connection between the submarine mine and the lights on shore?—A. That might have been.

By Mr. TURPIE:

Q. Judging from your experience in torpedo explosions, what would be the effect upon the water were a mine of the size and weight competent to make this destruction of the *Maine* lighted and exploded under a vessel of the size of the *Maine*, with metallic bottom? Would it be a disturbance in the nature of a wave or would it throw up the water in spouts?—A. I am very glad you asked that question. I had intended to say something about that, but had become interested in other matters and forgot it. The effect of the explosion of a mine in regard to the column of water thrown up depends, curiously enough, upon its depth from the surface.

The explosion of a mine near the surface—3 or 4 or 6 feet below the surface—will throw up a terrific column of water. The explosion of a mine at a depth of 30 feet would hardly make an ebullition, even when there is nothing on the surface. That was the case in removing the reefs at Hell Gate and elsewhere, where there were terrific explosions. Admiral Matthews's attention was called to this fact early in the day, and mine also. I confess it surprised me. I had supposed that the deeper a torpedo, the deeper and heavier it was tamped, the deeper and heavier would be the effect, and I was astonished to find that it was not so.

In the shallow water in Mobile Bay I could not go very deep, the deepest I could go was 15 feet. When I got below 4, or 5, or 6 feet, the smaller the water column thrown up, and Admiral Matthews will testify that at 30, or 35, or 40 feet, hardly a disturbance on the surface, even to bubbling.

STATEMENT OF HONORÉ FRANÇOIS LAINÉ, APRIL 7, 1898.

Honoré FRANÇOIS LAINÉ, being duly sworn, testified as follows:

Senator GRAY. Mr. Lainé, you were in Havana on the night of the disaster to the United States battle ship *Maine?*

Mr. LAINÉ. Yes, sir.

Senator GRAY. Please state how long you had been there and what was your occupation.

Mr. LAINÉ. I arrived in Havana on the 1st of January of this year at 6 o'clock in the morning, on the steamship *Olivette*, as correspondent of the New York Sun, and I was in that capacity in Havana until the 4th of March, when I was expelled by the Spanish authorities, who have never notified me why they have done so.

Senator GRAY. You had been a resident of Havana before that time, had you not?

Mr. LAINÉ. Yes, sir; I was born in Cuba and I lived in Cuba until I was 10 years old.

Senator GRAY. Who was your father?

Mr. LAINÉ. Damaco Lainé.

Senator GRAY. A planter?

Mr. LAINÉ. A planter in the Province of Matanzas.

Senator LODGE. And your mother was an American?

Mr. LAINÉ. My mother was an American, from Wilmington, Del.

Senator GRAY. What was her name, please?

Mr. LAINÉ. Mary Garesché.

Senator GRAY. The family had lived in Wilmington before?

Mr. LAINÉ. Yes, sir; the Du Pont Powder Works used to belong to them. They had powder works.

Senator LODGE. Your father was a French citizen?

Mr. LAINÉ. Yes, sir.

Senator LODGE. You were a French citizen?

Mr. LAINÉ. Yes, sir. When I was 10 years old they sent me to Georgetown College. Then I studied veterinary medicine in New York.

Senator LODGE. Veterinary surgery?

Mr. LAINÉ. Yes, sir; veterinary surgery. When I was 19 years old I graduated, March 4, 1885. I studied that as a sort of sport. I am very fond of horses and thought it best to study that. As to my work in Cuba, I own patents in machinery down there—sugar machinery patents. That was my business, and for that reason I traveled all over the Island of Cuba, and on the whole island. When the war broke out, not having anything to do, I accepted the position of correspondent of the New York Sun.

Senator GRAY. You are familiar with Cuba and with the Spanish language?

Mr. LAINÉ. Oh, yes, sir.

Senator GRAY. And French well as English?

Mr. LAINÉ. Yes, sir; French.

Senator GRAY. Now, please recur to the night of the explosion. Where were you at the time the explosion occurred?

Mr. LAINÉ. The American correspondents at Havana at that time had the habit of congregating in the park known as Isabel la Cotólica, in front of the Hotel Inglaterra. We used to sit down there and talk and exchange notes. That night I had just returned from the Captain General's palace, the censor's office, and was sitting in the park with some friends when we saw the skies get red, and two or three seconds afterwards we heard a terrific detonation. We took a cab and drove down Obispo street to the wharf of Caballería.

Senator GRAY. Will you be good enough to indicate on this map [exhibiting] by a cross with a pencil where you were sitting in the park?

Mr. LAINÉ [indicating]. Right here, sir. Here is the Hotel Ingleterra [indicating]. From there we took a cab and came down this street [indicating]. There is the Captain-General's palace [indicating]. The cab stopped there [indicating]. This is a gate [indicating].

Senator FORAKER. The cab stopped where?

Mr. LAINÉ. At the entrance of the wharf of Caballeria.

Senator FORAKER. At the water?

Senator GRAY. On the water front?

Mr. LAINÉ. On the water front. Then we passed through the iron door there [indicating] and we were on the wharves.

Senator FORAKER. Did you leave your cab there?

Mr. LAINÉ. Yes, we paid the man and left the carriage there. Right at the entrance of it there is a large electric pole, what you call——

Senator FORAKER. A lamp?

Mr. LAINÉ. An arc light. That was extinguished.

Senator FORAKER. The light was extinguished?

Mr. LAINÉ. The light was extinguished.

Senator FORAKER. Then what did you do after leaving your carriage?

Mr. LAINÉ. Then we got on the wharf, on the water side.

Senator GRAY. On the water side?

Mr. LAINÉ. On the water side. There are about 25 or 30 feet, you know. You can walk all around the wharves. These are on the wharves [indicating] and you go inside. There are long wharves.

Senator GRAY. All along the water front?

Mr. LAINÉ. Yes, sir; all along the water front. We got to the water front. I saw by the light that it was the *Maine* that had been blown up.

Senator GRAY. By what light?

Mr. LAINÉ. By the light of the *Maine*. She was burning already; at least, something was burning on the deck that showed me her mast. I could see by that that it was the *Maine*.

Senator GRAY. Did you notice any other electric lights extinguished than the one at the entrance?

Mr. LAINÉ. Every one of them all along here [indicating] was extinguished.

Senator FORAKER. Please state what you did after you left your carriage?

Mr. LAINÉ. After I left my carriage I saw everybody running in this direction [indicating].

Senator FORAKER. In what direction?

Mr. LAINÉ. In the direction of the machina.

Senator DANIEL. What is the machina?

Mr. LAINÉ. The machina is big shears that they have.

Senator LODGE. A great pair of tongs for the purpose of lifting masts out of vessels.

Senator FORAKER. How many squares were there from where you left your carriage to the machina?

Mr. LAINÉ. About six squares.

Senator GRAY. After you entered the iron gate you turned to your right and went along the water front?

Mr. LAINÉ. Yes, sir.

Senator GRAY. To the machina?

Mr. LAINÉ. Yes, sir.

Senator GRAY. And that was toward the *Maine?*

Mr. LAINÉ. Yes, sir; it was toward the *Maine*.

Senator LODGE. That is where the admiral's house is [indicating]?

Mr. LAINÉ. It is where the admiral's house is.

Senator GRAY. You say when you first entered the gate there was a tall iron pole that had an electric light on it which had been extinguished?

Mr. LAINÉ. Yes, sir. There are several around here; but this one was distinguished because it was right in the center here [indicating], and I had it in front of me. It was so dark that I noticed it.

Senator GRAY. Were those around it extinguished?

Mr. LAINÉ. All were extinguished around there.

Senator GRAY. Were there a number of electric-light poles along the water front that you traversed on your way to the machina?

Mr. LAINÉ. I will mark them here [indicating]. There are about twelve all along here.

Senator GRAY. On the road you traveled?

Mr. LAINÉ. Yes, sir.

Senator GRAY. Were they all extinguished?

Mr. LAINÉ. They were all extinguished. The wharf was very dark.

Senator GRAY. Is this part of the city [indicating] lighted largely by electricity?

Mr. LAINÉ. Only on the wharves, sir.

Senator GRAY. What is the lighting here [indicating]?

Mr. LAINÉ. Gas.

Senator GRAY. Was that extinguished?

Mr. LAINÉ. I did not notice that. My attention was not turned that way.

Senator FORAKER. Did you see any electric lights burning at all along the wharves?

Mr. LAINÉ. No, sir.

Senator GRAY. They were all out?

Mr. LAINÉ. Yes, sir.

Senator FORAKER. Were you ever down there at any other time in the night time?

Mr. LAINÉ. Yes, sir.

Senator FORAKER. Did you ever see them out before?

Mr. LAINÉ. No, sir; I never did. The wharves are always lit up at night, because goods are kept down there and they have to be well watched.

Senator FORAKER. Was this the first time you ever saw them out?

Mr. LAINÉ. Yes, sir; it was the first time.

Senator FORAKER. In the nighttime?

Mr. LAINÉ. Yes, sir.

Senator GRAY. Did you hear any remark at that time or the next day about the extinguishment of the electric lights at the time of the explosion?

Mr. LAINÉ. I believe the papers mentioned that fact the next day, but mentioned it as the effect of the big explosion. I remember reading also that in a café near by $3,000 worth of damage had been done by the breaking of glass and such things. But I am going to get those Spanish papers and try to send them to you.

Senator LODGE. Do you know whether the gas lights went out?

Mr. LAINÉ. I do not, sir.

Senator LODGE. You have no reason to suppose that they did?

Mr. LAINÉ. I could not tell you that, sir. When I got down to the wharf my main idea was to look toward the *Maine* and get a boat to go there. I paid no attention to the city or anything. But I saw this arc light fluttering; I can remember that distinctly.

Senator GRAY. You saw it fluttering?

Mr. LAINÉ. You know when an electric light goes out the carbon remains for some time red hot. I just saw that and that made the whole thing look dark. Then that crowd of excited Spaniards hallooing, and all that, impressed me with the darkness of the place.

Senator LODGE. You drove down Obispo street, which is lighted by gas?

Mr. LAINÉ. Yes, sir; it is lighted by gas.

Senator LODGE. In driving down that street, did you notice whether the lights were out?

Mr. LAINÉ. I did not. I could not tell you.

Senator LODGE. If they had been out, would you have been likely to have noticed it?

Mr. LAINÉ. Yes; I think if they had all gone out I certainly would have noticed it.

ADDITIONAL STATEMENT OF HONORÉ FRANÇOIS LAINÉ, APRIL 7. 1898.

Honoré FRANÇOIS LAINÉ, having been previously sworn, further testified as follows:

The CHAIRMAN (Senator Davis). Mr. Lainé, you are a native of Cuba?

Mr. LAINÉ. Yes, sir.

The CHAIRMAN. What is your age?

Mr. LAINÉ. Thirty-three.

The CHAIRMAN. Your father is a French subject?

Mr. LAINÉ. A French citizen, sir.

The CHAIRMAN. You were educated in this country?

Mr. LAINÉ. In this country.

The CHAIRMAN. Where?

Mr. LAINÉ. At Georgetown College and Philadelphia.

The CHAIRMAN. What is your profession?

Mr. LAINÉ. I have studied veterinary medicine, but my profession in Cuba—I own patents in connection with sugar machinery, sugar-making establishments there.

The CHAIRMAN. Is your father a planter?

Mr. LAINÉ. Yes, sir.

The CHAIRMAN. How far from Havana?

Mr. LAINÉ. Ninety miles.

The CHAIRMAN. What became of his plantation?

Mr. LAINÉ. It has been burned.

The CHAIRMAN. By whom?

Mr. LAINÉ. By the Spaniards.

The CHAIRMAN. When?

Mr. LAINÉ. In the month of October, 1896.

The CHAIRMAN. Where did you go then?

Mr. LAINÉ. I was in prison then.

The CHAIRMAN. What became of your father and mother?

Mr. LAINÉ. They have come to this country. They are living in Tampa now.

The CHAIRMAN. Your mother is a native of the United States?

Mr. LAINÉ. Yes, sir.

The CHAIRMAN. Born at Wilmington, Del.?

Mr. LAINÉ. At Wilmington, Del.

The CHAIRMAN. What was her maiden name?

Mr. LAINÉ. Mary Garesché.

The CHAIRMAN. You went from New York to Havana as a correspondent in 1897; did you not?

Mr. LAINÉ. On the 1st of January, 1898.

The CHAIRMAN. As a correspondent?

Mr. LAINÉ. Of the New York Sun.

The CHAIRMAN. For what paper?

Mr. LAINÉ. The New York Sun.

The CHAIRMAN. Did you make inquiry of the Spanish authorities whether you would be safe in doing so?

Mr. LAINÉ. I spoke to the Spanish consul in New York, and I spoke to Secretary Congosto when I arrived there.

The CHAIRMAN. What assurance, if any, did you receive?

Mr. LAINÉ. Secretary Congosto told me that as long as he would be there nothing would happen to me.

The CHAIRMAN. Did you enter upon your duties at Havana?

Mr. LAINÉ. Yes, sir.

The CHAIRMAN. You used to exchange notes with other correspondents for the purpose of furnishing each other news?

Mr. LAINÉ. Yes, sir.

The CHAIRMAN. Did you know a newspaper correspondent by the name of Diaz?

Mr. LAINÉ. Francesco Diaz?

The CHAIRMAN. An old friend of yours?

Mr. LAINÉ. Well, an acquaintance. A reporter has a great many.

The CHAIRMAN. Was he engaged in Havana at that time?

Mr. LAINÉ. He was engaged in reporting for the Union Constitucionel.

The CHAIRMAN. Was that a Weylerite paper?

Mr. LAINÉ. Yes, sir; a Weylerite paper.

The CHAIRMAN. Very radical?

Mr. LAINÉ. Very radical.

The CHAIRMAN. You have stated to me heretofore some events connected with a letter or a copy of a letter which you received from Mr. Diaz purporting to be a letter which General Weyler had sent to the editor of that newspaper. Now, I wish you to go on in your own way from the beginning, and state the history of that business and what happened to you on account of it.

Mr. LAINÉ. I met Diaz one night in a room of the Hotel Ingleterra, where the reporters used to congregate at night to talk and exchange notes. In talking with him he told me that General Weyler had acceded to become a candidate for the Cortes of Spain for the district of Havana. Asking him how he knew that, he told me he had a copy of a letter of General Weyler. The letter had been written by General Weyler to Santos Guzman, a lawyer, and head of the Spanish constitutional party in Cuba—the Weyler party. Mr. Santos Guzman had given the letter to Mr. Novo, editor of the paper, the Union Constitucionel.

The CHAIRMAN. Have you that copy of the letter with you now?

Mr. LAINÉ. I have not. It is in New York, sir.

The CHAIRMAN. Will you furnish it, or a copy of it, to this committee?

Mr. LAINÉ. Yes, sir. It is in Spanish.

The CHAIRMAN. And with it a translation?

Mr. LAINÉ. Yes, sir.

Senator GRAY. Both?

Mr. LAINÉ. Yes, sir.

The CHAIRMAN. Go on with your statement.

Mr. LAINÉ. This reporter, Diaz, saw the letter at the office of the paper there and took a copy of it, which copy he gave me. I do not remember the exact words of the letter.

Senator LODGE. State the purport of it.

Senator GRAY. Subject to correction when you send the committee a copy.

Mr. LAINÉ. In the letter Weyler said——

Senator FORAKER. In substance?

Mr. LAINÉ. Yes; Weyler said that after mature consideration he had decided to run as a candidate for a deputy of the Cortes in Spain. Of course the letter is much longer than that, you know.

Senator FORAKER. Just give the substance of it.

Mr. LAINÉ. And he gave his reasons why he ran as a candidate and gave some advice to Santos Guzman on that subject. Then he added that he had read that the Americans were intending to send a warship to Havana; that they had never dared to do so in his time, as he had the harbor well prepared for such emergencies——

Senator GRAY. Well prepared?

Mr. LAINÉ. Well prepared for such emergencies, and that he hoped there would be a Spanish hand who would chastise in a fitting way that offense.

The CHAIRMAN. Go on with your statement.

Mr. LAINÉ. The *Maine* not having arrived then, and knowing nothing at all about the arrival of American ships, that part of the letter had no importance at all.

Senator FORAKER. Was that before you had heard that the *Maine* was coming?

Mr. LAINÉ. Yes, sir; it was before that. This was so much so that as to that part of the letter I could hardly understand what he was referring to. The *Maine* arrived.

Senator FORAKER. What did you do with the letter?

Mr. LAINÉ. I have got the copy of the letter. I sent the news to this country that Weyler was willing to run as a candidate for the Spanish Cortes.

Senator LODGE. That was the part of the letter that interested you?

Mr. LAINÉ. That interested everybody then. Weyler had always said that he was not affiliated to any Spanish party. I kept the letter in my desk; I pigeonholed it in my desk and paid no more attention to it. The *Maine* arrived on the following day—two days after that.

Senator GRAY. Two days after you saw the copy of the letter?

Mr. LAINÉ. Yes; two days after I had the copy of the letter the *Maine* arrived.

Senator GRAY. Do you recollect about the date of the letter?

Mr. LAINÉ. I think it was the 24th, at nighttime——

Senator GRAY. The 24th of January?

Mr. LAINÉ. Of January, about 10 o'clock at night. At 10 or 11 o'clock at night he gave me the letter.

Senator GRAY. But do you recollect the date of the letter?

Mr. LAINÉ. The letter was written in Madrid on the 8th of January.

The CHAIRMAN. Proceed with your statement.

Mr. LAINÉ. The *Maine* arrived on the following day, and on the 15th of February it was blown up. I then recalled Weyler's letter. I took it out of my desk and read two or three times over his last paragraphs. I went to see Diaz three times, and tried to get at any price the original letter, and could not do it. A few days after that—— .

Senator GRAY. Did he deny the authenticity of the letter when you applied to him?

Mr. LAINÉ. Oh, no. I did not see Diaz after that until the time I am going to refer to now. A few days after the explosion of the *Maine* I met Diaz leaving the palace of the Captain-General as I was entering it. After saluting him he said to me, "Do you remember the copy of the letter of General Weyler I gave you?" I told him, "Yes." He said to me, "What do you think about what Weyler said of the American ship?" I answered that I thought someone had followed his advice. Diaz, being a Spaniard, looked at me very seriously in the face. I understood right then that I had made a false step. On the night of the 4th—let me see—Wednesday; if I had a calendar here——

The CHAIRMAN. There is a calendar here.

(A calendar was handed to the witness.)

Mr. LAINÉ (after examining the calendar). On the night of March 4, at 12 o'clock that night, as I was leaving the Hotel Ingleterra, I saw two figures on the sidewalk. They were the chief of police of Havana and a detective, who I afterwards ascertained had been following my footsteps for several days. As I passed the two figures the chief of police told me, " Stop, sir; you are under arrest." A cab was passing by. I was ordered to get in, and the detective took me to the jefatura, or police headquarters. There, after being searched for incriminating papers, I was locked in a small cell incommunicado. An hour after that the chief of police arrived, and said to me, " Well, we have you secure here at last." I made no reply to him, and he began to threaten me.

The CHAIRMAN. He spoke to you through the bars, did he not?

Mr. LAINÉ. Oh, yes; I was inside the cell.

The CHAIRMAN. What was his language in threatening you?

Mr. LAINÉ. I think I ought to refer to the cab again and the way.

The CHAIRMAN. Oh, yes.

Mr. LAINÉ. As the detective was paying for the cab that took us to jefatura I was able to signal to the cabman, who was an acquaintance of mine, to inform my friends that I had been detained. He nodded with his head and I knew that he had understood my sign. He was a Cuban, you know. When the chief of police began to threaten me——

The CHAIRMAN. What did he say?

Mr. LAINÉ. He said to me, "The secret that I know you know will never be known by others, as they will not know either what has happened to you." I then replied to him, "If you think, Colonel"—he is colonel of police—" that you can make me disappear as you did Posado and Ariza" (two young men who had been taken out of the place and killed in the outskirts of Havana by the Havana police) "you are very much mistaken, as by this time the French and the American consuls who were my friends know that I am detained." The chief of police changed his threatening attitude, ordered me out of the cell, ordered two chairs to be brought, and asked me to sit down as he wanted to have a talk with me. He then said, "I know all about a copy of a letter which you say you have of Weyler. That does not trouble me. What I want to know is what you said to Consul Lee on the 24th of February concerning the explosion of the Maine." I answered him that I had not spoken on that subject to Consul Lee. I was ordered to be locked up again in the cell. The next morning I was sent to the Fortress Las Cabañas. On Wednesday March 9, at 11 o'clock in the morning, I was taken out of my cell by a Spanish captain of the Fortress, put on board a Government boat, rowed to the steamer Olivette by Spanish sailors; and that is all. There is not anything more to it.

The CHAIRMAN. You were placed on board the Olivette?

Mr. LAINÉ. That is all. I do not know yet why I have been expelled.

The CHAIRMAN. You came to this country?

Mr. LAINÉ. I came to this country.

The CHAIRMAN. You have been here ever since?

Mr. LAINÉ. Yes, sir; I have been here ever since.

Senator GRAY. Did you bring that copy of the letter away with you?

Mr. LAINÉ. Yes, sir.

Senator GRAY. Where was it?

Mr. LAINÉ. Being a correspondent of an American newspaper and receiving all sorts of letters from the insurgents and people of that kind, I kept those documents in a secret corner of my room. The Spanish authorities, when they searched my room, were unable to find that. A friend of mine lived in the same house, the house of an American, Dr. Wilson, and knew where I kept my things. I was able to send him a message from the fortress and tell him to pack all my clothes and send all my papers. My clothes were sent to me, my valise, but the papers were given in a sealed envelop to the agent of the Plant Steamship Company, who delivered them to me on board the steamship *Olivette*, and I signed a receipt for them from this young man, named Mr. Miranda.

Senator FORAKER. You signed the receipt for this sealed package of papers on board the *Olivette?*

Mr. LAINÉ. Yes, sir; on board the *Olivette*.

Senator FORAKER. After the Spaniards had put you there?

Mr. LAINÉ. Yes, sir.

Senator GRAY. And that package contained this copy of Weyler's letter to which you have referred?

Mr. LAINÉ. Yes, sir; and it contained a great many things.

Senator FORAKER. Where is that copy of the Weyler letter now?

Mr. LAINÉ. I have it in New York.

Senator GRAY. And you will send us the original Spanish copy and a translation?

Mr. LAINÉ. Yes, sir.

The following is the copy of the letter referred to above with its translation:

MADRID, *Enero 8 de 1898.*

Sr. FRANCISCO DE LOS SANTOS GUZMAN, *Habana.*

MI DISTINGUIDO AMIGO Y CORRELIGIONARIO: Mi opinion sobre la actitud de nuestro partido en Cuba ha cambiado ante los ultimos sucesos.

Si yo creí antes que el partido debia dignamente abstenerse de entrar en la contienda electoral, ahora creo que es una necesidad patriotica y un deber que tome parte en esa elecciones.

No cabe dudar del exito ni de muestra mayoria en las listas; ni tampoco de que un programa fundado en la defensa del honor nacional habia de arrastrar junto con nosotros los elementos tibios; pero sinceramente españoles que se han dejado ilusionar por las combinaciones de Moret y Sagasta y que han tomado por buena moneda y como combinaciones cientificas la verdadera y deshonrosa humillacion de nuestro pueblo ante el de los Estados Unidos.

Inscriban Uds. en su bandera (la bandera de España) "revindicacion del decoro nacional" y yo me ofrezco como su candidato. Mi título mayor de gloria despues de haber mandado durante dos años doscientos mil heroes españoles en Cuba, será el de Diputado por la Habana.

Por cierto que he leido ultimamente que piensan los Americanos enviar un buque de guerra á esa ciudad. En mi tiempo ni lo soñaron siquiera.

Sabían el terrible castigo que les hubiera esperado.

Yo preparé ese puerto para esa contingencia haciendo obras que Martinez Campos había abandonado.

Si tal insulto llegara a realizarse, espero que no faltara una mano española que se levante para castigar tan ejemplarmente como merece la provocacion.

Romero está bien como nunca lo creimos sus amigos y aparte de los disgustos que esta atmosfera de humillaciones me impone lo esta tambien su afmo. amigo.

Y. S. S.

VALERIANO WEYLER.

Here is a copy of the letter:

His Excellency DON FRANCISCO DE LOS SANTOS GUZMAN,

Havana.

MY DISTINGUISHED PERSONAL AND POLITICAL FRIEND: Since the latest events, I have changed my views about the attitude which our political party in Cuba ought to assume.

I have thought before that it was more dignified for us to abstain from the electoral contest; I believe now that it is a patriotic duty for us to go to the polls. Our success can not be doubted; neither can be our majority of voters, nor that, with a programme of defense of the national honor, we will have side by side with us all those lukewarm politicians who, though Spaniards by heart, are deceived by the inside combinations of Moret and Sagasta, and take as scientific solutions of our colonial problems what are really dishonorable humiliations of our country before the United States.

Write on your flag, the flag of Spain, "Defense of national honor," and I offer you my name as your candidate.

After having commanded during two years 200,000 Spanish heroes in Cuba, the title I shall be more proud of is that of deputy from Havana at the Cortes of Spain.

By the way, I have read these days that the Americans are pondering about sending one of their war ships to that city. During my command in Cuba they did not even dare to dream about it. They knew the terrible punishment that awaited them.

I had Havana Harbor well prepared for such an emergency. I rapidly finished the work that Martinez Campos carelessly abandoned.

If the insult is made, I hope that there will be a Spanish hand to punish it as terribly as it deserves.

Romero is in better health than his friends could have expected, and notwithstanding how morally sick I feel breathing this humiliating atmosphere, is well, also your affectionate friend and servant.

VELERIANO WEYLER.

MADRID, *January 8, 1898.*

This letter was written to Guzman, who as leader of the Conservative party is Spanish as garlic, and was by him turned over to the editor of the ultra-Spanish paper, La Union Constitucional, in order that Weyler's candidacy might be announced and favorably commented upon.

This was before the *Maine* had gone to Havana, so there was no immediate significance in that portion of the letter that referred to the preparations to destroy American war ships.

Senator FORAKER. In whose handwriting is that copy of the letter?

Mr. LAINÉ. I believe it is in Diaz's handwriting.

Senator FORAKER. It is not in your handwriting?

Mr. LAINÉ. Oh, no, sir.

Senator GRAY. You will make affidavit that that is the copy you received from Diaz?

Mr. LAINÉ. Yes, sir.

Senator GRAY. And that it is given a proper translation? The translation, however, will show for itself.

Senator LODGE. You will also send us, if you can find them, those Spanish papers showing that the lights were turned out?

Mr. LAINÉ. Yes; I will try to get those Spanish papers which speak of the lights.

Senator GRAY. You spoke of being in prison at the time your father's plantation was burned?

Mr. LAINÉ. Yes, sir.

Senator GRAY. What was the nature of that imprisonment; was it political or otherwise?

Mr. LAINÉ. Political, sir.

Senator GRAY. Please state the causes and circumstances attending your imprisonment.

Senator FORAKER. And the duration of the same, and how it was terminated.

Mr. LAINÉ. When Gomez and Maceo were on their invading march; they invaded the whole island——

Senator GRAY. In what year?

Mr. LAINÉ. That was December 22, 1896. They passed near my father's place. I met a friend of mine, Brigadier Zayas, who induced me to accompany him for a few days. In order to see something of the war I consented, and I was with Gomez and Maceo for eight days. They were then making a circuit, and they promised that they would let me go home in the same place that they had taken me prisoner; that they had asked me to go with them, which was so.

Senator FORAKER. They were to return to the same place?

Mr. LAINÉ. Yes, just making a circle to see the Spanish forces. They were going back, you know; and eight days after that I came home. Convinced of what the Cubans were going to do in the island, I advised my family to leave the plantation and go to Havana, and they did, I accompanying them. Eight days after we were in Havana I was taken prisoner and accused by the Spanish of being an insurgent chief. I was tried twice by the Spanish authorities, once in Havana and the other time in Madrid, and I was acquitted in Madrid, as they had no charges against me, after being kept in prison for one year, one month, six days, and two hours.

Senator FORAKER. What was the nature of your imprisonment? Where were you imprisoned, and how?

Mr. LAINÉ. I was imprisoned until the 24th of June in the Cabañas fortress. General Lee one day appeared unexpectedly in the fortress to see the crew of the *Competitor*. This so worried Weyler that in order to avoid other visits of General Lee he forbade all foreigners from going to the fortress. My father, being a foreigner, was not allowed to go there. He had been going to see me for the last five months, you know.

Senator FORAKER. Were you present at the trial had in Havana when you were convicted?

Mr. LAINÉ. Yes, I was present there.

Senator FORAKER. Of what were you convicted?

Mr. LAINÉ. Well, I do not think I was convicted of anything, but I was accused of a good many things.

Senator FORAKER. You say you were accused of being an insurgent chief. Is that the charge which was made when you were tried?

Mr. LAINÉ. Yes, sir.

Senator FORAKER. They found you guilty?

Mr. LAINÉ. Yes, sir.

Senator FORAKER. Notwithstanding what the testimony was?

Mr. LAINÉ. Yes, sir.

Senator FORAKER. Then, you say you were acquitted at another trial, in Madrid?

Mr. LAINÉ. Yes, sir.

Senator FORAKER. Were you present in Madrid?

Mr. LAINÉ. No, sir.

Senator FORAKER. That trial was upon the record, I suppose?

Mr. LAINÉ. Yes, sir.

Senator FORAKER. They reversed the judgment of the court below?

Mr. LAINÉ. Yes, sir.

Senator FORAKER. What was the sentence pronounced upon you?

Mr. LAINÉ. Thirty years in chains.

Senator FORAKER. That was pronounced in Havana when you were found guilty?

Mr. LAINÉ. Yes, sir.

Senator FORAKER. When you were first arrested, where were you taken and how dealt with?

Mr. LAINÉ. I was taken to the jefatura, and from the jefatura to Cabañas fortress. I did not finish what I was saying just now. When my father protested he could not go to see me in the fortress, General

Weyler ordered me to be sent to the city jail, where my father could go to see me.

Senator FORAKER. Who interposed in your behalf, if anybody ?

Mr. LAINÉ. I have had a good many persons.

Senator FORAKER. I mean what official interposed.

Mr. LAINÉ. In my behalf?

Senator FORAKER. Yes.

Mr. LAINÉ. Mr. Eustis did a good deal for me, too, in Paris, and the French Government, of course.

Senator FORAKER. That is what I wanted to know, whether it was the French officials who interposed.

Mr. LAINÉ. Yes, the French Government got me out of that.

Senator FORAKER. Did you not, when arrested, call upon the representative in Havana of the French Government?

Mr. LAINÉ. Oh, yes, sir.

Senator FORAKER. Did he take any steps in your behalf?

Mr. LAINÉ. Unfortunately he was the only foreign representative who in the time of Weyler received a decoration from the Spanish Government, and it was not until after he had left Havana and my case went to Madrid that the French Government really took an interest in my case.

Senator DANIEL. He received a decoration from the Spanish Government?

Mr. LAINÉ. Yes, a decoration. He was given a cross.

Senator FORAKER. Were you at any time in incommunicado?

Mr. LAINÉ. Twenty-five days, sir.

Senator FORAKER. At what period of your confinement?

Mr. LAINÉ. The first twenty-five days.

Senator FORAKER. By incommunicado we are to understand that no one was allowed to see you?

Mr. LAINÉ. No one was allowed to see me. I could not write nor read, and I had no communication with the outside world.

Senator FORAKER. Can you us tell whether the Republic of Cuba has any headquarters; and if so, where located?

Mr. LAINÉ. They are located in the Province of Camaguey.

Senator FORAKER. At what place?

Mr. LAINÉ. In the mountains of Cubitas, at a place called Cubitas.

Senator FORAKER. What is the population of Cubitas, just roughly stated?

Mr. LAINÉ. I think about 800 to 1,000 persons. Of course the Cuban Government does not want to keep many women and children there. Fearing to be attacked, they prefer to have them dispersed around the prefectures.

Senator FORAKER. How long have the headquarters of the Cuban Republic been at Cubitas?

Mr. LAINÉ. Since June, 1895.

Senator FORAKER. Have you been at Cubitas since the headquarters were located there?

Mr. LAINÉ. Yes, sir.

Senator FORAKER. What officials of the Cuban Republic are there, if any at all?

Mr. LAINÉ. Well, there is the President, the Vice-President, the representatives of the constituent assembly, the secretary of war——

Senator FORAKER. The cabinet?

Mr. LAINÉ. Yes, sir; the cabinet.

Senator FORAKER. Let me ask you, so as to have it explicitly stated, whether it is or is not true that the assembly of representatives of the Cuban Republic, provided for in the constitution of that Republic, and the President, Vice-President, and the cabinet, provided for by that constitution, all reside at Cubitas during their official terms?

Mr. LAINÉ. Yes, sir; they all reside there during their official term, which is two years.

Senator FORAKER. State whether they have buildings set apart as the official buildings of the Republic of Cuba?

Mr. LAINÉ. They have; and I could get you a sketch of them.

Senator FORAKER. That is not necessary. You know this from your personal knowledge—from having visited the place?

Mr. LAINÉ. Yes, sir; I have seen them.

Senator FORAKER. Are those buildings occupied by these officials?

Mr. LAINÉ. Yes, sir.

Senator FORAKER. Do they conduct the business of their Government there and have archives?

Mr. LAINÉ. All the business of their Government is conducted there, and they have the archives, which are kept as I have seen them—I do not know that they have changed them since then—in cedar boxes, which are made in a way that they can be easily transported from one place to another in case of emergency.

Senator FORAKER. State what departments of that Government, if any, are in operation.

Mr. LAINÉ. Well, there is the legislative body there, and there is the war department; and the minister of finance is there.

Senator FORAKER. State whether they have a fiscal system.

Senator DANIEL. A secretary of the treasury?

Mr. LAINÉ. Yes, sir.

Senator FORAKER. And if so, by whom conducted.

Mr. LAINÉ. Yes, sir; the fiscal system is conducted by the department of the treasury there, which resides there, and taxes are collected by the Cubans all over the island, for which they always give a receipt.

Senator FORAKER. In the name of the Cuban Republic?

Mr. LAINÉ. In the name of the Cuban Republic; and the property of people who pay their taxes there is always respected. Only about two months ago a gentleman from New York, Mr. Louis Marx, asked me in Havana——

Senator FORAKER. Have they tax collectors throughout the island?

Mr. LAINÉ. Yes, sir; that is what I was going to say now. Mr. Marx owns a tobacco plantation near Alquizar. He informed me that the Cuban tax collector had come to his plantation and collected his taxes. He paid the contribution. He showed me the receipt and he asked me to inquire whether it was made in due form and by duly authorized persons.

Senator FORAKER. Is that the end of your statement on that point?

Mr. LAINÉ. I was going to give the proofs. I inquired of the prefect of Havana, who lives in the city of Havana, whether the said man was really the authorized man to do so, and when he saw the signature and——how do you call that thing they put on paper?

Senator FORAKER. The stamp?

Mr. LAINÉ. When he saw the signature and the stamp he informed me that it was correct.

Senator FORAKER. Then, as I understand you, they have a prefect in each subdivision of territory throughout the island?

Mr. LAINÉ. Yes, sir; throughout the Island of Cuba.

Senator FORAKER. What kind of an officer is a prefect?

S. Doc. 231, pt 7——54

Mr. LAINÉ. The prefect is generally chosen as a married man who knows how to read and write, and who has good conduct. He is the one who is in charge of all the petty civil charges of his neighborhood.

Senator FORAKER. Do you mean that he is a judicial officer?

Mr. LAINÉ. Yes, sir; he is one who has to take care of the children and see that they go to school, and protect the women and children. He has to furnish guides in traveling. It is a judicial and military title at the same time. He has to furnish guides to different bands or forces of Cubans who travel from one part of the island to another.

Senator FORAKER. And they have a prefect even in Havana?

Mr. LAINÉ. Yes, sir; in the city of Havana.

Senator FORAKER. They have them scattered throughout the island?

Mr. LAINÉ. All over the Island of Cuba.

Senator FORAKER. Are they in the constant discharge of their duties?

Mr. LAINÉ. Yes, sir.

Senator FORAKER. Is the prefect in the city of Havana appointed by the Republic of Cuba, known as such?

Mr. LAINÉ. He is known to all Cubans.

Senator FORAKER. He is known only to the Cubans?

Mr. LAINÉ. Yes, sir.

Senator FORAKER. He is not known to the Spanish authorities?

Mr. LAINÉ. No, sir.

Senator FORAKER. Now tell us as to their postal system, whether or not they have any in operation.

Mr. LAINÉ. They have a perfect postal system all over the island of Cuba.

Senator FORAKER. What is the nature of it?

Mr. LAINÉ. It is carried by special messengers in the provinces of Havana and Matanzas, in the trains of the Spanish Government, and through where there are no railroads by men on horseback. Do you wish me to describe how it is done?

Senator FORAKER. Yes.

Mr. LAINÉ. I do not know whether or not that would be interesting to put down, but I will just show you how it is done. There is a tree in Cuba called the royal palm, which gives a special bark, and these are the mail bags, because it is impervious to water. They make the bags out of this bark and carry them on horseback, and when the horse swims the stream the water does not cause damage.

Senator FORAKER. Are those the official mail bags that you speak of?

Mr. LAINÉ. No; that is the way that I have seen them carried.

Senator FORAKER. Have they any such thing as a postage stamp?

Mr. LAINÉ. Yes, sir.

Senator FORAKER. Who manufactures and furnishes that stamp?

Mr. LAINÉ. It is manufactured in this country.

Senator FORAKER. And furnished by whom?

Mr. LAINÉ. By the Cuban Government. If you wish, I can send you different postage stamps at different prices.

Senator FORAKER. That is not necessary. Are these postage stamps recognized as payment for the carrying of the mails in Cuba?

Mr. LAINÉ. Yes, sir; in the Cuban ranks.

Senator FORAKER. By the Cuban Republic?

Mr. LAINÉ. Yes, sir; by the Cuban Republic.

Senator FORAKER. How is it as to a system of education? Have they any?

Mr. LAINÉ. In these prefectures they have teachers who give lessons to Cuban children. Education, according to the rules of the Cuban Republic, is compulsory.

Senator FORAKER. It is compulsory?

Mr. LAINÉ. Yes, sir; compulsory.

Senator FORAKER. Is that system prevalent and in operation throughout the territory occupied by the Cubans?

Mr. LAINÉ. Throughout all the territory occupied by the Cuban forces.

Senator FORAKER. Where do they get their school books?

Mr. LAINÉ. They print them in Cuba themselves.

Senator FORAKER. In Cuba?

Mr. LAINÉ. Yes, sir; in Cuba, in the printing offices of the government.

Senator FORAKER. Has the government printing offices?

Mr. LAINÉ. Yes, sir.

Senator FORAKER. How many and where?

Mr. LAINÉ. They have one at Cubitas.

Senator FORAKER. Have they any other than that?

Mr. LAINÉ. I do not know of an official one, only that one.

Senator FORAKER. That is official?

Mr. LAINÉ. Yes, sir.

Senator FORAKER. Do I understand you to state that they have their public-school books?

Mr. LAINÉ. Yes, sir.

Senator FORAKER. Which are supplied under Government supervision and by Government direction?

Mr. LAINÉ. To the different prefectures.

Senator FORAKER. To the different prefectures?

Mr. LAINÉ. Yes, sir.

Senator FORAKER. And by the prefects distributed

Mr. LAINÉ. To the children.

Senator FORAKER. So, if I understand you, they have a system of collecting taxes, they have a postal system of the character described, and they have an educational system?

Mr. LAINÉ. Yes, sir.

Senator FORAKER. All in operation?

Mr. LAINÉ. Yes, sir.

Senator FORAKER. And this house of representatives is constantly in session, do I understand you to say?

Mr. LAINÉ. Yes, sir; in the town of Cubitas.

Senator FORAKER. The members of this house of representatives are elected by a direct vote of the people, as I understand you?

Mr. LAINÉ. Yes, sir.

Senator DANIEL. The council is the cabinet?

Mr. LAINÉ. The council.

Senator FORAKER. They have a president, a vice-president, and a cabinet or council?

Mr. LAINÉ. Yes, sir.

Senator FORAKER. And the house of representatives elect them, as I understand you?

Mr. LAINÉ. Yes, sir; the elections take place every two years.

Senator FORAKER. Who was the first President of the present Republic of Cuba?

Mr. LAINÉ. Salvador y Betancourt.

Senator DANIEL. That last is his mother's name?

Mr. LAINÉ. Yes, sir; his mother's name. In Cuba, and in Spain also, they always take the mother's and father's name to distinguish from cousins and others who may have the same name.

Senator FORAKER. Did you know him?

Mr. LAINÉ. I have seen him, but I do not know him personally?

Senator FORAKER. Do you know what his reputation is as a man of character?

Mr. LAINÉ. He is a man who belonged to a very good Cuban family. He has a title, Marquis Santa Lucia. He does not use his title.

Senator FORAKER. He does not use that title?

Mr. LAINÉ. He does not use that title.

Senator FORAKER. Is he an educated man?

Mr. LAINÉ. Yes, sir; he is an educated man. He was educated in this country and in England.

Senator FORAKER. He is a man of prominence in Cuba?

Mr. LAINÉ. Yes, sir.

Senator FORAKER. He was president for two years

Mr. LAINÉ. Yes, sir.

Senator FORAKER. Who is the present president?

Mr. LAINÉ. Bartolmé Masó.

Senator FORAKER. Do you know what his reputation is and what character of man he is in Cuba?

Mr. LAINÉ. He has been the only man I have known the Spaniards to speak in high terms of, because he was a man who had large business interests in Cuba—sugar interests. He was in the secrets of the coming revolution, and a few days before the revolution broke out he called all his creditors and paid them cash for his outstanding debts.

Senator FORAKER. And then went into the army?

Mr. LAINÉ. And then went into the army.

Senator FORAKER. Is he an educated man?

Mr. LAINÉ. Yes, sir.

Senator FORAKER. I call your attention to a short biographical sketch of him found in Senate Document No. 129, Fifty-fifth Congress, second session, at page 7. I will ask you to look at it and state whether that is a correct account of him, so far as you know?

Mr. LAINÉ (examining the document as indicated). It says here:

On the 24th of February, 1895, he settled his business affairs, paid his obligations even to the last penny, and with a tranquil conscience went to the field.

This is the thing, so well known, that impressed the Spaniards, of which I spoke a moment ago, about the honesty of the man.

Senator FORAKER. The question I ask you is whether the sketch as there given is correct?

Mr. LAINÉ. Yes, sir; to my knowledge it is correct.

Senator FORAKER. I wish you would also read the sketch immediately following of Dr. Domingo Mendez Capote, the vice-president of the Republic, and state whether or not it is correct, so that we may have before us some account of these officials.

Mr. LAINÉ (examining the document as indicated). Well, being acquainted with Mr. Domingo Mendez Capote I can say that all that is here stated is perfectly correct.

Senator FORAKER. He is a man of respectability, then, and of position, and was before the insurrection?

Mr. LAINÉ. That is proved by the positions which he held in Havana in foreign as well as in Spanish companies—corporations.

Senator DANIEL. Do you say that you knew him?

Mr. LAINÉ. Yes, sir.

Senator DANIEL. Did you state that you went to school with him?

Mr. LAINÉ. No; but I knew him very well in Havana. He was a man very well known by everybody by the positions he held.

Senator FORAKER. Here is a short biographical sketch of at least some members of the cabinet. Here is a sketch of Col. Ernesto Fonts y Sterling, secretary of the treasury.

Mr. LAINÉ. I know him very well.

Senator FORAKER. Please look at the biographical sketches of the members of the cabinet that follow in the same document and state whether or not they are correct. You can just glance through them and answer, so far as you know.

Mr. LAINÉ. Col. Ernesto Fonts y Sterling is a young man with whom I have been very well acquainted. I have known him very well for many years. He is an intimate friend. He is the secretary of the treasury of the Cuban Republic. He comes of an aristocratic Cuban family of lawyers. They have all been lawyers in that family. He has two brothers who are practicing law in Havana, one holding a Spanish Government position. His brother Carlos holds a government position under the new autonomist government.

Senator FORAKER. Then follows a sketch of Brigadier Jose B. Aleman, the secretary of war.

Mr. LAINÉ. I know his general reputation, but I am not personally acquainted with him.

Senator FORAKER. The sketch is in accord with his general reputation?

Mr. LAINÉ. Yes, sir.

Senator FORAKER. The next sketch is that of Andres Moreno de la Torre, secretary of foreign relations.

Mr. LAINÉ. I am personally acquainted with him, and know this sketch to be correct.

Senator FORAKER. The next is Dr. Manuel Ramón Silva, secretary of the interior. Are you personally acquainted with him?

Mr. LAINÉ. No, sir; I am not personally acquainted with him.

Senator FORAKER. Do you know his reputation?

Mr. LAINÉ. I know but little about him, sir.

Senator FORAKER. Can you tell us whether all these officials, the president, vice-president, and members of the cabinet, are white men?

Mr. LAINÉ. Yes, sir; they are all white men. They are all white men, belonging to the best Cuban families.

Senator FORAKER. We are much obliged to you, Mr. Lainé, for your attendance here.

STATEMENT OF BENJAMIN J. GUERRA, APRIL 8, 1898.

BENJAMIN J. GUERRA, being duly sworn, testified as follows:

Senator FORAKER. Please state your age and residence.

Mr. GUERRA. Forty-two years; residence, 104 West Sixty-first street, New York City.

Senator FORAKER. What is your occupation?

Mr. GUERRA. Merchant.

Senator FORAKER. What kind of a merchant?

Mr. GUERRA. I am a cigar manufacturer.

Senator FORAKER. To what extent have you engaged in the business of manufacturing cigars?

Mr. GUERRA. I have a cigar factory in Tampa, Fla., and one in Key West, Fla.

Senator FORAKER. Do you put your own product on the market?

Mr. GUERRA. Yes, sir; I have business relations in all the States of the Union.

Senator FORAKER. Of what nationality are you?

Mr. GUERRA. Cuban.

Senator FORAKER. You have resided in Cuba?

Mr. GUERRA. Yes, sir; all of my life until the year 1878.

Senator FORAKER. Where have you resided since then?

Mr. GUERRA. In New York City.

Senator FORAKER. Do you now hold any official relation to the Republic of Cuba? And if so, state what it is.

Mr. GUERRA. Yes, sir; I am the treasurer of the Cuban delegation.

Senator FORAKER. What do you mean by that term? What is the Cuban delegation and where is it located?

Mr. GUERRA. It is the representation of the Cuban Government in the United States.

Senator FORAKER. Who constitute that delegation?

Mr. GUERRA. Mr. Thomas Estrada Palma, Dr. Joaquin Castillo, sub-delegate; Antonio Gonzalez Lanuza, secretary, and myself, treasurer.

Senator FORAKER. There are four of you, then, in all?

Mr. GUERRA. Four in all.

Senator FORAKER. Are there any other official representatives of the Republic of Cuba in the United States?

Mr. GUERRA. Goncalo de Quesada, who is the chargé d'affaires at Washington.

Senator FORAKER. And anyone else?

Mr. GUERRA. Mr. Diaz Albertini, secretary of legation.

Senator FORAKER. By whom were you appointed to your present position, and have you any evidence of your appointment?

Mr. GUERRA. I was appointed by the President of the Republic of Cuba.

Senator FORAKER. With the approval of his cabinet?

Mr. GUERRA. With the approval of his cabinet.

Senator FORAKER. Have you the evidence of that appointment?

Mr. GUERRA. Yes, sir.

Senator FORAKER. Will you produce it and allow it to be copied into the record?

Mr. GUERRA. Yes [producing a paper]. I have it and now produce it. It is in Spanish. I will have it translated and a copy of it furnished for the record.

The paper was thereupon translated by Mr. Quesada and submitted, as follows:

[There is a seal which says,
"Republic of Cuba. Chancery.
Secretary of the Government."]

"JOSÉ CLEMENTE VIVANCO,
"Sec'y of the Government Council and
"Chancellor of the Republic of Cuba.

"I certify that on page two hundred and twenty-four of volume second of the minutes of the sessions of this council there is copied the following resolution, adopted by the council on the 6th of January: 'On motion of the secretary of foreign relations, it is resolved to appoint Citizen Benjamin J. Guerra treasurer of the plenipotentiary delegation abroad.'

"And at the request of the secretary of foreign relations I issued the present certificate. Country and liberty in the free town of Santa Lucia on the 28th of June, 1897.

"JOSÉ CLEMENTE VIVANCO.

[There is a seal Republic of Cuba, Presidency]

"Approved.
(Signed) "SALVADOR CISNEROS,
"*The President.*"

Senator FORAKER. Do you know whether the Republic of Cuba has issued any bonds at any time since its organization until the present?

Mr. GUERRA. Yes, sir.

Senator FORAKER. And if so, to what amount in money?

Mr. GUERRA. By the authority and direction of the Government of the Republic of Cuba, Mr. Estrada Palma and myself have caused to be printed bonds to the amount of $3,145,600.

Senator FORAKER. Who authorized the printing of those bonds?

Mr. GUERRA. The Government of the Republic of Cuba.

Senator FORAKER. Have you the authority of which you speak, that was given by the Government of the Republic of Cuba to yourself and Mr. Palma to issue those bonds?

Mr. GUERRA. Yes, sir.

Senator FORAKER. Will you produce it and allow it to be copied into the record?

Mr. GUERRA. Yes, sir; here it is [producing a paper].

Senator FORAKER. I will have a copy of it made for the record.

The paper referred to is as follows:

"REPUBLIC OF CUBA, PROVISIONAL GOVERNMENT.

"*I, Salvador Cisneros y Betancourt, President of the Republic of Cuba, to all whom these presents may come, greeting:*

"By virtue of the powers which have been conferred upon me by the constituent assembly, under date of the 18th of September, 1895, I hereby confer upon citizen Tomas Estrada Palma, delegate plenipotentiary of the Government of the Republic, the following powers:

"First. That personally, or by means of delegates, he represent the Republic of Cuba before the Government and people of all nations to which he may deem convenient to name a representative, giving him the powers he may deem adequate.

"Second. That he may contract one or more loans, to use the money in the service of the Republic, guaranteeing said loans with all the properties and public income, internal or of the customs, present and future, of the said Republic; issuing bonds, registered or to bearer, to the amount he may deem necessary, payable both as to interest and place of payment as he may deem convenient, hereby empowering him to fix the denominations, the rate of interest, conditions of payment of capital and interest, as he may deem most favorable, and to place said bonds on the most advantageous terms, and to pledge them.

"Third. To issue paper money in the name of the Republic of Cuba to the amount he may consider necessary, in the form and on conditions he may deem most adequate.

"Fourth. To issue postage stamps of the denominations he may judge convenient for the service of the Republic.

"Fifth. The bonds to be issued as well as the bills shall be signed by the delegate plenipotentiary or the person whom he shall delegate and by the treasurer of the 'Cuban Revolutionary Party,' and shall bear the seals and countermarks which the delegate believes necessary to avoid counterfeits.

"Sixth. (Relates to appointment of sub-delegate, who shall act in case of death or disability of delegate.)

"Seventh. (Authorizes substitution of power in whole or in part and authorizes appointment of employees.)

"Eighth. The delegate may receive, collect, and invest the funds which from any source whatever may come into his hands, doing so in the form which he may judge most favorable to the interests of the Republic, as well as the power to make concessions and celebrate in the name of the Republic all the agreements and contracts, which he may deem beneficial to the interests thereof, which from now on are declared ratified by the Government he represents.

"Given in Anton under my signature and that of the secretary of foreign relations and the treasury, the 21st day of November, one thousand eight hundred and ninety-five.

"SALAVADOR CISNEROS Y B.,
" The President.

"SEVERO PINA,
" The Secretary of the Treasury and
of Foreign Relations ad interim."

STATE OF NEW YORK,
City and County of New York, ss:

Leopoldo de Arrastia, being duly sworn, deposes and says:

That he is a notary public in and for the city and county of New York. That he is well acquainted with the English and Spanish languages and has often been employed as sworn translator from the Spanish into the English language, and that he is fully proficient to act as such.

That the above is a correct and accurate translation of the power of attorney given by the Government of the Republic of Cuba to Tomas Estrada Palma, under date of the 21st of November, 1895.

LEOPOLDO DE ARRASTIA.

Sworn to before me this 19th of March, 1896.

[SEAL.] LEON J. BENOIT,
Notary Public (377), New York County.

Senator FORAKER. Can you tell us to what extent the bonds which you say have been printed under this authority have been disposed of?

Mr. GUERRA. Yes, sir.

Senator FORAKER. Tell us in detail what has become of them—where they are now, if you know?

Mr. GUERRA. We have sold for cash, to several people, as per the book I present here to you (producing a record book), $94,050, and we have disposed of for merchandise, $28,350, which makes a total of bonds disposed of of $122,400.

Senator FORAKER. Have you any record of the bonds that you have disposed of for cash and merchandise?

Mr. GUERRA. Yes, sir.

Senator FORAKER. Where is that record?

Mr. GUERRA. Here it is [indicating the record book].

Senator FORAKER. You refer to a book which you have before you?

Mr. GUERRA. Yes, sir.

Senator FORAKER. What is the book? What is the name of it?

Mr. GUERRA. Sale of Bonds.

Senator FORAKER. Does it contain a complete record of every bond that has been disposed of by you and Mr. Palma?

Mr. GUERRA. Yes, sir.

Senator FORAKER. Please explain in detail what that record shows.

Mr. GUERRA. This book shows the date of the operation——

Senator FORAKER. Of the transaction?

Mr. GUERRA. Yes, of the transaction; number of the bonds that are sold, and then here [indicating] how many bonds; then denomination; then marks——

Senator FORAKER. By denomination you mean what amount the bond is?

Mr. GUERRA. Yes, sir; what amount.

Senator FORAKER. What do you mean by marks of the bond?

Mr. GUERRA. Marks by which we can identify them. Then rate at which the bond has been sold; the name of the buyer, street and number of his residence, city, and State. Here [indicating] are incidental remarks; amount; face value of the bond, and net realized.

Senator FORAKER. That is, the amount of the whole number of bonds sold in one transaction?

Mr. GUERRA. Yes, sir; in each transaction.

Senator FORAKER. Have you any objection to allowing this record to be copied?

Mr. GUERRA. No, sir; but most of it is in Spanish, except the names of Americans and their residence.

Senator FORAKER (examining record book). I observe that there are a little more than twelve closely written pages in this record book. On that account I will not take the trouble to have a complete copy of the record made, but I should be glad to have a quotation from this book running all the way through the record, showing one of these transactions, simply as a sample of the record that has been kept. I will call your attention to an entry dated May 26, 1896, on page 4. The one I indicate to you I ask you to read that it may be incorporated in the record.

Mr. GUERRA. (Reading.) Year, 1896; May 26; marks 18 to 37; twenty bonds of $100 each; marks 18 to 20, 21 to 25, 26 to 37; rate, 50 per cent; name of the buyer, A. Y. Gray, Rutland County, Middletown Springs, Vt., care of L. and A. Y. Gray, Middletown Springs Bank and Phœnix National Bank of New York; face value, $2,000; net realized, $1,000.

Senator FORAKER. Please state what rates were realized as shown by this record for the bonds which you have sold?

Mr. GUERRA. The different rates?

Senator FORAKER. Yes. What is the highest rate you have realized?

Mr. GUERRA. Par.

Senator FORAKER. How many of those bonds have you sold at par?

Mr. GUERRA. Some six or eight have sold for par. There are some at 62½.

Senator FORAKER. And they have sold at prices ranging all the way down from par to what as the lowest?

Mr. GUERRA. The lowest is 2 per cent. Some at 62½; some at 50; some at 75; some at 61; some at 80; some at 60, and others at 50 and 40, and of late, by order of the Government, we are not selling them at less than 40 per cent.

Senator FORAKER. Can you state without much trouble how many you have sold at 25 per cent?

Mr. GUERRA (examining record book). There are sixteen entries here at 25 per cent.

Senator FORAKER. What is the aggregate amount of the bonds at face value sold at 25 per cent in those sixteen transactions?

Mr. GUERRA. Thirteen thousand dollars.

Senator FORAKER. Give the date when those bonds were sold at 25 cents on the dollar, as shown by this record.

Mr. GUERRA. From September 12, 1896, to November 4 of the same year.

Senator FORAKER. What is the next entry there?

Mr. GUERRA. November 11, 1896.

Senator FORAKER. Run that entry through. What is it?

Mr. GUERRA (reading). November 11; No. 104; one bond of $100; mark 69,618; par; bought by Mr. Joaquin Fortune, of Jacksonville, Fla.; $100 face value; $100 net realized.

Senator FORAKER. Have you sold any bonds at 25 cents on the dollar since November 4, 1896?

Mr. GUERRA. Yes, sir; on January 13, 1897, I sold one for that amount.

Senator FORAKER. What prices have you realized usually since November, 1896, as shown by this record?

Mr. GUERRA. From 40 per cent up.

Senator FORAKER. So far as this record discloses, you have not made any sale since then for less than 40 cents on the dollar?

Mr. GUERRA. No, sir.

Senator FORAKER. This record, as I understand you, shows all the bonds that have been disposed of for either cash or merchandise?

Mr. GUERRA. For cash only.

Senator FORAKER. Is there a record of the bonds disposed of for merchandise?

Mr. GUERRA (producing a record book). Yes, sir; here is a book that shows all of the bonds that have gone out of my hands for which no cash has entered into the treasury.

Senator FORAKER. Is this a complete record for every such bond?

Mr. GUERRA. Yes, sir; of every such one.

Senator FORAKER. You have now accounted for bonds to the amount of $122,400, of which you have a record. Where are the rest of the bonds that were printed?

Mr. GUERRA. One million of those bonds is deposited in the safes of Messrs. August Belmont & Co.

Senator FORAKER. To whom do those bonds belong that are deposited with August Belmont & Co.?

Mr. GUERRA. To the Republic of Cuba, and the balance is in my possession.

Senator FORAKER. As treasurer?

Mr. GUERRA. As treasurer.

Senator FORAKER. Do any person or persons or any syndicate of any kind own or have any lien or claim upon any of the bonds that are still either in your possession or in the possession of August Belmont & Co.

Mr. GUERRA. No, sir.

Senator FORAKER. Are they the sole property of the Republic of Cuba?

Mr. GUERRA. They are.

Senator FORAKER. It has been stated in conversation, and possibly in the newspapers, that recently, in the city of New York, someone was offered $50,000 in bonds of the Republic of Cuba as a consideration for coming to New York and rendering some kind of political service. State whether there is any truth in such a statement.

Mr. GUERRA. I do not believe there is any truth in that, because nobody from the Cuban delegation has done it, and I do not think anybody has $50,000 of these bonds that can be offered.

Senator FORAKER. Would anyone, except Palma, Castillo, Lanuza, and yourself have authority to make such an offer on behalf of the Republic of Cuba?

Mr. GUERRA. Nobody else.

Senator FORAKER. Have any other bonds than those you have described ever been issued by the Republic of Cuba or authorized by the Republic of Cuba?

Mr. GUERRA. No other ones.

Senator FORAKER. Have any person or persons other than your delegation any authority to deal in the bonds of the Republic of Cuba?

Mr. GUERRA. No, sir.

Senator FORAKER. Then, as I understand you, the total amount of bonds that have been issued by the Republic of Cuba and outstanding is $122,400?

Mr. GUERRA. Yes, sir; that is all that have been sold.

Senator FORAKER. And all the remainder of the bonds are still in your possession?

Mr. GUERRA. They are all in my possession.

Senator FORAKER. Another story has been circulated to the effect that someone here in the city of Washington has been offered $3,000,000 of these bonds as a consideration for rendering some kind of political service, the kind of service not specified. Is there any truth in that story?

Mr. GUERRA. I do not believe there is any truth in it.

Senator FORAKER. Did anyone connected with your delegation make any such offer?

Mr. GUERRA. No, sir.

Senator FORAKER. Or have any authority to make any such offer?

Mr. GUERRA. No, sir; nobody has any authority to do it.

Senator FORAKER. In the House of Representatives, yesterday, Mr. Grosvenor, of Ohio, made the following statement, replying to Mr. Lentz, who had spoken on the Cuban question:

"Now, Mr. Speaker, let us see how this situation stands. The gentleman is greatly worried about bonds, and he read the name of John J. McCook in one of his raids this afternoon.

"Who is John J. McCook? Whom does he represent? What is he here for? How do he and the gentleman from Ohio stand with reference to this? I will show you that they are parties in a great conspiracy; one wittingly so, the other, I trust, ignorantly so. Who is John J. McCook? He is the legal representative of the Cuban Junta, of New York, behind which stands four hundred millions, more or less, of bonds that can be validated by the recognition of the independence of Cuba by the United States, and they will be destroyed by a policy that drives Spain out of Cuba in the interest of the American people."

Do you know John J. McCook, who is referred to here?

Mr. GUERRA. I do not know him personally.

Senator FORAKER. Has he any relation, official or otherwise, to your delegation?

Mr. GUERRA. Not to my knowledge.

Senator FORAKER. Has he any relation to the Government of the Republic of Cuba, official or otherwise?

Mr. GUERRA. Not to my knowledge.

Senator FORAKER. Does he have any relation whatever to the bonds that have been issued by the Republic of Cuba, concerning which you have testified?

Mr. GUERRA. None whatever.

Senator FORAKER. Do you know of any issue of $400,000,000 of bonds, more or less, by the Republic of Cuba?

Mr. GUERRA. I know nothing about it, and I do not think there has been any issued except those that I have described.

Senator FORAKER. Do you know anything about the syndicate and the bonds that are referred to by General Grosvenor in the remarks I have quoted?

Mr. GUERRA. No, sir.

Senator FORAKER. General Grosvenor further says in these same remarks:

" I will tell you who John J. McCook is. John J. McCook represents an interest running up into the hundreds of millions of dollars, and if he could get the United States to make a recognition of the independence of Cuba and then fight to establish it by the United States, at the cost of a thousand million dollars, the holders of these bogus bonds will realize $400,000,000 and collect the money. That is where the bonds come in."

I understand you to say there are no such issues of bonds?

Mr. GUERRA. I know there are not.

Senator FORAKER. Has the question of bonds or the validation of bonds anything whatever to do with the question of the recognition of the independence of Cuba or with the recognition of the Republic of Cuba as the government of Cuba?

Mr. GUERRA. None that I know. There were some gentlemen calling on me in my office a few days ago and asking me what we would take for ten millions of bonds.

Senator FORAKER. Did they say they wanted to buy?

Mr. GUERRA. Yes, sir. After consulting with Mr. Palma, I told him that the lowest price we could make them was 40 per cent. Then he made us an offer of 20 cents on the dollar, a cash offer, for the ten million—to give us two million for the ten million—which we refused.

Senator FORAKER. Are there any negotiations pending between your delegation as the representatives of the Republic of Cuba, and any person or persons for the sale of any bonds at this time?

Mr. GUERRA. Not to my knowledge.

Senator FORAKER. You are in such a relation to this whole matter that you would know about it if there were any such negotiations?

Mr. GUERRA. Yes, sir; the bonds have to pass through my hands; I have to sign the bonds.

The CHAIRMAN. Can you say that no such negotiations are being made?

Mr. GUERRA. None with my intervention.

Senator FORAKER. We want an answer that is not equivocal. State whether or not any such negotiations are pending.

Mr. GUERRA. I think there are not.

Senator FORAKER. If there are, you have no knowledge of them?

Mr. GUERRA. I have no knowledge of them at all.

Senator FORAKER. Could they be issued without your knowing about it and signing them?

Mr. GUERRA. They could not.

Senator FORAKER. I mean any large transactions.

Mr. GUERRA. The bonds could not be issued without my signature.

Senator FORAKER. What did you do with the cash realized from these bonds? I do not want an answer in detail, but just state it generally.

Mr. GUERRA. We employed it in the furtherance of the cause of Cuba in the revolution.

Senator FORAKER. Was all the money appropriated in that behalf which was realized from the sale of these bonds?

Mr. GUERRA. Yes, sir.

Senator FORAKER. How has the money necessary to carry on the war the insurgents have been making in Cuba been raised?

Mr. GUERRA. It has been contributed mostly by the Cubans. $472,617.42 have been received by me as treasurer of the Republic of Cuba from taxes paid by plantations in Cuba to the department of the treasury of the Cuban Republic.

Senator FORAKER. Are the taxes that are collected in Cuba by the Republic of Cuba sent to you?

Mr. GUERRA. Yes, sir.

Senator FORAKER. After collection?

Mr. GUERRA. Yes, sir.

Senator FORAKER. And you have received from taxes collected in Cuba the amount you have named?

Mr. GUERRA. Yes, sir.

Senator FORAKER. Over $400,000?

Mr. GUERRA. Yes, sir.

Senator FORAKER. How was that money expended; for the Cuban cause, or otherwise?

Mr. GUERRA. It was expended for the Cuban cause.

Senator FORAKER. Can you tell us what kind of a system of collecting taxes they have in Cuba?

Mr. GUERRA. Yes, sir. They have the department of the treasury organized. The secretary of the treasury is the head. In every one of the States there is what they call a ministrator of taxes, which corresponds to our collector of customs.

Senator FORAKER. What system of levying taxes has the Republic of Cuba in force there? You have told us of the official who does the collecting. What is the system?

Mr. GUERRA. The system on the sugar plantations is so much per bag of sugar produced. Sometimes it has been 40 cents, and in other years it has been 25 cents per bag. The Government imposed a war tax of 2 per cent on the value given to the plantations in the year 1894.

Senator FORAKER. Upon the value as given in 1894?

Mr. GUERRA. As given in 1894.

Senator FORAKER. When you say the Government you mean the Republic of Cuba?

Mr. GUERRA. The Republic of Cuba.

Senator FORAKER. Is that tax system uniform in its operation throughout the island?

Mr. GUERRA. Yes, sir.

Senator FORAKER. That is, every man is taxed alike, according to the same principle?

Mr. GUERRA. Yes, sir.

Senator FORAKER. And is this system enforced throughout the island?

Mr. GUERRA. It is.

Senator FORAKER. Have you tax collectors in all of the different States?

Mr. GUERRA. Yes, sir.

The CHAIRMAN. Is that done by virtue of a statute of the Cuban congress?

Mr. GUERRA. Yes, sir.

The CHAIRMAN. And not by a military regulation?

Mr. GUERRA. Not military at all; the army has nothing to do with it.

Senator FORAKER. Who appoints the tax collectors—the military or the civil government?

Mr. GUERRA. The civil government.

Senator FORAKER. Has that civil government, the Republic of Cuba, any other branch of government in operation except this fiscal branch of which you speak?

Mr. GUERRA. Yes, sir.

Senator FORAKER. What?

Mr. GUERRA. They have the interior department.

Senator FORAKER. What does that do?

Mr. GUERRA. The head of the interior department is the secretary of the interior, but there are governors and prefects and subprefects in the different states and districts.

Senator FORAKER. Are those officials whom you mention holding office now?

Mr. GUERRA. They are.

Senator FORAKER. In what way do they get their offices—by election or appointment?

Mr. GUERRA. By appointment.

Senator FORAKER. Who appoints them?

Mr. GUERRA. The President of the Republic.

Senator FORAKER. You say that they are appointed throughout the island?

Mr. GUERRA. Yes, sir.

Senator FORAKER. What is a prefect? What are his duties?

Mr. GUERRA. A prefect is a kind of a mayor of the district.

Senator FORAKER. Have you any other branch of the Government in operation?

Mr. GUERRA. The department of war.

Senator FORAKER. Aside from that? I will speak of that presently.

Mr. GUERRA. Well, the civil, I mean the interior department, assumes the post-office department.

Senator FORAKER. Has the Republic of Cuba a postal system?

Mr. GUERRA. Yes, sir.

Senator FORAKER. In operation?

Mr. GUERRA. Yes, sir.

Senator FORAKER. What is the nature of that system? How do they transport the mails?

Mr. GUERRA. They have post-houses in all the towns—the small towns—and they transmit the mails by horses—by couriers.

Senator FORAKER. Have they any postage stamps such as we have in this country?

Mr. GUERRA. Yes, sir; they have 2-cent, 5-cent, and 10-cent postage stamps.

Senator FORAKER. Have you any of those with you——

Mr. GUERRA. Yes, sir.

Senator FORAKER. That you could show as a sample?

Mr. GUERRA (producing a stamped envelope). Here is a letter addressed to me with two stamps on it, from Camaguey district, in Cuba.

Senator FORAKER. Will you allow us to put that envelope in the record as an exhibit.

Mr. GUERRA. Yes, sir.

Senator FORAKER. I ask that it be attached as a part of Mr. Guerra's evidence.

The envelope referred to is, in fac simile, as follows:

Senator FORAKER. How is it as to an educational system? Have they any?

Mr. GUERRA. Yes, sir; they have schools. That is also under the interior department.

Senator FORAKER. What is the system of education?

Mr. GUERRA. They have primary schools. They have some teaching books that have been printed there in our presses in Cuba.

Senator FORAKER. Do I understand you to say that the Government of the Republic of Cuba has a printing office?

Mr. GUERRA. Yes, sir; they have. There are several newspapers printed there.

Senator FORAKER. Does the Government prescribe the books that shall be used in the schools?

Mr. GUERRA. Yes, sir. It appoints the teachers, the inspectors.

Senator FORAKER. Does the Government print the school books?

Mr. GUERRA. They print the school books—the primary books. We could, perhaps, supply the committee with some.

Senator FORAKER. How are those books distributed, by the Government?

Mr. GUERRA. By the Government.

Senator FORAKER. Is the attendance of children at school optional?

Mr. GUERRA. Compulsory.

Senator FORAKER. It is compulsory?

Mr. GUERRA. Yes, sir.

Senator FORAKER. All children in Cuba, then, under the Government of the Republic of Cuba, are required to attend school?

Mr. GUERRA. Yes, sir.

Senator FORAKER. And are required to be taught in the primary branches, for which the Government furnishes the books?

Mr. GUERRA. Yes, sir.

Senator FORAKER. What kind of a judicial system have they in Cuba, under the Republic of Cuba, if you know?

Mr. GUERRA. They have what they call the judiciary corps. That is attached to the army, though; it is a dependent of the war department. It is made so by the constitution.

Senator FORAKER. The constitution makes that provision?

Mr. GUERRA. Yes, sir; while the war lasts.

Senator FORAKER. Where is the capital of the Republic of Cuba located?

Mr. GUERRA. It is in the State of Camaguey, District of Cubitas. The town is called Agramonte.

Senator FORAKER. Is there a town named Cubitas also?

Mr. GUERRA. No, sir; Cubitas is the district where this town is.

Senater FORAKER. What is the population of Agramonte?

Mr. GUERRA. Agramonte may have about a thousand inhabitants.

Senator FORAKER. State whether the Republic of Cuba has at Agramonte, where its capital is located, any official Government buildings.

Mr. GUERRA. Yes, sir; there is one building for the President, and one for each of the departments of state, interior, treasury, and war.

Senator FORAKER. Are those buildings occupied for official business simply?

Mr. GUERRA. Yes, sir.

Senator FORAKER. What is the legislative body of the Republic of Cuba called? What is the name of it?

Mr. GUERRA. The council of government assumes the legislative faculties of the Government until every two years there is the constituent assembly to elect another President and another council body.

Senator FORAKER. The members of the constituent assembly are elected by a popular vote, I understand?

Mr. GUERRA. By the people; by popular vote.

Senator FORAKER. And then the constituent assembly thus elected chooses a President?

Mr. GUERRA. Yes, sir.

Senator FORAKER. And a Vice-President?

Mr. GUERRA. Yes, sir.

Senator FORAKER. And a cabinet?

Mr. GUERRA. And a cabinet.

Senator FORAKER. And the President, Vice-President, and cabinet conduct the Government?

Mr. GUERRA. Yes, sir. The assembly also elects a general in chief of the army.

Senator FORAKER. Who is the President now of the Republic of Cuba?

Mr. GUERRA. Bartolomé Masó.

Senator FORAKER. Do you know him personally?

Mr. GUERRA. Yes, sir.

Senator FORAKER. Tell us what kind of a man he is as to character and reputation.

Mr. GUERRA. He is a man of great character, known by his honesty and by his literary accomplishments.

Senator FORAKER. Is he an educated, cultivated man?

Mr. GUERRA. He is an educated man.

Senator FORAKER. Where was he educated, if you know?

Mr. GUERRA. In Cuba; at the University of Havana.

Senator FORAKER. What is his business?

Mr. GUERRA. He was a landowner in Cuba; he is a landowner.

The CHAIRMAN. A man of large means?

Mr. GUERRA. Yes, sir; of wealth.

Senator FORAKER. Did he own plantations?

Mr. GUERRA. He does own them.

Senator FORAKER. Who is the vice-president?

Mr. GUERRA. The vice-president is Dr. Mendez Capote.

Senator FORAKER. How old a man is he?

Mr. GUERRA. He must be about 45 years old.

Senator FORAKER. What was his business before?

Mr. GUERRA. He is a lawyer. He is a doctor in laws.

Senator FORAKER. Was he connected with any university?

Mr. GUERRA. The University of Havana.

Senator FORAKER. In what capacity?

Mr. GUERRA. He has been a professor in the University of Havana. Of the other members of the Government——

Senator FORAKER. Yes; speak of them.

Mr. GUERRA. There is the secretary of the interior, as we call him. He is a doctor, too—a doctor in medicine.

The CHAIRMAN. A doctor of medicine?

Mr. GUERRA. Yes, sir.

The CHAIRMAN. Did he graduate in this country?

Mr. GUERRA. He graduated in Havana.

The CHAIRMAN. Well, the secretary of war.

Mr. GUERRA. The secretary of war is General Aleman.

The CHAIRMAN. Tell us briefly about him.

Mr. GUERRA. He was a merchant there. He went into the revolution at the beginning and has been fighting until he was elected secretary of war. He is an educated man, also; a literary man.

The CHAIRMAN. What was his business before?

Mr. GUERRA. He was in business.

The CHAIRMAN. A merchant?

Mr. GUERRA. Yes; a merchant. The secretary of the treasury is Fonts y Sterling; he is a lawyer. He is a member of one of the most ancient and illustrious families in Cuba.

The CHAIRMAN. A graduate of the university?

Mr. GUERRA. A graduate of Havana University.

The CHAIRMAN. What is his profession?

Mr. GUERRA. Law.

Senator FORAKER. Tell us briefly about the secretary of foreign relations. What was his business before he was appointed to that office?

Mr. GUERRA. Moreno de la Torre is a doctor in medicine, educated in Spain. He is a young man, known for his eneigy in all revolutionary affairs in Cuba. He is of a conservative temper, though. That is all I can say about him.

Senator FORAKER. To what extent has the Republic of Cuba governmental control of the Island of Cuba, I mean territorially?

Mr. GUERRA. The Government has control, full control, of all the rural districts of the central and eastern parts of the island.

Senator FORAKER. That would be all of Santiago de Cuba?

Mr. GUERRA. And Camaguey.

Senator FORAKER. Puerto Principe?

Mr. GUERRA. Yes; Puerto Principe. The Spanish call it Puerto Principe, and we call it Camaguey; and Santiago de Cuba Province outside of a few cities that are held by the Spanish Government.

Senator FORAKER. What proportion of the population of Cuba responds to your Government or shows it allegiance?

Mr. GUERRA. In my opinion, 80 per cent of the population of the island are friendly to the revolution.

Senator FORAKER. What is the population in the provinces of Santiago de Cuba and Camaguey, where you say the Republic of Cuba is in complete control?

Mr. GUERRA. The population is about half a million.

Senator FORAKER. Are the people in those provinces friendly and satisfied, apparently, with the Government of the Republic of Cuba?

Mr. GUERRA. Yes, sir.

Senator FORAKER. Would or would not, in your opinion, the Government of the Republic of Cuba be able to administer satisfactorily the civil affairs of the Island of Cuba if they were let alone and allowed to discharge their functions of government without interference by the Spaniards?

Mr. GUERRA. I am positive that they would be able to do it satisfactorily.

The CHAIRMAN. State the extreme eastern limit in Cuba of the concentration of the inhabitants under Weyler's order.

Mr. GUERRA. The limit is the Jucaro-Moron trocha.

The CHAIRMAN. Is that trocha east or west of Havana?

Mr. GUERRA. That trocha is east of Havana.

The CHAIRMAN. That is the extreme eastern trocha?

Mr. GUERRA. That is the extreme eastern trocha.

The CHAIRMAN. East of that trocha is there any concentration at all?

Mr. GUERRA. No, there is no concentration east of that.

The CHAIRMAN. What provinces lie east of that trocha?

Mr. GUERRA. Camaguey and Santiago de Cuba.

Senator FORAKER. Can you give us the area in square miles of those two provinces?

Mr. GUERRA. It is more than half the island in territory—in superficial territory.

Senator FORAKER. To what extent is the Republic of Cuba in control in the outlying country districts in the other provinces of the island?

Mr. GUERRA. The Republic of Cuba is in control in about two-thirds of the rural districts.

Senator FORAKER. Outside of those two?

Mr. GUERRA. Outside of those two.

Senator FORAKER. They are in entire control in those two?

Mr. GUERRA. In entire control except those parts that are covered by the Spaniards.

The CHAIRMAN. Do you mean to say that in those portions you have just spoken of they collect taxes as you have previously stated?

Mr. GUERRA. Yes, sir.

The CHAIRMAN. What do you say as to schools in those portions?

Mr. GUERRA. There are less, if any, in those portions than in the others.

Senator FORAKER. Throughout the two provinces of which you have complete control you have your tax system and your school system and all these other functions of government in operation?

Mr. GUERRA. Yes, sir.

Senator FORAKER. Without interruption?

Mr. GUERRA. Yes, sir.

Senator FORAKER. Is there any other school system than that which the Republic of Cuba provides in those two provinces?

Mr. GUERRA. There is the Spanish system in the cities—the larger cities.

Senator FORAKER. But I mean outside the cities?

Mr. GUERRA. No.

The CHAIRMAN. Previous to the establishment of this common-school system by the Republic, what common-school system had Spain established?

Mr. GUERRA. A regular common-school system in the cities only; not in the rural districts.

The CHAIRMAN. A common-school system in the cities, but none whatever in the rural districts?

Mr. GUERRA. None.

The CHAIRMAN. As to the limits of concentration, I suppose that in the portions of Cuba which the Republic holds there is concentration in the cities which the Spanish happen to hold, is there not?

Mr. GUERRA. Yes; but almost all the country people are in the country in those districts.

The CHAIRMAN. Take Santiago de Cuba. Is there not concentration there?

Mr. GUERRA. I do not think there is much concentration in Santiago de Cuba, because in the beginning of the revolution all the country people went to the country, and the Spanish Government has no means of concentrating them there.

The CHAIRMAN. Would you be surprised to learn that the consular reports show that there is a great deal of concentration and death and misery there?

Mr. GUERRA. Those are the regular city people. I call it concentrating to bring those people who have always lived in the country to the cities and keep them there without any means, while if there is misery, on account of the war, among those people who have always lived in the city because they can not get any work or any supplies, I do not call that a concentration. There may be misery and all that among them, but they are not what we regularly call reconcentrados. We apply that term simply to country people, peasants, who have lived always by laboring in the soil and who have been brought by force to the cities and kept there. Those are what I call reconcentrados.

Senator FORAKER. You have told us who constitute the delegation and what other representatives of the Republic of Cuba there are in this country. You have also told us of various other officials who are conducting the Government of the Republic of Cuba. Can you tell us what salaries those officials receive for their services?

Mr. GUERRA. There is no Cuban in the service of the Republic who receives any salary.

Senator FORAKER. Do you mean to say that the President and Vice-President and cabinet, who are devoting all their time in the way you have indicated, receive no salaries?

Mr. GUERRA. They receive no salary.

Senator FORAKER. They receive no salary whatever?

Mr. GUERRA. No salary whatever.

Senator FORAKER. No official connected with the civil government receives any salary?

Mr. GUERRA. No official connected with the civil government receives any salary.

Senator FORAKER. How is it as to the army?

Mr. GUERRA. They receive no salary at all.

Senator FORAKER. Then no officer or soldier in the army of Gomez receives any salary?

Mr. GUERRA. No, sir; nor Gomez himself, either.

Senator FORAKER. How many soldiers has Gomez now in his command or under his command?

Mr. GUERRA. In my opinion, in the neighborhood of 35,000.

Senator FORAKER. Every man works simply for——

Mr. GUERRA. For patriotism.

Senator FORAKER. That is all. I am much obliged to you.

Mr. GUERRA. You are welcome, sir.

STATEMENT OF HON. FITZHUGH LEE, April 12, 1898.

Senator FRYE. General, you have just returned from Cuba?

Consul-General LEE. Yes, sir.

Senator FRYE. You sent to the State Department certain communications touching the ship *Maine.* Have you any information additional to that conveyed in those communications?

Consul-General LEE. I have not.

Senator FRYE. Have you any information in relation to torpedoes or anything of that kind in the harbor?

Consul-General LEE. I am informed on very good authority that they have placed within the last month two rows of torpedoes just at the mouth of the harbor by Morro Castle and the switch board is in a room in the Morro.

Senator FRYE. Had you any information as to the placing of any torpedoes before the *Maine* was destroyed?

Consul-General LEE. No, sir.

Senator FRYE. Have you any information in relation to purchases made abroad, or have any communications been made to you by reliable persons of purchases of torpedoes made abroad?

Consul-General LEE. No, sir.

Senator FRYE. Have you any reason to suppose that the harbor was mined at all before the blowing up of the Maine?

Consul-General LEE. No, sir. No; I had no reason to suspect any-thing of that sort up to that time.

Senator GRAY. But since then?

Senator FRYE. Have you since received any information which leads you to suppose that it was mined before the disaster?

Consul-General LEE. I have seen a letter, and probably you, gentle-men, have also seen it, published in one of the New York papers by a person named Laine, from General Weyler to Santos Guzman, a citizen of Havana, a very ultra Spaniard, in which General Weyler says that he went on with the placing of the mines in the harbor, which Martin Campos, his predecessor, should have done.

I saw afterwards that General Weyler pronounced the letter a for-gery, but I happen to know of a telegram received from Weyler since, and this is the only reason I have to suspect that there were some mines there previous to the entrance of the *Maine* into the harbor. You have probably seen the letter which Laine published.

The CHAIRMAN. We have a copy of it on file.

Consul-General LEE. I see that Santos Guzman, under date of March 18, 1898, says to the editor of the Herald:

I have not received General Weyler's letter dated January 8, to which the New York Herald makes reference in its cablegram of yesterday addressed to me.

A Madrid dispatch further says:

General Weyler denies the authenticity of the letter published in New York yes-terday in which the former Captain-General of Cuba is alleged to have said that the United States would not have dared to send a warship to Havana while he was in command there, as "they knew the terrible punishment that awaited them," adding that he had Havana Harbor "well prepared for such an emergency," having "rap-idly finished the work that Martinez Campos carelessly abandoned."

I knew Laine very well. He was expelled from the island about sev-eral weeks ago, but I always found him a very upright, honest, straight fellow; and when I saw that he had a copy of a letter from Weyler to Santos Guzman, of Havana, I thought the chances were that he had a copy of a genuine letter, and that the facts were as stated; so I put some machinery to work and I found this cablegram, which had never been given to the public in any way.

Eva Canel——

She is quite a noted Spanish woman there, who was a great admirer of General Weyler, during the mob and so on, the riots, hallooing "Viva la Weyler" and "Muera Blanco" (death to Blanco). General Blanco had her expelled from the island and sent to Mexico.

Eva Canel and Santos Guzman——

Which is the very one that Laine refers to in his letter. This is in Spanish, but the translation is as follows:

Grave circumstances cause me to ask you to destroy the last letter of February 18.

The CHAIRMAN. Signed by whom?

Consul-General LEE. Signed "Weyler."

The CHAIRMAN. Dated when?

Consul-General LEE. There is no date to the telegram I have here, but it says: "In consequence of the grave condition of affairs or circum-stances ('make without effect' the Spanish is) destroy the last letter of date 18th February."

The CHAIRMAN. Whence does the telegram purport to have been sent?

Consul-General LEE. From Barcelona, I think.

The CHAIRMAN. Have you any doubt that is a genuine copy of a telegram from Weyler?

Consul-General LEE. I am satisfied it is a genuine copy of a telegram received in Havana.

The CHAIRMAN. From Weyler?

Consul-General LEE. From Weyler.

Senator FRYE. What is the date of the letter which Laine talks about?

Senator FORAKER. January 18, I believe.

Consul-General LEE. Laine's letter was dated in January, sometime.

Senator GRAY. January 8?

Consul-General LEE. January 8. This asks Santos Guzman, in consequence of grave circumstances which have arisen, to destroy his last letters of the 18th of February. This is simply rather confirmatory. If he had written to Guzman on the 8th of January, it makes this telegram that much more probable, and that he has also written to him after the 8th of January, and probably there was a very important letter on the 18th of February, which he wanted destroyed.

Senator MORGAN. A few days after the ship was destroyed?

Consul-General LEE. Yes, sir; the ship was destroyed on the 15th. I suppose the news reached Spain probably on the 16th, or something of that sort, and Weyler telegraphed right over.

Senator FRYE. Have you learned anything about any wire, such as is ordinarily used for torpedo service, ordered from Great Britain, or anywhere else?

Consul-General LEE. I saw a copy of a telegram from Admiral Manterolla in Havana, to the Spanish commission, as he put it, in London stating: "Hurry up electrical cables." Whether that referred to wire for submarine mines or torpedoes I do not know. I tried to ascertain if any of the wire or electrical cables had arrived there, but they came on Spanish ships and I could not find out. I have always had an idea about the *Maine* that, of course, it was not blown up by any private individual or by any private citizen, but it was blown up by some of the officers who had charge of the mines and electrical wires and torpedoes in the arsenal there who thoroughly understood their business, for it was done remarkably well.

I do not think General Blanco, the present Captain and Governor General of the Island of Cuba, had anything to do with it. I do not think he had any knowledge of it. I saw him just shortly after the occurrence. I was sitting in my room at the hotel and from the balcony of the hotel I could hear this. I heard the explosion and saw a great column of fire go up in the air. A few moments after ascertaining that it was the *Maine*, I went right down to the palace and I asked for General Blanco. He came in directly by himself. He had just heard it and was crying; tears were coming out of his eyes. He seemed to regret it as much as anybody I saw in Havana; but I think it came from some of the subaltern officers who had been there under Weyler, and who were probably anti-Blanco anyhow, and who had full knowledge of the business.

Senator FRYE. General, what have been the orders prevailing in Havana as to the sale of explosives of various kinds?

Consul-General LEE. I have never heard of any explosives being on sale there, or any orders about it one way or the other.

Senator FRYE. Would they permit explosives to be sold in the ordinary way?

Consul-General LEE. No, sir; I think not. They are very careful about that; so much so——

Senator FRYE. And have you been so for a long time?

Consul-General LEE. Very; so much so that when Captain Sigsbee wanted to use a little dynamite for the purpose of getting the 10-inch guns from the *Maine*, they violently objected to it; they did not want him to have any dynamite. I do not think they would allow any private store in Havana to sell dynamite or any explosive materials of any kind.

Senator FRYE. Have you read the testimony taken by our naval board?

Consul-General LEE. I glanced at it. I have not read it over very carefully.

Senator FRYE. Were you present in Havana all the time when they were conducting their inquiry?

Consul-General LEE. Yes, sir.

Senator FRYE. Are you familiar with what was done and what was found?

Consul-General LEE. I am tolerably familiar with it. I knew nothing about the report of the board, of course, until it was published, although I saw the officers every day. I saw them sometimes in town, and I was on board ship almost every day. I do not suppose there was a day they were there that I did not see Sampson and Potter and Marix. You know courts of inquiry in the Navy are like courts-martial in the Army. The officers are sworn, and they do not tell anybody what the findings are.

Senator FRYE. From what you have observed and heard there, have you any doubt as to the explosion of the *Maine* having been from the outside?

Consul-General LEE. I am satisfied it was from the outside. I cabled to the State Department a few days after the board assembled that it was almost certain that the explosion took place from the outside. I got that from some of the divers and from Ensign Powelson, and people I happened to meet and talk to about it. I had some little drawings of the ship.

The CHAIRMAN. A moment ago you started to say something about a telegram from Admiral Manterolla respecting——

Consul-General LEE. It was a telegram to the Spanish commission in London to hurry up the electric cables.

The CHAIRMAN. What I want to know is, whether that was before or after the explosion?

Consul-General LEE. I had that telegram. I want to see if I can get the exact date of it. That statement about the Admiral is in my testimony before the board of inquiry. I thought I had a copy of that. I do not remember the date exactly. It was prior to the explosion of the *Maine*.

The CHAIRMAN. About how long prior?

Consul-General LEE. A very short while. You can find that telegram in my testimony before the board; and I think it is right to say that that testimony about the admiral telegraphing to London, and this dispatch I have just given out here from Weyler to Santos Guzman, were not sent to Congress and were not published, because I sent a telegram requesting the State Department not to do it, as I was afraid the Spanish papers there would republish it and they would probably kill the man that gave it to me, so to protect him I did not want that known at the time. I can get the exact date of it, however.

The CHAIRMAN. It is not material.

Consul-General LEE. They have the exact date of it at the State Department.

Senator GRAY. You gave it in your testimony before the board?

Consul-General LEE. Yes, sir.

Senator CLARK. But that is not printed. It was withheld at the General's request.

Consul-General LEE. At my request. I ought to state, in justice to the State Department, that I telegraphed the State Department asking them not to have the telegram published, or this one about Weyler, because I was afraid of getting my informant into trouble.

Senator FRYE. We can get that at the State Department, and I guess we had better do it.

Senator MORGAN. How long, or about how long, after the explosion was it that General Blanco called at your quarters that night?

Consul-General LEE. Before he called at my quarters?

Senator MORGAN. Yes.

Consul-General LEE. You are not referring to my statement that I called at his palace the night of the explosion?

Senator MORGAN. Probably I am.

Consul-General LEE. That was the night of the explosion.

Senator MORGAN. Was that before you went down to the wharf?

Consul-General LEE. The palace is between my hotel and the harbor, and on my way to the harbor I stopped at the palace, about ten or fifteen minutes after the explosion—as soon as I could get down there in a carriage. I called by to see General Blanco.

Senator MORGAN. After you had heard the explosion how long was it before you reached the water's edge?

Consul-General LEE. Ten minutes afterwards I was in the palace, and I spent about five or ten minutes talking to General Blanco. He gave me an order to the admiral to give me one of the admiral's boats to take me right out into the harbor.

Senator MORGAN. When you got down to the water's edge did you see any electric lights burning?

Consul-General LEE. I did not notice that, but I have made inquiries since, and I have ascertained that no electric lights went out. I sent for electric-light men and gas men. Some gas jets went out in one or two places, caused by the shock or something, but I could not ascertain from these men that a single electric light went out.

Senator GRAY. Captain Sigsbee, in his testimony before the committee, said he was told, shortly after the explosion, by Admiral Manterolla that the electric lights in Havana went out simultaneously with the explosion.

Senator FORAKER. In the vicinity of the harbor.

Senator GRAY. In the vicinity of the harbor. Mr. Laine, who has been before the committee, and who made a very good impression upon us—it corresponds with what you say of him—says he was in the park opposite, or near the Hotel Inglaterra, looking toward the water with another correspondent, and that immediately upon the explosion they took a cab and drove to the water front, about 500 yards away, and when he got there he did notice that the electric light on a tall pole at the gate as he went in and smaller ones at the water front to the number of a dozen or more were out.

Consul-General LEE. I did not notice that at all, but I called up the two electric-light men. One of them is a good friend of mine, Carbonel, and then he sent for the person who has charge of the electric lights in Havana, and I had a talk with him. He came to my office. He said he had not heard of any such thing. I said, "I want to know with certainty." He said, "I will go all around and make inquiries, if you please." He was gone but an hour or two in a cab, and came back and said that with the exception of one electric light at a place called Gesus del Monte, right near the harbor, and one other place he mentioned, one place not very far from the harbor, where he thought perhaps the lights might have gone out by the shock, no other electric lights went out.

Senator MORGAN. Could you feel the jar of the explosion at the hotel?

Consul-General LEE. No, sir; I was in my room at the hotel.

Senator FRYE. I wish to ask one more question in regard to the *Maine*, and then I shall be through, so far as that is concerned. Have you heard since the explosion of the *Maine* any expression by Spanish officers in relation to it, indicating their pleasure at the fact?

Consul-General LEE. I heard, two or three days afterwards, from various persons who came in, that there was a good deal of rejoicing among some of the officers. Every report I always got said they were drinking champagne, quite a thing to do in honor of the event, and in different portions of the city officers were making merry. I attributed it to the fact that what they considered almost an enemy's battle ship had been blown up, and it was that much in their favor.

Senator MORGAN. Before the explosion, had you heard any threats of or allusions to the destruction of the *Maine?*

Consul General LEE. No, sir.

Senator LODGE. General, did you hear anything of an attempt on the *Montgomery?*

Consul-General LEE. I heard that there was something of that sort one evening, but I believe upon investigation it was found that it did not amount to anything.

Senator FRYE. I have asked all I desire to ask about the *Maine*.

The CHAIRMAN. Does any member of the committee wish to ask any questions.

Senator FORAKER. You think that no novice could have destroyed the *Maine*.

Consul-General LEE. Oh, no, sir. The man who did that work was an officer thoroughly acquainted with explosives of all sorts and who knew all about it. It was very well done.

Senator FORAKER. A man who had expert knowledge, necessarily?

Consul-General LEE. Yes, sir.

Senator CLARK. And who must have had knowledge of the location of the torpedo?

Consul-General LEE. Yes. I never have been certain that the submarine mine was placed there prior to the entrance of the *Maine* into the harbor. It might have been done afterwards. The *Maine* was anchored to a buoy by some little chain. A vessel swinging around that way sometimes gets at various places all around the circle. When she would swing off that way, with the bow next to the buoy, and these boats plying about the harbor all the time, anybody could go pretty well in front of her on a dark night and drop one of these submarine mines of 500 pounds. They have fingers, as it were, and as the boat goes around it would touch the finger, which makes contact and explodes the mine. That might have been done after the *Maine* got in there.

Senator CULLOM. And not be discovered?

Consul-General LEE. Yes, sir; one or two men rowing quietly in a boat could drop it off the stern of the boat on a dark night, though Sigsbee had his patrols out—I do not know what they call them on men of war; sentinels. Still, it might not have been discovered. A boat would not have been noticed, because boats go there always.

Senator CULLOM. Day and night?

Consul-General LEE. Yes, sir; to a late hour of the night. The harbor is full of these little boats. A mine weighs about 500 pounds, and I suppose it would take two or three men—one man to row and probably three or four to handle the mine.

Senator CULLOM. Containing 500 pounds of gun cotton?

Senator LODGE. And the casing.

Senator CULLOM. And the casing, which weighs something more.

Senator GRAY. What is the population of Havana?

Consul-General LEE. About 250,000.

Senator GRAY. Of what is that composed, so far as nationality and nativity are concerned?

Consul-General LEE. I suppose about equal parts of Cubans and Spaniards, now. I suppose one-fourth of the population, possibly, are negroes.

Senator GRAY. Is the Spanish proportion especially hostile to this country?

Consul-General LEE. No, sir; I do not think they are now. They were. But the Spanish portion are principally the merchants, commission merchants, shopkeepers, and all this agitation is affecting very much their business. A great many of them, whilst they give expression to great loyalty, are really annexationists, because they think it is the only way out of the trouble, and they would much prefer annexation to the United States to a Cuban republic, fearing that discriminations would be made against them in some way, and would rather trust to the United States than to the Cubans.

Senator GRAY. How as to the Cuban part of the population?

Consul-General LEE. They are generally all for free Cuba.

Senator CULLOM. What is the condition of the reconcentrados out in the country?

Consul-General LEE. Just as bad as in General Weyler's day. It has been relieved a good deal by supplies sent from the United States, but that has ceased now.

The CHAIRMAN. How about the Spaniards?

Consul-General LEE. General Blanco published a proclamation rescinding General Weyler's bando, as they call it there, but it has had no practical effect, for in the first place these people have no place to which to go; the houses have been burned down; there is nothing but the bare land there, and it takes them two months before they can raise the first crop. In the next place, they are afraid to go out from the lines of the towns, because the roving bands of Spanish guerrillas, as they are called, would kill them. So they stick right in at the edges of towns just like they did.

Senator CULLOM. With nothing to eat?

Consul-General LEE. Nothing in the world, except what they can get from charity; and I am afraid now they are in a dreadful condition, because all they had was the American relief, and that is stopped, you know. The Spanish have nothing to give.

Senator LODGE. General, what does this cessation of hostilities spoken of in the last few days amount to?

Consul-General LEE. Nothing; practically nothing—the armistice, you mean?

Senator LODGE. Yes; so called.

Consul-General LEE. It amounts to nothing.

Senator DANIEL. Do you know the conditions of it?

Consul-General LEE. I saw General Blanco's proclamation, which said the Queen Regent, at the request of his holiness, the Pope, had issued an armistice; but that is not worth the paper it is written on, because a truce or armistice between two contending forces requires the consent of both before it can be of any practical effect, and it will not have the consent of the insurgents.

Senator LODGE. What offer did he make to the insurgents?

Consul-General LEE. This occurred just about the time I left, and I do not know. I suppose he just relies upon that proclamation. He says the various Spanish officers in different parts of the island will see that it goes into effect.

Senator FRYE. Why do you say, General, that it will not receive any attention from the insurgent forces?

Consul-General LEE. Because every attempt so far to make terms or to make peace or to buy the insurgents or their leaders has met with signal failure; and whatever may be said about old General Gomez, he is, in my humble opinion, fighting that war in the only way it can be done—scattering his troops out—because to concentrate would be to starve, having no commissary train and no way to get supplies. They come in sometimes for the purpose of making some little raid, where he thinks it will do something; but he has given orders, so I have always been informed, not to fight, not to become engaged, not to lose their cartridges; and sometimes when he gets into a fight each man is ordered not to fire more than two cartridges.

When General Weyler was there he went out after him sometimes, and they would move up a column and fire, and sometimes the flank of the column, and the Spanish soldiers would deploy and throw out skirmishers, and the Cubans, like Indians, would go into the woods, valleys, and mountain sides, and scatter out, and wait until the Spanish troops were gone. Then the Spanish troops would countermarch and go back to town, 3 men killed and 10 or 12 wounded.

Senator CLARK. You think the insurgents would not accept any such terms?

Consul-General LEE. No, sir; I do not think it would be safe for any Spanish officer to go out under a flag of truce. They could not buy the insurgents. Every time they went out to buy them they killed them.

Senator MILLS. How much provisions have they in store for the army? How long can they maintain their forces there without bringing in more provisions?

Consul-General LEE. Senator, they are living there almost from hand to mouth.

Senator GRAY. Who?

Consul-General LEE. The Spaniards, and the citizens in the town of Havana also. I made some inquiries on that point just before I left. They have a good many barrels of flour and a good deal of rice and some potatoes, but not a great many, and a little lard; but everything that the town of Havana has received in the last four or five or six months has been from the United States by steamers from New York, New Orleans, and Tampa.

Senator MILLS. Can they get no subsistence from the island?

Consul-General LEE. Nothing more than from this floor [indicating].

Senator MILLS. That is what I supposed.

Consul-General LEE. The way the insurgents do is this: They have little patches of sweet potatoes—everything grows there very abundantly in a short time—and Irish potatoes and fruits. They drive their pigs and cattle into the valleys and hillsides, and they use those and scatter out. That is the reason why they all scatter out. A great many are planting. The insurgents plant crops in many parts of the island.

Speaking about an armistice, they have not been interfered with much since General Blanco came there. With the exception of the campaign of General Pando in the eastern part of the island, there have been very few military operations inaugurated by the Spanish. So it has been practically a sort of a truce for some time—the insurgents because they did not want to fight and because it was against orders to fight, and the Spanish soldiers——

Senator MILLS. Suppose Havana was blockaded, so that no provisions could come in, the people there would have no way to get any?

Consul-General LEE. None whatever. The town would surrender in a short while.

Senator FORAKER. What percentage of the population of the island is Cuban?

Consul-General LEE. About one million five or six hundred thousand people. About one-third of those are negroes. Take off 500,000 and that will leave 1,000,000, the Cubans being out of that 1,000,000 all except about 300,000.

Senator FORAKER. About 70 per cent?

Consul-General LEE. Yes; I think all but about 300,000.

Senator FORAKER. Are all the Cubans friendly to the insurgents?

Consul-General LEE. I never saw one who was not.

Senator FORAKER. They are all friendly to them?

Consul-General LEE. Yes.

Senator FRYE. What kind of men are the Cubans in the city? What character of men are they?

Consul-General LEE. There are some very good ones there and some are very trifling. It is like almost every population. The wealthier classes and the best educated and all those have generally left the island. They left nearly three years ago, when the war broke out. They are in London and Paris and many of them are in New York. I understand that 40,000 of them are in the United States.

Senator MORGAN. I wish to ask you, if you please, about the people we have been feeding in Cuba, on your requisition, from the Treasury of the United States. About how much of the appropriation of $50,000 have you expended?

Consul-General LEE. Forty-five thousand dollars. There is $5,000 left.

Senator MORGAN. Who got the benefit of it?

Consul-General LEE. American citizens.

Senator MORGAN. Do you mean native or adopted?

Consul General LEE. Native American citizens and naturalized citizens.

Senator MORGAN. Were they in Havana chiefly or in the country?

Consul-General LEE. All over the whole island.

Senator MORGAN. Was it a matter of actual necessity to feed them, or was it just a matter of kindness?

Consul-General LEE. They were practically in the condition of all the other inhabitants of the island. They have had very little if any business to work at. There were not a great many sugar plantations in operation nor tobacco places and that kind, and they were suffering like everybody else. This money was applied for the relief of Americans, and then afterwards they got up a general relief for everybody, for the reconcentrados, as they call them.

Senator CULLOM. Did the Spanish army get any of the supplies sent from the United States?

Consul-General LEE. No, sir; occasionally they might have gotten a little here and there.

Senator MORGAN. We noticed that in one of your reports (I think it was a report made to you by a consul; I can not refer to it from memory at this moment of time) a statement was made to the effect that the people all through those settlements were not permitted to go outside of the line of concentration back to their homes.

Consul-General LEE. Yes, sir.

Senator MORGAN. That was the fact?

Consul-General LEE. Yes, sir; they have only recently been permitted to do so by a proclamation of General Blanco.

Senator MORGAN. How recently?

Consul General LEE. Not quite three weeks ago.

The CHAIRMAN. Has General Blanco begun to relieve the reconcentrados, as has been said?

Consul-General LEE. Very little, indeed. They distributed some down there when the matter was first agitated, but it was a drop in the bucket.

The CHAIRMAN. How long ago was that?

Consul-General LEE. That was possibly eight or ten months ago, when they were first considering the relief of those reconcentrados.

Senator FRYE. What is the condition of the Spanish soldiers there in the island?

Consul-General LEE. Very bad.

Senator FRYE. As to clothing and subsistence, how are they?

Consul-General LEE. They are badly clothed and very badly fed; not well organized; not drilled. Nobody ever saw Spanish soldiers drill.

Senator FRYE. If Spain has really appropriated $600,000 for the sustenance of the reconcentrados, as it is stated, do you believe that that will be given to those people, and that their own soldiers will be left to starve?

Consul-General LEE. Oh, no. There will be very little of it paid to anybody.

Senator FORAKER. What will become of it?

Consul-General LEE. They will divide it up here and there—a piece taken off here and a piece taken off there. I do not believe they have appropriated anything of the kind. I see those things on paper always.

Senator FRYE. You would have no confidence in it and would not advise us to have any confidence in it?

Consul-General LEE. Not a particle.

Senator MORGAN. Let me ask you, if you please, as to those persons whom you have been supplying with subsistence there from the Treasury of the United States. Now that you have come from the island, what provision is made for their support?

Consul-General LEE. Well, a great many of those, Senator, have departed from the island, but still there are a few scattered about here and there. There is no provision at all for them any more than there is for the reconcentrados.

Senator MORGAN. So they will be passed in among the starving classes unless they are relieved?

Consul-General LEE. Yes. If the $5,000 had been used before we came away, they would have that now; but they will just have to take their chances with the reconcentrados of what is there of food from the American relief fund.

Senator MORGAN. If it is our duty to feed those people there in Cuba, I suppose we shall have to be active about it in order to give them relief?

Consul-General LEE. Yes; they are suffering and starving there now every day. The Spanish can not feed them.

Senator CULLOM. Now that you and the other consuls have come away from the island, who would have charge of the distribution of food down there?

Consul-General LEE. I thought perhaps Miss Clara Barton would, because she came back there; but, very much to my surprise, she turned around and came out the same day we did, bringing every Red Cross. We had a warehouse from this fund that was contributed by the people of the United States, and I saw the warehouseman, a man named Elwell, that I had put there, on the boat. I asked him what he did about the warehouse. He said he just shut it up; that there was not a great deal left in it, and that he gave the key to the person who owned the property.

Senator FRYE. Did Miss Barton give any reason for leaving?

Consul-General LEE. She thought there was going to be war and she had better get out. She told me coming back that the Red Cross policy was to go behind the guns and not in front of them.

Senator FRYE What, in your judgment, is the possibility of Spain conquering the insurgents and restoring peace to the island?

Consul-General LEE. I do not think there is the slightest possibility of their doing it at all in any way.

Senator CULLOM. Provided they do not starve them all to death?

Consul-General LEE. The same condition of things existed when Mr. Cleveland asked me to go down there last June a year ago. I gave him a report three weeks after I got there in which I told him there was no chance in my opinion of the Spaniards ever suppressing that insurrection nor was there any chance of the insurrectionists expelling the Spanish soldiers from the island. That report is in the State Department somewhere to-day, and if I had to write it over I would not dot an "i" or cross a "t," although I have been there nearly two years since then.

Senator FORAKER. Let me call your attention in this connection to a letter written by you to the State Department on the 13th of December last. If you have no objection, I should like to have it go into the record.

Consul-General LEE. I have no objection at all. It is on the same line I have been talking upon.

The letter referred to is as follows:

UNITED STATES CONSULATE-GENERAL,
Havana, December 13, 1897.

Hon. WILLIAM R. DAY,
Assistant Secretary of State, Washington, D. C.

SIR: I have the honor to make the following report:

First. In my opinion there is no possibility of Spain terminating the war here by *arms*.

Second. Or by *autonomy*—real or pretended.

Third. Or by *purchasing the insurrection leaders,* as recently attempted.

Fourth. Or, as far as I can see, in any other way.

Fifth. The contest for and against autonomy is most unequal.

For it, there are five or six of the head officers at the palace, and twenty or thirty other persons here in the city, who, it is said, desire to hold the offices to be created under autonomatic forms; at least, such is my information.

Against it, first, are the insurgents, with or without arms, and the Cuban noncombatants. Second, the great mass of the Spaniards, bearing or nonbearing arms, the latter desiring, if there must be a change, annexation to the United States.

Indeed, there is the greatest apathy concerning autonomy in any form. No one asks what it will be, or when, or how it will come.

I do not see how it could be even put into operation by force, because as long as the insurgents decline to accept it, so long, the Spanish authorities say, the war must continue.

I am compelled to say, therefore, that in my opinion autonomy does not now, if it ever did, exist as a factor in the solution of the Cuban problem.

I am obliged to say, too, that in spite of published manifestoes the government of this island has not been able to relieve from starvation the Cuban population driven from their homes by the Weyler edict, and no longer attempts to do so.

I am, sir, your obedient servant,

FITZHUGH LEE,
Consul-General.

Senator MORGAN. I wish to call your attention to the inclosure in your dispatch of November 27, 1897. In your letter you say:

One of two gentlemen who visited the reconcentrados after they were concentrated in Las Fosos, or the ditches in this city, handed me to-day the inclosed paper. The names of the two gentlemen are not signed to it for obvious reasons.

I do not care about the names; I suppose they are of no value to us; but do you know the gentlemen?

Consul-General LEE. Oh, yes; they are very reliable. I did not give the names because I thought perhaps if the document was published, or something of the kind, as the Spanish papers repeat everything, these men would be possibly arrested.

Senator MORGAN. Have you any reason to doubt the entire accuracy of that statement?

Consul-General LEE. No, sir; it is correct, in my opinion.

Senator LODGE. General, what is your opinion of the insurgent government?

Consul-General LEE. I have never thought that the insurgents had anything except the skeleton form of a government—a movable capital. I asked them one day why they did not have some permanent capital, and I think they gave a very good reason. They said it would require a large force to protect it and defend it, and they could not afford to mass up their men there; that the capital and the government offices had to move where they could be safest.

Senator FORAKER. Do you know any of the officials connected with their civil government?

Consul-General LEE. No, sir.

Senator FORAKER. You do not know President Maso or Vice-President Capote or the cabinet?

Consul-General LEE. I never had any communication with the insurgents in any way, shape, or form while on the island, except when, to save Colonel Ruiz's life, I wrote a letter to Aranguren, the insurgent chief.

Senator CULLOM. What is, approximately, the armed force of the insurgents?

Consul-General LEE. I suppose, if you could get them all up and mass them, they would number probably 31,000 or 32,000. The number has been up probably as high as 36,000 or 37,000.

Senator FRYE. Are they well or decently armed?

Consul-General LEE. They are well armed.

Senator FRYE. Have they much ammunition on hand?

Consul-General LEE. The ammunition varies. I think now and then a filibustering expedition gets in in some way and resupplies them, but I do not think they have a great deal. I presume that must be so, because, as I told you, Gomez issued an order not to fire more than two cartridges.

Senator FRYE. What is the force of cavalry?

Consul-General LEE. They had at one time nearly one-third, but they have not so many now. The horses died; it has been hard to get horse feed, and so on; and they dismounted a great many of them.

Senator FORAKER. How many Spanish soldiers are in the island now?

Consul-General LEE. Capable of making a fight, possibly 55,000 or 56,000.

Senator FORAKER. And they are rather inadequately disciplined and drilled?

Consul-General LEE. Oh, yes; not drilled, not organized.

Senator MILLS. Not officered well?

Consul-General LEE. No.

Senator FORAKER. Are they now conducting any offensive military operations at all?

Consul-General LEE. No, sir; they have been going through some form with General Pando, down on the eastern division of the island, at Santiago de Cuba, but I think that has all stopped now. The last information was that Gomez was getting around to flank Pando, and there were some fears entertained for his safety.

Senator FORAKER. It is practically only an army of occupation?

Consul-General LEE. That is about it, sir.

Senator FORAKER. Are the Spaniards confined to the fortified cities?

Consul General LEE. Yes.

Senator FORAKER. All are confined to the cities?

Consul General LEE. They do not try to occupy the country.

Senator FORAKER. Not outside the cities?

Consul-General LEE. No, sir; and generally the seaports. They do not want to get outside of any seaports. The seaports on the southern coast and the northern part are occupied by the Spanish troops and some of the larger towns in the interior. In the rest are the insurgents.

Senator FORAKER. The insurgents have the rest all around?

Consul-General LEE. Oh, yes; you can go from Havana 4 or 5 miles any day and get to the insurgents.

Senator FORAKER. To what extent do the insurgents control the eastern part—Puerto Principe and Santiago de Cuba?

Consul-General LEE. Nearly the entire portion of both provinces.

Senator FORAKER. What is the population of those two provinces?

Consul-General LEE. I do not know what it is as compared to the others.

Senator LODGE. Puerto Principe has a population of about 60,000.

Consul-General LEE. Santiago de Cuba is the largest in the island, I suppose. It has always been considered that there were not many Spanish troops there.

Senator FORAKER. The insurgents practically have control?

Consul-General LEE. So when General Weyler published his proclamation stating that the four western provinces were pacified Gomez published a counter proclamation and said that the eastern provinces were pacified.

Senator FORAKER. Gomez seems to be a man of a great deal of ability?

Consul-General LEE. Yes; he commenced to fight the war in that way and never has varied, but has gone right on in a straight line. They can not get him off of it. He goes out a little way, moves in a circle, and comes back to the place where he started.

Senator FORAKER. There are probably 300,000 Spaniards in the island population?

Consul-General LEE. I saw it stated the other day at 280,000, and I have seen it stated at 360,000.

Senator FORAKER. Are all the Spaniards hostile to the Cubans?

Consul-General LEE. As a general thing they are.

Senator FORAKER. The Spaniards are hostile to the insurgent government, and the Cubans are friendly to it, I suppose?

Consul-General LEE. Yes, sir.

Senator FORAKER. The line runs about that way?

Consul General LEE. Yes, sir.

Senator FORAKER. You said a while ago that you were not sure whether this mine was planted before or after the *Maine* went there. Was there any place about Havana where private persons could have bought this mine and from which they could have taken it and placed it?

Consul-General LEE. No, sir.

Senator FORAKER. Have you any doubt but that it was put there by the Government?

Consul-General LEE. I do not think it was put there by the Government. I think probably it was the act of four or five subordinate officers.

Senator FORAKER. Spanish officers?

Consul-General LEE. Spanish officers, who had knowledge of the location and probably were experts, and had that branch of the service to look after. I do not think General Blanco gave any order about it.

Senator GRAY. What number of Spanish troops are on the island now, as you estimate the number?

Consul-General LEE. I suppose probably 97,000 or 98,000. There are some 37,000 there in hospitals, and about 50,000, probably 55,000, capable of bearing arms. A Spanish steamer goes back to Spain once every ten days, and they have taken off in the last year 500 or 800 or 900 and sometimes 1,000 Spanish soldiers three times a month. If they averaged only 700 on a steamer, in a month they would take off 2,100.

Senator FORAKER. What was the largest number they ever had there?

Consul-General LEE. They claimed about 210,000.

Consul SPRINGER. 237,000 have been sent over.

Consul-General LEE. Is that shown from the official records?

Consul SPRINGER. Yes, sir.

Senator DANIEL. When does the rainy season commence?

Consul-General LEE. It commences about the middle of June or the latter part.

Senator DANIEL. What effect would that have upon the Spaniards and the Cubans?

S. Doc. 231, pt 7——56

Consul-General LEE. The Spaniards do not conduct any operations at all during the rainy season. The Cubans are acclimated and get along better.

Senator DANIEL. Have any of the reconcentrados been put to work on public works, as has been intimated in the press?

Consul-General LEE. No, sir; there are no public works, and there is no money to pay for them.

Senator DANIEL. Could an American army of occupation go into Cuba with safety now?

Consul-General LEE. Yes, sir.

Senator DANIEL. I mean on account of climate, and so on.

Consul-General LEE. On account of climate and on account of everything else.

Senator FORAKER. Is the Spanish army paid up to date, or is it in arrears?

Consul-General LEE. When I left they informed me that the troops had not been paid for nine months, and the officers for about four.

Senator DANIEL. What has become of Miguel Viondi, who defended Sanguilly?

Consul-General LEE. He has been released. He was taken over and kept in one of those African prisons for a long time, but immediately after General Blanco came back he was released. They said they released a great many of those prisoners because they found difficulty in feeding them.

Senator DANIEL. Do you regard that General Blanco was lacking in courtesy to you on your leaving the Island?

Consul-General LEE. General Blanco and I always got along very well together. We were quite friends. I went into the palace the morning I left as a matter of official etiquette, to bid good-bye.

I went with the British consul-general. I saw Dr. Congosto, the secretary to the General. I told Dr. Congosto that I had received instructions to leave the island and go to the United States, and I called to pay my final respects and would like to see General Blanco. He asked me to sit down and said he would go and let him know. He went off and stayed about fifteen minutes and came back and said the General said please excuse him; he was not well and was lying down. I told Dr. Congosto then to say good-bye to him and turned around and left.

Senator DANIEL. Were there any demonstrations of ill will toward you as you left?

Consul-General LEE. When we were coming out on the steamer Saturday evening there was some hallooing, catcalling, and whistling, and some Spanish expressions, " Mean cowards, running away," and so on. I think that was confined to the lower order of men, however.

The CHAIRMAN. General, we are very much obliged to you.

CONCENTRATION AND OTHER PROCLAMATIONS OF GENERAL WEYLER.

PROCLAMATION.

Don Valeriano Weyler y Nicolau, Marquis of Teneriffe, Governor and Captain-General of the Island of Cuba, General in Chief of the Army, etc., desirous of warning the honest inhabitants of Cuba and those loyal to the Spanish cause, and in conformity to the laws, does order and command:

ARTICLE I. All inhabitants of the district of Sancti Spiritus and the provinces of Puerto Principe and Santiago de Cuba will have to concentrate in places which are the headquarters of a division, a brigade, a column, or a troop, and will have to be provided with documentary proof of identity, within eight days of the publication of this proclamation in the municipalities.

ART. 2. To travel in the country in the radius covered by the columns in operation, it is absolutely indispensable to have a pass from the mayor, military commandants, or chiefs of detachments. Any one lacking this will be detained and sent to headquarters of divisions or brigades, and thence to Havana, at my disposition, by the first possible means. Even if a pass is exhibited, which is suspected to be not authentic or granted by authority to person with known sympathy toward the rebellion, or who show favor thereto, rigorous measures will result to those responsible.

ART. 3. All owners of commercial establishments in the country districts will vacate them, and the chiefs of columns will take such measures as the success of their operations dictates regarding such places which, while useless for the country's wealth, serve the enemy as hiding places in the woods and in the interior.

ART. 4. All passes hitherto issued hereby become null and void.

ART. 5. The military authorities will see to the immediate publication of this proclamation.

VALERIANO WEYLER.

HAVANA, *February 16, 1896.*

PROCLAMATION.

Don Valeriano Weyler Nicolau, Marquis of Teneriffe, Governor and Captain-General of the Island of Cuba, General in Chief of the Army, etc.:

In order to avoid suffering and delay, other than that essential in time of war, and the summary proceedings initiated by the forces in operation, I dictate the following proclamation:

ARTICLE 1. In accordance with the faculties conceded to me by rule two, article thirty-one, of the military code of justice, I assume, as general in chief of the army operating in this island, the judicial attributes of H. E. Captain-General.

ART. 2. In virtue of rule two of said article, I delegate from this date these judicial attributes to the commanders in chief of the first and second army corps, and to the general commanding the third division; that is, in Puerto Principe.

ART. 3. Prisoners caught in action will be subjected to the most summary trial, without any other investigation except that indispensable for the objects of the trial.

ART. 4. When the inquiry is finished, subject to consultation with the judicial authorities, the proceedings will continue during the course of operations, and in the presence of the judicial authority, with an auditor, the sentence may be carried out. When said authority is not present, the process will be remitted to him and the culpable parties detained at the locality where the division or brigade headquarters is situated.

ART. 5. The military juridic functionary of whatever rank who accompanies in the operations the judicial authorities, when the latter thus decides, will act as auditor, dispensing with the assessors' assistance at court-martial, during operations, in cases where no other member of the juridic body is at hand.

ART. 6. When the sentence is pronounced, if the sentence be deprivation of liberty, the culprit will be brought to Havana, with the papers in the case, so that the testimony can be issued as to the penalty, and the sentence be carried into effect.

ART. 7. The said authorities will be acquainted with all cases initiated against the accused in war.

ART. 8. I reserve the right of promoting and sustaining all questions of competence, with other jurisdictions, as also with the military, and to determine inhibitions in all kinds of military processes, in the territory of the island.

ART. 9. I reserve likewise the faculty of assuming an inquiry into all cases, when it is deemed convenient.

ART. 10. No sentence of death shall be effected without the acknowledgment by my authority of the testimony of the judgment, which must be sent to me immediately, except when no means of communication exists, or when it is a case of insult to superiors, or of military sedition, in which case sentence will be carried out, and the information furnished to me afterwards.

ART. 11. All previous proclamations or orders, conflicting with this, on the question of the delegation of jurisdiction in this island, are hereby rendered null and void.

VALERIANO WEYLER.

HAVANA, *February 16, 1896.*

PROCLAMATION.

Don Valeriano Weyler y Nicolau, Marquis of Teneriffe, Governor and Captain-General of the Island of Cuba, general in chief of the army, etc.:

I make known that, taking advantage of the temporary insecurity of communication between the district capitals and the rest of the provinces, notices which convey uneasiness and alarm are invented and propagated, and some persons, more daring still, have taken advantage of this to draw the deluded and ignorant to the rebel ranks. I am determined to have the laws obeyed, and to make known by special means the dispositions ruling and frequently applied during such times as the present, through which the island is now passing, and to make clear how far certain points go, in adapting them to the exigencies of war and in use of the faculties conceded to me by number twelve, article seven, of the code of military justice and by the law of public order of April 23, 1870. And I make known, order, and command that the following cases are subject to military law, among others specified by the law:

CLAUSE 1. Those who invent or propagate by any means notices or assertions favorable to the rebellion shall be considered as being guilty of offenses against the integrity of the nation, and comprised in article two hundred and twenty-three, clause six, of the military code, whenever such notices facilitate the enemy's operations.

CLAUSE 2. Those who destroy or damage railroad lines, telegraph or telephone wires, or apparatus connected therewith, or those who interrupt communications, by opening bridges or destroying highways.

CLAUSE 3. Incendiaries in town or country, or those who cause damage, as shown in caption eight, article thirteen, volume two, of the penal code ruling in Cuba.

CLAUSE 4. Those who sell, facilitate, convey, or deliver arms or ammunition to the enemy, or who supply such by any other means, or those who keep such in their power, or tolerate or deal in such through the customs, and employees of customs who fail to confiscate such importations, will be held responsible.

CLAUSE 5. Telegraphists who divulge telegrams referring to the war, or who send them to persons who should not be cognizant of them.

CLAUSE 6. Those who, through the press or otherwise, revile the prestige of Spain, her army, the volunteers, or firemen, or any other force that cooperates with the army.

CLAUSE 7. Those who, by the same means, endeavor to extol the enemy.

CLAUSE 8. Those who supply the enemy with horses, cattle, or any other war resources.

CLAUSE 9. Those who act as spies; and to these the utmost rigor of the law will be applied.

CLAUSE 10. Those who serve as guides, unless surrendering at once and showing the proof of force majeure and giving the troops evidence at once of loyalty.

CLAUSE 11. Those who adulterate army food, or conspire to alter the prices of provisions.

CLAUSE 12. Those who, by means of explosives, commit the offenses referred to in the law of June 10, 1894, made to extend to this island by the royal order of October 17, 1895, seeing that these offenses affect the public peace, and the law of April 23, 1870, grants me power to leave to the civil authorities the proceedings in such cases as are comprised in captions four and five, and treatise three of volume two of the common penal code, when the culprits are not military, or when the importance of the offense renders such action advisable.

CLAUSE 13. Those who, by messenger pigeons, fireworks, or other signals, communicate news to the enemy.

CLAUSE 14. The offenses enumerated, when the law prescribes the death penalty or life imprisonment, will be dealt with most summarily.

CLAUSE 15. All other proclamations and orders previously issued in conflict with this are annulled by this.

VALERIANO WEYLER.

HAVANA, *February 16, 1896.*

EXTRACTS FROM CONSULAR REPORTS IN REGARD TO AFFAIRS ON THE ISLAND OF CUBA.

Mr. Lee to Mr. Day.

UNITED STATES CONSULATE GENERAL,
Havana, November 23, 1897.

SIR: I have the honor to briefly submit a statement of what appears to be the present condition of affairs in this island:

First. The insurgents will not accept autonomy.

Second. A large majority of the Spanish subjects who have commercial and business interests and own property here will not accept autonomy, but prefer annexation to the United States rather than an independent republic or genuine autonomy under the Spanish flag.

Third. The Spanish authorities are sincere in doing all in their power to encourage, protect, and promote the grinding of sugar. The grinding season commences in December.

Fourth. The insurgents, leaders have given instructions to prevent grinding, wherever it can be done, because by diminishing the export of sugar the Spanish Government revenues are decreased. It will be very difficult for the Spanish authorities to prevent cane burning, because one man at night can start a fire which will burn hundreds of acres, just as a single individual could ignite a prairie by throwing a match into the dry grass.

Fifth. I am confident that General Blanco and Pando, his chief of staff, as well as Dr. Congosto, the secretary-general, with all of whom I have had conversations, are perfectly conscientious in their desire to relieve the distress of those suffering from the effects of Weyler's reconcentration order, but, unfortunately, they have not the means to carry out such benevolent purposes.

I have read letters stating that charitable persons in the United States will send clothing, food, and some money to these unfortunate people, and I have arranged with the Ward line of steamers to provide free transportation from New York. I hope to secure the permission of the Spanish authorities here for such things to be entered free of duty. I am told, however, that they must come consigned to the Bishop of Havana. The sufferings of the "reconcentrados" class have been terrible, beyond description, but in Havana less than in other places on the island; yet Dr. Brunner, acting United States sanitary inspector here, informed me this morning that the death rate of the "reconcentrados" in this city was about 50 per cent of other places of the island, and when it is remembered that there have been several hundred thousands of these noncombatants or "pacificos," mainly women and children, who are concentrated under General Weyler's order, some idea can be formed of the mortality among them.

In this city matters are assuming better shape. Under charitable committees large numbers of them have been gathered together in houses, and are now fed and cared for by private subscriptions. I visited them yesterday and found their condition comparatively good, and there will be a daily improvement among them, though the lives of all can not be saved. I witnessed many terrible scenes and saw some die while I was present. I am told General Blanco will give $100,000 to the relief fund.

> I am, etc.,   FITZHUGH LEE,
> *Consul-General.*

Mr. Lee to Mr. Day.

UNITED STATES CONSULATE-GENERAL,
Havana, November 27, 1897.

SIR: One of two gentlemen who visited the "reconcentrados" after they were concentrated on Los Fosos (the ditches) in this city handed me to-day the inclosed paper. The names of these two gentlemen are not signed to it for obvious reasons.

I personally know the gentleman who brought the communication, and know that he stands high in this community as a man of integrity and character.

The number of "reconcentrados" here, as I had the honor to report already, have always been less than elsewhere. I am able to say now that they will be taken care of and fed by committees of charitably disposed persons.

* * * * * *

> I am, etc.,   FITZHUGH LEE,
> *Consul-General.*

[Inclosure referred to above.]

SIR: The public rumor of the horrible state in which the reconcentrados of the municipal council of Havana were found in the Fosos having reached us, we resolved to pay a visit there, and we will relate to you what we saw with our own eyes:

Four hundred and sixty women and children thrown on the ground, heaped pellmell as animals, some in a dying condition, others sick, and others dead, without the slightest cleanliness nor the least help, not even to give water to the thirsty, with neither religious or social help, each one dying wherever chance laid them. And for this limited number of reconcentrados the deaths ranged between 40 and 50 daily, giving relatively ten days of life for each person, with great joy to the authorities, who seconded fatidically the politics of General Weyler to exterminate the Cuban people; for these unhappy creatures received food only after having been for eight days in the Fosos, if during this time they could feed themselves with the bad food that the dying refused.

On this first visit we were present at the death of an old man who died through thirst. When we arrived he begged us for God's sake to give him a drink; we looked for it and gave it to him, and fifteen minutes afterwards he breathed his last, not having had even a drink of water for three days before. Among the many deaths we witnessed there was one scene impossible to forget. There is still alive the only living witness, a young girl of 18 years, whom we found seemingly lifeless on the ground. On her right-hand side was the body of a young mother cold and rigid, but with her young child still alive, clinging to her dead breast; on her left-hand side was also the corpse of a dead woman holding her son in a dead embrace. A little farther on, a poor, dying woman, having in her arms a daughter of 14 crazy with pain, who, after five or six days, also died in spite of the care she received.

In one corner a poor woman was dying, surrounded by her children, who contemplated in silence, without a lament or shedding a tear, they themselves being real specters of hunger, emaciated in a horrible manner. This poor woman augments the catalogue, already large, of the victims of the reconcentration in the Fosos.

The relation of the pictures of misery and horror which we have witnessed would be never-ending were we to narrate them all.

It is difficult and almost impossible to express by writing the general aspect of the inmates of the Fosos, because it is entirely beyond the line of what civilized humanity is accustomed to see; therefore no language can describe it.

The circumstances which the municipal authorities could reunite there are the following: Complete accumulation of bodies, dead and alive, so that it was impossible to take one step without walking over them; the greatest want of cleanliness, want of light, air, and water; the food lacking in quality and quantity, what was necessary to sustain life, thus sooner putting an end to these already broken-down systems; complete absence of medical assistance, and, what is more terrible than all, no consolation whatever, religious or moral.

If any young girl came in any way nice looking, she was infallibly condemned to the most abominable of traffics.

At the sight of such horrible pictures the two gentlemen who went there resolved, in spite of the ferocious Weyler, who was still Captain-General of the island, to omit nothing to remedy a deed so dishonorable to humanity and so contrary to all Christianity. They did not fail to find persons animated with like sentiments, who, putting aside all fear of the present situation, organized a private committee, with the exclusive end of aiding, materially and morally, the reconcentrados. This neither has been nor is at present an easy task. The great number of the poor and scarcity of means makes us encounter constant conflicts. This conflict is more terrible with the official elements, and in a special manner with the mayor of the city and the civil authorities, who try by all means to annihilate this good work.

The result of the collections are very insignificant if we bear in mind the thousands of people who suffer from the reconcentrations; but it serves for some consolation to see that in Havana some 159 children and 84 women are well cared for in the asylum erected in Cadiz street, No. 82; and 93 women and children are equally well located in a large saloon erected for them in the second story of the Fosos, with good food and proper medical assistance, as also everything indispensable to civilized life.

According to the information which we have been able to acquire since August until the present day, 1,700 persons have entered the Fosos proceeding from Jaruco, Campo Florido, Guanabo, and Tapaste, in the province of Havana. Of these only 243 are living now and are to be found in Cadiz street; 82 in the saloon already mentioned, and 61 in the Quinta del Rey and the Hospital Mercedes; the whole amounting to about 397, and of these a great many will die on account of the great sufferings and hunger they have gone through.

From all this we deduce that the number of deaths among the reconcentrados has amounted to 77 per cent.

––––––

Mr. Lee to Mr. Day.

UNITED STATES CONSULATE-GENERAL,
Havana, December 3, 1897.

SIR: Referring to my cipher telegram of the 1st instant, which I beg to confirm, reading as follows:

ASSISTANT SECRETARY OF STATE, ETC.:

Inform the Department that he has learned from the United States consul at Matanzas of an extensive and dangerous conspiracy under the ex-governor of the province, directed against Americans. Action against them to be contingent upon movement of the United States Government in favor of independence to Cuba.

I have the honor to state that rumors have been more or less frequent regarding the riotous intentions of some of the dissatisfied elements toward citizens of the United States dwelling here and in other parts of the island. Any riotous demonstrations here must come from the Spanish noncombatants or from the volunteer forces. I do not think there is any danger from the former, many of whom seem to be in favor of annexation rather than for real autonomy or for an independent Cuban republic; and I am inclined to think if General Blanco can manage the volunteers, as yesterday he said he could, the trouble from that source is diminishing. The origin of the mobs in this city in the past has always been located in the ranks of the volunteers, who alone have organization and arms.

The Governor and Captain-General is now investigating the Matanzas rumors and will, I am sure, deal promptly with any conspirators found there.

The Weyler police have all been changed and the officers of the volunteers, too, when the Government here has reason to doubt their loyalty.

In consequence of all this, and the assurance of the governmental authorities that American life and property will, if necessary, be protected by them at a moment's notice, I have declined to make an application for the presence of one or more war ships in this harbor, and have advised those of our people who have wives and children here not to send them away, at least for the present, because such proceedings would not, in my opinion, be justifiable at this time, from the standpoint of personal security.

I still think that two warships at least should be at Key West, prepared to move here at short notice, and that more of them should be sent to Dry Tortugas, and a coal station be established there. Such proceedings would seem to be in line with that prudence and foresight necessary to afford safety to the Americans residing on the island, and to their properties, both of which, I have every reason to know, are objects of the greatest concern to our Government.

I am, etc.,

FITZHUGH LEE,
Consul-General.

Mr. Lee to Mr. Day.

UNITED STATES CONSULATE-GENERAL,
Havana, December 3, 1897.

SIR: I have the honor to state that a representative of a Madrid paper here says that "Canalejas has said, upon his return from the Vuelta Abajo, or Pinar del Rio Province, after the recent combat there between the Spanish Generals Bernal and Hernandez de Calasco, in command of 2,300 men and two pieces of artillery, and Cuban forces under Pedro Diaz, that, although the Spanish troops have displayed once more their usual valor in said fight and the enemy must have suffered heavy losses, yet the province of Pinar del Rio is not pacified, and that there are numerous rebel forces still there; that out of about 14,000 Spanish regular troops in that province only about 3,000 or 4,000 are able to operate, the balance being sick at the hospitals, garrisoning towns, and otherwise distributed; that he believes autonomy premature, and inclines himself to the adoption of energetic military action for the purpose of finally pacifying said province; that he does not believe in altering facts and news; that the truth, no matter how painful and bitter it may be, must be known in the Peninsula, where public opinion and the press have been deceived regarding the annihilation of the war and the so-called pacification of the western provinces, among which that of Pinar del Rio has been included."

The Lucha to-day publishes that Canalejas has said "that the economic condition of the Pinar del Rio Province is deplorable, there being 40,000 'reconcentrados' absolutely destitute, 15,000 of which are children, most of whom are orphans; that they are unequally distributed throughout the different towns in the province, there being only 460 at the capital city of Pinar del Rio, while in small towns like Consolacion and Candelaria there are over 4,000. The municipalities can not incur any expense because the taxes can not be collected, because most of the taxpayers, if not all, have been ruined by the war."

I am, etc.,

FITZHUGH LEE,
Consul-General.

Mr. Lee to Mr. Day.

UNITED STATES CONSULATE-GENERAL,
Havana, December 7, 1897.

SIR: (The consul-general informs the Assistant Secretary of State that measures for the relief of the "reconcentrados" are not sufficiently energetic to be effective, and that he is advised by the Governor-General that authority to admit articles of food and clothing from the United States to Cuban ports free of duty rested with the authorities at Madrid).

I see no effects of the governmental distribution to the "reconcentrados." I am informed that only $12,500 in Spanish silver had been dedicated to the Havana Province out of the $100,000 said to have been set aside for the purpose of relieving them on the island, and that reports from all parts of the Province show that 50 per cent have already died and that many of those left will die. Most of these are women and children. I do not believe the Government here is really able to relieve the distress and sufferings of these people.

*　　*　　*　　*　　*　　*　　*

I am informed an order has been issued in some parts of the island suspending the distribution of rations to "reconcentrados." * * * The condition of these people is simply terrible.

I inclose herewith an official document copy of the comparative mortality in Havana for the six months ending November 30. It will be perceived that there has been a great increase in the death rate, and without adequate means in the future to prevent it the mortality will increase. I hear of much suffering in the Spanish hospitals for want of food, and among the Spanish soldiers. * * * I hear also that the Spanish merchants in some parts of the island are placing their establishments in the name of foreigners in order to avoid their provisions being purchased on credit by the military administration, and that the Spanish army is suffering much from sickness and famine, and that a great deal of money is needed at once to relieve their condition. In some parts of the island, I am told, there is scarcely any food for soldiers or citizens, and that even cats are used for food purposes, selling at 30 cents apiece.

It is a fair inference, therefore, to draw from the *existing conditions,* that it is not possible for the Governor-General of this island to relieve the present situation with the means at his disposal. * * *

I am, etc.,

FITZHUGH LEE,
Consul-General.

———

Mr. Lee to Mr. Day.

[Confidential.]

UNITED STATES CONSULATE-GENERAL,
Havana, December 13, 1897. (Received December 18.)

SIR: I have the honor to make the following report

*　　*　　*　　*　　*　　*

The contest for and against autonomy is most unequal.

For it there are 5 or 6 of the head officers at the palace, and 20 or 30 other persons here in the city.

*　　*　　*

Against it, first, are the insurgents, with or without arms, and the Cuban noncombatants; second, the great mass of the Spaniards, bearing or nonbearing arms—the latter desiring, if there *must* be a *change,* annexation to the United States.

Indeed, there is the greatest apathy concerning autonomy in any form. No one asks what it will be or when or how it will come.

I do not see how it could even be put into *operation* by *force,* because as long as the insurgents decline to accept it so long, the Spanish authorities say, the war must continue.

* * * * * *

I am obliged to say, too, that * * * the Government of this island has not been able to relieve from starvation the Cuban population driven from their homes by the Weyler edict, and no longer attempts to do so.

I am, etc., FITZHUGH LEE,
Consul-General.

Mr. Lee to Mr. Day.

UNITED STATES CONSULATE-GENERAL,
Havana, December 14, 1897.

SIR: I have the honor to report that I have received information that in the Province of Havana reports show that there have been 101,000 "reconcentrados," and that out of that 52,000 have died. Of the said 101,000, 32,000 were children. This excludes the city of Havana and seven other towns from which reports have not yet been made up. It is thought that the *total number* of "reconcentrados" in *Havana Province* will amount to 150,000, nearly all women and children, and that the death rate among their whole number from starvation alone will be over 50 per cent.

For the above number of "reconcentrados" $12,500, Spanish silver, was set aside out of the $100,000 appropriated for the purpose of relieving all the "reconcentrados" on the island. Seventy-five thousand of the 150,000 may be still living, so if *every* dollar appropriated of the $12,500 *reaches them* the distribution will average about 17 cents to a person, which, of course, will be rapidly exhausted, and, as I can hear of no further succor being afforded, it is easy to perceive what little practical relief has taken place in the condition of these poor people.

I am, etc., FITZHUGH LEE,
Consul-General.

Mr. Lee to Mr. Day.

UNITED STATES CONSULATE-GENERAL,
Havana, January 8, 1898.

SIR: I have the honor to state, as a matter of public interest, that the "reconcentrado order" of General Weyler, formerly Governor-General of this island, transformed about 400,000 self-supporting people, principally women and children, into a multitude to be sustained by the contributions of others or die of starvation or of fevers resulting from a low physical condition and being massed in large bodies without change of clothing and without food.

Their houses were burned, their fields and plant beds destroyed, and their live stock driven away or killed.

I estimate that probably 200,000 of the rural population in the Provinces of Pinar del Rio, Havana, Matanzas, and Santa Clara have died of staivation, or from resultant causes, and the deaths of whole families almost simultaneously, or within a few days of each other, and of mothers praying for their children to be relieved of their horrible sufferings by death, are not the least of the many pitiable scenes which were ever present. In the Provinces of Puerto Principe and Santiago de Cuba, where the "reconcentrado order" could not be enforced, the great mass of the people are self-sustaining.

A daily average of 10 cents' worth of food to 200,000 people would be an expenditure of $20,000 per day, and of course the most humane efforts upon the part of our citizens can not hope to accomplish such a gigantic relief, and a great portion of these people will have to be abandoned to their fate.

   *   *   *   *   *   *   ,

I am, etc.,   FITZHUGH LEE,
                                                  Consul-General.

Mr. Lee to Mr. Day.

UNITED STATES CONSULATE-GENERAL,
Havana, January 17, 1898.

SIR: I have the honor to transmit herewith some statistics sent me about the mortality in the town of Santa Clara, the capital of Santa Clara Province, situated about 33 miles south of Sagua, which numbers some 14,000 inhabitants. It will be noticed that there were about 5,489 deaths in that town in the seven years previous to 1897, which included 1,417 in one year from an epidemic of yellow fever, while in 1897, owing to the concentration order, there were 6,981. The concentration order went into effect in February. In that year, 1897, the month's death rate for January was 78, but in February, the first month of reconcentration, there were 114, and there has been a gradual increase since, as you will see, until in December, 1897, the number of deaths was 1,011. I refer to this as a specimen of the mortality on this island in consequence of the "reconcentrado order" of the late Captain and Governor-General Weyler.

I am, etc.,   FITZHUGH LEE,
                                                  Consul-General.

Consul-General Lee, February 10, 1898, incloses a statement of the condition of some small towns near Havana; says the reports were made by a person sent by him for the purpose.

MELENA DEL SUR

The unhealthy conditions of this town and the total want of resources make it impossible for the mayor to remedy the present miserable situation of the people, who die in great numbers from starvation, fever, and smallpox. * * * There are other towns in the same condition; Guines, Catalina, and Madruga, whose situation could be in a small degree relieved if the country people could be allowed to leave the town freely in search of food, which is very scarce. In some towns this is entirely prohibited; in others they are obliged to pay a tax; and not having anything to eat, how can they pay a tax? In every town you visit the first thing you notice is the unhealthy condition of the men and their total want of physical strength, which prevents them even from making an effort to procure the means of support.

CATALINE DE GUINES.

The condition of the reconcentrados in this town is very sad and desperate. There are no zones for cultivation, and they a·e therefore not allowed, even with a military pass, to leave the town in search of work or food, which latter is so scarce that one must walk 4 or 5 miles before finding a sweet potato. * * * In these districts the liberty given by General Blanco to the reconcentrados is a farce.

GUINES TOWN.

* * * In fifteen days 200 reconcentrados have died in Guines from starvation and total lack of resources. Many of the sick sleep on the floor and on piazzas.

General Lee, under date of March 14, incloses the following from Consul Barker:

"DEAR SIR: I will thank you to communicate to the Department as quickly as possible the fact that the military commander and other officers of the military positively refuse to allow the reconcentrados, to whom I am issuing food in its raw state, to procure fuel with which to cook this food. In addition, they prohibited this class of people (I am only giving food to about one-fifth of the destitute; the authorities have quit altogether) from gathering vegetables cultivated within the protection of the fort, telling them: 'The Americans propose to feed you, and to the Americans you must look.'"

General Lee, March 28:

"I have the honor to report that instructions have been given by the civil governor of Havana that the alcaldes and other authorities shall not give out any facts about the reconcentrados, and if any of the American relief committees should make any inquiries concerning them all such inquiries must be referred to him."

United States Consul Brice, Matanzas, November 17, 1897:

"* * * Starvation; no relief is yet afforded the starving thousands in this province. Several days ago an order from Captain Gin was given municipal authorities to issue rations and clothing, but no attention is paid to the order. * * * Death rate in this city over eighty persons daily, nearly all from want of food, medicines, and clothing. As I write this a dead negro woman lies in the street within 200 yards of this consulate, starved to death; died some time this morning, and will lie there maybe for days. The misery and destitution in this city and other towns in the interior are beyond description. A general order has been issued allowing reconcentrados to return to the country, but the restrictions placed in the order are such as to practically prohibit. If they went, what can they do without money, food, or shelter? The situation is indeed deplorable, and I am free to say no real help can be expected from the Spanish Government, and the fate of the remaining reconcentrados is lingering death from starvation."

Consul Brice, Matanzas, December 17, 1897:

"SIR: 1 have the honor to report the following Cuban news in this Province, taken from personal observation and reliable sources of information. Concentrados: Relief offered these and other poor people by Spanish authorities is only in name. * * * 2,000 rations were given out for a few days only to 8,000 persons. There are more than 12,000 starving in this city to-day. * * * Death rate has diminished somewhat; now about 63 daily. There are less people to die. The scenes of misery and distress daily are beyond belief. Here is one out of hundreds. In a family of seventeen living in an old lime-kiln all were found dead except three, and they barely alive. * * * General Blanco's order allowing reconcentrados, owners of plantations and farms, to return and cultivate crops, etc., is inoperative and of no avail. Several of our American citizens, owners of land, have repeatedly asked the civil governor of this Province for permission to return to their homes, and in every case refused or restrictions imposed impossible to comply with."

Consul Brice (from a circular letter dated January 8, 1898):

"* * * There are in Matanzas Province over 90,000 people who are in actual starvation condition. In addition to above, there are thousands of families of the better classes, formerly well to do, who to-day are living on one meal a day, and that very scant. They have sold or pawned their furniture, clothing, jewels, etc., to eke out an existence until all is gone, or nearly so. Too proud to beg, they suffer in silence, and many die of starvation. The daughter of a former governor of this Province was seen begging on the streets of the city. Many of these people call on me privately at my residence, praying for God's sake to be remembered when relief comes from the United States. It is to be hoped that this relief will come quickly, for hundreds are dying daily in this Province of starvation. Conditions are dreadful, and no relief afforded by Spanish authorities."

Santiago de Cuba, Consul Hyatt, December 21, 1897:

"I respectfully report that the sickness and the death rate on this island is appalling. Statistics make a grievous showing, but come far short of the truth. * * * Dr. Caminero, United States sanitary inspector, has just informed me that there are in this city over 12,000 people sick in bed, not counting those in military hospitals. This is at least 35 per cent of the present population. Quinine, the only remedy of avail, is sold ten times higher than in the States. Steamers coming to this port mostly give out soup once a day to the waiting throng. Fresh meat in our market sells from 50 cents to $1 a pound."

Consul Hyatt, of Santiago de Cuba, under date of January 8, 1898:

"Numerous dead bodies at the cemetery are carried over from day to day, because the sexton is unable to bury them, with his present corps of assistants, as fast as they come."

Consul Hyatt, Santiago de Cuba, January 12, 1898:

"* * * It is beyond the power of my pen to describe the situation in eastern Cuba. Squalidity, starvation, sickness, and death meet one in all places. Beggars swarm our doors and stop us on the street. The dead in large numbers remain over from day to day in the cemeteries unburied."

Consul Hyatt, Santiago de Cuba, January 22, 1898:

"* * * The military situation is completely overshadowed in importance by the starving, struggling mass whose cry is, 'Bread, or I perish.' This consulate is besieged to an extent that blocks the entrance and greatly retards business. They have heard that the people of the

United States are giving funds for their relief and have not the patience to wait. I could name three Americans here who contribute monthly over $300 toward feeding the poor, but it is nothing compared to the people's necessities. Men, women, and children, homeless and almost naked, roam the streets by day, begging of almost everyone they meet or door they pass, and sleeping at night almost anywhere they can find a place to lie down. If the present death rate is continued there would not be a soul left in the city at the end of five years. For the masses it is speedy help or sure death."

Same, under date of February 26, 1898:

"Rations are issued in a court attached to the consulate, the people being admitted by the police through a carriage driveway.

"As I write the street is blocked by the hungry throng for nearly a square above and below the entrance.

"Since writing this dispatch I have been informed that the ladies' relief committee have estimated that in this city alone the number who need help is 18,000."

(The rations referred to in the foregoing are the relief sent from the United States.)

Consul Barker, Sagua la Grande, November 20, 1897:

"While General Blanco has made known his purpose to relieve the concentrated people by allowing them to go out of the towns, I give the Department reasons why this permission will not give the relief claimed. While article 1 grants permission to this starving class to return to the country, article 3 abrogates it in exacting that to avail themselves of the privilege the places to which they go must be garrisoned. This will preclude over one-half of these poor unfortunates, for their homes are in ruins, and the sugar estates able to maintain a guard can care for but a small percentage of the whole. * * * I will not question the good intention of those now in power. It is a self-evident fact that the authorities are utterly helpless to extend any relief to those who have thus far survived the pangs of hunger. * * *

"So far as relates to this section of the island, the claim made by the Captain-General, in a letter to the Spanish minister in Washington, that 'extensive zones of cultivation had been organized, daily rations are provided by the State, work is furnished,' etc., is not borne out by my observation."

Consul Barker, Sagua la Grande, November 25, 1897:

"Sir: With reference to the distress and deaths in this consular district, embracing a large part of the territory of the province, appended is the official mortality list of each of the judicial districts comprising the province known as Cinco Villas (five towns), from January 1 to November 15, 1897, inclusive, as follows, viz:

Santa Clara	27,900
Sagua	16,583
Cienfuegos	14,263
Remedios	11,415
Sancti Espiritus	5,482
Trinidad	4,946
Total	80,589

"Add to this 25 per cent for the number of which no record has been kept, * * * I deem a conservative estimate will make the grand total 100,736 deaths. In truth, after talking with both military and judicial officers, I regard this rather under than above the actual deaths for the period stated. Undoubtedly one-half of the concentrated people have died, and to-day Spanish soldiers are companion victims to the surviving noncombatants. The inclosed slip (inclosure No. 1), showing the number of deaths—official—in the small municipal district of San Juan de la Yeras, will give some idea of the rapid increase from month to month, as will also the clippings (inclosure No. 2) cut from the local papers show that the authorities no longer conceal these facts, as was done under the retired Captain-General.

"This appalling death rate is mute, yet convincing proof of the terrible destruction of life under the *main* policy pursued in attempting to subjugate the island. The heavens, it would appear, weep for despoiled, distressed Cuba, for during the present month the fall of rain has been almost phenomenal. I have to reiterate, the authorities, however great the desire to do so, are utterly helpless to ameliorate the dire distress that must continue to increase.

" * * * Relative to furnishing protection to the mills to grind, how is it possible in view of the fact that the safeguard extended planters in making the previous crop enabled them to grind less than one-third of the usual yield, while the military force available to-day is not half in numbers as at that time. With me the conviction is firmly rooted that within sixty days 90 per cent of the populace will reach a state of craving hunger, without outside aid; nor do I feel that I am speaking chimerically when I include the rank and file of the Spanish army. The true status, as viewed at present, will bear out this opinion. The suffering among the troops, as well as the reconcentrados, simply beggars portrayal, while discontent ripens daily."

Consul Barker, Sagua la Grande, December 13, 1897:

" * * * I have within the past few days visited five of the principal railroad towns in this district. The destitution is simply too harrowing to recite, and must become intensified each day. The death rate for the last month shows an increase of about 25 per cent. In these towns I got my information from the mayors. I learned that while an issue of food running from three to five days had been made, beginning on the 28th ultimo, consisting of 3 ounces of bacon and jerked beef and 6 ounces rice for adults, with half this allowance for children under 14 years, the pittance was sufficient only for one-fourth to one-tenth of the starving.

"The mayors of Santa Clara, Cruces, and Santo Domingo are authority for stating the Captain-General had ordered that after the 8th instant any issue of food to the concentrados be discontinued. * * * The mayor of Santa Clara stated to me that the Captain-General directed him to call on the commissary of the army for 5,000 rations for relief purposes, which, he said, was sufficient to feed the suffering people but one day. The officer's answer was he could not do so, as all Government supplies on hand would be required to feed the army. The mayor stated also that, in presenting this order to the military commander, he was ordered by him under no circumstances to give food to anyone having relatives in the insurrection, which, he said, would exclude 75 per cent of the destitute. * * * All efforts so far to obtain relief by popular subscription have met with signal failure. The Cubans are too poverty stricken, while the Spaniards who own the wealth will contribute nothing. * * *"

Consul Barker, Sagua, December 8, 1897, states that food, medicine, and clothing are required by more than 50,000 persons in his consular district, and that a reliable estimate of the starving in the Sagua Province is 100,000. * * *

Consul Barker, Sagua la Grande, January 31, 1898:

"Relative to citizens of the United States residing in this consular district, the new administration's progress and repudiation concerning the abuses in vogue under the former régime reveal the following facts: Of those herded in the garrison towns none have been allowed to return to their landed estates. Some few did venture to go to their farms, under a pledge of protection from the military commander of the province, to whom I will not impute bad faith, and were driven off by guerrillas.

"At my suggestion several Americans returned to the American-owned 'Central Santiana,' the owner having been forced to abandon property. Although a Government guard is stationed at the place, they (former tenants) were ordered to leave. Application was made to the military commander for authority to return unmolested, and it was refused. Over two months since two of our citizens notified me they had discovered in possession of the local guerrillas ten or twelve head of their horses. I addressed the military commander, asking, on proof of ownership, their stock be restored. Nothing has been done, while these American citizens, both in affluence at the breaking out of the rebellion, are to-day dependent upon charity. * * *"

Consul Barker, Sagua la Grande, March 12, 1898:

" * * * About a week since I received the first shipment of supplies, about 20 $tons$, being sent from Havana under direction of the Red Cross branch in that city. All this I distributed among 10 of the 22 towns I had managed to investigate, using none for Sagua. * * * About sixty days ago the mayors of these towns furnished, by request, this office with the number they claimed as actually destitute in their several municipal districts, which footed up over 50,000 persons. Estimating a decrease from death of 10.000 would leave, say, 40,000. * * *"

Consul Barker, Sagua la Grande, March 14, 1898:

"The inclosed letter from Mr. Valle, whom I have every reason to believe will not misrepresent the case, * * * shows that I have underestimated the number in my jurisdiction in need of relief. I beg to increase the amount required, as stated in my No. 294, from 80 to 100 tons a month."

(Letter referred to implored medicines and provisions.)

Consul Barker, Sagua la Grande, March 24, 1898:

"Closer investigation discloses larger number destitute than estimate sent. Fifty tons needful now. Distress far greater than my reports show."

Consul Barker, Sagua la Grande, March 24, 1898:

"SIR: I visited seat of government of this province, Santa Clara, where I learned * * * that the number of persons in actual want exceeds any estimate I have sent to the Department. The distress is simply heartrending; whole families without clothing to hide nakedness, sleeping on the bare ground without bedding of any kind, without food save such as we have been able to reach with provisions sent by our noble people; and the most distressing feature is that fully 50 per cent are ill, without medical attention or medicine. * * * I have found the civil governor willing to lend every aid in his power, but he admits he can do nothing but assist with his civil officers in expediting the relief sent from the United States. The military obstruct in every way possible."

Translation of the articles of General Blanco's proclamation of the 30th March, 1898, suspending the reconcentration.

ARTICLE 1. From the publication of the present proclamation (bando) in the Gazette of Havana the reconcentration of country people throughout the island is hereby terminated, and they are authorized to return with their families to their homes, and to dedicate themselves to all kinds of agricultural labors.

ARTICLE 2. The boards of relief and all civil and military authorities shall furnish them the means within their power to enable the rural population to return to their former places of residence, or those which they may now select, facilitating them the aid which they may respectively dispose.

ARTICLE 3. At the instance of the council of secretaries, and through the department of public works, the preparation and immediate realization of all public works necessary and useful to furnish work and food to the country people and their families who, through lack of means, truck farms, or want of agricultural implements, may not be able to return immediately to the fields, shall be proceeded with, as well as the establishment of soup kitchens, which may settle and cheapen such services.

ARTICLE 4. The expenses which the compliance with this proclamation (bando) may originate, as far as they may exceed the means disposed of by the boards of relief, shall be charged to the extraordinary war credit.

ARTICLE 5. All previous instructions issued regarding the reconcentration of the country people, and all others which may be in opposition to the compliance of this proclamation, are hereby derogated.

Havana, March 3, 1898.

RAMON BLANCO.

REPORT OF THE SPANISH NAVAL BOARD OF INQUIRY AS TO THE CAUSE OF THE DESTRUCTION OF THE U. S. B. S. MAINE.

[Translation.]

No. 33.] LEGATION OF SPAIN IN WASHINGTON,
Washington, April 2, 1898.

MR. SECRETARY: I have the honor, by order of my Government, to transmit to your excellency the full testimony in the inquiry instituted by the maritime authority of the Havana station by reason of the catastrophe which befell the United States ironclad *Maine* in that port in the night of the 15th of February last, which awful misfortune to the American people has been so deeply and sincerely lamented by the Spanish Government and people.

I improve this opportunity, Mr. Secretary, to reiterate to your excellency the assurances of my highest consideration.

LOUIS POLO DE BERNABE.

To the Hon. JOHN SHERMAN,
Secretary of State of the United States of America, etc.

[Translation.]

STATION OF HAVANA, 1898.

COMPLETE EVIDENCE IN THE PRELIMINARY PROCEEDINGS IN-AUGURATED ON THE OCCASION OF THE CATASTROPHE WHICH BEFELL THE NORTH AMERICAN IRONCLAD MAINE, IN THE HARBOR OF HAVANA, ON THE NIGHT OF FEBRUARY 15, 1898.

Judge in charge of the preparation of the case: Captain Don Pedro del Peral y Caballero.

Secretary: Lieutenant Don Javier de Salas y Gonzalez.

I, Don Francisco Javier de Salas y Gonzalez, lieutenant of the first class, secretary of the preliminary proceedings instituted in consequence of the blowing up of the North American ironclad *Maine*, of which court Captain Don Pedro Peral y Caballero is the judge in charge, proceeded to take the whole evidence in the case, which I certify, and it is as follows:

STATION OF HAVANA, 1898.

PRELIMINARY PROCEEDINGS INSTITUTED IN CONSEQUENCE OF THE EXPLOSION WHICH TOOK PLACE ON THE NORTH AMERICAN IRON-CLAD MAINE ON THE NIGHT OF FEBRUARY 15, 1898.

The proceedings began on the same date. The judge in charge, Captain Don Pedro de Peral. Secretary, Lieutenant Don Javier de Salas. A seal with the words: "Office of the Naval Commandant-General of the Station of Havana. Department of Justice."

An explosion, followed by the burning of the North American ironclad *Maine*, having occurred in this harbor at thirty-five minutes past nine o'clock to-night, and in view of the urgency of the case and the want of officers, aides of the naval commandant, at the present moment, your excellency will proceed, in the capacity of judge in charge, to institute the proper proceedings, in conformity with the provisions of the law of naval military procedure now in force; and you will designate an officer to act in the capacity of secretary of the proceedings.

God preserve your excellency.

Havana, February 15, 1898. Captain Don Pedro del Peral y Caballero.

HAVANA, *February 15, 1898.*

Let this be recorded as the beginning of these proceedings.

PEDRO DEL PERAL. [Rubricated.]

APPOINTMENT OF SECRETARY.

By virtue of the powers conferred upon me by the authority having jurisdiction in the case in appointing me judge in charge, I hereby appoint Lieutenant Don Francisco Javier de Salas, who possesses the necessary qualifications, secretary to act as such in this case.

Havana, February 15, 1898. PEDRO DEL PERAL. [Rubricated.]

SECRETARY'S OATH.

HAVANA, *February 15, 1898.*

Lieutenant Don Francisco de Salas being present, I notified him of the appointment given him; and he, upon being informed of it, accepts it and swears to discharge its duties well and faithfully, and signs these presents in witness thereof.

PEDRO DEL PERAL. [Rubricated.]
JAVIER DE SALAS. [Rubricated.]

DECREE.

HAVANA, *February 15, 1898.*

The judge in charge ordered the letter of appointment of the judge in charge to be annexed to these proceedings, and directed that the eye-witnesses of the occurrence and those persons who, by reason of their duties, ought to be best informed as to the event, be summoned. His honor gave this order before me, the secretary, who certify it.

PEDRO DEL PERAL. [Rubricated.]
JAVIER DE SALAS. [Rubricated.]

RECORD.

HAVANA, *February 15, 1898.*

A respectful letter was addressed to the authority having jurisdiction in the case, notifying him that Lieutenant Don Javier de Salas has been appointed secretary for these proceedings, and requesting his approval. I certify it.

PERAL. [Rubricated.]
JAVIER DE SALAS. [Rubricated.]

DECREE.

HAVANA, *February 15, 1898.*

His honor ordered that his excellency, the governor-general of the island, be requested to furnish an official interpreter that he may render assistance at the time of the depositions of the officers and sailors of the American man-of-war *Maine*, if he has one available. His honor gave this order before me, the secretary, who certify it.

JAVIER DE SALAS. [Rubricated.]
PEDRO DEL PERAL. [Rubricated.]

PROCEEDINGS.

HAVANA, *February 15, 1898.*

A respectful letter was addressed to the superior authority of the island in execution of the foregoing decree. I certify it.

JAVIER DE SALAS. [Rubricated.]
PERAL. [Rubricated.]

TESTIMONY OF ENSIGN DON MANUEL TAMAYO.

At Havana, February 15, 1898, the officer mentioned in the margin appeared before the judge in the presence of the secretary. His honor admonished him of his duty, to be truthful, and reminded him of the penalties which he would incur for the crime of perjury; after which he took the proper oath, and being questioned in conformity with article 142 of the Law of Naval Military Procedure, said that his name is Don Manuel Tamayo y Orellano, unmarried, 26 years of age, a native of Cadiz, and that he has no interest in the case which is being tried.

Being asked to state all that he knows with regard to the explosion which occurred an hour ago on the American man-of-war *Maine*, he said that, happening to be the officer of the deck on board the cruiser *Alfonso XII*, he heard, at about half past nine o'clock, an explosion in some place very near his ship, which turned out to proceed from the ironclad *Maine*, which was anchored very near, and which at that moment was on the port side (of the *Alfonso XII*). Immediately cries for help were heard, whereupon all the boats which were in the water, together with the fifth boat, were sent to the place of the disaster, as well as all the private boats which were within hail of the ship, and succeeded in rescuing from the water twenty-nine persons, most of them severely injured, who were conducted to the sick bay of the ship and were properly attended to.

All the efforts made to save more persons proved fruitless, as no others were seen in the water and nobody replied to the shouts which the boats directed to the ironclad, it being impossible to jump on board on account of the continuous explosions and the imminent danger incurred in the vicinity of the vessel owing to the increase of the flames, as, for a few minutes after the first explosion, which was the loudest, the ship remained in utter darkness, without any flames on the outside, though they appeared a little afterwards. When the first boats returned with the injured men they said that the ship had sunk by the bow, with a great deal of injury to the rigging and on the outside, and that boats from the *Legaspi* had come to her aid. The wounded men, when questioned by the witness, said that they could not imagine how the catastrophe had occurred. Being asked whether the boats of his ship patrolled the bay every day, the witness said that one boat of the *Alfonso XII* patrolled every day from sunset to dawn, and that at the time of the explosion the eighth boat, commanded by the second-class sailor, José Lopez Sanchez, was on guard.

Being asked what instructions that commander had, he said that he had general instructions to keep watch in the bay to prevent the traffic of boats not subject to the provisions of the law, and special instructions to pay the greatest attention to the vicinity of the new floating dock.

Being asked whether any violent quivering was felt on board his ship at the moment of the explosion, similar to that which is experienced during earthquakes, he said that nothing was felt except the concussion of the noise, but that the ship experienced no violent shock.

Being asked whether he has any clue by which he can form an opinion as to the cause of the explosion, either from what he has heard or from what he himself has seen, he replied that, although he saw the explosion, he can not say what caused it, nor has he heard anyone say anything that could throw any light on the matter.

Being asked whether the *Maine* was lighted by electricity, he replied that she was.

Being asked whether he knows whether any exercise was being practiced on board the American vessel at the time of the accident, he said he did not know, but that during the day they appeared to him to be drilling, as he saw movements among her guns.

At this point this deposition was suspended, with the reservation of the right to continue it if necessary. The witness read it for himself, affirmed and ratified its contents, and signed it in witness thereof, together with the judge, in the presence of the secretary, who certifies it.

MANUEL TAMAYO. [Rubricated.]
PEDRO DEL PERAL. [Rubricated.]
JAVIER DE SALAS. [Rubricated.]

TESTIMONY OF THE CHIEF BOATSWAIN, DON NICANOR MAURIS.

At Havana on the 15th February, 1898, appeared the person mentioned in the margin, who, being informed as to what he was about to be questioned, swore to tell the truth, the judge calling his attention to the penalties incurred by those giving false testimony, and being asked the usual questions prescribed by the law, he said that his name is Nicanor Mauris y Garrote, chief boatswain, married, a native of Galicia, of full age, employed in the San Fernando Shears-House with the duties of his rank, and that he is not directly or indirectly interested in the case which is being tried.

Being asked to state all that he knows with regard to the explosion which took place on the North American ship *Maine*, he said that, after 9.30 p. m., he heard a violent explosion in the bay; that he left his house immediately, and saw that it had taken place on the *Maine;* he noticed that a number of lights were ascending in a nearly vertical direction, lights of red and blue colors, which exploded with little noise and without much force. The ship was in the dark at that moment, but, a little afterwards, flames became visible, and detonation resembling those of small shells, like revolver shells, began to be heard. Immediately after the explosion the boats were manned by order of the commandant of the shears, and went to the place of the accident, returning with two wounded men in one boat and four in another, and on the second trip, with three in one boat and two in the other. These injured men were immediately attended to in the barracks of the shears.

Being asked whether, at the moment of the explosion, he perceived a violent agitation of the ground, similar, if not in its intensity, at least in its effects, to that produced by earthquakes, he said that he did not, that he noticed only the noise and the brightness (illumination).

Being asked whether any articles hurled up by the explosion fell in the shears yard, he replied, "No, nor in the neighborhood either."

Being asked whether he knows anything or has heard anything said as to the causes of the catastrophe, he replied that he knew nothing and has heard nothing said.

At this point this deposition was suspended, with the reservation of the right to continue it, if necessary. The witness read it, affirmed and ratified its contents, and signed it, with the judge, in the presence of the secretary, who certifies it.

NICANOR MAURIS. |Rubricated.]
PEDRO DEL PERAL. [Rubricated.]
JAVIER DE SALAS. [Rubricated.]

TESTIMONY OF FIRST LIEUTENANT DON JULIO PEREZ Y PERERA.

At Havana, on the 15th February, 1898, appeared in this court the officer mentioned in the margin, who, after being informed as to what he was about to be questioned, swore to tell the truth, and was admonished as to the penalties incurred by those giving false testimony.

Being asked the questions prescribed by the law, he said that his name is Don Julio Perez y Perera, first lieutenant in the navy, now in command of the machina (shears) of San Fernando, married, and of full age.

Being requested to state all that he knew with regard to the explosion on the *Maine*, he said that he was standing at the door of his house, situated facing the bay, of one story, on the lands of the navy, near the machina of San Fernando, and that, as he was necessarily looking toward the place where the *Maine* was anchored, he saw a most brilliant illumination ascending from the ship at the same time that a terrible explosion occurred; that afterwards, hearing shrieks and seeing smoke, he took the necessary steps to succor the victims who might be found.

Being asked whether he had any clue from which the causes of the catastrophe might be conjectured, he said that he had none, but that he thought that it had its origin in one of the magazines of the ship, from the shape in which he saw the smoke, the illumination, and the colored gases rise in the air.

Being asked if he noticed any upward movement in the water around the vessel, he replied that the bay was perfectly smooth, and that he saw no movement in the water nor any disturbance.

At this point the present deposition was suspended, the witness read it, affirmed and ratified its contents, and signed it, with the judge, in the presence of the secretary, who certifies it.

                          JULIO PEREZ Y PERERA. [Rubricated.]
PEDRO DEL PERAL. [Rubricated.]
JAVIER DE SALAS. [Rubricated.]

TESTIMONY OF ENSIGN DON JUAN RAPALLO.

At Havana, on the 15th February, 1898, appeared in this court the officer mentioned in the margin, who was notified as to what he was about to be questioned, and swore to tell the truth, his attention being called to the penalties incurred by those giving false testimony, and, being asked the questions prescribed by the law, he said that his name is Don Juan Rapallo y Ortis, ensign in the navy, serving on the cruiser *Alfonso XII*, unmarried, of full age.

Being requested to state what he knew with regard to the event in question, he said that while he was resting in the cabin of the ship he heard a tremendous explosion, the locality of which he could not even conjecture; that he went on deck immediately, and saw the *Maine* sending up flames and heard loud shrieks for help coming from her; that all the available boats were sent from his ship and the projectors were lighted.

Being asked whether he had formed any opinion as to the causes of the catastrophe, he replied that he thought that an explosion had been begun in the magazines of the ship, more probably in the torpedo magazine than in that of the shells and ammunition.

Being asked whether he had seen that day any manœuvre or movement indicating that some drill was being conducted, he said that he had seen to-day a kind of preparation for battle, in which all the guns and the boat drill had a part.

At this point this deposition was suspended; the witness read it, affirmed and ratified its contents, and signed it with the judge in charge, in the presence of the secretary, who certifies it.

                          JUAN RAPALLO. [Rubricated.]
PEDRO DEL PERAL. [Rubricated.]
JAVIER DE SALAS. [Rubricated.]

TESTIMONY OF THE SAILOR JOSÉ BALECIRO REY.

At Havana, on the 15th February, 1898, appeared the person mentioned in the margin, who was informed as to what he was about to be questioned, and swore to tell the truth. His attention was called to the penalties incurred by those giving false testimony, and being asked the questions prescribed by law, he said that his name is José Baleciro Rey, sailor of the second class in the crew of the *Alfonso XII*, unmarried, 20 years of age, and that he has no direct or indirect interest in this case.

Being asked to state all that he knew with regard to the explosion on the *Maine*, he said that he was on duty in the port gangway and saw the *Maine* on her starboard side; that, at exactly half past nine o'clock, he heard a drum beat (toque) on board the American, as if for silence, and that it wanted a few minutes of being a quarter to 10 o'clock, when he heard a tremendous explosion, and saw a very great blaze, like that of many skyrockets, going directly upwards, and then they scattered; that it ascended from about the center of the ship, although, at first, he did not know, and had no idea, whence it came; that the ship then became dark, and that, near the gangway where he was, a thing resembling a large splinter fell in the water, and that, immediately afterwards, he saw fire on the American man-of-war, which was already sinking, although it did not appear so at first, and that all the boats were immediately sent from his ship, and brought back injured men.

Being asked whether he noticed any movement in the water, he said that he did not.

At this point, this deposition was suspended; the witness read it for himself, affirmed and ratified its contents, and signed it with the judge and secretary, who certifies it.

JOSÉ BALECIRO REY. [Rubricated.]

PEDRO DEL PERAL. [Rubricated.]
JAVIER DE SALAS. [Rubricated.]

TESTIMONY OF THE SAILOR JOSÉ CRESTAR ZARALDO.

At Havana, on the 15th February, 1898, appeared in this court the person mentioned in the margin, who was informed as to what he was about to be questioned and swore to tell the truth. His attention was called to the penalties incurred by those giving false testimony, and being asked the questions prescribed by law, he said that his name is José Crestar Zaraldo, sailor of the second class, apprentice gunner in the crew of the *Alfonso XII*, 19 years of age.

Being requested to state what he knew as to the catastrophe which occurred on board the *Maine*, he said that he was on duty at the castle since 8 o'clock at night, and that all at once, at a little past half past nine, he heard a very loud explosion, and saw a very bright blaze, which dazzled him at first, but that he then saw that it was on the *Maine*.

At this moment the ship was seen to sink, and then explosions were heard, continuing for some time; boats were ordered off from the vessel and returned with wounded men. Being asked whether he noticed any movement in the water, he replied that he did not; that it continued as calm as before.

Thereupon this declaration was closed, and having read it through, and having affirmed and sworn to its contents, and signed the same in proof thereof, together with the judge and the undersigned secretary, who certifies to the same.

JOSÉ CRESTAR. [Rubric.]

PEDRO DEL PERAL. [Rubric.]
JAVIER DE SALAS. [Rubric.]

DECLARATION OF THE SEAMAN JOSÉ GALLEGO CARRERAS.

At Havana on February 15, 1898, appeared before the judge the person named in the margin who, being advised of the interrogatories to be put to him, swore that he would give true testimony and also having been warned of the penalty of perjury and being asked the general interrogatories required by law, declared that his name was José Gallego Carreras, first-class seaman of the crew of the *Alfonso XII*, and artillery apprentice; that he was 19 years old, a native of Mesgardos, province of Coruña.

Being requested to tell what he knew concerning the *Maine* disaster, he replied that he was on watch at the starboard gangway, and that, as the *Maine* was on the other side, he only noticed a very loud explosion, a great deal of smoke mingled with shining sparks and that he heard and saw nothing more.

Thereupon this declaration was closed, which the declarant read, and affirmed and swore to the same and signed the same with the judge and the undersigned secretary who certifies to the same.

JOSÉ GALLEGO. [Rubric.]

PEDRO DEL PERAL. [Rubric.]
JAVIER DE SALAS. [Rubric.]

HAVANA, *February 16, 1898.*

NOTE.—Don Luis Freixedas, interpreter of the Government, having appeared in consequence of the summons on page 4, was ordered to appear on the next day, and note is made of the same to which I, as secretary, certify.

JAVIER DE SALAS. [Rubric.]
PERAL. [Rubric.]

ORDERS.

HAVANA, *February 16, 1898.*

His honor directed that the consul of the United States should be requested, through H. E. the commandant general, to allow the presence in this court of certain officers and seamen of the crew of the *Maine*, survivors of the catastrophe, in order that their testimony might be taken in the present case. Thus his honor directs, in the presence of me, secretary, to which I certify. The interlined part is genuine.

JAVIER DE SALAS. [Rubric.]
PEDRO DEL PERAL. [Rubric.]

HAVANA, *February 16, 1898.*

NOTE.—Due notice was given the supreme authority with a view to carrying out the previous orders of the court.

JAVIER DE SALAS. [Rubric.]
PERAL. [Rubric.]

NOTE OF THE TESTIMONY OF DEPUTY HEALTH INSPECTOR OF THE NAVY DON JUAN LOPEZ PEREZ.

At Havana, on February 16, 1898, appeared before the judge and the undersigned secretary, the officer named in the margin, who, being advised of the interrogatories which were to be put to him, swore that he would give true testimony, and having been warned of the punishment due to perjury, and having been asked the general interrogatories required by law, replied that his name was Don Juan Lopez Perez; that he was of age, and deputy health inspector of the first class of the navy, and at the present time chief of the branch at the station.

Being asked to declare what number of wounded men coming from the disaster on the *Maine* he attended during the last night, and in regard to the nature of the wounds which he tended, he said that he assisted in and directed the attendance of all the wounded that came to the "Machina," giving his attention on the arrival of an adequate medical personnel to organizing the ambulance and direction services as chief of the health service at the station. Being asked whether he was able to attend to all these cases with all the requisite implements, he said "Yes," for besides the supplies of the navy, the army, and the fire brigade several private pharmacists supplied at once whatever was needed. Being asked whether he has heard either the said wounded people or the persons communicating with them say anything in relation to the cause that may have occasioned the disaster, he said that he does not know English, but he heard one of the wounded men say that the cause of the event was the blowing up of the powder magazine, a declaration which I did not understand directly for the reason above given, but which I knew by the medium of a civilian acquainted with the language, who was there.

Being asked whether he can give any information as to who that civilian was and whether he remembered the wounded man who made the statement, he said that it was impossible for him to say accurately anything, for at that time of confusion he endeavored chiefly to attend to the organization of the service. Being asked whether he knows approximately the number of wounded men attended under his direction, he said that approximately some twenty-five were attended in the "Machina," he directing that the most seriously hurt be transported to the San Ambrosio hospital, and that those less hurt be transported to that of Alfonso XIII, the injuries being generally the result of wide but not deep burns.

At this stage this declaration was suspended, the witness reading it, fully affirming it, and ratifying its contents and signing it with the judge in the presence of the secretary, who certified it.

JUAN LOPEZ PEREZ. [Sign manual.]

PEDRO DEL PERAL. [Sign manual.]
JAVIER DE SAAS. [Sign manual.]

ORDER.

At Havana, on the sixteenth of February, one thousand eight hundred and ninety-eight, his honor determined to address a polite official note to the jurisdictional authority requesting for an examination of the bottom of the American ship the requisite authority and assistance. So his honor dictated before me, the secretary, who certifies.

JAVIER DE SAAS. [Sign manual.]
PERAL. [Sign manual.]

MINUTES.

At Havana, on the sixteenth of February, one thousand eight hundred and ninety-eight, there was delivered to the most excellent commander-general of the station a polite note, in compliance with and to the ends of the beforegoing order. I so certify.

JAVER DE SAAS. [Sign manual.]
PERAL. [Sign manual.]

DEPOSITION OF THE CHIEF SURGEON OF THE FLEET D, AUGUSTIN MACHORRO.

At Havana, on the sixteenth of February, one thousand eight hundred and ninety-eight, appeared before this court the officer named in the margin, who, being advised of the object for which his deposition was wanted, swore to tell the truth, he being reminded of the penalties incurred by those who give false testimony, and being asked the usual question, declared himself his name to be Don Augustin Machorro y Amenabar, of full age, physician in chief of the navy, employed on board of the gunboat *Magallanes*, and married.

When asked whether he treated any of the wounded men from the *Maine*, and was directed, if so, to tell the number and kind of the wounds, as well as all that he knew in connection with the disaster, he said that from the first moment when he was present on board of the Machina he treated several of the wounded, all of them belonging to the crew of the ironclad *Maine*, that they presented, as their general character, extensive and superficial burns, which covered almost all the exposed parts, principally face, arms, and legs; that after he had finished treating those who were on board of the Machina, in which he was assisted by several other physicians belonging to the staff, that they likewise went on board of the cruiser *Alfonso XII*, where he also treated persons who had received similar injuries; that he afterwards went on board of the American steamer *City of Washington*, where he saw 24 seamen who had received slight wounds, almost all of them being burns and contusions which had been treated by the physicians attached to the *Maine*, who was already there; that those who were treated by him personally were 4 or 5 on board of the Machina and the same number on board of the *Alfonso XII*, although we can not state the precise number. As to the causes, he was unable to say what they were, and when he asked the surgeon on board the American war ship, that surgeon told him the same thing.

This deposition stopped here and the deponent read it and ratified its contents, signing it with his honor the judge and with me, the clerk of the court, who certify.

AUGUSTIN MACHORRA. [Flourish.]

PEDRO DEL PARAL. [Flourish.]

JAVIER DE SALAS. [Flourish.]

DEPOSITION OF THE PHYSICIAN IN CHIEF OF THE NAVY, DON GABRIEL LOPEZ MARTIN.

In the city of Havana, on the 16th of February, 1898, appeared before this court the aforesaid officer, who, being reminded of the reason why his deposition was needed, made oath that he would tell the truth, and having been informed of the penalties incurred by a person who bears false testimony, he was asked the usual preliminary questions. He said that his name was Don Gabriel Lopez Martin; that he was physician in chief of the navy, employed at this naval station; that he was married, and of full age.

Being asked whether he attended the wounded men yesterday who had received their wounds in consequence of the disaster to the *Maine*, and what was the number and kind of said wounds, and being requested to tell all that he knew in connection with the matter, he said that when he heard the explosion, in his house in the navy-yard where he was, and suspecting that it might be some accident of importance in the bay, which he did judging from the direction in which he saw the light of the explosion, he went to the commandant of the navy-yard, and having there been informed of the orders received from the commandant-general, he went on board of the Machina and went to her commander, placing himself at his orders, and went to the part of the vessel occupied by the sailors where the wounded were lodged, treating those who were brought on board after he arrived at 2 o'clock a. m., treating some 15 or 20 extensive burns of all grades and in all parts of the body, caused, for the most part, by the direct action of the flames; he observed in some of them the implantation of grains of powder in various parts of their bodies.

When asked whether he had seen in any seaman or wounded man anything that could throw light upon the causes of the disaster, he said that he heard from a person who acted as interpreter that the causes of the disaster were not known, and that he heard 3 or 4 of the wounded men say that they had no precise knowledge of the fact; that only one, the last one treated, whose wound was less serious, said that it must have been caused by the explosion of a powder magazine; that he did not remember who the person was who acted as interpreter, nor did he remember who the wounded man was; but he thought that he was taken immediately afterwards to the Hospital of San Ambrosio.

This deposition stopped here; deponent read it, ratified its contents, and signed it with his honor the judge and with me, the clerk of the court, who certifies.

GABRIEL LOPEZ. [Flourish.]
PEDRO DEL PARAL. [Flourish.]
JAVIER DE SALAS. [Flourish.]

DEPOSITION OF DON GUILLERMO FERRAGUT, NAVAL ENSIGN.

In the city of Havana, on the 16th of February, 1898, appeared the aforesaid officer, who, being admonished concerning that which he was to be questioned upon, made oath that he would tell the truth. He was then reminded of the penalties incurred by anyone who testifies falsely, and being asked the usual preliminary questions, he said that his name was Don Guillermo Ferragut y Sbort, a native of Palma, Majorca, 22 years of age, unmarried, naval ensign, doing duty on board of the war transport *Legazpi*, which anchored in the bay last night near to the *Maine*.

When asked to state what he knew concerning the case before the court, he said that he was doing guard duty on board of his vessel, which was anchored very near the *Maine*, and that being in the officers' room at about half past 9 o'clock p. m., he heard a great noise, accompanied by a very bright light, which was caused beyond a doubt by a tremendous explosion, and also by the fall of objects on board and by the falling of a great number of glasses, which from the very first led him to suppose that a disaster had occurred on board. A moment's reflection, however, was sufficient to convince him that the disaster had not occurred on board of his own vessel. He immediately ran up on deck and got there in time to see the things thrown into the air by the explosion. It produced a horrible effect upon him to see the *Maine* all on fire, while continual detonations and explosions of minor importance were going on, these latter explosions succeeding the first great one. He quickly ran to rouse the crew and they were already up and came to meet him, all of them without one exception, being desirous to lend their services at once. They immediately went in the fishing boat and the fifth boat, being unable to go in the third boat because that was entirely submerged. They got into the boats with extraordinary rapidity; less than five minutes elapsed between the time of the explosion and the time when the last of the boats was there rendering aid. It was afterwards learned that our boats were the first to arrive. We sent our small boat to the side of the Machina in case the captain of that vessel desired to come on board. Being asked whether at the time when the explosion took place, or soon afterwards, he had observed any motion in the water and whether the vessel suffered any shock or shaking up thereby, he said that he had not noticed anything of the kind whatever. Being asked what further measures he took, he said: That with the men who remained with him he cleared the vessel to make ready for a fire because many inflammable objects kept falling on board of the *Legazpi.*

As soon as these precautions had been taken, he observed that the third boat was sinking because a board had been knocked out of it, whereupon he ordered that every effort should be made to prevent its loss; that the damage was caused by a piece of iron apparently from a platform such as those which are used for getting on board, and that also a large piece fell on the awning, which, owing to the fact that it was seen at once, caused only a few burns and other slight injuries; moreover, many glasses in the skylights were broken. The boats of the vessel lent, according to the statements of the men in charge of them, the following services: The first made fast to the *Maine* aft, took up a wounded man, three of the third boat, and three more from one of the American boats, without allowing it to make fast alongside; in view of the fact that the surgeon of the vessel was on shore, he sent it to the infirmary of the Machina. He made another trip without any result. The fifth, which was the first that left, found on its trip two men in the water, whom it picked up, and on reaching the vessel, another, whom it turned over to the first boat.

After an explosion, which was one of those that followed, an officer of the ship from the *Maine,* speaking Spanish, ordered them not to remain fastened alongside. The *Chinchorro* (fishing boat) took up 7 men, one of whom was very seriously wounded, and took them on board; they were supplied with clothing and were sent to the Machina to have their wounds treated. All the boats, moreover, went around the vessel several times for the purpose of exploration and then they all retired; ours did the same. A boat of the *Maine* afterwards came alongside with 4 sailors in it, who were supplied with clothing by the Spanish seamen, who gave them their own, and who also gave them brandy, and sent them to the Machina in one of the ship's boats, the boat of the *Maine* remaining on board.

This deposition stopped here. Deponent read all of it, ratified its contents, and signed it with his honor the judge and with the present clerk of the court who certifies.

Guillermo Ferragut. [Flourish.]

Pedro del Paral. [Flourish.]
Javier de Salas. [Flourish.]

JUDICIAL ACT.

In the city of Havana, on the 16th of February, 1898, the bay was searched in order to see if anything from the explosion could be found. Remnants of the vessel were found, but no dead fish, which formed the principal object of this inspection, the result of which is hereby judicially stated.

Javier de Salas. [Flourish.]
Paral. [Flourish.]

ORDER.

In the city of Havana, on the 16th of February, 1898, his honor the judge having received a communication from the warden of the morgue stating that it was extremely urgent that the bodies which had accumulated in that establishment from on board the *Maine* should be buried at once, his honor decided to append said communication to the other papers in this case, and to state in reply that in anticipation of this case his excellency the commandant-general of the naval station has already, in all probability, made suitable arrangements, he having been consulted in concert with the United States consul. His honor so ordered before me the notary who certifies.

JAVIER DE SALAS. [Flourish.]
PARAL. [Flourish.]

JUDICIAL ACT.

HAVANA, February 16, 1898.

A communication was sent to the officer in charge of the morgue, containing the foregoing order, and his communication was added to the other papers in this case. I certify.

JAVIER DE SALAS. [Flourish.]

DEPOSITION OF JOSÉ LOPEZ SANCHEZ, SEAMAN.

In the city of Havana, on the 16th of February, 1898, appeared before this court the above-named person, who, having been told concerning what he was to be questioned about, made oath that he would tell the truth, having been warned of the penalty incurred by any witness who declares falsely. Having been asked the usual preliminary questions, he said that his name was José Lopez Sanchez; a second-class seaman belonging to the crew of the *Alfonso XII;* 21 years of age, and unmarried. He stated that he had no interest whatever in the case before the court.

Being asked whether he was in charge of the boat which made the round, he said "Yes." Being asked what instructions he had and whether he was under instructions to watch the bay, he said "Yes, and principally near to the dock." That near the dock and without seeing the *Maine* they heard the explosion, thinking that it was in the dock; but as soon as they saw that it was the American ship they went near it to see if their assistance was needed. When asked whether he observed any motion of the waters he said that he had observed none.

This deposition stopped here. It was then read by the clerk of the court and the deponent ratified it, making the sign of the cross, because he was unable to write, with his honor the judge and the present clerk of the court, who certifies.

[A cross.]

PEDRO DEL PARAL. [Flourish.]
JAVIER DE SALAS. [Flourish.]

ORDER.

In the city of Havana, on the 16th of February, 1898, his honor the judge, thinking proper to hear the commandants of engineers and artillery of the naval station and the commandant of the torpedo brigade, in order that he might form a more correct opinion of the fact, resolved to convoke them in a meeting on the 17th instant at 9 a. m. It was so ordered by his honor before me, the secretary, who certifies.

JAVIER DE SALAS. [Flourish.]
PARAL. [Flourish.]

JUDICIAL ACT.

HAVANA, *February 16, 1898.*

Communications were addressed to the commandant of the navy-yard and the commandant of the torpedo brigade for the purpose stated in the foregoing order. I certify.

JAVIER DE SALAS. [Flourish.]
PARAL. [Flourish.]

DEPOSITION OF ENQIQUE IGLESIAS, FIRST-CLASS SEAMAN.

In the city of Havana, on the 16th of February, 1898, appeared the person above named, who, being told what he was going to be questioned about, made oath that he would tell the truth, and being warned of the penalties incurred by any witness who gives false testimony, and being asked the usual preliminary questions, he said that his name was Enqique Iglesias Anido, 21 years of age, and a first-class seaman on board the *Legazpi.*

Being requested to state all that he knew about the explosion on board the *Maine,* he said that he was on watch on deck, and that shortly after half past 9 o'clock he heard a tremendous report and saw fire near the center of the ship, which was sinking, and that he then heard separate reports for some little time.

This deposition stopped here, it being read to him by the clerk, and he ratifying its contents, making the sign of the cross, being unable to write, with the judge and with the secretary, who certifies.

[A cross.]

PEDRO DEL PARAL. [Flourish.]
JAVIER DE SALAS. [Flourish.]

JUDICIAL ACT.

In the city of Havana, on the 17th February, 1898, the commandant of engineers, the commandant of artillery, and the commandant of the torpedo brigade of the naval station having met, his honor the judge and the present clerk of the court went in a boat belonging to the *Alfonso XII,* which had been assigned to them for this purpose, near to the American war ship *Maine* for the purpose of making such an ocular inspection as should furnish data that should render it possible to form a correct opinion, or an approximately correct one, of the occurrence concerning which they will sign a separate paper or certificate.

In testimony whereof, this fact is stated, to which I, the clerk of the court, certify.

JAVIER DE SALAS. [Flourish.]
PARAL. [Flourish.]

OFFICE OF THE WARDEN OF THE MORGUE,
Havana, February 16, 1898.

I have the honor to inform your honor that there being a large number of dead bodies from the *Maine* in the establishment under my charge, and the decomposition of these bodies being not only injurious to public health but the agglomeration of corpses likewise being dangerous, I trust your Excellency will order their burial, or if not, that you will issue suitable orders.

God guard your honor many years.

FRANCISCO OBREGON MAYON.

To his honor the Examining Judge.

JUDICIAL ACT.

In the city of Havana on the 17th February, 1898. Don Elias Iriarte, commandant of artillery, of the navy, and chief officer of this branch in the naval station, Don Ambrosio Monterro, engineer, chief officer of engineers of the naval station, and Don Francisco Benavente, naval lieutenant, acting commander of the torpedo brigade of the naval station, before the examining judge and the secretary, said: That from the ocular inspection which they were able to make from the boat there was reason to conclude that the explosion was one of the greatest magnitude, and that it took place in one of the forward powder magazines, situated between the foremast and the forward bulkheads of the boiler room; by this explosion the upper deck throughout the said extent was torn off and hurled backwards, knocking down the smokestacks and crushing the superstructure which it found, and the foremast and a portion of the deck was hurled forward. The hinder part apparently sustained no injury, for even the glasses of the skylights are intact, and it may be stated by way of recapitulation, from the effects observed, that the explosion was on the inside. Until a minute examination of the inside and outside of the hull can be made, and until data are available concerning the interior service of the vessel at the time of the occurrence—until then the undersigned can not state with precision the form and manner in which the explosion took place.

FRANCISCO DENAVENTE. [Flourish.]
AMBROSIO MONTERRO. [Flourish.]
ELIAS DE IRIARTE. [Flourish.]
PEDRO DEL PARAL. [Flourish.]

Before me, JAVIER DE SALAS. [Flourish.]

ORDER.

In the city of Havana on the 17th of February, 1898, his honor, the judge, knowing that on board the mail steamer *Colon* anchored in the bay several wounded persons from the *Maine* had been treated, resolved to go on board of the aforesaid vessel, accompanied by the clerk of the court, for the purpose of receiving the depositions of the captain and physician, with a view to investigating whether it was possible to learn the causes of the disaster from the statements of the wounded men. As the persons in question were not then on board, his honor, the judge, ordered that they should be summoned to appear before the court to-morrow.

It was so ordered by his honor before me, the clerk of the court, who certifies.

JAVIER DE SALAS. [Flourish.]
PARAL. [Flourish.]

HAVANA, *February 17, 1898.*

A communication was sent to the consignees of the mail steamers of Lopez for the purpose mentioned in the foregoing judicial act.
I certify.

JAVIER DE SALAS. [Flourish.]
PARAL. [Flourish.]

DEPOSITION OF DON LUIS CAMPS, CAPTAIN OF THE MAIL STEAMER COLON.

In the city of Havana, on the 18th February, 1898, appeared before this court the person above named, who, being informed of the matter concerning which he was to be questioned, made oath that he would tell the truth, he being warned of the penalties incurred by anyone who bears false witness, and being asked the usual preliminary questions, he said that his name was Don Luis Camps y Hechevarria, a native of Santiago de Cuba; of full age, and captain of the mail steamer *Colon,* owned by the Transatlantic Company; he said that he had no interest in the case before the court, either direct or indirect. Being asked concerning the number of wounded from the *Maine* who were cared for on board of the vessel under his command, he said that they were three in number; that they were brought by the boat of the mail steamer *Mexico,* of the same company, two of them being very severely wounded, and the removal of one of them to the shore being impossible; he said that the other two were sent ashore after they had received the first treatment.

Being asked whether any of those wounded men had made any statement with regard to the disaster, he said that at first they said nothing, but that on the next day the man who had remained on board of his vessel said that the disaster had been caused by the explosion of the boiler of the dynamo. When asked whether he knew the name of the wounded man who made this statement and in what capacity he was employed on board of the *Maine,* he said that he thought his name was Frank Freixa, and that he was a Swede by birth and a seaman by profession. When asked whether the boats of his vessel went to the scene of the disaster, he said that at the first moment the boat that was in the water was sent, but that it withdrew when the second explosion took place without having effected anything.

This deposition stopped here, and deponent read and ratified it, signing it with his honor the judge, and the present clerk of the court, who certifies.

L. CAMPS. [Flourish.]

PEDRO DEL PARAL. [Flourish.]
JAVIER DE SALAS. [Flourish.]

DEPOSITION OF THE PHYSICIAN ON BOARD OF THE MAIL STEAMER COLON, DON JOSÉ MARÍA ACUÑA.

In the city of Havana, on the 18th of February, 1898, appeared before this court the person above named, who, being informed of the matter concerning which he was to be questioned, made oath that he would tell the truth, being reminded of the penalties incurred by anyone who declares falsely, and being asked the usual preliminary questions, he said that his name was Don José María Acuña y Suarez;

a native of Cadiz; married; of full age, and at the present time a physician on board the mail steamer *Colon;* he further stated that he was not interested, either directly or indirectly, in the case now before the court.

Being asked whether he had treated any of the wounded men from the *Maine,* he said that he treated all who were brought on board the steamer *Colon,* who were three in number, and all of whom had received extensive burns of the first and second grade, and one of whom had received contusions in the occipital region and a fracture of the left clavicle, and that there was another who could not be taken ashore, in whom a crepitation was observed in the movement of the heel of the right foot, which led him to suspect that there was a fracture.

Being asked whether he heard statements from any of them that could show the cause of the disaster, he said "No." Being asked whether the state of the wounded man was then such as to permit his removal to the shore, he said "Yes." Being asked whether any officer or person from the ironclad *Maine* or from any other American vessel or any person sent by the American consul had come on board of the *Colon* for the purpose of ascertaining the name and class of the wounded man, he said "No," so far as he knew. Being asked whether he knew the names of the wounded men, he said that he thought he remembered only that of the man who was still on board, which was Frank Freixas.

The deposition stopped here, the witness reading it thoroughly, affirming and ratifying its contents and signing it, with the judge and secretary present, which I certify.

JOSE MARIA SOUNA. [Flourish.]

PADRO DEL PERAL. [Flourish.]
JAVIER DE SALAS. [Flourish.]

ORDER.

At Havana, on the eighteenth of February, one thousand eight hundred and ninety-eight, the honorable Judge ordered, to prevent the approach of vessels to the wreck of the *Maine,* excepting war vessels, Spanish and American, and those bearing especial permit, fixing an extent of a hundred meters as a line of protection round the vessel, sending to that effect a polite letter to the superior authority, in order that he should provide what was proper with respect to the patrol service and other guard duty, so that one or several officers appointed for the purpose might watch those boats and recognize suspicious vessels.

His honor thus ordered before me, the secretary. I certify.

JAVIER DE SALAS. [Flourish.]
PERAL. [Flourish.]

MINUTE.

Havana, the eighteenth of February, one thousand eight hundred and ninety-eight, two letters were dispatched to the commander-general of the port, to the ends indicated in the above order. I certify.

JAVIER DE SALAS. [Flourish.]
PERAL. [Flourish.

DEPOSITION OF PASCUAL FERRER, PORT PILOT.

At Havana, on the eighteenth of February, one thousand eight hundred and ninety-eight, appeared in this court the individual named in the margin, who, notified of the subject on which he was to be questioned, swore to tell the truth. He appeared, summoned orally a few moments previous, and he was informed of the penalties incurred by anyone giving false testimony, and questioned as to his legal competency to testify. He said his name was Pascual Ferrer y Juan, a native of Palma de Mallorca, a bachelor, and of age, who stated that he had no interest, direct or indirect, in the cause being tried.

Asked if he belonged to the corporation of Pilots of the Port of Havana, he said no, but he is an auxiliary and coast pilot.

Asked if it was he that brought in the American steamer *City of Washington* on the night of the fifteenth of February, and, if so, at what o'clock did he do it, he said that, as auxiliary and substitute, it was his turn to admit the steamer *City of Washington*, about eight o'clock entering it into port and leaving it fastened to the buoy on the port side of the *Maine* about nine o'clock.

Asked if he noticed anything irregular on the *Maine*, he said no, that the *Maine* was lighted with electricity, and music of accordions and people's voices were heard.

Asked to state what he may know about the explosion, he said that after anchoring the *Washington* a Cuban young lady, who spoke English and who was a passenger, went to the cabin (cámara), where she began to play the piano, and shortly after half past nine o'clock, while listening to her, he heard on the *Maine* a noise as of many rockets, but nothing came outside; that on looking he saw a light towards the bow and simultaneously a noise like two cannon reports; likewise inside, followed by a tremendous noise and by the flight through the air, in a most vivid fire, of the foremast, the deck, and a thousand things; that then he retired, as did all those who were outside, to shelter themselves from the shower of things that were falling upon the steamer, and when they looked again at the *Maine* they saw her on fire, the bow submerged; that this was seen at the time of the great explosion, and they heard the cries of the victims.

Asked what did his vessel do on seeing this, he said that it was ordered to lower the boats to give help in the disaster, and while lowering the first there arrived a felucca and longboat from the *Maine* with captains (Jefes), officers, and seamen; and after the commander of the *Maine*, who was in uniform and without his cap, had spoken with the captain, the latter came to declarer and asked if he could change his anchorage, as he did not like being there, to which the deponent replied there was no objection, loosening the chain and anchoring in front of the first post of the wharf of San Jose. Asked if after the explosion he saw dead fish or knows if there had been any, he said no. Asked if at the moment of the explosion or some instants after there was felt any violent motion in the water, he said no.

At this point this declaration was suspended, it being read by deponent, its contents being affirmed and ratified, he signing it with the judge and secretary present. I certify.

PASCUAL F. JUAN. [Flourish.]

JAVIER DE SALAS. [Flourish.]

ORDER.

At Havana, on the eighteenth of February, one thousand eight hundred and ninety-eight, his honor directed to request the commander-general of the station to obtain from the commander of the *Maine* direct, or through the consul of the United States at this capital, exact particulars as to the quantity of explosive materials that still remain in the unburnt portion of the *Maine*, in order to proceed, if necessary, to the extraction by divers of the material still existing, advising him to represent to the consul the urgency for his reply. His honor proceeded to do so, before me, the secretary. I certify.

JAIRES DE SALAS. [Flourish.]
PERAL. [Flourish.]

MINUTE.

At Havana, the eighteenth of February, one thousand eight hundred and ninety-eight, the letter referred to in the above order was dispatched. I certify.

JAIRES DE SALAS. [Flourish.]
PERAL. [Flourish.]

MINUTE.

At Havana, on the eighteenth of February, one thousand eight hundred and ninety-eight, at two o'clock p. m., news was received of the death of those of the crew of the *Maine* that were left on the steamer *Colon*. This is made to appear in the proceeding. I certify.

JAIRES DE SALAS. [Flourish.]
PERAL. [Flourish.]

MINUTE.

Havana, on the eighteenth of February, one thousand eight hundred and ninety-eight, letters were sent to the commanders of *Alfonso XII* and *Legaspi* in order to forward to the court a report of the members of the crew of the *Maine* saved by the men of their vessels and of the individuals on their boats who may have distinguished themselves in this work. I certify.

JAIRES DE SALAS. [Flourish.]
PERAL. [Flourish.]

WAR TRANSPORT LEGAZPI, COMMANDER'S OFFICE.

In answer to your respected letter of to-day I have the honor to state that the number of the wrecked men picked up by the boats of this vessel belonging to the complement of the battle ship *Maine* were: The first boat went alongside the stern of the *Maine* and picked up from there a wounded man, three from the third boat, and three others from one of the American boats, who were sent to the Shears House. The fifth boat found on the way two men in the water, and on reaching the other boat those that delivered it to the first boat leaving the side of the *Maine* and in obedience to orders from an American officer. The fishing smack picked up seven men, who were brought on board. Assistance was given them and clothing furnished. They were afterwards sent to the Machina.

A boat from the *Maine* containing four of the wrecked sailors came to the side of the ship. They were taken on board and clothing given to them. Afterwards they were rubbed with rum, and a glass of brandy was given to each one of them. After this they were sent to the cockpit of the Machina, as some of them were quite bruised. The boat was left on board. The doctor of this vessel, second physician Don Ramón Robles, as well as the assistant, Don Juan Aragon, rendered from the very first moment all necessary aid in the infirmary that was established on the Machina. Among those who distinguished themselves I will mention in the first place the officer on guard, Midshipman Don Guillermo Farragut, who, through timely orders, succeeded in having in a few moments all the boats alongside of the *Maine*, and the success of saving the wrecked crew was due to this rapid action. Regarding the boat's crew, I will mention, among those who contributed efficaciously to this end, the following: The carpenter of the vessel, Jesús Pencla, who, without having any official position in the service, contributed effectively to the rescue, being the first one to take a boat; the third boatswains Niconte Cortés and Andrés Posada, who commanded the first and second boats; the coxswains Juán García and Sebastian Martinez, who commanded the fishing smack and the fifth boat; the first coxswain Rudesindo Beeciro; the second coxswains José García Quinteros and José Pena, and the sailors Pedro Cervantes, Miguel Escondell, Ygnacio Bastarrechea, Manuel Vasquez, Gregorio Perez, Diego Navarro, Manuel Soto, Bernardo Mauris, José Dominguez, Andrés Otero, Felix Rodriguez, Domingo Arenos, Francisco Pomares, Gaspar Melgar, Lorenzo Toxer, Santiago Prega, and fireman Manuel Casal, all of whom went in the boats; and regarding the rest of the crew I can state that all did, to the best of their ability, whatever they could, not only in rendering assistance to the *Maine*, but in preventing this vessel from suffering the consequences of the explosion, helping in the manoeuvre that I deemed opportune, namely, to leave the buoy nearest the seat of the disaster. All the personnel that were on land returned to the vessel at the earliest moment.

I must also state that very timely aid was rendered to this vessel by the gunboat *Antonio Lopez*, which towed us until we reached the channel.

God preserve your honor many years.

On board, at Havana, February 18, 1898.

FRANCISCO F. TISCAL. [Rubric.]
Señor Don PEDRO DEL PERAL,
Captain of Frigate (Capitan de Fragata),
Judge of the Court of Inquiry (Juez Instructor).

MINUTE.

HAVANA, *February 18, 1898.*

Answer was received to the communication sent to the commandant of the *Legazpu*, of which reference was made in the preceding minute, and it is filed with the proceedings.

ORDER.

HAVANA, *February 18, 1898.*

The judge of the court decided to establish the position of the vessel in the chart of the port, and in order to facilitate this work and to gain time he requested the commandant of the cruiser *Alfonso XII* to have it done by the navigator of his ship.

It was so ordered by his honor, and to this I, as secretary, certify.

JAVIER DE SALAS. [Rubric.]
PERAL. [Rubric.]

MINUTE.

HAVANA, *February 18, 1898.*

A communication was delivered to the commandant of the *Alfonso XII* for the purpose indicated in the preceding decree.

I certify to this.

JAVIER DE SALAS. [Rubric.]
PERAL. [Rubric.]

MINUTE.

HAVANA, *February 18, 1898.*

· The captain of the Spanish steamer *Martin Saenz* was summoned to appear and give a deposition in this affair. A communication to this effect was put in the hands of his consignees.

I certify to this.

JAVIER DE SALAS. [Rubric.]
PERAL. [Rubric.]

MINUTE.

HAVANA, *February 19, 1898.*

Answer was received to the communication referred to in the preceding minute, said consignee stating that the steamer *Martin Saenz* had left the port. In view of this a new communication was addressed, requesting that they inform this court of the itinerary of said vessel, in order to summon her captain.

I certify to this.

JAVIER DE SALAS. [Rubric.]
PERAL. [Rubric.]

ORDER.

HAVANA, *February 19, 1898.*

Having received a communication from the consignees of the steamer *Martin Saenz*, his honor ordered that it be filed with these proceedings, and that the naval aid of Matanzas be instructed to take the deposition of the captain of the said steamer; and, in order that it be done without delay, the judge ordered that a telegram be sent to the naval aid, informing him of this resolution.

It was so ordered by his honor, and I, as secretary, certify to it.

JAVIER DE SALAS. [Rubric.]
PERAL. [Rubric.]

MINUTE.

HAVANA, *February 19, 1898.*

Everything contained in the preceding order was carried out, and a communication was sent to the naval aid of Matanzas, inclosing a copy of the questions to be answered.

I certify to this.

JAVIER DE SALAS. [Rubric.]
PERAL. [Rubric.]

MINUTE.

HAVANA, *February 19, 1898.*

The coxswains of the boats of the *Alfonso XII* and *Legazpu*, who went to the rescue of the victims, were summoned to give their depositions in this matter.

I certify to this.

> JAVIER DE SALAS. [Rubric.]
> PERAL. [Rubric.]

MINUTE.

HAVANA, *February 19, 1898.*

The captain-inspector of the house of M. Pinillos & Company appeared in person and verbally repeated all that he previously said in writing regarding the departure and itinerary of the steamer *Martin Saenz,* and that the boat which the captain took was that of the coxswain, Andrés Mugica, called *Alfonsito.*

I certify to this.

> JAVIER DE SALAS. [Rubric.]
> PERAL. [Rubric.]

MINUTE.

HAVANA, *February 19, 1898.*

The coxswain of the boat *Alfonsito,* Andrés Mugica, was verbally summoned to appear and give his deposition.

I certify to this.

> JAVIER DE SALAS. [Rubric.]
> PERAL. [Rubric.]

MINUTE.

HAVANA, *February 19, 1898.*

Several communications were filed with these proceedings, viz, four from his excellency the naval commander of the province; another approving the appointment of secretary; another from the commander of the cruiser *Alfonso XII,* giving an account of the accident, and referred to the court by the proper authorities, and another of this court, which was returned to be filed with these proceedings after having been passed upon by the proper authorities. The communications of his excellency the naval commandant of the province are: First, inclosing another from the naval subdelegate of Casa Blanca, accompanied by a list of articles; second, accompanying a death certificate of one of the crew of the *Maine* on board of the *Colon,* and giving account of same; third, transmitting an official communication accompanied by a report of the action of the captain of the said steamer, and, fourth, requesting, as a representative of the life-savers, a list of those distinguishing themselves.

I certify thereto.

> JAVIER DE SALAS. [Rubric.]
> PERAL. [Rubric.]

OFFICE OF THE COMMANDANT-GENERAL OF THE NAVY
OF THE STATION OF HAVANA. BUREAU OF JUSTICE.

I approve your appointment of Lieutenant Don Francisco Javier de Salas y Gonzalez as secretary of the court having in hand the proceedings brought about by the explosion on board the American war ship *Maine*, which I say to Y. H. that it may be recorded in the said proceedings and in reply to your communication of the 15th instant.

God preserve Y. H. many years.

MANTEROLA. [Rubric.]

HAVANA, *February 16, 1898.*

To the Judge Don Pedro del Peral, captain of frigate, commander of the cruiser *Marques de la Ensenada.*

COURT OF INQUIRY.

I beg you will so provide that the captain of the Spanish steamer *Martin Saenz* consigned to you shall appear in this court at 2 p. m. to-day, to depose in the proceedings I am conducting by reason of the catastrophe of the *Maine.*

God preserve you many years.

Havana, February 19, 1898.

PEDRO DEL PERAL, *Judge.* [Rubric.]

Messrs. Saenz y Compañia.

Communication nineteen.

We can not grant the request of Y. H., as we would gladly do, because the steamer *Martin Saenz* left this port a moment ago for Matanzas.

God preserve Y. H. many years.

Havana, February 19, 1898.   L. SAENZ Y COMPAÑIA. [Rubric.]

To the judge.

COURT OF INQUIRY, OFFICE OF THE
COMMANDANT-GENERAL OF THE STATION.

I beg you will furnish me with the itinerary to be followed by the steamer consigned to you, *Martin Saenz,* and the probable time of her arrival and departure at and from the ports where she will touch, so as to summon her captain.

God preserve you many years.

Havana, February 19, 1898.

PEDRO DEL PERAL, *Judge.* [Rubric.]

Messrs. Saenz y Compañia.

Communication nineteen.

She will reach Matanzas to-night; will leave there to-morrow, the twentieth, in the afternoon for Cienfuegos, where she will arrive on the twenty-third, remaining one day. From here she will go to New Orleans, whence we do not yet know with certainty whether she will go to Europe or return to this port.

God preserve Y. H. many years.

L. SAENZ Y COMPAÑIA.

To the judge.

Office of the naval commandant and harbor master of the port of Havana transmits a communication from a naval subdelegate of Casa Blanca regarding the assistance rendered the crew of the battle ship *Maine,* accompanied some articles and a list of the saved.

Most Excellent Sir: The naval subdelegate of Casa Blanca, in a communication dated on yesterday, writes me as follows:

Most Excellent Sir: Last night, at about nine thirty-five o'clock, there was heard a heavy detonation in the harbor, and supposing that some unfortunate accident had occurred, I immediately proceeded, accompanied by Doctor Don Baltazar Moas, of this ward, to the cruiser *Alfonso XII,* in order to render such assistance as might be necessary, sending at the same time bandages from the fire department, as well as some stretchers, for any service that might be required.

I returned a short time afterwards and invited Dr. Don Amado de los Cuetos to join me. He gracefully offered his services, and having noticed that, due to the prevailing wind, the whole shore was covered with objects belonging to the man-of-war *Maine*, where the catastrophe had occurred, I requested the authorities of this place to render whatever assistance they could to prevent abuses, and the military commander ordered that some of the volunteers of the marine corps belonging to this section should go on guard at different posts. The commander of public order also placed a half dozen policemen, with the same object in view. I afterwards joined the watchman of this ward and the commandant of the public order already mentioned, both of whom aided me the whole day and night, as they are thoroughly acquainted with this coast, until six o'clock in the morning, when I put six men, paid out of my own purse, in three small boats in order to save everything belonging to the vessel already referred to, and to pick up the bodies that might be floating. Five of these and a piece of the chest of another were picked up; all of which I sent to the Machina. I also sent in a launch that was lent to me by the heirs of P. Gamíz the articles contained in the list, which I have the honor to send to your excellency.

These articles were transferred in the afternoon to the lighter attached to the stern of the cruiser *Alfonso XII*. Besides these articles, there was a package of letters and documents in foreign language, a watch case, apparently of gold, and a piece of white kid. The captain of the cutter *Olaya* (folio 1019), Don Manuel Villegas, and his companion, D. Rosendo Martinez, delivered at this subdelegation an undershirt in bad condition, inside of which there was a watch and chain, apparently of gold, bearing the number 331134 on both sides, and marked B. W. C. x C. Warranted, 14 K, with the glass completely broken, and the works stopped. Also two caps, a leather case, with a wooden one inside, containing surgical instruments; this box bears the name of the makers, George Tiernaum & Company, 107 Park Row, New York. I send these articles to your excellency, with the exception of the two caps and the undershirt, which were delivered with the others mentioned in the list to the cruiser *Alfonso XII*. All of which I have the honor to bring to the knowledge of your excellency for such action as you may deem expedient.

I have the honor to refer all this matter to your excellency, with the original list mentioned above; the last six articles named in said list I send you, the others having been taken yesterday to the Machina and transferred to the launch belonging to the stern of the *Alfonso XII*. And conceived it a duty, of which the fulfilment gives him much pleasure, to recommend to the superior authority of your excellency both the conduct observed by the subdelegate of marine of Casa Blanca, Don Emilio Labade, who has demonstrated once more in this occasion the interest and great zeal which distinguishes him in all the acts of the service, and in a manner very special the honorable conduct of Manuel Villegas and Rosendo Martinez, master and mate respectively of the guard-ship *Olalla*.

God guard your excellency many years.

Havana, the 16th of February, 1898.

LUIS PASTOR Y LANDONE. [Flourish.]

His excellency the Sr. Commandante-General of the station, Providencia.

With the annexed report is forwarded to the Sr. Fiscal of the same Havana, the 18th of February, 1898.

MANTEROLA. [Flourish.]

Report of the effects collected on the shore by the Casa Blanca and conveyed by the launch *Salvador* to the war ship *Alfonso XII*, belonging to the American cruiser *Maine*, destroyed by an explosion the night of February, 1898.

A case conserves containing 12 boxes.
A case conserves, with 10 boxes.
48 boxes biscuit.
12 biscuit boxes, empty.
1 American flag.
1 Italian flag.
2 signal flags, with staff.
1 signal flag, American, with staff.
1 bucket twisted tobacco.
2 empty barrels.
2 cloths.
1 square copper jug.
1 cane chair in bad condition.
10 mattresses.
4 pillows.
1 rudder.
3 painted stuffs for awning.
5 painted canvass for clothing.
2 sailcloth awnings with masts.
1 broom.
1 sailcloth hammock.
1 empty case containing a flowered jug.
A roll of goods and several pieces of sail.
2 whisks.
8 brushes for bitumen.
An empty valise.
A pair of spatterdashes.
15 black caps.
6 pair socks.
1 pair shoes.
1 pair boots.
Small empty box with broken hinges.
1 sail-cloth pouch.
1 sail-cloth bag.
Sponge of cannon.
6 blankets.

18 white sail-cloth trousers.
16 white sail-cloth shirts.
17 blue-cloth shirts.
16 jackets blue drill.
14 pair blue woolen trousers.
2 uniform jackets.
2 cloth caps.
Sundry pieces linen.
4 pieces of regalia.
6 fragments of hammock.
An empty jar.
A small cuartel.
94 small bags with 24 salvidadas.
A cloth (hayaja).
A compound of metallic cloth.
A piece of canister.
A wooden stanchion.
A piece stanchion.
A plane.
A scale.
A piece of painted wood.
A leather case enclosing one of wood containing surgical instruments, a metal plate in the upper part having the following inscription: "Genito - Urinari. Case Medicinal, department U. S. N."
A watch with chain, apparently gold, with the number on both lids 331134, mark B. W. C. X. C. Warranted, with crystal completely broken and works stopped.
A memorandum book.
Package papers and letters and sundry photographs.
A watch case, apparently gold, with the number 603273.
A piece white kid.

CASA BLANCA, *17th February, 1898.*

The Subdelegado EMILIO LAVATE: [Flourish.]
A seal which says Subdelegation de Marine of Casa Blanca. Military Commandancy of Marine and Captaincy of the Port of Havana.

NOTICE OF THE DEATH OF THE SAILOR OF THE AMERICAN WAR-
SHIP MAINE, FRANK FISCHER.

Your Excellency: I regret to have to inform your excellency of the death, at 12.30 this day, of heart failure, of the sailor of the American warship *Maine*, Frank Fischer, who was brought to this ship on the night of the blowing up of the said ship. Which I have the honor to communicate to Y. E. for your superior resolution, adding that as soon as the said information was communicated to this ship a special boat from this vessel received the corpse and brought it to the vessel for the disposition of the judge instructor in the matter of the catastrophe of the *Maine*.

God guard your excellency many years.

Havana, February 18, 1898.

LUIS PASTOS. [Flourish.]

His Excellency Comandante-General of the Station Providence.
The accompanying document addressed to the Sr. Fiscal, of Havana,
February 18, 1898.

MANTEROLA. [Flourish.]

Steamer *Colon.*

The undersigned, physicians of this ship, declare that at 12.30 to day
there died in our hospital Franck Ficher, who was wounded in the accident to the *Maine*, in consequence of heart failure, which, by sudden
complications, caused his decease. He received the last spiritual min-
istrations appropriate to his failing condition, to which witness is given
with regret.

God guard your excellency many years.

Bay of Havana, February 18, 1898.

JOSE MARIA ACUNA. [Flourish.]
AMADEO ARIAS. [Flourish.]
Sr. Captain of the Steamer Colon.

Cruiser *Alfonso XII* Captaincy. Number 909:

Your Excellency: I regret to inform your excellency that last night
the American war ship *Maine* exploded and sank in the neighborhood
of this vessel. Immediately seven vessels were sent to render the necessary assistance, together with the guard ship *Alonsito*, the property of
Andres Mogica Chacharra, which, from the first moment, was placed
under our orders. Twenty-nine persons were rescued from the water,
most of them with severe wounds and bruises, who were relieved by the
Martin Saez and the *Casa Blanca*, and others arriving afterwards, to
offer assistance.

The increasing heat made it impossible to board the American vessel or to rescue a great number in spite of the most desperate exertions,
and the incessant explosions of war material endangered their lives.
As we were about quitting the scene of the catastrophe Y. E.'s order
arrived to watch the ship, for which purpose Antonio Lopez was placed
under my orders, who towed us and anchored us to ground ways No. 1.
During all the night the fire continued on the *Maine*, watch being kept
around her. In the morning more aids were sent. This is what I have
the honor to communicate to your excellency in fulfillment of my duty.

God guard your excellency many years.

A bordo,

Havana, 16th February, 1898.

MANUEL DE ELISA. [Flourish.]

His excellency commander-general of the station.
Providence. Address to the Sr. Fiscal of the same. Havana, February 18, 1898. [Flourish.] Military command of marine and captaincy
of the port of Havana.

OFFICIAL REPORT OF THE CAPTAIN OF THE MAIL STEAMER COLON
OF EFFECTUAL SUCCORS TO THE SAILORS OF THE CRUISER
MAINE.

Your Excellency: The captain of the Government mail boat *Colon*
under date of to-day writes to me as follows:

Your Excellency: The undersigned, captain of the mail boat *Colon*, has
the honor to inform Y. E. that at 10 o'clock last night, after the explosion
on the American battle ship *Maine*, aids were dispatched from this boat

and the *Mejico*, and the latter brought three wounded sailors, John Cafbe, gunner, Washington Cook, who were brought to this hospital, and Frank Fischer, sailor, who remained on board because the surgeon of the vessel did not think him fit to be moved. According to the report made to me to-day that the gravest symptoms have disappeared he may be removed at the pleasure of Y. E. Annexed I have the honor to add the medical reports which I have the honor to communicate to Y. E. for what action he may deem proper in the matter of the unfortunate accident to the war ship *Maine*.

It is my duty to add that the captain of the ship informed me verbally that the wounded man was in a very serious condition, for which reason he was not disposed to disembark him.

God guard Y. E. many years.

February 16, 1898.

LUIS PASTOR. [Flourish.]

His excellency Sr. commander-general of the station.

Providence. With the annexed documents presented to the Sr. Fiscal.

Havana, February 18, 1898.

MONTEROLA. [Flourish.]

At 2 this morning the wounded man, Frank Fischer, showed a reaction, which, at this hour, 8 in the morning, still continues. Being no longer in the immediate danger which caused his presence in our hospital it is deemed expedient to remove him to whatever place you may decree. Which is communicated for your information and other effects.

God guard your excellency many years.

Bay of Havana, February 16, 1898.

The surgeons,

AMADEO ARIAS. [Flourish.]
JOSÉ MARÍA ACUNA. [Flourish.]

In the hospital of this ship, and about 10 o'clock last night, we attended for the first time two white and one colored sailor of the North American battle ship *Maine*, whose cases present: The white, Frank Fischer, burns of first and second grade all over his face, anterior part of chest and abdomen, upper extremities, and both feet. There is observed also a great swelling of the right tarso-tibio joint, extending all over the foot which prevented us from localizing the seat of the malignant soft rattling which was perceptible on the movements communicated by the extension and flexion of the foot over the leg, and perceived more distinctly toward the heel. The second of the sailors, John Coffe, white, like the former, presented in the upper portion of the head and near the occiput and on the left side two contused wounds, one lineal, about four centimeters in length, extending over all the soft parts except the periostio. The other contiguous to the first and more to the left and lower down, was of irregular outline and bruised, anfractuous and extended to the bone including the periostio.

No perceptible wound or symptom of cerebral disturbance. The same person had in the anterior part of the head a slight erosion of small importance and a fracture of the outer extremity of the left clavicula. There were also burns of the first grade on the arms and shoulders. The negro named Washington has wounds of first and second grade over his whole face, neck, and anterior region of chest and upper extremities. The general condition of the two last wounded men was sufficiently good for them to be removed to a convenient place. On the contrary, the condition of Frank Fischer is such that, considering the possible grave contingencies of a removal, we have ordered that he be placed in the hospital, which, with the natural regret that we feel, is communicated to you.

God guard your excellency many years.

Bay of Havana, February 13, 1898.

The surgeons,

AMADES ARIAS. [Rubric.]
JOSE MARIA ACUÑIA. [Rubric.]

EXAMINING COURT OF THE
COMMANDING GENERAL OF DOCK-YARDS.

Excellency: I have the honor to inform Y. E. that, in order to continue the hearings in the matter of the lamentable accident to the North American battle ship *Maine*, it has been necessary to take the depositions of the survivors of the said ship, and having received notice that among these were the commander of the vessel and various officers, it would be proper to take the declaration of the first and the declarations of two or three of the officers. For this purpose I address myself to Y. E., in order that you may be good enough to decide.

God guard Y. E. many years.

Havana, February 16, 1898.

PEDRO DEL PERAL. [Rubric.]

His Excellency the Commander-General of the Dockyard.

ORDERS.

The presents shall be transmitted to H. E. the illustrious Governor-General of this island, requesting the appearance of all the parties in interest, and that the present document be returned to the examining judge in the case.

Havana, February 16, 1898.

MANTEROLA. [Rubric.]

Office of the military commandant of marines and of the captain of the port of Havana. To duly comply with the wish of the Spanish society for saving the lives of sailors, which I represent in this island, and in order that the distinguished deeds may not remain unknown and unrewarded, performed by those who at the risk of their lives had been enabled to take part in the rescue of the survivors of the *Maine*, as the result of its explosion, I address myself to you in order that you might be good enough to inform me of their names and acts which were worthy of reward.

God guard you, etc.,

Representative general, LUIS PASTOR,
Examining judge, in the investigation concerning
the explosion on the Maine.

Havana, February 18, 1898.

DECLARATION OF CABO DE MAR DE PRIMERA MIGUEL BARBAR.

Havana, February 19, 1898, there appeared in this court the person named in the margin, who, having been advised concerning the interrogatories to be made, declared on oath that he would speak the truth, and having been further advised of the punishment incurred by one swearing falsely and having had the usual questions required by law put to him, declared as follows: That his name was Miguel Barbar y Soriano, Cabo de mar de primera, employed as one of the crew of the cruiser *Alfonso XII;* that he was 31 years old, married, and declared that he had no interest direct or indirect in the investigation which was now being conducted.

Being asked whether he proceeded in command of any boat from the vessel on which he was employed for the purpose of assisting the victims of the *Maine*, and that he should tell what he did for them, he replied that on hearing the explosion he sprang up and, on learning what had occurred and hearing the order to man the boats, he went by the "*tangón*" to the first lifeboat of his vessel, of which he was the captain, in which six mariners and second gunner's mate Dominguez embarked.

The declarant going in his drawers and shirt, as no time was allowed for him to dress himself. That he reached the American vessel with difficulty, since there was much timber and wreckage floating in the water, and that on reaching it they passed to the port side about mid-ships, passing for this purpose over the remains of the vessel, across the prow and between what remained of the vessel and the foremast, which was now in the water; that he passed under the stern of the sixth lifeboat of the *Alfonso XII*, which was likewise there, and which delivered to him eight wounded men, all taken from on board the *Maine* by the sailors of the *Alfonso XII;* that he then proceeded with them to his vessel in order that they might receive attention, and going all the sooner because a sailor of the *Maine*, whom he could not see, but whom he thought was a machinist of the first class, told them that they should leave and get out of the way, because there was danger. On reaching his vessel, after placing the wounded on board, they undertook the task of unmooring their vessel in order that it might change its anchorage.

Being asked whether he noticed any movement in the water, he answered that as they were going he did notice it, caused by the rain of articles which fell, still on fire, and by the commotion of the explosion. Thereupon this declaration was closed, and having read it he affirmed the same and swore to its contents, signing it with the judge and the secretary now present, who certified the same.

MIGUEL BARBAR. [Rubric.]

PEDRO DEL PERAL. [Rubric.]
JAVIER DE SALAS. [Rubric.]

DECLARATION OF ROGALIO UFORT Y ECHEVERRIA.

Havana, on February 19, 1898, appeared in this court the person named in the margin, who, having been advised of the interrogatories to be put to him, swore that he would speak the truth, and who, likewise warned of the danger incurred by perjury and being asked the usual questions required by law, declared that his name was Rogalio Ufort y Echeverria, a native of Maniños, Ferrol Road, 26 years old, a bachelor, and brother of the owner of the boat *Carmen*, which was manned that same night, having declared that he had no interest in the examination now being conducted, he was asked whether on the night of the 15th he carried the captain of the steamer *Martin Saenz* to the *Eustraro*. He replied that on that day, at 4 in the evening, he proceeded from the San José wharf, where the *Martin Saenz* was moored, to the *Eustraro*, which was moored at Friscornia, opposite to the Belot sugar refinery, and that on his way there he passed round the *Maine*, without perceiving anything.

Being asked at what hour he returned from the *Eustraro*, and whether he knew anything of the *Maine* explosion, he replied that on that day about 9 o'clock he was carrying the captain of the *Martin Saenz* from the *Eustraro* to the San José wharf, when, being at a distance of about 50 or 60 meters from the *Maine*, and in a line therewith on the port side, he felt the explosion, and some of the objects began to fall around the boat, but none therein; and that they splashed the captain and the declarant, but that they did not notice any more movement in the water than that, he and the captain sheltering themselves under the awning and proceeding slowly toward the San José wharf on seeing that nothing further occurred. He did not see whether the vessel sank or no, as they were only occupied in getting out of the way. Thereupon this declaration was closed, and he, having read the same, and affirmed and sworn to the truth of its contents, signed with the judge in the presence of the secretary who certifies.

ROGILIO USFORT. [Sign manual.]
PEDRO DEL PERAL. [Sign manual.]
JAVIER DE SALAS. [Sign manual.]

DEPOSITION OF THE BOATMAN AURELIANO MUGICA.

At Havana, the nineteenth day of February, eighteen hundred and ninety-eight, appeared the individual named in the margin, who, being informed as to what he was to be interrogated about, swore to tell the truth with a knowledge of the penalties imposed upon those who give false testimony, and the usual questions being put to him, he said that he is and calls himself Aureliano Mugica y Valencia, native of Bermeo, thirty-three years old, married, boatman, manning the boat called *Alonsito*, who declared that he had no interest whatever in the cause which is being investigated.

Being asked to declare what he knew about the explosion occurring in the *Maine*, he said that shortly after half-past six, with another companion, he went toward the *Eustrara* to see if the machinists, his countrymen, should want to come to land. They told him no, and that he eat and drank there a little, coming, shortly after a quarter past nine, towards land, hearing that from the *Segaspo* they gave him the boat ahoy, replying loud, perceiving at this moment a very vivid flash and a very great detonation, such as has never been greater, and when he recovered from the flight he heard cries and went towards the *Alfonso XII*, where he gave the alarm and where they called him to go in aid of the victims; that there embarked there an officer and a petty officer and they went towards the *Maine*, picking up at its larboard side two wounded who were swimming and supported on tables on the water, taking them to the *Alfonso*. And in this state this deposition was suspended, reading it, and signing it, and ratifying it in full, signing it with the judge and secretary present, which I certify.

AURELIANO MUGACI. [Sealed.]
PEDRO DEL PERAL. [Sealed.]
JAVIER DE SALAS. [Sealed.]

DEPOSITION OF THE CABO DE MAR, THE FIRST JOSE ENSENATA.

At Havana, the nineteenth February, eighteen hundred and eighty-eight, appeared in this court the individual mentioned above, who being informed of what he was to be interrogated, swore to tell the truth, and doing so with a knowledge of the penalties visited upon those who swear falsely. Being asked the general questions, he said he was and called himself Jose Ensenata Rubio, first Cabo de Mar, enlisted in the crew of the *Alfonso XII*, who declared that he had no interest, direct or indirect, in the cause under investigation. Being asked what he knew about the explosion occurring in the *Maine*, he said that he was lying down, although awake, in the cockpit, and that upon hearing the detonation he went up on deck, embarking, by order of the officer of the guard, in the boat of which he is master, going immediately to the *Maine*.

Being the first boat to arrive, coming alongside its starboard side, at the fashion pieces; that in the roundhouse of the American (vessel) there were some ten or twelve men that he saw who had been thrown into the water, grasped at the *bosa* of his boat; that he took them out of water and already in his boat he saw that they had been wounded; that at this moment arrived Alferez de Navio D. Guillermo Colmenares in a *Quadraa* and he jumped aboard remaining already at his orders; sheering off in a little while because no one more was seen going aboard; and in this state this deposition was suspended, being read by himself, signing and ratifying it in full and signing it with the judge and secretary present; which I certify.

Jose Ensenata. [Sealed.]
Pedro del Peral. [Sealed.]
Javier de Salas. [Sealed.]

DECREE.

At Havana, nineteenth of February, eighteen hundred and ninety-eight, coming the judge, who from the depositions of the sailing masters could deduce nothing as to the cause of what happened, all of their depositions being to the same effect, he decided not to take the depositions of the rest of the cabos de mar (petty officers) in charge of the boats of the cruiser *Alfonso XII* and *Segazpi*. He decided as well to take the deposition of the quartermaster of the steamship *Colon* and certain persons of the *Alfonso XII*, who were on the left-hand side, according to advices of the court. His lordship thus decreed before me, the secretary, which I certify.

Javier de Salas. [Sealed.]
Peral. [Sealed.]

PROCEDURE.

Havana, *February 19, 1898.*

There were cited, by official notification, the quartermaster of the *Colon*, through his consignees, and verbally, the persons on the cruiser *Alfonso XII*. I certify.

Javier de Salas. [Sealed.]
Peral. [Sealed.]

PROCEDURE.

Havana, *February 20, 1898.*

It appears judicially that the quartermaster of the steamship *Colon* did not appear at nine o'clock in the morning of to-day, February twentieth, according to the summons issued. I certify.

Javier de Salas. [Sealed.
Peral. [Sealed.]

DECREE.

At Havana, February twentieth, eighteen hund.'ed and ninety-eight, the presiding judge resolved to send a private communication to the jurisdictional authority, giving it an account of the general aspect of the case and of the resumé of impressions that can be deduced from the work in this case, in order, if it should be thought proper, to turn it over to the Government of His Majesty, and to annex to these proceedings a copy of this letter as proof. Thus his lordship declared before me, his secretary, which I certify.

JAVIER DE SALAS. [Sealed.]
PERAL. [Sealed.]

COURT OF INSTRUCTION.

Excellent Sir: Thinking it proper, in view of the importance of the unfortunate accident occurring to the North American ironclad *Maine* to anticipate, although in reserved character, something of that which in brief will form part of the opinion of the fiscal (attorney-general) upon that which I undersign, and in case your excellency should think it opportune and proper to inform the Government of Her Majesty thereof, I have the honor to express to your excellency that from the judicial proceedings up to to-day in the matter, with the investigation of which you charged me immediately after the occurrence of the catastrophe, it is disclosed in conclusive manner that the explosion was not caused by any action exterior to the boat, and that the aid lent by our officers and marines was brought about with true interest by all and in a heroic manner by some.

It alone remains to terminate this dispatch that when the court can hear the testimony of crew of the *Maine* and make investigation of its interior some light may be attained to deduce, if it is possible, the true original cause of the event produced in the interior of the ship. God guard your excellency many years.

Havana, April 20, 1898.

PEDRO DEL PERAL. [Sealed.]
ESCOPIA JAVIER DE SALAS. [Sealed.]

Excellent sir, Commandant-general of the apostadero adjutancy of marine of the district and captaincy of the port of Matanzas:

I return to Your Excellency the annexed extract finished in the captain of the Spanish ship *Martin Sainz*. D. Jose Manuel Ozamiz. God guard your excellency many years.

Matanzas, February 20, 1898.

JUAN VIGNAN. [Sealed.]

Judge instructor, Captain of the Frigate Don Pedro Peral; Don Pedro del Peral y Caballona, captain of the frigate of the Armada, judge instructor of the proceedings instituted with regard to the explosion which took place on board the North American ironclad *Maine:*

To the military adjutant of marine of the district of Matanzas, I respectfully salute and make known that in the indicated proceedings it has been decided to receive the deposition of the captain of the steamship *Martin Sainz*, who has his residense therein, and to this end I address your excellency this letter in order to exhort and require you in the name of Her Majesty, and to ask and charge you in mine, that as soon as it is within your power you acknowledge receipt and devote yourself to carrying it out, taking the deposition in conformity to the annexed interrogatory in accordance with the questions set forth in it, and others which may be derived therefrom and may be pertinent, and when sworn to return the same to me with its results; then having done this you will administer justice which I giving obligation to another as well as to your excellency when it should be necessary.

Havana, February 19, 1898.

PEDRO DEL PERAL. [Sealed.]

Questions to which the person interrogated, whose examination is solicited, must be subjected: First, the usual general legal questions. Second, if he went to visit in the night of the fifteenth of the present month the captain of the steamship *Euskaro,* and at what hour. Third, at what distance did you pass from the North American ironclad *Maine* when you went toward the *Eustaro,* and if you observed anything on the *Maine* which attracted your attention? Fourth, in what boat did you go, and the name or names of its crew? Fifth, at what hour did you return to the *Eustraro,* if you did so in the same boat; at what distance did you pass from the *Maine ;* if you observed fire signals, how much time approximately did you see the fire before the explosion; who talked with the member or members of the crew of the boat, and tell all the phenomena that were presented, with the largest number of details possible. The chief (jefe) having charge of the taking of these interrogatories will ask such questions as he may consider pertinent and which may be deduced from the declarations of the captain.

Havana, February 19, 1898.

PEDRO DEL PERAL. [Seal.]

Don Juan Vignan y Vigmor, Captain of Frigate of the Amada, adjutant of marine of the district, and captain of the port of Matanzas:

Nomination of secretary having to undertake the annexed command in the captain of the steamer *Martin Sainz,* anchored to-day, day of the date in this port, I have nominated secretary of this cause M. Antonio Marzol y Rosa, who is possessed of the necessary qualifications.

Matanzas, February 20, 1898.

JUAN VIGNAN. [Seal.]

ACCEPTATION AND OATH OF SECRETARY, AT MATANZAS, FEBRUARY 20, 1898.

Present, the secretary.

He caused to be made known the nomination which resulted, and being informed thereof, as well as the duties of his office, he took oath to discharge them well and faithfully, subscribing with me these presents for record.

ANTONIO MONZEL. [Sealed.]
JUAN VIGNAN. [Sealed.]

ORDER.

MATANZAS, *February 20, 1898.*

Annex the interrogatories to this record and summon the captain of the steamer *Martin Saenz* to appear to give evidence as is proper.

JUAN VIGNAN. [Rubric.]

MINUTE.

In Matanzas, on February 20, 1898, I record that the said captain of the steamer *Martin Saenz* was summoned to answer the interrogatories at the head of these proceedings. I certify thereto.

ANTONIO MARZAL. [Rubric.]
VIGNAN. [Rubric.]

DEPOSITION OF DON JOSE MANUEL OZAMIZ.

In Matanzas, on the 20th of February of 1898, before the judge and me, the secretary, appeared Don José Manuel Ozamiz. His honor, after instructing the deponent of his obligation to tell the truth, and of the penalty inflicted by the code on the offense of false swearing in a criminal cause, administered to him the oath, which he took according to law, and replying to the first question of the interrogatories, said that his name was José Manuel Ozamiz, a native of Bilboa; the son of Manuel; 43 years of age; married; a member of the Roman Apostolic Catholic Church, and at present captain of the Spanish steamer *Martin Saenz.*

Being interrogated in the words of the second question, he said that the day about which he was asked, he went to visit the captain of the steamer *Eustraro* about 4 p. m., on which vessel he dined.

Being interrogated with the words of the third, he said that he passed near the Regla warehouses and about a cable's length from the battle ship *Maine,* and he saw nothing to attract his attention.

Being interrogated in the words of the fourth, he said that the cutter in the service of the company (and he is ignorant of the name of the master, although the house to which the vessel was consigned there—Messrs. L. Sainz & Compania ought to know it—which house can also give the name of the master, the only one on board) (sic).

Being interrogated in the terms of the fifth, he answered that he left the *Eustraro* to go on board his own vessel about 9.30 at night on the same cutter and with the same master.

On passing the Regla warehouses, as he was coming from the direction of Triscornia, where the steamer was anchored, to his own, which was at the San Jose warehouses, he passed about a cable's length from the *Maine,* and he suddenly saw a great light bursting from the vessel and almost instantly heard a great explosion. The man at the oars arose frightened, embraced the deponent, and got under the awning of the cutter, and after he had recovered from his fright they proceeded to the *Martin Saenz,* at the San Jose wharf. Being asked if he heard one explosion or more, he replied that he only heard one, and that afterwards flames were seen all over the vessel.

Being interrogated if he had anything further to state, he said he had not; that what he had stated is the truth under the oath taken.

And his deposition being read, he found it correct and signed it for record, together with the judge and the subscribing secretary.

JOSE MANUEL DE OZAMIS. [Rubric.]
JUAN VIGNAN. [Rubric.]
ANTONIO MARSAL. [Rubric.]

MINUTE.

MATANZAS, *February 20, 1898.*

The judge ordered these proceedings to be sent to the judge who issued the interrogatories. An entry was made.

ANTONIO NARSAL. [Rubric.]
VIGNAN. [Rubric.]

MINUTE.

HAVANA, *February 20, 1898.*
The communication to which the foregoing proceedings refer was sent together with the said copy. I certify thereto.

JAVIER DE SALAS. [Rubric.]
PERAL. [Rubric.]

MINUTE.

HAVANA, *February 20, 1898.*
An official communication was sent to the commandant of the navy-yard and the commandant of the *Magallenes* requesting them to trans mit to this court a statement of the assistance rendered to the victims of the *Maine* and of the men that may have distinguished themselves. I certify thereto.

JAVIER DE SALAS. [Rubric.]
PERAL. [Rubric.]

ORDER.

In Havana, on February twentieth of 1898, his honor ordered that several photographs, conveying an idea of the effects of the explosion, be attached to the proceedings. I certify thereto.

JAVIER DE SALAS. [Rubric.]
PERAL. [Rubric.]

ORDER.

In Havana, on February twentieth of 1898, the chart of the port of Havana, showing the location of the *Maine*, and the interrogatories answered by the captain of the Spanish steamer *Martin Saenz* having been received in this court, his honor ordered that they be annexed to the proceedings. He also ordered that the chief diver of the port be summoned to appear and depose as to the nature of the bottom and depth of the harbor at the place where the *Maine* rests, and as to the prevailing wind at the time of the catastrophe. His honor so ordered before me, the secretary, who certifies thereto.

JAVIER DE SALAS. [Rubric.]
PERAL. [Rubric.]

MINUTE.

HAVANA, *February 20, 1898.*
Everything contained in the foregoing order has been complied with, and I certify thereto.

JAVIER DE SALAS. [Rubric.]
PERAL. [Rubric.]

MINUTE.

HAVANA, *February 20, 1898.*
After notice from the commander of the *Maine*, the court, at 10.30 a. m. went on board the North American steamship *Mangrove* to confer with the said gentleman, who expressed his desire that his honor shoul.!

witness, in the vicinity of the *Maine*, the work of the official diver who would go down on that day to begin the inspection of the bottom toward the bow, completely submerged. The court was transferred to the said vicinity in a boat from the Machina of San Fernando, and witnessed the descent of the diver at 11.15 o'clock, who reappeared at 11.45. The second officer of the *Maine*, who arrived at this moment, stated, after speaking with the diver, that the latter had seen a good deal of mud, adding that the work would be continued at 1 p.m. At the said hour the court again met at the same place, and at 1.50 the diver went down again, coming up at 3.15, bringing up with him a copper cylindrical tube of thin plates, some 40 cen. in length by 15 in diameter. The diver again went down, coming up in a short while, without making any statement whatever of importance. And in order that a record be made, a minute is entered, to which I, the secretary, certify

JAVIER DE SALAS. [Rubric.]
PERAL. [Rubric.]

ORDER.

In Havana, on the twenty-first day of February of 1898, his honor ordered that an attentive official communication be sent to the commandant-general of the station, requesting him to again authorize the inspection of the bottom of the *Maine* by the divers from the navy-yard, and to annex a copy of that communication to these proceedings for record. His honor so ordered before me, the secretary, who certifies thereto.

JAVIER DE SALAS. [Rubric.]
PERAL. [Rubric.]

MINUTE.

HAVANA, *February 21, 1898.*
The foregoing order was complied with. I certify thereto.

JAVIER DE SALAS. [Rubric.]
PERAL. [Rubric.]

DEPOSITION OF THE CHIEF DIVER OF THE PORT, DON FRANCISCO ALDAO.

In Havana, on the twenty-second day of February, 1898, there appeared in this court the party summoned on the margin, who, being advised of the matters upon which he was to be interrogated, made oath to tell the truth, he being also informed of the penalties incurred by him who declares falsely under oath.

Being asked the usual preliminary questions, he said that he was named Francisco Aldao y Sixto, a native of Galicia, of lawful age, the chief pilot of the port, and that he had no interest whatever, direct or indirect, in the matter in hand. Being asked the draft of the battle ship *Maine*, the depth of water at the anchorage, the class of moorings, the nature of the bottom, the fluctuation of the tide, the state of the latter on the night and hour of the occurrence and the prevailing wind at that moment, he answered that according to the statement of the commander to the pilot who brought him in, the vessel drew 23 feet; that at the anchorage, at the place of mooring, which was Government buoy No. 4, there were 28 feet at low tide, and in the neighborhood as much as 36 feet; that the bottom, where the forward part of the vessel now rests, is muddy, and that the fluctuation of the tide is, generally, a foot and a half; that he does not remember the state of the tide at the time of the occurrence, and that the prevailing wind then was very light from the fourth quadrant, the bay being absolutely calm.

Being asked if after the occurrence he made any inspection in the vicinity of the *Maine* and in the west of the bay, and whether he has observed or has any information through his subordinates of any dead fish being found in the harbor, he said that at daybreak of the day following the occurrence he himself went, together with another numbered pilot of the port, to sound around the vessel and to see whether the vessel had lost her moorings when blown up; that he found them in the same place and did not notice, as a result of the soundings, any obstacle in the port other than the vessel itself; he did not find a single dead fish in his excursion, and having asked of all the pilots and many boatmen and people of the bay, no one saw them.

Being asked whether fish was plentiful in the bay and if there was anyone engaged in this calling in the interior of the harbor, he said that small fish is very plentiful in the interior of the harbor and that there are several engaged in fishing there.

Being asked whether he has heard or knows anything which may assist in the elucidation of the event which occurred on the *Maine*, he said that he neither knows nor has heard absolutely anything, and at this stage this deposition was suspended, the witness reading it, affirming and ratifying the same and its contents, and signing it with the judge in the presence of the secretary, who certifies it.

FRANCISCO ALDAO. [Sign manual.]
JAVIER DE SALAS. [Sign manual.]

MINUTES.

HAVANA, *February 22, 1898.*

The judge, accompanied by the secretary, repaired to the steamer *Mangrove*, where he conferred for a long while with the captain of the said steamer and the commander of the *Maine*, Mr. Sigsbee. On his return, he inspected the wreck of the American ship, where the divers were at work, and in order that it may be of record it is set forth by means of minutes which I, the secretary, certify.

JAVIER DE SALAS. [Sign manual.]
PERAL. [Sign manual.]

MINUTES.

HAVANA, *February 23, 1898.*

The most excellent inspector of military health was officially written to and requested to submit an account of the assistance rendered by the military medical professors and the names of the same for the records of the proceedings. I so certify.

JAVIER DE SALAS. [Sign manual.]
PERAL. [Sign manual.]

DEPOSITION OF THE "CABO DE MAR" OF THE SECOND CLASS ANTONIO VARELA LOPEZ.

At Havana, on the twenty-third of February, one thousand eight hundred and ninety-eight, appeared before the court the person named in the margin, who being informed of that about which he was to be interrogated, swore to tell the truth, being reminded of the penalties incurred by those who give false testimony; being asked the usual questions of the law declared himself in his name to be Antonio Varela Lopez, "Cabot de Mar" of the first class, on duty at the navy-yard, a bachelor twenty-six years old, and declared that he had no interests whatever in the case under investigation.

Being asked to depose when and why he went to the *Maine* in the night of the 15th instant, he said that by order of the adjutant major of the navy-yard shortly after the explosion he set out in a rowing boat with the adjutant major on board towards the *Maine*, but as they came near a certain number of shells exploded and by order of the officer whom he carried he then went to the Machina, he remaining there waiting for the adjutant major, who was in conference with the chief of staff; that at that time a civilian arrived who he thinks was an officer of the *Maine*, and that by order of the commander of the Machina he transported him to his ship; on coming near it he heard cries and then he came nearer, against the opinion of the American official who did not want to approach, and in the forward part, wholly under water and from which emerged several fragments of plating already blown up, he saw a man who was the one who was crying whom he picked up, carrying him to the Machina, for he was wounded, and he neither saw, heard, nor met in that neighborhood any other.

On the way the wounded man, who was lying down, exchanged a few words with the American officer, and it seems told him that there were still wounded men thereabouts, for on our arrival, after landing the seaman, he spoke to one of the aids of the admiral, then returned in his boat carrying again the same officer and two physicians, as he believes civilians; that they came alongside the *Maine* on the starboard side, jumping on board and seeing that the water had reached to the height of the deck on which they walked, but they run over it—the upper deck—as far as the very seat of the fire without seeing or hearing anything. They went up into the top without either finding anything; that they then withdrew, carrying the officer and physicians to the steamer *City of Washington*. The witness returned to the Machina, where he was ordered to go back to the navy-yard. And at this stage this deposition was suspended, the witness reading it, affirming and ratifying its contents, and subscribing it with the judge in the presence of the secretary, who certifies.

ANTONIO VARELA. [Sign manual.]
PEDRO DEL PARAL. [Sign manual.]
JAVIER DE SAAS. [Sign manual.]

Court of investigation.

Most Excellent Sir: It being deemed necessary for the elucidation of the facts in the case which I am investigating in regard to the explosion which occurred on the war ship of the United States *Maine* to make an examination of its bottom, I request that your excellency take the proper measures to authorize me to that effect, as well as to procure from the arsenal the assistance of divers and barges that may be requisite.

God guard your excellency for many years.

Havana, February 16, 1898.

PEDRO DEL PARAL. [Sign manual.]

Most Excellent Commander-General of the Station Providential: Let the most excellent and illustrious governor-general of this island be officially written to that he may be pleased to obtain from the most excellent consul of the United States of America the assent for the action referred to and to issue the necessary orders to the commander of the navy-yard, so that the assistance required be extended, and let the present letter be returned to the judge-advocate who signs it for the records in the case.

Havana, February 16, 1898.

MONTEROLA. [Sign manual.]

Court of investigation.

Most Excellent Sir: It being certain in the opinion of this court that there remains in the part under water that was not burned of the iron-clad *Maine* all the magazines appertaining to the afterpart in which there had been stored not only the ammunition belonging to a part of its ordnance, but also that for the torpedoes and other explosives that they might carry, I request your excellency to inquire of the commander of the *Maine*, whether directly or through the medium of his consulate, what he carried on board and what in his judgment remains that is liable to explode, in order that we may in case of necessity proceed to take out of the ship, through the divers, those substances and empty the magazines in order to avoid subsequent catastrophe similar to those which, in the case of the blowing up of the steamer *Cabo Machichaco,* occurred even after the boat had been under water for some time.

I ask your excellency that in order to save my responsibility you demand of the consul answer to this report of great interest in the present investigation. God save your excellency's life many years.

Havana, February 18, 1898.

PEDRO DEL PERAL. [Rubric.]
The judge of the court of inquiry (El Juez Instructor).

To his excellency the COMMANDER-GENERAL OF THE PROVIDENCIA STATION (APOSTADERO).

Let the attorney be informed that as agreed with the consul of the United States and the commander of the cruiser *Maine* the work for which a permit has been solicited shall be conducted as soon as said gentlemen receive the supplies of material and divers they have asked from their Government, and let this communication be filed.

Havana, February 19, 1898.

MANTEROLA. [Rubric.]

Court of inquiry (Juzgado de instruccion).

Most Excellent Sir: Having been previously called by the commander of the *Maine,* I personally went to-day on board of the American steamer *Mangrove,* at ten thirty o'clock, and had a conference with the above-mentioned gentleman, who informed me of his desire that I should be present in the neighborhood of the *Maine* to witness the work of the official divers who would, during the day, go down to begin the work of surveying the bottom of the part of the prow totally submerged. To comply with the gentleman's wishes, as well as to see if I could gain any light from him as to the result of said work, I went to the neighborhood of the *Maine* around its prow, and I witnessed the descent of the diver, at eleven fifteen o'clock. He came up again at eleven forty-five. The second commander of the *Maine,* who arrived at this last moment, told me, after having spoken to the diver, that he had seen much mud, and he informed me that he would descend again at one o'clock. I then withdrew. At the aforesaid hour I was again in the same place, the diver descending at one fifty o'clock and coming up again at three fifteen o'clock.

These operations were not witnessed by any officer, class, or person of any significance, but only by sailors who worked on the air pump and another who took care of the pipe of the helmet and the movements of the diver. Nothing was told to me, but I could notice that the diver brought up with him something in the shape of a cylindrical, thin plate copper pipe about forty centimeters in length by fifteen diameter. Shortly after this the diver descended again, and upon his ascending I was told by one of the mentioned sailors that there were six or seven corpses among the submerged débris, but that their removal was difficult as, on account of their state of decomposition, they had become soft. At four o'clock, the work for the day being finished, as I was informed, I left the place, and being convinced that if I do not make an investigation in the very near future of the bottom of the American ship, the proceedings I am to institute shall be incomplete and will not be closed for a very long time, I ask from your excellency to obtain from the proper authorities a permit to commence immediately said investigation with the divers of the arsenal, in order to proceed to work at once, and submit to your excellency the complete report of the proceedings in my charge, the prompt termination of which interests not only the credit of the navy, but of the whole nation as well.

God save your excellency many years.

Havana, February twenty-first, eighteen hundred and ninety-eight.

The judge of the court of inquiry (El Juez de Instrución). Pedro del Peral. [Rubric.]

This is a copy. JAVIER DE SALAS. [Rubric.]

To His Excellency the Commander-General of the Station, office of the commander-general of the navy at the station of Havana, secretary of justice:

In reply to the courteous communication of your excellency, dated yesterday, relative to the expediency of extracting, by means of divers, the explosive substances in the armored ship *Maine*, emptying the coal bins, in order to prevent further disaster, ·I beg to inform you that in accordance with the consul of the United States and the commander of the above-mentioned ship this operation will take place as soon as the supply of divers and materials said gentlemen have solicited from their Government arrive.

God save your excellency many years.

Havana, February nineteenth, eighteen hundred and ninety-eight.

MANTEROLA. [Rubric.]

To the captain of frigate (*Capitan de Fragata*) Don Pedro del Peral y Caballero. Auditor for a Process (Fiscal de una causa). Cruiser *Magallanes*, office of the commander.

In reply to the courteous dispatch of your lordship of this date, I must state that from the first moments of the *Maine's* disaster, the persons expressed in inclosed report went to the Machina, under command of the chief of staff, and that they rendered all the service that was requested from them until three o'clock in the morning, when they returned on board. I must commend, in the first place, the work of Don Agustin Machorra Amenabar, physician of this ship; the third practitioner (practicante), D. José Rodriguez Valencia, and the nurse, Juan Ramirez Pedrote, who were the first to arrive at the spot, and after having done their professional duties at the Machina, the cruiser *Alfonso XII* and the steamer *Washington*, remained at the Machina on watch until the next day to attend the wounded and burnt that were coming.

God save your lordship many years.

On board. Havana, February twenty-first, eighteen hundred and ninety-eight.

VICENTE PEREZ. [Rubric.]

To the judge of the court of inquiry on the process on account of the disaster of the *Maine*, cruiser *Magallanes:*

LIST OF THE OFFICERS, CLASSES, AND PERSONS IN THIS SHIP WHO LENT THEIR AID IN THE DISASTER OF THE MAINE.

Head physician, Don Agustin Machorra y Amenabar. Third boatswain, Manuel Muiñas. Third practitioner, D. José Rodriguez Valencia. Coxswain of the second class (cabo de mar de segunda), Antonio Martinez Lopez. First-class seamen, Manuel Guardado Fandiñu. Ditto, Manuel Abad y Abad. Ditto, Antonio Fernandez Costas. Ditto, Máximo Perin Rodriguez. Second class seamen, Juan Ramirez Pedrote, José Fernandez Rodal, José Sucira Rivademar, Enrique Lozano Huertas, Juan Planell Torres, José Orquin Galiana, Antonio Nuñez Varela, Manuel Lamela Gonzalez, José Pequeño Lolla, Antonio Iturbe Agoitu, José Subía Egaña. First-class firemen, Manuel Ferreira Sucira. Ditto second class, Manuel Pantin Dopico, Juan Perez Pico, Manuel Dapina Martinez, José Montero y Diaz, Tomás Boa Seguin, José Sucira Sardiña.

All of whom distinguished themselves.

On board, Havana, February twenty-first, eighteen hundred and ninety eight.

VINCENTE PEREZ. [Rubric.]

Cruiser *Alfonso XII*, Office of the Commander, No. nine hundred and fourteen:

In order to reply in due form to the communication of your lordship requesting a list of the persons of this crew (dotacíon) who distin-guished themselves in the rescue of the crew of the armored *Maine*, which took fire in this port on the evening of the fifteenth instant, I have caused a verbal investigation to be made on board relative to the movements of this ship during the first moments of the disaster. The result is that the first boats to arrive to the *Maine* were all belonging to this ship; first, those which were floating, then those which were hanging, which were immediatdly lowered; all of this is easy to un-derstand, if it is remembered that this ship was distant only 150 meters from the burning one, and consequently the one nearest. Said boats went alongside the *Maine*, their crew boarded the ship, saving from a probable death many of the unhappy men who were some wounded, some stunned, and all exposed on account of the large increase of the fire and the rapid foundering of the armored vessel.

I have been acquainted with many noble deeds done by the hands and seamen of this crew; some of them had to jump into the water to save the wounded, and others remaining on board of the *Maine* when she was foundering and had to hail their boat. As it is not possible to make the description inside the limits of this already lengthy communi-cation of the noble interest displayed by all, I inclose herewith, as requested by your excellency, a list of the names of those whom I believe more worthy of mention, stating at the margin their deeds. In regard to the officers, on the first moments the ensigns Don Guillermo Colmenares y Ortíz, Don Luis Ponce de Leon, and Don Juan Rapallo y Orts went on board. The first mentioned arrived in a private boat which was on board, compelling to be taken there, he being perhaps the first person to arrive. All the others helped on board as much as circumstances required, many wounded having been picked up and cured, and the anchorage of the ship being changed with great exactness under the effective danger of incessant small explosions from the *Maine*. Happily, no misfortune took place on board this ship.

God save your excellency many years.

On board, Havana, February nineteenth, eighteen hundred and ninety-eight.

MANUEL DE ELISA. [Rubric.]

To the captain of frigate (*Capitán de Fragata*), Don Pedro Peral, judge:

At folio ninety-seven of this report is to be found a statement of the personnel of the cruiser *Alfonso XII* who distinguished themselves most in saving the victims of the ironclad *Maine* in the night of the 15th of February, 1898.

MINUTES.

Havana, twenty-third of February, one thousand eight hundred and ninety-eight, an official letter of this court, ordered by his excellency, in regard to the permission solicited for the examination of the bottom of the *Maine*, is made part of these records.

An official letter of this court, ordered by the superior authorities in answer to the request for the removal of the explosives and ammunition which are still in the afterpart of the *Maine;* a copy of the official letter addressed to the superior authority reporting that the works of the official American diver have been witnessed, and on the subject of the necessity for examining without delay by means of divers designated by this court the bottom of the *Maine;* an official letter from the superior authority in reply to one of the foregoing, and two official letters of the commanders of the *Alfonso XII* and of the *Magallanes* on the subject of the assistance and service rendered by the personnel of their ships to the victims of the *Maine* are also made part of the record, and that it may be of record it is entered by means of minutes.

I so certify.

JAVIER DE SALAS. [Sign manual.]
PERAL. [Sign manual.]

DEPOSITION OF THE "CABOT DE MAR" OF THE FIRST CLASS, MANUAL ANDUJAR GUERRERO.

At Havana on the twenty-fifth of February, one thousand eight hundred and ninety-eight, appeared before this court the person named in the margin, whose deposition his honor thought fit to take, cautioning him as to the obligation under which he is to be truthful, and the penalties incurred by those who give false testimony; he swore to tell the truth, and being asked the usual questions of the law, declared himself and his name to be Manuel Rodriguez Guerrero, native of Ferrol, twenty-three years old, a bachelor, and Cabot de Mar of the first class, doing duty on the torpedo brigade; declared that he had no interest whatever in the case under investigation; being asked to depose how, when, and on what ground he went to the *Maine* in the night of the disaster, he said:

That a short while after the explosion, a little before ten in the night, he was by superior order sent out in a boat of the brigade, carrying the foreman major of the arsenal in the direction of the *Maine*, turning around it several times looking for floating objects that they met for the event of their finding some wounded men, and seeing nor hearing nothing unusual, they went to the Machina; there the foreman jumped out and they took on board the commander of the *Caridad* in civilian clothes, a physician from the relief house, another civilian, a captain of firemen, and two firemen, again returning with all to the *Maine*, which was burning, jumping on board on the starboard side; that the water was not yet on the deck, but it came very near it; and that the ship was flooded in the inside; that they carried their examination as far as possible, climbing on thereto, and seeing nor hearing anything, they returned to the Machina with all these same gentlemen whom he had carried and thence conducted to the *City of Washington*, some of them.

Here the declaration was ended, and after having been read was sworn to and ratified, and signed, with the judge and the secretary, who certifies to the same.

MANUEL RODRIGUEZ. [Rubric.[
PEDRO DEL PERAL. [Rubric.]
JAVIER DE SALAS. [Rubric.]

DECLARATION OF THE GUNNER'S MATE, MANUEL DOMINGUEZ.

In Havana, the twenty-fourth of February, 1898, appeared on being cited the below named, and after being warned of the duty of speaking the truth and the punishment incurred by those giving false testimony, he swore to tell the truth; and being questioned as to his qualifications, said that he was named Manuel Rodriguez Diaz, born in the province of Huelva, having attained his majority, gunner's mate of the fleet, in the service of the cruiser *Alfonso XII*, and declared that he had no direct or indirect interest in the case in question.

Being asked to declare all that he knew in regard to the aid rendered by his vessel to the *Maine*, he said that immediately after the explosion he went as he was into the boat that was in the water, to go in and of the victims; arriving, with other boats from his vessel, first at the side of the *Maine*, and finding themselves at the larboard side almost under the prow; that from the center came cries of the crew, and hence that they went there; that they mounted to the deck near the large iron davit, picked up seven wounded men, who were transferred to the *Alfonso XII*, leaving the coxswain, Garruche, on the *Maine*, who had lost his way while engaged in picking up the wounded.

That they saw as they reached the American ship, the captain's gig of the *Maine* with men in the poop, one of whom called, as well as he could make out, since he spoke in pigeon Spanish, that he was a doctor. That when they reached the *Alfonso XII*, his boat remained in the task of unmooring the ship, so as to change its position and remove it further from the scene of the catastrophe, where grenades were continually exploding.

Here the statement stopped, which he read, sworn to and ratified the contents, subscribing the same with the judge and the secretary, who certifies to the same.

ANTONIO DOMINGUEZ. [Seal.]

PEDRO DEL PERAL. [Rubric.]
JAVIER DE SALAS. [Rubric.]

CRUISER ALFONSO XII, COMMAND No. 916.

On the annexed plan is found the present position of the American battle ship *Maine*, as Y. H. state in your communication of yesterday, and I have the honor of placing it in your hands.

God guard your excellency.

MANUEL DE ELISA. [Seal.]

Havana, February 19, 1898.

Senor D. Pedro del Peral, captain of the frigate, judge of instruction.

On page 101 of this statement will be found a map of the port of Havana, in which the position of the *Maine* is plainly shown.

GENERAL GOVERNMENT OF THE ISLAND OF CUBA.

His excellency the consul-general of the United States officially said to me on this date: In reply to the courteous communication of your excellency, dated the 16th instant, transmitting another from his excellency, the general-commander of the navy, asking the acquiescence of this consulate in the request of Senor Inez, instructor, to have an inquiry made into the causes of the accident to the *Maine*, I have the honor to say that, having consulted the commander of the same, the latter informs me that he hopes to exercise all action necessary for the inquiry regarding the ship under his own direction, according to orders from the United States Navy Department.

I have the honor to transmit to your excellency for your information and subsequent action.

God guard your excellency.

RAMON BLANCO. [Seal.]

Havana, February 17, 1898.

His excellency the general-commander of the navy of the station.

ORDER.

Refer to the fiscal of the case for incorporation in the same.

MANTEROLA. [Rubric.]

Havana, February 22, 1898.

COURT OF INQUIRY.

Esteemed Sir: This court not having received an answer to the communication in which it requested permission to inquire into the causes of the accident to the *Maine*, and it being of the highest importance that while this investigation is taking place, the approach of boats of any class, even those under the American flag (except war ships and those which have special authorization from this court) to the spot in question should be prohibited, begs your excellency to have the goodness to order that a patrol of vessels shall prevent the approach of the said boats that have not been authorized within a distance of 100 meters from the wreck. In order to avoid friction, and in case you deem it advisable, it asks at the same time that the United States consul and the commanders of the American men-of-war in port should be made acquainted with this determination of the court, which has been adopted with the object of avoiding future confusion.

God guard your excellency.

Havana, February 18, 1898.

PEDRO DEL PERAL. [Seal.]

His excellency the commander general of the station.

Refer to the chief of the general staff, that he may order what he may deem advisable in the premises in furtherance of the matter in interest and return the same.

Havana, February 18, 1898.   MANTEROLA. [Rubric.]

Esteemed Sir: Having ordered what is advisable, I have the honor to return to Y. E. this record, as you have been pleased to order.

Havana, February 18, 1898.

By order.   GABRIEL RODERIGUEZ. [Rubric.]

Order: With the previous report refer to the fiscal for incorporation.

Havana, February 22, 1898.   MANTEROLA. [Seal.]

Court of instruction. Private.

Esteemed Sir: In order that the patrol vessels may keep a suitable watch in the vicinity of the *Maine*, I have the honor to ask your excellency to appoint one or more officials, to exercise in turn the same duty, keeping guard from sunset to dawn over the movements of the vessels that may approach the wreck, watching closely those that they may consider worthy of suspicion.

God guard your excellency.

Havana, February 18, 1898.   PEDRO DEL PERAL. [Seal.]

His Excellency the general, commander of the station.

Order: Refer to the chief of the staff, in order that he may take the action necessary in the premises, and return.

Havana, February 18, 1898.

                              MANTEROLA. [Rubric.]

Esteemed Sir: The proper action having been taken, I have the honor to return to your excellency the dispatch as you have ordered.

Havana, February 18, 1898.

By order.   GABRIEL RODRIGUEZ. [Rubric.]

Order: Refer to the Fiscal to be incorporated.

                              MANTEROLA. [Rubric.]

DECLARATION OF THE INSPECTOR OF POLICE OF THE INSPECTION OF VESSELS.

In Havana, February 24, 1898, appeared in court the inspector, having been cited, who having been warned of the duty of speaking the truth and of the penalty for telling falsehoods, swears that he will speak truth, and being questioned as to his qualifications, says that he is and is called D. Antonio Perez Lopez, born in Zaragoza, being of age, married and residing at Industria, 62, at present inspector of police of the examination of boats of the port of Havana and annexes thereof.

Being asked to state what he knows in regard to the explosion that occurred on the *Maine* and the causes thereof, he said that at the time he was standing on the balcony of his flagstand on the Machina looking at the place where the *Washington* was anchored, the latter having just made entrance, and witnessed a tremendous explosion within the *Maine*, rising to a great height and then disappearing, causing the subsequent conflagration of the vessel; that followed by the chief of police he went in a boat to the scene of the catastrophe, and that small explosions continued until half past twelve or one o'clock. That he was ignorant of the causes of the disaster, but that partly through information he had received, partly through that of his subordinates and other agents of police, boatmen, and many people with whom he was thrown in daily contact in his office he could not in any way believe that it occurred intentionally.

Here the declaration ceases; which, after he has read, sworn to, and ratified, he signs before the judge and secretary, who certifies to the same.

ANTONIO PEREZ. [Rubric.]

PEDRO DEL PERAL. [Rubric.]
JAVIER DE SALAS. [Rubric.]

MINUTE.

In Havana, the twenty-fourth of February, 1898, there is attached to these proceedings a map of the port of Havana with the actual position of the *Maine*, accompanied by the official communication of the commander of the *Alfonso XII*. Communication transmitted from the general government of the island, showing the answer of the consul of the United States, together with that of the commander of the *Maine*, in regard to the inquiry into the cause of the sinking of the boat. Two communications of this court, decreed by authority in regard to keeping watch in the vicinity of the wreck of the *Maine*.

I certify to the same.

JAVIER DE SALAS. [Rubric.]
PERAL. [Rubric.]

DEPOSITION OF THE PILOT, JULIAN GARCIA LOPEZ.

In Havana, February 24, 1898, appeared, after being cited, the above-named individual; being instructed as to the duty of telling the truth and the penalties incurred in giving false testimony, declared that he would speak truth, and, being questioned as to qualifications, said that he was and was called Julian Garcia Lopez, native of the province of Oviedo, of age, pilot of the port of Havana, and that he had no interest, direct or indirect, in the case in question.

Being asked if he had entered the battle ship *Maine* in the port, and if he had, to tell what he knew in regard to the matter, he said that on the 20th of last January he was on duty and it fell to him to receive an American man-of-war; but that, as it was not expected, he did not know what vessel it was; that it passed into port, and, according to the general instructions for all ships of war, after showing on the map to the *Maine's* captain the buoy of section No. 4, which was vacant, and receiving his approval, the pilot fastened the vessel there between the German man-of-war which was in port and the *Alfonso XII*, in 36 feet of water, the ship drawing 22, as he was informed. Being asked if he had anything more to add or declare, he said no, since he considered of no importance the inquiries made by the commander as to whether the boat was expected, to which he answered no; whether he considered himself capable of bringing the vessel in, to which he answered yes; and whether they would be well received, to which he answered yes, since Havana was a cultured town, and they need not fear anything if they behaved themselves.

This examination was then suspended; he read the same, affirming and ratifying it, and signing it with the judge and the secretary, who hereby certifies.

JULIAN GARCIA LOPEZ. [Rubric.]

PEDRO DEL PERAL. [Rubric.]
JAVIER DE SALAS. [Rubric.]

NAVAL HEADQUARTERS OF THE STATION OF HAVANA
AND THE SQUADRON OF THE ANTILLES.
GENERAL STAFF. SECTION SECOND. BUREAU OF EQUIPMENT.

I transmit to Y. H. the annexed invoice furnished by "La Balear," of the medicines furnished by it for the use of the wounded of the American battle ship *Maine* on the night that the explosion of said vessel occurred, in order that you may provide that the amount thereof, which reaches one hundred and seven pesos and sixty-five cents, be charged to the expenses incurred in this matter, as you have been pleased to order heretofore.

God preserve your honor.

Havana, February 28, 1898.

JOSE MARENCA, [Rubric.]
Captain of frigate Don Pedro del Parel,
judge of the Maine Court of Inquiry.

At folio 112 of these proceedings appears an invoice of medicines furnished by " La Balear," pharmacy, for the use of the wounded of the *Maine*, amounting to 117 pesos and 75 centimes gold.

OFFICE OF THE NAVAL COMMANDANT AND HARBOR MASTER OF HAVANA, REPORTING ARTICLES FOUND BELONGING TO THE BATTLE SHIP MAINE.

Most Excellent Sir: The naval subdelegate of Casa Blanca, in an official communication dated yesterday, writes me as follows:

Most Excellent Sir: I have the honor to transmit to Y. E., having found the same floating on the shores near the Friscornia Beach, a canvas ventilator, eleven meters sixty centimeters long by sixty-five centimeters wide, with four wooden rings, which was found enclosed in a canvas cover. At the Gandon wharf there was found a wooden box without a cover, with two cans, apparently of copper, which were empty and appeared to have contained varnish or oil, with their screw tops, measuring 35 centimeters in length by 45 in width, and as they may belong to the battle ship *Maine* I inform you thereof, that you may order what you may deem expedient in the premises. Which I have the honor to transmit to Y. E. for your superior information, adding that besides the articles mentioned the employees of this office recovered a torpedo skid and a compass, which, together with the articles already enumerated for your excellency to order their disposition, considering that they all belong to the battle ship *Maine*. God preserve Y. E. many years.

Havana, February 21, 1898. LUIS PASTOR. [Rubric.]

Most excellent COMMANDANT-GENERAL OF THE STATION.

Order: Refer to the fiscal that it may be incorporated in the record herein.

Havana, February 24, 1898. MANTEROLA. [Rubric.]

Office of the naval commandant and harbor master of the port of Havana reports bodies found on the Casa Blanca Beach belonging to the battle ship *Maine*.

Most Excellent Sir: The naval subdelegate of Casa Blanca, in an official communication of yesterday, informs me as follows:

Most Excellent Sir: I have the honor to make known to your excel

lency that from six until ten thirty a. m. to-day there have been found
floating on these shores 16 bodies, apparently of the white race; one leg,
a portion of another, and other parts of an arm which may belong to
the victims of the American battle ship *Maine*, which have been sent—
nine, the portion of the leg, and other parts of an arm, by men from
the Spanish cruiser *Alfonso XII*, and the other seven, and a leg, by the
boat belonging to me (folio 854) to the Machina. Which I have the
honor to transmit to Y. E. for your superior information. God preserve
Y. E. many years.

Havana, February 19, 1898.   LUIS PASTOR. [Rubric.]
Most excellent COMMANDANT-GENERAL OF THE STATION.

Order: Refer to the fiscal that he may incorporate it in the records
herein.

Havana, February 24, 1898.   MANTEROLA. [Rubric.]

OFFICE OF THE SUBINSPECTOR OF THE MILITARY
BOARD OF HEALTH OF THE ISLAND OF CUBA.
SECTION 4. No. 1252.

In reply to your communication of the 23rd instant, I transmit you
the reports of the parties who, as a result of the unfortunate accident
to the battle ship *Maine*, were cared for in the military hospitals of this
station where they were taken, stating at the same time that from the
very moment the accident occurred orders were issued that the entire
medical corps not in service should repair to the wharf or the cruiser
Alfonso XII, to offer their services should they be necessary, as also
the ambulances on hand, and which were utilized in the premises. God
preserve you many years.

Havana, February 24, 1898.   MAS. [Rubric.]
To the fiscal of the harbor master's office, Don PEDRO DEL PERAL.

At folio 118 of this record appears a statement showing that there
were entered in the military hospital of Alfonso XIII 5 individuals from
the *Maine*, wounded and burnt.

At folio 119 of the same appears another statement, showing that
there entered the hospital of San Ambrosio twenty-eight individuals
from the same vessel in a serious condition.

OFFICE OF THE COMMANDANT OF
THE NAVY-YARD OF HAVANA.
No. 660.

The chief adjutant of this garrison, to whom I sent the communication of Y. H. of the 21st instant, relating to the assistance given the
victims of the *Maine*, day before yesterday informed me as follows:

In compliance with what your honor has been pleased to order, I
have the honor to state that the assistance given by the men of this
navy-yard to the battle ship *Maine* on the night of the 15th was: The
first boat of this yard, carrying the undersigned, the Coxswain Antonio
Narela Lopez and a crew of ten; a boat of the torpedo squadron with
the Quartermaster Antonio Manjibar Rafart, Coxswain Manuelo Rodriguez Guerrero, and six in the crew; the auxiliary launch, with the
Second Quartermaster Jose Prache Otera, Coxswain Mattias Bestand,
and a crew of ten.

These boats being prepared with the alacrity which the case demanded,
they proceeded to the place of the disaster, remaining there a long
while; and the undersigned observing that the watchfulness of the
three boats was unnecessary, ordered the launch to go to the Machina

to receive further orders, and engaging it in carrying the wounded from the cruiser *Alfonso XII* to the barracks of the Machina. The undersigned, with the first boat, went to the Machina to receive orders from the commanding officer, the torpedo-squadron boat remaining under the quartermaster, Mangibar, on the lookout at the place of the disaster until further orders. On the second trip of the first boat from the navy-yard to the *Maine* it carried an officer from said vessel and succeeded in saving the last wounded man on board, to do which this boat had to moor alongside a dangerous place of the burning wreck, and in so doing lost its rudder.

The long time that the boat from the torpedo squadron remained rowing around the burning wreck at a short distance, constitutes, in the judgment of the subscriber, a distinguished action on the part of the quartermaster Mengibar and the crew of the said boat; distinguished also is the action of the chief of the first boat, Varela, and the crew, who, fighting the flames of the burning wreck, made fast to the bow of the *Maine* in order to save from certain death the last wounded man of the American crew. This is all I have the honor to impart to Y. H., and under separate cover I transmit a list of the names of the three crews who rivaled each other in the most humane of services. And with a copy of the statement mentioned, I transmit this to Y. H., having to add that, for my own part, I can not make individual mention of actions that may be considered distinguished, since from the very moment of the catastrophe the entire personnel of officers of this navy-yard went to the site of the danger, the only one remaining here being the chief of the torpedo squadron, in compliance with my orders.

The health officers voluntarily left to offer their services, as did the chief medical officer of the yard, who took the ambulances and surgical appliances on hand. God preserve Y. H. many years.

Navy-Yard, February 24, 1898.

ESTEBAN ALMEDA. [Rubric.]

To the Judge Don PEDRO DEL PERAL.

At folio 124 of this record appears a list of the men from the navy-yard who, manning three boats, rendered assistance on the night of the catastrophe to the battle ship *Maine.*

At folios 125, 126, 127, 128, and 129 of the said record appear five photographs.

OFFICE OF THE SUBINSPECTOR OF THE MILITARY BOARD OF HEALTH OF THE ISLAND OF CUBA.

In addition to the communication of this office, No. 1252, which I had the honor to address Y. H. under date of the 24th instant, referring to the assistance rendered by the military medical corps to the wounded in the catastrophe to the battle ship *Maine,* I have to inform Y. H. that the following distinguished themselves by reason of their energy, zeal, and their spontaneous presence at the necessary points, offering their professional and personal services, as well on the wharf, asylums, inns, and hospitals:

The medical subinspector, second class, Don Agustin Muniozguren, Dr. Clemente Senar y Vicente, Dr. Don Jose Locute y Gallego, and Dr. Don Enrique Solana y Alemany. Which I have the satisfaction of communication to Y. H. for the purposes you may deem expedient.

God preserve Y. H. many years.

Havana, Feb. 28, 1898.

CRISTOBAL MAS, *Inspector.* [Rubric.]

To the fiscal of the office of the harbor master.

GENERAL GOVERNMENT OF THE ISLAND OF CUBA.

Most Excellent Sir: Under date of to-day this office says to the consul of the United States in this city as follows: In order to close the record of the investigation being made by the Spanish Government of the causes which brought about the catastrophe to the *Maine* there only remains to proceed to an inspection of the exterior and interior of the vessel where the explosion occurred, to which end it is deemed indispensable (in order to give the investigation greater legal weight) that our divers in their inspection be accompanied by those of the American Government, and no conclusive reply having been yet received from Y. H. so as to proceed as indicated, I pray you to be pleased to order or request the proper party to see that the said American divers unite with the Spaniards for the purpose of making a minute of the inspection, permitting myself also to beg you to fix a time as soon as possible. Which I have the honor to transmit to Y. E. for the purposes indicated.

God preserve Y. E. many years.
Havana, February 25, 1898.

             RAMON BLANCO. [Rubric.]

ORDER.

Most Excellent Commandant-General of the station:
Refer to the captain of frigate *Don Pedro del Peral*, fiscal, for proper disposition.
Havana, Mar. 1, 1898.

             MANTEROLA. [Rubric.]

MINUTE.

HAVANA, *February twenty-five of 1898.*

These proceedings are suspended to await the reply to see whether the bottom of the *Maine* may be inspected by the divers of our Government. Certified.

          JAVIER DE SALAS. [Rubric.]
          PERAL.   [Rubric.]

MINUTE.

HAVANA, *March first, eighteen hundred and ninety eight.*

There are appended to these proceedings: A communication from the chief of the general staff enclosing an invoice of medicines furnished by *La Balear*, pharmacy, amounting to one hundred and seven pesos (sixty-five cents) gold, two communications sent by the head of the office of the harbor master of Havana, relating to bodies and articles found in the bay. A communication from the office of the subinspector of the military board of health, accompanied by a statement of the wounded of the *Maine*, cared for in the hospitals of this place. A communication from the office of the commandant of the navy-yard, accompanied by a statement, in reply to a communication from this court; five photographs of the *Maine* taken from different points after the catastrophe.

A communication from the general government of the island, transmitted by the same, informing that it had communicated with the consul of the United States regarding the necessary of proceeding to the inspection of the bottom of the *Maine*, by Spanish divers. Certified.

          JAVIER DE SALAS. [Rubric.]
          PERAL. [Rubric.]

In Havana, on the first of March, of eighteen hundred and ninety-eight, the judge ordered the continuing of these proceedings by reason of having received verbal authority from the Captain-General's office to proceed to the inspection of the bottom of the *Maine*, by this court. His honor so ordered, before me, the secretary, who certifies.

JAVIER DE SALAS. [Rubric.]
PERAL. [Rubric.]

MINUTE.

HAVANA, *March first, eighteen hundred and ninety-eight.*

I have received a communication from the office of the subinspector of the military board of health, amplifying a former one, already attached to the case.

Certified.

JAVIER DE SALAS. [Rubric.]
PERAL. [Rubric.]

MINUTE.

HAVANA, *March first, eighteen hundred and ninety-eight.*

One of the navy-yard divers being ill, for greater comfort and dispatch in the work, the office of the Captain-General was requested to ask the board of harbor works to send the official divers under them.

Certified.

JAVIER DE SALAS. [Rubric.]
PERAL. [Rubric.]

MINUTE.

In Havana, on the second of March of eighteen hundred and ninety-eight, the court moved to the vicinity of the *Maine*, where the divers and material of the board of harbor works were located, the diver Ramon Gonzalez going down at 9 and coming up at 9.30, and inspecting the port quarter.

Certified.

JAVIER DE SALAS. [Rubric.]
PERAL. [Rubric.]

MINUTE.

In Havana, on the second of March of eighteen hundred and ninety-eight, the court again moved to the vicinity of the *Maine*, where were the divers of the board of harbor works and that of the navy-yard, all with the necessary equipment, witnessing the descent of the said Juan Hernandez and Ramón Gonzales, the former on the port side toward the middle and the latter at the same part of the starboard side, remaining under water from one o'clock until fifteen minutes after three.

And in order that it may be of record, it is set forth by means of minutes which I, the secretary, certify.

JAVIER DE SALAS. [Sign manual.]
PERAL. [Sign manual.]

Havana, the second of March, one thousand eight hundred and ninety-eight, the judge determined to communicate orally to the superior authorities the result of the preliminary examination made by the divers on this day, in the event of its being deemed expedient to transmit the same to the Government of His Majesty, reporting that the one who inspected the port side did not reach the point where the vessel is broken, and that the one on the starboard side saw about the middle large pieces of plates bent outward, as well as coal strewn on the outside; the findings of the day not being more extensive by reason of the deep mine, which impeded progress, and of the wreckage, which caused stumbling.

So dictated his honor before me, the secretary, who certifies.

JAVIER DE SALAS. [Sign manual.]
PERAL. [Sign manual.]

GENERAL NAVY HEADQUARTERS OF THE HAVANA
STATION AND SQUADRON OF THE ANTILLES,
STAFF THIRD DIVISION, SECTION 2.

The commander of the ironclad is hereby directed to be pleased to order that the diver of his ship be present at seven to-morrow at the Machina of San Fernando, at the disposal of your honor, with the requisite equipment, to assist in the work of examining the bottom of the United States ironclad *Maine.* I state this to your honor for your information and as the consequence of your note of this date.

God guard your honor for many years.

Havana, March 2, 1898.

MANTEROLA. [Sign manual.]

The investigating judge,
Captain Don PEDRO DEL PERAL Y CABALLERO.

MINUTES.

HAVANA, *March 3, 1898.*

It is made of record by means of minutes that owing to the prevailing rain and in consequence of the turbidness of the water the work of the divers has been suspended for this day. I so certify.

JAVIER DE SALAS. [Sign manual.]
PERAL. [Sign manual.]

MINUTES.

HAVANA, *March 3, 1898.*

It was requested of the superior authorities that the diver of the *Vizcaya* be directed to assist, with the equipment of his occupation, in the work of the divers of the navy-yard and of the harbor works. I so certify.

JAVIER DE SALAS. [Sign manual.]
PERAL. [Sign manual.]

MINUTES.

HAVANA, *March 4, 1898.*

The court repaired to the location of the *Maine* and witnessed the descent of the divers Hernandez and Gonzalez of the harbor works, and Alvarez and Abellieras of the navy-yard, who proceeded with their examination, remaining under water, two at a time alternately, from 7 to 9 in the forenoon and from 12 to 3½ in the afternoon. It is made of record by means of minutes, which I, the secretary, certify.

JAVIER DE SALAS. [Sign manual.]
PERAL. [Sign manual.]

DEPOSITION OF DON FRANCISCO ALDRES Y CASAMES.

Havana, on the fourth of March, one thousand eight hundred and ninety-eight, appeared in this court, on verbal summons, the person named in the margin, who, being cautioned as to the obligation of speaking the truth and the penalty provided by law for false testimony, swore to tell the truth, and being asked the usual questions in the law, declared himself and his name to be D. Francisco Aldres y Casames, of age, married, a graduated assistant engineer of Public Works, an industrial engineer presently in the employ of the Board of Harbor Works, without any interest whatever in the case under investigation. Being asked whether he had effected works for the removal of sunken hulls in the bay, said that he effected the removal of sunken hulls at Tallapiedra, that of the hull of the American steamer *City of Rionda*, done the work required for the site of the dry dock and that recently concluded to blow up the shoal Feliciano.

Being asked what explosives he used for the purpose, in what quantity, and what were the effect and consequences, said that he used an American explosive called Rancka—rock similar to dynamite number 3; that he used it in quantities of from 5 to 25 pounds; that the effects of small quantities have been insignificant on the outside when the cartridges were placed more than two meters deep, and that with the medium and larger charges it was observed that there were projections of water, more or less high, according to the charge and depth; it drags considerable mire from the bottom and with it a greater or less number of dead fish, which appear on the surface sometimes one hundred meters distant from the place where the explosion took place, there always being found a larger number dead at the bottom or within the hulls worked on; that flames were never seen to issue at the surface, nor was there any volume of smoke sufficient to be perceived, as it were, the color being white in every case; that the effects of the explosions were always felt by the vessels near the spot where they took place, and that at distances of from 500 to 1,000 meters the hulls felt as if they had been struck a hard blow, but without consequences.

And at this stage this deposition was suspended, read by the witness, who affirmed and ratified its contents, subscribing it with the judge and in the presence of the secretary, who certifies.

FRANCISCO ALDOYS. [Sign manual.]
PEDRO DEL PERAL. [Sign manual.]
JAVIER DE SALAS. [Sign manual.]

MINUTES.

HAVANA, *March 4, 1898.*

Copy was made of the plans of the *Maine*, furnished by her late commander, Mr. Sigsbee, a draftsman of the navy-yard, doing duty at the artillery headquarters, being sent for to do the work. Saw plans, which will be appended to these proceedings, were examined to the end of dividing and distributing the work of the divers. I so certify.

JAVIER DE SALAS. [Sign manual.]
PERAL. [Sign manual.]

DEPOSITION OF THE MERCHANT NAVIGATING OFFICER DON MIGUEL
GONZALAZ FRAVIESO.

At Havana, on the fourth of March, one thousand eight hundred
and ninety-eight, appeared before the court the officer named in the
margin, who, being cautioned as to the interrogatories about to be put
to him and the penalties incurred by those who give false testimony,
swore to tell the truth, and, being asked the usual questions, declared
himself and his name to be Don Miguel Gonzalez Fravieso, twenty-
seven years old, of age, native of Castropol, Asturias, merchant navigating officer, and at present in the position of first officer of the steamer
San Juan.

Being asked whether in the night of the 15th of February, of the
present year, he was in the harbor and witnessed the blowing up of the
Maine, as well as such particulars in connection therewith as might
throw light on the proceedings, he said that he was on board the *San
Juan,* then under repairs at Regla, lying in his bunk; that he awoke at
the sound of the explosion, imagining that some misfortune had happened
in the bay, and believing that it might well be on one of our war vessels. That he ordered the boat to be manned by four men and proceeded
toward the channel of the harbor, when he saw flames beginning to
issue from a certain point which he approached, the *Maine* turning
out to be the vessel on fire; that on arriving he found there four boats
from our war vessels, and one which he believes might have been
from the *Mexico,* some being very near and others fastened to the
stern of the *Maine,* picking up and giving assistance to wounded men;
that of American boats he only saw one, a merchant *yoste,* which I
suppose was from the *Washington,* whither the wounded men were
likely taken, for one could hear the moaning and crying coming from
that vessel; that he was unable to pick up any wounded man or seaman, and after a short while withdrew, leaving the boats from the war
vessels.

Being asked whether he saw any boat from the *Washington* other than
that above mentioned, he said that he saw no other, and that at the same
moment the *Washington* weighed anchor and moored at San Jose.

And this deposition was suspended and read by the witness, who
affirmed and ratified its contents, subscribing it with the judge in the
presence of the secretary, who certifies.

MIGUEL GONZALEZ FRAIVESO. [Sign manual.]
PEDRO DEL PERAL. [Sign manual.]
JAVIER DE SALA. [Sign manual.]

DEPOSITION OF COMMODORE DON MANUEL ELISA Y VERGARA.

At Havana, on the fourth of March, one thousand eight hundred and
ninety-eight, appeared, on summons, the officer named in the margin,
who, being advised of the obligation resting on him to tell the truth and
of the penalties incurred by those who give false testimony, swore to tell
the truth, and being asked the usual questions, under the law, declared
himself and his name to be Don Manuel Elisa y Vergara, commodore;
married; of age; declaring to have no interest whatever, direct or
indirect, in the case under investigation.

Being asked whether, during the time while the ship under his command was moored to one of the buoys near to the site for the dry dock,
he felt any perceptible or considerable trepidations resulting from the
submarine explosions that took place there, he said that toward the

month of August or thereabout there took place small submarine explo-sions for the purpose, as he believed, of blowing up some rocks which impeded the work of the dredges on the site of the dry dock.

His ship, which is the cruiser *Alfonso XII*, experienced trepidations which alarmed him at first, and he reported to the admiral of the squadron for his opinion as to whether he thought it expedient that his mooring should be changed so as to avoid injury to his ship from the repetition of this effect, and in consequence made fast to the buoy at Friscornia, belonging to the steamers of the French line. Being asked in regard to the thickness of the plates on the sides of his ship at the bottom, he said that it is approximately a half inch (Spanish). And at this point this declaration was suspended, and after reading, affirming, and ratifying it, he subscribed it with the judge and the secretary, who certifies.

MANUEL DE ELISA. [Sign manual.]

PEDRO DEL PERAL. [Sign manual.]
JAVIER DE SALAS. [Sign manual.]

MINUTES.

HAVANA, March 5, 1898.

The court repaired to the location of the *Maine* and witnessed the descent of the divers Hernandez and Gonzales, of the harbor works, and Alvarez and Abelliera, of the navy-yard, who proceeded with the examination, remaining under water two at a time, alternately, toward the bow, all on the starboard side, from 7 to 9 in the forenoon and from 12 to 3½ in the afternoon.

It is made of record by means of minutes which I, the secretary, certify.

JAVIER DE SALAS. [Sign manual.]
PERAL. [Sign manual.]

MINUTES.

HAVANA, March 5, 1898.

There was submitted to the superior authorities, for their approval, an account of the expenses of this court up to this day, amounting to one hundred and eighty dollars (Spanish) sixty-five cents, gold. I so certify.

JAVIER DE SALAS. [Sign manual.]
PERAL. [Sign manual.]

MINUTES.

HAVANA, March 6, 1898.

The divers did not work, this being a holiday. I so certify.

JAVIER DE SALAS. [Sign manual.]
PERAL. [Sign manual.]

ORDER.

HAVANA, March 7, 1898.

The judge, with the plans of the *Maine* under his eyes, determined to make a distribution of the work to the divers, charging them espe-cially to direct their work to the finding the stem of the ship and the forward turret in order to take these at once for starting points and keep up the full examination of the submerged part.

So dictated his honor before me, the secretary, who certifies.

JAVIER DE SALAS. [Sign manual.]
PERAL. [Sign manual.]

MINUTES.

HAVANA, *March 8, 1898.*

The court repaired to the location of the *Maine* and witnessed the descent of the divers Hernandez and Gonzalez, of the board of harbor works, and Alvarez and Abelliera, of the navy-yard, who proceeded with their examination, remaining under the water from 7 to 9 in the forenoon and 12 to 3 in the afternoon.

It is made of record by means of minutes which I, the secretary, certify.

JAVIER DE SALAS. [Sign manual.]
PERAL. [Sign manual.]

MINUTES.

HAVANA, *March 9, 1898.*

The court repaired to the location of the *Maine* and witnessed the descent of the divers Gonzalez and Hernandez of the board of harbor works, and Alvares and Abelliera, of the navy-yard, who proceeded with the examination, remaining under water from 7 to 9 in the forenoon and from 12 to 3 in the afternoon. It is made of record by means of minutes which I, the secretary, certify.

JAVIER DE SALAS. [Sign manual.]
PERAL. [Sign manual.]

MINUTES.

HAVANA, *March 10, 1898.*

The court repaired to the location of the *Maine* and witnessed the descent of the divers Gonzalez and Hernandez, alternating from 12 to 3 in the afternoon. I so certify.

JAVIER DE SALAS. [Sign manual.]
PERAL. [Sign manual.]

MINUTES.

HAVANA, *March 11, 1898.*

The court repaired to the location of the *Maine* and witnessed the descent of the divers Gonzalez and Hernandez of the board of harbor works, who worked alternately from 12 to 3 in the afternoon. I so certify. JAVIER DE SALAS. [Sign manual.]
PEDRO DEL PERAL. [Sign manual.]

MINUTES.

HAVANA, *March 12, 1898.*

A report of the salient occurrences and facts of the night of the *Maine* disaster was asked officially of the chiefs of the companies of firemen in this capital.

MINUTES.

HAVANA, *March 12, 1898.*

The court repaired to the location of the *Maine* and witnessed the descent of the divers Gonzalez and Hernandez, of the board of harbor works, who worked alternately from 12 to 3 in the afternoon. I so certify.

JAVIER DE SALAS. [Sign manual.]
PERAL. [Sign manual.]

NAVY GENERAL HEADQUARTERS OF THE HAVANA STATION
AND SQUADRON OF THE ANTILLES.
STAFF DIVISION 3, SECTION 2, "CLASES."

I have to say to your honor, in reply to your polite note of this day, that I have obtained from the chief of harbor works here two divers, with the necessary equipment, who are to be at your disposal to-morrow at 7 in the forenoon, near the ironclad *Maine.*
God guard your honor for many years.
Havana, first of March, 1898.

MANTEROLA. [Sign manual.]
The investigating judge, Captain DON PEDRO DEL PERAL Y BABALLERO.

[Confidential.]

NAVY GENERAL HEADQUARTERS OF THE HAVANA STATION
AND SQUADRON OF THE ANTILLES. STAFF-DIVISION.

The most excellent minister in a cipher cablegram dated the 10th instant, writes as follows: Advisable you expedite as much as you can the conclusion report *Maine* so that it precede Americans. In transmitting this to your honor I do so to the end that, taking into consideration the wishes of the national government you may use, if that be possible, more expedition than has been done heretofore, in order to comply with the cablegram.
God guard your honor for many years.
Havana, 11 March, 1898.

MANTEROLA. [Sign manual.]
Captain D. PEDRO DEL PERAL,
Investigating Judge in the case of the Ironclad Maine.

[Telegram.]

OFFICE OF THE GOVERNOR-GENERAL OF THE ISLAND OF CUBA,
Washington, February 19, 1898.
Consul-General LEE, *Havana:*
The Government of the United States has already commenced an investigation concerning the causes which occasioned the disaster of the *Maine* through the medium of naval officers appointed especially for the purpose, who will conduct this investigation independently. This Government will extend every possible facility to the Spanish authorities for the investigations they may wish to make on their part.

DAY.
A true copy. JOSE CONGOSTO. [Sign manual.]

[Telegram]

OFFICE OF THE GOVERNOR-GENERAL OF THE ISLAND OF CUBA,
Havana, February 18, 1898.
Sigsbee begins work to-morrow with divers who have been sent him from the United States to recover the bodies that still remain in the

Maine, as well as personal effects of the officers and crew, and also any other article that may be secured. After this the Spanish Government wishes to unite with ours, to the end of examining the hull of the ship and the bottom of the harbor around the same.

LEE.

A true copy.

J. CONGOSTO. [Sign manual.]

OFFICE OF THE GOVERNOR-GENERAL
OF THE ISLAND OF CUBA.

Most Excellent Sir: The consul-general of the United States at this capital has just addressed me the following note:

"I have the honor to acknowledge the receipt of your communication of the 25th instant. In reply I take the liberty of inclosing a copy of my telegram to the Assistant Secretary of State at Washington, referring to the subject, and also the reply of that Department. It is to be observed that the Government of the United States thinks that the investigation by the two governments is to be independent, but that every kind of facilities will be granted to your Government for the prosecution of such investigation as it may think expedient. I shall confer with Captain Sigsbee on the matter and will suggest that he call on the admiral of the naval station, and I do not doubt that these two officers may agree upon some plan that will be satisfactory to all. I am sure that neither Government has any other object than to eluci-. date all the facts connected with the explosion on the *Maine,* and that the main desire of both Governments is to proceed in harmony with the investigations."

I have the honor to transmit the foregoing to your honor with the translated copies of the two telegrams referred to, for such ends as may be expedient.

God guard your honor for many years.

Havana, February 26, 1898.

RAMON BLANCO. [Sign manual.]

Most excellent naval commander-general of the station Providencia.

With the two annexed copies of the telegrams, let the present letter be turned over to Captain D. Pedro del Peral, prosecuting attorney (judge-advocate), for the ends thereto appertaining.

Havana, March 15, 1898.

COURT OF INVESTIGATION.

Most Excellent Sir: In the investigation conducted by me in the matter of the catastrophe of the *Maine* there are needed certain data which this court does not know where to find. I therefore turn to your excellency and beg that you may secure the same from the proper quarter. The said data are as follows: Ordnance carried by the ship, parts of the ship where the same was placed, quantity and nature of ammunition, and powder in the forward magazines.

God guard your excellency for many years.

Havana, March 16, 1898.

PEDRO DEL PERAL. [Sign manual.]

Most excellent commander-general of the station, Apostadero.

Let the present be transmitted to the most excellent and illustrious Governor-General of the island, and let him be asked to be pleased to secure from the consul of the United States the requested data, and let the present letter be returned to the judge-advocate, who signs it, for the ends thereto appertaining.

Havana, March 16, 1898.

MENTEROLA. [Sign manual.]

MINUTES.

HAVANA, *March 12, 1898.*

An official note from the superior authority transmitting a cipher telegram from the most excellent minister of the navy was received and is made part of these proceedings. I so certify.

JAVIER DE SALAS. [Sign manual.]
PERAL. [Sign manual.]

MINUTES.

HAVANA, *March 12, 1898.*

An official letter from the superior authority announcing that the help in equipment and divers has been secured from the board of works of the harbor, as requested, is made part of the proceedings. I so certify.

JAVIER DE SALAS. [Sign manual.]
PERAL. [Sign manual.]

MINUTES.

HAVANA, *March 13, 1898.*

This being a holiday the work of the divers is suspended. I so certify.

JAVIER DE SALAS. [Sign manual.]
PERAL. [Sign manual.]

MINUTES.

HAVANA, *March 14, 1898.*

The court repaired to the location of the *Maine* and witnessed the descent of the divers Hernandez and Gonzalez, of the board of harbor works, and Alvarez and Abellieras, of the navy-yard, who worked from 12 to 3½ in the afternoon. I so certify.

JAVIER DE SALAS. [Sign manual.]

MINUTES.

HAVANA, *March 15, 1898.*

The court repaired to the location of the *Maine* and witnessed the descent of the divers Hernandez and Gonzalez, of the harbor works, and Alvarez and Abelleira, of the navy-yard, who worked from 12 to 3½ in the afternoon. I so certify.

JAVIER DE SALAS. [Sign manual.]
PERAL. [Sign manual.]

MINUTES.

HAVANA, *March 16, 1898.*

Copies of two telegrams, one from the Secretary of State of the United States to the consul of his country at this capital, and the other from said consul to the Government of Washington, accompanied by an official letter of the Governor-General of the island transmitting the reply of the consul to previous official correspondence, were received and are made part of these proceedings. I so certify.

> JAVIER DE SALAS. [Sign manual.]
> PERAL. [Sign manual.]

MINUTES.

HAVANA, *March 16, 1898.*

An official letter went to the most excellent commander general of the station, asking him to obtain from the proper quarter certain data as to the ordnance carried by the *Maine,* the location of the same; the quantity and kinds of ammunition and powder in the forward magazines. I so certify.

> JAVIER DE SALAS. [Sign manual.]
> PERAL. [Sign manual.]

MINUTES.

MARCH 16, 1898.

A reply to the official note in the foregoing minutes is received and made part of the proceedings. I so certify.

> JAVIER DE SALAS. [Sign manual.
> PERAL. Sign manual.

MINUTES.

HAVANA, *March 16, 1898.*

The court repaired to the location of the *Maine* and witnessed the descent of the divers Hernandez and Gonzalez, of the board of harbor works, and Alverez and Abelliera, of the navy-yard, who worked from 12 to $3\frac{1}{2}$ in the afternoon, alternately. I so certify.

> JAVIER DE SALAS. |Sign manual.]
> PERAL. [Sign manual.]

MINUTES.

MARCH 17, 1898

The court repaired near the *Maine,* witnessing the descent of the divers of the arsenal and of the board of works of the port, who worked from 12 to $3\frac{1}{2}$ p. m. I certify.

> JAVIER DE SALAS. [Flourish.]
> PERAL. [Flourish.]

OFFICIAL ACT OR PROCEEDING.

HAVANA, *March 18, 1898.*

The court went near to the place where the *Maine* was, and witnessed the descent of the divers, who worked alternately from 12 to $3\frac{1}{2}$ p. m. I certify.

> JAVIER DE SALAS. [Flourish.]
> PERAL. [Flourish.]

HAVANA, *February 19, 1898.*

His honor ordered that the work of the divers in examining the *Maine* should be considered as ended, and proceeded to take their depositions, for which purpose they were summoned to appear on Monday, the 21st. Thus his honor ordered before me, the clerk of the court, who certify.

JAVIER DE SALAS. [Flourish.]
PERAL. [Flourish.]

· DEPOSITION OF RAMON GONZALEZ, DIVER.

In the city of Havana, on the 21st day of March, 1898, appeared, having been duly summoned, the diver above named, who, having been admonished that he was under strict obligations to tell the truth, and having been warned of the penalties to which any person subjected himself by bearing false witness, made oath that he would tell the truth, and, being asked the usual preliminary questions, said that his name was Ramon Gonzalez y Gravote; that he was a native of Santa Cruz de Teneriffe, married, 38 years of age, and a diver in the employ of the board of works of the port; he said that he had no interest, either direct or indirect, in the case now before the court.

When asked whether he had worked in the examination of the bottom and the sunken portion of the American ironclad *Maine*, and if so, how many days, and with what result, he said that he had, indeed, worked in the examination of the sunken portion of the *Maine* from the 2d day of the current month until the 18th without interruption, except on holidays, and on one day when the rain prevented him from working; that he had been every day, and that he could recapitulate what he had seen in the following;.that he began the examination on the port side, aft, but did not find any serious damage there; that he examined the spaces occupied by the boilers, forward, on both sides, and found that all the plates, which had apparently formed the sides, were bent outwards; that, in the center of the hull, there was such a mass of plates, irons, cable conductors (apparently for electric light), pieces of wood (projectiles, some whole and others broken) together with other objects, that it was impossible to get down into the hull of the vessel.

That in examining the forward part, on the starboard side, he found a small anchor, broken on one side; that, throughout an extent of two or three fathoms, it was found to be intact, although bulging outwards; continuing the same examination, forward, on the same port side, a double bottom was found in which there was apparently no break whatever; that, moreover, there were found on the port side of the same double bottom an orlop-gangway, the sides of which were intact, and within several pieces of iron, melted and broken, which had evidently stopped there; that, when the water around the vessel was examined, in a radius of from 50 to 60 metres, remnants of plates, handrails, and shapeless masses of all kinds and sizes were found, it being impossible to tell from what part of the vessel they were.

The bottom was found to be full of mud, without any cavity whatever except those caused by objects which fell during the explosion; that the bilge and keel of the vessel, throughout its entire extent, were buried in the mud, but did not appear to have suffered any damage; that he did not find the large turret on the starboard side, forward, nor could he form a correct idea of anything more, because the confusion of objects prevented him from penetrating into the interior portion of the vessel; that the point of rupture was at the same height, both on the port and starboard sides; that the rupture was caused by the uniting of two plates, the aft plate remaining intact, and the rivets which fastened it having been broken in two, their heads remaining in their places on the inside, and the rest outside of their orifices.

That some coal was found outside of the coal bunkers, on the mud, on both sides; that on the port side there was a boat of the kind propelled by steam, apparently uninjured, or at most with but slight injuries. There was another boat, farther aft, hanging from its davits in the uninjured portion of the vessel.

Here the deposition ended, and deponent read it and ratified its contents, and signed it with his honor the judge, and with the clerk of the court, who certifies.

RAMON GONZALEZ GARABOTE (sic). [Flourish.]
PEDRO DEL PERAL. [Flourish.]
JAVIER DE SALAS. [Flourish.]

DEPOSITION OF JUAN HERNANDÉZ, DIVER.

In the city of Havana, on the 21st day of March, 1898, appeared the aforesaid diver, who, having been admonished that he was under strict obligations to tell the truth, and was warned of the penalties incurred by any person who bears false witness, made oath that he would tell the truth, and being asked the usual preliminary questions, he said that his name was Juan Hernandez y Cabrera, a native of Santa Cruz, in Teneriffe, married, 29 years of age, a diver in the employ of the board of works of the port. He declared that he had no interest, either direct or indirect, in the case before the court.

He was then asked whether he had worked in examining the bottom of the *Maine* and the submerged portion of that vessel, how many days he had worked, and with what result. In reply to which he said that he had worked from the 2d to the 18th day of the current month without any interruption except on holidays and rainy days, and that he had seen the following: That he began to examine on the starboard side of the vessel, beginning aft and going forward, but found nothing remarkable until the point of rupture marked in the plan, which corresponds exactly to the forward side of the coal bunkers in the center from port to starboard; that the rupture of the side is perfectly well marked in the joining of the vertical plates; that the plates which run aft are intact, their rivets being preserved, together with their heads on the inner side, and the separated plate without the riveted portion or head which belonged to it; that in the portion comprised between the rupture and the rear portion of the vessel there was a boat hanging from its davits with a canvas cover, and that he examined from the point of rupture, going aft without finding any side or plates of that kind for a distance from the prow of 5 or 6 meters; that it was almost intact, although not down toward the outside portion.

That he there found an anchor broken in the side and a chain which went from the hawsehole, which is in the chain box; that in the place in which ———— was the plates are seen which have fallen upon the mud, always toward the outside; that on a more careful examination a part was found which had apparently belonged to the hold of the vessel, because there appeared a double bottom, one portion of which was detached from the other by vertical plates which divided it into small compartments communicating with each other through large oval holes; that near to the coal bunkers, on that side toward the forward part of the rupture, a quantity of coal was found scattered over the mud; that projectiles for the cannon were likewise seen of ten inches, and also of 6, and also for rapid-firing guns and even of Mauser rifles, some of them having burst and others being whole; that when examined on the outside throughout an extent equal to one-half of the length of the vessel around the hull remnants were found, more or less large, of plates, timbers, utensils, etc., at the bottom, which consists of loose mud, without any hole or cavity, presenting a uniform aspect.

That, examining the side on the starboard, the rupture was found at the same height as on the other side, with the difference that the forward part does not exist, and that on this side the remnants hurled out of the vessel are less numerous; that the part of the side which exists is knocked down on to the mud as far as the point of rupture; that on the inside of the vessel it has been impossible to make a careful examination on account of the pile of plates, irons, electric cables, and fragments of all kinds which prevent this; the filthy condition of the water likewise renders such work difficult; that they saw jars of powder, some of which had burst, and another—only one—was entire with the bag inside. This deposition stopped here and deponent signed it, after having read it and having ratified it; he signed it with his honor the judge and with the clerk of the court, who certifies.

JUAN HERNANDEZ.   [Flourish.]

PEDRO DEL PERAL. [Flourish.]
JAVIER DE SALAS. [Flourish.]

DEPOSITION OF JOSÉ MANUEL ALVAREZ.

In the city of Havana, on the 21st day of March, 1898, appeared the above-named diver, who, having been admonished that he was under strict obligation to tell the truth, and being warned of the penalties incurred by any person who bears false witness, made oath that he would tell the truth, and being asked the usual preliminary questions he said that his name was José Manuel Alvarez Muñiz, a native of Asturias, 37 years of age, and married, and that he had been a diver in the navy since the year 1887; he said that he was not interested, either directly or indirectly, in the case before the court. Being asked whether he had worked in the examination of the bottom and the submerged portion of the North American ironclad *Maine*, he said that he had indeed worked from the 2d day of the current month until the 18th, except on holidays and the 3d day of the month, which was rainy, and also the 11th, 12th, and 10th, when they were working on a Norwegian steamer in the dock.

He said that he began the examination at the point of rupture on the starboard side, and that he could not distinguish or reconstruct any portion of the vessel from that point, because the plates were in different positions and many of them were buried; that of the iron plates he only saw a few on the port side toward the middle; that the vessel in her forward half was broken up, and that in her inner portion the examination was difficult, especially when they were at work, because the American divers were working there; that the lowest portion of the vessel must be buried, and that among the plates and scattered pieces there is not one that can appear or be of the keel; that there were no cavities or rough places or large holes in the bottom, and that on the starboard side this appears higher than on the ———, which leads to the presumption that it was buried more on this side.

S. Doc. 231, pt 7——61

That he did not find the turret; that on the starboard side, forward, he had the vessel attempting to look for it by soundings and examinations for more than 30 meters away from the vessel without any result whatever; that he found a steamboat which had been knocked out of the vessel on the port side that was apparently uninjured; that he could not catch the stem of the boat or with the ————, to which the vessel was tied, or with any cannon; that he saw large pieces of the deck and of the side of the steamer lying at the bottom and being inverted. For instance, the wooden portion of the deck lay at the bottom and the wrong side was exposed, showing the beams; that they thought they had found the stem, but on a careful examination it appeared that it was not the stem; that he found the foremast forward and on the port side, away from the vessel, without yards and broken, and they saw on the starboard side forward a large anchor without stock, but with its chain whole.

That he saw on the starboard side, about 20 meters from the hull, a number of hand rails, and a gun carriage with its wheels; that on the inside it was impossible for him to see anything more, not only on account of the confusion with which things were piled up but because the American divers prevented him from working or from undertaking to work there.

This deposition stopped here, and deponent read it, ratifying and signing it, together with his honor the judge, and with me, the clerk of the court, who certifies.

JOSE MANUEL ALVAREZ. [Flourish.]

PEDRO DEL PERAL. [Flourish.]
JAVIER DE SALAS. [Flourish.]

DEPOSITION OF CRISTOBAL ABELLEIRAS.

In the city of Havana, on the 21st day of March, 1898, appeared the above-named diver, who, being admonished that he was under strict obligations to be truthful, and warned of the penalties incurred by any person who bears false witness, made oath that he would tell the truth; and being asked the usual preliminary questions, he said that his name was Cristobal Abelleiras Serantes, that he was a native of Ferrol, 34 years of age, married, and that he had been a diver in the navy since 1891. He said that he had no interest, either direct or indirect, in the matter before the court.

Being asked whether he had worked in the examinations of the bottom and the submerged portions of the North American ironclad *Maine*, he said that he had; that from the 2d to the 18th instant he had been employed in that way, with the exception of the holidays and of the 3d instant, which was a rainy day, and also of the 10th, 11th, and 12th instant, on which days they were working on a Norwegian steamer in the dock; that he began to examine from the point of rupture on the port side, and from that point no side was found and no plan whatever could be followed, there being everywhere an indescribable confusion of plates and pieces of the vessel; that it was impossible to see much on the bottom, because the water is very filthy, and moreover because when any motion is made there the mud becomes agitated and more roily.

That on the inside where he descended they found forward a mass of pipes which he thinks belonged to the torpedo chamber; that at the bottom there was no cavity, no crevices, and no holes worth mentioning, and that the entire vessel forward appears open, having undoubtedly burst toward the outside; that on the port side, forward, he found an appliance for casting anchor attached to its block on the side, and on the starboard side he found an anchor without stock with its chain. This deposition stopped here, and deponent signed it after having read it and ratified it with his honor, his judge, and with me, the secretary, who certifies.

CRISTOBAL ABELLEIRA. [Flourish.]
PEDRO DEL PERAL. [Flourish.]
JAVIER DE SALAS. [Flourish.]

On folios 160 and 161 of this examination are two plans. On folios 162 and 163 of the same are two statements of expenditures supplied and to be supplied for the account of the examining court in connection with the disaster to the ironclad *Maine.* The former amount to $180.65 and the second to $74.

Statements of the persons who distinguished themselves most on the night of February 15, 1898, in connection with the disaster to the *Maine,* they having been the persons who first came to render assistance to the victims:

The Illustrious Marquis of Esteban, municipal alcalde of Havana; Don Enrique Solano, second brig. gen'l. and maj. gen'l. chief of staff of the army of operations in this island.

Don Julio Perez, lieut. in the navy, and

[Here follow the names of about seventy-five soldiers and sailors, with their ranks, and civilians, with their occupations.]

Havana, Mch. 22, 1898.

PEDRO DEL PERAL. [Flourish.]

Judicial act. Havana, Mch. 22, 1898. Three communications have been sent to the superior authorities, one of them stating the impossibility of the continuation of the work of our divers, who are impeded by the labors which are being performed by the American divers; and another, giving a statement of the expense caused by this business from the 5th instant up to date; and another, containing a list of the persons who most distinguished themselves on the night of the disaster by the promptness and efficiency with which they hastened to the scene of the disaster. I certify.

JAVIER DE SALAS. [Flourish.]
PERAL. [Flourish.]

Judicial act, Havana, Mch. 22, 1898.

Copies are subjoined of the statement of expenses and of the list of the persons who most distinguished themselves on the night of the disaster which are referred to in the foregoing judicial act. I certify.

JAVIER DE SALAS. [Flourish.]
PARAL. [Flourish.]

DEPOSITION OF DON ENRIQUE FREIXAS, NAVAL LIEUTENANT.

In the city of Havana, on the 22d day of March, 1898, appeared, having been duly summoned, the above-named officer, who, having been admonished of the obligation under which he was to be truthful and of the penalties incurred by any person who bears false witness, made oath that he would tell the truth, and being the usual preliminary questions, he said that his name was Don Enrique Freixas y Ferran; that he was of full age; married; a lieutenant in the navy; employed in the office of the captain of the port of Havana. He declared that he was not interested, either directly or indirectly, in the case before the court.

Being requested to tell all that he knew with regard to the blowing up of the American ironclad *Maine*, he said that he heard a passenger, the Rev. Father Marizosa, a native of Mexico, who was on board the steamer *City of Washington*, enroute for Mexico, who witnessed the disaster from the steamer on board of which he was, and which had just anchored—that he heard Father Marizoza say that slight detonations were at first heard, similar to those of fireworks, which kept on increasing, and that he also saw light on board of the vessel greater than would have been afforded by the vessel's ordinary lights. Soon after the great explosion followed by the phenomena already known, which were seen by most of the witnesses.

He further stated that he heard another passenger who was on board of the same vessel, and whose name he does not know, state the fact in the same manner. He added that he asked both of the aforesaid witnesses whether they had observed any motion of the water, any liquid column, or trembling on board of the vessel on which they were, and that they answered No. This deposition stopped here, and after he had read it the deponent signed it, with his honor, the judge, and with me, the clerk of the court, who certifies.

ENRIQUE FREXAS. [Flourish.]

PEDRO DEL PARAL. [Flourish.]
JAVIER DE SALAS. [Flourish.]

YOUR EXCELLENCY:

On the night of February 15 last a dreadful and extraordinary event disturbed the usual tranquillity and internal order of this bay. A mournful catastrophe had occurred on board the North American ironclad *Maine*.

Having been instructed by your excellency, in the letter which gave rise to the present proceedings, to proceed with all possible promptitude and energy to the investigation of the matter in question, I began my preliminary proceedings while the flames produced by the explosion were still rising from the vessel, and while some lesser (explosions), caused, no doubt, by the action of the heat upon the shells and other explosives, were heard at intervals.

The undersigned immediately ordered all persons to be summoned who, owing to their being in the vicinity of the said vessel, could give any explanation or information with regard to the disaster, or any account of its effects, and I requested the attendance of an official interpreter of the Government in order that he might act as such in the taking of such depositions as might necessitate his services, and I wrote to the consul of the United States of America in this capital, requesting the attendance of such of the principal officers and men of the crew of the *Maine* as might be in a condition to testify.

As Don Francisco Javier de Salas, a lieutenant in the navy, the secretary of the court of enquiry, was asked by an American officer, a few minutes before the beginning of the proceedings, whether the explosion could have been caused by a torpedo, notwithstanding the emphatic expressions of public opinion, which immediately rejected this supposition as absurd, and which were corroborated by arguments easily understood by every naval officer, I thought it expedient 'to direct the investigation along this line on account of the facility of obtaining sufficient data to show the external action during the moments following submarine explosions, which are so peculiar in their character, and so well known to all who have witnessed them and studied them in their effects.

The North American man-of-war *Maine*, of 6,682 tons displacement, made of steel, 318 feet in length, 57 feet beam, and 22 feet in depth, having double engines of 9,293 indicated horsepower, launched in New York in 1890, entered this port on the 24th January of this year, and anchored at buoy No. 4 (see the part of the plan at folio 101).

The undersigned has heard unofficially the reason of the arrival and stay in these waters of the ironclad in question. For this it was sufficient to call to mind the royal order of August 11, 1882, which permits, in ordinary times of peace, the entrance of foreign squadrons and single vessels into our ports without any other restrictions than those prescribed by the Ordinances of the navy, and that of obedience to the police regulations established in those ports.

Taking the said Buoy No. 4 as the centre, the depth of the bay varies, within a radius of a hundred metres, from thirty to thirty-six feet, with a bottom of loose mud. The *Maine*, when she came in, drew 22 feet, and the depth of the water at the place where she is sunk is 32 feet at the bow and 30 feet at the stern.

On the night of the sad occurrence the Spanish cruiser *Alfonso XII* was anchored at Buoy No. 3 and the naval steam transport *Legaspi* at No. 2, distant 140 and 240 metres, respectively, from the said Buoy No. 4.

At the moment of the explosion there was no wind and the water was very smooth, as it usually is in this bay at that hour.

The rise of the tide in the harbor is one and a half feet, and high tide on that day was at 4 p. m.

Before proceeding to the consideration of other data, I think it well to recall to your excellency's enlightened mind the phenomena which accompany the explosion of a submarine mine, meaning thereby what is known under the generic term of torpedo, and leaving aside all that can apply exclusively to a subterranean mine, on account of the utter impossibility that such a mine could have been prepared without batteries (elementos), or even with batteries, without the knowledge of the authorities and of the public generally.

The ignition of the torpedo must necessarily have been produced either by collision or by an electrical discharge, and as the state of the sea and the wind did not allow of any motion in the vessel the hypothesis of a collision at that moment must be rejected, and we must consider that of an electric current sent by a cable (wire) from a station; but no traces or signs of any wire or station have been discovered.

The phenomena observed in submarine explosions are as follows: When the ignition takes place, the explosive substance is converted into a gaseous one and forms a bubble, which, owing to its ascensional force, tends usually to rise to the surface in a vertical line, producing a detonation more or less loud in proportion to the quantity of explosive material employed and the depth at which it is placed, and accompanied by a column of water, the height of which is likewise in proportion to the two circumstances mentioned.

At the same time a certain quaking (trepidacion) is noticed on the shore, which varies directly in proportion to the amount of explosive matter used, its greater immersion, and its nearness to the bottom; and, besides, a very peculiar shock is observed against the sides of vessels, which varies according to the distance, and which, owing to the incompressibility of the water, does not, according to experiments, diminish in inverse proportion to the square of the distance.

Another important phenomenon, to which great weight should be attached in this case, on account of the peculiar nature of the harbor, is the presence of dead fish on the surface (of the water), usually caused by the rupture of the natatory bladder.

'The action of torpedoes on vessels is very variable, and depends, besides, on the resistance of the hull which it strikes, the quantity of explosive matter, and the distance.

No known case has yet been recorded where the explosion of a torpedo against the side of a vessel has caused the explosion of the magazines.

As is seen by the plans (diagrams), there was nothing but powder and shells in the forward magazines of the *Maine*.

It appears from the examination of witnesses:

Don Julio Peres y Perera, naval lieutenant of the first class, states in his deposition that he was in his shears house (casa de la machina), about four hundred yards from the said vessel, when, at about 9.35 p. m., he saw an enormous blaze of fire rise toward the zenith and to a great height followed by a terrible explosion. He adds that almost the whole of the ironclad was covered by a thick smoke, that the illumination was instantaneously extinguished, and that an infinite number of colored lights passed away into space. The moment after the explosion all was dark until, a little later, the awful scene was illuminated by the brightness of the fire, which was certainly caused by the explosion

The witness says that other explosions, apparently of shells, followed, which continued until two o'clock in the morning, at which hour the fire began to diminish

The witness saw the bow sink a few minutes after the explosion, and he asserts that there was no column of water nor the least movement in the water (mar), and that there was no shaking of the land on the shore

The other depositions of witnesses confirm the description of the explosion given by this officer, and they all agree that they noticed no movement in the water, and that they felt no shock of the water, although some of them were on board vessels as near the *Maine* as the *Alfonso XII.*

During the early hours of the morning the undersigned, accompanied by the secretary, made a close examination of the bay without finding any dead fish, or injuries of any kind on the piles of the piers.

Don Francisco Aldao, the head pilot, testifies (page 80 and back) that the harbor of Havana abounds in fish, and that there are persons who devote themselves to this industry with profit, and the technical assistant of the junta of the harbor works, Señor Ardois, who has been engaged upon them for many years, states that, without any exception, whenever small blasts have been made with charges (of powder) varying from five to twenty-five pounds, for the purpose of blowing up hulls of vessels, loose rock, and even shoals in the bay, a great number of dead fish have been found inside the hulls or floating on the surface of the water.

For the purpose of procuring the greatest possible number of data, several experiments were made, to which the diagrams at pages 160 and 161 refer.

In continuation of the investigation, on the 16th February the United States consul was requested, through your excellency, to procure the attendance of some of the surviving officers and sailors of the *Maine*, in order to receive such testimony as they might see fit to give with regard to the occurrence. On the same day, through the same medium, permission was requested to examine the bottom of the vessel. On the 18th February I again applied to your excellency to procure from the commander of the *Maine*, either directly or through his consul, exact information as to the quantity of explosives still existing in that part of the vessel which had not been buint. On the 21st I went to the American steamer *Mungus*(?) for the purpose of having an interview with Mr. Sigsbee, the commander of the *Maine*, who expressed to me his wish that the Spanish investigators might be present at the operations of the American official diver. On the same day I again wrote, asking for permission to proceed to the examination of the ironclad. On the 22nd I repeated my visit to the *Mangrove*.

On the 19th February the authorities had replied, stating that by agreement with the commander of the *Maine* and the United States consul-general the examination requested in my letter of the 18th would be made as soon as those gentlemen received the appliances and divers whom they had asked for.

On the 24th I received an important communication, dated February 17, enclosing one from his excellency the Governor-General of this island, stating that the commander of the *Maine*, upon being consulted as to the steps necessary to the success of this investigation, had replied that he expected to execute all the operations necessary to the examination of the vessel which had been under his command under his own supervision, in accordance with the provisions of the regulations of the American Navy.

It was at last possible to make use of the new mode of investigation offered by the work of the divers, as it was discovered from what they have accomplished up to this date that the hull of the wrecked vessel is apparently buried in the mud, and that the examination of the outside is impracticable, but that it may be possible to examine the inside when the multitude of articles of all kinds which are lying in confusion in it have been removed.

The divers, having been instructed to examine and describe everything that they might notice at the bottom of the bay and nearest to the sunken vessel, reported that they had not found in the mud which forms the bottom any inequalities or fissures—such as the examination of the bottom of the bay at the place occupied by the *Maine* and the hull (calado) of the vessel would doubtless have brought to light, on the supposition that a torpedo had been the cause of the catastrophe. This imaginary explosive apparatus (artificio) must necessarily, in this case, have been placed at the very bottom of the bay or very near it, and when it exploded would have caused the gases to react upon it, and, at the same time that it produced a greater effect upon the water upward it would have made large fissures (deformaciones) in the mud.

It appears from the examination of the wreck of the *Maine*, part of which is afloat, made by the undersigned, the commandants of artillery, the commandant of engineers, and the commander of the torpedo brigade, the report of which appears at page 24, that whatever may have been the original cause of the disaster, there is no doubt that there was an explosion in the forward magazine, which entirely destroyed the decks and bulkheads, which now display the appearance of a shapeless mass of boards, bars, and pipes of metal, very difficult to describe. In particular, may be noticed a large fragment of the forward deck, which must have been raised in the most violent manner and bent double toward the stern by the forward stack house, like an immense sheet of iron, with a considerable inclination to starboard, which, upon turning over, hurled out of the ship the forward turret containing two guns, which was situated on the starboard side, and another gun with a shield which was placed within the ship on the second deck. When the deck was bent double, as has been said, the smokestacks must have fallen. On the present upper side of this deck may be seen the beams and the knees which fastened them to the sides of the ship.

The whole stern is submerged, with the mainmast in place and intact, so much of it as can be seen above the surface of the water, including the lights (glasses) of the skylights of the cabin hatchways, and the glasses of one projector (proyector).

The gentlemen above mentioned assert that the injuries described could only have been caused by the explosion of the forward magazine.

In order to give a better idea of the general appearance presented by that part of the ship which has been described, photographs were taken, which are shown at page 125 and following.

Notwithstanding what has been stated, it is proper to insist upon the fact that there is not a single instance on record, as has been already said, where the external action of a torpedo against the side of a vessel has caused the explosion of its magazines, although many vessels are recorded as having been totally destroyed by torpedoes, as may be proved by C. Sleeman's work entitled Torpedoes and Torpedo Warfare, published in London in 1880, in which treatise there is a detailed account, extending from page 330 to page 338, inclusive, of the principal events of this nature which have occurred from 1585 to 1885; and this inventory of marine disasters includes a great number of United States men-of-war which destroyed Confederate vessels by means of torpedoes.

H. W. Wilson's treatise, Volume II, published in 1896, and entitled Ironclads in Action. Naval Warfare from 1855 to 1895 may also be consulted on this subject.

On the other hand, there are recorded in the history of all the nations in the world, and especially in modern times, a proportionate number of events sufficing to prove the comparative facility with which ships of war are liable to become the victims of unknown and fatal accidents, owing to combinations which may result from the various and complicated materials employed in their construction and armament, as it is, in many cases, impossible to guard against them except at the cost of terrible calamities.

The knowledge of the spontaneous combustion of the coal in the coal bunkers is within the reach of all, and there is not a navy officer who can not relate some sad episode attributed to this cause.

This danger is increased when the coal bunkers are separated from the powder and ammunition magazines only by a bulkhead of iron or steel, and it becomes imminent when the heat developed in the coal is conveyed to the magazines, as has happened in several cases. To prevent them recourse has been had to the study of a ventilation sufficient to prevent the accumulation of gases and the development of caloric, taking, in addition, the temperature of the coal bunkers at proper intervals. In spite of all this, cases of spontaneous combustion have occurred repeatedly, and it is astonishing that the powder and shell magazines should still continue to be placed in immediate contact with the coal bunkers.

Don Saturnino Montojo, an illustrious lieutenant in our navy, relates a very remarkable case which happened to the unfortunate *Reina Regente* when she was being built at Clydebank. Señor Montojo says that the shafts of the screws passed through several water-tight compartments, which together formed a tunnel for the passage of the shaft. The compartment on the port side of that of the wheel of the helm was furnished with a register (registro) for the purpose of inspecting the shaft, and upon a workman attempting to draw out a small screw there was an explosion causing a small fracture of the side on the exterior, and filling the stern compartments of the vessel with water; but the ship did not sink entirely, thanks to the other water-tight compartments and to the powerful pumps with which the ship was provided, which were set to work, and kept her afloat.

This accident was attributed to the fact that the compartment in question had no ventilation. It is evident that gases are formed in any of the places mentioned by the electric action developed by the fatty substances combined with the paint, the water, etc.

If there is any ventilation, these gases have an outlet, but if there is none they accumulate and finally acquire a certain tension, and when they are brought into contact with a light or sufficient heat their explosion follows, as frequently occurs in mines and coal bunkers. The eighty or ninety (coal bunkers) of the *Reina Regente* had each a ventilation pipe and a temperature pipe. If, notwithstanding all this, any accident should obstruct or clog the ventilation, or if due attention is not paid to the temperature, or even when such attention is paid, if its indications are not good, the adoption of urgent measures of safety will merely diminish the danger, without making it disappear entirely.

The loss of the English vessel the *Dotterel*, which has been so much studied and discussed, was due to the use of a drier (drying oil) employed in painting and known under the name of the "zerotina drier."

In trade some of the varnishes and ingredients used in the painting of vessels are now recommended by protecting them with patents as not liable to produce inflammable gases.

The English scientific magazine The Engineer, No. 2189, of December 10, 1897, publishes an important article entitled "Shell accident at Bull Point," showing the possibility of the explosion of a shell, not by the fuse, but by the spontaneous breaking of the shell itself. The shell of which the author of the article speaks was made for a 4-inch gun, weighed 25 pounds, used the Leadenham fuse, and had a hardened point, tempered in water.

These instances suffice to prove that, in spite of all the precautions that may be taken, there may occur on board of modern vessels, especially war vessels, many unforeseen accidents, arising from the combination of such diverse substances as those which are employed in their armament, so difficult and dangerous to manage, accumulated in large quantities and exposed to the action of heat and electricity almost constantly, each unhappy accident serving to regulate services on the basis of precautions, and to cause precautions to be taken, so far as possible, with every new agent which necessity compels us to accept in the most recent constructions.

Consequently, in view of the result of the proceedings and the merits of the observations submitted, the undersigned considers it his imperative duty to state the following conclusions:

First. That on the night of February 15 last an explosion of the first order, in the forward magazine of the American ironclad *Maine*, caused the destruction of that part of the ship and its total submersion in the same place in this bay at which it was anchored.

Second. That it is learned, from the diagrams of the vessel, that there were no other explosive substances or articles in that magazine, the only one which exploded, than powder and shells of various calibers.

Third. That the same diagrams prove that said magazine was surrounded on the port side, the starboard side, and partly aft, by coal bunkers containing bituminous coal, and which were in compartments adjoining the said magazine, and apparently separated from it only by metal bulkheads.

Fourth. That the important facts connected with the explosion, in its external appearances, at every moment of its duration, having been described by witnesses, and the absence of all the circumstances which necessarily accompany the explosion of a torpedo, having been proved by these witnesses and experts, it can only be honestly asserted that the catastrophe was due to internal causes.

Fifth. That the character of the proceedings undertaken and respect for the law which establishes the principle of the absolute extraterritoriality of a foreign war vessel, have prevented the determination, even by conjecture, of the said internal origin of the disaster, to which, also, the impossibility of establishing the necessary communication, either with the crew of the wrecked vessel or with the officials of their Government commissioned to investigate the causes of the said event, or with those subsequently entrusted with the issue, has contributed.

Sixth. That the interior and exterior examination of the bottom of the *Maine* whenever it is possible, unless the bottom of the ship and that of the place in the bay where it is sunk are altered by the work which is being carried on for the total or partial recovery of the vessel, will prove the correctness of all that is said in this report; but this must not be understood to mean that the accuracy of these present conclusions requires such proof.

Believing that I have fulfilled all the requirements of article 246, Title XIV, Chapter I, of the Law of Military Procedure of the Navy, in accordance with which, and with your excellency's orders, this investigation has been made, I have the honor to transmit this report to your excellency's hands that you may come to a correct decision on the subject.

PEDRO DEL PERAL. [Rubricated.]

HAVANA, *March 22, 1898.*

DECREE.

HAVANA, *March 22, 1898.*

His excellency ordered the investigation intrusted to him to be closed and the proceedings to be transmitted to the superior authority for his action. His excellency gave this order before me, the secretary, who certify it.

JAVIER DE SALAS. [Rubricated.]
PEDRO DEL PERAL. [Rubricated.]

MINUTE.

HAVANA, *March 22, 1898.*

His excellency went, accompanied by me, the secretary, to deliver to his excellency the commandant general of the station, these proceedings, consisting of 181 written folios, without counting the blank ones or the covers. It is recorded, which I, the secretary, certify.

JAVIER DE SALAS. [Rubricated.]
PERAL. [Rubricated.]

The present evidence is transmitted by superior verbal order, which I, the secretary, certify, with the counter-signature of the judge, at Havana, March 28, 1898.

JAVIER DE SALAS.

Approved:
PERAL.

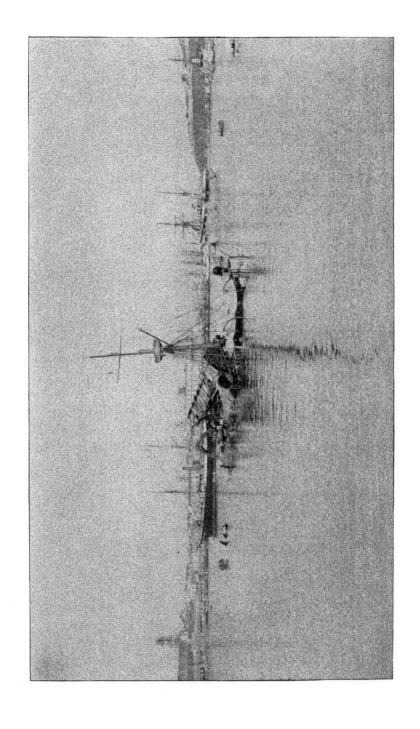

U.S.S. MAINE
LONGITUDINAL SECTION
SCALE ¼ INCH = 2 FEET.
NAVY YARD N.Y.   AUG. — 897.

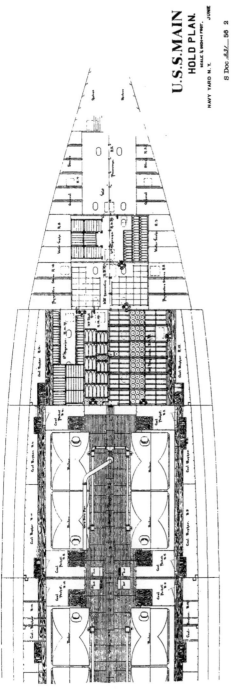

U.S.S. MAIN
HOLD PLAN.

SCALE ½ INCH=1 FOOT.

NAVY YARD N. Y. JUNE

S Doc 981 56 2

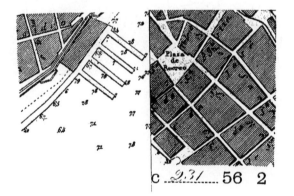

FIFTY-SIXTH CONGRESS, FIRST SESSION.

February 14, 1900.

[Senate Report No. 392.]

Mr. Foraker, from the Committee on Foreign Relations, submitted the following report:

The Committee on Foreign Relations, to whom was referred the bill (S. 1580) to provide for the punishment of violations of treaty rights of aliens, submit the following report:

The bill provides that any act committed in any State or Territory of the United States in violation of the rights of a citizen or subject of a foreign country, secured to such citizen or subject by treaty between the United States and such foreign country, which shall constitute a crime under the laws of such State or Territory, shall constitute a crime against the peace and dignity of the United States, and be punishable in like manner and by the same penalty as in the courts of said States or Territories, and the party offending may be prosecuted in the courts of the United States, and, upon conviction, sentence shall be executed in like manner as sentences for the conviction of crimes under the laws of the United States.

The purpose of the bill is manifest. It is to enable the United States, as such, to enforce, for the benefit of aliens, that protection to which they may be entitled under our treaties with other countries while they may be within the United States; and to provide, in this behalf, that the United States courts shall have jurisdiction to entertain prosecutions in all cases of crimes when against aliens under the State or Territorial criminal laws as though they were crimes against the laws of the United States, the United States courts, for that purpose, adopting the local criminal laws and administering them.

The propriety of such legislation has been suggested by a number of unfortunate experiences. Chief among them are the following:

1. The riot at New Orleans fn 1851, occasioned by the arrest and execution of some American filibusterers in the island of Cuba, in which citizens of New Orleans inflicted injury on the houses and business establishments and also on the persons of various Spanish subjects.

2. The riot against the Chinese in Colorado in 1880, in which two Chinamen were beaten to death and quite a number were seriously maltreated.

3. The riot at Rock Springs, Wyo., in September, 1885, in which 764 Chinamen were killed and wounded.

4. The riot at Seattle, Wash., in October, 1885, when three Chinamen were killed and three others wounded, and all the residences of the Chinese miners in that city were burned.

5. The riot of 1891 in New Orleans, occasioned by the failure of a jury to convict some Italians, or Sicilians, who belonged to a secret oath-bound order called the Mafia, and who were tried for the murder of the chief of police of that city. The rioters seized the Italians, who were imprisoned in jail, and put eleven of them to death, three of whom were subjects of the King of Italy.

6. The riot of March, 1895, in Colorado, in which three Italian prisoners were put to death.

7. The riot of August, 1896, at Hahnville, La., in which six Italians confined in the parish jail, charged with murder, were taken therefrom and three of them lynched.

8. The riot at Tallulah, La., in 1889, in which five Italians were taken from jail and hanged by a mob.

In each of these instances it was found impossible, on account of local sentiment, to successfully prosecute the perpetrators of these outrages in the local courts, and, in most instances, it was impossible to even institute a prosecution.

In each case the foreign country interested insisted and demanded of the United States Government that it should assert its authority and bring the offenders to justice, and seemed incapable of understanding why the United States Government should be powerless to act directly in the premises.

The contention of our Government has always been, in answer to these claims, that the only guaranty provided by the treaty stipulations in question is that aliens residing in this country shall have the same protection under the laws and in the courts provided for our own citizens.

Mr. Webster, as Secretary of State, said in his letter of November 13, 1857, to the Spanish minister, speaking on this point in relation to the New Orleans riot of 1851:

Private individuals, subjects of Her Catholic Majesty, coming to reside voluntarily in the United States, have certainly no cause for complaint if they are protected by the same law and the same administration of law as native-born citizens of this country.

Mr. Evarts said, as Secretary of State, in his letter to the Chinese minister of December 30, 1880, speaking on this point in regard to the Colorado mob of that year:

I know of no principle of national obligation, and there certainly is none arising from treaty stipulation, which renders it incumbent on the Government of the United States to make indemnity to the Chinese residents of Denver who, in common with the citizens of the United States, suffered losses from the operations of the mob. Whatever remedies may be offered to the citizens of Colorado or to the citizens of the United States from other States of the Union resident in Colorado for losses resulting from that occurrence are equally open to the Chinese residents of Denver who may have suffered from the lawlessness of the mob.

Mr. Blaine said, as Secretary of State, in his letter to the Spanish minister, speaking on this point with reference to the New Orleans riot of 1891:

The United States did not by the treaty (with Italy) become the insurer of lives and property of Italian subjects residing within our territory. The foreign resident must be content to share the same redress that is offered by the law to the citizen, and has no just cause of complaint or right to ask interposition of his country if the courts are equally open to him for the redress of his injuries. Foreign residents are not made a favored class.

While the position our Government has taken in all these matters has been tenable, and, in a strictly legal sense, justifiable, yet we have in almost every instance deemed it advisable, as a matter of equity and justice and good policy, to pay indemnities and make reparation.

These occurrences have been so frequent and the discussions with respect to the duty of our Government in such cases have been so intense, and, in some instances, so threatening, that President Harrison called attention to the subject in his message to Congress of December 9, 1891, and recommended that Congress enact the necessary legislation giving the courts of the United States jurisdiction in such cases, and in the last annual message of President McKinley occurs the following general discussion of the subject, including a reference to the recommendation of President Harrison and the unsuccessful attempt to legislate that followed:

For the fourth time in the present decade question has arisen with the Government of Italy in regard to the lynching of Italian subjects. The latest of these deplorable events occurred at Tallulah, La., whereby five unfortunates of Italian origin were taken from jail and hanged.

The authorities of the State and a representative of the Italian embassy having separately investigated the occurrence, with discrepant results, particularly as to the alleged citizenship of the victims, and it not appearing that the State had been able to discover and punish the violators of the law, an independent investigation has been set on foot, through the agency of the Department of State, and is still in progress. The result will enable the Executive to treat the question with the Government of Italy in a spirit of fairness and justice. A satisfactory solution will doubtless be reached.

The recurrence of these distressing manifestations of blind mob fury directed at dependents or natives of a foreign country suggests that the contingency has arisen for action by Congress in the direction of conferring upon the Federal courts jurisdiction in this class of international cases where the ultimate responsibility of the Federal Government may be involved. The suggestion is not new. In his annual message of December 9, 1891, my predecessor, President Harrison, said:

"It would, I believe, be entirely competent for Congress to make offenses against the treaty rights of foreigners domiciled in the United States cognizable in the Federal courts. This has not, however, been done, and the Federal officers and courts have no power in such cases to intervene either for the protection of a foreign citizen or for the punishment of his slayers. It seems to me to follow, in this state of the law, that the officers of the State charged with police and judicial powers in such cases must, in the consideration of international questions growing out of such incidents, be regarded in such sense as Federal agents as to make this Government answerable for their acts in cases where it would be answerable if the United States had used its constitutional power to define and punish crimes against treaty rights."

A bill to provide for the punishment of violations of treaty rights of aliens was introduced in the Senate March 1, 1892, and reported favorably March 30. Having doubtless in view the language of that part of Article III of the treaty of February 26, 1871, between the United States and Italy, which stipulates that "The citizens of each of the high contracting parties shall receive, in the States and Territories of the other, most constant protection and security for their persons and property, and shall enjoy in this respect the same rights and privileges as are or shall be granted to the natives, on their submitting themselves to the conditions imposed upon the natives," the bill so introduced and reported provided that any act committed in any State or Territory of the United States in violation of the rights of a citizen or subject of a foreign country secured to such citizen or subject by treaty between the United States and such foreign country and constituting a crime under the laws of the State or Territory shall constitute a like crime against the United States and be cognizable in the Federal courts. No action was taken by Congress in the matter.

I earnestly recommend that the subject be taken up anew and acted upon during the present session. The necessity for some such provision abundantly appears. Precedent for constituting a Federal jurisdiction in criminal cases where aliens are sufferers is rationally deducible from the existing statute, which gives to the district and circuit courts of the United States jurisdiction of civil suits brought by aliens where the amount involved exceeds a certain sum. If such jealous solicitude be shown for alien rights in cases of merely civil and pecuniary import, how much greater should be the public duty to take cognizance of matters affecting the life and the rights of aliens under the settled principles of international law no less than under treaty stipulation, in cases of such transcendent wrongdoing as mob murder, especially when experience has shown that local justice is too often helpless to punish the offenders.

So far as strict legal right and obligation may be concerned, it is a sufficient answer in all such cases to say that aliens have no right to complain of a failure on our part to secure to them the enjoyment of all the rights that they have under treaty stipulations so long as they enjoy the same protection as our own citizens enjoy and have the same redress in our courts that is provided for our own citizens. But the fact remains that it has always been necessary, not to say difficult, for our Government to satisfactorily explain how it is that, under our system, the National Government has no courts of its own authorized and no power to compel the State courts to punish or even bring to trial such offenders.

This is because they know and deal only with our national sovereignty. They do not concern themselves about our distribution of powers or our political divisions, and, therefore, for the enforcement of treaty stipulations they look only to the Government of the United States; and it naturally appears to them that we are evading our responsibilities and our duties when we plead a lack of power or authority on the part of the General Government to take action directly, and insist that the whole subject must be remitted to the local courts and local authorities, with which foreign governments have nothing to due and of which they have but little knowledge, and with which they could not have and are not allowed to have any direct communication. Out of all this grows the propriety—not to say necessity—for the legislation that is proposed.

That Congress has the constitutional power so to legislate is not open to argument. By the sixth article of the Constitution it is declared that—

All Treaties made, or which shall be made under the authority of the United States shall be, together with the Constitution and laws enacted by Congress in pursuance thereof, the supreme law of the land.

If a treaty stipulation be a part of the supreme law of the land, it is not only the right, but it is the duty of Congress to provide for its enforcement and for the enjoyment of it by those who are entitled thereto.

In the case of Baldwin v. Franks (120 U. S., 678) it was expressly held that Congress might provide for the protection of aliens in the enjoyment of treaty rights. But it was also held that Congress had not done so in the section (5519) there under consideration, except, perhaps, by a provision that would be capable of that construction if standing alone, but which was not separable from an unconstitutional provision, and therefore not enforceable.

The question is not, therefore, one of power, but simply one of propriety, and this question is not, in view of our experiences, longer debatable.

If it be shown by experience, as it has been shown, that where by mob violence the treaty rights of aliens are violated, the State courts are liable to be indifferent or inefficient because of local prejudice or for any other reason, to punish or even undertake to punish the offenders, good faith requires that Congress shall take the matter in hand and provide a way, independently of the State courts and beyond the reach of local prejudice and improper influences, for the satisfactory discharge of our international duty.

In accordance with the recommendation of President Harrison an effort was made in the Fifty-second Congress to enact legislation similar to that now under consideration. Senate bill 2409, of that Congress, contained the same general provisions that are found in this bill. It was reported favorably from the Committee on Foreign Relations, but was opposed in the Senate and its passage prevented. The chief ground of this opposition was not that Congress lacked power to so legislate, but that it was unnecessary to confer such jurisdiction on the United States courts, and, therefore, impolitic, because the prosecution of such offenses could be safely intrusted to the State courts.

It was urged that instead of the United States prescribing a criminal code that would apply to all the States, we would, if that legislation should be adopted, have 45 different codes, one for each State, and each liable to be changed, modified, or repealed as the State in each instance might see fit, without consulting the United States; and it was also further insisted that giving jurisdiction, as proposed, to the United States courts would have a tendency to oust the State courts in practice, although not in law, of that jurisdiction; or, if that did not occur, then the effect would be to put such offender twice in jeopardy for the same offense, since they would be liable to be twice tried for the same acts—once in the State and once in the United States courts.

These objections are easily answered. Surely it can not be contended that it is not competent for the Congress, instead of enacting one general law applicable to all the States, to adopt the criminal laws of each State in so far as they may be applicable, as and for the criminal laws on the subject, of the United States, and authorize the courts of the United States to administer them. There are numerous precedents for such legislation.

In the Fifty-second Congress, first session, page 4556 of the Congressional Record, Senator Davis said, speaking on this point:

This Government has been adopting State legislation and State procedure from the beginning. The competency of witnesses is measured and settled by State law. The rules of practice and proceeding, the laws of evidence in cases at common law, are settled by the State laws by 44 different codes, by 44 different rules of right and property in as many different States, adopted by the Federal statutes. What charm and magic are there in this proposed statute which ought to exempt its subject from the same specific method of enactment?

The United States have over and over again, not only in principle and by analogy, but actually, proceeded as this bill intends to proceed. Take the act of 3d of March, 1825, chapter 65, section 3, volume 4, of the statutes of that year, page 115, as amended on the 5th of April, 1866, chapter 24, section 5391, of the Revised Statutes.

This section reads as follows:

SEC. 5391. If any offense be committed in any place which has been or may hereafter be ceded to and under the jurisdiction of the United States, which offense is not prohibited, or the punishment thereof is not specially provided for by any law of the United States, such offense shall be liable to receive the same punishment as the laws of the State in which such place is situated now in force provide for the like offense when committed in the jurisdiction of such State, and no subsequent repeal of any such State law shall affect any prosecution for such offense in any court of the United States.

He made other citations to the same effect, and others might be given in addition to those referred to by him. (Sections 858, 867, 914, 915, 916, 933, 966, 977, 988, 990, 991, 992, 993.)

Speaking as to the policy or the effect of having 44 different criminal statutes, one for each State, instead of one general statute applicable to all States, Senator Davis, in that same debate, said:

Is it not better and will it not more tend to harmony to have the same identical body of Federal and State criminal law in each State, adjusted to its customs and ways of considering things, than to have one body of Federal laws in every State, as to crimes, differing from the laws of the several States in definition and possibly more severe in penalties, and in the case, for instance, of Louisiana, more severe than has been esteemed by its legislators necessary to be? * * * It strikes me this is a better scheme. I think it far better that the criminal laws of the States and of the United States be correlative in each State as far as practicable.

As to the objection that the tendency will be, if this legislation be enacted, to, in practice at least, oust the State courts of jurisdiction in these cases and confine such prosecutions to the United States courts, that can not be anything more than opinion or speculation. Such a result does not necessarily follow. All offenses that are punishable by the laws of the State will continue punishable according to those laws in the courts of the States, respectively. They will also, however, if this legislation be enacted, be, in a case where the rights of aliens are affected, punishable in the courts of the United States, but in such instance according to the laws and penalties prescribed by the State legislature.

No one claims that the fact that the United States courts will have this jurisdiction will, in legal effect, oust the State courts of their jurisdiction; nor can it be claimed that, while an offender will be liable to punishment by each sovereignty against the peace and dignity of which he may have offended, it is likely that he will be twice so prosecuted. It will rather be, as in all other cases where there are two sovereignties offended against, while the action of the court of one does not oust the other, yet it generally, by common consent, satisfies the requirements of the spirit of the law, and there will seldom, if ever, be a second prosecution predicated on the same act or offense.

To recapitulate: experience has shown that there is much propriety in this legislation, if not a necessity for it.

Congress unquestionably has power to enact the legislation. There is abundant precedent for it.

To confer this jurisdiction upon the United States courts does not interfere with the jurisdiction of the State courts. That will remain unaffected and may be invoked wherever desirable, and the offending party is not twice put in jeopardy within the meaning of the provisions prohibiting the same, for it is not twice putting a man in jeopardy for each sovereignty to put him to trial against which he may have offended: but it will in practice, no doubt, result, as the practice has heretofore been in all like instances, that a prosecution in one court will be all that a defendant will be required to meet. But, however this may be, it seems so obvious that the Government of the United States should be in a situation to enforce its treaty stipulations and accord the protection to aliens which it guarantees that, in the opinion of the committee, the bill should pass.

FIFTY-SIXTH CONGRESS, FIRST SESSION.

February 14, 1900.

[Senate Report No. 391.]

Mr. Money, from the Committee on Foreign Relations, submitted the following report:

The Committee on Foreign Relations, to whom was referred the bill (S. 2931) to incorporate the American National Red Cross and to protect its insignia, having carefully considered same, beg leave to submit the following report with the recommendation that the bill do pass:

The accompanying bill to incorporate the American National Red Cross and to protect its insignia (the red cross on a white ground) is a bill which has, in different forms, but all having the same object, been reported favorably many times within the past fifteen years by both Houses of Congress, and has failed of becoming a law through lack of attention and not from opposition. The treaty of the Red Cross, the articles and purposes of which are fully set out in the accompanying bill, was entered into August 22, 1864, at Geneva, Switzerland, by plenipotentiaries representing Italy, Baden, Belgium, Denmark, Spain, Portugal, France, Prussia, Saxony, and Wurttemberg, and the Federal Council of Switzerland, and was the result of a conference which convened in Geneva, Switzerland, October 26, 1863, at which fourteen governments were represented by official delegates, and there were also present five members of the Geneva committee, six delegates of different associations, and some unaccredited visitors.

This conference was called to find out and agree upon humane and reasonable methods upon which the civilized nations might agree for the treatment of the unfortunate and helpless victims of war; and a series of resolutions looking to this object, and providing the methods by which they should be carried out, were adopted. These resolutions are the basis of the Red Cross treaty of August 22, 1864, and provided, among other things, that there shall be in every country that comes into the treaty a national committee to act in times of emergency with whatever arm of the Government may need its services; and the red cross on the white ground was adopted as the sacred international insignia of the humane work. The United States gave its adherence to this treaty March 1, 1882, being the thirty-second country to come into its provisions; and since then 11 more countries have accepted the treaty, making in all 43 countries who have become parties to it.

While originally formed to give its aid in times of war, through the efforts of Miss Clara Barton, there has been added an article enlarging the work of the Red Cross to all cases of national emergency and disaster, known in foreign countries as the "American amendment," and in accordance with this article this country has already, under the leadership of this same woman, given its aid to Russia at the time of the famine in 1892, to Armenia and Turkey in 1896, and to the sufferers in Cuba in 1897, 1898, and 1899. In our country the Red Cross has led in ameliorating and relieving the sufferings arising from the fires in Michigan in 1881; the Mississippi floods in 1882 and 1883; the Mississippi cyclone of 1883; the Ohio and Mississippi floods of 1884; the Charleston earthquake of 1886; the Mount Vernon, Ill., cyclone of 1888; the Florida yellow-fever epidemic of 1888; the Johnstown disaster in 1889; the Pomeroy, Iowa, cyclone of 1893, and the South Carolina Islands hurricane of 1893 and 1894.

S. Doc. 231, pt 7——62

The work done by the Red Cross in the late Spanish-American war in Cuba and in the hospitals and camps in the United States exceeded in its extent all its previous records, and in its benefactories included officers and men, friend and foe alike.   This is in brief the history of the Red Cross in the United States.

All meetings of the international conferences of the Red Cross have recommended to the Governments concerned the importance of the protection of the Red Cross as the sacred insignia of this humane work, and also urged the necessity for the incorporation of their National Red Cross committees.   In pursuance of this recommendation every signatory country except ours has so protected its National Red Cross, most of them with measures much stronger than those embraced in the accompanying bill.

The bill is, therefore, favorably reported with amendments noted with the recommendation that it pass.

[See pp. 5, 33, and p. 120, Vol. VI.]

FIFTY-SIXTH CONGRESS, FIRST SESSION.

May 3, 1900.

[Senate Report No. 1202.]

Mr. Lodge, from the Committee on Foreign Relations, submitted the following report:

The Committee on Foreign Relations, to whom was referred the bill (S. 2661) to provide for the reorganization of the consular and diplomatic service, submit the following report:

The following report was made by Mr. Morgan on February 6, 1895, to accompany a similar bill when it was reported to the Senate at that time. It covers so many of the essential points in regard to the proposed reorganization that it is here reprinted:

The consular service of the United States, like that of other nations, developed gradually out of the necessities of commerce and the willingness of merchants in foreign countries to represent other governments than their own, and to discharge certain fiscal and other duties for the sake of the fees to be collected for such services. While the other great commercial nations of the world have at intervals down to recent times been active in the improvement of their consular service, in order to meet satisfactorily the exigencies of a steadily increasing competition in international trade, the consular system of the United States has remained practically unchanged since the time it was called into existence on a small scale by the acts of July 1, 1790, and of April 14, 1792, and kept alive by a number of subsequent unimportant acts.

The act "to remodel the diplomatic and consular system" of March 1, 1855, is entitled to be regarded as an improvement only so far as it slightly enlarged the service and corrected certain abuses therein by a closer supervision of the fees. It in no way, however, effected a change in the principle of consular representation or in the system of appointment. Apart, therefore, from the act of June 20, 1864, which provided for the establishment of a small body of thirteen consular clerks with a permanent tenure of office, a measure which at its inception was intended to form the nucleus of an entire reform of the service on that basis, this institution, so important to our foreign trade, has suffered the oversight and indifference of Congress.

This neglect is the more striking and the less excusable when our foreign trade of half a century ago is contrasted with that of to-day. In 1850 the combined value of our imports and domestic exports amounted to $308,409,759; in 1893 it reached the figure of $1,697,431,707. But notwithstanding these present vastly increased and far more intricate commercial relations indicated by these figures, no step whatever to increase the efficiency of the consular service, to which the direction and fostering of these relations are intrusted, has been taken. That this has entailed a great loss annually to our foreign trade can not be questioned; that there is also an urgent necessity to correct this want of efficiency is equally apparent.

Even more applicable to the industrial and commercial conditions of to-day, but with reference to those of a decade ago, Secretary Frelinghuysen said in 1884:

"Until recently the demands of Europe, which consumed the greater portion of our exports, and the condition of the producing countries, were such as to give us control in the supply of certain products, such as breadstuffs, provisions, cotton, petroleum, etc. The demands of Europe for all these products, and of the other continents for petroleum especially, were so positive, and our producing conditions so favorable, as to give us practically a monopoly for their supply.

"These conditions of international demand and supply are undergoing radical changes, which the near future will intensify.

"The efforts which have been made and which are being made by Europe to enlarge the field of supply in the above-mentioned products, aided by the ambition which prevails in all countries for the development of natural and artificial resources to meet their own wants and to supply the wants of others, have resulted in awakening competition for the supply even of those products which we have heretofore controlled. It is true that thus far this competition has not affected our trade to any appreciable extent, but the desire for development which is now abroad, and the ambition which prevails to increase the production (outside of the United States) of the foregoing articles, render consular supervision of absolute importance. *The complex commercial relations and industrial interests which now prevail in Europe have originated hostility to American products in many countries, and afford additional reasons for the enlargement and perfection of the consular service.*" [1]

In 1888 Mr. Cleveland, in his message to Congress, expresses himself to the same effect when he says: "The reorganization of the consular service is a matter of serious importance to our national interests," and in 1893 he again refers to the subject as follows:

"During my former administration I took occasion to recommend a recast of the laws relating to the consular service, in order that it might become a more efficient agency in the promotion of the interests it was intended to subserve. The duties and powers of consuls have been expanded with the growing requirements of our foreign trade. Discharging important duties affecting our commerce and American citizens abroad, and in certain countries exercising judicial functions, these officers should be men of character, intelligence, and ability."

In addition to these expressions from a high official source, the necessity of a reform has been recognized by men of letters, eminent statesmen, journalists, and important boards of trade of this country.

It must be admitted that the present management of our foreign service is burdened with many drawbacks to its efficacy by considerations that relate to domestic politics. Partisan policy, when strictly carried out in making appointments in our foreign service, has no other meaning than that the consular offices are primarily regarded as rewards for political services. The real capacity and usefulness of a consul is too often a secondary consideration.

This important and indispensable part of the machinery by which our foreign intercourse is conducted is often employed to pension political favorites. That to subserve the interests of the service ought to be the sole end in view in the selection of incumbents can not be disputed. To consider the offices merely as sources from which these partisan officeholders may derive four years of maintenance is as absurd as it would be to construct a navy to defend the country and to intrust its command to landsmen without experience for whom we might desire to provide a living and comfortable quarters.

Such a purpose, or one not more gratifying, has often been put into practice in our diplomatic and consular service. To protect and promote in time of peace our varied foreign interests through the agency of a trained personnel is not a less-important subject for legislative consideration and provision than in time of war to defend them by the most efficient means at our command.

The object of this act is to provide a system by which persons shall be trained for the duties of the consular service, so that they shall be able to perform them in the best possible way at a reasonable expense to the Government. That this can not be obtained without removing the selection of persons for this service from the control of party politics is shown by our experience, if any proof were required to establish a conclusion so entirely true and indisputable.

Fitness of the candidate, permanency of tenure during good behavior, and an

---

[1] Communication of the Secretary of State to the President, March 20, 1884.

impartial method of selection and to govern promotion as reward for efficiency are the principles on which a useful consular service can alone be based, with an expectation of the best results.

Under our present system a consular or diplomatic officer has no sooner familiarized himself with the duties of his office and begun to acquire a knowledge of its business and fitness for his duties than he is removed to make room for another novice, who is likewise superseded as soon as his experience begins to enable him to discharge the duties of his office to the satisfaction of himself and others. Thus, in one generation the same post is frequently filled by a number of men, who are successively displaced as soon as they have learned to transact the business of their offices with something of professional knowledge and skill.

This system is not only unjust to the people, but it is equally unjust to the agents, who are thrown back upon their own resources just at the time when a three or four years' preparation has fitted them to devote their energies and capacity with advantage to the foreign service.

To compete successfully with the agents of foreign powers, and to conduct advantageously the political and commercial affairs of our own country, the appointee to this service should be familiar not only with the laws, customs, industries, manufactures, and natural products of our own land, but they should be instructed in the laws, pursuits, language, the contributions to commerce, and the character of the people to whom they are accredited. To this should be added a competent knowledge of the law of nations and of commercial law. As long as these officers are transferred from pursuits and associations which have no connection with commerce or the foreign service, however able and skillful they may be in other things, they can not possess the special knowledge and skill which will render their labors either useful or creditable to the consular service.

The foreign service of European governments for many years has been the object of careful solicitude on their part. An outline statement of them will better enable us to understand the disadvantage we suffer from a defective system.

The French consular service is composed of—

40 consuls-general, at a salary each $3,600
50 consuls of the first class, each 2,800
80 consuls of the second class, each 2,000
100 vice-consuls 1,400
24 pupil consuls 800

The conditions for admission to the diplomatic and consular service of France are prescribed in a decree of October 15, 1892, and, to show how important France considers its foreign service, attention is called to the fact that over thirty decrees have been issued since 1880 tending to perfect the system.

The pupil consuls are appointed by the minister of foreign affairs. They can only be drawn from the body of attachés on probation who have passed a competitive examination for admission into the service and who have served not less than one year in the home office.

Before being assigned to a diplomatic or consular post they are required to spend at least one year at one of the principal chambers of commerce, where they are to acquire a thorough knowledge of the methods and needs of commerce, and whence they must send the minister periodical reports on the trade of the district. After three years of service, half of which time must be rendered abroad, the pupil consul becomes eligible for vice-consul, and after a service of three years in each subsequent grade he becomes eligible for promotion to a higher one.

Candidates for admission in the French diplomatic and consular service must be under 27 years of age and must have taken a collegiate degree in law, science, or letters, or must have passed certain other examinations, or be the holders of commissions in the army or navy.

The examination for entrance into the service is either written or oral, as may be required.

The written test consists of a composition on public and private international law and a translation into French from English and German, which is dictated. Those candidates who aspire to the diplomatic career are to write also a composition on a subject of diplomatic history that occurred since 1648; those destined for the consular service must write a composition on a subject of political economy or of political and commercial geography.

Those whose papers are sufficiently creditable in the opinion of the examiners to warrant their going any further are then subjected to a public oral examination on public and private international law, political and commercial geography, political economy, and a conversation in English and German. Candidates for the diplomatic career are further examined orally in diplomatic history since 1648, and candidates for the consular service are examined on maritime and customs laws.

The French foreign service is under very strict discipline, and for misconduct or inefficiency there are the following penalties:

(1) Reprimand.

(2) Withholding a part of the salary, not exceeding one-half thereof and not for a longer period than two months.

(3) Suspension from the service without salary for two or more years.

(4) Dismissal.

The last three penalties are imposed by the minister of foreign affairs, with the consent of the council of directors, and after a written or oral hearing of the party under censure.

In addition to their regular salaries, the French consular officers are entitled to traveling expenses and allowances for house and office rent, and for entertaining where it is necessary.

Such a course of training and discipline must produce thorough efficiency; and the generous rewards given for faithful and profitable service must encourage a good class of men to adopt such employment as a profession to which all their energies and abilities are industriously devoted. The permanency of employment, during good behavior, gives confidence to the officer and constantly increasing benefit to the Government.

The British system of regulations for the admission of applicants to the consular service are as follows:

"Persons selected for the consular service, whenever the circumstance of their being resident in England, on their first appointment, or of their passing through England on their way to take up such first appointment, may admit of their being subject to examination, will be expected to satisfy the civil service commissioners—

"(1) That they have a correct knowledge of the English language, so as to be able to express themselves clearly and correctly in writing.

"(2) That they can write and speak French correctly and fluently.

"(3) That they have a sufficient knowledge of the current language, as far as commerce is concerned, of the port at which they are appointed to reside, to enable them to communicate directly with the authorities and natives of the place; a knowledge of the German language, being taken to meet this requirement for ports in northern Europe; of the Spanish or Portuguese language, as may be determined by the secretary of state, for ports in Spain, Portugal, Morocco, and South or Central America; and of the Italian language for ports in Italy, Greece, Turkey, Egypt, and on the Black Sea or Mediterranean, except those in Morocco or Spain.

"(4) A sufficient knowledge of British mercantile and commercial law to enable them to deal with questions arising between British shipowners, shipmasters, and seamen. As regards this head of examination, candidates must be prepared to be examined in Smith's Compendium of Mercantile Law.

"(5) A sufficient knowledge of arithmetic for the nature of the duties which consuls are required to perform in drawing up commercial tables and reports. As regards this head of examination, candidates must be prepared to be examined in Bishop Colenso's Arithmetic.

"Moreover, all persons on their first nomination to consulships, and after having passed their examination before the civil service commissioners, will be required, as far as practicable, to attend for at least three months in the foreign office, in order that they may become acquainted with the forms of business as carried on there.

"Limit of age for candidates, 25 and 50, both years inclusive. (Fee for examination, £1 to £6.)"

Mr. Henry White, formerly secretary of legation at London, in an article contributed to the North American Review, makes the following instructive statements concerning the British consular service:

"The British service was established in its present form by act of Parliament in 1825 (6 Geo. IV, cap. 87). Up to that time its members had been appointed, on no regular system, by the King, and were paid from his civil list. This act placed the service under the foreign office, and provided for its payment out of funds to be voted by Parliament. Since then it has been the subject of periodical investigation by royal commissions and Parliamentary committees, with a view to the improvement of its efficiency. The evidence taken on these occasions is published in voluminous blue books, the perusal of which I recommend to those interested in the reform in our service.

"Appointments are made by the secretary of state for foreign affairs. Candidates must be recommended by someone known to him, and their names and qualifications are thereupon entered on a list, from which he selects a name when a vacancy occurs.   The candidate selected, whose age must be between 25 and 50, is then required to pass an examination before the civil service commissioners.

"The salaries of British consular officers are fixed, under the act of Parliament of July 21, 1891 (54 and 55 Vict.; cap. 36), by the secretary of state, with the approval of the treasury, and no increase can be made in any salary without the approval of the latter.   They average about £600 ($3,000) a year, but, of course, some of the important posts are much more highly paid, the salary of the consul-general at New York being £2,000 (nearly $10,000), with an office allowance besides of £1,660, and a staff consisting of a consul at £600 and two vice-consuls at £400 and £250, respectively; that of the consul at San Francisco, £1,200 (nearly $6,000), with an office allowance of £600 besides.

"British consular officials are retired at the age of 70 with a pension.

"There is also an unpaid branch of the service, consisting chiefly of vice-consuls, appointed at places which are not of sufficient importance to merit a paid official. They are usually British merchants, but may be foreigners.   They are not subjected to an examination, and are rarely promoted to a paid appointment.

"Consular clerks are required to pass an examination in handwriting and orthography, arithmetic, and one foreign language (speaking, translating, and copying)."

Mr. White through a series of years was our secretary of legation at London, and is thoroughly informed on the subject of consular duties and the acquirements that are essential to an efficient and respectable service.   His approval of the plan adopted in this bill for the reformation of our consular system and service is a strong recommendation of its future advantages.

In Germany persons are appointed to the office of consular chancellor who have passed their examinations as "referendary," a title which requires graduation at a German university and requires a thorough knowledge of law, political science, statistics, etc.   The chancellor of the consulate is promoted gradually until he reaches the rank of consul-general.

As a rule the personnel of our consular establishment is not in unfavorable contrast with that of the leading European States as to intelligence and sagacity; but our consuls have not usually the liberal education characteristic of the consular representatives of the great European States, nor are they so well informed as to commerce and its great variety of contributory pursuits, or with the exact business methods employed in conducting the commerce of the leading nations.   This seems to be our point of most serious deficiency.

It is proper, and may be necessary, that the laws should designate the places at which consulates are established, but discretion should be given to the President to send consuls to other places, at least temporarily, to meet the demands of trade and intercourse that may arise in new and unexpected quarters.   Especially is this necessary in cases where other countries are engaged in war, and a sudden emergency calls for the protection of our citizens in places which are not designated by law as the location of consular establishments.

But the laws should not designate the individual who is to be the consul at any particular locality.   That matter should be left to the discretion of the President, so that he can at all times have the right man at the right place, to meet any demand of trade, or to secure the adequate protection of the persons and property of our citizens in any emergency, or for any public reason.

The arrangement of the fixed residences of consuls of the several classes is not attempted in this bill.   The laws and the practice of the Department of State are, for the present at least, a sufficient guide in that matter.

The President should, however, be left free in his authority to send a consul of any class to any consulate when he may consider that the demands of the public service require such transfers.

The reasons for such a provision of law are many and cogent, and they are so obvious as not to require any elaboration in this report.   They relate as well to the fitness of consular officers for the particular duties of the occasion as to their usefulness because of their experience as to the condition of the people, the trade, and the language of the particular locality where their services are required.

The consular establishments thus mobilized would soon show a great growth in useful knowledge of the affairs of various parts of foreign countries, and our trade with many foreign countries would be greatly increased and rendered more secure.

The following statements, showing the present condition of our consular service, will show that the change in the organization of the system will add materially to the revenue derived from that source, without a material increase of the expenditures:

Expenditures for salaries of consular officers and amount of compensation in fees, where the officer has no salary, for the year 1894.

26 consuls-general (not including those also commissioned ministers resident)	$98,000.00
188 salaried consuls	371,500.00
11 salaried commercial agents	22,000.00
13 salaried consular clerks	15,000.00
62 feed consuls (personal perquisites in official fees)	36,152.85
33 feed commercial agents (personal perquisites in official fees)	36,505.53
Notarial and unofficial fees retained by consular officers as personal perquisites (lowest estimate)	250,000.00
333 Total	829,158.38

Officers of the diplomatic service embraced in this bill.

6 secretaries of embassy	$13,875.00
17 secretaries of legation	31,975.00
23 Total	45,850.00

According to the Annual Report of the Fifth Auditor of the Treasury for the year ended June 30, 1894—

The expenses for last year of the consular service were	$1,055,417.43
The consular fees received for official services were	758,410.81
Excess of expenditures over receipts	297,006.62

This excess of expenses is larger than it has been for ten years. In 1893 it only amounted to $96,042. The difference is not due to an increase of expenditures, but, no doubt, may be found to a great extent in the changes of our tariff laws. This excess, though larger than customary, is, after all, a small sum when considered with reference to the important purposes for which it is disbursed, and, with the payment into the Treasury of the unofficial fees, as proposed under this bill, it is likely to be greatly reduced, if not changed into a balance in favor of the income from that source.

The entire excess of expenditures for salaries in the Department of State and in the diplomatic and consular service over the receipts amounts to only $615,909.19, the smallest amount expended by any of the great powers of the world. The expenditures of the foreign service of Great Britain, Russia, Germany, Italy, and Spain exceed this amount by very considerable figures, and the report of the ministry of foreign affairs of France for the year 1893 shows only $240,000 receipts and $3,266,960 expenditures, a sum almost double that expended by the United States, including even the incidental and contingent expenses of the consular and diplomatic service of the latter country.

This bill adopts the principle of permanent official tenure, so far as the laws can control that subject, but permanent only as it is of benefit to the service. It leaves the power of removal from office to the discretion of the President. The position of each employee of the service is protected against the uncertain and demoralizing effects of changes for merely political reasons in the administration of the Government as far as Congress can control the subject. But this protection is as necessary in practice for efficient work as it is just in theory, and if the plan is adopted of appointing consuls after they are found to be qualified for the respective classifications of the consular service they will seldom, if ever, be dropped from the service for the purpose of supplying their places with political favorites.

The required examination for appointment and promotion creates an impediment in the way of those who may demand office as a reward for political partisanship, without having adequate knowledge of the duties of this peculiar branch of the public service.

Each consul must, on frequent occasions, be the judge of his proper line of action without aid or direction from the minister to whom he is required to report or from the Department of State. In such cases it is requisite to the honor and security of the Government that the consul should be well informed as to his duties.

The right of the President to select from the whole body of consuls any man for any place he may prefer, and to assign him to such place for duty, and to transfer him at pleasure to another place, is the full equivalent of the power of appointment to a particular office.

These functions are to be exercised in foreign countries, for the most part distant from the United States, and disconnect the incumbents from participation in our home politics.

In so far as they may be given as rewards for party services, they are a sort of pension system for men who have not been successful in getting offices at home, or who have failed of success in the usual channels of business.

The consular system should be based upon the plan of personal qualification for its important and peculiar duties, ascertained by the examination and experience of those employed in it, rather than upon the plan of selecting those for this service who have failed in other pursuits, or those who desire to go abroad for purposes of travel, recreation, or amusement.

This is the only branch of the public service that has been used, to any great extent, for the gratification of the incumbents, without regard to their capacity to render efficient service to the country, and it is time that our policy in respect of these offices was changed.

Taken in the aggregate, there is no class of representatives of our Government who can so seriously affect our commerce with other countries, in their actual and direct conduct and dealings, as our consuls and commercial agents.

We should encourage our best classes of people to qualify themselves for this important service by giving them just compensation for their work and by securing them in these offices during good behavior.

They have much to do with the dignity of our Government, its credit in foreign lands, the honor of its flag, and the safety of its citizens.

Since Mr. Morgan made the report which has just been given, the need for a reorganization of the consular service has become more apparent with each succeeding year. This is particularly true of the last two years, which have witnessed such an enormous increase in American exports, this increase occurring chiefly in manufactured articles of the most varied kind. The development of our industrial system has reached a point where its production is far in excess of the demands of the home market, and the expansion of our export trade is the result of the necessity of finding consumption for our surplus production. It is clearly in the interest of our industry and commerce that everything which the Government can do to facilitate this expansion of our export trade should be done, and no argument is needed to show that the consular service ought to be a most efficient instrument in promoting American exports and in aiding our industry and commerce to find new markets.

No one who has examined this question can fail to be convinced that we might and ought to obtain a much higher degree of efficiency in our consular service in these directions than is now the case. The chief trouble lies not in the character or ability of our consuls, but in the defective system under which they are appointed. A consul, as a rule, is most valuable to our business interests in proportion to his experience in the consular service, yet under the existing system experience is no guaranty for retention in the service, and when a man has attained experience the time has usually been reached for his removal, on account of a political change at Washington, and for replacing him with an inexperienced man who has the entire lesson to learn afresh from the beginning.

The bill reported from the committee aims to correct this evil by assuring a greater permanency of tenure, promotion for good service, and original appointments to the lowest grade of consulates of men whose fitness for the service has been, in a measure, tested by examination. The work of examining candidates is intrusted by the bill to a board composed of officers of the State Department and of the consular service to whom the requirements of that service are most familiar.

The bill also makes an important and much-needed change by abolishing all fees, wherever practicable, and giving to the consuls a proper salary. If all fees are turned into the Treasury of the United States it is believed that, despite the increase of salaries carried by the bill, the service will be practically self-supporting, certainly more nearly so than it is now, and that thus a better system will not only be obtained, but there will be a direct saving to the Government.

The bill also simplifies the present organization by bringing all commercial agents who are citizens of the United States into the regular service. It further requires that all persons now in the service shall be recalled and examined for reappointment in such manner as the board may prescribe; their record, to which great weight will be given, of course, will be examined at the same time. This provision, the committee believe, will lead to a marked improvement in the general character of the service, and will put all members of the service under the reorganization on the same plane.

The consular clerks, who must not be confounded with the clerks employed in consulates, but who now form a body of officers established by law, and who are sent out in various exigencies to take temporary charge of consulates, are, by this bill, to be graded as consuls and brought within the scheme of reorganization.

The committee have aimed to make the scheme of reorganization as simple as possible, and to seek only to give to the consular service a greater permanency of tenure and a higher degree of efficiency. Your committee believe that the consular service, reorganized as is proposed by this bill, will be of very great service to the business interests of the country and in advancing the development of our export trade. The industry and commerce of the United States have a right to demand the best consular system which the Government can provide. It is difficult to estimate the importance to our business interests of the information which an energetic and thoroughly organized consular service could furnish them. Many large firms and corporations now maintain agents in all parts of the world to gather this information for them, but smaller firms and corporations, unable to go to this expense, are put at a disadvantage because the consular service fails to give them what they have a right to expect. Representatives of chambers of commerce and of other commercial bodies from all over the country appeared before your committee to urge the passage of this bill. The attention of the Senate is especially invited to the statements made by these gentlemen which are appended to this report.

Your committee feel that, in response to the demand of our business men and as a potent means of promoting our export trade, the legislation embodied in this bill should receive prompt action at the hands of Congress.

REORGANIZATION OF THE CONSULAR SERVICE.

STATEMENT MADE BY MR. HARRY A. GARFIELD, REPRESENTING THE CHAMBER OF COMMERCE OF CLEVELAND, OHIO.

MR. GARFIELD. The organizations here present are not here to antagonize the advocates of the Adams bill. Both bills seek a common end, differing only in detail, the Lodge bill being fuller in provision; but we come here, gentlemen, with no desire to present to you a bill, and urge the report and passage of a bill calculated merely to effect a reform for reform's sake. We are business men, or the associates and representatives of business men, and it is through those associations that we have been led to take an interest in this subject. Our attention was called several years ago to the efforts made by Senator Lodge and Senator Morgan in the introduction of their bills for the reorganization of the consular service and of the failure of Congress at that time to take affirmative action by the passage of the bills. The Cleveland Chamber of Commerce took an active interest in this subject, or began to do so, about 1896. Some of us, individually, before that had had experiences which led us to see the necessity for a reorganization of the service.

The thing that impressed us, and I understand the same is true of the organizations represented here from elsewhere than Cleveland, was the fact that a change is liable to be made every four years in the personnel of the service and that these changes operate most unsatisfactorily both to the official and the citizen. A fair degree of efficiency is reached in the service, and then, a change of Administration occurring, new men take the place of old ones and must work up from inefficiency to comparative efficiency again. As a business proposition that did not appeal to anybody. There seemed to be no reason why the service could not be put on a permanent basis, nor did there seem to be any reason why the consular service should not be truly representative of America—composed of men experienced in affairs, and also, what you gentlemen readily appreciate is a greater necessity abroad than in our own home country, acceptable to the people among whom they are located. Not that the consul is in any sense a minister or called upon to perform the social duties of a minister, yet he certainly is expected to make himself sufficiently agreeable to those among whom he moves as to take a position on an equality with the representatives from other countries.

All of those things being impressed upon our minds, the Cleveland Chamber of Commerce, along with almost all of the chambers of commerce of the country, in 1898 took part in urging the introduction of a bill for the reorganization of the service. I speak more particularly of the Cleveland chamber, not because it was especially a leader, but because I personally know of its action. We sent a committee here, of which General Garrison and myself were two, to ask the President to deal with the matter in his annual message to Congress. The message was then being prepared; the President stated to us that he believed thoroughly in the necessity for reorganization, but that there was not sufficient time before Congress met to reach a satisfactory conclusion as to what was needed. He said that Mr. Chilton, of the Consular Bureau, was a man to be consulted, and he authorized us to say that he desired Mr. Chilton to take the matter up with us and suggest what should be done. This was about December 1, 1898. Without reciting all the steps taken, we did confer with Mr. Chilton. We called upon the Secretary of State, Mr. Hay, and more particularly we conferred with Dr. Hill, First Assistant Secretary of State. Between them and one or two others in the State Department, especially Mr. Hunt, of the Passport Bureau, who had formerly been in the Consular Bureau, a bill was drafted—this bill which is before you now. After it was drafted and had been passed around among a number of the commercial organizations of the country it was sent on here; in fact, I took it to Dr. Hill and put it in his hands, and asked him if he would please go over the bill and make such suggestions as occurred to him.

Dr. Hill, I believe, examined the bill very thoroughly, and Mr. Hunt, and also ex-Secretary of State John W. Foster (Mr. Chilton being ill). Important amendments were made and the bill then returned to us, representatives of the Department saying that while of course they could not speak officially, yet unofficially they approved of the bill as a practical measure. It was also submitted to ex-Secretary Day, whose experience, we felt assured, would be of value. So highly did he approve of our movement that he consented to address the Cleveland Chamber of Commerce on the subject. Unfortunately he was prevented from doing this, and was compelled to send us a letter of regret at the last moment, adding, however, a word commendatory of our efforts.

The CHAIRMAN. That is this bill which is now before this committee?

Mr. GARFIELD. Yes, sir.

The CHAIRMAN. As revised by the Assistant Secretary of State and others?

Mr. GARFIELD. Yes, sir. This bill now before you—the one introduced by Senator Lodge. With reference to the Adams bill, the chambers of commerce sent a committee to Washington a year ago for the purpose of getting a bill introduced. At that time we found that Mr. Adams had introduced a bill which had been favorably reported by the Committee on Foreign Affairs of the House. We had a conference with Mr. Adams and decided there was not time to get another bill through; at any rate, that it would not be wise to attempt it, that being the short session, and that the best we could do was to concentrate our efforts in behalf of Mr. Adams's bill. The various chambers of commerce passed resolutions favoring the Adams bill on our recommendation. The delegation which visited Washington, acting as an executive committee, sent out a statement to the leading boards of trade and kindred organizations, reciting what had been done as a reason for the recommendation. We told Mr. Adams that there were certain features which did not accord with our views, and especially that the first clause, providing for the organization of a commission to assist the President in framing a bill, was unnecessary and undesirable. The commission, I believe, was to be made up of two Senators and three members of the House and a member from the State Department—perhaps two from the Department. The objection was not merely that unnecessary delay would be occasioned, but that the commission so appointed would do work already accomplished. The State Department knows to-day all that a commission of that kind could get hold of, gathered from the reports of the consuls and agents.

I am informed that there is at the State Department a bushel basket full of reports and correspondence on the subject. The work of the commission can all be done in a committee room; in fact, Senate bill 2661 has in it now provisions which are born of the experience of the State Department, and based upon the information in the possession of the State Department, gathered from the reports I refer to, so that that work is done. The number of consuls-general and consuls provided for in this bill exactly covers the field to-day. The salaries and classifications are so arranged as to put in the first class, without naming them in the bill, all posts that ought to be in the first class. Some changes will be necessary in the present classification, but that is a matter which, of course, ought to be left to the Secretary of State and the President, who know most of the necessities of the service.

Two or three things presented themselves to the business men back of this movement as constituting possible objections to a bill of this sort. One of the first was that while seeking to attain a permanent service it was most undesirable to make it so permanent as to lead to dry rot in the service; also, it should not be so permanent as to leave a man at a post during his entire tenure of office without change of grade. Again, by one of the provisions of the bill, I do not recall the section, an appointment made to the lowest class is an appointment on probation. The President appoints to the lowest class in the service, and there the appointee remains during one year. If, at any time during that year, the President finds that he is not fitted—he may have passed the best examination possible, but he may prove to be unsuited in other and important respects—to fill the place satisfactorily, he may be dismissed without a reason being given. After that year his position becomes permanent, dependent, of course, upon good behavior; and he then progresses from grade to grade by passing the required examinations, and as his services merit promotion.

There is to be, by the provisions of the bill, no leaping over from one grade to another, but, to meet emergencies, the President is given authority to send a consul of one class to a post within another class, without, however, change of salary. This change is to be temporary only. For instance, suppose it should seem expedient to the President to send a consul-general to Pretoria temporarily. Under the provisions of this bill it would be possible without any disturbance of the system. Also, the President may call a consul home and put him in the home field, but not oftener than once in four years, and for not longer than one year at a time. That provision meets the objection that by keeping men constantly in the field and making the service permanent we run the risk of making our consuls mere tea-drinking functionaries, unfamiliar with the affairs of their own country. The President might call a man home (for instance, the consul at Birmingham) and send him to the steel manufacturing districts of this country that he might see what was going on, and at the expiration of his year send him back with a fair knowledge of the situation here; or, the consul so called home could be sent to the various chambers of commerce and manufacturing centers for the purpose of posting local institutions as to the foreign trade.

By these provisions we believe that sufficient elasticity is given to the service, and the dangers pointed out in connection with a permanent service are avoided.

One other point. In connection with candidates for admission to the service the bill provides for an eligible list of five. The five highest who shall pass the entrance examinations are to be certified to the President, and from this list he may appoint, subject, of course, to the approval of the Senate. This gives the President leeway, and at the same time puts the service on a merit basis. We very seriously considered the wisdom of requiring competitive examinations at all; but with an eligible list of five it seemed to us that we avoided the objectionable features and at the same time put into the bill a requirement almost essential to its usefulness. As you are very well aware there is now in existence, and has been since 1895, an Executive order which provides for the examination of applicants, but the custom is to appoint first and examine afterwards, and the examination amounts to what might be expected—nothing.

Senator WOLCOTT. I was quite impressed by what you said that our Government should be represented abroad socially on the plane with representatives of other governments, and, as gentlemen, bring credit to the service, which is undoubtedly very true. Is it your opinion that any man who presents himself, and is physically, mentally, and morally presentable, and passes an examination, is by reason of those facts a creditable representative of this country abroad?

Mr. GARFIELD. No; I can see that he may not be.

Senator WOLCOTT. Then, inasmuch as any man by this bill may present himself, are you of the opinion that the Government would be as well represented as if, for instance, the President should designate the man who might pass the examination? Do you not think there is something in the personality of a man outside of his mental qualifications?

Mr. GARFIELD. Very much.

Senator WOLCOTT. How are you to protect that?

Mr. GARFIELD. By the provision of the bill which allows the President at any time, within one year after the appointment has been made, to recall the appointment.

Senator WOLCOTT. A man does not like to do that. He is without justification if the appointee is mentally able. We must have as our consuls abroad a creditable lot of fellows, and the ability to pass the examination is one of the lesser qualifications, if our representatives are to meet the representatives of other countries and deal with them. Do you think you protect yourself by letting anybody come in if the basis of the examination is merely a mental and moral qualification?

Mr. GARFIELD. Anybody may take the examination, but the President has five out of which to select.

Senator WOLCOTT. He must appoint out of the five.

Mr. GARFIELD. Yes, sir; but that diminishes by four-fifths the difficulty you speak of. It is hardly to be supposed that out of five men, all five would be unsatisfactory, except for their mental attainments. That was the reason why we specified five for the eligible list.

Senator WOLCOTT. There is no opportunity to determine among the five, except by physical appearance. Five gentlemen come, and I look them over, and I say, that fellow looks like a gentleman——

Mr. GARFIELD. It seems to me that the practical method is of another sort. For instance, you gentlemen who are representing States in Congress—a man comes as a candidate from your State—you, or somebody from your State, will know something about the man.

Senator WOLCOTT. It is not, as a rule, true of the appointments of the civil service. A man comes from Massachusetts as an applicant, and I should say that Senator Lodge, knowing this man and his friends, would be the fittest person to designate who should take the examination. If you open the doors to the whole world to be consuls, as you do here, you eliminate from the appointment of consul that element of personal fitness. That is the only thing to my mind.

The CHAIRMAN. A man who can pass an examination in German, French, Spanish, and other branches is liable to be a pretty well qualified man in the respects you mention.

Senator WOLCOTT. If that is so, it is an answer to my question.

Mr. GARFIELD. That answer, of course, covers it, and the attempt on the part of the business men and business organizations was to put into the bill a provision which would give the best service, and I think we have in this bill provisions which will amply secure it.

Without taking more time than is necessary, I desire to call your attention to a pamphlet, copies of which I will leave with the committee. We have here put together excerpts from magazine articles and clippings from newspapers from all over the country, which will indicate better than we can by word of mouth the interest that business organizations are taking in this movement. I also have with me my scrapbook, from which these were taken. It will make my point still clearer. A little over a year ago, when we first started this movement, I made an arrangement with a clipping agency to send me everything referring to the consular movement, and these clippings are those which have been received during the past year. They simply go to show that this movement is not confined to a committee of men who come before you to urge the passage of this bill, but that we speak to you for commercial organizations generally over the country. Here is a list of resolutions and letters which I shall not take time to read to you. They have reference to this particular bill. They have come in since about the 1st of February, when this bill was introduced. We have them from the Chamber of Commerce of Denver, the Chamber of Commerce of Boston, the Memphis Produce Exchange, the Board of Trade of Baltimore, the Chamber of Commerce of San Francisco, the Board of Trade of Scranton, Pa., the Merchants' Exchange of St. Louis, the Chamber of Commerce of Portland, Oreg., and the boards of trade of Peoria, Detroit, and Washington, and of Wilmington, Del., and they are still coming in.

The CHAIRMAN. Will you leave those with us?

Mr. GARFIELD. Yes, sir; I will leave the original resolutions. They belong to the Cleveland Chamber of Commerce, and I would like to have them returned. They will indicate to you the attitude of the chambers of commerce. Colonel Ela has other resolutions and letters which he will present to you. The fact is, the business world has awakened to its opportunities. Extension of trade is an undoubted fact. We must push forward, and by every worthy means at our command seize the markets of the world. The opportunity is here, and we are ready to take it. The first question asked by your manufacturer or exporter who has not been in the field long enough to have agents of his own, is, What can I learn about my particular branch in this, that, or the other country? And his first point of inquiry is the United States consul. One does not need to go outside the limits of his own State to be impressed with the fact that manufacturers everywhere are taking an interest in this question that they have never taken before. They are reading the consular advance sheets, of the very existence of which they knew nothing until within the last year or two. Merchants have come to me and others have written me letters expressing their interest, often relating personal experiences reflecting on our consuls, and urging that we do everything possible, saying, "If your committee needs money or backing of any kind, or letters from our company, we will give them to you." The interest on the part of the business public is very much greater than I appreciated at the time we began our work, although I knew it was considerable.

We come to present to you the facts in the case to let you know what we know about the interest of business men in this country in the consular service, to urge that a favorable report be made, and that if by any means possible this bill be passed at this session of Congress. The reason why bills have not heretofore gone any further than the Senate or House, backed by a favorable report from committee, is that the business interests of the country have not appreciated what it means to them; now they know and are acting.

One word with reference to the observation made, I think, by Senator Frye, during a conversation before I began my statement, to the effect that the personnel of the service at the present time is the most satisfactory he has ever known it to be. That is true. At the end of every four years the personnel is satisfactory. It is impossible to put 1,100 men in the field and give them four years' experience and not have a rather satisfactory result, even when men are appointed by purely political methods. But the difficulty lies not in the fact that the service is at present good—that is why our organizations think a movement to reorganize the service will be well received at this time. We do not complain of the personnel of the service now, or of the service as a whole to-day; it has weak spots and many more than we believe it would have under permanent tenure of office with proper limitations; but sometime within the next few years that service is to be very materially changed by reason of the fact that an entirely new set of consuls will come into office. Out of the 1,100, 100 may hold over—perhaps not more than a dozen. That has been the rule.

The CHAIRMAN. It is the bottom of the ladder?

Mr. GARFIELD. Yes, sir; the percentage to hold over is very small indeed. With the exception of a very few, like Mr. Mason at Berlin, consuls have not held their places longer than a single Administration. Many now in office were in office under the Republican Administration prior to that of Mr. Cleveland, but of those now in office not much more than 12 were there four years ago. Thanking you for your attention, I will not now take further time. Mr. Schwab, of New York, will speak to you next.

Senator WOLCOTT. You can not by examination secure judgment and discretion and ability to deal with men. I am a strong believer in civil service, but I have much doubt whether there should not be men designated to pass the examination by somebody. A man fresh from the high school is a nice fellow and can pass an examination, but he is not a man fitted to deal with the questions which arise at Lyons, for instance, as to French manufactures and our business needs. It requires discretion and judgment and wisdom.

Mr. GARFIELD. Yes, sir.

Senator WOLCOTT. If there were only some way in which we could be secured by naming people to pass examination or by some test of fitness——

Mr. GARFIELD. If it is possible to do so by an amendment, such an amendment would be well worth putting in. There is absolutely no desire among our representatives here to seek anything but the best for the service. There is absolutely no desire on our part to bring to you a civil-service measure, because we are interested in civil service. All we want is a result.

The CHAIRMAN. You might put in an amendment stating that unless grave or other reasons existed, when all could be rejected.

Mr. GARFIELD. The same thing would be true—the President having appointed one of the five. It would be hardly more difficult to call home one of the five than to reject them all before appointment.

Senator WOLCOTT. These applicants may be just out of high school or college.

Mr. GARFIELD. There is an age limit of twenty-five years.

Senator WOLCOTT. There is no doubt but that such men make good material for public service; but it seems to me, if there is some way possible, we ought to be able to have a selection that would give discretion, wisdom, and judgment.

Mr. GARFIELD. I have letters here from Mr. Boyle, our consul at Liverpool, and Mr. Halstead, sending me typewritten copies of what the different papers have said. I was impressed with this fact. The commendation of the English press is almost always not so much of the personnel of our service, outside of the compliments they pay to the local representative, as it is of our advance sheets. In England, as you undoubtedly know, the consular reports are printed and distributed once a month. That was considered a great advance over the publication of once in six months, or a year, as they formerly were. They did that because our consular service publishes their advance sheets daily. I have analyzed comments of that sort, and I have found that the praise is of the advance sheets, and not so much of the service generally.

Senator FORAKER. I do not remember that they were mentioned in any of the articles sent me. The articles sent me by Mr. Halstead related particularly to himself. Mr. Boyle's articles were in general praise of the service, and they pointed out that the American consuls were appointed, and were ambitious to make a record and do successful work, and that inspirited them to be very industrious, and the defect in their service was that it was a sort of life business, and they did not have the opportunities or the desire to work for promotion.

Senator FRYE. What do you say to an amendment like this: That no man shall be appointed a consul to a country from which he was an emigrant?

Mr. GARFIELD. That might work, sometimes, a hardship. For example, we find, so I am told at the State Department, that there is difficulty in some of the South and Central American States. Here is a consul in a little town in Chile, perhaps, and we find the utmost difficulty in getting some one who is not a native who fully understands the language and people to occupy the position; and in regard to our commercial agents, we employ a great many of the natives, and included in this bill is provision for such use, but the Department finds great difficulty in getting anybody except local people.

Senator LODGE. Senator Frye did not mean the persons we appoint locally as commercial agents, but those who have emigrated to this country and are then sent back, perhaps to their native town, as consuls.

Mr. GARFIELD. It would avoid the situation which sometimes occurs, when we send a man back, perhaps for a little vacation, to go to his people in his own country——

Senator FRYE. It almost invariably creates trouble. If a German comes here and is afterwards appointed consul to the town, perhaps, where he was born, he goes there and is clothed with dignity and power as a consul of the United States, and he shows what can be done by moving to this country, and he creates trouble.

Senator BACON. I have known a very notable exception of this in the case of the consul appointed to Christiania. The general rule may be as you state, but in this case the man had come here and was appointed consul at that place, and was retained there under both Mr. Harrison and Mr. Cleveland. I was there a few years ago, and the testimony was unanimously in favor of his case.

Mr. SCHWAB. By sending such a man back, you send a man who can talk the language of the country.

Senator MORGAN. You have stricken out the provision which makes a school of languages. These consular clerks are appointed, practically, for life and taken into the State Department on a very close examination as to character and education, and an examination for languages.

Mr. GARFIELD. That is omitted by the desire of the State Department—at its own suggestion. They say that it was started as a sort of West Point for the consular service, but has come to nothing.

Senator MORGAN. I know a clerk in the service who can be transferred from Germany to China and knows the language of both countries. They are men like Federal soldiers and sailors, subject to the command of their general in chief to go anywhere, at any time, and stay as long as required. There is no preference or patronage in it, except the good of the service. I think that school ought to be encouraged instead of being broken up.

Senator FRYE. My experience is that they relieve the consul himself from obtaining any knowledge of the language of the country to which he is sent.

Mr. GARFIELD. This bill does not disturb those now in.

Senator MORGAN. I understand that, but I think the number ought to be increased.

Mr. GARFIELD. In connection with Senator Wolcott's question, I had occasion, speaking of the advance sheet—I took pains to go through the report of the consuls for 1898, analyzing the articles and the authors of the articles. We have about 1,100 consuls in the field, not counting clerks and smaller offices. There were only 229 who had published a single article in the advance sheets, and of the 229, 50 consuls contributed much more than one-half the articles, and the most of these were from consuls like Mr. Bailey and Mr. Listoe, from the important points.

STATEMENT OF MR. GUSTAVE SCHWAB, REPRESENTING THE CHAMBER OF COMMERCE OF NEW YORK.

Mr. Schwab. Gentlemen, I represent the New York Chamber of Commerce, and have been authorized to say that that chamber is very cordially in favor of this bill. I should like to be permitted to say in reply to the question raised by one of the members of the committee, that the experience of the New York Chamber of Commerce is that those men who are able to command, or who have acquired the use of foreign languages, are generally the men particularly adapted for this consular service and for these commercial agencies. I take it that we wish to extend our markets, and that is the chief reason we are anxious to have such a bill passed, and for such positions, men commanding foreign languages are generally best adapted. And not only should they know these languages, but also be men of some liberal education. I believe that would meet the objection raised.

I do not wish to enlarge upon the arguments advanced by Mr. Garfield. I think he has pretty fully covered the ground. But I wish to say this, the New York Chamber of Commerce has for fifteen or twenty years been continually in favor of a reform in the consular service. Of course we recognize that a very large number of our present consuls are fully efficient and send in very valuable reports. But we take the ground that this efficiency can be extended, and it is absolutely necessary that the consuls should be able to use the language of the country to which they are accredited, or at least a language common to them, and for this reason we believe that this bill would introduce very salutary reforms. I do not know that I have anything more to say, except to second fully what Mr. Garfield has said.

The Chairman. I suggest that after these gentlemen have made their statements we may have a talk with them on any points that may suggest themselves to us.

STATEMENT OF MR. JOHN W. ELA, REPRESENTING THE NATIONAL BUSINESS LEAGUE.

Mr. Ela. The suggestions from Senator Frye in regard to not sending back men to the countries from which they have emigrated has one objection, and that is that they know the language better than any foreigner can learn it from study. The school for languages will never teach any man to speak German, or any other language, as a man has learned it in his own country and has talked it until he is 21 years of age, perhaps. That is not a sufficient consideration to my mind. I am not going to take much of your time, fortunately for you. We, all of us, know that you know more about the history and defects of the consular service than we do, and when men like Senator Morgan and Senator Lodge have introduced bills along the same lines as ours, and your committee has recommended them, and they have not gone any farther than the Senate, it is not because men on the Committee on Foreign Relations of the Senate do not understand the situation.

Therefore, it is not necessary for us to spend any time in educating you gentlemen. We are here to say, do not be discouraged, but that the mercantile world is alive now to the situation, and that if you will report to the Senate this bill, or a bill similar in character—we would like to have this bill, because it has been most carefully prepared, as Mr. Garfield has explained to you—that the representatives of the great mercantile associations and firms of the country will take care of it that the Senators and Representatives from the districts of the different States over the country are educated during this session, and if they, when educated, can be brought to believe that the country needs it, we will have a bill passed.

I represent the National Business League of Chicago. The name is rather a large one, its history is not a long one, and its location in the West—three considerations which may perhaps detract from the title, "national." While that is true, and the organization is supported by Chicago business firms, in order to be honest about naming it a national association, we have what we call an advisory committee, consisting of three prominent business men in every large city or town in the country, generally a banker, a manufacturer, and a merchant. We have, therefore, two or three hundred of these that now represent, I think, every State but two in the country; and it is through these gentlemen that we present matters upon which we ask legislation to their neighbors, and from them that we get either the condemnation or the commendation of whatever we propose.

The object of the association is to influence legislation in an educational way—in a way of presenting subjects and asking consideration for them at the hands of Congress. We have taken up questions such as this new proposed department of commerce, which Senator Frye has had under consideration, and other matters, and in every case we have simply gotten the desires and the opinions of the business men throughout the country through this machinery of ours. We have taken this subject up in connection—at least our organization has—in connection with the Cleveland and New York chambers of commerce, represented here to-day. They took it up before we did, and we joined with them this year. We have had this bill printed and sent over the country, and we have here to present to you letters and resolutions passed by these gentlemen and organizations to which I have referred. I am not going to read them. I have had copies made to leave with the committee. In addition to that, we have sent out, and have asked them to send out, copies of this bill which we have had printed, and have asked the gentlemen and organizations to whom they were sent—and they were always prominent business men or boards of trade—to write their honest opinions and convictions. We have about 150 letters from these prominent business men and concerns, and perhaps fifteen or twenty or twenty-five series of resolutions passed by boards of trade and commercial associations. I will say to you that during the whole of this correspondence there has not been a single letter or resolution in opposition to the bill. Everything has been unanimously in favor of this particular bill, calling attention often, as you will see if you take pains to look over the correspondence (which is put up in good shape and indexed to get at easily) to the different provisions of the bill, showing they favor this particular bill as it stands, and this particular remedy as contained in this bill. I am simply speaking to you—and I will speak but a few moments longer—as to what the interests demand, so far as we have felt it and know it.

It would be inexcusable for me to waste your time by rehearsing the reasons why the reorganization of the consular service is urgently demanded. The members of this committee are much more familiar with the disgraceful condition of that service than I am. It is perhaps sufficient to say that the grade of our commercial representation in foreign countries is below that of any other civilized country and that the necessity of prompt reform, in view of our enlarged desire for new markets, is simply imperative.

There is no comparison between England's foreign commercial service and ours. Our public statistics are crude and useless compared with hers. Therefore it is that she is so much better equipped to utilize an "open door," into whatever part of the globe it opens.

I will say that our business men who have come back this last year from abroad, without a single exception—I will not say without a single exception, but so far as they have expressed themselves, and it has been very general—have been extremely disgusted, I might almost say, with our commercial representatives abroad. It is true, undoubtedly, as several Senators have stated, that we have some good men, but they are so comparatively few that it shows the system, or want of system, is a bad one. We have one firm in Chicago which has a representative in every important commercial point in the world, who sends by cable to his employer frequently a regular report, the same class as sent by the consuls of at least three or four countries through their regular consular service, all of which it seems to us we ought to have sent to us through our consuls for the benefit of all the business men in the country. When we open the door of the trade of the world we want to be so fitted that we can meet the representatives of countries who have trained men on the ground, and have had for years, and can have our commercial agents and exporters, and importers, for that matter, put in possession of the information necessary to enable them to contend with other countries. In that respect the comparison with English consuls—I think a careful comparison will show that there is not a possibility of comparing with those they have abroad as commercial agents. As Mr. Garfield says, we have some who will make a good showing; but from such examination as we have made we believe that even the reports that do come in, and are intelligent in some respects, are written by the clerk, who is a native of the country, and who understands the language of the country, and who has been the clerk not only of this consul, but of half a dozen before him, and goes over with the office from term to term, and that our representatives scarcely know the contents of the reports.

Senator WOLCOTT. Have you any evidence of that?

Mr. ELA. No, sir.

Senator WOLCOTT. Do you think you are justified in making such a wholesale charge?

Mr. ELA. Those statements are simply the remarks I have heard.

Senator WOLCOTT. Have you any evidence as to them?

Mr. ELA. No, sir; I am giving my reasons simply why there is a general evidence in favor——

Senator WOLCOTT. These manufacturers and bankers in every town have come back to say this?

Mr. ELA. I have just said that I have no evidence of this kind, but men who come back state that the reason we get such poor reports is owing to this fact, which they state is a fact. I do not attempt to guarantee it at all.   The examination now at the State Department is, I believe, largely a failure so far as any thorough examination to ascertain the fitness of the men is concerned; and the fact that they are examined after they are appointed does not help it out any.   We were addressed—the Manufacturers' Club at Chicago—by a man who has been consul at an important point in Germany, and who has been replaced recently by this Administration, and he said that the man who replaced him did not understand a word of the German language, and he asked him: "How happens it that you come here without understanding the language? I thought you had to pass an examination in which that was a requirement." The new appointee replied: "I believe that was true, and I did pass an examination, but I was considered sufficiently qualified and intelligent to represent this port without understanding the language."

These examinations, which are of the same character as former examinations from time to time under orders of the different Presidents and Secretaries of State, do not amount to very much; they are not what we are after.   I think as many as thirty or forty years ago Secretary Seward made an order of that kind, and again in 1866 and in 1872, I think we had them, but they never amounted to anything.   The idea is, unless there is an act of Congress directing, or in some way making it a rule, that such a thing shall be done, and through a board of examination properly appointed, that we never shall get it.   That is to say, we never shall get it if it is left to Presidential or departmental orders. I want to suggest that in the provisions of this bill these appointments go to the Senate, and have to take the chance of rejection, as under the present system, and of course the Senate will have an opportunity to look up the general character of the appointee.

Two things are necessary to make our consular service efficient. First, the application of the merit system to appointments and promotions, and, second, an increase of salaries and abolition of all fees to consuls.

This bill (S. 2661) will accomplish both purposes.   It provides that the President shall classify the entire service according to salaries; that the present consuls shall be gradually called for examination, and go back into the service in the same classes they now occupy if they pass the examination; that all applicants shall be subjected to an examination to test their fitness, and those who pass the test shall go onto the eligible list; that when there is a vacancy in the lowest grade the five who obtain the highest credit in the examination shall be certified for appointment to fill the vacancy, and the President may nominate one of the five to the Senate; that if the vacancy is in any grade above the lowest it is to be filled by a promotional examination of the members of the next lower grade.   It also provides that the Secretary of State, or a member of his Department, and a consul shall, with the Civil Service Commission, compose the examination board, which board shall formulate the rules and methods and make the certifications; and it also provides that the appointees shall serve for a probationary period of one year, after which they can only be removed upon the filing of charges and a hearing.

As to salaries and fees, the bill provides for graded salaries from 20 to 30 per cent higher than the present salaries, and that fees, official and unofficial, shall be turned over to the Government.

This is an outline of the bill.   There are other minor provisions, all of which have been carefully worked out by experienced members of the State Department.

This matter of salaries and fees is important, as you know. The present salaries do not secure competent men even now, and to attract men to train themselves for an examination such as is required by this bill there must be a substantial increase in salaries.

The fee system is indefensible. Those consuls who get the highest salaries also get the most fees. The minister to England is paid a salary of $17,500, while the consul-general of London receives a salary of $5,000 and fees, which he is allowed to pocket, aggregating about $35,000. So that the consul's compensation is more than double that of the minister, although it costs the minister ten times as much to maintain his social position. In Paris the minister receives the same salary, $17,500, and the consul-general $5,000 and about $20,000 fees. At Liverpool and Berlin the fees received by the consul-general are about $8,000 in addition to his salary. There have been several attempts to correct this worse than absurdity and they have all failed so far.

We do not object to House bill No. 1026 so far as it goes. But it goes such a little way. It is modeled on Senator Morgan's bill of 1894, but does not go even as far as that bill did, and it would seem as if we could afford to go much farther now. It provides for a committee—which you will observe must be a political committee—to assist the President in reorganizing the consular service, and allows two years in which to report a plan. The plan shall provide for a board of examiners, who shall determine a method of conducting examinations for entrance and promotion and shall conduct the examinations; but it does not prescribe what shall be the character of the examinations, except that "they shall chiefly, but not exclusively," relate to the duties of the service, and that candidates who pass the examination "shall be eligible" for appointment to the lowest grade according to their respective standing. It does not say that anybody shall or may appoint these examined candidates. It provides that in promotions no grade shall be overstepped, and for an increase of salary—somewhat less than that in Senate bill No. 2661—and abolishes fees. It does not provide for examination of present incumbents.

It will be seen that this House bill provides for a commission to assist the President to investigate and report in two years the plan of reorganization, and that the plan shall contain a board of examiners of persons who apply, and who shall, if they pass, be eligible for appointments. Nobody is directed or requested to appoint these persons, and no method of appointment is suggested. While a board might in this way furnish a list of fit applicants, if it chose to do so of its own accord, the fear would be that there would not be definiteness about it such as to induce a President to avail himself of the list or such as to furnish him a shield against the direct and definite demand to continue the old plan of political appointments.

The bill before you reorganizes the service now and establishes a definite system of examinations and appointments and furnishes the machinery by which the fitness of all applicants is required to be established. Having done this, by direct requirement of law it provides that the President may appoint the men furnished to him through this machinery, or, at least, the one whom he selects from the five so furnished. This provides such a shield against the demands of politicians, and indicates to the President so thoroughly what the Congress has decided shall be done, that it is not to be questioned but that the President will be governed by it.

As to the constitutionality of the bill we think there is no question, and we have had that matter carefully examined into. And whether constitutional or not, if the President will execute the provisions of the bill so far as they apply to him the question of constitutionality will not be raised.

To indicate to you something of what the demand is by business men for the prompt passage of this particular bill, I hand to you letters from 137 prominent business firms throughout the different States and several series of resolutions of business associations, such as commercial clubs, boards of trade, etc.

These communications are in response to letters from the National Business League, inclosing copies of this bill and asking for opinions upon the same; and, as you will see, they are unanimous in urging the passage of the bill. In fact, no letters to the contrary have yet been received, and resolutions and letters of the same character as these are still coming in daily and will be forwarded to you later.

STATEMENT OF MR. W. R. WARNER.

Mr. WARNER. I speak to you as a manufacturer who, in common with the other manufacturers of this country, has been largely increasing his trade with foreign countries. A few years ago either my partner or myself made it a point to go over to Europe every two or three years, and then we went every year, and now we send our superintendents over every little while to feel the pulse of trade on the other side.

The CHAIRMAN. What is your business; what do you make?

Mr. WARNER. Machinery for electrical supplies; such types as the Brown & Sharpe and Whitney. We find it advantageous to send our men over to Europe to learn what they most need there, and how we can adapt our work and our supplies to their requirements. We are shipping our manufactures abroad to the extent that more than half our entire product goes over, and it is our instructions to our men, and my practice when I go over, to visit the consuls of the United States in the several places. I want to see who is there to help us, and what he can do for us, and in many instances my experience with them has been so satisfactory that I have been proud of my country and of its representatives, and I want to emphasize this in regard to such appointees as we have, for instance, now in Berlin, Mr. Mason. He is commended by manufacturers all over this country, and the wish is frequently expressed that we could have such men representing our country everywhere. He gives us points and information that we could not get anywhere else. I believe one reason for this is on account of his long service. I do not know how long he has been there, but ever since I began to do business, and I believe that kind of service is being more and more emphasized in the consular appointments.

Another point, and that is as to the practice of foreign consuls and representatives here. In my little factory we have received not only consuls, but members of the legations from several different countries, who have come on just such service as our consuls should make a point of. We have had representatives from the German legations and those of other countries, who have come to our factory to see how we are doing it, and what we are making, to report to their people at home. All of this, in my estimation, perhaps because my experience has been quite limited, is becoming more and more important each year, as we are becoming more and more an exporting nation. Our trade, especially in machinery, is increasing every year, and there is a counter-influence being brought to bear very strongly, especially in Germany, for they are taking the especial manufactures of Americans and adapting them and making exact copies. One firm in Berlin started a factory, and in it invested 14,000,000 marks, for making American machinery, and they came over to America for their equipment, which they are now duplicating. I went last summer into their great engine room with their manager, and I saw there what appeared to be an American machine, and I said to him, "You compliment us very greatly, our manufacturers; I see that you have a copy of the Reynolds-Corliss engine, made in Milwaukee," and he said, "O, no; it is a Reynolds-Corliss engine, made in Milwaukee." They have the best that we can produce, and then they duplicate them and sell them in their own markets. In order to compete with them, we need just such men as Mason and Covert to send us their reports, and then have them supplement that by continual visits, in order to keep thoroughly up to the needs of the people, so that we might adapt our work to them, which is being done by the best manufacturers in this country.

Senator WOLCOTT. Do you think conditions would be best subserved by permitting anybody who might come along to take the examinations provided for in this bill?

Mr. WARNER. I do not know how to bar anyone from trying, but I should emphasize such points as are brought out here, that they should understand the language and should be thoroughly alive to the necessities of our manufacturers. Several of the consuls whom I have visited in my trips did not understand the language of the country where they are stationed, and that ought to be one of the eminent qualifications. But I believe largely in experience and good common sense. They will qualify a man, even if he has not had all the qualifications here.

Senator FORAKER. Where is Mr. Covert located?

Mr. WARNER. At Lyons, France.

Senator LODGE. You believe in permanency of tenure?

Mr. WARNER. Yes, sir. That is why Frank Mason is complimented so highly. He was consul for years and years at Frankfort—I do not know how many. When I saw him at Berlin I complimented him on his advancement, and he said he had been so long at Frankfort that he knew everybody there and all about the needs of the people and their requirements, and that he was afraid he would have to begin all over anew at Berlin.

Senator BACON. I am particularly interested in your statement, a natural statement it appears, that under the present system, even where it is especially desirable, competent men are retained in these consular positions through varying changes in political administration; for instance, Mr. Mason, whom you mention, has been there under Democratic and Republican rule. That has been done in a number of cases, as the consul at Christiania, whom I mentioned, and the consul-general at Brussels, who has, I think, been there for probably twenty years, and Mr. Williams at Habana, who was also probably there for over twenty years, and so on through.   The point I am wishing to direct your attention to is this: You gentlemen are trying to get a change in the law, and the question I wish to ask is whether the difficulty is, not so much with the present law as with those who are called upon to administer it, in looking rather to the reward of political work done and effort given than to the real good of the service?

Mr. WARNER. It seems to me that these gentlemen mentioned, these consuls, to whom reference has been made, are exceptions which might and should be made the rule, so that they could develop.   Now, when they are just beginning to reach efficiency, they are too often dropped aside for the purpose of appointing some one else, while it should be the rule to keep them in office.

Senator BACON. If the proper influence could be brought to bear to keep them there in their places without regard to party, but recognizing the importance of keeping men in office who are found to be efficient, that would be a much more efficient civil service, would it not?

Mr. WARNER. That is the purpose of this bill.

STATEMENT OF MR. S. A. HARRIS.

Mr. HARRIS. I merely wish to say that I have had quite an interest in the revision of the consular service for some years, my interest antedating the Spanish-American war, which gave rise to the present interest, almost universal, of the business men of the country.   I come from Minneapolis, Minn., the State of your chairman, and am directly engaged in banking, but also am interested in the grain business and the manufacture of agricultural implements, and on all sides I get this testimony, that there seems to be a lack of equality of opportunity for the American business man.   When he enters the foreign field, all he asks is equality of opportunities, and, that being granted, the business men will take care of the balance.   I am going to say that my own personal opinions have been modified in certain directions, owing to some correspondence I have had during the past three years with a cousin of mine, who is a consul at Nagasaki, Japan, appointed by President McKinley, and I have come to believe that the lack in our consular service is owing more to the short tenure of office than to the quality of material that is originally appointed, and any bill that will give opportunity for our consuls to perfect themselves in the requirements, which all must gain when they take the field, will add to the efficiency of the service.

I will also say that I believe it is quite important that this service should be based in some way upon merit; in no other way can we get the service in our foreign field that the American business men feel they are entitled to.   I would call your attention also to the fact that more and more as opportunities are offered to our young business men of the country you can not expect, through political channels, to get permanently for this consular service the class that you need.   You need a class of educated young men who will write up their reports as to business needs and requirements in a competent way.   The information I get through my correspondent is that the German and English representatives abroad, especially those two—the ones the Americans are thrown in competition with to the largest extent in foreign trade—

both the English and the German consular service is stated to me to be distinctly superior to our American representatives.

Senator WOLCOTT. How is the German consular service appointed?

Mr. HARRIS. I think upon the system based upon permanency and merit.

Senator WOLCOTT. Do you think experience should count as a factor or knowledge of languages?

Mr. HARRIS. If discretion is used in the original appointment of men to take the line in this branch of the service—I have a great deal of confidence in the ability of the ordinary mind to acquire efficiency through experience, and it seems to me that it is largely through experience and service that we will get efficiency.

STATEMENT OF MR. CHARLES P. MOSER, REPRESENTING THE CHAMBER OF COMMERCE OF AUBURN, N. Y.

Mr. MOSER. I will simply say that I come from the central part of New York State—from the town of Auburn. Not a very large city, but quite a manufacturing city. Our manufacturers and business men are interested in this bill. I talked with our largest manufacturer Monday morning. He represents a concern whose pay roll last year amounted to nearly a million of dollars for labor, and he said he was most emphatically in favor of this bill. This firm has its agents in foreign countries, so they do not need the work of the consular service so much; and he said he also got reports from a Philadelphia agency, but the better the reports made by the consuls, the better reports they would get in the country. He said one-fifth of his whole business is export business, and he proposes to make it one-quarter of the business of this year.

STATEMENT MADE BY HON. THOMAS W. CRIDLER, THIRD ASSISTANT SECRETARY OF STATE, BEFORE THE COMMITTEE ON FOREIGN RELATIONS, ON WEDNESDAY, APRIL 18, 1900, ON SENATE BILL 2661, TO REORGANIZE THE CONSULAR SERVICE OF THE UNITED STATES.

Senator LODGE. We will be glad, Mr. Cridler, if you will take up this bill by sections and give us the benefit of your information and views in regard to those sections and the bill generally.

Mr. CRIDLER. I shall be glad to do so; and, in order that my meaning may be clear, I shall read each section so that it may precede my remarks and be understood in connection with them, wherever it is necessary for me to dwell on the section.

As to section 1 no remarks whatever are necessary.

SEC. 2. That the offices of consular agents, deputy consuls, commercial agents, and vice-consuls, except when such offices are held by citizens of the United States, shall be excluded from this reorganization, and such officers shall not be in the line of promotion under this Act.

This section when read in connection with sections 15 and 16 is not clear. It would seem to mean that consular agents, deputy consuls, commercial agents, and vice-consuls are not included in the reorganization if they are not American citizens; yet nowhere does it provide in what way these officers *who are citizens* of the United States are to be appointed, compensated, or promoted. It is clear that the officers *who are not citizens* are to be appointed as heretofore. Under existing legislation vice-consuls and deputy consuls receive no salaries as such officers except during the absence beyond a stated period of the principal officer. Their only compensation as a rule is as clerk, in case there is an allowance for clerk hire. If it is the intention to place vice and deputy consuls, vice and deputy consuls-general and vice and deputy commercial agents, who are citizens of the United States, on a footing with other consular officers in respect to compensation, promotion and tenure, it should be distinctly so stated in the bill.

The part of the bill relating to commercial agents appears to be all right, leaving as it does the appointment as heretofore where the appointee is not a citizen, and placing him under the reorganization where he is a citizen.

The provision in regard to consular agents, however, leaves the appointment to be made as heretofore in case the appointee is not a citizen, but makes no provision for appointment of citizens of the United States to the position of consular agent.

Senator LODGE. That is true.

Mr. CRIDLER. The bill should be more explicit upon this subject. It is inferred that consular agents who may be citizens are not in line of promotion, and are to be appointed as heretofore, but if this is the intention of the proposed law it should be distinctly stated.

Senator LODGE. The idea was that consular agents and commercial agents ought not to be included under the reorganization.

Mr. CRIDLER. That is so, but the bill does not say so as I read it. I spent the time until after midnight last night in going over this bill, and I desire to say that this is absolutely the only bill to which I have given any attention, and the reason I have examined into this is because the Secretary wishes to oblige the Foreign Relations Committee, and especially one of its members who had personally requested information on the subject.

SEC. 3. That the reorganization shall include all offices of the consular service; and the offices of consular clerk are hereby transformed into consulates of the sixth class.

The first part of this section is not as clear as it should be, and might be advantageously considered in connection with my remarks as to section 2. The latter part of the section is commendable. It is highly important, however, that in making consuls of consular clerks, they should be placed in a higher class than class 6 ($1,500). Long experience and the well-known character of these men entitle them to favorable consideration in any reorganization, and it would seem that they should receive at least $1,800 or $2,000. Moreover, it may be pertinently observed that, although the salary of these offices, excepting five, is now $1,200, they make something beyond that sum annually by their assignments to consulates where they are permitted to share in certain of the unofficial fees. Of these five two have been in some twelve or fourteen months and the other three have several months yet to run.

When this is taken into account, it seems only just that in fixing a salary, as is proposed in this bill, it should be commensurate with their experience and sufficient to live upon comfortably, since they are usually men of limited financial means. I have known some consular clerks to realize more than it is now proposed to give them: others are annually receiving less, it is true.

SEC. 4. That there shall be not more than four consuls-general of the first class, at eight thousand dollars each per annum; not more than thirteen consuls-general of the second class, at six thousand dollars each per annum; not more than nineteen consuls-general of the third class, at five thousand dollars each per annum. That there shall be not more than thirty-seven consuls of the first class, at five thousand dollars each per annum; not more than thirty-five consuls of the second class, at four thousand dollars each per annum; not more than sixty consuls of the third class, at three thousand dollars each per annum; not more than forty consuls of the fourth class, at two thousand dollars each per annum; not more than thirty consuls of the fifth class, at one thousand eight hundred dollars each per annum; not more than fifty consuls of the sixth class, at one thousand five hundred dollars each per annum.

Senator LODGE. That is in regard to the arrangement of consuls?

Mr. CRIDLER. Yes, sir; and this section is for the most part to be commended. Excluding the seven consuls-general not subject to the reorganization on account of also being diplomatic officers (secretaries of legation or ministers resident) at Bogota, Cairo, Bangkok, Monrovia, Seoul, Teheran, Stockholm, and 44 feed consuls and commercial agents, whose official fees do not exceed $1,000, at the following places:

Algiers	$663.50	La Paz, Mexico	$367.30
Alicante		Madrid	
Antofagasta	199.50	Maskat	165.00
Arica	188.00	Moscow	760.00
Bagdad	443.00	Niuchwang	
Bathurst		Puerto Plata	678.68
Batoum	176.00	Riga	518.50
Belgrade		Rouen	415.00
Belleville	393.00	St. Martin	103.80
Budapest	947.75	Teneriffe	
Bucharest		Tunis	54.50
Carthagena		Turks Island	424.25
Colonia		Tuxpan	458.42
Cordoba	67.50	Warsaw	253.50
Corunna		Paysandu	32.00
Falmouth	650.00	Port Rowan	436.00
Gorée-Dakar	101.50	Stanbridge	137.50
Helsingfors	22.50	Saigon	75.00
Hobart		St. Christopher	900.14
Iquique	806.08	Samana	137.50
La Paz, Bolivia		Suva	

There are, subject to the reorganization bill, the following officers under the existing system:

6 consuls-general, at $5,000	$30,000.00
1 consul-general, at $4,500	4,500.00
6 consuls-general, at $4,000	24,000.00
2 consuls-general, at $3,500	7,000.00
12 consuls-general, at $3,000	36,000.00
1 consul-general, at $2,500	2,500.00
4 consuls-general, at $2,000	8,000.00
1 consul-general, at $1,500	1,500.00
1 consul, at $5,000	5,000.00
5 consuls, at $3,500	17,500.00
23 consuls, at $3,000	69,000.00
36 consuls, at $2,500	90,000.00
69 consuls, at $2,000	138,000.00
77 consuls and commercial agents, at $1,500	115,500.00
11 consuls, at $1,000	11,000.00
42 consuls and commercial agents, fees	19,939.53

579,439.53

The bill now under consideration provides for not more than the following salaried officers:

4 consuls-general, first class, at $8,000	$32,000
13 consuls-general, second class, at $6,000	78,000
19 consuls-general, third class, at $5,000	95,000
37 consuls, first class, at $5,000	185,000
35 consuls, second class, at $4,000	140,000
60 consuls, third class, at $3,000	180,000
40 consuls, fourth class, at $2,000	80,000
30 consuls, fifth class, at $1,800	54,000
50 consuls, sixth class, at $1,500	75,000
288	919,000

This schedule, in my judgment, is open to objection in the salaries provided for the consuls-general of the first class and the consuls of the fifth and sixth classes. In apportioning the four consulates-general at $8,000 each it is not unlikely that they would be given to London, Paris, Berlin, and say St. Petersburg. There are consulates-general in China and Japan that are entitled to be placed in this grade also. If I were to make a suggestion I would say that the consulate-general at London and at Paris should be given $10,000, and that a sufficient number of $8,000-officers be provided to make it possible to place Shanghai and Yokohama—Shanghai certainly—in that grade.

The compensation at present enjoyed by the consuls-general at London and Paris amply justify $10,000 as a compromise, to say the least. They annually cover into the Treasury of the United States many thousand dollars over and above the compensation they now receive, and it is much more than $10,000. The office at Berlin does not net so much, but it annually covers into the Treasury more than $8,000—I think $11,000 or $12,000, perhaps. St. Petersburg is the least fortunate. Its salary is less than one-half of that named, and its official fees considerably below either of the other three places indicated. It is, however, a more expensive place to live in than any one of them.

In regard to class 5 and 6 ($1,500 and $1,800), the salaries appear too small. The bill takes away the consul's share of official fees collected at agencies under his office, and all notarial or unofficial fees at his own office. He is thus left with nothing beyond the meager salary of $1,500 or $1,800, as the case may be, and on this he is expected to uphold the dignity of the United States and further American trade. It is not sufficient, nor in the main fair. If only the salary remains, it should afford the officer a fair living. I would suggest that class 4 be made $2,500, class 5, $2,000, and class 6, $1,800. The two grades last named might with propriety be raised still higher. I should not, however, recommend the abolishment of any of the grades, for the reason that they would act as a stimulus to the service and promote efficiency by competing for promotions.

SEC. 5. That all fees, official or unofficial, received by any officer in the consular service for services rendered in connection with the duties of his office or otherwise, shall be accounted for and paid into the Treasury of the United States, and the sole and only compensation of such officers shall be by salaries fixed by law; but this shall not apply to consular agents who shall be paid by one-half of the fees received in their offices, the other half being accounted for and paid into the Treasury of the United States.

Senator LODGE. That is the one abolishing fees?

Mr. CRIDLER. Yes, sir; abolishing all official fees; and a mighty good thing it is, too. This section can be commended in every way.

It will abolish the fee question, which has always been demoralizing to the service and of incalculable trouble to the Department. The President's order of August 28, 1898, partly relieves the situation at present, by stating how the fees at consular agencies shall be divided. That order was as follows:

COMPENSATION OF CONSULAR AGENTS.

DEPARTMENT OF STATE,
Washington, August 26, 1898.

To the consular officers of the United States.

GENTLEMEN. The following is hereby communicated to you for your information and guidance.

EXECUTIVE ORDER.

It is hereby prescribed that consular agents, as compensation for their services to American vessels and seamen, and for other official acts, shall receive one-half the official fees collected for such services, provided such compensation shall not exceed in any fiscal year the sum of $1,000, and all such fees in excess of such compensation shall be remitted to the consul in whose district the agency is located. No other arrangement with consular agents will be allowed.

Remittances from agents to consuls covering these fees are to be made quarterly, and consuls will be required to send agents' receipts for their share with their accounts. This order is to take effect on and after July 1, 1898, and applies to all fees included in the Tariff of Official Fees. Fees for notarial and unofficial services may be all retained by the consular agent collecting them.

WILLIAM McKINLEY.

Consular officers will be required to observe strictly the terms of this order in every respect.

Respectfully, yours, WILLIAM R. DAY.

Moreover, in regard to this section, it strengthens the Department's position that living salaries should be paid to consular officers embraced in this proposed reorganization. The order of the President I have just given cuts the fees right in two up to $2,000, and when the fees amounted to that sum the consular agent received $1,000 and the consul $1,000, and if there were any fees in excess of that amount they go into the Treasury. Some years ago the consul used to take all the fees of the office.

SEC. 6. That within one year after the date of the passage of this act the President shall classify the consulates-general and the consulates in accordance with the provisions of section three, and after such classification shall have been made any consulate-general or consulate may be abolished or its classification changed, or a new consulate-general or consulate created and placed in any class, the complement of which is not filled, by Executive order of the President

No remarks are necessary. One year will be sufficient time in which to make the classification called for by that section.

SEC. 7. That immediately after the classification required by the foregoing section shall have been made the incumbents of the consulates-general and consulates then holding office may be assigned by the President to the various classes as nearly as possible in accord with the salaries they were receiving when said classification was made. Commercial agents, wherever the agent is an American citizen, shall be brought into consulates on the same basis as consuls.

Nothing at present need be said about this section, except that in case the suggestions under section 2 are acted upon this section should be considered in that connection.

Senator LODGE. You think commercial agents and consular agents should be included?

Mr. CRIDLER. As to commercial and consular agents, I think I have covered that very fully under section 2.

SEC. 8. That the present incumbents of the consulates-general, consulates, and commercial agencies shall be gradually recalled for examination within two years from the date of the passage of this Act, and readmitted to the same classes which they respectively occupied on passing the prescribed examination, provided they are deemed competent, and anyone who shall fail to pass said examination shall thereupon be dropped from the consular service, but no consular officer shall be recalled for the purpose of said examination within six months after the passage of this Act.

Such examinations shall be conducted by the board of examiners provided for by this Act and under rules formulated by it, and their scope and method shall be determined by such board, but such examinations shall embrace at least all such subjects as may be required in the case of examinations for original appointment to the consular service in accordance with the provisions of this Act.

Here is where you are going to experience a good deal of difficulty, and it will necessarily increase the expense of reorganization. Under this section eighteen months are given within which to recall and examine the 267 officers. The examiners must during this time examine more than 15 persons a month. The bill makes no provision for expenses, and in order to be effective should be accompanied or immediately followed by an appropriation act, making provision for the traveling expenses of consuls who shall be members of the examining board, and for the officers who shall be recalled for examination. It would be unreasonable to expect consuls to pay their own expenses from their posts to the United States and return in order to be examined.

The additional work hereby entailed upon the Department is necessarily large, and ample provision should be made by law to meet proposed new conditions. As at present framed the bill is radically deficient in this respect. It simply says that a thing shall be done, without making any provision for the additional expense necessary in connection with the doing of it or for the method of doing it, and with the present limited force of the office it will be awfully trying to attempt to do it. Further on I shall again go into this matter.

SEC. 9. That a consul-general or a consul may be transferred by the President's order from one place to another in the same class according to the needs of the service, and a consul-general or consul may, in like manner, be assigned to act temporarily in a class above or below that in which he holds his commission, and his salary shall not be affected by such temporary assignment; but no consul-general or consul shall be transferred to a country in which the United States exercises extraterritorial jurisdiction until he shall have passed an examination in the fundamental principles of the common law, the rules of evidence, and the trial of civil and criminal cases.

Senator LODGE. That is about transfers?

Mr. CRIDLER. Yes, sir; in regard to transfers, and I think that this section is commendable in every way. It should, however, be amended by inserting after the word "commission," line 16, page 4, the words "or as specified in paragraph 2 of section 13;" and I will explain what I mean as to this when I come to remark on that paragraph of section 13. This would permit the President to avail himself of the benefit of the experience and service of such consular officer in the Department of State or in any other of the Executive Departments should it be thought necessary. It is not difficult to imagine a case where the services of such a person might be utilized with credit to the officer and advantage to the public service. You provide for the interchange over there, and speak of it here, and this amendment would simply make them interchangeable under section 13 as well.

In order to make this section effective it should be accompanied or followed by legislation providing for the compensation of the vice-consuls left in charge of the office during the absence of the consul. Under existing legislation vice-consuls receive no salary during the presence at the consulate of the principal officer.   During his absence on leave the vice-consular officer receives one-half the principal's salary, unless such absence should continue longer than sixty days in any one year, in addition to the statutory allowance for transit if the principal comes to the United States.   In such case the vice-consul receives the whole salary for the time in excess of the legal period. As this bill provides that the principal's absence from his post shall not affect his salary, the vice-consul can not be compensated from the principal's salary, and a special provision for his compensation is accordingly necessary.

As a rule they make an agreement between the principal and his vice as to what shall be the salary of the latter.   In some cases the former waive everything, and in some cases the vice gets a certain portion of the fees, but it is usually by a special arrangement between the two that the matter of salary is determined.

SEC. 10. That whenever a vacancy shall occur in the office of consul-general, or consul above the sixth class, members of the class next below that in which the vacancy occurred shall be deemed eligible to be selected to fill such vacancy.   But whenever the interests of the service demand it a member of a class not immediately below that in which such vacancy has occurred may, for exceptional reasons, which shall be published when the vacancy is filled, be deemed eligible to be selected to fill such vacancy.

Here is the weakness of this section in these words " But whenever the interests of the service demand," etc.   Although the spirit of this section is to be commended, I am unable to agree with it as a whole. It seems to me that it permits promotions to be made from a low grade to a place in a grade several degrees higher without regard to the efficiency of consuls in the grade immediately below that to which the promotion is made.

Senator LODGE. I agree with you in that entirely.

Mr. CRIDLER. It clearly opens the way, if one may be pardoned for saying so, to an abuse of power through favoritism, that should be eliminated or rather reduced to a minimum.   The "exceptional reasons" should be of the strongest possible character, based upon the record of the officer, and conclusively show his peculiar fitness for these higher duties to which he is to be promoted.   For these reasons it seems to me this section should be carefully safeguarded unless it is thought that the publication of the reasons therefor may be amply sufficient.   I admire the spirit of the thing, and I may be wrong, but that is the way it strikes me.

Senator MONEY. You propose that a man from class 6 shall not be permitted to be promoted to class 4, for instance?

Mr. CRIDLER. Yes, sir.

Senator CULLOM. That he shall not jump a grade?

Mr. CRIDLER. Yes, sir; without some very good reason given.

Senator MONEY. If the Secretary thinks he can find a man in the sixth class who can do the business of the fourth class better than anyone in the fifth class, he should have the opportunity to do so.

Mr. CRIDLER. It is practically so in the Navy that no grades shall be jumped.

Senator MONEY. It is practically so in the Navy, and in the Army also, but that does not show the necessity of having it practically so in this service; they are not deadly parallels.

Mr. CRIDLER. Very nearly so.

Senator MONEY. Why not let the President select?

Mr. CRIDLER. I haveyno desire to curtail the President's power.

Senator MONEY. I understand that it is the suggestion of the bill itself that promotions may be made in this way?

Mr. CRIDLER. Yes, sir.

The CHAIRMAN. Let us get through with Mr. Cridler's statements and suggestions, and then we can study that matter.

Mr. CRIDLER—

SEC. 11. That the Assistant Secretary of State, or such person in the Department of State as the President shall designate, and a consul-general or consul of the United States and an officer of the Department of State whom the President shall designate shall constitute a board of examiners for admission to the consular service.

I am in accord with this provision of the bill, leaving the examinations entirely in the hands of the President and the officials of the Department of State. While it will undoubtedly entail upon the board of examiners herein provided for a difficult and responsible task, yet I am confident the results will prove quite as satisfactory as by any other method that might be adopted. This board will be certainly familiar with the requirements of the consular service, and therefore in some degree better able to judge of the fitness of candidates who desire to enter into it. It will be necessary, however, to provide machinery for holding such examinations, as well as appropriate the required funds to pay for printing and for such other incidental expenses as are inseparable from such work.

Senator LODGE. That would come in any way?

Mr. CRIDLER. Yes, sir; of course it would. Section 12 does not seem to call for any observations. It will regulate itself if the measure becomes a law.

Senator LODGE. That simply provides for the examinations?

Mr. CRIDLER. Yes, sir.

SEC. 13. That anyone who has been continuously employed in the classified civil service of the Department of State for at least two years next preceding shall be eligible for nomination for and appointment to a consulship without previous examination by the board of examiners, in a class paying a salary not greater than that which he may be receiving in the Department of State when his appointment to the consular service is made.

Any consul-general or consul who has served continuously for a period of not less than two years next preceding in a consular capacity abroad may be assigned to duty in any bureau of the Department of State or on special duty in or for that Department, or by arrangement with the head of any other Department in or for such other Department in such position as may be desirable for the improvement of the service; but assignment under this clause shall in no case extend over a period of more than one year in any of four consecutive years.

This section does not seem to require any remarks. My understanding of it is that an employee in the classified service of the Department of State who has had not less than two years' service immediately preceding his appointment, may be transferred at the same salary into the consular service.

Senator LODGE. That relates back to section 2?

Mr. CRIDLER. Yes, sir. These employees may be transferred to the consular service—is that the meaning of it?

Senator LODGE. Yes, sir.

Mr. CRIDLER. It is the second paragraph of section 13 that has reference to section 2.

Senator LODGE. The idea is to make the service more or less interchangeable with the work in the Department.

Mr. CRIDLER.

SEC. 14. That after appointment and assignment to a consulate under the provisions of this Act a consul may be recalled at any time within twelve months and his place become vacant.

After service of twelve months in a consulate no consul shall be dismissed from the service except for due cause, presented to him in writing.

The first paragraph of this section contemplates a probationary appointment of twelve months, before the expiration of which any consul may be recalled and his place become vacant. I think the law should be specific. It should state that the board of examiners or the Secretary of State, upon their report, shall report to the President the standing of any consul before the expiration of the probationary period, with reasons for his recall, if that course be thought necessary for the good of the public service.

Senator LODGE. That ought to be in.

Mr. CRIDLER. The second paragraph of the section is not, in my judgment, as full as it should be. It should go further. A consul should have an opportunity to answer any charges preferred against him, and only after full consideration of the charges should action be taken by the President, in case the present measure contemplates a permanent service, similar to that of the Army and Navy. It is just as important to have a well-trained and efficient permanent consular service as to have such a military and naval service, while the civil official deserves equal treatment with his brother in the other service so far as his tenure of office is concerned.

Section 15. No statement in regard to this section seems to be necessary, except to call attention to the remarks under section 2.

Section 16. The remarks under section 2 apply also to this section.

Section 17. No remarks necessary.

I did not know but that you might be glad to have a comparative statement as to the conditions existing at some of the ports and places where consuls of the various nations are stationed with reference to salaries paid, etc., and I will give it to you in a few words. I shall include the United States, Great Britain, Germany, and France, and it will bear careful consideration in connection with section 4 and the remarks I have made in regard to that section. In order to make the consular service attract the best talent, the salaries paid must be larger than they are under existing conditions and legislation.

Senator CULLOM. Do the consuls of these foreign countries get anything but a fixed salary?

Mr. CRIDLER. Yes, sir; they often get allowances for entertainments, houses, etc.

Senator MONEY. What does this statement show?

Mr. CRIDLER. The comparative salaries of the consuls of various countries at these different important places. The statement does not purport to be minutely exact as to the total compensation of the officers mentioned, but has been compiled from official publications of the respective Governments on file in the Department of State, and is believed to be substantially correct.

Place.	Great Britain.	Germany.	France.	United States.
Pretoria		$7,140	$2,702	$2,000
Buenos Ayres	$4,866	5,712		2,500
Budapest	4,866	6,420	4,825	Fees.
Trieste	2,920	4,570	4,246	2,000
Antwerp	4,866	4,760	3,860	3,000
Rio de Janeiro	5,353	5,712	5,790	5,00.
Valparaiso	4,379	5,712	4,825	3,000
Amoy	4,866	5,712	(a)	3,500
Canton	5,840	5,712	4,825	3,500
Shanghai	7,300	7,140	9,650	5,000
Tientsin	4,866	8,570	5,018	3,500
Cairo	29,199	7,140	3,470	5,000
Odessa	4,380	6,420	3,860	2,000
Amsterdam	486	4,760	4,246	1,500
Constantinople	3,893	5,712	4,632	3,000
Montevideo		5,712		3,000
New York	9,733	11,424	10,615	
London		9,520	7,720	5,000
Paris	3,406	3,570		5,000

a Consular agent.

It is hardly fair to place Cairo and Paris in this list, owing to the difference in the importance of those places to European Governments and the United States.

Senator LODGE. Does the salary of the consul at Rio Janeiro cover all his receipts?

Mr. CRIDLER. No, sir; in addition to his salary of $5,000 he receives $756.75 unofficial, and one-half of the official fees collected at the agency under his office, amounting in all to in the neighborhood of $6,000.

Senator LODGE. The man there from the United States is paid better than the other consuls?

Mr. CRIDLER. As the salaries go, he is; but there may be other compensations for them. At London the German consul réceives $9,520 actual salary; ours, $5,000. But the actual compensation of our consul-general is more than that, it is safely $20,000, including all unofficial fees from every source.

Senator CULLOM. What is given him under the bill?

Mr. CRIDLER. It gives him $8,000; but I say that London and Paris ought to be $10,000. In Paris now the compensation that the consul-general receives is perhaps $20,000 all told.

I would also like to make a statement as to the amount of official and notarial fees to be deposited in the Treasury under the provisions of this bill if it shall be adopted.

Senator LODGE. We should very much like to have that.

Mr. CRIDLER. I worked until late last night in order to be able to state them to you, and am glad to be able to do so.

If this bill is to be interpreted as placing within the classification all salaried consulates, and all feed consulates whose compensation exceeds $1,000 a year, there will be deposited in the Treasury, in addition to the amount now turned into the Treasury, the following:

Official fees $67,251
Notarial fees 105,952

Total.. 173,203

These figures do not purport to be exact, but show in a general way the additional receipts of the Government under the proposed reorganized system.

The total expenses for salaries as provided by the new bill is:

For 288 offices	$919,000
The existing system, 267 officers	579,439
Increased cost under new bill	339,561
Less additional receipts above	173,203
Approximate actual increased cost	166,358

As stated above, these figures are merely intended to convey an idea of the total increased cost to the Government of the system provided for by the proposed reorganization bill. They show that the actual increase in the cost of the service under the new bill will be about $166,358. This does not, of course, include the expense of paying vice-consuls during the absence of the principal, traveling expenses, etc.

Senator FRYE. How will the additional fees compare with the increased cost?

Mr. CRIDLER. They will be a good deal more, with the official fees, which will be about $173,000, but the actual increased cost is $339,000, less the amount of these fees, which would make the increase of cost about $166,000 more than the actual cost now, over and above everything.

Senator FYRE. There are a good many consulates now where the fees paid are larger than the salary?

Mr. CRIDLER. That equalizes itself, because at some of them they are not.

Senator FRYE. The cost to the United States——

Mr. CRIDLER. Would be in excess of the present service——

Senator FRYE. In excess of all fees?

Mr. CRIDLER. Yes, sir; that includes everything. You see, if this bill is to be interpreted as placing all consulates on a salary basis, there will be deposited in the Treasury, in addition to the amount now deposited——

Senator FRYE. I understand the fees collected now are paid to the consular service.

Mr. CRIDLER. Not entirely.

Senator FRYE. How much?

Mr. CRIDLER. If you want to know what the amount of official fees covered into the Treasury is now, I can easily furnish that, although I do not have it with me at this moment.

Senator LODGE. Is the service self-supporting?

Mr. CRIDLER. It is not absolutely. Do you want to know the amount of consular fees which would be paid into the Treasury under this bill in addition to the amount now turned in?

The CHAIRMAN. We want to know how much additional the scheme will cost than it now does.

Senator FRYE. What is the net cost under this bill as compared with the present?

Mr. CRIDLER. You will have to take the fees of all kinds and add them together, and then subtract them from the extra amount paid in salaries, and the additional cost, if any, will be the difference.

Senator LODGE. I would suggest that Mr. Cridler take a copy of the proposed bill with him and make such amendments as he would suggest. There are parts of the bill which seem to be contradictory, perhaps, and he can point out the defects, and give us his suggestions in the form of amendments to the bill.

Mr. CRIDLER. I will do that very cheerfully.

Senator LODGE. If you will put the bill in shape——

Mr. CRIDLER. Redraft it as I think it should be?

Senator LODGE. Yes, sir; and you will also please give us the additional figures mentioned.

Mr. CRIDLER. Yes, sir; I will send you, either by telegram or by letter, the additional figures to include with my statement.

Senator FRYE. The net cost now and as it would be under the new system.

Mr. CRIDLER. The only way I see is to take all the official fees covered into the Treasury from all sources, add to them the unofficial fees now received, and the notarial fees which go to the various officers; add them together and subtract them from $919,000, the net cost under this bill as proposed. My ideas as to some matters will increase the cost somewhat, for I think the consuls-general at London and Paris ought to have $10,000, and also that there ought to be six, or perhaps eight, of the higher class.

Senator LODGE. You will also have to make a class of consular agents and commercial agents?

Senator FRYE. What is the difference between them?

Mr. CRIDLER. The difference is this: A commercial agent is appointed by the Secretary of State, without confirmation by the Senate, but he is as much a consular officer, except in the matter of confirmation, as any. The consular agent is subordinate to the consul or commercial agent, and is appointed by the Secretary of State on the recommendation of the principal officer. The consular agent is allowed one-half of the fees collected at his agency not in excess of $1,000 a year.

Senator LODGE. What I mean is this. We provide here that those consular agents and commercial agents shall be here, and yet make no provision for their appointment.

Mr. CRIDLER. That is included in my memoranda. I will tell the Secretary what you desire me to do, and I have no doubt he will permit it; but he told me before I came up here that while he had great sympathy for any effort for the betterment of the consular service, yet that he must not be considered as committed to any particular bill now before Congress.

Senator BACON. I do not know that it is necessary for him to be so, but it his business to administer the law after we shall make it.

Mr. CRIDLER. The following will show the expenditures and receipts for the consular service during the fiscal year ended June 30, 1899, under the present system, and a rough estimate of the probable cost of the service as contemplated by this bill. It is impossible to reach anything like accuracy in estimating the expenditures and receipts under the proposed reorganized service without a greater amount of labor and painstaking calculation than I am able, in justice to my other duties, to give the matter.   Attention is invited to the increased receipts under the reorganized system.

	Present system—expenses year ended June 30, 1899.	Proposed system—estimated expenditures.
Expenditures.		
Salaries, consular officers	$519,870.19	$923,000.00
Salaries, instruction, etc	10,146.91	
Salaries, consular clerks	13,407.51	
Interpreters, China, Korea, etc	14,835.02	14,835.02
Marshals for consular courts	8,800.00	8,800.00
Interpreters and guards	7,360.30	7,360.30
Prisons for American convicts	4,975.54	4,975.54
Contingent expenses	220,835.33	220,835.33
Services to American vessels	7,291.88	7,291.88
Clerks at consulates	99,358.87	99,358.87
Compensation from fees, Revised Statutes, 1703, 1730, 1732	165,574.42	165,574.42
Office rent and clerk hire from fees, Revised Statutes, 1732	1,075.76	
	1,073,531.73	1,452,031 36
Receipts·		
Consular fees	915,088 30	1,088,291 30
Excess of expenditures over receipts	158,443.43	363,740.06

It will be noticed that no provision is made in the foregoing estimate for compensation of vice-consuls during the absence of the consul, traveling expenses, etc., because there is no basis upon which to make such an estimate.   Irrespective of these items, the cost to the Government of the new system, approximately, and the old system, would be:

Reorganized system $363,740.06
Existing system... 158,443.43

Increased cost of new system 205,296.63

In explanation of this increased cost it is necessary to take into consideration that there are under the reorganization bill—

Salaried offices not affected...................................... 2
Salaried offices classified by bill 288
Feed offices not classified by bill 44

Total 334

Total number of offices under existing system compensated from consular appropriation or from fees 313

Increased number of offices under this bill...................... 21

This increased number of offices made by the bill under consideration will partly account for the increased expenditure estimated for the reorganized system.

Moreover, it seems to me proper to add that the difference may still be slightly greater since, in drafting a new bill or suggesting needed amendments to the one proposed, London and Paris may, and ought to be, included at $10,000 per year each, while perhaps six or eight places should, in justice to the public service and the constantly growing American commercial interests, be provided with annual salaries of not less than $8,000 each.

Until the new draft is actually formulated, it is impossible to be more specific than in the present instance, which according to my understanding is only intended as a tentative statement for the information of this committee as showing approximately the cost of the consular service as at present constituted and as proposed.

With reference to the increase in the number of offices, it is presumed that the bill does not make it obligatory upon the President to immediately classify the full complement of offices. If this be true, the actual expenditure would probably be considerably reduced in practice, because it is not likely it would be found necessary to instantly classify and establish the full number of additional offices for which provision may be made.

[See p. 189.]

May 14, 1900.

[Senate Report No. 1305.]

Mr. Daniel, from the Committee on Foreign Relations, submitted the following report:

The Committee on Foreign Relations, to whom was referred Senate bill 4650, respectfully report the same, with the recommendation that it pass.

This bill is recommended by the Secretary of the Treasury to carry out the provisions of "An act to provide a government for the Territory of Hawaii," approved April 30, 1900, and in fulfillment of the joint resolution "To provide for the annexing the Hawaiian Islands to the United States," approved July 7, 1898.

By the joint resolution approved as aforesaid it is provided, among other things, as follows:

The public debt of the Republic of Hawaii, lawfully existing at the date of the passage of this joint resolution, including the amounts due to depositors in the Hawaiian Postal Savings Bank, is hereby assumed by the Government of the United States, but the liability of the United States in this regard shall in no case exceed four million dollars. So long, however, as the existing government and the present commercial relations of the Hawaiian Islands are continued as hereinbefore provided, said government shall continue to pay the interest on said debt.

It appears that the gross public debt of Hawaii on August 12, 1898, as shown by the report of the minister of finance, was $4,603,747.34, and that there was cash in the treasury, certified to by the registrar, to the amount of $546,739.04.

It appears also that the bonded debt of Hawaii at the same time was $3,689,700, all of which, except $562,000, is now redeemable— that is to say, $3,127,700.

It appears also that the Hawaiian Postal Savings Bank, which was established in 1884, had at that time $836,297.34 on deposit due to 10,555 depositors of various nationalities; and in addition deposits of sums exceeding $500 due to 68 special depositors, amounting to $77,750, a total of $914,047.34.

Section 102 of "An act to provide a government for the Territory of Hawaii," approved April 30, 1900, is as follows:

SEC. 102. That the laws of Hawaii relating to the establishment and conduct of any postal savings bank or institution are hereby abolished. And the Secretary of the Treasury, in the execution of the agreement of the United States as expressed in an act entitled "Joint resolution to provide for annexing the Hawaiian Islands to the United States," approved July seventh, eighteen hundred and ninety-eight, shall pay the amounts on deposit in the Hawaiian Postal Savings Bank to the persons entitled thereto, according to their respective rights, and he shall make all needful orders, rules, and regulations for paying such persons and for notifying such persons to present their demands for payment. So much money as is necessary to pay said demands is hereby appropriated out of any money in the Treasury not otherwise appropriated, to be available on and after the first day of July, nineteen hundred, when such payments shall begin, and none of said demands shall bear interest after said date; and no deposit shall be made in said bank after said date. Said demands of such persons shall be certified to by the chief executive of Hawaii as being genuine and due to the persons presenting the same, and his certificate shall be sealed with the official seal of the Territory, and countersigned by its secretary, and shall be approved by the Secretary of the Interior, who shall draw his warrant for the amount due upon the Treasurer of the United States, and when the same are so paid no further liabilities shall exist in respect of the same against the Governments of the United States or of Hawaii.

Your committee recommend that this section be amended so as to read as follows:

SEC. 102. That the laws of Hawaii relating to the establishment and conduct of any postal savings bank or institution are hereby abolished. And the Secretary of the Treasury, in the execution of the agreement of the United States as expressed in an act entitled "Joint resolution to provide for annexing the Hawaiian Islands to the United States," approved July seventh, eighteen hundred and ninety-eight, shall pay the amounts on deposit in the Hawaiian Postal Savings Bank to the persons entitled thereto, according to their respective rights, and he shall make all needful orders, rules, and regulations for paying such persons and for notifying such persons to present their demands for payment. So much money as is necessary to pay said demands is hereby appropriated out of any money in the Treasury not otherwise appropriated, to be available on and after the first day of July, nineteen hundred, when such payments shall begin. and none of said demands shall bear interest after said date, and no deposit shall be made in said bank after said date. Said demands of such persons shall be certified to by the chief executive of Hawaii as being genuine and due to the persons presenting the same, and his certificate shall be sealed with the official seal of the Territory and countersigned by the secretary, and when the same are paid in the manner respecting payment from the Treasury no further liabilities shall exist in respect of the same against the Governments of the United States or Hawaii.

The section as amended in Senate bill 4650 omits the following words: "and shall be approved by the Secretary of the Interior, who shall draw his warrant for the amount due upon the Treasurer of the United States." It leaves the payment to be made by the Secretary of the Treasury without the intervention of the Secretary of the Interior. It was thought needless to require the Secretary of the Interior to approve the certificate of the executive of Hawaii and to draw his warrant for the amount due, as the Secretary of the Treasury is otherwise given charge of the whole matter and can appropriately attend to it.

Section 103 of "An act to provide a government for the Territory of Hawaii," approved April 30, 1900, provides as follows:

SEC. 103. That any money of the Hawaiian Postal Savings Bank that shall remain unpaid to the persons entitled thereto on the first day of July, nineteen hundred and one, and any assets of said bank shall be turned over by the government of Hawaii to the Treasurer of the United States. and the Secretary of the Treasury shall cause an account to be stated, as of said date. between such government of Hawaii and the United States in respect to said Hawaiian Postal Savings Bank.

SEC. 104. This act shall take effect forty-five days from and after the date of the approval thereof. excepting only as to section fifty-two, relating to appropriations, which shall take effect upon such approval.

Your committee recommend that this section be amended so as to read as follows:

SEC. 103. All money on deposit in the Hawaiian Postal Savings Bank shall, on the first day of July, nineteen hundred, be turned over by the government of Hawaii to the Treasurer of the United States; and the Secretary of the Treasury is hereby authorized to assume charge of all the assets of said bank and to convert the same into money, in such manner and in such time as may, in his judgment, best subserve the public interests. and by such agents as he may appoint. Such agents shall give good and sufficient bond to the United States for the faithful performance of their duties, in such form and in such penalty as the Secretary of the Treasury may prescribe. The moneys so turned over to the Treasurer of the United States, and those collected from the assets of said bank, shall be deposited in the Treasury of the United States to the credit of the Treasurer of the United States.

And it is further provided, That the Secretary of the Treasury in the execution of the agreement of the United States expressed in a "Joint resolution to provide for annexing the Hawaiian Islands to the United States." approved July seventh, eighteen hundred and ninety-eight, at the earliest practicable period shall pay of the public debt of the Republic of Hawaii, lawfully existing at the date of the passage of said joint resolution, an amount not exceeding in all four million dollars, including the sum required to pay the depositors in the Hawaiian Postal Savings Bank, as provided in the act entitled "An act to provide a government for the Territory of Hawaii, approved April thirtieth, nineteen hundre 1. as above amended; and so much money as shall be necessary to pay the same is hereby appropriated out of any money in the Treasury of the United States not otherwise appropriated.

There is also hereby appropriated in like manner such amount as may be necessary to pay any accruing interest on said public debt for which the United States may be liable under joint resolution of Congress, approved July seventh, eighteen hundred and ninety-eight, entitled "Joint resolution to provide for annexing the Hawaiian Islands to the United States;" and in addition thereto an amount not exceeding twenty thousand dollars, or so much thereof as may be necessary, to pay the expenses of executing this resolution.

The amended section requires all money on deposit in the Hawaiian Postal Savings Bank to be turned over to the Treasurer of the United States on the 1st of July of this year instead of next year.

It places the Secretary in charge of all of the assets of the bank, with authority to convert the same into money and to appoint proper agents, such agents to give a sufficient bond.

It further provides that the money so turned over to the Treasurer of the United States and that collected from the assets of the bank shall be deposited in the Treasury to the credit of the Treasurer of the United States.

It is further provided by Senate bill 4650 that in execution of the agreement of the United States in the joint resolution of July 7, 1898, the Secretary of the Treasury shall pay of the public debt of the Republic of Hawaii, existing at the date of the passage of the said joint resolution, an amount not exceeding in all $4,000,000, including the sum required to pay the depositors in the Hawaiian Postal Savings Bank as provided in the act of April 30, 1900, as amended by this bill.

It appropriates so much money as shall be necessary to pay the same, and also appropriates such an amount as may be necessary to pay any accruing interest on the public debt for which the United States may be liable under the joint resolution of July 7, 1898, and in addition thereto an amount not exceeding $20,000, or so much as may be necessary to pay the expenses of executing this resolution.

It will be observed that the joint resolution of July 7, 1898, which assumes the public debt of the Republic of Hawaii, including the amount due depositors in the Postal Savings Bank, to the extent of $4,000,000, requires that the Hawaiian Government shall continue to pay the interest on said debt "so long as the existing Government and the present commercial relations of the Hawaiian Islands are continued." This obligation upon the Hawaiian Government ceases when the government of July 7, 1898, is superseded by the government provided for in "An act to provide a government for the Territory of Hawaii," approved April 30, 1900—that is to say, forty-five days after the approval of said act, to wit, June 15, 1900. (See section 104 of act of April 30, 1900.) The interest after that date is left unprovided for, and should be assumed by the United States if, indeed, it is not assumed by fair construction of the act of July 7, 1898.

If this is promptly done, it will be a small matter, as only $562,000 of the public debt is not now redeemable, and that amount is redeemable in 1901. Only a small portion of the deposits in the Hawaiian Postal Savings Bank—that is to say, $77,750—carries interest, and all of these deposits in the Postal Savings Bank are to be met by deposits and assets of the bank.

Hereunto annexed as a part of this report is the statement of the public debt of Hawaii by Mr. Samuel M. Damon, minister of finance, which was reported to Hon. Shelby M. Cullom, chairman of the Hawaiian Commission, by Hon. Sanford B. Dole, as the report of the commission on the public debt on September 2, 1898, which is found in the report of the Hawaiian Commission.

REPORT OF COMMITTEE ON THE PUBLIC DEBT.

Hon. SHELBY M. CULLOM,
Chairman of the Hawaiian Commission:

I have the honor to present the accompanying statement on the public debt of Hawaii by Mr. Samuel M. Damon. the minister of finance, which I adopt as the report of the committee on the public debt.

SANFORD B. DOLE.

HONOLULU, *September 2, 1898.*

Hon. S. B. DOLE, *of the Hawaiian Commission.*

SIR: In response to the request for information on the public debt and matters relative thereto of the Government of Hawaii on the 12th of August of the present year, I have the honor to make the following report:

The financial obligations of this Government on that date I find to be as follows, not taking into consideration, however, the current monthly expenditures, salary lists, and pay rolls that are settled by warrants of the auditor-general on the treasury, drawn during the month, and all of which have been paid as presented.

The obligations of the Government are comprised under the heads of "Bonded debt" and "Postal Savings Bank."

Detailed statement of bonded debt August 12, 1898.

[Act of Aug. 5, 1892. Redeemable after 1887. Payable in 25 years]

Stock A, 6 per cent bonds	$14,000	
Stock E, 6 per cent bonds	8,000	
Stock O, 6 per cent bonds	2,200	
Stock U, 6 per cent bonds	10,000	
		$34,200

[Act of Oct. 15, 1886. Redeemable in and after 1897. Payable in 20 years.]

Loan in London	$980,000	
Stock A, 6 per cent bonds	373,000	
Stock E, 6 per cent bonds	124,000	
Stock O, 6 per cent bonds	18,000	
Stock U, 6 per cent bonds	505,000	
		2,000,000

[Act of Aug. 15, 1888 Redeemable after 1893 Payable in 20 years]

Stock A, 6 per cent bonds	$140,000	
Stock U, 6 per cent bonds	50,000	
		190,000

[Act of Aug. 6, 1890. Redeemable after 1895. Payable in 10 years.]

Stock A, 5 per cent bonds	$18,000
Stock E, 5 per cent bonds	9,000
Stock O, 5 per cent bonds	2,100
	$29,100

[Act of Oct. 24, 1890. Redeemable after 1895. Payable in 10 years]

Stock A, 6 per cent bonds	95,000

[Act of Sept. 7, 1892. Redeemable after 1897. Payable in 20 years.]

Stock A, 6 per cent bonds	$26,000
Stock E, 6 per cent bonds	31,500
Stock O, 6 per cent bonds	11,700
Stock A, 5 per cent bonds	8,000
Stock E, 5 per cent bonds	33,500
Stock O, 5 per cent bonds	8,700
Stock A, 4½ per cent bonds	1,000
Stock E, 4½ per cent bonds	7,000
Stock O, 4½ per cent bonds	2,000
	129,400

[Acts of Jan. 11 and Feb. 18, 1893. Redeemable in 1898. Payable in 20 years.]

Stock A, 6 per cent bonds	650,000

[Act of June 30, 1896. Redeemable in 1901. Payable in 20 years.]

Stock A, 5 per cent bonds	$352,000
Stock E, 5 per cent bonds	9,000
Stock O, 5 per cent bonds	1,000
Stock U, 5 per cent bonds	200,000
	562,000
	3,689,700

The proceeds of sales of bonds have been, with few exceptions of a minor nature, confined to expenditures on public buildings, harbor improvements, new roads and bridges, and the encouragement of immigration.

HAWAIIAN POSTAL SAVINGS BANK.

This institution was established by act of the legislature in 1884, to encourage the deposit of small savings at interest, with the security of the Government for repayment thereof, and was opened for business July 1, 1886, with His Majesty Kalakaua as the first depositor.

On the 12th day of August, 1898, the amount due to 10,555 depositors, classified by nationalities, was as follows:

Americans	602
British	526
Germans	329
Hawaiians	1,291
Portuguese	495
Sundry nationalities	221
Chinese under the board of immigration	7,091
Total	10,555

Amounted to	$836,297.34
And to 68 special depositors for sums exceeding $500, the sum of	77,750.00
A total of	914,047.34

These deposits bear interest at 4½ per cent per annum, and interest is credited to the several accounts on the 31st day of December of each year, and is a charge on the current revenues of the Government.

The present cash reserve to meet the demands is $112,409.23, of which $105,000 is on special deposit at the treasury.

The surplus over the requirement of the cash minimum reserve of $50,000 has been used by the Government for public works and permanent improvements.

During the twelve years of its existence every call by depositors has been promptly met, and the general confidence and usefulness to the community has been shown in its use by all nationalities.

The foregoing shows the gross public debt on August 12, 1898, to be $4,603,747.34. On the same date there was cash in the treasury to the credit of the following accounts, certified to by the register of—

Public accounts $546,739.04

Cash on hand in the Hawaiian treasury on August 12, 1898.

Current account, balance $284,014.51
Loan fund account, balance.. 38,370.17
                                                                     _____
    Total. 322,384.68

Special deposits.

Land sales $66,026.23
Road tax.. 53,270.83
School tax.. 54.30
Hawaiian Postal Savings Bank 105,000.00
                                                                     _____
    Total... 224,354.36

I hereby certify that the above is a true and correct statement as of above date.

W. G. ASHLEY,
Registrar of Public Accounts.

I would add, in relation to the Postal Savings Bank, that deposits up to $500 only are credited with interest.

Any deposit of three months' standing may, at the option of the depositor, be withdrawn and exchanged for a 5-20 Government bond, with interest at 4½ per cent.

Besides these provisions the bank may, at its discretion, issue what are called "term certificates," for not over three months, for any amount up to $5,000, and not to exceed in all $150,000 at any one time, at 4½ per cent.

Deposits amounting to over $100 may be withdrawn at ninety days' notice; under $100 without notice.

I have the honor to be, sir, your most obedient servant,

S. M. DAMON, *Minister of Finance.*

INDEX.

1023

S.

T.

U.

V.

W.

O

Lightning Source UK Ltd.
Milton Keynes UK
UKHW020607251118
332796UK00003B/407/P